Guide
to
Career
Colleges

2005

THOMSON

PETERSON'S

Australia • Canada • Mexico • Singapore • Spain • United Kingdom • United States

About the Career College Association

The Career College Association (CCA) is a voluntary membership organization of private postsecondary schools, institutes, colleges, and universities that comprise the for-profit sector of higher education. CCA's 1,270 members educate, prepare, and support nearly 1 million students each year for employment in more than 200 occupational fields.

For more information, contact Career College Association:
10 G Street NE, Suite 750
Washington, DC 20002
202-336-6700
www.career.org

About the Career College Foundation

The Career College Foundation, a CCA affiliate, is a District of Columbia not-for-profit corporation established in 1982. The Foundation provides scholarships and awards to assist high school graduates and military's active duty, honorable discharged, and retired veterans interested in attending CCA member schools, institutes, colleges, and universities through its award-winning *Imagine America* scholarship program and *Imagine America* Military Award Program (MAP). The Foundation also provides scholarships through the *Imagine America II* adult scholarship program and the *Imagine America* LDRSHIP (Loyalty, Duty, Respect, Selfless Service, Honor, Integrity, and Personal Courage) award program.

For more information, contact Career College Foundation:
10 G Street NE, Suite 750
Washington, DC 20002
202-336-6800
www.careercollegefoundation.org

About Thomson Peterson's

Thomson Peterson's (www.petersons.com) is a leading provider of education information and advice, with books and online resources focusing on education search, test preparation, and financial aid. Its Web site offers searchable databases and interactive tools for contacting educational institutions, online practice tests and instruction, and planning tools for securing financial aid. Thomson Peterson's serves 110 million education consumers annually.

For more information, contact Peterson's, 2000 Lenox Drive, Lawrenceville, NJ 08648;
800-338-3282; or find us on the World Wide Web at www.petersons.com/about.

Copyright © 2005 by Peterson's, a division of Thomson Learning, Inc.
Thomson Learning™ is a trademark used herein under license.

Previous editions © 2001, 2002, 2003, 2004

Editor: Fern A. Oram; Production Editor: L.A. Wagner; Copy Editors: Bret Bollmann, Jim Colbert, Michael Haines, Michele N. Firestone, Jill C. Schwartz, Pam Sullivan, Sally Ross, and Valerie Bolus Vaughan; Research Project Manager: Christine Lucas; Research Associate: Kristina Moran; Programmer: Phyllis Johnson; Manufacturing Manager: Ray Golaszewski; Composition Manager: Gary Rozmierski; Client Relations Representatives: Mimi Kaufman, Lois Regina Milton, Mary Ann Murphy, Michael Schwartz, Jim Swinarski, and Eric Wallace; Cover Design: Chris Chattin.

ISSN 1544-239X
ISBN 0-7689-1568-6

Printed in the United States of America

10 9 8 7 6 5 4 3 2   06 05

Fifth Edition

Contents

Introduction to Career Colleges

About Career College Association and Career College Foundation

CAREER COLLEGE ASSOCIATION

The Career College Association (CCA) is a voluntary membership organization made up of private postsecondary schools, institutes, colleges, and universities that comprise the for-profit sector of higher education. CCA's 1,270 members educate, prepare and support nearly 1 million students each year for employment in more than 200 occupational fields.

CCA member institutions cover the full spectrum of postsecondary education from short-term certificate and diploma programs, to two- and four-year associate and baccalaureate degrees, to master's and doctoral programs. Some of the occupational fields for which CCA institutions provide programs include accounting; allied medical; automotive technology; business administration; commercial art; culinary and hospitality management; information technology; mechanical engineering; and radio and television broadcasting.

Most CCA member institutions participate in federal student financial assistance programs under Title IV of the Higher Education Act. In order to participate, the institution must be licensed by the state in which it is located, accredited by a recognized national or regional accrediting body, and approved by the U.S. Department of Education. Many CCA member colleges also participate in other federal, state, and local education and workforce-training programs.

Career schools and colleges graduate approximately one-half of the technically trained workers who enter the U.S. workforce each year and also provide retraining for displaced workers and skills upgrading for a wide variety of public and private employers.

CAREER COLLEGE FOUNDATION

The Career College Foundation is a District of Columbia not-for-profit affiliate of CCA established in 1982. The Foundation's by-laws direct its resources to:

- demonstrate the value of specialized career training and improve public understanding of the role of career-training colleges and schools;
- present instructional opportunities for career school staff training and development;
- prepare reports on various aspects of career training for the use of schools, educators, researchers, government officials, and the public;
- conduct studies dealing with various aspects of career training and education and publish reports and educational material;
- establish scholarship programs; and
- recognize outstanding individual and organizations in the field of career training.

Over the past six years, the Foundation has provided more than $27 million in scholarships to high school graduates attending CCA member schools, institutes, colleges, and universities through its *Imagine America* scholarship program. *Imagine America* has received several awards from the American Society of Association Executives, including the Award of Excellence and the Summit Award for innovative education and training initiatives. Additionally, the Foundation has created an adult scholarship program, *Imagine America II*, funded through partnerships with key industry leaders such as Bridgestone/Firestone Trust, Dell Computer Corporation, Lockhead Martin, Mercedes Benz Corporation, Northrop Grumman Litton, and Sallie Mae Fund. The Foundation recently also created an *Imagine America* Military Award Program (MAP).

Accrediting Agencies

ccreditation is a status granted to an institution that meets or exceeds the stated criteria of educational quality. The purposes of accreditation are to assess and enhance the educational quality of an institution, assure consistency in institutional operations, promote institutional improvement, and provide for public accountability.

Accreditation functions specifically to:

- evaluate whether an institution meets or exceeds minimum standards of quality;
- assist students in determining acceptable institutions for enrollment;
- assist institutions in determining acceptability of transfer credits;
- assist employers in determining validity of programs of study and the acceptability of graduate qualifications;
- assist employers in determining eligibility for employee tuition reimbursement programs;
- enable graduates to sit for certification examinations;
- involve staff and faculty members, students, graduates, and advisory boards in institutional evaluation and planning;
- create goals for institutional self-improvement;
- provide a self-regulatory alternative for state oversight functions; and
- provide a basis for determining eligibility for federal student assistance.

Accreditation is a deliberate and thorough process and is entered into voluntarily for purposes of quality assessment and institutional enhancement. Accrediting agencies assess compliance with published administrative and academic standards and seek a continuous pursuit of excellence on the part of the institutions they accredit. As such, the accrediting agencies serve students, society, and higher education as well as their accredited institutions and entities by striving to ensure academic excellence and ethical standards. Providing appropriate accrediting criteria and enhancement services to its membership are key elements in achieving these goals. Accrediting agencies perform peer assessment, pay close attention to educational trends, and maintain a commitment to require both ethical business and educational practices at institutions in order to promote qualitative standards, policies, and procedures leading to institutional and organizational effectiveness.

All of the institutions listed in this publication are accredited by at least one of the national or regional accrediting agencies recognized by the U.S. Department of Education. A listing of these agencies follows.

National Accrediting Agencies

Accrediting Bureau of Health Education Schools (ABHES)
7777 Leesburg Pike, Suite 314 N.
Falls Church, Virginia 22043
Phone: 703-917-9503
Web: http://www.abhes.org

Accrediting Commission of Career Schools and Colleges of Technology (ACCSCT)
2101 Wilson Boulevard, Suite 302
Arlington, Virginia 22201
Phone 703-247-4212
Web: http://www.accsct.org

Accrediting Council for Continuing Education & Training (ACCET)
1722 N Street, N.W.
Washington, DC 20036
Phone: 202-955-1113
Web: http://www.accet.org

Accrediting Council for Independent Colleges and Schools (ACICS)
750 First Street, NE, Suite 980
Washington, DC 20002-4241
Phone: 202-336-6780
Web: http://www.acics.org

ACCREDITING AGENCIES

Council on Occupational Education (COE)
41 Perimeter Center East, NE, Suite 640
Atlanta, Georgia 30346
Phone: 800-917-2081
Web: http://www.council.org

The Distance Education and Training Council
(DETC)
1601 18th Street, N.W.
Washington, DC 20009
Phone: 202-234-5100
Web: http://www.detc.org

National Accrediting Commission of
Cosmetology Arts & Sciences (NACCAS)
4401 Ford Avenue, Suite 1300
Alexandria, Virginia 22302
Phone: 703-600-7600
Web: http://www.naccas.org

Regional Accrediting Agencies

Middle States Commission on Higher
Education
3624 Market Street
Philadelphia, Pennsylvania 19104
Phone: 267-284-5000
Web: http://www.msache.org

New England Association of Schools and
Colleges (NASC)
209 Burlington Road
Bedford, Massachusetts 01730-1433
Phone: 781-271-0022
Web: http://www.neasc.org

North Central Association of Colleges and
Schools (NCACS)
The Higher Learning Commission
30 North LaSalle Street, Suite 2400
Chicago, Illinois 60602-2504
Phone: 800-621-7440
Web: http://www.ncahigherlearning
commission.org

Northwest Commission on Colleges &
Universities (NWCCU)
8060 165th Avenue, NE, Suite 100
Redmond, Washington 98052
Phone: 425-558-4224
Web: http://www.nwccu.org

Southern Association of Colleges and Schools
(SACS)
Commission on Colleges
1866 Southern Lane
Decatur, Georgia 30033
Phone: 404-679-4500
Web: http://www.sacscoc.org

Western Association of Schools & Colleges
(WASC)
985 Atlantic Avenue, Suite 100
Alameda, California 94501
Phone: 510-748-9001
Web: http://www.wascweb.org/senior

How Career, Income, and Education Relate: The Bottom Line for Your Future

The relationship between education and work—the fact that the more you invest in your education, the more you will earn—probably has been repeated so often it virtually has become background noise. At the risk of boring you, here are educational attainment figures from the Census Bureau data:

Level of Education Attained	Average Annual Income
Bachelor's Degree	$43,782
Associate Degree	32,468
Regardless of Education, the Average Income	32,717
High School Graduate	23,594
Not a High School Graduate	16,053

U.S. Department of Commerce, Bureau of Census Statistical Abstract of United States, 2000, Washington, D.C.

Reliable data on the incomes of career school graduates is not available, but there are other data that might provide some clues as to what these might be. A 1986 study[1] of two-year college graduates showed that associate degree earners who took vocational programs had higher incomes than graduates from nonvocational programs. This difference in incomes expanded from 16 percent greater within five years after graduation to 37 percent greater within nine years after

---

[1] Ghazalah, Ismail. **1979 Vocational Education Graduates in 1986: A Longitudinal Study Based on Federal Income Tax Data**. 1991, Ohio University: Athens, Ohio.

graduation. Approximately 59 percent of two-year college graduates in 1992 earned degrees in vocational programs.

As to the income of the 49 percent of career college graduates from programs at schools other than two-year colleges (except with respect to certification for certain fields that demands graduation from accredited programs), we have not heard of vocations where there is a difference in earnings based on the particular school where one's skills were learned. We assume that there is no difference in income based on the category of school one attended.

FASTEST-GROWING OCCUPATIONS REQUIRE CAREER COLLEGE TRAINING

It is estimated that between 2000 and 2010, positions requiring an associate degree will increase by 24.1%. Tables 1a, 1b, and 1c have the latest projections from the Bureau of Labor Statistics of the fastest-growing occupations in the ten years from 2000 to 2010. Programs for many of these occupations are offered by schools that are represented in this book.

COLLEGE IS NOT FOR EVERYBODY

Thirty years ago, most young people went directly to work. Today, most young people first go to school for more training after high school. The figures on income and education demonstrate why this is a good idea. They also demonstrate that earning a bachelor's degree is a better option than going to vocational-technical school, but we know that college is not for everybody.

HOW CAREER, INCOME, AND EDUCATION RELATE

Table 1a. Industries with the Fastest Wage and Salary Employment Growth, 2000–2010

Industry Description	Thousands of Jobs 2000	2010	Change 2000–2010	Average Annual Rate of Change 2000–2010
Computer and data processing services	2,095	3,900	1,805	6.4
Residential care	806	1,318	512	5.0
Health services (not elsewhere classified)	1,210	1,900	690	4.6
Cable and pay television services	216	325	109	4.2
Personnel supply services	3,887	5,800	1,913	4.1
Warehousing and storage	206	300	94	3.8
Water and sanitation	214	310	96	3.8
Miscellaneous business services	2,301	3,305	1,004	3.7
Miscellaneous equipment rental and leasing	279	397	118	3.6
Management and public relations	1,090	1,550	460	3.6

U.S. Bureau of Labor Statistics. Occupational Employment Projections to 2010.

Life events often can interfere with plans to attend college. Responsibilities to a family may materialize that make it impossible to delay earning an income for four years. One may have to work and go to school. In this situation, career training that is measured in months, instead of years, can be the best choice.

Also, let's be real. College demands certain conventions, behaviors, and attitudes that do not fit every kind of person. Whether rooted in personality or upbringing, for some individuals, the intellectual path of college life and years of strict time management and postponed rewards is unsatisfying. On the other hand, the clear structure and demands of a worker in a real career might be an appealing alternative.

Certainly, the college world has made great attempts to be more inclusive. It is no longer a world of kids under the age of 23, but at its heart, from its standardized tests through to its campus social life, most colleges are defined by the standards and norms of the majority culture, which remains largely under age 23. Adults who have lived in the real world, although aware of the rewards that are promised by spending a few years in college, may not want to go through the years of self-denial, isolation, and cultural displacement of a college experience.

Table 1b. Fastest Growing Occupations, 2000–2010
Numbers in thousands of jobs

Occupation	Employment 2000	2010	Change Number	Percent
Computer software engineers, applications	380	760	380	100
Computer support specialists	506	996	490	97
Computer software engineers, systems software	317	601	284	90
Network and computer systems administrators	229	416	187	82
Network systems and data communications analysts	119	211	92	77
Desktop publishers	38	63	25	67
Database administrators	106	176	70	66
Personal and home care aides	414	672	258	62
Computer systems analysts	431	689	258	60
Medical assistants	329	516	187	57

U.S. Bureau of Labor Statistics. Occupational Employment Projections to 2010.

Table 1c. Occupations with the Largest Job Growth, 2000–2010
Numbers in thousands of jobs

Occupation	Employment 2000	2010	Change Number	Percent
Combined food preparation and serving workers, including fast food	2,206	2,879	673	30
Customer service representatives	1,946	2,577	631	32
Registered nurses	2,194	2,755	561	26
Retail salespersons	4,109	4,619	510	12
Computer support specialists	506	996	490	97
Cashiers, except gaming	3,325	3,799	474	14
Office clerks, general	2,705	3,135	430	16
Security guards	1,106	1,497	391	35
Computer software engineers, applications	380	760	380	100

U.S. Bureau of Labor Statistics. Occupational Employment Projections to 2010.

CAREER COLLEGE STUDENTS ACHIEVE THEIR GOALS

A truly positive aspect of career education is that most students who go into it are likely to complete their educational goals. Fifty-five percent of all students working toward an educational certificate (the category defining vo-tech students) complete their educational program. By contrast, only 24 percent of all students working toward an associate degree completed their degree work, while 54 percent of all students working toward a bachelor's degree completed their degree work. As the following chart demonstrates, these differences become even more dramatic when such factors as delaying one's education for more than a year after high school, studying part-time, or working while studying are factored in.

For most students, career education programs offer a truer chance of achievement than other alternative paths of education. The careers that can be entered provide the satisfaction of a fulfilling work life with exceptional compensation. Vocational-technical education can be a lifesaver for the men and women who choose to refrain from, or postpone, going to a four-year or two-year college.

Postsecondary Students Who Attained Their Initial Degree Objective

	Vocational-Technical Certificate Programs	Associate Degree Programs	Bachelor's Degree Programs
Enrollment More Than a Year after High School	54%	14%	50%
Part-Time Student	41%	18%	13%
Also Worked 1–20 Hours per Week	75%	42%	51%
Also Worked More Than 20 Hours per Week	47%	28%	40%

U.S. Department of Education, National Center for Education Statistics. *1990 Beginning Postsecondary Students Longitudinal Study (BPS 90/94)*, 1996, Washington, D.C.

Returning to School: Advice for Adult Students

many adults think about returning to school for a long time without taking any action. One purpose of this article is to help the "thinkers" finally make some decisions by examining what is keeping them from action. Another purpose is to describe not only some of the difficulties and obstacles that adult students may face when returning to school but also tactics for coping with them.

If you have been thinking about going back to college, and believing that you are the only person your age contemplating college, you should know that approximately 7 million adult students are currently enrolled in higher education institutions. This number represents 50 percent of total higher education enrollments. The majority of adult students are enrolled at two-year colleges.

There are many reasons why adult students choose to attend a two-year college. Studies have shown that the three most important criteria that adult students consider when choosing a college are location, cost, and availability of the major or program desired. Most two-year colleges are public institutions that serve a geographic district, making them readily accessible to the community. Costs at most two-year colleges are far less than at other types of higher education institutions. For many students who plan to pursue a bachelor's degree, completing their first two years of college at a community college is an affordable means to that end. If you are interested in an academic program that will transfer to a four-year institution, most two-year colleges offer the "general education" courses that comprise most freshman and sophomore years. If you are interested in a vocational or technical program, two-year colleges excel in providing this type of training.

UNCERTAINTY, CHOICE, AND SUPPORT

There are three different "stages" in the process of adults returning to school. The first stage is uncertainty. Do I really want to go back to school? What will my friends or family think? Can I compete with those 18-year-old whiz kids? Am I too old? The second stage is choice. Once the decision to return has been made, you must choose where you will attend. There are many criteria to use in making this decision. The third stage is support. You have just added another role to your already-too-busy life. There are, however, strategies that will help you accomplish your goals—perhaps not without struggle, but with grace and humor. Let's look at each of these stages.

UNCERTAINTY

Why are you thinking about returning to school? Is it to:

- fulfill a dream that had to be delayed?
- become more educationally well-rounded?
- fill an intellectual void in your life?

These reasons focus on *personal growth*.

If you are returning to school to:

- meet people and make friends
- attain and enjoy higher social status and prestige among friends, relatives, and associates
- understand/study a cultural heritage, or
- have a medium in which to exchange ideas,

you are interested in *social and cultural opportunities*.

If you are like most adult students, you want to:

- qualify for a new occupation
- enter or reenter the job market
- increase earnings potential, or

- qualify for a more challenging position in the same field of work.

You are seeking *career growth*.

Understanding the reasons why you want to go back to school is an important step in setting your educational goals and will help you to establish some criteria for selecting a college. However, don't delay your decision because you have not been able to clearly define your motives. Many times, these aren't clear until you have already begun the process, and they may change as you move through your college experience.

Assuming that you agree that additional education will be of benefit to you, what is it that keeps you from returning to school? You may have a litany of excuses running through your mind:

- I don't have time.
- I can't afford it.
- I'm too old to learn.
- My friends will think I'm crazy.
- The teachers will be younger than I.
- My family can't survive without me to take care of them every minute.
- I'll be X years old when I finish.
- I'm afraid.
- I don't know what to expect.

And that is just what these are—excuses. You can make school, like anything else in your life, a priority or not. If you really want to return, you can. The more you understand your motivation for returning to school and the more you understand what excuses are keeping you from taking action, the easier your task will be.

If you think you don't have time: The best way to decide how attending class and studying can fit into your schedule is to keep track of what you do with your time each day for several weeks. Completing a standard time-management grid (each day is plotted out by the half hour) is helpful for visualizing how your time is spent. For each 3-credit-hour class you take, you will need to find 3 hours for class plus 6 to 9 hours for reading-studying-library time. This study time should be spaced evenly throughout the week, not loaded up on one day. It is not possible to learn or retain the material that way. When you examine your grid, see where there are activities that could be replaced with school and study time. You may decide to give up your bowling league or some time in front of the TV. Try not to give up sleeping, and don't cut out every moment of free time. Here are some suggestions that have come from adults who have returned to school:

- Enroll in a time-management workshop. It helps you rethink how you use your time.
- Don't think you have to take more than one course at a time. You may eventually want to work up to taking more, but consider starting with one. (It is more than you are taking now!)
- If you have a family, start assigning those household chores that you usually do to them—and don't redo what they do.
- Use your lunch hour or commuting time for reading.

If you think you can not afford it: As mentioned earlier, two-year colleges are extremely affordable. If you cannot afford the tuition, look into the various financial aid options. Most federal and state funds are available to full- and part-time students. Loans are also available. While many people prefer not to accumulate a debt for school, these same people will think nothing of taking out a loan to buy a car. After five or six years, which is the better investment? Adult students who work should look into whether their company has a tuition-reimbursement policy. There are also an increasing number of private scholarships, available through foundations, service organizations, and clubs, that are focused on adult learners. Your public library and a college financial aid adviser are two excellent sources for reference materials regarding financial aid.

If you think you are too old to learn: This is pure myth. A number of studies have shown that adult learners perform as well as or better than traditional-age students.

If you are afraid your friends will think you're crazy: Who cares? Maybe they will, maybe they won't. Usually, they will admire your courage and be just a little jealous of your ambition (although they'll never tell you that). Follow your dreams, not theirs.

If you are concerned because the teachers or students will be younger than you: Don't be. The age differences that may be apparent in other settings evaporate in the classroom. If anything, an adult in the classroom strikes fear into the hearts of some 18-year-olds because adults have been known to be prepared, ask questions, be truly motivated, and be there to learn!

If you think your family will have a difficult time surviving while you are in school: If you have done everything for them up to now, they might struggle. Consider this an opportunity to help them become independent and self-sufficient. Your family can only make you feel guilty if you let them. You are not abandoning them; you are becoming an educational role model. When you are happy and working toward your goals, everyone benefits. Admittedly, it sometimes takes time for them to realize this. For single parents, there are schools that have begun to offer support groups, child care, and cooperative babysitting.

If you're appalled at the thought of being X years old when you graduate in Y years: How old will you be in Y years if you don't go back to school?

If you are afraid or don't know what to expect: Know that these are natural feelings when one encounters any new situation. Adult students find that their fears usually dissipate once they begin classes. Fear of trying is usually the biggest roadblock to the reentry process.

No doubt you have dreamed up a few more reasons for not making the decision to return to school. Keep in mind that what you are doing is making up excuses, and you are using these excuses to release you from the obligation to make a decision about your life. The thought of returning to college can be scary. Anytime anyone ventures into unknown territory, there is a risk, but taking risks is a necessary component of personal and professional growth. It is your life, and you alone are responsible for making the decisions that determine its course. Education is an investment in your future.

CHOICE

Once you have decided to go back to school, your next task is to decide where to go. If your educational goals are well defined (e.g., you want to pursue a degree in order to change careers), then your task is a bit easier. But even if your educational goals are still evolving, do not deter your return. Many students who enter higher education with a specific major in mind change that major at least once.

Most students who attend a public two-year college choose the community college in the district in which they live. This is generally the closest and least expensive option if the school offers the programs you want. If you are planning to begin your education at a two-year college and then transfer to a four-year school, there are distinct advantages to choosing your four-year school early. Many community and four-year colleges have "articulation" agreements that designate what credits from the two-year school will transfer to the four-year college and how. Some four-year institutions accept an associate degree as equivalent to the freshman and sophomore years, regardless of the courses you have taken. Some four-year schools accept two-year college work only on a course-by-course basis. If you can identify which school you will transfer to, you can know in advance exactly how your two-year credits will apply, preventing an unexpected loss of credit or time.

Each institution of higher education is distinctive. Your goal in choosing a college is to come up with the best student-institution fit—matching your needs with the offerings and characteristics of the school. The first step in choosing a college is to determine what criteria are most important to you in attaining your educational goals. Location, cost, and program availability are the three main factors that influence an adult student's college choice. In considering location, don't forget that some colleges have conveniently located branch campuses. In considering cost, remember to explore your financial aid options before ruling out an institution because of its tuition. Program availability should include not only the major in which you are interested, but also whether or not classes in that major are available when you can take them.

Some additional considerations beyond location, cost, and programs are:

- Does the school have a commitment to adult students and offer appropriate services, such as child care, tutoring, and advising?
- Are classes offered at times when you can take them?
- Are there academic options for adults, such as credit for life or work experience, credit by examination (including CLEP and PEP), credit for military service, or accelerated programs?
- Is the faculty sensitive to the needs of adult learners?

Once you determine which criteria are vital in your choice of an institution, you can begin to narrow your choices. There are myriad ways for you to locate the information you desire. Many urban newspapers publish a "School Guide" several times a year in which colleges and universities advertise to an adult student market. In addition, schools themselves publish catalogs, class schedules, and promotional materials that contain much of the information you need, and they are yours for the asking. Many colleges sponsor information sessions and open houses that allow you to visit the campus and ask questions. An appointment with an adviser is a good way to assess the fit between you and the institution. Be sure to bring your questions with you to your interview.

SUPPORT

Once you have made the decision to return to school and have chosen the institution that best meets your needs, take some additional steps to ensure your success during your crucial first semester. Take advantage of institutional support and build some social support systems of your own. Here are some ways of doing just that:

- Plan to participate in any orientation programs. These serve the threefold purpose of providing you with a great deal of important information, familiarizing you with the campus and its facilities, and giving you the opportunity to meet and begin networking with other students.

- Take steps to deal with any academic weaknesses. Take mathematics and writing placement tests if you have reason to believe you may need some extra help in these areas. It is not uncommon for adult students to need a math refresher course or a program to help alleviate math anxiety. Ignoring a weakness won't make it go away.
- Look into adult reentry programs. Many institutions offer adults workshops focusing on ways to improve study skills, textbook reading, test-taking, and time-management skills.
- Build new support networks by joining an adult student organization, making a point of meeting other adult students through workshops, or actively seeking out a "study buddy" in each class—that invaluable friend who shares and understands your experience.
- You can incorporate your new status as "student" into your family life. Doing your homework with your children at a designated "homework time" is a valuable family activity and reinforces the importance of education.
- Make sure you take a reasonable course load in your first semester. It is far better to have some extra time on your hands and to succeed magnificently than to spend the entire semester on the brink of a breakdown. Also, whenever possible, try to focus your first courses not only on requirements, but also in areas of personal interest.
- Faculty members, advisers, and student affairs personnel are there to help you during difficult times—let them assist you as often as necessary.

After completing your first semester, you will probably look back in wonder at why you thought going back to school was so imposing. Certainly, it's not without its occasional exasperations. But, as with life, keeping things in perspective and maintaining your sense of humor make the difference between just coping and succeeding brilliantly.

Sandra Cook, Ph.D., is Director, University Advising Center, San Diego State University.

Paying for Your Education

The decision to attend a career college is an extremely important one. The specialized education and training will provide you with the necessary tools and knowledge needed to be successful in the career of your choice. You will have the opportunity to grow in many areas, and you will learn the skills needed to prosper in the career of your choice.

Education is an investment in your future. Before you choose your career, it is necessary to consider how much time, money, and commitment you have to prepare yourself for a career. Remember, your career goals should be reasonable and realistic in terms of your ability, interests, and values. All students are encouraged to think about the amount of financial debt that may be necessary to achieve their educational goals and objectives. In addition, students should also look at the effect that student loan indebtedness can have on their future lifestyle. Choosing the right career and paying for college takes planning, forethought, dedication, and commitment.

This article is designed to familiarize you with the various kinds of financial aid programs available to help you meet the costs of attending a career college. Understanding the policies and procedures necessary to obtain financial assistance is essential. Although the process may seem confusing and complicated, financial aid helps many students pay for an education. The purpose of financial aid is to assist students with their educational expenses so that financial barriers do not prevent them from achieving their educational goals.

WHAT IS FINANCIAL AID?

Financial aid is the monetary assistance available to help students pay for the costs of attending an educational institution. Such aid is provided by federal, state, institutional, or private sources and may consist of grants, loans, work, or scholar-ships. Qualified students may be offered combinations of the various types of aid or aid from a single source. Each year, billions of dollars are given or lent to students, and about half of all students receive some sort of financial aid.

Most financial aid is awarded based on an individual's financial need, education costs, and the availability of funds. This aid is provided to students because neither they nor their families have all of the necessary resources needed to pay for an education. This kind of aid is referred to as *need-based aid*.

Merit-based aid is awarded to students who may or may not have financial need. Students are given assistance because they have a special skill or ability, display a particular talent, have a certain grade point average, or are enrolled in a specific program.

TYPES AND SOURCES OF FINANCIAL AID

There are several types of financial aid offered to help pay for educational expenses: grants, loans, student employment (work), and scholarships. Grants and scholarships are "gifts" and do not have to be repaid. Loans are borrowed money that the borrower must pay back over a period of time, usually after the student leaves school. Student employment is normally part-time work arranged for a student during the school year. Wages received by the student are used for specific college expenses.

The primary source of aid for students attending a career college is the federal government, offering both grant and loan financial aid programs. Another source of aid is state assistance. Many states across the country provide some aid for students attending colleges in their own home states. Most state aid programs are grants, although there are a few states that offer special loan and work-study programs. Other sources of aid that award money to students are private foundations, such as corporations, civic associations, unions, fraternal organizations, and religious groups. Most of these awards are not based solely on need, although the amount of the award may vary depending on financial need.

In addition, many companies offer tuition reimbursement to their employees and/or their employees' dependents. The Human Resources department at either your or your parent's place of employment can tell you whether or not the company offers this benefit and who may be eligible. Lastly, there are some colleges that offer awards from their own funds or from money received from various organizations. This type of aid is often referred to as "institutional aid."

GRANTS

Federal Pell Grant
Funded by the federal government, this need-based grant is available for undergraduate students who have financial need. Award amounts vary according to an eligibility index. The maximum award amount for the 2005-06 award year is $4,050 per year.

Federal Supplemental Educational Opportunity Grant (FSEOG)

Funded by the federal government, this need-based grant is available for undergraduate students who have exceptional financial need. Although the maximum award per year can be $4000, few career colleges have an abundance of FSEOG funds, and therefore award amounts usually range from $100 to $400 per year.

LOANS

Federal Perkins Loan
The Federal Perkins Loan is awarded on the basis of demonstrated financial need. The interest rate is 5 percent and the first payment is due nine months after leaving school. The maximum award is $3000 but, like the FSEOG funds, most career colleges have limited Perkins funding and will award what they can to the most needy students.

Subsidized Federal Stafford Student Loans
Subsidized Federal Stafford Student Loans are for students who demonstrate financial need.

Federal Family Education Stafford Loans (FFEL) are made to students through lending institutions such as banks and credit unions. Direct Stafford Loans are made to students through the school's financial aid office by the Department of Education. A college may participate in either or both of these loan programs. The interest rate on either Stafford loan is variable but cannot exceed 8.25 percent. Up to a 4 percent origination fee may be deducted, and loan repayment begins six months after leaving school or dropping below half-time status. The government pays the interest while you are in school and during the six-month grace period. Both FFEL and Direct Stafford Loans have a basic ten-year repayment period, but both also have several other extended repayment plans.

Unsubsidized Federal Stafford Loans
Unsubsidized Federal Stafford Loans are for students who do not demonstrate financial need. Students may borrow within the same loan limits and at the same interest rates as the regular Stafford Loan program. Up to a 4 percent origination fee may be deducted, and interest payments begin immediately. Most lenders allow students to defer payments while in school, but interest continues to accrue and is added to the principal balance. Regular payments begin six months after leaving school or dropping below half-time status.

Borrowers of additional unsubsidized loan amounts must meet the federal definition of an independent student or have exceptional circumstances as documented by the financial aid office. (Note: The loan amounts for which you are eligible may be prorated if your program is less than thirty weeks in length.)

Federal Parent Loans for Undergraduate Students (PLUS)
The Federal PLUS Loan program enables parents of dependent students to obtain loans to pay for their child's educational costs. The interest rate for this loan is set once each year with a maximum rate of 9 percent. Parents may borrow up to the cost of attendance minus any other financial aid received by the student.

WORK STUDY

Federal Work-Study (FWS)

The Federal Work-Study program provides jobs for students with financial aid eligibility. It gives students a chance to earn money to help pay for educational expenses while also providing valuable work experience. Eligible students are also afforded the opportunity to perform community service work. Many career schools offer FWS, but the number of jobs available tends to be limited.

UNDERSTANDING THE COST OF ATTENDANCE

Every career college establishes an estimate of what it will cost the student to attend the school. The expenses included in the cost of attendance are tuition and fees, books and supplies, room and board (includes food, rent, and utilities), personal expenses, and transportation. The total educational expenses or budgets are referred to as the student's cost of attendance.

DETERMING FINANCIAL AID ELIGIBILITY AND FINANCIAL NEED

Eligibility for financial aid is determined by subtracting the amount you and your parents can contribute from the cost of attendance. An assessment of your family's ability to contribute toward educational expenses is made based on the information you provide when applying for financial aid. Income, assets, size of family, and number of family members in college are some of the factors considered in this calculation. This assessment, referred to as need analysis, determines your financial need. Financial need is defined as the difference between the total cost of attendance and what you are expected to pay. The need analysis uses a formula mandated by federal legislation. It determines the ability, not the willingness, of the student and parents to finance the cost of attendance. Everyone who applies is treated equally under this analysis. The end result of the need analysis is your expected family contribution (EFC) and represents the amount your family should be able to contribute toward the cost of attendance. The cost of attendance will vary at each college, but the amount your family is expected to contribute should stay the same. Financial need will vary between colleges because of each school's different costs of attendance.

DETERMINING STUDENT STATUS: INDEPENDENT OR DEPENDENT?

If you are considered dependent by federal definition, then your parents' income and assets, as well as yours, will be counted toward the family contribution. If you are considered independent of your parents, only your income (and that of your spouse, if you are married) will count in the need analysis formula.

In order to be considered independent for financial aid, you must meet one of the following criteria:

- Be at least 24 years old;
- Be a veteran of the U.S. armed forces;
- Be married;
- Be an orphan or ward of the court;
- Have legal dependents other than a spouse; or
- Be a graduate or professional student.

If you can document extraordinary circumstances that might indicate independent status, you will need to show this information to the financial aid administrator at the college you will be attending. Only the financial aid administrator has the authority to make exceptions to the requirements listed above.

APPLYING FOR FINANCIAL AID

To apply for financial aid, it is essential that you properly complete the necessary forms so that your individual financial need can be evaluated. It is important to read all application materials and instructions very carefully. The application process can be a bit confusing, so remember to take it one step at a time. If you run into any problems or have specific questions, contact the financial aid office administrator at the college you will be attending. The financial aid office administrator will be happy to provide you with guidance and assistance.

Most career colleges use just one financial aid application—the Free Application for Federal

Student Aid (FAFSA). This form is a four-page application available at your college's financial aid office, local high school guidance office, and state education department offices. Students can apply for federal student aid via the Internet by using FAFSA on the Web (http://www.fafsa.ed. gov). The process is self-paced and interactive with step-by-step guidance. Depending on the availability of information about your income and financial situation, the process can take as little as 20 minutes to complete. The FAFSA that students use to apply for aid for each school year becomes available in the December prior to the year in which aid is needed. However, do not fill the form out until after January 1. (Note: You should complete the FAFSA as soon as possible after January 1. Although you may apply for aid at any time during the year, many state agencies have early cut-off dates for state aid funding.)

To complete this application, you will need to gather specific family information and financial records, such as tax forms, if they are available. If they are not, you can use estimates and make corrections later. Be sure to answer all questions. Omitted information may delay processing of your application. Be sure that you and your parents (if applicable) have signed the form and that you keep a copy of the form for your records. If applying online, you and one parent (if dependent) will need to get a Personal Identification Number (PIN) to sign the application. You can get the PIN at www.fafsa.ed.gov. Most students now use the Web-based application to apply for financial aid.

The FAFSA processing center will calculate your expected family contribution and will distribute the information back to the college.

About two to four weeks after you submit your completed FAFSA, you will receive a Student Aid Report (SAR) that shows the information you reported on the FAFAA and your calculated EFC. The colleges you listed on the FAFSA will receive the same information. If you need to make any corrections, you may do so at this time. If you applied on-line or supplied an e-mail address, you will be notified electronically. It is very important to ensure the e-mail address

REPAYMENT OPTIONS

A number of repayment options are available to borrowers of federally guaranteed student loans.

- **The Standard Repayment Plan**—requires fixed monthly payments (at least $50) over a fixed period of time (up to ten years). The length of the repayment period depends on the loan amount. This plan usually results in the lowest total interest paid because the repayment period is shorter than that of other plans.

- **The Extended Repayment Plan**—allows loan repayment to be extended over a period, generally from twelve to thirty years, depending on the total amount borrowed. Borrowers still pay a fixed amount each month (at least $50), but usually monthly payments will be less than under the Standard Repayment Plan. This plan may make repayment more manageable; however, borrowers usually will pay more interest because the repayment period is longer.

- **The Graduated Repayment Plan**—allows payments to start out low and increase every two years. This plan may be helpful to borrowers whose incomes are low initially but will increase steadily. A borrower's monthly payments must be at least half, but may not be more than one-and-a-half times, of what he or she would pay under Standard Repayment. As in the Extended Repayment Plan, the repayment period will usually vary from twelve to thirty years, depending on the total amount borrowed. Again, monthly payments may be more manageable at first because they are lower, but borrowers will pay more interest because the repayment period is longer.

- **The Income Contingent Repayment Plan**—bases monthly payments on adjusted gross income (AGI) and the total amount borrowed. This is currently only available to students who participate in the Direct Loan program; however, some FFEL lenders and guaranty agencies provide income-sensitive repayment plans. As income rises or falls each year, monthly payments are adjusted accordingly. The required monthly payment will not exceed 20 percent of the borrower's discretionary income, as calculated under a published formula. Borrowers have up to twenty-five years to repay; after twenty-five years, any unpaid amount will be discharged, and borrowers must pay taxes on the amount discharged. In other words, if the federal government forgives the balance of a loan, the amount is considered to be part of the borrower's income for that year.

you supply is accurate and that you notify the FAFSA processor if it changes.

If you are selected for verification by the school, you may be asked to submit documentation that will verify the information you reported on the FAFSA. Once the financial aid office is satisfied that all of the information is correct, the college can then determine your financial need and provide you with a financial aid offer for funding your education. If you are eligible to receive aid, most schools will either mail you an award letter or ask you to come into the financial aid office to discuss your financial aid eligibility. (Note: Financial aid is not renewed automatically; you must apply each year. Often, if you are in a program that lasts for more than one year, a renewal application or electronic notification will automatically be mailed to you by the federal processor.)

STUDENT LOANS AND DEBT MANAGEMENT

More than ever before, loans have become an important part of financial assistance. The majority of students find that they must borrow money to finance their education. If you accept a loan, you are incurring a financial obligation. You will have to repay the loan in full, along with all of the interest and any additional fees (collection, legal, etc.). Since you will be making loan payments to satisfy the loan obligation, carefully consider the burden your loan amount will impose on you after you leave college. Defaulting on a student loan can jeopardize your financial future. Borrow intelligently.

Common Questions Answered

q *Are a student's chances of being admitted to a college reduced if the student applies for financial aid?*

a Generally not. Nearly all colleges have a policy of "need-blind" admissions, which means that a student's financial need is not taken into account in the admission decision. There are a few selective colleges, however, that do consider ability to pay before deciding whether or not to admit a student. Some colleges will mention this in their literature; others may not. The best advice is to apply for financial aid if the student needs assistance to attend college.

q *Are parents penalized for saving money for college?*

a No. As a matter of fact, families that have made a concerted effort to save money for college are in a much better position than those that have not. For example, a student from a family that has saved money may not have to borrow as much. Furthermore, the "taxing rate" on savings is quite low—only about 5 percent of the parents' assets are assessed and neither home equity nor retirement savings are included. For example, a single 40-year-old parent who saved $40,000 for college expenses will have about $1100 counted as part of the parental contribution. Two parents, if the older one is 40 years old (a parent's age factors into the formulation), would have about $150 counted. (Note: The "taxing rate" for student assets is much higher—35 percent— compared to about 5 percent for parents.)

q *How does the financial aid system work in cases of divorce or separation? How are stepparents treated?*

a In cases of divorce or separation, the financial aid application(s) should be completed by the parent with whom the student lived for the longest period of time in the last twelve months (the custodial parent). If the custodial parent has remarried, the stepparent is considered a family member and must complete the application, along with the natural parent. If your family has any special circumstances, you can discuss these directly with the financial aid office. (Note: Colleges that award their own aid may ask the noncustodial natural parent to complete a separate aid application and will then calculate a contribution.)

q *When are students considered independent of parental support in applying for financial aid?*

a The student must be at least 24 years of age in order to be considered independent. If younger than 24, the student must be married, a graduate or professional student, have legal dependents other than a spouse, be an orphan or ward of the court, or a veteran of the armed forces. However, in very unusual situations, students who can clearly document estrangement from their parents can appeal to the financial aid office for additional consideration.

q *What can a family do if a job loss occurs?*

a Financial aid eligibility is based on the previous year's income. So the family's 2004 income would be reported to determine eligibility for the 2005-2006 academic year. In that way, the family's income can be verified with an income tax return. But the previous year's income may not accurately reflect the current financial situation, particularly if a parent lost a job or retired. In these instances, the projected income for the coming year can be used instead. Families should discuss the situation directly with the financial aid office and be prepared to provide appropriate documentation. The financial aid office will determine the most accurate estimate of current income and use this to determine eligibility for aid.

q *When my daughter first went to college, we applied for financial aid and were denied because our expected family contribution was too high. Now, my son is a high school senior, and we will soon have two in college. Will we get the same results?*

a The results will definitely be different. Both your son and your daughter should apply. As described earlier, need-based financial aid is based on your expected family contribution, or EFC. When you have two children in college, the parental portion of the EFC is divided in half for each child. For example, if the parent contribution for a family with one child in college is $6,000, it will be about $3,000 when there are two in college. The number of children in college has a big impact on determining the EFC.

q *I've heard about the "middle income squeeze" in regard to financial aid. What is it?*

a The so-called "middle-income squeeze" is the idea that low income families qualify for aid, high-income families have adequate resources to pay for education, and those in the middle are caught in between, not eligible for aid but also not able to pay full college costs. There is no provision in the Federal Methodology that treats middle-income students differently than others (such as an income cutoff for eligibility). The Expected Family Contribution rises proportionately as income and assets increase. If a middle-income family does not qualify for aid, it is because the need analysis formula yields a contribution that exceeds college costs. But keep in mind that if a $60,000-income family does not qualify for aid at a public university with a $10,000 budget, the same family will likely be eligible for aid at a private college with a cost of $25,000 or more. Also, there are now a number of loan programs available to parents and students that are not based on need. Since many of the grant programs funded by federal and state governments are directed at lower-income families, it is likely that a larger share of an aid package for a middle-income student will consist of loans rather than grants.

q *Given our financial condition, my daughter will be receiving financial aid. We will help out as much as we can, and, in fact, we ourselves will be borrowing. But I am concerned that she will have to take on a lot of loans in order to go to the college of her choice. Does she have any options?*

a She does. If offered a loan, she can decline all or part of it. One option is for her to ask the financial aid office to have some of the loan changed to a work-study job. If this is not possible, she can find her own part-time work. Often there is an employment office on campus that can help her locate a job. In most cases, the more she works, the less she has to borrow. It is important to remember that the educational loans offered to students have very attractive terms and conditions, with extremely flexible repayment options. Students should look upon these loans as a long-term investment that will reap significant rewards. Another way to pose the question: Is your daughter willing to take out a loan for a car? A car has a relatively short asset life, while the value of the college degree will reap financial benefits for the rest of her life.

q *Is it possible to change your financial aid package?*

a Yes. Most colleges have an appeal process. A request to change a need-based loan to a work-study job is usually approved if funds are available. A request to consider special financial circumstances may also be granted. At most colleges, a request for more grant money is rarely approved unless it is based on a change in the information reported. Applicants should speak with the financial aid officer if they have a concern about their financial appeal. Some colleges may even respond to a competitive appeal, that is, a request to match another college's offer.

q *My son was awarded a Federal Stafford Loan as part of his financial aid package. His award letter also indicated that we could take out a PLUS loan. How do we go about choosing our lender? Do we go to our local bank?*

a Read the material that came with the financial aid award letter. It is likely that the college has a "preferred lender" list for Stafford and PLUS Loans. Although you can borrow from any bank, your loan application will be processed more quickly if you use a lender recommended by the college. Also, some states have programs that offer better terms than the PLUS loan, so take a few minutes to check out this option with the financial aid officer.

q *I'm struggling with the idea that all students should apply to the college of their choice, regardless of cost, because financial aid will level the playing field. I feel I will be penalized because I have saved for college. My son has been required to save half of his allowance since age six for his college education. Will that count against him when he applies for financial aid? It's difficult to explain to him that his college choices may be limited because of the responsible choices and sacrifices we have made as a family. What can we do to make the most of our situation?*

a In general, it is always better to have planned ahead for college by saving. Families that have put away sufficient funds to pay for college will quickly realize that they have made the burden easier for themselves and their children. In today's college financing world, schools assume that the paying for higher education is a 10-year commitment, similar to a 30-year mortgage on a home, or a 4-year loan for a car. So by saving when your child is young, you reap significant advantages from compound interest on the assets and reduce the need to borrow as much while in school. This should reduce the number of years after college that you will be burdened with student and parent loans. We advise families to spend the student's assets first, since the financial aid formulas count these assets more heavily than parental assets. Then, after the first year, you can explain to the college how you spent these assets, and why you might now need assistance. When looking at parental information, the income of the family is by far the most important component. Contrary to popular belief however, parental assets play a relatively minor role in the calculation of the EFC. With this strategy, you have done the right thing, and in the long run, it should prove to be a wise financial plan.

q *My son was awarded a $2500 scholarship. This can be split and used for two years. When filling out the FAFSA, do we have to claim the full amount, or just the $1250 he plans to use the first year?*

a Congratulations to your son on the scholarship. Nowhere on the FAFSA should you report this scholarship. It is not considered income or an asset. However, once you choose a school to attend, you must notify the financial aid office for their advice on how to take the funds. But remember, do NOT report it on the FAFSA.

q *I will be receiving a scholarship from my local high school. How will this scholarship be treated in my financial aid award?*

a Federal student aid regulations specify that all forms of aid must be included within the defined level of need. This means that additional aid such as outside scholarships must be combined with any need-based aid you receive; it may not be kept separate and used to reduce your family's contribution. If the college has not filled 100 percent of your need, it will usually allow outside scholarships to close the "unmet need" gap. Once your total need has been met, however, the college must reduce other aid and replace it with the outside award. Most colleges will allow you to use some, if not all, of an outside scholarship to replace self-help aid (loans and Federal Work-Study) rather than grant or other scholarship aid.

q *I know we're supposed to apply for financial aid as soon as possible after January 1. What if I don't have my W-2's yet and my tax return isn't done?*

a The first financial aid application deadlines usually fall in early February, and many are later, usually March 1ˢᵗ or 15ᵗʰ. Chances are you'll have your W-2 forms by then, but you won't have a completed tax return. If that is the case, complete the financial aid application using your best estimates. Then, when you receive the Student Aid Report (SAR), you can use your completed tax return to make corrections. One trick is to use your prior year's tax return and make whatever adjustments you think are applicable and then complete the FAFSA with this estimated information.

q *Is there enough aid available to make it worthwhile for me to consider colleges that are more expensive than I can afford?*

a Definitely. More than $65 billion in aid is awarded to undergraduates every year. With more than half of all enrolled students qualifying for some type of assistance, this totals more than $5500 per student. You should view financial aid as a large, national system of tuition discounts, some given according to a student's ability and talent, others based on what a student's family can afford to pay. If you qualify for need-based financial aid, you will essentially pay only your calculated family contribution, regardless of the cost of the college. You will not pay the "sticker price" (the cost of attendance listed in the college catalog) but a lower rate that is reduced by the amount of aid you receive. No college should be ruled out until after financial aid is considered. In addition, when deciding which college to attend, consider that the short-term cost of a college education is only one criterion. If the college meets your educational needs and you are convinced it can launch you on an exciting career, a significant up-front investment may turn out to be a bargain over the long run.

q *If I don't qualify for need-based aid, what options are available?*

a You should try to put together your own aid package to help reduce your parents' share. There are three sources to look into. First is to search for merit scholarships. Second is to seek employment during both the summer and the academic year. The student employment office should be able to help you find a campus job. Third is borrowing. Even if you don't qualify for the need-based loan programs, the unsubsidized Federal Stafford and Direct Loans are available to all students. The terms and conditions are the same as the subsidized loan programs except that interest accrues while you are in college. After you have contributed what you can through scholarships, employment, and loans, your parents will be faced with their share of the college bill. Many colleges have monthly payment plans that allow families to spread their payments over the academic year. If these monthly payments turn out to be more than your parents can afford, they can take out a parent loan. By borrowing from the college itself, from a commercial agency or lender, or through PLUS, parents can extend the college payments over a ten-year period or longer. Borrowing reduces the monthly obligation to its lowest level, but the total amount paid will be the highest due to principal and interest payments. Contact the financial aid officer for the many alternatives that are available.

Families' Guide to Education Tax Cuts

many new tax benefits for adults who want to return to school and for parents who are sending or planning to send their children to college are now available due to the tax changes signed into law in August 1997. These tax cuts effectively make the first two years of college affordable and give many working Americans the financial means to go back to school if they want to choose a new career or upgrade their skills. About 13.1 million students benefit—5.9 million under the HOPE Scholarship tax credit and 7.2 million under the Lifetime Learning tax credit. The following is a guide to these tax incentive programs. For more detailed information, refer to IRS Publication 970, "Tax Benefits for Education."

HOPE SCHOLARSHIP TAX CREDIT FOR STUDENTS STARTING COLLEGE

The HOPE Scholarship program helps make the first two years of college or career school affordable by providing up to $1,500 as a non-refundable tax credit. Students receive a 100 percent tax credit for the first $1000 of tuition and required fees and a 50 percent credit on the second $1000. This credit is available for tuition and required fees less grants, scholarships, and other tax-free educational assistance.

This credit is phased out for joint filers who have between $83,000 and $103,000 of adjusted gross income and for single filers who have between $41,000 and $51,000 of adjusted gross income. These limits are adjusted each year for inflation. The credit can be claimed in two years for students who are in their first two years of college or career school and who are enrolled on at least a half-time basis in a degree or certificate program for any portion of the year. The taxpayer can claim a credit for his or her own tuition expense or for the expenses of his or her spouse or dependent children. Students must be enrolled at least half-time for at least one academic period and pursuing an undergraduate or other recognized educational credential. This credit can be claimed for more than one family member since there is no limit on the amount available to be claimed in any one year.

LIFETIME LEARNING TAX CREDIT

This tax credit is targeted at adults who want to go back to school, change careers, or take a course or two to upgrade their skills and to college juniors and seniors and to graduate and professional degree students. A family will receive a 20 percent tax credit for the first $10,000 of tuition and required fees paid each year for a maximum non-refundable tax credit of $2,000. Just like the HOPE Scholarship tax credit, the Lifetime Learning tax credit is available for tuition and required fees less grants, scholarships, and other tax-free educational assistance. The maximum credit is determined on a per-taxpayer (family) basis, regardless of the number of postsecondary students in the family, and is phased out at the same income levels as the HOPE Scholarship tax credit. Families will be able to claim the Lifetime Learning tax credit for some members of their family and the HOPE Scholarship tax credit for others who qualify in the same year. An eligible taxpayer must file a tax return and owe taxes to claim the credit. The taxpayer must also claim the eligible student as a dependent unless the credit is for the taxpayer or the taxpayer's spouse. Students are not required to pursue a degree or other recognized educational credential and can enroll for as few as one or more courses. The maximum amount that can be claimed in any year is $2,000.

STUDENT LOAN INTEREST DEDUCTION

Those who have paid interest on a student loan in 2003 may be eligible to deduct up to $2,500 of the interest paid on qualified student loans. To qualify, the loan must have been taken out solely to pay qualified educational expenses and cannot be from a related person or made under a qualified employer program. This program phases out for single taxpayers with incomes between $50,000 to $65,000, and joint filers with incomes between $100,000 to $130,000.

TUITION AND FEE DEDUCTION

College students may be able to deduct qualified tuition and related expenses paid during the year for himself or herself, a spouse, or a dependent. The tuition and expenses must be for higher education but cannot include living, personal, family, or related expenses. The tuition and fees deduction can reduce the student's income, subject to taxes, by up to $4,000. This tax deduction is currently scheduled to expire after the 2005 tax year. This program is limited for single taxpayers with incomes up to $65,000, and joint filers with incomes up to $130,000 and generally helps those taxpayers who are often not eligible for the HOPE or Lifetime programs.

INDIVIDUAL RETIREMENT ACCOUNTS/ COVERDALE EDUATION SAVINGS ACCOUNT

Since January 1, 1998, taxpayers have been able to withdraw funds from an IRA, without penalty, for their own higher education expenses or those of their spouse or child or even their grandchild. In addition, for each child under age 18, families may deposit $2,000 per year into an education IRA in the child's name. Earnings in the education IRA will accumulate tax-free and no taxes are due upon withdrawal if the money is used to pay for postsecondary tuition and required fees (less grants, scholarships, and other tax-free educational assistance), books, equipment, and eligible room and board expenses. Once the child reaches age 30, his or her education IRA must be closed or transferred to a younger member of the family.

A taxpayer's ability to contribute to an education IRA is phased out when the taxpayer is a joint filer with an adjusted gross income between $190,000 and $220,000 or a single filer with an adjusted gross income between $95,000 and $110,000.

STATE TUITION PLANS/QUALIFIED TUITION PROGRAMS (QTPS)

Effective January 2002, withdrawals taken for qualified educational expenses from 529 plans are free from federal income tax through 2010 when a family uses a qualified state-sponsored tuition plan to save for college. Families can now use these plans to save not only for tuition but also for certain room and board expenses for students who attend college on at least a half-time basis. Tuition and required fees paid with withdrawals from a qualified state tuition plan are eligible for the HOPE Scholarship tax credit and Lifetime Learning tax credit. These benefits became available on January 1, 1998. These programs and other prepayment programs (529 plans) are currently undergoing significant changes. Many states are taking a careful look at how these programs can be modified to ensure their long-term viability. Check with the state agency that is offering the plan for further information.

GOING TO SCHOOL WHILE YOU WORK

Section 127 of the federal tax code allows workers to exclude up to $5250 of employer-provided education benefits from their income. For courses beginning after January 1, 2002, the payments may be for either undergraduate or graduate-level courses. The payments do not have to be for work-related courses. Expenses include tuition, fees, books, equipment, and supplies. Workers may be able to deduct some of the costs related to education as a business expense. This provision enables many Americans to pursue their goals of lifelong learning.

COMMUNITY SERVICE LOAN FORGIVENESS

This provision excludes from income tax student loan amounts forgiven by nonprofit, tax-exempt charitable or educational institutions for borrowers who take community-service jobs that address unmet community needs. For example, a recent graduate who takes a low-paying job in a rural school will not owe any additional income tax if in recognition of this service her college or another charity forgives a loan it made to her to help pay her college costs. This provision applies to loans forgiven after August 5, 1997.

The AMERICORPS program also offers a number of attractive options to either help finance a college education or pay back federal student loans for students who dedicate a few years to community service. For additional information, call 800-942-2677 or visit their Web site at http://www.americorps.org/.

For information on additional student aid programs that will help meet the costs of college and lifelong learning, call 800-4FED-AID.

EARLY IRA DISTRIBUTIONS

Students can take distributions from their IRAs for qualified educational expenses without having to pay the 10 percent additional tax for an early distribution. They may owe income tax on at least part of the amount distributed, but they may not have to pay the 10 percent additional tax. The part not subject to the additional tax is generally the amount of the distribution that is not more than the adjusted qualified expenses for the year. See IRS Publication 970 for more information.

EDUCATIONAL SAVINGS BOND PROGRAM

Students may be able to cash in qualified U.S. savings bonds without having to include in their income some or all of the interest earned on the bonds. A qualified U.S. savings bond is a series EE bond issued after 1989 or a series I bond. The bond must be issued either in the student's name or in the name of both the student and his or her spouse. The owner must be at least 24 years old before the bond's issue date. The issue date is printed on the front of the savings bond. See IRS Publication 970 for more information.

SUMMARY

There are numerous tax incentive and related programs available to help students who are either planning for college, currently enrolled in higher education, or who have graduated with student loan debt. To get further information, contact the school's financial aid office, the federal government at 800-4FED AID, or an accountant or financial planner. The information presented here is offered as a guide to the many options available but should not be considered as a comprehensive explanation of the specific qualifications of each program. Please check with a qualified tax preparer for current regulations and benefits.

The *Imagine America* Scholarship Program

ach year, every high school in the United States and Puerto Rico can select up to three graduating seniors to each receive a $1,000 *Imagine America* Scholarship to attend any participating private postsecondary institution that is accredited by the U.S. Department of Education.

WHAT INSTITUTIONS HONOR THE SCHOLARSHIPS?

More than 490 career colleges voluntarily participate in this program. Within the **PROFILES OF CAREER COLLEGES** section of this guide, you will notice that some school profiles contain an 🅐 icon. This indicates that the school is a participating institution. In addition, the **INDEXES** list participating institutions in boldface.

HOW DO I APPLY?

Go online to www.petersons.com/cca/apply.asp and follow the instructions listed there. If your school does not have Internet access, you may request a paper application by writing to:

Career College Foundation
Imagine America Scholarships
10 G Street NE, Suite 750
Washington, DC 20002

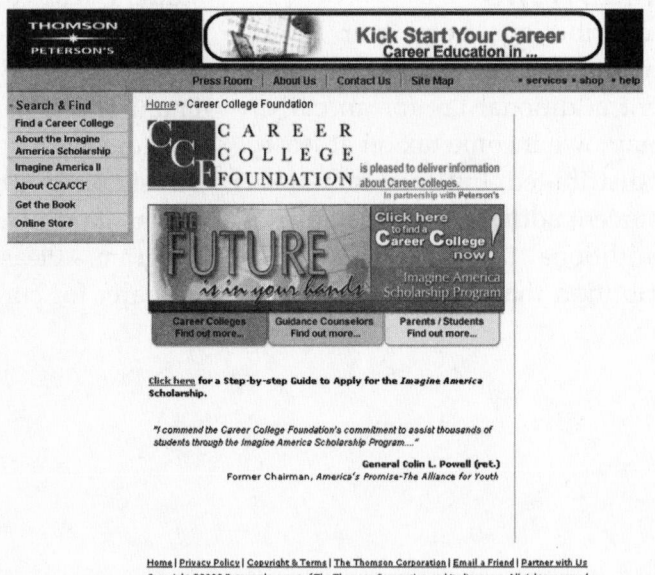

How to Use This Guide

eterson's *Guide to Career Colleges* profiles more than 1,000 private postsecondary schools, colleges, and universities that provide career-specific educational programs. They offer a wide variety of postsecondary education options from short-term certificate and diploma programs to two- and four-year associate and baccalaureate degrees to master's and doctoral programs in the U.S. The programs included are defined as instructional and are designed to prepare individuals with the entry-level skills and training required for employment in a specific trade, occupation, or profession. The institutions profiled in this book are all licensed by the state in which they are located and accredited by at least one of the national or regional accrediting agencies recognized by the U.S. Department of Education and are all members of the Career College Association.

WHAT'S INSIDE

Useful Articles The first section of this book contains articles covering topics such as accreditation, information for adults going back to school, financing your education, and federal tax breaks for education.

State Association Directory This directory includes a listing of state associations related to career education. Highlighted are the associations that offer scholarships to students wishing to pursue a career education.

Financial Advisory Council Here are members from the financial and investment communities who have an interest in the for-profit career sector of higher education.

Profiles of Allied Members This listing provides information about organizations that directly serve the career college market. These include financial aid institutions, recruiters, career consultants, and other related organizations.

Profiles of Career Colleges The meat of this book, this section provides the main features of the institutions listed in this directory. A sample profile appears in the box on this page.

Imagine America (IA) This icon represents career schools that offer the *Imagine America* Scholarship Program.

Enrollment Figures In most cases, career colleges report their enrollment by campus. However, in some instances, schools with many campuses may have chosen to report enrollment on an institution-wide basis.

In-Depth Descriptions Additional details on career college offerings are provided by participating institutions. Each one-page entry provides details about the institution, special features, financial aid and scholarship programs available, admissions and graduation requirements, tuition, and any degrees and certificates offered.

Indexes Six indexes are offered in this book. The first two provide a quick alphabetical- and geo-

---

Peterson's (IA)

2000 Lenox Drive
Lawrenceville, NJ 08648
Web: http://www.petersons.com

Accreditation: Accrediting Bureau of Health Education Schools

Programs Offered: dental assistant; medical administrative assistant/secretary; medical assistant; medical laboratory technician; pharmacy technician/assistant; respiratory therapy technician

Enrollment: 235 Students

Institution Contact: Campus Director
Phone: 609-896-1800 *Fax:* 609-896-4545
E-mail: campus.director@petersons.com

Admission Contact: Director of Recruitment
Phone: 609-896-1800 *Fax:* 609-896-4545
E-mail: director.recruitment@petersons.com

graphical-by-institution glance at who's in this book and on what page. If you know a specific school name or are looking to attend school in a particular state, these two indexes are a good place to start your search. The next index, "Alphabetical Listing of Programs," is organized by profession/career objectives, allowing you to search by a given discipline to see which career schools offer programs in your field of interest. The "Alphabetical Listing of Allied Members" and "Alphabetical Listing of *Imagine America* Scholarship Program Participants" follow. Finally, the last index lists those schools with military recruiting programs.

In all indexes, you will notice that some career schools appear in boldface while others do not. The boldface type indicates that the school is a participating institution in the *Imagine America* Scholarship Program.

DATA COLLECTION PROCEDURES

The data contained in the college indexes and college profiles were researched during the fall of 2004. Online surveys were made available to over 1,000 career college member institutions. With minor exceptions, data included in this edition have been submitted by officials (usually admissions officers or headquarters personnel) at the career colleges themselves. All usable information received in time for publication has been included. The omission of any particular item from **PROFILES** or **INDEXES** signifies that the information is either not applicable to that institution, not available, or not provided by the school. Because of Peterson's comprehensive editorial review and because all material comes directly from school officials, Peterson's believes that the information presented in this guide is accurate. Nonetheless, errors and omissions are possible in a data collection and processing endeavor of this scope. You should check with a specific career college at the time of application to verify pertinent data, which may have changed since publication.

State Association Directory

State Association Directory

The following are state associations related to career education. Those associations offering scholarships are indicated with a dollar sign ($).

Alabama
Alabama Association of Private Colleges and
    Schools
5355 Vaughn Road
Montgomery, Alabama 36116
Phone: 334-395-8800
Fax: 334-395-8859
Contact Person: Victor Biebighauser

Alaska
Alaska Association of Private Career Educators
1415 East Tudor Road
Anchorage, Alaska 99507-1033
Phone: 907-563-7575
Fax: 907-563-8330
Contact Person: Jennifer Deitz
E-mail: jdeitz@careeracademy.net

$Arizona
Arizona Private School Association
202 East. McDowell Road, Suite 273
Phoenix, Arizona 85004
Phone: 602-254-5199
Fax: 602-254-5073
Web: http://www.arizonapsa.org
Contact Person: Frederick Lockhart
E-mail: apsa@syspac.com

$California
California Association of Private Postsecondary
    Schools
921 11th Street, Suite 619
Sacramento, California 95814-2821
Phone: 916-447-5500
Fax: 916-440-8970
Web: http://www.cappsonline.org
Contact Person: Robert Johnson, Executive
    Director
E-mail: Robert@cappsonline.org

Contact Person: Jamie Strong, Assistant to the
    Executive Director
E-mail: Jamie@cappsoline.org

Colorado
Colorado Private School Association
1301 Pennsylvania Street, Suite 900
Denver, Colorado 80203
Phone: 303-866-8366
Fax: 303-860-0175
Contact Person: Steven J. Durham

Connecticut
Association of Connecticut Career Schools
342 North Main Street
W. Hartford, Connecticut 06117-2507
Phone: 860-586-7501
Fax: 860-586-7550
Contact Person: Tessa O'Sullivan
E-mail: Patrickfox@aol.com

$Florida
Florida Association of Postsecondary Schools
    and Colleges
150 South Monroe Street, Suite 303
Tallahassee, Florida 32301
Phone: 850-577-3139
Fax: 850-577-3133
Web: http://www.fapsc.org
Contact Person: Cecil Kidd
E-mail: mail@FAPSC.org

Illinois
Illinois Career College Association
1235 West Fullerton Avenue
Chicago, Illinois 60614-2102
Phone: 773-935-2522 Ext. 242
Fax: 773-935-2920
Contact Person: Russell Freeman

Indiana
Indiana Association of Private Career Schools
7302 Woodland Drive
Indianapolis, Indiana 46278-1736
Phone: 317-299-6001
Fax: 317-298-6342
Contact Person: Richard Weiss

Kentucky
Kentucky Association of Career Colleges and
   Schools
350 Village Drive
Frankfort, Kentucky 40601-8661
Phone: 502-848-0311
Fax: 502-848-0311
Contact Person: Betsie Taylor

Louisiana
Louisiana Career College Association
13944 Airline Highway
Baton Rouge, Louisiana 70817
Phone: 225-752-4233
Fax: 225-756-0903
Contact Person: Mark Worthy

$Maryland
Maryland Association of Private Colleges and
   Career Schools
3100 Dunglow Road
Baltimore, Maryland 21222
Phone: 410-282-4012
Contact Person: Diane MacDougall
E-mail: mdapcs@yahoo.com

Massachusetts
Massachusetts Association of Private Career
   Schools
P.O. Box 407
North Reading, Massachusetts 01864
Phone: 978-664-5146
Fax: 978-664-5154
Web: http://www.mapcs.org
Contact Person: Donna Carriker
E-mail: admin@mapcs.org

Michigan
Michigan Association of Career Schools
P.O. Box 292
Clarkston, Michigan 48347
Phone: 248-399-0220
Fax: 248-625-4864
Web: http://www.careerschoolsmi.com
Contact Person: Howard Weaver

$Minnesota
Minnesota Career College Association
c/o Globe College
7166 10th Street North
Oakdale, Minnesota 55128-5939
Phone: 651-730-5100
Fax: 651-730-5151

Web: http://www.mncareercolleges.org
Contact Person: Mike Hughes

Missouri
Missouri Association of Private Career Schools
c/o Metro Business College
10777 Sunset Office Drive, Suite 330
Saint Louis, Missouri 63127-1019
Phone: 314-966-3000
Fax: 314-966-3414
Contact Person: George Holske

Nebraska
Nebraska Council of Private Postsecondary
   Career Schools
636 Circle Drive
Seward, Nebraska 68434-1031
Phone: 402-643-2639
Fax: 402-643-6512
Contact Person: Ralph Hansen

$New Jersey
Private Career School Association of New Jersey
P.O. Box 11795
New Brunswick, New Jersey 08906
Web: http://www.pcsanj.com
Contact Person: Edith K. Giniger
Phone: 732-545-1399
Fax: 732-545-1527
Contact Person: L. Terry Nighan
Phone: 732-885-1580
Fax: 732-885-0424

New York
Association of Proprietary Colleges
1259 Central Avenue
Albany, New York 12205
Phone: 518-437-1867
Fax: 518-437-1048
Web: http://www.apc-colleges.org
Contact Person: Ellen Hollander
E-mail: LNHOL@aol.com

The Coalition of New York State Career Schools
437 Old Albany Post Road
Garrison, New York 10524
Phone: 845-788-5070
Fax: 845-788-5071
Web: http://www.
   coalitionofnewyorkstatecareerschools.com
Contact Person: Terence M. Zaleski
E-mail: tzaleski@sprynet.com

$Ohio

Ohio Association of Career Colleges and Schools
1857 Northwest Boulevard û Annex
Columbus, Ohio 43212
Phone: 614-487-8180
Fax: 614-487-8190
Web: http://www.ocpcs.org
Contact Person: Max J. Lerner

Oklahoma

Oklahoma Private School Association
2620 South Service Road
Moore, Oklahoma 73160
Phone: 405-329-5627
Fax: 405-321-2763
Contact Person: Thorpe A. Mayes
E-mail: tmawes@citycollegeinc.com

Oregon

Oregon Career College Association
10426 180th Court, NE
Redmond, Washington 98052
Phone: 425-376-0369
Fax: 425-881-1580
Contact Person: Gena Wikstrom

Pennsylvania

Pennsylvania Association of Private School
   Administrators
2090 Wexford Court
Harrisburg, Pennsylvania 17112
Phone: 717-540-9010
Fax: 717-540-7121
Web: http://www.papsa.org
Contact Person: Richard Dumaresq
E-mail: CCDQ@aol.com

Tennessee

Tennessee Association of Independent Colleges
   and Schools
3880 Priest Lake Drive, #78
Nashville, Tennessee 37217-4639
Phone: 615-399-3763
Fax: 615-366-9590
Web: http://www.taics.org
Contact Person: Sandy Robert
E-mail: taics@comcast.net

$Texas

Career Colleges and Schools of Texas
P.O. Box 11539
Austin, Texas 78711-1539
Phone: 866-909-2278
Web: http://www.colleges-schools.org
Contact Person: Jerry Valdez/ Linda Pavlik
E-mail: info@colleges-schools.org

$Virginia

Virginia Career College Association
108 East Main Street, Suite 904
Richmond, Virginia 23219
Pone: 804-346-2783
Fax: 804-346-8287
Web: http://www.va-cca.org
Contact Person: Mark Singer
E-mail: marksinger@va-cca.org

Washington

Washington Federation of Private Career Schools
   and Colleges
10426 180th Court NE
Redmond, Washington 98052
Phone: 425-376-0369
Fax: 425-881-1580
Web: http://www.washingtonschools.org
Contact Person: Gena Wikstrom
E-mail: exec@washingtonschools.org

West Virginia

West Virginia Association of Independent
   Colleges and Schools
144 Willey Street
Morgantown, West Virginia 26505
Phone: 304-296-8284
Fax: 304-296-5612
Contact Person: Michael K. Callen

Wisconsin

Wisconsin Council for Independent Education
5218 East Terrace Drive
Madison, Wisconsin 53718
Phone: 608-249-6611
Fax: 608-249-8593
Contact Person: Don Madelung

financial
Advisory Council

Financial Advisory Council

The Financial Advisory Council is comprised of members from the financial and investment communities who have a substantial interest in the for-profit career sector of higher education. Omer Waddles, President and Chief Operating Officer of ITT-Educational Services Inc., serves as chairman.

Omer Waddles
FAC Chairman
ITT Educational Services, Inc.
13000 North Meridian Street
Carmel, Indiana 46032-1404
Phone: 317-706-9200
E-mail: owaddles@ittesi.com

Gary Bisbee
Lehman Brothers
745 7th Avenue, 17th Floor
New York, New York 10019
Phone: 212-526-3047
Fax: 646-758-4720
E-mail: gbisbee@lehman.com

James Burke, Jr.
Stonington Partners, Inc.
767 Fifth Avenue
New York, New York 10153
Phone: 212-339-8502
Fax: 212-339-8585
E-mail: jburke@stonington.com

Gregory Cappelli
Credit Suisse First Boston
AT&T Corporate Center
227 W Monroe Street, 41st Floor
Chicago, Illinois 60606-5016
Phone: 312-750-3138
Fax: 312-750-1833
E-mail: eric.sledgister@csfb.com

Richard C. Close
Jeffries & Co
2525 West End Avenue, Suite 1150
Nashville, Tennessee 37203
Phone: 615-963-8335
Fax: 615-963-8399
E-mail: rclose@jefco.com

John Cozzi
Arena Capital Partners, LLC
540 Madison Avenue, Floor 25
New York, New York 10022-3242
Phone: 212-735-8520
Fax: 212-735-8585
E-mail: jcozzi@arenafund.com

Ryan Craig
Warburg Pincus
466 Lexington Avenue, 10th Floor
New York, New York 10017
Phone: 212-878-0633
Fax: 212-716-5142
E-mail: rcraig@warburgpincus.com

Kelly Flynn
UBS Warburg
1285 Ave. of the Americas
New York, New York 10019
Phone: 212-713-1037
Fax: 212-969-7740
E-mail: kelly.flynn@ubsw.com

Mark Hughes
Equity Research
SunTrust Robinson Humphrey
800 Nashville City Center
Nashville, Tennessee 37219-1743
Phone: 615-780-9334
Fax: 615-780-9400
E-mail: mark_hughes@rhco.com

Louis Kenter
Prospect Partners
200 W. Madison, Suite 2710
Chicago, Illinois 60606
Phone: 312-782-7400
Fax: 312-782-7410
E-mail: lkenter@prospect-partners.com

Celeste Lee-Bobroff
Lombard Investments, Inc.
600 Montgomery Street, Floor 36
San Francisco, California 9411
Phone: 415-397-5900
Fax: 415-397-5820
E-mail: cleebobroff@lombardinvestments.com

Mark Marostica
U.S. Bancorp Piper Jaffray
800 Nicollet Mall, Suite 800
Minneapolis, Minnesota 55402
Phone: 612-303-5572
Fax: 612-303-6360
E-mail: mmarostica@pjc.com

Gerald Odening
GRO Capital
151 Library Place
Princeton, New Jersey 8540
Phone: 609-921-3758
Fax: 609-021-0797
E-mail: godening@jefco.com or
   grocapital@mail.com

Alexander Paris
Barrington Research
161 N. Clark Street, Suite 2950
Chicago, Illinois 60601
Phone: 312-634-6352
Fax: 312-634-6350
E-mail: aparis@brai.com

James Rowan
Legg Mason Wood Walker, Inc.
100 Light Street, 34th Floor
Baltimore, Maryland 21202
Phone: 410-454-5102
Fax: 410-454-4508
E-mail: jarowan@leggmason.com

Tim Schenk
Blue Ridge Capital
122 A East Main Street
Charlottesville, Virginia 22902
Phone: 434-923-8901
Fax: 434-923-8903
E-mail: tim@blueridgelp.com

John Smart
Harris Nesbitt
111 W. Monroe Street, 20th Floor East
Chicago, Illinois 60603
Phone: 312-461-6022
Fax: 312- 293-4278
E-mail: john.smart@harrisbank.com

Lara Vaughan Gordon
Parchman, Vaughan & Compnay
717 Light Street, Suite 200
Baltimore, Maryland 21230-3851
Phone: 410-244-8971
Fax: 410-244-0877
E-mail: lara@parchmanvaughan.com

Gregory Wilson
CIVC Partners, LLC
231 South LaSalle Street, 7th Floor
Chicago, Illinois 60697
Phone: 312-828-5322
Fax: 312-987-0887
E-mail: gregory.w.wilson@bankofamerica.com

Profiles of Allied Members

Abacus Mergers & Acquisitions

11404 Harbor Boulevard
Suite 101
Frisco, Texas 75035
Phone: 972-731-7890
Fax: 972-692-8887
Contact: Mr. Philip Balis
Service: Consulting
Special Message: Abacus Mergers & Acquisitions specializes in school sales, mergers, and acquisitions. Its services include valuing schools, preparing marketing packages, finding prospective buyers or sellers, advising owners who are contemplating selling, assisting with negotiations, locating acquisition financing, and assisting with issues arising with due diligence, the definitive agreement, and closing. Abacus works with its clients from start to finish. Additional information is available at the Web site (http://www.abacusma.com/).

Abramson Pendergast & Company

3000 Northup Way, Suite 200
Bellevue, Washington 98004
Phone: 425-828-9420
Fax: 425-827-6884
E-mail: sfelts@apccpa.com
Contact: Mr. Beull Felts, Principal
Service: Certified Public Accountants
Special Message: Abramson Pendergast & Company is a full-service audit, tax, and consulting firm with a diverse clientele of career schools. With more than ten years of experience performing school audits and SFA attestations, Abramson Pendergast & Company emphasizes development and maintenance of a strong system of internal controls as a school's best defense against compliance lapses. For more information, visit the Web site (http://www.apccpa.com).

ACT, Inc.

2201 North Dodge Street
Iowa City, Iowa 52243-0001
Phone: 319-337-1660
Fax: 319-337-1790
E-mail: endel@act.org
Contact: Dr. Barbara Endel, Consultant
Service: Testing Tools/Equipment
Special Message: The Career Programs Assessment Test (CPAT) from ACT (a nonprofit testing organization) is a complete basic skills assessment for career colleges to use as an admissions and advising tool. CPAT was developed specifically to meet the needs of career colleges.

ADx, Inc.

23172 Plaza Pointe Drive, Suite 135
Laguna Hills, California 92653
Phone: 949-581-5377 Ext. 212
E-mail: JudyM@adxinc.net
Contact: Judith Munoz, Vice President, Marketing
Service: Advertising/Marketing/Recruitment
Special Message: ADx is an advertising agency specializing in print materials designed to boost enrollment, enhance recruitment and create dynamic product marketing programs for educational schools and corporations. Their services include ad campaigns, brochures, billboards, stand-alone pieces, public relations, media placement, and other related capabilities. More information about ADx can be found on the Web at http://www.adxinc.net.

Affiliated Computer Services

One World Trade Center, Suite 2200
Long Beach, California 90831
Phone: 315-738-2237
Fax: 315-824-1257
E-mail: heather.ficarra@acs-inc.com
Contact: Ms. Heather Ficarra, Vice President
Service: Student Financial Aid/Financial Aid/ Administrative Services/Consulting/IT Solutions
Special Message: Affiliated Computer Services (ACS) provides career colleges with enrollment optimization and financial aid performance improvements by improving the number of award packages, financial aid cash flow, student service, and processing cycle time. ACS's compliance experts and Title IV knowledge reduce risk and improves scalability. ACS processed financial aid for more than 200,000 students and disbursed $1.3 billion in financial aid in 2003. During a three-month pilot for one client, ACS increased enrollment by 411 students, resulting in $2.7 million in financial aid and an 80 percent improvement in processing-cycle time. ACS also provides information technology outsourcing, imaging, student call centers, loan servicing, finance and accounting, and other services to serve 1,047 colleges.

AlaQuest International, Inc.

28 Molasses Hill Road
Lebanon, New Jersey 08833-3206
Phone: 908-713-9399
Fax: 908-713-9288
E-mail: sales@alaquest.com
Contact: Ms. Marsha Magazzu, President

---

* indicates that the member is an Allied Plus Member.

Service: Software/Administrative Services

Special Message: AlaQuest International is solely dedicated to the research, development, sales, and support of administrative software products for the postsecondary educational marketplace. AlaQuest has products for admissions, scheduling, grades, attendance, student accounts, financial aid, placement, housing, alumni, book sales, and more. Additional information is available at http://www.alaquest.com.

Almich & Associates

19000 MacArthur Boulevard, Suite 610
Irvine, California 92612
Phone: 949-495-5410
Fax: 949-475-5412
E-mail: leighann@almichcpa.com

Contact: Mr. Robin Almich, Managing Partner

Service: Certified Public Accountants/Consulting/ Financial Aid

Special Message: Almich & Associates is a certified public accounting and business services firm that specializes in the education, healthcare, and not-for-profit industries. It offers a variety of valuable accounting and business solutions and has been nationally acknowledged as one of the foremost experts providing professional services in this highly regulated market. Some of its services include financial statement analysis and financial statement audits; Title IV planning and audits; income tax planning and preparation services; and acquisition, divestiture and change of ownership planning and implementation. Additional information is available at the Web site (http://www.almichcpa.com).

AMDG

2859 Paces Ferry Road
Overlook III, Suite 120
Atlanta, Georgia 30339
Phone: 770-431-5115
Fax: 770-234-5299
E-mail: gregmorse@amdg.ws

Contact: Mr. Gregory M. Morse, Chairman

Service: Placement/Training Providers/Recruitment/ Miscellaneous/Education Management/e-Learning Providers/Distance Education/Education Training

Special Message: AMDG is one of the nation's most comprehensive education institutions providing student-centered Internet and site-based education programs to learners of all ages. These programs include integrated solutions for accredited online curriculum, high school diplomas, certified training, recruiting, screening, and job placement services for government and Fortune 500 organizations. AMDG graduates are better qualified, better trained, more motivated, and enjoy a consistent job placement rate of 98 percent. Additional information is available at http://www.amdg.ws.

American Medical Technologists

710 Higgins Road
Park Ridge, Illinois 60068-5737
Phone: 847-823-5169
Fax: 847-823-0458
E-mail: mail@amt1.com

Contact: Christopher A Damon, J.D., Executive Director

Service: Certification

Special Message: Established in 1939, American Medical Technologists (AMT) has become one of the nation's largest and most established certification agencies for clinical laboratory practitioners and other allied health professionals. AMT provides certification for medical technologists, medical laboratory technicians, office laboratory technicians, laboratory consultants, phlebotomy technicians, medical and dental assistants, and allied health instructors.

Ball & McGraw, P.C.

351 West Hatcher
Phoenix, Arizona 85021
Phone: 602-942-3435
Fax: 602-942-8555
E-mail: ballmcgraw@worldnet.att.net

Contact: Mr. Douglas Ball, Director

Service: Certified Public Accountants

Special Message: Ball & McGraw, P.C., are certified public accountants that provide financial statement audits, Title IV compliance audits, composite score calculation and analysis, change of ownership audits and consulting, file reviews, and internal auditing.

Becker Media

374 17th Street
Oakland, California 94612
Phone: 415-621-1070
Fax: 510-465-6056
E-mail: rogerbecker@earthlink.net

Contact: Mr. Roger Becker, President

Service: Marketing

Special Message: Becker Media creates full-service advertising campaigns for schools including TV, radio, print, and the Web. Becker Media specializes in strategic media selection, strategic planning, and creativity that generates results.

* indicates that the member is an Allied Plus Member.

Best Associates

2200 Ross Avenue, Suite 3800
Dallas, Texas 75201
Phone: 214-438-4100
Fax: 214-438-4133
E-mail: leisenbraun@bestassociates.com

Contact: Lezlie Eisenbraun

Service: Investment Banking

Special Message: Best Associates has a strong commitment to the education industry and a track record of exceptional results. The for-profit education sector is expected to continue to grow rapidly over the next decade. Best Associates is investing in both the K-12 and postsecondary markets here and abroad. The firm acquires companies with proven leadership and a global vision, and founds companies in the sector. Additional information is available at http://www.bestassociates.com.

The Boston Educational Network

399 US Highway 4
Barrington, New Hampshire 03825
Phone: 603–868–8184
Fax: 603–868–3906
E-mail: pzocchi@boston-ed.com

Contact: Mr. Paul Zocchi, President

Service: Consulting/Software/Financial Aid/Administrative Services

Special Message: The Boston Educational Network is a career-school consulting/processing firm that assists schools in the pursuit of educational excellence. Initially specializing in managing and processing federal student aid, Boston Educational Network has diversified its team to all aspects of school consulting and administrative software. Additional information is available at http://www.boston-ed.com.

Boston Search Group, Inc.

224 Clarendon Street
Boston, Massachusetts 02116
Phone: 617-266-4633
Fax: 781-735-0562
E-mail: rprotsik@bostonsearchgroup.com

Contact: Mr. Ralph Protsik, Managing Director

Service: Consulting/Management Search

Special Message: Boston Search Group (BSG), Inc. is a national leader in retained executive search within the career education and eLearning domains. The company specializes in providing leaders for both public and private companies, and it does so with a keen appreciation for the unique requirements of each type of organization. Since 1994 its principals have been engaged to fill more than 100 senior-management positions at the VP level and above. Additional information is available at the Web site (http://www.bostonsearchgroup.com).

Business Solutions Group

John Wiley & Sons, Inc.
111 River Street
Hoboken, New Jersey 07030
Phone: 201-748-5802
Fax: 201-748-6118
E-mail: jpowers@wiley.com

Contact: Ms. Jennifer Powers, Market Solutions Manager, Business Solutions Group

Service: Education Training/Financial Aid/Consulting

Special Message: As part of John Wiley & Sons, Inc., the Business Solutions Group creates customized educational solutions for the specialized needs of Wiley's for-profit clients.

The company provides university-wide revenue-enhancement consulting services to assist its clients in achieving their organizational goals of recruitment, retainment, and revenue with private-labeled print editions. Wiley provides curricula and content development services, sales of regular titles through a low-returns discount structure, e-learng solutions, and customized textbooks utilizing all of Wiley's rich resources of print and electronic content.

Established in 1807, Wiley is a global publisher of print and electronic products, specializing in scientific, technical, and medical books and journals; professional and consumer books and subscription services; and textbooks and other educational materials for undergraduate and graduate students as well as lifelong learners. Wiley has approximately 22,700 active titles and about 400 journals, and it publishes about 2,000 new titles in a variety of print and electronic formats each year.

Campus Management Corporation*

777 Yamato Road, Suite 400
Boca Raton, Florida 33431
Phone: 561-999-9904
Fax: 561-923-2750
E-mail: chuckt@campusmgmt.com

Contact: Chuck Thompson

Service: Software

Special Message: Campus Management Corporation is a leading provider of software and systems technology to the postsecondary education community. More than 900 colleges across the nation have

---

* indicates that the member is an Allied Plus Member.

chosen Campus Management's fully integrated administrative software systems to manage their daily operations.

CCAssure*

MIMS International
901 Dulaney Valley Road, Suite 610
Towson, Maryland 21204
Phone: 800-899-1399 (toll-free)
Fax: 410-296-1741
E-mail: jsgoff@mimsintl.com
Contact: Jon Stone Goff
Service: Insurance
Special Message: CCAssure–Career College Insurance allows clients to put their insurance program to the test. Coverages include complete liability, property, automobile, and crime as well as fiduciary. MIMS International, the program's administrator, has also developed a surety program to meet clients' needs. Visit http://www.ccassure.com for more information.

Chase Education First

5100 West Lemon Street
Suite 150
Tampa, Florida 33609
Phone: 813–281–3320
Fax: 813–281–3366
E-mail: mmyers@edfirst.com
Contact: Mrs. Michelle Myers, Executive Director of Market Services
Service: Financial Aid
Special Message: Chase is a leading national lender in the Federal Family Education Loan Program. In addition to Federal Stafford and PLUS Loans, Chase offers a variety of alternative loans that can be used to cover up to the full cost of education. Chase borrowers benefit from flexible repayment options, money-saving repayment benefits for on-time payments, combined billing of loans, and online and toll-free access to account information. When clients choose Chase as a lender, they and the families they serve can count on outstanding service and benefits. For a Chase application, clients should contact 800–242–7339 or visit http://www.ChaseStudentLoans.com.

Cisco Systems, Inc. Networking Academy Program

42984 Chesterton Street
Ashburn, Virginia 20147
Phone: 703-724-1619
E-mail: eloos@cisco.com
Contact: Mrs. Ellen Loos, National Manager, Cisco Networking Academy Program for Accredited Career Colleges
Service: Educational Training
Special Message: Launched in 1997, the Cisco Networking Academy Program offers a comprehensive that trains students and in-transition workers to design, build, secure, and maintain networks. The courses prepare students for industry-standard certifications including CCNA, CompTIA A+, CompTIA Network+, CCNP, Cisco Firewall Specialist, CompTIA Security+, and Cisco Wireless LAN Support Specialist. Additional information is available at the Web site (http://cisco.netacad.net/public/index.html).

Clairvest Group, Inc.

22 St. Clair Avenue East
Toronto, Ontario M4T 253
Phone: 416-925-9270
Fax: 416-925-5753
E-mail: dennisd@clairvest.com
Contact: Mr. Dennis Dussin, Associate
Service: Consulting
Special Message: Clairvest is a private equity firm that forms investment partnerships with entrepreneurial corporations in a variety of industries. It traditionally invests $10 to $20 million in its partners' businesses, and prefers to take a minority shareholder position. Clairvest seeks to be a value-added investor supporting a management team in the education industry that is aggressively growing a business, either organically or through acquisition. Additional information is available at the Web site (http://www.clairvest.com).

The CollegeBound Network

1200 South Avenue, Suite 202
Staten Island, New York 10314
Phone: 718-761-4800, Ext 17
Fax: 718-761-3300
E-mail: mlupia@collegebound.net
Contact: Mr. Mario Lupia, Director of Online Marketing
Service: Advertising/Marketing
Special Message: The CollegeBound Network's CollegeSurfing division specializes in marketing retention and lead generation solutions for the career education industry. Services include e-marketing, direct marketing, event marketing, and print media solutions to help clients build their brand and reach America's leading candidates looking to further their professional growth with a degree in career education.

* indicates that the member is an Allied Plus Member.

CollegeSurfing's expertise lies in today's most desirable markets, including culinary, health care, technology, art/fashion design, and business. The seasoned staff of industry professionals strives to develop long standing partnerships with their clients in an effort to understand their businesses and work with them to develop the most profitable programs to meet their growth-solution needs. Additional information is available at http://www.collegesurfing.com/ce/search and http://www.collegebound.net.

College Executives

5155 Martinique Drive
Lakeland, Florida 33813
Phone: 863–646–6471
Fax: 868–533–3475
E-mail: fmorris@collegeexecutives.com
Contact: Mr. Frances J. Morris, Ph.D.
Service: Consulting
Special Message: College Executives provides executive recruitment services that are targeted specifically to the needs of colleges and schools within the for-profit sector of higher education. College Executives provides the highest-quality candidates for corporate positions as well as midman-agement positions at the campus level. Additional information is available on the Web at http://www.collegeexecutives.com.

CONTACT Direct Marketing

2091 East Murray-Holladay Road, Suite 21
Salt Lake City, Utah 84117
Phone: 866-USE-CONTACT (873-2668)
Fax: 801-942-9282
E-mail: contact@contactdm.com
Contact: Eric Schanz, President
Service: Advertising/Marketing
Special Message: CONTACT Direct Marketing is a full-service direct-marketing company. CONTACT Direct Marketing offers innovative direct mail packages and publication advertising, quality production at a lower cost, cutting-edge Internet and telecommunication services, targeted mailing lists that get results, thorough market analysis, and effective admissions training. Customers can count on CONTACT Direct Marketing for expeditious turnaround and superior customer service. For more information, customers should visit www.contactdm.com.

* indicates that the member is an Allied Plus Member.

Corporate Educational Resources, Inc.

4255 Gulf Shore Boulevard, Suite 702
Naples, Florida 34103
Phone: 239-263-1200
     888-861-9001 (toll-free)
E-mail: john@corp-ed.com

Contact: John Huston, President

Service: Admissions/Recruitment/Student Retention/
Information Technology Solutions/Consulting/
Miscellaneous

Special Message: Corporate Educational Resources
(CER), Inc., provides colleges with services to improve processes and efficiencies in their admissions,
operations, and academic departments. Prospect
Manager (PMx) software improves management of
leads, conversion rates, and electronic target-market-
ing follow-up of leads. Document Retrieval System
(DRS) improves management of student information
files and brings efficiencies to all departments. DRS
produces efficiency in document storage, time of
development, and retrieval time and reduces chances
of lost documents. Classroom Performance System
(CPS) stimulates class discussion with subjective and
objective questions using CPS's ad hoc or formal
question-authoring capabilities. Research gives
evidence of students' learning process, cognitive
engagement, and an improved desire to attend class.
CPS software gives access to easy test development,
electronic grading, and Gradebook, leaving the
faculty time for other important responsibilities.

Corvus, LLC dba GradMax

53 East North Street
York, Pennsylvania 17401
Phone: 717–845–5600
Fax: 717–845–5620
E-mail: lorenkroh@corvusllc.com

Contact: Mr. Loren H. Kroh, President

Service: Retention

Special Message: GradMax is a Web-based software
application designed to measure student stress and
offer early intervention for at-risk students, thereby
increasing retention. Additional information is
available at the Web site (http://www.corvusllc.com).

Craft & Associates

801 North Elmwood Avenue
Sioux Falls, South Dakota 57104-1942
Phone: 605-334-9558
Fax: 605-334-9693

Contact: Mr. Terry Craft, President

Service: Advertising/Marketing

Special Message: Craft & Associates specializes in
marketing and advertising for career schools and
colleges.

CUnet

445 West Main Street
Wyckoff, New Jersey 07481
Phone: 201–560–1230
Fax: 201–560–1677
E-mail: Tom@CUnetCorp.com

Contact: Mr. Tom Ferrara, CEO

Service: Admissions/Advertising/Consulting/
Employee Assessment/Marketing/Miscellaneous/
Software

Special Message: CUnet, an established industry
leader and innovator, currently provides more than
230 schools—online and on campus—with performance-based advertising and lead generation, acting
either as a high-quality lead provider or as a firm's
Agency of Record. In addition, industry-leading
assessments (motivational and career-based) and
professional services help education clients improve
their lead to enrollment conversion rates as well as
schoolwide/systemwide student-retention rates. Each
month, approximately 1,000,000 users browse CUnet's
client schools listed on their flagship education portal,
http://www.CollegeandUniversity.net. Its unique
position as traditional media's largest and most
geographically diverse network of interactive education directories is driven via its positioning as the
education "Sections/Directories" for more than 170
geographically targeted major media portals, such as
newspapers, network TV stations, and industry
portals, along with their large network of independent education directories, career portals and partners. CUnet can provide schools with access to highly
specific, relevant, and targeted education leads and
marketing services.

Datamark*

2305 Presidents Drive
Salt Lake City, Utah 84120
Phone: 801-886-1001
Fax: 801-886-0102
E-mail: info@datamark-inc.com

Contact: Mr. Arthur Benjamin, Chairman and CEO

Service: Advertising/Marketing/Media/Recruiting/
Retention/Admissions

Special Message: Datamark is the nation's leading
strategic marketing company exclusively for colleges
and proprietary schools. It offers comprehensive
recruiting, enrollment, retention, and business-growth

---

* indicates that the member is an Allied Plus Member.

solutions that include direct mail, e-marketing, media placement, custom research, admissions training, and student retention.

For more than sixteen years, Datamark's marketing experts have produced unparalleled results through Datamark's hallmark research- and technology-based strategies.

David S. Shefrin and Associates, LLC

7950 East Redfield Road, Suite 120
Scottsdale, Arizona 85260-6913
Phone: 480-556-0631
Fax: 480-556-0638
E-mail: mail@dshefrin.com
Contact: Mr. David Shefrin
Service: Consulting/Recruitment
Special Message: David S. Shefrin and Associates is a private career school consulting group that provides executive search services as well as merger and acquisition services to both buyer and seller, primarily to the career college sector. David Shefrin has more than twenty-five years of industry experience; previously he owned one of the largest computer training school operations in the Northeast. Offices on both West and East coasts allow David S. Shefrin and Associates to effectively handle their clients' needs. A list of the company's most-recently sold schools and their buyers, as well as a list of the most recent placements, are available at the Web site (http://www.careerschoolconsulting.com).

Deborah John & Associates, Inc.

108 West Main Street
Mulvane, Kansas 67110-1763
Phone: 800-242-0977 (toll-free)
Fax: 316-777-1703
E-mail: djainfo@gotodja.com
Contact: Mr. Alan John, CEO
Service: Financial Aid
Special Message: Deborah John & Associates (DJA) offers comprehensive financial aid servicing and consulting to Title IV institutions across the U.S. Electronic Financial Aid Servicing provides institutions with a streamlined approach to administering Title IV programs, such as Pell Grants, SEOG, CWS, FFEL, and direct loans. Additional information can be obtained on the Web site (http://www.gotodja.com).

Dell Computer Corporation*

1 Dell Way
Round Rock, Texas 78682-7000
Phone: 512-725-1346
Fax: 512-283-1111
E-mail: david_lundquist@dell.com
Contact: David Lundquist
Service: Computer Hardware/Consulting/Distance Education/e-Learning Providers/Educational Training/Information Technology Solutions
Special Message: The world's leading direct computer systems company, Dell offers an exclusive discount-pricing program to CCA members for institutional and personal purchases. The newest product lines, including switches and projectors; information about the Dell/EMC alliance; and a customized, online catalog are available at http://www.dell.com/hied/cca or by calling the personal account team at 800-274-7799 (toll-free). Dell works to provide CCA members with high-quality computer equipment and award winning service for the best price.

Deltak edu, Inc.

15 Salt Creek Lane, Suite 410
Hinsdale, Illinois 60521
Phone: 603-455-7105 Ext. 18
Fax: 630-455-9968
E-mail: gfogel@deltakedu.com
Contact: George E. Fogel
Service: Distance Education/e-Learning Providers
Special Message: Deltak invests in career-oriented colleges and provides world-class online resources to enable the company's school investments as well as its school partners to rapidly build, support, and go to market with online and blended educational programs. For more information, visit the Web site (http://www.deltakedu.com).

Diamond D, Inc.

P.O. Box 235
Kingsburg, California 93631
Phone: 559-897-7872
Fax: 559-596-1030
E-mail: dianna@diamondd.biz
Contact: Ms. Dianna Atwood, President
Service: Software
Special Message: Diamond D, Inc. was founded on the thought that its school management database system has many facets, like a diamond, that all fit together and become one high-quality gem. That

* indicates that the member is an Allied Plus Member.

gives Diamond D's customers the clarity of where their school is going. Among these, Diamond D considers the quality of its software, the support provided by its staff, and its setup and end-user training services to be most critical. Additional information is available at http://www.Diamond-D.biz.

Dickstein Shapiro Morin & Oshinsky, LLP

2101 L Street, N.W.
Washington, DC 20037
Phone: 202-828-2260
Fax: 202-887-0689
E-mail: lefkowitzn@dsmo.com
Contact: Mr. Neil Lefkowitz, Partner
Service: Legal Services
Special Message: Dickstein Shapiro Morin & Oshinsky, LLP, founded in 1953, is a multiservice law firm with more than 325 attorneys in offices in Washington, D.C., and New York City. Dickstein Shapiro has significant experience in representing postsecondary proprietary educational companies in merger and acquisition and finance transactions. Dickstein Shapiro also advises postsecondary proprietary educational companies on a full range of legal matters, including insurance coverage; litigation, including securities litigation; employment and employee benefits; tax; and intellectual property. Additional information is available on the Web (http://www.DicksteinShapiro.com).

Dow Lohnes & Albertson, PLLC

1200 New Hampshire Avenue NW, Suite 800
Washington, DC 20036-6802
Phone: 202-776-2000
Fax: 202-776-2222
E-mail: mgoldstein@dowlohnes.com
Contact: Mr. Michael Goldstein, Member
Service: Consulting/Distance Education/Financial Aid/Legal Services/Student Financial Aid
Special Message: Dow, Lohnes & Albertson offers comprehensive legal services to all segments of the education industry. Services for career colleges include advice on student financial aid; accreditation; licensure; acquisitions; finance; telecommunications; and information technology.

Drinker Biddle & Reath

1500 K Street NW, Suite 1100
Washington, DC 20005-1209
Phone: 202-842-8858
Fax: 202-842-8465
E-mail: john.przypyszny@dbr.com
Contact: Mr. John R. Przypyszny

Service: Legal Services
Special Message: Drinker Biddle & Reath is full-service law firm founded in 1849 and headquartered in Philadelphia, with offices in Washington, D.C.; New York; Princeton and Florham Park, NJ; and Berwyn, PA. Drinker Biddle & Reath provides legal services in mergers and acquisitions, joint ventures, and restructuring as well as advice on institutional eligibility and certification matters and Title IV programs.

eCollege.com*

4900 South Monaco Street, Suite 200
Denver, Colorado 80237
Phone: 303-873-3893
Fax: 303-873-7449
E-mail: saral@ecollege.com
Contact: Ms. Sara LaBounty, Events Manager
Service: Distance Education/Training Providers/e-Learning Providers
Special Message: eCollege provides, in an integrated approach, all the technology and services that are necessary for powering the profitable growth of online distance programs. The company designs, builds, and supports many of the most successful, fully online degree programs in the country. It supports more online degree programs and hosts more student enrollments through its data center than any other eLearning provider. eCollege's outsource solution includes course management system software; program administrative applications; a secure, reliable, and scalable hosted environment; and an array of support services for administrator, faculty, and student success. Additional information is available at http://www.ecollege.com.

EDFUND

3300 Zinfandel Drive
Rancho Cordova, California 95670
Phone: 877-261-2387
E-mail: vshankli@edfund.org
Contact: Ventrice Shanklin, Director of Corporate Clients
Service: Student Financial Aid/Financial Aid/Default Management
Special Message: EDFUND, a nonprofit public benefit corporation, is the nation's second-largest provider of student loan guarantee services under the Federal Family Education Loan Program. Operating as an auxiliary corporation of the California Student Aid Commission, EDFUND offers students a wide range of financial aid and debt management information, while supporting schools with advanced loan processing solutions and default prevention techniques.

* indicates that the member is an Allied Plus Member.

ED MAP, Inc.

296 Harper Street
Nelsonville, Ohio 45764
Phone: 740–753–3439 Ext 304
Fax: 740–753–9402
E-mail: ajherd@edmap.biz
Contact: Mr. Andrew J. Herd, Director of Business
Development
Service: Miscellaneous
Special Message: ED MAP is a company dedicated to
providing an array of support services to career
colleges in the area of textbook and learning materials
distribution. ED MAP has created software and
processes that ease the burden of procuring, managing, and distributing course materials by bringing
together faculty members, administrators, and
students under one virtual roof, thus allowing the
institution to generate greater financial rewards and
academic control. Additional information is available
on the Web (http://www.edmap.biz).

EdRecruit

P.O. Box 222
Dewittville, New York 14728-0222
Phone: 716-386-5415
Fax: 509-271-5313
E-mail: bjones@cecomet.net
Contact: Mr. Brad Jones, President
Service: Management Search
Special Message: EdRecruit is fully dedicated to selec-
tive management searches for all levels of management
in private postsecondary education. Every effort is made
to exercise selectivity, confidentiality, and professional-
ism to achieve a true match. This is EdRecruit's only
business; it's conducted with full-time focus.

Educational Financial Services

18757 Burbank Boulevard, Suite 330
P.O. Box 7031
Tarzana, California 91357-7031
Phone: 818-881-3710
Fax: 818-881-2446
E-mail: info@efs-nlsc.com
Contact: Mr. Leonard Rosen, President
Service: Tuition Financing
Special Message: Educational Financial Services (EFS)
provides financing for students attending colleges and
schools throughout the U.S., usually at no cost to the
school. EFS financing enables colleges to enroll
students by offering affordable payment programs
and providing up-front money. Additional informa-
tion is available at http://www.efs-nlsc.com.

Education Systems & Solutions, LLC

5521 Greenville, Suite 104-268
Dallas, Texas 75206
Phone: 214-827-5403
Fax: 214-887-4810
E-mail: jfriedheim@aol.com
sfriedheim@aol.com
Contact: Mr. Stephen and Jan Friedheim, Strategic
Coaches
Service: Consulting
Special Message: Education Systems & Solutions
provides management strategies relating to administration, admissions, accreditation, curriculum development, marketing, retention, placement, and public
relations. The principals have more than sixty years
of combined experience on the front lines of career
college operations as well as having served in
national leadership positions. References and propos-
als are provided upon request.

Eduventures, Inc.

20 Park Plaza, Suite 1300
Boston, Massachusetts 02116
Phone: 617–426–5622 Ext 17
E-mail: bbright@educentures.com
Contact: Mr. Brian S. Bright, M.Ed., Manager-Business
Development
Service: Consulting/Miscellaneous
Special Message: The worldwide authority on the
education industry, Eduventures supports the growth
of organizations operating in the pre-K–12, postsec-
ondary, and corporate-learning markets. Eduventures'
market forecasts, competitive assessments, analysis of
financial transactions, and buyer data provide clients
with the analysis and insight necessary to develop
and execute organizational strategy. Founded in 1993,
Eduventures is privately held and is headquartered in
Boston, Massachusetts. Additional information is
available at http://www.eduventures.com.

Elsevier Health Science

11830 Westline Industrial Drive
St. Louis, Missouri 63146
Phone: 800-222-9570 (toll-free)
Contact: Faculty Support
Service: Educational Training
Special Message: Elsevier Health Science is the
world's leading publisher of texts for health careers,
with Saunders, Mosby, Churchill Livingstone, and
Butterworth-Heinemann imprints. Elsevier Health
Science is committed to career school education.

* indicates that the member is an Allied Plus Member.

EMB Medical Services, Inc.

P.O. Box 20876
Keizer, Oregon 97307
Phone: 503-390-0995
Fax: 503-390-1130
Contact: Mr. Tom Pierson, President
Service: Medical Services
Special Message: EMB Medical Services is a full health service company specializing in the trade school industry. EMB provides a wide range of health services that schools and their students may need while in school and prior to heading into the health-care workforce. Along with complete reporting services for both the school and its students, EMB can also provide background checks, scrubs, and stetho-scopes. Additional information is available at http://www.EMBMedical.com.

EMCC, Inc.

33 Riverside Drive
Pembroke, Massachusetts 02359
Phone: 781-829-1800
Fax: 781-829-1802
Contact: Mr. Arthur Levine, President
Service: Investment Management/Receivables Management
Special Message: With offices throughout the country, EMCC is one of the nation's leading pur-chasers of paying/performing/reperforming receiv-ables, currently administering more that $900 million in consumer accounts. For nearly 25 years, EMCC, Inc., has been providing world-class receivables management solutions to the credit-granting commu-nity. EMCC's products, technology, services, and corporate capacity give it the unique ability to provide innovative solutions for a broad range of clients. As an affiliate of Schottenstein Stores Corpora-tion, a leading Midwest retailer, EMCC, Inc., pos-sesses the financial resources needed to purchase resources quickly and at a fair and competitive price.

Executive Search Group

750 Boston Neck Road, Suite 14
Narragansett, Rhode Island 02882
Phone: 401-788-9373
Fax: 401-788-0707
E-mail: esearch@att.net
Contact: Mr. Michael Cobb
Service: Consulting/Management Serarchs/Miscella-neous
Special Message: Executive Search Group (ESG) has more than 20 years experience in the education/recruiting fields. The company conducts executive searches for proprietary, college, and university positions, such as presidents, COOs, executive directors, corporate management, regional directors, school presidents/directors, directors of admissions, academic deans/directors of education, directors of financial aid and various management and staffing positions. ESG specializes in the brokerage, purchase, and sale of career colleges and assists owners and buyers in the sale and purchase of their institutions. Visit www.esearchgroup.net for further information.

FAME

5301 North Dixie Highway
Fort Lauderdale, Florida 33334-3403
Phone: 954-772-5883
Fax: 954-772-6257
E-mail: fame@fameinc.com
Contact: Ms. Julia Brown, Senior Vice President, Marketing and Client Relations
Service: Financial Aid/Software
Special Message: FAME is the largest financial aid servicing company in the nation. FAME offers school administrative software, a full range of financial aid services, and student loan management for more than 700 institutions nationwide. FAME also provides highly acclaimed financial aid training programs.

Financial Aid Services, Inc./Genesis: SMSS

90 Stiles Road
Suite #101
Salem, New Hampshire 03079-4884
Phone: 603-328-1550
    800-4-FAS-INC (432-7462) (toll-free)
Fax: 603-328-1560
E-mail: fas@fastinc.net
Contact: Mr. Albert Gillis, President/CEO
Service: Financial Aid/Software/Consulting
Special Message: Founded in 1980, Financial Aid Services, Inc. (FAS) remains the only nationwide servicing company that provides a customized approach of personalized consulting and professional management of proprietary institution's federal student aid programs. FAS enables schools to com-pletely automate processing using FASLine©, its internet-based software.

FAS can also integrate its financial aid servicing with its own school administrative software, Genesis-SMS©, an entirely Windows-based program that completely automates and generates reports on admissions, academics, attendance, accounting, placement, and compliance.

* indicates that the member is an Allied Plus Member.

Both FAS and Genesis-SMC© have raised the standards in meeting the challenges of school management and Title IV processing.

1st Student Financial

671 E. Delagado Drive
Palatine, Illinois 60074
Phone: 847-963-8161
      847-722-3807 (cell)
Fax: 847-574-7601
E-mail: dwhitaker@1student.org
Contact: Dan Whitaker, Vice President of National Accounts
Service: Default Management/Financial Aid/Student Financial Aid/Tuition Financing
Special Message: 1st Student Financial is a not-for-profit student lender offering Federal Stafford, PLUS, and Consolidation Loans. 1st Student Financial also provides a full suite of gap financing and alternative-loan products, serving postsecondary students across the country. 1st Student Financial's mission is to educate students about financial matters and assure their future financial fitness. The vision at 1st Student Financial is to reduce student loan default rates at career colleges to less than 1 percent. Additional information is available at http://www.1student.org.

Fred W. Jurash & Company, P.C.

175 West Old Marlton Pike
Marlton, New Jersey 08053-2033
Phone: 856-596-9600
Fax: 856-985-9086
E-mail: jurashcpa@aol.com
Contact: Mr. Fred Jurash, President
Service: Certified Public Accountant
Special Message: Fred W. Jurash & Co., P.C. is a full-service tax, audit, and consulting firm that specializes in education and not-for-profit industries, including OMB 133 audits. The firm concentrates on education support services and provides consulting services related to change of ownership, acquisitions, financial analysis, file reviews, internal auditing, and year-end planning.

Froehle & Co., Inc., P.C.

8401 Claude Thomas Road, Suite 45
Franklin, Ohio 45005–1475
Phone: 937–746–3999
Fax: 937–746–1556
E-mail: froehle@froehle.com
Contact: Mr. Jeffery Froehle, President
Service: Certified Public Accountants

Special Message: Froehle & Co., Inc. is a CPA firm specializing in services to postsecondary educational institutions, providing audits of Title IV and financial statements, state financial aid programs, consultation, and compliance reviews. Additional information is available at http://www.froehle.com.

GEMCOR, Inc.

400 Quadrangle Drive
Bolingbrook, Illinois 60440
Phone: 888-GEMCOR8 (436-2678)
Fax: 888-9GEMCOR (943-6267)
E-mail: info@gemcorinc.com
Contact: Mr. Donald Grybas, President
Service: Financial Aid
Special Message: GEMCOR, Inc. is one of the largest third-party servicers in the country, administering federal aid for more than 150 institutions. Daily grant and loan processing, cash management, and complete reconciliation and consulting services are available as is TRAX school administrative software. Visit gemcorinc.com for more information. Additional information is available at http://www.gemcorinc.com.

Global Financial Aid Services, Inc.

10467 Corporate Drive
Gulfport, Mississippi 39503
Phone: 228-523-1000
Fax: 228-523-1722
E-mail: jaddison@globalfas.com
Contact: Mr. Edward Addison, President
Service: Financial Aid
Special Message: Global Financial Aid Services, Inc., is a nationally recognized third-party financial aid servicer that provides the postsecondary community with a variety of outsourcing options for Title IV processing, including its comprehensive Platinum Service, its Virtual Financial Aid Office for distance/nationally recruited students, and a wide range of consulting services. The state-of-the-art, Internet-driven services are flexible and designed to meet the clients' needs. Additional information is available at the Web site (http://www.globalfas.com).

Gordon, Niles & Company, P.A.

3041 Monument Road, Suite 2
Jacksonville, Florida 32225
Phone: 904-642-7456
Fax: 904-642-7474
E-mail: kgordon@gordonnilescpa.com
Contact: T. Kip Gordon, CPA

* indicates that the member is an Allied Plus Member.

Service: Certified Public Accountants

Special Message: For more than 20 years, Gordon, Niles & Company has provided accounting and auditing services, including financial statement audits and Title IV compliance attestations, for private schools and colleges.

Gragg Advertising & Design

4049 Pennsylvania Avenue, Suite 201
Kansas City, Missouri 64111-3021
Phone: 816-931-0050
Fax: 816-931-0051
E-mail: chuck@graggadv.com
Contact: Mr. Gregory Gragg
Service: Admissions/Advertising/Marketing/Media/Recruitment/Retention
Special Message: Gragg has a reputation of generating results-oriented recruitment advertising programs for career schools. Gragg specializes in lead and enrollment flow and admission strategies through turnkey recruitment campaigns, media analysis, Web development, admission training, and strategic direct-mail programs.

Graymark International, Inc.

P.O. Box 2015
Tustin, California 92781
Phone: 800-854-7393 (toll-free)
Fax: 714-544-2323
E-mail: sales@graymarkint.com
Contact: Mr. Riad A. El Masri, President
Service: Educational/Training Materials
Special Message: Graymark International, Inc., is a leading manufacturer of quality courseware and hardware-based IT trainers, electronic component kits, and projects. Graymark proudly celebrates its 40th anniversary of developing trainers that provide a stimulating real-world working experience for students and a simple-to-complex, success-oriented curriculum for instructors. Additonal information is available at the Web site (http://www.graymarkint.com).

Hands On, Inc.*

College Services
2901 North 78th Street, Suite 200
Scottsdale, Arizona 85251
Phone: 480-947-7375
        800-761-7376 (toll-free)
Fax: 480-947-7374
E-mail: marylynh@handsonmgmt.com
Contact: Ms. Mary Lyn Hammer, President/CEO

Service: Default Management/Placement

Special Message: Hands On, Inc. is the nation's leader and largest provider of default prevention services for federally guaranteed student loans. By combining proprietary, automated state-of-the-art computer software with proven and effective techniques, Hands On, Inc. delivers extraordinary results and performance that exceed its clients' expectations.

In response to client requests, Hands On, Inc. has added Skip Trace Assistance and Placement Verification to its portfolio of services. These professional services aid in-house collection efforts and reporting abilities for accreditation-, state-, and/or federally required data.

High Voltage Interactive

80 Rancho Drive
Tiburon, California 94920
Phone: 415-332-1591
        866-383-8161 (toll-free)
Fax: 415-383-3152
E-mail: matt@highvoltageinteractive.com
Contact: Mr. Matt McAllister, Marketing Manager
Service: Admissions/Advertising/Educational Training Materials/Marketing and Media
Special Message: High Voltage Interactive is the leading online marketing and management solutions company, specializing in lead generation services for the education industry. High Voltage Interactive's performance-based enrollment marketing services leverage its own user-based Web portal, www.SearchForClasses.com, as well as its vast media network to generate timely, high-quality, and cost-effective leads that convert to active students at unprecedented levels. With a reputation built on strategic direction and precise execution, High Voltage Ineractive delivers an exceptional return on its clients' marketing investment. Additional information, including management of complete, end-to-end enrollment marketing needs, is available at http://www.highvoltageinteractive.com.

Homer & Bonner, P.A.

1200 Four Seasons Tower
1441 Brickell Avenue
Miami, Florida 33131
Phone: 305-350-5188
Fax: 305-372-2738
E-mail: kjacobs@homerbonner.com
Contact: Mr. Kevin Jacobs, Esq.
Service: Legal Services
Special Message: Homer & Bonner, P.A. represents publicly and privately owned postsecondary educa-

* indicates that the member is an Allied Plus Member.

tion companies in connection with student, employee, and regulatory disputes, including putative class actions, in federal, state, and arbitral forums throughout the nation. The firm has substantial experience in defending student class actions, securities suits, regulatory inquiries, and all manner of employee disputes. The firm also represents private education companies in connection with the acquisition of other such companies and on the range of legal matters associated with the operation of such companies. More information is available at Homer & Bonner, P.A.'s Web site (http://www.homerbonner.com).

Integrated Enrollment Solutions

422 East Main, #210
Nacogdoches, Texas 75961
Phone: 888–676–5524 (toll-free)
E-mail: susan.backofen@enroll2grad.org
Contact: Susan Backofen, President
Service: Consulting
Special Message: Integrated Enrollment Solutions provides consulting services to educational institutions in designing customized SRM programs aimed specifically at increasing student graduation. Its team of experts has nearly 100 of years combined experience in areas such as enrollment management, enrollment forecasting, process automation, admissions, financial aid, advising, registration, career services, information systems, data integration, report development, data analysis, and staff training. Additional information is available at http://www.enroll2grad.org.

Jones e-global library

9697 East Mineral Avenue
Centennial, Colorado 80112
Phone: 800-701-6463 Ext 8236 (toll-free)
Fax: 303-784-8533
E-mail: somalley@jonesknowledge.com
Contact: Susan O'Malley, Manager, e-global library
Service: Library Services
Special Message: Jones e-global library® offers a comprehensive suite of online research tools that provide access to a vast range of academic and business literature. Developed and maintained by professional librarians, elements of this collection can provide an entire online library solution or be selected on an individual basis to complement existing offerings. Additional information is available at the Web site (http://www.egloballibrary.com).

Jopling, Inc.

3 Gateway Center, Suite 1840
Pittsburgh, Pennsylvania 15222
Phone: 412-765-3044
Fax: 412-765-3497
E-mail: mjopling@joplinginc.com
Contact: J. Mark Jopling, President
Service: Investment Banking
Special Message: Jopling, Inc. was founded in 1990 to provide investment-banking services to middle-market companies and larger corporations needing assistance with their middle-market operations. The firm advises and assists clients in selling, buying, and valuing companies and securities (including fairness opinions). Additional information is available at the Web site (http://www.joplinginc.com).

Jostens, Inc.*

26 Cross Point Drive
Owings, Maryland 20736
Phone: 410-257-6294
E-mail: marty.murphy@jostens.com
Contact: Mr. Marty Murphy, National Strategic Accounts Manager
Service: Promotional/Recognition/Miscellaneous
Special Message: Minneapolis-based Jostens, founded in 1897, is a leading provider of products, programs, and services that help people celebrate important moments, recognize achievements, and build affiliation. The company's products include graduation products, class rings, diplomas, certificates, diploma frames, graduation announcements, and achievement awards. Clients should visit www.jostens.com for more information.

Journey Education Marketing, Inc.

13755 Hutton Drive, Suite 500
Dallas, Texas 75234
Phone: 800-874-9001 (toll-free)
Fax: 972-481-2100
E-mail: schoolsales@journeyed.com
Contact: Greg Lamkin
Service: Computer Hardware/Software
Special Message: Journey Education Marketing is the leading provider of business, digital video, animation, engineering/CAD, Web publishing, and digital publishing software to educational institutions, faculty members, and students nationwide. In addition, Journey offers eStore solutions to schools, currently operating more than 1,900 software eStores. Journey specializes in serving the private career postsecondary sector. Customers should visit http://www.JourneyEd.com for more information.

* indicates that the member is an Allied Plus Member.

Kavanagh and Associates, PC

7935 Perry Highway
Pittsburgh, Pennsylvania 45237
Phone: 412-364-6644
Fax: 412-364-8012
E-mail: jayalex@kavcpa.com
Contact: Mr. John H. Alexander, CPA
Service: Certified Public Accountant
Special Message: Kavanagh and Associates are certified public accountants specializing in trade and technical schools as well as non-profit educational institutions. Services provided by the firm include, but are not limited to, financial aid audits; consulting; financial statement audits, including OMB 133 audits; and retirement plan implementation and reporting, including 401k plans.

Kaye, Rose & Maltzman, LLP

402 Broadway, 21st Floor
San Diego, California 92101-3542
Phone: 619-232-6555
Fax: 619-232-6577
E-mail: kzakarin@kayerose.com
Contact: Mr. Keith Zakarin, Esq.
Service: Legal Services
Special Message: Kay, Rose & Maltzman, Inc. represents California and Florida private post-secondary and vocational schools and colleges in all of the many facets of their complex and specialized businesses. The firm handles student and employee claims and lawsuits, from simple disputes to large class actions and private-attorney general suits. The firm also represents schools before state and federal regulatory and accrediting bodies, as well as in purchase and sale transactions of the schools themselves. The firm places particular emphasis on the creation and implementation of sound risk management and claim prevention strategies, and works in partnership with its clients to structure their admissions, financial aid, and instructor guidelines to maximize profitability while minimizing risk. Additional information is available at the Web site (http://www.kayrose.com).

Kessler, Orlean, Silver & Company, P.C.

7400 North Oak Park Avenus
Niles, Illinois 60714-3818
Phone: 847-647-6600
Fax: 847-647-7554
E-mail: sfa@koscpa.com
Contact: Mr. Sanford Alper, Principal

Service: Certified Public Accountants
Special Message: Kessler, Orlean, Silver & Company, P.C., (KOS) is a full-service accounting firm located in Niles, Illinois, specializing in institutional audits, year-end planning, consulting, income taxes, 90/10 ratios, and other major financial information. KOS is licensed across the United States.

Knutte & Associates, P.C.

7900 South Cass Avenue, Suite 210
Darien, Illinois 60561-5073
Phone: 630-960-3317
Fax: 630-960-9960
E-mail: kathyh@knutte.com
Contact: Ms. Kathleen Hays, Marketing Director
Service: Certified Public Accountants
Special Message: Knutte & Associates (K&A) has been providing career colleges with guidance and solutions for more than ten years. The range of services to career colleges includes financial audits, SFA compliance audits and attestations, monthly financial statements, business valuations, regulatory ratio monitoring, tax planning and preparation, and profit sharing and retirement plans. K&A is licensed nationwide and is committed to providing and maintaining service excellence for every client. Additional information is available at http://www.k-nute.com.

LaSalle Bank National Association

135 South LaSalle Street, Suite 1743
Chicago, Illinois 60603
Phone: 312-904-6570
Fax: 312-606-8423
E-mail: chris.o'brien@abnamro.com
Contact: Mr. Christopher J. O'Brien, Senior Vice President
Service: Consulting/Financial Aid and Investment Management/Investment Banking/Student Financial Aid/Tuition Financing
Special Message: LaSalle Bank is one of the largest middle-market commercial banks in the Midwest. Through its Educational Services Division, it offers financial products and services (e.g., lines of credit, term loans, leasing, cash management services, advisory services, investment services, and trust services) tailored to the needs of participants in the postsecondary education industry. Through its Consumer Lending Division, LaSalle Bank makes it easy to finance education costs by offering Stafford and PLUS loans to students and their parents and should be contacted to discuss borrower benefit

* indicates that the member is an Allied Plus Member.

options that help students with their financing needs. LaSalle Bank also offers extremely competitive home equity loan options throughout the United States. Additional information is available at the Web site (http://www.lasallebanks.com/commercial/educational_services.html).

Lead Advantage, Inc.

1519 South Bowman Road, Suite A
Little Rock, Arkansas 72211
Phone: 501-687-5323
Fax: 501-225-8163
E-mail: phillip@leadadvantage.us
Contact: Mr. Phillip More, Managing Partner
Service: Advertising/Consulting/Marketing/Admissions
Special Message: Lead Advantage Inc. is a full-service direct-response advertising agency and video production company specializing in lead generation and admission training for the proprietary school industry. Its team of professionals has more than fifty years combined experience in direct response advertising, television production, media placement, and admissions training. Lead Advantage believes that its unique approach to lead generation and recruiter training truly differentiates it from its peers. The corporate office is located in Little Rock, Arkansas. Additional information is available at http://www.leadadvantage.us.

Making Your Mark/LDF Publishing, Inc.

P.O. Box 45
Port Perry, Ontario L9L 1A2
Canada
Phone: 905–985–9990 or 877–492–6845
Fax: 905–985–0713
E-mail: info@makingyourmark.com
Contact: Mr. Don Fraser, Vice President, Retention
Service: Retention
Special Message: LDF Publishing has been helping colleges develop student success and retention strategies since 1992. Its college success book, *Making Your Mark,* is used in more 1,500 educational institutions across North America and has sold more than 750,000 copies. LDF Publishing also offers faculty training seminars in student retention and student motivation. More than 7,000 college staff members have attended their workshops—"The Right Start to College" and "Student Motivation: From Day 1 to Graduation." Additional information is available at http://www.makingyourmark.com.

Marketing & Design Team

9 Southeast 9th Avenue, Suite 3
Fort Lauderdale, Florida 33301-2047
Phone: 800-424-7397
Fax: 954-764-5853
E-mail: mitch@mdtdirect.com
Contact: Mr. Mitch Talenfeld
Service: Admissions/Advertising/Consulting/Marketing/Media/Recruitment/Training Providers
Special Message: MDT Direct, a division of Custom Cuts Printing, Inc., provides its customers with products and services that improve sales efforts and advertising effectiveness. Visit www.mdtdirect.com for details.

Marketing Solutions, Inc.

1601 Westpark Drive, Suite 3
Little Rock, Arkansas 72204-2432
Phone: 501-663-3433
Fax: 501-801-5100
E-mail: dewitt@msileads.com
Contact: Mr. Dewitt Shotts, President
Service: Advertising/Marketing
Special Message: Marketing Solutions specializes in direct response advertising for private career schools. The company assists schools with developing strategic marketing plans and television and direct mail production. Additional information is available at the Web site (http://www.msileads.com).

MaxKnowledge, Inc.

601 N. Parkcenter Drive, Suite 208
Santa Ana, California 92705
Phone: 714-505-0901
Fax: 714-505-1517
E-mail: amirm@maxknowledge.com
Contact: Mr. Amir Moghadam, Ph.D., Executive Director
Service: Admissions/Distance Learning/Distance Education/Educational,Training Materials/e-Learning Providers/Financial Aid/Marketing/Placement/Retention/Training Providers
Special Message: In partnership with the Career College Association, MaxKnowledge offers a wide variety of online and blended training courses to enhance the knowledge and skills of career school personnel. Subject areas include accreditation, admissions, education (instructor training), e-learning, financial aid, marketing, operations, placement, and retention. The training courses are facilitated by leading career education experts, and participants

* indicates that the member is an Allied Plus Member.

receive continuing education units upon completion of training. MaxKnowledge also offers a large selection of free courses in soft skills areas such as communications, management, leadership, creativity, and innovation. Its ultimate objective is to increase the efficiency and quality of career college operations through effective training of personnel.

MBS Direct

2711 West Ash Street
Columbia, Missouri 65203-4613
Phone: 800-325-3249
Fax: 573-446-5242
E-mail: krust@mbsdirect.com
Contact: Mr. Kenneth Rust
Service: Education Training/IT Solutions/Miscellaneous
Special Message: MBS Direct provides a Virtual Bookstore course materials fulfillment program that handles all inventory, receiving student orders, shipping course materials directly to students, a book buyback program, and excellent customer service. College profitability on textbooks is guaranteed. School staff members are able to focus on student recruitment and education without the challenges and costs of course material distribution. MBS Direct offers solutions for student financial aid orders and can ship course materials directly to students or the classroom when textbook fees are bundled within tuition.

McClintock & Associates, CPAs

1370 Washington Pike, Suite 201
Bridgeville, Pennsylvania 15017-2839
Phone: 412-257-5980
Fax: 412-257-2549
E-mail: bmcclintock@mcclintockcpa.com
Contact: Mr. Bruce McClintock, President
Service: Certified Public Accountants
Special Message: McClintock & Associates is a CPA and consulting firm with a nationwide practice in the education industry, specializing in financial aid audits, financial statement audits, mergers and acquisitions, tax consulting and preparation, management consulting, computer consulting, and financial aid consulting.

McGraw-Hill Career College Group*

2043 Woodland Parkway, Suite 115
Saint Louis, Missouri 63146
Phone: 314-993-4623
Fax: 314-993-4786
E-mail: dennis_spisak@mcgraw-hill.com
Contact: Mr. Dennis Spisak, Senior Vice President

Service: Educational Training Materials/eLearning Resources
Special Message: Glencoe/McGraw-Hill publishes postsecondary occupational textbooks and software in computer education, allied health, office technology and keyboarding, criminal justice, student success and professional development, and trades and technology. It also publishes the *McGraw-Hill Higher Education* series in general education. Additional information is available at the Web site (http://www.mhhe.com).

Military Advantage*

799 Market Street, Suite 700
San Francisco, California 94103
Phone: 415-820-3466
E-mail: Josh@MilitaryAdvantage.com
Contact: Mr. Josh Brody, Director of Sales
Service: Advertising/Financial Aid/Marketing/Media/Recruitment/Retention
Special Message: Military Advantage, the nation's largest military affinity marketing firm, has more than 4 million members, 3 million newsletter subscribers, and the world's largest online military destination at http:www.military.com. Military Advantage connects mature, motivated servicemembers and veterans with GI Bill and tuition assistance benefits to educational institutions through targeted, measurable advertising vehicles, qualified lead generation programs, and the *Directory of Military-Friendly Schools*.

Muno, Summers & Associates

P.O. Box 882
Oldsmar, Florida 34667
Phone: 813-925-8410
Fax: 813-925-8420
Contact: Ms. Deborah Muno, Partner
Service: Consulting/Education Management/Employee Assessment/Recruitment/Retention/Testing Tools, Equipment/Training Providers
Special Message: The products and services of Muno, Summers & Associates help put the right person in the right job and the right student in the right curriculum to obtain the right job. By working with faculty and staff members and students, Muno, Summers & Associates provides results in recruitment, retention, development, and placement. More information can be found on the Web at http://www.munosummers.com.

* indicates that the member is an Allied Plus Member.

National Allied Health Credentialing Association

P.O. Cox 1473
Chino, California 91708
Phone: 626–252–2562
Fax: 909–627–2156
E-mail: nahcc1@netscape.net

Contact: Mr. Santos Vera, D.O.

Service: Certification

Special Message: NAHCA offers certifications in their area of study to students or graduates of medical assisting, dental assisting, medical billing, medical coding, and pharmacy technician programs. Additional information is available at http://www.nahcc.com.

National Center for Competency Testing (NCCT)

7007 College Boulevard, Suite 250
Overland Park, Kansas 66211
Phone: 913-498-1000
Fax: 913-498-1243
E-mail: bruce@ncctinc.com

Contact: Bruce Brackett, President

Service: Certification/Advertising

Special Message: National Center for Competency Testing (NCCT) is a national certification agency for individuals in the allied health and business fields. NCCT is an agent for Multiskilled Medical Certifications Institution, Inc. All NCCT examinations are validated by psychometricians using both item response and classical test theories. Additional information is available at the Web site (http://www.ncctinc.com).

NIIT

1050 Crown Point Parkway
Suite 500
Atlanta, Georgia 30338
Phone: 888-454-6448 Ext 6021
Fax: 770-551-9229
E-mail: lawimberly@niit.com

Contact: LeeAnne Wimberly, Marketing Manager

Service: Training Providers/e-Learning Providers/Distance Education/Educational Training/IT Solutions

Special Message: NIIT has more than twenty years of experience developing and imparting education and has a student body of 500,000 in thirty-one countries. NIIT can help career colleges secure their competitive advantage with custom solutions that include: custom educational materials—textbooks, courseware, companion sites, instructor guides, and online courses; custom program development; technology infrastructure for online education; and IT instructors for online and classroom delivery. More information is available at the Web site (http://www.niit.com).

The Pacific Institute

1230 South Southlake Drive
Hollywood, Florida 33019-1825
Phone: 954-926-5668
Fax: 954-926-5667
E-mail: drjpace@msn.com

Contact: Dr. Joe Pace, Managing Partner, Education Initiative

Service: Retention/Admissions/Consulting and Training/Development/Training Providers/Educational and Training Materials

Special Message: The Pacific Institute, a world leader in high achievement, peak performance, and change management training, has designed a process for career schools. The process, Success Strategies for Effective Colleges and Schools, results in greater student success and increased admissions and retention rates.

The Palmer Group

3600 Market Street, Suite 530
Philadelphia, Pennsylvania 19104-2649
Phone: 215-243-2590
Fax: 215-243-2593
E-mail: gfrancois@palmer-group.co

Contact: Mr. Gerard Francois, Principal

Service: Investment Management

Special Message: The Palmer Group is a private investment firm based in Philadelphia that invests in small and medium-sized career colleges to help them achieve leadership in their markets and develop a reputation for excellence in their communities.

Pearson Education*

555 West Iron Avenue
Suite 101
Mesa, Arizona 85210
Phone: 480-786-1505
Fax: 480-610-7937
E-mail: Pat.Sullivan@PearsonEd.com

Contact: Patrick Sullivan, Director of National Accounts

* indicates that the member is an Allied Plus Member.

Service: Educational/Training Materials

Special Message: Pearson Custom Publishing is the largest custom publisher in North America, providing classroom materials in all formats and media and representing the content offerings of Prentice Hall, Allyn & Bacon, Addison Wesley Longman, Benjamin Cummings, and Penguin Books in customized formats.

People Resources, Inc.

9338 Olive Boulevard
St. Louis, Missouri 63132
Phone: 314–222–4020 Ext 3015
　　　866–500–2327 Ext 3015 (toll-free)
E-mail: jmug@peopleresourceseap.com

Contact: Janet Mug, M.A., LPC, CEAP; President and Owner

Service: Consulting/Retention/e-Learning Providers/Admissions

Special Message: People Resources, Inc. has focused more than twenty years on developing and delivering customized Student Resource Program (SRP) services for adult students and Employee Assistance Program (EAP) services for employees worldwide. SRP is designed for career colleges seeking to enhance student retention and graduation rates. The SRP program can support the documentation process for reaccreditation, meet student needs, and provide a better return on student-acquisition costs. SRP services are delivered through First Clinical Coordination, with licensed professionals available 24 hours a day, seven days a week. Confidential telephone coaching and counseling and face-to-face counseling are provided where the student resides. In addition to the counseling options, extensive Web-based services are available. By providing direct access to all available resources, students can have solutions to life's unexpected events and crises. This full-access approach allows students to find around-the-clock solutions for a wide range of personal, housing, financial, and family difficulties. This full-access approach increases the number of students seeking services, thereby addressing the students' personal worries and challenges in a confidential manner and improving the overall success rate of students. Additional information is available at the Web site (http://www.peopleresourceseap.com).

PlattForm Advertising*

500 North Rogers Road
Olathe, Kansas 66062
Phone: 913-254-6061
Fax: 913-764-4043
E-mail: bradg@plattformad.com

Contact: Mr. Brad Gibbs, Vice President Marketing and Sales

Service: Admissions/Advertising/Consulting/Marketing/Media/Recruitment/Training Providers

Special Message: PlattForm Advertising is a full-service, integrated marketing communications agency specializing in direct-response advertising within the school industry. With its headquarters in Olathe, Kansas, the agency provides all aspects of advertising campaigns in house. These services include strategic media planning and buying, creative production, Web design, full-service Web marketing, interactive cost per lead programs, and direct mail. PlattForm Advertising specializes in the proprietary school market, servicing more than 1,000 campus locations across the U.S. and Canada. For more information, visit www.PlattFormAd.com.

PNC Bank

2312 Montego Drive
Arlington, Texas 76002
Phone: 817-375-8272
Fax: 817-417-5919
E-mail: jennie.hargrove@pncbank.com

Contact: Mrs. Jennie Hargrove, Campus Relations Manager

Service: Financial Aid

Special Message: As one of the nation's top education lenders, PNC Bank provides a complete range of financial products and services, from Federal Stafford and PLUS Loans to alternative lending programs, such as its Continuing Education Loan. Visit http://www.eduloans.pncbank.com for more information.

Powers, Pyles, Sutter & Verville, P.C.

1875 Eye Street, NW, 12th Floor
Washington, DC 20006
Phone: 202-466-6550
Fax: 202-785-1756
E-mail: sfreeman@ppsv.com

Contact: Mr. Stanley Freeman, Attorney-at-Law

Service: Education Training/Legal Services

Special Message: Powers, Pyles, Sutter & Verville (PPS&V) is a group of education lawyers representing both privately owned and publicly traded career colleges across the country. The company provides advice on federal regulatory compliance, program review and audit resolution, state licensure, accreditation, acquisitions, and more.

QuinStreet, Inc.

301 Constitution Drive
Menlo Park, California 94205
Phone: 650-475-7705
Fax: 650-578-7605
E-mail: cmancini@quinstreet.com

Contact: Mr. Chris Mancini

* indicates that the member is an Allied Plus Member.

Service: Marketing

Special Message: QuinStreet helps companies acquire new customers cost effectively through online lead-generation programs that target and qualify customers while they research purchase options online. QuinStreet is one of the few lead-generation businesses that operates strictly on a pay-for-performance basis, tests and optimizes lead quality continuously, and delivers lead volumes according to clients' requests. Additional information is available at the Web site (http://www.quinstreet.com).

Ritzert & Leyton, P.C.

11350 Random Hills Road, Suite 400
Fairfax, Virginia 22030
Phone: 703-934-2660
Fax: 703-934-9840
E-mail: pleyton@ritzert-leyton.com
Contact: Mr. Peter Leyton, Attorney-at-Law
Service: Legal Services
Special Message: Ritzert & Leyton, a D.C. area law firm, offers all sectors of higher education counseling and representation before federal and state agencies, accrediting agencies, and federal and state courts, regarding compliance with federal student financial assistance requirements, institutional eligibility and certification, program review and audit resolution, OIG audits and investigations, acquisitions and restructuring, accreditation, and licensure.

Sallie Mae, Inc.*

12061 Bluemont Way
Reston, Virginia 20190
Phone: 703-984-6211
Fax: 703-984-5132
E-mail: laura.w.hardman@slma.com
Contact: Ms. Laura Hardman, Manager, Education Loan Product Management
Service: Student Financial Aid
Special Message: Sallie Mae provides low-cost federal and private education loans for students, whether they attend full-time, half-time, or part-time. Sallie Mae's federal loans offer money-saving benefits and flexible repayment options, while the private loans feature low rates, high approvals, and extended repayment terms. More information is available at http://www.salliemae.com/partners/cca.html.

Salmon, Beach & Company, P.C.

12720 Hillcrest Road, Suite 900
Dallas, Texas 75230-2035
Phone: 972-392-1143
Fax: 972-934-1269
E-mail: rsalmon@salmonbeach.com
Contact: Mr. Ronald Salmon, President

Service: Certified Public Accountants

Special Message: Salmon, Beach & Company, P.C., is dedicated to providing a full range of professional services to career colleges and schools. Services include financial audits, SFA compliance audits and attestations, monthly financial statements, regulatory ratio consulting, and accounting software solutions.

Sapienza & Associates

3020 Annandale Drive
Presto, Pennsylvania 15142
Phone: 412-279-0802
Fax: 412-279-0876
E-mail: sapienza@aol.com
Contact: Mr. Thomas Sapienza
Service: Investment Management
Special Message: Sapienza & Associates is an investment consulting services company.

School Guide Publications

210 North Avenue
New Rochelle, New York 10801
Phone: 800-433-7771 (toll-free)
Fax: 914-632-3412
E-mail: mridder@schoolguides.com
Contact: Mr. Myles Ridder, President
Service: Advertising
Special Message: School Guide Publications has produced high-quality student inquiries for colleges for more than 65 years. In print, their directories include *School Guide* and *Veterans Education Guide*. *School Guide* reaches high school students and their families as they are beginning to plan for college. *Veterans Education Guide* reaches men and women as they are leaving the service with education benefits. These veterans are looking for education that prepares them for careers. The Web site, SchoolGuides.com, offers a searchable database of colleges, nursing schools, and business and career schools. The site effectively directs traffic to advertisers' Web sites. Other publications include *College Transfer Guide*, *College Conference Manuals*, and *Graduate School Guide*. GraduateGuide.com is an additional Web site.

Security Credit Systems, Inc.

1250 Niagara Street
Buffalo, New York 14213
Phone: 716-882-4515
Fax: 716-884-2577
E-mail: rdixon@securitycreditsystems.com
Contact: Mr. Robert Dixon, Vice President of Sales and Marketing

* indicates that the member is an Allied Plus Member.

Service: Advertising/Marketing/Media

Special Message: Security Credit System, Inc., is a nationwide college debt recovery service specializing in the recovery of student loan and tuition receivables. Since 1983, SCS has represented colleges and universities across the country and is recognized as an industry leader in higher education receivables.

Shughart Thomson & Kilroy, P.C.

Twelve Wyandotte Plaza, Suite 1800
120 West 12th Street
Kansas City, Missouri 64105-1929
Phone: 816-421-3355
Fax: 816-374-0509
E-mail: rholt@stklaw.com

Contact: Mr. Ronald Holt, Partner

Service: Legal Services

Special Message: Shughart Thomson & Kilroy, a business law firm with more than 170 lawyers in offices in 7 cities, including Kansas City, Denver, and Phoenix, provides counsel to institutions of higher learning across the nation on regulatory compliance; representation in lawsuits and agency proceedings concerning accrediting disputes, program reviews, LS&T proceedings, and student disputes; labor and employment issues; change of ownership transactional and regulatory work; and tax and corporate matters. Information on the firm's education practice, can be found at http://www.stklaw.com/practicegroups/education.html).

Signature

5115 Parkcenter Avenue
Dublin, Ohio 43017
Phone: 614-766-5101
       800-398-0518 (toll-free)
Fax: 614-766-9419
E-mail: barryhimmel@legendary.net

Contact: Mr. Barry Himmel, Executive Vice President

Service: Admissions/Training Providers

Special Message: Signature is a leading provider of legendary training solutions tailored to educational institutions. Signature's training programs increase student satisfaction, student retention, and enrollment rates. The concepts taught at the training events are reinforced through a variety of methods, including mystery phone shops, on-site shops, personalized coaching, and continual on-site training. Those interesting in learning about staff member training should call Signature's toll-free number. Visit http://www.legendary.net/edu/index.htm for more information.

Sonnenschein Nath & Rosenthal, LLP

8000 Sears Tower
Chicago, Illinois 60606
Phone: 312-876-2569
Fax: 312-876-7934
E-mail: edecator@sonnenschein.com

Contact: Mr. Eric R. Decator, Partner

Service: Legal Services

Special Message: Sonnenschein, with 600 attorneys in nine U.S. cities and a global reach throughout Europe, Asia, and Latin America, serves the legal needs of many of the world's largest and best-known businesses, nonprofits, and individuals. The firm's attorneys have extensive experience representing colleges and universities in all aspects of their operations. Sonnenschein advises clients in both the proprietary and not-for-profit sectors of the higher-education industry. In the past few years, they have represented clients in connection with the acquisition and disposition of numerous colleges, universities, and other postsecondary schools. Sonnenschein's higher-education lawyers routinely collaborate with the firm's lawyers in its corporate, health-care, taxation, litigation, antitrust, employment, employee benefits, bankruptcy, environmental, and real estate practice groups in Sonnenschein's continuing effort to provide its clients with a broad range of legal expertise. For more information on services, customers should visit the Web site (http://www.sonnenschein.com).

The Source for Training, Inc.

2875 South Delaney Avenue
Orlando, Florida 32806
Phone: 407-420-1010
Fax: 407-420-9500
E-mail: sourcetran@aol.com

Contact: Ms. Nancy Rogers, President

Service: Admissions and Performance Training

Special Message: For more than twenty-five years, the Source has worked with private postsecondary schools in providing support and training throughout the admissions process. Schools can increase productivity and achieve exceptional growth using the Source's highly effective recruiting tools, techniques, and proven systems.

Spectrum Industries, Inc.

1600 Johnson Street
P.O. Box 400
Chippewa Falls, Wisconsin 54729-1468
Phone: 800-235-1262 (toll-free)
Fax: 800-335-0473 (toll-free)
E-mail: spectrum@spectrumfurniture.com

Contact: Mr. James Lloyd, National Sales Representative

---

* indicates that the member is an Allied Plus Member.

Service: Miscellaneous

Special Message: Leaders in modernizing the learning environment, Spectrum Industries offers furniture for computer labs, technology classrooms, and multimedia centers. Sold direct from the factory, the furnishings are durable, flexible, and ergonomically correct. Using their exclusive Cable-Guard™ wire management system, Spectrum's solutions to furniture needs are economical and look great.

Sterling Education Properties

1033 Skokie Boulevard, Suite 600
Northbrook, Illinois 60062
Phone: 847-412-6220
Fax: 847-480-0199
E-mail: jperelman@sterlingpartners.us
Contact: Mr. Jeffrey Perelman, Managing Director
Service: Real Estate
Special Message: Sterling Education Properties, a private equity firm, focuses their investments on educational real estate and, with its capital, provides a one-stop solution to the real estate needs of education companies in the form of sale leaseback of company-owned real estate, build-to-suit opportunities, and forward commitments to purchase. Sterling works with companies to enable them to use their real estate to evolve and enhance their ability to fulfill their core missions and grow their enrollments.

Student Loan Xpress*

12770 High Bluff Drive, Suite 340
San Diego, California 92130
Phone: 866-759-7737
Fax: 866-289-7737
Contact: Mr. Fabrizio Balestri
Service: Student Financial Aid/Financial Aid
Special Message: Student Loan Xpress, Inc. offers a new way to look at lending with an experienced and dedicated team providing smart solutions for the financing of educational expenses. Student Loan Xpress® offers Federal Stafford Loans for students and Parent Loans for Undergraduate Students (PLUS Loans) for parents. In addition to Stafford and PLUS loans, Student Loan Xpress® offers a variety of private loans to meet any additional funding needs its clients may experience. Student Loan Xpress® provides help with easy-to-use tools and student loan programs and services for students, parents, and schools. Its commitment emphasizes early awareness, debt management, and individual financial responsibility for parents and students alike. In cooperation with the Career College Foundation, the Consolidation Assistance Program (CAP®) is offered to CCA member schools. Additional information is available at http://www.studentloanexpress.com.

SunTrust Education Loans

1001 Semmes Avenue, RVW 7900
Richmond, Virginia 23224
Phone: 804-319-1339
Fax: 804-319-4823
E-mail: sherrye.ward@suntrust.com
Contact: Sherrye A. Ward. National Sales Manager
Service: Financial Aid/Student Financial Aid/Tuition Financing
Special Message: SunTrust is a leading national provider of education loans with a commitment to serving the needs of private career schools and their students. SunTrust offers Federal Stafford, PLUS, and consolidation loans, all with money-saving repayment benefits. SunTrust also offers alternative loan products, including its eCareer® education loan that gives students greater flexibility in paying for school since it is not subject to the lending limits and eligibility requirements of many federal loan programs. Students may find more information at http://www.SunTrustEducation.com.

Susan F. Schulz & Associates, Inc.

Schools for Sale International, Inc.
2831 NW 23 Court
Boca Raton, Florida 33431
Phone: 561-483-9554
Fax: 561-451-4602
E-mail: susan@susanfschulz.com
Contact: Dr. Susan F. Schulz, President
Service: Consulting/Educational Training
Special Message: Susan F. Schulz & Associates, Inc. provides consulting services to career schools and colleges in the area of licensing, accreditation, curriculum and school development, continuing education, operations assessment, and more. Through its professional and licensed affiliate, Schools for Sale International, Inc., it offers intermediary and consulting services specializing in the purchase and sale of privately held schools and education entities. Additional informatin can be found online at http://www.schoolsforsaleinternational.com.

Synergistic Strategies Consulting

1550 Woodrose Court
Colorado Springs, Colorado 80921–3717
Phone: 719-481-5999
Fax: 719-481-5999
E-mail: rrroehrich@adelphia.net
Contact: Mr. Robert Roehrich

* indicates that the member is an Allied Plus Member.

Service: Consulting/Development/Distance Education/e-Learning/Educational Management/Management Search/Placement/Recruitment/Retention/Training Providers/Miscellaneous/

Special Message: Synergistic Strategies Consulting specializes in serving career schools and colleges in achieving their strategic and operational goals. Services include strategies planning, SWOT analysis, academic planning, product development, accreditation, and executive recruiting. Recent projects have included e-learning, corporate training, retention plans, DACUM, and board development and training activities. Additional information is available at http://www.synergisticstrat.com.

Target Direct Marketing

185 Main Street
Gloucester, Massachusetts 01930-1802
Phone: 978-281-5967
Fax: 978-282-0311
E-mail: tdm@shore.net

Contact: Mr. John Pirroni, President

Service: Marketing/Advertising

Special Message: Target Direct Marketing (TDM) can help clients systematically generate cost-effective quality leads and starts through its proven direct-mail programs. TDM does market analysis, campaign planning, list procurement, creative design and copy, mailing, training, and evaluation of results. Additonal information is available at http://www.targetdirectmarketing.com.

TFC Credit Corporation

199 Jericho Turnpike, Suite 300
Floral Park, New York 11001-2100
Phone: 800-358-1900
Fax: 516-358-6357
E-mail: info@tfccredit.com

Contact: Mr. Stanley Sobel, President

Service: Student Financial Aid/Tuition Finance

Special Message: TFC provides tuition financing for students attending both accredited and non-accredited schools. Interest rates are comparable to federal loans for amounts up to $15,000. Students may use TFC's tuition financing to supplement or replace other financing options. Information is available through the school's financial aid office. Additional information is available at http://www.tfccredit.com.

Thomson/Delmar Learning

Executive Woods
5 Maxwell Drive
Clifton Park, New York 12065-2919
Phone: 518-348-2300
Fax: 518-881-1250
E-mail: john.young@thomson.com

Contact: Mr. John Young, VP, Career Education Sales

Service: Educational/Training Materials/e-Learning

Special Message: Thomson/Delmar Learning is a leading provider of skills-based learning solutions for all areas of study in general education, health care, automotive, computer and information technologies, business, criminal justice, and paralegal studies. Offering a range of solutions from individual products to comprehensive curriculum packages, the wealth of vocational and technical print, CD-ROM, DVD, and online products work individually or together to allow clients to choose the best combination for their needs. Thomson/Delmar Learning's ability to bring knowledge the way clients want to receive it makes them the obvious choice for learning and teaching materials.

TMP Worldwide Educational Marketing Group

205 Hudson Street, 5th Floor
New York, New York 10013
Phone: 646-613-2000
Fax: 646-613-9752
E-mail: steve.ehrlich@tmp.com

Contact: Mr. Steven Ehrlich, Director

Service: Marketing

Special Message: TMP Worldwide's Educational Marketing Group is a trusted guide, a thought-provoking partner, and a strategic leader. Its goal is to collaborate with its clients to create innovative solutions that traverse the evolving student-recruitment landscape. It's a lofty aspiration—one that TMP Worldwide believes in wholeheartedly. Its desire to form a dynamic relationship with each of its clients compels it to understand its client's individual challenges as well as the global dynamics swaying the educational market today. When it comes to selecting a marketing communications and solutions partner, there is really only one word that matters: Delivery. Additional information is available at the Web site (http://www.timp.com).

Top-Colleges.com by Affiliate CREW

6415 South 3000 E.
Suite 200
Salt Lake City, Utah 84121
Phone: 801–993–2222
Fax: 801–993–2295
E-mail: pharrison@affiliatecrew.com

Contact: Mr. Peter Harrison, President

Service: Marketing/Advertising

Special Message: Top-Colleges.com provides colleges and universities with a cost-effective alternative to traditional offline lead generation. Its online education directory provides a customized experience for each student, based on geography and degree type.

* indicates that the member is an Allied Plus Member.

The result is a highly qualified prospect, matched to the right school in the right location. Additional information is available at http://www. top-colleges.com.

Training Masters, Inc.

1017 Country Club Road
Camp Hill, Pennsylvania 17011
Phone: 877-885-3276
Fax: 800-882-8574
E-mail: docrita@trainingmasters.com
Contact: Dr. Rita Girondi, President
Service: Admissions/Consulting/Education Management/Education, Training Materials/Information Technology Solutions/Placement/Retention/Software/Training Providers
Special Message: Training Masters is a training and consulting company specializing in products and services designed for career schools and colleges. Training Masters' distinction is its direct experience in successfully operating and owning schools. To improve starts, retention, and other key operational areas, Training Masters brings best practices to schools and keeps compliance and profitability in focus. STARS (Student Tracking, Accounting, and Record System) is a complete administrative software solution that combines information technology tools with internal procedures to create a proven, comprehensive school operational system. PIE (Pursuing International Excellence) is a computer-based interactive instructor-training CD library covering topics such as active learning, motivational strategies, classroom management, adult learning, the new instructor's guide to career schools, and more. Admissions presentations for the high school market, school retention programs, school director training, high-performance team building, and numerous other services and tools that support schools' goals are available. More information about Training Masters can be found on the Web (http://www.trainingmasters.com).

Trudeau & Trudeau Associates, Inc.

400 Washington Street
Braintree, Massachusetts 02184
Phone: 781-843-6699 Ext. 111
Fax: 781-843-6583
E-mail: wrtrudeau@trudeau-trudeau.com
Contact: Mr. William Trudeau, President
Service: Investment Banking
Special Message: Trudeau & Trudeau Associates, Inc. (T&T) is a full service M&A firm based on the South Shore of Boston, providing merger and acquisition, corporate finance, and strategic consulting services to client companies and equity groups. The firm was founded in 1982 and has affiliate offices located in the major markets throughout Western Europe and Southeast Asia as well as an extensive network of industry specialists. The T&T founders believe that effective M&A advisory services must be driven by an effective strategic initiative that is focused on the long-term goals and objectives of their clients. Additional information is available at the Web site (http://www.Trudeau-Trudeau.com).

Wells Fargo Education Financial Services (EFS)

829 Bethel Road, PMB 305
Columbus, Ohio 4321
Phone: 614-447-0076
Fax: 614-447-0182
E-mail: kate.barton@wellsfargoefs.com
Contact: Mrs. Kate Barton, Account Executive
Service: Financial Aid/Tuition Finance
Special Message: Wells Fargo Education Financial Services (EFS) originates more than $2.3 billion each year in federal and private educational lending. EFS serves 770,000 students and family customers in all 50 states. It has a variety of loan products, including a private alternative loan designed for the career education sector. Additional information is available at the Web site (http://www.wellsfargo.com/student).

West & Company

2938 N.W. 50th
Oklahoma City, Oklahoma 73112
Phone: 405-949-9730
Fax: 405-949-9738
E-mail: westandcompany@aol.com
Contact: Mr. William West, President
Service: Certified Public Accountant
Special Message: West & Company, a certified public accounting firm specializing in the educational industry, provides services in the fields of financial aid audits and attestation engagements, financial statement audits, tax planning and compliance, systems consulting services, and compliance consulting services.

Weworski & Associates

Certified Public Accountants and Business Consultants
4660 La Jolla Village Drive, Suite 880
San Diego, California 92122
Phone: 858-546-1505
Fax: 858-546-1405
E-mail: jweworski@weworski.com
Contact: Joseph Weworski

* indicates that the member is an Allied Plus Member.

Service: Certified Public Accountant

Special Message: Weworski & Associates is a certified public accounting firm that was formed specifically to service the proprietary school industry. The firm has built a solid reputation for providing quality and timely services to its clients. Weworski & Associates provides a wide array of services, including financial statement audits, student financial aid audits, income tax planning and preparation, acquisition due diligence, and other management advisory services, to more than 100 proprietary schools.

Whiteford, Taylor & Preston

1025 Connecticut Avenue N.W., Suite 400
Washington, D.C. 20036
Phone: 202-659-6800
Fax: 202-331-0573
E-mail: kingram@wtplaw.com
Contact: Mr. Kenneth J. Ingram, Partner
Service: Legal Services
Special Message: Whiteford, Taylor & Preston represents a number of private nonprofit accrediting agencies, including ACICS, ABHES, ACCET, MEAC, and CSWE.

Wonderlic, Inc.

1795 North Butterfield Road
Libertyville, Illinois 60048
Phone: 800-323-3742 (toll-free)
Fax: 847-680-9492
E-mail: justin.long@wonderlic.com
Contact: Mr. Justin Long, Director, Educational Relations
Service: Consulting/Retention/Recruitment/Testing Tools/Equipment/Administrative Services/Distance Education
Special Message: Wonderlic, Inc., has been a leader in the test publishing, consulting, and information gathering business since 1937. Wonderlic is a found-

ing member of the Association of Test Publishers and is approved by both the U.S. Department of Education and the American Council on Education. More than 130-million individuals have taken Wonderlic assessments and satisfaction surveys at nearly 60,000 schools, government agencies, and businesses worldwide. Additional information is available at http://www.wonderlic.com.

WorkForce Communications

627 Bay Shore Drive, Suite 100
Oshkosh, Wisconsin 54901-4975
Phone: 800-558-8250
Fax: 920-231-9977
E-mail: mcooney@workforce-com.com
Contact: Mr. Michael Cooney, Vice President
Service: Advertising/Marketing
Special Message: Workforce Communications offers fast, responsive, and cost-effective production of response-driven career college brochures and TV commercials. WorkForce's veteran media placement team provides high-accountability lead generation. Since 1926, the Career Education Review has served as the independent trade publication serving private career colleges.

Wright International Student Services

6405 Metcalf
Shawnee Mission, Kansas 66202
Phone: 800-257-4757 (toll-free)
Fax: 913-677-0977
Contact: Mr. John Beal, President
Service: Default Management
Special Message: Wright International Student Services (WISS) is the industry leader in default management services. More than 300 institutions, both private and public, utilize WISS for their default reduction needs. The average default rate of WISS' client schools is 4.69 percent.

* indicates that the member is an Allied Plus Member.

Profiles of Career Colleges

alabama

Capps College

200 Vulcan Way
Dothan, AL 36303
Web: http://www.medcareers.net

Programs Offered: massage therapy; medical/clinical assistant; medical office management; medical transcription; pharmacy technician

Institution Contact: *Phone:* 334-677-2832 *Fax:* 334-677-3756

Capps College

914 North McKenzie Street
Foley, AL 36535
Web: http://www.medcareers.net

Accreditation: Accrediting Bureau of Health Education Schools

Programs Offered: medical/clinical assistant

Institution Contact: Mr. Travis R. Townsend, Director *Phone:* 251-970-1460 *Fax:* 251-970-1660 *E-mail:* ttownsend@medcareers.net

Admission Contact: Ms. Kimberly Bateman, Admissions Advisor *Phone:* 251-970-1460 *Fax:* 251-970-1660

Capps College

Capps College, 3590 Pleasant Valley Road
Mobile, AL 36609

Accreditation: Accrediting Bureau of Health Education Schools

Programs Offered: massage therapy; medical administrative assistant and medical secretary; medical/clinical assistant; pharmacy technician

Enrollment: 223 students

Institution Contact: Mr. Glen King, Campus Director *Phone:* 251-344-1203 ext. 11 *Fax:* 251-344-1299 *E-mail:* gking@medcareers.net

Admission Contact: Mrs. Vicki Green, Admissions Advisor *Phone:* 251-344-1203 ext. 12 *Fax:* 251-344-1299 *E-mail:* info@medcareers.net

Capps College

Capps College, 3736 Atlanta Highway
Montgomery, AL 36109

Accreditation: Accrediting Bureau of Health Education Schools

Programs Offered: medical administrative assistant and medical secretary; medical/clinical assistant; pharmacy technician

Enrollment: 231 students

Institution Contact: Mr. Wayne Currie, Campus Director *Phone:* 334-272-3857 *Fax:* 334-272-3859 *E-mail:* wcurrie@medcareers.net

Admission Contact: Mrs. Andrea Johnson, Admissions Advisor *Phone:* 334-272-3857 *Fax:* 334-272-3859 *E-mail:* info@medcareers.net

Herzing College Ⓐ

280 West Valley Avenue
Birmingham, AL 35209-4816
Web: http://www.herzing.edu/birmingham

Accreditation: Accrediting Commission of Career Schools and Colleges of Technology; North Central Association of Colleges and Schools

Programs Offered: business administration and management; communications technology; computer and information systems security; computer engineering technology; computer/information technology administration and management; computer/information technology services administration related; computer programming; computer programming (specific applications); computer programming (vendor/product certification); computer systems analysis; computer systems networking and telecommunications; computer technology/computer systems technology; data processing and data processing technology; e-commerce; electrical, electronic and communications engineering technology; electromechanical technology; health/health care administration; health information/medical records administration; health information/medical records technology; industrial electronics technology; information technology; medical administrative assistant and medical secretary; medical insurance coding; medical insurance/medical billing; medical office computer specialist; medical office management; system administration; system, networking, and LAN/WAN management; technology management; telecommunications; telecommunications technology; web page, digital/multimedia and information resources design

Enrollment: 445 students

Institution Contact: Mr. Donald Lewis, President *Phone:* 205-916-2800 *Fax:* 205-916-2807 *E-mail:* donl@bhm.herzing.edu

Admission Contact: Ms. Tess L. Anderson, Director of Admissions *Phone:* 205-916-2800 *Fax:* 205-916-2807 *E-mail:* info@bhm.herzing.edu

See full description on page 280.

Ⓐ indicates that the school is a participating institution in the *Imagine America* Scholarship Program.

ITT Technical Institute Ⓐ

500 Riverhills Business Park
Birmingham, AL 35242
Web: http://www.itt-tech.edu

Accreditation: Accrediting Council for Independent Colleges and Schools

Programs Offered: accounting and business/management; animation, interactive technology, video graphics and special effects; business administration and management; CAD/CADD drafting/design technology; communications technology; computer and information systems security; computer engineering technology; computer software and media applications; computer software engineering; computer systems networking and telecommunications; criminal justice/police science; digital communication and media/multimedia; electrical, electronic and communications engineering technology; technology management; web page, digital/multimedia and information resources design

Enrollment: 586 students

Institution Contact: Mr. Allen Rice, Director *Phone:* 205-991-5410

Admission Contact: Mr. Jesse L. Johnson, Director of Recruitment *Phone:* 205-991-5410

See full description on page 281.

Remington College–Mobile Campus Ⓐ

828 Downtowner Loop West
Mobile, AL 36609-5404
Web: http://www.remingtoncollege.edu

Accreditation: Accrediting Commission of Career Schools and Colleges of Technology

Programs Offered: allied health and medical assisting services related; business administration and management; computer engineering technology; computer installation and repair technology; computer programming; electrical, electronic and communications engineering technology; pharmacy technician

Enrollment: 454 students

Institution Contact: Mr. Micheal Ackerman, Campus President *Phone:* 251-343-8200 ext. 209 *Fax:* 251-343-0577 *E-mail:* michael.ackerman@remingtoncollege.edu

Admission Contact: Mr. Chris Jones, Director of Recruitment *Phone:* 251-343-8200 ext. 221 *Fax:* 251-343-0577 *E-mail:* chris.jones@remingtoncollege.com

See full description on page 282.

South University

5355 Vaughn Road
Montgomery, AL 36116-1120
Web: http://www.southuniversity.edu/

Accreditation: Southern Association of Colleges and Schools

Programs Offered: accounting; business administration and management; health/health care administration; information technology; legal assistant/paralegal; medical/clinical assistant; physical therapist assistant; pre-law studies

Enrollment: 400 students

Institution Contact: Mr. Victor K. Biebighauser, President *Phone:* 334-395-8800 *Fax:* 334-395-8859 *E-mail:* vbiebighauser@southuniversity.edu

Admission Contact: Ms. Anna M. Pearson, Director of Admissions *Phone:* 334-395-8800 *Fax:* 334-395-8859 *E-mail:* apearson@southuniversity.edu

VC Tech

2790 Pelham Parkway
Pelham, AL 35124
Web: http://www.vc.edu

Accreditation: Accrediting Council for Independent Colleges and Schools

Programs Offered: autobody/collision and repair technology; automobile/automotive mechanics technology; welding technology

Institution Contact: Mr. J. Kregg Pruitt, Campus Director *Phone:* 205-943-2100 ext. 2926 *Fax:* 205-943-2097 *E-mail:* kpruitt@vc.edu

Admission Contact: Mr. Dean Mahaffey, National Director of Admissions *Phone:* 205-943-2100 ext. 2920 *Fax:* 205-943-2097 *E-mail:* dmahaffey@vc.edu

Virginia College at Birmingham Ⓐ

PO Box 19249
Birmingham, AL 35219-9249
Web: http://www.vc.edu

Accreditation: Accrediting Council for Independent Colleges and Schools

Programs Offered: accounting; accounting and business/management; accounting related; accounting technology and bookkeeping; administrative assistant and secretarial science; advertising; allied health and medical assisting services related; animation, interactive technology, video graphics and special effects; architectural drafting and CAD/CADD; autobody/collision and repair technology; automobile/automotive mechanics technology; baking and pastry arts; business administration and management; CAD/

Ⓐ indicates that the school is a participating institution in the *Imagine America* Scholarship Program.

Virginia College at Birmingham *(continued)*

CADD drafting/design technology; computer and information sciences; computer and information systems security; computer graphics; computer/information technology services administration related; computer programming; computer programming (specific applications); cosmetology; cosmetology, barber/styling, and nail instruction; criminal justice/law enforcement administration; culinary arts; diagnostic medical sonography and ultrasound technology; executive assistant/executive secretary; general studies; graphic communications; health information/medical records administration; human resources management; interior design; legal assistant/paralegal; management information systems; massage therapy; medical/clinical assistant; medical insurance coding; medical office management; nursing (licensed practical/vocational nurse training); surgical technology; telecommunications technology; web/multimedia management and webmaster; word processing

Enrollment: 2,850 students

Institution Contact: Dr. James Hutton, Chief Operating Officer *Phone:* 205-802-1200 *Fax:* 205-802-1597 *E-mail:* jdh@vc.edu

Admission Contact: Mrs. Bibbie McLaughlin, Senior Vice President of Admissions *Phone:* 205-802-1200 ext. 1207 *Fax:* 205-802-7045 *E-mail:* bibbie@vc.edu

See full description on page 283.

Virginia College at Huntsville Ⓐ

2800A Bob Wallace Avenue
Huntsville, AL 35805
Web: http://www.vc.edu

Accreditation: Accrediting Council for Independent Colleges and Schools

Programs Offered: accounting technology and bookkeeping; administrative assistant and secretarial science; business administration and management; CAD/CADD drafting/design technology; computer graphics; computer installation and repair technology; computer systems networking and telecommunications; computer technology/computer systems technology; criminal justice/law enforcement administration; criminal justice/police science; drafting and design technology; health information/medical records technology; legal administrative assistant/secretary; legal assistant/paralegal; massage therapy; medical administrative assistant and medical secretary; medical/clinical assistant; medical insurance/medical billing; medical office assistant; medical office management; office management; system administration; system, networking, and LAN/WAN management; web/multimedia management and webmaster

Enrollment: 680 students

Institution Contact: Mr. James Foster, Director *Phone:* 256-533-7387 *Fax:* 256-533-7785 *E-mail:* jfoster@vc.edu

Admission Contact: Ms. Tricia L. Smith, Admissions Assistant *Phone:* 256-533-7387 *Fax:* 256-533-7785 *E-mail:* tsmith@vc.edu

See full description on page 284.

Virginia College at Mobile

5901 Airport Boulevard
Mobile, AL 36608
Web: http://www.medcci.com

Accreditation: Accrediting Bureau of Health Education Schools; Accrediting Council for Independent Colleges and Schools

Programs Offered: accounting technology and bookkeeping; administrative assistant and secretarial science; human resources management; legal administrative assistant/secretary; medical/clinical assistant; medical insurance coding; medical insurance/medical billing; surgical technology

Institution Contact: Mrs. Joy Harden, Campus Administrator *Phone:* 251-343-7227 ext. 2405 *Fax:* 251-343-7287 *E-mail:* jharden@vc.edu

Admission Contact: Mrs. Tracy McManus, Director of Admissions *Phone:* 251-343-7227 ext. 2402 *Fax:* 251-343-7287 *E-mail:* tmcmanus@vc.edu

Career Academy

1415 East Tudor Road
Anchorage, AK 99507-1033
Web: http://www.careeracademy.edu

Accreditation: Accrediting Commission of Career Schools and Colleges of Technology

Programs Offered: airline pilot and flight crew; business operations support and secretarial services related; massage therapy; medical/clinical assistant; medical insurance coding; medical insurance/medical billing; office management; phlebotomy; tourism and travel services management

Enrollment: 653 students

Institution Contact: Ms. Jennifer Deitz, President *Phone:* 907-563-7575 *Fax:* 907-563-8330 *E-mail:* jdeitz@careeracademy.edu

Ⓐ indicates that the school is a participating institution in the *Imagine America* Scholarship Program.

Admission Contact: Ms. Lisa Spencer, Director of Admissions *Phone:* 907-563-7575 *Fax:* 907-563-8330 *E-mail:* lspencer@careeracademy.edu

Charter College

2221 East Northern Lights Boulevard, Suite 120
Anchorage, AK 99508-4140
Web: http://www.chartercollege.edu

Accreditation: Accrediting Council for Independent Colleges and Schools

Programs Offered: accounting; accounting technology and bookkeeping; administrative assistant and secretarial science; architectural drafting and CAD/CADD; business administration and management; business administration, management and operations related; CAD/CADD drafting/design technology; civil drafting and CAD/CADD; computer engineering related; computer engineering technologies related; computer engineering technology; computer graphics; computer hardware technology; computer/information technology administration and management; computer/information technology services administration related; computer software technology; computer systems networking and telecommunications; computer technology/computer systems technology; health and medical administrative services related; information technology; medical office management; web/multimedia management and webmaster

Enrollment: 489 students

Institution Contact: Dr. Milton Byrd, President *Phone:* 907-777-1304 *Fax:* 907-274-3342 *E-mail:* mbyrd@chartercollege.edu

Admission Contact: Miss Brenda O'Neill, Associate Director of Academic Services *Phone:* 907-777-1342 *Fax:* 907-274-3342 *E-mail:* bo'neill@chartercollege.edu

Academy of Radio Broadcasting

4914 East McDowell Road, #107
Phoenix, AZ 85008
Web: http://www.arbradio.com

Accreditation: Accrediting Council for Continuing Education and Training

Programs Offered: cinematography and film/video production; radio and television

Institution Contact: Mr. Thomas Gillenwater, President *Phone:* 602-267-8001 *Fax:* 602-273-6411

Admission Contact: Mr. Brian Jewett, Admissions Director *Phone:* 602-267-8001 *Fax:* 602-273-6411 *E-mail:* jewettbrianm@aol.com

American Institute of Technology

440 South 54th Avenue
Phoenix, AZ 85043-4729
Web: http://www.ait-schools.com

Accreditation: Accrediting Commission of Career Schools and Colleges of Technology

Programs Offered: truck and bus driver/commercial vehicle operation

Enrollment: 147 students

Institution Contact: Mr. R. Wade Murphree, President *Phone:* 602-233-2222 *Fax:* 602-278-4849 *E-mail:* wade@ait-schools.com

Admission Contact: Mrs. Julie Wirth, Assistant to the Vice President *Phone:* 602-233-2222 *Fax:* 602-278-4849 *E-mail:* admissions@ait-schools.com

Apollo College—Phoenix, Inc. Ⓐ

8503 North 27th Avenue
Phoenix, AZ 85051
Web: http://www.apollocollege.com

Accreditation: Accrediting Bureau of Health Education Schools

Programs Offered: clinical/medical laboratory technology; dental assisting; medical administrative assistant and medical secretary; medical/clinical assistant; pharmacy technician; veterinary/animal health technology

Institution Contact: Mr. Randy Utley, Campus Director *Phone:* 602-864-1571 *Fax:* 602-864-8207 *E-mail:* rutley@apollocollege.com

See full description on page 286.

Apollo College—Tri-City, Inc. Ⓐ

630 West Southern Avenue
Mesa, AZ 85210
Web: http://www.apollocollege.com

Accreditation: Accrediting Bureau of Health Education Schools

Programs Offered: dental assisting; massage therapy; medical administrative assistant and medical secretary; medical/clinical assistant; pharmacy technician; respiratory care therapy; veterinary/animal health technology

Ⓐ indicates that the school is a participating institution in the *Imagine America* Scholarship Program.

Apollo College–Tri-City, Inc. (*continued*)

Institution Contact: Mr. James Miller, Campus Director *Phone:* 480-831-6585 *Fax:* 480-827-0022 *E-mail:* jmiller@apollocollege.com

See full description on page 285.

Apollo College–Tucson, Inc. Ⓐ

3550 North Oracle Road
Tucson, AZ 85705
Web: http://www.apollocollege.com

Accreditation: Accrediting Bureau of Health Education Schools

Programs Offered: computer/information technology administration and management; computer/information technology services administration related; computer technology/computer systems technology; dental assisting; massage therapy; medical administrative assistant and medical secretary; medical/clinical assistant; pharmacy technician; veterinary/animal health technology

Institution Contact: Mr. Jeff Turner, Campus Director *Phone:* 520-888-5885 *Fax:* 520-887-3005 *E-mail:* jeffturner@apollocollege.com

See full description on page 287.

Apollo College–Westside, Inc. Ⓐ

2701 West Bethany Home Road
Phoenix, AZ 85017
Web: http://www.apollocollege.com

Accreditation: Accrediting Bureau of Health Education Schools

Programs Offered: computer/information technology services administration related; computer programming; computer software and media applications; computer software engineering; health information/medical records administration; information technology; massage therapy; medical office computer specialist; physical therapist assistant; radiologic technology/science

Institution Contact: Mr. Patrick Lydick, Campus Director *Phone:* 602-433-1333 *Fax:* 602-433-1222 *E-mail:* cnestor@apollocollege.com

See full description on page 288.

Arizona Automotive Institute Ⓐ

6829 North 46th Avenue
Glendale, AZ 85301
Web: http://www.azautoinst.com

Accreditation: Accrediting Commission of Career Schools and Colleges of Technology

Programs Offered: automobile/automotive mechanics technology; automotive engineering technology; diesel mechanics technology; heating, air conditioning, ventilation and refrigeration maintenance technology

Enrollment: 858 students

Institution Contact: Mr. Alan Kluger, Executive Director *Phone:* 623-934-7273 *Fax:* 623-937-5000 *E-mail:* akluger@atienterprises.com

Admission Contact: Mr. Mark LaCaria, Director of Admissions *Phone:* 623-934-7273 *Fax:* 623-937-5000 *E-mail:* mlacaria@atienterprises.com

See full description on page 289.

Arizona College of Allied Health

4425 West Olive Avenue, Suite 300
Glendale, AZ 85302
Web: http://www.arizonacollege.edu

Accreditation: Accrediting Bureau of Health Education Schools

Programs Offered: dental assisting; health information/medical records technology; massage therapy; medical/clinical assistant; medical insurance/medical billing; pharmacy technician

Enrollment: 200 students

Institution Contact: Mr. Larkin Hicks, President *Phone:* 602-222-9300 *Fax:* 623-298-1329 *E-mail:* lhicks@arizonacollege.edu

Admission Contact: Ms. Renee Fabig, Campus Director *Phone:* 602-222-9300 *Fax:* 602-200-8726 *E-mail:* rfabig@arizonacollege.edu

The Art Institute of Phoenix

2233 West Dunlap Avenue
Phoenix, AZ 85021
Web: http://www.aipx.edu

Accreditation: Accrediting Council for Independent Colleges and Schools

Programs Offered: advertising; animation, interactive technology, video graphics and special effects; apparel and accessories marketing; apparel and textile marketing management; audiovisual communications technologies related; baking and pastry arts; CAD/CADD drafting/design technology; cinematography and film/video production; commercial and advertising art; computer graphics; culinary arts; desktop publishing and digital imaging design; digital communication and media/multimedia; graphic communications; graphic communications related; interior design; intermedia/multimedia; photographic and film/video technology; restaurant, culinary, and catering management; web/multimedia management

Ⓐ indicates that the school is a participating institution in the *Imagine America* Scholarship Program.

and webmaster; web page, digital/multimedia and information resources design

Enrollment: 1,200 students

Institution Contact: Ms. Karen A. Bryant, President *Phone:* 800-474-2479 ext. 7501 *Fax:* 602-331-5300 *E-mail:* kabryant@aii.edu

Admission Contact: Mr. Jerry Driskill, Director of Admissions *Phone:* 800-474-2479 ext. 7502 *Fax:* 602-331-5300 *E-mail:* jdriskill@aii.edu

The Bryman School

2250 West Peoria Avenue
Phoenix, AZ 85029
Web: http://www.hightechinstitute.com/

Accreditation: Accrediting Bureau of Health Education Schools; Accrediting Commission of Career Schools and Colleges of Technology

Programs Offered: dental assisting; health unit coordinator/ward clerk; massage therapy; medical/clinical assistant; medical radiologic technology; surgical technology

Institution Contact: Mr. Glen M. Tharp, Director *Phone:* 602-274-4300 *Fax:* 602-248-9087 *E-mail:* gtharp@hightechschools.com

Admission Contact: Ms. Kelly McDermid, Director of Admissions *Phone:* 602-274-4300 *Fax:* 602-248-9087 *E-mail:* kmcdermid@hightechinstitue.com

Chaparral College

4585 East Speedway Boulevard, Suite 204
Tucson, AZ 85712
Web: http://www.chap-col.edu

Accreditation: Accrediting Council for Independent Colleges and Schools

Programs Offered: accounting; business administration and management; computer systems networking and telecommunications; computer technology/computer systems technology; criminal justice/law enforcement administration; information science/studies

Enrollment: 400 students

Institution Contact: Mr. Richard L. Melin, Marketing/Public Relations Director *Phone:* 520-327-6866 *Fax:* 520-325-0108 *E-mail:* rmelin@chap-col.edu

Admission Contact: Ms. Becki Rossini, Admissions Director *Phone:* 520-327-6866 *Fax:* 520-325-0108 *E-mail:* becki@chap-col.edu

CollegeAmerica–Flagstaff

1800 South Milton Road
Flagstaff, AZ 86001
Web: http://www.collegeamerica.edu

Accreditation: Accrediting Bureau of Health Education Schools

Programs Offered: computer technology/computer systems technology; medical/clinical assistant

Institution Contact: Mr. Pascal Berlioux, Executive Director *Phone:* 800-977-5455 *E-mail:* pberlioux@collegeamerica.edu

Admission Contact: Ms. Nicole Dieter, Director of Admissions *Phone:* 800-977-5455 *E-mail:* ndieter@collegeamerica.edu

Collins College: A School of Design and Technology

1140 South Priest Drive
Tempe, AZ 85281-5206
Web: http://www.collinscollege.edu/

Accreditation: Accrediting Commission of Career Schools and Colleges of Technology

Programs Offered: animation, interactive technology, video graphics and special effects; business administration and management; business administration, management and operations related; cinematography and film/video production; commercial and advertising art; computer programming (specific applications); computer systems networking and telecommunications; computer/technical support; design and visual communications; digital communication and media/multimedia; graphic communications related; information technology; interior design; system, networking, and LAN/WAN management; web/multimedia management and webmaster; web page, digital/multimedia and information resources design

Enrollment: 2,000 students

Institution Contact: Mr. John Calman, President *Phone:* 480-966-3000 *Fax:* 480-966-2599 *E-mail:* jcalman@collinscollege.edu

Admission Contact: Ms. Wendy Johnston, Vice President of Marketing and Admissions *Phone:* 480-966-3000 *Fax:* 480-966-2599 *E-mail:* wjohnston@collinscollege.edu

Conservatory of Recording Arts and Sciences Ⓐ

2300 East Broadway Road
Tempe, AZ 85282-1707
Web: http://www.audiorecordingschool.com

Accreditation: Accrediting Commission of Career Schools and Colleges of Technology

Ⓐ indicates that the school is a participating institution in the *Imagine America* Scholarship Program.

Conservatory of Recording Arts and Sciences (*continued*)

Programs Offered: audiovisual communications technologies related; computer software and media applications related; digital communication and media/multimedia; music management and merchandising; recording arts technology

Enrollment: 408 students

Institution Contact: Mr. Kirt R. Hamm, Administrator *Phone:* 800-562-6383 *Fax:* 480-829-1332 *E-mail:* hamm@cras.org

Admission Contact: Mr. John F. McJunkin, Director of Admissions *Phone:* 800-562-6383 *Fax:* 480-829-1332 *E-mail:* john@cras.org

See full description on page 290.

Everest College Ⓐ

10400 North 25th Avenue, Suite 190
Phoenix, AZ 85021-1641
Web: http://everest-college.com/

Accreditation: North Central Association of Colleges and Schools

Programs Offered: accounting; accounting technology and bookkeeping; administrative assistant and secretarial science; business administration and management; criminal justice/law enforcement administration; criminal justice/police science; executive assistant/executive secretary; legal administrative assistant/secretary; legal assistant/paralegal; medical insurance coding; medical insurance/medical billing; office management; office occupations and clerical services; web page, digital/multimedia and information resources design

Enrollment: 500 students

Institution Contact: Mr. Todd McDonald, Academic Dean *Phone:* 602-942-4141 *Fax:* 602-943-0960 *E-mail:* tmcdonal@cci.edu

Admission Contact: Melissa Agee, Director of Admissions *Phone:* 602-942-4141 *Fax:* 602-943-0960 *E-mail:* magee@cci.edu

See full description on page 291.

High-Tech Institute

1515 East Indian School Road
Phoenix, AZ 85014
Web: http://www.hightechinstitute.edu

Accreditation: Accrediting Commission of Career Schools and Colleges of Technology

Programs Offered: animation, interactive technology, video graphics and special effects; CAD/CADD drafting/design technology; computer and information systems security; electrical, electronic and

communications engineering technology; medical/ clinical assistant; medical insurance coding; medical insurance/medical billing; system administration; system, networking, and LAN/WAN management; web page, digital/multimedia and information resources design

Enrollment: 1,326 students

Institution Contact: Rich Craven, Director *Phone:* 602-279-9700 *Fax:* 602-279-2999 *E-mail:* rcraven@hightechinstitute.edu

Admission Contact: Holly Kast, Director of Admissions *Phone:* 602-279-9700 *Fax:* 602-279-2999 *E-mail:* kkast@hightechinstitute.edu

High-Tech Institute

2250 West Peoria Avenue
Phoenix, AZ 85029
Web: http://www.hightechinstitute.edu

Accreditation: Accrediting Commission of Career Schools and Colleges of Technology

Programs Offered: CAD/CADD drafting/design technology; computer and information sciences and support services related; computer and information systems security; computer graphics; computer/ information technology administration and management; computer/information technology services administration related; computer installation and repair technology; computer software and media applications; computer software and media applications related; computer software technology; computer systems networking and telecommunications; computer/technical support; computer technology/ computer systems technology; data processing and data processing technology; design and visual communications; digital communication and media/ multimedia; drafting and design technology; electrical/electronics equipment installation and repair; electromechanical technology; industrial radiologic technology; information technology; intermedia/ multimedia; medical administrative assistant and medical secretary; medical/clinical assistant; medical insurance coding; robotics technology; telecommunications technology; web/multimedia management and webmaster; web page, digital/multimedia and information resources design

Enrollment: 1,300 students

Institution Contact: Ms. Carole Miller, Vice President *Phone:* 602-328-2800 ext. 2803 *Fax:* 602-264-8391 *E-mail:* cmiller@hightechschools.com

Admission Contact: Mr. Todd Rash, Director of Marketing *Phone:* 602-328-2800 *Fax:* 602-264-8391 *E-mail:* dkullman@hightechschools.com

Ⓐ indicates that the school is a participating institution in the *Imagine America* Scholarship Program.

International Import-Export Institute

2432 West Peoria, Suite 1026
Phoenix, AZ 85029
Web: http://www.iiei.edu

Accreditation: Distance Education and Training Council

Programs Offered: business administration and management; entrepreneurship; international business/trade/commerce; logistics and materials management; marketing/marketing management

Institution Contact: Barbara Ann Baderman, Executive Director *Phone:* 602-648-5750 *Fax:* 602-648-5755 *E-mail:* don.burton@expandglobal.com

Admission Contact: Melissa Jensen, Student Services Coordinator *Phone:* 602-648-5750 *Fax:* 602-648-5755 *E-mail:* info@expandglobal.com

International Institute of the Americas

925 South Gilbert Road, Suite 201
Mesa, AZ 85204-4448
Web: http://www.aibtonline.com

Accreditation: Accrediting Council for Independent Colleges and Schools

Programs Offered: accounting technology and bookkeeping; business administration and management; computer systems networking and telecommunications; computer technology/computer systems technology; health information/medical records administration; medical administrative assistant and medical secretary; medical/clinical assistant; medical office management; system, networking, and LAN/WAN management

Institution Contact: *Phone:* 480-545-8755 *Fax:* 480-926-1371 *E-mail:* info@aibt.edu

International Institute of the Americas

4136 North 75th Avenue, Suite 211
Phoenix, AZ 85033
Web: http://www.iia.edu

Accreditation: Accrediting Council for Independent Colleges and Schools

Programs Offered: accounting; administrative assistant and secretarial science; business administration and management; business/corporate communications; computer technology/computer systems technology; criminal justice/law enforcement administration; legal assistant/paralegal; medical/clinical assistant; medical/health management and clinical assistant; medical transcription; nursing assistant/aide and patient care assistant; phlebotomy; security and loss prevention

Enrollment: 1,369 students

Institution Contact: Dr. Lynda K. Angel, Vice President *Phone:* 602-242-6265 *Fax:* 602-589-1348 *E-mail:* langel@iia.edu

Admission Contact: Mr. John Pechota, Director of Admissions *Phone:* 623-849-7830 *Fax:* 623-849-7835 *E-mail:* jpechota@iia.edu

International Institute of the Americas

6049 North 43rd Avenue
Phoenix, AZ 85019
Web: http://www.iia.edu

Accreditation: Accrediting Council for Independent Colleges and Schools

Programs Offered: accounting technology and bookkeeping; business administration and management; clinical/medical laboratory assistant; computer systems networking and telecommunications; computer technology/computer systems technology; criminal justice/law enforcement administration; health information/medical records administration; hospital and health care facilities administration; medical administrative assistant and medical secretary; medical/clinical assistant; medical insurance coding; medical insurance/medical billing; medical office assistant; medical office management; medical reception; nursing (licensed practical/vocational nurse training); nursing (registered nurse training); system, networking, and LAN/WAN management

Enrollment: 315 students

Institution Contact: Mr. Joseph A. Brickman, Campus Director *Phone:* 602-242-6265 ext. 210 *Fax:* 602-589-1353 *E-mail:* jbrickman@iia.edu

Admission Contact: Mr. John Pechota, Director of Admissions and Marketing *Phone:* 623-463-6812 *Fax:* 623-849-7835 *E-mail:* jpechota@iia.edu

International Institute of the Americas

5441 East 22nd Street, Suite 125
Tucson, AZ 85711
Web: http://www.iia.edu

Accreditation: Accrediting Council for Independent Colleges and Schools

Programs Offered: accounting; business administration and management; computer/information technology services administration related; computer technology/computer systems technology; criminal justice/law enforcement administration; health/health care administration; medical/clinical assistant

Institution Contact: Mrs. Leigh Anne Pechota, Director *Phone:* 520-748-9799 *Fax:* 520-748-9355 *E-mail:* lpechota@iia.edu

Ⓐ indicates that the school is a participating institution in the *Imagine America* Scholarship Program.

International Institute of the Americas (*continued*)

Admission Contact: Ms. Tracy Ebeling, Admissions Representative *Phone:* 520-748-9799 *Fax:* 520-748-9355 *E-mail:* tebeling@iia.edu

ITT Technical Institute ⓐ

5005 South Wendler
Tempe, AZ 85282
Web: http://www.itt-tech.edu
Accreditation: Accrediting Council for Independent Colleges and Schools
Programs Offered: accounting and business/management; animation, interactive technology, video graphics and special effects; business administration and management; CAD/CADD drafting/design technology; communications technology; computer and information systems security; computer engineering technology; computer software and media applications; computer software engineering; computer systems networking and telecommunications; criminal justice/police science; digital communication and media/multimedia; electrical, electronic and communications engineering technology; technology management; web page, digital/multimedia and information resources design
Enrollment: 617 students
Institution Contact: Mr. Chuck Wilson, Director *Phone:* 602-437-7500
Admission Contact: Mr. Gene McWhorter, Director of Recruitment *Phone:* 602-437-7500
See full description on page 292.

ITT Technical Institute ⓐ

1455 West River Road
Tucson, AZ 85704
Web: http://www.itt-tech.edu
Accreditation: Accrediting Council for Independent Colleges and Schools
Programs Offered: accounting and business/management; animation, interactive technology, video graphics and special effects; business administration and management; CAD/CADD drafting/design technology; communications technology; computer and information systems security; computer engineering technology; computer software and media applications; computer software engineering; computer systems networking and telecommunications; criminal justice/police science; digital communication and media/multimedia; electrical, electronic and communications engineering technology; technology management; web page, digital/multimedia and information resources design

Enrollment: 456 students
Institution Contact: Mr. Timothy Riordan, Director *Phone:* 520-408-7488
Admission Contact: Ms. Linda Lemken, Director of Recruitment *Phone:* 520-408-7488
See full description on page 293.

Long Technical College

13450 North Black Canyon Highway, Suite 104
Phoenix, AZ 85029
Web: http://www.longtechnicalcollege.com
Accreditation: Accrediting Commission of Career Schools and Colleges of Technology
Programs Offered: legal assistant/paralegal; medical/clinical assistant; pharmacy technician; respiratory care therapy; sports medicine; veterinary/animal health technology
Enrollment: 410 students
Institution Contact: Mr. Michael S. Savely, Executive Director *Phone:* 602-548-1955 *Fax:* 602-548-1956 *E-mail:* msavely@longtechnicalcollege.com
Admission Contact: Ms. Joyce McCullough, Director of Admissions *Phone:* 602-548-1955 ext. 126 *Fax:* 602-548-1956 *E-mail:* jmccullough@longtechnicalcollege.com

Long Technical College—East Valley

111 West Monroe Street, Suite 800
Phoenix, AZ 85003
Web: http://www.phoenixparalegal.com
Accreditation: Accrediting Council for Independent Colleges and Schools
Programs Offered: legal assistant/paralegal
Institution Contact: Mr. Dennis Del Valle, Executive Director *Phone:* 602-252-2171 *Fax:* 602-252-1891 *E-mail:* ddelvalle@phoenixcareercollege.com

Motorcycle Mechanics Institute ⓐ

2844 West Deer Valley Road
Phoenix, AZ 85027-2399
Web: http://www.uticorp.com
Accreditation: Accrediting Commission of Career Schools and Colleges of Technology
Programs Offered: marine maintenance and ship repair technology; motorcycle maintenance and repair technology
Enrollment: 2,200 students
Institution Contact: Mr. Bryan Fishkind, Campus Director *Phone:* 623-869-9644 *Fax:* 623-581-2871 *E-mail:* bfishkind@uticorp.com

ⓐ indicates that the school is a participating institution in the *Imagine America* Scholarship Program.

Admission Contact: Ms. Angie Murphy, Admissions Office Manager *Phone:* 623-869-9644 *Fax:* 623-516-7660 *E-mail:* amurphy@uticorp.com
See full description on page 294.

Pima Medical Institute

957 South Dobson Road
Mesa, AZ 85202
Web: http://www.pmi.edu
Accreditation: Accrediting Bureau of Health Education Schools
Programs Offered: dental assisting; massage therapy; medical administrative assistant and medical secretary; medical/clinical assistant; pharmacy technician; phlebotomy; physical therapist assistant; radiologic technology/science; respiratory care therapy; veterinary/animal health technology
Enrollment: 592 students
Institution Contact: Mr. Christopher Luebke, Admissions Support Center Director *Phone:* 888-898-9048 *E-mail:* asc@pmi.edu
Admission Contact: Admissions Support Representative *Phone:* 888-898-9048

Pima Medical Institute

3350 East Grant Road, Suite 200
Tucson, AZ 85716
Web: http://www.pmi.edu
Accreditation: Accrediting Bureau of Health Education Schools
Programs Offered: dental assisting; health unit coordinator/ward clerk; medical administrative assistant and medical secretary; medical/clinical assistant; pharmacy technician; phlebotomy; physical therapist assistant; radiologic technology/science; respiratory care therapy; veterinary/animal health technology
Enrollment: 567 students
Institution Contact: Mr. Christopher Luebke, Admissions Support Center Director *Phone:* 888-898-9048 *E-mail:* asc@pmi.edu
Admission Contact: Admissions Support Representative *Phone:* 888-898-9048 *E-mail:* asc@pmi.edu

The Refrigeration School Ⓐ

4210 East Washington Street
Phoenix, AZ 85034
Web: http://www.refrigerationschool.com/
Accreditation: Accrediting Commission of Career Schools and Colleges of Technology

Programs Offered: electrician; electromechanical technology; heating, air conditioning and refrigeration technology; heating, air conditioning, ventilation and refrigeration maintenance technology; mechanical engineering/mechanical technology
Enrollment: 336 students
Institution Contact: Ms. Elizabeth Cline, President/Director *Phone:* 602-275-7133 *Fax:* 602-267-4811 *E-mail:* liz@rsiaz.org
Admission Contact: Ms. Mary Simmons, Admissions Director *Phone:* 602-275-7133 *Fax:* 602-267-4805 *E-mail:* mary@rsiaz.org
See full description on page 295.

Remington College–Tempe Campus Ⓐ

875 West Elliot Road, Suite 126
Tempe, AZ 85284
Web: http://www.educationamerica.com/
Accreditation: Accrediting Council for Independent Colleges and Schools
Programs Offered: computer programming (specific applications); computer systems networking and telecommunications; criminal justice/law enforcement administration; information science/studies; internet information systems
Institution Contact: Mr. Joe Drennen, Campus President *Phone:* 480-834-1000 *Fax:* 480-491-2970 *E-mail:* jdrennen@edamerica.com
Admission Contact: Mr. Steve Schwartz, Director of Recruitment *Phone:* 480-834-1000 *Fax:* 480-491-2970 *E-mail:* sschwart@edamerica.com
See full description on page 296.

Scottsdale Culinary Institute

8100 East Camelback Road, Suite 1001
Scottsdale, AZ 85251-3940
Web: http://www.scichefs.com/
Accreditation: Accrediting Commission of Career Schools and Colleges of Technology
Programs Offered: baking and pastry arts; culinary arts
Institution Contact: Mr. Jon Alberts, President *Phone:* 480-990-3773 *Fax:* 480-990-0351
Admission Contact: Ms. Leslie Idaspe, Director of Admissions *Phone:* 480-990-3773 *Fax:* 480-990-0351 *E-mail:* leslie.idaspe@scichefs.com

Sonoran Desert Institute

10245 East Via Linda, Suite 102
Scottsdale, AZ 85258
Web: http://www.sonoranlearning.com
Accreditation: Distance Education and Training Council

Ⓐ indicates that the school is a participating institution in the *Imagine America* Scholarship Program.

Sonoran Desert Institute (*continued*)

Programs Offered: building/home/construction inspection; gunsmithing
Institution Contact: *Phone:* 480-314-2102 *Fax:* 480-314-2138 *E-mail:* info@sonoranlearning.com

Universal Technical Institute

10695 West Pierce Street
Avondale, AZ 85323
Web: http://www.uticorp.com
Accreditation: Accrediting Commission of Career Schools and Colleges of Technology
Programs Offered: automotive engineering technology; diesel mechanics technology
Enrollment: 2,200 students
Institution Contact: Mike Klackle, Director *Phone:* 623-245-4600 *Fax:* 623-245-4601 *E-mail:* mklackle@uticorp.com
Admission Contact: Ms. Jennifer Clifford, Director *Phone:* 623-245-4600 *Fax:* 623-245-4601 *E-mail:* jclifford@uticorp.com
See full description on page 297.

arkansas

Eastern College of Health Vocations

6423 Forbing Road
Little Rock, AR 72209
Accreditation: Accrediting Bureau of Health Education Schools
Programs Offered: dental assisting; medical/clinical assistant
Institution Contact: Mr. Don E. Enroth, Jr., Director of Operations *Phone:* 228-831-3863 *Fax:* 228-831-3589 *E-mail:* denroth@echv.com
Admission Contact: Cyndi Chrisman, Admissions Officer *Phone:* 501-568-0211 *Fax:* 501-565-4076 *E-mail:* cchriisman@echv.com

ITT Technical Institute

4520 South University Avenue
Little Rock, AR 72204
Web: http://www.itt-tech.edu
Accreditation: Accrediting Council for Independent Colleges and Schools

ⓐ indicates that the school is a participating institution in the *Imagine America* Scholarship Program.

Programs Offered: animation, interactive technology, video graphics and special effects; CAD/CADD drafting/design technology; communications technology; computer and information systems security; computer engineering technology; computer software and media applications; computer software engineering; computer systems networking and telecommunications; digital communication and media/multimedia; electrical, electronic and communications engineering technology; technology management; web page, digital/multimedia and information resources design

Enrollment: 433 students

Institution Contact: Mr. Thomas Crawford, Director *Phone:* 501-565-5550

Admission Contact: Mr. Reed W. Thompson, Director of Recruitment *Phone:* 501-565-5550

See full description on page 298.

Remington College—Little Rock Campus Ⓐ

19 Remington Road
Little Rock, AR 72204
Web: http://www.remingtoncollege.edu

Accreditation: Accrediting Commission of Career Schools and Colleges of Technology

Programs Offered: business operations support and secretarial services related; computer technology/computer systems technology; criminal justice/police science; medical/clinical assistant; pharmacy technician

Enrollment: 368 students

Institution Contact: Mr. David Cunningham, Campus President *Phone:* 501-312-0007 *Fax:* 501-225-3819 *E-mail:* david.cunningham@remingtoncollege.edu

Admission Contact: Ms. Carla Larson, Director of Recruitment *Phone:* 501-312-0007 *Fax:* 501-225-3819 *E-mail:* carla.larson@remingtoncollege.edu

See full description on page 299.

alifornia

Academy of Art University Ⓐ

79 New Montgomery Street
San Francisco, CA 94105
Web: http://www.academyart.edu

Accreditation: Accrediting Council for Independent Colleges and Schools

Programs Offered: advertising; animation, interactive technology, video graphics and special effects; architectural drafting and CAD/CADD; ceramic arts and ceramics; cinematography and film/video production; commercial and advertising art; computer graphics; computer software and media applications related; desktop publishing and digital imaging design; English as a second language; fashion/apparel design; fashion merchandising; fiber, textile and weaving arts; fine/studio arts; furniture design and manufacturing; interior design; painting; photography; printmaking; visual and performing arts

Enrollment: 7,700 students

Institution Contact: Mr. Joe Vollaro, Executive Vice President of Financial Aid and Compliance *Phone:* 415-274-8688 *Fax:* 415-296-2098 *E-mail:* jvollaro@academyart.edu

Admission Contact: Mr. John Meurer, Director of Admissions *Phone:* 415-263-5518 *Fax:* 415-263-4130 *E-mail:* jmeurer@academyart.edu

See full description on page 300.

Academy of Professional Careers

45-691 Monroe Avenue, Suite 11
Indio, CA 92201
Web: http://www.academyofhealthcareers.com

Accreditation: Accrediting Council for Continuing Education and Training

Programs Offered: massage therapy; medical administrative assistant and medical secretary; medical/clinical assistant; pharmacy technician

Institution Contact: Raelene Vanek, Director *Phone:* 800-400-1005 *Fax:* 760-347-0535 *E-mail:* rvanek@academyofhealthcareers.com

Academy of Professional Careers

8376 Hercules Street
La Mesa, CA 91942
Web: http://www.apcschool.edu

Accreditation: Accrediting Council for Continuing Education and Training

Programs Offered: massage therapy; medical/clinical assistant; medical reception; pharmacy technician

Institution Contact: Ms. Cathy Tobin, Vice President of Compliance *Phone:* 559-735-3818 ext. 1012 *Fax:* 559-733-7831 *E-mail:* ctatcorp@aol.com

Admission Contact: Admissions Representative *Phone:* 619-461-5100 *Fax:* 619-461-1401 *E-mail:* info@academyofhealthcareers.com

Ⓐ indicates that the school is a participating institution in the *Imagine America* Scholarship Program.

Academy of Radio Broadcasting

16052 Beach Boulevard, Suite 263
Huntington Beach, CA 92647
Web: http://www.arbradio.com

Accreditation: Accrediting Council for Continuing
Education and Training

Programs Offered: cinematography and film/video
production; radio and television

Institution Contact: Mr. Thomas Gillenwater, President *Phone:* 714-842-0100 *Fax:* 714-842-1858 *E-mail:*
arbradio@earthlink.net

Admission Contact: Mr. Mike Kelly, Admissions
Director *Phone:* 714-842-0100 *Fax:* 714-842-1858 *E-mail:*
arbradio@earthlink.net

Academy Pacific Travel College Ⓐ

1777 North Vine Street
Los Angeles, CA 90028
Web: http://www.academypacific.com

Accreditation: Accrediting Commission of Career
Schools and Colleges of Technology

Programs Offered: airline flight attendant; transportation management

Institution Contact: Daniel Gilreath, Information
Contact *Phone:* 323-462-3211 *Fax:* 323-462-7755 *E-mail:*
apsws@aol.com

See full description on page 301.

Advanced Training Associates

1900 Joe Crosson Drive
El Cajon, CA 92020
Web: http://www.advancedtraining.net

Accreditation: Council on Occupational Education

Programs Offered: aircraft powerplant technology;
airframe mechanics and aircraft maintenance technology; air traffic control; avionics maintenance technology; computer and information systems security;
computer installation and repair technology; computer systems networking and telecommunications;
customer service support/call center/teleservice
operation; electrical and electronic engineering
technologies related; electrical/electronics equipment
installation and repair; information technology;
telecommunications

Institution Contact: *Phone:* 619-596-2766 *Fax:* 619-596-
4526 *E-mail:* edproinc@aol.com

American Career College

1200 North Magnolia Avenue
Anaheim, CA 92801
Web: http://www.americancareer.com

Programs Offered: business administration and
management; dental assisting; health/medical claims

examination; medical/clinical assistant; nursing
(licensed practical/vocational nurse training); optometric technician; pharmacy technician

Institution Contact: *Phone:* 877-809-8686 *E-mail:*
info@americancareer.com

American Career College, Inc.

4021 Rosewood Avenue
Los Angeles, CA 90004
Web: http://www.americancareer.com

Accreditation: Accrediting Bureau of Health Education Schools

Programs Offered: computer/information technology
administration and management; dental assisting;
medical/clinical assistant; medical insurance/medical
billing; nursing (licensed practical/vocational nurse
training); opticianry; pharmacy technician

Institution Contact: Rita Totten, Executive Director of
Campus Operations *Phone:* 323-906-2299 *Fax:* 323-953-
3654 *E-mail:* rita@americancareer.com

Admission Contact: Susan Pailet, Executive Director
of Admissions *Phone:* 323-906-2263 *Fax:* 323-666-3519
E-mail: susan@americancareer.com

American InterContinental University

12655 West Jefferson Boulevard
Los Angeles, CA 90066
Web: http://www.aiula.com

Accreditation: Southern Association of Colleges and
Schools

Programs Offered: business administration and
management; commercial and advertising art;
educational/instructional media design; fashion/
apparel design; fashion merchandising; information
technology; interior design; international business/
trade/commerce; web page, digital/multimedia and
information resources design

Institution Contact: Steven E. Tartaglini, President
Phone: 310-302-2000 *Fax:* 310-302-2402 *E-mail:*
startaglini@la.aiuniv.edu

Admission Contact: Brian Willingham, Director of
Admissions *Phone:* 888-248-7390 *Fax:* 310-302-2000
E-mail: bwillingham@la.aiuniv.edu

The Art Institute of California—Los Angeles

2900 31st Street
Santa Monica, CA 90405-3035
Web: http://www.aicala.artinstitutes.edu

Accreditation: Accrediting Council for Independent
Colleges and Schools

Ⓐ indicates that the school is a participating institution in the *Imagine America* Scholarship Program.

Programs Offered: animation, interactive technology, video graphics and special effects; cinematography and film/video production; commercial and advertising art; culinary arts; marketing/marketing management; web page, digital/multimedia and information resources design

Institution Contact: Dr. Gregory J. Strick, President *Phone:* 310-752-4700 *Fax:* 310-314-6050 *E-mail:* strickg@aii.edu

Admission Contact: Ms. Patti Drace, Director of Admissions *Phone:* 310-752-4700 *Fax:* 310-752-4708 *E-mail:* dracep@aii.edu

The Art Institute of California–Orange County ⓐ

3601 West Sunflower Avenue
Santa Ana, CA 92704
Web: http://www.aicaoc.artinstitutes.edu

Accreditation: Accrediting Council for Independent Colleges and Schools

Programs Offered: animation, interactive technology, video graphics and special effects; commercial and advertising art; computer graphics; culinary arts; interior design; web/multimedia management and webmaster; web page, digital/multimedia and information resources design

Institution Contact: Mr. Ken Post, Vice President/ Director of Admissions *Phone:* 714-830-0200 *Fax:* 714-556-1923 *E-mail:* postk@aii.edu

See full description on page 302.

The Art Institute of California–San Diego

7650 Mission Valley Road
San Diego, CA 92108
Web: http://www.aica.artinstitutes.edu

Accreditation: Accrediting Commission of Career Schools and Colleges of Technology

Programs Offered: advertising; animation, interactive technology, video graphics and special effects; baking and pastry arts; commercial and advertising art; computer graphics; culinary arts; digital communication and media/multimedia; interior design; web page, digital/multimedia and information resources design

Institution Contact: Ms. Sandy Park, Director of Admissions *Phone:* 858-546-0602 *Fax:* 858-457-0903 *E-mail:* parks@aii.edu

The Art Institute of California–San Francisco ⓐ

1170 Market Street
San Francisco, CA 94102
Web: http://www.aicasf.artinstitutes.edu

Accreditation: Accrediting Council for Independent Colleges and Schools

Programs Offered: animation, interactive technology, video graphics and special effects; commercial and advertising art; computer graphics; computer programming (specific applications); fashion/apparel design; graphic communications; interior design; web/multimedia management and webmaster; web page, digital/multimedia and information resources design

Enrollment: 875 students

Institution Contact: Mr. Charles Nagele, President *Phone:* 415-865-0198 *Fax:* 415-863-5831 *E-mail:* cnagele@aii.edu

Admission Contact: Mr. Daniel Cardenas, Director of Admissions *Phone:* 888-493-3261 *Fax:* 415-863-6344 *E-mail:* cardenad@aii.edu

See full description on page 303.

Brooks College

4825 East Pacific Coast Highway
Long Beach, CA 90804
Web: http://www.brookscollege.edu

Accreditation: Western Association of Schools and Colleges

Programs Offered: commercial and advertising art; computer/information technology administration and management; computer software and media applications; computer systems networking and telecommunications; fashion/apparel design; fashion merchandising; interior design

Enrollment: 1,200 students

Institution Contact: Mr. Al Nederhood, President *Phone:* 800-421-3775 *Fax:* 562-985-1381

Admission Contact: Michael Selter, Vice President of Admissions *Phone:* 800-421-3775 *Fax:* 562-597-2591 *E-mail:* mselter@brookscollege.edu

Brooks College

1120 Kifer Road
Sunnyvale, CA 94086-5303
Web: http://www.brooks-sv.com

Accreditation: Western Association of Schools and Colleges

Programs Offered: fashion/apparel design; fashion merchandising; graphic communications; system,

---

ⓐ indicates that the school is a participating institution in the *Imagine America* Scholarship Program.

Brooks College *(continued)*

networking, and LAN/WAN management; web page, digital/multimedia and information resources design

Institution Contact: James H. Mack Nair, Dean of Education *Phone:* 408-328-5700 *Fax:* 408-328-5790 *E-mail:* jmacknair@brooks-sv.com

Brooks Institute of Photography

801 Alston Road
Santa Barbara, CA 93108-2399
Web: http://www.brooks.edu

Accreditation: Accrediting Council for Independent Colleges and Schools

Programs Offered: cinematography and film/video production; photography

Institution Contact: Mr. John Calman, President *Phone:* 805-966-3888 *Fax:* 805-564-1475 *E-mail:* president@brooks.edu

Admission Contact: Miss Inge Kautzmann, Director of Admissions *Phone:* 805-966-3888 *Fax:* 805-564-1475 *E-mail:* admissions@brooks.edu

Bryman College Ⓐ

2215 West Mission Road
Alhambra, CA 91803
Web: http://www.bryman-college.com

Accreditation: Accrediting Commission of Career Schools and Colleges of Technology

Programs Offered: business administration and management; dental assisting; massage therapy; medical administrative assistant and medical secretary; medical/clinical assistant; medical insurance coding; medical insurance/medical billing; pharmacy technician

Institution Contact: Mr. Randy Morales, School President *Phone:* 626-979-4940 *Fax:* 626-280-4011 *E-mail:* rmorales@cci.edu

See full description on page 304.

Bryman College Ⓐ

511 North Brookhurst Street, Suite 300
Anaheim, CA 92801
Web: http://www.cci.edu

Accreditation: Accrediting Commission of Career Schools and Colleges of Technology

Programs Offered: dental assisting; massage therapy; medical administrative assistant and medical secretary; medical/clinical assistant; medical insurance coding; medical insurance/medical billing; pharmacy technician

Institution Contact: Ms. Susie Reed, President *Phone:* 714-953-6500 *Fax:* 714-953-4163 *E-mail:* sreed@cci.edu

Admission Contact: Mr. Daniel Valdez, Admissions Director *Phone:* 714-953-6500 *Fax:* 714-953-4163 *E-mail:* dvaldez@cci.edu

See full description on page 305.

Bryman College Ⓐ

12801 Crossroad Parkway
City of Industry, CA 91746
Web: http://www.bryman-college.com

Accreditation: Accrediting Commission of Career Schools and Colleges of Technology

Programs Offered: administrative assistant and secretarial science; business administration and management; business/corporate communications; clinical/medical laboratory technology; dental assisting; diagnostic medical sonography and ultrasound technology; massage therapy; medical administrative assistant and medical secretary; medical/clinical assistant; medical insurance/medical billing; medical office management; medical radiologic technology; phlebotomy

Institution Contact: Ms. Lillian Gonzalez, Director of Admissions *Phone:* 562-908-2500 *Fax:* 562-908-7656 *E-mail:* lilliang@cci.edu

See full description on page 306.

Bryman College Ⓐ

1045 West Redondo Beach Boulevard, Suite 275
Gardena, CA 90247
Web: http://www.cci.edu

Accreditation: Accrediting Commission of Career Schools and Colleges of Technology

Programs Offered: dental assisting; dialysis technology; massage therapy; medical administrative assistant and medical secretary; medical/clinical assistant; medical insurance coding; medical insurance/medical billing

Enrollment: 660 students

Institution Contact: Mrs. Pat Martin, President *Phone:* 310-527-7105 *Fax:* 310-523-3766 *E-mail:* smartin@cci.edu

Admission Contact: Ms. Hasani Thompson, Director of Admissions *Phone:* 310-527-7105 *Fax:* 310-523-3766 *E-mail:* hgorden@cci.edu

See full description on page 307.

Ⓐ indicates that the school is a participating institution in the *Imagine America* Scholarship Program.

Bryman College ⓐ

22336 Main Street, First Floor
Hayward, CA 94541
Web: http://www.bryman-college.com
Accreditation: Accrediting Commission of Career
Schools and Colleges of Technology
Programs Offered: massage therapy; medical administrative assistant and medical secretary; medical/clinical assistant; medical insurance coding; medical insurance/medical billing; surgical technology
Institution Contact: Ms. Nina Kamatani, Director of Admissions *Phone:* 510-582-9500 *Fax:* 510-582-9645 *E-mail:* kamatan@cci.edu
See full description on page 308.

Bryman College ⓐ

3000 South Robertson Boulevard, 3rd Floor
Los Angeles, CA 90034
Web: http://bryman-college.com
Accreditation: Accrediting Commission of Career
Schools and Colleges of Technology
Programs Offered: administrative assistant and secretarial science; clinical/medical laboratory assistant; dental assisting; diagnostic medical sonography and ultrasound technology; massage therapy; medical/clinical assistant; medical insurance/medical billing; medical office management; medical radiologic technology
Institution Contact: Director of Admissions *Phone:* 310-840-5777 *Fax:* 310-287-2344
See full description on page 316.

Bryman College ⓐ

3460 Wilshire Boulevard, Suite 500
Los Angeles, CA 90010
Web: http://www.bryman-college.com
Accreditation: Accrediting Commission of Career
Schools and Colleges of Technology
Programs Offered: dental assisting; medical administrative assistant and medical secretary; medical/clinical assistant; medical insurance coding; medical insurance/medical billing; pharmacy technician
Institution Contact: Marie Guerrero, Director of Admissions *Phone:* 213-388-9950 *Fax:* 313-388-9907 *E-mail:* mguerrer@cci.edu
See full description on page 309.

Bryman College ⓐ

1460 South Milliken Avenue
Ontario, CA 91761
Web: http://bryman-college.com/
Accreditation: Accrediting Commission of Career
Schools and Colleges of Technology
Programs Offered: business administration and management; dental assisting; massage therapy; medical/clinical assistant; medical insurance coding; medical insurance/medical billing; medical radiologic technology
Enrollment: 537 students
Institution Contact: Dan Day, Campus President *Phone:* 909-984-5027 *Fax:* 909-988-9339 *E-mail:* dday@cci.edu
Admission Contact: Mr. Alfred M. Desrosiers, Director of Admissions *Phone:* 909-984-5027 *Fax:* 909-988-9339 *E-mail:* adesrosiers@cci.edu
See full description on page 310.

Bryman College ⓐ

18040 Sherman Way, Suite 400
Reseda, CA 91335
Web: http://bryman-college.com/
Accreditation: Accrediting Bureau of Health Education Schools; Accrediting Commission of Career Schools and Colleges of Technology
Programs Offered: dental assisting; interior design; massage therapy; medical administrative assistant and medical secretary; medical/clinical assistant; pharmacy technician; surgical technology
Enrollment: 800 students
Institution Contact: Lani Townsend, President *Phone:* 818-774-0550 *Fax:* 818-774-1577
Admission Contact: Ms. Paula Dorsey, Director of Admissions *Phone:* 818-774-0550 *Fax:* 818-774-1577
See full description on page 311.

Bryman College ⓐ

217 Club Center Drive, Suite A
San Bernardino, CA 92408
Web: http://www.bryman-college.com
Accreditation: Accrediting Council for Independent Colleges and Schools
Programs Offered: health information/medical records technology; massage therapy; medical administrative assistant and medical secretary; medical/clinical assistant; medical insurance/medical billing; medical office management; office occupations and clerical services
Admission Contact: Mrs. Mary Beth Coutts, Director of Admissions *Phone:* 909-777-3300 *Fax:* 909-777-3313 *E-mail:* mcook@cci.edu
See full description on page 312.

ⓐ indicates that the school is a participating institution in the *Imagine America* Scholarship Program.

Bryman College Ⓐ

814 Mission Street, Suite 500
San Francisco, CA 94103
Web: http://www.cci.edu

Accreditation: Accrediting Commission of Career
Schools and Colleges of Technology

Programs Offered: dental assisting; massage therapy;
medical administrative assistant and medical secretary; medical/clinical assistant; medical insurance
coding; pharmacy technician

Enrollment: 724 students

Institution Contact: Mr. Cary Kaplan, President
Phone: 415-777-2500 ext. 243 *Fax:* 415-495-3457 *E-mail:*
ckaplan@cci.edu

Admission Contact: Earon B. Mackey, Admissions
Director *Phone:* 415-777-2500 ext. 284 *Fax:* 415-495-3457
E-mail: emackey@cci.edu

See full description on page 313.

Bryman College Ⓐ

1245 South Winchester Boulevard, Suite 102
San Jose, CA 95128
Web: http://www.bryman-college.com

Accreditation: Accrediting Commission of Career
Schools and Colleges of Technology

Programs Offered: dental assisting; massage therapy;
medical administrative assistant and medical secretary; medical/clinical assistant; medical insurance
coding; pharmacy technician

Institution Contact: George Grayeb, Regional Vice
President of Operations *Phone:* 408-246-4171 *Fax:*
408-557-9874 *E-mail:* ggrayeb@cci.edu

Admission Contact: Ms. Jo Ann Andre, Director of
Admissions *Phone:* 408-246-4171 ext. 103 *Fax:* 408-557-
9874 *E-mail:* jandre@cci.edu

See full description on page 314.

Bryman College Ⓐ

1231 Cabrillo Avenue, Suite 201
Torrance, CA 90501

Accreditation: Accrediting Council for Continuing
Education and Training

Programs Offered: massage therapy; pharmacy
technician

Enrollment: 130 students

Institution Contact: Ms. Carol J. Jacobs, College
President *Phone:* 310-320-3200 *Fax:* 310-320-3070
E-mail: cjacobs@cci.edu

Admission Contact: Ms. Sandy Ock, Director of
Admissions *Phone:* 310-320-3200 *Fax:* 310-320-3070
E-mail: sock@cci.edu

See full description on page 315.

California Culinary Academy

625 Polk Street
San Francisco, CA 94102
Web: http://www.baychef.com/

Accreditation: Accrediting Commission of Career
Schools and Colleges of Technology

Programs Offered: baking and pastry arts; culinary
arts; hospitality administration; restaurant/food
services management

Enrollment: 1,900 students

Institution Contact: Ms. Nancy Seyfert, Director of
Admissions *Phone:* 415-771-3500 *Fax:* 415-771-2194
E-mail: admissions@baychef.com

California Design College

3440 Wilshire Boulevard, 10th Floor
Los Angeles, CA 90010
Web: http://www.aicdc.artinstitutes.edu

Accreditation: Accrediting Council for Independent
Colleges and Schools

Programs Offered: design and visual communications; fashion and fabric consulting; fashion/apparel
design; fashion merchandising; fiber, textile and
weaving arts; interior design; intermedia/multimedia;
web page, digital/multimedia and information
resources design

Enrollment: 352 students

Institution Contact: Elizabeth Erickson, President
Phone: 213-251-3636 *Fax:* 213-385-3545 *E-mail:*
eerickson@aii.edu

Admission Contact: Josh Pond, Director of Admissions *Phone:* 213-251-3636 *Fax:* 213-385-3545 *E-mail:*
jpond@aii.edu

California Healing Arts College

12217 Santa Monica Boulevard, Suite 206
Los Angeles, CA 90025
Web: http://www.chac.edu

Accreditation: Accrediting Commission of Career
Schools and Colleges of Technology

Programs Offered: massage therapy

Institution Contact: Dr. Paul Schwinghamer, Director
Phone: 310-826-7622 *E-mail:* drpaul@chac.edu

Ⓐ indicates that the school is a participating institution in the *Imagine America* Scholarship Program.

Admission Contact: Lucinda Chrisman, Director of Admissions *Phone:* 310-826-7622 *E-mail:* lucinda@chac.edu

California School of Culinary Arts

521 East Green Street
Pasadena, CA 91101
Web: http://calchef.com

Accreditation: Accrediting Council for Independent Colleges and Schools

Programs Offered: baking and pastry arts; culinary arts; hospitality administration; hotel/motel administration

Institution Contact: Mr. Chris Becker, President *Phone:* 888-900-2433 *Fax:* 626-585-0486 *E-mail:* chris@scsca.com

Admission Contact: Mr. Mike Darnell, Vice President of Admissions *Phone:* 888-900-2433 *Fax:* 626-585-0486 *E-mail:* mdarnell@scsca.com

Career Networks Institute

3420 Bristol Street, Suite 209
Costa Mesa, CA 92626
Web: http://www.cniworks.com

Accreditation: Accrediting Bureau of Health Education Schools

Programs Offered: health information/medical records technology; massage therapy; medical administrative assistant and medical secretary; medical/clinical assistant; medical insurance/medical billing; medical office management; medical reception; nursing (licensed practical/vocational nurse training); surgical technology

Enrollment: 312 students

Institution Contact: Mr. James Buffington, AIA, President *Phone:* 714-437-9697 *Fax:* 714-437-9356 *E-mail:* jim@cniworks.com

Admission Contact: Patrick O'Hara, Admissions Director *Phone:* 714-437-9697 *Fax:* 714-437-9356 *E-mail:* patrick@cniworks.com

Central Coast College Ⓐ

480 South Main Street
Salinas, CA 93901
Web: http://www.centralcoastcollege.edu

Accreditation: Accrediting Council for Continuing Education and Training

Programs Offered: accounting; accounting technology and bookkeeping; administrative assistant and secretarial science; business machine repair; computer/information technology administration and management; computer installation and repair technology; computer systems networking and telecommunications; computer/technical support; computer technology/computer systems technology; data entry/microcomputer applications; data entry/ microcomputer applications related; executive assistant/executive secretary; health information/ medical records administration; health unit coordinator/ward clerk; information technology; medical administrative assistant and medical secretary; medical/clinical assistant; medical insurance coding; medical insurance/medical billing; medical office management; medical reception; medical transcription; office occupations and clerical services; phlebotomy; receptionist; system administration; word processing

Enrollment: 205 students

Institution Contact: Ms. Elaine M. Giuliano, Compliance Officer/Administrative Coordinator *Phone:* 831-753-6660 ext. 17 *Fax:* 831-753-6485 *E-mail:* giuel@cccbus.com

Admission Contact: Ms. Cathy Del Fante, Admissions Coordinator *Phone:* 831-753-6660 ext. 14 *Fax:* 831-753-6485 *E-mail:* delca@cccbus.com

See full description on page 317.

Clarita Career College

27125 Sierra Highway, Suite 329
Canyon Country, CA 91351
Web: http://www.claritacareercollege.com/

Accreditation: Accrediting Commission of Career Schools and Colleges of Technology

Programs Offered: clinical/medical laboratory assistant; dental assisting; legal assistant/paralegal; massage therapy; medical administrative assistant and medical secretary; medical/clinical assistant; pharmacy technician

Enrollment: 160 students

Institution Contact: Julie Ha, President *Phone:* 661-252-1864 *Fax:* 661-252-2153 *E-mail:* ha_julie@claritacareercollege.com

Admission Contact: Mike Bell, School Director *Phone:* 661-252-1864 *Fax:* 661-252-2153 *E-mail:* bell_michael@claritacareercollege.com

Coleman College

7380 Parkway Drive
La Mesa, CA 91942
Web: http://www.coleman.edu

Accreditation: Accrediting Council for Independent Colleges and Schools

---

Ⓐ indicates that the school is a participating institution in the *Imagine America* Scholarship Program.

Coleman College (*continued*)

Programs Offered: accounting; computer graphics; computer programming; computer programming related; computer systems analysis; computer systems networking and telecommunications; computer/technical support; information science/studies; office management; web page, digital/multimedia and information resources design

Institution Contact: Mr. Pritpal S. Panesar, President *Phone:* 619-465-3990 ext. 130 *Fax:* 619-463-0162 *E-mail:* panesar@coleman.edu

Admission Contact: Tana Sanderson, Director of Admissions *Phone:* 619-465-3990 ext. 109 *Fax:* 619-463-0162 *E-mail:* tsanderson@coleman.edu

Coleman College

1284 West San Marcos Boulevard
San Marcos, CA 92069
Web: http://www.coleman.edu/

Accreditation: Accrediting Council for Independent Colleges and Schools

Programs Offered: computer and information sciences; computer and information systems security; computer graphics; computer programming; computer systems networking and telecommunications; general studies

Enrollment: 230 students

Institution Contact: Ms. Darlene Ankton, Site Manager *Phone:* 760-747-3990 *Fax:* 760-752-9808 *E-mail:* dankton@coleman.edu

Empire College

3035 Cleveland Avenue
Santa Rosa, CA 95403
Web: http://www.empcol.edu

Accreditation: Accrediting Council for Independent Colleges and Schools

Programs Offered: accounting; accounting technology and bookkeeping; administrative assistant and secretarial science; business automation/technology/data entry; clinical/medical laboratory assistant; clinical/medical laboratory technology; computer hardware engineering; computer/information technology administration and management; computer/information technology services administration related; computer systems networking and telecommunications; computer/technical support; computer technology/computer systems technology; data entry/microcomputer applications; data processing and data processing technology; executive assistant/executive secretary; gene therapy; health information/medical records administration; health information/medical records technology; hospitality administration; information technology; legal assistant/paralegal; medical administrative assistant and medical secretary; medical/clinical assistant; medical/health management and clinical assistant; medical insurance coding; medical insurance/medical billing; medical office computer specialist; medical office management; medical reception; medical transcription; office occupations and clerical services; pre-law studies; receptionist; securities services administration; system administration; system, networking, and LAN/WAN management; tourism and travel services management; word processing

Enrollment: 645 students

Institution Contact: Mr. Roy Hurd, President *Phone:* 707-546-4000 *Fax:* 707-546-4058 *E-mail:* rhurd@empcol.com

Admission Contact: Ms. Dahnja Barker, Director of Admissions *Phone:* 707-546-4000 ext. 238 *Fax:* 707-546-4058 *E-mail:* dahnja@empirecollege.com

Everest College ⓐ

9616 Archibald Avenue, Suite 100
Rancho Cucamonga, CA 91730
Web: http://www.cci.edu

Accreditation: Accrediting Council for Independent Colleges and Schools

Programs Offered: accounting; business administration and management; criminal justice/law enforcement administration; legal assistant/paralegal

Enrollment: 1,000 students

Institution Contact: Richard Mallow, President *Phone:* 909-484-4311 *Fax:* 909-484-1162

Admission Contact: Greg Lam, Director of Admissions *Phone:* 909-484-4311 *Fax:* 909-484-1162 *E-mail:* glam@cci.edu

See full description on page 318.

Four-D Success Academy

1020 East Washington Street
Colton, CA 92324
Web: http://www.4Dcollege.com

Accreditation: Accrediting Bureau of Health Education Schools

Programs Offered: adult and continuing education; dental assisting; medical/clinical assistant; medical insurance coding; medical insurance/medical billing; nursing assistant/aide and patient care assistant; pharmacy technician

Enrollment: 275 students

ⓐ indicates that the school is a participating institution in the *Imagine America* Scholarship Program.

Institution Contact: Pebble Thomas, Executive Administrative Assistant *Phone:* 909-783-9331 *Fax:* 909-783-6529 *E-mail:* 4dadmin.asst@friendsof4d.org

Admission Contact: Paula Herman, Admissions Representative *Phone:* 909-783-9331 ext. 254 *Fax:* 909-783-9334 *E-mail:* pherman@4dcollege.com

Galen College of California, Inc.

1325 North Wishon Avenue
Fresno, CA 93728

Accreditation: Accrediting Commission of Career Schools and Colleges of Technology

Programs Offered: dental assisting; health aide; medical/clinical assistant

Institution Contact: Ms. Stella Mesple, President *Phone:* 559-264-9700 *E-mail:* galencollege@pfny.com

Admission Contact: Mrs. Sandra Marquez, Assistant School Director *Phone:* 559-264-9700 *E-mail:* galencollege@pfny.com

Galen College of California, Inc.

1604 Ford Avenue
Modesto, CA 95350

Accreditation: Accrediting Commission of Career Schools and Colleges of Technology

Programs Offered: dental assisting; medical/clinical assistant

Institution Contact: Mrs. Kellie Thornhill, Director *Phone:* 559-527-5084 *E-mail:* galencollege@pfny.com

Admission Contact: Ms. Betsy Johns, Enrollment Officer *Phone:* 209-527-5100

Galen College of California, Inc.

3908 West Caldwell Avenue, Suite A
Visalia, CA 93277

Accreditation: Accrediting Commission of Career Schools and Colleges of Technology

Programs Offered: dental assisting; medical/clinical assistant

Institution Contact: Mrs. Stella Mesple, President *Phone:* 559-732-5200 *E-mail:* galencollege@pfny.com

Admission Contact: Ms. Beth Esquivel, Admissions *Phone:* 559-732-5200 *E-mail:* galencollege@psnw.com

Gemological Institute of America, Inc. Ⓐ

5345 Armada Drive
Carlsbad, CA 92008
Web: http://www.gia.edu

Accreditation: Accrediting Commission of Career Schools and Colleges of Technology; Distance Education and Training Council

Programs Offered: applied art; business administration and management; metal and jewelry arts

Enrollment: 347 students

Institution Contact: Ms. Christine Galdston, JD, Accreditation and Compliance Officer *Phone:* 760-603-4182 *Fax:* 760-603-4596 *E-mail:* cgaldsto@gia.edu

Admission Contact: Mr. Jason Drake, Manager, Admissions *Phone:* 760-603-4000 ext. 7327 *Fax:* 760-603-4003 *E-mail:* jadrake@gia.edu

See full description on page 319.

Gemological Institute of America, Inc. Ⓐ

550 South Hill Street, Suite 901
Los Angeles, CA 90013
Web: http://www.gia.edu

Accreditation: Accrediting Commission of Career Schools and Colleges of Technology

Programs Offered: metal and jewelry arts

Institution Contact: Ms. Veronica Clark-Hudson, Director *Phone:* 213-833-0115 *Fax:* 213-622-7374 *E-mail:* laedu@gia.edu

Admission Contact: Ms. Maritza Fuentes, Administrative Assistant *Phone:* 213-833-0115 *Fax:* 213-622-7374 *E-mail:* laedu@gia.edu

See full description on page 319.

Glendale Career College

1015 Grandview Avenue
Glendale, CA 91201
Web: http://www.success.edu

Accreditation: Accrediting Council for Continuing Education and Training

Programs Offered: administrative assistant and secretarial science; instrumentation technology; massage therapy; medical/clinical assistant; medical office management; nursing (licensed practical/vocational nurse training); surgical technology

Enrollment: 480 students

Institution Contact: Mr. Tim O'Neil, Campus Director *Phone:* 818-243-1131 *Fax:* 818-243-6028

Admission Contact: Mr. Robert Ramirez, Admissions Director *Phone:* 818-243-1131 *Fax:* 818-243-6028 *E-mail:* rramirez@success.edu

Glendale Career College—Oceanside

Tri-City Medical Center, 4002 Vista Way
Oceanside, CA 92056

Accreditation: Accrediting Council for Continuing Education and Training

Ⓐ indicates that the school is a participating institution in the *Imagine America* Scholarship Program.

Glendale Career College–Oceanside (*continued*)

Programs Offered: surgical technology

Institution Contact: Ms. Cindy Harris, Director *Phone:* 760-945-9896 *Fax:* 760-945-9970

Golden State College

3356 South Fairway
Visalia, CA 93277

Accreditation: Accrediting Council for Continuing Education and Training

Programs Offered: accounting; computer and information sciences related; corrections; dental assisting; massage therapy; medical administrative assistant and medical secretary; medical/clinical assistant

Institution Contact: Mr. Dan Serna, Career Services Director *Phone:* 800-400-1005 *Fax:* 559-735-3808

Admission Contact: Ms. Stephanie Farias, Director of Admissions *Phone:* 800-400-1005 *Fax:* 559-735-3808 *E-mail:* sfarias@goldenstatecollege.com

High-Tech Institute

1111 Howe Avenue, #250
Sacramento, CA 95825
Web: http://www.hightechschools.com

Accreditation: Accrediting Bureau of Health Education Schools; Accrediting Commission of Career Schools and Colleges of Technology

Programs Offered: dental assisting; information technology; medical/clinical assistant; surgical technology

Institution Contact: Mr. Richard Dyer, School Director *Phone:* 916-929-9700 *Fax:* 916-929-9703 *E-mail:* rdyer@hightechschools.com

Admission Contact: Mrs. Sarah Maskovich, Director of Admissions *Phone:* 916-929-9700 *Fax:* 916-929-9703 *E-mail:* smaskovich@hightechschools.com

Institute of Computer Technology

3200 Wilshire Boulevard, Suite 400
Los Angeles, CA 90010-1308
Web: http://www.ICTCollege.edu

Accreditation: Accrediting Council for Independent Colleges and Schools

Programs Offered: accounting; business administration and management; computer and information sciences related; computer and information systems security; computer graphics; computer hardware engineering; computer hardware technology; computer/information technology administration and management; computer/information technology services administration related; computer installation and repair technology; computer programming; computer programming related; computer programming (specific applications); computer programming (vendor/product certification); computer science; computer software and media applications; computer software and media applications related; computer software engineering; computer software technology; computer systems analysis; computer systems networking and telecommunications; computer/technical support; computer technology/computer systems technology; data entry/microcomputer applications; entrepreneurship; graphic communications; graphic communications related; information science/studies; information technology; marketing/marketing management; photographic and film/video technology; photography; system, networking, and LAN/WAN management; taxation; web page, digital/multimedia and information resources design; word processing

Enrollment: 230 students

Institution Contact: Dr. K. C. You, President *Phone:* 213-381-3333 *Fax:* 213-383-9369 *E-mail:* kcyou@ictcollege.edu

Admission Contact: Mr. Randy Doten, Admissions Director *Phone:* 800-574-6428 *Fax:* 213-383-9369 *E-mail:* rdoten@ictcollege.edu

ITT Technical Institute Ⓐ

525 North Muller Street
Anaheim, CA 92801-9938
Web: http://www.itt-tech.edu

Accreditation: Accrediting Council for Independent Colleges and Schools

Programs Offered: accounting and business/management; animation, interactive technology, video graphics and special effects; business administration and management; CAD/CADD drafting/design technology; communications technology; computer and information systems security; computer engineering technology; computer software and media applications; computer software engineering; computer systems networking and telecommunications; criminal justice/police science; digital communication and media/multimedia; electrical, electronic and communications engineering technology; technology management; web page, digital/multimedia and information resources design

Enrollment: 738 students

Institution Contact: Mr. Louis Osborn, Director *Phone:* 714-535-3700

Admission Contact: Mr. Albert A. Naranjo, Director of Recruitment *Phone:* 714-535-3700

See full description on page 329.

Ⓐ indicates that the school is a participating institution in the *Imagine America* Scholarship Program.

ITT Technical Institute

16916 South Harlan Road
Lathrop, CA 95330
Web: http://www.itt-tech.edu

Accreditation: Accrediting Council for Independent Colleges and Schools

Programs Offered: accounting and business/management; animation, interactive technology, video graphics and special effects; business administration and management; CAD/CADD drafting/design technology; communications technology; computer and information systems security; computer engineering technology; computer software and media applications; computer software engineering; computer systems networking and telecommunications; criminal justice/police science; digital communication and media/multimedia; electrical, electronic and communications engineering technology; technology management; web page, digital/multimedia and information resources design

Enrollment: 565 students

Institution Contact: Mr. W. Donald Fraser, Director
Phone: 209-858-0077

Admission Contact: Ms. Kathy Paradis, Director of Recruitment *Phone:* 209-858-0077

ITT Technical Institute Ⓐ

2051 North Solar Drive, Suite 150
Oxnard, CA 93030
Web: http://www.itt-tech.edu

Accreditation: Accrediting Council for Independent Colleges and Schools

Programs Offered: accounting and business/management; animation, interactive technology, video graphics and special effects; business administration and management; CAD/CADD drafting/design technology; communications technology; computer and information systems security; computer engineering technology; computer software and media applications; computer software engineering; computer systems networking and telecommunications; criminal justice/police science; digital communication and media/multimedia; electrical, electronic and communications engineering technology; technology management; web page, digital/multimedia and information resources design

Enrollment: 591 students

Institution Contact: Ms. Lorraine Bunt, Director
Phone: 805-988-0143 ext. 112

Admission Contact: Mr. Dean K. Dunbar, Director of Recruitment *Phone:* 805-988-0143

See full description on page 330.

ITT Technical Institute Ⓐ

10863 Gold Center Drive
Rancho Cordova, CA 95670-6034
Web: http://www.itt-tech.edu

Accreditation: Accrediting Council for Independent Colleges and Schools

Programs Offered: accounting and business/management; animation, interactive technology, video graphics and special effects; business administration and management; CAD/CADD drafting/design technology; communications technology; computer and information systems security; computer engineering technology; computer software and media applications; computer software engineering; computer systems networking and telecommunications; criminal justice/police science; digital communication and media/multimedia; electrical, electronic and communications engineering technology; technology management; web page, digital/multimedia and information resources design

Enrollment: 589 students

Institution Contact: Mr. Mark Garland, Director
Phone: 916-851-3900

Admission Contact: Mr. Robert Menszer, Director of Recruitment *Phone:* 916-851-3900

See full description on page 331.

ITT Technical Institute Ⓐ

630 East Brier Drive, Suite 150
San Bernardino, CA 92408-2800
Web: http://www.itt-tech.edu

Accreditation: Accrediting Council for Independent Colleges and Schools

Programs Offered: accounting and business/management; animation, interactive technology, video graphics and special effects; business administration and management; CAD/CADD drafting/design technology; communications technology; computer and information systems security; computer engineering technology; computer software and media applications; computer software engineering; computer systems networking and telecommunications; criminal justice/police science; digital communication and media/multimedia; electrical, electronic and communications engineering technology; technology management; web page, digital/multimedia and information resources design

Enrollment: 1,078 students

Institution Contact: Mr. Terry Lorenz, Director *Phone:* 909-889-3800 ext. 20

Admission Contact: Mr. Tyron Cooley, Director of Recruitment *Phone:* 909-889-3800 ext. 11

See full description on page 332.

Ⓐ indicates that the school is a participating institution in the *Imagine America* Scholarship Program.

ITT Technical Institute (A)

9680 Granite Ridge Drive, Suite 100
San Diego, CA 92123
Web: http://www.itt-tech.edu

Accreditation: Accrediting Council for Independent Colleges and Schools

Programs Offered: accounting and business/management; animation, interactive technology, video graphics and special effects; business administration and management; CAD/CADD drafting/design technology; communications technology; computer and information systems security; computer engineering technology; computer software and media applications; computer software engineering; computer systems networking and telecommunications; criminal justice/police science; digital communication and media/multimedia; electrical, electronic and communications engineering technology; technology management; web page, digital/multimedia and information resources design

Enrollment: 1,150 students

Institution Contact: Mr. David Parker, Director *Phone:* 858-571-8500

Admission Contact: Mr. Robert Dutton, Director of Recruitment *Phone:* 858-571-8500

See full description on page 333.

ITT Technical Institute (A)

12669 Encinitas Avenue
Sylmar, CA 91342-3664
Web: http://www.itt-tech.edu

Accreditation: Accrediting Council for Independent Colleges and Schools

Programs Offered: accounting and business/management; animation, interactive technology, video graphics and special effects; business administration and management; CAD/CADD drafting/design technology; communications technology; computer and information systems security; computer engineering technology; computer software and media applications; computer software engineering; computer systems networking and telecommunications; computer technology/computer systems technology; criminal justice/police science; digital communication and media/multimedia; electrical, electronic and communications engineering technology; technology management; web page, digital/multimedia and information resources design

Enrollment: 891 students

Institution Contact: Mr. Nader Mojtabai, Director *Phone:* 818-364-5151

Admission Contact: Ms. Kelly Christensen, Director of Recruitment *Phone:* 818-364-5151

See full description on page 334.

ITT Technical Institute (A)

20050 South Vermont Avenue
Torrance, CA 90502
Web: http://www.itt-tech.edu

Accreditation: Accrediting Council for Independent Colleges and Schools

Programs Offered: accounting and business/management; animation, interactive technology, video graphics and special effects; business administration and management; CAD/CADD drafting/design technology; communications technology; computer and information systems security; computer engineering technology; computer software and media applications; computer software engineering; computer systems networking and telecommunications; criminal justice/police science; digital communication and media/multimedia; electrical, electronic and communications engineering technology; technology management; web page, digital/multimedia and information resources design

Enrollment: 757 students

Institution Contact: Ms. Anne Marie Koerin, Director *Phone:* 310-380-1555

Admission Contact: Mr. Freddie Polk, Director of Recruitment *Phone:* 310-380-1555

See full description on page 335.

ITT Technical Institute (A)

1530 West Cameron Avenue
West Covina, CA 91790-2711
Web: http://www.itt-tech.edu

Accreditation: Accrediting Council for Independent Colleges and Schools

Programs Offered: accounting and business/management; animation, interactive technology, video graphics and special effects; business administration and management; CAD/CADD drafting/design technology; communications technology; computer and information systems security; computer engineering technology; computer software and media applications; computer software engineering; computer systems networking and telecommunications; criminal justice/police science; digital communication and media/multimedia; electrical, electronic and communications engineering technology; industrial technology; technology management; web page, digital/multimedia and information resources design

Enrollment: 854 students

Institution Contact: Ms. Maria Alamat, Director *Phone:* 626-960-8681

Admission Contact: Ms. JoAnn Meron, Director of Recruitment *Phone:* 626-960-8681

See full description on page 336.

(A) indicates that the school is a participating institution in the *Imagine America* Scholarship Program.

Maric College

1360 South Anaheim Boulevard
Anaheim, CA 92805

Accreditation: Accrediting Council for Independent Colleges and Schools

Programs Offered: business administration and management; computer and information sciences related; information technology; legal administrative assistant/secretary; legal assistant/paralegal; medical administrative assistant and medical secretary; medical/clinical assistant

Institution Contact: Mr. Gene M. Villarin, Student Services Director *Phone:* 714-758-1500 ext. 115 *Fax:* 714-758-1220 *E-mail:* gene@mariccollege.com

Admission Contact: Mrs. Dora Tellez, Director of Admissions *Phone:* 714-758-1500 ext. 117 *Fax:* 714-758-1220 *E-mail:* dora@mariccollege.edu

Maric College

25361 Commercentre Drive, Suite 100
Lake Forest, CA 92630

Programs Offered: business administration and management; computer and information sciences related; information technology; legal administrative assistant/secretary; legal assistant/paralegal; medical administrative assistant and medical secretary; medical/clinical assistant

Institution Contact: *Phone:* 949-472-4192 *Fax:* 949-609-1567

Maric College

6180 Laurel Canyon Boulevard, #101
North Hollywood, CA 91606
Web: http://www.moderntec.com

Accreditation: Accrediting Commission of Career Schools and Colleges of Technology

Programs Offered: diagnostic medical sonography and ultrasound technology; electrocardiograph technology; health information/medical records administration; information technology; medical/clinical assistant; medical insurance/medical billing; medical radiologic technology; radiologic technology/science

Institution Contact: Mr. Mark Newman, Executive Director *Phone:* 818-763-2563 ext. 240 *Fax:* 818-763-1623 *E-mail:* mark@moderntec.com

Admission Contact: Mr. Roger Cranmer, Director of Admissions *Phone:* 818-763-2563 ext. 229 *Fax:* 818-763-1623 *E-mail:* roger@moderntec.com

Maric College

4330 Watt Avenue, Suite 400
Sacramento, CA 95660
Web: http://www.californiacollegetech.com

Accreditation: Accrediting Council for Independent Colleges and Schools

Programs Offered: computer systems networking and telecommunications; information technology; interior design; medical/clinical assistant

Institution Contact: Mr. Tapas Ghosh, Executive Director *Phone:* 916-649-8168 *Fax:* 916-649-8344 *E-mail:* tghosh@californiacollegetech.com

Admission Contact: Mr. Charlie Reese, Director of Admissions *Phone:* 916-649-8168 *Fax:* 916-649-8344 *E-mail:* creese@californiacollegetech.com

Maric College

5172 Kiernan Court
Salida, CA 95368
Web: http://www.mariccollege.edu

Accreditation: Accrediting Bureau of Health Education Schools; Accrediting Commission of Career Schools and Colleges of Technology

Programs Offered: allied health and medical assisting services related; medical administrative assistant and medical secretary; medical/clinical assistant

Enrollment: 496 students

Institution Contact: Mrs. MaryAnn Crone, Executive Director *Phone:* 209-543-7000 *Fax:* 209-543-1755 *E-mail:* mcrone@mariccollege.edu

Admission Contact: Mrs. Linda Stovall, Director of Admissions *Phone:* 209-543-7020 *Fax:* 209-543-1755 *E-mail:* lstovall@mariccollege.edu

Maric College

3666 Kearny Villa Road, Suite 100
San Diego, CA 92123
Web: http://www.mariccollege.edu

Accreditation: Accrediting Bureau of Health Education Schools; Accrediting Commission of Career Schools and Colleges of Technology

Programs Offered: criminal justice/law enforcement administration; criminal justice/police science; information technology; legal assistant/paralegal; medical administrative assistant and medical secretary; medical insurance coding; medical insurance/medical billing; medical office assistant; medical office management; medical radiologic technology; nursing assistant/aide and patient care assistant; nursing (licensed practical/vocational nurse training); nursing (registered nurse training)

⊛ indicates that the school is a participating institution in the *Imagine America* Scholarship Program.

Maric College *(continued)*

Enrollment: 1,273 students

Institution Contact: Mr. Michael Seifert, Executive Director *Phone:* 858-279-4500 *Fax:* 858-279-4885 *E-mail:* mseifert@mariccollege.edu

Admission Contact: Ms. Angela Robertson, Director of Admissions *Phone:* 858-279-4500 ext. 3623 *Fax:* 858-279-4885 *E-mail:* arobertson@mariccollege.edu

Maric College

722 West March Lane
Stockton, CA 95207
Web: http://www.mariccollege.edu

Accreditation: Accrediting Bureau of Health Education Schools; Accrediting Commission of Career Schools and Colleges of Technology

Programs Offered: dental assisting; health aide; medical administrative assistant and medical secretary; medical/clinical assistant

Enrollment: 250 students

Institution Contact: Bill Jones, Executive Director *Phone:* 209-462-8777 ext. 207 *Fax:* 209-462-3219 *E-mail:* bjones@mariccollege.edu

Admission Contact: Eric Lopez, Director of Admissions *Phone:* 209-462-8777 ext. 208 *Fax:* 209-462-3219 *E-mail:* elopez@mariccollege.edu

Maric College

2022 University Drive
Vista, CA 92083
Web: http://www.mariccollege.edu

Accreditation: Accrediting Bureau of Health Education Schools; Accrediting Commission of Career Schools and Colleges of Technology

Programs Offered: computer/information technology administration and management; health aide; legal assistant/paralegal; medical administrative assistant and medical secretary; medical/clinical assistant; medical insurance coding; nursing assistant/aide and patient care assistant; nursing (licensed practical/vocational nurse training); system administration; system, networking, and LAN/WAN management

Institution Contact: Ms. Jann Underwood-Hemphill, Executive Director *Phone:* 760-630-1555 *Fax:* 760-630-1656 *E-mail:* junderwood@maric.org

Admission Contact: Mrs. Nancie Froning, Director of Admissions *Phone:* 760-630-1555 *Fax:* 760-630-1656 *E-mail:* nfroning@maric.org

MTI Business College of Stockton Inc.

6006 North El Dorado Street
Stockton, CA 95207-4349
Web: http://www.mtistockton.com

Accreditation: Accrediting Commission of Career Schools and Colleges of Technology

Programs Offered: accounting; administrative assistant and secretarial science; business administration and management; business automation/technology/data entry; clinical/medical laboratory assistant; computer/technical support; data entry/microcomputer applications; executive assistant/executive secretary; gene therapy; health/health care administration; health information/medical records administration; internet information systems; legal administrative assistant/secretary; management information systems; medical administrative assistant and medical secretary; medical/clinical assistant; medical office computer specialist; medical office management; medical reception; medical transcription; office management; office occupations and clerical services; receptionist; web page, digital/multimedia and information resources design; word processing

Institution Contact: Mr. Steven J. Brenner, Director *Phone:* 209-957-3030 ext. 313 *Fax:* 209-474-8705 *E-mail:* mtistockton@hotmail.com

Admission Contact: Ms. Sally M. Lofthus, Associate Director *Phone:* 209-957-3030 ext. 314 *Fax:* 209-474-8705 *E-mail:* mtistockton@hotmail.com

National Institute of Technology Ⓐ

2161 Technology Place
Long Beach, CA 90810
Web: http://www.nitschools.com

Accreditation: Accrediting Commission of Career Schools and Colleges of Technology

Programs Offered: automobile/automotive mechanics technology; electrician; heating, air conditioning and refrigeration technology; industrial electronics technology; massage therapy; medical/clinical assistant; plumbing technology

Enrollment: 879 students

Institution Contact: Mr. Dana K. Martin, President *Phone:* 562-437-0501 *Fax:* 562-432-3721 *E-mail:* dmartin@cci.edu

Admission Contact: Miss Therese El Khoury, Director of Admissions *Phone:* 562-437-0501 *Fax:* 562-432-3721 *E-mail:* telkhoury@cci.edu

See full description on page 337.

Ⓐ indicates that the school is a participating institution in the *Imagine America* Scholarship Program.

Newschool of Architecture & Design ⒶⒶ

1249 F Street
San Diego, CA 92101-6634
Web: http://www.newschoolarch.edu/
Accreditation: Accrediting Council for Independent Colleges and Schools
Programs Offered: architectural engineering technology
Enrollment: 320 students
Institution Contact: Mr. Gil Cooke, President *Phone:* 619-235-4100 ext. 108 *Fax:* 619-235-4651 *E-mail:* gcooke@newschoolarch.edu
Admission Contact: Mr. Armin Geiger, Director of Admissions *Phone:* 619-235-4100 ext. 123 *Fax:* 619-235-4651 *E-mail:* ageiger@newschoolarch.edu
See full description on page 338.

Pima Medical Institute

780 Bay Boulevard, Suite 101
Chula Vista, CA 91910
Web: http://www.pmi.edu
Accreditation: Accrediting Bureau of Health Education Schools
Programs Offered: dental assisting; medical administrative assistant and medical secretary; medical/clinical assistant; pharmacy technician; radiologic technology/science; respiratory care therapy; veterinary/animal health technology
Enrollment: 500 students
Institution Contact: Mr. Christopher Luebke, Admissions Support Center Director *Phone:* 888-898-9048 *E-mail:* asc@pmi.edu
Admission Contact: Admissions Support Representative *Phone:* 888-898-9048 *E-mail:* asc@pmi.edu

Platt College ⒶⒶ

3901 MacArthur Boulevard, Suite 101
Newport Beach, CA 92660
Web: http://www.plattcollege.edu
Accreditation: Accrediting Commission of Career Schools and Colleges of Technology
Programs Offered: animation, interactive technology, video graphics and special effects; commercial and advertising art; computer engineering technology; computer/information technology administration and management; computer/information technology services administration related; computer systems networking and telecommunications; computer technology/computer systems technology; desktop publishing and digital imaging design; information science/studies; information technology; legal

assistant/paralegal; system administration; web page, digital/multimedia and information resources design
Enrollment: 215 students
Institution Contact: Ms. Lisa Rhodes, Campus President *Phone:* 949-851-4991 ext. 222 *Fax:* 949-833-0269 *E-mail:* lrhodes@plattcollege.edu
Admission Contact: Ms. Christina Varon, Director of Admissions *Phone:* 949-851-4991 ext. 227 *Fax:* 949-833-0269 *E-mail:* cvaron@plattcollege.edu
See full description on page 340.

Platt College ⒶⒶ

3700 Inland Empire Boulevard
Ontario, CA 91764
Web: http://www.plattcollege.edu
Accreditation: Accrediting Commission of Career Schools and Colleges of Technology
Programs Offered: animation, interactive technology, video graphics and special effects; commercial and advertising art; computer graphics; computer/information technology administration and management; computer/information technology services administration related; computer/technical support; computer technology/computer systems technology; design and visual communications; information science/studies; information technology; intermedia/multimedia; legal assistant/paralegal; system administration; web page, digital/multimedia and information resources design
Enrollment: 425 students
Institution Contact: Mr. Alan Purvis, Executive Director *Phone:* 909-941-9410 *Fax:* 909-941-9660 *E-mail:* apurvis@plattcollege.edu
Admission Contact: Ms. Carmen Conceicao, Director of Admissions *Phone:* 909-941-9410 *Fax:* 909-941-9660 *E-mail:* cconceicao@plattcollege.edu
See full description on page 341.

Platt College—Los Angeles, Inc ⒶⒶ

1000 South Fremont A9W
Alhambra, CA 91803
Web: http://www.plattcollege.edu
Accreditation: Accrediting Commission of Career Schools and Colleges of Technology
Programs Offered: commercial and advertising art; computer systems networking and telecommunications; information technology; legal assistant/paralegal; web page, digital/multimedia and information resources design

Ⓐ indicates that the school is a participating institution in the *Imagine America* Scholarship Program.

Platt College–Los Angeles, Inc *(continued)*

Institution Contact: Manfred Rodriguez, Director
Phone: 626-300-5444 *Fax:* 626-300-3978 *E-mail:*
mrodriguez@plattcollege.edu
See full description on page 339.

Platt College San Diego
6250 El Cajon Boulevard
San Diego, CA 92115-3919
Web: http://www.platt.edu
Accreditation: Accrediting Commission of Career
Schools and Colleges of Technology
Programs Offered: advertising; animation, interactive
technology, video graphics and special effects;
cinematography and film/video production; commercial and advertising art; computer graphics; computer
software and media applications; design and visual
communications; desktop publishing and digital
imaging design; digital communication and media/
multimedia; education; graphic and printing equipment operation/production; graphic communications;
graphic communications related; intermedia/multime-
dia; photographic and film/video technology; visual
and performing arts; web/multimedia management
and webmaster; web page, digital/multimedia and
information resources design
Enrollment: 350 students
Institution Contact: Mr. Steve Gallup, Director of
Marketing *Phone:* 619-265-0107 *Fax:* 619-308-0570
E-mail: sgallup@platt.edu
Admission Contact: Ms. Carly Westerfield, Admissions Coordinator *Phone:* 619-265-0107 *Fax:* 619-308-
0570 *E-mail:* cwesterfield@platt.edu

Remington College–San Diego Campus Ⓐ
123 Camino De La Reina, Suite 100 North
San Diego, CA 92108
Web: http://www.remingtoncollege.edu
Accreditation: Accrediting Council for Independent
Colleges and Schools
Programs Offered: allied health and medical assisting
services related; business administration and management; computer systems networking and telecommunications; computer/technical support; criminal
justice/law enforcement administration; criminal
justice/police science; massage therapy; system,
networking, and LAN/WAN management; word
processing
Enrollment: 600 students

Institution Contact: Jose Cisneros, Campus President
Phone: 619-686-8600 ext. 225 *Fax:* 619-686-8669 *E-mail:*
jose.cisneros@remingtoncollege.edu
Admission Contact: Mr. Lennor Johnson, Director of
Recruitment *Phone:* 619-686-8600 ext. 229 *Fax:* 619-686-
8684 *E-mail:* lennor.johnson@remingtoncollege.edu
See full description on page 342.

San Joaquin Valley College Ⓐ
201 New Stine Road
Bakersfield, CA 93309
Web: http://www.sjvc.edu
Accreditation: Western Association of Schools and
Colleges
Programs Offered: administrative assistant and
secretarial science; business administration and
management; computer engineering technology;
computer/information technology services administration related; computer installation and repair
technology; computer systems networking and
telecommunications; computer technology/computer
systems technology; corrections; criminal justice/law
enforcement administration; dental assisting; executive assistant/executive secretary; health information/
medical records technology; heating, air conditioning
and refrigeration technology; information science/
studies; insurance; medical administrative assistant
and medical secretary; medical/clinical assistant;
medical office management; office occupations and
clerical services; receptionist; respiratory care therapy;
security and loss prevention; surgical technology
Institution Contact: Mr. Joseph Holt, Director of
Marketing and Admissions *Phone:* 559-651-2500 *Fax:*
559-651-4864 *E-mail:* josephh@sjvc.edu
Admission Contact: Mr. David Baker, Campus
Director *Phone:* 661-834-0126 *Fax:* 661-834-1021 *E-mail:*
davidb@sjvc.edu
See full description on page 344.

San Joaquin Valley College Ⓐ
295 East Sierra Avenue
Fresno, CA 93710
Web: http://www.sjvc.edu
Accreditation: Western Association of Schools and
Colleges
Programs Offered: business administration and
management; computer/technical support; criminal
justice/law enforcement administration; dental
assisting; electrical, electronic and communications
engineering technology; health/health care administration; heating, air conditioning and refrigeration
technology; hospitality administration; medical

Ⓐ indicates that the school is a participating institution in the *Imagine America* Scholarship Program.

administrative assistant and medical secretary; medical office management; pharmacy technician; tourism and travel services management

Institution Contact: Director, Fresno Campus *Phone:* 559-229-7800 *Fax:* 559-448-8250

Admission Contact: Admissions Director *Phone:* 559-229-7800 *Fax:* 559-448-8250

See full description on page 345.

San Joaquin Valley College Ⓐ

4985 East Anderson Avenue
Fresno, CA 93727
Web: http://www.sjvc.edu

Accreditation: Western Association of Schools and Colleges

Programs Offered: airframe mechanics and aircraft maintenance technology; avionics maintenance technology

Enrollment: 57 students

Institution Contact: Bob Loogman, Executive Director, Aviation Campus *Phone:* 559-453-0123 *Fax:* 559-453-0133 *E-mail:* bobl@sjvc.edu

Admission Contact: Bob Loogman, Director, Aviation Campus *Phone:* 559-453-0123 *Fax:* 559-453-0133 *E-mail:* bobl@sjvc.edu

See full description on page 343.

San Joaquin Valley College

1700 McHenry Village Way
Modesto, CA 95350
Web: http://www.sjvc.edu

Accreditation: Western Association of Schools and Colleges

Programs Offered: business administration and management; medical/clinical assistant; medical office management

Institution Contact: *Phone:* 866-808-9387

San Joaquin Valley College Ⓐ

10641 Church Street
Rancho Cucamonga, CA 91730
Web: http://www.sjvc.edu

Accreditation: Western Association of Schools and Colleges

Programs Offered: business administration and management; corrections; dental hygiene; medical administrative assistant and medical secretary; medical/clinical assistant; pharmacy technician

Enrollment: 500 students

Institution Contact: Ms. Sherril Hein, Director, Rancho Cucamonga Campus *Phone:* 909-948-7582 *Fax:* 909-948-3860 *E-mail:* sherrilh@sjvc.edu

Admission Contact: Mr. Ramon Abreu, Enrollment Services Director *Phone:* 909-948-7582 *Fax:* 909-948-3860 *E-mail:* ramona@sjvc.edu

See full description on page 346.

San Joaquin Valley College Ⓐ

8400 West Mineral King Avenue
Visalia, CA 93291-9283
Web: http://www.sjvc.edu

Accreditation: Western Association of Schools and Colleges

Programs Offered: accounting; administrative assistant and secretarial science; business administration and management; business automation/technology/data entry; computer installation and repair technology; computer systems networking and telecommunications; computer technology/computer systems technology; corrections; criminal justice/law enforcement administration; data processing and data processing technology; dental assisting; dental hygiene; executive assistant/executive secretary; health information/medical records technology; medical administrative assistant and medical secretary; medical/clinical assistant; medical office management; nursing assistant/aide and patient care assistant; nursing (licensed practical/vocational nurse training); office occupations and clerical services; physician assistant; receptionist; respiratory care therapy

Institution Contact: Mr. Mark Perry, President *Phone:* 559-651-2500 *Fax:* 559-651-0574 *E-mail:* president@sjvc.edu

Admission Contact: Ms. Wendi Oliviera, Admissions Director *Phone:* 559-651-2500 *Fax:* 559-651-0574 *E-mail:* wendio@sjvc.edu

See full description on page 347.

Santa Barbara Business College

211 South Real Road
Bakersfield, CA 93309
Web: http://www.sbbcollege.com/

Accreditation: Accrediting Bureau of Health Education Schools; Accrediting Council for Independent Colleges and Schools

Programs Offered: accounting technology and bookkeeping; business administration and management; computer programming (vendor/product certification); computer systems networking and telecommunications; computer/technical support;

Ⓐ indicates that the school is a participating institution in the *Imagine America* Scholarship Program.

Santa Barbara Business College (*continued*)

criminal justice/law enforcement administration; legal administrative assistant/secretary; legal assistant/paralegal; medical/clinical assistant; medical insurance/medical billing; medical office management; pharmacy technician; web page, digital/multimedia and information resources design

Enrollment: 400 students

Institution Contact: Mr. Dean Johnston, President *Phone:* 805-967-0483 *Fax:* 805-683-5861 *E-mail:* deanj@sbbcollege.net

Admission Contact: Mr. Ron League, Director of Admissions *Phone:* 805-835-1100 *Fax:* 805-835-0242 *E-mail:* ronl@sbbcollege.edu

Santa Barbara Business College

5266 Hollister Avenue
Santa Barbara, CA 93111

Accreditation: Accrediting Council for Independent Colleges and Schools

Programs Offered: accounting; administrative assistant and secretarial science; business administration and management; computer/information technology administration and management; computer/technical support; criminal justice/law enforcement administration; legal administrative assistant/secretary; legal assistant/paralegal; medical/clinical assistant; medical insurance/medical billing; pharmacy technician; web/multimedia management and webmaster

Enrollment: 250 students

Institution Contact: Mr. Dean Johnston, President *Phone:* 805-967-0483 *Fax:* 805-683-5861 *E-mail:* deanj@sbbcollege.edu

Admission Contact: Mrs. Denise Evans, Director of Admissions *Phone:* 805-967-9677 *Fax:* 805-683-5861 *E-mail:* denisee@sbbcollege.edu

Santa Barbara Business College

305 East Plaza Drive
Santa Maria, CA 93454
Web: http://www.sbbcollege.com

Accreditation: Accrediting Council for Independent Colleges and Schools

Programs Offered: accounting; business administration and management; computer systems networking and telecommunications; computer/technical support; criminal justice/law enforcement administration; legal assistant/paralegal; medical/clinical assistant; medical insurance/medical billing; medical office manage-

ment; pharmacy technician; web page, digital/multimedia and information resources design

Enrollment: 300 students

Institution Contact: Mr. Dean Johnston, President *Phone:* 805-967-0483 *Fax:* 805-683-5861

Admission Contact: Mrs. Holly Ortiz, Director of Admissions *Phone:* 805-922-8256 *E-mail:* hollyo@sbbcollege.edu

Silicon Valley College ⓐ

1400 65th Street, Suite 200
Emeryville, CA 94608
Web: http://www.svcollege.com

Accreditation: Accrediting Commission of Career Schools and Colleges of Technology

Programs Offered: commercial and advertising art; drafting and design technology; information technology; medical/clinical assistant

Enrollment: 550 students

Institution Contact: Elvie Engstrom, Executive Director *Phone:* 510-601-0133 *Fax:* 510-601-0793 *E-mail:* eengstrom@svcollege.com

Admission Contact: Mr. Robert Zayed, Director of Admissions *Phone:* 510-601-0133 *Fax:* 510-601-0793 *E-mail:* rzayed@svcollege.com

See full description on page 348.

Silicon Valley College ⓐ

41350 Christy Street
Fremont, CA 94538
Web: http://www.siliconvalley.edu

Accreditation: Accrediting Commission of Career Schools and Colleges of Technology

Programs Offered: commercial and advertising art; computer graphics; computer/information technology administration and management; computer/information technology services administration related; computer systems networking and telecommunications; drafting and design technology; information science/studies; information technology; intermedia/multimedia; massage therapy; medical/clinical assistant; medical office management; pharmacy technician; system administration; system, networking, and LAN/WAN management

Institution Contact: Chuck Ericson, Executive Director *Phone:* 510-623-9966 *Fax:* 510-623-9822

Admission Contact: *Phone:* 510-623-9966 *Fax:* 510-623-9822

See full description on page 349.

ⓐ indicates that the school is a participating institution in the *Imagine America* Scholarship Program.

Silicon Valley College Ⓐ

6201 San Ignacio Avenue
San Jose, CA 95119
Web: http://www.siliconvalley.edu

Accreditation: Accrediting Commission of Career Schools and Colleges of Technology

Programs Offered: CAD/CADD drafting/design technology; commercial and advertising art; computer graphics; computer/information technology administration and management; design and visual communications; drafting and design technology; health information/medical records administration; information science/studies; information technology; internet information systems; massage therapy; medical/clinical assistant; medical office management; pharmacy technician; system administration; system, networking, and LAN/WAN management

Institution Contact: Mr. Steve Ashab, Executive Director *Phone:* 408-360-0840 *Fax:* 408-360-0848 *E-mail:* sjwebleads@svcollege.com

Admission Contact: *Phone:* 408-360-0840 *Fax:* 408-360-0848

See full description on page 350.

Silicon Valley College Ⓐ

2800 Mitchell Drive
Walnut Creek, CA 94598
Web: http://www.siliconvalley.edu

Accreditation: Accrediting Bureau of Health Education Schools; Accrediting Commission of Career Schools and Colleges of Technology

Programs Offered: business administration and management; commercial and advertising art; computer graphics; computer/information technology administration and management; computer systems networking and telecommunications; health/health care administration; health information/medical records administration; information science/studies; information technology; intermedia/multimedia; massage therapy; mechanical design technology; medical administrative assistant and medical secretary; medical/clinical assistant; medical office computer specialist; medical office management; pharmacy technician; system administration; system, networking, and LAN/WAN management

Enrollment: 500 students

Institution Contact: Mr. Mark J. Millen, Executive Director *Phone:* 925-280-0235 *Fax:* 925-280-9567 *E-mail:* mmillen@svcollege.com

Admission Contact: Mr. Mark Millen, Campus Director *Phone:* 925-280-0235 *Fax:* 925-280-0267 *E-mail:* vpsvc@aol.com

See full description on page 351.

Software Education of America College of Technology

265 South Randolph Avenue, #230
Brea, CA 92821
Web: http://www.seacollege.edu

Accreditation: Accrediting Commission of Career Schools and Colleges of Technology

Programs Offered: accounting; administrative assistant and secretarial science; computer engineering technology; computer graphics; computer/information technology administration and management; computer/information technology services administration related; computer installation and repair technology; computer programming; computer systems networking and telecommunications; medical administrative assistant and medical secretary; web/multimedia management and webmaster; web page, digital/multimedia and information resources design

Institution Contact: Mr. Daniel C. Day, President/CEO *Phone:* 714-257-3095 *Fax:* 714-256-1549 *E-mail:* dday@seaed.com

Admission Contact: Mr. Pablo Hojberg, Director of Admissions *Phone:* 714-257-3095 *Fax:* 714-256-2549 *E-mail:* phojberg@seaed.com

Trinity College

804 West Texas Street
Fairfield, CA 94533
Web: http://www.trinitycollege.com

Accreditation: Accrediting Council for Continuing Education and Training

Programs Offered: corrections; massage therapy; medical administrative assistant and medical secretary; medical/clinical assistant; pharmacy technician

Institution Contact: Ms. Karen Keden, School Director *Phone:* 707-424-6017 *Fax:* 707-425-3383 *E-mail:* kkeden@trinitycollege.com

Admission Contact: Mr. Eric Grayson, Admissions Director *Phone:* 707-425-2288 *Fax:* 707-424-6027 *E-mail:* egrayson@trinitycollege.com

United Education Institute

310 3rd Avenue, Suite C6/C7
Chula Vista, CA 91910
Web: http://www.uei-edu.com

Accreditation: Accrediting Council for Continuing Education and Training

Programs Offered: business administration and management; dental assisting; medical/clinical

Ⓐ indicates that the school is a participating institution in the *Imagine America* Scholarship Program.

United Education Institute *(continued)*

assistant; system administration; system, networking, and LAN/WAN management

Institution Contact: Ms. Fia Afalava, Executive Director *Phone:* 619-409-4111 *Fax:* 619-409-4114 *E-mail:* afalavaf@iecglobal.com

Admission Contact: Ms. Nancy Fellciano, Director of Admissions *Phone:* 619-409-4111 *Fax:* 619-409-4114 *E-mail:* fellcianon@iecglobal.com

United Education Institute, Huntington Park

6812 Pacific Boulevard
Huntington Park, CA 90255
Web: http://www.uei-edu.com

Accreditation: Accrediting Council for Continuing Education and Training

Programs Offered: business administration and management; dental assisting; medical/clinical assistant; system administration; system, networking, and LAN/WAN management

Institution Contact: Ms. Myra Hadley, Executive Director *Phone:* 323-277-8000 *Fax:* 323-588-5484 *E-mail:* hadleym@iecglobal.com

Admission Contact: Ms. Dora Tellez, Director of Admissions *Phone:* 323-277-8000 *Fax:* 323-588-5484 *E-mail:* tellezd@iecglobal.com

United Education Institute, Los Angeles

3020 Wilshire Boulevard, #250
Los Angeles, CA 90010
Web: http://www.uei-edu.com

Accreditation: Accrediting Council for Continuing Education and Training

Programs Offered: business administration and management; computer systems networking and telecommunications; medical/clinical assistant; medical insurance/medical billing; pharmacy technician

Enrollment: 305 students

Institution Contact: Mr. Brian Lahargoue, Executive Director *Phone:* 213-427-3700 ext. 410 *Fax:* 213-487-1090 *E-mail:* lahargoueb@ueiglobal.com

Admission Contact: Director of Admissions *Phone:* 213-427-3700 *Fax:* 213-487-1090

United Education Institute, Ontario Campus

3380 Shelby Street, Suite 150
Ontario, CA 91764
Web: http://www.uei-edu.com

Accreditation: Accrediting Council for Continuing Education and Training

Programs Offered: business administration and management; dental assisting; medical/clinical assistant; pharmacy technician; system administration; system, networking, and LAN/WAN management

Institution Contact: Ms. Jacky Ford, Executive Director *Phone:* 909-476-2424 *Fax:* 909-484-8748 *E-mail:* fordj@iecglobal.com

Admission Contact: Mr. Juan Tellez, Director of Admissions *Phone:* 909-476-2424 *Fax:* 909-484-8748 *E-mail:* tellezj@iecglobal.com

United Education Institute, San Bernardino Campus

295 East Caroline Street, Suite E
San Bernardino, CA 92408
Web: http://www.uei-edu.com

Accreditation: Accrediting Council for Continuing Education and Training

Programs Offered: business administration and management; dental assisting; medical/clinical assistant; medical insurance coding; medical insurance/medical billing; pharmacy technician; system, networking, and LAN/WAN management

Institution Contact: Mr. Robert Cios, Executive Director *Phone:* 909-554-1999 *Fax:* 909-554-1991 *E-mail:* ciosr@iecglobal.com

Admission Contact: Ms. Elisabeth Miller, Director of Admissions *Phone:* 909-554-1999 *Fax:* 909-554-1991 *E-mail:* millere@iecglobal.com

United Education Institute, San Diego Campus

1323 6th Avenue
San Diego, CA 92101
Web: http://www.uei-edu.com

Accreditation: Accrediting Council for Continuing Education and Training

Programs Offered: business administration and management; computer/technical support; dental assisting; medical/clinical assistant; pharmacy technician

Collins College > A School of Design & Technology

Main Campus - Tempe, Arizona > West Campus - Phoenix, Arizona

How bad do you wanna get good?

by Gabe Turner

by Ryan Heuett

by David Mazey

DEGREE PROGRAMS:

MEDIA ARTS
> Digital Video/Television & Cinema Production
> Film & HDTV
> Motion Graphics & Visual FX

GRAPHIC DESIGN

VISUAL COMMUNICATION

INTERIOR DESIGN

GAME DESIGN

ANIMATION

NETWORK TECHNOLOGY

MANAGEMENT

APPLIED TECHNOLOGY MANAGEMENT

TAKE YOUR CREATIVITY TO THE NEXT LEVEL.

Start your design, technology or management career training at Collins College. With job-focused training that's interactive. Industry-driven. And in demand for today's global marketplace. We offer Bachelor & Associate degree programs at two convenient valley locations.

Call now for a free brochure **1-800-906-1700**
www.CollinsCollege.edu

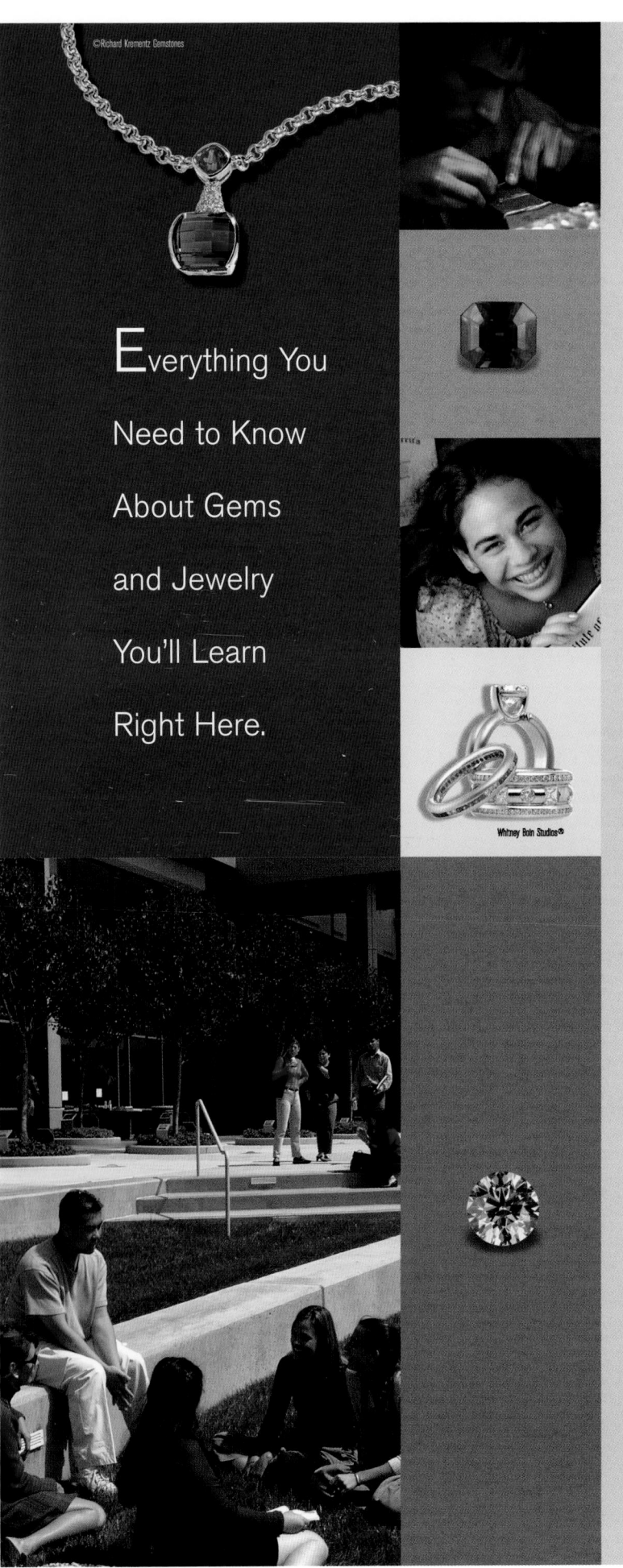

The Gemological Institute of America

For more than 70 years, the nonprofit Gemological Institute of America has educated the world's leading jewelers, gemologists and jewelry designers, offering the most comprehensive and respected gem and jewelry education available anywhere. Find out how GIA can prepare you for a rich and rewarding career in the fine jewelry industry with:

Diploma programs and courses in gemology, jewelry design, manufacturing, sales, and jewelry business management

On Campus, Distance Education, Online Web Enhanced Courses, Traveling Extension Classes, and Seminars

Year-round admission

Financial assistance programs and scholarships for qualifying students

On-going career support

Campus locations in Carlsbad, Los Angeles, New York City, and 10 major gem and jewelry centers around the world

To learn more, call today for a free course catalog: 800-421-7250 ext. 4001 or visit www.gia.edu

Learn from the World's Foremost Authority in Gemology™

World Headquarters
The Robert Mouawad Campus
5345 Armada Drive | Carlsbad, CA 92008

PGCC05

Institution Contact: Ms. April Bjornsen, Executive Director *Phone:* 619-544-9800 *Fax:* 619-233-3028 *E-mail:* bjornsena@iecglobal.com

Admission Contact: Ms. Mike Wynn, Director of Admissions *Phone:* 619-544-9800 *Fax:* 619-233-3028 *E-mail:* wynnm@iecglobal.com

United Education Institute, Van Nuys Campus

7335 Van Nuys Boulevard
Van Nuys, CA 91405
Web: http://www.uei-edu.com

Accreditation: Accrediting Council for Continuing Education and Training

Programs Offered: business administration and management; dental assisting; medical/clinical assistant; medical insurance/medical billing; pharmacy technician; system administration; system, networking, and LAN/WAN management

Institution Contact: Ms. Carolann Hartmann, Executive Director *Phone:* 818-756-1200 *Fax:* 818-994-2607 *E-mail:* hartmannc@iecglobal.com

Admission Contact: Ms. Jackie Azizyan, Director of Admissions *Phone:* 818-756-1200 *Fax:* 818-994-2607 *E-mail:* azizyanj@iecglobal.com

Universal Technical Institute Ⓐ

9494 Haven Avenue
Rancho Cucamonga, CA 91730
Web: http://www.uticorp.com

Accreditation: Accrediting Commission of Career Schools and Colleges of Technology

Programs Offered: automobile/automotive mechanics technology; automotive engineering technology

Institution Contact: Mr. Eric Oster, School Director *Phone:* 909-484-1929 *Fax:* 909-484-6639 *E-mail:* eoster@uticorp.com

See full description on page 352.

Western Career College Ⓐ

380 Civic Drive, Suite 300
Pleasant Hill, CA 94523
Web: http://www.westerncollege.com

Accreditation: Accrediting Commission of Career Schools and Colleges of Technology; Western Association of Schools and Colleges

Programs Offered: dental assisting; massage therapy; medical administrative assistant and medical secretary; medical/clinical assistant; medical insurance/

medical billing; nursing (licensed practical/vocational nurse training); pharmacy technician; veterinary technology

Institution Contact: LaShawn Wells, Executive Director *Phone:* 925-609-6650 *Fax:* 925-609-6666 *E-mail:* phwebleads@westerncollege.com

See full description on page 353.

Western Career College Ⓐ

8909 Folsom Boulevard
Sacramento, CA 95826
Web: http://www.westerncollege.com

Accreditation: Accrediting Commission of Career Schools and Colleges of Technology; Western Association of Schools and Colleges

Programs Offered: dental assisting; massage therapy; medical administrative assistant and medical secretary; medical/clinical assistant; medical insurance coding; nursing (licensed practical/vocational nurse training); pharmacy technician; veterinary/animal health technology

Institution Contact: Ms. Sue Fleming, Executive Director *Phone:* 916-361-1660 ext. 605 *Fax:* 916-361-6666 *E-mail:* sfleming@westerncollege.com

Admission Contact: Mr. Bobby Grainger, Director of High School Admissions *Phone:* 916-361-1660 ext. 615 *Fax:* 916-361-6666 *E-mail:* bgrainger@westerncollege.com

See full description on page 354.

Western Career College Ⓐ

170 Bayfair Mall
San Leandro, CA 94578
Web: http://www.westerncollege.com

Accreditation: Accrediting Commission of Career Schools and Colleges of Technology; Western Association of Schools and Colleges

Programs Offered: dental assisting; massage therapy; medical administrative assistant and medical secretary; medical/clinical assistant; medical insurance/ medical billing; nursing (licensed practical/vocational nurse training); pharmacy technician; veterinary/ animal health technology

Institution Contact: Ms. Dawn Matthews, Executive Director *Phone:* 510-276-3888 *Fax:* 510-276-3654 *E-mail:* slwebleads@westerncollege.com

See full description on page 355.

Ⓐ indicates that the school is a participating institution in the *Imagine America* Scholarship Program.

Western State University College of Law

1111 North State College Boulevard
Fullerton, CA 92831
Web: http://www.wsulaw.edu

Accreditation: Western Association of Schools and Colleges

Programs Offered: pre-law studies

Enrollment: 510 students

Institution Contact: Mrs. Gloria Switzer, Assistant Dean of Admission *Phone:* 714-459-1101 *Fax:* 714-441-1748 *E-mail:* gswitzer@wsulaw.edu

Westwood College–Anaheim Ⓐ

1551 South Douglass Road
Anaheim, CA 92806
Web: http://www.westwood.edu

Accreditation: Accrediting Commission of Career Schools and Colleges of Technology

Programs Offered: accounting and business/management; animation, interactive technology, video graphics and special effects; business, management, and marketing related; CAD/CADD drafting/design technology; computer engineering technology; computer software engineering; criminal justice/law enforcement administration; information technology; interior design; marketing/marketing management; technology management; web/multimedia management and webmaster; web page, digital/multimedia and information resources design

Enrollment: 735 students

Institution Contact: Mr. Frederick Holland, Executive Director *Phone:* 714-704-2721 ext. 200 *Fax:* 714-939-2011 *E-mail:* fholland@westwood.edu

Admission Contact: Emily Yost, Director of Admissions *Phone:* 714-704-2721 ext. 100 *Fax:* 714-456-9971 *E-mail:* eyost@westwood.edu

See full description on page 357.

Westwood College–Inland Empire Ⓐ

20 West 7th Street
Upland, CA 91786
Web: http://www.westwood.edu/

Accreditation: Accrediting Commission of Career Schools and Colleges of Technology

Programs Offered: accounting; accounting and business/management; animation, interactive technology, video graphics and special effects; business administration and management; CAD/CADD drafting/design technology; commercial and advertising art; computer and information systems security; computer programming; computer software and media applications; computer software engineering; computer software technology; computer systems networking and telecommunications; computer technology/computer systems technology; criminal justice/law enforcement administration; e-commerce; finance; interior design; marketing/marketing management; system, networking, and LAN/WAN management; web page, digital/multimedia and information resources design

Enrollment: 1,050 students

Institution Contact: Ms. Kathy Allin, Executive Director *Phone:* 909-931-7599 ext. 200 *Fax:* 909-946-6304 *E-mail:* kallin@westwood.edu

Admission Contact: Lyle Seavers, Director of Admissions *Phone:* 909-931-7550 ext. 100 *Fax:* 909-931-5962 *E-mail:* lseavers@westwood.edu

See full description on page 358.

Westwood College–Long Beach Ⓐ

3901 Via Oro Avenue, Suite 103
Long Beach, CA 90810
Web: http://www.westwood.edu

Accreditation: Accrediting Commission of Career Schools and Colleges of Technology

Programs Offered: animation, interactive technology, video graphics and special effects; CAD/CADD drafting/design technology; computer/information technology administration and management; computer technology/computer systems technology; criminal justice/law enforcement administration; information technology; interior design; technology management

Enrollment: 300 students

Institution Contact: Ms. Vicki L. Bowles, Executive Director *Phone:* 310-522-2088 ext. 200 *Fax:* 310-522-4318 *E-mail:* vbowles@westwood.edu

Admission Contact: Mr. Steve Maloof, Assistant Director of Admissions *Phone:* 310-522-2088 ext. 104 *Fax:* 310-522-4318 *E-mail:* smaloof@westwood.edu

See full description on page 359.

Westwood College–Los Angeles Ⓐ

8911 Aviation Boulevard
Inglewood, CA 90301
Web: http://www.westwood.edu

Accreditation: Council on Occupational Education

Programs Offered: aircraft powerplant technology; airframe mechanics and aircraft maintenance technology

Enrollment: 636 students

Ⓐ indicates that the school is a participating institution in the *Imagine America* Scholarship Program.

Institution Contact: Mr. Mitch J. Thomas, Executive Director *Phone:* 310-642-5440 ext. 200 *Fax:* 310-642-3716 *E-mail:* mthomas@westwood.edu

Admission Contact: Ms. Alexandra Fi, Director of Admissions *Phone:* 310-642-5440 ext. 240 *Fax:* 310-337-1176 *E-mail:* afi@westwood.edu

See full description on page 356.

Westwood College—Los Angeles

3460 Wilshire Boulevard, Suite 700
Los Angeles, CA 90010
Web: http://www.westwood.edu

Accreditation: Accrediting Council for Independent Colleges and Schools

Programs Offered: animation, interactive technology, video graphics and special effects; business, management, and marketing related; computer engineering technology; computer graphics; computer/information technology administration and management; computer programming; criminal justice/law enforcement administration; e-commerce; information technology; technology management; web page, digital/multimedia and information resources design

Enrollment: 539 students

Institution Contact: Mr. William Frank, Executive Director *Phone:* 213-739-9999 ext. 200 *Fax:* 213-382-2468 *E-mail:* bfrank@westwood.edu

Admission Contact: Mr. Ron Milman, Director of Admissions *Phone:* 213-739-9999 ext. 100 *Fax:* 213-382-2468 *E-mail:* rmilman@westwood.edu

See full description on page 360.

WyoTech ⓐ

200 Whitney Place
Fremont, CA 94539-7663
Web: http://www.wyotech.com

Accreditation: Accrediting Commission of Career Schools and Colleges of Technology

Programs Offered: automobile/automotive mechanics technology; heating, air conditioning and refrigeration technology; plumbing technology

Enrollment: 1,631 students

Institution Contact: Mr. Ric Kimbell, President *Phone:* 510-580-6735 *Fax:* 510-770-3873 *E-mail:* rkimbell@cci.edu

Admission Contact: Mr. Joseph File, Director of Admissions *Phone:* 510-580-3507 *Fax:* 510-490-8599 *E-mail:* jfile@sequoiainstitute.edu

See full description on page 361.

WyoTech

9636 Earhart Road, Oakland International Airport
Oakland, CA 94621
Web: http://www.wyotech.com

Programs Offered: airframe mechanics and aircraft maintenance technology

Institution Contact: *Phone:* 510-569-8436 *Fax:* 510-635-3936

WyoTech

980 Riverside Parkway
West Sacramento, CA 95605
Web: http://www.wyotech.com

Accreditation: Accrediting Commission of Career Schools and Colleges of Technology

Programs Offered: automobile/automotive mechanics technology

Enrollment: 300 students

Institution Contact: Jeanette M. Prickett, President *Phone:* 916-376-8888 ext. 201 *Fax:* 916-617-2069 *E-mail:* jprickett@wyotech.edu

Admission Contact: Mr. Steve Coffee, Director of Admissions *Phone:* 916-376-8888 ext. 202 *Fax:* 916-376-8888 ext. 95605 *E-mail:* scoffee@wyotech.edu

Colorado

The Art Institute of Colorado ⓐ

1200 Lincoln Street
Denver, CO 80203
Web: http://www.aic.artinstitutes.edu

Accreditation: Accrediting Council for Independent Colleges and Schools

Programs Offered: advertising; art; baking and pastry arts; cinematography and film/video production; commercial and advertising art; commercial photography; computer graphics; culinary arts; hospitality administration; industrial design; interior design; intermedia/multimedia; photography; restaurant, culinary, and catering management; web/multimedia management and webmaster; web page, digital/multimedia and information resources design

Enrollment: 2,000 students

Institution Contact: Mr. Steve Mansdoerfer, President *Phone:* 303-837-0825 *Fax:* 303-860-8520 *E-mail:* smansdoerfer@aii.edu

ⓐ indicates that the school is a participating institution in the *Imagine America* Scholarship Program.

The Art Institute of Colorado *(continued)*

Admission Contact: Mr. Brian Parker, Director of Admissions *Phone:* 800-275-2420 *Fax:* 303-860-8520 *E-mail:* baparker@aii.edu

See full description on page 362.

Bel—Rea Institute of Animal Technology ⓐ

1681 South Dayton Street
Denver, CO 80247
Web: http://www.bel-rea.com

Accreditation: Accrediting Commission of Career Schools and Colleges of Technology

Programs Offered: veterinary/animal health technology; veterinary technology

Enrollment: 700 students

Institution Contact: Mr. Marc Schapiro, Controller *Phone:* 303-751-8700 *Fax:* 303-751-9969 *E-mail:* schapiro@bel-rea.com

Admission Contact: Ms. Paulette Kaufman, Director *Phone:* 800-950-8001 *Fax:* 303-751-9969 *E-mail:* kaufman@bel-rea.com

See full description on page 363.

Blair College ⓐ

1815 Jetwing Drive
Colorado Springs, CO 80916
Web: http://www.cci.edu

Accreditation: Accrediting Council for Independent Colleges and Schools

Programs Offered: accounting; administrative assistant and secretarial science; business administration and management; computer programming (specific applications); criminal justice/law enforcement administration; legal assistant/paralegal; medical administrative assistant and medical secretary; medical/clinical assistant; medical insurance/ medical billing; security and loss prevention; system, networking, and LAN/WAN management

Institution Contact: Mr. Tom Andron, President *Phone:* 719-638-6580 ext. 105 *Fax:* 719-638-6818 *E-mail:* tandron@cci.edu

Admission Contact: Ms. Dawn Collins, Director of Admissions *Phone:* 719-638-6580 ext. 102 *Fax:* 719-638-6818 *E-mail:* mcollins@cci.edu

See full description on page 364.

Cambridge College

12500 East Iliff Avenue
Aurora, CO 80014
Web: http://www.hightechschools.com/

Accreditation: Accrediting Bureau of Health Education Schools; Accrediting Commission of Career Schools and Colleges of Technology

Programs Offered: computer/information technology administration and management; massage therapy; medical/clinical assistant; medical radiologic technology; surgical technology

Institution Contact: Ms. Sandi Parks, College Director *Phone:* 303-338-9700 *Fax:* 303-338-9701 *E-mail:* sparks@hightechschools.com

Admission Contact: Mr. Mitch Hauer, Director of Admissions *Phone:* 303-338-9700 *Fax:* 303-338-9701 *E-mail:* mhauer@hightechschools.com

CollegeAmerica—Colorado Springs

3645 Citadel Drive South
Colorado Springs, CO 80909
Web: http://www.CollegeAmerica.com

Accreditation: Accrediting Commission of Career Schools and Colleges of Technology

Programs Offered: accounting; business administration and management; computer and information sciences related; computer programming; e-commerce; gene therapy; health/health care administration; medical administrative assistant and medical secretary; medical/clinical assistant; medical insurance coding; medical insurance/medical billing; medical office management; pharmacy technician; respiratory therapy technician; system administration; system, networking, and LAN/WAN management

Institution Contact: Mr. Mark E. Duda, Executive Director *Phone:* 719-637-0600 *Fax:* 719-637-0806 *E-mail:* mduda@collegeamerica.com

Admission Contact: Ms. Cristina Reyna, Director of Admissions *Phone:* 719-637-0600 *Fax:* 719-637-0806 *E-mail:* creyna@collegeamerica.edu

CollegeAmerica—Denver

1385 South Colorado Boulevard, 5th Floor
Denver, CO 80222
Web: http://www.collegeamerica.com

Accreditation: Accrediting Commission of Career Schools and Colleges of Technology

Programs Offered: accounting; acupuncture; administrative assistant and secretarial science; business administration and management; clinical/medical laboratory technology; computer/information technology administration and management; computer/

ⓐ indicates that the school is a participating institution in the *Imagine America* Scholarship Program.

information technology services administration related; computer installation and repair technology; computer programming; computer programming (specific applications); computer systems networking and telecommunications; computer/technical support; computer technology/computer systems technology; data entry/microcomputer applications; desktop publishing and digital imaging design; executive assistant/executive secretary; health information/medical records administration; marketing/marketing management; medical administrative assistant and medical secretary; medical/clinical assistant; nursing assistant/aide and patient care assistant; pharmacy technician; system, networking, and LAN/WAN management; telecommunications; web/multimedia management and webmaster; web page, digital/multimedia and information resources design; word processing

Institution Contact: Ms. Barbara W. Thomas, President *Phone:* 303-691-9756 *Fax:* 303-692-9156 *E-mail:* collegeamerica@aol.com

CollegeAmerica–Fort Collins

4601 South Mason Street
Fort Collins, CO 80525
Web: http://www.collegeamerica.edu

Accreditation: Accrediting Commission of Career Schools and Colleges of Technology

Programs Offered: accounting; business administration and management; commercial and advertising art; computer and information sciences related; computer programming; computer technology/computer systems technology; health/health care administration; medical/clinical assistant

Institution Contact: Ms. Anna DiTorrice-Mull, Director of Admission *Phone:* 970-223-6060 *Fax:* 970-225-6059 *E-mail:* anna@collegeamerica.edu

Colorado School of Trades

1575 Hoyt Street
Lakewood, CO 80215-2996
Web: http://schooloftrades.com

Accreditation: Accrediting Commission of Career Schools and Colleges of Technology

Programs Offered: gunsmithing; horseshoeing

Enrollment: 120 students

Institution Contact: Mr. Robert Martin, Director *Phone:* 303-233-4697 ext. 14 *Fax:* 303-233-4723 *E-mail:* robert@schooloftrdades.com

Admission Contact: Admissions *Phone:* 303-233-4697 ext. 15 *Fax:* 303-233-4723 *E-mail:* info@schooloftrades.com

Colorado Technical University

4435 North Chestnut Street
Colorado Springs, CO 80907
Web: http://www.coloratech.edu

Accreditation: North Central Association of Colleges and Schools

Programs Offered: business administration and management; communications technology; computer and information sciences related; computer and information systems security; computer engineering technology; computer software engineering; criminal justice/law enforcement administration; design and visual communications; e-commerce; electrical, electronic and communications engineering technology; entrepreneurship; human resources management; information technology; insurance; logistics and materials management; marketing/marketing management; technology management

Institution Contact: Dr. David E. Leasure, Vice President of Academic Affairs *Phone:* 719-590-6716 *Fax:* 719-590-6817 *E-mail:* dleasure@coloradotech.edu

Admission Contact: Mr. Ron Begora, Director of Admissions *Phone:* 719-590-6718 *Fax:* 719-598-3740 *E-mail:* rbegora@coloradotech.edu

Colorado Technical University Denver Campus

5775 Denver Tech Center Boulevard
Greenwood Village, CO 80111-3258
Web: http://www.ctu-denver.com

Accreditation: North Central Association of Colleges and Schools

Programs Offered: accounting; business administration and management; computer and information sciences related; computer and information systems security; criminal justice/law enforcement administration; electrical, electronic and communications engineering technology; graphic communications related; information technology

Enrollment: 580 students

Institution Contact: Dr. Michael Basham, President *Phone:* 303-694-6600 *Fax:* 303-694-6673 *E-mail:* mbasham@coloradotech.edu

Admission Contact: Ms. Jennifer Schmidt, Director of Admissions *Phone:* 303-694-6600 *Fax:* 303-694-6673 *E-mail:* jschmidt@coloradotech.edu

Denver Automotive and Diesel College Ⓐ

460 South Lipan Street, PO Box 9366
Denver, CO 80223-9960
Web: http://www.dadc.com

Accreditation: Accrediting Commission of Career Schools and Colleges of Technology

Ⓐ indicates that the school is a participating institution in the *Imagine America* Scholarship Program.

Denver Automotive and Diesel College (*continued*)

Programs Offered: automotive engineering technology; diesel mechanics technology
Enrollment: 1,100 students
Institution Contact: Mr. Marty Cieslak, Executive Director *Phone:* 303-722-5724 ext. 109 *Fax:* 303-778-8264 *E-mail:* mcieslak@lincolntech.com
Admission Contact: Mr. Levi Myers, Director of Admissions *Phone:* 303-722-5724 *Fax:* 303-778-8264 *E-mail:* lmyers@lincolntech.com
See full description on page 365.

Denver Career College

500 East 84th Avenue, W-200
Thornton, CO 80229
Web: http://www.denvercareercollege.com
Accreditation: Accrediting Commission of Career Schools and Colleges of Technology
Programs Offered: business administration and management; criminal justice/law enforcement administration; legal assistant/paralegal; massage therapy; medical/clinical assistant; medical office assistant; pharmacy technician
Enrollment: 210 students
Institution Contact: Mr. Ken Sigmon, Regional Director *Phone:* 402-572-8500 *Fax:* 402-408-1909 *E-mail:* ksigmon@khec.com
Admission Contact: Ms. Stephanie Parys, Executive Director *Phone:* 303-736-0030 ext. 231 *Fax:* 303-295-0102 *E-mail:* sparys@denvercareercollege.com

ITT Technical Institute Ⓐ

500 East 84 Avenue, Suite B12
Thornton, CO 80229
Web: http://www.itt-tech.edu
Accreditation: Accrediting Council for Independent Colleges and Schools
Programs Offered: accounting and business/management; animation, interactive technology, video graphics and special effects; business administration and management; CAD/CADD drafting/design technology; communications technology; computer and information systems security; computer engineering technology; computer software and media applications; computer software engineering; computer systems networking and telecommunications; criminal justice/police science; digital communication and media/multimedia; electrical, electronic and communications engineering technology; technology management; web page, digital/multimedia and information resources design

Enrollment: 512 students
Institution Contact: Mr. Fred Hansen, Director *Phone:* 303-288-4488
Admission Contact: Ms. Niki Donahue, Director of Recruitment *Phone:* 303-288-4488
See full description on page 366.

Jones International University

9697 East Mineral Avenue
Englewood, CO 80112
Web: http://www.jonesinternational.edu
Accreditation: North Central Association of Colleges and Schools
Programs Offered: business administration and management; business/corporate communications; business, management, and marketing related; communications technology; education; global management
Institution Contact: *Phone:* 303-784-8904 *Fax:* 303-784-8547 *E-mail:* info@jonesinternational.edu

National American University

5125 North Academy Boulevard
Colorado Springs, CO 80918
Web: http://www.national.edu
Accreditation: North Central Association of Colleges and Schools
Programs Offered: accounting; allied health and medical assisting services related; business, management, and marketing related; computer/information technology administration and management; computer programming (specific applications); computer systems networking and telecommunications; hospital and health care facilities administration; information technology
Enrollment: 250 students
Institution Contact: Ms. Jeanne M. Liepe, Campus Director *Phone:* 719-277-0588 *Fax:* 719-277-0589 *E-mail:* jliepe@national.edu
Admission Contact: Mrs. Markita McKamie, Director of Admissions *Phone:* 719-277-0588 *Fax:* 719-277-0589 *E-mail:* mmckamie@national.edu

National American University

1325 South Colorado Boulevard
Denver, CO 80222
Web: http://www.national.edu
Accreditation: North Central Association of Colleges and Schools

Ⓐ indicates that the school is a participating institution in the *Imagine America* Scholarship Program.

Programs Offered: accounting; business administration and management; computer/information technology administration and management; computer programming; computer systems networking and telecommunications; general studies; health/health care administration; information science/studies; information technology; management information systems; medical administrative assistant and medical secretary; medical/clinical assistant

Enrollment: 200 students

Institution Contact: Mr. Nathan M. Larson, Colorado Regional President *Phone:* 303-758-6700 *Fax:* 303-758-6810 *E-mail:* nlarson@national.edu

Admission Contact: Mr. Casey Crist, Director of Admissions *Phone:* 303-758-6700 *Fax:* 303-758-6810 *E-mail:* ccrist@national.edu

Parks College ⓐ

14280 East Jewell Avenue, Suite 100
Aurora, CO 80012
Web: http://www.parks-college.com

Accreditation: Accrediting Council for Independent Colleges and Schools

Programs Offered: accounting; assistive/augmentative technology and rehabilitation engineering; business administration and management; computer and information sciences related; criminal justice/law enforcement administration; legal assistant/paralegal; medical/clinical assistant; medical insurance coding; system administration; system, networking, and LAN/WAN management; web/multimedia management and webmaster

Enrollment: 686 students

Institution Contact: Mr. Rick Harding, Director of Admissions *Phone:* 303-745-6244 *Fax:* 303-745-6245 *E-mail:* rharding@cci.edu

See full description on page 367.

Parks College ⓐ

9065 Grant Street
Denver, CO 80229
Web: http://www.cci.edu/

Accreditation: Accrediting Council for Independent Colleges and Schools

Programs Offered: accounting; business administration and management; computer and information sciences related; computer/information technology services administration related; computer technology/computer systems technology; criminal justice/law enforcement administration; legal assistant/paralegal;

medical administrative assistant and medical secretary; medical/clinical assistant; medical insurance coding

Enrollment: 927 students

Institution Contact: Mr. Allan Short, President *Phone:* 303-457-2757 *Fax:* 303-457-4030 *E-mail:* ashort@cci.edu

Admission Contact: Mr. James Henig, Director of Admissions *Phone:* 303-457-2757 *Fax:* 303-457-4030 *E-mail:* jhenig@cci.edu

See full description on page 368.

Pima Medical Institute

370 Printers Parkway
Colorado Springs, CO 80910
Web: http://www.pmi.edu

Accreditation: Accrediting Bureau of Health Education Schools

Programs Offered: dental assisting; medical administrative assistant and medical secretary; medical/clinical assistant; pharmacy technician; veterinary/animal health technology

Enrollment: 370 students

Institution Contact: Mr. Christopher Luebke, Admissions Support Center Director *Phone:* 888-898-9048 *E-mail:* asc@pmi.edu

Admission Contact: Admissions Support Representative *Phone:* 888-898-9048 *E-mail:* asc@pmi.edu

Pima Medical Institute

1701 West 72nd Avenue, Suite 130
Denver, CO 80221
Web: http://www.pmi.edu

Accreditation: Accrediting Bureau of Health Education Schools

Programs Offered: dental assisting; medical administrative assistant and medical secretary; medical/clinical assistant; ophthalmic technology; pharmacy technician; phlebotomy; physical therapist assistant; radiologic technology/science; respiratory care therapy; veterinary/animal health technology

Enrollment: 724 students

Institution Contact: Mr. Christopher Luebke, Admissions Support Center Director *Phone:* 888-898-9048 *E-mail:* asc@pmi.edu

Admission Contact: Admissions Support Representative *Phone:* 888-898-9048 *E-mail:* asc@pmi.edu

ⓐ indicates that the school is a participating institution in the *Imagine America* Scholarship Program.

Remington College—Colorado Springs Campus (A)

6050 Erin Park Drive
Colorado Springs, CO 80918-3401
Web: http://www.remingtoncollege.edu

Accreditation: Accrediting Council for Independent Colleges and Schools

Programs Offered: computer systems networking and telecommunications; criminal justice/law enforcement administration; medical/clinical assistant; pharmacy technician

Enrollment: 272 students

Institution Contact: Mr. Shibu Thomas, Campus President *Phone:* 719-532-1234 ext. 202 *Fax:* 719-264-1234 *E-mail:* shibu.thomas@remingtoncollege.edu

See full description on page 369.

Remington College—Denver Campus (A)

11011 West 6th Avenue
Lakewood, CO 80215-5501
Web: http://www.remingtoncollege.edu

Accreditation: Accrediting Council for Independent Colleges and Schools

Programs Offered: computer systems networking and telecommunications; criminal justice/law enforcement administration; medical/clinical assistant; operations management; pharmacy technician

Enrollment: 239 students

Institution Contact: Dr. Bill Cathey, Director of Education *Phone:* 303-445-0500 *Fax:* 303-445-0090 *E-mail:* bill.cathey@remingtoncollege.edu

Admission Contact: Mr. Rob Dillman, Director of Recruitment *Phone:* 303-445-0500 *Fax:* 303-445-6839 *E-mail:* robert.dillman@remingtoncollege.edu

See full description on page 370.

Remington College—Online Campus

55 Madison Street, Suite 700
Denver, CO 80206
Web: http://www.remingtoncollege.edu

Accreditation: Accrediting Commission of Career Schools and Colleges of Technology; Accrediting Council for Independent Colleges and Schools

Programs Offered: criminal justice/law enforcement administration; operations management

Institution Contact: Dr. Linda Coyle, Director of Internet Learning *Phone:* 501-376-6300 ext. 501 *Fax:* 501-374-7266 *E-mail:* linda.coyle@remingtonadmin.edu

Admission Contact: Ms. Cynthia Sabin, Internet Learning Representative *Phone:* 303-780-7777 *Fax:* 303-780-0099 *E-mail:* cynthia.sabin@remingtoncollegeonline.edu

Sage Technical Services

647 4th Avenue
Grand Junction, CO 81501
Web: http://www.sageschools.com

Programs Offered: driver and safety teacher education; transportation technology; truck and bus driver/commercial vehicle operation

Enrollment: 134 students

Institution Contact: Mr. Jerry Dudley, Director *Phone:* 800-523-0492 *Fax:* 970-257-1593 *E-mail:* gj@sageschools.com

Admission Contact: Mrs. Lisa Gordon, Staff Assistant *Phone:* 970-257-7243 *Fax:* 970-257-1593

Sage Technical Services

9690 Dallas Street, Suite L
Henderson, CO 80640
Web: http://www.sageschools.com

Accreditation: Accrediting Commission of Career Schools and Colleges of Technology

Programs Offered: truck and bus driver/commercial vehicle operation

Enrollment: 24 students

Institution Contact: Mr. Robert Lyons, Director *Phone:* 800-867-9856 *Fax:* 303-289-1933 *E-mail:* rlyons@wcox.com

Westwood College—Denver (A)

10851 West 120th Avenue
Broomfield, CO 80021-3465
Web: http://www.westwood.edu

Accreditation: Accrediting Commission of Career Schools and Colleges of Technology

Programs Offered: aircraft powerplant technology; airframe mechanics and aircraft maintenance technology; aviation/airway management; avionics maintenance technology

Enrollment: 412 students

Institution Contact: Mr. Kevin Paveglio, Executive Director *Phone:* 303-464-2300 *Fax:* 303-466-2052 *E-mail:* kpaveglio@westwood.edu

Admission Contact: Ms. Vicki Middeker, New Student Advisor *Phone:* 303-464-2308 *Fax:* 303-469-3797 *E-mail:* vmiddeker@westwood.edu

See full description on page 371.

(A) indicates that the school is a participating institution in the *Imagine America* Scholarship Program.

Westwood College—Denver North

7350 North Broadway
Denver, CO 80221-3653
Web: http://www.westwood.edu

Accreditation: Accrediting Commission of Career Schools and Colleges of Technology

Programs Offered: accounting; animation, interactive technology, video graphics and special effects; architectural drafting and CAD/CADD; automobile/ automotive mechanics technology; aviation/airway management; business administration and management; business, management, and marketing related; CAD/CADD drafting/design technology; commercial and advertising art; computer engineering technology; computer programming; computer software technology; e-commerce; heating, air conditioning and refrigeration technology; hotel/motel administration; information technology; interior design; marketing/ marketing management; medical administrative assistant and medical secretary; medical/clinical assistant; medical transcription; survey technology; system, networking, and LAN/WAN management; technology management; web page, digital/multimedia and information resources design

Enrollment: 1,304 students

Institution Contact: Mr. Anthony Caggiano, Executive Director *Phone:* 303-426-7000 ext. 200 *Fax:* 303-426-4647 *E-mail:* tcaggiano@westwood.edu

Admission Contact: Mr. Ben Simms, Director of Admissions *Phone:* 303-426-7000 ext. 100 *Fax:* 303-426-1832 *E-mail:* bsimms@westwood.edu

See full description on page 372.

Westwood College—Denver South

3150 South Sheridan Boulevard
Denver, CO 80227
Web: http://www.westwood.edu

Accreditation: Accrediting Commission of Career Schools and Colleges of Technology

Programs Offered: accounting; animation, interactive technology, video graphics and special effects; architectural drafting and CAD/CADD; business administration and management; commercial and advertising art; computer and information systems security; computer engineering technology; computer programming; computer software engineering; criminal justice/law enforcement administration; e-commerce; finance; information technology; interior design; marketing/marketing management; system, networking, and LAN/WAN management; technology management; web page, digital/multimedia and information resources design

Enrollment: 386 students

Institution Contact: Mr. Wayne Fletcher, Executive Director *Phone:* 303-934-1122 ext. 200 *Fax:* 303-934-2583 *E-mail:* wfletcher@westwood.edu

Admission Contact: Mr. Ron Dejong, Director of Admissions *Phone:* 303-934-1122 ext. 100 *Fax:* 303-934-2583 *E-mail:* rdejong@westwood.edu

See full description on page 374.

Westwood Online

7350 North Broadway
Denver, CO 80221
Web: http://www.westwoodonline.edu

Accreditation: Accrediting Commission of Career Schools and Colleges of Technology

Programs Offered: animation, interactive technology, video graphics and special effects; business administration and management; business/commerce; commercial and advertising art; computer engineering technology; computer graphics; computer/information technology administration and management; computer software engineering; computer systems networking and telecommunications; e-commerce; graphic communications; interior design; web page, digital/multimedia and information resources design

Enrollment: 2,000 students

Institution Contact: Shaun McAlmont, President *Phone:* 303-410-7990 *Fax:* 720-542-5721 *E-mail:* smcalmont@westwood.edu

Admission Contact: David Eby, Senior Director of Admissions *Phone:* 303-410-7901 *Fax:* 303-410-7996 *E-mail:* deby@westwood.edu

See full description on page 373.

Connecticut

Gibbs College

10 Norden Place
Norwalk, CT 06855
Web: http://www.gibbscollege.com/

Accreditation: Accrediting Council for Independent Colleges and Schools

Programs Offered: administrative assistant and secretarial science; computer graphics; computer/ information technology services administration related; computer programming; computer/technical support; digital communication and media/multime-

Gibbs College (*continued*)

dia; e-commerce; fashion/apparel design; fashion merchandising; visual and performing arts

Enrollment: 1,125 students

Institution Contact: Ms. Lorren West, President *Phone:* 203-663-2314 *Fax:* 203-854-2936 *E-mail:* lwest@gibbsnorwalk.com

Admission Contact: Mr. Ted Havelka, Vice President of Marketing and Admissions *Phone:* 203-663-2311 *Fax:* 203-854-2936 *E-mail:* thavelka@gibbsnorwalk.com

Porter and Chester Institute

138 Weymouth Road
Enfield, CT 06082
Web: http://www.porterchester.com

Accreditation: Accrediting Bureau of Health Education Schools; Accrediting Commission of Career Schools and Colleges of Technology

Programs Offered: automobile/automotive mechanics technology; CAD/CADD drafting/design technology; computer systems networking and telecommunications; computer technology/computer systems technology; dental assisting; electrical and electronic engineering technologies related; heating, air conditioning, ventilation and refrigeration maintenance technology; medical/clinical assistant

Institution Contact: *Phone:* 860-741-2561

Porter and Chester Institute

670 Lordship Boulevard
Stratford, CT 06497
Web: http://www.porterchester.com

Accreditation: Accrediting Bureau of Health Education Schools; Accrediting Commission of Career Schools and Colleges of Technology

Programs Offered: automobile/automotive mechanics technology; CAD/CADD drafting/design technology; computer systems networking and telecommunications; computer technology/computer systems technology; dental assisting; electrical and electronic engineering technologies related; heating, air conditioning, ventilation and refrigeration maintenance technology; medical/clinical assistant

Institution Contact: *Phone:* 203-375-4463

Porter and Chester Institute

320 Sylvan Lake Road
Watertown, CT 06779-1400
Web: http://www.porterchester.com

Accreditation: Accrediting Bureau of Health Education Schools; Accrediting Commission of Career Schools and Colleges of Technology

Programs Offered: automobile/automotive mechanics technology; CAD/CADD drafting/design technology; computer systems networking and telecommunications; computer technology/computer systems technology; dental assisting; electrical and electronic engineering technologies related; heating, air conditioning, ventilation and refrigeration maintenance technology; medical/clinical assistant

Institution Contact: *Phone:* 860-274-9294

Porter and Chester Institute

125 Silas Deane Highway
Wethersfield, CT 06109
Web: http://www.porterchester.com

Accreditation: Accrediting Bureau of Health Education Schools; Accrediting Commission of Career Schools and Colleges of Technology

Programs Offered: automobile/automotive mechanics technology; CAD/CADD drafting/design technology; computer systems networking and telecommunications; computer technology/computer systems technology; dental assisting; electrical and electronic engineering technologies related; heating, air conditioning, ventilation and refrigeration maintenance technology; medical/clinical assistant

Institution Contact: *Phone:* 860-529-2519

delaware

Dawn Training Centre, Inc.

3700 Lancaster Pike, Suite 105
Wilmington, DE 19805

Accreditation: Accrediting Commission of Career Schools and Colleges of Technology

Programs Offered: aesthetician/esthetician and skin care; home health aide/home attendant; legal assistant/paralegal; massage therapy; medical/clinical assistant; medical insurance coding; medical insurance/medical billing; medical office computer specialist; medical transcription; nursing assistant/aide and patient care assistant; pharmacy technician

Enrollment: 182 students

Institution Contact: Mr. Hollis C. Anglin, President/Director *Phone:* 302-633-9075 *Fax:* 302-633-9077 *E-mail:* hcanglin@earthlink.net

Admission Contact: Ms. Mary Anglin, Director of Admissions/Student Services *Phone:* 302-633-9075 ext. 10 *Fax:* 302-633-9077 *E-mail:* admissions@dawntrainingcentre.com

⊛ indicates that the school is a participating institution in the *Imagine America* Scholarship Program.

Harrison Career Institute

631 West Newport Pike, Graystone Plaza
Wilmington, DE 19804
Web: http://www.hci.edu

Accreditation: Accrediting Commission of Career Schools and Colleges of Technology

Programs Offered: cardiovascular technology; dialysis technology; medical/clinical assistant; medical office assistant; pharmacy technician

Enrollment: 200 students

Institution Contact: Mr. Rodney D. Bailey, Director *Phone:* 302-999-7827 *Fax:* 302-999-7983 *E-mail:* rbailey@hci-inst.net

Admission Contact: Ms. Holly Bott, Career Representative *Phone:* 302-999-7827 *Fax:* 302-999-7983 *E-mail:* hollyhci@yahoo.com

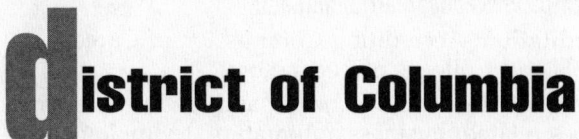

district of Columbia

Potomac College

4000 Chesapeake Street, NW
Washington, DC 20016
Web: http://www.potomac.edu/

Accreditation: Accrediting Council for Independent Colleges and Schools; Middle States Association of Colleges and Schools

Programs Offered: business administration and management; e-commerce; information science/studies; information technology

Enrollment: 165 students

Institution Contact: Ms. Florence Tate, President *Phone:* 202-686-0876 *Fax:* 202-686-0818 *E-mail:* ftate@potomac.edu

Admission Contact: Mr. Marcus Palmore, Assistant Director of Admissions *Phone:* 202-686-0876 *Fax:* 202-686-0818 *E-mail:* mpalmore@potomac.edu

Strayer University

1133 15th Street NW, Suite 200
Washington, DC 20005
Web: http://www.strayer.edu

Accreditation: Middle States Association of Colleges and Schools

Programs Offered: accounting; business administration and management; communications technology; computer/information technology administration and management; computer programming; computer systems networking and telecommunications; data modeling/warehousing and database administration; economics; general studies; information science/studies; information technology; international business/trade/commerce; marketing/marketing management; purchasing, procurement/acquisitions and contracts management

Institution Contact: Dr. J. Chris Toe, University President *Phone:* 202-419-0400 *Fax:* 202-419-1425 *E-mail:* jct@strayer.edu

Admission Contact: Mr. Melvin Menns, Campus Manager *Phone:* 202-408-2400 *Fax:* 202-419-1425 *E-mail:* washington@strayer.edu

Strayer University at Takoma Park

6830 Laurel Street, Northwest
Washington, DC 20012
Web: http://www.strayer.edu

Accreditation: Middle States Association of Colleges and Schools

Programs Offered: accounting; business administration and management; communications technology; computer/information technology administration and management; computer programming; computer systems networking and telecommunications; data modeling/warehousing and database administration; economics; general studies; information science/studies; information technology; international business/trade/commerce; marketing/marketing management; purchasing, procurement/acquisitions and contracts management

Institution Contact: Dr. J. Chris Toe, University President *Phone:* 202-408-2424 *Fax:* 202-789-0387 *E-mail:* jct@strayer.edu

Admission Contact: Campus Manager *Phone:* 202-722-8100 *Fax:* 202-722-8108 *E-mail:* takomapark@strayer.edu

florida

Advanced Career Training

3563 Phillips Highway, Suite 300
Jacksonville, FL 32207
Web: http://www.actglobal.com

Accreditation: Accrediting Commission of Career Schools and Colleges of Technology; Accrediting

Ⓐ indicates that the school is a participating institution in the *Imagine America* Scholarship Program.

Advanced Career Training (*continued*)

Council for Continuing Education and Training; Accrediting Council for Independent Colleges and Schools

Programs Offered: business administration and management; computer technology/computer systems technology; dental assisting; medical/clinical assistant

Enrollment: 328 students

Institution Contact: Mr. Scott Nelowet, Executive Director *Phone:* 904-737-6911 *Fax:* 904-448-0280 *E-mail:* nelowets@actglobal.com

Admission Contact: Mr. Montrez Lucas, Director of Admissions *Phone:* 904-737-6911 *Fax:* 904-448-0280 *E-mail:* lucasm@actglobal.com

American InterContinental University

2250 North Commerce Parkway, Fourth Floor
Weston, FL 33326
Web: http://www.aiufl.edu

Accreditation: Southern Association of Colleges and Schools

Programs Offered: business administration and management; commercial and advertising art; educational/instructional media design; fashion/apparel design; information technology; interior design; international business/trade/commerce

Institution Contact: Mr. Tod Gibbs, President *Phone:* 954-446-6100 *E-mail:* tgibbs@aiufl.edu

AMI, Inc. (A)

3042 West International Speedway Boulevard
Daytona Beach, FL 32124
Web: http://www.amiwrench.com

Accreditation: Accrediting Council for Continuing Education and Training

Programs Offered: marine maintenance and ship repair technology; marine technology; motorcycle maintenance and repair technology

Enrollment: 250 students

Institution Contact: Carey Brown, Director of Admissions *Phone:* 800-881-2264 *Fax:* 386-252-3523 *E-mail:* carey@amiwrench.com

See full description on page 375.

The Art Institute of Fort Lauderdale (A)

1799 Southeast 17th Street
Fort Lauderdale, FL 33316-3000
Web: http://www.aifl.edu

Accreditation: Accrediting Council for Independent Colleges and Schools

Programs Offered: advertising; animation, interactive technology, video graphics and special effects; broadcast journalism; culinary arts; fashion/apparel design; graphic communications related; industrial design; interior design; marine technology; photography; visual and performing arts; web/multimedia management and webmaster; web page, digital/multimedia and information resources design

Institution Contact: Director of Admissions *Phone:* 954-527-1799 *Fax:* 954-728-8637

See full description on page 376.

ATI Career Training Center (A)

2880 Northwest 62nd Street
Fort Lauderdale, FL 33309-9731
Web: http://www.aticareertraining.edu

Accreditation: Accrediting Commission of Career Schools and Colleges of Technology

Programs Offered: allied health and medical assisting services related; business automation/technology/data entry; CAD/CADD drafting/design technology; civil drafting and CAD/CADD; communications systems installation and repair technology; communications technology; computer and information sciences; computer and information sciences and support services related; computer and information sciences related; computer engineering related; computer engineering technology; computer hardware engineering; computer hardware technology; computer/information technology administration and management; computer/information technology services administration related; computer installation and repair technology; computer programming; computer programming related; computer programming (specific applications); computer software technology; computer systems analysis; computer systems networking and telecommunications; computer/technical support; computer technology/computer systems technology; drafting and design technology; electrical and electronic engineering technologies related; electrical, electronic and communications engineering technology; electrical/electronics drafting and CAD/CADD; electrical/electronics equipment installation and repair; engineering technology; health/health care administration; health information/medical records administration; health information/medical records technology; hospital and health care facilities administration; information technology; medical administrative assistant and medical secretary; medical/clinical assistant; medical/health management and clinical assistant; medical insurance coding; medical insurance/medical billing; medical office assistant; medical office computer specialist; medical office management; medical

(A) indicates that the school is a participating institution in the *Imagine America* Scholarship Program.

reception; medical transcription; office management; telecommunications technology; word processing

Enrollment: 350 students

Institution Contact: Ms. Connie Bailus, Executive Director *Phone:* 954-973-4760 *Fax:* 954-973-6422 *E-mail:* cbailus@atienterprises.edu

See full description on page 378.

ATI Career Training Center Ⓐ

1 Northeast 19th Street
Miami, FL 33132
Web: http://www.aticareertraining.com

Accreditation: Accrediting Commission of Career Schools and Colleges of Technology

Programs Offered: appliance installation and repair technology; automobile/automotive mechanics technology; CAD/CADD drafting/design technology; computer/information technology administration and management; electrical and electronic engineering technologies related; heating, air conditioning and refrigeration technology; information technology

Institution Contact: Errol Stephenson, School Director *Phone:* 305-573-1600 *Fax:* 305-576-8365 *E-mail:* estephenson@atienterprises.edu

See full description on page 379.

ATI Career Training Center Ⓐ

3501 Northwest 9th Avenue
Oakland Park, FL 33309-5900
Web: http://www.aticareertraining.com

Accreditation: Accrediting Commission of Career Schools and Colleges of Technology

Programs Offered: automobile/automotive mechanics technology; heating, air conditioning and refrigeration technology

Enrollment: 300 students

Institution Contact: Ms. Cindy Gordon, Director *Phone:* 954-563-5899 *Fax:* 954-568-0874 *E-mail:* cgordon@atienterprises.com

Admission Contact: Mr. Donald Robinson, Assistant Director of Admissions *Phone:* 954-563-5899 *Fax:* 954-568-0874 *E-mail:* cgordon@atienterprises.com

See full description on page 380.

ATI Health Education Center Ⓐ

Plaza Executive Center, 1395 Northwest 167th Street, Building #1
Miami, FL 33169-5745
Web: http://www.aticareertraining.com

Accreditation: Accrediting Commission of Career Schools and Colleges of Technology

Programs Offered: dental assisting; diagnostic medical sonography and ultrasound technology; medical/clinical assistant; pharmacy technician; respiratory care therapy

Enrollment: 330 students

Institution Contact: Ms. Barbara Woosley, Executive Director *Phone:* 305-628-1000 *Fax:* 305-628-1461 *E-mail:* bwoosley@atienterprises.edu

Admission Contact: Ms. Mercedes Segal, Director of Admissions *Phone:* 305-628-1000 *Fax:* 305-628-1461 *E-mail:* msegal@atienterprises.edu

See full description on page 377.

Barbara Brennan School of Healing

500 Northeast Spanish River Boulevard, Suite 108
Boca Raton, FL 33431-4559
Web: http://www.barbarabrennan.com

Programs Offered: alternative and complementary medical support services related; energy and biologically based therapies related

Enrollment: 500 students

Institution Contact: Ms. Bonnie J. Brandt, Director of Academic Affairs *Phone:* 561-620-8767 *Fax:* 561-620-9028 *E-mail:* bonnie.brandt@barbarabrennan.com

Admission Contact: Ms. Jean Bellegarde, Admissions Representative *Phone:* 800-924-2564 *Fax:* 561-620-9028 *E-mail:* jean.bellegarde@barbarabrennan.com

Capps College

6420 North 9th Avenue
Pensacola, FL 32504
Web: http://www.medcareers.net

Programs Offered: massage therapy; medical/clinical assistant; medical office management; medical transcription; pharmacy technician

Institution Contact: *Phone:* 850-476-7607 *Fax:* 850-475-5955

Career Training Institute

2463 East Semoran Boulevard
Apopka, FL 32703-5806
Web: http://www.centralfloridacollege.edu

Accreditation: Accrediting Commission of Career Schools and Colleges of Technology

Programs Offered: barbering; cosmetology; cosmetology, barber/styling, and nail instruction; facial treatment/facialist; nail technician and manicurist

Institution Contact: Ms. Nancy Bradley, Owner/Director *Phone:* 407-884-1816 *Fax:* 407-889-8083 *E-mail:* nbradley@centralfloridacollege.edu

Ⓐ indicates that the school is a participating institution in the *Imagine America* Scholarship Program.

Career Training Institute (continued)

Admission Contact: Mr. Michael Murray, Director of Admissions *Phone:* 407-884-1816 *Fax:* 407-889-8083 *E-mail:* mmurray@centralfloridacollege.edu

Central Florida College

1573 West Fairbanks Avenue
Winter Park, FL 32789
Web: http://www.centralfloridacollege.edu

Accreditation: Accrediting Commission of Career Schools and Colleges of Technology

Programs Offered: accounting; business administration and management; criminal justice/law enforcement administration; health aide; management information systems; medical administrative assistant and medical secretary; medical/clinical assistant; medical insurance coding; pharmacy technician

Enrollment: 450 students

Institution Contact: Ms. Nancy Bradley, Owner/ Director *Phone:* 407-843-3984 *Fax:* 407-843-9828 *E-mail:* nbradley@centralfloridacollege.edu

Admission Contact: Mrs. Gladys Secada, Director of Admissions *Phone:* 407-843-3984 *Fax:* 407-843-9828 *E-mail:* gsecada@centalfloridacollege.edu

Florida Career College

1321 Southwest 107th Avenue, Suite 201B
Miami, FL 33174
Web: http://www.careercollege.edu

Accreditation: Accrediting Council for Independent Colleges and Schools

Programs Offered: computer engineering technology; computer graphics; computer installation and repair technology; computer programming; computer programming (specific applications); computer software and media applications; computer systems networking and telecommunications; computer technology/computer systems technology; massage therapy; medical/clinical assistant; medical insurance coding; pharmacy technician; web/multimedia management and webmaster; web page, digital/ multimedia and information resources design

Institution Contact: Mr. David Knobel, Chief Executive Officer *Phone:* 305-825-3231 *Fax:* 305-825-3436 *E-mail:* dknobel@careercollege.edu

Admission Contact: Ms. Niki Rodriguez, Director of Admissions *Phone:* 305-553-6065 *Fax:* 305-225-0128 *E-mail:* nrodriguez@careercollege.edu

Florida College of Natural Health ⓐ

616 67th Street Circle East
Bradenton, FL 34208
Web: http://steinered.com

Accreditation: Accrediting Commission of Career Schools and Colleges of Technology

Programs Offered: aesthetician/esthetician and skin care; facial treatment/facialist; massage therapy

Enrollment: 125 students

Institution Contact: Mr. Wayne Dawson, Campus Director *Phone:* 941-744-1244 *Fax:* 941-744-1242 *E-mail:* wayned@fcnh.com

Admission Contact: Admissions Department *Phone:* 941-744-1244 *Fax:* 941-744-1242 *E-mail:* sarasota@fcnh.com

See full description on page 381.

Florida College of Natural Health ⓐ

2600 Lake Lucien Drive, Suite 140
Maitland, FL 32751
Web: http://steinered.com

Accreditation: Accrediting Commission of Career Schools and Colleges of Technology

Programs Offered: aesthetician/esthetician and skin care; facial treatment/facialist; massage therapy

Enrollment: 325 students

Institution Contact: Mr. Steve Richards, Campus Director *Phone:* 407-261-0319 *Fax:* 407-261-0342 *E-mail:* orlando@fcnh.com

Admission Contact: Admissions Department *Phone:* 407-261-0319 *Fax:* 407-261-0342 *E-mail:* orlando@fcnh.com

See full description on page 381.

Florida College of Natural Health ⓐ

7925 NW 12th Street, Suite 201
Miami, FL 33126
Web: http://steinered.com

Accreditation: Accrediting Commission of Career Schools and Colleges of Technology

Programs Offered: aesthetician/esthetician and skin care; facial treatment/facialist; massage therapy

Enrollment: 240 students

Institution Contact: Ms. Debra J. Starr, Campus Director *Phone:* 305-597-9599 *Fax:* 305-597-9110 *E-mail:* dstarr@fcnh.com

Admission Contact: Admissions Department *Phone:* 305-597-9599 *Fax:* 305-597-9110 *E-mail:* miami@fcnh.com

See full description on page 381.

ⓐ indicates that the school is a participating institution in the *Imagine America* Scholarship Program.

Florida College of Natural Health

2001 West Sample Road, Suite 100
Pompano Beach, FL 33064
Web: http://steinered.com

Accreditation: Accrediting Commission of Career Schools and Colleges of Technology

Programs Offered: aesthetician/esthetician and skin care; facial treatment/facialist; massage therapy

Enrollment: 275 students

Institution Contact: Darren Teigue, Campus Director *Phone:* 954-975-6400 *Fax:* 954-975-9633 *E-mail:* darrent@fcnh.com

Admission Contact: Admissions Department *Phone:* 954-975-6400 *Fax:* 954-975-9633 *E-mail:* ftlauderdale@fcnh.com

See full description on page 381.

Programs Offered: accounting; business administration and management; computer/information technology services administration related; computer software and media applications; criminal justice/law enforcement administration; legal assistant/paralegal; marketing/marketing management; medical/clinical assistant; medical insurance/medical billing; pharmacy technician; surgical technology

Enrollment: 1,301 students

Institution Contact: Mr. Stephen Backman, II, President *Phone:* 813-621-0041 *Fax:* 813-623-5769 *E-mail:* sbackman@cci.edu

Admission Contact: Mr. Jarad Held, Director of Admissions *Phone:* 813-621-0041 *Fax:* 813-628-0919 *E-mail:* jheld@cci.edu

See full description on page 382.

Florida Metropolitan University—Brandon Campus

3924 Coconut Palm Drive
Tampa, FL 33619
Web: http://www.fmu.edu

Accreditation: Accrediting Council for Independent Colleges and Schools

Florida Metropolitan University—Fort Lauderdale Campus

225 North Federal Highway
Pompano Beach, FL 33062
Web: http://www.fmu.edu

Accreditation: Accrediting Council for Independent Colleges and Schools

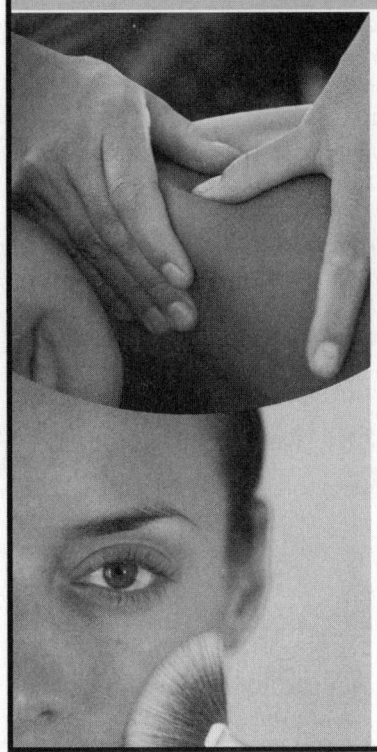

 indicates that the school is a participating institution in the *Imagine America* Scholarship Program.

Florida Metropolitan University–Fort Lauderdale Campus
(continued)

Programs Offered: accounting; business administration and management; computer and information sciences related; criminal justice/law enforcement administration; hospitality administration; information science/studies; international business/trade/commerce; legal assistant/paralegal; management science; marketing/marketing management; medical/clinical assistant

Institution Contact: Fran Heaston, Director of Admissions *Phone:* 954-783-7339 *Fax:* 954-783-7964 *E-mail:* fheaston@cci.edu

See full description on page 389.

Florida Metropolitan University–Jacksonville Campus ⓐ

8226 Phillips Highway
Jacksonville, FL 32256
Web: http://www.fmu.edu

Accreditation: Accrediting Council for Independent Colleges and Schools

Programs Offered: accounting; business administration and management; computer and information sciences related; computer/information technology administration and management; criminal justice/law enforcement administration; information science/studies; medical/clinical assistant

Enrollment: 900 students

Institution Contact: Peter Neigler, President *Phone:* 904-731-4949 *Fax:* 904-731-0599 *E-mail:* pneigler@cci.edu

Admission Contact: Admissions *Phone:* 904-731-4949 *Fax:* 904-731-0599

See full description on page 383.

Florida Metropolitan University–Lakeland Campus ⓐ

995 East Memorial Boulevard, Suite 110
Lakeland, FL 33801-1919
Web: http://www.cci.edu

Accreditation: Accrediting Council for Independent Colleges and Schools

Programs Offered: accounting; administrative assistant and secretarial science; business administration and management; business, management, and marketing related; computer and information sciences related; computer programming (vendor/product certification); computer software and media applications; criminal justice/law enforcement administra-

tion; executive assistant/executive secretary; health/health care administration; information science/studies; legal assistant/paralegal; marketing/marketing management; massage therapy; medical administrative assistant and medical secretary; medical/clinical assistant; medical insurance coding; office management; pharmacy technician

Enrollment: 760 students

Institution Contact: Ms. Diane Y. Walton, President *Phone:* 863-686-1444 *Fax:* 863-688-9881 *E-mail:* dwalton@cci.edu

Admission Contact: Ms. Jodi DeLaGarza, Director of Admissions *Phone:* 863-686-1444 ext. 101 *Fax:* 863-688-9881 *E-mail:* astenbec@cci.edu

See full description on page 384.

Florida Metropolitan University–Melbourne Campus ⓐ

2401 North Harbor City Boulevard
Melbourne, FL 32935
Web: http://www.fmu.edu

Accreditation: Accrediting Council for Independent Colleges and Schools

Programs Offered: accounting; business administration and management; cinematography and film/video production; computer and information sciences related; criminal justice/law enforcement administration; health and medical administrative services related; health/health care administration; legal assistant/paralegal; medical/clinical assistant; pharmacy technician; web page, digital/multimedia and information resources design

Enrollment: 912 students

Institution Contact: T. Michael Barlow, President *Phone:* 321-253-2929 *Fax:* 321-255-2017 *E-mail:* tbarlow@cci.edu

Admission Contact: Mr. Timothy J. Alexander, Interim Director of Admissions *Phone:* 321-253-2929 ext. 11 *Fax:* 321-255-2017 *E-mail:* talexand@cci.edu

See full description on page 385.

Florida Metropolitan University–North Orlando Campus ⓐ

5421 Diplomat Circle
Orlando, FL 32810
Web: http://www.cci.edu

Accreditation: Accrediting Council for Independent Colleges and Schools

Programs Offered: accounting; assistive/augmentative technology and rehabilitation engineering; business administration and management; cinematog-

ⓐ indicates that the school is a participating institution in the *Imagine America* Scholarship Program.

raphy and film/video production; commercial and advertising art; computer and information sciences related; criminal justice/law enforcement administration; health/health care administration; information science/studies; legal assistant/paralegal; marketing/ marketing management; medical/clinical assistant; pharmacy technician; web page, digital/multimedia and information resources design

Enrollment: 1,481 students

Institution Contact: Ms. Ouida Kirby, President *Phone:* 407-628-5870 ext. 101 *Fax:* 407-628-1344 *E-mail:* okirby@cci.edu

Admission Contact: Mr. David Ritchie, Director of Admissions *Phone:* 407-628-5870 ext. 108 *Fax:* 407-628-1344 *E-mail:* okirby@cci.edu

See full description on page 386.

Florida Metropolitan University—Orange Park Campus (A)

805 Wells Road
Orange Park, FL 32073
Accreditation: Accrediting Council for Independent Colleges and Schools
Programs Offered: business administration and management; criminal justice/law enforcement administration; medical/clinical assistant

Enrollment: 194 students

Institution Contact: Dr. Roxanne Jordan, President *Phone:* 904-264-9122 ext. 101 *Fax:* 904-264-9952

Admission Contact: Jeff Sherman, Director of Admissions *Phone:* 904-264-9122 ext. 108 *Fax:* 904-264-9952 *E-mail:* jsherman@cci.edu

See full description on page 387.

Florida Metropolitan University—Pinellas Campus (A)

2471 McMullen Booth Road
Clearwater, FL 33759
Web: http://www.fmu.edu
Accreditation: Accrediting Council for Independent Colleges and Schools
Programs Offered: accounting; business administration and management; criminal justice/law enforcement administration; health/health care administration; information science/studies; information technology; legal assistant/paralegal; marketing/ marketing management; medical/clinical assistant; medical insurance coding; medical insurance/medical billing

Admission Contact: Ms. Yvonne Hunter, Director of Admissions *Phone:* 727-725-2688 *Fax:* 727-796-3722 *E-mail:* yhunter@cci.edu

See full description on page 388.

Florida Metropolitan University—South Orlando Campus (A)

9200 South Park Center Loop
Orlando, FL 32819
Web: http://www.fmu.edu
Accreditation: Accrediting Council for Independent Colleges and Schools
Programs Offered: accounting; business administration and management; computer and information sciences related; computer engineering related; computer systems networking and telecommunications; criminal justice/law enforcement administration; health/health care administration; legal assistant/paralegal; management science; marketing/ marketing management; medical/clinical assistant; medical insurance coding; medical insurance/medical billing

Institution Contact: Mrs. Annette Cloin, Director of Admissions *Phone:* 407-851-2525 *Fax:* 407-354-7946 *E-mail:* acloin@cci.edu

See full description on page 390.

Florida Metropolitan University—Tampa Campus (A)

3319 West Hillsborough Avenue
Tampa, FL 33614
Web: http://www.fmu.edu
Accreditation: Accrediting Council for Independent Colleges and Schools
Programs Offered: accounting; art; business administration and management; computer systems networking and telecommunications; criminal justice/law enforcement administration; hospital and health care facilities administration; information science/studies; legal assistant/paralegal; marketing/marketing management; massage therapy; medical/clinical assistant; medical insurance coding; medical insurance/medical billing; pharmacy technician

Institution Contact: Mr. Donnie Broughton, Director of Admissions *Phone:* 813-879-6000 *Fax:* 813-871-2063 *E-mail:* dbrought@cci.edu

See full description on page 391.

(A) indicates that the school is a participating institution in the *Imagine America* Scholarship Program.

Florida Technical College (A)

298 Havendale Boulevard
Auburndale, FL 33823
Web: http://www.flatech.edu

Accreditation: Accrediting Council for Independent Colleges and Schools

Programs Offered: business automation/technology/ data entry; CAD/CADD drafting/design technology; computer engineering technology; computer programming (vendor/product certification); electrical, electronic and communications engineering technology; health information/medical records technology; medical administrative assistant and medical secretary; medical/clinical assistant; system administration; system, networking, and LAN/WAN management

Enrollment: 165 students

Institution Contact: Chris Georgeti, School Director
Phone: 863-967-8822 *Fax:* 863-967-4972

Admission Contact: Gregory Pelz, Director of Admissions *Phone:* 863-967-8822 *Fax:* 863-967-4972 *E-mail:* gpelz@flatech.edu

See full description on page 392.

Florida Technical College (A)

1199 South Woodland Boulevard
DeLand, FL 32720
Web: http://www.flatech.edu

Accreditation: Accrediting Council for Independent Colleges and Schools

Programs Offered: allied health and medical assisting services related; architectural drafting and CAD/ CADD; business administration and management; business administration, management and operations related; business, management, and marketing related; business operations support and secretarial services related; CAD/CADD drafting/design technology; civil drafting and CAD/CADD; computer and information sciences; computer and information sciences and support services related; computer and information sciences related; computer engineering technology; computer graphics; computer hardware technology; computer/information technology administration and management; computer/information technology services administration related; computer installation and repair technology; computer programming; computer programming related; computer programming (specific applications); computer programming (vendor/product certification); computer software and media applications; computer software and media applications related; computer/technical support; computer technology/ computer systems technology; design and visual communications; desktop publishing and digital imaging design; drafting and design technology; drafting/design engineering technologies related; electrical and electronic engineering technologies related; electrical/electronics drafting and CAD/ CADD; health and medical administrative services related; health services/allied health/health sciences; health unit coordinator/ward clerk; hematology technology; information technology; intermedia/ multimedia; management information systems; management information systems and services related; mechanical drafting and CAD/CADD; medical administrative assistant and medical secretary; medical/clinical assistant; medical insurance coding; medical insurance/medical billing; medical office assistant; medical office computer specialist; medical office management; medical reception; medical transcription; office management; system administration; system, networking, and LAN/WAN management; web/multimedia management and webmaster; web page, digital/multimedia and information resources design

Enrollment: 304 students

Institution Contact: Mr. Bill Atkinson, Director *Phone:* 386-734-3303 *Fax:* 386-734-5150 *E-mail:* batkinson@flatech.edu

Admission Contact: Mrs. Teri DelVecchio, Director of Admissions *Phone:* 386-734-3303 *Fax:* 386-734-5150 *E-mail:* tdelvecchio@flatech.edu

See full description on page 393.

Florida Technical College (A)

8711 Lone Star Road
Jacksonville, FL 32211
Web: http://www.flatech.edu

Accreditation: Accrediting Council for Independent Colleges and Schools

Programs Offered: CAD/CADD drafting/design technology; computer programming; computer technology/computer systems technology; electrical, electronic and communications engineering technology; medical/clinical assistant; system administration; system, networking, and LAN/WAN management

Institution Contact: Mr. Barry Durden, Director
Phone: 904-724-2229 *Fax:* 904-720-0920 *E-mail:* bdurden@flatech.edu

See full description on page 394.

Florida Technical College (A)

12689 Challenger Parkway
Orlando, FL 32826
Web: http://www.flatech.edu

Accreditation: Accrediting Council for Independent Colleges and Schools

(A) indicates that the school is a participating institution in the *Imagine America* Scholarship Program.

Programs Offered: CAD/CADD drafting/design technology; computer engineering technology; computer programming (vendor/product certification); health information/medical records technology; medical administrative assistant and medical secretary; medical/clinical assistant; medical insurance coding; medical office computer specialist; medical reception; system administration; system, networking, and LAN/WAN management; web page, digital/multimedia and information resources design
Institution Contact: Ann Melone, Director *Phone:* 407-447-7300 *Fax:* 407-447-7301 *E-mail:* amelone@flatech.edu
See full description on page 395.

Full Sail Real World Education

3300 University Boulevard
Winter Park, FL 32792-7429
Web: http://www.fullsail.com
Accreditation: Accrediting Commission of Career Schools and Colleges of Technology
Programs Offered: animation, interactive technology, video graphics and special effects; cinematography and film/video production; digital communication and media/multimedia; recording arts technology; web page, digital/multimedia and information resources design
Enrollment: 4,325 students
Institution Contact: Mr. Edward Haddock, Jr., Co-Chairman and Chief Executive Officer *Phone:* 407-679-0100 *Fax:* 407-679-8810 *E-mail:* ehaddock@fullsail.com
Admission Contact: Mary Beth Plank, Vice President of Admissions *Phone:* 407-679-0100 *Fax:* 407-679-8810 *E-mail:* mbplank@fullsail.com

Galiano Career Academy

1140E Altamonte Drive, #1020
Altamonte Springs, FL 32701
Web: http://www.galianocareeracademy.com
Accreditation: Accrediting Council for Independent Colleges and Schools
Programs Offered: administrative assistant and secretarial science; airline flight attendant; anatomy; business administration and management; business automation/technology/data entry; business/corporate communications; clinical/medical laboratory assistant; computer/information technology administration and management; computer/information technology services administration related; customer service management; data entry/microcomputer applications; data entry/microcomputer

applications related; executive assistant/executive secretary; gene therapy; health information/medical records administration; health information/medical records technology; hospitality administration; hotel/motel administration; human resources management; human services; medical administrative assistant and medical secretary; medical/clinical assistant; medical/health management and clinical assistant; medical insurance coding; medical insurance/medical billing; medical office computer specialist; medical reception; medical transcription; nursing assistant/aide and patient care assistant; office occupations and clerical services; receptionist; tourism and travel services management; word processing
Institution Contact: Dr. Michael Gagliano, School Administrator *Phone:* 407-331-7443 ext. 201 *Fax:* 407-834-6189 *E-mail:* mgagliano@galianocareeracademy.com
Admission Contact: Ms. Josie Teresi, Lead Career Counselor *Phone:* 407-331-7443 ext. 209 *Fax:* 407-834-6189 *E-mail:* jteresi@galianocareeracademy.com

Herzing College Ⓐ

1595 South Semoran Boulevard, Suite 1501
Winter Park, FL 32792
Web: http://www.herzing.edu
Accreditation: Accrediting Council for Independent Colleges and Schools; North Central Association of Colleges and Schools
Programs Offered: business administration and management; computer and information systems security; computer/information technology administration and management; massage therapy; medical/clinical assistant; medical insurance coding; medical office management
Institution Contact: Mr. Randy G. Atwater, President *Phone:* 407-478-0500 *Fax:* 407-478-0501 *E-mail:* randya@orl.herzing.edu
Admission Contact: Ms. Karen Mohamad, Vice President/Director of Admissions *Phone:* 407-478-0500 *Fax:* 407-478-0501 *E-mail:* info@orl.herzing.edu
See full description on page 396.

High-Tech Institute

3710 Maguire Boulevard
Orlando, FL 32803
Web: http://www.hightechinstitute.edu
Accreditation: Accrediting Commission of Career Schools and Colleges of Technology
Programs Offered: computer and information systems security; dental assisting; massage therapy; medical/

Ⓐ indicates that the school is a participating institution in the *Imagine America* Scholarship Program.

High-Tech Institute *(continued)*

clinical assistant; medical insurance/medical billing; medical radiologic technology; pharmacy technician; surgical technology

Institution Contact: Elizabeth Beseke, Campus President *Phone:* 407-893-7400 *Fax:* 407-895-1804 *E-mail:* ebeseke@hightechinstitute.edu

Admission Contact: Sheryl Ferguson, Director of Admissions *Phone:* 407-893-7400 *Fax:* 407-895-1804 *E-mail:* sferguson@hightechinstitute.edu

International Academy of Design & Technology ⓐ

5959 Lake Ellenor Drive
Orlando, FL 32809
Web: http://www.iadt.edu

Accreditation: Accrediting Council for Independent Colleges and Schools

Programs Offered: commercial and advertising art; computer graphics; design and visual communications; fashion/apparel design; fashion merchandising; interior design; intermedia/multimedia; web page, digital/multimedia and information resources design

Enrollment: 809 students

Institution Contact: Mr. Mark A. Page, President *Phone:* 407-857-2300 ext. 5920 *Fax:* 407-888-5941 *E-mail:* mpage@iadt.edu

Admission Contact: Dr. John Dietrich, Vice President of Admissions and Marketing *Phone:* 877-753-0007 ext. 5934 *Fax:* 407-251-0465 *E-mail:* jdietrich@idat.edu

See full description on page 397.

International Academy of Design & Technology

5225 Memorial Highway
Tampa, FL 33634
Web: http://www.academy.edu

Accreditation: Accrediting Council for Independent Colleges and Schools

Programs Offered: commercial and advertising art; computer graphics; fashion/apparel design; interior design; system, networking, and LAN/WAN management; web page, digital/multimedia and information resources design

Institution Contact: Mr. Steve R. Wood, Director of Financial Aid *Phone:* 813-880-8056 *Fax:* 813-885-4695 *E-mail:* steve@academy.edu

Admission Contact: Mr. Brandon Barnhill, Vice President of Admissions and Marketing *Phone:* 813-880-8029 *Fax:* 813-889-3442 *E-mail:* brandonb@academy.edu

ITT Technical Institute

3401 South University Drive
Fort Lauderdale, FL 33328-2021
Web: http://www.itt-tech.edu

Accreditation: Accrediting Council for Independent Colleges and Schools

Programs Offered: accounting and business/management; animation, interactive technology, video graphics and special effects; business administration and management; CAD/CADD drafting/design technology; communications technology; computer and information systems security; computer engineering technology; computer software and media applications; computer software engineering; computer systems networking and telecommunications; criminal justice/police science; digital communication and media/multimedia; electrical, electronic and communications engineering technology; technology management; web page, digital/multimedia and information resources design

Enrollment: 160 students

Institution Contact: Ms. Nanell Lough, Director *Phone:* 954-476-9300

Admission Contact: Mr. Robert Bixler, Director of Recruitment *Phone:* 954-476-9300

ITT Technical Institute

6600 Youngerman Circle, Suite 10
Jacksonville, FL 32244-6630
Web: http://www.itt-tech.edu

Accreditation: Accrediting Council for Independent Colleges and Schools

Programs Offered: accounting and business/management; animation, interactive technology, video graphics and special effects; business administration and management; CAD/CADD drafting/design technology; communications technology; computer and information systems security; computer engineering technology; computer software and media applications; computer software engineering; computer systems networking and telecommunications; criminal justice/police science; digital communication and media/multimedia; electrical, electronic and communications engineering technology; technology management; web page, digital/multimedia and information resources design

Enrollment: 660 students

ⓐ indicates that the school is a participating institution in the *Imagine America* Scholarship Program.

Institution Contact: Mr. Brian Quirk, Director *Phone:* 904-573-9100

Admission Contact: Mr. Jorge Torres, Director of Recruitment *Phone:* 904-573-9100

ITT Technical Institute Ⓐ

1400 International Parkway South
Lake Mary, FL 32746
Web: http://www.itt-tech.edu

Accreditation: Accrediting Council for Independent Colleges and Schools

Programs Offered: accounting and business/management; animation, interactive technology, video graphics and special effects; business administration and management; CAD/CADD drafting/design technology; communications technology; computer and information systems security; computer engineering technology; computer software and media applications; computer software engineering; computer systems networking and telecommunications; criminal justice/police science; digital communication and media/multimedia; electrical, electronic and communications engineering technology; technology management; web page, digital/multimedia and information resources design

Enrollment: 441 students

Institution Contact: Mr. Gary Cosgrove, Director *Phone:* 407-660-2900

Admission Contact: Mr. Larry S. Johnson, Director of Recruitment *Phone:* 407-660-2900

See full description on page 398.

ITT Technical Institute

7955 Northwest 12th Street
Miami, FL 33126
Web: http://www.itt-tech.edu

Accreditation: Accrediting Council for Independent Colleges and Schools

Programs Offered: accounting and business/management; animation, interactive technology, video graphics and special effects; business administration and management; communications technology; computer and information systems security; computer engineering technology; computer software engineering; computer systems networking and telecommunications; criminal justice/police science; digital communication and media/multimedia; electrical, electronic and communications engineering technology; technology management; web page, digital/multimedia and information resources design

Enrollment: 500 students

Institution Contact: Mr. Robert T. Hayward, Director *Phone:* 305-477-3080

Admission Contact: Mrs. Rosa Sacarello Daratany, Director of Recruitment *Phone:* 305-477-3080

ITT Technical Institute Ⓐ

4809 Memorial Highway
Tampa, FL 33634-7151
Web: http://www.itt-tech.edu

Accreditation: Accrediting Council for Independent Colleges and Schools

Programs Offered: accounting and business/management; animation, interactive technology, video graphics and special effects; business administration and management; CAD/CADD drafting/design technology; communications technology; computer and information systems security; computer engineering technology; computer software and media applications; computer software engineering; computer systems networking and telecommunications; computer technology/computer systems technology; criminal justice/police science; digital communication and media/multimedia; electrical, electronic and communications engineering technology; technology management; web page, digital/multimedia and information resources design

Enrollment: 606 students

Institution Contact: Mr. Dennis Alspaugh, Director *Phone:* 813-885-2244

Admission Contact: Mr. Joseph E. Rostkowski, Director of Recruitment *Phone:* 813-885-2244

See full description on page 399.

Keiser Career College

12520 Pines Boulevard
Pembroke Pines, FL 33027
Web: http://www.keisercareer.com

Accreditation: Accrediting Bureau of Health Education Schools; Council on Occupational Education

Programs Offered: business administration and management; computer graphics; computer/information technology administration and management; massage therapy; medical/clinical assistant; pharmacy technician

Institution Contact: Mr. Mark Levine, Executive Director *Phone:* 954-252-0002 *Fax:* 954-252-0003 *E-mail:* markl@keisercollege.cc.fl.us

Admission Contact: Director of Admissions *Phone:* 954-252-0002 *Fax:* 954-252-0003

Ⓐ indicates that the school is a participating institution in the *Imagine America* Scholarship Program.

Keiser Career College

2085 Vista Parkway
West Palm Beach, FL 33411
Web: http://www.keisercareer.com

Accreditation: Accrediting Bureau of Health Education Schools; Accrediting Commission of Career Schools and Colleges of Technology; Council on Occupational Education

Programs Offered: business administration and management; computer graphics; computer/information technology administration and management; massage therapy; medical/clinical assistant; pharmacy technician

Institution Contact: Ms. Colleen Rupp, Vice President *Phone:* 561-547-5472 *Fax:* 561-547-6609 *E-mail:* colleenr@keisercollege.edu

Admission Contact: Ms. Danielle Shrank, Director of Admissions *Phone:* 561-547-5472 *Fax:* 561-547-6609 *E-mail:* danielles@keisercollege.edu

Keiser College

1800 Business Park Boulevard
Daytona Beach, FL 32114
Web: http://www.keisercollege.edu

Accreditation: Accrediting Bureau of Health Education Schools; Southern Association of Colleges and Schools

Programs Offered: accounting; business administration and management; computer graphics; computer/information technology administration and management; criminal justice/law enforcement administration; diagnostic medical sonography and ultrasound technology; hospital and health care facilities administration; legal assistant/paralegal; medical/clinical assistant; radiologic technology/science

Institution Contact: Ms. Maxine Stine, Vice President *Phone:* 386-274-5060 *Fax:* 386-274-2745 *E-mail:* maxines@keisercollege.edu

Admission Contact: Mr. Eugene Moreno, Director of Admissions *Phone:* 386-274-5060 *Fax:* 386-274-2725 *E-mail:* eugenem@keisercollege.edu

Keiser College

1500 Northwest 49th Street
Fort Lauderdale, FL 33309-9722
Web: http://www.keisercollege.edu

Accreditation: Accrediting Bureau of Health Education Schools; Southern Association of Colleges and Schools

Programs Offered: accounting; business administration and management; clinical/medical laboratory technology; commercial and advertising art; computer engineering technology; computer graphics; computer/information technology administration and management; computer programming; criminal justice/law enforcement administration; diagnostic medical sonography and ultrasound technology; e-commerce; health/health care administration; hospitality administration; legal assistant/paralegal; medical/clinical assistant; nursing (registered nurse training); occupational therapist assistant; physical therapist assistant; radiologic technology/science

Institution Contact: Mr. Todd DeAngelis, Director of Public Relations *Phone:* 954-776-4476 ext. 314 *Fax:* 954-489-2974 *E-mail:* toddd@keisercollege.edu

Admission Contact: Ms. Linda Ebeling, Admissions Assistant *Phone:* 954-776-4456 *Fax:* 954-351-4043 *E-mail:* lindae@keisercollege.edu

Keiser College

3515 Aviation Drive
Lakeland, FL 33811
Web: http://www.keisercollege.edu

Accreditation: Southern Association of Colleges and Schools

Programs Offered: accounting; business administration and management; computer graphics; computer/information technology services administration related; criminal justice/law enforcement administration; health/health care administration; legal assistant/paralegal; massage therapy; medical/clinical assistant; radiologic technology/science

Enrollment: 300 students

Institution Contact: Ms. Rebecca Rodgers, Vice President *Phone:* 863-701-7789 *Fax:* 863-701-8758 *E-mail:* rebeccar@keisercollege.edu

Admission Contact: Mr. Walter Bequette, Director of Admissions *Phone:* 863-701-7789 *Fax:* 863-701-8758 *E-mail:* wbequette@keisercollege.edu

Keiser College

900 South Babcock Street
Melbourne, FL 32901
Web: http://www.keisercollege.cc.fl.us

Accreditation: Accrediting Bureau of Health Education Schools; Southern Association of Colleges and Schools

Programs Offered: accounting; business administration and management; commercial and advertising art; computer graphics; computer/information technology administration and management; computer programming; e-commerce; hospital and health care facilities administration; hospitality administra-

⊛ indicates that the school is a participating institution in the *Imagine America* Scholarship Program.

tion; legal assistant/paralegal; medical/clinical assistant; nursing (registered nurse training); occupational therapist assistant; radiologic technology/science

Institution Contact: Ms. Rhonda Fuller, Vice President *Phone:* 321-255-2255 *Fax:* 321-725-3766 *E-mail:* rhondaf@keisercollege.edu

Admission Contact: Mr. Larry DelVecchio, Director of Admissions *Phone:* 321-255-2255 *Fax:* 321-725-3766 *E-mail:* larryd@keisercollege.edu

Keiser College

8505 Mills Drive
Miami, FL 33183
Web: http://www.keisercollege.edu

Accreditation: Southern Association of Colleges and Schools

Programs Offered: accounting; business administration and management; computer and information systems security; criminal justice/law enforcement administration; health services administration; legal assistant/paralegal; medical/clinical assistant; nuclear medical technology; nursing (registered nurse training); radiologic technology/science

Enrollment: 550 students

Institution Contact: Mr. Gary Markowitz, Vice President *Phone:* 305-596-2226 *Fax:* 305-596-7077 *E-mail:* garym@keisercollege.edu

Admission Contact: Mr. Ted Weiner, Director of Admissions *Phone:* 305-596-2226 *Fax:* 305-596-7077 *E-mail:* tedw@keisercollege.edu

Keiser College

5600 Lake Underhill Road
Orlando, FL 32807
Web: http://www.keisercollege.edu

Accreditation: Southern Association of Colleges and Schools

Programs Offered: accounting; business administration and management; computer and information sciences related; computer graphics; computer systems networking and telecommunications; criminal justice/law enforcement administration; health/health care administration; hospitality administration; legal assistant/paralegal; medical/clinical assistant; radiologic technology/science

Institution Contact: Dr. David M. Hubbard, Vice President *Phone:* 407-273-5800 *Fax:* 407-382-2201 *E-mail:* davidh@keisercollege.edu

Keiser College

9468 South US Highway 1
Port St. Lucie, FL 34952
Web: http://www.keisercollege.edu

Accreditation: Accrediting Bureau of Health Education Schools; Accrediting Commission of Career Schools and Colleges of Technology; Council on Occupational Education; Southern Association of Colleges and Schools

Programs Offered: accounting; business administration and management; computer graphics; criminal justice/law enforcement administration; health/health care administration; legal assistant/paralegal; massage therapy; medical/clinical assistant; pharmacy technician; surgical technology

Enrollment: 290 students

Institution Contact: Mr. Jay Lambeth, Vice President *Phone:* 772-398-9990 ext. 104 *Fax:* 772-335-9619 *E-mail:* jayl@keisercollege.edu

Admission Contact: Mr. Robert Andriola, Director of Admissions *Phone:* 772-398-9990 ext. 111 *Fax:* 772-335-9619 *E-mail:* randriola@keisercollege.edu

Keiser College

6151 Lake Osprey Drive
Sarasota, FL 34240
Web: http://www.keisercollege.edu

Accreditation: Accrediting Bureau of Health Education Schools; Southern Association of Colleges and Schools

Programs Offered: accounting; business administration and management; computer graphics; computer/information technology administration and management; computer programming; criminal justice/law enforcement administration; emergency medical technology (EMT paramedic); fire science; hospital and health care facilities administration; legal assistant/paralegal; massage therapy; medical/clinical assistant; nursing (registered nurse training); radiologic technology/science; respiratory therapy technician

Institution Contact: Ms. Michele I. Sterner, Vice President *Phone:* 941-907-3900 *Fax:* 941-907-2016 *E-mail:* micheles@keisercollege.edu

Admission Contact: Ms. Barbara Doran, Director of Admissions *Phone:* 941-907-3900 *Fax:* 941-907-2016 *E-mail:* bdoran@keisercollege.edu

◑ indicates that the school is a participating institution in the *Imagine America* Scholarship Program.

Keiser College

1700 Halstead Boulevard
Tallahassee, FL 32309
Web: http://www.keisercollege.edu

Accreditation: Accrediting Bureau of Health Education Schools; Southern Association of Colleges and Schools

Programs Offered: accounting; business administration and management; computer and information systems security; computer graphics; computer/information technology administration and management; criminal justice/law enforcement administration; culinary arts; hospital and health care facilities administration; legal assistant/paralegal; medical/clinical assistant; radiologic technology/science

Enrollment: 625 students

Institution Contact: Mr. Mark Gutmann, Vice President *Phone:* 850-906-9494 *Fax:* 850-906-9497 *E-mail:* markg@keisercollege.edu

Admission Contact: Mr. Guy Pierce, Director of Admissions *Phone:* 850-906-9494 *Fax:* 850-906-9497 *E-mail:* gpierce@keisercollege.edu

Key College

5225 West Broward Boulevard
Fort Lauderdale, FL 33317
Web: http://www.keycollege.edu

Accreditation: Accrediting Council for Independent Colleges and Schools

Programs Offered: computer programming (specific applications); court reporting; drafting and design technology; legal assistant/paralegal; medical administrative assistant and medical secretary; medical transcription

Institution Contact: Mr. Ronald H. Dooley, President *Phone:* 954-923-4440 *Fax:* 954-583-9458 *E-mail:* rdooley@keycollege.edu

La Belle Beauty School

775 West 49th Street, Suite #5
Hialeah, FL 33012

Accreditation: Accrediting Commission of Career Schools and Colleges of Technology

Programs Offered: aesthetician/esthetician and skin care; cosmetology; nail technician and manicurist

Institution Contact: Mr. Humberto Balboa, Director *Phone:* 305-558-0562 *Fax:* 305-362-0665 *E-mail:* labellehia@beautyacademy.com

Admission Contact: Mrs. Anna Garcia, Admissions *Phone:* 305-558-0562 *Fax:* 305-362-0665

Le Cordon Bleu College of Culinary Arts Miami

2841 Corporate Way, MPC 15
Miramar, FL 33025
Web: http://www.miamiculinary.com

Programs Offered: culinary arts

Marine Mechanics Institute Ⓐ

9751 Delegates Drive
Orlando, FL 32837-9835
Web: http://www.uticorp.com

Accreditation: Accrediting Commission of Career Schools and Colleges of Technology

Programs Offered: marine maintenance and ship repair technology; motorcycle maintenance and repair technology

Enrollment: 1,788 students

Institution Contact: Ms. Dianne Ely, Director *Phone:* 407-240-2422 ext. 1610 *Fax:* 407-240-1318 *E-mail:* dely@uticorp.com

Admission Contact: Mr. Dwight Berry, Admissions Office Manager *Phone:* 407-240-2422 ext. 1128 *Fax:* 407-240-1318 *E-mail:* dberry@uticorp.com

See full description on page 400.

MedVance Institute

170 JFK Drive
Atlantis, FL 33462-6607
Web: http://www.medvance.org

Accreditation: Council on Occupational Education

Programs Offered: dental assisting; gene therapy; medical/clinical assistant; nursing assistant/aide and patient care assistant; pharmacy technician

Institution Contact: Ms. Brenda P. Cortez, Campus Director *Phone:* 561-304-3466 *Fax:* 561-304-3471 *E-mail:* bcortez@medvance.org

Admission Contact: *Phone:* 561-304-3466 *Fax:* 561-304-3471

MedVance Institute

4101 Northwest 3rd Court, Suite 9
Fort Lauderdale, FL 33317-2857
Web: http://www.medvance.edu

Accreditation: Accrediting Bureau of Health Education Schools

Programs Offered: medical/clinical assistant; medical insurance coding; medical radiologic technology; medical staff services technology; pharmacy technician; surgical technology

Institution Contact: *Phone:* 954-587-7100 *Fax:* 954-587-7704

Ⓐ indicates that the school is a participating institution in the *Imagine America* Scholarship Program.

MedVance Institute

9035 Sunset Drive, Suite 200
Miami, FL 33173
Web: http://www.medvance.edu

Accreditation: Council on Occupational Education

Programs Offered: massage therapy; medical administrative assistant and medical secretary; medical/clinical assistant; medical insurance coding; medical radiologic technology; medical staff services technology; nursing (licensed practical/vocational nurse training); pharmacy technician; surgical technology

Institution Contact: *Phone:* 305-596-5553 *Fax:* 305-596-0552

MedVance Institute

10792 U.S. 1
Port St. Lucie, FL 34592
Web: http://www.medvance.edu

Accreditation: Accrediting Bureau of Health Education Schools

Programs Offered: massage therapy; medical administrative assistant and medical secretary; medical/clinical assistant; medical insurance coding; medical radiologic technology; medical staff services technology; nursing (licensed practical/vocational nurse training); pharmacy technician; surgical technology

Institution Contact: *Phone:* 772-221-9799 *Fax:* 772-223-0522

Miami International University of Art & Design

1501 Biscayne Boulevard, Suite 100
Miami, FL 33132
Web: http://www.aimiu.aii.edu

Accreditation: Southern Association of Colleges and Schools

Programs Offered: advertising; apparel and accessories marketing; apparel and textile marketing management; apparel and textiles related; applied art; art; ceramic arts and ceramics; cinematography and film/video production; commercial and advertising art; computer graphics; digital communication and media/multimedia; drawing; fashion/apparel design; fashion merchandising; graphic and printing equipment operation/production; interior design; photographic and film/video technology; retailing; sculpture; visual and performing arts

Enrollment: 1,200 students

Institution Contact: Ms. Elsia Suarez, Director of Admissions *Phone:* 800-225-9023 *Fax:* 305-374-5933 *E-mail:* suareze@aii.edu

Admission Contact: Ms. Elisa Suarez, Director of Admissions *Phone:* 800-225-9023 *Fax:* 305-374-5933 *E-mail:* suareze@aii.edu

National School of Technology, Inc. Ⓐ

1040 Bayview Drive
Fort Lauderdale, FL 33304
Web: http://www.nst.cc

Accreditation: Accrediting Bureau of Health Education Schools

Programs Offered: massage therapy; medical/clinical assistant; medical insurance coding

Institution Contact: Ashly Miller, Director of Admissions *Phone:* 954-630-0066 *Fax:* 954-630-0076 *E-mail:* amiller@cci.edu

See full description on page 401.

National School of Technology, Inc. Ⓐ

4410 West 16th Avenue, Suite 52
Hialeah, FL 33012

Accreditation: Accrediting Bureau of Health Education Schools

Programs Offered: cardiovascular technology; diagnostic medical sonography and ultrasound technology; massage therapy; medical/clinical assistant; medical insurance coding; pharmacy technician; surgical technology

Enrollment: 846 students

Institution Contact: Dr. Gilbert Delgado, Campus President *Phone:* 305-558-9500 *Fax:* 305-558-4419 *E-mail:* gdelgado@cci.edu

Admission Contact: Mr. Daniel Alonso, Director of Admission *Phone:* 305-558-9500 *Fax:* 305-558-4419 *E-mail:* dalonso@cci.edu

See full description on page 402.

National School of Technology, Inc. Ⓐ

9020 Southwest 137th Avenue, Suite 200
Miami, FL 33186

Accreditation: Accrediting Bureau of Health Education Schools

Programs Offered: cardiovascular technology; legal assistant/paralegal; massage therapy; medical/clinical assistant; medical insurance/medical billing; pharmacy technician; surgical technology

Ⓐ indicates that the school is a participating institution in the *Imagine America* Scholarship Program.

National School of Technology, Inc. *(continued)*

Institution Contact: Mr. Randy Kaufman, Academic Dean *Phone:* 305-386-9900 ext. 130 *Fax:* 305-388-1740 *E-mail:* rkaufman@cci.edu

Admission Contact: Mr. John Rios, Director of Admissions *Phone:* 305-386-9900 ext. 109 *Fax:* 305-388-1740 *E-mail:* jrios@cci.edu

See full description on page 403.

National School of Technology, Inc. Ⓐ

111 Northwest 183rd Street, 2nd Floor
Miami, FL 33169
Web: http://www.nst.cc

Accreditation: Accrediting Bureau of Health Education Schools

Programs Offered: health aide; massage therapy; medical/clinical assistant; medical insurance coding; pharmacy technician; surgical technology

Enrollment: 830 students

Institution Contact: Dr. Mario Paul Miro, School President *Phone:* 305-949-9500 *Fax:* 305-949-7303 *E-mail:* mmiro@cci.edu

Admission Contact: Mr. Walter McQuade, Director of Admissions *Phone:* 305-949-9500 *Fax:* 305-956-5758 *E-mail:* wmcquade@cci.edu

See full description on page 404.

New England Institute of Technology at Palm Beach

2410 Metrocentre Boulevard
West Palm Beach, FL 33407
Web: http://www.newenglandtech.com

Accreditation: Accrediting Council for Independent Colleges and Schools; Council on Occupational Education

Programs Offered: architectural drafting and CAD/CADD; automobile/automotive mechanics technology; baking and pastry arts; business administration and management; CAD/CADD drafting/design technology; computer systems networking and telecommunications; cosmetology; culinary arts; dental assisting; drafting and design technology; electrical, electronic and communications engineering technology; heating, air conditioning and refrigeration technology; legal assistant/paralegal; medical/clinical assistant; medical insurance coding; restaurant, culinary, and catering management; web/multimedia management and webmaster

Enrollment: 2,000 students

Institution Contact: Mr. Charles H. Halliday, President *Phone:* 561-712-5100 *Fax:* 561-842-9503 *E-mail:* challiday@newenglandtech.com

Admission Contact: Mr. Kevin Cassidy, Director of Admissions *Phone:* 561-688-2001 *Fax:* 561-842-9503 *E-mail:* kcassidy@newenglandtech.com

North Florida Institute

560 Wells Road
Orange Park, FL 32073

Accreditation: Accrediting Council for Independent Colleges and Schools

Programs Offered: accounting; accounting and business/management; allied health and medical assisting services related; business administration and management; business, management, and marketing related; clinical laboratory science/medical technology; criminal justice/law enforcement administration; criminal justice/police science; gene therapy; health information/medical records administration; health information/medical records technology; health professions related; information technology; medical/clinical assistant; medical insurance coding; medical insurance/medical billing; medical office assistant; medical office management; medical staff services technology; nursing assistant/aide and patient care assistant; nursing related; pharmacy technician; phlebotomy; surgical technology

Enrollment: 388 students

Institution Contact: Dr. Ray Diaz, Jr., Director *Phone:* 904-269-7086 *Fax:* 904-269-6664 *E-mail:* rdiaz@northfloridainstitute.edu

Admission Contact: Ms. Jan Allen, Admissions *Phone:* 904-269-7086 *Fax:* 904-269-6664 *E-mail:* janallen@northfloridainstitute.edu

Orlando Culinary Academy

8511 Commodity Circle
Orlando, FL 32819
Web: http://www.orlandoculinary.com

Accreditation: Accrediting Council for Independent Colleges and Schools

Programs Offered: culinary arts

Institution Contact: Mrs. Debbie Taylor, Director of Career Services *Phone:* 407-313-8793 *Fax:* 407-888-4019 *E-mail:* detaylor@orlandoculinary.com

Admission Contact: Ms. Leigh Hughes, Director of Admissions *Phone:* 407-313-8701 *Fax:* 407-888-4019 *E-mail:* lhughes@orlandoculinary.com

Ⓐ indicates that the school is a participating institution in the *Imagine America* Scholarship Program.

Remington College–Jacksonville Campus (A)

7011 A.C. Skinner Parkway, Suite 140
Jacksonville, FL 32256
Web: http://www.remingtoncollege.edu

Accreditation: Accrediting Commission of Career Schools and Colleges of Technology

Programs Offered: allied health and medical assisting services related; business administration, management and operations related; computer and information sciences related; computer engineering technology; computer/information technology services administration related; computer installation and repair technology; computer software and media applications; computer systems networking and telecommunications; computer/technical support; computer technology/computer systems technology; criminal justice/law enforcement administration; criminal justice/police science; information technology; massage therapy; medical/clinical assistant; medical office assistant; pharmacy administration/pharmaceutics; pharmacy technician; phlebotomy; securities services administration

Enrollment: 425 students

Institution Contact: Mr. Tony Galang, Campus President *Phone:* 904-296-3435 *Fax:* 904-296-3474 *E-mail:* tony.galang@remingtoncollege.edu

Admission Contact: Chantel Whidbee, Registrar *Phone:* 904-296-3435 *Fax:* 904-296-9097 *E-mail:* chantel.whidbee@remingtoncollege.edu

See full description on page 405.

Remington College–Pinellas Campus (A)

8550 Ulmerton Road, Unit 100
Largo, FL 33771
Web: http://www.remingtoncollege.edu

Accreditation: Accrediting Commission of Career Schools and Colleges of Technology

Programs Offered: business administration and management; business administration, management and operations related; business automation/technology/data entry; business machine repair; business operations support and secretarial services related; computer engineering technology; computer/information technology services administration related; computer installation and repair technology; computer programming; computer programming related; computer programming (specific applications); computer programming (vendor/product certification); computer systems networking and telecommunications; computer technology/computer systems technology; criminal justice/law enforcement administration; data modeling/warehousing and database

administration; electrical, electronic and communications engineering technology; information science/studies; information technology; internet information systems; massage therapy; medical/clinical assistant; pharmacy technician

Enrollment: 342 students

Institution Contact: Ms. Edna Higgins, Campus President *Phone:* 727-532-1999 *Fax:* 727-530-7710 *E-mail:* edna.higgins@remingtoncollege.edu

See full description on page 406.

Remington College–Tampa Campus (A)

2410 East Busch Boulevard
Tampa, FL 33612
Web: http://www.remingtoncollege.edu

Accreditation: Accrediting Commission of Career Schools and Colleges of Technology

Programs Offered: accounting; art; business administration and management; business automation/technology/data entry; commercial and advertising art; commercial photography; computer and information systems security; computer engineering related; computer engineering technology; computer graphics; computer/information technology administration and management; computer/information technology services administration related; computer programming; computer systems networking and telecommunications; desktop publishing and digital imaging design; electrical, electronic and communications engineering technology; engineering technology; information science/studies; information technology; internet information systems; management information systems; operations management; system, networking, and LAN/WAN management; web/multimedia management and webmaster; web page, digital/multimedia and information resources design

Institution Contact: Mr. William D. Polmear, Campus President *Phone:* 813-932-0701 *Fax:* 813-935-7415 *E-mail:* william.polmear@remingtoncollege.edu

Admission Contact: Ms. Kathy Miller, Director of Recruitment *Phone:* 813-932-0701 *Fax:* 813-935-7415 *E-mail:* kathy.miller@remingtoncollege.edu

See full description on page 407.

Ross Medical Education Center

6847 Taft Street
Hollywood, FL 33024

Programs Offered: medical/clinical assistant

Institution Contact: Barbara Franklin, Director *Phone:* 954-963-0043 *Fax:* 954-963-0211

(A) indicates that the school is a participating institution in the *Imagine America* Scholarship Program.

Ross Medical Education Center

2601 South Military Trail, Suite 29
West Palm Beach, FL 33415-9141
Programs Offered: medical/clinical assistant
Institution Contact: Ms. Linda Materazzi, Director
Phone: 561-433-1288 *Fax:* 561-641-8477

Sanford-Brown Institute

10255 Fortune Parkway, Unit 501
Jacksonville, FL 32256
Web: http://www.sbjacksonville.com
Accreditation: Accrediting Bureau of Health Education Schools; Accrediting Council for Independent Colleges and Schools
Programs Offered: dental assisting; health information/medical records technology; massage therapy; medical/clinical assistant; surgical technology
Enrollment: 350 students
Institution Contact: Mr. Wyman A. Dickey, Campus President *Phone:* 904-363-6221 *Fax:* 904-363-6824
E-mail: wdickey@sbjacksonville.com
Admission Contact: Mr. Sean McHaney, Director of Admissions *Phone:* 904-363-6221 *Fax:* 904-363-6824
E-mail: smchaney@sbjacksonville.com

Sanford-Brown Institute

4780 North State Road 7, #100-E
Lauderdale Lakes, FL 33319-5860
Web: http://www.sbftlaud.com
Accreditation: Accrediting Bureau of Health Education Schools
Programs Offered: cardiovascular technology; dental assisting; diagnostic medical sonography and ultrasound technology; health information/medical records technology; massage therapy; medical/clinical assistant; surgical technology
Enrollment: 750 students
Institution Contact: Ms. Mary-Jo Greco, President *Phone:* 954-733-8900 ext. 2229 *Fax:* 954-733-8994 *E-mail:* mgreco@sbftl.com
Admission Contact: Mr. Chris George, Director of Admissions *Phone:* 954-733-8900 ext. 2225 *Fax:* 954-733-8994 *E-mail:* cgeorge@sbftlaud.com

Sanford-Brown Institute

5701 East Hillsborough Avenue
Tampa, FL 33610
Web: http://www.ultrasounddiagnosticschool.com/default.htm
Accreditation: Accrediting Bureau of Health Education Schools; Accrediting Council for Independent Colleges and Schools

Programs Offered: cardiovascular technology; diagnostic medical sonography and ultrasound technology; medical/clinical assistant; medical insurance coding; surgical technology
Institution Contact: Dr. Mary Smith, Executive Director *Phone:* 813-621-0072 *Fax:* 813-626-0392
Admission Contact: Mrs. Angela Panter, Director of Admissions *Phone:* 813-621-0072 *Fax:* 813-626-0392

South University

1760 North Congress Avenue
West Palm Beach, FL 33409
Web: http://www.southuniversity.edu/
Accreditation: Southern Association of Colleges and Schools
Programs Offered: accounting; business administration and management; computer/information technology services administration related; computer programming (specific applications); computer systems networking and telecommunications; legal administrative assistant/secretary; legal assistant/paralegal; medical/clinical assistant; nursing (registered nurse training); physical therapist assistant
Institution Contact: Dr. Thomas Bloom, President *Phone:* 561-697-9200 ext. 7227 *Fax:* 561-697-9944 *E-mail:* tbloom@southuniversity.edu
Admission Contact: Mr. Peter Grosfeld, Director of Admissions *Phone:* 561-697-9200 *Fax:* 561-697-9944 *E-mail:* pgrosfeld@southuniversity.edu

Southwest Florida College (A)

1685 Medical Lane
Fort Myers, FL 33907
Web: http://www.swfc.edu
Accreditation: Accrediting Council for Independent Colleges and Schools
Programs Offered: accounting; business administration and management; CAD/CADD drafting/design technology; commercial and advertising art; computer graphics; computer/information technology services administration related; computer installation and repair technology; computer programming; computer software and media applications; computer systems networking and telecommunications; computer/technical support; criminal justice/law enforcement administration; drafting and design technology; forensic science and technology; health information/medical records administration; hospitality administration; legal assistant/paralegal; medical/clinical assistant; medical office management; medical transcription; pharmacy technician; restaurant, culinary, and catering management; surgical technology

(A) indicates that the school is a participating institution in the *Imagine America* Scholarship Program.

Enrollment: 1,300 students

Institution Contact: Mr. Gregory H. Jones, President *Phone:* 239-939-4766 *Fax:* 239-939-1332 *E-mail:* gjones@swfc.edu

Admission Contact: Mrs. Carmen E. King, Director of Admissions *Phone:* 239-939-4766 *Fax:* 239-936-4040 *E-mail:* cking@swfc.edu

See full description on page 408.

Southwest Florida College

3910 Riga Boulevard
Tampa, FL 33619
Web: http://www.swfc.edu/

Accreditation: Accrediting Bureau of Health Education Schools; Accrediting Council for Independent Colleges and Schools

Programs Offered: accounting; allied health and medical assisting services related; architectural drafting and CAD/CADD; business, management, and marketing related; CAD/CADD drafting/design technology; computer and information sciences; computer and information systems security; computer graphics; computer systems networking and telecommunications; computer/technical support; criminal justice/law enforcement administration; information technology; legal assistant/paralegal; marketing/marketing management; medical administrative assistant and medical secretary; medical/clinical assistant; medical office assistant; medical office management; medical transcription; pharmacy technician; surgical technology; technology management

Enrollment: 550 students

Institution Contact: Mr. Wayne Slater, Chief Operating Officer *Phone:* 813-630-4401 *Fax:* 813-623-8154 *E-mail:* wslater@sunstate.edu

Admission Contact: Ms. Stephanie Schweihofer, Director of Admissions *Phone:* 813-630-4401 *Fax:* 813-630-4272 *E-mail:* sschweihofer@swfc.edu

Tulsa Welding School Ⓐ

3500 Southside Boulevard
Jacksonville, FL 32216
Web: http://www.weldingschool.edu

Accreditation: Accrediting Commission of Career Schools and Colleges of Technology

Programs Offered: welding technology

Enrollment: 145 students

Institution Contact: Mr. Roger Hess, President/Co-CEO *Phone:* 904-646-9353 ext. 222 *Fax:* 904-646-9467 *E-mail:* r3h4@aol.com

Admission Contact: Mr. Bob Lutz, Director of Admissions *Phone:* 904-646-9353 ext. 242 *Fax:* 904-646-9956 *E-mail:* tws@ionet.net

See full description on page 409.

Virginia College at Pensacola

19 West Garden Street
Pensacola, FL 32502
Web: http://www.medcci.com

Accreditation: Accrediting Bureau of Health Education Schools; Accrediting Council for Independent Colleges and Schools

Programs Offered: accounting technology and bookkeeping; administrative assistant and secretarial science; human resources management; legal administrative assistant/secretary; medical/clinical assistant; medical insurance coding; medical insurance/medical billing; nursing (licensed practical/vocational nurse training); surgical technology

Institution Contact: Ms. Linda Weldon, President *Phone:* 850-436-8444 ext. 2302 *Fax:* 850-436-8470 *E-mail:* lweldon@vc.edu

Admission Contact: Mrs. Bunty Cantwell, Director of Admissions *Phone:* 850-436-8444 *Fax:* 850-436-8470 *E-mail:* bcantwell@vc.edu

Webster College

2127 Grand Boulevard
Holiday, FL 34691
Web: http://www.webstercollege.com

Accreditation: Accrediting Council for Independent Colleges and Schools

Programs Offered: accounting; business administration and management; computer systems networking and telecommunications; information technology; management science; medical/clinical assistant

Enrollment: 236 students

Institution Contact: Mrs. Claire Walker, Executive Director *Phone:* 727-942-0069 *Fax:* 727-938-5709 *E-mail:* cwalker@webstercollege.com

Webster College

2221 SW 19th Avenue Road
Ocala, FL 34474
Web: http://www.webstercollege.com

Accreditation: Accrediting Council for Independent Colleges and Schools

Programs Offered: accounting; business administration and management; computer/information technology services administration related; medical/clinical assistant

Ⓐ indicates that the school is a participating institution in the *Imagine America* Scholarship Program.

Webster College *(continued)*

Institution Contact: Ms. Peggy Meyers, Associate Director *Phone:* 352-629-1941 *Fax:* 352-629-0926 *E-mail:* pmeyers@webstercollege.com

Webster College

3910 US Highway 301 North, Suite 200
Tampa, FL 33619-1259
Web: http://www.webstercollege.com/

Accreditation: Accrediting Council for Independent Colleges and Schools

Programs Offered: computer/information technology administration and management; computer technology/computer systems technology; medical/clinical assistant; tourism and travel services management

Enrollment: 146 students

Institution Contact: Mr. Todd Matthews, Executive Director *Phone:* 813-620-1446 *Fax:* 813-620-1641 *E-mail:* tmatthews@webstercollege.com

Admission Contact: Mr. Gregory Bell, Director of Admissions *Phone:* 813-620-1446 *Fax:* 813-620-1641 *E-mail:* gbell@webstercollege.com

georgia

Advanced Career Training

2 Executive Park Drive, NW, Building 2, Suite #100
Atlanta, GA 30329
Web: http://www.therightskills.com

Accreditation: Accrediting Council for Continuing Education and Training

Programs Offered: business administration and management; dental assisting; medical/clinical assistant; technology management

Enrollment: 300 students

Institution Contact: Dr. John A. England, Executive Director *Phone:* 404-321-2929 ext. 210 *Fax:* 404-633-0028 *E-mail:* englandj@actglobal.com

Admission Contact: Director of Admissions *Phone:* 404-321-2929 ext. 220 *Fax:* 404-633-0028

Advanced Career Training

7165 Georgia Highway 85
Riverdale, GA 30274
Web: http://www.therightskills.com

Accreditation: Accrediting Council for Continuing Education and Training

Programs Offered: business administration and management; dental assisting; medical/clinical assistant; technology management

Institution Contact: Mr. John Mills, Executive Director *Phone:* 770-991-9356 *Fax:* 770-991-2472 *E-mail:* millsj@actglobal.com

Admission Contact: Mr. John Payton, Director of Admissions *Phone:* 770-991-9356 *Fax:* 770-991-2472

American InterContinental University

3330 Peachtree Road, NE
Atlanta, GA 30326
Web: http://www.aiubuckhead.com

Accreditation: Southern Association of Colleges and Schools

Programs Offered: cinematography and film/video production; commercial and advertising art; fashion/apparel design; fashion merchandising; interior design; international business/trade/commerce

Institution Contact: Mr. Rafael Lago, President *Phone:* 404-965-5700 *Fax:* 404-965-5701 *E-mail:* rlago@buckhead.aiuniv.edu

Admission Contact: Ms. Knitra Watson Norwood, Vice President of Admissions and Marketing *Phone:* 888-999-4248 *Fax:* 404-965-5701 *E-mail:* kwatson@buckhead.aiuniv.edu

American InterContinental University

6600 Peachtree-Dunwoody Road, 500 Embassy Row
Atlanta, GA 30328
Web: http://www.aiudunwoody.com

Accreditation: Southern Association of Colleges and Schools

Programs Offered: business administration and management; business/corporate communications; commercial and advertising art; computer and information sciences and support services related; computer technology/computer systems technology; criminal justice/law enforcement administration; health/health care administration; human resources management; information technology; intermedia/multimedia; marketing/marketing management; marketing related

Enrollment: 1,470 students

Institution Contact: Mr. Peter Buswell, President *Phone:* 404-965-6500 *Fax:* 404-965-6501 *E-mail:* pbuswell@aiuniv.edu

Admission Contact: Ms. Joy Marks, Vice President of Admissions *Phone:* 800-353-1744 *Fax:* 404-965-6501 *E-mail:* jmarks@aiuniv.edu

🅐 indicates that the school is a participating institution in the *Imagine America* Scholarship Program.

The Art Institute of Atlanta

6600 Peachtree-Dunwoody Road, 100 Embassy Row
Atlanta, GA 30328
Web: http://www.aia.artinstitutes.edu

Accreditation: Southern Association of Colleges and Schools

Programs Offered: advertising; animation, interactive technology, video graphics and special effects; audiovisual communications technologies related; baking and pastry arts; cinematography and film/video production; commercial and advertising art; culinary arts; design and visual communications; drawing; interior design; photography; restaurant, culinary, and catering management; web page, digital/multimedia and information resources design

Enrollment: 2,700 students

Institution Contact: Mrs. Janet S. Day, President *Phone:* 770-394-8300 *Fax:* 770-394-8813 *E-mail:* aiaadm@aii.edu

Admission Contact: Ms. Donna Scott, Director of Admissions *Phone:* 770-394-8300 *Fax:* 770-394-8813 *E-mail:* aiaadm@aii.edu

Asher School of Business

4975 Jimmy Carter Boulevard, Suite 600
Norcross, GA 30093

Programs Offered: accounting technology and bookkeeping; business administration and management; CAD/CADD drafting/design technology; computer and information sciences related; computer programming; computer software technology; criminal justice/law enforcement administration; legal assistant/paralegal; medical/clinical assistant

Institution Contact: *Phone:* 888-301-3670

Bauder College

Phipps Plaza, 3500 Peachtree Road
Atlanta, GA 30326
Web: http://www.bauder.edu

Accreditation: Southern Association of Colleges and Schools

Programs Offered: business administration and management; commercial and advertising art; criminal justice/law enforcement administration; fashion/apparel design; fashion merchandising; fashion modeling; information technology; interior design; marketing/marketing management

Institution Contact: Mrs. Jo Ann Wilson, President and Chief Executive Officer *Phone:* 404-237-7573 ext. 262 *Fax:* 404-237-1642 *E-mail:* jwilson@bauder.edu

Admission Contact: Mr. Del McCormick, Director of Admissions *Phone:* 404-237-7573 ext. 223 *Fax:* 404-237-1619 *E-mail:* dmccormick@bauder.edu

Computer-Ed Institute Ⓐ

2359 Windy Hill Road
Marietta, GA 30067
Web: http://www.ceitraining.com

Accreditation: Accrediting Council for Independent Colleges and Schools

Programs Offered: medical administrative assistant and medical secretary; medical/clinical assistant; system administration

Institution Contact: Executive Director *Phone:* 770-226-0056 *Fax:* 770-226-0084 *E-mail:* execdirmarietta@lincolntech.com

See full description on page 410.

Computer-Ed Institute Ⓐ

5675 Jimmy Carter Boulevard, Suite 100
Norcross, GA 30071
Web: http://www.ceitraining.com

Accreditation: Accrediting Council for Independent Colleges and Schools

Programs Offered: business administration and management; computer systems networking and telecommunications; computer/technical support; massage therapy; medical administrative assistant and medical secretary; medical/clinical assistant; system administration

Enrollment: 400 students

Institution Contact: Mr. Bryan Gulebian, Executive Director *Phone:* 678-966-9411 *Fax:* 678-966-9687 *E-mail:* bgulebian@ceitraining.com

Admission Contact: Mr. Thomas Trahan, Director of Admissions *Phone:* 678-966-9411 *Fax:* 678-966-9687 *E-mail:* ttrahan@ceitraining.com

See full description on page 411.

The Creative Circus, Inc.

812 Lambert Drive, NE
Atlanta, GA 30324
Web: http://www.creativecircus.com

Accreditation: Council on Occupational Education

Programs Offered: advertising; art; design and visual communications; photography

Enrollment: 220 students

Institution Contact: Mr. Bret Johnson, Executive Director *Phone:* 800-728-1590 *Fax:* 404-875-1590 *E-mail:* bjohnson@creativecircus.com

Ⓐ indicates that the school is a participating institution in the *Imagine America* Scholarship Program.

The Creative Circus, Inc. *(continued)*

Admission Contact: Mr. Dan Benner, Senior Admissions Representative, International Admissions *Phone:* 800-728-1890 *Fax:* 404-875-1590 *E-mail:* dbenner@creativecircus.com

Decker School of Construction Crafts

3700 Dekalb Technology Parkway, Suite A
Atlanta, GA 30340
Accreditation: Council on Occupational Education
Programs Offered: carpentry; electrician; heating, air conditioning and refrigeration technology
Institution Contact: Andrew Wynes, Office Manager *Phone:* 770-457-4545 *Fax:* 770-457-3337 *E-mail:* awynes@compassedu.com
Admission Contact: Jessica Darby, Admissions Representative *Phone:* 770-457-4545 *Fax:* 770-457-3337 *E-mail:* jdarby@deckercollege.com

Georgia Medical Institute Ⓐ

1750 Beaver Ruin Road, Suite 500
Norcross, GA 30093
Web: http://www.georgia-med.com/
Accreditation: Accrediting Commission of Career Schools and Colleges of Technology
Programs Offered: dental assisting; massage therapy; medical administrative assistant and medical secretary; medical/clinical assistant
Enrollment: 350 students
Institution Contact: Christine Knouff, School President *Phone:* 770-921-1085 *Fax:* 770-923-4533 *E-mail:* cknouff@cci.edu
Admission Contact: Sandra Williams, Director of Admissions *Phone:* 770-921-1085 *Fax:* 770-923-4533
See full description on page 416.

Georgia Medical Institute–Atlanta Ⓐ

101 Marietta Street, Suite 600
Atlanta, GA 30303
Web: http://www.georgia-med.com
Accreditation: Accrediting Bureau of Health Education Schools
Programs Offered: medical administrative assistant and medical secretary; medical/clinical assistant; medical insurance coding; pharmacy technician
Institution Contact: Ms. Sonya Jabriel, Director of Admissions *Phone:* 404-525-1111 *Fax:* 404-525-0966 *E-mail:* sjabriel@cci.edu
See full description on page 412.

Georgia Medical Institute–DeKalb Ⓐ

1706 Northeast Expressway
Atlanta, GA 30329
Web: http://www.georgia-med.com
Accreditation: Accrediting Commission of Career Schools and Colleges of Technology
Programs Offered: dialysis technology; massage therapy; medical/clinical assistant; medical insurance coding; medical insurance/medical billing; respiratory care therapy
Enrollment: 476 students
Institution Contact: Mr. Rodney Amadori, School President *Phone:* 404-327-8787 *Fax:* 404-327-8980 *E-mail:* ramadori@cci.edu
Admission Contact: Ms. Trish Sherwood, Director of Admissions *Phone:* 404-327-8787 *Fax:* 404-327-8980 *E-mail:* tsherwood@cci.edu
See full description on page 413.

Georgia Medical Institute–Jonesboro Ⓐ

6431 Tara Boulevard
Jonesboro, GA 30236
Web: http://www.georgia-med.com
Accreditation: Accrediting Bureau of Health Education Schools
Programs Offered: dental assisting; health aide; massage therapy; medical administrative assistant and medical secretary; medical/clinical assistant; medical insurance coding; medical insurance/medical billing; pharmacy technician
Admission Contact: Mr. Victor Tedoff, Director of Admissions *Phone:* 770-603-0000 *Fax:* 770-210-3259 *E-mail:* vtedoff@cci.edu
See full description on page 414.

Georgia Medical Institute–Marietta Ⓐ

1600 Terrell Mill Road, Suite G
Marietta, GA 30067
Web: http://www.cci.edu
Accreditation: Accrediting Bureau of Health Education Schools
Programs Offered: massage therapy; medical administrative assistant and medical secretary; medical/clinical assistant; medical insurance/medical billing; pharmacy technician; surgical technology
Enrollment: 532 students
Institution Contact: Dr. Doris O'Keefe, President *Phone:* 770-303-7997 *Fax:* 770-303-4422 *E-mail:* dokeefe@cci.edu

Ⓐ indicates that the school is a participating institution in the *Imagine America* Scholarship Program.

Admission Contact: Ms. Lynn M. Jones, Director of Admissions *Phone:* 770-303-7997 *Fax:* 770-303-4422 *E-mail:* ljones@cci.edu

See full description on page 415.

Herzing College ⒶΙ

3355 Lenox Road, Suite 100
Atlanta, GA 30326
Web: http://www.herzing.edu

Accreditation: Accrediting Council for Independent Colleges and Schools; North Central Association of Colleges and Schools

Programs Offered: accounting; business administration and management; computer installation and repair technology; computer programming; computer programming (specific applications); computer programming (vendor/product certification); computer software and media applications; computer systems analysis; computer systems networking and telecommunications; computer/technical support; computer technology/computer systems technology; electrical, electronic and communications engineering technology; insurance; medical administrative assistant and medical secretary; system administration; web page, digital/multimedia and information resources design

Enrollment: 320 students

Institution Contact: Ms. Kasi Robinson, Registrar *Phone:* 404-816-4533 *Fax:* 404-816-5576 *E-mail:* kasir@atl.herzing.edu

Admission Contact: Mr. Frank Webster, Campus President *Phone:* 404-816-4533 *Fax:* 404-816-5576 *E-mail:* fwebster@atl.herzing.edu

See full description on page 417.

High-Tech Institute

1090 Northchase Parkway, Suite 150
Marietta, GA 30067
Web: http://www.hightechinstitute.edu

Accreditation: Accrediting Commission of Career Schools and Colleges of Technology

Programs Offered: computer and information systems security; digital communication and media/multimedia; massage therapy; medical/clinical assistant; medical insurance coding; medical insurance/medical billing; pharmacy technician; surgical technology

Enrollment: 600 students

Institution Contact: Myra Hadley, Campus President *Phone:* 678-279-9000 *Fax:* 770-988-8824 *E-mail:* mhadley@hightechinstitute.edu

Admission Contact: Ron Brandt, Director of Admissions *Phone:* 678-279-7000 *Fax:* 770-988-8824 *E-mail:* rbrandt@hightechinstitute.edu

ITT Technical Institute ⒶΙ

10700 Abbotts Bridge Road, Suite 190
Duluth, GA 30097
Web: http://www.itt-tech.edu

Accreditation: Accrediting Council for Independent Colleges and Schools

Programs Offered: CAD/CADD drafting/design technology; communications technology; computer and information systems security; computer engineering technology; computer software and media applications; computer systems networking and telecommunications; digital communication and media/multimedia; electrical, electronic and communications engineering technology; technology management; web page, digital/multimedia and information resources design

Enrollment: 291 students

Institution Contact: Ms. Sue Schmith, Director *Phone:* 678-957-8510

Admission Contact: Mr. Chip Hinton, Director of Recruitment *Phone:* 678-957-8510

See full description on page 418.

Kerr Business College ⒶΙ

2528 Centerwest Parkway, Building A
Augusta, GA 30909
Web: http://www.kerrbusinesscollege.com

Accreditation: Accrediting Council for Independent Colleges and Schools

Programs Offered: accounting; administrative assistant and secretarial science; business administration and management; computer engineering technology; computer/information technology services administration related; medical administrative assistant and medical secretary; medical/clinical assistant; medical insurance/medical billing; nursing assistant/aide and patient care assistant

Enrollment: 277 students

Institution Contact: Mr. Darryl H. Kerr, President *Phone:* 706-738-5046 *Fax:* 706-736-3599 *E-mail:* dhkerr@kerrbusinesscollege.com

Admission Contact: Ms. Dawn M. McCraith, Director *Phone:* 706-738-5046 *Fax:* 706-736-3599 *E-mail:* mccraith@kerrbusinesscollege.com

See full description on page 419.

Ⓐ indicates that the school is a participating institution in the *Imagine America* Scholarship Program.

Le Cordon Bleu College of Culinary Arts, Atlanta

1927 Lakeside Parkway
Tucker, GA 30084
Web: http://www.atlantaculinary.com

Accreditation: Accrediting Commission of Career Schools and Colleges of Technology

Programs Offered: culinary arts

Enrollment: 508 students

Institution Contact: Mr. Doug Solomon, Director of Education *Phone:* 770-723-3575 *Fax:* 770-938-4571 *E-mail:* dsolomon@atlantaculinary.com

Admission Contact: Terri Holte, Director of Admissions *Phone:* 770-938-4711 *Fax:* 770-938-4571 *E-mail:* tholte@atlantaculinary.com

Medix School Ⓐ

2108 Cobb Parkway
Smyrna, GA 30080
Web: http://www.medixschool.edu

Accreditation: Accrediting Bureau of Health Education Schools

Programs Offered: dental assisting; emergency medical technology (EMT paramedic); massage therapy; medical administrative assistant and medical secretary; medical/clinical assistant; nursing assistant/aide and patient care assistant; pharmacy technician

Enrollment: 550 students

Institution Contact: Mr. Larry Ritchie, Director *Phone:* 770-980-0002 *Fax:* 770-980-0467 *E-mail:* lritchie@medixschool.com

Admission Contact: Ms. Crystal Henry, Director of Admissions *Phone:* 770-980-0002 *Fax:* 770-980-0811 *E-mail:* chenry@medixschool.com

See full description on page 420.

Roffler–Moler Hairstyling College

1311 Roswell Road
Marietta, GA 30062
Web: http://www.roffler.net/

Accreditation: Accrediting Commission of Career Schools and Colleges of Technology

Programs Offered: barbering; cosmetology; cosmetology, barber/styling, and nail instruction

Enrollment: 137 students

Institution Contact: Mr. Dale Sheffield, Director *Phone:* 770-565-3285 *Fax:* 770-477-0136 *E-mail:* info@roffler.net

Admission Contact: Ms. Becky Sheffield, Administrative Director *Phone:* 770-565-3285 *Fax:* 770-477-0136 *E-mail:* info@roffler.net

Ross Medical Education Center

2645 North Decatur Road
Decatur, GA 30033

Programs Offered: medical/clinical assistant

Institution Contact: Valencia White, Director *Phone:* 404-377-5744 *Fax:* 404-377-6692

Ross Medical Education Center

2534 Cobb Parkway
Smyrna, GA 30080

Programs Offered: medical/clinical assistant

Institution Contact: Eileen Menefee, Director *Phone:* 770-951-9255 *Fax:* 770-951-9722

Sanford-Brown Institute

1140 Hammond Drive, Suite 1150-A
Atlanta, GA 30328
Web: http://www.sb-atlanta.com

Accreditation: Accrediting Bureau of Health Education Schools

Programs Offered: cardiovascular technology; diagnostic medical sonography and ultrasound technology; medical/clinical assistant; medical insurance coding; medical insurance/medical billing

Institution Contact: Mr. Clifton W. Phillips, President *Phone:* 770-576-4545 *Fax:* 770-576-4547 *E-mail:* cphillips@sb-atlanta.com

Admission Contact: Mr. Chris Key, Director of Admissions *Phone:* 770-576-4542 *Fax:* 770-350-0640 *E-mail:* ckey@sb-atlanta.com

South University

709 Mall Boulevard
Savannah, GA 31406
Web: http://www.southuniversity.edu

Accreditation: Southern Association of Colleges and Schools

Programs Offered: accounting; athletic training; business administration and management; computer and information sciences related; computer/information technology administration and management; computer/information technology services administration related; computer programming; computer programming related; computer programming (specific applications); computer programming

Ⓐ indicates that the school is a participating institution in the *Imagine America* Scholarship Program.

(vendor/product certification); computer software engineering; computer systems analysis; computer systems networking and telecommunications; computer/technical support; computer technology/computer systems technology; general studies; health/health care administration; hospital and health care facilities administration; internet information systems; legal administrative assistant/secretary; legal assistant/paralegal; management information systems; medical administrative assistant and medical secretary; medical/clinical assistant; medical/health management and clinical assistant; medical office management; occupational therapist assistant; physical therapist assistant; physician assistant; pre-law studies; system administration; system, networking, and LAN/WAN management; technology management

Institution Contact: Mr. Stephen E. Weeks, Director of Communications *Phone:* 912-201-8026 *Fax:* 912-201-8070 *E-mail:* sweeks@southuniversity.edu

Admission Contact: Mr. Robin Manning, Director of Admissions *Phone:* 912-201-8014 *Fax:* 912-201-8070 *E-mail:* rmanning@southuniversity.edu

Strayer University

3101 Towercreek Parkway, SE, Suite 700
Atlanta, GA 30339-3256
Web: http://www.strayer.edu

Programs Offered: accounting; business administration and management; education; health services administration; information technology

Institution Contact: Haroon Mokel, Campus Manager *Phone:* 770-612-2170 *Fax:* 770-956-7241 *E-mail:* cobbcounty@strayer.edu

Strayer University

3355 Northeast Expressway, Suite 100
Atlanta, GA 30339-3256
Web: http://www.strayer.edu

Programs Offered: accounting; business administration and management; education; health services administration; information technology

Institution Contact: Ayanna Martin, Campus Manager *Phone:* 770-454-9270 *Fax:* 770-457-6958 *E-mail:* chamblee@strayer.edu

Westwood College—Atlanta Campus Ⓐ

1100 Spring Street, Suite 101A
Atlanta, GA 30309
Web: http://www.westwood.edu

Accreditation: Accrediting Council for Independent Colleges and Schools

Programs Offered: accounting; animation, interactive technology, video graphics and special effects; business administration and management; CAD/CADD drafting/design technology; commercial and advertising art; computer engineering related; computer software engineering; insurance; interior design; web/multimedia management and webmaster

Enrollment: 107 students

Institution Contact: Mr. Bill Armour, Executive Director *Phone:* 404-745-9862 ext. 14200 *Fax:* 404-892-7253

Admission Contact: Mr. Rory Laney, Director of Admissions *Phone:* 404-745-9862 ext. 14100 *Fax:* 404-892-7253 *E-mail:* rlaney@westwood.edu

See full description on page 421.

Westwood College—Atlanta Northlake Ⓐ

2220 Parklake Drive Northeast
Atlanta, GA 30345
Web: http://www.westwoodcollege.net

Accreditation: Accrediting Council for Independent Colleges and Schools

Programs Offered: animation, interactive technology, video graphics and special effects; business administration and management; business, management, and marketing related; communications technology; computer engineering related; computer/information technology administration and management; computer systems networking and telecommunications; digital communication and media/multimedia

Institution Contact: Admissions Representative *Phone:* 877-558-2083

See full description on page 422.

hawaii

Hawaii Business College

33 South King Street, 4th Floor
Honolulu, HI 96813
Web: http://www.hbc.edu

Accreditation: Accrediting Council for Independent Colleges and Schools

Programs Offered: accounting; business administration and management; e-commerce; legal administrative assistant/secretary; medical/clinical assistant; medical office management; system, networking, and LAN/WAN management; tourism and travel services

Ⓐ indicates that the school is a participating institution in the *Imagine America* Scholarship Program.

Hawaii Business College (*continued*)

management; web/multimedia management and webmaster; web page, digital/multimedia and information resources design

Institution Contact: Admissions Department *Phone:* 808-524-4014 *Fax:* 808-524-8652 *E-mail:* admin@hbc.edu

New York Technical Institute of Hawaii

1375 Dillingham Boulevard
Honolulu, HI 96817-4415

Accreditation: Accrediting Commission of Career Schools and Colleges of Technology

Programs Offered: automobile/automotive mechanics technology; heating, air conditioning, ventilation and refrigeration maintenance technology

Institution Contact: Mr. Brian Hamilton, Principal and Second Vice President *Phone:* 808-841-5827 *Fax:* 808-841-5829 *E-mail:* nytih@gte.net

Remington College—Honolulu Campus Ⓐ

1111 Bishop Street, Suite 400
Honolulu, HI 96813
Web: http://www.remingtoncollege.edu

Accreditation: Accrediting Council for Independent Colleges and Schools

Programs Offered: computer/technical support; criminal justice/law enforcement administration; hospitality administration related; international business/trade/commerce; massage therapy; medical/clinical assistant; operations management

Enrollment: 650 students

Institution Contact: Mr. Kenneth G. Heinemann, Campus President *Phone:* 808-942-1000 *Fax:* 808-533-3064 *E-mail:* ken.heinemann@remingtoncollege.edu

Admission Contact: Mr. Paul Billington, Director of Recruitment *Phone:* 808-942-1000 *Fax:* 808-550-4802 *E-mail:* paul.billington@remingtoncollege.edu

See full description on page 424.

Idaho

Academy of Professional Careers

8590 West Fairview Avenue
Boise, ID 83704

Accreditation: Accrediting Council for Continuing Education and Training

Programs Offered: dental assisting; massage therapy; medical administrative assistant and medical secretary; medical/clinical assistant; pharmacy technician

Enrollment: 320 students

Institution Contact: Barbara DeHaan, Campus Director *Phone:* 208-672-9500 *Fax:* 208-322-8207 *E-mail:* bdehaan@apcschools.edu

Admission Contact: Joni Griffin, Director of Admissions *Phone:* 208-672-9500 *Fax:* 208-322-8207 *E-mail:* jgriffin@apcschools.edu

Academy of Professional Careers

1021 West Hemingway
Nampa, ID 83651

Accreditation: Accrediting Council for Continuing Education and Training

Programs Offered: dental assisting; massage therapy; medical administrative assistant and medical secretary; medical/clinical assistant

Institution Contact: Barbara DeHaan, Campus Director *Phone:* 208-672-9500 *Fax:* 208-322-8207 *E-mail:* bdehaan@apcschools.edu

Admission Contact: Joni Griffin, Director of Admissions *Phone:* 208-672-9500 *Fax:* 208-322-8207 *E-mail:* jgriffin@apcschools.edu

American Institute of Health Technology Ⓐ

1200 North Liberty Street
Boise, ID 83704
Web: http://www.aiht.com

Accreditation: Accrediting Bureau of Health Education Schools

Programs Offered: dental assisting; dental hygiene; emergency medical technology (EMT paramedic); massage therapy; medical administrative assistant and medical secretary; medical/clinical assistant; medical insurance/medical billing; pharmacy technician

Enrollment: 530 students

Institution Contact: Mr. Jeff Akens, Executive Director *Phone:* 208-377-8080 *Fax:* 208-322-7658 *E-mail:* jakens@aiht.com

Admission Contact: Director of Admissions *Phone:* 208-377-8080 *Fax:* 208-322-7658 *E-mail:* receptionist@aiht.com

See full description on page 425.

ITT Technical Institute Ⓐ

12302 West Explorer Drive
Boise, ID 83713
Web: http://www.itt-tech.edu

Accreditation: Accrediting Council for Independent Colleges and Schools

---

Ⓐ indicates that the school is a participating institution in the *Imagine America* Scholarship Program.

Programs Offered: accounting and business/management; animation, interactive technology, video graphics and special effects; business administration and management; CAD/CADD drafting/design technology; communications technology; computer and information systems security; computer engineering technology; computer software and media applications; computer software engineering; computer systems networking and telecommunications; criminal justice/police science; digital communication and media/multimedia; electrical, electronic and communications engineering technology; technology management; web page, digital/multimedia and information resources design

Enrollment: 430 students

Institution Contact: Mrs. Jennifer Kandler, Director *Phone:* 208-322-8844

Admission Contact: Mr. Terry G. Lowder, Director of Recruitment *Phone:* 208-322-8844

See full description on page 426.

Sage Technical Services

207 South 34th Avenue
Caldwell, ID 83605
Web: http://www.sageschools.com/

Programs Offered: truck and bus driver/commercial vehicle operation

Enrollment: 5 students

Institution Contact: Mr. Wayne Rogers, Director *Phone:* 800-858-6304 *Fax:* 208-454-1159 *E-mail:* caldwell@sageschools.com

Sage Technical Services

1420 East 3rd Avenue
Post Falls, ID 83854
Web: http://www.sageschools.com/

Accreditation: Accrediting Commission of Career Schools and Colleges of Technology

Programs Offered: truck and bus driver/commercial vehicle operation

Institution Contact: Mr. Alan Coldwell, Director *Phone:* 800-400-0779 *Fax:* 208-773-4690 *E-mail:* postfalls@sageschools.com

Stevens-Henager College

730 Americana Boulevard
Boise, ID 83702
Web: http://www.stevenshenager.edu

Accreditation: Accrediting Commission of Career Schools and Colleges of Technology

Programs Offered: accounting; advertising; business administration and management; cardiovascular technology; commercial and advertising art; computer and information sciences related; computer graphics; computer programming; e-commerce; emergency medical technology (EMT paramedic); health/health care administration; information science/studies; insurance; medical/clinical assistant; medical insurance coding; medical insurance/medical billing; medical transcription; pharmacy technician; system, networking, and LAN/WAN management

Institution Contact: Ms. Vicky Dewsnup, President *Phone:* 801-622-1550 *Fax:* 801-394-1149 *E-mail:* vdewsnup@stevenshenager.edu

Illinois

American Academy of Art

332 South Michigan Avenue
Chicago, IL 60604
Web: http://www.aaart.edu/

Accreditation: Accrediting Commission of Career Schools and Colleges of Technology

Programs Offered: animation, interactive technology, video graphics and special effects; art; commercial and advertising art; computer graphics; design and visual communications; drawing; fine/studio arts; painting; web/multimedia management and webmaster; web page, digital/multimedia and information resources design

Enrollment: 368 students

Institution Contact: Mr. Stuart Rosenblom, Director of Admissions *Phone:* 312-461-0600 *Fax:* 312-294-9570

American InterContinental University Online

5550 Prairie Stone Parkway, Suite 400
Hoffman Estates, IL 60192
Web: http://www.aiuonline.edu

Accreditation: Southern Association of Colleges and Schools

Programs Offered: accounting and finance; business administration and management; computer and information sciences related; computer/information technology administration and management; computer systems networking and telecommunications; criminal justice/law enforcement administration;

Ⓐ indicates that the school is a participating institution in the *Imagine America* Scholarship Program.

Guide to Career Colleges 2005 www.petersons.com **129**

American InterContinental University Online (continued)

digital communication and media/multimedia; education; educational/instructional media design; health/health care administration; human resources management; information technology; marketing/marketing management; operations management

Institution Contact: Marilyn Parry, Director of Regulatory Affairs *Phone:* 847-586-4560 *Fax:* 847-586-6519 *E-mail:* mparry@aiuonline.edu

Admission Contact: Mr. Steve Fireing, Senior Vice President of Admissions and Marketing *Phone:* 877-701-3800 *E-mail:* info@aiuonline.edu

Cardean University

500 Lake Cook Road, Suite 150
Deerfield, IL 60015-5609
Web: http://www.cardean.edu

Programs Offered: accounting; business administration and management; e-commerce; economics; finance; global management; health/health care administration; human resources management; management information systems; marketing/marketing management; technology management

Institution Contact: *Phone:* 847-405-5000 *Fax:* 847-940-2521 *E-mail:* admissions@cardean.edu

The Chubb Institute

25 East Washington Street
Chicago, IL 60602
Web: http://www.chubbinstitute.com

Accreditation: Accrediting Council for Continuing Education and Training

Programs Offered: allied health and medical assisting services related; computer and information sciences and support services related; computer and information sciences related; computer and information systems security; computer engineering technologies related; computer graphics; computer programming; computer programming related; computer programming (specific applications); computer programming (vendor/product certification); computer software and media applications; computer systems networking and telecommunications; computer/technical support; desktop publishing and digital imaging design; digital communication and media/multimedia; graphic communications; graphic communications related; health and medical administrative services related; health/health care administration; health information/medical records administration; health information/medical records technology; health professions related; health services/allied health/health sciences; health unit coordinator/ward

clerk; massage therapy; medical administrative assistant and medical secretary; medical/clinical assistant; medical/health management and clinical assistant; medical insurance/medical billing; medical office assistant; medical pharmacology and pharmaceutical sciences; medical radiologic technology; medical reception; pharmacy technician; phlebotomy; surgical technology

Enrollment: 150 students

Institution Contact: Mr. Carlos Llarena, Campus President *Phone:* 312-821-7561 *Fax:* 312-821-7581 *E-mail:* cllarena@chubbinstitute.com

Admission Contact: Ms. Maegan Kirby, Director of Admissions *Phone:* 312-821-7567 *Fax:* 312-821-7581 *E-mail:* mkirby@hightechinstitute.edu

Commonwealth Business College

1527 47th Avenue
Moline, IL 61265

Accreditation: Accrediting Council for Independent Colleges and Schools

Programs Offered: accounting; business administration and management; computer and information sciences related; computer programming; computer software and media applications; legal assistant/paralegal; medical/clinical assistant

Enrollment: 175 students

Institution Contact: Ms. Ann M. Sandoval, Senior Admissions Representative *Phone:* 309-762-2100 *Fax:* 309-762-2374 *E-mail:* asandoval@amedcts.com

The Cooking and Hospitality Institute of Chicago Ⓐ

361 West Chestnut
Chicago, IL 60610-3050
Web: http://www.chicnet.org

Accreditation: Accrediting Commission of Career Schools and Colleges of Technology; North Central Association of Colleges and Schools

Programs Offered: baking and pastry arts; culinary arts

Enrollment: 965 students

Institution Contact: Mr. Lloyd Kirsch, President *Phone:* 877-828-7772 *Fax:* 312-944-8557 *E-mail:* lkirsch@chicnet.org

Admission Contact: Mr. David McDaniel, Vice President of Admissions *Phone:* 877-828-7772 *Fax:* 312-944-8557 *E-mail:* dmcdaniel@chicnet.org

See full description on page 427.

Ⓐ indicates that the school is a participating institution in the *Imagine America* Scholarship Program.

Coyne American Institute  ⒶⒾ

1235 West Fullerton Avenue
Chicago, IL 60614-2186
Web: http://www.coyneamerican.edu

Accreditation: Accrediting Commission of Career Schools and Colleges of Technology

Programs Offered: administrative assistant and secretarial science; business automation/technology/data entry; computer installation and repair technology; computer systems networking and telecommunications; computer/technical support; computer technology/computer systems technology; data processing and data processing technology; electrical, electronic and communications engineering technology; electrical/electronics equipment installation and repair; electrician; electromechanical technology; health and medical administrative services related; health/health care administration; health information/medical records administration; health information/medical records technology; health/medical claims examination; health services administration; health services/allied health/health sciences; heating, air conditioning and refrigeration technology; industrial electronics technology; information science/studies; medical administrative assistant and medical secretary; medical insurance coding; medical insurance/medical billing; medical office assistant; medical office management; medical reception; medical transcription; office occupations and clerical services; receptionist; system, networking, and LAN/WAN management; word processing

Enrollment: 639 students

Institution Contact: Mr. Peter Pauletti, Director of Admissions *Phone:* 800-999-5220 *Fax:* 773-935-2920 *E-mail:* ppauletti@coyneamerican.edu

See full description on page 428.

Fox College

4201 West 93rd Street
Oak Lawn, IL 60453
Web: http://www.foxcollege.edu/

Accreditation: Accrediting Council for Independent Colleges and Schools

Programs Offered: accounting; administrative assistant and secretarial science; computer software and media applications related; computer software technology; executive assistant/executive secretary; medical administrative assistant and medical secretary; medical/clinical assistant; medical office assistant

Enrollment: 240 students

Ⓐ indicates that the school is a participating institution in the *Imagine America* Scholarship Program.

Fox College (*continued*)

Institution Contact: Mr. Carey Cranston, President *Phone:* 708-636-7700 *Fax:* 708-636-8078 *E-mail:* ccranston@foxcollege.edu

Admission Contact: Ms. Susan Szala, Admissions Representative *Phone:* 708-636-7700 *Fax:* 708-636-8078 *E-mail:* sszala@foxcollege.edu

Harrington College of Design Ⓐ

200 West Madison, Suite 200
Chicago, IL 60606
Web: http://www.interiordesign.edu/

Accreditation: Accrediting Council for Independent Colleges and Schools

Programs Offered: interior design; photography

Enrollment: 1,555 students

Institution Contact: Mr. Patrick W. Comstock, President *Phone:* 312-939-4975 *Fax:* 312-697-8032 *E-mail:* pcomstock@interiordesign.edu

Admission Contact: Ms. Wendi Franczyk, Vice President of Admissions *Phone:* 312-939-4975 *Fax:* 312-697-8032 *E-mail:* wfranczyk@interiordesign.edu

See full description on page 429.

The Illinois Institute of Art

350 North Orleans, Suite 136
Chicago, IL 60654-1593
Web: http://www.ilia.artinstitutes.edu

Accreditation: Accrediting Commission of Career Schools and Colleges of Technology

Programs Offered: advertising; animation, interactive technology, video graphics and special effects; apparel and textile manufacturing; apparel and textile marketing management; apparel and textiles related; applied art; art; baking and pastry arts; CAD/CADD drafting/design technology; commercial and advertising art; computer graphics; culinary arts; design and visual communications; digital communication and media/multimedia; fashion and fabric consulting; fashion/apparel design; fashion merchandising; food preparation; interior design; merchandising; retailing; selling skills and sales; visual and performing arts; web page, digital/multimedia and information resources design

Institution Contact: Mr. John C. Becker, Dean of Education *Phone:* 312-280-3500 ext. 6851 *Fax:* 312-280-8562 *E-mail:* beckerj@aii.edu

Admission Contact: Ms. Janice Anton, Director of Admissions *Phone:* 800-351-3450 *Fax:* 312-280-8562 *E-mail:* antonj@aii.edu

The Illinois Institute of Art-Schaumburg

1000 Plaza Drive
Schaumburg, IL 60173
Web: http://www.ilia.aii.edu

Accreditation: Accrediting Commission of Career Schools and Colleges of Technology

Programs Offered: animation, interactive technology, video graphics and special effects; digital communication and media/multimedia; interior design; web page, digital/multimedia and information resources design

Institution Contact: Mr. Sam T. Hinojosa, Director of Admissions *Phone:* 800-314-3450 *Fax:* 847-619-3064 *E-mail:* hinojost@aii.edu

Illinois School of Health Careers Ⓐ

220 South State Street, Suite 600
Chicago, IL 60604
Web: http://www.ishc.edu

Accreditation: Accrediting Bureau of Health Education Schools

Programs Offered: dental assisting; massage therapy; medical/clinical assistant; medical insurance coding

Enrollment: 457 students

Institution Contact: Mr. Jeffrey Jarmes, Executive Director *Phone:* 312-913-1230 *Fax:* 312-913-1113 *E-mail:* jjarmes@ishc.edu

Admission Contact: Mr. Charles Woods, Director of Admissions *Phone:* 312-913-1230 *Fax:* 312-913-1113 *E-mail:* cwoods@ishc.edu

See full description on page 430.

International Academy of Design & Technology

1 North State Street, Suite 400
Chicago, IL 60602-9736
Web: http://www.iadtchicago.edu

Accreditation: Accrediting Council for Independent Colleges and Schools

Programs Offered: advertising; CAD/CADD drafting/design technology; commercial and advertising art; computer graphics; computer/information technology administration and management; computer systems analysis; computer/technical support; fashion/apparel design; fashion merchandising; information technology; interior design; intermedia/multimedia; system administration; system, networking, and LAN/WAN management; web/multimedia management and webmaster; web page, digital/multimedia and information resources design

Ⓐ indicates that the school is a participating institution in the *Imagine America* Scholarship Program.

Institution Contact: Mrs. Robyn Palmersheim, Vice President of Marketing/Admissions *Phone:* 312-980-9200 *Fax:* 312-541-3929 *E-mail:* info@iadtchicago.com

Admission Contact: Mrs. Nikee Carnagey, Director of Admissions *Phone:* 312-980-9200 *Fax:* 312-541-3929 *E-mail:* info@iadtchicago.com

International Academy of Design and Technology

915 National Parkway
Schaumburg, IL 60173
Web: http://www.iadtschaumburg.com

Accreditation: Accrediting Council for Independent Colleges and Schools

Programs Offered: digital communication and media/multimedia; fashion/apparel design; interior design; intermedia/multimedia

ITT Technical Institute (A)

7040 High Grove Boulevard
Burr Ridge, IL 60521
Web: http://www.itt-tech.edu

Accreditation: Accrediting Council for Independent Colleges and Schools

Programs Offered: computer and information systems security; computer engineering technology; computer software and media applications; computer systems networking and telecommunications; digital communication and media/multimedia; technology management; web page, digital/multimedia and information resources design

Enrollment: 359 students

Institution Contact: Ms. Aida Carpenter, Director *Phone:* 630-455-6470

Admission Contact: Mr. Andrew Mical, Director of Recruitment *Phone:* 630-455-6470

See full description on page 431.

ITT Technical Institute (A)

600 Holiday Plaza Drive
Matteson, IL 60443
Web: http://www.itt-tech.edu

Accreditation: Accrediting Council for Independent Colleges and Schools

Programs Offered: CAD/CADD drafting/design technology; computer engineering technology; computer software and media applications; computer systems networking and telecommunications; digital

communication and media/multimedia; technology management; web/multimedia management and webmaster

Enrollment: 442 students

Institution Contact: Ms. Lillian Williams-McClain, Director *Phone:* 708-747-2571

Admission Contact: Ms. Lillian Wiliams-McClain, Director *Phone:* 708-747-2571

See full description on page 432.

ITT Technical Institute (A)

1401 Feehanville Drive
Mount Prospect, IL 60056
Web: http://www.itt-tech.edu

Accreditation: Accrediting Council for Independent Colleges and Schools

Programs Offered: CAD/CADD drafting/design technology; computer and information systems security; computer engineering technology; computer software and media applications; computer systems networking and telecommunications; digital communication and media/multimedia; electrical, electronic and communications engineering technology; technology management; web page, digital/multimedia and information resources design

Enrollment: 561 students

Institution Contact: Mr. Elvis Parker, Director *Phone:* 847-375-8800

Admission Contact: Mr. Ernest Lloyd, Director of Recruitment *Phone:* 847-375-8800

See full description on page 433.

Lincoln Technical Institute (A)

8317 West North Avenue
Melrose Park, IL 60160
Web: http://www.lincolntech.com

Accreditation: Accrediting Commission of Career Schools and Colleges of Technology

Programs Offered: automobile/automotive mechanics technology; electrical/electronics equipment installation and repair; medical/clinical assistant

Enrollment: 1,065 students

Institution Contact: Ms. Helen M. Carver, Executive Director *Phone:* 708-344-4700 *Fax:* 708-345-4065 *E-mail:* hcarver@lincolntech.com

Admission Contact: Mr. Joseph Painter, Director of Admissions *Phone:* 708-344-4700 *Fax:* 708-345-4065 *E-mail:* jpainter@lincolntech.com

See full description on page 434.

(A) indicates that the school is a participating institution in the *Imagine America* Scholarship Program.

Olympia College (A)

6880 North Frontage Road, Suite 400
Burr Ridge, IL 60527
Web: http://www.olympia-college.com

Accreditation: Accrediting Commission of Career Schools and Colleges of Technology

Programs Offered: massage therapy; medical administrative assistant and medical secretary; medical/clinical assistant

Enrollment: 550 students

Institution Contact: Mr. David Profita, Director of Admissions *Phone:* 630-920-1102 *Fax:* 630-920-9012 *E-mail:* dprofita@cci.edu

See full description on page 435.

Olympia College (A)

247 South State Street, Suite 400
Chicago, IL 60604
Web: http://www.olympia-college.com

Accreditation: Accrediting Commission of Career Schools and Colleges of Technology

Programs Offered: massage therapy; medical administrative assistant and medical secretary; medical/clinical assistant; pharmacy technician

Institution Contact: Nikee Carnagey, Director of Admissions *Phone:* 312-913-1616 *Fax:* 312-913-9422 *E-mail:* ncarnage@cci.edu

See full description on page 436.

Olympia College (A)

9811 Woods Drive, Second Floor
Skokie, IL 60077
Web: http://www.olympia-college.com

Accreditation: Accrediting Commission of Career Schools and Colleges of Technology

Programs Offered: massage therapy; medical/clinical assistant; medical insurance coding; medical insurance/medical billing

Enrollment: 588 students

Institution Contact: Mr. Mark E. Sullivan, President *Phone:* 847-470-0277 *Fax:* 847-470-0266 *E-mail:* msulliva@cci.edu

Admission Contact: Ms. Romona Ewing, Director of Admissions *Phone:* 847-470-0277 *Fax:* 847-470-0266 *E-mail:* rewing@cci.edu

See full description on page 437.

Rockford Business College

730 North Church Street
Rockford, IL 61103
Web: http://www.rockfordbusinesscollege.edu

Accreditation: Accrediting Council for Independent Colleges and Schools

Programs Offered: accounting; administrative assistant and secretarial science; business administration and management; computer/information technology administration and management; computer/information technology services administration related; computer installation and repair technology; computer programming; computer systems networking and telecommunications; data processing and data processing technology; executive assistant/executive secretary; legal administrative assistant/secretary; legal assistant/paralegal; marketing/marketing management; medical/clinical assistant; medical transcription; office occupations and clerical services

Enrollment: 513 students

Institution Contact: Miss Barbara Holliman, President *Phone:* 815-965-8616 ext. 223 *Fax:* 815-965-0360 *E-mail:* bholliman@rbcsuccess.com

Admission Contact: Mr. Manuel Carrasquillo, Director of Enrollment *Phone:* 815-965-8616 ext. 263 *Fax:* 815-965-0360 *E-mail:* cmanuel@rbcsuccess.com

Sanford-Brown College

1101 Eastport Plaza Drive
Collinsville, IL 62234
Web: http://www.sanford-brown.com

Accreditation: Accrediting Bureau of Health Education Schools; Accrediting Council for Independent Colleges and Schools

Programs Offered: accounting and business/management; business administration and management; computer/technical support; massage therapy; medical/clinical assistant; medical insurance coding

Enrollment: 415 students

Institution Contact: Ms. Carole Underwood, Executive Director *Phone:* 618-344-5600 *Fax:* 618-421-5256 *E-mail:* cunderwood@sbc-collinsville.com

Admission Contact: Ms. Ladon Harris, Director of Admissions *Phone:* 618-344-5600 *Fax:* 618-421-5256 *E-mail:* lharris@sbc-collinsville.com

The Soma Institute, The National School of Clinical Massage Therapy

14 East Jackson Boulevard, Suite 1300
Chicago, IL 60604
Web: http://www.thesomainstitute.com

Accreditation: Accrediting Council for Continuing Education and Training

(A) indicates that the school is a participating institution in the *Imagine America* Scholarship Program.

Programs Offered: massage therapy

Enrollment: 330 students

Institution Contact: Dr. Helen J. Robinson, Vice President, Compliance *Phone:* 312-939-2723 ext. 18 *Fax:* 312-939-0171 *E-mail:* hjrobinson@thesomainstitute.com

Admission Contact: Ms. Tilda Williams, Admissions Assistant *Phone:* 312-939-2723 ext. 10 *Fax:* 312-939-0171 *E-mail:* info@thesomainstitute.com

Universal Technical Institute, Inc. Ⓐ

601 Regency Drive
Glendale Heights, IL 60139
Web: http://www.uticorp.com

Accreditation: Accrediting Commission of Career Schools and Colleges of Technology

Programs Offered: automobile/automotive mechanics technology; diesel mechanics technology

Institution Contact: Mr. Karl Lewandowski, Director *Phone:* 630-529-2662 *Fax:* 630-529-7567 *E-mail:* karllewandowski@uticorp.com

Admission Contact: Mr. Alan Schultz, Admissions Director *Phone:* 800-441-4248 *Fax:* 630-529-7567 *E-mail:* aschultz@uticorp.com

See full description on page 438.

Vatterott College Ⓐ

501 North 3rd Street
Quincy, IL 62301
Web: http://www.vatterott-college.edu

Accreditation: Accrediting Commission of Career Schools and Colleges of Technology

Programs Offered: CAD/CADD drafting/design technology; computer technology/computer systems technology; data entry/microcomputer applications; electrician; heating, air conditioning, ventilation and refrigeration maintenance technology; medical/clinical assistant

Enrollment: 200 students

Institution Contact: Ms. Katrina L. Houser, Director *Phone:* 217-224-0600 *Fax:* 217-223-6771 *E-mail:* khouser@vatterott-college.edu

Admission Contact: Mr. David A. Stickney, Director of Admissions *Phone:* 217-224-0600 *Fax:* 217-223-6771 *E-mail:* vattqcy@adams.net

See full description on page 439.

Westwood College–Chicago Du Page Ⓐ

7155 Janes Avenue
Woodridge, IL 60517
Web: http://www.westwood.edu

Accreditation: Accrediting Council for Independent Colleges and Schools

Programs Offered: animation, interactive technology, video graphics and special effects; business administration and management; CAD/CADD drafting/design technology; commercial and advertising art; computer and information systems security; computer graphics; computer software and media applications; computer software engineering; computer systems networking and telecommunications; criminal justice/law enforcement administration; graphic communications; interior design; web page, digital/multimedia and information resources design

Enrollment: 626 students

Institution Contact: Kelly Thumm Moore, Executive Director *Phone:* 630-434-8244 ext. 200 *Fax:* 630-434-8255 *E-mail:* kmoore@westwood.edu

Admission Contact: Scott Kawall, Director of Admissions *Phone:* 630-434-8244 ext. 100 *Fax:* 630-434-8255 *E-mail:* skawall@westwood.edu

See full description on page 442.

Westwood College–Chicago Loop Campus Ⓐ

17 North State Street, Suite 300
Chicago, IL 60602
Web: http://www.westwood.edu

Accreditation: Accrediting Council for Independent Colleges and Schools

Programs Offered: animation, interactive technology, video graphics and special effects; architectural drafting and CAD/CADD; CAD/CADD drafting/design technology; commercial and advertising art; computer/information technology administration and management; computer software engineering; computer systems networking and telecommunications; criminal justice/police science; design and visual communications; e-commerce; interior design; internet information systems; marketing/marketing management; marketing related; web page, digital/multimedia and information resources design

Enrollment: 300 students

Institution Contact: Ms. Jeanne Glielmi, Executive Assistant *Phone:* 312-739-0850 ext. 10201 *Fax:* 312-739-1004 *E-mail:* jglielmi@westwood.edu

Admission Contact: Mr. Bruce E. Jones, Director of Admissions *Phone:* 312-739-0850 ext. 10100 *Fax:* 312-739-1004 *E-mail:* bjones@westwood.edu

See full description on page 440.

Ⓐ indicates that the school is a participating institution in the *Imagine America* Scholarship Program.

Westwood College—Chicago O'Hare Airport ⓐ

8501 West Higgins Road, Suite 100
Chicago, IL 60631
Web: http://www.westwood.edu

Accreditation: Accrediting Commission of Career Schools and Colleges of Technology; Accrediting Council for Independent Colleges and Schools

Programs Offered: advertising; business administration and management; business, management, and marketing related; CAD/CADD drafting/design technology; commercial and advertising art; computer engineering technology; computer programming; computer software technology; corrections; criminal justice/law enforcement administration; criminal justice/police science; drafting and design technology; interior design; intermedia/multimedia; medical administrative assistant and medical secretary; system, networking, and LAN/WAN management; technology management

Enrollment: 510 students

Institution Contact: Mr. Lou Pagano, Executive Director *Phone:* 877-877-8857 ext. 201 *E-mail:* lpagano@westwood.edu

Admission Contact: Mr. David Traub *Phone:* 877-877-8857 ext. 100 *E-mail:* dtraub@westwood.edu

See full description on page 441.

Westwood College—Chicago River Oaks ⓐ

80 River Oaks Center, Suite 111
Calumet City, IL 60409
Web: http://www.westwood.edu

Accreditation: Accrediting Council for Independent Colleges and Schools

Programs Offered: allied health and medical assisting services related; animation, interactive technology, video graphics and special effects; architectural drafting and CAD/CADD; CAD/CADD drafting/design technology; computer and information systems security; computer engineering related; computer engineering technology; criminal justice/law enforcement administration; e-commerce; system, networking, and LAN/WAN management; technology management

Enrollment: 600 students

Institution Contact: Mr. Bruce McKenzie, Executive Director *Phone:* 708-832-1988 ext. 200 *Fax:* 708-832-6525 *E-mail:* bmckenzie@westwood.edu

Admission Contact: Mr. Tash Uray, Director of Admissions *Phone:* 708-832-1988 ext. 100 *Fax:* 708-832-9342 *E-mail:* turay@westwood.edu

See full description on page 443.

Indiana

Commonwealth Business College

1000 East 80th Place, Suite 101 North
Merrillville, IN 46410

Accreditation: Accrediting Bureau of Health Education Schools; Accrediting Council for Independent Colleges and Schools

Programs Offered: accounting; CAD/CADD drafting/design technology; computer programming; computer/technical support; criminal justice/law enforcement administration; legal assistant/paralegal; medical/clinical assistant

Institution Contact: Mrs. Sheryl Elston, Director of Admissions *Phone:* 219-769-3321 *Fax:* 219-738-1076 *E-mail:* selston@amedcts.com

Commonwealth Business College

325 East US Highway 20
Michigan City, IN 46360

Accreditation: Accrediting Bureau of Health Education Schools; Accrediting Council for Independent Colleges and Schools

Programs Offered: accounting; CAD/CADD drafting/design technology; computer programming; computer/technical support; criminal justice/law enforcement administration; legal assistant/paralegal; medical/clinical assistant

Institution Contact: Mrs. Sheryl L. Elston, Director of Admissions *Phone:* 219-769-3321 *Fax:* 219-738-1076 *E-mail:* selston@amedcts.com

Decker College

6825 Hillsdale Court
Indianapolis, IN 46250
Web: http://www.deckercollege.com

Accreditation: Council on Occupational Education

Programs Offered: accounting; computer and information sciences related; computer systems networking and telecommunications; finance; medical office computer specialist

Institution Contact: *Phone:* 800-333-9844 *E-mail:* admissions@deckercollege.com

ⓐ indicates that the school is a participating institution in the *Imagine America* Scholarship Program.

Indiana Business College (A)

140 East 53rd Street
Anderson, IN 46013-1717
Web: http://www.ibcschools.edu

Accreditation: Accrediting Council for Independent Colleges and Schools

Programs Offered: accounting; administrative assistant and secretarial science; business administration and management; medical/clinical assistant; medical insurance coding; medical insurance/medical billing

Institution Contact: Ms. Charlene Stacy, Executive Director *Phone:* 765-644-7514 *Fax:* 765-644-5724

See full description on page 444.

Indiana Business College (A)

2222 Poshard Drive
Columbus, IN 47203
Web: http://www.ibcschools.edu

Accreditation: Accrediting Council for Independent Colleges and Schools

Programs Offered: accounting; administrative assistant and secretarial science; business administration and management; computer/technical support; information technology; medical/clinical assistant; medical insurance coding; medical insurance/medical billing

Institution Contact: Angela Rentmeesters, Assistant Executive Director *Phone:* 812-379-9000 *Fax:* 812-375-0414

See full description on page 445.

Indiana Business College (A)

4601 Theater Drive
Evansville, IN 47715
Web: http://www.ibcschools.edu

Accreditation: Accrediting Council for Independent Colleges and Schools

Programs Offered: accounting; administrative assistant and secretarial science; business administration and management; health/medical claims examination; information technology; medical administrative assistant and medical secretary; medical/clinical assistant; medical insurance coding; medical insurance/medical billing

Institution Contact: Mr. Steve Hardin, Executive Director *Phone:* 812-476-6000 *Fax:* 812-471-8576

See full description on page 446.

Indiana Business College (A)

6413 North Clinton Street
Fort Wayne, IN 46825
Web: http://www.ibcschools.edu

Accreditation: Accrediting Council for Independent Colleges and Schools

Programs Offered: accounting; administrative assistant and secretarial science; business administration and management; medical/clinical assistant; medical insurance coding; medical insurance/medical billing; medical office assistant; surgical technology

Institution Contact: Ms. Janet Hein, Executive Director *Phone:* 219-471-7667 *Fax:* 219-471-6918

See full description on page 447.

Indiana Business College (A)

550 East Washington Street
Indianapolis, IN 46204
Web: http://www.ibcschools.edu

Accreditation: Accrediting Council for Independent Colleges and Schools

Programs Offered: accounting; administrative assistant and secretarial science; business administration and management; communications systems installation and repair technology; computer/information technology services administration related; computer installation and repair technology; computer/technical support; fashion merchandising; information technology; legal administrative assistant/secretary; medical transcription

Institution Contact: Pat Mozley, Executive Director *Phone:* 317-264-5656 *Fax:* 317-264-5640

See full description on page 448.

Indiana Business College (A)

2 Executive Drive
Lafayette, IN 47905-4859
Web: http://www.ibcschools.edu

Accreditation: Accrediting Council for Independent Colleges and Schools

Programs Offered: accounting; administrative assistant and secretarial science; business administration and management; information technology

Institution Contact: Mr. Gregory P. Reger, Executive Director *Phone:* 765-447-9550 *Fax:* 765-447-0868

See full description on page 450.

Indiana Business College (A)

830 North Miller Avenue
Marion, IN 46952
Web: http://www.ibcschools.edu

Accreditation: Accrediting Council for Independent Colleges and Schools

(A) indicates that the school is a participating institution in the *Imagine America* Scholarship Program.

Indiana Business College *(continued)*

Programs Offered: accounting; administrative assistant and secretarial science; business administration and management; health information/medical records technology; medical insurance coding

Institution Contact: Mr. Richard Herman, Executive Director *Phone:* 765-662-7497 *Fax:* 765-651-9421

See full description on page 451.

Indiana Business College (A)

411 West Riggin Road
Muncie, IN 47303-6413
Web: http://www.ibcschools.edu

Accreditation: Accrediting Council for Independent Colleges and Schools

Programs Offered: accounting; administrative assistant and secretarial science; business administration and management; computer/technical support; health information/medical records technology; information technology; medical/clinical assistant; medical insurance coding

Institution Contact: Mr. Greg Bond, Executive Director *Phone:* 765-288-6413 *Fax:* 765-288-8797

See full description on page 452.

Indiana Business College (A)

3175 South Third Place
Terre Haute, IN 47802
Web: http://www.ibcschools.edu

Accreditation: Accrediting Council for Independent Colleges and Schools

Programs Offered: accounting; administrative assistant and secretarial science; business administration and management; computer systems networking and telecommunications; health information/medical records technology; medical/clinical assistant; medical insurance coding; medical insurance/medical billing

Institution Contact: Ms. Laura Hale, Executive Director *Phone:* 812-232-4458 *Fax:* 812-234-2361

See full description on page 453.

Indiana Business College-Medical (A)

8150 Brookville Road
Indianapolis, IN 46239
Web: http://www.ibcschools.com

Accreditation: Accrediting Council for Independent Colleges and Schools

Programs Offered: health information/medical records administration; health information/medical records technology; health/medical claims examination; massage therapy; medical administrative assistant and medical secretary; medical/clinical assistant; medical insurance coding; medical transcription

Institution Contact: Mr. Rod Allee, Director of Admissions *Phone:* 317-375-8000 *Fax:* 317-351-1871

See full description on page 449.

International Business College

5699 Coventry Lane
Fort Wayne, IN 46804
Web: http://www.ibcfortwayne.edu

Accreditation: Accrediting Council for Independent Colleges and Schools

Programs Offered: accounting; administrative assistant and secretarial science; business administration and management; commercial and advertising art; computer programming; finance; hospitality administration; industrial technology; legal administrative assistant/secretary; legal assistant/paralegal; medical/clinical assistant; retailing; tourism and travel services management

Enrollment: 575 students

Institution Contact: Mr. Jim Zillman, President *Phone:* 219-459-4555 *Fax:* 219-436-1896 *E-mail:* jzillman@ibcfortwayne.edu

Admission Contact: Mr. Steve M. Kinzer, Director *Phone:* 219-459-4513 *Fax:* 219-436-1896 *E-mail:* skinzer@ibcfortwayne.edu

International Business College

7205 Shadeland Station
Indianapolis, IN 46256
Web: http://www.intlbusinesscollege.com/

Accreditation: Accrediting Council for Independent Colleges and Schools

Programs Offered: accounting; administrative assistant and secretarial science; commercial and advertising art; computer programming; computer software and media applications related; data entry/microcomputer applications; graphic and printing equipment operation/production; legal administrative assistant/secretary; legal assistant/paralegal; medical/clinical assistant; tourism and travel services management

Enrollment: 337 students

Institution Contact: Ms. Kathy Chivdioni, Director *Phone:* 317-841-6400 *Fax:* 317-841-6419 *E-mail:* info@ibcindianapolis.edu

(A) indicates that the school is a participating institution in the *Imagine America* Scholarship Program.

ITT Technical Institute Ⓐ

4919 Coldwater Road
Fort Wayne, IN 46825-5532
Web: http://www.itt-tech.edu

Accreditation: Accrediting Council for Independent Colleges and Schools

Programs Offered: accounting and business/management; animation, interactive technology, video graphics and special effects; business administration and management; CAD/CADD drafting/design technology; communications technology; computer and information systems security; computer engineering technology; computer software and media applications; computer software engineering; computer systems networking and telecommunications; criminal justice/police science; digital communication and media/multimedia; electrical, electronic and communications engineering technology; industrial technology; technology management; web page, digital/multimedia and information resources design

Enrollment: 538 students

Institution Contact: Alois Johnson, Director *Phone:* 219-484-4107 ext. 244

Admission Contact: Mr. Michael D. Frantom, Director of Recruitment *Phone:* 219-484-4107

See full description on page 454.

ITT Technical Institute Ⓐ

9511 Angola Court
Indianapolis, IN 46268-1119
Web: http://www.itt-tech.edu

Accreditation: Accrediting Council for Independent Colleges and Schools

Programs Offered: accounting and business/management; animation, interactive technology, video graphics and special effects; business administration and management; CAD/CADD drafting/design technology; communications technology; computer and information systems security; computer engineering technology; computer software and media applications; computer software engineering; computer systems networking and telecommunications; criminal justice/police science; digital communication and media/multimedia; electrical, electronic and communications engineering technology; industrial technology; technology management; web page, digital/multimedia and information resources design

Enrollment: 878 students

Institution Contact: Mr. James Horner, Director *Phone:* 317-875-8640 *Fax:* 317-875-8641 *E-mail:* jhorner@itt-tech.edu

Admission Contact: Martha Watson, Director of Recruitment *Phone:* 317-875-8640 *Fax:* 317-875-8641

See full description on page 455.

ITT Technical Institute Ⓐ

10999 Stahl Road
Newburgh, IN 47630-7430
Web: http://www.itt-tech.edu

Accreditation: Accrediting Council for Independent Colleges and Schools

Programs Offered: animation, interactive technology, video graphics and special effects; CAD/CADD drafting/design technology; communications technology; computer and information systems security; computer engineering technology; computer software and media applications; computer software engineering; computer systems networking and telecommunications; digital communication and media/multimedia; electrical, electronic and communications engineering technology; industrial technology; technology management; web page, digital/multimedia and information resources design

Enrollment: 394 students

Institution Contact: Mr. Ken Butler, Director *Phone:* 812-858-1600

Admission Contact: Mr. Tom Campbell, Director of Recruitment *Phone:* 812-858-1600

See full description on page 456.

Lincoln Technical Institute Ⓐ

7225 Winton Drive, Building 128
Indianapolis, IN 46268
Web: http://www.lincolntech.com

Accreditation: Accrediting Commission of Career Schools and Colleges of Technology

Programs Offered: architectural drafting and CAD/CADD; automobile/automotive mechanics technology; automotive engineering technology; diesel mechanics technology; electrical and electronic engineering technologies related; mechanical drafting and CAD/CADD

Institution Contact: Director of Admissions *Phone:* 317-632-5553 *Fax:* 317-687-0475 *E-mail:* doaindy@lincolnedu.com

See full description on page 457.

MedTech College

6612 East 75th Street, Suite 300
Indianapolis, IN 46250
Web: http://www.medtechcollege.com

Accreditation: Accrediting Council for Independent Colleges and Schools

Programs Offered: massage therapy; medical/clinical assistant; medical insurance coding

Enrollment: 70 students

Ⓐ indicates that the school is a participating institution in the *Imagine America* Scholarship Program.

MedTech College (continued)

Institution Contact: Mr. Joe Davis, President Phone: 317-845-0100 ext. 207 Fax: 317-845-1800 E-mail: jdavis@medtechcollege.com

Admission Contact: Ms. Cindy Andrews, Executive Vice President of Marketing and Recruitment Phone: 317-845-0100 ext. 202 Fax: 317-845-1800 E-mail: candrews@medtechcollege.com

Michiana College

4422 East State Boulevard
Fort Wayne, IN 46815
Web: http://www.michianacollege.com/

Programs Offered: business administration and management; CAD/CADD drafting/design technology; computer and information sciences related; pre-law studies

Institution Contact: Phone: 888-300-6802

Michiana College

1030 East Jefferson Boulevard
South Bend, IN 46617
Web: http://www.michianacollege.com

Accreditation: Accrediting Council for Independent Colleges and Schools

Programs Offered: accounting; business administration and management; CAD/CADD drafting/design technology; computer installation and repair technology; computer programming; computer software technology; computer systems networking and telecommunications; criminal justice/law enforcement administration; legal assistant/paralegal; medical/clinical assistant; occupational therapist assistant; physical therapist assistant

Institution Contact: Ms. Connie S. Adelman, Campus Director Phone: 574-237-0774 Fax: 574-237-3585 E-mail: cadelman@amedcts.com

Admission Contact: Ms. Laurie Johannesen-Oliver, Director of Admissions Phone: 574-237-0774 Fax: 574-237-3585 E-mail: ljohannesen@amedcts.com

Olympia College Ⓐ

707 East 80th Place, Suite 200
Merrillville, IN 46410
Web: http://www.olympia-college.com

Accreditation: Accrediting Bureau of Health Education Schools

Programs Offered: massage therapy; medical administrative assistant and medical secretary; medical/

clinical assistant; nursing (licensed practical/vocational nurse training); surgical technology

Institution Contact: Sandy Kaup, Director of Admissions Phone: 219-756-6811 E-mail: skaup@cci.edu

See full description on page 458.

Professional Careers Institute Ⓐ

7302 Woodland Drive
Indianapolis, IN 46278-1736
Web: http://www.pcicareers.com

Accreditation: Accrediting Commission of Career Schools and Colleges of Technology

Programs Offered: administrative assistant and secretarial science; computer/information technology administration and management; computer programming; computer programming (specific applications); dental assisting; legal assistant/paralegal; massage therapy; medical administrative assistant and medical secretary; medical/clinical assistant; medical office management

Enrollment: 500 students

Institution Contact: Mr. Richard Weiss, President Phone: 317-299-6001 Fax: 317-298-6342 E-mail: rick.weiss@pcicareers.com

See full description on page 459.

Sawyer College

3803 East Lincoln Highway
Merrillville, IN 46410

Accreditation: Accrediting Council for Independent Colleges and Schools

Programs Offered: accounting; administrative assistant and secretarial science; computer engineering technology; computer hardware engineering; computer programming; computer software and media applications; computer/technical support; data processing and data processing technology; executive assistant/executive secretary; health/health care administration; hospital and health care facilities administration; legal administrative assistant/secretary; massage therapy; medical/clinical assistant; medical office computer specialist

Institution Contact: Mrs. Mary Jo Dixon, President Phone: 219-736-0436 Fax: 219-942-3762 E-mail: mary.j.dixon@att.net

Admission Contact: Mrs. Linda J. Yednak, Director of Operations Phone: 219-736-0436 Fax: 219-942-3762 E-mail: lyednak@sawyercollege.edu

Ⓐ indicates that the school is a participating institution in the *Imagine America* Scholarship Program.

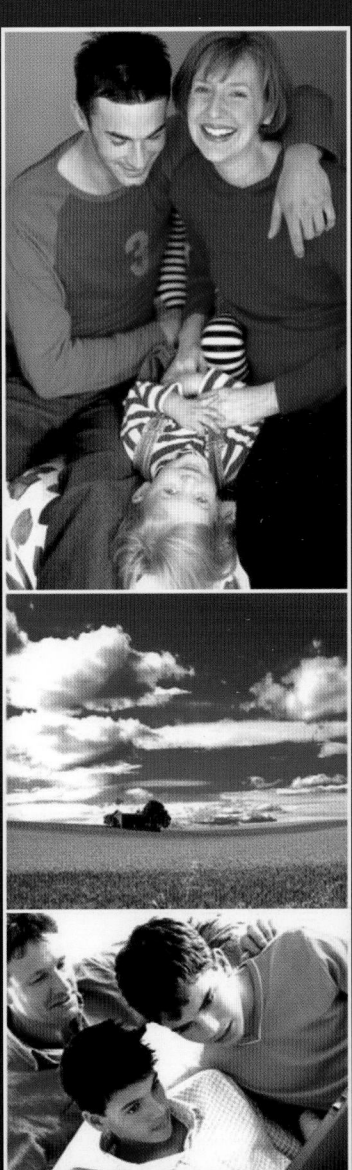

Iowa

Hamilton College

3165 Edgewood Parkway, SW
Cedar Rapids, IA 52404
Web: http://www.hamiltonia.edu

Accreditation: North Central Association of Colleges and Schools

Programs Offered: accounting; administrative assistant and secretarial science; business administration and management; computer systems networking and telecommunications; computer/technical support; criminal justice/law enforcement administration; information science/studies; medical/clinical assistant; medical transcription; multi-/interdisciplinary studies related; tourism and travel services management

Institution Contact: Lori L. Canning, Bookstore Manager *Phone:* 319-363-0481 *Fax:* 319-363-3812 *E-mail:* canningl@hamiltonia.edu

Admission Contact: Mr. Brad Knudson, Director of Admissions *Phone:* 319-363-0481 *Fax:* 319-363-3812 *E-mail:* knudsobr@hamiltonia.edu

Kaplan College

1801 East Kimberly Road, Suite 1
Davenport, IA 52807
Web: http://www.kaplancollegeia.com

Accreditation: North Central Association of Colleges and Schools

Programs Offered: accounting; business administration and management; computer programming; computer systems analysis; computer/technical support; criminal justice/law enforcement administration; data modeling/warehousing and database administration; legal assistant/paralegal; medical/clinical assistant; medical transcription; system, networking, and LAN/WAN management; tourism and travel services management; web/multimedia management and webmaster

Enrollment: 750 students

Institution Contact: Ms. Judy M. Howard, Assistant to the Executive Director *Phone:* 563-441-2492 *Fax:* 563-355-1320 *E-mail:* judy@kaplancollegeia.com

Admission Contact: Mr. Robert Hoffmann, Director of Admissions *Phone:* 563-441-2496 *Fax:* 563-355-1320 *E-mail:* hoffmanro@kaplancollegeia.edu

Vatterott College

6100 Thornton, Suite 290
Des Moines, IA 50321
Web: http://www.vatterott-college.edu

Accreditation: Accrediting Commission of Career Schools and Colleges of Technology

Programs Offered: CAD/CADD drafting/design technology; computer programming; computer systems networking and telecommunications; dental assisting; drafting and design technology; information science/studies; medical office computer specialist

Enrollment: 168 students

Institution Contact: Mr. Henry Franken, Co-Director *Phone:* 515-309-9000 *Fax:* 515-309-0366 *E-mail:* hfranken@vatterott-college.edu

Admission Contact: Ms. Jodi Clendenen, Co-Director *Phone:* 515-309-9000 *Fax:* 515-309-0336 *E-mail:* jclendenen@vatterott-college.edu

See full description on page 460.

Kansas

The Brown Mackie College

2106 South 9th Street
Salina, KS 67401

Programs Offered: business administration and management; computer and information sciences related

Institution Contact: *Phone:* 888-242-2971

The Brown Mackie College–Lenexa Campus

9705 Lenexa Drive
Lenexa, KS 66215
Web: http://www.bmcaec.com

Accreditation: North Central Association of Colleges and Schools

Programs Offered: accounting; accounting technology and bookkeeping; business administration and management; CAD/CADD drafting/design technology; computer engineering technology; computer programming (specific applications); computer software and media applications; computer systems networking and telecommunications; criminal justice/law enforcement administration; criminal justice/police science; data processing and data

Ⓐ indicates that the school is a participating institution in the *Imagine America* Scholarship Program.

The Brown Mackie College–Lenexa Campus (continued)

processing technology; electrical/electronics equipment installation and repair; legal administrative assistant/secretary; legal assistant/paralegal; medical/clinical assistant; medical office management; pre-law studies; system, networking, and LAN/WAN management

Institution Contact: Mr. Richard M. Thome, President *Phone:* 913-768-1900 *Fax:* 913-495-9555 *E-mail:* rthome@amedcts.com

Admission Contact: Ms. Julia M. Denniston, Director of Admissions *Phone:* 913-768-1900 *Fax:* 913-495-9555 *E-mail:* jdenniston@amedcts.com

Bryan College

1527 SW Fairlawn Road
Topeka, KS 66604

Accreditation: Accrediting Council for Independent Colleges and Schools

Programs Offered: business administration and management; computer installation and repair technology; computer programming; medical/clinical assistant; medical office assistant; tourism and travel services marketing

Enrollment: 135 students

Institution Contact: Mrs. Rebecca A. Cox, Executive Director *Phone:* 785-272-0889 *Fax:* 785-272-4538 *E-mail:* bcox@bryancc.com

Admission Contact: Mrs. Angela Tyroler, Director of Admissions *Phone:* 785-272-0889 *Fax:* 785-272-4538 *E-mail:* atyroler@bryancc.com

National American University

10310 Mastin
Overland Park, KS 66212
Web: http://www.national.edu

Accreditation: North Central Association of Colleges and Schools

Programs Offered: accounting; accounting and business/management; business administration and management; business, management, and marketing related; information technology; legal assistant/paralegal; medical administrative assistant and medical secretary; medical/clinical assistant; medical office assistant

Enrollment: 150 students

Institution Contact: Ms. Mari Jane O'Donnell, Director of Admissions *Phone:* 913-217-2900 *Fax:* 913-217-2909 *E-mail:* modonnell@national.edu

Pinnacle Career Institute (A)

1601 West 23rd Street, Suite 200
Lawrence, KS 66046
Web: http://www.pcitraining.edu

Accreditation: Accrediting Council for Independent Colleges and Schools

Programs Offered: business operations support and secretarial services related; massage therapy; medical/clinical assistant; medical office computer specialist

Institution Contact: Angie Kelso, Financial Aid Director *Phone:* 785-841-9640 ext. 203 *Fax:* 785-841-4854 *E-mail:* akelso@pcitraining.edu

Admission Contact: Karen Stewart, Admissions *Phone:* 785-841-9640 ext. 206 *Fax:* 785-841-4854 *E-mail:* kstewart@pcitrainin.edu

See full description on page 461.

Vatterott College (A)

3639 North Comotara
Wichita, KS 67226
Web: http://www.vatterott-college.edu

Accreditation: Accrediting Commission of Career Schools and Colleges of Technology

Programs Offered: CAD/CADD drafting/design technology; computer programming; computer technology/computer systems technology; electrician; heating, air conditioning and refrigeration technology; medical/clinical assistant

Institution Contact: Office of Admissions *Phone:* 316-634-0066 *Fax:* 316-634-0002 *E-mail:* wichita@vatterott-college.edu

See full description on page 462.

Wichita Technical Institute

2051 South Meridian
Wichita, KS 67213-1681
Web: http://www.wti.edu

Accreditation: Accrediting Commission of Career Schools and Colleges of Technology

Programs Offered: computer technology/computer systems technology; electrical, electronic and communications engineering technology; heating, air conditioning and refrigeration technology

Enrollment: 350 students

Institution Contact: J. Barry Mannion, Director of Administration *Phone:* 316-943-2241 *Fax:* 316-943-5438 *E-mail:* bmannion@wti.edu

Admission Contact: Chris Windham, Admissions Representative *Phone:* 316-943-2241 *Fax:* 316-943-5438 *E-mail:* cwindham@wti.edu

(A) indicates that the school is a participating institution in the *Imagine America* Scholarship Program.

WTI The Electronic School

1710 Southwest Topeka Boulevard
Topeka, KS 66612
Web: http://www.wtielectronics.com

Accreditation: Accrediting Commission of Career Schools and Colleges of Technology

Programs Offered: electrical, electronic and communications engineering technology; electrical/electronics equipment installation and repair

Institution Contact: Ms. Alisa Bowhay, Director *Phone:* 785-354-4568 *Fax:* 785-354-4541 *E-mail:* abowhay@wtielectronics.com

Admission Contact: Mr. Gary Hively, Vice President/Director of Admissions *Phone:* 785-354-4568 *Fax:* 785-354-4541 *E-mail:* ghively@wtielectronics.com

Kentucky

AEC Southern Ohio College, Northern Kentucky Campus

309 Buttermilk Pike
Fort Mitchell, KY 41017
Web: http://socaec.com

Accreditation: Accrediting Council for Independent Colleges and Schools

Programs Offered: accounting technology and bookkeeping; business administration and management; CAD/CADD drafting/design technology; computer and information sciences related; computer programming; computer software technology; criminal justice/law enforcement administration; legal assistant/paralegal; medical/clinical assistant

Enrollment: 476 students

Institution Contact: Mr. Ricky Dean Lemmel, President *Phone:* 859-341-5627 ext. 5009 *Fax:* 859-341-6483 *E-mail:* rlemmel@edmc.edu

Admission Contact: Ms. Joanne Dellefield, Director of Admissions *Phone:* 859-341-5627 *Fax:* 859-341-6483 *E-mail:* jdellefield@edmc.edu

Daymar College Ⓐ

4400 Breckenridge Lane, Suite 415
Louisville, KY 40218
Web: http://www.daymarcollege.edu

Accreditation: Accrediting Council for Independent Colleges and Schools

Programs Offered: business administration and management; computer systems networking and telecommunications; health information/medical records administration; health information/medical records technology; legal assistant/paralegal; medical transcription

Institution Contact: Mr. Patrick Carney, Director of Admissions *Phone:* 502-495-1040 *Fax:* 502-495-1518 *E-mail:* pcarney@daymarcollege.edu

See full description on page 463.

Daymar College Ⓐ

3361 Buckland Square
Owensboro, KY 42301
Web: http://www.daymarcollege.edu

Accreditation: Accrediting Council for Independent Colleges and Schools

Programs Offered: business administration and management; computer/information technology services administration related; computer software and media applications related; computer systems networking and telecommunications; e-commerce; legal assistant/paralegal; medical/clinical assistant

Institution Contact: Ms. Vickie McDougal, Director of Admissions *Phone:* 270-926-4040 *Fax:* 270-685-4090

See full description on page 464.

Decker College

981 South 3rd Street
Louisville, KY 40203

Accreditation: Council on Occupational Education

Programs Offered: computer/information technology administration and management; legal assistant/paralegal; medical office assistant

Enrollment: 368 students

Institution Contact: Gay St. Mary, Dean of Operations/Campus Director *Phone:* 502-583-2860 *Fax:* 502-583-5800 *E-mail:* gstmary@deckercollege.com

Admission Contact: Kenneth Washington, Director of Admissions *Phone:* 502-583-6900 *Fax:* 502-583-5800 *E-mail:* kwashington@deckercollege.com

Draughons Junior College Ⓐ

2421 Fitzgerald Industrial Drive
Bowling Green, KY 42101
Web: http://www.draughons.edu

Accreditation: Accrediting Council for Independent Colleges and Schools

Programs Offered: accounting; business administration and management; computer/information technol-

---

Ⓐ indicates that the school is a participating institution in the *Imagine America* Scholarship Program.

Draughons Junior College (*continued*)

ogy administration and management; computer technology/computer systems technology; criminal justice/law enforcement administration; e-commerce; health/health care administration; legal assistant/paralegal; medical/clinical assistant; pharmacy technician

Enrollment: 450 students

Institution Contact: Mrs. Melva P. Hale, Director *Phone:* 270-843-6750 *Fax:* 270-843-6976 *E-mail:* mhale@draughons.edu

Admission Contact: Mrs. Amye Melton, Director of Admissions *Phone:* 270-843-6750 *Fax:* 270-843-6976 *E-mail:* amelton@draughons.edu

See full description on page 465.

ITT Technical Institute (A)

10509 Timberwood Circle, Suite 100
Louisville, KY 40223-5392
Web: http://www.itt-tech.edu

Accreditation: Accrediting Council for Independent Colleges and Schools

Programs Offered: accounting and business/management; animation, interactive technology, video graphics and special effects; business administration and management; CAD/CADD drafting/design technology; communications technology; computer and information systems security; computer engineering technology; computer software and media applications; computer software engineering; computer systems networking and telecommunications; criminal justice/police science; digital communication and media/multimedia; electrical, electronic and communications engineering technology; technology management; web page, digital/multimedia and information resources design

Enrollment: 633 students

Institution Contact: Mr. Alan Crews, Director *Phone:* 502-327-7424

Admission Contact: Mr. Steve Allen, Director of Recruitment *Phone:* 502-327-7424

See full description on page 466.

Louisville Technical Institute (A)

3901 Atkinson Square Drive
Louisville, KY 40218-4528
Web: http://www.louisvilletech.com

Accreditation: Accrediting Council for Independent Colleges and Schools

Programs Offered: animation, interactive technology, video graphics and special effects; architectural

drafting and CAD/CADD; architectural engineering technology; CAD/CADD drafting/design technology; commercial and advertising art; computer and information systems security; computer engineering related; computer engineering technology; computer graphics; computer/information technology administration and management; computer/information technology services administration related; computer installation and repair technology; computer systems networking and telecommunications; computer/technical support; computer technology/computer systems technology; design and visual communications; desktop publishing and digital imaging design; drafting and design technology; drafting/design engineering technologies related; drawing; electrical and electronic engineering technologies related; electrical/electronics equipment installation and repair; engineering technology; graphic communications; hydraulics and fluid power technology; industrial design; industrial electronics technology; industrial mechanics and maintenance technology; industrial technology; information technology; instrumentation technology; interior design; intermedia/multimedia; internet information systems; marine maintenance and ship repair technology; mechanical design technology; mechanical drafting and CAD/CADD; mechanical engineering/mechanical technology; mechanical engineering technologies related; robotics technology; web/multimedia management and webmaster; web page, digital/multimedia and information resources design

Enrollment: 630 students

Institution Contact: Mr. David B. Keene, Executive Director *Phone:* 502-456-6509 *Fax:* 502-456-2341 *E-mail:* dkeene@louisvilletech.com

Admission Contact: Mr. David Ritz, Director of Admissions *Phone:* 502-456-6509 *Fax:* 502-456-2341 *E-mail:* dritz@louisvilletech.com

See full description on page 467.

National College of Business & Technology (A)

115 East Lexington Avenue
Danville, KY 40422
Web: http://www.ncbt.edu

Accreditation: Accrediting Council for Independent Colleges and Schools

Programs Offered: accounting; administrative assistant and secretarial science; business administration and management; computer and information sciences related; medical/clinical assistant; medical insurance coding; medical transcription

Institution Contact: Admissions Department *Phone:* 859-236-6991 *Fax:* 859-236-1063

See full description on page 468.

(A) indicates that the school is a participating institution in the *Imagine America* Scholarship Program.

National College of Business & Technology Ⓐ

7627 Ewing Boulevard
Florence, KY 41042
Web: http://www.ncbt.edu

Accreditation: Accrediting Council for Independent Colleges and Schools

Programs Offered: accounting; administrative assistant and secretarial science; business administration and management; computer and information sciences related; medical/clinical assistant; medical insurance coding; medical transcription; pharmacy technician

Institution Contact: Admissions Department *Phone:* 859-525-6510 *Fax:* 859-525-8961

See full description on page 469.

National College of Business & Technology Ⓐ

628 East Main Street
Lexington, KY 40508
Web: http://www.ncbt.edu

Accreditation: Accrediting Council for Independent Colleges and Schools

Programs Offered: accounting; administrative assistant and secretarial science; business administration and management; computer and information sciences related; executive assistant/executive secretary; legal administrative assistant/secretary; medical administrative assistant and medical secretary; medical/clinical assistant; medical insurance coding; medical transcription; pharmacy technician

Enrollment: 325 students

Institution Contact: Ms. Tracy Harris, Director of Institutional Reporting *Phone:* 540-986-1800 *Fax:* 540-444-4198 *E-mail:* tharris@ncbt.edu

Admission Contact: Ms. Carolyn Howard *Phone:* 859-253-0621 *Fax:* 859-233-3054 *E-mail:* choward@educorp.edu

See full description on page 470.

National College of Business & Technology Ⓐ

4205 Dixie Highway
Louisville, KY 40216
Web: http://www.ncbt.edu

Accreditation: Accrediting Council for Independent Colleges and Schools

Programs Offered: accounting; business administration and management; computer and information

sciences related; health information/medical records technology; medical administrative assistant and medical secretary; medical/clinical assistant; medical insurance coding; medical transcription; pharmacy technician

Institution Contact: Admissions Department *Phone:* 502-447-7634 *Fax:* 502-447-7665

See full description on page 471.

National College of Business & Technology Ⓐ

288 South Mayo Trail, Suite 2
Pikeville, KY 41501
Web: http://www.ncbt.edu

Accreditation: Accrediting Council for Independent Colleges and Schools

Programs Offered: accounting; administrative assistant and secretarial science; business administration and management; computer and information sciences related; medical/clinical assistant; medical insurance coding; medical transcription; pharmacy technician

Enrollment: 225 students

Institution Contact: Ms. Tracy Harris, Director of Institutional Reporting *Phone:* 540-986-1800 *Fax:* 540-444-4198 *E-mail:* tharris@ncbt.edu

Admission Contact: Mr. Jerry Lafferty, Campus Director *Phone:* 606-432-5477 *Fax:* 606-437-4952 *E-mail:* lafferty@educorp.edu

See full description on page 472.

National College of Business & Technology Ⓐ

139 South Killarney Lane
Richmond, KY 40475
Web: http://www.ncbt.edu

Accreditation: Accrediting Council for Independent Colleges and Schools

Programs Offered: accounting; administrative assistant and secretarial science; business administration and management; computer and information sciences related; medical administrative assistant and medical secretary; medical/clinical assistant; medical insurance coding; medical transcription; pharmacy technician

Enrollment: 343 students

Institution Contact: Ms. Tracy Harris, Director of Institutional Reporting *Phone:* 540-986-1800 ext. 108 *Fax:* 540-444-4199 *E-mail:* tharris@ncbt.edu

Ⓐ indicates that the school is a participating institution in the *Imagine America* Scholarship Program.

National College of Business & Technology (*continued*)

Admission Contact: Ms. Keeley Gadd, Campus Director *Phone:* 859-623-8956 *Fax:* 859-624-5544 *E-mail:* kgadd@educorp.edu

See full description on page 473.

RETS Institute of Technology

300 High Rise Drive
Louisville, KY 40213
Web: http://www.retsaec.com

Programs Offered: business administration and management; CAD/CADD drafting/design technology; computer and information sciences related; pre-law studies

Institution Contact: *Phone:* 888-476-1266

RETS Medical and Business Institute

4001 Ft. Campbell Boulevard
Hopkinsville, KY 42240
Web: http://www.retsmbi.com

Accreditation: Accrediting Council for Independent Colleges and Schools

Programs Offered: accounting; business administration and management; CAD/CADD drafting/design technology; computer programming; computer software technology; computer systems networking and telecommunications; criminal justice/law enforcement administration; legal assistant/paralegal; medical/clinical assistant

Institution Contact: *Phone:* 888-296-0262

Southwestern College of Business Ⓐ

8095 Connector Drive
Florence, KY 41042
Web: http://www.swcollege.net

Accreditation: Accrediting Council for Independent Colleges and Schools

Programs Offered: accounting; accounting technology and bookkeeping; administrative assistant and secretarial science; business administration and management; computer science; computer software and media applications; medical administrative assistant and medical secretary; medical/clinical assistant; medical insurance coding; medical insurance/medical billing; phlebotomy

Admission Contact: Laura Paletta, Director of Admissions *Phone:* 859-282-9999 *Fax:* 859-282-7940 *E-mail:* doaflorence@lincolnedu.com

See full description on page 474.

Spencerian College

4627 Dixie Highway, PO Box 16418
Louisville, KY 40256-0418

Accreditation: Accrediting Council for Independent Colleges and Schools

Programs Offered: accounting; administrative assistant and secretarial science; business administration and management; computer/information technology services administration related; executive assistant/executive secretary; gene therapy; health unit coordinator/ward clerk; medical administrative assistant and medical secretary; medical/clinical assistant; medical insurance coding; medical insurance/medical billing; medical office management; medical radiologic technology; medical transcription; nursing (licensed practical/vocational nurse training); nursing (registered nurse training); surgical technology

Institution Contact: Ms. Jan M. Gordon, Executive Director *Phone:* 502-447-1000 *Fax:* 502-447-4574 *E-mail:* jmgordon@spencerian.edu

Admission Contact: Ms. Terri Thomas, Director of Admissions *Phone:* 502-447-1000 *Fax:* 502-447-4574 *E-mail:* tthomas@spencerian.edu

Spencerian College—Lexington

2355 Harrodsburg Road
Lexington, KY 40504
Web: http://www.spencerian.edu

Programs Offered: computer engineering technology; computer graphics; computer technology/computer systems technology; mechanical design technology

Admission Contact: Ms. Peggy O'Donell, Director of Admissions *Phone:* 859-223-9608 *Fax:* 859-224-7744 *E-mail:* podonnell@spencerian.edu

Sullivan University

2355 Harrodsburg Road
Lexington, KY 40504
Web: http://www.sullivan.edu

Accreditation: Southern Association of Colleges and Schools

Programs Offered: accounting; administrative assistant and secretarial science; business administration and management; child care and support services management; computer and information sciences related; computer programming; computer programming (specific applications); computer/technical support; executive assistant/executive secretary; human resources management; information technology; legal administrative assistant/secretary; legal assistant/paralegal; marketing/marketing manage-

Ⓐ indicates that the school is a participating institution in the *Imagine America* Scholarship Program.

ment; medical administrative assistant and medical secretary; medical/clinical assistant; medical office management; medical radiologic technology; office management; receptionist; tourism and travel services management

Enrollment: 1,219 students

Institution Contact: Mr. David McGuire, Executive Director *Phone:* 859-276-4357 *Fax:* 859-276-1153 *E-mail:* dmcguire@sullivan.edu

Admission Contact: Ms. Sue Michael, Director of Admissions *Phone:* 859-276-4357 *Fax:* 859-276-1153 *E-mail:* smichael@sullivan.edu

Sullivan University (A)

3101 Bardstown Road
Louisville, KY 40205
Web: http://www.sullivan.edu

Accreditation: Southern Association of Colleges and Schools

Programs Offered: accounting; administrative assistant and secretarial science; baking and pastry arts; business administration and management; child care and support services management; child care provision; computer/information technology administration and management; computer installation and repair technology; computer programming; computer programming (specific applications); computer software engineering; computer systems networking and telecommunications; computer/technical support; culinary arts; executive assistant/executive secretary; finance; food preparation; hospitality administration; hotel/motel administration; information technology; internet information systems; legal administrative assistant/secretary; legal assistant/paralegal; logistics and materials management; marketing/marketing management; medical administrative assistant and medical secretary; medical office management; restaurant, culinary, and catering management; tourism and travel services management; word processing

Institution Contact: Mr. Stephen Coppock, EdD *Phone:* 502-456-6506 *Fax:* 502-456-0040 *E-mail:* gscoppock@sullivan.edu

Admission Contact: Mr. Greg Cawthon, Director of Admissions *Phone:* 502-456-6505 *Fax:* 502-456-0040 *E-mail:* gcawthon@sullivan.edu

See full description on page 475.

Louisiana

American Commercial College

3014 Knight Street
Shreveport, LA 71105
Web: http://www.acc-careers.com

Accreditation: Accrediting Council for Independent Colleges and Schools

Programs Offered: accounting; administrative assistant and secretarial science; business administration and management; data entry/microcomputer applications; legal administrative assistant/secretary; medical office computer specialist; medical transcription

Institution Contact: Judy Killough, Director *Phone:* 318-861-2112 *Fax:* 318-861-2119 *E-mail:* jkillough@acc-careers.com

Admission Contact: Jamie Waites, Instructor *Phone:* 318-861-2112 *Fax:* 318-261-2119

Ayers Institute, Inc.

PO Box 3941
Shreveport, LA 71133-3941

Accreditation: Council on Occupational Education

Programs Offered: heating, air conditioning and refrigeration technology; medical/clinical assistant

Institution Contact: Mr. Bruce Busada, President *Phone:* 318-635-0280 *Fax:* 318-636-9736 *E-mail:* response@ayersinstitute.com

Blue Cliff College

3501 Severn Avenue, Suite 20
Metairie, LA 70002

Accreditation: Accrediting Commission of Career Schools and Colleges of Technology

Programs Offered: massage therapy

Enrollment: 180 students

Institution Contact: Mr. Doug Robertson, Director of Education *Phone:* 504-456-3141 ext. 104 *Fax:* 504-456-7849 *E-mail:* dougr@bluecliff.com

Admission Contact: Ms. Cathy Goodwin, Director of Admissions *Phone:* 504-456-3141 ext. 122 *Fax:* 504-456-7849 *E-mail:* cathyg@bluecliffcollege.com

(A) indicates that the school is a participating institution in the *Imagine America* Scholarship Program.

Blue Cliff College—Lafayette

100 Asma Boulevard, Suite 350
Lafayette, LA 70508
Web: http://www.bluecliffcollege.com

Accreditation: Accrediting Commission of Career Schools and Colleges of Technology

Programs Offered: information technology; massage therapy

Institution Contact: Admissions *Phone:* 337-269-0620 *E-mail:* admissions_laf@bluecliffcollege.com

Blue Cliff College—Shreveport

200 North Thomas Street
Shreveport, LA 71107

Accreditation: Accrediting Commission of Career Schools and Colleges of Technology

Programs Offered: massage therapy; medical/clinical assistant

Institution Contact: Admissions Officer *Phone:* 318-425-7941 *Fax:* 318-425-3740

Bryman College ⓐ

1201 Elmwood Park Boulevard, Suite 600
New Orleans, LA 70123
Web: http://www.bryman-college.com

Accreditation: Accrediting Commission of Career Schools and Colleges of Technology

Programs Offered: dental assisting; medical administrative assistant and medical secretary; medical/clinical assistant; medical insurance coding; medical insurance/medical billing; pharmacy technician

Enrollment: 545 students

Institution Contact: Mr. Tom Bonesteel, President *Phone:* 504-733-7117 ext. 101 *Fax:* 504-734-1217 *E-mail:* mbonesteel@cci.edu

Admission Contact: Richard Beard, Director of Admissions *Phone:* 504-733-7117 *Fax:* 504-734-1217 *E-mail:* rbeard@cci.edu

See full description on page 476.

Career Technical College

2319 Louisville Avenue
Monroe, LA 71201
Web: http://www.careertc.com

Accreditation: Council on Occupational Education

Programs Offered: business administration and management; computer/information technology services administration related; health information/medical records technology; massage therapy; medical administrative assistant and medical secretary; medical/clinical assistant; medical insurance coding; phlebotomy; radiologic technology/science; surgical technology

Enrollment: 555 students

Institution Contact: Rose M. Steptoe, College Director *Phone:* 318-323-2889 *Fax:* 318-324-9883 *E-mail:* rsteptoe@careertc.com

Delta School of Business & Technology ⓐ

517 Broad Street
Lake Charles, LA 70601
Web: http://www.deltatech.edu

Accreditation: Accrediting Council for Independent Colleges and Schools

Programs Offered: accounting; administrative assistant and secretarial science; business administration and management; CAD/CADD drafting/design technology; clinical/medical laboratory technology; computer/information technology administration and management; computer/information technology services administration related; computer software technology; computer systems analysis; computer systems networking and telecommunications; computer/technical support; computer technology/computer systems technology; drafting and design technology; executive assistant/executive secretary; health information/medical records technology; information technology; legal administrative assistant/secretary; medical administrative assistant and medical secretary; medical/clinical assistant; medical office management; medical transcription; nursing assistant/aide and patient care assistant; office occupations and clerical services; physical therapist assistant; receptionist

Enrollment: 420 students

Institution Contact: Mr. Gary Holt, President *Phone:* 337-439-5765 *Fax:* 337-436-5151 *E-mail:* gholt@deltatech.edu

See full description on page 477.

Eastern College of Health Vocations

3321 Hessmer Avenue, Suite 200
Metairie, LA 70002

Institution Contact: *Phone:* 504-885-3353 *Fax:* 504-885-6721

Grantham University

34641 Grantham College Road
Slidell, LA 70460
Web: http://www.grantham.edu

Accreditation: Distance Education and Training Council

ⓐ indicates that the school is a participating institution in the *Imagine America* Scholarship Program.

Programs Offered: business administration and management; computer and information sciences related; computer engineering technology; computer software engineering; criminal justice/law enforcement administration; electrical, electronic and communications engineering technology; engineering technology; general studies; information science/studies; information technology

Enrollment: 5,000 students

Institution Contact: Ms. Beth Alexander, Marketing Assistant *Phone:* 985-649-4191 ext. 267 *Fax:* 985-649-1812 *E-mail:* beth@grantham.edu

Admission Contact: Ms. DeAnn Wandler, Director of Admissions *Phone:* 985-649-4191 ext. 322 *Fax:* 985-649-1812 *E-mail:* deann@grantham.edu

Gretna Career College

1415 Whitney Avenue
Gretna, LA 70053
Web: http://www.gretnacareercollege.edu

Accreditation: Accrediting Commission of Career Schools and Colleges of Technology

Programs Offered: accounting technology and bookkeeping; administrative assistant and secretarial science; adult development and aging; business automation/technology/data entry; clinical/medical laboratory assistant; computer/information technology services administration related; data entry/microcomputer applications related; executive assistant/executive secretary; gene therapy; health aide; health information/medical records technology; home health aide/home attendant; medical administrative assistant and medical secretary; medical/clinical assistant; medical office management; nursing assistant/aide and patient care assistant; receptionist; word processing

Institution Contact: Mr. Nick Randazzo, President *Phone:* 504-366-5409 *Fax:* 504-365-1004 *E-mail:* admissions@gretnacareercollege.com

Admission Contact: Ms. Ava Himes, Admissions Representative *Phone:* 504-366-5409 *Fax:* 504-365-1004 *E-mail:* admissions@gretnacareercollege.com

Herzing College Ⓐ

2400 Veterans Boulevard, Suite 410
Kenner, LA 70062
Web: http://www.herzing.edu

Accreditation: Accrediting Council for Independent Colleges and Schools; North Central Association of Colleges and Schools

Programs Offered: business administration and management; CAD/CADD drafting/design technol-

ogy; computer programming; computer systems networking and telecommunications; legal assistant/paralegal; medical insurance coding; pre-law studies; technology management

Enrollment: 279 students

Institution Contact: Ms. Darla Chin, Campus President *Phone:* 504-733-0074 *Fax:* 504-733-0020 *E-mail:* dchin@nor.herzing.edu

Admission Contact: Ms. Genny Bordelon, Admissions Director *Phone:* 504-733-0074 *Fax:* 504-733-0020 *E-mail:* genny@nor.herzing.edu

See full description on page 478.

ITI Technical College

13944 Airline Highway
Baton Rouge, LA 70817-5998
Web: http://www.iticollege.edu

Accreditation: Accrediting Commission of Career Schools and Colleges of Technology

Programs Offered: business automation/technology/data entry; business/corporate communications; business machine repair; CAD/CADD drafting/design technology; civil engineering technology; computer and information systems security; computer engineering technology; computer hardware engineering; computer/information technology administration and management; computer/information technology services administration related; computer installation and repair technology; computer programming; computer programming related; computer programming (specific applications); computer software and media applications; computer software and media applications related; computer software technology; computer systems analysis; computer systems networking and telecommunications; computer/technical support; computer technology/computer systems technology; data entry/microcomputer applications; data entry/microcomputer applications related; data modeling/warehousing and database administration; data processing and data processing technology; desktop publishing and digital imaging design; digital communication and media/multimedia; drafting and design technology; drawing; electrical, electronic and communications engineering technology; electrical/electronics equipment installation and repair; electrician; engineering technology; heating, air conditioning and refrigeration technology; heating, air conditioning, ventilation and refrigeration maintenance technology; hydraulics and fluid power technology; industrial design; industrial electronics technology; industrial mechanics and maintenance technology; industrial radiologic technology; industrial technology; information science/studies; information technology; instrumentation technology; internet information systems; management information

Ⓐ indicates that the school is a participating institution in the *Imagine America* Scholarship Program.

ITI Technical College (*continued*)

systems; mechanical design technology; mechanical engineering/mechanical technology; petroleum technology; system administration; system, networking, and LAN/WAN management; telecommunications; telecommunications technology; web/multimedia management and webmaster; web page, digital/multimedia and information resources design; word processing

Enrollment: 358 students

Institution Contact: Mr. Mark Worthy, Vice President *Phone:* 225-752-4230 ext. 212 *Fax:* 225-756-0903 *E-mail:* mworthy@iticollege.edu

Admission Contact: Mr. Joe Martin, III, President *Phone:* 225-752-4230 ext. 213 *Fax:* 225-756-0903 *E-mail:* jmartin@iticollege.edu

ITT Technical Institute Ⓐ

140 James Drive East
Saint Rose, LA 70087
Web: http://www.itt-tech.edu

Accreditation: Accrediting Council for Independent Colleges and Schools

Programs Offered: animation, interactive technology, video graphics and special effects; communications technology; computer and information systems security; computer engineering technology; computer software and media applications; computer software engineering; computer systems networking and telecommunications; digital communication and media/multimedia; electrical, electronic and communications engineering technology; technology management; web page, digital/multimedia and information resources design

Enrollment: 571 students

Institution Contact: Ms. Brenda Nash, Director *Phone:* 504-463-0338

Admission Contact: Ms. Heidi Munoz, Director of Recruitment *Phone:* 504-463-0338

See full description on page 479.

MedVance Institute

9255 Interline Avenue
Baton Rouge, LA 70809

Accreditation: Accrediting Bureau of Health Education Schools; Council on Occupational Education

Programs Offered: clinical/medical laboratory technology; gene therapy; medical/clinical assistant; medical insurance coding; pharmacy technician; radiologic technology/science

Institution Contact: Ms. Doris Hick, Campus Director *Phone:* 225-248-1015 ext. 206 *Fax:* 225-248-9517 *E-mail:* dhick@medvance.org

Admission Contact: Ms. Donna Hathaway, Admissions Representative *Phone:* 225-248-1015 ext. 219 *Fax:* 225-248-9517 *E-mail:* dhathaway@medvance.org

Remington College—Baton Rouge Campus Ⓐ

1900 North Lobdell Boulevard
Baton Rouge, LA 70806
Web: http://www.remingtoncollege.edu

Accreditation: Accrediting Council for Independent Colleges and Schools

Programs Offered: business administration and management; computer engineering related; computer systems networking and telecommunications; criminal justice/police science; medical/clinical assistant; medical insurance coding; pharmacy technician

Enrollment: 384 students

Institution Contact: Ms. Midge Jacobson, Campus President *Phone:* 225-922-3990 *Fax:* 225-922-9569 *E-mail:* midge.jacobson@remingtoncollege.edu

Admission Contact: Mr. Roger Moore, Director of Recruitment *Phone:* 225-922-3990 *Fax:* 225-922-9569 *E-mail:* roger.moore@remingtoncollege.edu

See full description on page 480.

Remington College—Lafayette Campus Ⓐ

303 Rue Louis XIV
Lafayette, LA 70508
Web: http://www.remingtoncollege.edu

Accreditation: Accrediting Council for Independent Colleges and Schools

Programs Offered: accounting; computer systems networking and telecommunications; computer/technical support; electrical, electronic and communications engineering technology; medical/clinical assistant; medical insurance coding; medical insurance/medical billing

Enrollment: 427 students

Institution Contact: Dr. Rosalie Lampone, Campus President *Phone:* 337-981-4010 *Fax:* 337-983-7130 *E-mail:* rosalie.lampone@remingtoncollege.edu

Admission Contact: Mr. William Duncan, Director of Recruitment *Phone:* 337-981-4010 *Fax:* 337-983-7130 *E-mail:* william.duncan@remingtoncollege.edu

See full description on page 481.

Ⓐ indicates that the school is a participating institution in the *Imagine America* Scholarship Program.

Remington College—New Orleans Campus

321 Veterans Memorial Boulevard
Metairie, LA 70005
Web: http://www.remingtoncollege.edu

Accreditation: Accrediting Commission of Career Schools and Colleges of Technology

Programs Offered: administrative assistant and secretarial science; commercial and advertising art; computer/information technology administration and management; drafting and design technology; electrical, electronic and communications engineering technology; engineering technology; system, networking, and LAN/WAN management

Institution Contact: Mr. Gregg Falcon, Campus President *Phone:* 504-831-8889 ext. 246 *Fax:* 504-831-6803 *E-mail:* gregg.falcon@remingtoncollege.edu

Admission Contact: Mr. Roy Kimble, Director of Recruitment *Phone:* 504-831-8889 *Fax:* 504-831-6803 *E-mail:* roy.kimble@remingtoncollege.edu

See full description on page 482.

maine

New England School of Communications

1 College Circle
Bangor, ME 04401-2999
Web: http://www.nescom.edu

Accreditation: Accrediting Commission of Career Schools and Colleges of Technology

Programs Offered: advertising; broadcast journalism; business/corporate communications; cinematography and film/video production; communications technology; computer software and media applications; desktop publishing and digital imaging design; marketing/marketing management; radio and television broadcasting technology; recording arts technology; speech and rhetoric; web/multimedia management and webmaster; web page, digital/multimedia and information resources design

Enrollment: 285 students

Institution Contact: Mr. Benjamin E. Haskell, Dean *Phone:* 207-941-7176 ext. 1094 *Fax:* 207-947-3987 *E-mail:* haskellb@nescom.edu

Admission Contact: Mrs. Louise G. Grant, Director of Admissions *Phone:* 207-941-7176 ext. 1093 *Fax:* 207-947-3987 *E-mail:* grantl@nescom.edu

maryland

Baltimore School of Massage

6401 Dogwood Road
Baltimore, MD 21207
Web: http://steinered.com

Accreditation: Accrediting Commission of Career Schools and Colleges of Technology

Programs Offered: massage therapy

Enrollment: 315 students

Institution Contact: Ms. Angela DenHerder, Campus Director *Phone:* 410-944-8855 *Fax:* 410-944-8859 *E-mail:* adenherder@steinerleisure.com

Admission Contact: Admissions Department *Phone:* 410-944-8855 *Fax:* 410-944-8859 *E-mail:* adenherder@steinerleisure.com

See full description on page 483.

Hagerstown Business College

18618 Crestwood Drive
Hagerstown, MD 21742
Web: http://www.hagerstownbusinesscol.org

Accreditation: Accrediting Council for Independent Colleges and Schools

Programs Offered: accounting; administrative assistant and secretarial science; business administration and management; commercial and advertising art; computer graphics; computer/information technology administration and management; computer/information technology services administration related; computer installation and repair technology; computer programming; computer programming related; computer programming (specific applications); computer programming (vendor/product certification); computer software and media applications; computer software and media applications related; computer software technology; computer/technical support; computer technology/computer systems technology; criminal justice/law enforcement administration; customer service management; executive assistant/executive secretary; forensic science and technology; health information/medical records administration; health information/medical records technology; health unit coordinator/ward clerk; information technology; legal administrative assistant/secretary; legal assistant/paralegal; marketing/marketing management; medical administrative assistant and medical secretary; medical/clinical assistant; medical insurance coding; medical insur-

Hagerstown Business College (*continued*)

ance/medical billing; medical office management; medical reception; medical transcription; office occupations and clerical services; receptionist; system administration

Enrollment: 950 students

Institution Contact: Mr. W. Christopher Motz, Executive Director *Phone:* 301-739-2680 ext. 128 *Fax:* 301-791-7661 *E-mail:* cmotz@hagerstownbusinesscol.org

Admission Contact: Ms. Jessica Border, Admissions Representative *Phone:* 800-422-2670 *Fax:* 301-791-7661 *E-mail:* info@hagerstownbusinesscol.org

See full description on page 485.

Harrison Career Institute

1040 Park Avenue, Suite 10
Baltimore, MD 21201
Web: http://www.hci.edu

Accreditation: Accrediting Commission of Career Schools and Colleges of Technology

Programs Offered: cardiovascular technology; electrocardiograph technology; medical/clinical assistant; medical insurance coding; medical insurance/medical billing; medical office computer specialist; medical transcription; phlebotomy

Enrollment: 290 students

Institution Contact: Lorene Pryor, Director *Phone:* 410-962-0303 *E-mail:* lpryor@hci-inst.net

Lincoln Technical Institute Ⓐ

9325 Snowden River Parkway
Columbia, MD 21046
Web: http://www.lincolntech.com

Accreditation: Accrediting Commission of Career Schools and Colleges of Technology

Programs Offered: automobile/automotive mechanics technology; automotive engineering technology; computer/technical support; electrical and electronic engineering technologies related; heating, air conditioning and refrigeration technology

Institution Contact: Director of Admissions *Phone:* 410-290-7100 *Fax:* 410-290-7880 *E-mail:* doacolumbia@lincolnedu.com

See full description on page 486.

Medix School Ⓐ

700 York Road
Towson, MD 21204-2511
Web: http://www.medixschooltowson.com

Accreditation: Accrediting Bureau of Health Education Schools

Programs Offered: dental assisting; medical administrative assistant and medical secretary; medical/clinical assistant

Enrollment: 531 students

Institution Contact: Mr. Sean London, Director *Phone:* 410-337-5155 *Fax:* 410-337-5104 *E-mail:* slondon@medixsch.com

Admission Contact: Ms. Joan Verfuerth, Director of Admissions *Phone:* 410-337-5155 *Fax:* 410-337-5104 *E-mail:* admissions@medixsch.com

See full description on page 487.

Sanford-Brown Institute

8401 Corporate Drive, Suite 500
Landover, MD 20785
Web: http://www.ultrasounddiagnosticschool.com/default.htm

Accreditation: Accrediting Bureau of Health Education Schools

Programs Offered: cardiovascular technology; diagnostic medical sonography and ultrasound technology; medical/clinical assistant

Institution Contact: Ms. Janet L. Stanley, Executive Director *Phone:* 301-918-8221 *Fax:* 301-918-8278 *E-mail:* janet.stanley@wix.net

Admission Contact: Mr. Kerry Haley, Director of Admissions *Phone:* 301-918-8221 *Fax:* 301-918-8278 *E-mail:* kerry.haley@wix.net

Strayer University at Anne Arundel Campus

1111 Benfield Boulevard, Suite 100
Millersville, MD 21108
Web: http://www.strayer.edu

Accreditation: Middle States Association of Colleges and Schools

Programs Offered: accounting; business administration and management; communications technology; computer/information technology administration and management; computer programming; computer systems networking and telecommunications; data modeling/warehousing and database administration; economics; general studies; information science/studies; information technology; international business/trade/commerce; marketing/marketing management; purchasing, procurement/acquisitions and contracts management

Institution Contact: Dr. J. Chris Toe, President *Phone:* 202-408-2424 *Fax:* 202-789-0387 *E-mail:* jct@strayer.edu

Admission Contact: Mr. James Derdock, Campus Manager *Phone:* 410-923-4500 *E-mail:* annearundel@strayer.edu

Ⓐ indicates that the school is a participating institution in the *Imagine America* Scholarship Program.

Strayer University at Montgomery Campus

20030 Century Boulevard, Suite 300
Germantown, MD 20874
Web: http://www.strayer.edu

Accreditation: Middle States Association of Colleges and Schools

Programs Offered: accounting; business administration and management; communications technology; computer/information technology administration and management; computer programming; computer systems networking and telecommunications; data modeling/warehousing and database administration; economics; general studies; information science/studies; information technology; international business/trade/commerce; marketing/marketing management; purchasing, procurement/acquisitions and contracts management

Institution Contact: Dr. J. Chris Toe, President *Phone:* 202-408-2424 *Fax:* 202-789-0387 *E-mail:* jct@strayer.edu

Admission Contact: Campus Manager *Phone:* 301-540-8066 *E-mail:* montgomery@strayer.edu

Strayer University at Prince George's County

4710 Auth Place, 1st Floor
Suitland, MD 20746
Web: http://www.strayer.edu

Accreditation: Middle States Association of Colleges and Schools

Programs Offered: accounting; business administration and management; communications technology; computer/information technology administration and management; computer programming; computer systems networking and telecommunications; data modeling/warehousing and database administration; economics; general studies; information science/studies; information technology; international business/trade/commerce; marketing/marketing management; purchasing, procurement/acquisitions and contracts management

Institution Contact: Dr. J. Chris Toe, University President *Phone:* 202-408-2424 *Fax:* 202-789-0387 *E-mail:* jct@strayer.edu

Admission Contact: Charles Davis, Campus Manager *Phone:* 301-423-3600 *Fax:* 301-423-3999 *E-mail:* princegeorges@strayer.edu

Strayer University at Owings Mills Campus

500 Redland Court, Suite 100
Owings Mills, MD 21117
Web: http://www.strayer.edu

Accreditation: Middle States Association of Colleges and Schools

Programs Offered: accounting; business administration and management; communications technology; computer/information technology administration and management; computer programming; computer systems networking and telecommunications; data modeling/warehousing and database administration; economics; general studies; information science/studies; information technology; international business/trade/commerce; marketing/marketing management; purchasing, procurement/acquisitions and contracts management

Institution Contact: Dr. J. Chris Toe, University President *Phone:* 202-408-2424 *Fax:* 202-789-0387 *E-mail:* jct@strayer.edu

Admission Contact: Paula Khanal, Campus Manager *Phone:* 443-394-3339 *E-mail:* owingsmills@strayer.edu

Strayer University at White Marsh Campus

9409 Philadelphia Road
Baltimore, MD 21237
Web: http://www.strayer.edu

Accreditation: Middle States Association of Colleges and Schools

Programs Offered: accounting; business administration and management; communications technology; computer/information technology administration and management; computer programming; computer systems networking and telecommunications; data modeling/warehousing and database administration; economics; general studies; information science/studies; information technology; international business/trade/commerce; marketing/marketing management; purchasing, procurement/acquisitions and contracts management

Institution Contact: Dr. J. Chris Toe, University President *Phone:* 202-408-2424 *Fax:* 202-789-0387 *E-mail:* jct@strayer.edu

Admission Contact: Campus Manager *Phone:* 410-238-9000 *Fax:* 410-238-9099 *E-mail:* whitemarsh@strayer.edu

🅐 indicates that the school is a participating institution in the *Imagine America* Scholarship Program.

TESST College of Technology

1520 South Caton Avenue
Baltimore, MD 21227-1063
Web: http://www.tesst.com

Accreditation: Accrediting Commission of Career Schools and Colleges of Technology

Programs Offered: computer/information technology administration and management; computer/information technology services administration related; computer programming related; drafting and design technology; electrical, electronic and communications engineering technology; heating, air conditioning and refrigeration technology; information technology

Institution Contact: Ms. Susan Sherwood, Director
Phone: 410-644-6400 *Fax:* 410-644-6481 *E-mail:* ssherwood@tesst.com

TESST College of Technology

4600 Powder Mill Road, Suite 500
Beltsville, MD 20705
Web: http://www.tesst.com

Accreditation: Accrediting Commission of Career Schools and Colleges of Technology

Programs Offered: business automation/technology/data entry; business/corporate communications; CAD/CADD drafting/design technology; communications technology; computer engineering technology; computer/information technology services administration related; computer installation and repair technology; computer software and media applications; computer software engineering; computer systems networking and telecommunications; computer/technical support; computer technology/computer systems technology; criminal justice/law enforcement administration; data entry/microcomputer applications; data entry/microcomputer applications related; data processing and data processing technology; desktop publishing and digital imaging design; drafting and design technology; electrical, electronic and communications engineering technology; electrician; engineering technology; information science/studies; information technology; massage therapy; medical/clinical assistant; telecommunications; web page, digital/multimedia and information resources design; word processing

Enrollment: 611 students

Institution Contact: Mr. Reginald M. Morton, Executive Director *Phone:* 301-937-8448 *Fax:* 301-937-5327 *E-mail:* rmorton@tesst.com

Admission Contact: Miss Tina Turk, Director of Admissions *Phone:* 301-937-8448 *Fax:* 301-937-5327 *E-mail:* tturk@tesst.com

TESST College of Technology

803 Glen Eagles Court
Towson, MD 21286
Web: http://www.tesst.com

Accreditation: Accrediting Commission of Career Schools and Colleges of Technology

Programs Offered: administrative assistant and secretarial science; computer/information technology services administration related; computer installation and repair technology; computer systems networking and telecommunications; computer technology/computer systems technology; electrical, electronic and communications engineering technology; information science/studies; massage therapy; medical/clinical assistant; telecommunications

Institution Contact: Mr. Ray Joll, Executive Director *Phone:* 410-296-5350 *Fax:* 410-296-5356 *E-mail:* rjoll@tesst.com

Admission Contact: Ms. Alicia Hayman, Director of Admissions *Phone:* 410-296-5350 *Fax:* 410-296-5356 *E-mail:* ahayman@tesst.com

massachusetts

Bay State College

122 Commonwealth Avenue
Boston, MA 02116
Web: http://www.baystate.edu

Accreditation: New England Association of Schools and Colleges

Programs Offered: accounting; business administration and management; computer and information sciences related; criminal justice/law enforcement administration; fashion/apparel design; fashion merchandising; general studies; medical/clinical assistant; physical therapist assistant; tourism and travel services management

Enrollment: 750 students

Institution Contact: *Phone:* 617-236-8000 *Fax:* 617-536-1735

Bryman Institute ⓐ

1505 Commonwealth Avenue
Brighton, MA 02135
Web: http://www.bryman-institute.com

Accreditation: Accrediting Commission of Career Schools and Colleges of Technology

---

ⓐ indicates that the school is a participating institution in the *Imagine America* Scholarship Program.

Programs Offered: dental assisting; massage therapy; medical administrative assistant and medical secretary; medical/clinical assistant

Admission Contact: Mr. Arthur Banaster, Director of Admissions *Phone:* 617-783-9955 *Fax:* 617-783-1166 *E-mail:* abanaste@cci.edu

See full description on page 488.

Bryman Institute Ⓐ

70 Everett Avenue, 4th Floor
Chelsea, MA 02150
Web: http://Http://www.bryman-institute.com

Accreditation: Accrediting Commission of Career Schools and Colleges of Technology

Programs Offered: massage therapy; medical/clinical assistant; pharmacy technician

Institution Contact: Kim Villarreal, School President *Phone:* 617-889-5999 *Fax:* 617-889-0340 *E-mail:* kvillarr@cci.edu

Admission Contact: Mr. Carl Williams, Director of Admissions *Phone:* 617-889-5999 *Fax:* 617-889-0340

See full description on page 489.

Career Education Institute Ⓐ

375 Westgate Drive
Brockton, MA 02301-1818
Web: http://www.ceitraining.com

Accreditation: Accrediting Council for Independent Colleges and Schools

Programs Offered: administrative assistant and secretarial science; anatomy; animation, interactive technology, video graphics and special effects; blood bank technology; business automation/technology/data entry; business machine repair; clinical/medical laboratory assistant; clinical/medical laboratory technology; computer and information systems security; computer graphics; computer/information technology administration and management; computer/information technology services administration related; computer installation and repair technology; computer programming; computer programming (specific applications); computer programming (vendor/product certification); computer software technology; computer systems networking and telecommunications; computer/technical support; computer technology/computer systems technology; data entry/microcomputer applications; data entry/microcomputer applications related; data processing and data processing technology; e-commerce; electrocardiograph technology; electroneurodiagnostic/electroencephalographic technology; executive assistant/executive secretary; gene therapy; health

information/medical records administration; health information/medical records technology; hematology technology; hospital and health care facilities administration; information technology; legal administrative assistant/secretary; management information systems; massage therapy; medical administrative assistant and medical secretary; medical/clinical assistant; medical insurance coding; medical insurance/medical billing; medical office computer specialist; medical office management; medical radiologic technology; medical reception; medical transcription; office occupations and clerical services; physician assistant; receptionist; system administration; system, networking, and LAN/WAN management; web/multimedia management and webmaster; web page, digital/multimedia and information resources design; word processing

Enrollment: 300 students

Institution Contact: Mr. Wayne H. Mullin, Executive Director *Phone:* 508-941-0730 *Fax:* 508-587-8436 *E-mail:* wmullin@ceitraining.com

Admission Contact: Mr. Steve Giddings, Director of Admissions *Phone:* 508-941-0730 *Fax:* 508-587-8436 *E-mail:* sgiddings@ceitraining.com

See full description on page 490.

Career Education Institute Ⓐ

211 Plain Street
Lowell, MA 01852
Web: http://www.ceitraining.com

Accreditation: Accrediting Council for Independent Colleges and Schools

Programs Offered: computer and information sciences and support services related; massage therapy; medical administrative assistant and medical secretary; medical/clinical assistant; pharmacy technician; system, networking, and LAN/WAN management

Institution Contact: Executive Director *Phone:* 978-458-4800 *Fax:* 978-458-1287 *E-mail:* execdirlowell@lincontech.com

See full description on page 491.

Computer-Ed Institute

477 Washington Street
Boston, MA 02111
Web: http://www.computered.com

Accreditation: Accrediting Council for Independent Colleges and Schools

Programs Offered: computer programming (specific applications); computer software and media applications related; computer software technology; computer/technical support; medical administrative

---

Ⓐ indicates that the school is a participating institution in the *Imagine America* Scholarship Program.

Computer-Ed Institute (*continued*)

assistant and medical secretary; system administration; system, networking, and LAN/WAN management; web page, digital/multimedia and information resources design

Institution Contact: Mr. Jeffrey Malkin, Executive Director *Phone:* 617-348-9857 *Fax:* 617-348-9864 *E-mail:* jmalkin@lincolntech.com

Admission Contact: Ms. Laura Forgays, Admissions Director *Phone:* 617-348-9857 *Fax:* 617-348-9864 *E-mail:* lforgays@lincolntech.com

Computer-Ed Institute Ⓐ

5 Middlesex Avenue
Somerville, MA 02145
Web: http://www.ceitraining.com

Accreditation: Accrediting Council for Independent Colleges and Schools

Programs Offered: computer/technical support; massage therapy; medical administrative assistant and medical secretary; medical/clinical assistant; pharmacy technician; system administration

Institution Contact: Executive Director *Phone:* 617-776-3500 *Fax:* 617-776-1899 *E-mail:* execdirsomerville@lincolntech.com

See full description on page 492.

Gibbs College

126 Newbury Street
Boston, MA 02116
Web: http://www.gibbsboston.com

Accreditation: Accrediting Council for Independent Colleges and Schools

Programs Offered: accounting; business administration and management; commercial and advertising art; computer/information technology administration and management; legal administrative assistant/secretary; medical administrative assistant and medical secretary

Institution Contact: Mr. David J. Waldron, President *Phone:* 617-578-7117 *Fax:* 617-578-7181 *E-mail:* dwaldron@gibbsboston.net

Admission Contact: Mr. David Arce Toledo, Director of Admissions *Phone:* 617-578-7100 *Fax:* 617-578-7163 *E-mail:* dtoledo@gibbsboston.net

Hallmark Institute of Photography Ⓐ

PO Box 308
Turners Falls, MA 01376-0308
Web: http://www.hallmark.edu

Accreditation: Accrediting Commission of Career Schools and Colleges of Technology

Programs Offered: photography

Enrollment: 220 students

Institution Contact: Mr. George Rosa, III, President *Phone:* 413-863-2478 *Fax:* 413-863-4118 *E-mail:* george@hallmark.edu

Admission Contact: Ms. Tammy L. Murphy, Director of Admissions *Phone:* 413-863-2478 *Fax:* 413-863-4118 *E-mail:* tammy@hallmark.edu

See full description on page 493.

ITT Technical Institute Ⓐ

333 Providence Highway
Norwood, MA 02062
Web: http://www.itt-tech.edu

Accreditation: Accrediting Council for Independent Colleges and Schools

Programs Offered: CAD/CADD drafting/design technology; computer engineering technology; computer software and media applications; computer systems networking and telecommunications; digital communication and media/multimedia; web page, digital/multimedia and information resources design

Enrollment: 289 students

Institution Contact: Mr. Dennis Saccoia, Director *Phone:* 781-278-7200

Admission Contact: Mr. Thomas F. Ryan, Director of Recruitment *Phone:* 781-278-7200

See full description on page 494.

ITT Technical Institute Ⓐ

10 Forbes Road
Woburn, MA 01801
Web: http://www.itt-tech.edu

Accreditation: Accrediting Council for Independent Colleges and Schools

Programs Offered: CAD/CADD drafting/design technology; computer engineering technology; computer software and media applications; computer systems networking and telecommunications; digital communication and media/multimedia; web page, digital/multimedia and information resources design

Enrollment: 303 students

Institution Contact: Mr. Steve Carter, Director *Phone:* 781-937-8324

Admission Contact: Mr. David Lundgren, Director of Recruitment *Phone:* 781-937-8324

See full description on page 495.

Ⓐ indicates that the school is a participating institution in the *Imagine America* Scholarship Program.

The New England Institute of Art

10 Brookline Place, West
Brookline, MA 02445
Web: http://www.neia.aii.edu

Accreditation: New England Association of Schools and Colleges

Programs Offered: animation, interactive technology, video graphics and special effects; commercial and advertising art; computer graphics; interior design; radio and television; recording arts technology; web/multimedia management and webmaster; web page, digital/multimedia and information resources design

Enrollment: 1,250 students

Institution Contact: Ms. Stacy Sweeney, President *Phone:* 617-739-1700 *Fax:* 617-582-4520 *E-mail:* sweeneys@aii.edu

Admission Contact: Ms. Deborah Brent, Director of Admissions *Phone:* 800-903-4425 *Fax:* 617-582-4500 *E-mail:* brentd@aii.edu

Porter and Chester Institute

134 Dulong Circle
Chicopee, MA 01022
Web: http://www.porterchester.com

Accreditation: Accrediting Bureau of Health Education Schools; Accrediting Commission of Career Schools and Colleges of Technology

Programs Offered: automobile/automotive mechanics technology; CAD/CADD drafting/design technology; computer systems networking and telecommunications; computer technology/computer systems technology; dental assisting; electrical and electronic engineering technologies related; heating, air conditioning, ventilation and refrigeration maintenance technology; medical/clinical assistant

Institution Contact: *Phone:* 413-593-3339

RETS Technical Center

570 Rutherford Avenue
Charlestown, MA 02129
Web: http://www.retstech.com

Accreditation: Accrediting Commission of Career Schools and Colleges of Technology

Programs Offered: allied health and medical assisting services related; clinical/medical laboratory assistant; computer hardware technology; electrical/electronics equipment installation and repair; health professions related; health services/allied health/health sciences; heating, air conditioning and refrigeration technology; heating, air conditioning, ventilation and refrigeration maintenance technology; industrial electronics

technology; medical administrative assistant and medical secretary; medical/clinical assistant; medical office assistant; medical office computer specialist; medical reception; medical transcription

Enrollment: 291 students

Institution Contact: Mr. Douglas R. Dunn, Executive Director *Phone:* 617-580-4010 ext. 4012 *Fax:* 617-580-4074 *E-mail:* ddunn@khec.com

Admission Contact: Ms. Julie English, Director of Admissions *Phone:* 617-580-4010 *Fax:* 617-580-4074 *E-mail:* julie@retstech.com

Sanford-Brown Institute

365 Cadwell Drive, 1st Floor
Springfield, MA 01104-1739
Web: http://www.ultrasounddiagnosticschool.com/default.htm

Accreditation: Accrediting Bureau of Health Education Schools

Programs Offered: criminal justice/law enforcement administration; massage therapy; medical/clinical assistant; medical insurance coding

Enrollment: 350 students

Institution Contact: Mr. Winn Sanderson, President *Phone:* 413-739-4700 *Fax:* 413-739-4800 *E-mail:* wsanderson@sbmass.com

Admission Contact: Ms. Susan Dillon, Director of Admissions *Phone:* 413-739-4700 *Fax:* 413-739-4800 *E-mail:* sdillon@sbmass.com

WyoTech ⓐ

150 Hanscom Drive
Bedford, MA 01730
Web: http://www.wyotech.com

Accreditation: Accrediting Commission of Career Schools and Colleges of Technology

Programs Offered: aircraft powerplant technology; airframe mechanics and aircraft maintenance technology

Enrollment: 250 students

Institution Contact: Mr. John Buck, School President *Phone:* 781-274-8448 *Fax:* 781-274-8490 *E-mail:* jbuck@cci.edu

Admission Contact: Mr. Don Keeney, Jr., Director of Admissions *Phone:* 781-274-8448 *Fax:* 781-274-8490 *E-mail:* dkeeney@cci.edu

See full description on page 496.

ⓐ indicates that the school is a participating institution in the *Imagine America* Scholarship Program.

ichigan

Carnegie Institute Ⓐ

550 Stephenson Highway, Suite 100
Troy, MI 48083-1159
Web: http://www.carnegie-institute.com

Accreditation: Accrediting Commission of Career Schools and Colleges of Technology

Programs Offered: cardiovascular technology; electroneurodiagnostic/electroencephalographic technology; massage therapy; medical administrative assistant and medical secretary; medical/clinical assistant; medical insurance/medical billing; medical transcription

Enrollment: 295 students

Institution Contact: Mr. Robert McEachern *Phone:* 248-589-1078 *Fax:* 248-589-1631 *E-mail:* carnegie47@aol.com

See full description on page 497.

Dorsey Schools

30821 Barrington Avenue
Madison Heights, MI 48071
Web: http://www.dorseyschools.com

Accreditation: Accrediting Council for Independent Colleges and Schools

Programs Offered: accounting; accounting technology and bookkeeping; administrative assistant and secretarial science; computer engineering related; computer engineering technology; computer hardware engineering; computer/information technology administration and management; computer/information technology services administration related; computer installation and repair technology; computer programming (vendor/product certification); computer software and media applications; computer systems networking and telecommunications; computer/technical support; computer technology/computer systems technology; data entry/microcomputer applications; data processing and data processing technology; executive assistant/executive secretary; information technology; legal administrative assistant/secretary; medical administrative assistant and medical secretary; medical/clinical assistant; medical/health management and clinical assistant; medical insurance/medical billing; medical office computer specialist; medical office management; medical reception; medical transcription; office occupations and clerical services; receptionist; word processing

Enrollment: 220 students

Institution Contact: Miss Wendy Mathis, Director *Phone:* 248-588-9660 *Fax:* 248-583-4153 *E-mail:* wmathis@dorseyschools.com

Dorsey Schools

31542 Gratiot Avenue
Roseville, MI 48066
Web: http://www.dorseyschools.com

Accreditation: Accrediting Council for Independent Colleges and Schools

Programs Offered: accounting; administrative assistant and secretarial science; data entry/microcomputer applications; data processing and data processing technology; executive assistant/executive secretary; legal administrative assistant/secretary; medical administrative assistant and medical secretary; medical/clinical assistant; medical/health management and clinical assistant; medical insurance coding; medical insurance/medical billing; medical office computer specialist; medical office management; medical reception; medical transcription; receptionist; word processing

Institution Contact: Ms. Kim Peck, Director *Phone:* 586-296-3225 *Fax:* 586-296-6840 *E-mail:* kpeck@dorseyschools.com

Dorsey Schools

15755 Northline Road
Southgate, MI 48195
Web: http://www.dorseyschools.com

Accreditation: Accrediting Council for Independent Colleges and Schools

Programs Offered: accounting; administrative assistant and secretarial science; data entry/microcomputer applications; data processing and data processing technology; executive assistant/executive secretary; legal administrative assistant/secretary; medical administrative assistant and medical secretary; medical/clinical assistant; medical/health management and clinical assistant; medical insurance/medical billing; medical office computer specialist; medical office management; medical transcription; receptionist; word processing

Enrollment: 165 students

Institution Contact: Ms. Golda Szydlowski, Director *Phone:* 734-285-5400 *Fax:* 734-285-8877 *E-mail:* gszyd@dorseyschools.com

Ⓐ indicates that the school is a participating institution in the *Imagine America* Scholarship Program.

Dorsey Schools

34841 Veteran's Plaza
Wayne, MI 48184
Web: http://www.dorseyschools.com

Accreditation: Accrediting Council for Independent Colleges and Schools

Programs Offered: accounting; administrative assistant and secretarial science; data entry/micro-computer applications; data processing and data processing technology; executive assistant/executive secretary; medical administrative assistant and medical secretary; medical/clinical assistant; medical/health management and clinical assistant; medical insurance/medical billing; medical office computer specialist; medical office management; medical transcription; receptionist; word processing

Enrollment: 200 students

Institution Contact: Ms. Barbara Bubnikovich, Director *Phone:* 734-595-1540 *Fax:* 734-595-6010 *E-mail:* bbubnikovich@dorseyschools.com

Flint Institute of Barbering

3214 Flushing Road
Flint, MI 48504-4395

Accreditation: Accrediting Commission of Career Schools and Colleges of Technology

Programs Offered: barbering

Enrollment: 41 students

Institution Contact: Ms. Martha Poulos, Director *Phone:* 810-232-4711 *Fax:* 810-232-3132 *E-mail:* barber@tir.com

International Academy of Design & Technology

1850 Research Drive, Suite 375
Troy, MI 48083

Accreditation: Accrediting Council for Independent Colleges and Schools

Programs Offered: commercial and advertising art; fashion/apparel design; interior design

Institution Contact: Rosemary Couser, Director of Student Management *Phone:* 248-526-1700 ext. 225 *E-mail:* rcouser@iadtdetroit.com

Admission Contact: Anthony Amato, Director of Admissions *Phone:* 248-526-1700 ext. 237 *Fax:* 248-526-1710 *E-mail:* tamato@iadtdetroit.com

ITT Technical Institute Ⓐ

1905 South Haggerty Road
Canton, MI 48188-2025
Web: http://www.itt-tech.edu

Accreditation: Accrediting Council for Independent Colleges and Schools

Programs Offered: CAD/CADD drafting/design technology; computer engineering technology; computer software and media applications; computer systems networking and telecommunications; digital communication and media/multimedia; web page, digital/multimedia and information resources design

Enrollment: 708 students

Institution Contact: Ms. Nadine Palazzolo, Director *Phone:* 734-397-7800

Admission Contact: Mr. Dudley Layfield, Director of Recruitment *Phone:* 734-397-7800

See full description on page 498.

ITT Technical Institute Ⓐ

4020 Sparks Drive, Southeast
Grand Rapids, MI 49546
Web: http://www.itt-tech.edu

Accreditation: Accrediting Council for Independent Colleges and Schools

Programs Offered: CAD/CADD drafting/design technology; computer engineering technology; computer software and media applications; computer systems networking and telecommunications; digital communication and media/multimedia; web page, digital/multimedia and information resources design

Enrollment: 643 students

Institution Contact: Mr. Dennis Hormel, Director *Phone:* 616-956-1060

Admission Contact: Mr. Todd Peuler, Director of Recruitment *Phone:* 616-956-1060

See full description on page 499.

ITT Technical Institute Ⓐ

1522 East Big Beaver Road
Troy, MI 48083-1905
Web: http://www.itt-tech.edu

Accreditation: Accrediting Council for Independent Colleges and Schools

Programs Offered: CAD/CADD drafting/design technology; computer engineering technology; computer software and media applications; computer systems networking and telecommunications; digital communication and media/multimedia; web page, digital/multimedia and information resources design

Enrollment: 690 students

Ⓐ indicates that the school is a participating institution in the *Imagine America* Scholarship Program.

ITT Technical Institute (*continued*)

Institution Contact: Dr. Stephen Goddard, Director
Phone: 248-524-1800
Admission Contact: Ms. Patricia Hyman, Director of
Recruitment *Phone:* 248-524-1800
See full description on page 500.

Lawton School
20755 Greenfield Road, Suite 300
Southfield, MI 48075
Accreditation: Accrediting Commission of Career
Schools and Colleges of Technology
Programs Offered: administrative assistant and
secretarial science; computer software and media
applications; legal assistant/paralegal; medical/
clinical assistant
Enrollment: 111 students
Institution Contact: Miss Tamiko Strange, Executive
Director *Phone:* 248-569-7787 *Fax:* 248-569-6974 *E-mail:*
strangetamiko@hotmail.com
Admission Contact: Mr. Oliver Hunter, Jr., Admission Director *Phone:* 248-569-7787 *Fax:* 248-569-6974

National Institute of Technology ⓐ
300 River Place Drive, Suite 1000
Detroit, MI 48207
Web: http://www.nitschools.com
Accreditation: Accrediting Commission of Career
Schools and Colleges of Technology
Programs Offered: massage therapy; medical/clinical
assistant; medical insurance/medical billing; pharmacy technician
Enrollment: 331 students
Institution Contact: Mr. Joseph M. Egelski, School
President *Phone:* 313-567-5350 ext. 101 *Fax:* 313-567-
2095 *E-mail:* jegelski@cci.edu
Admission Contact: Mr. Mike Draheim, Director of
Admissions *Phone:* 313-567-5350 ext. 102 *Fax:* 313-567-
2095 *E-mail:* mdraheim@cci.edu
See full description on page 502.

National Institute of Technology ⓐ
26111 Evergreen Road, Suite 201
Southfield, MI 48076-4491
Web: http://www.cci.edu
Accreditation: Accrediting Commission of Career
Schools and Colleges of Technology
Programs Offered: computer engineering technology;
computer/information technology services adminis-

tration related; computer installation and repair
technology; computer systems networking and
telecommunications; electrical, electronic and communications engineering technology; information
science/studies; massage therapy; medical administrative assistant and medical secretary; medical/clinical
assistant; medical insurance coding; medical insurance/medical billing; system administration; system,
networking, and LAN/WAN management
Enrollment: 850 students
Institution Contact: Mrs. Marchelle Weaver, President
Phone: 248-799-9933 *Fax:* 248-799-2912 *E-mail:*
mweaver@cci.edu
Admission Contact: Santiago Rocha, Director of
Admissions *Phone:* 248-799-9933 ext. 118 *Fax:* 248-799-
2912 *E-mail:* srocha@cci.edu
See full description on page 503.

National Institute of Technology—Dearborn ⓐ
23400 Michigan Avenue, Suite 200
Dearborn, MI 48124
Web: http://www.nitschools.com
Accreditation: Accrediting Commission of Career
Schools and Colleges of Technology
Programs Offered: computer/information technology
administration and management; computer systems
networking and telecommunications; massage
therapy; medical/clinical assistant; medical insurance/medical billing
Enrollment: 630 students
Institution Contact: Mr. Joseph Belliotti, Jr., President
Phone: 313-562-4228 ext. 102 *Fax:* 313-562-5774 *E-mail:*
jbelliotti@cci.edu
Admission Contact: Ms. Kathy Galasso, Director of
Admissions *Phone:* 313-562-4228 ext. 101 *Fax:* 313-562-
5774 *E-mail:* kgalasso@cci.edu
See full description on page 501.

Olympia Career Training Institute ⓐ
1750 Woodworth Street, NE
Grand Rapids, MI 49525
Accreditation: Accrediting Bureau of Health Education Schools
Programs Offered: computer technology/computer
systems technology; dental assisting; information
technology; massage therapy; medical administrative
assistant and medical secretary; medical/clinical
assistant; nursing (licensed practical/vocational nurse
training); surgical technology
Enrollment: 790 students

ⓐ indicates that the school is a participating institution in the *Imagine America* Scholarship Program.

Institution Contact: Mrs. Ruth Stewart, President *Phone:* 616-364-8464 ext. 10 *Fax:* 616-364-5454 *E-mail:* rstewart@cci.edu

Admission Contact: Ms. Bobbi Blok, Director of Admissions *Phone:* 616-364-8464 ext. 34 *Fax:* 616-364-5454 *E-mail:* rblok@cci.edu

See full description on page 504.

Olympia Career Training Institute Ⓐ

5349 West Main Street
Kalamazoo, MI 49009
Web: http://www.olympia-institute.com

Accreditation: Accrediting Bureau of Health Education Schools

Programs Offered: dental assisting; massage therapy; medical administrative assistant and medical secretary; medical/clinical assistant; medical insurance coding; pharmacy technician

Enrollment: 450 students

Institution Contact: Ms. Gloria Stender, Director of Admissions *Phone:* 269-381-9616 *Fax:* 269-381-2513 *E-mail:* gstender@cci.edu

Admission Contact: Ms. Susan Smith, Director of Admissions *Phone:* 269-381-9616 *Fax:* 269-381-2513 *E-mail:* susans@cci.edu

See full description on page 505.

Ross Medical Education Center

4741 Washtenaw
Ann Arbor, MI 48108-1411

Programs Offered: medical/clinical assistant

Institution Contact: Pat Sadler, Director *Phone:* 734-434-7320 *Fax:* 734-434-8579

Ross Medical Education Center

5757 Whitmore Lake Road, Suite 800
Brighton, MI 48116

Programs Offered: medical/clinical assistant

Institution Contact: Sharon Tremuth, Director *Phone:* 810-227-0160 *Fax:* 810-227-9582

Ross Medical Education Center

1036 Gilbert Street
Flint, MI 48532

Programs Offered: medical/clinical assistant

Institution Contact: Ms. Martha Watts, Director *Phone:* 810-230-1100 *Fax:* 810-230-6755

Ross Medical Education Center

2035 28th Street, SE
Grand Rapids, MI 49508

Programs Offered: medical/clinical assistant

Institution Contact: Brooksie Smith, Director *Phone:* 616-243-3070 *Fax:* 616-243-2937

Ross Medical Education Center

913 West Holmes, Suite 260
Lansing, MI 48910

Programs Offered: medical/clinical assistant

Institution Contact: Kelly Byrnes, Director *Phone:* 517-887-0180 *Fax:* 517-887-2393 *E-mail:* kbyrnes@rosslearning.com

Ross Medical Education Center

3568 Pine Grove
Port Huron, MI 48060

Programs Offered: medical/clinical assistant

Institution Contact: Kristine Furtaw, Director *Phone:* 810-982-0454 *Fax:* 810-982-0590 *E-mail:* kfurtaw@rosslearning.com

Ross Medical Education Center

9327 Telegraph Road
Redford, MI 48239

Programs Offered: medical/clinical assistant

Institution Contact: Merrideth Perry-Moore, Director *Phone:* 313-794-6448 *Fax:* 313-794-6573

Ross Medical Education Center

950 Norton Avenue
Roosevelt Park, MI 49441

Programs Offered: medical/clinical assistant

Institution Contact: Marge Scheneman, Director *Phone:* 231-739-1531 *Fax:* 231-739-7456

Ross Medical Education Center

27120 Dequindre
Warren, MI 48092

Programs Offered: medical/clinical assistant

Institution Contact: Terri Charison, Director *Phone:* 586-574-0830 *Fax:* 586-574-0851

Ⓐ indicates that the school is a participating institution in the *Imagine America* Scholarship Program.

Ross Medical Education Center—Saginaw Campus

4054 Bay Road
Saginaw, MI 48603

Programs Offered: medical/clinical assistant

Institution Contact: Kathy Leach, Director *Phone:* 989-793-9800 *Fax:* 989-793-0003 *E-mail:* kleach@rosslearning.com

Specs Howard School of Broadcast Arts Inc. Ⓐ

19900 West Nine Mile Road
Southfield, MI 48075-3953
Web: http://www.specshoward.edu

Accreditation: Accrediting Commission of Career Schools and Colleges of Technology

Programs Offered: radio and television

Enrollment: 535 students

Institution Contact: Mr. Jonathan Liebman, President/CEO *Phone:* 248-358-9000 *Fax:* 248-746-9772 *E-mail:* jliebman@specshoward.edu

Admission Contact: Ms. Nancy Shiner, Director of Admissions *Phone:* 248-358-9000 ext. 225 *Fax:* 248-746-9772 *E-mail:* nshiner@specshoward.edu

See full description on page 506.

Minnesota

Academy College

1101 East 78th Street, Suite 100
Minneapolis, MN 55420
Web: http://www.academycollege.edu

Accreditation: Accrediting Council for Independent Colleges and Schools

Programs Offered: accounting; aircraft pilot (private); airline pilot and flight crew; animation, interactive technology, video graphics and special effects; art; aviation/airway management; business administration and management; commercial and advertising art; computer and information systems security; computer graphics; computer installation and repair technology; computer programming; computer programming (specific applications); computer science; computer software and media applications; computer systems networking and telecommunications; computer/technical support; digital communi-

cation and media/multimedia; human resources management; legal administrative assistant/secretary; medical administrative assistant and medical secretary; medical insurance coding; medical office assistant; medical transcription; office management; safety/security technology; system administration; taxation; web/multimedia management and webmaster; web page, digital/multimedia and information resources design

Institution Contact: Ms. Nancy Grazzini-Olson, President *Phone:* 952-851-0066 *Fax:* 952-851-0094 *E-mail:* ngo@academycollege.edu

Admission Contact: Mr. Paul Burkhartzmeyer, Director of Admissions *Phone:* 952-851-0066 *Fax:* 952-851-0094 *E-mail:* admissions@academycollege.edu

The Art Institutes International Minnesota Ⓐ

15 South 9th Street
Minneapolis, MN 55402
Web: http://www.aim.artinstitutes.edu

Accreditation: Accrediting Council for Independent Colleges and Schools

Programs Offered: advertising; animation, interactive technology, video graphics and special effects; baking and pastry arts; commercial and advertising art; computer graphics; culinary arts; design and visual communications; digital communication and media/multimedia; food service and dining room management; interior design; photography; web/multimedia management and webmaster; web page, digital/multimedia and information resources design

Enrollment: 1,380 students

Institution Contact: Anjila Kozel, Director of Public Relations and Marketing *Phone:* 800-777-3643 ext. 6862 *Fax:* 612-338-2417 *E-mail:* akozel@aii.edu

Admission Contact: Mr. Russ Gill, Director of Admissions *Phone:* 800-777-3643 ext. 6820 *Fax:* 612-332-3934 *E-mail:* rgill@aii.edu

See full description on page 507.

Brown College

1440 Northland Drive
Mendota Heights, MN 55120-1004
Web: http://www.browncollege.edu

Accreditation: Accrediting Commission of Career Schools and Colleges of Technology

Programs Offered: business administration and management; commercial and advertising art; communications technology; computer and information sciences related; computer/information technology administration and management; computer

---

Ⓐ indicates that the school is a participating institution in the *Imagine America* Scholarship Program.

programming; computer systems networking and telecommunications; criminal justice/law enforcement administration; culinary arts; digital communication and media/multimedia; graphic communications related; information technology; interior design; medical office assistant; medical office management; radio and television; radio and television broadcasting technology; system administration; system, networking, and LAN/WAN management; web page, digital/multimedia and information resources design

Enrollment: 1,652 students

Institution Contact: Dr. Ronald A. Swanson, Chancellor/CEO *Phone:* 651-905-3409 *Fax:* 651-905-3510 *E-mail:* rswanson@browncollege.edu

Admission Contact: Ms. Mary Strand, Director of High School Admissions *Phone:* 651-905-3485 *Fax:* 651-905-3540 *E-mail:* mstrand@browncollege.edu

Bryman Institute (A)

1000 Blue Gentian Road, Suite 250, Spectrum Commerce Center
Eagan, MN 55121
Web: http://www.bryman-institute.com

Accreditation: Accrediting Commission of Career Schools and Colleges of Technology

Programs Offered: massage therapy; medical/clinical assistant; medical insurance/medical billing

Enrollment: 125 students

Institution Contact: Mr. Kevin L. Sanderson, President *Phone:* 651-668-2145 ext. 102 *Fax:* 651-686-8029 *E-mail:* ksanderson@cci.edu

Admission Contact: Mr. Douglas Lockwood, Director of Admissions *Phone:* 651-688-2145 ext. 103 *Fax:* 651-686-8029 *E-mail:* dlockwood@cci.edu

See full description on page 508.

Capella University

222 South 9th Street, 20th Floor
Minneapolis, MN 55402
Web: http://www.capellauniversity.edu

Accreditation: North Central Association of Colleges and Schools

Programs Offered: adult and continuing education; business administration and management; computer and information systems security; computer graphics; computer/information technology administration and management; computer/information technology services administration related; computer programming; computer programming related; computer programming (specific applications); computer software and media applications; computer software and media applications related; computer software

engineering; computer systems analysis; computer systems networking and telecommunications; corrections; counselor education/school counseling and guidance; criminal justice/law enforcement administration; criminal justice/police science; digital communication and media/multimedia; e-commerce; education; educational/instructional media design; educational leadership and administration; education (specific levels and methods) related; elementary education; health/health care administration; human resources development; human resources management; human services; information technology; insurance; management information systems; marketing/marketing management; mental health counseling; quality control technology; secondary education; selling skills and sales; substance abuse/addiction counseling; system, networking, and LAN/WAN management; technology management; web/multimedia management and webmaster; web page, digital/multimedia and information resources design

Enrollment: 10,800 students

Institution Contact: Mr. Gregory Thom, Vice President of Government Affairs *Phone:* 612-659-5470 *Fax:* 612-659-5057 *E-mail:* greg.thom@capella.edu

Admission Contact: Enrollment Services *Phone:* 888-227-3552 ext. 8 *Fax:* 612-339-8022 *E-mail:* info@capella.edu

Duluth Business University (A)

4724 Mike Colalillo Drive
Duluth, MN 55807
Web: http://www.dbumn.edu

Accreditation: Accrediting Council for Independent Colleges and Schools

Programs Offered: accounting; administrative assistant and secretarial science; business administration and management; graphic communications related; massage therapy; medical/clinical assistant; medical insurance/medical billing; office management; veterinary/animal health technology; veterinary technology

Enrollment: 350 students

Institution Contact: Ms. Bonnie Kupczynski, Director *Phone:* 218-722-4000 *Fax:* 218-628-2127 *E-mail:* bonniek@dbumn.edu

Admission Contact: Mr. Mark Truax, Director of Admissions *Phone:* 218-740-4345 *Fax:* 218-628-2127 *E-mail:* markt@dbumn.edu

See full description on page 509.

(A) indicates that the school is a participating institution in the *Imagine America* Scholarship Program.

Globe College

7166 10th Street North
Oakdale, MN 55128
Web: http://www.globecollege.edu

Accreditation: Accrediting Council for Independent Colleges and Schools

Programs Offered: accounting; accounting technology and bookkeeping; administrative assistant and secretarial science; business administration and management; commercial and advertising art; computer engineering technology; computer graphics; computer/information technology administration and management; computer/information technology services administration related; computer software engineering; computer/technical support; cosmetology; e-commerce; information technology; legal administrative assistant/secretary; legal assistant/paralegal; massage therapy; medical administrative assistant and medical secretary; medical/clinical assistant; music management and merchandising; nail technician and manicurist; veterinary technology; web/multimedia management and webmaster

Enrollment: 900 students

Institution Contact: Mr. Mike Hughes, Director *Phone:* 651-730-5100 ext. 329 *Fax:* 651-730-5151 *E-mail:* mhughes@globecollege.edu

Admission Contact: Mr. Rob Harker, Director of Admissions *Phone:* 651-730-5100 ext. 313 *Fax:* 651-730-5151 *E-mail:* rharker@globecollege.edu

Herzing College, Lakeland Medical–Dental Division ⓐ

5700 West Broadway
Minneapolis, MN 55428
Web: http://www.herzing.edu

Accreditation: Accrediting Commission of Career Schools and Colleges of Technology

Programs Offered: dental assisting; dental hygiene; massage therapy; medical/clinical assistant; medical insurance coding; medical insurance/medical billing

Admission Contact: Mr. James Decker, Director of Admissions *Phone:* 763-535-3000 *Fax:* 763-535-9205 *E-mail:* info@mpls.herzing.edu

See full description on page 510.

Herzing College, Minneapolis Drafting School Division ⓐ

5700 West Broadway
Minneapolis, MN 55428-3548
Web: http://www.herzing.edu

Accreditation: Accrediting Commission of Career Schools and Colleges of Technology; North Central Association of Colleges and Schools

Programs Offered: CAD/CADD drafting/design technology; computer systems networking and telecommunications; dental assisting; dental hygiene; drafting and design technology; medical/clinical assistant; medical insurance coding; technology management; web page, digital/multimedia and information resources design

Enrollment: 400 students

Institution Contact: Mr. Thomas Kosel, President *Phone:* 763-535-3000 ext. 151 *Fax:* 763-535-9205 *E-mail:* tkosel@mpls.herzing.edu

Admission Contact: Mr. James Decker, Director of Admissions *Phone:* 763-535-3000 ext. 152 *Fax:* 763-535-9205 *E-mail:* jdecker@mpls.herzing.edu

See full description on page 511.

High-Tech Institute

5100 Gamble Drive
St. Louis Park, MN 55416
Web: http://www.hightechinstitute.edu

Accreditation: Accrediting Bureau of Health Education Schools; Accrediting Commission of Career Schools and Colleges of Technology

Programs Offered: computer systems networking and telecommunications; massage therapy; medical/clinical assistant; medical insurance coding; medical insurance/medical billing; medical radiologic technology; pharmacy technician; surgical technology

Enrollment: 750 students

Institution Contact: Mr. Todd Brown, Campus President *Phone:* 952-417-2200 *Fax:* 952-545-6149 *E-mail:* tbrown@hightechinstitute.edu

Admission Contact: Mr. Paul Keprios, Director of Admissions *Phone:* 952-417-2200 *Fax:* 952-545-6149 *E-mail:* pkeprios@hightechinstitute.edu

ITT Technical Institute

8911 Columbine Road
Eden Prairie, MN 55347-4143
Web: http://www.itt-tech.edu

Accreditation: Accrediting Council for Independent Colleges and Schools

Programs Offered: animation, interactive technology, video graphics and special effects; CAD/CADD drafting/design technology; communications technology; computer and information systems security; computer engineering technology; computer software and media applications; computer software engineering; computer systems networking and telecommunications; digital communication and media/multimedia; electrical, electronic and communications

ⓐ indicates that the school is a participating institution in the *Imagine America* Scholarship Program.

engineering technology; technology management; web page, digital/multimedia and information resources design

Enrollment: 160 students

Institution Contact: Michele Ernst, Director *Phone:* 952-914-5300

Admission Contact: John Nelson, Director of Recruitment *Phone:* 952-914-5300

Minneapolis Business College

1711 West County Road B
Roseville, MN 55113
Web: http://www.minneapolisbusinesscollege.edu

Accreditation: Accrediting Council for Independent Colleges and Schools

Programs Offered: accounting; administrative assistant and secretarial science; commercial and advertising art; computer programming (specific applications); computer systems networking and telecommunications; hotel/motel administration; legal administrative assistant/secretary; medical/clinical assistant; tourism and travel services management

Enrollment: 304 students

Institution Contact: Mr. David Blair Whitman, President *Phone:* 651-604-4118 *Fax:* 651-636-8185 *E-mail:* dwhitman@minneapolisbusinesscollege.edu

Minnesota School of Business—Brooklyn Center

5910 Shingle Creek Parkway, Suite 200
Brooklyn Center, MN 55430
Web: http://www.msbcollege.edu

Accreditation: Accrediting Council for Independent Colleges and Schools

Programs Offered: accounting; business administration and management; computer engineering related; computer graphics; computer programming related; executive assistant/executive secretary; legal administrative assistant/secretary; legal assistant/paralegal; massage therapy; medical administrative assistant and medical secretary; medical/clinical assistant; veterinary technology

Enrollment: 850 students

Institution Contact: Ms. Susan Lynne Cooke, Director *Phone:* 763-585-5225 *Fax:* 763-566-7030 *E-mail:* scooke@msbcollege.edu

Admission Contact: Mr. Jeffrey Lee Georgeson, Director of Admissions *Phone:* 763-585-5206 *Fax:* 763-566-7030 *E-mail:* jgeorgeson@msbcollege.edu

Minnesota School of Business-Plymouth

1455 County Road 101 N
Plymouth, MN 55447
Web: http://www.msbcollege.edu

Accreditation: Accrediting Council for Independent Colleges and Schools

Programs Offered: accounting; administrative assistant and secretarial science; business administration and management; clinical/medical laboratory assistant; commercial and advertising art; computer graphics; computer/information technology administration and management; computer/information technology services administration related; computer programming; computer programming (specific applications); computer software and media applications; computer systems networking and telecommunications; digital communication and media/multimedia; e-commerce; information technology; legal assistant/paralegal; marketing/marketing management; massage therapy; medical administrative assistant and medical secretary; medical/clinical assistant; music management and merchandising; sport and fitness administration; system administration; veterinary/animal health technology; veterinary technology; web/multimedia management and webmaster; web page, digital/multimedia and information resources design

Enrollment: 700 students

Institution Contact: Mr. Jeff Myhre, Campus Director *Phone:* 763-476-2000 *Fax:* 763-476-1000 *E-mail:* jmyhre@msbcollege.edu

Admission Contact: Mr. Don Baker, Admissions Director *Phone:* 763-476-2000 *Fax:* 763-476-1000 *E-mail:* dbaker@msbcollege.edu

Minnesota School of Business-Richfield

1401 West 76th Street
Richfield, MN 55423

Accreditation: Accrediting Council for Independent Colleges and Schools

Programs Offered: accounting; business administration and management; computer graphics; e-commerce; legal administrative assistant/secretary; legal assistant/paralegal; massage therapy; medical administrative assistant and medical secretary; medical/clinical assistant; veterinary technology

Institution Contact: Mr. George Teagarden, Director *Phone:* 612-861-2000 *Fax:* 612-861-5548 *E-mail:* gteagarden@msbcollege.edu

Admission Contact: Ms. Patricia Murray, Director of Admissions *Phone:* 612-861-2000 ext. 720 *Fax:* 612-861-5548 *E-mail:* pmurray@msbcollege.edu

🅐 indicates that the school is a participating institution in the *Imagine America* Scholarship Program.

National American University

W112 West Market
Bloomington, MN 55425
Web: http://www.national.edu

Accreditation: North Central Association of Colleges and Schools

Programs Offered: accounting; business administration and management; information technology

Institution Contact: Ms. Mary Ellen Schmidt, Regional President *Phone:* 952-883-0439 *Fax:* 952-883-0106 *E-mail:* mschmidt@national.edu

National American University

6120 Earle Brown Drive, Suite 100
Brooklyn Center, MN 55430
Web: http://www.national.edu

Accreditation: North Central Association of Colleges and Schools

Programs Offered: accounting; business administration and management; information science/studies; information technology; legal assistant/paralegal; marketing/marketing management

Enrollment: 230 students

Institution Contact: Dr. Jeffrey S. Allen, Campus Vice President *Phone:* 763-560-8377 *Fax:* 763-549-9955 *E-mail:* jallen@national.edu

Admission Contact: Ms. Claudia Tomlin, Director of Admissions *Phone:* 763-560-8377 *Fax:* 763-549-9955 *E-mail:* ctomlin@national.edu

National American University

1550 West Highway 36
Roseville, MN 55113
Web: http://www.national.edu

Accreditation: North Central Association of Colleges and Schools

Programs Offered: accounting; business administration and management; information technology; massage therapy; medical administrative assistant and medical secretary; medical/clinical assistant; medical reception

Enrollment: 248 students

Institution Contact: Mr. Gene Muilenburg, Campus Director *Phone:* 651-644-1265 *Fax:* 651-644-0690 *E-mail:* gmuilenburg@national.edu

Admission Contact: Bay Vang, Admissions Representative *Phone:* 651-644-1265 *Fax:* 651-644-0690 *E-mail:* bvang@national.edu

Northwest Technical Institute

11995 Singletree Lane
Eden Prairie, MN 55344-5351
Web: http://www.nti.edu

Accreditation: Accrediting Commission of Career Schools and Colleges of Technology

Programs Offered: architectural drafting and CAD/CADD; CAD/CADD drafting/design technology; drafting and design technology; electrical/electronics drafting and CAD/CADD; engineering technology

Enrollment: 90 students

Institution Contact: Mr. Michael E. Kotchevar, President *Phone:* 952-944-0080 ext. 101 *Fax:* 952-944-9274 *E-mail:* mkotchevar@nti.edu

Admission Contact: Mr. John K. Hartman, Director of Marketing and Admissions *Phone:* 952-944-0080 ext. 103 *Fax:* 952-944-9274 *E-mail:* jhartman@nti.edu

Rasmussen College Eagan

3500 Federal Drive
Eagan, MN 55122
Web: http://www.rasmussen.edu

Accreditation: Accrediting Council for Independent Colleges and Schools; North Central Association of Colleges and Schools

Programs Offered: accounting; administrative assistant and secretarial science; banking and financial support services; business administration and management; business/corporate communications; child care and support services management; child care provision; computer and information systems security; computer/information technology administration and management; computer/information technology services administration related; computer systems networking and telecommunications; computer/technical support; data entry/microcomputer applications; data entry/microcomputer applications related; health information/medical records technology; information science/studies; information technology; marketing/marketing management; medical administrative assistant and medical secretary; medical insurance coding; medical office management; medical transcription; restaurant, culinary, and catering management; retailing; selling skills and sales; system, networking, and LAN/WAN management; web page, digital/multimedia and information resources design; word processing

Institution Contact: Ms. Tawnie L. Cortez, Campus Director *Phone:* 651-687-9000 *Fax:* 651-687-0507 *E-mail:* tawniec@rasmussen.edu

Admission Contact: Ms. Jacinda Miller, Admission Coordinator *Phone:* 651-687-9000 *Fax:* 651-687-0507 *E-mail:* jacindam@rasmussen.edu

---

Ⓐ indicates that the school is a participating institution in the *Imagine America* Scholarship Program.

Rasmussen College Mankato

501 Holly Lane
Mankato, MN 56001-6803
Web: http://www.rasmussen.edu/

Accreditation: Accrediting Council for Independent Colleges and Schools; North Central Association of Colleges and Schools

Programs Offered: accounting; accounting and business/management; administrative assistant and secretarial science; banking and financial support services; business administration and management; business, management, and marketing related; criminal justice/law enforcement administration; health information/medical records technology; health unit coordinator/ward clerk; human resources management; massage therapy; pharmacy technician; selling skills and sales; system, networking, and LAN/WAN management

Enrollment: 400 students

Institution Contact: Mr. Douglas Gardner, Director *Phone:* 507-625-6556 *Fax:* 507-625-6557 *E-mail:* dougg@rasmussen.edu

Admission Contact: Kathy Clifford, Director of Admissions *Phone:* 507-625-6556 *Fax:* 507-625-6557 *E-mail:* kathyc@rasmussen.edu

Rasmussen College Minnetonka

12450 Wayzata Boulevard, Suite 315
Minnetonka, MN 55305-1928
Web: http://www.rasmussen.edu

Accreditation: Accrediting Council for Independent Colleges and Schools; North Central Association of Colleges and Schools

Programs Offered: accounting; accounting technology and bookkeeping; administrative assistant and secretarial science; banking and financial support services; business administration and management; business/corporate communications; child care and support services management; child care provision; computer and information systems security; computer/information technology administration and management; computer/information technology services administration related; computer software and media applications; computer systems networking and telecommunications; computer/technical support; criminal justice/law enforcement administration; data entry/microcomputer applications; e-commerce; health/health care administration; health information/medical records administration; health information/medical records technology; health unit coordinator/ward clerk; health unit management/ward supervision; human resources management; information science/studies; information technology; legal administrative assistant/secretary; marketing/

marketing management; medical administrative assistant and medical secretary; medical insurance coding; medical office management; medical reception; medical transcription; office management; office occupations and clerical services; receptionist; retailing; selling skills and sales; system, networking, and LAN/WAN management; tourism and travel services management; web page, digital/multimedia and information resources design; word processing

Enrollment: 370 students

Institution Contact: Ms. Kathy P. Howe, Campus Director *Phone:* 952-545-2000 *Fax:* 952-545-7038 *E-mail:* kathyh@rasmussen.edu

Rasmussen College St. Cloud

226 Park Avenue, South
St. Cloud, MN 56301-3713
Web: http://www.rasmussen.edu/

Accreditation: Accrediting Council for Independent Colleges and Schools; North Central Association of Colleges and Schools

Programs Offered: accounting; accounting and business/management; accounting and finance; administrative assistant and secretarial science; banking and financial support services; business administration and management; business operations support and secretarial services related; child care and support services management; child care provision; computer hardware technology; computer/information technology services administration related; computer systems networking and telecommunications; computer/technical support; computer technology/computer systems technology; criminal justice/law enforcement administration; criminal justice/police science; desktop publishing and digital imaging design; e-commerce; executive assistant/executive secretary; health information/medical records administration; health information/medical records technology; health unit coordinator/ward clerk; hotel/motel administration; information technology; insurance; internet information systems; legal administrative assistant/secretary; marketing/marketing management; massage therapy; medical insurance coding; medical insurance/medical billing; medical office management; medical pharmacology and pharmaceutical sciences; medical reception; medical transcription; office management; pharmacy technician; receptionist; system, networking, and LAN/WAN management; tourism and travel services management

Enrollment: 503 students

Institution Contact: Ms. Cathy Wogen, Director *Phone:* 320-251-5600 *Fax:* 320-251-3702 *E-mail:* cathyw@rasmussen.edu

---

Ⓐ indicates that the school is a participating institution in the *Imagine America* Scholarship Program.

Rasmussen College St. Cloud (continued)

Admission Contact: Ms. Andrea Peters, Director of Admissions *Phone:* 320-251-5600 *Fax:* 320-251-3702 *E-mail:* andreap@rasmussen.edu

Walden University

155 Fifth Avenue South
Minneapolis, MN 55401
Web: http://www.waldenu.edu

Accreditation: North Central Association of Colleges and Schools

Programs Offered: business administration and management; education; health/health care administration; human services; information science/studies; marketing/marketing management

Institution Contact: Mr. Jonathan Kaplan, Vice President, Business and Regulatory Affairs *Phone:* 800-925-3368 *Fax:* 612-338-5092

Admission Contact: *Phone:* 800-925-3368 *Fax:* 612-338-5092

Mississippi

Blue Cliff College

942 Beach Drive
Gulfport, MS 39507
Web: http://www.bluecliffcollege.com

Accreditation: Accrediting Commission of Career Schools and Colleges of Technology

Programs Offered: massage therapy

Institution Contact: Admissions *Phone:* 228-896-9727 *E-mail:* admissions_glf@bluecliffcollege.com

Virginia College at Jackson Ⓐ

5360 I-55 North
Jackson, MS 39211
Web: http://www.vc.edu

Accreditation: Accrediting Council for Independent Colleges and Schools

Programs Offered: accounting; administrative assistant and secretarial science; aesthetician/esthetician and skin care; biomedical technology; business administration and management; computer engineering related; computer hardware engineering; computer/information technology administration and management; computer installation and repair technology; computer programming related; computer technology/computer systems technology; cosmetology; cosmetology, barber/styling, and nail instruction; criminal justice/law enforcement administration; electrical, electronic and communications engineering technology; human resources management; human resources management and services related; massage therapy; medical/clinical assistant; medical insurance/medical billing; medical office management; nail technician and manicurist; surgical technology

Enrollment: 1,200 students

Institution Contact: Mrs. Madeline Little, President *Phone:* 601-977-0960 *Fax:* 601-956-4325 *E-mail:* mtlittle@vc.edu

Admission Contact: Mr. Bill Milstead, Director of Admissions *Phone:* 601-977-0960 *Fax:* 601-956-4325 *E-mail:* bmilstead@vc.edu

See full description on page 512.

Missouri

Allied College

1227 Water Tower Place
Arnold, MO 63010
Web: http://www.alliedcollege.edu

Accreditation: Accrediting Bureau of Health Education Schools

Programs Offered: dental assisting; massage therapy; medical/clinical assistant; medical insurance coding; medical insurance/medical billing; pharmacy technician

Institution Contact: Admissions *Phone:* 866-502-2627

Allied College

500 Northwest Plaza Tower, Suite 400
St. Ann, MO 63074
Web: http://www.alliedcollege.edu

Accreditation: Accrediting Bureau of Health Education Schools

Programs Offered: dental assisting; health aide; health/health care administration; health information/medical records technology; massage therapy; medical/clinical assistant; pharmacy technician

Institution Contact: Mr. Larkin Hicks, President *Phone:* 314-739-4450 *Fax:* 314-739-5133 *E-mail:* lhicks@alliedmedicalcollege.com

Ⓐ indicates that the school is a participating institution in the *Imagine America* Scholarship Program.

Admission Contact: Ms. Donna Pettigrew, Director of Admissions *Phone:* 314-739-4450 *Fax:* 314-739-5133 *E-mail:* dpettigrew@alliedmedicalcollege.com

Bryan College

237 South Florence Avenue
Springfield, MO 65806
Web: http://www.bryancollege.com

Accreditation: Accrediting Council for Independent Colleges and Schools

Programs Offered: allied health and medical assisting services related; business administration and management; clinical/medical laboratory assistant; computer and information sciences; computer and information sciences and support services related; computer and information sciences related; computer programming; computer programming related; computer programming (specific applications); computer science; computer systems analysis; computer systems networking and telecommunications; computer/technical support; computer technology/computer systems technology; human resources management; information science/studies; information technology; medical/clinical assistant; medical office assistant; sport and fitness administration; system administration; system, networking, and LAN/WAN management; tourism and travel services management

Enrollment: 225 students

Institution Contact: Mr. Brian Stewart, President/CEO *Phone:* 417-862-5700 *Fax:* 417-862-9554 *E-mail:* bstewart@bryancollege.com

Admission Contact: Ms. Jamie Carpenter, Director of Admissions *Phone:* 417-862-5700 *Fax:* 417-865-7144 *E-mail:* jcarpenter@bryancollege.com

Hickey College

940 West Port Plaza
St. Louis, MO 63146
Web: http://www.hickeycollege.edu

Accreditation: Accrediting Council for Independent Colleges and Schools

Programs Offered: accounting; administrative assistant and secretarial science; business administration and management; business operations support and secretarial services related; commercial and advertising art; computer graphics; computer programming; computer programming (specific applications); computer software technology; computer systems networking and telecommunications; computer/technical support; information resources management; legal administrative assistant/secretary; legal assistant/paralegal

Enrollment: 450 students

Institution Contact: Mr. Christopher Gearin, President *Phone:* 314-434-2212 *Fax:* 314-434-1974 *E-mail:* admin@hickeycollege.com

High-Tech Institute

9001 State Line Road
Kansas City, MO 64114
Web: http://www.hightechinstitute.edu

Accreditation: Accrediting Commission of Career Schools and Colleges of Technology

Programs Offered: dental assisting; massage therapy; medical/clinical assistant; medical insurance coding; surgical technology

Institution Contact: Mr. Peter Hogaboom, Campus Director *Phone:* 816-444-4300 *Fax:* 816-444-4494 *E-mail:* phogaboom@hightechinstitute.edu

Admission Contact: Ms. Barbette Hatcher, Director of Admission *Phone:* 816-444-4300 *Fax:* 816-444-4494 *E-mail:* bhatcher@hightechinstitute.edu

ITT Technical Institute Ⓐ

1930 Meyer Drury Drive
Arnold, MO 63010
Web: http://www.itt-tech.edu

Accreditation: Accrediting Council for Independent Colleges and Schools

Programs Offered: accounting and business/management; animation, interactive technology, video graphics and special effects; business administration and management; CAD/CADD drafting/design technology; communications technology; computer and information systems security; computer engineering technology; computer software and media applications; computer software engineering; computer systems networking and telecommunications; criminal justice/police science; digital communication and media/multimedia; electrical, electronic and communications engineering technology; technology management; web page, digital/multimedia and information resources design

Enrollment: 621 students

Institution Contact: Ms. Paula Jerden, Director *Phone:* 636-464-6600

Admission Contact: Mr. James R. Rowe, Director of Recruitment *Phone:* 636-464-6600

See full description on page 513.

ITT Technical Institute Ⓐ

13505 Lakefront Drive
Earth City, MO 63045-1412
Web: http://www.itt-tech.edu

Accreditation: Accrediting Council for Independent Colleges and Schools

Ⓐ indicates that the school is a participating institution in the *Imagine America* Scholarship Program.

ITT Technical Institute *(continued)*

Programs Offered: accounting and business/management; animation, interactive technology, video graphics and special effects; business administration and management; CAD/CADD drafting/design technology; communications technology; computer and information systems security; computer engineering technology; computer software and media applications; computer software engineering; computer systems networking and telecommunications; criminal justice/police science; digital communication and media/multimedia; electrical, electronic and communications engineering technology; technology management; web page, digital/multimedia and information resources design

Enrollment: 629 students

Institution Contact: Ms. Karen Finkenkeller, Director *Phone:* 314-298-7800

Admission Contact: Ms. Karla Milla, Director of Recruitment *Phone:* 314-298-7800

See full description on page 514.

Metro Business College

1732 North Kings Highway
Cape Girardeau, MO 63701
Web: http://www.metrobusinesscollege.edu

Accreditation: Accrediting Council for Independent Colleges and Schools

Programs Offered: administrative assistant and secretarial science; business automation/technology/data entry; computer/information technology administration and management; massage therapy; medical administrative assistant and medical secretary

Enrollment: 149 students

Institution Contact: Ms. Jan Reimann, Director *Phone:* 573-334-9181 *Fax:* 573-334-0617 *E-mail:* jan@metrobusinesscollege.edu

Admission Contact: Mrs. Denise Acey, Admissions Representative *Phone:* 573-334-9181 *Fax:* 573-334-0617 *E-mail:* denise@metrobusinesscollege.edu

Metro Business College

1407 Southwest Boulevard
Jefferson City, MO 65109
Web: http://www.metrobusinesscollege.edu

Accreditation: Accrediting Council for Independent Colleges and Schools

Programs Offered: administrative assistant and secretarial science; business automation/technology/data entry; computer/information technology administration and management; massage therapy; medical administrative assistant and medical secretary; medical reception

Enrollment: 142 students

Institution Contact: Ms. Cheri Chockley, Campus Director *Phone:* 573-635-6600 *Fax:* 573-635-6999 *E-mail:* cheri@metrobusinesscollege.edu

Admission Contact: Ms. Patti Sander, Admission Representative *Phone:* 573-635-6600 *Fax:* 573-635-6999 *E-mail:* patti@metrobusinesscollege.edu

Metro Business College

1202 East Highway 72
Rolla, MO 65401
Web: http://www.metrobusinesscollege.edu

Accreditation: Accrediting Council for Independent Colleges and Schools

Programs Offered: administrative assistant and secretarial science; business automation/technology/data entry; computer/information technology administration and management; massage therapy; medical/health management and clinical assistant; medical office computer specialist; medical reception

Enrollment: 125 students

Institution Contact: Ms. Cristie Barker, Director *Phone:* 573-364-8464 *Fax:* 573-364-8077 *E-mail:* cbarker76@hotmail.com

Missouri College Ⓐ

10121 Manchester Road
St. Louis, MO 63122
Web: http://www.missouricollege.com

Accreditation: Accrediting Commission of Career Schools and Colleges of Technology

Programs Offered: administrative assistant and secretarial science; computer software engineering; computer systems networking and telecommunications; data entry/microcomputer applications; dental assisting; executive assistant/executive secretary; information technology; massage therapy; medical administrative assistant and medical secretary; medical/clinical assistant; medical office management; selling skills and sales

Institution Contact: Ms. Erin Cunningham, Admissions Director *Phone:* 314-821-7700 *Fax:* 314-821-0891 *E-mail:* info@missouricollege.com

See full description on page 515.

Ⓐ indicates that the school is a participating institution in the *Imagine America* Scholarship Program.

Missouri Tech Ⓐ

1167 Corporate Lake Drive
St. Louis, MO 63132-2907
Web: http://www.motech.edu

Accreditation: Accrediting Commission of Career Schools and Colleges of Technology

Programs Offered: artificial intelligence and robotics; computer and information sciences related; computer and information systems security; computer engineering related; computer engineering technology; computer graphics; computer hardware engineering; computer/information technology administration and management; computer/information technology services administration related; computer installation and repair technology; computer programming; computer programming related; computer programming (specific applications); computer programming (vendor/product certification); computer software and media applications; computer software and media applications related; computer software engineering; computer software technology; computer systems analysis; computer systems networking and telecommunications; computer/technical support; computer technology/computer systems technology; digital communication and media/multimedia; electrical, electronic and communications engineering technology; engineering technology; information science/studies; management information systems; system administration; system, networking, and LAN/WAN management; technology management; telecommunications; telecommunications technology

Enrollment: 200 students

Institution Contact: Mr. Paul Dodge, Director *Phone:* 314-569-3600 *Fax:* 314-569-1167 *E-mail:* pdodge@motech.edu

Admission Contact: Mr. Robert Honaker, Director of Student Affairs *Phone:* 314-569-3600 *Fax:* 314-569-1167 *E-mail:* bob@motech.edu

See full description on page 516.

National American University

4200 Blue Ridge Boulevard
Kansas City, MO 64133

Accreditation: North Central Association of Colleges and Schools

Programs Offered: accounting; business administration and management; business, management, and marketing related; computer programming; computer software technology; computer/technical support; e-commerce; general studies; information technology; legal assistant/paralegal; management information systems; nursing related; web/multimedia management and webmaster

Enrollment: 327 students

Institution Contact: Ms. Michelle Holland, Regional President *Phone:* 816-353-4554 *Fax:* 816-353-1176 *E-mail:* mholland@national.edu

Admission Contact: Mr. Marcus Smith, Director of Admissions *Phone:* 816-343-4554 *Fax:* 816-353-1176 *E-mail:* msmith2@national.edu

Pinnacle Career Institute

15329 Kensington Avenue
Kansas City, MO 64147
Web: http://www.pcitraining.com

Programs Offered: computer programming; medical/clinical assistant; telecommunications

Institution Contact: *Phone:* 816-331-5700

St. Louis College of Health Careers

4044 Butler Hill Road
St. Louis, MO 63129
Web: http://www.slchc.com

Programs Offered: massage therapy; medical/clinical assistant; medical insurance/medical billing; medical staff services technology; nursing (licensed practical/vocational nurse training); phlebotomy

Institution Contact: *Phone:* 314-845-6100 *Fax:* 314-845-6406

St. Louis College of Health Careers

909 South Taylor
St. Louis, MO 63110

Accreditation: Accrediting Bureau of Health Education Schools

Programs Offered: massage therapy; medical administrative assistant and medical secretary; medical/clinical assistant; medical insurance/medical billing; nursing assistant/aide and patient care assistant; nursing (licensed practical/vocational nurse training); ophthalmic and optometric support services and allied professions related; pharmacy technician; phlebotomy

Enrollment: 320 students

Institution Contact: Dr. Rush L. Robinson, President *Phone:* 314-652-0300 ext. 2001 *Fax:* 314-652-4825 *E-mail:* rrobinson@slchcmail.com

Admission Contact: Ms. Stephanie Todd, Admissions Director *Phone:* 314-652-0300 ext. 2100 *Fax:* 314-652-4825 *E-mail:* stodd@slchcmail.com

Ⓐ indicates that the school is a participating institution in the *Imagine America* Scholarship Program.

Sanford-Brown College Ⓐ

1203 Smizer Mill Road
Fenton, MO 63026
Web: http://www.sanford-brown.edu

Accreditation: Accrediting Council for Independent Colleges and Schools

Programs Offered: accounting; business administration and management; computer/information technology administration and management; computer systems networking and telecommunications; computer/technical support; health information/medical records technology; legal assistant/paralegal; massage therapy; medical/clinical assistant; medical insurance coding; medical insurance/medical billing; nursing (licensed practical/vocational nurse training); radiologic technology/science; respiratory care therapy; surgical technology; web page, digital/multimedia and information resources design

Institution Contact: Ms. Sarah Squires, Director of High School Admissions Support *Phone:* 636-349-4900 *Fax:* 636-349-9317

See full description on page 517.

Sanford-Brown College

75 Village Square
Hazelwood, MO 63042
Web: http://www.sanford-brown.edu

Accreditation: Accrediting Bureau of Health Education Schools; Accrediting Council for Independent Colleges and Schools

Programs Offered: accounting; administrative assistant and secretarial science; business administration and management; computer programming related; computer systems networking and telecommunications; legal assistant/paralegal; medical/clinical assistant

Institution Contact: Ms. Melissa Uding, Executive Director *Phone:* 314-731-5200 *Fax:* 314-731-7044

Admission Contact: Mr. Ken Thomas, Director of Admissions *Phone:* 314-731-5200 *Fax:* 314-731-7044 *E-mail:* kenneth.thomas@wix.net

Sanford-Brown College

520 East 19th Avenue
North Kansas City, MO 64116-3614
Web: http://www.sanford-browncollege.com

Accreditation: Accrediting Bureau of Health Education Schools; Accrediting Council for Independent Colleges and Schools

Programs Offered: business administration and management; computer/information technology administration and management; criminal justice/law enforcement administration; health/health care administration; marketing/marketing management; massage therapy; medical/clinical assistant; medical insurance/medical billing; nursing (licensed practical/vocational nurse training); radiologic technology/science; surgical technology

Enrollment: 560 students

Institution Contact: Mr. Dennis L. Townsend, Campus President *Phone:* 816-472-0275 *Fax:* 816-472-0688 *E-mail:* dtownsend@kc.sanfordbrown.com

Admission Contact: Mr. Micheal Murdie, Director of Admissions *Phone:* 816-472-0275 *Fax:* 816-472-0688 *E-mail:* micheal.murdie@wix.net

Sanford-Brown College

3555 Franks Drive
St. Charles, MO 63301
Web: http://www.sanford-brown.edu

Accreditation: Accrediting Council for Independent Colleges and Schools

Programs Offered: accounting; business administration and management; computer systems networking and telecommunications; data entry/microcomputer applications; health/health care administration; intermedia/multimedia; legal assistant/paralegal; nursing (licensed practical/vocational nurse training); nursing (registered nurse training); web page, digital/multimedia and information resources design

Institution Contact: Julia A. Leeman, President *Phone:* 636-949-2620 *Fax:* 636-925-9827 *E-mail:* jleeman@sbc-stcharles.com

Admission Contact: Mr. Doug Goodwin, Director of Admissions *Phone:* 636-949-2620 *Fax:* 636-949-5081 *E-mail:* dgoodwin@sbc-stcharles.com

Springfield College Ⓐ

1010 West Sunshine
Springfield, MO 65807
Web: http://www.Springfield-college.com

Accreditation: Accrediting Council for Independent Colleges and Schools

Programs Offered: accounting; business administration and management; computer programming (specific applications); dental assisting; legal assistant/paralegal; medical/clinical assistant; medical insurance/medical billing; medical office management; medical transcription

Enrollment: 600 students

Institution Contact: Mr. Gerald F. Terrebrood, President *Phone:* 417-864-7220 *Fax:* 417-864-5697 *E-mail:* gterrebr@cci.edu

Ⓐ indicates that the school is a participating institution in the *Imagine America* Scholarship Program.

Admission Contact: Mr. Scott Lester, Director of Admissions *Phone:* 417-864-7220 *Fax:* 417-864-5697 *E-mail:* slester@cci.edu

See full description on page 518.

Vatterott College Ⓐ

5898 North Main
Joplin, MO 64801
Web: http://www.vatterott-college.edu

Accreditation: Accrediting Commission of Career Schools and Colleges of Technology

Programs Offered: accounting; CAD/CADD drafting/design technology; computer/information technology administration and management; computer installation and repair technology; computer programming; computer software and media applications; cosmetology; medical administrative assistant and medical secretary; nail technician and manicurist

Institution Contact: Office of Admissions *Phone:* 417-781-5633 *Fax:* 417-781-6437 *E-mail:* joplin@vatterott-college.edu

See full description on page 519.

Vatterott College Ⓐ

8955 East 38th Terrace
Kansas City, MO 64129
Web: http://www.vatterott-college.edu

Accreditation: Accrediting Commission of Career Schools and Colleges of Technology

Programs Offered: administrative assistant and secretarial science; business automation/technology/data entry; computer installation and repair technology; computer programming; computer systems networking and telecommunications; drafting and design technology; electrician; heating, air conditioning and refrigeration technology; medical/clinical assistant; pharmacy technician

Institution Contact: Office of Admissions *Phone:* 816-861-1000 *Fax:* 816-861-1400 *E-mail:* kc@vatterott-college.edu

See full description on page 520.

Vatterott College Ⓐ

927 East Terra Lane
O'Fallon, MO 63366
Web: http://www.vatterott-college.edu

Accreditation: Accrediting Commission of Career Schools and Colleges of Technology

Programs Offered: building/property maintenance and management; computer systems networking and telecommunications; computer technology/computer systems technology; electrical/electronics equipment installation and repair; electrician; heating, air conditioning and refrigeration technology; heating, air conditioning, ventilation and refrigeration maintenance technology; medical administrative assistant and medical secretary; medical/clinical assistant; medical office assistant

Enrollment: 150 students

Institution Contact: Mr. Ray Flacke, Director *Phone:* 636-978-7488 *Fax:* 636-978-5121 *E-mail:* rflacke@vatterott-college.edu

Admission Contact: Jerry Martin, Director of Admissions *Phone:* 636-978-7488 *Fax:* 636-978-5121 *E-mail:* jmartin@vatterott-college.edu

See full description on page 521.

Vatterott College Ⓐ

3925 Industrial Drive
St. Ann, MO 63074
Web: http://www.vatterott-college.edu

Accreditation: Accrediting Commission of Career Schools and Colleges of Technology

Programs Offered: CAD/CADD drafting/design technology; computer engineering technology; computer programming; computer systems analysis; computer systems networking and telecommunications; computer technology/computer systems technology; electromechanical technology; heating, air conditioning and refrigeration technology; welding technology

Institution Contact: Director *Phone:* 888-370-7955 *Fax:* 314-428-5956

Admission Contact: Office of Admissions *Phone:* 888-370-7955 *Fax:* 314-428-5956 *E-mail:* saintann@vatterott-college.edu

See full description on page 522.

Vatterott College Ⓐ

3131 Frederick Boulevard
St. Joseph, MO 64506
Web: http://www.vatterott-college.edu

Accreditation: Accrediting Commission of Career Schools and Colleges of Technology

Programs Offered: administrative assistant and secretarial science; computer programming; computer technology/computer systems technology; cosmetology; drafting and design technology; health information/medical records technology; massage therapy; medical administrative assistant and medical secretary; medical/clinical assistant; medical office man-

Ⓐ indicates that the school is a participating institution in the *Imagine America* Scholarship Program.

Vatterott College *(continued)*

agement; medical transcription; nail technician and manicurist; office occupations and clerical services

Enrollment: 440 students

Institution Contact: Mr. Wayne Major, Director *Phone:* 816-364-5399 *Fax:* 816-364-1593 *E-mail:* wmajor@vatterott-college.edu

Admission Contact: Mrs. Sandra Wisdom, Director of Admissions *Phone:* 816-364-5399 *Fax:* 816-364-1593 *E-mail:* swisdom@vatterott-college.edu

See full description on page 524.

Vatterott College ⓐ
12970 Maurer Industrial Drive
St. Louis, MO 63127
Web: http://www.vatterott-college.edu

Accreditation: Accrediting Commission of Career Schools and Colleges of Technology

Programs Offered: building/property maintenance and management; CAD/CADD drafting/design technology; computer programming; computer technology/computer systems technology; electrical, electronic and communications engineering technology; heating, air conditioning and refrigeration technology; heating, air conditioning, ventilation and refrigeration maintenance technology; medical/clinical assistant

Institution Contact: Mr. James Rund, Co-Director *Phone:* 314-843-4200 *Fax:* 314-843-1709 *E-mail:* jrund@vatterott-college.edu

Admission Contact: Ms. Lee Ann Edwards, Director of Admissions *Phone:* 314-843-4200 *Fax:* 314-843-1709 *E-mail:* leeannb@vatterott-college.edu

See full description on page 525.

Vatterott College ⓐ
1258 East Trafficway
Springfield, MO 65802
Web: http://www.vatterott-college.edu

Accreditation: Accrediting Commission of Career Schools and Colleges of Technology

Programs Offered: administrative assistant and secretarial science; computer software and media applications; computer technology/computer systems technology; dental assisting; drafting and design technology; medical administrative assistant and medical secretary; medical/clinical assistant; pharmacy technician

Enrollment: 201 students

Institution Contact: Mrs. Cheryl Tilley, Director *Phone:* 417-831-8116 *Fax:* 417-831-5099 *E-mail:* ctilley@vatterott-college.edu

Admission Contact: Admissions *Phone:* 417-831-8116 *Fax:* 417-831-5099 *E-mail:* springfield@vatterott-college.edu

See full description on page 523.

Sage Technical Services
3044 Hesper Road
Billings, MT 59102
Web: http://www.sageschools.com

Accreditation: Accrediting Commission of Career Schools and Colleges of Technology

Programs Offered: transportation technology; truck and bus driver/commercial vehicle operation

Enrollment: 2 students

Institution Contact: Mr. Lew Grill, Director *Phone:* 406-652-3030 *Fax:* 406-652-3129 *E-mail:* lew@lewgrill.com

College of Hair Design
304 South 11th Street
Lincoln, NE 68508-2199
Web: http://www.collegeofhairdesign.com

Accreditation: Accrediting Commission of Career Schools and Colleges of Technology

Programs Offered: barbering; cosmetology

Enrollment: 125 students

Institution Contact: Mrs. Alyce Howard, President *Phone:* 402-477-4040 ext. 110 *Fax:* 402-474-4075 *E-mail:* greg@collegeofhairdesign.com

Admission Contact: Mr. Greg Howard, Vice President *Phone:* 402-477-4040 *Fax:* 402-474-4075 *E-mail:* greg@collegeofhairdesign.com

ⓐ indicates that the school is a participating institution in the *Imagine America* Scholarship Program.

Hamilton College-Lincoln

1821 K Street
Lincoln, NE 68508
Web: http://www.lincolnschoolofcommerce.com

Accreditation: Accrediting Council for Independent Colleges and Schools

Programs Offered: accounting; administrative assistant and secretarial science; business administration and management; computer programming; criminal justice/law enforcement administration; information technology; legal assistant/paralegal; medical/clinical assistant; office occupations and clerical services; tourism and travel services management

Institution Contact: Mr. Todd Lardenoit, Executive Director *Phone:* 402-474-5315 *Fax:* 402-474-5302 *E-mail:* tlardenoit@lincolnschoolofcommerce.com

Admission Contact: Mr. Andy Bossaller, Director of Admissions *Phone:* 402-474-5315 *Fax:* 402-474-0896 *E-mail:* abossaller@lincolnschoolofcommerce.com

Hamilton College-Omaha Ⓐ

3350 North 90th Street
Omaha, NE 68134
Web: http://www.hamiltonomaha.edu

Accreditation: Accrediting Council for Independent Colleges and Schools; North Central Association of Colleges and Schools

Programs Offered: accounting; business administration and management; computer systems networking and telecommunications; criminal justice/law enforcement administration; dental assisting; legal assistant/paralegal; massage therapy; medical/clinical assistant; nursing (licensed practical/vocational nurse training)

Enrollment: 711 students

Institution Contact: Mr. Michael D. Abdouch, Executive Director *Phone:* 402-572-8500 *Fax:* 402-573-1341 *E-mail:* mabdouch@hamiltonomaha.edu

Admission Contact: Mr. Mark Stoltenberg, Director of Admissions *Phone:* 402-572-8500 *Fax:* 402-573-1341 *E-mail:* mstoltenberg@hamiltonomaha.edu

See full description on page 526.

ITT Technical Institute

9814 M Street
Omaha, NE 68127-2056
Web: http://www.itt-tech.edu

Accreditation: Accrediting Council for Independent Colleges and Schools

Programs Offered: accounting and business/management; business administration and management; CAD/CADD drafting/design technology; communications technology; computer and information systems security; computer engineering technology; computer software and media applications; computer systems networking and telecommunications; criminal justice/police science; digital communication and media/multimedia; electrical, electronic and communications engineering technology; technology management; web page, digital/multimedia and information resources design

Enrollment: 419 students

Institution Contact: Mr. Jerome S. Padak, Director *Phone:* 402-331-2900

Admission Contact: Ms. Trish Miller, Director of Recruitment *Phone:* 402-331-2900

Vatterott College Ⓐ

225 North 80th Street
Omaha, NE 68114
Web: http://www.vatterott-college.edu

Accreditation: Accrediting Commission of Career Schools and Colleges of Technology

Programs Offered: dental assisting; heating, air conditioning and refrigeration technology; medical administrative assistant and medical secretary; veterinary technology

Institution Contact: Office of Admissions *Phone:* 402-392-1300

See full description on page 528.

Vatterott College Ⓐ

5318 South 136th Street
Omaha, NE 68137
Web: http://www.vatterott-college.edu

Accreditation: Accrediting Commission of Career Schools and Colleges of Technology

Programs Offered: CAD/CADD drafting/design technology; commercial and advertising art; computer engineering technology; computer programming; computer systems networking and telecommunications; drafting and design technology

Institution Contact: Office of Admissions *Phone:* 402-891-9411 *Fax:* 402-891-9413 *E-mail:* deerfield@vatterott-college.edu

See full description on page 527.

Ⓐ indicates that the school is a participating institution in the *Imagine America* Scholarship Program.

evada

American Institute of Technology

4610 Vanderberg Drive
North Las Vegas, NV 85043-4729
Web: http://www.ait-schools.com

Accreditation: Accrediting Commission of Career Schools and Colleges of Technology; Accrediting Council for Continuing Education and Training

Programs Offered: truck and bus driver/commercial vehicle operation

Institution Contact: Ms. Sandra Turkington, Director *Phone:* 702-644-1234 *Fax:* 702-632-0167 *E-mail:* lvdirector@ait-schools.com

The Art Institute of Las Vegas

2350 Corporate Circle
Henderson, NV 89074
Web: http://www.ailv.artinstitutes.edu

Accreditation: Accrediting Commission of Career Schools and Colleges of Technology

Programs Offered: animation, interactive technology, video graphics and special effects; commercial and advertising art; culinary arts; drafting and design technology; interior design; web/multimedia management and webmaster; web page, digital/multimedia and information resources design

Institution Contact: Mr. Steve Brooks, President *Phone:* 702-369-9944 *Fax:* 702-992-8555 *E-mail:* brookss@aii.edu

Admission Contact: Assistant Director of Admissions *Phone:* 702-369-9944 *Fax:* 702-992-8458

Career College of Northern Nevada

1195-A Corporate Boulevard
Reno, NV 89502
Web: http://www.ccnn4u.com

Accreditation: Accrediting Commission of Career Schools and Colleges of Technology

Programs Offered: business automation/technology/data entry; computer/information technology administration and management; data processing and data processing technology; electrical, electronic and communications engineering technology; legal administrative assistant/secretary; medical/clinical assistant; medical insurance coding; medical insurance/medical billing

Enrollment: 316 students

Institution Contact: Mr. L. Nathan Clark, President *Phone:* 775-856-2266 *Fax:* 775-856-0935 *E-mail:* nclark@ccnn4u.com

Admission Contact: laura Goldhammer, Director of Admissions *Phone:* 775-856-2266 *Fax:* 775-856-0935 *E-mail:* admissions2@ccnn4u.com

Career Education Institute Ⓐ

2290 Corporate Circle Drive, Suite 100
Henderson, NV 89074
Web: http://www.ceitraining.com

Accreditation: Accrediting Council for Independent Colleges and Schools

Programs Offered: business administration and management; computer/information technology administration and management; massage therapy; medical administrative assistant and medical secretary; medical/clinical assistant; system, networking, and LAN/WAN management

Enrollment: 250 students

Institution Contact: Mr. David L. Evans, Executive Director *Phone:* 702-269-7600 ext. 201 *Fax:* 702-269-7676 *E-mail:* devans@lincolntech.com

Admission Contact: Mr. David L. Evans, Admissions Director *Phone:* 702-269-7600 *Fax:* 702-269-7676 *E-mail:* devans@lincolntech.com

See full description on page 529.

Heritage College

3305 Spring Mountain Road, Suite 7
Las Vegas, NV 89102

Programs Offered: business administration and management; legal assistant/paralegal; medical/clinical assistant; pharmacy technician

Institution Contact: *Phone:* 702-368-2338 *Fax:* 702-638-3853

High-Tech Institute

2320 South Rancho Drive
Las Vegas, NV 89102
Web: http://www.hightechinstitute.edu

Accreditation: Accrediting Commission of Career Schools and Colleges of Technology

Programs Offered: dental assisting; massage therapy; medical/clinical assistant; medical insurance/medical billing; pharmacy technician; surgical technology

Enrollment: 455 students

Ⓐ indicates that the school is a participating institution in the *Imagine America* Scholarship Program.

Institution Contact: Mr. David Moore, Campus President *Phone:* 702-385-6700 *Fax:* 702-388-4463 *E-mail:* dmoore@hightechinstitute.edu

Admission Contact: Ms. Amy Tu, Director of Admissions *Phone:* 702-385-6700 *Fax:* 702-388-4463 *E-mail:* atu@hightechinstitute.edu

International Academy of Design and Technology

2495 Village View Drive
Henderson, NV 89074
Web: http://www.iadtvegas.com

Accreditation: Accrediting Council for Independent Colleges and Schools

Programs Offered: design and visual communications; fashion/apparel design; interior design

Enrollment: 270 students

Institution Contact: Mr. Jason A. Smith, President *Phone:* 702-990-0150 ext. 5911 *Fax:* 702-269-1981 *E-mail:* jsmith@iadtvegas.com

Admission Contact: Ms. Jocelyn Y. Vasquez, Vice President of Admissions *Phone:* 702-990-0150 ext. 5914 *Fax:* 702-990-0161 *E-mail:* jvasquez@iadtvegas.com

ITT Technical Institute (A)

168 North Gibson Road
Henderson, NV 89014
Web: http://www.itt-tech.edu

Accreditation: Accrediting Council for Independent Colleges and Schools

Programs Offered: accounting and business/management; animation, interactive technology, video graphics and special effects; business administration and management; CAD/CADD drafting/design technology; communications technology; computer and information systems security; computer engineering technology; computer software and media applications; computer software engineering; computer systems networking and telecommunications; criminal justice/police science; digital communication and media/multimedia; electrical, electronic and communications engineering technology; technology management; web page, digital/multimedia and information resources design

Enrollment: 527 students

Institution Contact: Mr. Donn Nimmer, Director *Phone:* 702-558-5404

Admission Contact: Ms. Anne Buzak, Director of Recruitment *Phone:* 702-558-5404

See full description on page 530.

Las Vegas College (A)

170 North Stephanie Street, Suite 145
Henderson, NV 89014

Accreditation: Accrediting Council for Independent Colleges and Schools

Programs Offered: business administration and management; criminal justice/law enforcement administration; medical/clinical assistant; medical office assistant

Enrollment: 137 students

Institution Contact: Mr. Joel D. Boyd, President *Phone:* 702-567-1920 *Fax:* 702-566-9725 *E-mail:* jboyd@cci.edu

Admission Contact: Mr. Bart Van Ry, Director of Admissions *Phone:* 702-567-1920 *Fax:* 702-566-9725 *E-mail:* bvanry@cci.edu

See full description on page 531.

Las Vegas College (A)

4100 West Flamingo Road, #2100
Las Vegas, NV 89103
Web: http://www.cci.edu

Accreditation: Accrediting Council for Independent Colleges and Schools

Programs Offered: accounting; administrative assistant and secretarial science; business administration and management; business automation/technology/data entry; court reporting; criminal justice/law enforcement administration; legal assistant/paralegal; medical administrative assistant and medical secretary; medical/clinical assistant; medical insurance coding; medical insurance/medical billing; word processing

Institution Contact: Mr. Sam A. Gentile, President *Phone:* 702-368-6200 *Fax:* 702-368-6464 *E-mail:* sgentile@cci.edu

Admission Contact: Mr. Shawn Saunders, Admissions Director *Phone:* 702-368-6200 *Fax:* 702-368-6464 *E-mail:* ssaunder@cci.edu

See full description on page 532.

Le Cordon Bleu College of Culinary Arts, Las Vegas

1451 Center Crossing Road
Las Vegas, NV 89144
Web: http://www.VegasCulinary.com

Accreditation: Accrediting Commission of Career Schools and Colleges of Technology

Programs Offered: culinary arts

Enrollment: 650 students

(A) indicates that the school is a participating institution in the *Imagine America* Scholarship Program.

Le Cordon Bleu College of Culinary Arts, Las Vegas
(continued)

Institution Contact: Ms. Tyka Burton, Director of NS
Admission *Phone:* 866-450-2433 *Fax:* 702-365-7690
E-mail: tburton@vegasculinary.com

Morrison University

10315 Professional Circle, Second Floor, Reno-Tahoe Tech
 Center
Reno, NV 89521
Web: http://www.morrison.northface.edu
Accreditation: Accrediting Council for Independent
Colleges and Schools
Programs Offered: accounting; accounting and
business/management; business administration and
management; computer and information sciences
related
Enrollment: 88 students
Institution Contact: Ms. Barbara Andersen, Director
of Admissions *Phone:* 775-850-0700 ext. 108 *Fax:*
775-850-0711 *E-mail:*
bandersen@morrison.northface.edu

Nevada Career Academy

950 Industrial Way
Sparks, NV 89431
Web: http://www.nevadacareeracademy.com
Accreditation: Accrediting Council for Continuing
Education and Training
Programs Offered: computer software and media
applications; massage therapy; medical/clinical
assistant; medical reception; pharmacy technician
Institution Contact: Ms. Cathy Tobin, Vice President
of Compliance *Phone:* 559-735-3818 ext. 1012 *Fax:*
559-733-7831 *E-mail:* ctatcorp@aol.com
Admission Contact: Admissions Representative
Phone: 775-348-7200 *Fax:* 775-359-7227 *E-mail:*
infonca@nevadacareeracademy.com

Nevada Career Institute

3025 East Desert Inn Road, Suite A
Las Vegas, NV 89121
Web: http://www.nevadacareerinstitute.com
Accreditation: Accrediting Council for Continuing
Education and Training
Programs Offered: massage therapy; medical/clinical
assistant; medical office management; surgical
technology
Enrollment: 250 students

Institution Contact: Ms. Joanne Q. Leming, Director
Phone: 702-893-3300 *Fax:* 702-893-3881 *E-mail:*
jqleming@success.edu

Pima Medical Institute

3333 East Flamingo Road
Las Vegas, NV 89121
Web: http://www.pmi.edu
Accreditation: Accrediting Bureau of Health Educa-
tion Schools
Programs Offered: dental assisting; medical adminis-
trative assistant and medical secretary; medical/
clinical assistant; pharmacy technician; phlebotomy;
radiologic technology/science; respiratory care
therapy; veterinary/animal health technology
Enrollment: 303 students
Institution Contact: Mr. Christopher Luebke, Admis-
sions Support Center Director *Phone:* 888-898-9048
E-mail: asc@pmi.edu
Admission Contact: Admissions Support Representative *Phone:* 888-898-9048 *E-mail:* asc@pmi.edu

New Hampshire

Hesser College

3 Sundial Avenue
Manchester, NH 03103
Web: http://www.hesser.edu/
Accreditation: New England Association of Schools
and Colleges
Programs Offered: accounting; athletic training;
business administration and management; business/
corporate communications; commercial and advertising art; communications systems installation and
repair technology; computer engineering technology;
computer programming (specific applications);
computer systems networking and telecommunications; computer technology/computer systems
technology; criminal justice/law enforcement administration; fashion/apparel design; fashion merchandising; hospitality administration; interior design;
kindergarten/preschool education; legal assistant/
paralegal; marketing/marketing management;
massage therapy; medical/clinical assistant; pharmacy
technician; physical therapist assistant; radio and
television; tourism and travel services management

*indicates that the school is a participating institution in the *Imagine America* Scholarship Program.*

Institution Contact: Dr. Paul F. Tero, Dean of Academic Affairs *Phone:* 603-668-6660 ext. 2154 *Fax:* 603-666-4722 *E-mail:* ptero@hesser.edu

Admission Contact: Mr. Robert S. Moon, President *Phone:* 603-668-6660 ext. 2102 *Fax:* 603-666-4722 *E-mail:* rmoon@hesser.edu

McIntosh College

23 Cataract Avenue
Dover, NH 03820-3990
Web: http://www.gomcintosh.com

Accreditation: New England Association of Schools and Colleges

Programs Offered: accounting; accounting and business/management; accounting and finance; advertising; allied health and medical assisting services related; apparel and accessories marketing; business administration and management; business administration, management and operations related; clinical laboratory science/medical technology; clinical/medical laboratory assistant; clinical/medical laboratory science and allied professions related; clinical/medical laboratory technology; commercial and advertising art; computer graphics; corrections; criminal justice/law enforcement administration; criminal justice/police science; desktop publishing and digital imaging design; drawing; fashion merchandising; graphic communications; graphic communications related; health/health care administration; health information/medical records administration; health services administration; health services/allied health/health sciences; kinesiotherapy; marketing/marketing management; marketing related; massage therapy; medical/clinical assistant; medical/health management and clinical assistant; medical office assistant; medical office management; merchandising; merchandising, sales, and marketing operations related (general); merchandising, sales, and marketing operations related (specialized); phlebotomy; photography; web/multimedia management and webmaster; web page, digital/multimedia and information resources design; word processing

Enrollment: 1,200 students

Institution Contact: Mrs. Marylin Newell, President *Phone:* 800-521-3995 *Fax:* 603-743-0060 *E-mail:* mnewell@mcintoshcollege.edu

Admission Contact: Mrs. Jody LaBrie, Director of High School Admissions *Phone:* 800-521-3995 *Fax:* 603-743-0060 *E-mail:* jlabrie@mcintoshcollege.edu

ew Jersey

Berdan Institute (A)

265 Route 46 West
Totowa, NJ 07512-1819
Web: http://www.berdaninstitute.com

Accreditation: Accrediting Bureau of Health Education Schools; Accrediting Commission of Career Schools and Colleges of Technology

Programs Offered: dental assisting; massage therapy; medical administrative assistant and medical secretary; medical/clinical assistant; medical insurance/medical billing; nursing assistant/aide and patient care assistant; pharmacy technician

Enrollment: 345 students

Institution Contact: Mr. E. Lynn Thacker, Director *Phone:* 973-256-3444 *Fax:* 973-256-0816 *E-mail:* lthacker@berdaninstitute.com

Admission Contact: Mr. Alan Concha, Director of Admissions *Phone:* 973-256-3444 *Fax:* 973-256-0816 *E-mail:* aconcha@berdaninstitute.com

See full description on page 533.

Berkeley College

44 Rifle Camp Road
West Paterson, NJ 07424
Web: http://www.BerkeleyCollege.edu

Accreditation: Middle States Association of Colleges and Schools

Programs Offered: accounting; business administration and management; fashion merchandising; interior design; international business/trade/commerce; legal assistant/paralegal; marketing/marketing management; system, networking, and LAN/WAN management; web page, digital/multimedia and information resources design

Enrollment: 2,200 students

Institution Contact: Dr. Mildred Garcia, President *Phone:* 212-986-4343 ext. 4101 *Fax:* 212-986-8901 *E-mail:* millieg@berkeleycollege.edu

Admission Contact: Ms. Carol Covino, Director of High School Admissions *Phone:* 973-278-5400 *Fax:* 973-278-9141 *E-mail:* info@berkeleycollege.edu

(A) indicates that the school is a participating institution in the *Imagine America* Scholarship Program.

The Chubb Institute

2100 Route 38 and Mall Drive
Cherry Hill, NJ 08002
Web: http://www.chubbinstitute.edu

Accreditation: Accrediting Council for Independent Colleges and Schools

Programs Offered: administrative assistant and secretarial science; computer and information systems security; computer engineering related; computer engineering technology; computer graphics; computer hardware engineering; computer/information technology administration and management; computer/information technology services administration related; computer installation and repair technology; computer programming; computer programming (specific applications); computer programming (vendor/product certification); computer software and media applications; computer software engineering; computer systems analysis; computer systems networking and telecommunications; computer/technical support; computer technology/computer systems technology; data entry/microcomputer applications; data entry/microcomputer applications related; information science/studies; information technology; medical administrative assistant and medical secretary; system administration; system, networking, and LAN/WAN management; web page, digital/multimedia and information resources design

Enrollment: 258 students

Institution Contact: Ms. Michelle Bonocore, Executive Director *Phone:* 856-755-4831 *Fax:* 856-755-4802 *E-mail:* mbonocore@chubbinstitute.edu

Admission Contact: Ms. Dina Gentile, Director of Admissions *Phone:* 856-755-4827 *Fax:* 856-755-4801 *E-mail:* dgentile@chubbinstitute.edu

The Chubb Institute

40 Journal Square
Jersey City, NJ 07306-4009
Web: http://www.chubbinstitute.com/

Accreditation: Accrediting Commission of Career Schools and Colleges of Technology

Programs Offered: computer/information technology administration and management; computer programming; computer programming related; computer programming (specific applications); computer software and media applications related; computer systems networking and telecommunications; computer/technical support; computer technology/computer systems technology; design and visual communications; graphic communications related; information technology; medical administrative assistant and medical secretary; medical insurance coding; medical insurance/medical billing; medical

office assistant; medical office computer specialist; medical office management; system administration; web page, digital/multimedia and information resources design

Enrollment: 319 students

Institution Contact: Mr. Gary E. Duchnowski, Campus President *Phone:* 201-876-3801 *Fax:* 201-656-2091 *E-mail:* gduchnowski@chubbinstitute.edu

Admission Contact: Mr. Julio Nieto, Admissions Director *Phone:* 201-876-3816 *Fax:* 201-656-2091 *E-mail:* jnieto@chubbinstitute.edu

The Chubb Institute

651 US Route 1 South
North Brunswick, NJ 08902
Web: http://www.chubbinstitute.com/

Accreditation: Accrediting Commission of Career Schools and Colleges of Technology

Programs Offered: computer and information sciences related; computer engineering technology; computer graphics; computer/information technology administration and management; computer/information technology services administration related; computer installation and repair technology; computer programming; computer programming related; computer programming (specific applications); computer programming (vendor/product certification); computer software and media applications; computer software and media applications related; computer software engineering; computer systems networking and telecommunications; computer/technical support; computer technology/computer systems technology; data entry/microcomputer applications; data entry/microcomputer applications related; data processing and data processing technology; information technology; medical administrative assistant and medical secretary; medical insurance coding; medical insurance/medical billing; medical office assistant; system administration; system, networking, and LAN/WAN management; web page, digital/multimedia and information resources design

Enrollment: 500 students

Institution Contact: Mr. Dennis Mascali, Campus President *Phone:* 732-448-2637 *Fax:* 732-448-2665

Admission Contact: Mr. Rudolf Rangel, Director of Admissions *Phone:* 732-448-2600 *Fax:* 732-448-2665 *E-mail:* rthornton@chubbinstitute.com

The Chubb Institute

8 Sylvan Way
Parsippany, NJ 07054-0342
Web: http://www.chubbinstitute.com/

Accreditation: Accrediting Commission of Career Schools and Colleges of Technology; Accrediting

---

Ⓐ indicates that the school is a participating institution in the *Imagine America* Scholarship Program.

Council for Continuing Education and Training; Accrediting Council for Independent Colleges and Schools

Programs Offered: administrative assistant and secretarial science; computer and information sciences related; computer and information systems security; computer engineering technology; computer graphics; computer hardware engineering; computer/information technology administration and management; computer/information technology services administration related; computer installation and repair technology; computer programming; computer programming related; computer programming (specific applications); computer programming (vendor/product certification); computer software engineering; computer systems analysis; computer systems networking and telecommunications; computer/technical support; computer technology/computer systems technology; data entry/microcomputer applications; data entry/microcomputer applications related; health information/medical records administration; information science/studies; information technology; medical administrative assistant and medical secretary; medical insurance coding; medical insurance/medical billing; system administration; system, networking, and LAN/WAN management; web page, digital/multimedia and information resources design

Institution Contact: Mr. Thomas Hull, School Director *Phone:* 973-630-4900 *Fax:* 973-630-4218

Admission Contact: Mr. Carl Berne, Director of Admissions *Phone:* 973-630-4977 *Fax:* 973-630-4218 *E-mail:* cberne@chubbinstitute.com

The Cittone Institute ⓐ

1697 Oak Tree Road
Edison, NJ 08820
Web: http://www.cittone.com/

Accreditation: Accrediting Council for Independent Colleges and Schools

Programs Offered: business administration and management; massage therapy; medical administrative assistant and medical secretary; medical/clinical assistant; pharmacy technician; system, networking, and LAN/WAN management; web page, digital/multimedia and information resources design

Enrollment: 642 students

Institution Contact: Mr. John Joseph Willie, Executive Director *Phone:* 732-548-8798 *Fax:* 732-548-9682 *E-mail:* jwillie@cittone.com

Admission Contact: Mr. Ron Barone, Admissions Director *Phone:* 732-548-8798 *Fax:* 732-548-9682 *E-mail:* rbarone@cittone.com

See full description on page 534.

The Cittone Institute ⓐ

1000 Howard Boulevard
Mount Laurel, NJ 08054
Web: http://www.cittone.com

Accreditation: Accrediting Council for Independent Colleges and Schools

Programs Offered: business administration and management; computer systems networking and telecommunications; medical administrative assistant and medical secretary; medical/clinical assistant; pharmacy technician; system administration; web page, digital/multimedia and information resources design

Institution Contact: Executive Director *Phone:* 856-722-9333 *Fax:* 856-722-1110 *E-mail:* execdirmtlaurel@lincolntech.com

See full description on page 535.

The Cittone Institute ⓐ

160 East Route 4
Paramus, NJ 07652
Web: http://www.cittone.com

Accreditation: Accrediting Council for Independent Colleges and Schools

Programs Offered: administrative assistant and secretarial science; business administration and management; computer installation and repair technology; computer/technical support; massage therapy; medical administrative assistant and medical secretary; medical/clinical assistant; medical insurance coding; medical reception; pharmacy technician; system administration; system, networking, and LAN/WAN management

Enrollment: 550 students

Institution Contact: Mr. Alan Shikowitz, Executive Director *Phone:* 201-845-6868 *Fax:* 201-368-0736 *E-mail:* ashikowitz@cittone.com

Admission Contact: Mr. Ron Barone, Director of Admissions *Phone:* 201-845-6868 *Fax:* 201-529-3229 *E-mail:* rbarone@cittone.com

See full description on page 536.

Divers Academy International

2500 South Broadway
Camden, NJ 08104-2431
Web: http://www.diversacademy.com

Accreditation: Accrediting Commission of Career Schools and Colleges of Technology

Programs Offered: diving, professional and instruction

Enrollment: 154 students

ⓐ indicates that the school is a participating institution in the *Imagine America* Scholarship Program.

Divers Academy International (*continued*)

Institution Contact: Ms. Tamara Brown, Executive Director *Phone:* 800-238-3483 *Fax:* 856-541-4355 *E-mail:* tamara@diversacademy.com

Admission Contact: Ms. Kim Sweeney, Director of Admissions *Phone:* 800-238-3483 *Fax:* 856-541-4355 *E-mail:* kim@diversacademy.com

Dover Business College

East 81, Route 4 West
Paramus, NJ 07652
Web: http://www.doverbusinesscollege.org

Accreditation: Accrediting Council for Independent Colleges and Schools

Programs Offered: accounting; accounting and business/management; computer/information technology administration and management; massage therapy; medical/clinical assistant; medical insurance coding; medical insurance/medical billing; medical office computer specialist; system, networking, and LAN/WAN management

Enrollment: 255 students

Institution Contact: Mr. Timothy Luing, Executive Director *Phone:* 201-843-8500 *Fax:* 201-843-3896 *E-mail:* tluing@doverbusinesscollege.org

Admission Contact: Mr. Mike Russo, Admissions Director *Phone:* 201-843-8500 *Fax:* 201-843-3896 *E-mail:* mrusso@doverbusinesscollege.org

Gibbs College

630 West Mount Pleasant Avenue
Livingston, NJ 07039

Programs Offered: accounting; computer programming; computer systems networking and telecommunications; criminal justice/law enforcement administration; medical/clinical assistant

Institution Contact: *Phone:* 973-369-1360

Gibbs College

50 Church Street
Montclair, NJ 07042
Web: http://www.njgibbscollege.net

Accreditation: Accrediting Council for Independent Colleges and Schools

Programs Offered: accounting; administrative assistant and secretarial science; business administration and management; commercial and advertising art; computer programming; computer systems networking and telecommunications; computer/technical support; hospitality administration; hotel/

motel administration; legal administrative assistant/secretary; marketing/marketing management; medical administrative assistant and medical secretary; restaurant, culinary, and catering management; system, networking, and LAN/WAN management; telecommunications; visual and performing arts; web page, digital/multimedia and information resources design

Institution Contact: Ms. Mary-Jo Greco, President *Phone:* 201-744-2010 *Fax:* 201-744-2298 *E-mail:* mgreco@njgibbscollege.net

Admission Contact: Mr. Mike Russo, Director of High School Admissions *Phone:* 201-744-6962 ext. 3050 *Fax:* 201-744-0333 *E-mail:* mrusso@njgibbscollege.net

Harrison Career Institute

1227-31 Main Avenue
Clifton, NJ 07011
Web: http://www.hci.edu

Accreditation: Accrediting Commission of Career Schools and Colleges of Technology

Programs Offered: electrocardiograph technology; medical/clinical assistant; medical insurance coding; medical insurance/medical billing; medical transcription; phlebotomy

Enrollment: 250 students

Institution Contact: Joe Amalbert, Director *Phone:* 973-253-0444 *E-mail:* jamalbert@hci-inst.net

Harrison Career Institute

4000 Route 130 North, Suite A, 2nd Floor
Delran, NJ 08075
Web: http://www.hci.edu

Accreditation: Accrediting Commission of Career Schools and Colleges of Technology

Programs Offered: cardiovascular technology; dental assisting; electrocardiograph technology; medical/clinical assistant; medical insurance/medical billing; medical office computer specialist; medical transcription; pharmacy technician; phlebotomy

Enrollment: 120 students

Institution Contact: Mrs. Dawn L. Mack, Director *Phone:* 856-764-8933 *Fax:* 856-764-8829 *E-mail:* dmack@hci-inst.net

Harrison Career Institute

The Plaza at Deptford, 1450 Clements Bridge Road
Deptford, NJ 08096
Web: http://www.hci.edu

Accreditation: Accrediting Commission of Career Schools and Colleges of Technology

---

⋒ indicates that the school is a participating institution in the *Imagine America* Scholarship Program.

Programs Offered: cardiovascular technology; dental assisting; dialysis technology; electrocardiograph technology; gene therapy; medical/clinical assistant; medical insurance/medical billing; medical office computer specialist; nursing (licensed practical/vocational nurse training); pharmacy technician; phlebotomy

Enrollment: 200 students

Institution Contact: Ms. Cheryl L. Papa, Director *Phone:* 856-384-2888 *Fax:* 856-384-1063 *E-mail:* cpapa@hci-inst.net

Admission Contact: Ms. Keri Krapsho, Admissions Representative *Phone:* 856-384-2888 *Fax:* 856-384-1063

Harrison Career Institute

1001 Spruce Street
Ewing, NJ 08628
Web: http://www.hci.edu

Accreditation: Accrediting Commission of Career Schools and Colleges of Technology

Programs Offered: cardiovascular technology; dental assisting; medical administrative assistant and medical secretary; medical/clinical assistant; medical office assistant; medical transcription; pharmacy technician

Enrollment: 240 students

Institution Contact: Ms. Carole M Heininger, Director *Phone:* 609-656-4303 *Fax:* 609-656-4373 *E-mail:* cheininger@hci-inst.net

Admission Contact: Ms. Debbie Miller-Moore, Career Advisor *Phone:* 609-656-4303 *Fax:* 609-656-4373

Harrison Career Institute

600 Pavonia Avenue
Jersey City, NJ 07306
Web: http://www.hci.edu

Accreditation: Accrediting Commission of Career Schools and Colleges of Technology

Programs Offered: cardiovascular technology; dialysis technology; medical/clinical assistant; medical insurance/medical billing; medical office computer specialist; pharmacy technician

Enrollment: 200 students

Institution Contact: Mr. Israel Delgado, Director *Phone:* 201-222-1700 *Fax:* 201-222-9645 *E-mail:* idelgado@hci-inst.net

Admission Contact: Miss Ysolde Miranda, Career Representative *Phone:* 201-222-1700 *Fax:* 201-222-9645 *E-mail:* ysolde@hci-inst.net

Harrison Career Institute

2105 Highway 35
Oakhurst, NJ 07755
Web: http://www.hci.edu

Accreditation: Accrediting Commission of Career Schools and Colleges of Technology

Programs Offered: allied health and medical assisting services related; clinical/medical laboratory technology; dialysis technology; electrocardiograph technology; health/health care administration; health information/medical records administration; health information/medical records technology; health/medical claims examination; medical administrative assistant and medical secretary; medical/clinical assistant; medical insurance/medical billing; medical office assistant; medical transcription; phlebotomy; surgical technology

Enrollment: 270 students

Institution Contact: Mr. Scott H. Applegate, Director *Phone:* 732-493-1660 *Fax:* 732-493-2283 *E-mail:* hcioakh@aol.com

Admission Contact: Mr. Scott Applegate, Director *Phone:* 732-493-1660 *Fax:* 732-493-2283

Harrison Career Institute

525 South Orange Avenue
South Orange, NJ 07079
Web: http://www.hci.edu

Accreditation: Accrediting Commission of Career Schools and Colleges of Technology

Programs Offered: cardiovascular technology; dental assisting; electrocardiograph technology; medical/clinical assistant; medical insurance coding; medical insurance/medical billing; medical office computer specialist; medical transcription; pharmacy technician; phlebotomy

Enrollment: 225 students

Institution Contact: Ms. Lynn M. Lockamy, Director *Phone:* 973-763-9484 *Fax:* 973-763-4645 *E-mail:* llockamy@hci-inst.net

Harrison Career Institute

1386 South Delsea Drive
Vineland, NJ 08360-6210
Web: http://www.hci.edu

Accreditation: Accrediting Commission of Career Schools and Colleges of Technology

Programs Offered: cardiovascular technology; customer service management; dialysis technology; electrocardiograph technology; health professions related; medical administrative assistant and medical

Ⓐ indicates that the school is a participating institution in the *Imagine America* Scholarship Program.

Harrison Career Institute (*continued*)

secretary; medical/clinical assistant; medical insurance/medical billing; medical office assistant; medical office computer specialist; medical office management; medical transcription; phlebotomy; renal/dialysis technology

Enrollment: 260 students

Institution Contact: Ms. Arline M. Pillows, Director *Phone:* 856-696-0500 *Fax:* 856-691-0701 *E-mail:* jgmannion@aol.com

Admission Contact: Mrs. Arline M. Pillows, Director *Phone:* 856-696-0500 *Fax:* 856-691-0701 *E-mail:* hcivineland@aol.com

Hohokus Hackensack School of Business and Medical Sciences

66 Moore Street
Hackensack, NJ 07601-7197
Web: http://www.hohokushackensack.com

Accreditation: Accrediting Council for Independent Colleges and Schools

Programs Offered: accounting technology and bookkeeping; administrative assistant and secretarial science; business administration and management; computer software and media applications related; executive assistant/executive secretary; legal assistant/paralegal; medical/clinical assistant; medical insurance coding; medical office management

Enrollment: 225 students

Institution Contact: Mrs. Kim Staudt, Director *Phone:* 201-488-9400 ext. 23 *Fax:* 201-488-1007 *E-mail:* kstaudt66@yahoo.com

Admission Contact: Mrs. Sandra O'Hagan, Director of Admissions *Phone:* 201-488-9400 ext. 24 *Fax:* 201-488-1007

HoHoKus School

10 South Franklin Turnpike
Ramsey, NJ 07446
Web: http://www.hohokus.com

Accreditation: Accrediting Council for Independent Colleges and Schools

Programs Offered: business administration and management; cardiovascular technology; computer and information sciences related; diagnostic medical sonography and ultrasound technology; medical/clinical assistant; medical insurance coding; medical insurance/medical billing; nursing (licensed practical/vocational nurse training)

Enrollment: 503 students

Institution Contact: Mr. Thomas M. Eastwick, President *Phone:* 201-327-8877 *Fax:* 201-327-9054 *E-mail:* hohokus_school@www.hohokus.com

Admission Contact: Ms. Ruth Zayas, Director of Admissions *Phone:* 201-327-8877 ext. 226 *Fax:* 201-825-2115 *E-mail:* hohokus_school@www.hohokus.com

Joe Kubert School of Cartoon and Graphic Art Inc.

37 Myrtle Avenue
Dover, NJ 07801-4054
Web:
   http://www.kubertsworld.com/kubertschool/KubertSchool.htm

Accreditation: Accrediting Commission of Career Schools and Colleges of Technology

Programs Offered: animation, interactive technology, video graphics and special effects; applied art; commercial and advertising art; computer graphics; computer software and media applications; design and visual communications; drawing

Enrollment: 120 students

Institution Contact: Mrs. Debby Kubert, Director *Phone:* 973-361-1327 *Fax:* 973-361-1844 *E-mail:* kubert@earthlink.net

Katharine Gibbs School

180 Centennial Avenue
Piscataway, NJ 08854
Web: http://www.gibbseducation.com

Accreditation: Accrediting Council for Independent Colleges and Schools

Programs Offered: administrative assistant and secretarial science; business administration and management; communications systems installation and repair technology; computer graphics; computer/technical support; executive assistant/executive secretary; fashion merchandising; legal assistant/paralegal; medical/clinical assistant; system administration; system, networking, and LAN/WAN management; web/multimedia management and webmaster; web page, digital/multimedia and information resources design

Enrollment: 1,200 students

Institution Contact: Ms. L. Terry Nighan, President *Phone:* 732-885-1580 *Fax:* 732-885-0448 *E-mail:* tnighan@gibbsnj.edu

Admission Contact: Mr. Steven Weinstein, Vice President of Marketing *Phone:* 732-885-1580 *Fax:* 732-885-0448 *E-mail:* sweinstein@gibbsnj.edu

ⓘ indicates that the school is a participating institution in the *Imagine America* Scholarship Program.

Lincoln Technical Institute (A)

70 McKee Drive
Mahwah, NJ 07430
Web: http://www.lincolntech.com

Accreditation: Accrediting Commission of Career Schools and Colleges of Technology

Programs Offered: automobile/automotive mechanics technology; automotive engineering technology; electrical and electronic engineering technologies related; electrical, electronic and communications engineering technology; electrical/electronics equipment installation and repair; heating, air conditioning and refrigeration technology; industrial electronics technology

Enrollment: 1,225 students

Institution Contact: Mr. Thomas E. Lynch, Executive Director *Phone:* 201-529-1414 ext. 106 *Fax:* 201-529-5295 *E-mail:* tlynch@lincolntech.com

Admission Contact: Mr. Rick Strage, Director of Admissions *Phone:* 201-529-1414 *Fax:* 201-529-5295 *E-mail:* rstrage@lincolntech.com

See full description on page 537.

Lincoln Technical Institute (A)

2299 Vauxhall Road
Union, NJ 07083
Web: http://www.lincolntech.com

Accreditation: Accrediting Commission of Career Schools and Colleges of Technology

Programs Offered: automotive engineering technology; electrical, electronic and communications engineering technology; heating, air conditioning and refrigeration technology

Enrollment: 1,291 students

Institution Contact: Mr. Kevin Kirkley, Executive Director *Phone:* 908-964-7800 *Fax:* 908-964-3035 *E-mail:* kkirkley@lincolntech.com

Admission Contact: Mr. Carl Berne, Admissions Director *Phone:* 908-964-7800 *Fax:* 908-964-3035 *E-mail:* cberne@lincolntech.com

See full description on page 538.

Pennco Tech

99 Erial Road, PO Box 1427
Blackwood, NJ 08012-9961
Web: http://www.penncotech.com

Accreditation: Accrediting Commission of Career Schools and Colleges of Technology

Programs Offered: autobody/collision and repair technology; automobile/automotive mechanics technology; automotive engineering technology; computer installation and repair technology; diesel mechanics technology; drafting and design technology; heating, air conditioning and refrigeration technology; marine technology; medical administrative assistant and medical secretary; system, networking, and LAN/WAN management

Institution Contact: Mr. Doug Johnson, Director *Phone:* 856-232-0310 *Fax:* 856-232-2032 *E-mail:* dougbristol@yahoo.com

RETS Institute (A)

103 Park Avenue
Nutley, NJ 07110-3505
Web: http://www.rets-institute.com

Accreditation: Accrediting Commission of Career Schools and Colleges of Technology

Programs Offered: administrative assistant and secretarial science; allied health and medical assisting services related; business administration and management; business machine repair; business operations support and secretarial services related; communications technology; computer engineering technology; computer installation and repair technology; computer/technical support; computer technology/computer systems technology; data processing and data processing technology; electrical, electronic and communications engineering technology; health professions related; industrial technology; medical/clinical assistant; medical office assistant; office occupations and clerical services

Enrollment: 300 students

Institution Contact: Mr. Martin Klangasky, Director *Phone:* 973-661-0600 *Fax:* 973-661-2954 *E-mail:* director@rets-institute.com

Admission Contact: Mr. Dominic Zampella, High School Admissions Director *Phone:* 973-661-0600 *Fax:* 973-661-2954 *E-mail:* zampella@rets-institute.com

See full description on page 539.

Sanford-Brown Institute

675 US Route 1, Second Floor
Iselin, NJ 08830

Programs Offered: cardiovascular technology; diagnostic medical sonography and ultrasound technology; medical/clinical assistant; medical insurance/medical billing; surgical technology

Institution Contact: *Phone:* 732-634-1131

Stuart School of Business Administration

2400 Belmar Boulevard
Wall, NJ 07719
Web: http://www.stuartschool.com

Accreditation: Accrediting Council for Independent Colleges and Schools

(A) indicates that the school is a participating institution in the *Imagine America* Scholarship Program.

Stuart School of Business Administration *(continued)*

Programs Offered: accounting; administrative assistant and secretarial science; adult and continuing education; business administration and management; computer software and media applications; data entry/microcomputer applications; executive assistant/executive secretary; legal administrative assistant/secretary; medical administrative assistant and medical secretary; medical office management

Enrollment: 90 students

Institution Contact: Mr. Joe Davis, President *Phone:* 317-845-0100 *Fax:* 317-845-1800 *E-mail:* jdavis@medtechcollege.com

Admission Contact: *Phone:* 732-681-7200 *Fax:* 732-681-7205

Teterboro School of Aeronautics, Inc.

Teterboro Airport, 80 Moonachie Avenue
Teterboro, NJ 07608-1083
Web: http://www.teterboroschool.com

Accreditation: Accrediting Commission of Career Schools and Colleges of Technology

Programs Offered: aircraft powerplant technology; airframe mechanics and aircraft maintenance technology

Enrollment: 173 students

Institution Contact: Mr. Donald Hulse, President *Phone:* 201-288-6300 *Fax:* 201-288-5609 *E-mail:* tsanj@bellatlantic.net

Admission Contact: Mr. Richard Ciasulli, Director of Admissions *Phone:* 201-288-6300 *Fax:* 201-288-5609 *E-mail:* tsanj@bellatlantic.net

New Mexico

Apollo College Ⓐ

5301 Central Avenue, Northeast, Suite 101
Albuquerque, NM 87108-1513
Web: http://www.apollocollege.com

Accreditation: Accrediting Bureau of Health Education Schools

Programs Offered: clinical/medical laboratory technology; dental assisting; health information/ medical records administration; massage therapy; medical administrative assistant and medical secretary; medical/clinical assistant; pharmacy technician

Enrollment: 350 students

Institution Contact: Mr. Patrick King, Campus Director *Phone:* 505-254-7777 *Fax:* 505-254-1101 *E-mail:* pking@apollocollege.com
See full description on page 540.

International Institute of the Americas

4201 Central Avenue, NW, #J
Albuquerque, NM 87105
Web: http://www.iia.edu

Accreditation: Accrediting Council for Independent Colleges and Schools

Programs Offered: business administration and management; criminal justice/law enforcement administration; medical/clinical assistant

Institution Contact: Mr. Rick Rickel, Campus Director *Phone:* 505-880-2877 *Fax:* 505-352-0199 *E-mail:* rrickel@iia.edu

Admission Contact: Ms. Dorian Kreiling, Admissions Director *Phone:* 602-589-1382 *Fax:* 602-589-1300 *E-mail:* dkreiling@iia.edu

ITT Technical Institute Ⓐ

5100 Masthead Street, NE
Albuquerque, NM 87109-4366
Web: http://www.itt-tech.edu

Accreditation: Accrediting Council for Independent Colleges and Schools

Programs Offered: accounting and business/management; animation, interactive technology, video graphics and special effects; business administration and management; CAD/CADD drafting/design technology; communications technology; computer and information systems security; computer engineering technology; computer software and media applications; computer software technology; computer systems networking and telecommunications; criminal justice/police science; digital communication and media/multimedia; electrical, electronic and communications engineering technology; technology management; web page, digital/multimedia and information resources design

Enrollment: 607 students

Institution Contact: Ms. Marianne Rittner, Director *Phone:* 505-828-1114

Admission Contact: Mr. John Crooks, Director of Recruitment *Phone:* 505-828-1114
See full description on page 541.

Ⓐ indicates that the school is a participating institution in the *Imagine America* Scholarship Program.

National American University

4775 Indian School Road, NE, Suite 200
Albuquerque, NM 87110
Web: http://www.national.edu

Accreditation: North Central Association of Colleges and Schools

Programs Offered: accounting; business administration and management; computer/information technology services administration related; computer programming; computer systems networking and telecommunications; computer technology/computer systems technology; education (specific levels and methods) related; engineering-related technologies; information technology; management information systems; medical/clinical assistant

Enrollment: 532 students

Institution Contact: Mr. J. P. Foley, Associate Director *Phone:* 505-265-7517 *Fax:* 505-265-7542 *E-mail:* jpfoley@national.edu

Admission Contact: Ms. Nancy Pointer, Director of Admissions *Phone:* 512-301-4901 *Fax:* 512-301-4902 *E-mail:* npointer@national.edu

National American University

Highway 528 and Sara Road
Rio Rancho, NM 87124

Accreditation: North Central Association of Colleges and Schools

Programs Offered: accounting; advertising; allied health and medical assisting services related; business administration and management; business, management, and marketing related; computer and information sciences; engineering/industrial management; engineering-related technologies; engineering technology; general studies; human resources management; information technology; selling skills and sales

Enrollment: 325 students

Institution Contact: Ms. Lisa Knigge, Regional President *Phone:* 505-891-1111 *Fax:* 505-896-2818 *E-mail:* lknigge@national.edu

Admission Contact: Ms. Wanda Butler, Senior Admissions Representative/Office Manager *Phone:* 505-891-1111 *E-mail:* wbutler@national.edu

Pima Medical Institute

2201 San Pedro, NE, Suite 100
Albuquerque, NM 87110
Web: http://www.pmi.edu

Accreditation: Accrediting Bureau of Health Education Schools

Programs Offered: dental assisting; medical administrative assistant and medical secretary; medical/clinical assistant; ophthalmic technology; pharmacy technician; physical therapist assistant; radiologic technology/science; respiratory care therapy; veterinary/animal health technology

Enrollment: 513 students

Institution Contact: Mr. Christopher Luebke, Admissions Support Center Director *Phone:* 888-898-9048 *E-mail:* asc@pmi.edu

Admission Contact: Admissions Support Representative *Phone:* 888-898-9048 *E-mail:* asc@pmi.edu

New York

Apex Technical School

635 Avenue of the Americas
New York, NY 10011
Web: http://www.ApexTechnicalSchool.com

Accreditation: Accrediting Commission of Career Schools and Colleges of Technology

Programs Offered: autobody/collision and repair technology; automotive engineering technology; heating, air conditioning and refrigeration technology; welding technology

Enrollment: 1,281 students

Institution Contact: Mr. William Cann, CEO *Phone:* 212-989-5656 *Fax:* 212-463-7510 *E-mail:* wzc@apexschool.net

Admission Contact: Mr. William Ott, Admissions Director *Phone:* 212-645-3300 *Fax:* 212-645-6985

See full description on page 542.

The Art Institute of New York City

75 Varick Street, 16th Floor
New York, NY 10013
Web: http://www.ainyc.aii.edu

Accreditation: Accrediting Council for Independent Colleges and Schools

Programs Offered: advertising; baking and pastry arts; cinematography and film/video production; commercial and advertising art; culinary arts; design and visual communications; digital communication and media/multimedia; fashion/apparel design; hotel/motel administration; interior design; web page, digital/multimedia and information resources design

Enrollment: 1,600 students

indicates that the school is a participating institution in the *Imagine America* Scholarship Program.

The Art Institute of New York City (*continued*)

Institution Contact: Mr. Michael R. Iannacone, President *Phone:* 212-226-5500 ext. 6003 *Fax:* 212-966-0706 *E-mail:* miannacone@edmc.edu

Admission Contact: Mr. Rich Clark, Director of Admissions *Phone:* 212-226-5500 ext. 6005 *Fax:* 212-226-5644 *E-mail:* rjclark@edmc.edu

See full description on page 543.

Berkeley College-New York City Campus
3 East 43rd Street
New York, NY 10017
Web: http://www.BerkeleyCollege.edu
Accreditation: Middle States Association of Colleges and Schools
Programs Offered: accounting; business administration and management; fashion merchandising; international business/trade/commerce; legal assistant/paralegal; marketing/marketing management
Enrollment: 1,872 students
Institution Contact: Dr. Mildred Garcia, President *Phone:* 212-986-4343 ext. 4101 *Fax:* 212-986-8901 *E-mail:* millieg@berkeleycollege.edu
Admission Contact: Mr. Stuart Siegman, Director, High School Admissions *Phone:* 212-986-4343 *Fax:* 212-818-1079 *E-mail:* nycampus@berkeleycollege.edu

Berkeley College-Westchester Campus
99 Church Street
White Plains, NY 10601
Web: http://www.BerkeleyCollege.edu
Accreditation: Middle States Association of Colleges and Schools
Programs Offered: accounting; business administration and management; fashion merchandising; international business/trade/commerce; legal assistant/paralegal; marketing/marketing management; office management
Enrollment: 623 students
Institution Contact: Dr. Mildred Garcia, President *Phone:* 212-986-4343 ext. 4101 *Fax:* 212-986-8901 *E-mail:* millieg@berkeleycollege.edu
Admission Contact: Mr. Dave Bertone, Director of High School Admissions *Phone:* 914-694-1122 ext. 3110 *Fax:* 914-328-9469 *E-mail:* wpcampus@berkeleycollege.edu

Briarcliffe College
1055 Stewart Avenue
Bethpage, NY 11714-3545
Web: http://www.Briarcliffe.edu
Accreditation: Middle States Association of Colleges and Schools
Programs Offered: accounting; accounting related; administrative assistant and secretarial science; art; business administration and management; business administration, management and operations related; business automation/technology/data entry; business, management, and marketing related; business operations support and secretarial services related; commercial and advertising art; communications systems installation and repair technology; computer and information sciences; computer and information sciences and support services related; computer and information sciences related; computer and information systems security; computer engineering technology; computer graphics; computer/information technology administration and management; computer/information technology services administration related; computer installation and repair technology; computer programming; computer programming related; computer programming (specific applications); computer software and media applications; computer software and media applications related; computer systems analysis; computer systems networking and telecommunications; computer/technical support; computer technology/computer systems technology; criminal justice/law enforcement administration; criminal justice/police science; data entry/microcomputer applications; data entry/microcomputer applications related; data processing and data processing technology; executive assistant/executive secretary; health and medical administrative services related; health/health care administration; health information/medical records administration; information science/studies; information technology; legal administrative assistant/secretary; legal assistant/paralegal; marketing/marketing management; medical administrative assistant and medical secretary; system administration; system, networking, and LAN/WAN management; telecommunications; web/multimedia management and webmaster; web page, digital/multimedia and information resources design; word processing
Enrollment: 4,310 students
Institution Contact: Ms. Theresa Donohue, Vice President of Marketing and Admissions *Phone:* 516-918-3600 ext. 3705 *Fax:* 516-470-6020 *E-mail:* tdonohue@bcl.edu

indicates that the school is a participating institution in the *Imagine America* Scholarship Program.

Briarcliffe College

10 Lake Street
Patchogue, NY 11772
Web: http://www.briarcliffe.edu

Accreditation: Middle States Association of Colleges and Schools

Programs Offered: accounting; administrative assistant and secretarial science; applied art; business administration and management; business automation/technology/data entry; commercial and advertising art; communications systems installation and repair technology; computer and information sciences related; computer graphics; computer hardware engineering; computer/information technology administration and management; computer/information technology services administration related; computer installation and repair technology; computer programming; computer programming related; computer programming (specific applications); computer programming (vendor/product certification); computer software and media applications; computer software technology; computer systems analysis; computer systems networking and telecommunications; computer/technical support; computer technology/computer systems technology; criminal justice/law enforcement administration; data entry/microcomputer applications; data entry/microcomputer applications related; data processing and data processing technology; desktop publishing and digital imaging design; drafting and design technology; drawing; executive assistant/executive secretary; graphic and printing equipment operation/production; health information/medical records administration; health information/medical records technology; information science/studies; information technology; intermedia/multimedia; internet information systems; legal administrative assistant/secretary; legal assistant/paralegal; marketing/marketing management; medical reception; medical transcription; office occupations and clerical services; receptionist; retailing; selling skills and sales; system administration; system, networking, and LAN/WAN management; telecommunications; telecommunications technology; visual and performing arts; web/multimedia management and webmaster; web page, digital/multimedia and information resources design; word processing

Institution Contact: Mr. James Swift, Director of High School and National Admissions *Phone:* 631-654-5300 *Fax:* 631-654-5082 *E-mail:* jswift@bcl.edu

Admission Contact: Ms. Kathy McDermott, Director of Admissions *Phone:* 631-730-2010 *Fax:* 631-730-1244 *E-mail:* kmcdermott@bcl.edu

Caliber Training Institute

500 7th Avenue, 2nd Floor
New York, NY 10018
Web: http://www.caliberny.edu

Accreditation: Accrediting Commission of Career Schools and Colleges of Technology; Accrediting Council for Independent Colleges and Schools

Programs Offered: banking and financial support services; child care provision; health information/medical records technology; medical administrative assistant and medical secretary; medical/clinical assistant; nursing assistant/aide and patient care assistant; securities services administration; tourism and travel services management

Enrollment: 1,000 students

Institution Contact: Mr. Ben Lokos, President *Phone:* 212-564-0500 *Fax:* 212-564-0694 *E-mail:* caliberny@aol.com

Admission Contact: Mr. John Daniel, Director of Admissions *Phone:* 212-564-0500 *Fax:* 212-564-0694 *E-mail:* jdaniel@caliberny.edu

The Chubb Institute

498 7th Avenue, 17th Floor
New York, NY 10018
Web: http://www.chubbinstitute.edu

Accreditation: Accrediting Commission of Career Schools and Colleges of Technology; Accrediting Council for Continuing Education and Training

Programs Offered: computer and information sciences; computer and information sciences related; computer and information systems security; computer graphics; computer installation and repair technology; computer software engineering; computer systems networking and telecommunications; computer/technical support; computer technology/computer systems technology; health and medical administrative services related; health/health care administration; health information/medical records administration; health information/medical records technology; health professions related; health services administration; information technology; medical administrative assistant and medical secretary; medical insurance/medical billing; medical office assistant; medical office management; medical reception; system administration; system, networking, and LAN/WAN management; web page, digital/multimedia and information resources design

Enrollment: 386 students

Institution Contact: Ms. Diane Gilles, Executive Director *Phone:* 212-659-2122 *Fax:* 212-659-2175 *E-mail:* dgilles@chubbinstitute.edu

⚫ indicates that the school is a participating institution in the *Imagine America* Scholarship Program.

The Chubb Institute *(continued)*

Admission Contact: Ms. Tara Dorsey, Director of Admissions *Phone:* 212-659-2126 *Fax:* 212-659-2175 *E-mail:* tdorsey@chubbinstitute.edu

The Chubb Institute
1400 Old Country Road
Westbury, NY 11590
Web: http://www.chubbinstitute.com
Accreditation: Accrediting Council for Continuing Education and Training
Programs Offered: computer systems networking and telecommunications; graphic communications; graphic communications related; medical insurance coding; medical insurance/medical billing; medical office assistant; system, networking, and LAN/WAN management; web page, digital/multimedia and information resources design
Enrollment: 205 students
Institution Contact: Ms. Eileen Jackson, School Director *Phone:* 516-997-1400 *Fax:* 516-997-1496 *E-mail:* ejackson@chubbinstitute.com
Admission Contact: Mr. Nick Buffardi, Director of Admissions *Phone:* 516-997-1400 *Fax:* 516-997-1496 *E-mail:* nbuffardi@chubbinstitute.com

Computer Career Center
200 Garden City Plaza, Suite 519
Garden City, NY 11530
Web: http://www.ccctraining.edu
Accreditation: Accrediting Council for Independent Colleges and Schools
Programs Offered: accounting technology and bookkeeping; automobile/automotive mechanics technology; computer and information systems security; computer engineering technology; computer hardware engineering; computer systems networking and telecommunications; computer technology/computer systems technology; customer service management; electrical/electronics equipment installation and repair; electrician; electrocardiograph technology; information technology; internet information systems; medical administrative assistant and medical secretary; medical/clinical assistant; medical insurance coding; medical insurance/medical billing; medical office assistant; system, networking, and LAN/WAN management; web/multimedia management and webmaster
Enrollment: 1,000 students

Institution Contact: Mr. Kenneth G. Barrett, President *Phone:* 516-877-1225 ext. 1105 *Fax:* 516-877-1329 *E-mail:* kenb@ccctraining.edu
Admission Contact: Ms. Mary Miller, Director of Admissions *Phone:* 516-877-1225 *Fax:* 516-877-1959 *E-mail:* marym@ccctraining.edu

Computer Career Center
95-25 Queens Boulevard, Suite 600
Rego Park, NY 11374
Web: http://www.ccctraining.net
Accreditation: Accrediting Council for Independent Colleges and Schools
Programs Offered: computer and information sciences related; computer engineering technology; medical insurance coding; system, networking, and LAN/WAN management; web/multimedia management and webmaster
Institution Contact: Ms. Barbara Patterson, Director *Phone:* 516-877-1225 *Fax:* 516-877-1959 *E-mail:* barbarap@ccctraining.net
Admission Contact: Ms. Mary Miller, Admissions Director *Phone:* 516-877-1225 *Fax:* 516-877-1959 *E-mail:* marym@ccctraining.net

The French Culinary Institute Ⓐ
462 Broadway
New York, NY 10013
Web: http://www.frenchculinary.com
Accreditation: Accrediting Commission of Career Schools and Colleges of Technology
Programs Offered: baking and pastry arts; culinary arts; restaurant, culinary, and catering management
Enrollment: 900 students
Institution Contact: Mary Caldwell, Marketing Manager *Phone:* 212-219-8890 *Fax:* 212-226-0672 *E-mail:* mcaldwell@frenchculinary.com
Admission Contact: Mr. David Waggoner, Dean of Enrollment *Phone:* 212-219-8890 *Fax:* 212-226-0672 *E-mail:* admission@frenchculinary.com
See full description on page 544.

Gemological Institute of America, Inc. Ⓐ
270 Madison Avenue, 2nd Floor
New York, NY 10016-0601
Web: http://www.gia.edu
Accreditation: Accrediting Commission of Career Schools and Colleges of Technology
Programs Offered: applied art; metal and jewelry arts
Enrollment: 106 students

Ⓐ indicates that the school is a participating institution in the *Imagine America* Scholarship Program.

Institution Contact: Mr. Daniel Campbell, Director
Phone: 212-944-5900 *Fax:* 212-719-9563 *E-mail:*
dcampb@gia.edu
See full description on page 319.

Institute of Audio Research

64 University Place
New York, NY 10003-4595
Web: http://www.audioschool.com
Accreditation: Accrediting Commission of Career
Schools and Colleges of Technology
Programs Offered: recording arts technology
Enrollment: 500 students
Institution Contact: Ms. Muriel H. Adler, Director
Phone: 212-677-7580 *Fax:* 212-677-6549 *E-mail:*
murieliar@aol.com
Admission Contact: Mr. Mark L. Kahn, Director of
Admissions *Phone:* 212-777-8550 *Fax:* 212-677-6549
E-mail: iarny@aol.com

Island Drafting and Technical Institute (A)

128 Broadway
Amityville, NY 11701-2704
Web: http://www.idti.edu
Accreditation: Accrediting Commission of Career
Schools and Colleges of Technology
Programs Offered: architectural drafting and CAD/
CADD; CAD/CADD drafting/design technology;
civil drafting and CAD/CADD; computer engineering
technology; computer/information technology
administration and management; computer installation and repair technology; computer systems
networking and telecommunications; computer/
technical support; computer technology/computer
systems technology; data entry/microcomputer
applications; drafting and design technology; draft-
ing/design engineering technologies related; electrical, electronic and communications engineering
technology; engineering technology; information
technology; mechanical design technology; mechanical
drafting and CAD/CADD; system, networking, and
LAN/WAN management; word processing
Enrollment: 345 students
Institution Contact: Mr. James DiLiberto, President
Phone: 631-691-8733 *Fax:* 631-691-8738 *E-mail:*
dilibertoj@idti.edu
Admission Contact: Mr. John G. DiLiberto, Vice
President *Phone:* 631-691-8733 *Fax:* 631-691-8738
E-mail: johng@idti.edu
See full description on page 545.

ITT Technical Institute (A)

13 Airline Drive
Albany, NY 12205
Web: http://www.itt-tech.edu
Accreditation: Accrediting Council for Independent
Colleges and Schools
Programs Offered: computer engineering technology;
computer software and media applications; computer
systems networking and telecommunications; digital
communication and media/multimedia; web page,
digital/multimedia and information resources design
Enrollment: 419 students
Institution Contact: Mr. Christopher Chang, Director
Phone: 518-452-9300
Admission Contact: Mr. John Henebry, Director of
Recruitment *Phone:* 518-452-9300
See full description on page 546.

ITT Technical Institute (A)

2295 Millersport Highway, PO Box 327
Getzville, NY 14068
Web: http://www.itt-tech.edu
Accreditation: Accrediting Council for Independent
Colleges and Schools
Programs Offered: CAD/CADD drafting/design
technology; computer engineering technology;
computer software and media applications; computer
systems networking and telecommunications; digital
communication and media/multimedia; web page,
digital/multimedia and information resources design
Enrollment: 671 students
Institution Contact: Mr. Lester Burgess, Director
Phone: 716-689-2200
Admission Contact: Mr. Scott Jaskier, Director of
Recruitment *Phone:* 716-689-2200
See full description on page 547.

ITT Technical Institute (A)

235 Greenfield Parkway
Liverpool, NY 13088
Web: http://www.itt-tech.edu
Accreditation: Accrediting Council for Independent
Colleges and Schools
Programs Offered: computer engineering technology;
computer software and media applications; computer
systems networking and telecommunications; digital
communication and media/multimedia; web page,
digital/multimedia and information resources design
Enrollment: 364 students

(A) indicates that the school is a participating institution in the *Imagine America* Scholarship Program.

ITT Technical Institute *(continued)*

Institution Contact: Mr. Terry Riesel, Director of Recruitment *Phone:* 315-461-8000
See full description on page 548.

Katharine Gibbs School

320 South Service Road
Melville, NY 11747
Web: http://www.gibbsmelville.com
Accreditation: Accrediting Council for Independent Colleges and Schools
Programs Offered: accounting; administrative assistant and secretarial science; animation, interactive technology, video graphics and special effects; business administration and management; commercial and advertising art; computer graphics; computer/information technology administration and management; computer installation and repair technology; computer software and media applications; computer systems networking and telecommunications; computer/technical support; computer technology/computer systems technology; executive assistant/executive secretary; information technology; marketing/marketing management; medical administrative assistant and medical secretary; medical transcription; receptionist; system, networking, and LAN/WAN management; web page, digital/multimedia and information resources design
Enrollment: 700 students
Institution Contact: Mrs. Tammi D. Palms, Director of Compliance *Phone:* 631-370-3300 ext. 3390 *Fax:* 631-293-4849 *E-mail:* tpalms@gibbsmelville.com
Admission Contact: Mrs. Patricia Martin, President *Phone:* 631-370-3300 *Fax:* 631-293-2709

Katharine Gibbs School

200 Park Avenue
New York, NY 10166
Web: http://www.katharinegibbs.com/
Accreditation: Accrediting Council for Independent Colleges and Schools
Programs Offered: accounting; administrative assistant and secretarial science; business administration and management; business/corporate communications; commercial and advertising art; computer/information technology administration and management; computer/information technology services administration related; computer/technical support; desktop publishing and digital imaging design; digital communication and media/multimedia; executive assistant/executive secretary; fashion/apparel design; fashion merchandising; hospitality administration; hotel/motel administration; legal administrative assistant/secretary; marketing/marketing management; medical administrative assistant and medical secretary; office occupations and clerical services; system, networking, and LAN/WAN management; web page, digital/multimedia and information resources design
Institution Contact: Ms. Pat Martin, President *Phone:* 212-867-9300 *Fax:* 212-338-9606

Mandl School ⓐ

254 West 54th Street
New York, NY 10019-5516
Web: http://www.mandlschool.com
Accreditation: Accrediting Bureau of Health Education Schools; Accrediting Commission of Career Schools and Colleges of Technology
Programs Offered: clinical/medical laboratory technology; dental assisting; electrocardiograph technology; gene therapy; home health aide/home attendant; medical/clinical assistant; medical insurance/medical billing; nursing assistant/aide and patient care assistant; ophthalmic technology
Enrollment: 850 students
Institution Contact: Mr. Melvyn Weiner, President *Phone:* 212-247-3434 *Fax:* 212-247-3617 *E-mail:* melweiner2@aol.com
Admission Contact: Mr. Stuart Weiner, Vice President *Phone:* 212-247-3434 *Fax:* 212-247-3617 *E-mail:* stu.mandl@prodigy.net
See full description on page 549.

New York Institute of Massage

PO Box 645
Buffalo, NY 14231
Web: http://www.nyinstituteofmassage.com
Accreditation: Accrediting Commission of Career Schools and Colleges of Technology
Programs Offered: adult and continuing education; massage therapy
Enrollment: 180 students
Institution Contact: Ms. Diane Dinsmore, RN, Director *Phone:* 716-633-0355 *Fax:* 716-633-0213 *E-mail:* nyimdirector@adelphia.net
Admission Contact: *Phone:* 716-633-0355

Rochester Business Institute ⓐ

1630 Portland Avenue
Rochester, NY 14621
Web: http://www.rochester-institute.com
Accreditation: Accrediting Council for Independent Colleges and Schools

ⓐ indicates that the school is a participating institution in the *Imagine America* Scholarship Program.

Programs Offered: accounting; administrative assistant and secretarial science; business administration and management; computer programming; executive assistant/executive secretary; legal administrative assistant/secretary; legal assistant/paralegal; medical administrative assistant and medical secretary; medical/clinical assistant

Enrollment: 1,200 students

Institution Contact: Mr. Carl A. Silvio, President *Phone:* 585-266-0430 ext. 112 *Fax:* 585-266-8243 *E-mail:* csilvio@cci.edu

Admission Contact: Deanna Pfluke, Director of Admissions *Phone:* 585-266-0430 ext. 101 *Fax:* 585-266-8243 *E-mail:* dpfluke@cci.edu

See full description on page 550.

Sanford-Brown Institute

1 Old Country Road, LL1
Carle Place, NY 11514
Web: http://www.ultrasounddiagnosticschool.com/default.htm

Accreditation: Accrediting Bureau of Health Education Schools

Programs Offered: cardiovascular technology; diagnostic medical sonography and ultrasound technology; medical/clinical assistant

Institution Contact: Mr. Steve Dumerve, Executive Director *Phone:* 516-248-6060 *Fax:* 516-294-9336

Admission Contact: Mr. Ed Perez, Director of Admissions *Phone:* 516-248-6060 *Fax:* 516-248-9336

Sanford-Brown Institute

120 East 16th Street, 2nd Floor
New York, NY 10003
Web: http://www.sbnewyork.com

Accreditation: Accrediting Bureau of Health Education Schools

Programs Offered: cardiovascular technology; diagnostic medical sonography and ultrasound technology; health services/allied health/health sciences; medical/clinical assistant; medical insurance coding; medical insurance/medical billing

Enrollment: 658 students

Institution Contact: Lynn D. Salvage, President *Phone:* 646-313-4556 *Fax:* 212-253-6507 *E-mail:* lsalvage@sbnewyork.com

Admission Contact: Mr. Aldwyn Cook, Director of Admissions *Phone:* 646-313-4510 *Fax:* 212-253-6701

Sanford-Brown Institute

333 Westchester Avenue, West Building
White Plains, NY 10604

Accreditation: Accrediting Bureau of Health Education Schools; Accrediting Council for Independent Colleges and Schools

Programs Offered: cardiovascular technology; diagnostic medical sonography and ultrasound technology; medical/clinical assistant; medical insurance coding; medical insurance/medical billing

Enrollment: 355 students

Institution Contact: Mr. Larry Stieglitz, Campus President *Phone:* 914-874-2506 *Fax:* 914-347-5466 *E-mail:* lstieglitz@sbwhiteplains.com

Admission Contact: Mr. Emilio Noble, Director of Admissions *Phone:* 914-874-2510 *Fax:* 914-347-5466 *E-mail:* enoble@sbwhiteplains.com

TCI-The College of Technology

320 West 31st Street
New York, NY 10001
Web: http://www.tcicollege.net

Programs Offered: accounting; administrative assistant and secretarial science; appliance installation and repair technology; building/property maintenance and management; business administration and management; business automation/technology/data entry; business machine repair; carpentry; clinical/medical laboratory technology; communications systems installation and repair technology; communications technology; computer engineering technology; computer graphics; computer/information technology administration and management; computer/information technology services administration related; computer installation and repair technology; computer programming; computer programming related; computer programming (specific applications); computer software and media applications; computer software and media applications related; computer software engineering; computer software technology; computer systems networking and telecommunications; computer/technical support; computer technology/computer systems technology; construction engineering technology; data entry/microcomputer applications; data entry/microcomputer applications related; data processing and data processing technology; design and visual communications; digital communication and media/multimedia; e-commerce; electrical, electronic and communications engineering technology; electrical/electronics equipment installation and repair; electrician; engineering technology; English as a second language; environmental engineering technology; executive assistant/executive secretary; health information/medical records

⚫ indicates that the school is a participating institution in the *Imagine America* Scholarship Program.

TCI-The College of Technology *(continued)*

administration; heating, air conditioning and refrigeration technology; heating, air conditioning, ventilation and refrigeration maintenance technology; industrial electronics technology; information science/studies; information technology; instrumentation technology; internet information systems; legal administrative assistant/secretary; management information systems; medical administrative assistant and medical secretary; medical insurance coding; medical insurance/medical billing; medical office computer specialist; medical office management; office occupations and clerical services; pipefitting and sprinkler fitting; receptionist; system administration; technology management; telecommunications; telecommunications technology; web/multimedia management and webmaster; web page, digital/multimedia and information resources design; word processing

Institution Contact: Mr. Thomas Coleman, President *Phone:* 212-594-4000 ext. 201 *Fax:* 212-330-0898 *E-mail:* tcoleman@tcicollege.net

Admission Contact: Mr. Larry Stieglitz, Vice President of Admissions *Phone:* 212-594-4000 ext. 437 *Fax:* 212-330-0891 *E-mail:* lstieglitz@tcicollege.net

Technical Career Institute

320 West 31st
New York, NY 10001
Web: http://www.tcicollege.com

Accreditation: Middle States Association of Colleges and Schools

Programs Offered: accounting and business/management; accounting technology and bookkeeping; building/property maintenance and management; computer and information systems security; computer systems networking and telecommunications; computer technology/computer systems technology; digital communication and media/multimedia; electrical and electronic engineering technologies related; health information/medical records technology; heating, air conditioning, ventilation and refrigeration maintenance technology; industrial electronics technology; medical office management; office management; telecommunications technology; transportation technology

Institution Contact: Admissions *Phone:* 800-878-8246 *E-mail:* admissions@tcicollege.edu

Wood Tobe–Coburn School

8 East 40th Street
New York, NY 10016-0190
Web: http://www.woodtobecoburn.com

Programs Offered: accounting; administrative assistant and secretarial science; clinical/medical laboratory assistant; commercial and advertising art; computer graphics; computer programming; computer programming (specific applications); computer software and media applications; executive assistant/executive secretary; fashion and fabric consulting; fashion/apparel design; fashion merchandising; hospitality administration; medical administrative assistant and medical secretary; medical/clinical assistant; medical office management; medical transcription; retailing; system, networking, and LAN/WAN management; tourism and travel services management; web page, digital/multimedia and information resources design

Institution Contact: Ms. Sandi Gruninger, President *Phone:* 212-686-9040 *Fax:* 212-686-9171 *E-mail:* info@woodtobecoburn.com

Admission Contact: Ms. Sandra Wendland, Director of Admissions *Phone:* 212-686-9040 *Fax:* 212-686-9171 *E-mail:* info@woodtobecoburn.com

North Carolina

The Art Institute of Charlotte ⒶⓅ

Three LakePointe Plaza, 2110 Water Ridge Parkway
Charlotte, NC 28217-4536
Web: http://www.aich.artinstitutes.edu

Accreditation: Accrediting Council for Independent Colleges and Schools

Programs Offered: commercial and advertising art; culinary arts; desktop publishing and digital imaging design; fashion merchandising; interior design; web/multimedia management and webmaster; web page, digital/multimedia and information resources design

Institution Contact: Mrs. Elizabeth Guinan, College President *Phone:* 704-357-8020 ext. 2541 *Fax:* 704-357-1144 *E-mail:* guinane@aii.edu

Admission Contact: Mr. George Garcia, Director of Admissions *Phone:* 800-872-4417 ext. 5872 *Fax:* 704-357-1133 *E-mail:* garciag@aii.edu

See full description on page 551.

Ⓐ indicates that the school is a participating institution in the *Imagine America* Scholarship Program.

Brookstone College of Business (A)

10125 Berkeley Place Drive
Charlotte, NC 28262-1294
Web: http://www.brookstone.edu

Accreditation: Accrediting Council for Independent Colleges and Schools

Programs Offered: accounting; accounting technology and bookkeeping; administrative assistant and secretarial science; allied health and medical assisting services related; computer installation and repair technology; computer systems networking and telecommunications; medical administrative assistant and medical secretary; medical/clinical assistant; medical insurance coding; medical insurance/medical billing; medical office assistant; medical transcription

Enrollment: 210 students

Institution Contact: Mr. F. Jack Henderson, III, President *Phone:* 704-547-8600 *Fax:* 704-547-8887 *E-mail:* jhenderson@brookstone.edu

Admission Contact: Admissions Department *Phone:* 704-547-8600 *Fax:* 704-547-8887 *E-mail:* admissions@brookstone.edu

See full description on page 552.

Brookstone College of Business (A)

7815 National Service Road, Suite 600
Greensboro, NC 27409-9423
Web: http://www.brookstone.edu

Accreditation: Accrediting Council for Independent Colleges and Schools

Programs Offered: accounting; administrative assistant and secretarial science; business automation/technology/data entry; computer hardware technology; computer/information technology services administration related; computer installation and repair technology; computer software technology; computer/technical support; computer technology/computer systems technology; health information/medical records technology; information technology; medical administrative assistant and medical secretary; medical/clinical assistant; medical insurance coding; medical insurance/medical billing; medical office assistant; medical office computer specialist; medical reception; medical transcription; word processing

Enrollment: 240 students

Institution Contact: Mrs. Bridget Handley, Community Relations Coordinator *Phone:* 336-668-2627 ext. 18 *Fax:* 336-668-2717 *E-mail:* bhandley@brookstone.edu

See full description on page 553.

ECPI College of Technology (A)

4800 Airport Center Parkway
Charlotte, NC 28208
Web: http://www.ecpi.edu

Accreditation: Southern Association of Colleges and Schools

Programs Offered: business administration and management; business automation/technology/data entry; computer and information systems security; computer engineering technology; computer installation and repair technology; computer technology/computer systems technology; electrical, electronic and communications engineering technology; health information/medical records administration; health information/medical records technology; information science/studies; medical administrative assistant and medical secretary; medical/clinical assistant; medical transcription; nursing (licensed practical/vocational nurse training); office occupations and clerical services; telecommunications; web page, digital/multimedia and information resources design

Enrollment: 517 students

Institution Contact: Mr. Victor Riley, Provost *Phone:* 704-399-1010 *Fax:* 704-399-9144 *E-mail:* vriley@ecpi.edu

See full description on page 554.

ECPI College of Technology (A)

7802 Airport Center Drive
Greensboro, NC 27409
Web: http://www.ecpi.edu

Accreditation: Southern Association of Colleges and Schools

Programs Offered: administrative assistant and secretarial science; business administration and management; business automation/technology/data entry; computer engineering technology; computer installation and repair technology; computer systems networking and telecommunications; computer/technical support; computer technology/computer systems technology; health information/medical records administration; health information/medical records technology; information science/studies; information technology; medical/clinical assistant; medical insurance coding; medical insurance/medical billing; medical office computer specialist; office occupations and clerical services; telecommunications; web page, digital/multimedia and information resources design

Enrollment: 358 students

Institution Contact: Ms. Melinda J. Catron, Provost *Phone:* 336-665-1400 *E-mail:* mcatron@ecpi.edu

See full description on page 555.

(A) indicates that the school is a participating institution in the *Imagine America* Scholarship Program.

ECPI College of Technology Ⓐ

4101 Doie Cope Road
Raleigh, NC 27613
Web: http://www.ecpi.edu

Accreditation: Accrediting Commission of Career Schools and Colleges of Technology; Southern Association of Colleges and Schools

Programs Offered: administrative assistant and secretarial science; business administration and management; business automation/technology/data entry; computer engineering technology; computer/information technology administration and management; computer installation and repair technology; computer systems networking and telecommunications; computer/technical support; computer technology/computer systems technology; health information/medical records technology; information science/studies; information technology; office occupations and clerical services; system administration; telecommunications; web page, digital/multimedia and information resources design

Enrollment: 300 students

Institution Contact: Ms. Susan Wells, Provost *Phone:* 919-571-0057 *Fax:* 919-571-0780 *E-mail:* swells@ecpi.edu

See full description on page 556.

King's College

322 Lamar Avenue
Charlotte, NC 28204
Web: http://www.kingscollege.org

Accreditation: Accrediting Council for Independent Colleges and Schools

Programs Offered: accounting; administrative assistant and secretarial science; commercial and advertising art; computer programming; computer/technical support; legal administrative assistant/secretary; legal assistant/paralegal; medical/clinical assistant; tourism and travel services management

Institution Contact: Ms. Barbara Rockecharlie, School Director *Phone:* 704-688-3613 *Fax:* 704-348-2029 *E-mail:* brockecharlie@kingscollege.org

Admission Contact: Mrs. Diane Ryon, School Director *Phone:* 704-372-0266 ext. 3600 *Fax:* 704-348-2029 *E-mail:* dryon@kingscollege.org

Miller-Motte Technical College

5000 Market Street
Wilmington, NC 28405
Web: http://www.miller-motte.com

Accreditation: Accrediting Council for Independent Colleges and Schools

Programs Offered: accounting; administrative assistant and secretarial science; aesthetician/esthetician and skin care; business administration and management; computer software and media applications; computer systems networking and telecommunications; cosmetology; massage therapy; medical/clinical assistant; medical office assistant; nail technician and manicurist; office management; surgical technology

Institution Contact: *Phone:* 800-784-2110

NASCAR Technical Institute Ⓐ

220 Byers Creek Road
Mooresville, NC 28117

Accreditation: Accrediting Commission of Career Schools and Colleges of Technology

Programs Offered: automobile/automotive mechanics technology

Enrollment: 1,588 students

Institution Contact: Mr. Mike Fritz, School Director *Phone:* 704-658-1950 ext. 17401 *Fax:* 704-658-1952 *E-mail:* mfritz@uticorp.com

Admission Contact: Mr. Mike Gavin, Admissions Director *Phone:* 704-658-1950 ext. 17417 *Fax:* 704-658-1952 *E-mail:* mgavin@uticorp.com

See full description on page 557.

South College-Asheville

1567 Patton Avenue
Asheville, NC 28806-1748

Accreditation: Accrediting Council for Independent Colleges and Schools

Programs Offered: accounting; administrative assistant and secretarial science; business administration and management; computer systems networking and telecommunications; data entry/microcomputer applications; executive assistant/executive secretary; legal assistant/paralegal; medical/clinical assistant; medical transcription; surgical technology

Enrollment: 112 students

Institution Contact: Ms. Elaine Cue, Executive Director *Phone:* 828-252-2486 *Fax:* 828-252-8558 *E-mail:* ecue@southcollegenc.com

Admission Contact: Mr. Michael Darnell, Director of Admissions *Phone:* 828-252-2486 *Fax:* 828-252-8558 *E-mail:* mdarnell@southcollegenc.com

Strayer University at Cary

3200 Gateway Centre Boulevard, Suite 105
Morrisville, NC 27560
Web: http://www.strayer.edu

Accreditation: Middle States Association of Colleges and Schools

Ⓐ indicates that the school is a participating institution in the *Imagine America* Scholarship Program.

Programs Offered: accounting; business administration and management; communications technology; computer/information technology administration and management; computer programming; computer systems networking and telecommunications; data modeling/warehousing and database administration; economics; general studies; information science/studies; information technology; international business/trade/commerce; marketing/marketing management; purchasing, procurement/acquisitions and contracts management

Institution Contact: Dr. J. Chris Toe, University President *Phone:* 202-419-0400 *Fax:* 202-419-1425 *E-mail:* jct@strayer.edu

Admission Contact: Tricia Kokolis, Campus Manager *Phone:* 919-466-1150 *E-mail:* cary@strayer.edu

Strayer University at North Charlotte

8335 IBM Drive, Suite 150
Charlotte, NC 28262
Web: http://www.strayer.edu

Accreditation: Middle States Association of Colleges and Schools

Programs Offered: accounting; business administration and management; communications technology; computer/information technology administration and management; computer programming; computer systems networking and telecommunications; data modeling/warehousing and database administration; economics; general studies; information science/studies; information technology; international business/trade/commerce; marketing/marketing management; purchasing, procurement/acquisitions and contracts management

Institution Contact: Dr. J. Chris Toe, University President *Phone:* 202-408-2424 *Fax:* 202-789-0387 *E-mail:* jct@strayer.edu

Admission Contact: Carter Smith, Campus Manager *Phone:* 704-717-2380 *E-mail:* northcharlotte@strayer.edu

Strayer University at Raleigh

3200 Spring Forest Road, Suite 214
Raleigh, NC 27616
Web: http://www.strayer.edu

Accreditation: Middle States Association of Colleges and Schools

Programs Offered: accounting; business administration and management; communications technology; computer/information technology administration and management; computer programming; computer systems networking and telecommunications; data modeling/warehousing and database administration; economics; general studies; information science/

studies; information technology; international business/trade/commerce; marketing/marketing management; purchasing, procurement/acquisitions and contracts management

Institution Contact: Dr. J. Chris Toe, University President *Phone:* 202-408-2424 *Fax:* 202-789-0387 *E-mail:* jct@strayer.edu

Admission Contact: Cherry Clark, Campus Manager *Phone:* 919-878-9900 *Fax:* 919-878-6625 *E-mail:* northraleigh@strayer.edu

Strayer University at South Charlotte

2430 Whitehall Park Drive
Charlotte, NC 28273
Web: http://www.strayer.edu

Accreditation: Middle States Association of Colleges and Schools

Programs Offered: accounting; business administration and management; communications technology; computer/information technology administration and management; computer programming; computer systems networking and telecommunications; data modeling/warehousing and database administration; economics; general studies; information science/studies; information technology; international business/trade/commerce; marketing/marketing management; purchasing, procurement/acquisitions and contracts management

Institution Contact: Dr. J. Chris Toe, University President *Phone:* 202-408-2424 *Fax:* 202-789-0387 *E-mail:* jct@strayer.edu

Admission Contact: Helen Houser, Campus Manager *Phone:* 704-587-5360 *E-mail:* southcharlotte@strayer.edu

North Dakota

Aakers Business College

4012 19th Avenue, SW
Fargo, ND 58103

Accreditation: Accrediting Council for Independent Colleges and Schools

Programs Offered: accounting; accounting and finance; banking and financial support services; computer/information technology administration and management; computer/technical support; executive assistant/executive secretary; legal administrative assistant/secretary; marketing/marketing management; medical administrative assistant and medical

Aakers Business College (*continued*)

secretary; medical insurance coding; medical office assistant; medical reception; medical transcription; receptionist; tourism and travel services management

Enrollment: 490 students

Institution Contact: Ms. Elizabeth N. Largent, Director *Phone:* 701-277-3889 *Fax:* 701-277-5604 *E-mail:* blargent@aakers.edu

Admission Contact: Ms. Britta Sundberg, Director of Admissions *Phone:* 701-277-3889 *Fax:* 701-277-5604 *E-mail:* bsundberg@aakers.edu

Ohio

AEC Southern Ohio College

1320 West Maple Street, NW
North Canton, OH 44720-2854
Web: http://www.ETITech.Com

Accreditation: Accrediting Council for Independent Colleges and Schools

Programs Offered: accounting; business administration and management; business/corporate communications; CAD/CADD drafting/design technology; computer programming; computer software and media applications related; computer software technology; computer systems networking and telecommunications; computer technology/computer systems technology; criminal justice/law enforcement administration; electrical, electronic and communications engineering technology; legal administrative assistant/secretary; legal assistant/paralegal; medical administrative assistant and medical secretary; medical/clinical assistant

Enrollment: 736 students

Institution Contact: Mr. Peter Perkowski, Director *Phone:* 330-494-1214 *Fax:* 330-494-8112 *E-mail:* peterp@amedcts.com

Admission Contact: Mr. Greg Laudermilt, Director of Admissions *Phone:* 330-494-1214 *Fax:* 330-494-8112 *E-mail:* elaudermilt@amedcts.com

AEC Southern Ohio College, Akron Campus

2791 Mogadore Road
Akron, OH 44312

Accreditation: Accrediting Council for Independent Colleges and Schools

Programs Offered: accounting and business/management; CAD/CADD drafting/design technology; computer programming; computer programming related; computer programming (specific applications); computer programming (vendor/product certification); computer science; computer software and media applications related; computer software technology; computer systems networking and telecommunications; criminal justice/law enforcement administration; electrical and electronic engineering technologies related; electrical, electronic and communications engineering technology; legal assistant/paralegal; mechanical drafting and CAD/CADD; medical/clinical assistant

Enrollment: 481 students

Institution Contact: Ms. Sandra A. Wilk, Campus Director *Phone:* 330-733-8766 *Fax:* 330-733-5853 *E-mail:* swilk@amedcts.com

Admission Contact: Mr. Seamus White, Director of Admissions *Phone:* 330-733-8766 *Fax:* 330-733-5853 *E-mail:* swhite@amedcts.com

AEC Southern Ohio College, Cincinnati Campus

1011 Glendale Milford Road
Cincinnati, OH 45215
Web: http://www.socaec.com

Accreditation: Accrediting Council for Independent Colleges and Schools

Programs Offered: accounting; allied health and medical assisting services related; audiovisual communications technologies related; business, management, and marketing related; CAD/CADD drafting/design technology; computer programming (specific applications); computer software technology; computer systems networking and telecommunications; criminal justice/law enforcement administration; legal assistant/paralegal; medical/clinical assistant; nursing (registered nurse training); opticianry

Enrollment: 1,121 students

Institution Contact: Danny Finuf, President *Phone:* 513-771-2424 *Fax:* 513-771-3413 *E-mail:* dfinuf@edmc.edu

Admission Contact: Joanne Dellefield, Director of Admissions *Phone:* 513-771-2424 *Fax:* 513-771-3413 *E-mail:* jdellefield@edmc.edu

Ⓘ indicates that the school is a participating institution in the *Imagine America* Scholarship Program.

AEC Southern Ohio College, Findlay Campus

1700 Fostoria Avenue, Suite 100
Findlay, OH 45847
Web: http://www.socaec.edu

Accreditation: Accrediting Council for Independent Colleges and Schools

Programs Offered: accounting technology and bookkeeping; business administration and management; CAD/CADD drafting/design technology; computer programming (specific applications); computer software and media applications; computer systems networking and telecommunications; criminal justice/law enforcement administration; electrical, electronic and communications engineering technology; legal assistant/paralegal; medical/clinical assistant; nursing (licensed practical/vocational nurse training)

Admission Contact: Kathy Pichacz, Admissions Director *Phone:* 513-771-2424 *Fax:* 419-423-0725

Akron Institute Ⓐ

1625 Portage Trail
Cuyahoga Falls, OH 44223
Web: http://www.akroninstitute.com

Accreditation: Accrediting Commission of Career Schools and Colleges of Technology

Programs Offered: business administration and management; computer technology/computer systems technology; dental assisting; medical/clinical assistant; medical insurance/medical billing

Enrollment: 256 students

Institution Contact: Mr. David L. LaRue, Campus President *Phone:* 330-928-3400 *Fax:* 330-928-1906 *E-mail:* director@akroninstitute.com

Admission Contact: Mr. Richard Fuller, Director of Admissions *Phone:* 330-928-3400 *Fax:* 330-928-1906 *E-mail:* rfuller@akroninstitute.com

See full description on page 558.

American School of Technology

2100 Morse Road, #4599
Columbus, OH 43229

Accreditation: Accrediting Commission of Career Schools and Colleges of Technology

Programs Offered: computer and information sciences related; heating, air conditioning and refrigeration technology; medical/clinical assistant; medical insurance coding

Enrollment: 635 students

Institution Contact: Mrs. Susan Stella, Director and Chief Executive Officer *Phone:* 614-436-4820

Admission Contact: Mrs. Tera Wilson, Director of Admissions *Phone:* 614-436-4820

Bradford School

2469 Stelzer Road
Columbus, OH 43219
Web: http://www.bradfordschoolcolumbus.edu

Accreditation: Accrediting Council for Independent Colleges and Schools

Programs Offered: accounting; administrative assistant and secretarial science; commercial and advertising art; computer graphics; computer programming; computer systems networking and telecommunications; executive assistant/executive secretary; hospitality administration; legal administrative assistant/secretary; legal assistant/paralegal; medical/clinical assistant; tourism and travel services management

Enrollment: 354 students

Institution Contact: Mr. Dennis Bartels, President *Phone:* 614-416-6200 *Fax:* 614-416-6210 *E-mail:* dbartels@bradfordschoolcolumbus.edu

Admission Contact: Ms. Raeann Lee, Director of Admissions *Phone:* 614-416-6200 *Fax:* 614-416-6210 *E-mail:* rlee@bradfordschoolcolumbus.edu

Bryman Institute

825 Tech Center Drive
Gahanna, OH 43230-6653

Programs Offered: medical/clinical assistant; medical insurance coding; medical insurance/medical billing

Davis College

4747 Monroe Street
Toledo, OH 43623-4307
Web: http://www.daviscollege.edu

Programs Offered: administrative assistant and secretarial science; massage therapy; medical/clinical assistant; medical insurance coding; medical transcription

Institution Contact: *Phone:* 419-473-2700 *Fax:* 419-473-2472 *E-mail:* learn@daviscollege.edu

EduTek College

3855 Fishcreek Road
Stow, OH 44224
Web: http://www.edutekcollege.com

Accreditation: Accrediting Council for Independent Colleges and Schools

Ⓐ indicates that the school is a participating institution in the *Imagine America* Scholarship Program.

EduTek College (*continued*)

Programs Offered: adult and continuing education; computer engineering technology; medical insurance coding; medical insurance/medical billing; medical office assistant; medical office management; medical transcription; office management; pharmacy technician

Institution Contact: Angela J. Daniel, Executive Director *Phone:* 330-677-4667 *Fax:* 330-677-4560 *E-mail:* adaniel@edutekcollege.com

Admission Contact: Christopher Caraway, Director of Admissions *Phone:* 330-677-4667 *Fax:* 330-677-4560 *E-mail:* ccaraway@edutekcollege.com

ETI Technical College of Niles ⓐ

2076 Youngstown-Warren Road
Niles, OH 44446

Accreditation: Accrediting Commission of Career Schools and Colleges of Technology

Programs Offered: accounting; computer engineering technology; data processing and data processing technology; electrical, electronic and communications engineering technology; heating, air conditioning and refrigeration technology; legal administrative assistant/secretary; medical/clinical assistant; web page, digital/multimedia and information resources design

Enrollment: 279 students

Institution Contact: Ms. Diane Marsteller, Director of Admissions *Phone:* 330-652-9919 *Fax:* 330-652-4399 *E-mail:* etiadmissionsdir@hotmail.com

See full description on page 559.

Gallipolis Career College

1176 Jackson Pike, Suite 312
Gallipolis, OH 45631-2600
Web: http://www.gallipoliscareercollege.com/

Accreditation: Accrediting Council for Independent Colleges and Schools

Programs Offered: accounting; business administration and management; computer technology/computer systems technology; data entry/microcomputer applications; executive assistant/executive secretary; medical administrative assistant and medical secretary; medical office management

Institution Contact: Mr. Robert L. Shirey, President *Phone:* 740-446-4367 *Fax:* 740-446-4124 *E-mail:* gcc@gallipoliscareercollege.com

Admission Contact: Mr. Jack L. Henson, Director of Admissions *Phone:* 740-446-4367 *Fax:* 740-446-4124 *E-mail:* admissions@gallipoliscareercollege.com

Hondros College

4140 Executive Parkway
Westerville, OH 43081
Web: http://www.hondros.com

Programs Offered: financial planning and services; insurance; real estate; sales, distribution and marketing; securities services administration

Institution Contact: *Phone:* 614-508-7277 *Fax:* 614-508-7279

International College of Broadcasting

6 South Smithville Road
Dayton, OH 45431
Web: http://www.icbcollege.com

Accreditation: Accrediting Commission of Career Schools and Colleges of Technology; Accrediting Council for Independent Colleges and Schools

Programs Offered: broadcast journalism; communications technology; radio and television; recording arts technology

Institution Contact: Mr. J. Michael LeMaster, Director and Vice President of Operations *Phone:* 937-258-8251 ext. 201 *Fax:* 937-258-8714 *E-mail:* micicb@aol.com

Admission Contact: Mr. Aan McIntosh, Director of Admissions *Phone:* 937-258-8251 ext. 202 *Fax:* 937-258-8714

International College of Broadcasting ⓐ

6 South Smithville Road
Dayton, OH 45431
Web: http://www.icbcollege.com

Accreditation: Accrediting Commission of Career Schools and Colleges of Technology

Programs Offered: broadcast journalism; communications technology; radio and television; recording arts technology

Institution Contact: Mr. Chuck O. Oesterle, Director of Admissions *Phone:* 937-258-8251 *Fax:* 937-258-8714

See full description on page 560.

ITT Technical Institute ⓐ

3325 Stop Eight Road
Dayton, OH 45414-3425
Web: http://www.itt-tech.edu

Accreditation: Accrediting Council for Independent Colleges and Schools

Programs Offered: CAD/CADD drafting/design technology; computer engineering technology; computer software and media applications; computer

ⓐ indicates that the school is a participating institution in the *Imagine America* Scholarship Program.

systems networking and telecommunications; digital communication and media/multimedia; web page, digital/multimedia and information resources design

Enrollment: 470 students

Institution Contact: Mr. Michael S. Shaffer, Director *Phone:* 937-454-2267

Admission Contact: Mr. Joe G. Graham, Director of Recruitment *Phone:* 937-454-2267

See full description on page 561.

ITT Technical Institute ⒜

3781 Park Mill Run Drive
Hilliard, OH 43026
Web: http://www.itt-tech.edu

Accreditation: Accrediting Council for Independent Colleges and Schools

Programs Offered: accounting and business/management; business administration and management; CAD/CADD drafting/design technology; computer engineering technology; computer software engineering; computer systems networking and telecommunications; criminal justice/police science; digital communication and media/multimedia; web page, digital/multimedia and information resources design

Enrollment: 303 students

Institution Contact: Mr. James Vaas, Director *Phone:* 614-771-4888

See full description on page 562.

ITT Technical Institute ⒜

4750 Wesley Avenue
Norwood, OH 45212
Web: http://www.itt-tech.edu

Accreditation: Accrediting Council for Independent Colleges and Schools

Programs Offered: CAD/CADD drafting/design technology; computer engineering technology; computer software and media applications; computer systems networking and telecommunications; digital communication and media/multimedia; web page, digital/multimedia and information resources design

Enrollment: 627 students

Institution Contact: Mr. Bill Bradford, Director *Phone:* 513-531-8300

Admission Contact: Mr. Greg Hitt, Director of Recruitment *Phone:* 513-531-8300

See full description on page 563.

ITT Technical Institute ⒜

14955 Sprague Road
Strongsville, OH 44136
Web: http://www.itt-tech.edu

Accreditation: Accrediting Council for Independent Colleges and Schools

Programs Offered: accounting and business/management; business administration and management; CAD/CADD drafting/design technology; computer engineering technology; computer software and media applications; computer systems networking and telecommunications; criminal justice/police science; digital communication and media/multimedia; web page, digital/multimedia and information resources design

Enrollment: 653 students

Institution Contact: Mr. Scott Behmer, Director *Phone:* 440-234-9091

Admission Contact: Ms. Joanne Dyer, Director of Recruitment *Phone:* 440-234-9091

See full description on page 564.

ITT Technical Institute ⒜

1030 North Meridian Road
Youngstown, OH 44509-4098
Web: http://www.itt-tech.edu

Accreditation: Accrediting Council for Independent Colleges and Schools

Programs Offered: CAD/CADD drafting/design technology; computer engineering technology; computer software and media applications; computer systems networking and telecommunications; digital communication and media/multimedia; web page, digital/multimedia and information resources design

Enrollment: 484 students

Institution Contact: Mr. Frank Quartini, Director *Phone:* 330-270-1600

Admission Contact: Mr. Tom Flynn, Director of Recruitment *Phone:* 330-270-1600

See full description on page 565.

Miami–Jacobs College

110 North Patterson Boulevard
Dayton, OH 45402
Web: http://www.miamijacobs.edu

Accreditation: Accrediting Council for Independent Colleges and Schools

Programs Offered: business administration and management; computer systems networking and telecommunications; criminal justice/law enforcement

Ⓐ indicates that the school is a participating institution in the *Imagine America* Scholarship Program.

Miami–Jacobs College (*continued*)

administration; massage therapy; medical/clinical assistant; medical office management; surgical technology

Enrollment: 527 students

Institution Contact: Ms. Darlene R. Waite, President *Phone:* 937-461-5174 *Fax:* 937-461-3384 *E-mail:* darlene.waite@miamijacobs.edu

Admission Contact: Mr. Sean Kuhn, Director of Admissions *Phone:* 937-461-5174 ext. 123 *Fax:* 937-461-3384 *E-mail:* sean.kuhn@miamijacobs.edu

National College of Business and Technology

1837 Woodman Center Drive
Kettering, OH 45420-1157

Programs Offered: accounting; business administration and management; health information/medical records technology; medical/clinical assistant; pharmacy technician; surgical technology

Ohio Institute of Photography and Technology Ⓐ

2029 Edgefield Road
Dayton, OH 45439
Web: http://www.oipt.com

Accreditation: Accrediting Commission of Career Schools and Colleges of Technology

Programs Offered: commercial and advertising art; digital communication and media/multimedia; medical/clinical assistant; medical office management; photographic and film/video technology; photography

Institution Contact: Mr. David McDaniel, Information Contact *Phone:* 800-932-9698 *Fax:* 937-294-2259

See full description on page 566.

Ohio Valley College of Technology Ⓐ

16808 St. Clair Avenue, PO Box 7000
East Liverpool, OH 43920
Web: http://www.ovct.edu

Accreditation: Accrediting Council for Independent Colleges and Schools

Programs Offered: accounting; computer installation and repair technology; computer software and media applications related; dental assisting; medical/clinical assistant; medical office management

Enrollment: 166 students

Institution Contact: Ms. Debra Sanford, Director of Education *Phone:* 330-385-1070 *Fax:* 330-385-4606 *E-mail:* dsanford@ovct.edu

Admission Contact: Mr. Scott S. Rogers, Director *Phone:* 330-385-1070 *Fax:* 330-385-4606 *E-mail:* srogers@ovct.edu

See full description on page 568.

Remington College–Cleveland Campus Ⓐ

14445 Broadway Avenue
Cleveland, OH 44125
Web: http://www.remingtoncollege.edu

Accreditation: Accrediting Commission of Career Schools and Colleges of Technology

Programs Offered: computer/information technology administration and management; computer programming (specific applications); information science/studies; internet information systems; medical/clinical assistant; medical insurance/medical billing; pharmacy technician; system, networking, and LAN/WAN management

Institution Contact: Mr. Todd A. Zvaigzne, Campus President *Phone:* 216-475-7520 *Fax:* 216-475-6055 *E-mail:* todd.zvaigzne@remingtoncollege.edu

Admission Contact: Mr. William Cassidy, Director of Recruitment *Phone:* 216-475-7520 *Fax:* 216-475-6055 *E-mail:* william.cassidy@remingtoncollege.edu

See full description on page 569.

Remington College–Cleveland West Campus Ⓐ

26350 Brookpark
North Olmstead, OH 44070
Web: http://www.remingtoncollege.edu

Accreditation: Accrediting Commission of Career Schools and Colleges of Technology

Programs Offered: computer systems analysis; criminal justice/law enforcement administration; dental assisting; medical/clinical assistant; pharmacy technician

Institution Contact: Mr. Gary Azotea, Vice President *Phone:* 440-777-2560 *Fax:* 440-777-3238 *E-mail:* gary.azotea@remingtoncollege.edu

Admission Contact: Mr. Vic Hart, Director of Recruitment *Phone:* 440-777-2560 *Fax:* 440-777-3238 *E-mail:* vic.hart@remingtoncollege.edu

See full description on page 570.

Ⓐ indicates that the school is a participating institution in the *Imagine America* Scholarship Program.

RETS Tech Center (A)

555 East Alex Bell Road
Centerville, OH 45459
Web: http://www.retstechcenter.com

Accreditation: Accrediting Commission of Career Schools and Colleges of Technology

Programs Offered: computer/information technology administration and management; electrical, electronic and communications engineering technology; heating, air conditioning and refrigeration technology; legal assistant/paralegal; medical/clinical assistant; medical insurance coding; nursing (licensed practical/vocational nurse training); robotics technology; tourism and travel services management

Enrollment: 574 students

Institution Contact: Mr. Michael LeMaster, President *Phone:* 937-433-3410 *Fax:* 937-435-6516 *E-mail:* rets@erinet.com

Admission Contact: Mr. Rich Elkin, Director of Admissions *Phone:* 937-433-3410 *Fax:* 937-435-6516 *E-mail:* rets@erinet.com

See full description on page 571.

Sanford-Brown Institute

17535 Rosbough Drive, Suite 100
Middleburg Heights, OH 44130
Web: http://www.wix.net

Accreditation: Accrediting Bureau of Health Education Schools

Programs Offered: cardiovascular technology; criminal justice/law enforcement administration; diagnostic medical sonography and ultrasound technology; massage therapy; medical/clinical assistant; medical insurance/medical billing

Enrollment: 480 students

Institution Contact: Ms. Christine Smith, President *Phone:* 440-239-9640 *Fax:* 440-239-9648 *E-mail:* csmith@sbc-cleveland.com

Admission Contact: Ms. Lorna Martin, Director of Admissions *Phone:* 440-239-9640 *Fax:* 440-239-9648

Southeastern Business College

1855 Western Avenue
Chillicothe, OH 45601
Web: http://www.southeasternbusinesscollege.com

Accreditation: Accrediting Council for Independent Colleges and Schools

Programs Offered: accounting; business administration and management; information technology; medical administrative assistant and medical secretary; office management

Enrollment: 100 students

Institution Contact: Betty McAdow, Director *Phone:* 740-774-6300 *Fax:* 740-774-6317 *E-mail:* betty_sbc@yahoo.com

Admission Contact: Tressa Strausbaugh, Admissions Representative *Phone:* 740-774-6300 *Fax:* 740-774-6317 *E-mail:* admit2_chillicothe@yahoo.com

Southeastern Business College

504 McCarty Lane
Jackson, OH 45640
Web: http://www.southeasternbusinesscollege.com

Accreditation: Accrediting Council for Independent Colleges and Schools

Programs Offered: accounting; administrative assistant and secretarial science; business administration and management; computer software and media applications; information technology; medical administrative assistant and medical secretary

Enrollment: 65 students

Institution Contact: Karen Osborne, Director/Director of Education *Phone:* 740-286-1554 *Fax:* 740-286-4476 *E-mail:* dir_jackson@yahoo.com

Admission Contact: Ronda Smith, Admissions Representative *Phone:* 740-286-1554 *Fax:* 740-286-4476

Southeastern Business College

1522 Sheridan Drive
Lancaster, OH 43130-1368

Accreditation: Accrediting Council for Independent Colleges and Schools

Programs Offered: accounting; administrative assistant and secretarial science; business administration and management; information technology; medical administrative assistant and medical secretary

Institution Contact: Ms. Mary Gang, Director *Phone:* 740-687-6126 *Fax:* 740-687-0431 *E-mail:* dir_lanc@yahoo.com

Admission Contact: Mr. Bret Fannin *Phone:* 740-687-6126 *Fax:* 740-687-0431 *E-mail:* bret_sbc@yahoo.com

Southeastern Business College

3879 Rhodes Avenue
New Boston, OH 45662
Web: http://www.careersohio.com/

Accreditation: Accrediting Council for Independent Colleges and Schools

Programs Offered: accounting; administrative assistant and secretarial science; business administra-

(A) indicates that the school is a participating institution in the *Imagine America* Scholarship Program.

Southeastern Business College *(continued)*

tion and management; computer software and media applications; information technology; medical administrative assistant and medical secretary

Enrollment: 74 students

Institution Contact: Mrs. Teresa L. Roe, Director of Education *Phone:* 740-456-4124 *Fax:* 740-456-5163 *E-mail:* dir_nb@yahoo.com

Admission Contact: Mrs. Rebecca Mowery, Admissions Representative *Phone:* 740-456-4124 *Fax:* 740-456-5163 *E-mail:* admit_nb@yahoo.com

Southwestern College of Business Ⓐ

149 Northland Boulevard
Cincinnati, OH 45246
Web: http://www.swcollege.net

Accreditation: Accrediting Council for Independent Colleges and Schools

Programs Offered: accounting; accounting technology and bookkeeping; administrative assistant and secretarial science; business administration and management; computer science; computer software and media applications; medical administrative assistant and medical secretary; medical/clinical assistant; medical insurance coding; medical insurance/medical billing; phlebotomy

Admission Contact: Roy Kimble, Director of Admissions *Phone:* 513-874-0432 *Fax:* 513-874-1330 *E-mail:* doatri-county@lincolnedu.com

See full description on page 574.

Southwestern College of Business Ⓐ

632 Vine Street
Cincinnati, OH 45246
Web: http://www.swcollege.net

Accreditation: Accrediting Council for Independent Colleges and Schools

Programs Offered: accounting; administrative assistant and secretarial science; business administration and management; computer science; computer software and media applications; medical administrative assistant and medical secretary; medical/clinical assistant; medical insurance coding; medical insurance/medical billing; phlebotomy

Admission Contact: Betty Streber, Director of Admissions *Phone:* 513-421-3212 *Fax:* 513-421-8325 *E-mail:* doavinestreet@lincolnedu.com

See full description on page 575.

Southwestern College of Business Ⓐ

111 West First Street
Dayton, OH 45402
Web: http://www.swcollege.net

Accreditation: Accrediting Council for Independent Colleges and Schools

Programs Offered: accounting; accounting technology and bookkeeping; administrative assistant and secretarial science; business administration and management; computer science; computer software and media applications; medical administrative assistant and medical secretary; medical/clinical assistant; medical insurance coding; medical insurance/medical billing; phlebotomy

Admission Contact: Curtis Kirby, Director of Admissions *Phone:* 937-224-0061 *Fax:* 937-224-0065 *E-mail:* doadayton@lincolnedu.com

See full description on page 572.

Southwestern College of Business Ⓐ

201 East Second Street
Franklin, OH 45005
Web: http://www.swcollege.net

Accreditation: Accrediting Council for Independent Colleges and Schools

Programs Offered: accounting; administrative assistant and secretarial science; business administration and management; computer science; computer software and media applications; medical administrative assistant and medical secretary; medical/clinical assistant; medical insurance coding; medical insurance/medical billing; phlebotomy

Admission Contact: Lynne Reilly, Director of Admissions *Phone:* 937-746-6633 *Fax:* 937-746-6754 *E-mail:* doafranklin@lincolnedu.com

See full description on page 573.

TDDS, Inc.

1688 North Pricetown Road, SR 534, PO Box 506
Lake Milton, OH 44429
Web: http://www.tdds.edu

Accreditation: Accrediting Commission of Career Schools and Colleges of Technology

Programs Offered: diesel mechanics technology; truck and bus driver/commercial vehicle operation

Enrollment: 515 students

Institution Contact: Mr. Richard A. Rathburn, Jr., President *Phone:* 330-538-2216 *Fax:* 330-538-2905 *E-mail:* rick@tdds.edu

Ⓐ indicates that the school is a participating institution in the *Imagine America* Scholarship Program.

Admission Contact: Mr. Michael A. Rouzzo, Admissions Director *Phone:* 330-538-2216 *Fax:* 330-538-2905 *E-mail:* michael@tdds.edu

Technology Education College

2745 Winchester Pike
Columbus, OH 43232-2087
Web: http://www.teccollege.com

Accreditation: Accrediting Commission of Career Schools and Colleges of Technology

Programs Offered: accounting; computer programming; computer technology/computer systems technology; criminal justice/law enforcement administration; drafting and design technology; engineering technology; medical/clinical assistant

Institution Contact: Mr. Thomas Greenhouse, Director *Phone:* 614-759-7700 *Fax:* 614-759-7747 *E-mail:* tgreenhouse@teceducation.com

Admission Contact: Rhonda Frazier *Phone:* 614-456-4600 *Fax:* 800-838-3233 *E-mail:* rfrazier@teceducation.com

Trumbull Business College Ⓐ

3200 Ridge Road
Warren, OH 44484
Web: http://www.tbc-trumbullbusiness.com

Accreditation: Accrediting Council for Independent Colleges and Schools

Programs Offered: accounting; business administration and management; computer software and media applications; executive assistant/executive secretary; legal administrative assistant/secretary; medical administrative assistant and medical secretary; word processing

Enrollment: 425 students

Institution Contact: Mr. D. J. Griffith, Vice President *Phone:* 330-369-3200 ext. 11 *Fax:* 330-369-6792 *E-mail:* djgriffith@tbc-trumbullbusiness.com

Admission Contact: Mrs. Amy Gazdik, Admissions Director/High School Coordinator *Phone:* 330-369-3200 ext. 14 *Fax:* 330-369-6792 *E-mail:* agazdik@tbc-trumbullbusiness.com

See full description on page 576.

Vatterott College Ⓐ

5025 East Royalton Road
Broadview Heights, OH 44147
Web: http://www.vatterott-college.edu

Accreditation: Accrediting Commission of Career Schools and Colleges of Technology

Programs Offered: building/property maintenance and management; computer technology/computer systems technology; electrician; heating, air conditioning, ventilation and refrigeration maintenance technology

Enrollment: 240 students

Institution Contact: Mr. Bob Martin, Director *Phone:* 440-526-1860 *Fax:* 440-526-1933 *E-mail:* bmartin@vatterott-college.edu

Admission Contact: Mr. Kevin Pugely, High School Admissions Coordinator *Phone:* 440-526-1860 *Fax:* 440-526-1933 *E-mail:* kevin.pugely@vatterott-college.edu

See full description on page 577.

Virginia Marti College of Art and Design Ⓐ

11724 Detroit Avenue
Lakewood, OH 44107
Web: http://www.virginiamarticollege.com

Accreditation: Accrediting Commission of Career Schools and Colleges of Technology

Programs Offered: commercial and advertising art; fashion/apparel design; fashion merchandising; interior design

Enrollment: 320 students

Institution Contact: Mr. Dennis Marti, Assistant School Director *Phone:* 216-221-8584 *Fax:* 216-221-2311 *E-mail:* qmarti@virginiamarticollege.com

Admission Contact: Mr. Quinn E. Marti, Admissions *Phone:* 216-221-8584 *Fax:* 216-221-2311 *E-mail:* qmarti@virginiamarticollege.com

See full description on page 578.

Oklahoma

City College, Inc.

2620 South Service Road
Moore, OK 73160
Web: http://www.citycollegeinc.com

Accreditation: Accrediting Council for Continuing Education and Training

Programs Offered: accounting; child care provision; computer technology/computer systems technology; legal administrative assistant/secretary; legal assistant/paralegal; medical insurance coding

ⒶÂ indicates that the school is a participating institution in the *Imagine America* Scholarship Program.

City College, Inc. *(continued)*

Enrollment: 250 students

Institution Contact: Mr. Andrew Moore *Phone:* 405-329-5627 *Fax:* 405-321-2763 *E-mail:* jmoore@citycollegeinc.com

Community Care College

4242 South Sheridan
Tulsa, OK 74145
Web: http://www.communitycarecollege.com

Accreditation: Accrediting Bureau of Health Education Schools

Programs Offered: dental assisting; massage therapy; medical/clinical assistant; pharmacy technician; phlebotomy; surgical technology; veterinary/animal health technology

Enrollment: 850 students

Institution Contact: Ms. Teresa L. Knox, Chief Executive Officer *Phone:* 918-610-0027 ext. 205 *Fax:* 918-622-9696 *E-mail:* tknox@communitycarecollege.com

Admission Contact: Ms. April Straly, Director of Admissions *Phone:* 918-610-0027 ext. 220 *Fax:* 918-610-0029 *E-mail:* astraly@communitycarecollege.com

Dickinson Business School/Career Point Business School

3138 South Garnett Road
Tulsa, OK 74146-1933
Web: http://www.career-point.org

Accreditation: Accrediting Council for Independent Colleges and Schools

Programs Offered: accounting technology and bookkeeping; administrative assistant and secretarial science; clinical/medical laboratory assistant; computer systems networking and telecommunications; electrocardiograph technology; legal administrative assistant/secretary; medical administrative assistant and medical secretary; medical/clinical assistant; medical insurance coding; medical insurance/medical billing; medical office assistant; medical office computer specialist; office occupations and clerical services

Enrollment: 400 students

Institution Contact: James J. D. Endsley, Director of Admissions *Phone:* 918-627-8074 *Fax:* 918-627-4007 *E-mail:* tadmdir@career-point.org

Oklahoma Health Academy

1939 North Moore Avenue
Oklahoma City, OK 73160-3667
Institution Contact: Ms. Kayla Kanyeur

Oklahoma Health Academy

2865 East Skelly Drive
Tulsa, OK 74105-6233
Institution Contact: Mr. Jim Wolfenberger

Platt College

112 Southwest 11th Street
Lawton, OK 73501
Web: http://www.plattcollege.org

Accreditation: Accrediting Commission of Career Schools and Colleges of Technology

Programs Offered: dental assisting; medical/clinical assistant; nursing (licensed practical/vocational nurse training)

Institution Contact: Ms. Kirsten Sellens, Director *Phone:* 580-355-4416 *Fax:* 580-355-4526 *E-mail:* kirstens@plattcollege.org

Admission Contact: Ms. Lisa Hannah, Admissions Representative *Phone:* 580-355-4416 *Fax:* 580-355-4526

Platt College

2727 West Memorial Road
Oklahoma City, OK 73134

Accreditation: Accrediting Commission of Career Schools and Colleges of Technology

Programs Offered: culinary arts; medical/clinical assistant; nursing (registered nurse training)

Enrollment: 287 students

Institution Contact: Ms. Mollie F. Hager, Director *Phone:* 405-749-2433 *Fax:* 405-748-4150 *E-mail:* mollieh@plattcollege.org

Platt College ⓐ

309 South Ann Arbor
Oklahoma City, OK 73128

Accreditation: Accrediting Commission of Career Schools and Colleges of Technology

Programs Offered: dental assisting; medical administrative assistant and medical secretary; medical/clinical assistant; nursing (licensed practical/vocational nurse training); pharmacy technician; surgical technology

Enrollment: 300 students

ⓐ indicates that the school is a participating institution in the *Imagine America* Scholarship Program.

Institution Contact: Ms. Jane Nowlin, Director *Phone:* 405-946-7799 *Fax:* 405-943-2150 *E-mail:* janen@plattcollege.org
Admission Contact: Ms. Renee Jackson, Director of Admissions *Phone:* 405-946-7799 *Fax:* 405-943-2150 *E-mail:* reneej@plattcollege.org
See full description on page 579.

Platt College Ⓐ

3801 South Sheridan Road
Tulsa, OK 74145-1132
Web: http://www.plattcollege.org
Accreditation: Accrediting Commission of Career Schools and Colleges of Technology
Programs Offered: dental assisting; medical/clinical assistant; nursing (licensed practical/vocational nurse training); pharmacy technician; surgical technology
Enrollment: 450 students
Institution Contact: Mrs. Susan Rone, Director *Phone:* 918-663-9000 *Fax:* 918-622-1240 *E-mail:* susanr@plattcollege.org
Admission Contact: Mrs. Renee Jackson, Director of Admissions *Phone:* 918-663-9000 *Fax:* 918-622-1240 *E-mail:* reneej@plattcollege.org
See full description on page 580.

State Barber and Hair Design College Inc.

2514 South Agnew
Oklahoma City, OK 73108-6220
Accreditation: Accrediting Commission of Career Schools and Colleges of Technology
Programs Offered: barbering
Enrollment: 38 students
Institution Contact: Ms. Elaine Gunn, Director *Phone:* 405-631-8621 *Fax:* 405-632-2738 *E-mail:* statebarber2514@aol.com

Tulsa Welding School Ⓐ

2545 East 11th Street
Tulsa, OK 74104-3909
Web: http://www.weldingschool.edu
Accreditation: Accrediting Commission of Career Schools and Colleges of Technology
Programs Offered: welding technology
Enrollment: 390 students
Institution Contact: Mr. R. Michael Harter, Chairman and Chief Executive Officer *Phone:* 918-587-6789 ext. 223 *Fax:* 918-295-6821 *E-mail:* mharter641@aol.com

Admission Contact: Mr. Mike Thurber, Director of Admissions *Phone:* 918-587-6789 ext. 240 *Fax:* 918-587-8170 *E-mail:* tws@ionet.net
See full description on page 581.

Vatterott College Ⓐ

4629 Northwest 23rd Street
Oklahoma City, OK 73127
Web: http://www.vatterott-college.edu
Accreditation: Accrediting Commission of Career Schools and Colleges of Technology
Programs Offered: CAD/CADD drafting/design technology; computer engineering technology; computer programming; computer programming (specific applications); computer technology/computer systems technology; drafting and design technology; electrician; heating, air conditioning, ventilation and refrigeration maintenance technology; medical administrative assistant and medical secretary; medical/clinical assistant; medical insurance coding; medical insurance/medical billing; medical office computer specialist
Institution Contact: Office of Admissions *Phone:* 405-945-0088 *Fax:* 405-945-0788 *E-mail:* okcity@vatterott-college.edu
See full description on page 582.

Vatterott College Ⓐ

555 South Memorial Drive
Tulsa, OK 74112
Web: http://www.vatterott-college.edu
Accreditation: Accrediting Commission of Career Schools and Colleges of Technology
Programs Offered: computer programming; computer technology/computer systems technology; electrician; heating, air conditioning and refrigeration technology; medical office computer specialist; web page, digital/multimedia and information resources design
Institution Contact: Office of Admissions *Phone:* 918-835-8288 *Fax:* 918-836-9698 *E-mail:* tulsa@vatterott-college.edu
See full description on page 583.

Ⓐ indicates that the school is a participating institution in the *Imagine America* Scholarship Program.

regon

Apollo College Ⓐ

2004 Lloyd Center
Portland, OR 97232
Web: http://www.apollocollege.edu

Accreditation: Accrediting Bureau of Health Education Schools

Programs Offered: clinical/medical laboratory technology; dental assisting; medical administrative assistant and medical secretary; medical/clinical assistant; medical/health management and clinical assistant; medical insurance/medical billing; pharmacy technician; veterinary/animal health technology

Enrollment: 380 students

Institution Contact: Ms. Micaela Sieracki, Campus Director *Phone:* 503-761-6100 *Fax:* 503-761-3351 *E-mail:* msieracki@apollocollege.edu

See full description on page 584.

The Art Institute of Portland

1122 Northwest Davis Street
Portland, OR 97209
Web: http://www.aipd.artinstitutes.edu

Accreditation: Northwest Association of Schools and Colleges

Programs Offered: advertising; animation, interactive technology, video graphics and special effects; applied art; art; CAD/CADD drafting/design technology; commercial and advertising art; computer graphics; design and visual communications; digital communication and media/multimedia; drawing; fashion/apparel design; interior design; web/multimedia management and webmaster; web page, digital/multimedia and information resources design

Enrollment: 1,497 students

Institution Contact: Lori Murray, Director of Admissions *Phone:* 503-228-6528 *Fax:* 503-227-1945 *E-mail:* murrayl@aii.edu

Admission Contact: Lori Murray, Admissions Office *Phone:* 888-228-6528 *Fax:* 503-227-1945 *E-mail:* aipdadm@aii.edu

Ashmead College Ⓐ

9600 Southwest Oak Street, Suite 400
Tigard, OR 97223
Web: http://www.ashmeadcollege.com

Accreditation: Accrediting Council for Continuing Education and Training

Programs Offered: massage therapy

Institution Contact: Director of Admissions *Phone:* 503-892-8100 *Fax:* 503-892-8871

See full description on page 585.

ITT Technical Institute Ⓐ

6035 Northeast 78th Court
Portland, OR 97218-2854
Web: http://www.itt-tech.edu

Accreditation: Accrediting Council for Independent Colleges and Schools

Programs Offered: animation, interactive technology, video graphics and special effects; CAD/CADD drafting/design technology; communications technology; computer and information systems security; computer software and media applications; computer software engineering; computer systems networking and telecommunications; digital communication and media/multimedia; electrical, electronic and communications engineering technology; industrial technology; technology management; web page, digital/multimedia and information resources design

Enrollment: 575 students

Institution Contact: Mr. Edward Yakimchick, Director *Phone:* 503-255-6500

Admission Contact: Mr. Cliff Custer, Director of Recruitment *Phone:* 503-255-6500

See full description on page 587.

Pioneer Pacific College

8800 SE Sunnyside Road
Clackamas, OR 97015

Programs Offered: accounting; business administration and management; information technology; legal assistant/paralegal; medical/clinical assistant

Pioneer Pacific College Ⓐ

27501 Southwest Parkway Avenue
Wilsonville, OR 97070-9296
Web: http://www.pioneerpacific.edu

Accreditation: Accrediting Council for Independent Colleges and Schools

Programs Offered: accounting; administrative assistant and secretarial science; business administration and management; computer/information technology administration and management; criminal justice/law enforcement administration; health/health care administration; legal assistant/paralegal; medical/clinical assistant; medical insurance/medical billing; pharmacy technician; radiologic technology/

Ⓐ indicates that the school is a participating institution in the *Imagine America* Scholarship Program.

science; web/multimedia management and webmaster; web page, digital/multimedia and information resources design

Enrollment: 1,000 students

Institution Contact: Mr. David J. Hallett, JD, President *Phone:* 503-682-3903 *Fax:* 503-682-1514 *E-mail:* dhallett@pioneerpacific.edu

Admission Contact: Mrs. Mary Harris, Vice President of Admissions *Phone:* 503-654-8000 *Fax:* 503-659-6107 *E-mail:* mharris@pioneerpacific.edu

See full description on page 589.

Pioneer Pacific College-Eugene/Springfield Branch Ⓐ

3800 Sports Way
Springfield, OR 97477
Web: http://www.pioneerpacific.edu

Accreditation: Accrediting Council for Independent Colleges and Schools

Programs Offered: accounting; business administration and management; computer systems networking and telecommunications; criminal justice/law enforcement administration; health/health care administration; marketing/marketing management; medical/clinical assistant; medical insurance/medical billing

Institution Contact: Debra Marcus, Director *Phone:* 541-684-4644 *Fax:* 541-684-0665 *E-mail:* inquiries@pioneerpacific.edu

See full description on page 588.

Western Business College Ⓐ

425 Southwest Washington Street
Portland, OR 97204
Web: http://www.cci.edu

Accreditation: Accrediting Council for Independent Colleges and Schools

Programs Offered: accounting; administrative assistant and secretarial science; computer/information technology administration and management; data entry/microcomputer applications; executive assistant/executive secretary; hospitality administration; legal administrative assistant/secretary; legal assistant/paralegal; medical administrative assistant and medical secretary; medical/clinical assistant; medical insurance coding; medical insurance/medical billing; pharmacy technician; receptionist; tourism and travel services management

Enrollment: 758 students

Institution Contact: Mrs. Mardell Lanfranco, President *Phone:* 503-222-3225 *Fax:* 503-228-6926 *E-mail:* mlanfranc@cci.edu

Admission Contact: Ms. Laurel Coke, Director of Admissions *Phone:* 503-222-3225 *Fax:* 503-228-6926 *E-mail:* lbuchana@cci.edu

See full description on page 590.

Western Culinary Institute

921 SW Morrison Street, Suite 400
Portland, OR 97205
Web: http://www.wci.edu

Accreditation: Accrediting Commission of Career Schools and Colleges of Technology

Programs Offered: baking and pastry arts; culinary arts; food preparation; food services technology; hospitality administration; hotel/motel administration; restaurant, culinary, and catering management

Enrollment: 950 students

Institution Contact: Mrs. Zoya Kumar-Ufford, Director of Marketing *Phone:* 503-223-2245 ext. 587 *Fax:* 503-223-5554 *E-mail:* zufford@wci.edu

Admission Contact: Mrs. Janine Carnel, Vice President of Admissions and Marketing *Phone:* 503-223-2245 ext. 386 *Fax:* 503-223-5554 *E-mail:* jcarnel@wci.edu

Pennsylvania

Academy of Medical Arts and Business Ⓐ

2301 Academy Drive
Harrisburg, PA 17112-1012
Web: http://www.ACADcampus.com

Accreditation: Accrediting Bureau of Health Education Schools; Accrediting Commission of Career Schools and Colleges of Technology

Programs Offered: business automation/technology/data entry; child care and support services management; child care provision; computer and information systems security; computer graphics; computer/information technology administration and management; computer/information technology services administration related; computer programming; computer programming (specific applications); computer programming (vendor/product certification); computer software and media applications; computer software and media applications related; computer systems analysis; computer systems networking and telecommunications; computer

---

Ⓐ indicates that the school is a participating institution in the *Imagine America* Scholarship Program.

Academy of Medical Arts and Business (*continued*)

technology/computer systems technology; culinary arts; data processing and data processing technology; dental assisting; design and visual communications; desktop publishing and digital imaging design; digital communication and media/multimedia; electrocardiograph technology; health information/medical records administration; health information/medical records technology; home health aide/home attendant; information science/studies; information technology; legal administrative assistant/secretary; legal assistant/paralegal; massage therapy; medical administrative assistant and medical secretary; medical/clinical assistant; medical office management; medical transcription; office occupations and clerical services; receptionist; system administration; system, networking, and LAN/WAN management; web/multimedia management and webmaster; web page, digital/multimedia and information resources design; word processing

Enrollment: 250 students

Institution Contact: Mr. Gary Kay, President *Phone:* 717-545-4747 *Fax:* 717-901-9090 *E-mail:* info@acadcampus.com

See full description on page 591.

Allentown Business School

2809 East Saucon Valley Road
Center Valley, PA 18034
Web: http://www.chooseabs.com/

Accreditation: Accrediting Council for Independent Colleges and Schools

Programs Offered: accounting; business administration and management; child care and support services management; commercial and advertising art; computer programming; computer systems networking and telecommunications; criminal justice/law enforcement administration; fashion merchandising; hospitality administration; legal assistant/paralegal; massage therapy; medical administrative assistant and medical secretary; system, networking, and LAN/WAN management; tourism and travel services management; web/multimedia management and webmaster; web page, digital/multimedia and information resources design

Enrollment: 1,450 students

Institution Contact: Mr. Sam Jarvis, Director of Marketing *Phone:* 610-791-5100 *Fax:* 610-791-7810

Admission Contact: Jena Marx, Assistant Director of Admissions *Phone:* 610-625-5325 *Fax:* 610-791-7810 *E-mail:* scholarships@chooseabs.com

The Art Institute of Philadelphia Ⓐ

1622 Chestnut Street
Philadelphia, PA 19103-5119
Web: http://www.aiph.artinstitutes.edu

Accreditation: Accrediting Council for Independent Colleges and Schools

Programs Offered: animation, interactive technology, video graphics and special effects; cinematography and film/video production; commercial and advertising art; computer graphics; culinary arts; fashion/apparel design; fashion merchandising; industrial design; interior design; photography; web page, digital/multimedia and information resources design

Institution Contact: Mr. Tim Howard, Director of Admissions *Phone:* 215-567-7080 *Fax:* 215-405-6399

See full description on page 592.

The Art Institute of Pittsburgh Ⓐ

420 Boulevard of the Allies
Pittsburgh, PA 15219-1328
Web: http://www.aip.artinstitutes.edu

Accreditation: Accrediting Council for Independent Colleges and Schools; Middle States Association of Colleges and Schools

Programs Offered: advertising; animation, interactive technology, video graphics and special effects; applied art; art; baking and pastry arts; CAD/CADD drafting/design technology; ceramic arts and ceramics; cinematography and film/video production; commercial and advertising art; commercial photography; culinary arts; design and visual communications; desktop publishing and digital imaging design; drawing; food preparation; foodservice systems administration; graphic and printing equipment operation/production; graphic communications; graphic communications related; hotel/motel administration; industrial design; interior design; make-up artist; metal and jewelry arts; photography; restaurant, culinary, and catering management; web/multimedia management and webmaster; web page, digital/multimedia and information resources design

Enrollment: 3,839 students

Institution Contact: Mr. George L. Pry, President *Phone:* 412-291-6210 *Fax:* 412-263-3715 *E-mail:* gpry@aii.edu

Admission Contact: Mr. Newton Myvett, Director of Admissions *Phone:* 800-275-2470 *Fax:* 412-263-6667 *E-mail:* nmyvett@aii.edu

See full description on page 593.

Ⓐ indicates that the school is a participating institution in the *Imagine America* Scholarship Program.

Automotive Training Center Ⓐ

114 Pickering Way
Exton, PA 19341-1310
Web: http://www.autotraining.edu

Accreditation: Accrediting Commission of Career Schools and Colleges of Technology

Programs Offered: autobody/collision and repair technology; automobile/automotive mechanics technology; diesel mechanics technology; engine machinist

Enrollment: 600 students

Institution Contact: Mr. Steven Hiscox, President *Phone:* 610-363-6716 *Fax:* 610-363-8524 *E-mail:* schiscox@hotmail.com

Admission Contact: Mr. Donald S. VanDemark, Jr., Vice President/COO *Phone:* 610-363-6716 *Fax:* 610-363-8524 *E-mail:* donvan@autotraining.edu

See full description on page 594.

Baltimore School of Massage, York Campus Ⓐ

170 Red Rock Road
York, PA 17402
Web: http://steinered.com

Accreditation: Accrediting Commission of Career Schools and Colleges of Technology

Programs Offered: massage therapy

Enrollment: 130 students

Institution Contact: Ms. Anita Perry-Strong, Campus Director *Phone:* 717-268-1881 *Fax:* 717-268-1991 *E-mail:* anitas@steinerleisure.com

Admission Contact: Admissions Department *Phone:* 866-699-1881 *Fax:* 717-268-1991 *E-mail:* anitas@steinerleisure.com

See full description on page 595.

Berks Technical Institute Ⓐ

2205 Ridgewood Road
Wyomissing, PA 19610-1168
Web: http://www.berks.edu

Accreditation: Accrediting Commission of Career Schools and Colleges of Technology

Programs Offered: accounting; business administration and management; business automation/technology/data entry; CAD/CADD drafting/design technology; commercial and advertising art; computer and information sciences related; computer engineering technology; computer graphics; computer/information technology administration and management; computer installation and repair technology; computer programming; computer technology/computer systems technology; drafting and design technology; information science/studies; information technology; internet information systems; legal administrative assistant/secretary; legal assistant/paralegal; massage therapy; medical administrative assistant and medical secretary; medical/clinical assistant; medical/health management and clinical assistant; medical reception; web/multimedia management and webmaster; web page, digital/multimedia and information resources design

Enrollment: 550 students

Institution Contact: Mr. Adrian Clark, Executive Director *Phone:* 610-372-1722 *Fax:* 610-376-4684 *E-mail:* aclark@berkstech.com

Admission Contact: Mr. Jim Wunder *Phone:* 610-372-1722 *Fax:* 610-376-4684 *E-mail:* jwunder@berkstech.com

See full description on page 596.

Bradford School

Gulf Tower, 707 Grant Street
Pittsburgh, PA 15219
Web: http://www.bradfordpittsburgh.edu

Accreditation: Accrediting Council for Independent Colleges and Schools

Programs Offered: accounting; administrative assistant and secretarial science; business administration and management; business automation/technology/data entry; commercial and advertising art; computer graphics; computer/information technology administration and management; computer programming; computer programming (specific applications); computer software and media applications; computer systems networking and telecommunications; computer/technical support; computer technology/computer systems technology; data entry/microcomputer applications; data processing and data processing technology; fashion merchandising; health information/medical records administration; health unit management/ward supervision; hospitality administration; hotel/motel administration; legal administrative assistant/secretary; legal assistant/paralegal; medical administrative assistant and medical secretary; medical/clinical assistant; medical office management; medical transcription; office occupations and clerical services; receptionist; restaurant, culinary, and catering management; retailing; selling skills and sales; system, networking, and LAN/WAN management; tourism and travel services management; web/multimedia management and webmaster; web page, digital/multimedia and information resources design

Institution Contact: Mr. Vincent Graziano, President *Phone:* 412-391-6710 *Fax:* 412-471-6714 *E-mail:* info@bradfordpittsburgh.edu

Ⓐ indicates that the school is a participating institution in the *Imagine America* Scholarship Program.

Bradford School (continued)

Admission Contact: Director of Admissions *Phone:* 412-391-6710 *Fax:* 412-471-6714 *E-mail:* info@bradfordpittsburgh.edu

Bradley Academy for the Visual Arts Ⓐ

1409 Williams Road
York, PA 17402
Web: http://www.bradleyacademy.net

Accreditation: Accrediting Commission of Career Schools and Colleges of Technology

Programs Offered: animation, interactive technology, video graphics and special effects; apparel and textile marketing management; applied art; art; commercial and advertising art; computer graphics; computer software and media applications; design and visual communications; desktop publishing and digital imaging design; digital communication and media/multimedia; drawing; fashion/apparel design; fashion merchandising; interior design; internet information systems; merchandising; retailing; visual and performing arts; web/multimedia management and webmaster; web page, digital/multimedia and information resources design

Institution Contact: *Phone:* 800-864-7725 *Fax:* 717-840-1951 *E-mail:* info@bradleyacademy.net

See full description on page 597.

Business Institute of Pennsylvania

628 Arch Street, Suite B-105
Meadville, PA 16335
Web: http://www.biop.com

Accreditation: Accrediting Council for Independent Colleges and Schools

Programs Offered: accounting; administrative assistant and secretarial science; anatomy; business administration, management and operations related; business automation/technology/data entry; business/corporate communications; clinical/medical laboratory assistant; computer/information technology administration and management; computer/information technology services administration related; data entry/microcomputer applications related; data processing and data processing technology; executive assistant/executive secretary; health and medical administrative services related; legal administrative assistant/secretary; medical administrative assistant and medical secretary; medical/health management and clinical assistant; medical insurance coding; medical insurance/medical billing; medical office assistant; medical office computer specialist; medical reception; medical transcription; office occupations and clerical services; receptionist; web page, digital/multimedia and information resources design; word processing

Enrollment: 85 students

Institution Contact: Mrs. Patricia McMahon, President *Phone:* 814-724-0700 *Fax:* 814-724-2777 *E-mail:* info@biop.com

Admission Contact: Ms. Anne M. Burger, Acting Director *Phone:* 814-724-0700 *Fax:* 814-724-2777 *E-mail:* burgera@biop.com

Business Institute of Pennsylvania

335 Boyd Drive
Sharon, PA 16146
Web: http://www.biop.com

Accreditation: Accrediting Council for Independent Colleges and Schools

Programs Offered: accounting; administrative assistant and secretarial science; anatomy; business administration and management; business automation/technology/data entry; business/corporate communications; child care provision; clinical/medical laboratory assistant; computer/information technology administration and management; computer/information technology services administration related; data entry/microcomputer applications related; data processing and data processing technology; executive assistant/executive secretary; health/health care administration; health information/medical records technology; legal administrative assistant/secretary; marketing/marketing management; medical administrative assistant and medical secretary; medical/clinical assistant; medical/health management and clinical assistant; medical insurance coding; medical insurance/medical billing; medical reception; medical transcription; office occupations and clerical services; receptionist; web page, digital/multimedia and information resources design; word processing

Enrollment: 100 students

Institution Contact: Mrs. Kathleen McMahon Motolenich, Director *Phone:* 724-983-0700 *Fax:* 724-983-8355 *E-mail:* kaisim@biop.com

Admission Contact: Miss Shannon McNamara, Admission Officer *Phone:* 724-983-0711 *Fax:* 724-983-8355 *E-mail:* mac2002ten@yahoo.com

CHI Institute

Lawrence Park Shopping Center, 1991 Sproul Road, Suite 42
Broomall, PA 19008
Web: http://www.chi-institute.net/

Accreditation: Accrediting Commission of Career Schools and Colleges of Technology

---

Ⓐ indicates that the school is a participating institution in the *Imagine America* Scholarship Program.

Programs Offered: commercial and advertising art; computer installation and repair technology; computer programming; computer programming related; computer programming (vendor/product certification); computer systems networking and telecommunications; computer/technical support; computer technology/computer systems technology; electrician; gene therapy; health information/medical records administration; heating, air conditioning and refrigeration technology; heating, air conditioning, ventilation and refrigeration maintenance technology; information technology; medical administrative assistant and medical secretary; medical/clinical assistant; medical/health management and clinical assistant; surgical technology; system administration; system, networking, and LAN/WAN management

Enrollment: 800 students

Institution Contact: Mr. Robert G. Milot, Executive Director *Phone:* 610-353-7630 *Fax:* 610-359-1370 *E-mail:* bmilot@chi-institute.net

Admission Contact: Mr. Paul Richardson, Director of Admissions *Phone:* 610-353-7630 *Fax:* 610-359-1370 *E-mail:* prichardson@chi-institute.net

CHI Institute Ⓐ

520 Street Road
Southampton, PA 18966
Web: http://www.chitraining.com

Accreditation: Accrediting Commission of Career Schools and Colleges of Technology

Programs Offered: administrative assistant and secretarial science; business automation/technology/data entry; commercial and advertising art; communications systems installation and repair technology; computer engineering technology; computer graphics; computer/information technology services administration related; computer programming; computer programming (specific applications); computer software and media applications; computer systems networking and telecommunications; computer/technical support; computer technology/computer systems technology; criminal justice/law enforcement administration; data entry/microcomputer applications; electrical/electronics equipment installation and repair; electrician; medical administrative assistant and medical secretary; medical/clinical assistant; medical insurance coding; medical insurance/medical billing; medical office computer specialist; medical office management; medical pharmacology and pharmaceutical sciences; medical reception; office occupations and clerical services; pharmacy; pharmacy technician; phlebotomy; system administration; system, networking, and LAN/WAN management; telecommunications; telecommunications technology;

web/multimedia management and webmaster; web page, digital/multimedia and information resources design; word processing

Enrollment: 650 students

Institution Contact: Ms. Dale Anspach, Executive Director *Phone:* 215-357-5100 *Fax:* 215-357-4212 *E-mail:* d_anspach@chicareers.com

Admission Contact: Mr. Eric Heller, Director of Admissions *Phone:* 215-357-5100 *Fax:* 215-357-4212 *E-mail:* eheller@chicareers.com

See full description on page 598.

The Chubb Institute

Marple Crossroads, 400 South State Road
Springfield, PA 19064-3957
Web: http://www.chubbinstitute.edu

Accreditation: Accrediting Council for Independent Colleges and Schools

Programs Offered: administrative assistant and secretarial science; computer and information sciences related; computer and information systems security; computer graphics; computer/information technology administration and management; computer/information technology services administration related; computer programming; computer programming related; computer programming (specific applications); computer programming (vendor/product certification); computer software and media applications; computer software and media applications related; computer systems analysis; computer systems networking and telecommunications; computer/technical support; computer technology/computer systems technology; data entry/microcomputer applications; data entry/microcomputer applications related; data processing and data processing technology; information science/studies; information technology; medical administrative assistant and medical secretary; medical insurance coding; medical insurance/medical billing; medical office computer specialist; medical reception; system administration; system, networking, and LAN/WAN management; web page, digital/multimedia and information resources design

Institution Contact: Ms. Judith M. Cole, Campus President *Phone:* 610-338-2321 *Fax:* 610-338-2393 *E-mail:* jcole@chubbinstitute.edu

Admission Contact: Ms. Kimberly Ewing, Director of Admissions *Phone:* 610-338-2305 *Fax:* 610-338-2399 *E-mail:* kewing@chubbinstitute.edu

Ⓐ indicates that the school is a participating institution in the *Imagine America* Scholarship Program.

The Cittone Institute Ⓐ

2180 Hornig Road, Building A
Philadelphia, PA 19116
Web: http://www.cittone.com

Accreditation: Accrediting Council for Independent Colleges and Schools

Programs Offered: allied health and medical assisting services related; computer engineering related; computer engineering technology; computer graphics; computer hardware engineering; computer/information technology administration and management; computer/information technology services administration related; computer software and media applications related; health and medical administrative services related; health information/medical records administration; health information/medical records technology; massage therapy

Enrollment: 341 students

Institution Contact: Mr. James K. Tolbert, Executive Director *Phone:* 215-969-0869 ext. 207 *Fax:* 215-969-4023 *E-mail:* jtolbert@cittone.com

Admission Contact: Mr. Thomas A. Driscoll, III, Director of Admissions *Phone:* 215-969-0869 ext. 245 *Fax:* 215-969-3457 *E-mail:* tdriscoll@cittone.com

See full description on page 600.

The Cittone Institute Ⓐ

3600 Market Street
Philadelphia, PA 19104
Web: http://www.cittone.com

Accreditation: Accrediting Council for Independent Colleges and Schools

Programs Offered: computer systems networking and telecommunications; computer/technical support; medical administrative assistant and medical secretary; medical/clinical assistant; system administration

Institution Contact: Executive Director *Phone:* 215-382-1553 ext. 201 *Fax:* 215-382-3875 *E-mail:* execdirphilly@lincolntech.com

See full description on page 599.

The Cittone Institute Ⓐ

1 Plymouth Meeting, Suite 300
Plymouth Meeting, PA 19462
Web: http://www.cittone.com

Accreditation: Accrediting Council for Independent Colleges and Schools

Programs Offered: clinical laboratory science/medical technology; clinical/medical laboratory technology; computer engineering related; computer engineering technology; computer hardware engineering; com-puter/information technology administration and management; computer/information technology services administration related; computer installation and repair technology; computer programming; computer programming related; computer programming (specific applications); computer software engineering; computer software technology; computer systems analysis; computer systems networking and telecommunications; computer/technical support; computer technology/computer systems technology; health information/medical records administration; health information/medical records technology; massage therapy; medical administrative assistant and medical secretary; medical/clinical assistant; medical/health management and clinical assistant; medical insurance coding; medical insurance/medical billing; medical office computer specialist; medical office management; medical reception; pharmacy technician

Enrollment: 320 students

Institution Contact: Mr. Craig M. Avery, Executive Director *Phone:* 610-941-0319 ext. 156 *Fax:* 610-941-3367 *E-mail:* cavery@cittone.com

Admission Contact: Mr. Shawn Brady, Director of Admissions *Phone:* 610-941-0319 ext. 129 *Fax:* 610-941-4158 *E-mail:* sbrady@cittone.com

See full description on page 601.

Computer Learning Network Ⓐ

2900 Fairway Drive
Altoona, PA 16602-4457
Web: http://www.cln.edu

Accreditation: Accrediting Commission of Career Schools and Colleges of Technology

Programs Offered: business automation/technology/data entry; computer installation and repair technology; computer software and media applications; computer systems networking and telecommunications; legal administrative assistant/secretary; legal assistant/paralegal; massage therapy; medical office computer specialist; medical office management; medical transcription; office occupations and clerical services; pharmacy technician; receptionist; system, networking, and LAN/WAN management; word processing

Enrollment: 320 students

Institution Contact: Ms. Vickie J. Clements, Director *Phone:* 814-944-5643 *Fax:* 814-944-5309 *E-mail:* vclements@cln.edu

Admission Contact: Ms. Miriam Kratzer, Admissions Director *Phone:* 814-944-5643 *Fax:* 814-944-5309 *E-mail:* admissions@cln.edu

See full description on page 602.

Ⓐ indicates that the school is a participating institution in the *Imagine America* Scholarship Program.

Computer Learning Network Ⓐ

401 East Winding Hill Road, Suite 101
Mechanicsburg, PA 17055-4989
Web: http://www.clntraining.net

Accreditation: Accrediting Commission of Career Schools and Colleges of Technology

Programs Offered: administrative assistant and secretarial science; computer and information systems security; computer/information technology administration and management; computer/information technology services administration related; computer installation and repair technology; computer programming; computer programming related; computer programming (specific applications); computer programming (vendor/product certification); computer software and media applications; computer software and media applications related; computer systems networking and telecommunications; computer/technical support; computer technology/ computer systems technology; criminal justice/law enforcement administration; criminal justice/police science; data entry/microcomputer applications; data entry/microcomputer applications related; health information/medical records technology; information science/studies; information technology; massage therapy; medical administrative assistant and medical secretary; medical/clinical assistant; medical transcription; office occupations and clerical services; pharmacy technician; system administration; system, networking, and LAN/WAN management; web/multimedia management and webmaster; web page, digital/multimedia and information resources design; word processing

Enrollment: 367 students

Institution Contact: Mr. Robert J. Grohman, Director *Phone:* 717-761-1481 *Fax:* 717-761-0558 *E-mail:* rgrohman@clntraining.net

Admission Contact: Mr. Michael R. Wilson, Director of Admissions *Phone:* 717-761-1481 *Fax:* 717-761-0558 *E-mail:* mwilson@clntraining.net

See full description on page 603.

Dean Institute of Technology

1501 West Liberty Avenue
Pittsburgh, PA 15226
Web: http://home.earthlink.net/~deantech

Accreditation: Accrediting Commission of Career Schools and Colleges of Technology

Programs Offered: building/property maintenance and management; electrician; heating, air conditioning and refrigeration technology; welding technology

Institution Contact: Mr. James Dean, President *Phone:* 412-531-4433 *Fax:* 412-531-4435 *E-mail:* deantech@earthlink.net

Admission Contact: Mr. Burt Wolfe, Admissions Director *Phone:* 412-531-4433 *Fax:* 412-531-4435 *E-mail:* deantech@earthlink.net

Douglas Education Center

130 7th Street
Monessen, PA 15062-1097
Web: http://www.douglas-school.com/

Accreditation: Accrediting Council for Independent Colleges and Schools

Programs Offered: accounting; accounting related; accounting technology and bookkeeping; administrative assistant and secretarial science; aesthetician/ esthetician and skin care; allied health and medical assisting services related; anatomy; animation, interactive technology, video graphics and special effects; banking and financial support services; business administration and management; business automation/technology/data entry; clinical laboratory science/medical technology; clinical/medical laboratory assistant; clinical/medical laboratory science and allied professions related; clinical/medical laboratory technology; commercial and advertising art; computer graphics; cosmetology; cosmetology, barber/styling, and nail instruction; customer service management; data entry/microcomputer applications; data processing and data processing technology; desktop publishing and digital imaging design; digital communication and media/multimedia; executive assistant/ executive secretary; facial treatment/facialist; general studies; graphic communications; graphic communications related; health aide; health information/medical records administration; health information/medical records technology; health professions related; health unit coordinator/ward clerk; health unit management/ward supervision; home health aide/home attendant; legal administrative assistant/secretary; make-up artist; medical administrative assistant and medical secretary; medical/clinical assistant; medical/ health management and clinical assistant; medical insurance coding; medical insurance/medical billing; medical office assistant; medical office computer specialist; medical office management; medical reception; medical transcription; nail technician and manicurist; nursing assistant/aide and patient care assistant; office management; receptionist; robotics technology; sculpture; web/multimedia management and webmaster; web page, digital/multimedia and information resources design; word processing

Enrollment: 359 students

Institution Contact: Mr. Jeffrey Imbrescia, CPA, President *Phone:* 724-684-3684 *Fax:* 724-684-7463 *E-mail:* dec@douglas-school.com

Admission Contact: Ms. Sherry Lee Walters, Director of Enrollment Services *Phone:* 724-684-3684 *Fax:* 724-684-7463 *E-mail:* dec@douglas-school.com

Ⓐ indicates that the school is a participating institution in the *Imagine America* Scholarship Program.

Duff's Business Institute ⓐ

Kossman Building, Suite 1200
Pittsburgh, PA 15222
Web: http://www.duffs-institute.com

Accreditation: Accrediting Council for Independent Colleges and Schools

Programs Offered: accounting; administrative assistant and secretarial science; business administration and management; clinical laboratory science/medical technology; computer/information technology administration and management; computer/information technology services administration related; criminal justice/law enforcement administration; legal administrative assistant/secretary; legal assistant/paralegal; medical administrative assistant and medical secretary; medical/clinical assistant; medical insurance coding; medical staff services technology

Institution Contact: Lynn Fischer, Director of Admissions *Phone:* 412-261-4520 *Fax:* 412-261-4546 *E-mail:* lfischer@cci.edu

See full description on page 604.

Erie Business Center, Main

246 West 9th Street
Erie, PA 16501
Web: http://www.eriebc.edu

Accreditation: Accrediting Council for Independent Colleges and Schools

Programs Offered: accounting; administrative assistant and secretarial science; computer hardware engineering; computer programming; computer software and media applications related; computer systems networking and telecommunications; computer technology/computer systems technology; executive assistant/executive secretary; health information/medical records technology; insurance; legal administrative assistant/secretary; legal assistant/paralegal; marketing/marketing management; medical administrative assistant and medical secretary; medical/clinical assistant; medical transcription; tourism and travel services management; web page, digital/multimedia and information resources design

Enrollment: 450 students

Institution Contact: Mrs. Donna B. Perino, Director *Phone:* 814-456-7504 ext. 17 *Fax:* 814-456-6015 *E-mail:* perinod@eriebc.edu

Erie Business Center South

170 Cascade Galleria
New Castle, PA 16101-3950
Web: http://www.eriebc.edu

Accreditation: Accrediting Council for Independent Colleges and Schools

Programs Offered: accounting; administrative assistant and secretarial science; business administration and management; computer programming; data entry/microcomputer applications; health information/medical records technology; legal administrative assistant/secretary; medical administrative assistant and medical secretary; medical transcription; tourism and travel services management

Enrollment: 98 students

Institution Contact: Mrs. Irene Marburger, Director *Phone:* 800-722-6227 *Fax:* 724-658-3083 *E-mail:* marburgeri@eriebcs.com

Admission Contact: Mrs. Rose Hall, Admission Representative *Phone:* 800-722-6227 *Fax:* 724-658-3083 *E-mail:* hallr@eriebcs.com

Great Lakes Institute of Technology

5100 Peach Street
Erie, PA 16509
Web: http://www.glit.edu

Accreditation: Accrediting Commission of Career Schools and Colleges of Technology; National Accrediting Commission of Cosmetology Arts and Sciences

Programs Offered: cosmetology; cosmetology, barber/styling, and nail instruction; dental assisting; diagnostic medical sonography and ultrasound technology; massage therapy; medical administrative assistant and medical secretary; medical/clinical assistant; nail technician and manicurist; pharmacy technician; surgical technology; veterinary/animal health technology

Institution Contact: Mrs. Francine M. Steele, Director of Education *Phone:* 814-864-6666 ext. 225 *Fax:* 814-868-1717 *E-mail:* fran@glit.edu

Admission Contact: Barbara Bolt, Director of Admissions *Phone:* 814-864-6666 ext. 242 *Fax:* 814-868-1717 *E-mail:* barbb@glit.edu

Harrison Career Institute

2101 Union Boulevard
Allentown, PA 18109-1633
Web: http://www.hci.edu

Accreditation: Accrediting Commission of Career Schools and Colleges of Technology

Programs Offered: cardiovascular technology; medical administrative assistant and medical secretary; medical/clinical assistant; surgical technology

Enrollment: 175 students

Institution Contact: Ms. Nancy Seier, Director *Phone:* 610-434-9963 *Fax:* 610-434-8292 *E-mail:* nseier@hci-inst.net

ⓐ indicates that the school is a participating institution in the *Imagine America* Scholarship Program.

Harrison Career Institute

1619 Walnut Street, 3rd Floor
Philadelphia, PA 19103
Web: http://www.hci.edu

Accreditation: Accrediting Commission of Career Schools and Colleges of Technology

Programs Offered: cardiovascular technology; dental assisting; dialysis technology; medical/clinical assistant; medical office computer specialist; medical transcription; pharmacy technician; phlebotomy; surgical technology

Enrollment: 630 students

Institution Contact: Mr. Michael E. Seeherman, Director *Phone:* 215-640-0177 *Fax:* 215-640-0466 *E-mail:* mseeherman@hci-inst.net

Admission Contact: Ms. Jennifer Tarantino, Career Representative *Phone:* 215-640-0177 *Fax:* 215-640-0466 *E-mail:* jtarantino@hci-inst.net

Harrison Career Institute

645 Penn Street, 3rd Floor
Reading, PA 19601
Web: http://www.harrisoncareerinst.com

Accreditation: Accrediting Commission of Career Schools and Colleges of Technology

Programs Offered: cardiovascular technology; electrocardiograph technology; medical administrative assistant and medical secretary; medical/clinical assistant; medical office computer specialist

Enrollment: 90 students

Institution Contact: Ms. Monica S. Sokoloff, Director *Phone:* 610-374-2469 *Fax:* 610-374-4192 *E-mail:* msokoloff@hci-inst.net

Hussian School of Art

1118 Market Street
Philadelphia, PA 19107-3679
Web: http://www.hussianart.edu/

Accreditation: Accrediting Commission of Career Schools and Colleges of Technology

Programs Offered: commercial and advertising art

Enrollment: 150 students

Institution Contact: Lynne D. Wartman, Director of Admissions *Phone:* 215-981-0900 *Fax:* 215-864-9115 *E-mail:* hussian@pond.com

Admission Contact: Ms. Lynne D. Wartman, Director of Admissions *Phone:* 215-981-0900 *Fax:* 215-864-9115 *E-mail:* hussian@pond.com

ICM School of Business & Medical Careers ⓐ

10 Wood Street
Pittsburgh, PA 15222
Web: http://www.ICMschool.com

Accreditation: Accrediting Council for Independent Colleges and Schools

Programs Offered: accounting; business administration and management; computer and information systems security; computer engineering related; computer engineering technology; computer hardware engineering; computer/information technology administration and management; computer/information technology services administration related; computer installation and repair technology; computer programming; computer programming related; computer programming (specific applications); computer programming (vendor/product certification); computer systems networking and telecommunications; computer/technical support; computer technology/computer systems technology; corrections; criminal justice/law enforcement administration; data entry/microcomputer applications related; data modeling/warehousing and database administration; e-commerce; engineering technology; executive assistant/executive secretary; fashion merchandising; health information/medical records technology; legal administrative assistant/secretary; medical administrative assistant and medical secretary; medical/clinical assistant; medical/health management and clinical assistant; medical office management; medical transcription; occupational therapist assistant; office management; pre-law studies; system, networking, and LAN/WAN management; tourism and travel services management; web page, digital/multimedia and information resources design

Enrollment: 1,044 students

Institution Contact: Mr. Bobby Reese, Jr., Executive Director *Phone:* 412-261-2647 ext. 302 *Fax:* 412-261-6491 *E-mail:* breese@icmschool.com

Admission Contact: Mrs. Marcia Rosenberg, Director of Admissions *Phone:* 412-261-2647 ext. 229 *Fax:* 412-261-0998 *E-mail:* mrosenberg@icmschool.com

See full description on page 605.

International Academy of Design & Technology ⓐ

555 Grant Street, 5th Floor
Pittsburgh, PA 15219
Web: http://www.iadtpitt.com

Accreditation: Accrediting Council for Independent Colleges and Schools

ⓐ indicates that the school is a participating institution in the *Imagine America* Scholarship Program.

International Academy of Design & Technology *(continued)*

Programs Offered: business administration and management; commercial and advertising art; computer/information technology administration and management; computer/technical support; criminal justice/law enforcement administration; e-commerce; web page, digital/multimedia and information resources design

Enrollment: 670 students

Institution Contact: Ms. Vicci Essig, Admissions Coordinator *Phone:* 800-447-8324 ext. 296 *Fax:* 412-391-4224 *E-mail:* vessig@iadt-pitt.com

See full description on page 606.

Katharine Gibbs School

2501 Monroe Boulevard
Norristown, PA 19403
Web: http://www.pagibbs.com

Accreditation: Accrediting Council for Independent Colleges and Schools

Programs Offered: business administration and management; commercial and advertising art; computer/information technology administration and management; computer systems networking and telecommunications; criminal justice/law enforcement administration; fashion merchandising; medical/clinical assistant; system, networking, and LAN/WAN management; web page, digital/multimedia and information resources design

Institution Contact: Dr. David Goodwin, President *Phone:* 610-676-0500 *Fax:* 610-676-0530 *E-mail:* dgoodwin@pagibbs.com

Admission Contact: Kevin Puls, Director of Admissions *Phone:* 866-724-4227 *Fax:* 610-676-0530 *E-mail:* kpuls@pagibbs.com

Lansdale School of Business Ⓐ

201 Church Road
North Wales, PA 19454
Web: http://www.LSB.edu

Accreditation: Accrediting Council for Independent Colleges and Schools

Programs Offered: accounting; accounting and business/management; administrative assistant and secretarial science; advertising; allied health and medical assisting services related; anatomy; business administration and management; business automation/technology/data entry; business/corporate communications; business, management, and marketing related; business operations support and secretarial services related; clinical/medical laboratory assistant; commercial and advertising art; computer graphics; computer/information technology services administration related; computer software and media applications; computer software and media applications related; corrections; criminal justice/law enforcement administration; desktop publishing and digital imaging design; electrocardiograph technology; executive assistant/executive secretary; health information/medical records technology; insurance; intermedia/multimedia; legal administrative assistant/secretary; legal assistant/paralegal; marketing/marketing management; medical administrative assistant and medical secretary; medical/clinical assistant; medical office management; medical transcription; office occupations and clerical services; operations management; pharmacy technician; phlebotomy; telecommunications; web/multimedia management and webmaster; web page, digital/multimedia and information resources design; word processing

Enrollment: 475 students

Institution Contact: Mr. Marlon D. Keller, President *Phone:* 215-699-5700 *Fax:* 215-699-8770 *E-mail:* mkeller@lsb.edu

Admission Contact: Mrs. Marianne H. Johnson, Director of Admissions *Phone:* 215-699-5700 ext. 112 *Fax:* 215-699-8770 *E-mail:* mjohnson@lsb.edu

See full description on page 607.

Laurel Business Institute

11-15 Penn Street, PO Box 877
Uniontown, PA 15401
Web: http://www.laurelbusiness.edu

Accreditation: Accrediting Council for Independent Colleges and Schools

Programs Offered: accounting; administrative assistant and secretarial science; child care provision; computer programming; computer software technology; computer technology/computer systems technology; cosmetology; cosmetology, barber/styling, and nail instruction; executive assistant/executive secretary; hospitality administration; legal administrative assistant/secretary; massage therapy; medical administrative assistant and medical secretary; medical/clinical assistant; medical insurance/medical billing; medical transcription; office occupations and clerical services; tourism and travel services management; web/multimedia management and webmaster

Enrollment: 324 students

Institution Contact: Mrs. Nancy M. Decker, Director *Phone:* 724-439-4900 *Fax:* 724-439-3607 *E-mail:* ndecker@laurelbusiness.edu

Admission Contact: Miss Lisa Tressler, Enrollment Supervisor *Phone:* 724-439-4900 *Fax:* 724-439-3607 *E-mail:* ltressler@laurelbusiness.edu

Ⓐ indicates that the school is a participating institution in the *Imagine America* Scholarship Program.

Lebanon County Career School

18 East Weidman Street
Lebanon, PA 17046
Web: http://www.sageschools.com/

Accreditation: Accrediting Commission of Career Schools and Colleges of Technology

Programs Offered: driver and safety teacher education; transportation technology; truck and bus driver/commercial vehicle operation

Enrollment: 12 students

Institution Contact: Ms. Holly L. Reichert, Director *Phone:* 800-694-8804 *Fax:* 717-274-6036 *E-mail:* sage08lccs@aol.com

Admission Contact: Mr. James L. McClellan, Admissions Representative *Phone:* 800-694-8804 *Fax:* 717-274-6036 *E-mail:* sage08lccs@aol.com

Lincoln Technical Institute Ⓐ

5151 Tilghman Street
Allentown, PA 18104-3298
Web: http://www.lincolntech.com

Accreditation: Accrediting Commission of Career Schools and Colleges of Technology

Programs Offered: CAD/CADD drafting/design technology; computer systems networking and telecommunications; drafting and design technology; engineering technology; medical administrative assistant and medical secretary; medical/clinical assistant; pharmacy technician

Enrollment: 512 students

Institution Contact: Ms. Lisa Kuntz, Executive Director *Phone:* 610-398-5300 *Fax:* 610-395-2706 *E-mail:* lkuntz@lincolntech.com

Admission Contact: Mr. Walter Kowalczyk, Director of Admissions *Phone:* 610-398-5301 *Fax:* 610-395-2706 *E-mail:* wkowalczyk@lincolntech.com

See full description on page 608.

Lincoln Technical Institute Ⓐ

9191 Torresdale Avenue
Philadelphia, PA 19136
Web: http://www.lincolntech.com

Accreditation: Accrediting Commission of Career Schools and Colleges of Technology

Programs Offered: automobile/automotive mechanics technology; automotive engineering technology

Institution Contact: Executive Director *Phone:* 215-335-0800 *Fax:* 215-335-1443 *E-mail:* execdirphilly@lincolntech.com

Admission Contact: Director of Admissions *Phone:* 215-335-0800 *Fax:* 215-335-1443 *E-mail:* doaphilly@lincolnedu.com

See full description on page 609.

McCann School of Business

47 South Main Street
Mahanoy City, PA 17948

Accreditation: Accrediting Council for Independent Colleges and Schools

Programs Offered: accounting; accounting technology and bookkeeping; administrative assistant and secretarial science; anatomy; banking and financial support services; business administration and management; business automation/technology/data entry; business/corporate communications; clinical laboratory science/medical technology; computer and information sciences related; computer hardware engineering; computer/information technology administration and management; computer/information technology services administration related; computer installation and repair technology; computer programming; computer programming (specific applications); computer software and media applications; computer software technology; computer systems analysis; computer systems networking and telecommunications; computer/technical support; computer technology/computer systems technology; criminal justice/law enforcement administration; criminal justice/police science; data entry/microcomputer applications; data entry/microcomputer applications related; data processing and data processing technology; executive assistant/executive secretary; health information/medical records administration; health information/medical records technology; human resources management; information technology; legal administrative assistant/secretary; legal assistant/paralegal; marketing/marketing management; medical administrative assistant and medical secretary; medical/clinical assistant; medical/health management and clinical assistant; medical insurance coding; medical insurance/medical billing; medical office computer specialist; medical office management; medical reception; medical transcription; office management; office occupations and clerical services; receptionist; system, networking, and LAN/WAN management; web page, digital/multimedia and information resources design; word processing

Enrollment: 170 students

Institution Contact: Mrs. Barbara J. Reese, Director *Phone:* 570-773-1820 *E-mail:* bjr@mccannschool.com

Admission Contact: Mr. Michael S. Mazalusky, Jr., Admissions Representative *Phone:* 570-773-1820 *E-mail:* msm@mccannschool.com

Ⓐ indicates that the school is a participating institution in the *Imagine America* Scholarship Program.

McCann School of Business

201 Lackawanna Avenue
Scranton, PA
Web: http://www.mccannschool.com

Accreditation: Accrediting Council for Independent Colleges and Schools

Programs Offered: accounting; administrative assistant and secretarial science; business administration and management; computer and information sciences related; legal assistant/paralegal; medical/clinical assistant

Institution Contact: Ms. Mary Repasky, Campus Director *Phone:* 570-969-4330 *Fax:* 570-969-3139

Admission Contact: Mr. Matt McEney, Campus Director *Phone:* 570-969-4330 *Fax:* 570-969-3139

McCann School of Business

225 Market Street
Sunbury, PA 17801

Programs Offered: accounting; administrative assistant and secretarial science; computer and information sciences related; computer programming; computer software and media applications; computer systems networking and telecommunications; health information/medical records technology; legal administrative assistant/secretary; legal assistant/paralegal; marketing/marketing management; medical administrative assistant and medical secretary; medical/clinical assistant; medical office computer specialist; medical office management; word processing

Institution Contact: Ms. Susan Harmon *Phone:* 570-286-3058 *Fax:* 570-969-3139

McCann School of Business & Technology

2650 Woodglen Road
Pottsville, PA 17901
Web: http://www.mccannschool.com/

Accreditation: Accrediting Council for Independent Colleges and Schools

Programs Offered: accounting; administrative assistant and secretarial science; computer and information sciences related; computer systems networking and telecommunications; legal administrative assistant/secretary; legal assistant/paralegal; marketing/marketing management; massage therapy; medical administrative assistant and medical secretary; medical/clinical assistant; medical transcription; word processing

Institution Contact: Linda Walinsky, Regional Manager *Phone:* 570-622-3295 *Fax:* 570-622-7770

Admission Contact: Ms. Patsy Klouser, Admissions Representative *Phone:* 570-622-7622 *Fax:* 570-622-7770 *E-mail:* pak@mccannschool.com

New Castle School of Trades Ⓐ

4164 Route 422
Pulaski, PA 16143
Web: http://www.ncstrades.com

Accreditation: Accrediting Commission of Career Schools and Colleges of Technology

Programs Offered: automobile/automotive mechanics technology; construction engineering technology; electrician; heating, air conditioning and refrigeration technology; machine tool technology; truck and bus driver/commercial vehicle operation; welding technology

Enrollment: 435 students

Institution Contact: Mr. Rex Spaulding, Director *Phone:* 724-964-8811 *Fax:* 724-964-8177 *E-mail:* ncstrades@aol.com

Admission Contact: Mr. James Catheline, Admissions Director *Phone:* 724-964-8811 *Fax:* 724-964-8177 *E-mail:* ncstrades@aol.com

See full description on page 610.

Orleans Technical Institute

1330 Rhawn Street
Philadelphia, PA 19111-2899
Web: http://www.orleanstech.edu

Accreditation: Accrediting Commission of Career Schools and Colleges of Technology

Programs Offered: building/property maintenance and management; carpentry; computer and information sciences related; computer/information technology services administration related; electrician; food services technology; heating, air conditioning, ventilation and refrigeration maintenance technology; human development and family studies related; plumbing technology; word processing

Enrollment: 277 students

Institution Contact: Ms. Jayne Siniari, Director *Phone:* 215-728-4450 *Fax:* 215-745-4718 *E-mail:* trades@jevs.org

Admission Contact: Ms. Deborah M. Bello, Admissions Director *Phone:* 215-728-4700 *Fax:* 215-745-1689 *E-mail:* trades@jevs.org

Orleans Technical Institute-Center City Campus

1845 Walnut Street, 7th Floor
Philadelphia, PA 19103
Web: http://www.jevs.org

Accreditation: Accrediting Commission of Career Schools and Colleges of Technology

Programs Offered: court reporting

Enrollment: 166 students

Institution Contact: Ms. Delores Jefferson Swanson, Director *Phone:* 215-854-1846 *Fax:* 215-854-1880 *E-mail:* swansd@jevs.org

Admission Contact: Ms. Jacqueline Williams, Admissions Representative *Phone:* 215-854-1853 *Fax:* 215-854-1880 *E-mail:* courtreporting@jevs.org

Peirce College

1420 Pine Street
Philadelphia, PA 19102
Web: http://www.peirce.edu

Accreditation: Middle States Association of Colleges and Schools

Programs Offered: business administration and management; information technology; legal assistant/paralegal

Enrollment: 2,225 students

Institution Contact: Mr. James J. Mergiotti, Senior Vice President and COO *Phone:* 215-670-9372 *Fax:* 215-545-6588 *E-mail:* jjmergiotti@peirce.edu

Admission Contact: Ms. Nadine M. Maher, Manager, Enrollment Services *Phone:* 215-670-9236 *Fax:* 215-893-4347 *E-mail:* nmmaher@peirce.edu

Pennco Tech

3815 Otter Street
Bristol, PA 19007-3696
Web: http://www.penncotech.com

Accreditation: Accrediting Commission of Career Schools and Colleges of Technology

Programs Offered: autobody/collision and repair technology; automobile/automotive mechanics technology; computer systems networking and telecommunications; computer/technical support; electrician; executive assistant/executive secretary; heating, air conditioning and refrigeration technology; heating, air conditioning, ventilation and refrigeration maintenance technology; information technology; medical/clinical assistant; pharmacy technician

Enrollment: 453 students

Institution Contact: Mr. Alfred W. Parcells, Jr., School Director *Phone:* 800-575-9399 *Fax:* 215-785-1975 *E-mail:* fparcells@penncotech.com

Admission Contact: Mr. Glenn Slater, Director of Admissions and Marketing *Phone:* 215-824-3200 *Fax:* 215-785-1945 *E-mail:* admissions@penncotech.com

Pennsylvania Culinary Institute

717 Liberty Avenue
Pittsburgh, PA 15222
Web: http://www.paculinary.com

Accreditation: Accrediting Commission of Career Schools and Colleges of Technology

Programs Offered: baking and pastry arts; culinary arts; hotel/motel administration

Enrollment: 1,300 students

Institution Contact: Mrs. Jessica M. Sanders, Compliance Director *Phone:* 800-432-2433 ext. 4210 *Fax:* 412-201-1654 *E-mail:* jsanders@paculinary.com

Admission Contact: Mr. Bob Cappel, Vice President of Admissions *Phone:* 800-432-2433 *Fax:* 412-566-2434 *E-mail:* bcappel@paculinary.com

Pittsburgh Technical Institute

1111 McKee Road
Oakdale, PA 15071
Web: http://www.pti.edu

Accreditation: Middle States Association of Colleges and Schools

Programs Offered: accounting; animation, interactive technology, video graphics and special effects; architectural drafting and CAD/CADD; business administration and management; CAD/CADD drafting/design technology; commercial and advertising art; computer and information systems security; computer programming; computer/technical support; criminal justice/law enforcement administration; criminal justice/police science; drafting and design technology; e-commerce; electrical, electronic and communications engineering technology; forensic science and technology; graphic communications; hospitality administration; hotel/motel administration; information technology; marketing/marketing management; mechanical drafting and CAD/CADD; medical administrative assistant and medical secretary; medical/clinical assistant; medical insurance coding; medical office computer specialist; medical office management; safety/security technology; system, networking, and LAN/WAN management; tourism and travel services management; web/multimedia management and webmaster

Enrollment: 1,940 students

Institution Contact: Ms. Cynthia A. Reynolds, President *Phone:* 412-809-5100 *Fax:* 412-809-5320 *E-mail:* reynolds@pti.edu

Admission Contact: Ms. Marylu Zuk, Vice President of Admissions *Phone:* 412-809-5100 *Fax:* 412-809-5351 *E-mail:* zuk@pti.edu

◑ indicates that the school is a participating institution in the *Imagine America* Scholarship Program.

The PJA School Ⓐ

7900 West Chester Pike
Upper Darby, PA 19082-1926
Web: http://www.pjaschool.com

Accreditation: Accrediting Commission of Career Schools and Colleges of Technology

Programs Offered: accounting; accounting technology and bookkeeping; administrative assistant and secretarial science; business administration and management; computer graphics; computer/information technology administration and management; computer software and media applications; criminal justice/law enforcement administration; data entry/microcomputer applications; executive assistant/executive secretary; finance; legal administrative assistant/secretary; legal assistant/paralegal; real estate; word processing

Enrollment: 300 students

Institution Contact: Mr. David Hudiak, Director *Phone:* 610-789-6700 *Fax:* 610-789-5208 *E-mail:* pjaschool@dvol.com

Admission Contact: Mr. Daniel A. Alpert, Director of Institutional Development *Phone:* 610-789-6700 *Fax:* 610-789-5208 *E-mail:* pjaschool@dvol.com

See full description on page 611.

The Restaurant School at Walnut Hill College Ⓐ

4207 Walnut Street
Philadelphia, PA 19104
Web: http://www.walnuthillcollege.edu

Accreditation: Accrediting Commission of Career Schools and Colleges of Technology

Programs Offered: baking and pastry arts; culinary arts; hotel/motel administration; restaurant, culinary, and catering management; restaurant/food services management

Institution Contact: Office of Admissions *Phone:* 215-222-4200 *Fax:* 215-222-4219

See full description on page 612.

Sanford-Brown Institute

3600 Horizon Boulevard
Trevose, PA 19053
Web: http://www.careered.com

Accreditation: Accrediting Bureau of Health Education Schools

Programs Offered: cardiovascular technology; dental assisting; diagnostic medical sonography and ultrasound technology; massage therapy; medical/clinical assistant; medical insurance/medical billing

Enrollment: 600 students

Institution Contact: Mr. Joseph E. Nimerfroh, President *Phone:* 215-436-6928 *Fax:* 215-355-4909 *E-mail:* jnimerfroh@sbphilly.com

Admission Contact: Mr. Douglas Lingo, Director of Admissions *Phone:* 215-436-6921 *Fax:* 215-355-4909 *E-mail:* dlingo@sbphilly.com

Schuylkill Institute of Business and Technology Ⓐ

171 Red Horse Road
Pottsville, PA 17901
Web: http://www.sibt.edu

Accreditation: Accrediting Council for Independent Colleges and Schools

Programs Offered: accounting; accounting and business/management; administrative assistant and secretarial science; architectural drafting and CAD/CADD; business administration, management and operations related; CAD/CADD drafting/design technology; commercial and advertising art; computer and information systems security; computer graphics; computer software and media applications; computer software engineering; computer systems analysis; computer systems networking and telecommunications; computer/technical support; computer technology/computer systems technology; design and visual communications; desktop publishing and digital imaging design; digital communication and media/multimedia; drafting and design technology; executive assistant/executive secretary; health information/medical records technology; legal assistant/paralegal; massage therapy; mechanical drafting and CAD/CADD; medical administrative assistant and medical secretary; medical/clinical assistant; medical/health management and clinical assistant; medical office management; medical reception; office occupations and clerical services

Enrollment: 150 students

Institution Contact: Mr. Anthony H. Dooley, Executive Director *Phone:* 570-622-4835 *Fax:* 570-622-6563 *E-mail:* tdooley@sibt.edu

Admission Contact: Ms. Gina Gargano, Director of Admissions *Phone:* 570-622-4835 *Fax:* 570-622-6563 *E-mail:* ggargano@sibt.edu

See full description on page 614.

Strayer University

234 Mall Boulevard
King of Prussia, PA 19406-2954
Web: http://www.strayer.edu

Programs Offered: accounting; business administration and management; information technology

Ⓐ indicates that the school is a participating institution in the *Imagine America* Scholarship Program.

Institution Contact: Charles Baukman, Campus Manager *Phone:* 610-992-1700 *Fax:* 610-992-9777 *E-mail:* kingofprussia@strayer.edu

Strayer University at Delaware County

760 West Sproul Road
Springfield, PA 19064
Web: http://www.strayer.edu

Accreditation: Middle States Association of Colleges and Schools

Programs Offered: accounting; business administration and management; communications technology; computer/information technology administration and management; computer programming; computer systems networking and telecommunications; data modeling/warehousing and database administration; economics; general studies; information science/studies; information technology; international business/trade/commerce; marketing/marketing management; purchasing, procurement/acquisitions and contracts management

Institution Contact: Dr. J. Chris Toe, University President *Phone:* 202-408-2424 *Fax:* 202-789-0387 *E-mail:* jct@strayer.edu

Admission Contact: Diane Ford, Campus Manager *Phone:* 610-543-2500 *Fax:* 610-543-6599 *E-mail:* delco@strayer.edu

Strayer University at Lower Bucks County

3600 Horizon Boulevard, Suite 100
Trevose, PA 19053
Web: http://www.strayer.edu

Accreditation: Middle States Association of Colleges and Schools

Programs Offered: accounting; business administration and management; communications technology; computer/information technology administration and management; computer programming; computer systems networking and telecommunications; data modeling/warehousing and database administration; economics; general studies; information science/studies; information technology; international business/trade/commerce; marketing/marketing management; purchasing, procurement/acquisitions and contracts management

Institution Contact: Dr. J. Chris Toe, University President *Phone:* 202-408-2424 *Fax:* 202-789-0387 *E-mail:* jct@strayer.edu

Admission Contact: Fatima Arukwe, Campus Manager *Phone:* 215-953-5999 *Fax:* 215-953-9464 *E-mail:* bucks@strayer.edu

Thompson Institute

2593 Philadelphia Avenue
Chambersburg, PA 17201
Web: http://www.thompson.edu

Accreditation: Accrediting Council for Independent Colleges and Schools

Programs Offered: accounting; business administration and management; business operations support and secretarial services related; customer service support/call center/teleservice operation; data entry/microcomputer applications; electrical/electronics equipment installation and repair; electrician; electrocardiograph technology; health information/medical records technology; medical administrative assistant and medical secretary; medical/clinical assistant; medical insurance coding; medical insurance/medical billing; medical office assistant; pharmacy technician

Institution Contact: Mrs. Sherry Rosenberg, Executive Director *Phone:* 717-709-1311 *Fax:* 717-709-1332 *E-mail:* srosenberg@thompson.edu

Thompson Institute ⒶN

5650 Derry Street
Harrisburg, PA 17111
Web: http://www.thompson.edu

Accreditation: Accrediting Council for Independent Colleges and Schools

Programs Offered: accounting technology and bookkeeping; business administration and management; CAD/CADD drafting/design technology; computer/information technology administration and management; criminal justice/law enforcement administration; digital communication and media/multimedia; medical/clinical assistant; medical insurance coding

Enrollment: 434 students

Institution Contact: Mr. Roy Hawkins, Executive Director *Phone:* 800-272-4632 *Fax:* 717-564-3779 *E-mail:* rhawkins@thompson.edu

Admission Contact: Mr. Charles Zimmerman, Director of Admissions *Phone:* 717-901-5845 *Fax:* 717-564-3779 *E-mail:* czimmerman@thompson.edu

See full description on page 615.

Thompson Institute ⒶN

3010 Market Street, 2nd Floor
Philadelphia, PA 19104-3325
Web: http://www.thompsoninstitute.org

Accreditation: Accrediting Council for Independent Colleges and Schools

ⒶN indicates that the school is a participating institution in the *Imagine America* Scholarship Program.

Thompson Institute *(continued)*

Programs Offered: medical/clinical assistant; medical office management

Institution Contact: Mr. Scott Dams, Director of Admissions *Phone:* 215-594-4000 *Fax:* 215-594-4088 *E-mail:* sdams@thompsoninstitute.org

See full description on page 616.

Triangle Tech, Inc.—DuBois School Ⓐ

PO Box 551
DuBois, PA 15801-0551
Web: http://www.triangle-tech.edu

Accreditation: Accrediting Commission of Career Schools and Colleges of Technology

Programs Offered: CAD/CADD drafting/design technology; carpentry; electrician; welding technology

Institution Contact: Mrs. Deborah Hepburn, Director *Phone:* 814-371-2090 *Fax:* 814-371-9227 *E-mail:* dhepburn@triangle-tech.edu

See full description on page 617.

Triangle Tech, Inc.—Erie School Ⓐ

2000 Liberty Street
Erie, PA 16502-9987
Web: http://www.triangle-tech.edu

Accreditation: Accrediting Commission of Career Schools and Colleges of Technology

Programs Offered: CAD/CADD drafting/design technology; carpentry; electrician

Institution Contact: Mr. David McMutrie, Director *Phone:* 814-453-6016 *Fax:* 814-454-2818 *E-mail:* dmcmutrie@triangle-tech.edu

See full description on page 618.

Triangle Tech, Inc.—Greensburg School Ⓐ

222 East Pittsburgh Street
Greensburg, PA 15601-3304
Web: http://www.triangle-tech.edu

Accreditation: Accrediting Commission of Career Schools and Colleges of Technology

Programs Offered: CAD/CADD drafting/design technology; carpentry; electrician; heating, air conditioning and refrigeration technology

Institution Contact: Mr. Kurt Stridinger, Director *Phone:* 724-832-1050 *Fax:* 724-834-0325 *E-mail:* kstridinger@triangle-tech.edu

See full description on page 619.

Triangle Tech, Inc.—Pittsburgh School Ⓐ

1940 Perrysville Avenue
Pittsburgh, PA 15214-3897
Web: http://www.triangle-tech.edu

Accreditation: Accrediting Commission of Career Schools and Colleges of Technology

Programs Offered: CAD/CADD drafting/design technology; carpentry; electrician; heating, air conditioning and refrigeration technology; welding technology

Institution Contact: Mrs. Stacie D. Hendrickson, Director *Phone:* 412-359-1000 *Fax:* 412-359-1012 *E-mail:* shendrickson@triangle-tech.edu

See full description on page 620.

Triangle Tech, Inc.—Sunbury School Ⓐ

R.R.2, Performance Drive, Route 61 & 890
Sunbury, PA 17801
Web: http://www.triangle-tech.edu

Accreditation: Accrediting Commission of Career Schools and Colleges of Technology

Programs Offered: carpentry; electrician

Institution Contact: Mr. Jess Null, Director *Phone:* 570-988-0700 *Fax:* 570-988-4641 *E-mail:* jnull@triangle-tech.edu

See full description on page 621.

Tri-State Business Institute

5757 West 26th Street
Erie, PA 16506
Web: http://www.tsbi.org

Accreditation: Accrediting Council for Independent Colleges and Schools

Programs Offered: accounting; administrative assistant and secretarial science; business administration and management; computer and information systems security; computer installation and repair technology; computer programming; computer programming (specific applications); computer software and media applications; computer systems networking and telecommunications; computer/technical support; computer technology/computer systems technology; cosmetology; cosmetology, barber/styling, and nail instruction; information technology; legal assistant/paralegal; marketing/marketing management; medical transcription; office occupations and clerical services; system administration; system, networking, and LAN/WAN management; web/multimedia management and webmaster; web page, digital/multimedia and information resources design; word processing

Ⓐ indicates that the school is a participating institution in the *Imagine America* Scholarship Program.

Institution Contact: Mr. Guy Euliano, President *Phone:* 814-838-7673 *Fax:* 814-838-8642 *E-mail:* geuliano@tsbi.org

Admission Contact: Ms. Karen A. LaPaglia, Enrollment Coordinator *Phone:* 814-838-7673 *Fax:* 814-838-1047 *E-mail:* klapaglia@tsbi.org

Universal Technical Institute Ⓐ

750 Pennsylvania Avenue
Exton, PA 19341
Web: http://www.uticorp.com

Accreditation: Accrediting Commission of Career Schools and Colleges of Technology

Programs Offered: automobile/automotive mechanics technology

See full description on page 622.

Western School of Health and Business Careers

One Monroeville Center, Suite 125, Route 22
Monroeville, PA 15146-2142

Accreditation: Accrediting Bureau of Health Education Schools; Accrediting Commission of Career Schools and Colleges of Technology

Programs Offered: business administration and management; criminal justice/law enforcement administration; dental assisting; diagnostic medical sonography and ultrasound technology; legal assistant/paralegal; massage therapy; medical/clinical assistant; medical office computer specialist; pharmacy technician; radiologic technology/science; respiratory care therapy; surgical technology; veterinary technology

Enrollment: 338 students

Institution Contact: Mr. Michael C. Cole, Associate Director of Education *Phone:* 412-373-9038 ext. 224 *Fax:* 412-373-2544 *E-mail:* mcole@western-school.com

Admission Contact: Mr. Chris Moore, Director of Admissions *Phone:* 412-373-9038 ext. 233 *E-mail:* cmoore@western-school.com

Western School of Health and Business Careers

421 Seventh Avenue
Pittsburgh, PA 15219-1907

Programs Offered: business administration and management; dental assisting; diagnostic medical sonography and ultrasound technology; legal assistant/paralegal; massage therapy; medical/clinical assistant; medical office computer specialist; phar-

macy technician; radiologic technology/science; respiratory care therapy; surgical technology; veterinary technology

West Virginia Career Institute Ⓐ

PO Box 278
Mount Braddock, PA 15465
Web: http://www.wvjcmorgantown.edu

Accreditation: Accrediting Council for Independent Colleges and Schools

Programs Offered: accounting; administrative assistant and secretarial science; computer/information technology administration and management; computer software and media applications; computer/technical support; medical administrative assistant and medical secretary; medical/clinical assistant; medical office management; word processing

Institution Contact: Ms. Stephanie Franks, Admissions Representative *Phone:* 724-437-4600 *Fax:* 724-437-6053

See full description on page 623.

WyoTech Ⓐ

500 Innovation Drive
Blairsville, PA 15717
Web: http://www.wyotech.com/

Accreditation: Accrediting Commission of Career Schools and Colleges of Technology

Programs Offered: autobody/collision and repair technology; automobile/automotive mechanics technology

Enrollment: 696 students

Institution Contact: Brenda Heine, Director of Career Services *Phone:* 724-459-9500 ext. 281 *Fax:* 724-459-6499 *E-mail:* bheine@wyotech.com

Admission Contact: Wendy Hauser, Director of Admissions *Phone:* 427-459-9500 ext. 286 *Fax:* 724-459-6499 *E-mail:* whauser@wyotech.com

See full description on page 624.

York Technical Institute

1405 Williams Road
York, PA 17402-9017
Web: http://www.yti.edu

Accreditation: Accrediting Commission of Career Schools and Colleges of Technology

Programs Offered: accounting; baking and pastry arts; business administration and management; CAD/CADD drafting/design technology; computer/

Ⓐ indicates that the school is a participating institution in the *Imagine America* Scholarship Program.

York Technical Institute (*continued*)

technical support; computer technology/computer systems technology; criminal justice/law enforcement administration; culinary arts; drafting and design technology; emergency medical technology (EMT paramedic); heating, air conditioning and refrigeration technology; hospitality administration; hotel/motel administration; industrial technology; information science/studies; marketing/marketing management; mechanical design technology; motorcycle maintenance and repair technology; office management; robotics technology; system, networking, and LAN/WAN management; telecommunications; tourism and travel services management

Institution Contact: Mr. Harold Maley, President *Phone:* 717-757-1100 *Fax:* 717-757-4964 *E-mail:* hlm@yti.edu

Admission Contact: Ms. Cathi Bost, Executive Vice President *Phone:* 717-757-1100 *Fax:* 717-757-4964 *E-mail:* bostc@yti.edu

Yorktowne Business Institute Ⓐ

West 7th Avenue
York, PA 17404-9946
Web: http://www.ybi.edu

Accreditation: Accrediting Council for Independent Colleges and Schools

Programs Offered: accounting; administrative assistant and secretarial science; baking and pastry arts; business administration and management; culinary arts; medical administrative assistant and medical secretary; medical/clinical assistant; medical insurance/medical billing

Enrollment: 330 students

Institution Contact: Ms. Elizabeth Dreibelbis, Executive Director *Phone:* 717-846-5000 ext. 125 *Fax:* 717-848-4584 *E-mail:* betsyd@ybi.edu

Admission Contact: Ms. Deborah Bostic, Associate Director *Phone:* 717-846-5000 ext. 129 *Fax:* 717-848-4584 *E-mail:* financialaid@ybi.edu

See full description on page 625.

puerto Rico

A-1 Business and Technical College

Dr. Rufo Street, #14, PO Box 351
Caguas, PR 00725
Web: http://home.coqui.net/a1colleg/

Accreditation: Accrediting Commission of Career Schools and Colleges of Technology

Programs Offered: accounting; adult development and aging; computer installation and repair technology; computer programming; cosmetology, barber/styling, and nail instruction; legal administrative assistant/secretary; medical administrative assistant and medical secretary; photography

Antilles School of Technical Careers

Avenue Fernandez Juncos, 1851
Santurce, PR 00907

Accreditation: Accrediting Bureau of Health Education Schools

Programs Offered: dental assisting; funeral service and mortuary science; massage therapy; nursing (licensed practical/vocational nurse training); pharmacy technician; respiratory care therapy; surgical technology

Enrollment: 514 students

Institution Contact: Mr. Alexis R. De Jorge, President *Phone:* 787-268-2244 *Fax:* 787-268-1873 *E-mail:* antillesexe@aol.com

Admission Contact: Mrs. Lupe Milán, Admissions Director *Phone:* 787-268-2244 *Fax:* 787-268-1873 *E-mail:* antillesexe@aol.com

Automeca Technical College

PO Box 4999
Aguadilla, PR 00605-4999
Web: http://www.automeca.com

Accreditation: Accrediting Council for Continuing Education and Training

Programs Offered: automobile/automotive mechanics technology; diesel mechanics technology; electromechanical technology; marine technology

Enrollment: 285 students

Institution Contact: Mr. Enrique Caro, Director *Phone:* 787-882-2828 *Fax:* 787-891-5030 *E-mail:* ecaro@automeca.com

Ⓐ indicates that the school is a participating institution in the *Imagine America* Scholarship Program.

Admission Contact: Mrs. Mirelsa Cruz, Admissions Officer *Phone:* 787-882-2828 *Fax:* 787-891-5030 *E-mail:* aguadilla@automeca.com

Automeca Technical College

PO Box 8569
Bayamon, PR 00960-8569
Web: http://www.automeca.com
Accreditation: Accrediting Council for Continuing Education and Training
Programs Offered: automobile/automotive mechanics technology; diesel mechanics technology; electromechanical technology; marine technology
Institution Contact: Mrs. Carmen Estrada, Director *Phone:* 787-779-6161 *Fax:* 787-779-6100 *E-mail:* cestrada@automeca.com
Admission Contact: Mrs. Samira Saab, Admissions Officer *Phone:* 787-779-6161 *Fax:* 787-779-6100 *E-mail:* bayamon@automeca.com

Automeca Technical College

69 Calle Munoz Rivera
Caguas, PR 00725-3642
Web: http://www.automeca.com
Accreditation: Accrediting Council for Continuing Education and Training
Programs Offered: automobile/automotive mechanics technology; diesel mechanics technology; electromechanical technology; marine technology
Institution Contact: Mrs. Milagros Hernandez, Director *Phone:* 787-746-3429 *Fax:* 787-746-3472 *E-mail:* mhernandez@automeca.com
Admission Contact: Caipa Santa, Admissions Officer *Phone:* 787-746-3429 *Fax:* 787-746-3472 *E-mail:* caguas@automeca.com

Automeca Technical College

452 Calle Villa
Ponce, PR 00728-0402
Web: http://www.automeca.com
Accreditation: Accrediting Council for Continuing Education and Training
Programs Offered: automobile/automotive mechanics technology; diesel mechanics technology; electromechanical technology; marine technology
Institution Contact: Mr. Leo Bagildo Lopez-Saez, Director *Phone:* 787-840-7880 *Fax:* 787-259-2319 *E-mail:* aportalatin@automeca.com

Admission Contact: Mr. Juan Tiru, Admissions Officer *Phone:* 787-840-7880 *Fax:* 787-259-2319 *E-mail:* ponce@automeca.com

Bayamon Community College

PO Box 55176
Bayamon, PR 00960
Accreditation: Accrediting Commission of Career Schools and Colleges of Technology
Programs Offered: administrative assistant and secretarial science; data entry/microcomputer applications related
Institution Contact: Ms. Tanus J. Saad, Director *Phone:* 787-780-4370 *Fax:* 787-778-7447 *E-mail:* saadt@bccpr.org
Admission Contact: Ms. Rebecca Berrios, Financial Aid Administrator *Phone:* 787-780-4370 *Fax:* 787-778-7447 *E-mail:* rebeccaberrios@bccpr.org

Caguas Institute of Mechanical Technology

PO Box 6118, 39-40, B Street, West Industrial Park
Caguas, PR 00726
Accreditation: Accrediting Council for Continuing Education and Training
Programs Offered: adult and continuing education; appliance installation and repair technology; artificial intelligence and robotics; autobody/collision and repair technology; automobile/automotive mechanics technology; biomedical technology; CAD/CADD drafting/design technology; computer systems networking and telecommunications; diesel mechanics technology; electrical/electronics drafting and CAD/CADD; electrical/electronics equipment installation and repair; electrician; electromechanical and instrumentation and maintenance technologies related; electromechanical technology; heavy equipment maintenance technology; industrial electronics technology; industrial mechanics and maintenance technology; marine technology; tool and die technology; welding technology
Institution Contact: Mr. Edwin J. Colon, President *Phone:* 787-743-0484 *Fax:* 787-744-1035 *E-mail:* mechtech@caribe.net
Admission Contact: Mr. Ricardo Nieves, Admissions Director *Phone:* 787-743-0484 *Fax:* 787-744-1035 *E-mail:* admisiones@mechtechcollege.com

Colegio Mayor de Tecnologia

PO Box 1490
Arroyo, PR 00714
Accreditation: Accrediting Commission of Career Schools and Colleges of Technology

🅝 indicates that the school is a participating institution in the *Imagine America* Scholarship Program.

Colegio Mayor de Tecnologia (*continued*)

Programs Offered: computer installation and repair technology; computer programming (specific applications); culinary arts; data entry/microcomputer applications; dental assisting; electrician; emergency medical technology (EMT paramedic); hospitality administration; hotel/motel administration; legal administrative assistant/secretary; nursing assistant/aide and patient care assistant; nursing (licensed practical/vocational nurse training); nursing (registered nurse training)

Institution Contact: Mr. Mancio Vicente, President *Phone:* 787-839-5266 *Fax:* 787-839-0033 *E-mail:* mvicente@colegiomayortec.com

Admission Contact: Mrs. Julia Melendez, Admission Director *Phone:* 787-839-5266 *Fax:* 787-839-0033 *E-mail:* estudios@colegiomayortec.com

Columbia College Ⓐ

PO Box 8517
Caguas, PR 00726-8517
Web: http://www.columbiaco.edu

Accreditation: Accrediting Council for Independent Colleges and Schools

Programs Offered: administrative assistant and secretarial science; business administration and management; computer/information technology administration and management; electrical, electronic and communications engineering technology; nursing (registered nurse training)

Enrollment: 780 students

Institution Contact: Ms. Alex De Jorge, President *Phone:* 787-258-1501 ext. 212 *Fax:* 787-746-5616 *E-mail:* adejorge@columbiaco.edu

Admission Contact: Ms. Ana R. Burgos, Marketing and Admissions Manager *Phone:* 787-743-4041 ext. 211 *Fax:* 787-746-5616 *E-mail:* arburgos@columbiaco.edu

See full description on page 626.

Columbia College

PO Box 3062
Yauco, PR 00698

Accreditation: Accrediting Council for Independent Colleges and Schools

Programs Offered: administrative assistant and secretarial science; business administration and management; computer/information technology administration and management; nursing (registered nurse training)

Institution Contact: Mr. Alex De Jorge, President *Phone:* 787-258-1501 ext. 212 *Fax:* 787-746-5616

Admission Contact: Mr. Efrain Cruz, Admissions and Recruitment Coordinator *Phone:* 787-856-0845 *Fax:* 787-267-2335

Electronic Data Processing College of Puerto Rico

PO Box 192303
San Juan, PR 00919-2303

Accreditation: Accrediting Council for Independent Colleges and Schools

Programs Offered: administrative assistant and secretarial science; business administration and management; computer and information systems security; computer programming; e-commerce; emergency medical technology (EMT paramedic)

Enrollment: 1,021 students

Institution Contact: Ing. Gladys Nieves de Berríos, President *Phone:* 787-765-3560 ext. 240 *Fax:* 787-777-0025 *E-mail:* nievglad@edpcollege.edu

Admission Contact: Mrs. Wanda Santiago, Admissions Coordinator *Phone:* 787-765-3560 ext. 245 *Fax:* 787-777-0025 *E-mail:* wmsf@edpcollege.edu

Electronic Data Processing College of Puerto Rico–San Sebastian

PO Box 1674, Betances #49
San Sebastián, PR 00685

Accreditation: Accrediting Council for Independent Colleges and Schools

Programs Offered: administrative assistant and secretarial science; business administration and management; computer programming; emergency medical technology (EMT paramedic); nursing (registered nurse training); pharmacy technician

Institution Contact: Mrs. Mayra Rivera, Associate Director/Dean *Phone:* 787-896-2252 ext. 234 *Fax:* 787-896-0066 *E-mail:* mrivera@edpcollege.edu

Admission Contact: Mrs. Ingrid Gonzalez, Admissions Officer *Phone:* 787-896-2252 ext. 290 *Fax:* 787-896-0066 *E-mail:* igonzalez@edpcollege.edu

Escuela Hotelera de San Juan in Puerto Rico

Guayama Street, #229, Hato Rey
San Juan, PR 00917

Accreditation: Accrediting Commission of Career Schools and Colleges of Technology

Ⓐ indicates that the school is a participating institution in the *Imagine America* Scholarship Program.

Programs Offered: baking and pastry arts; bartending; culinary arts; food service and dining room management

Institution Contact: Mrs. Sylvia Cestero, President *Phone:* 787-766-0606 *Fax:* 787-281-6855 *E-mail:* hotelerasj@prtc.net

Admission Contact: Ms. Devalis Ortiz, Admissions Director *Phone:* 787-759-7599 *Fax:* 787-281-6855 *E-mail:* hotelerasj@prtc.net

Globelle Technical Institute

Marginal 114 Monte Carlo
Vega Baja, PR 00693

Institution Contact: Gloria E. Cruz Lugo, President

Admission Contact: Maria Torres, Admissions Department *Phone:* 787-858-0236 *Fax:* 787-855-7423 *E-mail:* globelle@caribe.net

Huertas Junior College

Box 8429
Caguas, PR 00726

Accreditation: Accrediting Council for Independent Colleges and Schools

Programs Offered: accounting technology and bookkeeping; administrative assistant and secretarial science; business administration and management; CAD/CADD drafting/design technology; computer installation and repair technology; computer programming; dental assisting; drafting and design technology; electrical, electronic and communications engineering technology; electrician; health information/medical records administration; heating, air conditioning and refrigeration technology; information technology; pharmacy technician; respiratory care therapy; tourism and travel services management

Enrollment: 1,833 students

Institution Contact: Dr. Rafael Ramirez-Rivera, President *Phone:* 787-743-0480 *Fax:* 787-747-0170 *E-mail:* rrramire@coqui.net

Admission Contact: Mrs. Barbara Hassim, Director of Admissions Office *Phone:* 787-743-1242 *Fax:* 787-743-0203 *E-mail:* huertas@huertas.org

ICPR Junior College—Arecibo Campus (A)

20 San Patricio Avenue, Box 140067
Arecibo, PR 00614-0067
Web: http://www.icprjc.edu

Accreditation: Middle States Association of Colleges and Schools

Programs Offered: accounting; administrative assistant and secretarial science; business administration and management; computer installation and repair technology; computer technology/computer systems technology; hospitality administration; information science/studies; marketing/marketing management; medical insurance/medical billing; office occupations and clerical services; tourism and travel services management

Enrollment: 440 students

Institution Contact: Mrs. Elsa N. Banos, Academic Dean *Phone:* 787-878-6000 *Fax:* 787-878-7750 *E-mail:* ebanos@icprjc.edu

Admission Contact: Mrs. Magdalena Vega, Admissions Director *Phone:* 787-878-6000 *Fax:* 787-878-7750 *E-mail:* mvega@icprjc.edu

See full description on page 627.

ICPR Junior College—Hato Rey Campus (A)

558 Munoz Rivera Avenue, PO Box 190304
San Juan, PR 00919-0304
Web: http://www.icprjc.edu

Accreditation: Middle States Association of Colleges and Schools

Programs Offered: accounting; administrative assistant and secretarial science; business administration and management; computer installation and repair technology; computer technology/computer systems technology; hospitality administration; information science/studies; marketing/marketing management; medical insurance/medical billing; office occupations and clerical services; tourism and travel services management

Enrollment: 485 students

Institution Contact: Ms. Maria Rivera, Dean/Director *Phone:* 787-753-6000 *Fax:* 787-763-7249 *E-mail:* mrivera@icprjc.edu

Admission Contact: M. Francisco Mena, Admissions Director *Phone:* 787-753-6000 *Fax:* 787-763-7249 *E-mail:* fmena@icprjc.edu

See full description on page 629.

ICPR Junior College—Mayaguez Campus (A)

80 West McKinley Street, PO Box 1108
Mayaguez, PR 00681-1108
Web: http://www.icprjc.edu

Accreditation: Middle States Association of Colleges and Schools

Programs Offered: accounting; administrative assistant and secretarial science; business administra-

(A) indicates that the school is a participating institution in the *Imagine America* Scholarship Program.

ICPR Junior College–Mayaguez Campus *(continued)*

tion and management; computer installation and repair technology; computer technology/computer systems technology; hospitality administration; information science/studies; marketing/marketing management; medical insurance/medical billing; office occupations and clerical services; tourism and travel services management

Enrollment: 550 students

Institution Contact: Mrs. Dorca Acosta-Ortiz, Dean/Director *Phone:* 787-832-6000 *Fax:* 787-833-2237 *E-mail:* dacosta@icprjc.edu

Admission Contact: Mr. Jose Ortiz, Admissions Director *Phone:* 787-832-6000 *Fax:* 787-833-2237 *E-mail:* jortiz@icprjc.edu

See full description on page 628.

Instituto Banca y Comercio

Calle Ruiz Belves #52 Alto
Caguas, PR 00725
Web: http://www.ibanca.net/

Accreditation: Accrediting Council for Independent Colleges and Schools

Programs Offered: banking and financial support services; barbering; computer programming; cosmetology; culinary arts; data entry/microcomputer applications; dental assisting; drafting and design technology; emergency medical technology (EMT paramedic); nursing (licensed practical/vocational nurse training); respiratory care therapy; tourism and travel services management

Institution Contact: *Phone:* 787-745-9525

Instituto Banca y Comercio

PO Box 37-2710
Cayey, PR 00737
Web: http://www.ibanca.net/

Accreditation: Accrediting Council for Independent Colleges and Schools

Programs Offered: computer programming; drawing; electrician; emergency medical technology (EMT paramedic); heating, air conditioning, ventilation and refrigeration maintenance technology; nursing (registered nurse training); respiratory care therapy

Institution Contact: Mrs. Lillian Diaz Aponte, Director *Phone:* 787-738-7144 *Fax:* 787-738-7629 *E-mail:* ibanca@caribe.net

Admission Contact: Mr. Alan Rodriguez Vázquez, Recruiting Director *Phone:* 787-738-7144 *Fax:* 787-738-7629 *E-mail:* ibanca@caribe.net

Instituto Banca y Comercio

PO Box 822
Fajardo, PR 00738
Web: http://www.ibanca.net/

Accreditation: Accrediting Council for Independent Colleges and Schools

Programs Offered: banking and financial support services; computer programming related; culinary arts; dental assisting; electrician; heating, air conditioning and refrigeration technology; medical administrative assistant and medical secretary; nursing (licensed practical/vocational nurse training); respiratory therapy technician; tourism and travel services management; word processing

Institution Contact: Ms. Claribel López, Director *Phone:* 787-860-6262 *Fax:* 787-860-6265 *E-mail:* ibancafd@coqui.net

Admission Contact: Mr. Luis Rivera, Admissions Director *Phone:* 787-860-6262 ext. 24 *Fax:* 787-860-6265 *E-mail:* ibancafd@coqui.net

Instituto Banca y Comercio

Derques Street, #4 Este
Guayama, PR 00784
Web: http://www.ibanca.net/

Accreditation: Accrediting Council for Independent Colleges and Schools

Programs Offered: banking and financial support services; computer programming; cosmetology, barber/styling, and nail instruction; dental assisting; drafting and design technology; electrician; emergency medical technology (EMT paramedic); medical reception; nursing (registered nurse training); respiratory care therapy; tourism and travel services management; word processing

Institution Contact: Mr. Hector J. Arroyo, Director *Phone:* 787-864-8040 *Fax:* 787-866-3238 *E-mail:* bancaguayama@prtc.net

Instituto Banca y Comercio

56 Carretera, #2
Manati, PR 00674
Web: http://www.ibanca.net

Accreditation: Accrediting Council for Independent Colleges and Schools

Programs Offered: banking and financial support services; barbering; CAD/CADD drafting/design technology; computer installation and repair technology; computer software technology; cosmetology; culinary arts; electrician; emergency medical technology (EMT paramedic); health information/medical records administration; heating, air conditioning and

---

⊕ indicates that the school is a participating institution in the *Imagine America* Scholarship Program.

refrigeration technology; nail technician and manicurist; nursing (registered nurse training); plumbing technology; tourism and travel services management; word processing

Enrollment: 1,125 students

Institution Contact: Mr. Benjamin Padilla, Director *Phone:* 787-854-6634 *Fax:* 787-884-3372 *E-mail:* bpadilla@ibancapr.com

Instituto Banca y Comercio

4 Ramos Antonini Street East
Mayaguez, PR 00680-4932
Web: http://www.ibanca.net

Accreditation: Accrediting Council for Independent Colleges and Schools

Programs Offered: administrative assistant and secretarial science; banking and financial support services; barbering; CAD/CADD drafting/design technology; computer programming; cosmetology; culinary arts; electrician; emergency medical technology (EMT paramedic); heating, air conditioning and refrigeration technology; medical administrative assistant and medical secretary; nursing assistant/ aide and patient care assistant

Institution Contact: Angel L. Lopez-Galarza, Director *Phone:* 787-833-4647 *Fax:* 787-833-4746 *E-mail:* mayaguez@ibanca.net

Admission Contact: Ms. Elizabeth Ramos-Rodriguez, Admissions Director *Phone:* 787-833-4647 *Fax:* 787-833-4746 *E-mail:* mayaguez@ibanca.net

Instituto Banca y Comercio

Box 7623
Ponce, PR 00731
Web: http://www.ibanca.net

Accreditation: Accrediting Council for Independent Colleges and Schools

Programs Offered: administrative assistant and secretarial science; baking and pastry arts; banking and financial support services; barbering; business automation/technology/data entry; CAD/CADD drafting/design technology; computer/information technology services administration related; computer programming; computer programming (specific applications); cosmetology; cosmetology, barber/ styling, and nail instruction; electrical, electronic and communications engineering technology; electrical/ electronics equipment installation and repair; electrician; emergency medical technology (EMT paramedic); food preparation; health aide; heating, air conditioning and refrigeration technology; heating, air conditioning, ventilation and refrigeration maintenance technology; home health aide/home attendant;

hotel/motel administration; machine shop technology; medical administrative assistant and medical secretary; nursing assistant/aide and patient care assistant; respiratory care therapy; respiratory therapy technician; tourism and travel services management

Institution Contact: Mr. Juan A. Orengo, Director *Phone:* 787-840-6119 *Fax:* 787-840-0530 *E-mail:* orengo_2000@yahoo.com

Admission Contact: Miss Daisy Sigueroa, Admissions Director *Phone:* 787-840-6119 *Fax:* 787-840-0530

Instituto Banca y Comercio

1660 Santa Ana Street
San Juan, PR 00909
Web: http://www.ibanca.net/

Accreditation: Accrediting Council for Independent Colleges and Schools

Programs Offered: administrative assistant and secretarial science; baking and pastry arts; banking and financial support services; computer programming; cosmetology, barber/styling, and nail instruction; data entry/microcomputer applications; dental assisting; drafting and design technology; electrician; emergency medical technology (EMT paramedic); heating, air conditioning, ventilation and refrigeration maintenance technology; medical administrative assistant and medical secretary; nursing (registered nurse training); respiratory care therapy; tourism and travel services management

Enrollment: 2,000 students

Institution Contact: Mr. Guillermo Nigaglioni, President/CEO *Phone:* 787-982-3000 *Fax:* 787-982-3075 *E-mail:* gnigaglioni@ibancapr.com

Admission Contact: Mr. Jose Padial, Vice President of Marketing *Phone:* 787-982-3000 *Fax:* 787-982-3003 *E-mail:* hrivera@ibancapr.com

Instituto Vocational y Commercial EDIC

Urb. Caguas Norte Calle Genova, Num 8, Corner 5, PO Box 9120
Caguas, PR 00726-9120

Accreditation: Accrediting Council for Independent Colleges and Schools

Programs Offered: cardiovascular technology; diagnostic medical sonography and ultrasound technology; emergency medical technology (EMT paramedic); medical administrative assistant and medical secretary; nursing (licensed practical/ vocational nurse training); radiologic technology/ science; respiratory care therapy; surgical technology; teacher assistant/aide

Enrollment: 457 students

Ⓐ indicates that the school is a participating institution in the *Imagine America* Scholarship Program.

Instituto Vocational y Commercial EDIC *(continued)*

Institution Contact: Mr. Jose A. Cartágena, President *Phone:* 787-746-2730 *Fax:* 787-744-8519 *E-mail:* edic@coqui.net

Admission Contact: Mrs. Virginia Cartagena, Admission Director *Phone:* 787-746-2732 *Fax:* 787-744-8519 *E-mail:* edic@coqui.net

Liceo de Arte y Tecnologia

405 Ponce De Leon Avenue, 4th Floor, PO Box 192346
San Juan, PR 00919-9955
Web: http://www.liceopr.com

Accreditation: Accrediting Commission of Career Schools and Colleges of Technology

Programs Offered: automobile/automotive mechanics technology; drafting and design technology; electrician; heating, air conditioning and refrigeration technology; office management

Enrollment: 987 students

Institution Contact: Mr. Carlos Manzanal, President *Phone:* 787-999-2473 ext. 456 *Fax:* 787-765-7210 *E-mail:* liceo@liceopr.com

Admission Contact: Ms. Annamalie Manzanal, Admissions Director *Phone:* 787-999-2473 ext. 245 *Fax:* 787-765-7210 *E-mail:* gmanzanal@liceopr.com

National College of Business and Technology

PO Box 4035, MSC452
Arecibo, PR 00614

Accreditation: Accrediting Council for Independent Colleges and Schools

Programs Offered: accounting; administrative assistant and secretarial science; business administration and management; business automation/technology/data entry; computer installation and repair technology; dental assisting; electrical, electronic and communications engineering technology; emergency/disaster science; hospitality administration; information science/studies; medical administrative assistant and medical secretary; nursing assistant/aide and patient care assistant; pharmacy technician; tourism and travel services management

Enrollment: 1,433 students

Institution Contact: Mr. Francisco Nunez, Executive Director of Arecibo Campus *Phone:* 787-879-5044 ext. 2513 *Fax:* 787-879-5047 *E-mail:* fnunez@nationalcollegepr.edu

Admission Contact: Mrs. Brenda Rivera, Admissions Director *Phone:* 787-879-5044 ext. 2504 *Fax:* 787-879-5047

National College of Business & Technology

PO Box 2036
Bayamon, PR 00960

Accreditation: Accrediting Council for Independent Colleges and Schools

Programs Offered: accounting; administrative assistant and secretarial science; business administration and management; computer installation and repair technology; computer programming; data entry/microcomputer applications; dental assisting; educational/instructional media design; emergency/disaster science; engineering technology; information technology; legal administrative assistant/secretary; medical administrative assistant and medical secretary; nursing (licensed practical/vocational nurse training); nursing (registered nurse training); pharmacy technician; tourism and travel services management

Enrollment: 2,300 students

Institution Contact: Mr. Desi Lopez, Vice President of Financial Aid and Compliance *Phone:* 787-780-5134 ext. 4400 *Fax:* 787-786-9093 *E-mail:* desil@nationalcollegepr.edu

Admission Contact: Mrs. Gloria Gonzalez, Vice President of Admissions, Marketing, and Human Resources *Phone:* 787-780-5134 *Fax:* 787-740-7360 *E-mail:* ggonzalez@nationalcollegepr.edu

National College of Business & Technology

PO Box 3064
Rio Grande, PR 00745

Accreditation: Accrediting Council for Independent Colleges and Schools

Programs Offered: accounting; entrepreneurship; information technology; nursing (licensed practical/vocational nurse training); office occupations and clerical services; pharmacy technician; tourism and travel services management

Enrollment: 746 students

Institution Contact: Ms. Lourdes Balseiro, Executive Director *Phone:* 787-888-8286

Admission Contact: Mr. Miguel Lopez, Admissions Director *Phone:* 787-888-8286

Ponce Paramedical College, Inc.

PO Box 106
Coto Laurel, PR 00780-0106

Accreditation: Accrediting Commission of Career Schools and Colleges of Technology

Programs Offered: child care provision; computer installation and repair technology; computer technology/computer systems technology; dental assisting; emergency medical technology (EMT paramedic); environmental/environmental health engineering; legal assistant/paralegal; massage therapy; medical administrative assistant and medical secretary; medical insurance coding; nursing (licensed practical/vocational nurse training); nursing (registered nurse training); pharmacy technician; respiratory care therapy; sports medicine

Institution Contact: Angel Quinones, President's Assistant *Phone:* 787-848-1589 *Fax:* 787-259-0169 *E-mail:* ppcadmin@coqui.net

Admission Contact: Mr. Arlin Mercado, Admission Director *Phone:* 787-848-1589 *Fax:* 787-259-0169

Trinity College of Puerto Rico

834 Hostos Avenue, PO Box 34360
Ponce, PR 00734-4360

Accreditation: Accrediting Council for Independent Colleges and Schools

Programs Offered: accounting technology and bookkeeping; administrative assistant and secretarial science; computer programming; computer systems networking and telecommunications; data entry/microcomputer applications; health aide; health information/medical records administration; nursing (registered nurse training)

Institution Contact: Mrs. María Isabel Colón, Director *Phone:* 787-842-0000 ext. 226 *Fax:* 787-284-2537 *E-mail:* dmramos@pucpr.edu

Admission Contact: Mrs. Jenny Ríos, Community Affairs Director *Phone:* 787-842-0000 ext. 238 *Fax:* 787-284-2537 *E-mail:* dmramos@pucpr.edu

rhode Island

Career Education Institute Ⓐ

622 George Washington Highway
Lincoln, RI 02865
Web: http://www.ceitraining.com

Accreditation: Accrediting Council for Independent Colleges and Schools

Programs Offered: computer/technical support; dental assisting; electrical/electronics equipment installation and repair; massage therapy; medical

administrative assistant and medical secretary; medical/clinical assistant; pharmacy technician

Enrollment: 400 students

Institution Contact: Executive Director *Phone:* 401-334-2430 *Fax:* 401-334-5087 *E-mail:* execdirlincoln@lincolntech.com

See full description on page 630.

Gibbs College - Cranston

85 Garfield Avenue
Cranston, RI 02920
Web: http://www.kgibbsprovidence.com

Accreditation: Accrediting Council for Independent Colleges and Schools

Programs Offered: administrative assistant and secretarial science; allied health and medical assisting services related; computer and information sciences and support services related; computer and information systems security; computer graphics; computer hardware technology; computer/information technology administration and management; computer/information technology services administration related; computer installation and repair technology; computer software and media applications; computer/technical support; computer technology/computer systems technology; criminal justice/law enforcement administration; criminal justice/police science; data processing and data processing technology; design and visual communications; desktop publishing and digital imaging design; digital communication and media/multimedia; executive assistant/executive secretary; graphic communications related; health information/medical records administration; health information/medical records technology; information technology; legal administrative assistant/secretary; medical administrative assistant and medical secretary; medical/clinical assistant; medical office assistant; medical office management; medical transcription; office management; office occupations and clerical services; phlebotomy; receptionist; system administration; system, networking, and LAN/WAN management; web page, digital/multimedia and information resources design; word processing

Institution Contact: Mr. Wynn F Blanton, President *Phone:* 401-824-5300 *Fax:* 401-824-5378 *E-mail:* wblanton@gibbsprovidence..com

Admission Contact: Mr. Ric Jackson, Vice President of Admissions *Phone:* 401-824-5300 *Fax:* 401-824-5378 *E-mail:* rjackson@gibbsprovidence.com

Ⓐ indicates that the school is a participating institution in the *Imagine America* Scholarship Program.

The International Yacht Restoration School

449 Thames Street
Newport, RI 02840
Web: http://www.iyrs.org

Accreditation: Accrediting Commission of Career Schools and Colleges of Technology

Programs Offered: marine maintenance and ship repair technology

Enrollment: 29 students

Institution Contact: Ms. Marti J. Kwon, Coordinator of Academic Services *Phone:* 401-848-5777 *Fax:* 401-842-0669 *E-mail:* mkwon@iyrs.org

New England Institute of Technology Ⓐ

2500 Post Road
Warwick, RI 02886-2266
Web: http://www.neit.edu

Accreditation: New England Association of Schools and Colleges

Programs Offered: administrative assistant and secretarial science; architectural drafting and CAD/CADD; architectural engineering technology; auto-body/collision and repair technology; automobile/automotive mechanics technology; automotive engineering technology; building/property maintenance and management; business administration and management; cabinetmaking and millwork; CAD/CADD drafting/design technology; carpentry; clinical/medical laboratory assistant; clinical/medical laboratory technology; communications technology; computer and information sciences; computer programming; computer programming (specific applications); computer systems networking and telecommunications; computer/technical support; computer technology/computer systems technology; construction engineering technology; desktop publishing and digital imaging design; digital communication and media/multimedia; drafting and design technology; electrical, electronic and communications engineering technology; electrician; executive assistant/executive secretary; heating, air conditioning and refrigeration technology; information science/studies; information technology; interior design; marine maintenance and ship repair technology; marine technology; mechanical design technology; mechanical engineering/mechanical technology; medical/clinical assistant; occupational therapist assistant; pipefitting and sprinkler fitting; plumbing technology; radio and television; radio and television broadcasting technology; surgical technology; telecommunications; transportation technology; web/multimedia management and webmaster; web page, digital/multimedia and information resources design

Institution Contact: Mr. Seth Kurn, Executive Vice President *Phone:* 401-739-5000 ext. 3323 *Fax:* 401-738-8990 *E-mail:* skurn@neit.edu

Admission Contact: Mr. Michael Kwiatkowski, Director of Admissions *Phone:* 800-736-7744 ext. 3308 *Fax:* 401-738-5122 *E-mail:* mickey_k@neit.edu

See full description on page 631.

South Carolina

ECPI College of Technology Ⓐ

15 Brendan Way, Suite 120
Greenville, SC 29615-3514
Web: http://www.ecpi.edu

Accreditation: Southern Association of Colleges and Schools

Programs Offered: business automation/technology/data entry; computer and information sciences; computer engineering technologies related; computer/information technology administration and management; computer systems networking and telecommunications; computer/technical support; computer technology/computer systems technology; information science/studies; information technology; medical administrative assistant and medical secretary; medical office assistant; office occupations and clerical services; system, networking, and LAN/WAN management; web page, digital/multimedia and information resources design

Enrollment: 330 students

Institution Contact: Mr. Patrick J. Donivan, Provost *Phone:* 864-288-2828 *Fax:* 864-288-2930 *E-mail:* pdonivan@ecpi.edu

Admission Contact: Ms. Wendy J. Donivan, Director of Admissions *Phone:* 864-288-2828 *Fax:* 864-288-2930 *E-mail:* wdonivan@ecpi.edu

See full description on page 633.

ECPI College of Technology Ⓐ

7410 Northside Drive, G101
North Charleston, SC 29420
Web: http://www.ecpi.edu

Accreditation: Southern Association of Colleges and Schools

Programs Offered: computer and information sciences; computer engineering technology; computer hardware technology; computer/information technol-

Ⓐ indicates that the school is a participating institution in the *Imagine America* Scholarship Program.

234 www.petersons.com/cca

Guide to Career Colleges 2005

ogy administration and management; computer installation and repair technology; computer science; computer technology/computer systems technology; health and medical administrative services related; information technology; medical/clinical assistant

Enrollment: 70 students

Institution Contact: Ms. Shirley Long, Admissions Director *Phone:* 843-414-0350 *Fax:* 843-572-8085 *E-mail:* slong@ecpi.edu

See full description on page 632.

ITT Technical Institute

6 Independence Pointe
Greenville, SC 29615
Web: http://www.itt-tech.edu

Accreditation: Accrediting Council for Independent Colleges and Schools

Programs Offered: animation, interactive technology, video graphics and special effects; CAD/CADD drafting/design technology; communications technology; computer and information systems security; computer engineering technology; computer software and media applications; computer software engineering; computer systems networking and telecommunications; digital communication and media/multimedia; electrical, electronic and communications engineering technology; technology management; web page, digital/multimedia and information resources design

Enrollment: 412 students

Institution Contact: Mr. David Murray, Director *Phone:* 864-288-0777 ext. 21

Admission Contact: Mr. Joseph Fisher, Director of Recruitment *Phone:* 864-288-0777

See full description on page 634.

Miller-Motte Technical College

8085 Rivers Avenue
North Charleston, SC 29406
Web: http://www.miller-motte.net/

Accreditation: Accrediting Council for Independent Colleges and Schools

Programs Offered: accounting; business administration and management; computer and information sciences related; computer software and media applications related; criminal justice/police science; data entry/microcomputer applications; international business/trade/commerce; legal assistant/paralegal; massage therapy; medical/clinical assistant; surgical technology

Enrollment: 576 students

Institution Contact: Ms. Julie Corner, Campus Director *Phone:* 843-574-0101 *Fax:* 843-266-3424 *E-mail:* juliasc@miller-motte.net

Admission Contact: Kerrie Tobias-Roth, Admissions Department Coordinator *Phone:* 843-574-0101 *Fax:* 843-266-3424 *E-mail:* kerriet@miller-motte.net

South University

3810 North Main Street
Columbia, SC 29203
Web: http://www.southuniversity.edu

Accreditation: Southern Association of Colleges and Schools

Programs Offered: accounting; business administration and management; computer/information technology administration and management; health/health care administration; health services administration; legal assistant/paralegal; medical/clinical assistant; pre-law studies

Enrollment: 400 students

Institution Contact: Mrs. Anne F. Patton, President *Phone:* 803-799-9082 *Fax:* 803-799-9038 *E-mail:* apatton@southuniversity.edu

Admission Contact: Ms. Vanessa DeBauche, Associate Director of Admissions *Phone:* 803-799-9082 *Fax:* 803-799-9038 *E-mail:* vdebauche@southuniversity.edu

Strayer University

555 North Pleasantburg Drive
Greenville, SC 29607-2194
Web: http://www.strayer.edu

Programs Offered: accounting; business administration and management; information technology

Institution Contact: Rodney Kruse, Campus Manager *Phone:* 864-232-4700 *Fax:* 864-235-5739 *E-mail:* greenville@strayer.edu

South Dakota

Colorado Technical University Sioux Falls Campus

3901 West 59th Street
Sioux Falls, SD 57108

Accreditation: North Central Association of Colleges and Schools

 indicates that the school is a participating institution in the *Imagine America* Scholarship Program.

Colorado Technical University Sioux Falls Campus
(*continued*)

Programs Offered: accounting; business administration and management; computer and information sciences related; computer software engineering; criminal justice/law enforcement administration; finance; human resources management; information technology; medical/clinical assistant; technology management

National American University

2700 Doolittle Drive
Ellsworth AFB, SD 57706
Accreditation: North Central Association of Colleges and Schools
Programs Offered: business administration and management; e-commerce; information technology
Institution Contact: Mr. Bruce Hamby, Academic and Student Success Coordinator *Phone:* 605-923-5856 *Fax:* 605-923-7674 *E-mail:* bhamby@national.edu

National American University

321 Kansas City Street
Rapid City, SD 57701
Web: http://www.national.edu
Accreditation: North Central Association of Colleges and Schools
Programs Offered: accounting; athletic training; business administration and management; computer/information technology administration and management; computer programming; computer systems networking and telecommunications; computer/technical support; e-commerce; equestrian studies; finance; general studies; information technology; international business/trade/commerce; legal assistant/paralegal; management information systems; marketing/marketing management; medical/health management and clinical assistant; veterinary/animal health technology; veterinary technology; web/multimedia management and webmaster
Institution Contact: Mr. Thomas O. Shea, Vice President for Enrollment Management *Phone:* 605-394-4902 *Fax:* 605-394-4871 *E-mail:* tshea@national.edu

National American University–Sioux Falls Branch

2801 South Kiwanis Avenue, Suite 100
Sioux Falls, SD 57105
Web: http://www.national.edu
Accreditation: North Central Association of Colleges and Schools

Programs Offered: accounting; business administration and management; computer/technical support; general studies; information technology; legal assistant/paralegal; massage therapy; medical/clinical assistant; pre-law studies
Enrollment: 400 students
Institution Contact: Mrs. Susan Watton, Campus Vice President *Phone:* 605-334-5430 *Fax:* 605-334-1575 *E-mail:* swatton@national.edu
Admission Contact: Mrs. Lisa L. Houtsma, Director of Admissions *Phone:* 605-334-5430 *Fax:* 605-334-1575 *E-mail:* lhoutsma@national.edu

tennessee

Draughons Junior College ⓐ

1860 Wilma Rudolph Boulevard
Clarksville, TN 37040
Web: http://www.draughons.org
Accreditation: Accrediting Council for Independent Colleges and Schools
Programs Offered: accounting; business administration and management; computer/information technology administration and management; computer/information technology services administration related; computer programming (specific applications); computer software and media applications; criminal justice/law enforcement administration; e-commerce; health/health care administration; legal assistant/paralegal; medical/clinical assistant; pharmacy technician
Enrollment: 663 students
Institution Contact: Mrs. Christie McCullough, Student Services Coordinator *Phone:* 931-552-7600 *Fax:* 931-552-3624 *E-mail:* cmccullough@draughons.org
Admission Contact: Mrs. Christi Nolder, Assistant Admissions Director *Phone:* 931-552-7600 *Fax:* 931-552-3624 *E-mail:* cnolder@draughons.org
See full description on page 635.

Draughons Junior College

1237 Commerce Park Drive
Mufreesboro, TN 37130
Web: http://www.draughons.org
Programs Offered: accounting technology and bookkeeping; business administration and management; computer/information technology administra-

tion and management; computer/technical support; criminal justice/police science; e-commerce; health information/medical records technology; legal assistant/paralegal; medical/clinical assistant; medical insurance coding; medical insurance/medical billing; medical transcription; pharmacy technician

Institution Contact: *Phone:* 615-217-9347

Draughons Junior College Ⓐ

340 Plus Park Boulevard
Nashville, TN 37217
Web: http://www.draughons.edu

Accreditation: Accrediting Council for Independent Colleges and Schools

Programs Offered: accounting; business administration and management; computer/information technology administration and management; computer systems networking and telecommunications; criminal justice/law enforcement administration; e-commerce; information technology; legal assistant/paralegal; medical/clinical assistant; medical transcription; pharmacy technician

Enrollment: 850 students

Institution Contact: Mr. Darrel E. Hanbury, Director of Admissions *Phone:* 615-361-7555 *Fax:* 615-367-2736 *E-mail:* dhanbury@draughons.edu

See full description on page 636.

Fountainhead College of Technology

3203 Tazewell Pike
Knoxville, TN 37918-2530
Web: http://www.fountainheadcollege.edu

Accreditation: Accrediting Commission of Career Schools and Colleges of Technology

Programs Offered: computer and information systems security; computer programming; electrical, electronic and communications engineering technology; forensic science and technology; information technology; technology management; web/multimedia management and webmaster

Enrollment: 153 students

Institution Contact: Mr. Richard Rackley, President *Phone:* 865-688-9422 *Fax:* 865-688-2419 *E-mail:* info@fountainheadcollege.com

Admission Contact: Ms. Casey Rackley, Director of Administration *Phone:* 865-688-9422 *Fax:* 865-688-2419 *E-mail:* admissions@fountainheadcollege.com

High-Tech Institute

5865 Shelby Oaks Circle, Suite 100
Memphis, TN 38134

Accreditation: Accrediting Commission of Career Schools and Colleges of Technology

Programs Offered: massage therapy; medical/clinical assistant; medical insurance/medical billing; surgical technology

Enrollment: 375 students

Institution Contact: Mr. Larry L. Collins, Campus President *Phone:* 901-432-3803 *Fax:* 901-387-1181 *E-mail:* cbaird@hightechinstitute.edu

Admission Contact: Ms. Cathy Baird, Director of Admissions *Phone:* 901-432-3803 *Fax:* 901-387-1181 *E-mail:* cbaird@hightechinstitute.edu

High-Tech Institute

2710 Old Lebanon Road, Suite 12
Nashville, TN 37214
Web: http://www.high-techinstitute.com

Accreditation: Accrediting Commission of Career Schools and Colleges of Technology

Programs Offered: computer/information technology administration and management; dental assisting; digital communication and media/multimedia; massage therapy; medical/clinical assistant; medical radiologic technology; surgical technology

Institution Contact: Ms. Lisa Bacon, Campus President *Phone:* 615-902-9705 *Fax:* 615-902-9766 *E-mail:* lbacon@hightechinstitute.edu

Admission Contact: Ms. Leslie Starks, Director of Admissions *Phone:* 615-902-9705 *Fax:* 615-902-9766 *E-mail:* lstarks@hightechinstitute.edu

International Academy of Design and Technology

One Bridgestone Park
Nashville, TN 37214
Web: http://www.iadtnashville.com

Accreditation: Accrediting Council for Independent Colleges and Schools

Programs Offered: commercial and advertising art; computer graphics; design and visual communications; fashion/apparel design; interior design; intermedia/multimedia

Enrollment: 130 students

Institution Contact: Mr. Richard D. Wechner, President *Phone:* 615-232-7384 ext. 4006 *Fax:* 615-883-5285 *E-mail:* rwechner@careered.com

Admission Contact: Mr. Ronald D. Binkley, Vice President of Admissions *Phone:* 615-232-7384 ext. 4008 *Fax:* 615-883-5285 *E-mail:* rbinkley@iadtnashville.com

Ⓐ indicates that the school is a participating institution in the *Imagine America* Scholarship Program.

ITT Technical Institute ⓐ

10208 Technology Drive
Knoxville, TN 37932
Web: http://www.itt-tech.edu

Accreditation: Accrediting Council for Independent Colleges and Schools

Programs Offered: CAD/CADD drafting/design technology; communications technology; computer and information systems security; computer engineering technology; computer software and media applications; computer systems networking and telecommunications; digital communication and media/multimedia; electrical, electronic and communications engineering technology; technology management; web page, digital/multimedia and information resources design

Enrollment: 634 students

Institution Contact: Mr. David Reynolds, Director
Phone: 865-671-2800

Admission Contact: Mr. Mike Burke, Director of Recruitment *Phone:* 865-671-2800

See full description on page 637.

ITT Technical Institute ⓐ

1255 Lynnfield Road, Suite 192
Memphis, TN 38119
Web: http://www.itt-tech.edu

Accreditation: Accrediting Council for Independent Colleges and Schools

Programs Offered: accounting and business/management; animation, interactive technology, video graphics and special effects; business administration and management; CAD/CADD drafting/design technology; communications technology; computer and information systems security; computer engineering technology; computer software and media applications; computer software engineering; computer systems networking and telecommunications; criminal justice/police science; digital communication and media/multimedia; electrical, electronic and communications engineering technology; technology management; web page, digital/multimedia and information resources design

Enrollment: 699 students

Institution Contact: Ms. Melinda Jo Catron, Director
Phone: 901-762-0556 ext. 101

Admission Contact: Mr. James R. Mills, Director of Recruitment *Phone:* 901-762-0556

See full description on page 638.

ITT Technical Institute ⓐ

2845 Elm Hill Pike
Nashville, TN 37214-3717
Web: http://www.itt-tech.edu

Accreditation: Accrediting Council for Independent Colleges and Schools

Programs Offered: accounting and business/management; animation, interactive technology, video graphics and special effects; business administration and management; CAD/CADD drafting/design technology; communications technology; computer and information systems security; computer engineering technology; computer software and media applications; computer software engineering; computer systems networking and telecommunications; criminal justice/police science; digital communication and media/multimedia; electrical, electronic and communications engineering technology; technology management; web page, digital/multimedia and information resources design

Enrollment: 812 students

Institution Contact: Mr. James Coakley, Director
Phone: 615-889-8700

Admission Contact: Mr. James Royster, Director of Recruitment *Phone:* 615-889-8700

See full description on page 639.

MedVance Institute

1025 Highway 111
Cookeville, TN 38501
Web: http://www.medvance.org

Accreditation: Council on Occupational Education

Programs Offered: clinical/medical laboratory technology; medical administrative assistant and medical secretary; medical/clinical assistant; medical insurance coding; pharmacy technician; radiologic technology/science; surgical technology

Enrollment: 226 students

Institution Contact: Mrs. Shirley Cole, Campus Director *Phone:* 931-526-3660 ext. 224 *Fax:* 931-372-2603 *E-mail:* slee@medvance.org

Admission Contact: Mrs. Sharon Mellott, Associate Director of Admissions *Phone:* 931-526-3660 ext. 223 *Fax:* 931-372-2603 *E-mail:* smellott@medvance.org

Miller-Motte Technical College

6020 Shallowford Road
Chattanooga, TN 37421
Web: http://www.miller-motte.com

Accreditation: Accrediting Council for Independent Colleges and Schools

ⓐ indicates that the school is a participating institution in the *Imagine America* Scholarship Program.

Programs Offered: business administration and management; computer engineering technology; criminal justice/law enforcement administration; massage therapy; medical/clinical assistant; office management; pharmacy technician; surgical technology

Enrollment: 370 students

Institution Contact: Ms. June O. Kearns, Executive Director *Phone:* 423-510-9675 ext. 200 *Fax:* 423-510-9675 *E-mail:* jkearns@miller-motte.com

Miller-Motte Technical College

1820 Business Park Drive
Clarksville, TN 37040
Web: http://www.miller-motte.com

Accreditation: Accrediting Council for Independent Colleges and Schools

Programs Offered: administrative assistant and secretarial science; business administration and management; electrician; legal assistant/paralegal; massage therapy; medical/clinical assistant

Institution Contact: *Phone:* 800-558-0071

Nashville Auto Diesel College Ⓐ

1524 Gallatin Road
Nashville, TN 37206
Web: http://www.nadcedu.com

Accreditation: Accrediting Commission of Career Schools and Colleges of Technology

Programs Offered: autobody/collision and repair technology; automobile/automotive mechanics technology; diesel mechanics technology

Institution Contact: Executive Director *Phone:* 615-226-3990 *Fax:* 615-262-8466 *E-mail:* execdirnashville@lincolntech.com

See full description on page 640.

National College of Business & Technology Ⓐ

8415 Kingston Pike
Knoxville, TN 37919
Web: http://www.ncbt.edu

Accreditation: Accrediting Council for Independent Colleges and Schools

Programs Offered: accounting; business administration and management; medical/clinical assistant

Institution Contact: Admissions Department *Phone:* 865-539-2011 *Fax:* 865-824-2778

See full description on page 641.

National College of Business & Technology Ⓐ

3748 Nolensville Pike
Nashville, TN 37211
Web: http://www.ncbt.edu

Accreditation: Accrediting Council for Independent Colleges and Schools

Programs Offered: business administration and management; computer software and media applications; medical/clinical assistant; office management

Institution Contact: Admissions Department *Phone:* 615-333-3344 *Fax:* 615-333-3429

See full description on page 642.

Remington College—Memphis Campus Ⓐ

2731 Nonconnah Boulevard
Memphis, TN 38132-2199
Web: http://www.remingtoncollege.edu

Accreditation: Accrediting Commission of Career Schools and Colleges of Technology

Programs Offered: computer/information technology administration and management; criminal justice/law enforcement administration; electrical, electronic and communications engineering technology; information technology; medical/clinical assistant; operations management; pharmacy technician; system, networking, and LAN/WAN management

Enrollment: 650 students

Institution Contact: Dr. Lori May, Campus President *Phone:* 901-291-4225 *Fax:* 901-396-8310 *E-mail:* lori.may@remingtoncollege.edu

Admission Contact: Mr. Preston King, Director of Recruitment *Phone:* 901-345-1000 *Fax:* 901-396-8310 *E-mail:* preston.king@remingtoncollege.edu

See full description on page 643.

Remington College—Nashville Campus Ⓐ

441 Donelson Pike, Suite 150
Nashville, TN 37214
Web: http://www.remingtoncollege.edu

Accreditation: Accrediting Commission of Career Schools and Colleges of Technology

Programs Offered: computer systems analysis; computer systems networking and telecommunications; electrical, electronic and communications engineering technology; internet information systems; medical/clinical assistant; operations management

Institution Contact: Mr. Joseph Rossberger, Campus President *Phone:* 615-889-5520 *Fax:* 615-889-5528 *E-mail:* joseph.rossberger@remingtoncollege.edu

Ⓐ indicates that the school is a participating institution in the *Imagine America* Scholarship Program.

Remington College–Nashville Campus (*continued*)

Admission Contact: Mr. Michael Johnson, Director of Recruitment *Phone:* 615-889-5520 *Fax:* 615-889-5528 *E-mail:* michael.johnson@remingtoncollege.edu
See full description on page 644.

South College

720 North 5th Avenue
Knoxville, TN 37917
Web: http://www.southcollegetn.edu
Accreditation: Southern Association of Colleges and Schools
Programs Offered: accounting; administrative assistant and secretarial science; business administration and management; computer software and media applications related; computer systems networking and telecommunications; data entry/microcomputer applications; elementary education; legal administrative assistant/secretary; legal assistant/paralegal; medical/clinical assistant; medical transcription; nursing (registered nurse training); occupational therapist assistant; physical therapist assistant; radiologic technology/science; system, networking, and LAN/WAN management
Enrollment: 510 students
Institution Contact: Mr. Stephen A. South, President *Phone:* 865-251-1800 *Fax:* 865-673-8019 *E-mail:* ssouth@southcollegetn.edu
Admission Contact: Mr. Walter Hosea, Director of Admissions *Phone:* 865-251-1800 *Fax:* 865-673-8019 *E-mail:* whosea@southcollegetn.edu

Southeastern Career College

2416 21st Avenue South, Suite 300
Nashville, TN 37212
Web: http://www.southeasterncareercollege.com
Accreditation: Council on Occupational Education
Programs Offered: legal assistant/paralegal; massage therapy; medical/clinical assistant
Enrollment: 324 students
Institution Contact: Ms. Donna M. Clarkin, Executive Director *Phone:* 615-269-9900 ext. 14 *Fax:* 615-297-6678 *E-mail:* dclarkin@southeasterncareercollege.com
Admission Contact: Ms. Kimberly A. Marino, Director of Admissions *Phone:* 615-269-9900 ext. 12 *Fax:* 615-297-6678 *E-mail:* kmarino@southeasterncareercollege.com

Strayer University

2620 Thousand Oaks Boulevard, Suite 1100
Memphis, TN 38118
Web: http://www.strayer.edu
Accreditation: Middle States Association of Colleges and Schools
Programs Offered: accounting; business administration and management; communications technology; computer programming; computer systems networking and telecommunications; data modeling/warehousing and database administration; economics; general studies; information science/studies; information technology; international business/trade/commerce; marketing/marketing management; purchasing, procurement/acquisitions and contracts management
Institution Contact: Dr. J. Chris Toe, University President *Phone:* 202-408-2424 *Fax:* 202-789-0387 *E-mail:* jct@strayer.edu
Admission Contact: Randy Jones, Campus Manager *Phone:* 901-369-0835 *Fax:* 901-565-9400 *E-mail:* thousandoaks@strayer.edu

Strayer University

6211 Shelby Oaks Drive, Suite 100
Memphis, TN 38134-7400
Web: http://www.strayer.edu
Programs Offered: accounting; business administration and management; information technology
Institution Contact: Darryl Daniels, Campus Manager *Phone:* 901-383-6750 *E-mail:* shelbyoaks@strayer.edu
Admission Contact: Daryl Daniels, Campus Manager *Phone:* 901-383-6750 *E-mail:* shelbyoaks@strayer.edu

Strayer University

30 Rachel Drive, Suite 200
Nashville, TN 37214
Web: http://www.strayer.edu
Accreditation: Middle States Association of Colleges and Schools
Programs Offered: accounting; business administration and management; communications technology; computer/information technology administration and management; data modeling/warehousing and database administration; economics; general studies; information science/studies; information technology; international business/trade/commerce; marketing/ marketing management; purchasing, procurement/ acquisitions and contracts management
Institution Contact: Dr. J. Chris Toe, University President *Phone:* 202-408-2424 *Fax:* 202-789-0387 *E-mail:* jct@strayer.edu

@ indicates that the school is a participating institution in the *Imagine America* Scholarship Program.

Admission Contact: Tonya Yancy, Campus Manager *Phone:* 615-871-2260 *Fax:* 615-391-5330 *E-mail:* nashville@strayer.edu

texas

Academy of Professional Careers

2201 South Western Street, Suite 102-103
Amarillo, TX 79109
Web: http://www.apcschool.edu

Accreditation: Accrediting Council for Continuing Education and Training

Programs Offered: dental assisting; massage therapy; medical/clinical assistant; medical reception; pharmacy technician

Institution Contact: Ms. Cathy Tobin, Vice President of Compliance *Phone:* 559-735-3818 ext. 1012 *Fax:* 559-733-7831 *E-mail:* ctatcorp@aol.com

Admission Contact: Admissions Representative *Phone:* 806-353-3500 *Fax:* 806-353-7172 *E-mail:* infoahctex@academyofhealthcareers.com

Vatterott College Ⓐ

6152 Macon Road
Memphis, TN 38134
Web: http://www.vatterott-college.edu

Accreditation: Accrediting Commission of Career Schools and Colleges of Technology

Programs Offered: computer technology/computer systems technology; drafting and design technology; electrician; heating, air conditioning, ventilation and refrigeration maintenance technology; medical/clinical assistant

Enrollment: 225 students

Institution Contact: Ms. Victoria Talley, Director *Phone:* 901-761-5730 *Fax:* 901-763-2897 *E-mail:* victoria.talley@vatterott-college.edu

Admission Contact: Mr. Joe Lockwood, Director of Admissions *Phone:* 901-761-5730 *Fax:* 901-763-2897 *E-mail:* joe.lockwood@vatterott-college.edu

See full description on page 645.

AEC Texas Institute

1500 Eastgate Drive
Garland, TX 75041
Web: http://www.texasinstitute.com/

Programs Offered: business administration and management; computer and information sciences related; pre-law studies

Institution Contact: *Phone:* 888-300-9346

AEC Texas Institute

301 Northeast Loop 820
Hurst, TX 76053

Accreditation: Accrediting Council for Independent Colleges and Schools

Programs Offered: accounting; business administration and management; CAD/CADD drafting/design technology; computer programming (specific applications); computer software and media applications; computer systems networking and telecommunications; electrical, electronic and communications engineering technology; legal assistant/paralegal; medical/clinical assistant

Institution Contact: Mr. William Holler, School Director *Phone:* 817-589-0505 *Fax:* 817-595-2595 *E-mail:* bholler@amedcts.com

Admission Contact: Ricky Watkins, Senior Admissions Representative *Phone:* 817-589-0505 *Fax:* 817-595-2595

West Tennessee Business College Ⓐ

1186 Highway 45 Bypass
Jackson, TN 38301
Web: http://www.wtbc.com

Accreditation: Accrediting Council for Independent Colleges and Schools

Programs Offered: accounting; administrative assistant and secretarial science; aesthetician/esthetician and skin care; cosmetology; medical administrative assistant and medical secretary; medical/clinical assistant; medical office computer specialist; nail technician and manicurist; office occupations and clerical services

Enrollment: 325 students

Institution Contact: Mrs. Charlotte Burch, President *Phone:* 731-668-7240 *Fax:* 731-668-3824 *E-mail:* cvburch@wtbc.com

Admission Contact: Miss Ann Record, Director of Admissions *Phone:* 731-668-7240 *Fax:* 731-668-3824 *E-mail:* arecord@wtbc.com

See full description on page 646.

Ⓐ indicates that the school is a participating institution in the *Imagine America* Scholarship Program.

American Commercial College

402 Butternut Street
Abilene, TX 79602
Web: http://www.acc-careers.com
Accreditation: Accrediting Council for Independent Colleges and Schools
Programs Offered: accounting; administrative assistant and secretarial science; CAD/CADD drafting/design technology; data processing and data processing technology; executive assistant/executive secretary; health information/medical records administration; medical administrative assistant and medical secretary; medical transcription; office occupations and clerical services; receptionist; word processing
Enrollment: 160 students
Institution Contact: Mr. Tony Delgado, Director *Phone:* 325-672-8495 *Fax:* 325-672-8497 *E-mail:* tdelgado@acc-careers.com

American Commercial College

2007 34th Street
Lubbock, TX 79411
Web: http://www.acc-careers.com
Accreditation: Accrediting Council for Independent Colleges and Schools
Programs Offered: accounting; administrative assistant and secretarial science; business administration and management; computer technology/computer systems technology; data entry/microcomputer applications; drafting and design technology; electrical/electronics equipment installation and repair; medical administrative assistant and medical secretary; medical/clinical assistant; medical transcription
Enrollment: 214 students
Institution Contact: Mr. Michael J. Otto, Director *Phone:* 806-747-4339 *Fax:* 806-765-9838 *E-mail:* mjotto@acc-careers.com

American Commercial College

2115 East 8th Street
Odessa, TX 76904
Web: http://www.acc-careers.com
Programs Offered: accounting; administrative assistant and secretarial science; CAD/CADD drafting/design technology; data entry/microcomputer applications; information technology; legal administrative assistant/secretary; medical administrative assistant and medical secretary; medical transcription
Institution Contact: *Phone:* 915-332-0768

American Commercial College

3177 Executive Drive
San Angelo, TX 76904
Web: http://www.acc-careers.com
Accreditation: Accrediting Council for Independent Colleges and Schools
Programs Offered: accounting; administrative assistant and secretarial science; business administration and management; business machine repair; computer/information technology services administration related; computer systems networking and telecommunications; drafting and design technology; information technology; legal administrative assistant/secretary; medical administrative assistant and medical secretary; medical office management; medical transcription; office occupations and clerical services; receptionist; system administration; system, networking, and LAN/WAN management
Institution Contact: Mr. B. A. Reed, Director *Phone:* 915-942-6797 *Fax:* 915-949-2330 *E-mail:* bareed@acc-careers.com

American InterContinental University

11830 Webb Chapel Road
Dallas, TX 75234
Web: http://www.aiuniv.edu
Programs Offered: business administration and management; digital communication and media/multimedia; fashion/apparel design; information technology
Institution Contact: *Phone:* 800-818-2995

American InterContinental University Ⓐ

9999 Richmond Avenue
Houston, TX 77042
Web: http://www.aiuhouston.com
Accreditation: Southern Association of Colleges and Schools
Programs Offered: business administration and management; commercial and advertising art; digital communication and media/multimedia; education; information technology
Enrollment: 305 students
Institution Contact: Ms. Jori Kadlec, President *Phone:* 832-201-3626 *Fax:* 832-201-3633 *E-mail:* jkadlec@aiuhouston.com
Admission Contact: Greg Garrett, Director of Admissions *Phone:* 832-201-3624 *Fax:* 832-201-3637 *E-mail:* ggarrett@aiu.houston.com
See full description on page 647.

Ⓐ indicates that the school is a participating institution in the *Imagine America* Scholarship Program.

American InterContinental University

4511 Horizon Hill Boulevard
San Antonio, TX 78229
Web: http://www.aiusanantonio.com

Programs Offered: business, management, and marketing related; fashion/apparel design; graphic communications; health/health care administration; human resources management; information resources management; information technology

Institution Contact: Dr. Alan Stutts, President *Phone:* 210-530-9449 *Fax:* 210-530-9463 *E-mail:* astutts@aiusanantonio.com

Admission Contact: Mr. Kenneth Thomas, Vice President, Marketing and Admissions *Phone:* 210-530-9449 *Fax:* 210-530-9463 *E-mail:* kthomas@aiusanantonio.com

American School of Business

4317 Barnett Road
Wichita Falls, TX 76310
Web: http://www.acc-careers.com

Accreditation: Accrediting Council for Independent Colleges and Schools

Programs Offered: accounting; administrative assistant and secretarial science; business automation/technology/data entry; computer systems networking and telecommunications; executive assistant/executive secretary; health information/medical records administration; medical administrative assistant and medical secretary; medical/clinical assistant; medical office assistant; medical reception; medical transcription; word processing

Enrollment: 148 students

Institution Contact: Mr. Don Dobbins, Director *Phone:* 940-691-0454 *Fax:* 940-691-0470 *E-mail:* ddobbins@acc-careers.com

The Art Institute of Dallas Ⓐ

2 North Park East, 8080 Park Lane, Suite 100
Dallas, TX 75231-9959
Web: http://www.aid.edu

Accreditation: Southern Association of Colleges and Schools

Programs Offered: art; commercial and advertising art; culinary arts; design and visual communications; fashion/apparel design; interior design; web page, digital/multimedia and information resources design

Enrollment: 1,460 students

Institution Contact: Mr. Paul McGuirk, President *Phone:* 800-275-4243 ext. 1173 *Fax:* 214-696-4898 *E-mail:* mcguirkp@aii.edu

Admission Contact: Mr. Keith Petovello, Director of Admissions *Phone:* 800-275-4243 ext. 1184 *Fax:* 214-754-9460 *E-mail:* petovelk@aii.edu

See full description on page 648.

The Art Institute of Houston Ⓐ

1900 Yorktown
Houston, TX 77056
Web: http://www.aih.artinstitutes.edu

Accreditation: Southern Association of Colleges and Schools

Programs Offered: applied art; commercial and advertising art; computer graphics; computer software and media applications; culinary arts; interior design; restaurant, culinary, and catering management; web page, digital/multimedia and information resources design

Enrollment: 1,650 students

Institution Contact: Dr. Kim Nugent, President *Phone:* 713-623-2040 ext. 4136 *Fax:* 713-966-2700 *E-mail:* nugentk@aii.edu

Admission Contact: Mr. Aaron McCardell, III, Director of Admissions *Phone:* 800-275-4244 *Fax:* 713-966-2792 *E-mail:* mccardea@aii.edu

See full description on page 649.

ATI Career Training Center Ⓐ

10003 Technology Boulevard West
Dallas, TX 75220
Web: http://www.aticareertraining.edu

Accreditation: Accrediting Commission of Career Schools and Colleges of Technology

Programs Offered: business administration and management; business automation/technology/data entry; CAD/CADD drafting/design technology; commercial and advertising art; dental assisting; electrical, electronic and communications engineering technology; information technology; massage therapy; medical/clinical assistant; respiratory care therapy

Enrollment: 800 students

Institution Contact: Mr. Gerald Parr, Director *Phone:* 214-902-8191 *Fax:* 214-358-7500 *E-mail:* gparr@atienterprises.edu

Admission Contact: Miss Debra Chapman, Director of Admissions *Phone:* 214-902-8191 *Fax:* 214-358-7500 *E-mail:* dchapman@atienterprises.edu

See full description on page 650.

Ⓐ indicates that the school is a participating institution in the *Imagine America* Scholarship Program.

ATI Career Training Center Ⓐ

6351 Grapevine Highway, Suite 100
North Richland Hills, TX 76180
Web: http://www.aticareertraining.edu

Accreditation: Accrediting Commission of Career Schools and Colleges of Technology

Programs Offered: administrative assistant and secretarial science; business automation/technology/data entry; CAD/CADD drafting/design technology; commercial and advertising art; computer technology/computer systems technology; dental assisting; electrical, electronic and communications engineering technology; information technology; medical/clinical assistant

Enrollment: 570 students

Institution Contact: Mr. Joe P. Mehlmann, Executive Director *Phone:* 817-284-1141 *Fax:* 817-284-2107 *E-mail:* jpmehlmann@atienterprises.edu

Admission Contact: Director of Admissions *Phone:* 817-284-1141 *Fax:* 817-284-2107

See full description on page 651.

ATI Technical Training Center Ⓐ

6627 Maple Avenue
Dallas, TX 75235-4623
Web: http://www.aticareertraining.com

Accreditation: Accrediting Commission of Career Schools and Colleges of Technology

Programs Offered: automobile/automotive mechanics technology; heating, air conditioning and refrigeration technology; welding technology

Enrollment: 425 students

Institution Contact: Mr. Darrell E. Testerman, Executive Director *Phone:* 214-352-2222 ext. 107 *Fax:* 214-350-3951 *E-mail:* d.testerman@atienterprises.edu

Admission Contact: Mrs. Judith Johnson, Director of Admissions *Phone:* 214-352-2222 ext. 104 *Fax:* 214-350-3951 *E-mail:* jjohnson@atienterprises.edu

See full description on page 652.

Austin Business College

2101 South IH 35, Suite 300
Austin, TX 78741
Web: http://www.austinbusinesscollege.org

Accreditation: Accrediting Council for Independent Colleges and Schools

Programs Offered: accounting; accounting technology and bookkeeping; administrative assistant and secretarial science; business automation/technology/data entry; data entry/microcomputer applications; executive assistant/executive secretary; health information/medical records administration; health information/medical records technology; legal administrative assistant/secretary; legal assistant/paralegal; medical administrative assistant and medical secretary; medical office management; medical reception; receptionist; word processing

Institution Contact: Mr. Paul Ellis, President *Phone:* 512-447-9415 *Fax:* 512-447-0194 *E-mail:* pellis@austinbusinesscollege.org

Admission Contact: Ms. Pam Binns, Director of Admissions *Phone:* 512-447-9415 *Fax:* 512-447-0194 *E-mail:* pambinns@austinbusinesscollege.org

Border Institute of Technology

9611 Acer Avenue
El Paso, TX 79925-6744
Web: http://www.bitelp.edu

Accreditation: Accrediting Commission of Career Schools and Colleges of Technology

Programs Offered: business administration and management; business/corporate communications; computer and information systems security; computer engineering technology; computer graphics; computer hardware engineering; computer/information technology administration and management; computer/information technology services administration related; computer installation and repair technology; computer programming; computer programming (specific applications); computer programming (vendor/product certification); computer software and media applications; computer software engineering; computer systems analysis; computer systems networking and telecommunications; computer/technical support; marketing/marketing management; safety/security technology; system administration; system, networking, and LAN/WAN management; telecommunications; web/multimedia management and webmaster; web page, digital/multimedia and information resources design; word processing

Enrollment: 230 students

Institution Contact: Mr. Stephen Simon, President *Phone:* 915-593-7328 ext. 17 *Fax:* 915-595-2507 *E-mail:* ssimon@bitelp.edu

Admission Contact: Ms. Kristie Navarette, Admissions Manager *Phone:* 915-593-7328 ext. 24 *Fax:* 915-595-2507 *E-mail:* knavarette@bitelp.edu

Bradford School of Business

4669 Southwest Freeway, Suite 300
Houston, TX 77027-7150
Web: http://www.BradfordSchoolHouston.edu

Accreditation: Accrediting Council for Independent Colleges and Schools

Ⓐ indicates that the school is a participating institution in the *Imagine America* Scholarship Program.

Programs Offered: accounting; administrative assistant and secretarial science; commercial and advertising art; legal administrative assistant/secretary; medical administrative assistant and medical secretary; medical/clinical assistant

Enrollment: 200 students

Institution Contact: Mr. Mark Stroeh, School President *Phone:* 713-629-1500 *Fax:* 713-629-0059 *E-mail:* mstroeh@bradfordschoolhouston.edu

Admission Contact: Mr. Mark Stroeh, President *Phone:* 713-629-8940 *Fax:* 713-629-0059 *E-mail:* mstroeh@bradfordschoolhouston.edu

Career Centers of Texas

8360 Burnham Road, Suite 100
El Paso, TX 79907
Web: http://www.cct-ep.com

Accreditation: Accrediting Commission of Career Schools and Colleges of Technology

Programs Offered: computer software and media applications; computer technology/computer systems technology; dental assisting; electrician; medical/clinical assistant; medical insurance/medical billing; medical office management; pharmacy technician; surgical technology

Enrollment: 775 students

Institution Contact: Ms. Sally Crickard, Executive Director *Phone:* 915-595-1935 ext. 122 *Fax:* 915-595-6619 *E-mail:* scrickard@cct-ep.com

Admission Contact: Mr. Aldo Melucci, Director of Admissions *Phone:* 915-595-1935 ext. 135 *Fax:* 915-595-6619 *E-mail:* amelucci@cct-ep.com

Career Point Business School

485 Spencer Lane
San Antonio, TX 78201
Web: http://www.career-point.org

Accreditation: Accrediting Council for Independent Colleges and Schools

Programs Offered: accounting; administrative assistant and secretarial science; computer systems networking and telecommunications; legal assistant/paralegal; medical administrative assistant and medical secretary; medical/clinical assistant; medical office management; office occupations and clerical services

Institution Contact: Ms. Carol Kendall, Director *Phone:* 210-732-3000 ext. 223 *Fax:* 210-734-9225 *E-mail:* sdirector@career-point.org

Admission Contact: Mr. David Murguia, Admissions/Marketing *Phone:* 210-732-3000 ext. 224 *Fax:* 210-734-9225

Career Quest

5430 Fredericksburg Road, Suite 310
San Antonio, TX 78229
Institution Contact: *Phone:* 210-366-2701

Court Reporting Institute of Dallas (A)

8585 North Stemmons Freeway, Suite 200N
Dallas, TX 75247-3821
Web: http://www.crid.com

Accreditation: Accrediting Council for Independent Colleges and Schools

Programs Offered: court reporting

Enrollment: 700 students

Institution Contact: Mr. Eric S. Juhlin, President *Phone:* 214-350-9722 *Fax:* 214-631-0143 *E-mail:* ejuhlin@crid.com

Admission Contact: Mrs. Debra Smith-Armstrong, Admissions Director *Phone:* 214-350-9722 *Fax:* 214-631-0143 *E-mail:* darmstrong@crid.com

See full description on page 653.

Court Reporting Institute of Houston (A)

13101 Northwest Freeway, Suite 100
Houston, TX 77040
Web: http://www.crid.com

Accreditation: Accrediting Council for Independent Colleges and Schools

Programs Offered: court reporting

Enrollment: 400 students

Institution Contact: Ms. Cindy Smith, Director *Phone:* 713-996-8300 *Fax:* 713-996-8360 *E-mail:* csmith@crid.com

See full description on page 654.

Everest College (A)

2801 East Division Street, Suite 250
Arlington, TX 76011
Web: http://www.everest-college.com

Accreditation: Accrediting Council for Independent Colleges and Schools

Programs Offered: business administration and management; criminal justice/law enforcement administration; medical/clinical assistant; medical insurance coding; medical insurance/medical billing

Enrollment: 409 students

Institution Contact: Bruce J. Schlee, Director of Admissions *Phone:* 817-652-7790 *Fax:* 817-649-6033 *E-mail:* bschlee@cci.edu

See full description on page 656.

(A) indicates that the school is a participating institution in the *Imagine America* Scholarship Program.

Everest College Ⓐ

6060 North Central Expressway, Suite 101
Dallas, TX 75206
Web: http://www.everest-college.com

Accreditation: Accrediting Council for Independent Colleges and Schools

Programs Offered: business administration and management; criminal justice/law enforcement administration; medical/clinical assistant; medical insurance coding; medical insurance/medical billing

Admission Contact: Mr. Jae Lee, Director of Admissions *Phone:* 214-234-4850 *Fax:* 214-696-6208 *E-mail:* jlee@cci.edu

See full description on page 655.

Everest College

5237 North Riverside Drive, Suite G101
Fort Worth, TX 76137

Programs Offered: business administration and management; medical/clinical assistant

Hallmark Institute of Aeronautics

10401 IH-10 West
San Antonio, TX 78230

Accreditation: Accrediting Commission of Career Schools and Colleges of Technology

Programs Offered: aircraft powerplant technology; airframe mechanics and aircraft maintenance technology; avionics maintenance technology

Enrollment: 210 students

Institution Contact: Mr. Joe Fisher, President *Phone:* 210-690-9000 ext. 244 *Fax:* 210-697-8225 *E-mail:* jfisher@hallmarkinstitute.com

Admission Contact: Mrs. Sonia Ross, Vice President of Admissions *Phone:* 210-690-9000 ext. 212 *Fax:* 210-697-8225 *E-mail:* sross@hallmarkinstitute.com

Hallmark Institute of Technology

10401 IH-10 West
San Antonio, TX 78230
Web: http://www.hallmarkinstitute.com

Accreditation: Accrediting Commission of Career Schools and Colleges of Technology

Programs Offered: accounting; business administration and management; computer technology/computer systems technology; electrical, electronic and communications engineering technology; medical administrative assistant and medical secretary; medical/clinical assistant

Institution Contact: Mr. Joe Fisher, President *Phone:* 210-690-9000 ext. 244 *Fax:* 210-697-8225 *E-mail:* jfisher@hallmarkinstitute.com

Admission Contact: Mrs. Sonia Ross, Vice President of Admissions *Phone:* 210-690-9000 ext. 212 *Fax:* 210-697-8225 *E-mail:* sross@hallmarkinstitute.com

High-Tech Institute

4250 North Beltline Road
Irving, TX 75038
Web: http://www.high-techinstitute.com

Accreditation: Accrediting Commission of Career Schools and Colleges of Technology

Programs Offered: computer systems networking and telecommunications; massage therapy; medical/clinical assistant; medical insurance/medical billing; pharmacy technician; surgical technology

Enrollment: 800 students

Institution Contact: Mrs. Claudia A. Stapleton, Campus Director *Phone:* 972-871-2824 *Fax:* 972-871-2860 *E-mail:* cstapleton@hightechschools.com

Admission Contact: Ms. Juanita Cherry, Director of Admissions *Phone:* 972-871-2824 *Fax:* 972-871-2860 *E-mail:* jchery@hightechschools.com

International Business College

5700 Cromo
El Paso, TX 79912
Web: http://www.ibcelpaso.edu

Accreditation: Accrediting Council for Independent Colleges and Schools

Programs Offered: accounting; administrative assistant and secretarial science; business administration and management; computer software and media applications; international business/trade/commerce; legal administrative assistant/secretary; medical administrative assistant and medical secretary; medical/clinical assistant

Enrollment: 551 students

Institution Contact: Mrs. Margie Aguilar, Vice President *Phone:* 915-779-0900 *Fax:* 915-779-1145 *E-mail:* maguilar@ibcelpaso.edu

Admission Contact: M. Abe Lincoln, Admissions Representative *Phone:* 915-566-8643 *Fax:* 915-585-2584 *E-mail:* alincoln@ibcelpaso.edu

International Business College

1155 North Zaragosa, Suite 100
El Paso, TX 79907-1806
Web: http://www.ibcelpaso.edu

Accreditation: Accrediting Council for Independent Colleges and Schools

Ⓐ indicates that the school is a participating institution in the *Imagine America* Scholarship Program.

Programs Offered: accounting; administrative assistant and secretarial science; business automation/technology/data entry; legal administrative assistant/secretary; medical administrative assistant and medical secretary; medical/clinical assistant

Enrollment: 668 students

Institution Contact: Mr. Don Chittenden, Director *Phone:* 915-859-3986 *Fax:* 915-859-4142 *E-mail:* donald.chittenden@ibcelpaso.edu

Admission Contact: Mr. Ernest Pettengill, Admissions Representative *Phone:* 915-859-3986 *Fax:* 915-859-4142 *E-mail:* ernest.pettengill@ibcelpaso.edu

ITT Technical Institute Ⓐ

551 Ryan Plaza Drive
Arlington, TX 76011
Web: http://www.itt-tech.edu

Accreditation: Accrediting Council for Independent Colleges and Schools

Programs Offered: CAD/CADD drafting/design technology; computer engineering technology; computer software and media applications; computer systems networking and telecommunications; digital communication and media/multimedia; web page, digital/multimedia and information resources design

Enrollment: 657 students

Institution Contact: Ms. Paulette Gallerson, Director *Phone:* 817-794-5100

Admission Contact: Mr. Edward Leal, Director of Recruitment *Phone:* 817-794-5100

See full description on page 657.

ITT Technical Institute Ⓐ

6330 Highway 290 East, Suite 150
Austin, TX 78723-1061
Web: http://www.itt-tech.edu

Accreditation: Accrediting Council for Independent Colleges and Schools

Programs Offered: CAD/CADD drafting/design technology; computer engineering technology; computer software and media applications; computer systems networking and telecommunications; digital communication and media/multimedia; web page, digital/multimedia and information resources design

Enrollment: 789 students

Institution Contact: Ms. Barbara Anthony, Director *Phone:* 512-467-6800

Admission Contact: Mr. Jim Branham, Director of Recruitment *Phone:* 512-467-6800

See full description on page 658.

ITT Technical Institute Ⓐ

15621 Blue Ash Drive, Suite 160
Houston, TX 77090-5821
Web: http://www.itt-tech.edu

Accreditation: Accrediting Council for Independent Colleges and Schools

Programs Offered: CAD/CADD drafting/design technology; computer engineering technology; computer software and media applications; computer systems networking and telecommunications; digital communication and media/multimedia; web page, digital/multimedia and information resources design

Enrollment: 437 students

Institution Contact: Mr. David Champlin, Director *Phone:* 281-873-0512

Admission Contact: Mr. Benjamin Moore, Director of Recruitment *Phone:* 281-873-0512

See full description on page 659.

ITT Technical Institute Ⓐ

2222 Bay Area Boulevard
Houston, TX 77058
Web: http://www.itt-tech.edu

Accreditation: Accrediting Council for Independent Colleges and Schools

Programs Offered: CAD/CADD drafting/design technology; computer engineering technology; computer software and media applications; computer systems networking and telecommunications; digital communication and media/multimedia; web page, digital/multimedia and information resources design

Enrollment: 372 students

Institution Contact: Mr. Robert Jeffords, Director *Phone:* 281-486-2630

Admission Contact: Mr. Derrick Sutton, Director of Recruitment *Phone:* 281-486-2630

See full description on page 660.

ITT Technical Institute Ⓐ

2950 South Gessner Road
Houston, TX 77063-3751
Web: http://www.itt-tech.edu

Accreditation: Accrediting Council for Independent Colleges and Schools

Programs Offered: CAD/CADD drafting/design technology; computer engineering technology; computer software and media applications; computer systems networking and telecommunications; digital communication and media/multimedia; web page, digital/multimedia and information resources design

Enrollment: 478 students

Ⓐ indicates that the school is a participating institution in the *Imagine America* Scholarship Program.

ITT Technical Institute (continued)

Institution Contact: Mr. Robert Van Elsen, Director
Phone: 713-952-2294

Admission Contact: Mr. Johnny Jackson, Director of
Recruitment *Phone:* 713-952-2294

See full description on page 661.

ITT Technical Institute

2101 Waterview Parkway
Richardson, TX 75080
Web: http://www.itt-tech.edu

Accreditation: Accrediting Council for Independent
Colleges and Schools

Programs Offered: CAD/CADD drafting/design
technology; computer engineering technology;
computer software and media applications; computer
systems networking and telecommunications; digital
communication and media/multimedia; electrical,
electronic and communications engineering technology; web page, digital/multimedia and information
resources design

Enrollment: 783 students

Institution Contact: Ms. Maureen Clements, Director
Phone: 972-690-9100

Admission Contact: Mr. Nate Wallace, Director of
Recruitment *Phone:* 972-690-9100

ITT Technical Institute (A)

5700 Northwest Parkway
San Antonio, TX 78249-3303
Web: http://www.itt-tech.edu

Accreditation: Accrediting Council for Independent
Colleges and Schools

Programs Offered: CAD/CADD drafting/design
technology; computer engineering technology;
computer software and media applications; computer
systems networking and telecommunications; digital
communication and media/multimedia; web page,
digital/multimedia and information resources design

Enrollment: 786 students

Institution Contact: Mr. Stephen Marks, Director
Phone: 210-694-4612

Admission Contact: Mr. Buddy Hoyt, Director of
Recruitment *Phone:* 210-694-4612

See full description on page 662.

Lincoln Technical Institute (A)

2501 East Arkansas Lane
Grand Prairie, TX 75052
Web: http://www.lincolntech.com

Accreditation: Accrediting Commission of Career
Schools and Colleges of Technology

Programs Offered: automobile/automotive mechanics
technology; automotive engineering technology; diesel
mechanics technology; heating, air conditioning and
refrigeration technology; heating, air conditioning,
ventilation and refrigeration maintenance technology

Enrollment: 1,100 students

Institution Contact: Mr. A. Michael Rowan, Executive
Director *Phone:* 972-660-5701 *Fax:* 972-660-6148 *E-mail:*
mrowan@lincolntech.com

Admission Contact: Mr. Charles Darling, Director of
High School Admission *Phone:* 972-660-5701 *Fax:*
972-660-6148 *E-mail:* cdarling@lincolntech.com

See full description on page 663.

MedVance Institute

6220 Westpark, Suite 180
Houston, TX 77057
Web: http://www.medvance.edu

Programs Offered: medical/clinical assistant; medical
insurance/medical billing; pharmacy technician;
radiologic technology/science; surgical technology

Institution Contact: Mr. Scott Jay Cotlar, Campus
Director *Phone:* 713-266-6594 *Fax:* 713-782-5873 *E-mail:*
scotlar@medvance.org

Admission Contact: Ms. Sonya Sanders, Director of
Admissions *Phone:* 713-266-6594 ext. 226 *Fax:* 713-782-
5873 *E-mail:* ssanders@medvance.edu

MTI College of Business and Technology (A)

1275 Space Park Drive, Suite 100
Houston, TX 77058
Web: http://www.mti.edu

Accreditation: Accrediting Commission of Career
Schools and Colleges of Technology

Programs Offered: accounting; administrative
assistant and secretarial science; business administration and management; business automation/technol-
ogy/data entry; computer and information systems
security; computer/information technology services
administration related; computer installation and
repair technology; computer systems analysis;
computer systems networking and telecommunications; computer/technical support; computer technol-
ogy/computer systems technology; electrical and
electronic engineering technologies related; English as
a second language; executive assistant/executive
secretary; health information/medical records
administration; information science/studies; instrumentation technology; medical administrative
assistant and medical secretary; medical insurance
coding; medical insurance/medical billing; medical

(A) indicates that the school is a participating institution in the *Imagine America* Scholarship Program.

office computer specialist; medical office management; medical transcription; office occupations and clerical services; receptionist; system administration; system, networking, and LAN/WAN management; web page, digital/multimedia and information resources design; word processing

Enrollment: 245 students

Institution Contact: Mr. John Springhetti, Director *Phone:* 281-333-3363 *Fax:* 281-333-4118 *E-mail:* john@mti.edu

Admission Contact: Mr. Derrell Beck, Admissions Director *Phone:* 281-333-3363 *Fax:* 281-333-4118 *E-mail:* derrell@mti.edu

See full description on page 666.

MTI College of Business and Technology ⓐ

7277 Regency Square Boulevard
Houston, TX 77036-3163
Web: http://www.mti.edu

Accreditation: Accrediting Commission of Career Schools and Colleges of Technology

Programs Offered: accounting; administrative assistant and secretarial science; business administration and management; business automation/technology/data entry; computer/information technology services administration related; computer installation and repair technology; computer systems analysis; computer systems networking and telecommunications; computer/technical support; computer technology/computer systems technology; electrical, electronic and communications engineering technology; English as a second language; health information/medical records administration; information science/studies; instrumentation technology; medical administrative assistant and medical secretary; medical insurance coding; medical insurance/medical billing; medical office computer specialist; medical office management; medical transcription; office occupations and clerical services; receptionist; system administration; system, networking, and LAN/WAN management; web page, digital/multimedia and information resources design; word processing

Enrollment: 666 students

Institution Contact: Mr. Robert Obenhaus, President *Phone:* 713-974-7181 *Fax:* 713-974-2090 *E-mail:* bob@mti.edu

Admission Contact: Mr. David Wood, Director of Admissions *Phone:* 713-974-7181 *Fax:* 713-974-2090 *E-mail:* davidw@mti.edu

See full description on page 665.

MTI College of Business and Technology ⓐ

11420 East Freeway
Houston, TX 77029
Web: http://www.mti.edu

Accreditation: Accrediting Commission of Career Schools and Colleges of Technology

Programs Offered: administrative assistant and secretarial science; business automation/technology/data entry; English as a second language; health information/medical records administration; health information/medical records technology; medical administrative assistant and medical secretary; medical insurance coding; medical office computer specialist; medical reception; office occupations and clerical services; receptionist; word processing

Enrollment: 104 students

Institution Contact: Mr. Ed Kessing, Director *Phone:* 713-979-1800 *Fax:* 713-979-1818 *E-mail:* ed@mti.edu

See full description on page 664.

National Institute of Technology ⓐ

9100 US Highway 290 East, Suite 100
Austin, TX 78754
Web: http://www.nitschools.com

Accreditation: Accrediting Commission of Career Schools and Colleges of Technology

Programs Offered: computer technology/computer systems technology; heating, air conditioning, ventilation and refrigeration maintenance technology; medical administrative assistant and medical secretary; medical/clinical assistant; pharmacy technician

Institution Contact: Ms. Kim Whitehead, Director of Admissions *Phone:* 512-928-1933 *Fax:* 512-927-8587 *E-mail:* kwhitehe@cci.edu

See full description on page 667.

National Institute of Technology ⓐ

4150 Westheimer Road, Suite 200
Houston, TX 77027
Web: http://www.nitschools.com

Accreditation: Accrediting Commission of Career Schools and Colleges of Technology

Programs Offered: computer engineering technology; electrical, electronic and communications engineering technology; information technology; medical/clinical assistant; medical insurance coding

Enrollment: 457 students

Institution Contact: Mr. Thomas C. Wilson, President *Phone:* 713-629-1637 *Fax:* 713-629-1643 *E-mail:* twilson@cci.edu

ⓐ indicates that the school is a participating institution in the *Imagine America* Scholarship Program.

National Institute of Technology (*continued*)

Admission Contact: Mr. Scott Morris, Director of Admissions *Phone:* 713-629-1637 ext. 102 *Fax:* 713-629-1643 *E-mail:* smorris@cci.edu

See full description on page 669.

National Institute of Technology Ⓐ

9700 Bissonnet, Suite 1400
Houston, TX 77036
Web: http://www.nitschools.com

Accreditation: Accrediting Commission of Career Schools and Colleges of Technology

Programs Offered: medical/clinical assistant; medical insurance coding; medical insurance/medical billing; pharmacy technician

Institution Contact: Vanessa Smith, Director of Admissions *Phone:* 713-772-4200 *Fax:* 713-772-4204 *E-mail:* vasmith@cci.edu

See full description on page 668.

National Institute of Technology Ⓐ

6550 First Park Ten Boulevard
San Antonio, TX 78213
Web: http://www.cci.edu

Accreditation: Accrediting Commission of Career Schools and Colleges of Technology

Programs Offered: business automation/technology/data entry; computer technology/computer systems technology; electrical, electronic and communications engineering technology; heating, air conditioning and refrigeration technology; medical administrative assistant and medical secretary; medical/clinical assistant; pharmacy technician; system administration

Enrollment: 626 students

Institution Contact: Mr. James Yeaman, President *Phone:* 210-733-6000 *Fax:* 210-733-3300 *E-mail:* jyeaman@cci.edu

Admission Contact: Mr. Jimmy Clontz, Director of Admissions *Phone:* 210-733-6000 *Fax:* 210-733-3300 *E-mail:* jimmyclontz@cci.edu

See full description on page 672.

National Institute of Technology—Greenspoint Ⓐ

255 Northpoint, Suite 100
Houston, TX 77060
Web: http://www.nitschools.com

Accreditation: Accrediting Commission of Career Schools and Colleges of Technology

Programs Offered: dental assisting; medical/clinical assistant; medical insurance coding; medical insurance/medical billing; pharmacy technician

Enrollment: 610 students

Institution Contact: Mr. Robert Bosic, President *Phone:* 281-447-7037 *Fax:* 281-447-6937 *E-mail:* rbosic@cci.edu

Admission Contact: Mr. Jeff Brown, Director of Admissions *Phone:* 281-447-7037 ext. 102 *Fax:* 281-447-6937 *E-mail:* jbrown@cci.edu

See full description on page 670.

National Institute of Technology—Hobby Ⓐ

7151 Office City Drive, Suite 100
Houston, TX 77087
Web: http://www.nitschools.com

Accreditation: Accrediting Commission of Career Schools and Colleges of Technology

Programs Offered: medical/clinical assistant; medical insurance/medical billing; pharmacy technician

Enrollment: 596 students

Institution Contact: Mrs. Barbara Andrews, School President *Phone:* 713-645-7404 ext. 101 *Fax:* 713-645-7346 *E-mail:* bandrews@cci.edu

Admission Contact: Mr. Greg Lotz, Director of Admissions *Phone:* 713-645-7404 ext. 102 *Fax:* 713-645-7346 *E-mail:* wlotz@cci.edu

See full description on page 671.

Ocean Corporation Ⓐ

10840 Rockley Road
Houston, TX 77099-3416
Web: http://www.oceancorp.com

Accreditation: Accrediting Commission of Career Schools and Colleges of Technology

Programs Offered: diving, professional and instruction; quality control technology

Enrollment: 162 students

Institution Contact: Mr. John Wood, President *Phone:* 800-321-0298 *Fax:* 281-530-9143 *E-mail:* johnswood@worldnet.att.net

Admission Contact: Mr. Mike Oden, Admissions *Phone:* 800-321-0298 *Fax:* 281-530-9143 *E-mail:* admissions@oceancorp.com

See full description on page 673.

PCI Health Training Center

8101 John W. Carpenter Freeway
Dallas, TX 75247-4720
Web: http://www.pcihealth.net

Accreditation: Accrediting Commission of Career Schools and Colleges of Technology

---

Ⓐ indicates that the school is a participating institution in the *Imagine America* Scholarship Program.

Programs Offered: medical/clinical assistant; medical office computer specialist; psychiatric/mental health services technology; substance abuse/addiction counseling

Enrollment: 640 students

Institution Contact: Mr. Don Wood, Director of Compliance and Financial Aid *Phone:* 214-630-0568 ext. 323 *Fax:* 214-630-1002 *E-mail:* dwood@pcihealth.net

Admission Contact: Kelly Drake, Director of Admissions *Phone:* 214-630-0568 ext. 305 *Fax:* 214-630-1002 *E-mail:* kdrake@pcihealth.net

Remington College Ⓐ

11310 Greens Crossing Road, Suite 300
Houston, TX 77067
Web: http://www.remingtoncollege.edu

Programs Offered: business administration and management; computer and information sciences; computer systems networking and telecommunications; criminal justice/law enforcement administration; medical/clinical assistant; medical insurance coding; pharmacy technician

Institution Contact: Mr. Christopher Tilley, Campus President *Phone:* 281-899-1240 *Fax:* 281-597-8466

Admission Contact: Mr. Lance Stribling, Director of Recruitment *Phone:* 281-899-1240 *Fax:* 281-597-8466

See full description on page 676.

Remington College—Dallas Campus Ⓐ

1800 Eastgate Drive
Garland, TX 75041
Web: http://www.remingtoncollege.edu

Accreditation: Accrediting Council for Independent Colleges and Schools

Programs Offered: business administration and management; computer software technology; computer systems networking and telecommunications; electrical, electronic and communications engineering technology; medical/clinical assistant

Enrollment: 796 students

Institution Contact: Mr. Skip Walls, Campus President *Phone:* 972-686-7878 *Fax:* 972-686-5116 *E-mail:* skip.walls@remingtoncollege.edu

Admission Contact: Ms. Shonda Whisenhunt, Director of Recruitment *Phone:* 972-686-7878 *Fax:* 972-686-5116 *E-mail:* shonda.whisenhunt@remingtoncollege.edu

See full description on page 674.

Remington College—Fort Worth Campus Ⓐ

300 East Loop 820
Fort Worth, TX 76112
Web: http://www.remingtoncollege.edu

Accreditation: Accrediting Commission of Career Schools and Colleges of Technology

Programs Offered: commercial and advertising art; computer systems analysis; electrical, electronic and communications engineering technology; information science/studies; medical/clinical assistant; system, networking, and LAN/WAN management

Institution Contact: Ms. Lynn Wey, Campus President *Phone:* 817-451-0017 *Fax:* 817-496-1257 *E-mail:* lynn.wey@remingtoncollege.edu

Admission Contact: Ms. Annette Latshaw, Director of Recruitment *Phone:* 817-451-0017 *Fax:* 817-496-1257 *E-mail:* annette.latshaw@remingtoncollege.edu

See full description on page 675.

Remington College—Houston Campus

3110 Hayes Road, Suite 380
Houston, TX 77082
Web: http://www.remingtoncollege.edu

Accreditation: Accrediting Commission of Career Schools and Colleges of Technology

Programs Offered: computer programming; computer systems analysis; computer systems networking and telecommunications; electrical, electronic and communications engineering technology; medical/clinical assistant; system, networking, and LAN/WAN management; web page, digital/multimedia and information resources design

Enrollment: 380 students

Institution Contact: Ms. Chris Tilley, Campus President *Phone:* 281-899-1240 *Fax:* 281-597-8466 *E-mail:* chris.tilley@remingtoncollege.edu

Admission Contact: Mr. Lance Stribling *Phone:* 281-899-1240 ext. 206 *Fax:* 281-597-8466 *E-mail:* lance.stribling@remingtoncollege.edu

San Antonio College of Medical and Dental Assistants

San Pedro Town Centre Phase II, 7142 San Pedro, Suite 100
San Antonio, TX 78216
Web: http://www.sacmda.com

Accreditation: Accrediting Bureau of Health Education Schools; Accrediting Commission of Career Schools and Colleges of Technology

Programs Offered: computer/technical support; dental assisting; medical administrative assistant and

Ⓐ indicates that the school is a participating institution in the *Imagine America* Scholarship Program.

San Antonio College of Medical and Dental Assistants
(*continued*)

medical secretary; medical/clinical assistant; pharmacy technician; phlebotomy

Enrollment: 804 students

Institution Contact: Mr. Art Rodriguez, Executive Director *Phone:* 210-733-0777 ext. 1545 *Fax:* 210-735-2431 *E-mail:* arodriguez@sac-mda.com

Admission Contact: Mr. Rey Torres, Admissions Director *Phone:* 210-733-0777 ext. 1540 *Fax:* 210-248-1566 *E-mail:* rtorres@sac-mda.com

Sanford-Brown Institute

1250 Mockingbird Lane, Suite 150
Dallas, TX 75247
Web: http://www.sbdallas.com

Accreditation: Accrediting Bureau of Health Education Schools

Programs Offered: cardiovascular technology; diagnostic medical sonography and ultrasound technology; medical/clinical assistant; medical insurance/medical billing; surgical technology

Institution Contact: Mr. Marcus McMellon, CPA, President *Phone:* 214-459-8490 *Fax:* 214-638-6401 *E-mail:* mmcmellon@sbdallas.com

Admission Contact: Mr. John Magombo, Director of Admissions *Phone:* 214-459-8490 *Fax:* 214-638-6006 *E-mail:* jmagombo@sbdallas.com

Sanford-Brown Institute

10500 Forum Place Drive, Suite 200
Houston, TX 77036
Web: http://www.sbhouston.com

Accreditation: Accrediting Bureau of Health Education Schools

Programs Offered: cardiovascular technology; diagnostic medical sonography and ultrasound technology; medical/clinical assistant; medical insurance/medical billing; surgical technology

Institution Contact: Mr. James C. Garrett, Executive Director *Phone:* 713-779-1110 *Fax:* 713-779-2408 *E-mail:* jgarrett@sbhouston.com

Admission Contact: Mrs. RoseAnne Heckman, Director of Admissions *Phone:* 713-779-1110 *Fax:* 713-779-2408 *E-mail:* rheckman@sbhouston.com

Southeastern Career Institute

5440 Harvest Hill, #200
Dallas, TX 75230
Web: http://www.southeasterncareerinstitute.com

Accreditation: Council on Occupational Education

Programs Offered: criminal justice/police science; legal assistant/paralegal

Enrollment: 247 students

Institution Contact: Ms. Cindy M. Lewellen, Executive Director *Phone:* 972-385-1446 *Fax:* 972-385-0641 *E-mail:* mlewellen@sci-education.com

Admission Contact: Ms. Carol L. Richardson, Director of Admissions *Phone:* 972-385-1446 *Fax:* 972-385-0641 *E-mail:* crichardson@sci-dallas.com

Southern Educational Alliance

6420 Richmond, Suite 345
Houston, TX 77057
Web: http://www.seainstantlearning.com

Programs Offered: allied health and medical assisting services related; business/corporate communications; cardiovascular technology; clinical/medical laboratory assistant; computer hardware engineering; computer programming (specific applications); English as a second language; medical administrative assistant and medical secretary; medical/clinical assistant; nursing assistant/aide and patient care assistant; nursing (licensed practical/vocational nurse training); pharmacy technician; phlebotomy; surgical technology

Institution Contact: Mr. Ron Daniels, Sr., President/CEO *Phone:* 713-975-9642 *Fax:* 713-975-9714 *E-mail:* rdaniels@instantlearning.edu

Admission Contact: Mrs. Sheila Daniels, Vice President *Phone:* 713-975-9642 *Fax:* 713-975-9714 *E-mail:* sdaniels@instantlearning.edu

Texas Careers-San Antonio

1015 Jackson Keller
San Antonio, TX 78213
Web: http://www.texascareers.com

Accreditation: Council on Occupational Education

Programs Offered: computer software technology; legal assistant/paralegal; medical/clinical assistant; medical office computer specialist; nursing assistant/aide and patient care assistant; nursing (registered nurse training)

Institution Contact: Ms. Laura M. Bledsoe, Executive Director *Phone:* 210-308-8584 *Fax:* 210-308-8985 *E-mail:* lbledsoe@texascareers.com

Admission Contact: Mr. Mike Maloto, Director of Admissions *Phone:* 210-308-8584 *Fax:* 210-308-8985 *E-mail:* mmaloto@texascareers.com

⬥ indicates that the school is a participating institution in the *Imagine America* Scholarship Program.

Texas Culinary Academy

11400 Burnet Road, Suite 2100
Austin, TX 78758
Web: http://www.tca.edu

Accreditation: Accrediting Council for Independent Colleges and Schools; Council on Occupational Education

Programs Offered: culinary arts

Institution Contact: Ms. Paula M. Paulette, Director of Admissions *Phone:* 512-837-2665 *Fax:* 512-977-9794 *E-mail:* ppaulette@txca.com

Admission Contact: Paula Paulette, Director of Admissions *Phone:* 888-553-2433 *Fax:* 512-837-2665 *E-mail:* ppaulette@txca.com

Texas School of Business—East Campus

711 East Airtex Drive
Houston, TX 77073
Web: http://www.tsb.edu/

Accreditation: Accrediting Council for Independent Colleges and Schools

Programs Offered: accounting; administrative assistant and secretarial science; business automation/technology/data entry; computer/information technology administration and management; data processing and data processing technology; executive assistant/executive secretary; health information/medical records administration; medical administrative assistant and medical secretary; medical/clinical assistant; medical office management; office occupations and clerical services; receptionist; word processing

Institution Contact: Mr. Kevin Keller, President *Phone:* 713-974-2593 ext. 301 *Fax:* 713-339-9081 *E-mail:* kkeller@tsb.edu

Admission Contact: Mr. Craig Dodson, Director of Admissions *Phone:* 281-443-8900 *Fax:* 281-443-0777 *E-mail:* cdodson@tsb.edu

Texas School of Business Friendswood

17164 Blackhawk Boulevard
Friendswood, TX 77546
Web: http://www.tsb.edu/

Accreditation: Accrediting Council for Independent Colleges and Schools

Programs Offered: accounting; administrative assistant and secretarial science; business automation/technology/data entry; computer/information technology administration and management; data processing and data processing technology; executive assistant/executive secretary; health information/medical records administration; medical administra-

tive assistant and medical secretary; medical/clinical assistant; medical office management; office occupations and clerical services; receptionist; word processing

Institution Contact: Mr. Kevin Keller, President *Phone:* 713-974-2593 ext. 301 *Fax:* 713-339-9081

Admission Contact: Mr. Bobby Wilmore, Director *Phone:* 281-648-0880 *Fax:* 281-648-0821

Texas School of Business, Inc.

711 Airtex Drive
Houston, TX 77073
Web: http://www.tsb.edu

Accreditation: Accrediting Council for Independent Colleges and Schools

Programs Offered: accounting; computer science; medical/clinical assistant; office occupations and clerical services

Institution Contact: *Phone:* 800-555-8012 *E-mail:* info@tsb.edu

Texas School of Business Southwest

6363 Richmond, Suite 500
Houston, TX 77057
Web: http://www.tsb.edu/

Accreditation: Accrediting Council for Independent Colleges and Schools

Programs Offered: accounting; administrative assistant and secretarial science; business automation/technology/data entry; computer/information technology administration and management; data processing and data processing technology; executive assistant/executive secretary; health information/medical records administration; medical administrative assistant and medical secretary; medical/clinical assistant; medical office management; office occupations and clerical services; receptionist; word processing

Institution Contact: Mr. Kevin Keller, President *Phone:* 713-974-2593 ext. 301 *Fax:* 713-339-9081

Admission Contact: Mrs. Diane Nguyen, Director of Admissions *Phone:* 713-975-7527 *Fax:* 713-339-9081

Universal Technical Institute Ⓐ

721 Lockhaven Drive
Houston, TX 77073
Web: http://www.uticorp.com

Accreditation: Accrediting Commission of Career Schools and Colleges of Technology

Ⓐ indicates that the school is a participating institution in the *Imagine America* Scholarship Program.

Universal Technical Institute (*continued*)

Programs Offered: autobody/collision and repair technology; automobile/automotive mechanics technology; diesel mechanics technology

Institution Contact: Mr. Ken Golaszewski, School Director *Phone:* 281-443-6262 *Fax:* 281-443-1866 *E-mail:* kgolaszewski@uticorp.com

See full description on page 677.

Virginia College at Austin Ⓐ

6301 East Highway 290, Suite 200
Austin, TX 78723
Web: http://www.vc.edu

Accreditation: Accrediting Council for Independent Colleges and Schools

Programs Offered: accounting technology and bookkeeping; administrative assistant and secretarial science; computer and information systems security; computer systems networking and telecommunications; diagnostic medical sonography and ultrasound technology; legal assistant/paralegal; medical/clinical assistant; medical insurance coding; medical insurance/medical billing; medical office management; office management; surgical technology

Enrollment: 540 students

Institution Contact: Mr. David B. Champlin, Campus President *Phone:* 512-371-3500 ext. 2802 *Fax:* 512-371-3502 *E-mail:* dchamplin@vc.edu

Admission Contact: Mrs. Charlotte A. Frohnhoefer, Director of Admissions *Phone:* 512-371-3500 ext. 2801 *Fax:* 512-371-3502 *E-mail:* cfrohnhoefer@vc.edu

See full description on page 678.

Western Technical Institute Ⓐ

1000 Texas Avenue
El Paso, TX 79901-1536
Web: http://www.wti-ep.com

Accreditation: Accrediting Bureau of Health Education Schools; Accrediting Commission of Career Schools and Colleges of Technology

Programs Offered: automobile/automotive mechanics technology; communications technology; computer/information technology administration and management; computer installation and repair technology; computer systems networking and telecommunications; computer technology/computer systems technology; electrical, electronic and communications engineering technology; health information/medical records administration; health information/medical records technology; heating, air conditioning and refrigeration technology; heating, air conditioning, ventilation and refrigeration maintenance technology; information technology; medical/clinical assistant; medical insurance coding; medical insurance/medical billing; medical transcription; sheet metal technology; telecommunications; telecommunications technology; welding technology

Enrollment: 822 students

Institution Contact: Mr. Bill Terrell, Chief Administrative Officer *Phone:* 915-532-3737 ext. 117 *Fax:* 915-532-6946 *E-mail:* bterrell@wti-ep.com

See full description on page 679.

Western Technical Institute

9451 Diana Drive
El Paso, TX 79924
Web: http://www.wti-ep.com

Accreditation: Accrediting Bureau of Health Education Schools; Accrediting Commission of Career Schools and Colleges of Technology

Programs Offered: automobile/automotive mechanics technology; computer/information technology administration and management; computer systems networking and telecommunications; computer technology/computer systems technology; electrical, electronic and communications engineering technology; health/health care administration; health information/medical records administration; heating, air conditioning, ventilation and refrigeration maintenance technology; industrial technology; medical/clinical assistant; telecommunications; welding technology

Enrollment: 960 students

Institution Contact: Mr. Bill Terrell, Chief Administrative Officer *Phone:* 915-532-3737 ext. 117 *Fax:* 915-532-6946 *E-mail:* bterrell@wti-ep.com

Admission Contact: Mr. Jerry Martin, Director, Office of Recruitment & School Relations *Phone:* 915-566-9621 ext. 123 *Fax:* 915-565-9903 *E-mail:* jmartin@wti-ep.com

Westwood Aviation Institute Ⓐ

8880 Telephone Road
Houston, TX 77061
Web: http://www.westwood.edu

Accreditation: Council on Occupational Education; Southern Association of Colleges and Schools

Programs Offered: aircraft powerplant technology; airframe mechanics and aircraft maintenance technology

Enrollment: 400 students

Institution Contact: Mr. Robert Pim, Executive Director *Phone:* 713-645-4444 *Fax:* 713-644-0902 *E-mail:* rpim@westwood.edu

Ⓐ indicates that the school is a participating institution in the *Imagine America* Scholarship Program.

Admission Contact: Mr. Glen Feist, Director of Admissions *Phone:* 713-644-7777 *Fax:* 713-644-0902 *E-mail:* gfeist@westwood.edu

See full description on page 680.

Westwood College—Dallas

8390 LBJ Freeway, Suite 100
Dallas, TX 75243

Accreditation: Accrediting Council for Independent Colleges and Schools

Programs Offered: CAD/CADD drafting/design technology; commercial and advertising art; computer engineering related; computer programming; interior design; medical office assistant

Enrollment: 512 students

Institution Contact: Mr. Vince Thomae, Executive Director *Phone:* 214-570-0100 ext. 200 *Fax:* 214-570-8502 *E-mail:* vthomae@westwood.edu

Admission Contact: Mr. Eric Southwell, Director of Admissions *Phone:* 214-570-0100 ext. 100 *Fax:* 214-570-8502 *E-mail:* esouthwell@westwood.edu

See full description on page 681.

Westwood College—Fort Worth

1331 Airport Freeway, Suite 402
Euless, TX 76040
Web: http://www.westwood.edu

Accreditation: Accrediting Council for Independent Colleges and Schools

Programs Offered: CAD/CADD drafting/design technology; commercial and advertising art; computer systems networking and telecommunications; information technology; medical/clinical assistant

Enrollment: 570 students

Institution Contact: Kelly Coates, Executive Director *Phone:* 817-685-9994 *Fax:* 817-685-8929 *E-mail:* kcoates@westwood.edu

See full description on page 682.

Westwood College—Houston South Campus

7322 Southwest Freeway, Suite 1900
Houston, TX 77074
Web: http://www.westwood.edu

Accreditation: Accrediting Commission of Career Schools and Colleges of Technology

Programs Offered: CAD/CADD drafting/design technology; commercial and advertising art; computer engineering technology; computer software engineering

Enrollment: 190 students

Institution Contact: Mr. Rick Skinner, Executive Director *Phone:* 713-219-2013 *Fax:* 713-219-2088 *E-mail:* rskinner@westwood.edu

Admission Contact: Mr. David Phillips, Regional Director of Admissions *Phone:* 303-691-5726 *Fax:* 303-691-5701 *E-mail:* dphillips@westwood.edu

See full description on page 683.

Utah

Certified Careers Institute

775 South 2000 East
Clearfield, UT 84015
Web: http://www.cciutah.edu

Accreditation: Accrediting Commission of Career Schools and Colleges of Technology

Programs Offered: administrative assistant and secretarial science; medical/clinical assistant; medical insurance coding; medical insurance/medical billing; medical office computer specialist

Institution Contact: Mr. Matthew W. Maxwell, Director *Phone:* 801-774-9900 *Fax:* 801-774-0111 *E-mail:* mmaxwell@cciutah.edu

Admission Contact: Blake Gardner, Admissions Representative *Phone:* 801-774-9900 *Fax:* 801-774-0111 *E-mail:* bgardner@cciutah.edu

Certified Careers Institute

1385 West 2200 South, Suite 100
Salt Lake City, UT 84119
Web: http://www.cciutah.edu

Accreditation: Accrediting Commission of Career Schools and Colleges of Technology

Programs Offered: medical/clinical assistant; medical office management

Enrollment: 60 students

Institution Contact: Mr. Matt Maxwell, School Director *Phone:* 801-973-7008 *Fax:* 801-973-6070 *E-mail:* mmaxwell@cciutah.edu

 indicates that the school is a participating institution in the *Imagine America* Scholarship Program.

Eagle Gate College

5588 South Green Street
Murray, UT 84123
Web: http://www.eaglegatecollege.com

Accreditation: Accrediting Council for Independent Colleges and Schools

Programs Offered: accounting; business administration and management; computer programming; computer systems networking and telecommunications; dental assisting; digital communication and media/multimedia; medical/clinical assistant; office management

Institution Contact: *Phone:* 801-268-9271

ITT Technical Institute Ⓐ

920 West Levoy Drive
Murray, UT 84123-2500
Web: http://www.itt-tech.edu

Accreditation: Accrediting Council for Independent Colleges and Schools

Programs Offered: accounting and business/management; animation, interactive technology, video graphics and special effects; business administration and management; CAD/CADD drafting/design technology; communications technology; computer and information systems security; computer engineering technology; computer software and media applications; computer software engineering; computer systems networking and telecommunications; criminal justice/police science; digital communication and media/multimedia; electrical, electronic and communications engineering technology; technology management; web page, digital/multimedia and information resources design

Enrollment: 639 students

Institution Contact: Dr. P. Michael Linzmaier, Director *Phone:* 801-263-3313

Admission Contact: Mr. Gary Wood, Director of Recruitment *Phone:* 801-263-3313

See full description on page 684.

Mountain West College Ⓐ

3280 West 3500 South
West Valley City, UT 84119
Web: http://www.cci.edu

Accreditation: Accrediting Council for Independent Colleges and Schools

Programs Offered: accounting; business administration and management; computer programming; computer systems networking and telecommunications; criminal justice/law enforcement administra-

tion; legal assistant/paralegal; medical/clinical assistant; medical insurance coding; medical insurance/medical billing; office management; surgical technology; tourism and travel services management

Enrollment: 797 students

Institution Contact: Mr. Larry Banks, PhD, President *Phone:* 801-840-4800 *Fax:* 801-969-0828 *E-mail:* lbanks@cci.edu

Admission Contact: Mr. Jason Lynn, Director of Admissions *Phone:* 801-840-4800 *Fax:* 801-969-0828 *E-mail:* jlynn@cci.edu

See full description on page 685.

Northface University

2755 East Cottonwood Parkway, 6th Floor
Salt Lake City, UT 84121
Web: http://www.northface.edu

Accreditation: Accrediting Council for Independent Colleges and Schools

Programs Offered: business administration and management; computer and information sciences related; computer software engineering

Institution Contact: Mr. Jamie Wyse, Senior Vice President, Strategic Development *Phone:* 801-438-1107 *Fax:* 801-438-1111 *E-mail:* jamie.wyse@northface.edu

Admission Contact: Mr. Jeff Marcus, Vice President, Enrollment *Phone:* 801-438-1114 *Fax:* 801-438-1111 *E-mail:* jeff.marcus@northface.edu

Provo College

1450 West 820 North
Provo, UT 84601
Web: http://www.provocollege.edu

Accreditation: Accrediting Commission of Career Schools and Colleges of Technology

Programs Offered: accounting; business administration and management; commercial and advertising art; computer programming related; computer systems networking and telecommunications; dental assisting; English as a second language; executive assistant/executive secretary; hotel/motel administration; massage therapy; medical/clinical assistant; physical therapist assistant

Enrollment: 550 students

Institution Contact: Mr. Gordon C. Peters, College Director *Phone:* 801-375-1861 *Fax:* 801-375-9728 *E-mail:* gordonp@provocollege.edu

Admission Contact: Mr. Kim T. Miller, Director of Admissions *Phone:* 801-375-1861 *Fax:* 801-375-9728 *E-mail:* kimm@provocollege.edu

Ⓐ indicates that the school is a participating institution in the *Imagine America* Scholarship Program.

Stevens-Henager College

755 South Main Street
Logan, UT 84321
Web: http://www.stevenshenager.edu

Accreditation: Accrediting Commission of Career Schools and Colleges of Technology

Programs Offered: accounting; administrative assistant and secretarial science; business administration and management; business automation/technology/data entry; clinical/medical laboratory assistant; computer and information sciences related; computer graphics; computer installation and repair technology; computer programming; computer programming related; computer programming (specific applications); computer programming (vendor/product certification); computer systems networking and telecommunications; computer technology/computer systems technology; data entry/microcomputer applications; desktop publishing and digital imaging design; emergency medical technology (EMT paramedic); health/health care administration; health information/medical records administration; health information/medical records technology; marketing/marketing management; medical administrative assistant and medical secretary; medical/clinical assistant; medical office management; medical radiologic technology; medical transcription; nursing assistant/aide and patient care assistant; pharmacy technician; receptionist; respiratory care therapy; surgical technology; system administration; system, networking, and LAN/WAN management; telecommunications; web page, digital/multimedia and information resources design; word processing

Institution Contact: Ms. Vicky Dewsnup, President *Phone:* 435-713-4777 *Fax:* 435-713-4799 *E-mail:* vdewsnup@stevenshenager.edu

Admission Contact: Katie Curtis, Director of Admissions *Phone:* 435-713-4777 *Fax:* 437-755-7611 *E-mail:* schclogan@yahoo.com

Stevens-Henager College

PO Box 9428
Ogden, UT 84409
Web: http://www.stevenshenager.edu

Accreditation: Accrediting Commission of Career Schools and Colleges of Technology

Programs Offered: accounting; advertising; business administration and management; cardiovascular technology; commercial and advertising art; computer and information sciences related; computer graphics; computer programming; e-commerce; emergency medical technology (EMT paramedic); health/health care administration; information science/studies; insurance; medical/clinical assistant; medical insur-

ance coding; medical insurance/medical billing; medical transcription; pharmacy technician; surgical technology; system, networking, and LAN/WAN management

Institution Contact: Ms. Vicky Dewsnup, President *Phone:* 801-394-7791 *E-mail:* vdewsnup@yahoo.com

Admission Contact: Ms. Wynn Hurtado, Director of Admissions *Phone:* 801-394-7791 *E-mail:* whurtado@stevenshenager.edu

Stevens-Henager College—Provo

25 East 1700 South
Provo, UT 84606

Accreditation: Accrediting Commission of Career Schools and Colleges of Technology

Programs Offered: accounting; business administration and management; clinical/medical laboratory assistant; clinical/medical laboratory technology; computer and information sciences related; computer graphics; computer hardware engineering; computer/information technology administration and management; computer/information technology services administration related; computer programming; computer programming (specific applications); computer systems networking and telecommunications; finance; gene therapy; health/health care administration; massage therapy; medical/clinical assistant; medical insurance coding; medical insurance/medical billing; medical radiologic technology; medical transcription; physical therapist assistant; physician assistant; real estate; word processing

Institution Contact: Ms. Carol Gastiger, President *Phone:* 801-375-5455 ext. 2000 *Fax:* 801-374-9454 *E-mail:* stevenprovo@aol.com

Admission Contact: Mr. Kenneth Plant *Phone:* 801-375-5455 ext. 2002 *Fax:* 801-375-9836

Stevens-Henager College—Salt Lake City

635 West 5300 South
Salt Lake City, UT 84123
Web: http://www.stevenshenager.edu

Accreditation: Accrediting Commission of Career Schools and Colleges of Technology; Accrediting Council for Independent Colleges and Schools

Programs Offered: accounting; administrative assistant and secretarial science; business administration and management; business automation/technology/data entry; clinical/medical laboratory assistant; computer and information sciences related; computer graphics; computer installation and repair technology; computer programming; computer programming related; computer programming (specific applications); computer programming (vendor/product

ⓐ indicates that the school is a participating institution in the *Imagine America* Scholarship Program.

Stevens-Henager College–Salt Lake City (*continued*)

certification); computer systems networking and telecommunications; computer technology/computer systems technology; data entry/microcomputer applications; desktop publishing and digital imaging design; emergency medical technology (EMT paramedic); health/health care administration; health information/medical records administration; health information/medical records technology; marketing/marketing management; medical administrative assistant and medical secretary; medical/clinical assistant; medical office management; medical radiologic technology; medical transcription; nursing assistant/aide and patient care assistant; pharmacy technician; receptionist; respiratory care therapy; surgical technology; system administration; system, networking, and LAN/WAN management; telecommunications; web page, digital/multimedia and information resources design; word processing

Institution Contact: Mr. Ron Moss, President *Phone:* 801-262-7600 *Fax:* 801-293-9024 *E-mail:* shcslc@aol.com

Admission Contact: Mr. Scott Sainsbury, Director of Admissions *Phone:* 801-262-7600 *Fax:* 801-293-9024 *E-mail:* ssainsbury@stevenshenager.edu

Utah Career College

1902 West 7800 South
West Jordan, UT 84088

Accreditation: Accrediting Commission of Career Schools and Colleges of Technology

Programs Offered: athletic training; business administration and management; commercial and advertising art; massage therapy; medical/clinical assistant; veterinary technology

Enrollment: 501 students

Institution Contact: Mr. Nate Herrmann, School Director *Phone:* 801-304-4224 *Fax:* 801-304-4229 *E-mail:* nherrmann@utahcollege.edu

Admission Contact: Mrs. Denice Dunker, Director of Admissions *Phone:* 801-304-4224 *Fax:* 801-304-4229 *E-mail:* ddunker@utahcollege.edu

Vermont

Distance Learning International, Inc.

80 North Main Street, PO Box 846
Saint Albans, VT 05478-0846
Web: http://www.dlilearn.com

Programs Offered: accounting; accounting technology and bookkeeping; business administration and management; computer programming; dental assisting; English as a second language; gunsmithing; health information/medical records administration; journalism; legal administrative assistant/secretary; legal assistant/paralegal; medical administrative assistant and medical secretary; medical/clinical assistant; medical office management; pharmacy technician; receptionist; word processing

Enrollment: 875 students

Institution Contact: Mr. Juergen Fitzgerald Williamson-Persh, President *Phone:* 802-524-2223 *Fax:* 802-524-2053 *E-mail:* jfwp@dlilearn.com

Admission Contact: Ms. Janie Gregory, Director of Admission *Phone:* 802-524-2223 *Fax:* 802-524-2053 *E-mail:* janieg@dlilearn.com

New England Culinary Institute Ⓐ

250 Main Street
Montpelier, VT 05602-9720
Web: http://www.neci.edu

Accreditation: Accrediting Commission of Career Schools and Colleges of Technology

Programs Offered: baking and pastry arts; culinary arts; restaurant, culinary, and catering management

Enrollment: 264 students

Institution Contact: Ms. Dawn Hayward, Director of Admissions *Phone:* 802-223-6324 *Fax:* 802-225-3280 *E-mail:* dawnh@neci.edu

See full description on page 686.

New England Culinary Institute at Essex

48 1/2 Park Street
Essex Junction, VT 05452
Web: http://www.neci.edu

Accreditation: Accrediting Commission of Career Schools and Colleges of Technology

Programs Offered: baking and pastry arts; culinary arts; restaurant, culinary, and catering management

Ⓐ indicates that the school is a participating institution in the *Imagine America* Scholarship Program.

Enrollment: 261 students

Institution Contact: Mr. Francis Voigt, Chief Executive Officer *Phone:* 802-223-6324 *Fax:* 802-225-3280 *E-mail:* emilys@neci.edu

Admission Contact: Ms. Dawn Hayward, Director of Admissions *Phone:* 877-223-6324 ext. 3211 *Fax:* 802-225-3280 *E-mail:* dawnh@neci.edu

Virginia

ACT College

6118 Franconia Road, Suite 200
Alexandria, VA 22310
Web: http://www.actcollege.edu

Accreditation: Accrediting Bureau of Health Education Schools

Programs Offered: dental assisting; massage therapy; medical/clinical assistant

Enrollment: 160 students

Institution Contact: Mr. Jeffrey S. Moore, President/CEO *Phone:* 703-527-6660 *Fax:* 703-528-4021 *E-mail:* jeffmoore@actcollege.edu

Admission Contact: Mr. Orlando Moore, Jr., Director of Admissions *Phone:* 703-719-0700 *Fax:* 703-719-9700 *E-mail:* omoore@actcollege.edu

ACT College

1100 Wilson Boulevard, Suite M780
Arlington, VA 22209-2297
Web: http://www.actcollege.edu

Accreditation: Accrediting Bureau of Health Education Schools

Programs Offered: dental assisting; health information/medical records administration; medical/clinical assistant; pharmacy technician

Enrollment: 360 students

Institution Contact: Mr. Jeffrey S. Moore, President/CEO *Phone:* 703-527-6660 *Fax:* 703-528-4021 *E-mail:* jeffmoore@actcollege.edu

Admission Contact: Mr. Orlando Moore, Jr., Director of Admissions *Phone:* 703-527-6660 *Fax:* 703-527-6688 *E-mail:* omoore@actcollege.edu

ACT College

8870 Rixlew Lane, Suite 201
Manassas, VA 20109-3795
Web: http://www.actcollege.edu

Accreditation: Accrediting Bureau of Health Education Schools

Programs Offered: medical/clinical assistant; medical radiologic technology

Enrollment: 78 students

Institution Contact: Mr. Jeffrey S. Moore, President/CEO *Phone:* 703-527-6660 *Fax:* 703-528-4021 *E-mail:* jeffmoore@actcollege.edu

Admission Contact: Mr. Orlando Moore, Jr., Director of Admissions *Phone:* 703-365-9286 *Fax:* 703-365-9288 *E-mail:* omoore@actcollege.edu

Advanced Technology Institute

5700 Southern Boulevard
Virginia Beach, VA 23462
Web: http://www.auto.edu

Accreditation: Accrediting Commission of Career Schools and Colleges of Technology

Programs Offered: automobile/automotive mechanics technology; automotive engineering technology; diesel mechanics technology; heating, air conditioning and refrigeration technology; heating, air conditioning, ventilation and refrigeration maintenance technology; heavy equipment maintenance technology; truck and bus driver/commercial vehicle operation

Enrollment: 500 students

Institution Contact: Mr. William M. Tomlin, Director *Phone:* 757-490-1241 *Fax:* 757-499-5929 *E-mail:* btomlin@auto.edu

Admission Contact: Mr. Michael S. Levy, Director of Admissions *Phone:* 757-490-1241 *Fax:* 757-499-5929 *E-mail:* mlevy@auto.edu

The Art Institute of Washington

1820 North Fort Myer Drive
Arlington, VA 22209
Web: http://www.aiw.aii.edu

Accreditation: Southern Association of Colleges and Schools

Programs Offered: advertising; animation, interactive technology, video graphics and special effects; art; commercial and advertising art; computer graphics; culinary arts; interior design; web/multimedia management and webmaster; web page, digital/multimedia and information resources design

Enrollment: 1,045 students

Ⓐ indicates that the school is a participating institution in the Imagine America Scholarship Program.

The Art Institute of Washington (*continued*)

Institution Contact: Lawrence E. McHugh, Director of Admissions *Phone:* 703-247-6850 *Fax:* 703-358-9759 *E-mail:* lmchugh@aii.edu

Admission Contact: Mr. Lawrence E. McHugh, Director of Admissions *Phone:* 703-247-6850 *Fax:* 703-358-9759 *E-mail:* lmchugh@aii.edu

The Chubb Institute

1515 North Courthouse Road, Sixth Floor
Arlington, VA 22201
Web: http://www.chubbinstitute.com

Accreditation: Accrediting Council for Continuing Education and Training

Programs Offered: administrative assistant and secretarial science; business administration and management; computer and information sciences related; computer and information systems security; computer engineering related; computer engineering technology; computer graphics; computer hardware engineering; computer/information technology administration and management; computer/information technology services administration related; computer installation and repair technology; computer programming; computer programming related; computer programming (specific applications); computer programming (vendor/product certification); computer software and media applications; computer software and media applications related; computer software engineering; computer systems analysis; computer systems networking and telecommunications; computer/technical support; computer technology/computer systems technology; data entry/microcomputer applications; data entry/microcomputer applications related; data processing and data processing technology; information science/studies; information technology; system administration; system, networking, and LAN/WAN management; web page, digital/multimedia and information resources design

Enrollment: 125 students

Institution Contact: Mr. Richard G. Rynders, Executive Director *Phone:* 703-908-8300 *Fax:* 703-908-8301 *E-mail:* rrynders@chubbinstitute.com

Admission Contact: Ms. Tina Turk, Director of Admissions *Phone:* 703-908-8300 *Fax:* 703-908-8301 *E-mail:* tturk@chubbinstitute.com

ECPI College of Technology

21010 Dulles Town Circle, #200
Dulles, VA 20166
Web: http://www.ecpi.edu

Accreditation: Southern Association of Colleges and Schools

Programs Offered: administrative assistant and secretarial science; biomedical technology; business automation/technology/data entry; computer/information technology administration and management; computer installation and repair technology; computer programming; computer programming (specific applications); computer systems networking and telecommunications; computer technology/computer systems technology; data processing and data processing technology; information science/studies; office occupations and clerical services; system administration; system, networking, and LAN/WAN management; telecommunications; telecommunications technology; web page, digital/multimedia and information resources design

Institution Contact: Mrs. Mary Barefoot, Executive Assistant *Phone:* 757-671-7171 ext. 205 *Fax:* 757-671-8661 *E-mail:* mbarefoot@ecpi.edu

Admission Contact: M. Pierce *Phone:* 703-421-9191 *Fax:* 703-671-2144 *E-mail:* mpierce@ecpi.edu

ECPI College of Technology Ⓐ

10021 Balls Ford Road, #100
Manassas, VA 20109
Web: http://www.ecpi.edu

Accreditation: Southern Association of Colleges and Schools

Programs Offered: administrative assistant and secretarial science; biomedical technology; business administration and management; business machine repair; clinical/medical laboratory assistant; computer and information sciences related; computer and information systems security; computer installation and repair technology; computer programming; computer programming (specific applications); computer systems analysis; computer technology/computer systems technology; criminal justice/law enforcement administration; data processing and data processing technology; health information/medical records administration; information science/studies; information technology; management information systems; medical administrative assistant and medical secretary; medical/clinical assistant; medical office computer specialist; nursing (licensed practical/vocational nurse training); receptionist; web/multimedia management and webmaster; word processing

Enrollment: 428 students

Institution Contact: Mrs. Judith Hughes, Provost *Phone:* 703-330-5300 *Fax:* 703-369-0530 *E-mail:* jhughes@ecpi.edu

See full description on page 688.

Ⓐ indicates that the school is a participating institution in the *Imagine America* Scholarship Program.

ECPI College of Technology (A)

1001 Omni Boulevard, #100
Newport News, VA 23606
Web: http://www.ecpi.edu

Accreditation: Southern Association of Colleges and Schools

Programs Offered: accounting; administrative assistant and secretarial science; business administration and management; business automation/technology/data entry; communications technology; computer and information systems security; computer engineering technology; computer/information technology administration and management; computer installation and repair technology; computer programming; computer systems networking and telecommunications; computer/technical support; computer technology/computer systems technology; criminal justice/law enforcement administration; data processing and data processing technology; information science/studies; information technology; medical administrative assistant and medical secretary; medical insurance coding; medical insurance/medical billing; medical office computer specialist; medical reception; medical transcription; security and loss prevention; system, networking, and LAN/WAN management; telecommunications; telecommunications technology; web/multimedia management and webmaster; web page, digital/multimedia and information resources design

Enrollment: 475 students

Institution Contact: Mr. John Olson, Provost *Phone:* 757-838-9191 *Fax:* 757-827-5351 *E-mail:* jolson@ecpi.edu

Admission Contact: Ms. Cheryl Lokey, Director of Recruitment *Phone:* 757-838-9191 *Fax:* 757-827-5351 *E-mail:* clokey@ecpi.edu

See full description on page 687.

ECPI College of Technology (A)

5555 Greenwich Road, #300
Virginia Beach, VA 23462-6542
Web: http://www.ecpi.edu

Accreditation: Southern Association of Colleges and Schools

Programs Offered: accounting; administrative assistant and secretarial science; biomedical technology; business automation/technology/data entry; computer and information systems security; computer engineering technology; computer/information technology administration and management; computer/information technology services administration related; computer installation and repair technology; computer programming; computer programming related; computer programming (specific applications); computer systems networking and telecommu-

nications; computer/technical support; computer technology/computer systems technology; criminal justice/law enforcement administration; data processing and data processing technology; information science/studies; information technology; office occupations and clerical services; system administration; system, networking, and LAN/WAN management; telecommunications; telecommunications technology; web page, digital/multimedia and information resources design

Enrollment: 980 students

Institution Contact: Mr. Mark Dreyfus, President *Phone:* 757-671-7171 ext. 218 *Fax:* 757-671-8661 *E-mail:* president@ecpi.edu

Admission Contact: Ms. Karie Edwards, High School Admissions *Phone:* 804-330-5533 *Fax:* 804-330-5577 *E-mail:* kedwards@ecpitech.edu

See full description on page 689.

ECPI Technical College (A)

4305 Cox Road
Glen Allen, VA 23060
Web: http://www.ecpitech.edu

Accreditation: Accrediting Commission of Career Schools and Colleges of Technology

Programs Offered: administrative assistant and secretarial science; business automation/technology/data entry; computer and information systems security; computer engineering technology; computer/information technology administration and management; computer installation and repair technology; computer programming; computer programming (specific applications); computer/technical support; computer technology/computer systems technology; data processing and data processing technology; information science/studies; information technology; management information systems; office occupations and clerical services; system administration; system, networking, and LAN/WAN management; telecommunications; web page, digital/multimedia and information resources design

Enrollment: 327 students

Institution Contact: Mr. Jacob Pope, Director *Phone:* 804-934-0100 *Fax:* 804-934-0054 *E-mail:* jpope@ecpitech.edu

Admission Contact: Ms. Karie Edwards, Director of Admissions *Phone:* 804-934-0100 *Fax:* 804-934-0054 *E-mail:* kedwards@ecpitech.edu

See full description on page 690.

(A) indicates that the school is a participating institution in the *Imagine America* Scholarship Program.

ECPI Technical College ⓐ

800 Moorefield Park Drive
Richmond, VA 23236
Web: http://www.ecpitech.edu

Accreditation: Accrediting Commission of Career Schools and Colleges of Technology

Programs Offered: administrative assistant and secretarial science; business automation/technology/data entry; computer engineering technology; computer/information technology administration and management; computer installation and repair technology; computer programming; computer programming (specific applications); computer systems networking and telecommunications; computer/technical support; computer technology/computer systems technology; criminal justice/law enforcement administration; data processing and data processing technology; information science/studies; medical administrative assistant and medical secretary; medical insurance coding; medical insurance/medical billing; medical office computer specialist; medical transcription; office occupations and clerical services; system administration; system, networking, and LAN/WAN management; telecommunications; telecommunications technology; web page, digital/multimedia and information resources design

Enrollment: 420 students

Institution Contact: Ms. Ada Gerard, Director *Phone:* 804-330-5533 *Fax:* 804-330-5577 *E-mail:* agerard@ecpitech.edu

Admission Contact: Ms. Kari Edwards, Admission Coordinator *Phone:* 804-330-5533 *Fax:* 804-330-5577 *E-mail:* kedward@ecpitech.edu

See full description on page 691.

ECPI Technical College ⓐ

5234 Airport Road
Roanoke, VA 24012
Web: http://www.ecpitech.edu

Accreditation: Accrediting Commission of Career Schools and Colleges of Technology

Programs Offered: administrative assistant and secretarial science; business administration and management; clinical laboratory science/medical technology; computer engineering technology; computer/information technology administration and management; computer installation and repair technology; computer systems networking and telecommunications; computer/technical support; computer technology/computer systems technology; information science/studies; medical/clinical assistant; nursing (licensed practical/vocational nurse training); office occupations and clerical services; telecommunications; telecommunications technology; web page, digital/multimedia and information resources design

Enrollment: 277 students

Institution Contact: Mr. Elmer Haas, Director *Phone:* 540-563-8080 ext. 205 *Fax:* 540-362-5400 *E-mail:* ehaas@ecpitech.edu

Admission Contact: Mr. Brad Kesner, Director of Admissions *Phone:* 540-563-8080 *Fax:* 540-362-5400 *E-mail:* bkesner@ecpitech.edu

See full description on page 692.

Gibbs School

1980 Gallows Road
Vienna, VA 22182
Web: http://www.gibbsva.edu

Accreditation: Accrediting Council for Independent Colleges and Schools

Programs Offered: business administration and management; computer programming; computer systems networking and telecommunications; criminal justice/law enforcement administration; medical/clinical assistant; visual and performing arts

Institution Contact: Mr. M. Lauck Walton, President *Phone:* 703-584-3163 *Fax:* 703-852-3917 *E-mail:* lwalton@gibbsva.edu

Admission Contact: Ms. Susan Riggs, Director of Admissions *Phone:* 703-584-3151 *Fax:* 703-559-0953 *E-mail:* sgriggs@gibbsva.edu

ITT Technical Institute

14420 Albemarle Point Place, Suite 100
Chantilly, VA 20151
Web: http://www.itt-tech.edu

Accreditation: Accrediting Council for Independent Colleges and Schools

Programs Offered: accounting and business/management; business administration and management; CAD/CADD drafting/design technology; communications technology; computer and information systems security; computer engineering technology; computer software and media applications; computer systems networking and telecommunications; criminal justice/police science; digital communication and media/multimedia; electrical, electronic and communications engineering technology; technology management; web page, digital/multimedia and information resources design

Enrollment: 251 students

Institution Contact: Ms. Peggy T. Payne, Director *Phone:* 703-263-2541

ⓐ indicates that the school is a participating institution in the *Imagine America* Scholarship Program.

Admission Contact: Mr. Vincent Terreri, Director of Recruitment *Phone:* 703-263-2541

ITT Technical Institute

863 Glenrock Road, Suite 100
Norfolk, VA 23502-3701
Web: http://www.itt-tech.edu

Accreditation: Accrediting Council for Independent Colleges and Schools

Programs Offered: accounting and business/management; business administration and management; CAD/CADD drafting/design technology; communications technology; computer and information systems security; computer engineering technology; computer software and media applications; computer software engineering; computer systems networking and telecommunications; criminal justice/police science; digital communication and media/multimedia; electrical, electronic and communications engineering technology; industrial technology; technology management; web page, digital/multimedia and information resources design

Enrollment: 559 students

Institution Contact: Mr. Calvin Lawrence, Director *Phone:* 757-466-1260

Admission Contact: Mr. Jack Keesee, Director of Recruitment *Phone:* 757-466-1260

ITT Technical Institute Ⓐ

300 Gateway Centre Parkway
Richmond, VA 23235
Web: http://www.itt-tech.edu

Accreditation: Accrediting Commission of Career Schools and Colleges of Technology; Accrediting Council for Independent Colleges and Schools

Programs Offered: accounting and business/management; animation, interactive technology, video graphics and special effects; business administration and management; CAD/CADD drafting/design technology; communications technology; computer and information systems security; computer engineering technology; computer software and media applications; computer software engineering; computer systems networking and telecommunications; criminal justice/police science; digital communication and media/multimedia; electrical, electronic and communications engineering technology; technology management; web page, digital/multimedia and information resources design

Enrollment: 350 students

Institution Contact: Mr. Doug Howard, Director *Phone:* 804-330-4992

Admission Contact: Ms. Elaine Bartoli, Director of Recruitment *Phone:* 804-330-4992

See full description on page 693.

ITT Technical Institute Ⓐ

7300 Boston Boulevard
Springfield, VA 22153
Web: http://www.itt-tech.edu

Accreditation: Accrediting Council for Independent Colleges and Schools

Programs Offered: accounting and business/management; business administration and management; CAD/CADD drafting/design technology; communications technology; computer and information systems security; computer engineering technology; computer software and media applications; computer systems networking and telecommunications; criminal justice/police science; digital communication and media/multimedia; electrical, electronic and communications engineering technology; technology management; web page, digital/multimedia and information resources design

Enrollment: 562 students

Institution Contact: Mr. Paul M. Ochoa, Director of Recruitment *Phone:* 703-440-9535

See full description on page 694.

Kee Business College Ⓐ

803 Diligence Drive
Newport News, VA 23606
Web: http://www.cci.edu

Accreditation: Accrediting Council for Independent Colleges and Schools

Programs Offered: accounting; allied health and medical assisting services related; computer/information technology services administration related; computer software and media applications; massage therapy; medical administrative assistant and medical secretary; medical/clinical assistant; medical insurance coding; medical insurance/medical billing; security and loss prevention

Enrollment: 340 students

Institution Contact: Mrs. Margaret Ortiz, President *Phone:* 757-873-1111 *Fax:* 757-873-0728 *E-mail:* mortiz@cci.edu

Admission Contact: Mr. Larry Veeneman, Jr., Director of Admissions *Phone:* 757-873-1111 *Fax:* 757-873-0728 *E-mail:* lveenema@cci.edu

See full description on page 696.

Ⓐ indicates that the school is a participating institution in the *Imagine America* Scholarship Program.

Kee Business College–Chesapeake Ⓐ

825 Greenbrier Circle, Suite 100
Chesapeake, VA 23320-2637
Web: http://kee-business-college.com/

Accreditation: Accrediting Council for Independent Colleges and Schools

Programs Offered: computer/information technology administration and management; dental assisting; massage therapy; medical administrative assistant and medical secretary; medical/clinical assistant; medical insurance coding; medical insurance/medical billing; safety/security technology

Enrollment: 524 students

Institution Contact: Ms. Lisa S. Scott, President *Phone:* 757-361-3900 *Fax:* 757-361-3917 *E-mail:* lscott@cci.edu

Admission Contact: Mr. Ed Flores, Director of Admission *Phone:* 757-361-3900 *Fax:* 757-361-3917 *E-mail:* eflores@cci.edu

See full description on page 695.

Medical Careers Institute Ⓐ

1001 Omni Boulevard, #200
Newport News, VA 23606-4215
Web: http://www.medical.edu

Accreditation: Council on Occupational Education

Programs Offered: dental assisting; health and medical administrative services related; massage therapy; medical administrative assistant and medical secretary; medical/clinical assistant; medical office computer specialist; nursing (licensed practical/vocational nurse training); nursing (registered nurse training)

Enrollment: 430 students

Institution Contact: Mrs. Laura Egatz, Director *Phone:* 757-873-2423 *Fax:* 757-873-2472 *E-mail:* legatz@medical.edu

Admission Contact: Ms. Laura Egatz, Director *Phone:* 757-873-2423 *Fax:* 757-873-2472 *E-mail:* legatz@medical.edu

See full description on page 697.

Medical Careers Institute Ⓐ

800 Moorefield Park Drive, #302
Richmond, VA 23236
Web: http://www.medical.edu

Accreditation: Council on Occupational Education

Programs Offered: health information/medical records administration; health information/medical records technology; massage therapy; medical/clinical assistant; medical insurance coding; medical insurance/medical billing; medical office computer

specialist; medical transcription; nursing (licensed practical/vocational nurse training)

Enrollment: 320 students

Institution Contact: Mr. Jeffrey T. Muroski, Campus Director *Phone:* 804-521-0400 *Fax:* 804-521-0406 *E-mail:* jmuroskimayle@medical.edu

Admission Contact: Mr. David K. Mayle, Director of Admissions *Phone:* 804-521-0400 *Fax:* 804-521-0406 *E-mail:* dmayle@medical.edu

See full description on page 698.

Medical Careers Institute Ⓐ

5501 Greenwich Road, #100
Virginia Beach, VA 23462
Web: http://www.medical.edu

Accreditation: Council on Occupational Education

Programs Offered: health information/medical records administration; health information/medical records technology; medical/clinical assistant; medical insurance coding; medical office computer specialist; medical reception; medical transcription; nursing (licensed practical/vocational nurse training); nursing (registered nurse training); physical therapist assistant

Enrollment: 350 students

Institution Contact: Ms. Joyce Wheatley, Director *Phone:* 757-497-8400 *Fax:* 757-497-8493 *E-mail:* jwheatley@medical.edu

See full description on page 699.

Miller-Motte Technical College

1011 Creekside Lane
Lynchburg, VA 24502
Web: http://www.miller-motte.com

Accreditation: Accrediting Council for Independent Colleges and Schools

Programs Offered: administrative assistant and secretarial science; business administration and management; criminal justice/law enforcement administration; massage therapy; medical administrative assistant and medical secretary; medical/clinical assistant; pharmacy technician; phlebotomy

Enrollment: 200 students

Institution Contact: Mr. G. David Tipps, Campus Director *Phone:* 434-239-5222 *Fax:* 434-239-1069 *E-mail:* dtipps@miller-motte.com

National College of Business & Technology Ⓐ

100 Logan Street
Bluefield, VA 24605
Web: http://www.ncbt.edu

Accreditation: Accrediting Council for Independent Colleges and Schools

Ⓐ indicates that the school is a participating institution in the *Imagine America* Scholarship Program.

Programs Offered: accounting; administrative assistant and secretarial science; business administration and management; computer software and media applications; medical/clinical assistant

Institution Contact: Admissions Department *Phone:* 276-326-3621 *Fax:* 276-322-5731

See full description on page 700.

National College of Business & Technology Ⓐ

300A Piedmont Avenue
Bristol, VA 24201
Web: http://www.ncbt.edu

Accreditation: Accrediting Council for Independent Colleges and Schools

Programs Offered: accounting; administrative assistant and secretarial science; business administration and management; computer/information technology services administration related; medical/clinical assistant; medical insurance coding; medical transcription

Institution Contact: Admissions Department *Phone:* 540-669-5333 *Fax:* 540-669-4793

See full description on page 701.

National College of Business & Technology Ⓐ

1819 Emmet Street
Charlottesville, VA 22901
Web: http://www.ncbt.edu

Accreditation: Accrediting Council for Independent Colleges and Schools

Programs Offered: accounting; administrative assistant and secretarial science; business administration and management; computer/information technology services administration related; computer software and media applications; medical/clinical assistant; medical insurance coding; medical transcription; pharmacy technician; tourism and travel services management

Enrollment: 168 students

Institution Contact: Mrs. Tracy Harris, Director of Institutional Reporting *Phone:* 540-986-1800 *Fax:* 540-444-4198 *E-mail:* tharris@educorp.edu

Admission Contact: Ms. Adrienne D. Granitz, Campus Director *Phone:* 434-295-0136 *Fax:* 434-979-8061 *E-mail:* agranitz@ncbt.edu

See full description on page 702.

National College of Business & Technology Ⓐ

734 Main Street
Danville, VA 24541
Web: http://www.ncbt.edu

Accreditation: Accrediting Council for Independent Colleges and Schools

Programs Offered: accounting; administrative assistant and secretarial science; business administration and management; computer/information technology services administration related; computer software and media applications; medical/clinical assistant; medical insurance coding; medical transcription

Institution Contact: Admissions Department *Phone:* 434-793-6822 *Fax:* 434-793-3634

See full description on page 703.

National College of Business & Technology Ⓐ

51 B Burgess Road
Harrisonburg, VA 22801
Web: http://www.ncbt.edu

Accreditation: Accrediting Council for Independent Colleges and Schools

Programs Offered: accounting; administrative assistant and secretarial science; business administration and management; computer and information sciences related; medical/clinical assistant; medical insurance coding; medical office assistant; medical transcription; pharmacy technician

Enrollment: 242 students

Institution Contact: Mrs. Tracy Harris, Director of Institutional Reporting *Phone:* 540-986-1800 *Fax:* 540-444-4198 *E-mail:* tharris@educorp.edu

Admission Contact: Kanika Shipe *Phone:* 540-432-0943

See full description on page 704.

National College of Business & Technology Ⓐ

104 Candlewood Court
Lynchburg, VA 24502
Web: http://www.ncbt.edu

Accreditation: Accrediting Council for Independent Colleges and Schools

Programs Offered: accounting; administrative assistant and secretarial science; business administration and management; computer and information

Ⓐ indicates that the school is a participating institution in the *Imagine America* Scholarship Program.

National College of Business & Technology *(continued)*

sciences related; medical/clinical assistant; medical insurance coding; medical transcription; pharmacy technician

Institution Contact: Admissions Department *Phone:* 434-239-3500 *Fax:* 434-239-3948

See full description on page 705.

National College of Business & Technology Ⓐ

10 Church Street
Martinsville, VA 24114
Web: http://www.ncbt.edu

Accreditation: Accrediting Council for Independent Colleges and Schools

Programs Offered: accounting; administrative assistant and secretarial science; business administration and management; computer and information sciences related; medical/clinical assistant; medical insurance coding; medical transcription

Institution Contact: Admissions Department *Phone:* 276-632-5621 *Fax:* 276-632-7915

See full description on page 706.

National College of Business & Technology Ⓐ

1813 East Main Street
Salem, VA 24153
Web: http://www.ncbt.edu

Accreditation: Accrediting Council for Independent Colleges and Schools

Programs Offered: accounting; business administration and management; computer engineering technology; computer software and media applications; hospitality administration; legal assistant/paralegal; medical/clinical assistant; office management; tourism and travel services management

Institution Contact: Admissions Department *Phone:* 540-986-1800 *Fax:* 540-986-1344

See full description on page 707.

Parks College Ⓐ

801 North Quincy Street, Suite 500
Arlington, VA 22203
Web: http://www.parks-college.com

Accreditation: Accrediting Council for Independent Colleges and Schools

Programs Offered: business administration and management; criminal justice/law enforcement administration; legal assistant/paralegal; securities services administration

Enrollment: 660 students

Institution Contact: Timothy Vogeley, President *Phone:* 703-248-8887 *Fax:* 703-351-2202 *E-mail:* tvogeley@cci.edu

Admission Contact: Edward Lubin, Director of Admissions *Phone:* 703-248-8887 *Fax:* 703-351-2202 *E-mail:* elubin@cci.edu

See full description on page 708.

Parks College

1430 Spring Hill Road, Suite 200
McLean, VA 22102
Web: http://www.parks-college.com

Accreditation: Accrediting Council for Independent Colleges and Schools

Programs Offered: business administration and management; criminal justice/police science; medical/clinical assistant; safety/security technology

Enrollment: 95 students

Institution Contact: Ms. Maxine H. Stine, Campus President *Phone:* 703-288-3131 *Fax:* 703-288-3757 *E-mail:* mstine@cci.edu

Potomac College

1029 Herndon Parkway
Herndon, VA 20170
Web: http://www.potomac.edu

Accreditation: Accrediting Council for Independent Colleges and Schools; Middle States Association of Colleges and Schools

Programs Offered: business administration and management; e-commerce; information science/studies; information technology

Enrollment: 59 students

Institution Contact: Ms. Florence Tate, President *Phone:* 202-686-0876 *Fax:* 202-686-0818 *E-mail:* ftate@potomac.edu

Admission Contact: Ms. Patricia Rodriguez, Director of Admissions *Phone:* 703-709-5875 *Fax:* 703-709-8972 *E-mail:* prodriguez@potomac.edu

Stratford University Ⓐ

7777 Leesburg Pike
Falls Church, VA 22043
Web: http://www.stratford.edu

Accreditation: Accrediting Council for Independent Colleges and Schools

Ⓐ indicates that the school is a participating institution in the *Imagine America* Scholarship Program.

Programs Offered: accounting; baking and pastry arts; business administration and management; computer and information systems security; computer graphics; computer/information technology administration and management; computer/information technology services administration related; computer programming; computer programming (specific applications); computer software and media applications; computer software engineering; computer systems analysis; computer systems networking and telecommunications; computer technology/computer systems technology; culinary arts; digital communication and media/multimedia; e-commerce; engineering technology; finance; food services technology; hotel/motel administration; information science/studies; information technology; international business/trade/commerce; internet information systems; marketing/marketing management; restaurant, culinary, and catering management; technology management; telecommunications; telecommunications technology; web/multimedia management and webmaster; web page, digital/multimedia and information resources design

Enrollment: 500 students

Institution Contact: Ms. Lavona Suppes, Dean of Undergraduate Studies *Phone:* 703-734-5321 *Fax:* 703-734-5335 *E-mail:* lsuppes@stratford.edu

Admission Contact: Ms. Nicole Kredel, Director of Admissions *Phone:* 703-821-8570 *Fax:* 703-734-5339 *E-mail:* nkredel@stratford.edu

See full description on page 709.

Stratford University Ⓐ

13576 Minnieville Road
Woodbridge, VA 22192
Web: http://www.stratford.edu

Accreditation: Accrediting Council for Independent Colleges and Schools; Council on Occupational Education

Programs Offered: business administration and management; computer and information systems security; computer engineering technology; computer/information technology services administration related; computer installation and repair technology; computer programming; computer systems networking and telecommunications; computer/technical support; web page, digital/multimedia and information resources design

Enrollment: 250 students

Institution Contact: Ms. Lavona Suppes, Dean of Undergraduate Studies *Phone:* 703-734-5321 *Fax:* 703-734-5335 *E-mail:* lsuppes@stratford.edu

Admission Contact: Ted Hart, Director of Admissions *Phone:* 703-821-8570 *E-mail:* admissions@stratford.edu

See full description on page 710.

Strayer University at Alexandria Campus

2730 Eisenhower Avenue
Alexandria, VA 22314
Web: http://www.strayer.edu

Accreditation: Middle States Association of Colleges and Schools

Programs Offered: accounting; business administration and management; communications technology; computer/information technology administration and management; computer programming; computer systems networking and telecommunications; data modeling/warehousing and database administration; economics; general studies; information science/studies; information technology; international business/trade/commerce; marketing/marketing management; purchasing, procurement/acquisitions and contracts management

Institution Contact: Dr. J. Chris Toe, President *Phone:* 202-408-2424 *Fax:* 202-789-0387 *E-mail:* jct@strayer.edu

Admission Contact: Oscar Mamaril, Campus Manager *Phone:* 703-329-9100 *Fax:* 703-329-9602 *E-mail:* alexandria@strayer.edu

Strayer University at Arlington Campus

2121 15th Street North
Arlington, VA 22201
Web: http://www.strayer.edu

Accreditation: Middle States Association of Colleges and Schools

Programs Offered: accounting; business administration and management; communications technology; computer/information technology administration and management; computer programming; computer systems networking and telecommunications; data modeling/warehousing and database administration; economics; general studies; information science/studies; information technology; international business/trade/commerce; marketing/marketing management; purchasing, procurement/acquisitions and contracts management

Institution Contact: Dr. J. Chris Toe, President *Phone:* 202-408-2424 *Fax:* 202-789-0387 *E-mail:* jct@strayer.edu

Admission Contact: Val Harvey, Campus Manager *Phone:* 703-892-5100 *Fax:* 703-769-2677 *E-mail:* arlington@strayer.edu

Strayer University at Chesapeake Campus

700 Independence Parkway, Suite 400
Chesapeake, VA 23320-5186
Web: http://www.strayer.edu

Accreditation: Middle States Association of Colleges and Schools

Ⓐ indicates that the school is a participating institution in the *Imagine America* Scholarship Program.

Strayer University at Chesapeake Campus (*continued*)

Programs Offered: accounting; business administration and management; communications technology; computer/information technology administration and management; computer programming; computer systems networking and telecommunications; data modeling/warehousing and database administration; economics; general studies; information science/studies; information technology; international business/trade/commerce; marketing/marketing management; purchasing, procurement/acquisitions and contracts management

Institution Contact: Dr. J. Chris Toe, University President *Phone:* 202-419-0400 *Fax:* 202-419-1423 *E-mail:* jct@strayer.edu

Admission Contact: Michael Camden, Campus Manager *Phone:* 757-382-9900 *E-mail:* chesapeake@strayer.edu

Strayer University at Chesterfield Campus

2820 Waterford Lake Drive, Suite 100
Midlothian, VA 23112
Web: http://www.strayer.edu

Accreditation: Middle States Association of Colleges and Schools

Programs Offered: accounting; business administration and management; communications technology; computer/information technology administration and management; computer programming; computer systems networking and telecommunications; data modeling/warehousing and database administration; economics; general studies; information science/studies; information technology; international business/trade/commerce; marketing/marketing management; purchasing, procurement/acquisitions and contracts management

Institution Contact: Dr. J. Chris Toe, University President *Phone:* 202-408-2424 *Fax:* 202-789-0387 *E-mail:* jct@strayer.edu

Admission Contact: Campus Manager *Phone:* 804-763-6300 *Fax:* 804-763-6304 *E-mail:* chesterfield@strayer.edu

Strayer University at Fredericksburg Campus

4500 Plank Road, Suite 220
Fredericksburg, VA 22407-0120
Web: http://www.strayer.edu

Accreditation: Middle States Association of Colleges and Schools

Programs Offered: accounting; business administration and management; communications technology; computer/information technology administration and management; computer programming; computer systems networking and telecommunications; data modeling/warehousing and database administration; economics; general studies; information science/studies; information technology; international business/trade/commerce; marketing/marketing management; purchasing, procurement/acquisitions and contracts management

Institution Contact: Dr. J. Chris Toe, University President *Phone:* 202-408-2424 *Fax:* 202-789-0387 *E-mail:* jct@strayer.edu

Admission Contact: Clay Orsborne, Campus Manager *Phone:* 540-785-8800 *Fax:* 540-785-8808 *E-mail:* fredericksburg@strayer.edu

Strayer University at Henrico Campus

11501 Nuckols Road, Suite D
Glen Allen, VA 23059
Web: http://www.strayer.edu

Accreditation: Middle States Association of Colleges and Schools

Programs Offered: accounting; business administration and management; communications technology; computer/information technology administration and management; computer programming; computer systems networking and telecommunications; data modeling/warehousing and database administration; economics; general studies; information science/studies; information technology; international business/trade/commerce; marketing/marketing management; purchasing, procurement/acquisitions and contracts management

Institution Contact: Dr. J. Chris Toe, University President *Phone:* 202-408-2424 *Fax:* 202-789-0387 *E-mail:* jct@strayer.edu

Admission Contact: Chris Stout, Campus Manager *Phone:* 804-527-1000 *E-mail:* henrico@strayer.edu

Strayer University at Loudoun Campus

45150 Russell Branch Parkway, Suite 200
Ashburn, VA 20147
Web: http://www.strayer.edu

Accreditation: Middle States Association of Colleges and Schools

Programs Offered: accounting; business administration and management; communications technology; computer/information technology administration and management; computer programming; computer systems networking and telecommunications; data modeling/warehousing and database administration;

♠ indicates that the school is a participating institution in the *Imagine America* Scholarship Program.

economics; general studies; information science/studies; information technology; international business/trade/commerce; marketing/marketing management; purchasing, procurement/acquisitions and contracts management

Institution Contact: Dr. J. Chris Toe, University President *Phone:* 202-408-2424 *Fax:* 202-789-0387 *E-mail:* jct@strayer.edu

Admission Contact: Campus Manager *Phone:* 703-729-8800 *Fax:* 703-729-8820 *E-mail:* loudoun@strayer.edu

Strayer University at Manassas Campus

9990 Battleview Parkway
Manassas, VA 20109
Web: http://www.strayer.edu

Accreditation: Middle States Association of Colleges and Schools

Programs Offered: accounting; business administration and management; communications technology; computer/information technology administration and management; computer programming; computer systems networking and telecommunications; data modeling/warehousing and database administration; economics; general studies; information science/studies; information technology; international business/trade/commerce; marketing/marketing management; purchasing, procurement/acquisitions and contracts management

Institution Contact: Dr. J. Chris Toe, President *Phone:* 202-408-2424 *Fax:* 202-789-0387 *E-mail:* jct@strayer.edu

Admission Contact: Campus Manager *Phone:* 703-330-8400 *Fax:* 703-330-8135 *E-mail:* manassas@strayer.edu

Strayer University at Newport News Campus

813 Diligence Drive, Suite 100
Newport News, VA 23606
Web: http://www.strayer.edu

Accreditation: Middle States Association of Colleges and Schools

Programs Offered: accounting; business administration and management; communications technology; computer/information technology administration and management; computer programming; computer systems networking and telecommunications; data modeling/warehousing and database administration; economics; general studies; information science/studies; information technology; international business/trade/commerce; marketing/marketing management; purchasing, procurement/acquisitions and contracts management

Institution Contact: Dr. J. Chris Toe, University President *Phone:* 202-408-2424 *Fax:* 202-789-0387 *E-mail:* jct@strayer.edu

Admission Contact: Campus Manager *Phone:* 757-873-3100 *E-mail:* newportnews@strayer.edu

Strayer University at Woodbridge Campus

13385 Minnieville Road
Woodbridge, VA 22192
Web: http://www.strayer.edu

Accreditation: Middle States Association of Colleges and Schools

Programs Offered: accounting; business administration and management; communications technology; computer/information technology administration and management; computer programming; computer systems networking and telecommunications; data modeling/warehousing and database administration; economics; general studies; information science/studies; information technology; international business/trade/commerce; marketing/marketing management; purchasing, procurement/acquisitions and contracts management

Institution Contact: Dr. J. Chris Toe, University President *Phone:* 202-408-2424 *Fax:* 202-789-0387 *E-mail:* jct@strayer.edu

Admission Contact: Campus Manager *Phone:* 703-878-2800 *Fax:* 703-878-2993 *E-mail:* woodbridge@strayer.edu

TESST College of Technology

6315 Bren Mar Drive
Alexandria, VA 22312
Web: http://www.tesst.com

Accreditation: Accrediting Commission of Career Schools and Colleges of Technology

Programs Offered: business automation/technology/data entry; business machine repair; communications systems installation and repair technology; computer engineering technology; computer hardware engineering; computer/information technology administration and management; computer/information technology services administration related; computer installation and repair technology; computer software and media applications; computer systems networking and telecommunications; computer/technical support; computer technology/computer systems technology; data processing and data processing technology; electrical, electronic and communications engineering technology; electrical/electronics equipment installation and repair; information science/studies; informa-

❀ indicates that the school is a participating institution in the Imagine America Scholarship Program.

TESST College of Technology (*continued*)

tion technology; system administration; system, networking, and LAN/WAN management; telecommunications; web/multimedia management and webmaster; web page, digital/multimedia and information resources design

Institution Contact: Mr. Bob Somers, Director *Phone:* 703-548-4800 *Fax:* 703-683-2765 *E-mail:* tesstal@erols.com

Admission Contact: Mr. William Scott, Admissions Director *Phone:* 703-548-4800 *Fax:* 703-683-2765 *E-mail:* alexandriaadmissions@tesst.com

Virginia School of Massage Ⓐ

2008 Morton Drive
Charlottesville, VA 22903
Web: http://steinered.com

Accreditation: Accrediting Commission of Career Schools and Colleges of Technology

Programs Offered: massage therapy

Enrollment: 125 students

Institution Contact: Suzanne Spear, Campus Director *Phone:* 434-293-4031 *Fax:* 434-293-4190 *E-mail:* suzanne@vasom.com

Admission Contact: Admissions Department *Phone:* 434-293-4031 *Fax:* 434-293-4190 *E-mail:* suzanne@vasom.com

See full description on page 711.

Virginia School of Technology

9210 Arboretum Parkway, Suite 190
Richmond, VA 23236
Web: http://www.vstsuccess.com

Accreditation: Accrediting Council for Independent Colleges and Schools

Programs Offered: court reporting; massage therapy; medical insurance/medical billing

Institution Contact: Mrs. Judy Katzen, Campus Director *Phone:* 804-323-1020 *Fax:* 804-560-5319 *E-mail:* judykatzen@vstsuccess.com

Admission Contact: Ms. Kriss Wagnor, Admissions Representative *Phone:* 804-323-1020 *Fax:* 804-560-5319 *E-mail:* kwagnor@vstsuccess.com

Virginia School of Technology

100 Constitution Drive, Suite 101
Virginia Beach, VA 23462
Web: http://www.vstsuccess.com

Accreditation: Accrediting Council for Independent Colleges and Schools

Programs Offered: computer/information technology administration and management; computer software and media applications; court reporting; massage therapy; nursing (licensed practical/vocational nurse training)

Institution Contact: Dr. James Barger, Campus Director *Phone:* 757-499-5447 *Fax:* 757-473-5735 *E-mail:* jbarger@vstsuccess.com

Admission Contact: Mrs. Chastity Jones, Director of Admissions *Phone:* 757-499-5447 *Fax:* 757-473-5735 *E-mail:* cjones@vstsuccess.com

Washington

Apollo College Ⓐ

10102 East Knox, Suite 200
Spokane, WA 99206
Web: http://www.apollocollege.com

Accreditation: Accrediting Bureau of Health Education Schools

Programs Offered: dental assisting; health information/medical records technology; medical administrative assistant and medical secretary; medical/clinical assistant; medical radiologic technology; pharmacy technician

Institution Contact: Mr. Ray Keevy, Campus Director *Phone:* 509-532-8888 *Fax:* 509-433-5983 *E-mail:* rkeevy@apollocollege.com

See full description on page 712.

The Art Institute of Seattle Ⓐ

2323 Elliott Avenue
Seattle, WA 98121
Web: http://www.ais.edu

Accreditation: Northwest Association of Schools and Colleges

Programs Offered: animation, interactive technology, video graphics and special effects; baking and pastry arts; cinematography and film/video production; commercial and advertising art; computer graphics; culinary arts; design and visual communications; desktop publishing and digital imaging design; digital communication and media/multimedia; fashion/apparel design; fashion merchandising; industrial design; interior design; photography; web/multimedia management and webmaster; web page, digital/multimedia and information resources design

Ⓐ indicates that the school is a participating institution in the *Imagine America* Scholarship Program.

Enrollment: 2,500 students

Institution Contact: Ms. Shelly C. DuBois, President *Phone:* 206-239-2314 *Fax:* 206-448-2501 *E-mail:* duboiss@aii.edu

Admission Contact: Ms. Karen Shea, Director of Admissions *Phone:* 206-239-2242 *Fax:* 206-448-2501 *E-mail:* kshea@aii.edu

See full description on page 713.

Ashmead College Ⓐ

3019 Colby Avenue
Everett, WA 98201
Web: http://www.ashmeadcollege.com

Accreditation: Accrediting Council for Continuing Education and Training

Programs Offered: massage therapy

Enrollment: 209 students

Institution Contact: Ms. Meredyth A. Given, College President *Phone:* 425-339-2678 ext. 15 *Fax:* 425-258-2670 *E-mail:* mgiven@ashmeadcollege.com

Admission Contact: Elizabeth Wade, Director of Admissions *Phone:* 425-339-2678 *Fax:* 425-258-2620 *E-mail:* ewade@ashmeadcollege.com

See full description on page 714.

Ashmead College Ⓐ

5005 Pacific Highway East, Suite 20
Fife, WA 98424
Web: http://www.ashmeadcollege.com

Accreditation: Accrediting Council for Continuing Education and Training

Programs Offered: massage therapy

Enrollment: 350 students

Institution Contact: Campus President

Admission Contact: Admissions Representative *Phone:* 253-926-1435 *Fax:* 253-926-0651

See full description on page 716.

Ashmead College Ⓐ

2111 North Northgate Way, Suite 218
Seattle, WA 98133
Web: http://www.ashmeadcollege.com

Accreditation: Accrediting Council for Continuing Education and Training

Programs Offered: massage therapy; sport and fitness administration

Institution Contact: Eric Rasmussen, College President *Phone:* 206-440-3090 *Fax:* 206-440-3239

Admission Contact: Juli Lau, Director of Admissions *Phone:* 206-440-3090 *Fax:* 206-440-3239

See full description on page 715.

Ashmead College School of Massage Ⓐ

120 Northeast 136th Avenue, Suite 220
Vancouver, WA 98684
Web: http://www.ashmeadcollege.com

Accreditation: Accrediting Council for Continuing Education and Training

Programs Offered: aromatherapy; massage therapy

Institution Contact: Lalitha Pataki, Director of Admissions *Phone:* 360-885-3152 *Fax:* 360-885-3151

See full description on page 717.

Bryman College Ⓐ

906 Southeast Everett Mall Way, Suite 600
Everett, WA 98208
Web: http://brymancollege.com

Accreditation: Accrediting Council for Independent Colleges and Schools

Programs Offered: dental assisting; medical/clinical assistant; medical insurance/medical billing; pharmacy technician

Institution Contact: Admissions Representative *Phone:* 425-789-7960 *Fax:* 425-789-7989

See full description on page 718.

Bryman College Ⓐ

19020 33rd Avenue West, Suite 250
Lynnwood, WA 98036
Web: http://www.bryman-college.com

Accreditation: Accrediting Commission of Career Schools and Colleges of Technology

Programs Offered: dental assisting; medical administrative assistant and medical secretary; medical/clinical assistant; medical insurance coding; medical insurance/medical billing

Institution Contact: Ms. Gynger Steele, Director of Admissions *Phone:* 425-778-9894 *Fax:* 425-778-9794 *E-mail:* gsteele@cci.edu

See full description on page 719.

Bryman College Ⓐ

3649 Frontage Road
Port Orchard, WA 98367
Web: http://brymancollege.com

Accreditation: Accrediting Council for Independent Colleges and Schools

---

Ⓐ indicates that the school is a participating institution in the *Imagine America* Scholarship Program.

Bryman College *(continued)*

Programs Offered: dental assisting; medical/clinical assistant; medical insurance/medical billing; pharmacy technician

Institution Contact: Sheila Austin, Director of Admissions *Phone:* 360-473-1120 *Fax:* 360-792-2404

See full description on page 720.

Bryman College Ⓐ

981 Powell Avenue, SW, Suite 200
Renton, WA 98055
Web: http://www.bryman-college.com

Accreditation: Accrediting Commission of Career Schools and Colleges of Technology

Programs Offered: dental assisting; medical administrative assistant and medical secretary; medical/clinical assistant; pharmacy technician

Admission Contact: Paige Mathis, Director of Admissions *Phone:* 425-255-3281 *Fax:* 425-255-9327 *E-mail:* pmathis@cci.edu

See full description on page 721.

Bryman College Ⓐ

2156 Pacific Avenue
Tacoma, WA 98402

Accreditation: Accrediting Council for Independent Colleges and Schools

Programs Offered: dental assisting; medical/clinical assistant; medical insurance/medical billing; pharmacy technician

Enrollment: 532 students

Institution Contact: Mr. Timothy E. Allen, President *Phone:* 253-207-4000 *Fax:* 253-207-4031 *E-mail:* t.allen@etontech.com

Admission Contact: Mrs. Lynette Rickman, Director of Admissions *Phone:* 253-207-4000 *Fax:* 253-207-4031 *E-mail:* l.rickman@etontech.com

See full description on page 722.

Emil Fries School of Piano Tuning and Technology

2511 East Evergreen Boulevard
Vancouver, WA 98661
Web: http://www.pianotuningschool.org

Accreditation: Accrediting Commission of Career Schools and Colleges of Technology

Programs Offered: musical instrument fabrication and repair

Enrollment: 8 students

Institution Contact: Mr. Len Leger, Executive Director *Phone:* 360-693-1511 *Fax:* 360-693-6891 *E-mail:* lenleger@pianotuningschool.org

Gene Juarez Academy of Beauty Ⓐ

2222 South 314th Street
Federal Way, WA 98003
Web: http://www.genejuarez.com

Accreditation: National Accrediting Commission of Cosmetology Arts and Sciences

Programs Offered: cosmetology; cosmetology, barber/styling, and nail instruction; nail technician and manicurist

Enrollment: 192 students

Institution Contact: Ms. Maryann Brathwaite *Phone:* 253-839-4338 *Fax:* 253-946-6560 *E-mail:* maryannb@genejuarez.com

See full description on page 724.

Gene Juarez Academy of Beauty Ⓐ

10715 8th Avenue, Northeast
Seattle, WA 98125
Web: http://www.genejuarez.com

Accreditation: National Accrediting Commission of Cosmetology Arts and Sciences

Programs Offered: cosmetology; cosmetology, barber/styling, and nail instruction; nail technician and manicurist

Enrollment: 204 students

Institution Contact: Ms. Maryann Brathwaite *Phone:* 253-839-4338 *Fax:* 253-946-6560 *E-mail:* maryannb@genejuarez.com

See full description on page 723.

International Academy of Design and Technology

645 Andover Park West
Tukwila, WA 98188
Web: http://www.iadtseattle.com

Accreditation: Accrediting Council for Independent Colleges and Schools

Programs Offered: fashion/apparel design; graphic communications; interior design

Institution Contact: Mr. Michael Gary Milford, President *Phone:* 206-575-1865 *Fax:* 206-575-1192 *E-mail:* mmilford@iadtseattle.com

Admission Contact: Mr. Bradley Tiehen, Vice President of Admissions *Phone:* 206-575-1865 *Fax:* 206-575-1192 *E-mail:* btiehen@iadtseattle.com

Ⓐ indicates that the school is a participating institution in the *Imagine America* Scholarship Program.

International Air Academy Ⓐ

2901 East Mill Plain Boulevard
Vancouver, WA 98661-4899
Web: http://www.airacademy.com

Accreditation: Accrediting Commission of Career Schools and Colleges of Technology

Programs Offered: airline flight attendant; tourism and travel services management

Enrollment: 250 students

Institution Contact: Ms. Lynn Rullman, School Director *Phone:* 360-695-2500 ext. 323 *Fax:* 360-992-4340 *E-mail:* lrullman@airacademy.com

Admission Contact: Ms. Colleen Piller, Director of Admissions *Phone:* 360-695-2500 ext. 319 *Fax:* 360-992-4340 *E-mail:* cpiller@airacademy.com

See full description on page 725.

ITT Technical Institute Ⓐ

Canyon Park East, 2525 223rd Street, SE
Bothell, WA 98021
Web: http://www.itt-tech.edu

Accreditation: Accrediting Council for Independent Colleges and Schools

Programs Offered: accounting and business/management; animation, interactive technology, video graphics and special effects; business administration and management; CAD/CADD drafting/design technology; communications technology; computer and information sciences related; computer and information systems security; computer engineering technology; computer software and media applications; computer software engineering; computer systems networking and telecommunications; criminal justice/police science; digital communication and media/multimedia; electrical, electronic and communications engineering technology; technology management; web page, digital/multimedia and information resources design

Enrollment: 303 students

Institution Contact: Mr. Mike Milford, Director *Phone:* 425-485-0303

Admission Contact: Mr. Jon L. Scherrer, Director of Recruitment *Phone:* 425-485-0303

See full description on page 726.

ITT Technical Institute Ⓐ

12720 Gateway Drive, Suite 100
Seattle, WA 98168-3333
Web: http://www.itt-tech.edu

Accreditation: Accrediting Council for Independent Colleges and Schools

Programs Offered: accounting and business/management; animation, interactive technology, video graphics and special effects; business administration and management; CAD/CADD drafting/design technology; communications technology; computer and information systems security; computer engineering technology; computer software and media applications; computer software engineering; computer systems networking and telecommunications; criminal justice/police science; digital communication and media/multimedia; electrical, electronic and communications engineering technology; technology management; web page, digital/multimedia and information resources design

Enrollment: 518 students

Institution Contact: Mr. Jack Kempt, Director of Recruitment *Phone:* 206-244-3300

See full description on page 727.

ITT Technical Institute

1050 North Argonne Road
Spokane, WA 99212-2682
Web: http://www.itt-tech.edu

Accreditation: Accrediting Council for Independent Colleges and Schools

Programs Offered: animation, interactive technology, video graphics and special effects; CAD/CADD drafting/design technology; communications technology; computer and information systems security; computer engineering technology; computer software and media applications; computer software engineering; computer systems networking and telecommunications; digital communication and media/multimedia; electrical, electronic and communications engineering technology; technology management; web page, digital/multimedia and information resources design

Enrollment: 460 students

Institution Contact: Mr. William King, Director *Phone:* 509-926-2900

Admission Contact: Mr. Gregory L. Alexander, Director of Recruitment *Phone:* 509-926-2900

Pima Medical Institute

555 South Renton Village Place, Suite 110
Renton, WA 98055
Web: http://www.pmi.edu

Accreditation: Accrediting Bureau of Health Education Schools

Programs Offered: dental assisting; health unit coordinator/ward clerk; medical administrative assistant and medical secretary; medical/clinical

Ⓐ indicates that the school is a participating institution in the *Imagine America* Scholarship Program.

Pima Medical Institute (*continued*)

assistant; pharmacy technician; phlebotomy; veterinary/animal health technology

Institution Contact: Mr. Christopher Luebke, Admissions Support Center Director *Phone:* 888-898-9048 *E-mail:* asc@pmi.edu

Admission Contact: Admissions Support Representative *Phone:* 888-898-9048 *E-mail:* asc@pmi.edu

Pima Medical Institute

1627 Eastlake Avenue East
Seattle, WA 98102
Web: http://www.pmi.edu

Accreditation: Accrediting Bureau of Health Education Schools

Programs Offered: dental assisting; health unit coordinator/ward clerk; medical administrative assistant and medical secretary; medical/clinical assistant; pharmacy technician; phlebotomy; radiologic technology/science; veterinary/animal health technology

Enrollment: 314 students

Institution Contact: Mr. Christopher Luebke, Admissions Support Center Director *Phone:* 888-898-9048 *E-mail:* asc@pmi.edu

Admission Contact: Admissions Support Representative *Phone:* 888-898-9048 *E-mail:* asc@pmi.edu

Western Business College Ⓐ

Stonemill Center, 120 Northeast 136th Avenue, Suite 130
Vancouver, WA 98684
Web: http://www.cci.edu

Accreditation: Accrediting Council for Independent Colleges and Schools

Programs Offered: accounting; administrative assistant and secretarial science; data entry/microcomputer applications; executive assistant/executive secretary; legal administrative assistant/secretary; legal assistant/paralegal; medical administrative assistant and medical secretary; medical/clinical assistant; medical insurance/medical billing; office occupations and clerical services

Institution Contact: Mr. Edward Leonard Yakimchick, President *Phone:* 360-254-3282 *Fax:* 360-254-3035 *E-mail:* eyakimch@cci.edu

Admission Contact: Ms. Renee Schiffhauer, Director of Admissions *Phone:* 360-254-3282 *Fax:* 360-254-3035 *E-mail:* rschiffhauer@cci.edu

See full description on page 728.

West Virginia

International Academy of Design & Technology

2000 Green River Drive
Fairmont, WV 26554
Web: http://www.iadtwv.com

Accreditation: Accrediting Council for Independent Colleges and Schools

Programs Offered: computer/information technology administration and management; computer/information technology services administration related; computer software and media applications; design and visual communications; legal administrative assistant/secretary; medical office assistant

Enrollment: 200 students

Institution Contact: Mr. Edward A. Schwartz, President *Phone:* 888-406-8324 *Fax:* 304-534-5669 *E-mail:* eschwartz@iadtwv.com

National Institute of Technology Ⓐ

5514 Big Tyler Road
Cross Lanes, WV 25313
Web: http://www.cci.edu

Accreditation: Accrediting Commission of Career Schools and Colleges of Technology

Programs Offered: computer engineering technology; computer systems networking and telecommunications; electrical, electronic and communications engineering technology; massage therapy; medical/clinical assistant; pharmacy technician; security and loss prevention

Enrollment: 540 students

Institution Contact: Dr. Robert L. Bliss, President *Phone:* 304-776-6290 *Fax:* 304-776-6262 *E-mail:* rbliss@cci.edu

Admission Contact: Ms. Karen Wilkinson, Admissions Director *Phone:* 304-776-6290 *Fax:* 304-776-6262 *E-mail:* kwilkins@cci.edu

See full description on page 729.

West Virginia Junior College

176 Thompson Drive
Bridgeport, WV 26330

Accreditation: Accrediting Council for Independent Colleges and Schools

Ⓐ indicates that the school is a participating institution in the *Imagine America* Scholarship Program.

Programs Offered: administrative assistant and secretarial science; computer/information technology services administration related; computer installation and repair technology; computer software and media applications; computer systems networking and telecommunications; computer/technical support; computer technology/computer systems technology; data entry/microcomputer applications; health information/medical records technology; medical administrative assistant and medical secretary; medical/clinical assistant; medical office management; medical transcription; web/multimedia management and webmaster; web page, digital/multimedia and information resources design; word processing

Enrollment: 216 students

Institution Contact: Ms. Sharron Stephens, Executive Director *Phone:* 304-842-4007 *Fax:* 304-842-8191 *E-mail:* sstephens@wvjcinfo.net

Admission Contact: Ms. Sharron Stephens, Director of Admissions *Phone:* 304-842-4007 *Fax:* 304-842-8191 *E-mail:* sstephens@wvjcinfo.net

West Virginia Junior College Ⓐ

1000 Virginia Street, East
Charleston, WV 25301
Web: http://www.wvjc.com

Accreditation: Accrediting Council for Independent Colleges and Schools

Programs Offered: computer/information technology administration and management; legal administrative assistant/secretary; medical administrative assistant and medical secretary; medical/clinical assistant; web page, digital/multimedia and information resources design

Enrollment: 162 students

Institution Contact: Mr. Thomas Crouse, President/Director *Phone:* 304-345-2820 *Fax:* 304-345-1425 *E-mail:* tacrouse@charter.net

Admission Contact: Mr. Tom Crouse, Director *Phone:* 304-345-2820 *Fax:* 304-345-1425 *E-mail:* tacrouse@charter.net

See full description on page 730.

West Virginia Junior College Ⓐ

148 Willey Street
Morgantown, WV 26505
Web: http://www.wvjcmorgantown.edu

Accreditation: Accrediting Council for Independent Colleges and Schools

Programs Offered: accounting; administrative assistant and secretarial science; business administration and management; computer/information technol-

ogy services administration related; computer installation and repair technology; computer software and media applications; computer systems networking and telecommunications; computer/technical support; computer technology/computer systems technology; data entry/microcomputer applications; legal assistant/paralegal; medical administrative assistant and medical secretary; medical/clinical assistant; medical office management; medical transcription; receptionist; web/multimedia management and webmaster; web page, digital/multimedia and information resources design; word processing

Enrollment: 195 students

Institution Contact: Ms. Patricia Callen, Executive Director *Phone:* 304-296-8282 *Fax:* 304-296-5612 *E-mail:* pcallen@wvjc.com

Admission Contact: Ms. Stephanie Franks, Admissions Director *Phone:* 304-296-8282 *Fax:* 304-296-5612 *E-mail:* sfranks@wvjcmorgantown.edu

See full description on page 731.

Wisconsin

Herzing College Ⓐ

5218 East Terrace Drive
Madison, WI 53718
Web: http://www.herzing.edu

Accreditation: Accrediting Commission of Career Schools and Colleges of Technology; North Central Association of Colleges and Schools

Programs Offered: banking and financial support services; business administration and management; business/corporate communications; CAD/CADD drafting/design technology; communications technology; computer and information systems security; computer engineering technology; computer/information technology administration and management; computer/information technology services administration related; computer programming; computer programming (specific applications); computer programming (vendor/product certification); computer systems analysis; computer systems networking and telecommunications; drafting and design technology; electrical, electronic and communications engineering technology; information technology; management information systems; marketing/marketing management; medical administrative assistant and medical secretary; medical insurance coding; medical insurance/medical billing; system

Ⓐ indicates that the school is a participating institution in the *Imagine America* Scholarship Program.

Herzing College *(continued)*

administration; web page, digital/multimedia and information resources design

Enrollment: 575 students

Institution Contact: Mr. Don Madelung, President *Phone:* 608-249-6611 *Fax:* 608-249-8593 *E-mail:* madelung@msn.herzing.edu

Admission Contact: Ms. Rebecca Abrams, Director of Admissions *Phone:* 608-249-6611 *Fax:* 608-249-8593 *E-mail:* rabrams@msn.herzing.edu

See full description on page 732.

ITT Technical Institute Ⓐ

470 Security Boulevard
Green Bay, WI 54313
Web: http://www.itt-tech.edu

Accreditation: Accrediting Council for Independent Colleges and Schools

Programs Offered: accounting and business/management; animation, interactive technology, video graphics and special effects; business administration and management; CAD/CADD drafting/design technology; communications technology; computer and information systems security; computer engineering technology; computer software and media applications; computer software engineering; computer systems networking and telecommunications; criminal justice/police science; digital communication and media/multimedia; electrical, electronic and communications engineering technology; technology management; web page, digital/multimedia and information resources design

Enrollment: 577 students

Institution Contact: Mr. Raymond Sweetman, Director of Recruitment *Phone:* 920-662-9000

See full description on page 733.

ITT Technical Institute Ⓐ

6300 West Layton Avenue
Greenfield, WI 53220-4612
Web: http://www.itt-tech.edu

Accreditation: Accrediting Council for Independent Colleges and Schools

Programs Offered: accounting and business/management; advanced/graduate dentistry and oral sciences related; animation, interactive technology, video graphics and special effects; business administration and management; CAD/CADD drafting/design technology; communications technology; computer and information systems security; computer engineering technology; computer software and media applications; computer software engineering; computer systems networking and telecommunications; criminal justice/police science; digital communication and media/multimedia; electrical, electronic and communications engineering technology; technology management; web page, digital/multimedia and information resources design

Enrollment: 645 students

Institution Contact: Mr. Jonathan L. Patterson, Director *Phone:* 414-282-9494

Admission Contact: Mr. Brian Guenther, Director of Recruitment *Phone:* 414-282-9494

See full description on page 734.

Madison Media Institute Ⓐ

2702 Agriculture Drive
Madison, WI 53718
Web: http://www.madisonmedia.com

Accreditation: Accrediting Commission of Career Schools and Colleges of Technology

Programs Offered: animation, interactive technology, video graphics and special effects; digital communication and media/multimedia; radio and television; recording arts technology

Enrollment: 316 students

Institution Contact: Mr. Chris K. Hutchings, President/Director *Phone:* 608-663-2000 *Fax:* 608-442-0141 *E-mail:* chutch@madisonmedia.com

Admission Contact: Mr. Steve W. Hutchings, Vice President/Director of Admissions *Phone:* 608-663-2000 *Fax:* 608-442-0141 *E-mail:* swh@madisonmedia.com

See full description on page 735.

Wyoming

Sage Technical Services

2368 Oil Drive
Casper, WY 82604
Web: http://www.sageschools.com

Accreditation: Accrediting Commission of Career Schools and Colleges of Technology

Programs Offered: driver and safety teacher education; transportation technology; truck and bus driver/commercial vehicle operation

Enrollment: 20 students

Ⓐ indicates that the school is a participating institution in the *Imagine America* Scholarship Program.

Institution Contact: Ms. Lisa Novotny, Director
Phone: 307-234-0242 *Fax:* 307-234-0552 *E-mail:*
casper@sageschools.com

WyoTech Ⓐ

4373 North 3rd Street
Laramie, WY 82072-9519
Web: http://www.wyotech.com
Accreditation: Accrediting Commission of Career
Schools and Colleges of Technology

Programs Offered: autobody/collision and repair
technology; automobile/automotive mechanics
technology; diesel mechanics technology; engine
machinist; upholstery
Enrollment: 1,873 students
Institution Contact: Ms. Helen Aro, Director of
Licensing and Accreditation *Phone:* 307-742-3776 *Fax:*
307-742-4354 *E-mail:* haro@wyotech.com
Admission Contact: Mr. Glenn Halsey, Director of
Admissions *Phone:* 307-742-3776 *Fax:* 307-742-4354
E-mail: ghalsey@wyotech.com
See full description on page 736.

Ⓐ indicates that the school is a participating institution in the *Imagine America* Scholarship Program.

In-Depth Descriptions

ALABAMA

Herzing College, Birmingham

About Our Institution
Herzing College, licensed by the Alabama State Department of Education, was founded in 1965 in Milwaukee, Wisconsin, by Henry Herzing. The Birmingham campus offers Associate of Science and Bachelor of Science degrees and diploma programs. The purpose of Herzing College is to provide a meaningful, high-quality education that prepares graduates for successful and rewarding technical, business, health-care, and public safety careers. The College fulfills this purpose by offering educational opportunities through bachelor's or associate degree curricula in technical, business, health-care, and public safety programs designed to prepare a student for employment. By accomplishing this, Herzing College believes that it effectively serves both the student and the larger economic community.

Special Features
Many students, at designated points in their curriculum, are prepared to take certification tests offered by NARTE, Microsoft, Professional Secretaries International, FCC, and ISCET. Another feature enjoyed by Herzing students is the fact that every student workstation is connected to the Internet and the College's Electric Library for research. Advisory boards for each of Herzing's curricula have been established to review the courses offered at the College. Those who sit on the advisory boards are professionals from the Birmingham area who are dedicated to assisting Herzing College make immediate changes as the job market dictates. Herzing students also have the benefit of a full-time Career Services Office that assists students with job placement while they are in school and upon graduation.

Financial Aid/Scholarships
Herzing College will help students develop financial plans to pay for their education through a combination of financial aid (if eligible), family contributions, and employer tuition reimbursement plans. Herzing Colleges are eligible to participate in the following five categories of programs: FPELL (Federal Pell Grant), FSEOG (Federal Supplemental Educational Opportunity Grant), FWS (Federal Work-Study), FFEL (Federal Family Education Loan Program, and the William D. Ford Direct Loan Program. Herzing College also has a number of institutional scholarships available.

Tuition and Fees
Tuition costs per credit hour are $295 for all technical courses and $255 for all other courses. Textbooks are included in the tuition charges, with the exception of students taking courses online.

Accreditation
Herzing College is accredited by the Higher Learning Commission of the North Central Association of Colleges and Schools. For more information,

Program Content
Business Administration; Computer Information Systems; Computer Network Technology; Computers, Electronics, and Telecommunications Technology; Homeland Security and Public Safety; Information Technology; Insurance Coding Specialist; Medical Office Administration; Technology Management

students should contact the Higher Learning Commission (telephone: 800-621-7440; Web site: http://www.ncahigherlearning commission.org).

Admissions
Prospective students are expected to complete an application and interview with a Herzing College admissions representative. The representative will provide information about programs, start dates, student services, and employment opportunities for graduates.

Graduation Requirements
The requirements for graduation include a cumulative grade point average of 2.0 or higher; completion of the required number of credit hours and passing all required courses; achievement of minimum skill levels in courses where applicable; and being current regarding financial obligations with the business office.

Contact
Tess L. Anderson, Director of Admissions
Herzing College
280 West Valley Avenue
Birmingham, AL 35209
Phone: (205) 916-2800
Fax: (205) 916-2807
E-mail: info@bhm.herzing.edu
Web: www.herzing.edu

Programs Eligible for Scholarship	Tuition and Fees*	Course Length/Credit Hours	Credential Earned
Business Administration	$4,080/semester	20/36 months	AS/BS
Computer Information Systems	$4,560/semester	20 months	AS
Computer Network Technology	$4,560/semester	20 months	AS
Computers, Electronics, and Telecommunications Technology	$4,560/semester	20 months	AS
Homeland Security and Public Safety	$4,080/semester	36 months	BS
Information Technology	$4,560/semester	36 months	BS
Technology Management	$4,080/semester	36 months	BS

*Semesters at Herzing College are sixteen weeks long. A full-time student generally completes 16 credits a semester.

ITT Technical Institute, Birmingham

About Our Institution
ITT Technical Institute is owned and operated by ITT Educational Services, Inc. (ESI), a leading private college system focused on technology-oriented programs of study. ESI operates seventy-six ITT Technical Institutes in twenty-nine states; they provided career-focused degree programs to approximately 38,000 students as of the spring of 2004. Headquartered in Carmel, Indiana, ESI has been actively involved in the higher education community in the United States since 1969. Curriculum offerings are designed to help students begin to prepare for career opportunities in fields of technology. Students attend classes year-round, with convenient breaks provided throughout the year. Classes are generally scheduled three days a week and are typically available in the morning and evening, depending on student enrollment. This class schedule offers flexibility to students to pursue part-time employment opportunities.

Special Features
Most ITT Technical Institute programs of study blend traditional academic content with applied learning concepts, with a significant portion devoted to practical study in a lab environment. Advisory committees, made up of representatives of local businesses and employers for each program of study, help each ITT Technical Institute periodically assess and update curricula, equipment, and laboratory design. Assistance with housing and part-time employment is available.

The degrees awarded are the Associate of Applied Science and the Bachelor of Science.

Financial Aid/Scholarships
ITT Technical Institute maintains a Finance Department on campus. The campus is designated as an eligible institution by the U.S. Department of Education for participation in the following programs: Federal Pell Grant, Federal Perkins Loan, Federal Stafford Student Loan, Federal PLUS Loan, and Federal Work-Study Program. The school also offers nonfederal loans made available through Bank One for eligible students.

Tuition and Fees
For tuition and fees information, students should refer to the school catalog.

Accreditation
Accrediting Council for Independent Colleges and Schools (ACICS).

Admissions
Admission requirements include a high school diploma or GED certificate; passage of an admission test, which may be waived (students should refer to the school catalog for details); and passage, in the school's discretion, of an interview with the registrar, should the registrar request one.

Graduation Requirements
Students should consult the school's catalog for graduation requirements.

Contact
Jesse Johnson, Director of Recruitment
ITT Technical Institute
500 Riverhills Business Park
Birmingham, AL 35242
Phone: (205) 991-5410
Fax: (205) 991-5025

Program Content
Business Accounting Technology, Business Administration, Computer Drafting and Design, Computer and Electronics Engineering Technology, Criminal Justice, Digital Entertainment and Game Design, Electronics and Communications Engineering Technology, Information Systems Security, Information Technology (options: Computer Network Systems, Multimedia, Software Applications and Programming, Web Development), Software Engineering Technology, Technical Project Management

Program Description
The Business Accounting Technology program blends acounting concepts and skills, financial applications and elements of business with accounting technology, such as business data interchange and migration and network technologies.

The Business Administration program offers a foundation to develop business knowledge and skills. It combines the study of fundamentals of marketing, finance, communications, and starategic management.

The Computer and Electronics Engineering Technology program prepares students for careers in modern electronics and computer technology.

The Computer Drafting and Design program combines computer-aided drafting with conventional methods of graphic communication to solve drafting and basic design-related problems.

The Criminal Justice program teaches the fundamentals of the criminal justice system and criminal justice skills. The program offers a foundation in criminal law, legal procedures, criminal evidence, and criminology.

The Digital Entertainment and Game Design program helps graduates prepare for career opportunities involving technology associated with designing and developing digital games and multimedia applications.

The Electronics and Communications Engineering Technology program prepares graduates for careers involving electronics engineering technology, including communication systems.

The Information Systems Security program gives students the opportunity to study the essentials of information security and the security aspects of common information technology platforms.

The IT Computer Network Systems program helps prepare students to perform tasks associated with installing, upgrading, and maintaining computer network systems.

The IT Multimedia program helps students prepare to perform tasks associated with designing and creating interactive multimedia communications.

The IT Software Applications and Programming program helps students prepare to perform tasks associated with developing and modifying software applications.

The IT Web Development program helps students prepare to perform tasks associated with designing, creating, and maintaining Web sites.

The Software Engineering Technology program emphasizes technical skills that are used to design and implement software-based solutions for business and consumer markets.

The Technical Project Management bachelor's program is designed to teach students IT/e-commerce project management skills.

Remington College, Mobile Campus, Mobile

About Our Institution
Remington College was founded in 1985 in an effort to meet the growing need for computer-related education and training in the technical and business fields. To date, Remington College consists of twenty campuses across the United States. It teaches a "career first" curriculum that allows students to concentrate on learning the necessary technical skills early in their program and build on them as they progress toward graduation.

Special Features
Remington College is uncompromisingly dedicated to high-quality, college-level, career-oriented education. Its primary objectives are to graduate a high percentage of students who enter career programs and to help them achieve relevant employment at the highest possible starting salary. Remington College's hands-on training is the foundation of its educational structure. Practical application in well-equipped labs, coupled with theoretical reinforcement in the classroom, allows students to acquire substantial knowledge in their chosen career field. When appropriate, externships are used to provide the student with real-world experience.

Financial Aid/Scholarships
Remington College–Mobile Campus maintains a Financial Services Office on campus, providing a variety of grants, loans, scholarships, work study, veterans' benefits, and vocational rehabilitation programs.

Tuition and Fees
Students should contact the campus for current tuition pricing. Textbook cost and lab fees are included in tuition. A $50 registration fee is required for all programs.

Accreditation
Remington College–Mobile Campus programs are accredited by the Accrediting Commission of Career Schools and Colleges of Technology (ACCSCT).

Admissions
A high school diploma or GED, along with an acceptance interview, is used to determine a candidate's potential for success. At some sites, an entrance test is also included.

Graduation Requirements
In order to graduate, a student must maintain an overall 2.0 cumulative grade point average for the entire program and complete all courses specified in the program catalog.

Contact
Mike Ackerman, Campus President
828 Downtowner Loop West
Mobile, AL 36609
Phone: (251) 343-8200
Fax: (251) 343-0577
Web: www.remingtoncollege.edu

Program Description
Business Information Systems: This program is designed to advance the student's knowledge in today's business environment.

Operations Management Technology: This program is designed to further develop the soft skills of decision-making and problem solving behaviors needed for professional administrators.

Computer Aided Drafting: This program is designed to provide the student with experience in applying drafting skills to Mechanical, Electrical, Piping, Civil, Structural and Architectural disciplines.

Computer Information Systems: The Computer Information Systems Program curriculum explores both the fundamentals and advanced theory in computer and programming, computer operations, system analysis, and system design.

Electronics and Computer Engineering Technology: This program provides students with a theoretical and practical understanding of basic electricity and electronics, semiconductors, digital logic gates in IC chips, and basic circuit construction.

Computer Networking Technology: This program is designed to provide comprehensive training in computer networking, including installation, configuration, and troubleshooting of local and wide area networks as well as intranets.

Virginia College at Birmingham, Birmingham

About Our Institution
Virginia College is a private proprietary institution of higher education that offers diploma courses, associate degree programs, and baccalaureate programs that strengthen the student's ability to enter or maintain a chosen career.

Special Features
Virginia College maintains vigilance on the ever-changing job market requirements and expansion of its program offerings. The College supports a progressive policy to prepare students as competitive employees in the local, regional, and multistate job market.

Financial Aid/Scholarships
Pell Grants, FFEL, FDSLP, work-study, FSEOG, VA assistance, and scholarships for graduating high school seniors and single working parents are offered.

Tuition and Fees
Tuition (which includes books and fees) varies based on the program and ranges from $14,710 to $24,930.

Accreditation
Virginia College is accredited by the Accrediting Council for Independent Colleges and Schools (ACICS).

Admissions
An entrance exam and a high school diploma or GED certificate are required.

Graduation Requirements
In order to graduate, a student must have earned a minimum cumulative grade point average of 2.0, earned the minimum credit hours as required by the program of study, and satisfied all financial obligations to the College.

Program Content
Administrative Office Management–Medical Office, Business Management, Computer-Aided Drafting and Design, Computer Networking, Computer Programming, Culinary Arts, Database Administration, Diagnostic Medical Sonography, Imaging and Animation, Interior Design, Internet Webmaster, Legal Assisting, Management Information Systems, Office Automation Management, Therapeutic Massage

Contact
Bibbie J. McLaughlin, Vice President of Marketing and Admissions
Virginia College at Birmingham
65 Bagby Drive
Birmingham, AL 35209
Phone: (205) 802-1200
Fax: (205) 802-7045
Web: www.vc.edu

Programs Eligible for Scholarship	Tuition and Fees	Course Length/Credit Hours	Credential Earned
Administrative Office Management-Medical	$16,835	91 credit hours	AAS
Business Management	$33,670	182 credit hours	BA
Computer-Aided Drafting and Design	$22,050	90 credit hours	AAS
Computer Networking	$26,950	110 credit hours	OA
Computer Programming	$24,500	100 credit hours	OA
Culinary Arts	$29,680	106 credit hours	OA
Database Administration	$28,420	116 credit hours	OA
Diagnostic Medical Sonography	$26,880	96 credit hours	AS
Imaging and Animation	$22,785	93 credit hours	AAS
Interior Design	$18,600	93 credit hours	AAA
Interior Design	$27,600	138 credit hours	Advanced AA
Interior Design	$36,000	180 credit hours	Bachelor of Applied Art
Internet Webmaster	$22,295	91 credit hours	AAS
Legal Assisting	$18,130	98 credit hours	AAS
Management Information Systems	$44,100	180 credit hours	BS
Office Automation Management	$17,020	92 credit hours	AAS
Therapeutic Massage	$17,760	96 credit hours	OA

Virginia College at Huntsville, Huntsville

About Our Institution
Virginia College is a private, proprietary institution of higher education committed to offering bachelor and associate degree programs and diploma courses that strengthen the student's ability to enter or maintain a chosen career.

Special Features
Virginia College maintains vigilance on the ever-changing job market requirements and the expansion of its program offerings. The College supports a progressive policy to prepare students as competitive employees in the local, regional, and multistate job market.

Financial Aid/Scholarships
Pell, FFEL, FDSLP, work-study, SEOG, VA assistance, and scholarships for graduating high school seniors and single working parents are offered.

Tuition and Fees
Tuition (which includes books and fees) varies based on the program and ranges from $8,980 to $41,458.

Accreditation
Virginia College is accredited by the Accrediting Council for Independent Colleges and Schools (ACICS).

Admissions
An entrance exam and a high school diploma or GED certificate are required.

Graduation Requirements
In order to graduate, a student must have earned a minimum cumulative grade point average of 2.0, earned the minimum credit hours as required by the program of study, and satisfied all financial obligations to the College.

Program Content
Accounting Assistant, Administrative Assistant, Administrative Office Management, Administrative Office Management-Medical, Business Management, Cisco Network Associate, Computer-Aided Imaging and Visualization, Computer-Aided Drafting and Design, Internet Webmaster, Internet Webmaster Technician, Legal Assistant, Medical Assistant, Medical Billing and Coding, Multimedia Management, Microsoft Network Engineer, Network Engineering, Therapeutic Massage

Program Description
Each program focuses on the needs of an individual desiring a specialized knowledge in their field of choice. Upon successful completion of the program, the student is ready for direct entry into the job market.

Contact
Pat Thomas Foster, Vice-President of Admissions
Virginia College at Huntsville
2800 Bob Wallace Avenue
Huntsville, AL 35805
Phone: (256) 533-7387
Fax: (256) 533-7785
Web: www.vc.edu

Programs Eligible for Scholarship	Tuition and Fees	Course Length/Credit Hours	Credential Earned
Accounting Assistant	$ 8,980	48 credit hours	Diploma
Administrative Assistant	$10,090	54 credit hours	Diploma
Administrative Office Management	$17,120	92 credit hours	AAS
Administrative Office Management-Medical	$16,935	91 credit hours	AAS
Business Management	$33,770	182 credit hours	Bachelor of Applied Arts
Cisco Network Associate	$12,840	52 credit hours	Diploma
Computer-Aided Drafting & Design	$22,150	90 credit hours	OA
Computer-Aided Imaging & Visualization	$22,885	93 credit hours	OA
Internet Webmaster	$11,860	48 credit hours	Diploma
Internet Webmaster Technician	$22,395	91 credit hours	OA
Legal Assistant	$18,230	98 credit hours	AAS
Medical Assistant	$10,390	56 credit hours	Diploma
Medical Billing and Coding	$10,900	54 credit hours	Diploma
Microsoft Network Engineer	$10,390	42 credit hours	Diploma
Multimedia Management	$41,458	183 credit hours	BA
Network Engineering	$27,050	110 credit hours	OA
Therapeutic Massage	$17,860	96 credit hours	OA

Apollo College, Mesa

About Our Institution

Apollo College, founded in 1976, is recognized in communities as a leader in high-quality career education, with hands-on orientation. Since then, the College has enjoyed a proud history of assisting people in becoming skilled professionals who go on to assume important positions in their communities. Highly trained, experienced faculty members present course materials that are relevant to current workforce needs; small class sizes ensure individualized attention for students. Programs begin on a monthly basis, with day and evening classes offered to accommodate busy schedules.

Special Features

The College's Advisory Board, composed of industry professionals, keeps Apollo abreast of the latest advances in their respective fields. Classrooms and labs are equipped with the latest technological equipment.

Career and academic counseling is available. Placement services, such as job fairs, assistance with resume and interview preparation, and on-campus recruiting are available through the Office of Student Services. The College also assists full-time students in finding part-time employment. Housing information is available through the Admissions Department. Apollo's Skills Advancement Program offers continuous refresher courses to graduates at no cost.

Financial Aid/Scholarships

Financial aid is available to those who qualify. Apollo participates in a variety of state and federal financial aid and alternate loan programs, including Pell, FFEL, FDSLP, SEOG, SSIG, and JTPA.

Tuition and Fees

There is a separate application fee.

Accreditation

Apollo is nationally accredited by the Accrediting Bureau of Education Schools to award diplomas and associate degrees. Additional accreditations and approvals include the American Association of Medical Assistants, ABHES, APSA, JRCERT, CoARC, CAAHEP, and AMTA.

Admissions

Students must submit a completed application and a registration fee. An interview with an admissions representative is required. For some programs, an interview with a program director or instructional staff member may also be required to determine eligibility.

Graduation Requirements

To graduate, students must have satisfied all financial obligations and successfully completed the course of study and externship, including course requirements.

Enrollment

There are 600 students enrolled.

Program Content

Dental Assistant, Medical Administrative Assistant, Medical Assistant, Massage Therapist, Pharmacy Technician, Respiratory Therapist, Veterinary Assistant

Program Description

Dental Assistant students are trained to work directly with patients and dentists and perform dental office administrative duties.

The Medical Administrative Assistant Program provides instruction in medical law, ethics, and terminology and computer and office skills that are critical to office practice.

Medical Assistant students are trained to aid physicians and other medical personnel as they treat patients and perform administrative tasks that keep a medical office running smoothly.

The Massage Therapist program, through classroom and clinical training, prepares students for the NCBTMB certification exam and rewarding careers as health-care professionals.

Pharmacy Technician students are provided a working knowledge of the pharmaceutical business and learn to apply technical and practical training in pharmaceutical and medical terminology, drug dispensing, and administration.

Respiratory Therapists learn to apply scientific knowledge and theory to the practical clinical problems of respiratory care and are qualified to assume responsibility for all respiratory care treatments.

Veterinary Assistants achieve the skills needed to succeed in a career with animals, meeting the strong demand for qualified animal-care services. Students learn up-to-date career skills and hands-on experience in today's veterinary technology.

Contact

James Miller, Campus Director
630 West Southern Avenue
Mesa, AZ 85210
Phone: (480) 831-6585
        (800) 36-TRAIN (toll-free)
Fax: (480) 827-0022
E-mail: jmiller@apollocollege.com
Web: www.apollocollege.com

Programs Eligible for Scholarship	Tuition and Fees	Course Length/Credit Hours	Credential Earned
Dental Assistant	Call campus for current pricing information.	720 hours/24 credits	Diploma
Massage Therapist		720 hours/36 credits	Diploma
Medical Administrative Assistant		720 hours/24 credits	Diploma
Medical Assistant		720 hours/24 credits	Diploma
Pharmacy Technician		836 hours/24 credits	Diploma
Respiratory Therapist		1,920 hours/84 credits	AOS
Veterinary Assistant		720 hours/24 credits	Diploma

Apollo College, Phoenix North, Phoenix

About Our Institution
Apollo College, founded in 1976, is recognized in communities as a leader in high-quality career education with a hands-on orientation. Since then, the College has enjoyed a proud history of assisting people in becoming skilled professionals who go on to assume important positions in their communities. Highly trained, experienced faculty members present course materials that are relevant to current workforce needs; small class sizes ensure individualized attention for students. Programs begin on a monthly basis, with day and evening classes offered to accommodate busy schedules.

Special Features
The College's Advisory Board, composed of industry professionals, keeps Apollo abreast of the latest advances in their respective fields. Classrooms and labs are equipped with the latest-technology equipment.

Career and academic counseling is available. Placement services, such as job fairs, assistance with resume and interview preparation, and on-campus recruiting are available through the Office of Student Services. The College also assists full-time students in finding part-time employment. Housing information is available through the Admissions Department.

Apollo's Skills Advancement Program offers continuous refresher courses to graduates at no extra cost.

Financial Aid/Scholarships
Financial aid is available to those who qualify. Apollo participates in a variety of state and federal financial aid and alternate loan programs, including Pell, FFEL, FDSLP, SEOG, SSIG, and JTPA.

Tuition and Fees
There is a separate application fee.

Accreditation
Apollo is nationally accredited by the Accrediting Bureau of Education Schools to award diplomas and associate degrees. Additional accreditations and approvals include the American Association of Medical Assistants, ABHES, APSA, JRCERT, CoARC, CAAHEP, and AMTA.

Admissions
Students must submit a completed application and a registration fee. An interview with an admissions representative is required. For some programs, an interview with a program director or instructional staff member may also be required to determine eligibility.

Graduation Requirements
To graduate, students must have satisfied all financial obligations and successfully completed the course of study and externship, including course requirements.

Enrollment
There are 700 students enrolled.

Program Content
Dental Assistant, Medical Administrative Assistant (Computerized Medical Office Secretary), Medical Assistant, Medical Laboratory Technician, Pharmacy Technician, Respiratory Therapist, Veterinary Assistant

Program Description
Dental Assistant students are trained to work directly with patients and dentists and perform dental office administrative duties.

The Medical Administrative Assistant Program provides instruction in medical law, ethics, and terminology and computer and office skills that are critical to office practice.

Medical Assistant students are trained to aid physicians and other medical personnel as they treat patients and perform administrative tasks that keep a medical office running smoothly.

The Medical Laboratory Technician Program trains students to perform various laboratory tests and procedures, understand body systems and their relationship to the tests and procedures, and determine the test/procedure outcomes.

Pharmacy Technician students are provided a working knowledge of the pharmaceutical business and learn to apply technical and practical training in pharmaceutical and medical terminology, drug dispensing, and administration.

Respiratory Therapists learn to apply scientific knowledge and theory to the practical clinical problems of respiratory care and are qualified to assume responsibility for all respiratory care treatments.

Veterinary Assistants achieve the skills needed to succeed in a career with animals, meeting the strong demand for qualified animal-care services. Students learn up-to-date career skills and hands-on experience in today's veterinary technology.

Contact
Randy Utley, Campus Director
8503 North 27th Avenue
Phoenix, AZ 85051
Phone: (602) 864-1571
          (800) 36-TRAIN (toll-free)
Fax: (602) 864-8207
E-mail: rutley@apollocollege.com
Web: www.apollocollege.com

Programs Eligible for Scholarship	Tuition and Fees	Course Length/Credit Hours	Credential Earned
Dental Assistant	Call campus for current pricing information.	720 hours/24 credits	Diploma
Medical Administrative Assistant (Comp. Medical Office Secretary)		720 hours/24 credits	Diploma
Medical Assistant		720 hours/24 credits	Diploma
Medical Laboratory Technician		1,500 hours/76 credits	AOS
Pharmacy Technician		836 hours/24 credits	Diploma
Veterinary Assistant		720 hours/24 credits	Diploma

Guide to Career Colleges 2005

Apollo College, Tucson

About Our Institution

Apollo College, founded in 1976, is recognized in communities as a leader in high-quality career education, with a hands-on orientation. Since then, the College has enjoyed a proud history of assisting people in becoming skilled professionals who go on to assume important positions in their communities. Highly trained, experienced faculty members present course materials that are relevant to current workforce needs; small class sizes ensure individualized attention for students. Programs begin on a monthly basis with day and evening classes offered to accommodate busy schedules.

Special Features

The College's Advisory Board, composed of industry professionals, keeps Apollo abreast of the latest advances in their respective fields. Classrooms and labs are equipped with the latest-technology equipment. Career and academic counseling is available. Placement services, such as job fairs, assistance with resume and interview preparation, and on-campus recruiting are available through the Office of Student Services. The College also assists full-time students in finding part-time employment. Housing information is available through the Admissions Department. Apollo's Skills Advancement Program offers continuous refresher courses to graduates at no extra cost.

Financial Aid/Scholarships

Financial aid is available to those who qualify. Apollo participates in a variety of state and federal financial aid and alternate loan programs, including Pell, FFEL, FDSLP, SEOG, SSIG, and JTPA.

Tuition and Fees

There is a separate application fee.

Accreditation

Apollo is nationally accredited by the Accrediting Bureau of Education Schools to award diplomas and associate degrees. Additional accreditations and approvals include the American Association of Medical Assistants, ABHES, APSA, JRCERT, CoARC, CAAHEP, and AMTA.

Admissions

Students must submit a completed application and a registration fee. An interview with an admissions representative is required. For some programs, an interview with a program director or instructional staff member may also be required to determine eligibility.

Graduation Requirements

Graduation requirements are the successful completion of the course of study and externship, including course requirements; a minimum grade of D (degree programs may require a minimum grade of C); and satisfaction of all financial obligations.

Enrollment

There are 450 students enrolled.

Program Content

Dental Assistant, Massage Therapist, Medical Administrative Assistant, Medical Assistant, Network and Database Administrator, Veterinary Assistant

Program Description

Dental Assistant students are trained to work directly with patients and dentists and perform dental office administrative duties.

The Massage Therapist program, through classroom and clinical training, prepares students for the NCBTMB certification exam and rewarding careers as health-care professionals.

The Massage Therapist Associate of Occupational Studies degree program provides students a comprehensive education and the personal critical skills needed to become successful practicing body workers.

The Medical Administrative Assistant Program provides instruction in medical law, ethics, and terminology and computer and office skills that are critical to office practice.

Medical Assistant students are trained to aid physicians and other medical personnel as they treat patients and perform administrative tasks that keep a medical office running smoothly.

Network and Database Administrators learn to design and configure personal computer networks and maintain and optimize systems that store large volumes of information. The program prepares students for the Microsoft® Certified Systems Engineer examinations.

Pharmacy Technician students learn to apply technical and practical training in pharmaceutical and medical terminology, drug dispensing, and administration.

Veterinary Assistants achieve the skills needed to succeed in a career with animals, learning up-to-date career skills and gaining hands-on experience in current veterinary technology.

Contact

Jeff Turner, Campus Director
3550 North Oracle Road
Tucson, AZ 85705
Phone: (520) 888-5885
(800) 36-TRAIN (toll-free)
Fax: (520) 887-3005
E-mail: jeffturner@apollocollege.com
Web: www.apollocollege.com

Programs Eligible for Scholarship	Tuition and Fees	Course Length/Credit Hours	Credential Earned
Dental Assistant	Call campus for current pricing information.	720 hours/24 credits	Diploma
Massage Therapist		720 hours/36 credits	Diploma
Massage Therapist Degree Program		1,122 hours/60 credits	AOS
Medical Administrative Assistant		720 hours/24 credits	Diploma
Medical Assistant		720 hours/24 credits	Diploma
Network and Database Administrator		1,136 hours/64 credits	AAS
Pharmacy Technician		836 hours/24 credits	Diploma
Veterinary Assistant		720 hours/24 credits	Diploma

Apollo College, Westside Campus, Phoenix

About Our Institution
Apollo College, founded in 1976, is recognized in communities as a leader in high-quality career education, with hands-on orientation. Since then, the College has enjoyed a proud history of assisting people in becoming skilled professionals who go on to assume important positions in their communities. Highly trained, experienced faculty members present course materials that are relevant to current workforce needs; small class sizes ensure individualized attention for students. Programs begin on a monthly basis, with day and evening classes offered to accommodate busy schedules.

Special Features
The College's Advisory Board, composed of industry professionals, keeps Apollo abreast of the latest advances in their respective fields. Classrooms and labs are equipped with the latest-technology equipment.

Career and academic counseling is available. Placement services, such as job fairs, assistance with resume and interview preparation, and on-campus recruiting are available through the Office of Student Services. The College also assists full-time students in finding part-time employment. Housing information is available through the Admissions Department.

Apollo's Skills Advancement Program offers continuous refresher courses to graduates at no extra cost.

Financial Aid/Scholarships
Financial aid is available to those who qualify. Apollo participates in a variety of state and federal financial aid and alternate loan programs, including Pell, FFEL, FDSLP, SEOG, SSIG, and JTPA.

Tuition and Fees
There is a separate application fee.

Accreditation
Apollo is nationally accredited by the Accrediting Bureau of Education Schools to award diplomas and associate degrees. Additional accreditations and approvals include the American Association of Medical Assistants, ABHES, APSA, JRCERT, CoARC, CAAHEP, and AMTA.

Admissions
Students must submit a completed application and a registration fee. An interview with an admissions representative is required. For some programs, an interview with a program director or instructional staff member may also be required to determine eligibility.

Graduation Requirements
To graduate, students must have satisfied all financial obligations and successfully completed the course of study and externship, including course requirements.

Enrollment
There are 500 students enrolled.

Program Content
Massage Therapist, Medical Radiography, Medical Records Specialist, Network and Database Administrator, and Physical Therapy Technician

Program Description
The Massage Therapist program, through classroom and clinical training, prepares students for the NCBTMB certification exam and rewarding careers as health-care professionals.

Students in Medical Records Specialist Program learn to maintain accurate, organized documentation of medical care to provide data for a variety of health information needs.

Medical Radiography students attend three 16-week semesters of classroom training that prepares them for an additional sixteen-week externship and a national certification examination.

Network and Database Administrators learn to design and configure personal computer networks and maintain and optimize systems that store large volumes of information. The program prepare students for the Microsoft® Certified Systems Engineer examinations.

Physical Therapy Technicians work in hospitals, rehabilitation centers, physician offices, nursing homes, home health agencies, adult day care programs, schools, wellness and community centers, and in private industry. Graduates may also choose to train and test as a personal trainer, opening many doors for a successful career in fitness.

Contact
Patrick Lydick, Campus Director
2701 West Bethany Home Road
Phoenix, AZ 85017
Phone: (602) 433-1333
          (800) 36-TRAIN (toll-free)
Fax: (602) 433-1222
E-mail: cnestor@apollocollege.com
Web: www.apollocollege.com

Programs Eligible for Scholarship	Tuition and Fees	Course Length/Credit Hours	Credential Earned
Massage Therapist	Call campus for current pricing information.	720 hours/36 credits	Diploma
Medical Records Specialist		860 hours/27 credits	Diploma
Physical Therapy Technician		720 hours/24 credits	Diploma
Medical Radiography		2,752 hours/106 credits	AAS
Network and Database Administrator		1,136 hours/64 credits	AAS

Arizona Automotive Institute, Glendale

About Our Institution

Arizona Automotive Institute (AAI) was founded in October 1968. In fall 1981, AAI became part of National Education Corporation, Irvine, California. In June 1997, Harcourt General Incorporated, which is located in Chestnut Hills, Massachusetts, acquired AAI. In April 1999, AAI became part of ATI Enterprises of Florida, Inc. Through these changes of ownership, AAI has remained on the original site.

The 7½-acre campus, conveniently located near public transportation and student housing, includes more than 77,000 square feet of air-conditioned classrooms, shops, work areas, offices, and a library containing reference and reading materials related to the programs taught. All classrooms are equipped with audiovisual aids such as overhead projectors, videotape monitors, slide projectors, and audiotape players.

The shop and work environments have been specially designed to simulate actual working conditions encountered in the industry. The shop equipment in all programs is current to the industry standards, such as can be found in current repair facilities. Both the industries the Institute serves and its Industry Advisory Council recommend the equipment AAI purchases, changes to the course content, and teaching procedures. Equipment and teaching aides provide real-world experience and the best training possible in the fields of automotive, autotronics, diesel technologies, and shop management.

Financial Aid/Scholarships

The Institute offers the Federal Pell Grant, Federal Family Education Loan Program, Federal Direct Loan Program, and Federal Work-Study Program.

Accreditation

AAI is accredited by the Accrediting Commission of Career Schools and Colleges of Technology (ACCSCT). It is licensed and authorized by the U.S. Department of Education, Veterans Administration, and Arizona State Board of Private-Post-Secondary Education.

Program Content

Automotive and Autotronics Technology; Automotive and Diesel Technology; Automotive Technology; Automotive Technology and Shop Management; Diesel Technology; Diesel Technology and Shop Management; Heating, Ventilation, Air Conditioning, and Refrigeration Technology

Contact

Alan Kluger, Director
Mark La Caria, Director of Admissions
Joe Wilson, Director of Education
Julie Hamilton, Director of Student Service
Carolyn Hardwick, Director of Financial Aid
Arizona Automotive Institute
6829 North 46th Avenue
Glendale, AZ 85301
Phone: (623) 934-7273
        (800) 528-0717

Programs Eligible for Scholarship	Tuition and Fees	Course Length/Credit Units	Credential Earned
Automotive Technology	$13,995	60 credit units/4 quarters 10 months/800 clock hours	Diploma
Diesel Technology	$13,995	64 credit units/4 quarters 10 months/800 clock hours	Diploma
Heating, Ventilation, Air Conditioning, and Refrigeration Technology	$11,796	64 credit units/4 quarters 10 months/800 clock hours	Diploma
Advanced Heating, Ventilation, Air Conditioning, and Refrigeration Technology	$17,644	94 credit units/6 quarters 14 months/1,200 clock hours	OA
Automotive & Autotronics Technology	$18,495	94 credit units/6 quarters 14 months/1,200 clock hours	OA
Automotive & Diesel Technology	$18,495	94 credit units/6 quarters 14 months/1,200 clock hours	OA
Automotive Technology & Shop Management	$18,495	100 credit units/6 quarters 14 months/1,200 clock hours	AAS
Diesel Technology & Shop Management	$18,495	100 credit units/6 quarters 14 months/1,200 clock hours	AAS

Conservatory of Recording Arts and Sciences, Tempe

About Our Institution

The Conservatory offers a thirty-seven-week (900 clock-hour) comprehensive course in audio technology featuring study in music recording, live sound reinforcement, MIDI and digital recording, troubleshooting, music business, postproduction for film and television, and Pro Tools and comprehensive instruction on Solid State Logic consoles. A 280 clock-hour internship is required for graduation. The courses are taught by award-winning professionals who care passionately about the industry.

Special Features

The Conservatory provides numerous manufacturer certifications that are not available anywhere else, increasing the likelihood for the employment of its graduates. Selective enrollment is practiced, yielding small classes that are populated with students who are academically capable and highly motivated. The Conservatory is the only school that requires an internship for graduation, and the student chooses the internship location.

Financial Aid/Scholarships

The Conservatory is approved for Title IV federal financial aid, and other private sources for student loans are also available.

Tuition and Fees

Tuition for Master Recording Program II is $13,500.

Accreditation

The Conservatory is accredited by the Accrediting Commission of Career Schools and Colleges of Technology.

Admissions

Applicants must be at least 18 years of age and possess a high school diploma or GED certificate. The Conservatory exclusively enrolls academically capable students with a high degree of motivation and appropriate, realistic goals.

Graduation Requirements

The Conservatory's students must maintain a minimum of 90 percent attendance and a cumulative GPA of at least 2.0 in order to graduate.

Contact

John F. McJunkin
2300 East Broadway Road
Tempe, AZ 85282
Phone: (800) 562-6383 (toll-free)
Fax: (480) 633-0916
E-mail: info@cras.org
Web: www.audiorecordingschool.com

Program Content

Master Recording Program II

Program Description

Comprehensive course in audio technology featuring manufacturer certifications and a required internship.

Everest College, Phoenix

About Our Institution
Everest College is an accredited, two-year college offering associate, diploma, and certificate programs in business, legal studies, and computer technology. Everest College has celebrated more than twenty years of excellence. Everest College, Phoenix, is one of more than eighty schools owned and operated by Corinthian Colleges, Inc., in the United States.

Special Features
The professional setting of the College prepares students for the work place and continuing education opportunities. Attractive surroundings, well-equipped classrooms, and computer labs set the tone for concentrated and dedicated study. The College is located in Phoenix, Arizona, which is conducive to all types of outdoor activities and sports. Trips to the famous Grand Canyon can easily be arranged. In addition, Phoenix is a metropolitan city offering a variety of cultural attractions. Parking is available adjacent to the campus, city buses are available for transportation, and affordable housing is nearby.

Financial Aid/Scholarships
The majority of financial aid available to students is provided by the federal government and is called Title IV Student Assistance. This includes the Federal Pell Grant, Federal Supplemental Educational Opportunity Grant (FSEOG), Federal Work-Study (FWS), Federal Family Educational Loan Program (subsidized and unsubsidized Stafford), and Federal Parent Loans for Undergraduate Students (PLUS). High school and other scholarships are also available for those who qualify.

Accreditation
Everest College is accredited by the Higher Learning Commission and is a member of the North Central Association (NCA) of Colleges and Schools (telephone: 312-263-0456). The Paralegal program is approved by the American Bar Association (ABA).

Admissions
Application for admission to Everest College may be granted to any person who meets one of the following criteria: has an advanced, bachelor's, or associate degree from a regionally accredited college with a minimum cumulative grade point average of 2.0 (on a 4.0 scale) or is a graduate of a regionally accredited high school as defined by the United States Office of Education or approved by a State Department of Education or other appropriate state educational agency or has a General Education Development (GED) certificate of high school equivalency.

Program Content
Accounting, Accounting Applications, Business Administration, Criminal Justice, Criminal Justice Administration, Homeland Security Specialist, Medical Insurance Billing/Coding, Office Administration, Office Management Technology, Paralegal, Web Administration

Graduation Requirements
All candidates must make application for graduation with the Registrar one term prior to graduation. To be eligible for graduation, the candidate must fulfill the following requirements: successfully complete all classes required within the maximum credits that may be attempted, achieve a 2.0 overall grade point average and have successfully passed all program courses, return all library books and pay any library fines, have all financial obligation satisfied and establish a complete career development file with the Career Development Coordinator, and earn at least 50 percent of the required credits at Everest College.

Enrollment
There are 500 students enrolled.

Contact
Melissa L. Agee
Director of Admissions
10400 N. 25th Avenue
Phoenix, AZ 85020
Phone (602) 942-4141
Fax: (602) 943-0960
E-mail: magee@cci.edu
Web: www.everest-college.com

Programs Eligible for Scholarship	Tuition and Fees	Course Length/Credit Hours	Credential Earned
Accounting	$249/credit hour	96 credit hours	Associate
Accounting Applications	$249/credit hour	48 credit hours	Diploma
Business Administration	$249/credit hour	96 credit hours	Associate
Criminal Justice	$249/credit hour	96 credit hours	Bachelor's
Criminal Justice Administration	$249/credit hour	96 credit hours	Associate
Homeland Security Specialist	$7,950	48 credit hours	Diploma
Medical Insurance Billing/Coding	$7,738	6 months	Diploma
Office Administration	$249/credit hour	46 credit hours	Diploma
Office Management and Technology	$249/credit hour	92 credit hours	Associate
Paralegal	$249/credit hour	96 credit hours	Associate
Web Administration	$7,738	36 credit hours	Diploma

ITT Technical Institute, Tempe

About Our Institution

The company: ITT Technical Institute is owned and operated by ITT Educational Services, Inc. (ITT/ESI), a leading private college system offering on technology-influenced programs of study. ITT/ESI operates seventy-seven ITT Technical Institutes in thirty states, providing career-focused degree programs to approximately 39,000 students as of spring 2004. Headquartered in Carmel, Indiana, ITT/ESI has been actively involved in the higher education community in the United States since 1969.

Curricula: Curriculum offerings are designed to prepare students for career opportunities in fields of technology. Students attend classes year-round, with convenient breaks provided throughout the year. A full-time student course load can have class meetings as often as three days per week and are typically available in the morning, afternoon, and evening, depending on student enrollment. General education courses may be available online. This class schedule offers students the flexibility to pursue part-time employment opportunities.

ITT Technical Institute, Tempe, awards the Associate of Applied Science, the Bachelor of Applied Science, and the Bachelor of Science degrees.

Special Features

Most ITT Technical Institute programs of study blend traditional academic content with applied learning concepts, with a significant portion devoted to practical study in a lab environment. Advisory committees, made up of representatives of local businesses help each ITT Technical Institute periodically review and update curricula, equipment, and laboratory design.

Financial Aid/Scholarships

ITT Technical Institute maintains a Financial Aid Department on the campus. The campus is designated as an eligible institution by the U.S. Department of Education for participation in the following programs: Federal Stafford Student Loan Program, Federal PLUS Loan Program, and Federal Work-Study Program. The school also offers nonfederal loans through Bank One for eligible students.

Tuition and Fees

March 2005 tuition is $386 per credit hour.

Accreditation

The Institute is accredited by the Accrediting Council for Independent Colleges and Schools (ACICS).

Admissions

For admission requirements, students should consult the school catalog.

Graduation Requirements

For graduation requirements, students should consult the school catalog.

Program Content

School of Information Technology: Information Systems Security, Data Communications Systems Technology, Software Engineering Technology, Information Technology–Computer Network Systems, Information Technology–Software Applications and Programming, Information Technology–Web Development

School of Electronics Technology: Electronics and Communications Engineering Technology, Computer and Electronics Engineering Technology

School of Drafting and Design: Digital Entertainment and Game Design, Computer Drafting and Design, Information Technology–Multimedia

School of Business: Business Administration, Business Accounting Technology, Technical Project Management

School of Criminal Justice: Criminal Justice

Contact

Chuck Wilson, Director
ITT Technical Institute
5005 South Wendler
Tempe, AZ 85282
Phone: (602) 437-7500
Fax: (602) 267-8727

ITT Technical Institute, Tucson

About Our Institution
The company: ITT Technical Institute is owned and operated by ITT Educational Services, Inc. (ITT/ESI), a leading private college system that offers technology-influenced programs of study. ITT/ESI operates seventy-seven ITT Technical Institutes in thirty states; they provide career-focused degree programs to approximately 39,000 students as of spring 2004. Headquartered in Carmel, Indiana, ITT/ESI has been actively involved in the higher education community in the United States since 1969.

Curricula: Curriculum offerings are designed to help students begin to prepare for career opportunities in the fields of technology. Students attend classes year-round, with convenient breaks provided throughout the year. A full-time student can have class meetings as often as three days a week, and they are typically available in the morning, afternoon, and evening, depending on student enrollment. General education courses may be available online. This schedule offers flexibility to allow students to pursue part-time employment opportunities.

ITT Technical Institute, Tucson, awards Associate of Applied Science and Bachelor of Science degrees.

Special Features
Most ITT Technical Institute programs of study blend traditional academic content with applied learning concepts, with a significant portion devoted to practical study in a lab environment. Advisory committees, made up of representatives of local businesses help each ITT Technical Institute periodically review and update curricula, equipment, and laboratory design.

Financial Aid/Scholarships
ITT Technical Institute maintains a Financial Aid Department on campus. The campus is designated as an eligible institution by the U.S. Department of Education for participation in the following programs: Federal Stafford Student Loan, Federal PLUS Loan, and Federal Work-Study. The school also participates in the California Grant Program and offers nonfederal loans through Bank One for eligible students.

Tuition and Fees
March 2005 tuition is $386 per credit hour.

Accreditation
Accrediting Council for Independent Colleges and Schools (ACICS).

Admissions
For admission requirements, students should contact the school for a catalog.

Graduation Requirements
For graduation requirements, students should consult the school catalog.

Program Content

School of Information Technology: Information Systems Security, Data Communication Systems Technology, Software Engineering Technology, Information Technology–Computer Network Systems, Information Technology–Software Applications and Programming, Information Technology–Web Development.

School of Electronics Technology: Electronics and Communications Engineering Technology, Computer and Electronics Engineering Technology.

School of Drafting and Design: Digital Entertainment and Game Design, Computer Drafting and Design, Information Technology–Multimedia Option.

School of Business: Business Administration, Business Accounting Technology, Technical Project Management.

School of Criminal Justice: Criminal Justice.

Contact
Tim Riordan, Director
ITT Technical Institute
1455 West River Road
Tucson, AZ 85704
Phone: (520) 408-7488
Fax: (520) 292-9899

Motorcycle Mechanics Institute, Phoenix

About Our Institution
Motorcycle Mechanics Institute (MMI) Arizona is a private postsecondary technical school that has provided students with the technical education needed for a successful career in the motorcycle industry since opening in 1973. MMI provides full student services, housing assistance, financial aid to those who qualify, campus activities, and both part-time and graduate employment assistance for as long as it is needed.

Special Features
MMI has developed strong industry relations and is endorsed by the top five major motorcycle manufacturers: Harley-Davidson, Honda, Kawasaki, Suzuki, and Yamaha. These agreements have created incredible training and career opportunities for MMI graduates. Many manufacturers and dealers, in addition to those listed above, also participate in MMI's TRIP program, wherein these companies agree to pay back the student tuition loans for the graduates they hire.

Financial Aid/Scholarships
MMI students are eligible to apply for various federal grants and loans. These include Federal Pell Grants, FSEOG, Federal Stafford Student Loans, Federal Perkins Loans, and PLUS Loans. MMI also participates in various scholarship programs and awards more than $500,000 in scholarships annually. These programs include VICA, CCA, Imagine America, Ford AAA, FFA, and UTI's National High School Scholarship competition.

Tuition and Fees
Tuition and fees vary by course content. Tuition prices include all workbooks, textbooks, and uniforms; there are no hidden costs. For specific tuition information, students should contact the Phoenix Admissions Office.

Accreditation
Motorcycle Mechanics Institute is accredited by the Accrediting Commission of Career Schools and Colleges of Technology (ACCSCT), which is listed by the U.S. Department of Education as a nationally recognized accrediting agency.

Admissions
Each student, at least 16 years of age, applying for admission must submit a completed application, a signed enrollment agreement, a registration fee, high school diploma or equivalent, and any other information that the applicant or Institute feels is pertinent to admission. Each applicant's qualifications for enrollment are reviewed and either approved, approved with stipulations, or denied.

Graduation Requirements
Students must receive a passing grade in each three-week course in order to be considered a candidate for graduation. All students are required to attend exit talks with Employment Services and Financial Aid. All monies owed must be paid in full three weeks prior to the student's graduation date.

Program Content
Motorcycle Technology

Program Description
MMI's Motorcycle Technology program prepares the graduate to service, repair, diagnose, and troubleshoot motorcycles. Students work in a professional, shop-like environment using the necessary equipment to prepare for an entry-level position in the industry. Students learn everything from machine shop to engine troubleshooting and noise diagnosis. Graduates have all the skills needed to start a challenging and rewarding career in the motorcycle industry.

Contact
Bryan Fishkind, School Director
Motorcycle Mechanics Institute
2844 West Deer Valley Road
Phoenix, AZ 85027
Phone: (623) 869-9644
(800) 528-7995 (toll-free)
Fax: (623) 581–2871
E-mail: bfishkind@uticorp.com
Web: www.uticorp.com

The Refrigeration School, Inc., Phoenix

About Our Institution

The Refrigeration School, Inc. (RSI), is a private institution specializing in heating, ventilation, air conditioning and refrigeration (HVAC/R), and electrical technology education and training. Serving primarily adult learners, this family-owned school has developed a reputation for high-quality service to students and industry since its founding in 1965. Although located in Phoenix, Arizona, the School enjoys relationships with employers from Alaska to Florida and from New York to California, helping to assure the ability to serve students' training and employment needs nationwide, making RSI one of the largest single sources for entry-level HVAC/R technicians in the country. Through accelerated classes that include hands-on training and taught by instructional staff members who are certified and represent well over 500 years cumulative experience, RSI strives to offer students the best value for their educational investment in the shortest time possible.

Special Features

Electrical circuitry troubleshooting is a key to career success in the HVAC/R field. The best technicians are the best troubleshooters. At RSI, specialty troubleshooting trainers have been developed for student training specifically to address the demand. Coupled with the environment of a family-owned institution, students expect to receive high-quality career preparation with personal attention from caring individuals, void of the typical corporate feel of larger schools. Students also appreciate the fact that within the course of training they are eligible for, and have the opportunity to pursue, multiple career-related certifications. Morning, afternoon, and evening classes and multiple start dates yearly offer maximum flexibility and work-friendly schedules. Graduates who wish to return and review course material may do so free of charge.

Financial Aid/Scholarships

State and federal programs available to qualified students include Federal Pell Grants, Federal and Direct Stafford Loans, Federal Plus Loans, Vocational Rehabilitation programs, Workforce Initiative Act–funded programs, TRA, TAA, SEOG, LEAP, and Veterans Affairs–funded programs. In addition, scholarship programs to individuals currently employed in a field related to their training and private scholarships are also available.

Tuition and Fees

Tuition ranges from $5,500 to $15,500 depending on the program chosen.

Accreditation

The Refrigeration School, Inc., is accredited by the Accrediting Commission of Career Schools and Colleges of Technology (ACCSCT).

Admissions

Students seeking a certificate must have a high school diploma, a GED (or equivalent), or may demonstrate the ability to benefit through a satisfactory score on a federally approved entrance examination. Students seeking an Associate of Occupational Studies (AOS) degree must have a high school diploma or GED (or equivalent). Applicants must also participate in a personal interview and tour facilities prior to attending classes.

Graduation Requirements

Students must maintain standards of the School's Satisfactory Progress Policy and pass all cumulative final exams with a minimum score of 70 percent.

Program Content

Certificate: Electrical Technologies; Electro-Mechanical Technologies; Refrigeration, Air Conditioning, and Heating Technologies

Associate of Occupational Studies: Mechanical Maintenance Engineering

Program Description

Electrical Technologies: This program teaches residential, commercial, and some industrial wiring and maintenance electrical applications and techniques.

Electro-Mechanical Technologies: This program combines the Electrical Technologies course with the Refrigeration, Air Conditioning, and Heating Technologies course to provide flexibility and employment security.

Refrigeration, Air Conditioning, and Heating Technologies: This program prepares students for installation, service, and maintenance of residential and light commercial comfort maintenance and refrigeration systems.

Mechanical Maintenance Engineering: This Associate of Occupational Studies degree program builds on the Electro-Mechanical Technologies program with upper-division courses in applied general education and heavy commercial applications.

Contact

Mary Simmons, Director of Admissions
4210 E. Washington Street
Phoenix, AZ 85034
Phone: (602) 275-7133
Fax: (602) 267-4805
E-mail: mary@rsiaz.org
Web: www.refrigerationschool.com

Programs Eligible for Scholarship	Tuition and Fees	Course Length/Credit Hours	Credential Earned
Electrical Technologies	$ 5,500	12 weeks/14 semester credits	Certificate
Electro-Mechanical Technologies	$ 9,500	40 weeks/42 semester credits	Certificate
Refrigeration, Air Conditioning, and Heating Technologies	$ 7,500	24 weeks/34 semester credits	Certificate
Mechanical Maintenance Engineering	$15,500	60 weeks/72 semester credits	AOS

Remington College, Tempe Campus, Tempe

About Our Institution

Remington College was founded in 1985 in an effort to meet the growing need for computer-related education and training in the technical and business fields. To date, Remington College consists of twenty campuses across the United States. Remington College teaches a "career first" curriculum that allows students to concentrate on learning the necessary technical skills early in their program and build on these skills as they progress toward graduation.

Special Features

Remington College is uncompromisingly dedicated to high-quality, college-level, career-oriented education. Its primary objectives are to graduate a high percentage of students who enter career programs and to help them achieve relevant employment at the highest possible starting salary. Remington College's hands-on training is the foundation of its educational structure. Practical application in well-equipped labs, coupled with theoretical reinforcement in the classroom, allows students to acquire substantial knowledge in their chosen career field. When appropriate, externships are used to provide the student with real-world experience.

Financial Aid/Scholarships

Remington College–Tempe Campus maintains a Financial Services Office on the campus, providing a variety of grants, loans, scholarships, work-study, veterans' benefits, and vocational rehabilitation programs.

Tuition and Fees

Students should contact the campus for current tuition pricing. Textbook cost and lab fees are included in the tuition. A $50 registration fee is required for all programs.

Accreditation

Remington College–Tempe Campus programs are accredited by the Accrediting Council for Independent Colleges and Schools (ACICS).

Admissions

A high school diploma or GED certificate, along with an acceptance interview, is used to determine a candidate's potential for success. At some sites, an entrance test is also included.

Graduation Requirements

In order to graduate, a student must maintain an overall cumulative grade point average of 2.0 or better for the entire program and complete all courses specified in the program catalog.

Contact

Jeff Gearhart, Campus President
875 West Elliot Road, Suite 126
Tempe, AZ 85284
Phone: (480) 834-1000
Fax: (480) 491-2970
Web: www.remingtoncollege.edu

Program Content

Business Computer Programming, Computer Systems Networking and Telecommunications, Criminal Justice/Law Enforcement Administration, Information Sciences and Systems, and Internet Information Systems

Program Description

Computer Information Systems: The objective of the program is to present the technology that integrates into information systems and provide the student with a framework of programming skills and a knowledge of local area networks.

Computer Networking Technology: The curriculum includes an intensive study of general computer science, including PC architecture, desktop operating systems, and related computer courses.

Criminal Justice: The program is designed to prepare the student for entry into or advancement within the criminal justice systems in any of the many areas existing within the career field.

Internet Information Systems: The program provides comprehensive training in the technology and techniques necessary to create, develop, market, and maintain a professional corporate Web site.

Universal Technical Institute, Phoenix

About Our Institution

UTI Phoenix is a private postsecondary technical school that has provided students with the technical education needed for a successful career in the automotive, diesel, and collision repair and refinishing industries since opening in 1965. UTI provides full student services, housing assistance, financial aid to those who qualify, campus activities, and both part-time and graduate employment assistance for as long as needed.

Special Features

UTI has developed strong industry relations with companies such as Audi, BMW, Ford, International Trucks, Jaguar, Mercedes-Benz, NASCAR, Porsche, Volkswagen, and Volvo. These agreements have created excellent training and career opportunities for UTI automotive and diesel graduates. From electives for upgraded UTI training to fully paid manufacturer-specific graduate training, UTI's connections and commitment to excellence place its graduates in the driver's seat in a career field that is in demand. Many manufacturers and dealers in addition to those listed above also participate in UTI's TRIP program, wherein these companies agree to pay back the student tuition loans for the graduates they hire.

Financial Aid/Scholarships

UTI students are eligible to apply for various federal grants and loans. These include Pell Grants, FSEOG, and Stafford, Perkins, and PLUS loans. UTI also sponsors, as well as administers, various scholarship programs and awards more than $500,000 in scholarships annually, including ones from SkillsUSA, CCA, Imagine America, Ford/AAA, FFA, and UTI's National High School Scholarship competition.

Tuition and Fees

Tuition and fees vary by course content. Tuition prices include all workbooks, textbooks, and uniforms; there are no hidden costs. For specific tuition information, students should contact the Phoenix Admissions Office.

Accreditation

UTI is accredited by the Accrediting Commission of Career Schools and Colleges of Technology (ACCSCT), which is listed by the U.S. Department of Education as a nationally recognized accrediting agency.

Admissions

Applicants must be at least 16 years of age, have a high school diploma or equivalent, and submit a completed application, a signed enrollment agreement, a registration fee, and any other information that the applicant or the Institute feels is pertinent to admission. Each applicant's qualifications for enrollment are reviewed and either approved, approved with stipulations, or denied.

Graduation Requirements

Students must achieve at least an overall 2.0 cumulative GPA and receive a satisfactory grade in all required courses in the selected program. Graduation must be achieved within a ratio of 1:5 attempted courses in a student's program. Students must have a zero balance in their student account and have attended UTI's Career Development Classes.

Program Content

Automotive Technology, Diesel and Industrial Technology, Automotive/Diesel and Industrial Technology; Ford Technology elective also available.

Program Description

UTI's Automotive and Diesel ASE Master Certified programs prepare the graduate to diagnose, troubleshoot, service, and repair foreign and domestic automobiles and diesel engines. Students work in a professional, shoplike environment using the latest engine analyzers, handheld scanners, and other computerized diagnostic equipment. Students learn everything from basic engine systems to computerized engine controls and from hydraulics to transport refrigeration.

Contact

Mike Klackle, School Director
10695 West Pierce Street
Avondale, AZ 85323
Phone: (800) 859-1202 (toll-free)
Fax: (623) 245-4600
E-mail: mklackle@uticorp.com
Web: www.uticorp.com

ITT Technical Institute, Little Rock

About Our Institution
The company: ITT Technical Institute is owned and operated by ITT Educational Services, Inc. (ITT/ESI), a leading private college system offering technology-influenced programs of study. ITT/ESI operates seventy-seven ITT Technical Institutes in thirty states, providing career-focused degree programs to approximately 39,000 students as of spring 2004. Headquartered in Carmel, Indiana, ITT/ESI has been actively involved in the higher education community in the United States since 1969.

Curricula: Curriculum offerings are designed to prepare students for career opportunities in fields of technology. Students attend classes year-round, with convenient breaks provided throughout the year. A full-time student course load can have class meetings as often as three days a week and are typically available in the morning, afternoon, and evening, depending on student enrollment. General education courses may be available online. This class schedule offers students the flexibility to pursue part-time employment opportunities.

ITT Technical Institute, Little Rock, awards the Associate of Applied Science and Bachelor of Science degrees.

Special Features
Most ITT Technical Institute programs of study blend traditional academic content with applied learning concepts, with a significant portion devoted to practical study in a lab environment. Advisory committees, made up of representatives of local businesses, help each ITT Technical Institute periodically review and update curricula, equipment, and laboratory design.

Financial Aid/Scholarships
ITT Technical Institute maintains a Financial Aid Department on the campus. The campus is designated as an eligible institution by the U.S. Department of Education for participation in the following programs: Federal Stafford Student Loan Program, Federal PLUS Loan Program, and Federal Work-Study Program. The school also offers nonfederal loans through Bank One for eligible students.

Tuition and Fees
March 2005 tuition is $386 per credit hour.

Accreditation
The Institute is accredited by the Accrediting Council for Independent Colleges and Schools (ACICS).

Admissions
For admission requirements, prospective students should consult the school catalog.

Graduation Requirements
For graduation requirements, prospective students should consult the school catalog.

Program Content
School of Information Technology: Information Systems Security, Data Communications Systems Technology, Software Engineering Technology, Information Technology–Computer Network Systems, Information Technology–Software Applications and Programming, Information Technology–Web Development

School of Electronics Technology: Electronics and Communications Engineering Technology, Computer and Electronics Engineering Technology

School of Drafting and Design: Digital Entertainment and Game Design, Computer Drafting and Design, Information Technology–Multimedia

School of Business: Technical Project Management

Contact
Tom Crawford, Director
ITT Technical Institute
4520 South University Avenue
Little Rock, AR 72204
Phone: (501) 565-5550
Fax: (501) 565-4747

Remington College, Little Rock Campus, Little Rock

About Our Institution

Remington College was founded in 1985 in an effort to meet the growing need for computer-related education and training in the technical and business fields. To date, Remington College consists of twenty campuses across the United States. Remington College teaches a "career first" curriculum that allows students to concentrate on learning the necessary technical skills early in their program and build on them as they progress toward graduation.

Special Features

Remington College is uncompromisingly dedicated to high-quality, college-level, career-oriented education. Its primary objectives are to graduate a high percentage of students who enter career programs and to help them achieve relevant employment at the highest possible starting salary. Remington College's hands-on training is the foundation of its educational structure. Practical application in well-equipped labs, coupled with theoretical reinforcement in the classroom, allows students to acquire substantial knowledge in their chosen career field. When appropriate, externships are used to provide the student with real-world experience.

Financial Aid/Scholarships

Remington College–Little Rock Campus maintains a Financial Services Office on the campus, providing a variety of grants, loans, scholarships, work-study, veterans' aid, and vocational rehabilitation programs.

Tuition and Fees

Students should contact the campus for current tuition pricing. Textbook cost and lab fees are included in tuition. A $50 registration fee is required for all programs.

Accreditation

Remington College–Little Rock Campus's programs are accredited by the Accrediting Commission of Career Schools and Colleges of Technology (ACCSCT).

Admissions

A high school diploma or GED, along with an acceptance interview, is used to determine a candidate's potential for success. At some sites, an entrance test is also required.

Graduation Requirements

In order to graduate, a student must maintain a minimum 2.0 cumulative grade point average for the entire program and complete all courses specified in the program catalog.

Contact

David Cunningham, Campus President
19 Remington Road
Little Rock, AR 72204
Phone: (501) 312-0007
Fax: (501) 225-3819
Web: www.remingtoncollege.edu

Program Description

Business Information Systems (A.A.S.): The program provides comprehensive training in the operation and effective use of various computer systems and software in DOS and Windows environments.

Computer Networking Technology (A.A.S.): Upon completion of the program, each student is able to install, configure, maintain, and troubleshoot local area networks, wide area networks, and intranets that use DOS and Windows-based network operating systems.

Electronics Engineering Technology (A.A.S.): The curriculum explores both the fundamentals and advanced theory in electronics, integrated circuits, microprocessors, and computer technology.

Medical Assisting (Diploma): The objective of the program is to provide graduates with the skills and knowledge that will enable them to qualify for entry-level positons as medical assistants.

Academy of Art University, San Francisco

About Our Institution

Academy of Art University (AAU) is the largest accredited private art and design school in the nation. Since its inception in 1929, the mission statement of the Academy has been "to provide aspiring artists and designers with career preparation, combined with academic excellence for the A.A., B.F.A., M.F.A., and Certificate Programs in the areas of art and design."

Graduates of the Academy, which has a job placement rate of more than 85 percent, embark upon successful careers in the art and design industry. Alumni of the Academy have been hired by prestigious companies all over the world, including Disney, Industrial Light + Magic, Pixar, LucasArts, DreamWorks SKG, Silicon Graphics, Hallmark, Oscar de la Renta, and Primo Angeli.

Special Features

The Academy is one of the leading schools in the country for providing students with the latest in technological advances, using constantly updated, industry-professional equipment. Students have the opportunity to learn from professionals at the top of their field from the biggest art, design, and studio companies in the industry. This allows students to learn the most sought-after techniques, in addition to making the contacts they need to obtain positions with such companies as Warner Brothers, Pixar, LucasFilm, and Donna Karan, who are known for recruiting AAU students. Students' work is constantly exposed to the public through many publications, the Academy's E-Gallery site (www.academyartgallery.com), four storefront art galleries, and the annual spring show in May. This allows students to showcase their artwork and gain firsthand knowledge of how to become working artists.

The demand for education to meet individuals' time and geographical restrictions led to the addition of an online education program in 2002. Students can take courses in fashion merchandising, interior design, drawing, animation, photography, advertising, and more, all from the convenience of a computer.

Financial Aid/Scholarships

Financial aid packages consisting of grants, loans, and work-study are offered to eligible students with a demonstrated need. Low-interest loans are available to all eligible students, regardless of need. Applicants should contact the Financial Aid Office for current requirements.

The Academy offers four scholarship programs: teacher grants, portfolio grants, and the high school Saturday and Summer Art Experience programs. Students should visit the Academy's Web site for details.

Tuition and Fees

Tuition is $550 per credit unit for undergraduates and $600 for graduates. There is a nonrefundable $130 registration fee, of which $100 is applicable toward tuition. Lab fees range from $25 to $400 per semester, depending on the class. Tuition and fees are subject to change at any time. Art supplies can run from $250 to $500 per semester, depending on the major.

Accreditation

The Academy is accredited by the Accrediting Council for Independent Colleges and Schools (ACICS), the Foundation for Interior Design Education Research (FIDER) for the B.F.A. in interior design, and the National Association of Schools of Art and Design (NASAD).

Admissions

Applicants for the B.F.A. program must have a high school diploma or GED equivalent. The application fee is $100 for undergraduates. A $500 tuition deposit applies to international applicants. Admission to the M.F.A. program requires official transcripts indicating the completion of at least a bachelor's degree, the submission of a portfolio of work, a statement of intent outlining graduate study goals, a resume, and two letters of recom-

Program Content

The Academy offers A.A., B.F.A., and M.F.A. degrees and certificates in the following majors: advertising (account planning, art direction, copywriting, and television commercials), computer arts (animation, digital imaging, graphic design, multimedia, new media, special effects, 2-D and 3-D modeling, and video games), fashion (costume design, fashion design, fashion illustration, knitwear design, merchandising, and textiles for fashion), fine art (drawing and painting, printmaking, and sculpture), graphic design (branding and print, corporate identity, and packaging design), illustration (cartooning, children's books, editorial, and feature film animation), industrial design (automotive design and product design), interior architecture and design (commercial and residential interior architecture and furniture design), motion pictures and television (acting, cinematography, editing, music videos, production/direction, and screenwriting), and photography (advertising, digital, documentary, fashion, fine art, photo illustration, and portraiture). Architecture is offered at the M.F.A. level only.

mendation. Graduate applicants should contact the Graduate Admissions Office for further details.

Graduation Requirements

To earn a B.F.A. degree, 132 credit units must be completed, consisting of 18 units of foundations courses, 60 units in the major, 12 units of art electives, and 42 units of liberal arts/art history courses. Students are advised to meet with departmental directors at least once during the academic year to have their progress assessed. Portfolios are reviewed before the junior year to determine whether or not a student has progressed sufficiently to continue study at the Academy.

Attainment of the M.F.A. degree requires the graduate candidate to successfully complete 63 credit units, including 27 units of studio courses, 18 units of directed study, 12 units of academic study, and 6 units of electives.

Enrollment

More than 7,000 students are enrolled.

Contact

Prospective Student Services
Academy of Art University
79 New Montgomery Street
San Francisco, CA 94105
Phone: (415) 274-2208
    (800) 544-ARTS (toll-free in the U.S.)
Fax: (415) 263-4130
Web: www.academyart.edu

Academy Pacific Travel College, Los Angeles

About Our Institution

Academy Pacific Travel College was founded in 1948 in Hollywood, California, as an Air Hostess Training School for Trans World Airlines and Western Airlines under the direction of Marsha Toy. The College has trained thousands of individuals for travel careers, which have opened the world to them and their families. As the general transportation industry grew in size and sophistication, Academy Pacific Travel College expanded its curriculum to meet the added demand for skilled ground personnel in the rewarding and stimulating careers offered by airlines, travel agencies, railroads, cruise lines, corporate travel divisions, and the hospitality industry.

Special Features

The College offers an English as a second language program and has a very active and successful job placement department.

Financial Aid/Scholarships

Financial aid is available via Federal Pell Grants, FFEL, FDLSP, Federal Perkins Loans, Federal Work-Study Program, FSEOG, and Veteran's Administration.

Tuition and Fees

Tuition and fees for the program in Transportation Management are $9,768.

Accreditation

Academy Pacific Travel College is accredited by ACCSCT.

Admissions

Applicants are accepted based on admission test scores, prior education, and personal interview.

Graduation Requirements

Students must complete all classes with a passing grade and have an overall minimum GPA of 2.0.

Contact

Daniel Gilreath
1777 North Vine Street
Los Angeles, CA 90028
Phone: (323) 462-3211
Fax: (323) 462-7755
E-mail: apsws@aol.com
Web: www.academypacific.com

Program Content

Transportation Management: Customer Service; Transportation Management: Flight Attendant

Program Description

The 30-week program covers all aspects of the travel industry, including airline operations and reservations, travel agency, rail, car, cruise lines, and hospitality management. Upon approval, students may take a four-week flight attendant program instead of hospitality management.

Customer Service: 30-week program covering all aspects of the travel industry with a four-week module covering hospitality management.

Flight Attendant: 30-week program covering all aspects of the travel industry with a four-week module covering flight attendant.

Programs Eligible for Scholarship	Tuition and Fees	Course Length/Credit Hours	Credential Earned
Transportation Management	$9,768	30 weeks/26 credit hours	Diploma

The Art Institute of California, Orange County, Santa Ana

About Our Institution

The Art Institute of California–Orange County is an educational institution for career preparation in the visual and practical arts. The school's mission is to provide postsecondary education programs that prepare students for entry-level positions in their chosen fields through a market-driven curricula. The school involves employers in the development of curricula that respond to industry needs. The Art Institute creates an environment that encourages academic freedom, responsible decision making, and critical thinking among students and faculty and staff members; fosters a collaborative environment that encourages personal and professional growth; and continually improves operations by promoting teamwork and communications through an institutional effectiveness process.

Special Features

The Art Institute is located in beautiful Southern California, within easy driving distance of local beaches and entertainment centers. The school affords students the opportunity to learn from top professionals in their industry, learning sought-after techniques, creating professional portfolios, and establishing networks that help lead them to their chosen career. The campus includes nine open computer labs, four professional kitchens, a student gallery, a learning resource center, and constantly-updated professional equipment. Students have access to student housing, public transportation, part-time job opportunities, and a wealth of leisure time activities.

Financial Aid/Scholarships

The Art Institute offers financial planning assistance for students. Financial aid, consisting of grants, loans, and work-study programs, is available for students who qualify. The school also offers scholarships to new and continuing students, based on merit, motivation, and financial need. Students should contact the Admissions Department for more information.

Tuition and Fees

The cost per credit is $331. The cost per academic year is $15,888. The application fee is $50 and there is a $100 enrollment fee. Culinary arts students pay a $300 lab fee per quarter. A starting kit, containing the majority of the first quarter books and supplies, is $505 for each program (except culinary arts, which costs $690). Culinary students are advised to budget $45 per month for textbooks. All other majors should budget $125 per month for books and supplies.

Accreditation

The Art Institute of California–Orange County is accredited by the Accrediting Council for Independent Colleges and Schools (ACICS) and by the Bureau of Private Postsecondary and Vocational Education Bureau as a California private postsecondary degree-granting institution. The school is a branch of The Art Institute of California–Los Angeles.

Admissions

A student seeking admission must be a high school graduate, hold a GED certificate, or have a bachelor's degree or higher from an accredited institution of postsecondary education. High school seniors who have not yet graduated should submit a partial transcript that indicates their expected graduation date. Each applicant is interviewed, either in person or by telephone by an Assistant Director of Admissions, and is required to write an essay of approximately 150 words explaining how an education at the Art Institute would help them attain their career goals.

Graduation Requirements

To graduate, students must achieve a minimum 2.0 GPA, earn a passing grade or credit for all required course work, earn the minimum required credits for the program of study, meet portfolio or other requirements outlined in the student handbook, and satisfy all financial obligations to The Art Institute.

Program Content

Culinary Arts, Culinary Management, Game Art and Design, Graphic Design, Industrial Design, Interior Design, Media Arts and Animation, Multimedia and Web Design

Program Description

Culinary Arts: The curriculum is based on the classical principals of Escoffier. Students are taught in modern kitchens and receive practical experience.

Culinary Management: Students learn to become competent in identified priorities of the food service industry.

Game and Art Design: Students develop skills in drawing, 2-D/3-D design, and animation. The game designer lays out the choices and options, with an underlying purpose or story in mind.

Graphic Design: Students develop basic skills in design, illustration, painting, and typography.

Industrial Design: Students learn to take a product (toy, phone, automobile) from a "great idea" to production, making it user-friendly and deciding how it looks, feels, and functions.

Interior Design: Students learn the art of creating mood, from the romantic supper club to a work-efficient office environment. Their canvas is space. Their tools are color, texture, fabric, and light.

Media Arts and Animation: Students develop skills as a visual communicators who combine artistic talent with technological expertise to create impressions in a moving-image format.

Multimedia and Web Design: Students develop a foundation in drawing and design, image manipulation, multimedia system design, scriptwriting, sound, video, and animation.

Contact

Ken Post, Director of Admissions
The Art Institute of California–Orange County
3601 W. Sunflower Avenue
Santa Ana, CA 92704-9888
Phone: (714) 830-0200
Fax: (714) 556-1923
E-mail: postk@aii.edu

Programs Eligible for Scholarship	Tuition and Fees	Course Length/Credit Hours	Credential Earned
Culinary Arts	$5,824/quarter	2 years/7 quarters/112 quarter credits	AS
Culinary Management	$5,824/quarter	3 years/12 quarters/192 quarter credits	BS
Game Art and Design	$5,824/quarter	3 years/12 quarters/192 quarter credits	BS
Graphic Design	$5,824/quarter	2 years/7 quarters/112 quarter credits	AS
Graphic Design	$5,824/quarter	3 years/12 quarters/192 quarter credits	BS
Industrial Design	$5,824/quarter	3 years/12 quarters/192 quarter credits	BS
Interior Design	$5,824/quarter	3 years/12 quarters/192 quarter credits	BS
Media Arts and Animation	$5,824/quarter	3 years/12 quarters/192 quarter credits	BS
Multimedia and Web Design	$5,824/quarter	2 years/7 quarters/112 quarter credits	AS
Multimedia and Web Design	$5,824/quarter	3 years/12 quarters/192 quarter credits	BS

The Art Institute of California, San Francisco

About Our Institution
The Art Institute of California–San Francisco is a leader in providing postsecondary education programs that prepare students for careers in art- and design-related fields. Graduates are trained for entry-level positions in their chosen fields through curricula that emphasize actual job skills and competencies necessary for success in the field. The curriculum is taught in an environment that encourages free expression, leadership, and responsible decision making by faculty members, many of whom are working professionals.

Special Features
The Art Institute of California–San Francisco is located in the Civic Center area of downtown San Francisco. The building's interior is designed with the creative student in mind. Light, spacious classrooms and equipped studios and computer labs offer a productive working atmosphere for students to explore their creativity. The school also includes library resources, a student gallery, a student lounge, staff offices, an art supply store, and other amenities. The Art Institute of California–San Francisco is one of The Art Institutes, a system of thirty-one education institutions located nationwide, providing an important source of design, media arts, fashion, and culinary professionals.

The school offers the following degrees: Associate of Science degrees in fashion design, fashion marketing, graphic design, and interactive media design; the Bachelor of Fine Arts degree in fashion design; and Bachelor of Science degrees in advertising, fashion marketing and management, game art and design, graphic design, interactive media design, interior design, media arts and animation, and visual and game programming.

Financial Aid/Scholarships
The Art Institute of California–San Francisco maintains a financial aid office at the school and participates in federal, state, and other financial aid programs. The school also participates in The Art Institute's scholarship competition and other scholarship programs.

Tuition and Fees
Tuition is charged on a per-credit basis. Tuition per quarter (based on 16 credits per quarter at $373 per credit hour) is $5,968 for both associate and bachelor's degree programs. There are an application fee of $50 and an enrollment fee of $100.

Accreditation
The Art Institute of California–San Francisco is accredited by the Accrediting Council for Independent Colleges and Schools (ACICS).

Admissions
A high school diploma or GED certificate or a bachelor's degree from an accredited institution of postsecondary education is a prerequisite for admission, as is a preadmission interview. A portfolio, previous work experience, and personal recommendations are also considered.

Graduation Requirements
To be qualified to graduate, students must receive a passing grade or credit for all required course work, earn the minimum required credits for the program, achieve a minimum cumulative GPA of 2.0, meet portfolio requirements as outlined by the student's degree program, and satisfy all financial obligations to the school.

Program Content
Bachelor of Science degree: Advertising, Fashion Marketing and Management, Game Art and Design, Graphic Design, Interactive Media Design, Interior Design, Media Arts and Animation, Visual and Game Programming

Bachelor of Fine Arts degree: Fashion Design

Associate of Science degree: Fashion Design, Fashion Marketing, Graphic Design, Interactive Media Design

Program Description
The advertising program provides graduates with the skills needed to work in the field of advertising—art direction, copywriting, and account supervision.

The fashion design and fashion marketing programs prepare students for successful entry into the industry in a variety of positions in design, production, merchandising, or marketing.

The game art and design program prepares graduates for entry-level positions, including texture artist, character animator, modeler, and level designer.

The graphic design programs prepare students to work in such fields as advertising, publishing, television, and graphic design, which offer great opportunities for trained visual communicators.

The interactive media design programs prepare graduates to apply the practical, creative, and technical skills they acquire for entry-level positions in the multimedia field.

The interior design program prepares graduates for entry-level positions in commercial and residential interior design such as residential designer, computer-aided draftsperson, facilities designer, and showroom manager.

The media arts and animation program equips students with the necessary skills to work in positions such as animation artist, special effects artist, or broadcast graphics designer.

The visual and game programming program trains students for entry-level positions such as technical artist, artist wizard, data wrangler, and 3-D tools programmer.

Contact
Department of Admissions
The Art Institute of California–San Francisco
1170 Market Street
San Francisco, CA 94102
Phone: (415) 865-0198
　　　(888) 493-3261 (toll-free)
Fax: (415) 863-6344
E-mail: aisfadm@aii.edu
Web: www.aicasf.aii.edu

Bryman College, Alhambra

About Our Institution

The Bryman Schools were founded in 1962 by Mrs. Esther Bryman as the Los Angeles Colleges of Medical and Dental Assistants. The Los Angeles campus was the original school. In December 1995, Corinthian Schools, Inc. (CSi), a division of Corinthian Colleges, Inc. (CCi), acquired the schools. CCi is one of the largest postsecondary school organizations in the United States, operating more than eighty colleges and institutions nationwide.

The College's philosophy is to provide high-quality programs that are sound in concept, implemented by a competent and dedicated faculty, and geared to serve those seeking a solid foundation in business or health-care fields. The programs emphasize hands-on training, are relevant to the needs of employers, and focus on areas that offer strong long-term employment opportunities. Upon completion, graduates are prepared for entry-level positions in medical, dental, or business fields.

Financial Aid/Scholarships

Information regarding Federal Pell Grants, FSEOG, FFEL, Federal Perkins Loans, VA funds, WIA, and other assistance can be obtained from the Finance Office. Financial aid is available for those who qualify.

Accreditation

Accrediting Commission of Career Schools and Colleges of Technology (ACCSCT)—all programs; Commission on Accreditation of Allied Health Education Programs (CAAHEP)—Medical Assisting; Registered Dental Assisting (RDA)—Dental Assisting.

Admissions

Successful candidates are selected based on admissions tests, interviews, and the completion and presentation of required documents. Enrollment is open to all high school graduates as well as those holding a GED certificate or its equivalency. Under certain circumstances, students who do not have a high school diploma or its equivalent may still be accepted for admission. Students should contact the Admissions Department for additional information.

Graduation Requirements

To be eligible for graduation, students must successfully complete all classroom modules with a grade of at least 70 percent or 2.0, finish an approved externship of 160 hours, receive satisfactory evaluations from the externship facility, and complete all other program requirements.

Program Content

Business Operations, Dental Assisting, Massage Therapy, Medical Administrative Assistant, Medical Assisting, Medical Insurance Billing/Coding, Pharmacy Technician

Contact

Randy Morales, School President
Bryman College, Alhambra
2215 West Mission Road
Alhambra, CA 91803
Phone: (626) 979-4940
Fax: (626) 280-4011
E-mail: rmorales@cci.edu
Web: www.bryman-college.com

Programs Eligible for Scholarship	Tuition and Fees	Course Length/Credit Hours	Credential Earned
Dental Assisting	$9,312	720 clock hours/47 credit hours	Diploma
Medical Administrative Assistant	$9,286	720 clock hours/47 credit hours	Diploma
Medical Assisting	$9,341	720 clock hours/47 credit hours	Diploma
Medical Insurance Billing/Coding	$6,539	480 clock hours/29 credit hours	Diploma
Pharmacy Technician	$9,820	720 clock hours/58 credit hours	Diploma
Business Operations	$9,166	720 clock hours/54 credit hours	Certificate

Bryman College, Anaheim

About Our Institution

The Bryman Schools were founded in 1962 by Mrs. Esther Bryman as the Los Angeles Colleges of Medical and Dental Assistants. The Los Angeles campus was the original school. In 1995, Corinthian Schools, Inc. (CSi), a division of Corinthian Colleges, Inc. (CCi), acquired the schools. CCi is one of the largest postsecondary school organizations in the United States, operating more than eighty colleges and institutions nationwide.

The College's philosophy is to provide high-quality programs that are sound in concept, implemented by a competent and dedicated faculty, and geared to serve those seeking a solid foundation in business or health-care fields. The programs emphasize hands-on training, are relevant to the needs of employers, and focus on areas that offer strong long-term employment opportunities. Upon completion, graduates are prepared for entry-level positions in both medical and dental practices.

The College is conveniently located near good public transportation and is easily accessible from the Santa Ana, Costa Mesa, Garden Grove, and Riverside freeways.

Special Features

Bryman College offers career development training throughout each program, with emphasis on resumes, interviewing, and the self-directed job search. Placement assistance is provided to each graduate.

Financial Aid/Scholarships

Information regarding Pell Grants, FSEOG, FFEL, FPLUS, Perkins, Federal Work-Study, VA funds, state grants, WIA, and other assistance can be obtained from the Finance Office. Financial aid is available for those who qualify.

Accreditation

All programs are accredited by the Accrediting Commission of Career Schools and Colleges of Technology (ACCSCT). The Medical Assisting program is also accredited by the Commission on Accreditation of Allied Health Education Programs (CAAHEP). The Dental Assisting program is also accredited by Registered Dental Assisting (RDA).

Admissions

Successful candidates are selected based on admissions tests, interviews, and the completion and presentation of required documents. Enrollment is open to all high school graduates as well as those holding a GED or its equivalency. Under certain circumstances, students who do not have a high school diploma or its equivalent may still be accepted for admission. Students should contact the Admissions Department for additional information.

Program Content

Dental Assisting, Massage Therapy, Medical Administrative Assistant, Medical Assisting, Medical Insurance Billing/Coding, Pharmacy Technician, Vocational Nursing

Graduation Requirements

To be eligible for graduation, students must successfully complete all classroom modules with a grade of at least 70 percent, finish an approved externship of 160 hours, and complete all other program requirements.

Contact

Danny Valdez, Director of Admissions
511 North Brookhurst
Suite 300
Anaheim, CA 92801
Phone: (714) 953-6500
Fax: (714) 953-4163
E-mail: dvaldez@cci.edu
Web: http://bryman-college.com

Programs Eligible for Scholarship	Tuition and Fees	Course Length/Credit Hours	Credential Earned
Dental Assisting	$10,211.54	720 clock hours/47 credit hours	Diploma
Massage Therapy	$11,364.58	720 clock hours/57 credit hours	Diploma
Medical Administrative Assistant	$10,127.61	720 clock hours/47 credit hours	Diploma
Medical Assisting	$ 9,983.39	720 clock hours/47 credit hours	Diploma
Medical Insurance Billing/Coding	$ 7,964.39	480 clock hours/29 credit hours	Diploma
Pharmacy Technician	$10,310.88	720 clock hours/58 credit hours	Diploma
Vocational Nursing	$22,917.17		

Bryman College, City of Industry

About Our Institution
NOVA Institute of Health Technology, previously known as Whittier Institute of Technology, was acquired by Educorp, Inc., in 1988. The institute had been in existence since 1969. In 2000, NOVA Institute of Health Technology was purchased by Corinthian Schools, Inc., a division of Corinthian Colleges, Inc. The school's name was then changed to Bryman College, City of Industry.

Special Features
Bryman College, City of Industry, is housed within a building consisting of 8,700 square feet of classroom space and 9,300 square feet of laboratory space, with a total area of 39,390 square feet. The facility is modern, air conditioned, and handicapped accessible. The facility can accommodate 300 students at any one time. Each classroom is equipped with supportive materials to enrich and broaden the students' knowledge and training. Classrooms and laboratories are equipped for a maximum class size of 30 students and usually average between 20 and 25 students for theory and 15 to 20 for laboratory.

Financial Aid/Scholarships
Financial assistance information may be obtained from the Financial Aid Office. To be eligible for some student assistant programs, students are required to demonstrate financial need.

Accreditation
The institute maintains all approvals from the Bureau for Private Postsecondary and Vocational Education as well as its accreditation by the ACCSCT (Accrediting Commission of Career Schools and Colleges of Technology).

Admissions
All applicants must have a high school diploma or the equivalent. However, the education requirement may also be met if the applicant is at least 18 years of age and can demonstrate the ability to benefit from the training. The ability to benefit is determined by passing the admission examination and by a personal interview with the school administrator. Applicants who possess a high school diploma or the equivalent take the SRA, published by NCS Pearson, Inc. Applicants without a high school diploma or the equivalent take the cPAT Career Programs Assessment Test, published by NCS Pearson, Inc. Applicants may apply for Diploma, Certificate, or Accelerated Programs. All applicants for degree programs must have a high school diploma or the equivalent. All applications are taken in person, with an appointment. Successful completion of an entrance examination is necessary. Students may enroll daily for upcoming start dates.

Program Contents
Business Management/Administrative Assistant, Dental Assistant, Massage Therapist, Medical Assistant, Medical Insurance Biller, Medical Laboratory Assistant/Phlebotomist, X-Ray Technician

Graduation Requirements
To qualify for graduation and a diploma, students must complete a prescribed course of study with a minimum average of 70 percent (C), meet the credit-hour and skills requirements for the program, meet the school's attendance and conduct policies, and satisfy their financial obligations to the school.

Contact
Lillian Gonzalez
Director of Admissions
12801 Crossroad Parkway
City of Industry, CA 91746
Phone: (562) 908-2500
Fax: (562) 908-7656
E-mail: lilliang@cci.edu
Web: www.bryman-college.com

Programs Eligible for Scholarship	Tuition	Course Length/Credit Hours	Credential Earned
Business Management/Administrative Assistant	$10,788	36 weeks/54 credit hours	Diploma
Dental Assistant	$10,650	32 weeks/47 credit hours	Diploma
Massage Therapist	$11,375	36 weeks/57 credit hours	Diploma
Medical Assistant	$10,415	32 weeks/47 credit hours	Diploma
Medical Insurance Biller	$ 8,190	24 weeks/35 credit hours	Diploma
Medical Laboratory Assistant/Phlebotomist	$10,810	32 weeks/47 credit hours	Diploma
X-Ray Technician	$12,160	36 weeks/39 credit hours	Diploma

Bryman College, Gardena

About Our Institution

The Bryman Schools were founded in 1962 by Mrs. Esther Bryman as the Los Angeles Colleges of Medical and Dental Assistants. The Los Angeles campus was the original school. In December 1995, Corinthian Schools, Inc. (CSi), a division of Corinthian Colleges, Inc. (CCi), acquired the schools. CCi is one of the largest postsecondary school organizations in the United States, operating more than eighty colleges and institutions nationwide.

The school's philosophy is to provide quality programs that are sound in concept, implemented by a competent and dedicated faculty and geared to serve those seeking a solid foundation in the health-care field. The programs emphasize hands-on training, are relevant to employer's needs and focus on areas that offer strong long-term employment opportunities. Upon completion, graduates are prepared for entry-level positions in both medical and dental practices.

Financial Aid/Scholarships

Information regarding Pell Grants, FSEOG, FFEL, FSL, FPLUS, Perkins, Federal Work-Study, and other assistance can be obtained from the Finance Office. Financial aid available for those who qualify.

Accreditation

All programs are accredited by the Accrediting Commission of Career Schools and Colleges of Technology (ACCSCT). The Medical Assisting program is also accredited by the Commission on Accreditation of Allied Health Education Programs (CAAHEP).

Admissions

Successful candidates are selected based on admissions tests, interviews, and the completion and presentation of required documents. Enrollment is open to all high school graduates as well as those holding a GED or its equivalency. Under certain circumstances, students who do not have a high school diploma or its equivalent may still be accepted for admission. Students should contact the Admissions Department for additional information.

Graduation Requirements

To be eligible for graduation, students must successfully complete all classroom modules with a grade of at least 70 percent, finish an approved externship of 160 hours, receive satisfactory evaluations from the externship facility, and complete all other program requirements.

Program Content

Dental Assisting, Dialysis Technician, Massage Therapy, Medical Administrative Assistant, Medical Assisting, Medical Insurance Billing/Coding

Contact

Hasani Thompson, Director of Admissions
1045 W. Redondo Beach Blvd.
Suite 275
Gardena, CA 90247
Phone: (310) 527-2040
Fax: (310) 527-7985
E-mail: hgorden@cci.edu
Web: www.bryman-college.com

Programs Eligible for Scholarship	Tuition and Fees	Course Length/Credit Hours	Credential Earned
Dental Assisting	$10,283.54	720 clock hours/47 credit hours	Diploma
Dialysis Technician	$13,119.42	760 clock hours/47 credit hours	Diploma
Massage Therapy	$11,506.79	720 clock hours/57 credit hours	Diploma
Medical Administrative Assistant	$10,129.79	720 clock hours/47 credit hours	Diploma
Medical Assisting	$10,251.00	720 clock hours/47 credit hours	Diploma
Medical Insurance Billing/Coding	$ 7,996.29	560 clock hours/35 credit hours	Diploma

Bryman College, Hayward

About Our Institution

The Bryman Schools were founded in 1962 by Mrs. Esther Bryman as the Los Angeles Colleges of Medical and Dental Assistants. The Los Angeles campus was the original school. In December 1995, Corinthian Schools, Inc. (CSi), a division of Corinthian Colleges, Inc. (CCi), acquired the schools. CCi is one of the largest postsecondary school organizations in the United States, operating more than eighty colleges and institutions nationwide.

The College's philosophy is to provide high-quality programs that are sound in concept, implemented by a competent and dedicated faculty, and geared to serve those seeking a solid foundation in the health-care field. The programs emphasize hands-on training, are relevant to the needs of employers, and focus on areas that offer strong long-term employment opportunities. Upon completion, graduates are prepared for entry-level positions in the health-care field.

Financial Aid/Scholarships

Information regarding Pell Grants, Perkins, WIA, and other assistance can be obtained from the Finance Office. Financial is aid available for those who qualify.

Accreditation

All programs are accredited by the Accrediting Commission of Career Schools and Colleges of Technology (ACCSCT).

Admissions

Successful candidates are selected based on admissions tests, interviews, and the completion and presentation of required documents. Enrollment is open to all high school graduates as well as those holding a GED or its equivalency. Under certain circumstances, students who do not have a high school diploma or its equivalent may still be accepted for admission. Students should contact the Admissions Department for additional information.

Graduation Requirements

To be eligible for graduation, students must successfully complete all classroom modules with a grade of at least 70 percent, finish an approved externship of 160 hours, and complete all other program requirements.

Contact

Nina Kamatani, Director of Admissions
22336 Main Street, First Floor
Hayward, CA 94541
Phone: (510) 582-9500
Fax: (510) 582-9645
E-mail: kamatan@cci.edu
Web: www.bryman-college.com

Program Content

Massage Therapy, Medical Administrative Assistant, Medical Assisting, Medical Insurance Billing/Coding

Programs Eligible for Scholarship	Tuition and Fees	Course Length/Credit Hours	Credential Earned
Massage Therapy	$12,197	720 clock hours/61 credit hours	Diploma
Medical Administrative Assistant	$12,071	720 clock hours/47 credit hours	Diploma
Medical Assisting	$12,380	720 clock hours/47 credit hours	Diploma
Medical Insurance Billing/Coding	$ 6,981	480 clock hours/29 credit hours	Diploma

Bryman College, Los Angeles

About Our Institution
The Bryman Schools were founded in 1962 by Mrs. Esther Bryman as the Los Angeles Colleges of Medical and Dental Assistants. The Los Angeles campus was the original school. In December 1995, Corinthian Schools, Inc. (CSi), a division of Corinthian Colleges, Inc. (CCi), acquired the schools. CCi is one of the largest postsecondary school organizations in the United States, operating more than eighty colleges and institutions nationwide.

Bryman's philosophy is to provide high-quality programs that are sound in concept, implemented by a competent and dedicated faculty and geared to serve those seeking a solid foundation in the health-care field. The programs emphasize hands-on training, are relevant to the needs of employers, and focus on areas that offer strong long-term employment opportunities. Upon completion, graduates are prepared for entry-level positions in both medical and dental practices. Upon completion, graduates are prepared for entry-level positions in medical, dental, and pharmacy technician practices.

The College is conveniently located near good public transportation and easily accessible from the Harbor, Santa Monica, and Hollywood freeways.

Financial Aid/Scholarships
Information regarding Pell Grants, FSEOG, FFEL, Perkins, Financing Vocational Rehab, Federal Work-Study, scholarships, and other assistance can be obtained from the Finance Office. Financial aid is available for those who qualify.

Accreditation
All programs are accredited by the Accrediting Commission of Career Schools and Colleges of Technology (ACCSCT). The Medical Assisting program is also accredited by the Commission on Accreditation of Allied Health Education Programs (CAAHEP).

Admissions
Successful candidates are selected based on admissions tests, interviews, and the completion and presentation of required documents. Enrollment is open to all high school graduates as well as those holding a GED or its equivalency. Under certain circumstances, students who do not have a high school diploma or its equivalent may still be accepted for admission under the ability to benefit criteria, with the exception of the Pharmacy Technician program. Students should contact the Admissions Department for additional information.

Graduation Requirements
To be eligible for graduation, students must successfully complete all classroom modules with a grade of at least 70 percent, finish an approved

Program Content
Dental Assisting, Medical Administrative Assistant, Medical Assisting, Medical Insurance Billing/Coding, Pharmacy Technician

externship of 160 hours, receive satisfactory evaluations from the externship facility, and complete all other program requirements.

Contact
Marie Guerrero, Director of Admissions
3460 Wilshire Boulevard, Suite 500
Los Angeles, CA 90010
Phone: (213) 388-9950
Fax: (213) 388-9907
E-mail: mguerrer@cci.edu
Web: www.bryman-college.com

Programs Eligible for Scholarship	Tuition and Fees	Course Length/Credit Hours	Credential Earned
Dental Assisting	$10,846.46	720 clock hours/47 credit hours	Diploma
Medical Administrative Assistant	$10,825.55	720 clock hours/47 credit hours	Diploma
Medical Assisting	$11,173.29	720 clock hours/47 credit hours	Diploma
Medical Insurance Billing/Coding	$ 8,655.93	560 clock hours/35 credit hours	Diploma
Pharmacy Technician	$11,094.78	720 clock hours/58 credit hours	Diploma

Bryman College, Ontario

About Our Institution
Bryman College, Ontario, was founded in 1986 as American Academy for Career Education. It was renamed Nova Institute of Health Technology and acquired in 1991 by Educorp, Inc. In 2000, it was purchased by Corinthian Schools, Inc., a division of Corinthian Colleges, Inc., which owns and operates more than eighty colleges and institutions nationwide. The school's name was then changed to Bryman College, Ontario. Bryman College, Ontario, offers traditional occupational and professional degrees and nondegree programs.

Special Features
The College occupies two floors of an office building consisting of 3,000 square feet of classroom space and 2,000 square feet of laboratory space with a total area of 7,500 square feet. The facilities are modern and air-conditioned. Each classroom is equipped with supportive materials to enrich and broaden the students' knowledge and training. Classroom and laboratories are equipped for a maximum class size of 30 students and usually average between 20 and 25 students for theory and 15 to 20 students for laboratory. The facility can accommodate 150 students at any one time. Ample parking is also available for students, with handicapped-accessible services provided.

Financial Aid/Scholarships
Financial assistance information may be obtained from the Financial Aid Office. To be eligible for some student assistant programs, students are required to demonstrate financial need. Eligibility for some types of financial aid is awarded on the basis of need only if the estimated cost of attending for a given period is greater than the student's expected family contribution (known as EFC).

Accreditation
The College maintains all approvals from the Bureau for Private Postsecondary and Vocational Education as well as its accreditation by the Accrediting Commission of Career Schools and Colleges of Technology (ACCSCT).

Admissions
All applicants must have a high school diploma or equivalent. However, the educational requirement may also be met if the applicant is at least 18 years of age and can demonstrate the ability to benefit from the training. The ability to benefit is determined by passing the admission examination and by a personal interview with the school administrator. Applicants who possess a high school diploma or equivalent take the PAR Aptitude Test published by the Irwin Corporation. Applicants without a high school diploma or equivalent take the Career Programs Assessment Test

Program Contents
Business Management/Administrative Assistant, Dental Assistant, Massage Therapist, Medical Assistant, Medical Insurance Biller, Medical Office Management, X-Ray Technician

(CPAt). Applicants may apply for diploma, certificate, or accelerated programs. All applications are taken in person. An appointment is necessary. Successful completion of an entrance examination is necessary. Students may enroll daily for upcoming start dates.

Graduation Requirements
To qualify for graduation and a diploma, a student must complete a prescribed course of study with a minimum average of 70 (C), meet the credit-hour and skills requirements for the program, meet the school's attendance and conduct policies, and satisfy his or her financial obligations to the school.

Enrollment
There are 500 to 600 students enrolled.

Contact
Alfred Mark Desrosiers
Director of Admissions
1460 South Milliken Avenue
Ontario, CA 91761
Phone: (909) 984-5027
Fax: (909) 988-9339
E-mail: adesrosiers@cci.edu
Web: www.bryman-college.com

Programs Eligible for Scholarship	Tuition and Fees	Course Length/Credit Hours	Credential Earned
Business Management/Administrative Assistant/Medical Office Management*	$11,566	9 months	Diploma
Dental Assistant	$11,138.28	8 months	Diploma
Massage Therapist	$12,502.04	9 months	Diploma
Medical Assisting	$11,042.09	8 months	Diploma
Medical Insurance Biller	$ 8,674.50	6 months	Diploma
X-Ray Technician	$12,648.84	9 months	Diploma

* Average cost for tuition and fees. Costs vary depending on Associate of Science emphasis.

Bryman College, Reseda

About Our Institution
The Bryman Schools were founded in 1962 by Mrs. Esther Bryman as the Los Angeles Colleges of Medical and Dental Assistants. The Los Angeles campus was the original school. In December 1995, Corinthian Schools, Inc. (CSi), a division of Corinthian Colleges, Inc. (CCi), acquired the schools. CCi is one of the largest postsecondary school organizations in the United States, operating more than eighty colleges and institutions nationwide.

Bryman's philosophy is to provide quality programs that are sound in concept, implemented by a competent and dedicated faculty and geared to serve those seeking a solid foundation in the health-care field. The programs emphasize hands-on training, are relevant to the needs of employers, and focus on areas that offer strong long-term employment opportunities. Upon completion, graduates are prepared for entry-level positions in the medical or dental fields.

Financial Aid/Scholarships
Information regarding Pell Grants, FSEOG, FFEL, Perkins, state grants, WIA, and other assistance can be obtained from the Finance Office. Financial aid is available for those who qualify.

Accreditation
All programs are accredited by the Accrediting Commission of Career Schools and Colleges of Technology (ACCSCT).

Admissions
Successful candidates are selected based on admissions tests, interviews, and the completion and presentation of required documents. Enrollment is open to all high school graduates as well as those holding a GED or its equivalency. Under certain circumstances, students who do not have a high school diploma or its equivalent may still be accepted for admissions under the Ability to Benefit criteria. Students should contact the Admissions Department for additional information.

Graduation Requirements
To be eligible for graduation, students must successfully complete all classroom modules with a grade of at least 70 percent, finish an approved externship/clinical requirement, and complete all other program requirements.

Program Content
Dental Assisting, Dialysis Technician, Massage Therapy, Medical Administrative Assistant, Medical Assisting, Surgical Technologist

Contact
Paula Dorsey, Director of Admissions
Bryman College
18040 Sherman Way, #400
Reseda, CA 91335
Phone: (818) 774-0550
Fax: (818) 774-1577
E-mail: pdorsey@cci.edu
Web: www.bryman-college.com

Programs Eligible for Scholarship	Tuition and Fees	Course Length/Credit Hours	Credential Earned
Dental Assisting	$11,485.40	720 clock hours/47 credit hours	Diploma
Dialysis Technician	$13,668.82	720 clock hours/47 credit hours	Diploma
Massage Therapy	$12,510.45	720 clock hours/47 credit hours	Diploma
Medical Administrative Assistant	$11,406.75	720 clock hours/47 credit hours	Diploma
Medical Assisting	$11,377.80	720 clock hours/47 credit hours	Diploma
Surgical Technologist	$22,813.20	1,280 clock hours/75 credit hours	Diploma

Bryman College, San Bernardino

About Our Institution

Bryman College, San Bernardino, is a part of Corinthian Schools, Inc. (CSi), a division of Corinthian Colleges, Inc. (CCi). CCi is one of the largest postsecondary school organizations in the United States, operating more than eighty colleges and institutions nationwide. Bryman College, San Bernardino, formerly Skadron College, is the oldest private business school in San Bernardino County.

The College's philosophy is to provide high-quality programs that are sound in concept, implemented by a competent and dedicated faculty, and geared to serve those seeking a solid foundation in the health-care and business fields. The programs emphasize hands-on training, are relevant to the needs of employers, and focus on areas that offer strong long-term employment opportunities. Upon completion, graduates are prepared for entry-level positions in health-care fields and business.

Financial Aid/Scholarships

Information regarding Pell Grants, FSEOG, Perkins, Cal Grants, and other assistance can be obtained from the Finance Office. Financial aid is available for those who qualify.

Accreditation

All programs are accredited by the Accrediting Council for Independent Colleges and Schools (ACICS). The Medical Assisting program is accredited by the Commission on Accreditation of Allied Health Education Programs (CAAHEP).

Admissions

Successful candidates are selected based on admissions tests, interviews, and the completion and presentation of required documents. Enrollment is open to all high school graduates as well as those holding a GED or its equivalent. Under certain circumstances, students who do not have a high school diploma or its equivalent may still be accepted for admissions. Students should contact the Admissions Department for additional information.

Graduation Requirements

To be eligible for graduation, students must successfully complete all classroom modules with a grade of at least 70 percent (or 2.0), finish an approved externship of 160 hours for some courses, and complete all other program requirements.

Program Content

Computerized Office Applications, Homeland Security, Massage Therapy, Medical Administrative Assistant, Medical Assistant, Medical Clinical Assistant

Contact

Mary Beth Coutts, Director of Admissions
217 Club Center Drive, Suite A
San Bernardino, CA 92408
Phone: (909) 777-3300
Fax: (909) 777-3313
E-mail: mcook@cci.edu
Web: www.bryman-college.com

Programs Eligible for Scholarship	Tuition and Fees	Course Length/Credit Hours	Credential Earned
Computerized Office Applications	$10,500	6 modules/720 clock hours/54 credit hours	Diploma
Homeland Security	$9,500	7 modules/560 clock hours/48 credit hours	Diploma
Massage Therapy	$11,525	9 modules/720 clock hours/57 credit hours	Diploma
Medical Administrative Assistant	$10,700	8 modules/720 clock hours/47 credit hours	Diploma
Medical Assistant	$11,025	8 modules/720 clock hours/47 credit hours	Diploma
Medical Clinical Assistant	$4,550	3 modules/360 clock hours/27 credit hours	Certificate

Bryman College, San Francisco

About Our Institution

The Bryman Schools were founded in 1962 by Mrs. Esther Bryman as the Los Angeles Colleges of Medical and Dental Assistants. The Los Angeles campus was the original school. In December 1995, Corinthian Schools, Inc. (CSi), a division of Corinthian Colleges, Inc. (CCi), acquired the schools. CCi is one of the largest postsecondary school organizations in the United States, operating more than eighty colleges and institutions nationwide.

The College's philosophy is to provide high-quality programs that are sound in concept, implemented by a competent and dedicated faculty, and geared to serve those seeking a solid foundation in the health-care field. The programs emphasize hands-on training, are relevant to the needs of employers, and focus on areas that offer strong long-term employment opportunities. Upon completion, graduates are prepared for entry-level positions in both medical and dental practices.

The school is centrally located in the heart of San Francisco and is near both bus routes and BART.

Financial Aid/Scholarships

Information regarding Federal Pell Grants, FSEOG, FFEL, FDSLP, Federal Perkins Loans, WIA, and other assistance can be obtained from the Finance Office. Financial aid is available for those who qualify.

Accreditation

All programs are accredited by the Accrediting Commission of Career Schools and Colleges of Technology (ACCSCT). The Medical Assisting program is also accredited by the Commission on Accreditation of Allied Health Education Programs (CAAHEP).

Admissions

Successful candidates are selected based on admissions tests, interviews, and the completion and presentation of required documents. Enrollment is open to all high school graduates as well as those holding a GED certificate or its equivalency. Under certain circumstances, students who do not have a high school diploma or its equivalent may still be accepted for admissions. Please contact our Admissions Department for additional information.

Graduation Requirements

To be eligible for graduation, students must successfully complete all classroom modules with a grade of at least 70 percent, finish an approved externship of 160 hours, and complete all other program requirements.

Program Content

Dental Assisting, Homeland Security Specialist, Massage Therapy, Medical Administrative Assistant, Medical Assisting, Medical Insurance Billing/Coding, Pharmacy Technician, X-Ray Technician Limited

Contact

Earon B. Mackey, Director of Admissions
814 Mission Street
Suite 500
San Francisco, CA 94103
Phone: (415) 777-2500
Fax: (415) 495-3457
E-mail: emackey@cci.edu
Web: www.bryman-college.com

Programs Eligible for Scholarship	Tuition and Fees	Course Length/Credit Hours	Credential Earned
Dental Assisting	$11,970	720 clock hours/47 credit hours	Diploma
Homeland Security Specialist	$10,000	560 clock hours/48 credit hours	Diploma
Massage Therapy	$11,288	720 clock hours/57 credit hours	Diploma
Medical Administrative Assistant	$11,970	720 clock hours/47 credit hours	Diploma
Medical Assisting	$11,970	720 clock hours/47 credit hours	Diploma
Medical Insurance Billing/Coding	$ 8,505	560 clock hours/35 credit hours	Diploma
Pharmacy Technician	$11,970	720 clock hours/58 credit hours	Diploma
X-Ray Technician Limited	$13,000	600 clock hours/48 credit hours	Diploma

Bryman College, San Jose

About Our Institution

The Bryman Schools were founded in 1962 by Mrs. Esther Bryman as the Los Angeles Colleges of Medical and Dental Assistants. The Los Angeles campus was the original school. In December 1995, Corinthian Schools, Inc. (CSi), a division of Corinthian Colleges, Inc. (CCi), acquired the schools. CCi is one of the largest postsecondary school organizations in the United States, operating more than eighty colleges and institutions nationwide.

Bryman's philosophy is to provide high-quality programs that are sound in concept, implemented by a competent and dedicated faculty, and geared to serve those seeking a solid foundation in the health-care field. The programs emphasize hands-on training, are relevant to the needs of employers, and focus on areas that offer strong long-term employment opportunities. Upon completion, graduates are prepared for entry-level positions in both medical and dental practices.

The College is located on the West Side of San Jose, accessible to public transportation and freeways.

Financial Aid/Scholarships

Information regarding Federal Pell Grants, FSEOG, FFEL, Federal Perkins Loans, Federal Work-Study Program, VA funds, WIA, and other assistance can be obtained from the Finance Office. Financial aid is available for those who qualify.

Accreditation

All program are accredited by the Accrediting Commission of Career Schools and Colleges of Technology (ACCSCT). Council on Accreditation of Allied Health Educational Programs (CAAHEP).

Admissions

Successful candidates are selected based on admissions tests, interviews, and the completion and presentation of required documents. Enrollment is open to all high school graduates as well as those holding a GED certificate or its equivalency. Under certain circumstances, students who do not have a high school diploma or its equivalent may still be accepted for admission. Students should contact Bryman's Admissions Department for additional information.

Graduation Requirements

To be eligible for graduation, students must successfully complete all classroom modules with a grade of at least 70 percent, finish an approved externship of 160 hours, receive satisfactory evaluations from the externship facility, and complete all other program requirements.

Program Content

Dental Assisting, Massage Therapy, Medical Administrative Assistant, Medical Assisting, Medical Insurance Billing/Coding, Pharmacy Technician

Contact

JoAnn Andre, Director of Admissions
Bryman College
Suite 102
1245 South Winchester Boulevard
San Jose, CA 95128
Phone: (408) 246-4171
Fax: (408) 557-9855
E-mail: jgenrich@cci.edu
Web: www.bryman-college.com

Programs Eligible for Scholarship	Tuition and Fees	Course Length/Credit Hours	Credential Earned
Dental Assisting	$13,131.50	720 clock hours/47 credit hours	Diploma
Massage Therapy	$13,815.50	720 clock hours/57 credit hours	Diploma
Medical Administrative Assistant	$13,409.50	720 clock hours/47 credit hours	Diploma
Medical Assisting	$13,341.50	720 clock hours/47 credit hours	Diploma
Medical Insurance Billing/Coding	$ 9,165.50	560 clock hours/35 credit hours	Diploma
Pharmacy Technician	$13,504.50	720 clock hours/58 credit hours	Diploma

Bryman College, Torrance

About Our Institution
The Bryman Schools were founded in 1962 by Mrs. Esther Bryman as the Los Angeles Colleges of Medical and Dental Assistants. The Los Angeles campus was the original school. In December 1995, Corinthian Schools, Inc. (CSi), a division of Corinthian Colleges, Inc. (CCi), acquired the schools. CCi is one of the largest postsecondary school organizations in the United States, operating more than eighty colleges and institutions nationwide.

Special Features
The campus is located on the second floor of the facility and has four spacious, air-conditioned classrooms for instruction, handicapped-accessible rest room facilities, administrative offices, a reception area, and an elevator that also provides access for the handicapped. The maximum occupancy of the facility is 240 students.

Financial Aid/Scholarships
This campus offers students several options for payment of tuition. Those able to pay tuition are given a plan to help reduce their fees upon entry. On the other hand, the school recognizes that many students lack the resources to begin their educational training. The campus participates in several types of federal, state, and institutional financial aid programs, most of which are based on financial need.

Accreditation
The College voluntarily undergoes periodic accrediting evaluations by teams of qualified examiners, including subject experts and specialists in occupational education and private school administration. The school is accredited by the Accrediting Council for Continuing Education and Training and is approved to operate by the Bureau for Private Postsecondary and Vocational Education.

Admissions
Applicants enrolling in the Pharmacy Technician program must be high school graduates or have a GED certificate.

Graduation Requirements
To be eligible for graduation, students must complete all required classroom modules with a grade of at least 2.0 and meet the grade requirements for the module components, if applicable. Students must successfully complete all hours (160) in an approved externship for the Pharmacy Technician program, receive satisfactory evaluations from the externship facility, and complete all program requirements.

Enrollment
There are 180 students enrolled.

Program Content
Massage Therapy, Pharmacy Technician

Contact
Sandy Ock, Director of Admissions
Bryman College
1231 Cabrillo Avenue, Suite 201
Torrance, CA 90501
Phone: (310) 320-3200
Fax: (310) 320-7030
E-mail: sock@cci.edu
Web: www.bryman-college.com

Programs Eligible for Scholarship	Tuition and Fees	Course Length/Credit Hours	Credential Earned
Massage Therapy	$10,520	720 clock hours/57 credit hours	Diploma
Pharmacy Technician	$ 9,820	720 clock hours/58 credit hours	Diploma

Bryman College, West Los Angeles

About Our Institution

In 2000, NOVA Institute of Health Technology was purchased by Corinthian Schools, Inc., a division of Corinthian Colleges, Inc. The school's name was then changed to Bryman College. The Institute has been in existence since 1969. In 1990, the Institute became a free-standing school, and in 1994, it moved to its current facility.

Special Features

Bryman College, Los Angeles campus, is located in the heart of the West Side in Los Angeles. The campus provides a healthy and comfortable learning environment and is close to a major health-care facility as well as a varied cultural and business center. The facility can accommodate 250 students at any one time. The Los Angeles campus occupies more than 20,000 square feet, including classrooms, administrative offices, and a laboratory section. Each classroom may hold between 25 and 35 students for theory and 15 to 20 students for laboratory. Audiovisual equipment and a wide assortment of subject-related recordings are available for use in the classrooms.

Financial Aid/Scholarships

Financial assistance information may be obtained from the Financial Aid Office. To be eligible for some student assistant programs, you will be required to demonstrate financial need. Eligibility for some types of financial aid is awarded on the basis of need only if the estimated cost of attending for a given period is greater than your expected family contribution (known as EFC).

Accreditation

The institute maintains all approvals from the Bureau for Private Postsecondary and Vocational Education as well as its accreditation by the ACCSCT (Accrediting Commission of Career Schools and Colleges of Technology).

Admissions

All applicants must have a high school diploma or equivalent. However, the educational requirement may also be met if the applicant is at least 18 years of age and can demonstrate the ability to benefit from the training. The ability to benefit is determined by passing the admission examination and by a personal interview with the school administrator. Applicants who possess a high school diploma or equivalent take the SRA Aptitude Test published by NCS Pearson, Inc. Applicants without a high school diploma or equivalent take the Career Placement Aptitude Test published by ACT, Inc. All applicants for degree programs must have a high school diploma or equivalent. All applications are taken in person, with appointment. Successful completion of an entrance examination is necessary. Students may enroll daily for upcoming start dates.

Programs Offered

Business Management/Administrative Assistant, Dental Assisting, Massage Therapist, Medical Assisting, Medical Insurance Biller, X-Ray Technician

Graduation Requirements

To qualify for graduation and a diploma, a student must complete a prescribed course of study with a minimum average of 70 percent (C), meet the credit-hour and skills requirements for the program, meet the school's attendance and conduct policies, and satisfy his/her financial obligations to the school.

Enrollment

There are 537 students enrolled.

Contact

Director of Admissions
Bryman College
3000 S. Robertson Blvd., Third Floor
Los Angeles, CA 90034
Phone: (310) 840-5777
Fax: (310) 287-2344
Web: www.bryman-college.com

Programs Eligible for Scholarship	Tuition and Fees	Course Length/Credit Hours	Credential Earned
Business Management/Administrative Assistant	$10,788	36 weeks/54 credit hours	Diploma
Dental Assisting	$10,650	36 weeks/47 credit hours	Diploma
Massage Therapist	$11,375	36 weeks/57 credit hours	Diploma
Medical Assisting	$10,415	36 weeks/47 credit hours	Diploma
Medical Insurance Biller	$ 8,190	24 weeks/35 credit hours	Diploma
X-Ray Technician	$12,160	36 weeks/39 credit hours	Diploma

Central Coast College, Salinas

About Our Institution

Central Coast College is a private, coeducational, career-training institution. The College provides a specialized curriculum to meet the needs of students interested in professional preparation for careers in medical assisting, computer office administration, medical office administration, accounting, and computer and networking technology.

Location: Central Coast College is located in Monterey County, one of California's most beautiful regions. Founded in the city of Salinas in 1983, the College is situated at the northern end of the world-famous Salinas Valley. It is approximately 20 miles from the scenic Monterey Peninsula, which is renowned for its picturesque coastline and world-famous golf courses.

History: The College began in 1983 with a single program in business data processing. Computer office administration and general accounting programs were added during the mid-1980s to meet the growing needs for technically competent workers. In 1993, an increased need for medical office workers led to programs in medical billing and medical office administration. The College added the medical assisting program in 1997 and the computer and network support specialist program in 2000.

Affiliations: Salinas Valley and Monterey Peninsula Chambers of Commerce, Hispanic Chamber of Commerce, Central Coast Human Resource Association, California Association of Private Postsecondary Schools, Career College Association, various other professional organizations.

Special Features

Learning is a holistic experience at the College. The focus is on preparing students for career employment in the shortest time possible, with intensive, career-oriented classes. Instruction emphasizes skill development through hands-on application and the development of responsible and mature work habits and attitudes—qualities that are essential to success on the job.

High standards for attendance, appearance, and behavior instill a strong work ethic and emphasize the re-creation of the work environment in the classroom. Regular evaluations are given, and students are expected to be on time, dressed, and ready for work. Internships and externships provide additional on-the-job training. The College comprises two buildings, with computer classrooms, an information technology laboratory, and a fully equipped medical assisting laboratory in addition to Student Services offices. A traditional library is supplemented by a high-speed Internet connection for research and other educational services. Students have a comfortable break area; free parking is available on or near the campus.

The College's mission is to provide high-quality career education that meets the needs of the students and community. Every individual deserves a high-quality education that enhances professionalism and employability while maintaining the College's integrity and standards. Learning should be a positive experience, and, in addition to learning specific skills, students should develop responsible, mature work attitudes and habits and a favorable self-image. There are 15 part- and full-time instructors, with an average of 17 years' work experience in their fields. Students benefit greatly from this depth of knowledge and workplace experience.

Financial Aid/Scholarships

Central Coast College participates in various programs of financial assistance. The College offers assistance in applying for the following federal programs: Federal Work-Study Program, Federal Supplemental Educational Opportunity Grants (FSEOG), Federal Stafford Student Loan (Subsidized and Unsubsidized), Federal Parent Loan for Undergraduate Students (PLUS), Federal Pell Grant, Workforce Investment Act (WIA), Approved Enrollment of Veteran's Administration Students for Educational Benefits, and is authorized by U.S. Department of Immigration to enroll nonimmigrant alien students.

Program Content

Accounting: General, Accounts Payable/Receivable, Payroll. Medical Office: Medical Assisting, Medical Administrative Assistant/Biller. Computer Specialist: Accounting. Computer Office Administration: Administrative Assistant. Information Technology: Computer and Network Support Specialist.

Program Description

Programs combine lecture and laboratory instruction, and emphasize hands-on, work-related skills. For specific program descriptions and objectives, prospective students should contact the office or visit the College Web site.

Tuition and Fees

Tuition varies by program and ranges from $6,900 to $10,400, which includes books and materials. A $75 registration fee is also charged. Prospective students should contact the school for up-to-date tuition information.

Accreditation

The school is nationally accredited by the Accrediting Council for Continuing Education and Training (ACCET). The Medical Assisting Program is also accredited by Accrediting Bureau of Health Education Schools (ABHES).

Admissions

Applicants for admission are required to demonstrate an aptitude for success through personal assessment by school staff members, which includes an enrollment interview and a passing score on the entrance exam. A high school diploma or GED is required for admission.

Graduation Requirements

Students must meet each of their program competencies and complete all classes with a passing grade (minimum GPA of 2.0), within 150 percent of the normal time allowed for their programs. Overall attendance must be 90 percent or better; students must satisfy all financial, academic, and other obligations to the school.

Contact

Elaine Giuliano, Administrative Coordinator
480 South Main Street
Salinas, CA 93901
Phone: (831) 424-6767
Fax: (831) 753-6485
E-mail: giuel@cccbus.com
Web: www.centralcoastcollege.edu

All programs listed above are eligible for scholarship.
Tuition and fees vary by program; contact the College for current information.
Course length varies from 18–54 weeks.
Credentials earned: Graduates of programs listed above receive a diploma.

Everest College, Rancho Cucamonga

About Our Institution
Everest College, Rancho Cucamonga, is a branch campus of Springfield College in Springfield, Missouri, with roots extending back to 1910. Everst College, Rancho Cucamonga is one of more than eighty schools owned and operated by Corinthian Colleges, Inc., in the United States.

Special Features
Everest College is dedicated to the ideal that every student should have the encouragement and opportunity to develop to the full potential, believing that most students succeed in a collegiate environment when receiving proper motivation. Faculty and staff members are dedicated to providing that motivation and assisting students in the achievement of personal, educational, career, and economic goals. The College is located in Rancho Cucamonga, one of the premier cities in the Inland Empire. Rancho Cucamonga can trace its beginning to the mid-1800s when it was a major wine grape– and citrus-growing area. Located about 40 miles east of downtown Los Angeles, Rancho Cucamonga lies within the county of San Bernadino. San Bernadino County, the largest county in the United States, is home to approximately 1.6 million residents and is one of the nation's fastest growing metropolitan areas.

Financial Aid/Scholarships
Everest College students are eligible to participate in Title IV Financial Aid Programs. Students' federal student financial aid eligibility and access to alternative funding sources are discussed with students in detail during the application and enrollment process.

Accreditation
Everest College is accredited by the Accrediting Council for Independent Colleges and Schools (ACICS) to award associate degrees.

Admissions
Prospective students must have a high school diploma or a recognized equivalency certificate (GED), and are required to furnish proof by providing the school with the official transcript or GED certificate. A copy of the document is placed in the student's file. The student must also achieve a passing score on a nationally normed, standardized test.

Graduation Requirements
Students at Everest College must have a minimum 2.0 cumulative grade point average and the required hours of the program they are pursuing to be eligible to graduate.

Enrollment
Eight hundred students are enrolled.

Program Content
Accounting, Business, Criminal Justice, Paralegal

Contact
Gregory K. Lam
Director of Admissions
9616 Archibald Avenue, Ste. 100
Rancho Cucamonga, CA 91730
Phone: (909) 484-4311
Fax: (909) 484-1162
Web: www.everest-college.com

Programs Eligible for Scholarship	Tuition and Fees	Course Length/Credit Hours	Credential Earned
Accounting	$249/credit hour	96 credit hours	AS
Business	$249/credit hour	96 credit hours	AS
Criminal Justice	$249/credit hour	96 credit hours	AS
Paralegal	$249/credit hour	96 credit hours	AS

Gemological Institute of America, Carlsbad

About Our Institution

Established in 1931, the Gemological Institute of America (GIA) is the world's foremost authority in gemology and the nonprofit educational and research center for the international gem and jewelry industry. Having trained more than 300,000 professionals around the world, GIA offers credentials that denote the highest level of professional training in the jewelry industry. Small class size and personalized instruction ensure that GIA students quickly develop highly valued technical skills in diamond grading, gem identification, fine jewelry sales, design, fabrication, repair, and jewelry business management.

Special Features

Held in the highest esteem all over the world, GIA attracts students from every corner of the globe. Students who study at GIA World Headquarters and Robert Mouawad Campus in Carlsbad, California, have access to some of the industry's most respected gem and jewelry authorities as well as the world's largest gemological library and information center. In addition to its headquarters in Carlsbad, GIA also has U.S. branch schools in New York and Los Angeles. GIA students also benefit from ongoing career support through the Career Services department, the GIA Alumni Association, and the twice-annual Career Fair, the largest recruiting event in the jewelry industry. The Student Services department assists students in finding local housing, medical and banking services, and entertainment and recreational facilities.

Financial Aid/Scholarships

For students who qualify, scholarships, grants, and loans may be available for certain On Campus programs to help pay for a portion of tuition and living expenses.

Tuition and Fees

Tuition and fees for the following On Campus programs are: Graduate Gemologist (G.G.): $13,495; Graduate Jeweler (G.J.): $13,495; Applied Jewelry Arts (A.J.A.): $13,495; Jewelry Design: $4,150; and Jewelry Business Management: $7,960. Combined programs are also available.

Accreditation

GIA Carlsbad is accredited by the Accrediting Commission of Career Schools and Colleges of Technology (ACCSCT). GIA Los Angeles and GIA New York are each accredited by the ACCSCT as branches of the main school in Carlsbad. GIA Carlsbad is also accredited by the Accrediting Commission of the Distance Education and Training Council (DETC).

Admissions

Admission to On Campus programs is year-round, with new classes beginning approximately each month. Prospective students must meet the minimum education requirement of a high school diploma or GED. Non-U.S. citizens must demonstrate English proficiency by a minimum TOEFL score of 500/173, by IELTS Band 5.0 or higher, by a minimum grade of B on the Cambridge CAE exam, by proof of graduation from a secondary school or college/university where English is the language of instruction, or by proof of completion of the ELS Language Center Level 109 course.

Graduation Requirements

Students must complete the specific requirements of each program in which they are enrolled and achieve the minimum passing scores on all assignments, quizzes, and exams.

Program Content

Gemology, Jewelry Business Management, Jewelry Design, Jewelry Manufacturing

Program Description

Not all programs are offered at each campus.

Graduate Gemologist Through extensive practice in a lab-like setting, students learn to grade and identify both diamonds and colored stones, to use gemological testing equipment, and to separate synthetic, treated, assembled, and imitations from natural gemstones.

Graduate Jeweler Working in karat gold, platinum, and sterling silver, students learn custom jewelry manufacturing, including stone-setting, assembly, fabrication, and jewelry repair.

Applied Jewelry Arts Students learn how to create beautiful jewelry with hands-on training in all design fundamentals, including: drawing, illustration, wax carving, casting, and state-of-the-art CAD/CAM computer renderings.

Jewelry Design Students learn the principles of design and develop the skills to create and illustrate jewelry designs for beauty, problem-free manufacturing, long wear, and comfort.

Jewelry Business Management In a business program tailored specifically for the gem and jewelry industry, students gain the executive leadership skills and insight needed to make profitable business decisions in the jewelry industry.

Contact

Jason Drake, Admissions Manager
Gemological Institute of America
The Robert Mouawad Campus
5345 Armada Drive
Carlsbad, CA 92008
Phone: (760) 603-4001
            (800) 421-7250 Ext. 4001 (toll-free)
Fax: (760) 603-4003
E-mail: eduinfo@gia.edu
Web: www.gia.edu

Programs Eligible for Scholarship	Tuition and Fees	Course Length/Credits	Credential Earned
Graduate Gemologist Program	$13,495	26 weeks	Diploma
Graduate Jeweler Program	$13,495	26 weeks	Diploma
Applied Jewelry Arts Program	$13,495	24 weeks	Diploma
Graduate Jeweler Gemologist Program	$26,990	12 months	Diploma
Graduate Jeweler with Design and Wax	$20,795	10 months	Diploma
Graduate Jeweler Gemologist with Design and Wax	$34,290	16 months	Diploma

Heald College, Concord Campus, Concord

About Our Institution

Heald College is a nonprofit, WASC-accredited institution with eleven campuses located in northern California, Hawaii, and Oregon. Heald College was founded in 1863 by Edward Payson Heald and for more than 140 years has helped students prepare for successful business, technical, and health-care careers.

Located in a 66,000-square-foot, fully networked facility that opened in January, 2001, the Heald College Concord location serves all of Contra Costa County. The building features a beautiful, multipurpose conference center with complete wireless capability. The Concord campus is conveniently located near the crossroads of Highways 242 and 4, with ample on-campus parking. It is also a short bus ride from the North Concord Bay Area Rapid Transit (BART) station. Programs in business, technology, and health care are offered.

Special Features

Heald College provides focused programs in business, technology, and health care that prepare students for success in the workplace in the shortest practical time. Heald College also provides personal attention every step of the way. From completion of the admissions application through navigation of financial aid options to ongoing academic assistance programs (workshops, individual tutoring, learning resource centers) to job placement assistance, the College believes that it succeeds only when its students succeed.

Financial Aid/Scholarships

A Financial Aid Adviser meets with students to assess each person's individual situation and eligibility for assistance. The adviser explains each option, guides the student to those that are appropriate, and assists in the proper completion of all the necessary paperwork. Financial aid options available include Federal Pell Grants, Federal SEOG, scholarships, state Cal Grants and private grants, Federal Work-Study, Federal Stafford Student Loans (subsidized and unsubsidized), Federal PLUS Loans, private loans, Workforce Investment Act (WIA) grants, and veterans' educational benefits. Students must qualify for financial aid and meet specific academic progress requirements to obtain and remain eligible for all federal and state financial assistance programs.

Tuition and Fees

Tuition and fees vary by program length. Students should contact the Admissions Department for additional information.

Accreditation

Heald is accredited by the Accrediting Commission for Community and Junior Colleges of the Western Association of Schools and Colleges (WASC). Heald's medical assisting program and its medical office program have both been approved by the American Medical Technologists (AMT), a nonprofit certification agency, and by the National Center for Competency Testing. These partnerships allow Heald's health-care graduates to sit for appropriate certification examinations. The Heald College accounting curriculum has been approved by the California Tax Education Council (CTEC) to offer course work that fulfills the 60-hour qualifying education requirement, imposed by the state, to become a tax preparer.

Admissions

Applicants must interview with an Admissions Adviser, indicate that they have a high school diploma or GED equivalent, complete an application, pass an admissions examination, and be recommended by an Admissions

Program Content

Most Heald campuses offer Associate in Applied Science (A.A.S.) degrees and diploma programs in accounting, business administration, criminal justice, office skills, office technologies, sales and marketing, electronics technology, software technologies, network systems administration, technical support, medical assisting, and medical office administration as well as opportunities to earn a second A.A.S. degree or certificate in CISCO and Microsoft Windows networking technology or in business accounting. Special diploma and certificate programs in medical assisting and office skills are also offered at some campuses.

Program Description

Heald College programs include both professional and general education courses, which together allow students to experience the integration of knowledge and skills. The general education courses offer students breadth in their experiences by introducing them to major areas of knowledge, thus expanding their understanding of the world and cultures around them. Furthermore, these courses foster a spirit of inquiry and provide for students' development of the skills, knowledge, and intellectual habits necessary to support their personal, professional, and public lives. Heald also provides hands-on training in all of its programs to ensure that students can successfully apply the skills they learn in the workplace after graduation.

Adviser to the Campus Director. Students should contact the Admissions Department for additional information.

Graduation Requirements

To be eligible for graduation, students must successfully complete all classes with a minimum 2.0 cumulative grade point average and complete all program, unit, and course requirements.

Contact

Lily Woo, Director of Admissions
5130 Commercial Circle
Concord, CA 94520
Phone: (925) 288-5800
        (800) 755-3550 (toll-free)
Fax: (925) 288-5892
E-mail: lily_woo@heald.edu
Web: www.heald.edu

Heald College, Fresno Campus, Fresno

About Our Institution
Heald College is a nonprofit, WASC-accredited institution with eleven campuses located in northern California, Hawaii, and Oregon. Heald College was founded in 1863 by Edward Payson Heald and for more than 140 years has helped students prepare for successful business, technical, and health-care careers.

The Fresno campus opened in 1891, and it has grown and evolved into a leading career college that offers a range of programs in business, technology, and health care. As San Joaquin Valley emerges as a market for new jobs, Heald College is proud to be providing uniquely qualified graduates. Heald Fresno offers a variety of business, technology, and health-care programs.

Special Features
Heald College provides focused programs in business, technology, and health care that prepare students for success in the workplace in the shortest practical time. Heald College also provides personal attention every step of the way. From completion of the admissions application through navigation of financial aid options to ongoing academic assistance programs (workshops, individual tutoring, learning resource centers) to job placement assistance, the College believes that it succeeds only when its students succeed.

Financial Aid/Scholarships
A Financial Aid Adviser meets with students to assess each person's individual situation and eligibility for assistance. The adviser explains each option, guides the student to those that are appropriate, and assists in the proper completion of all the necessary paperwork. Financial aid options available include Federal Pell Grants, Federal SEOG, scholarships, state Cal Grants and private grants, Federal Work-Study, Federal Stafford Student Loans (subsidized and unsubsidized), Federal PLUS Loans, private loans, Workforce Investment Act (WIA) grants, and veterans' educational benefits. Students must qualify for financial aid and meet specific academic progress requirements to obtain and remain eligible for all federal and state financial assistance programs.

Tuition and Fees
Tuition and fees vary by program length. Students should contact the Admissions Department for additional information.

Accreditation
Heald is accredited by the Accrediting Commission for Community and Junior Colleges of the Western Association of Schools and Colleges (WASC). Heald's medical assisting program and its medical office program have both been approved by the American Medical Technologists (AMT), a nonprofit certification agency, and by the National Center for Competency Testing. These partnerships allow Heald's health-care graduates to sit for appropriate certification examinations. The Heald College accounting curriculum has been approved by the California Tax Education Council (CTEC) to offer course work that fulfills the 60-hour qualifying education requirement, imposed by the state, to become a tax preparer.

Admissions
Applicants must interview with an Admissions Adviser, indicate that they have a high school diploma or GED equivalent, complete an application, pass an admissions examination, and be recommended by an Admissions

Program Content
Most Heald campuses offer Associate in Applied Science (A.A.S.) degrees and diploma programs in accounting, business administration, criminal justice, office skills, office technologies, sales and marketing, software technologies, network systems administration, technical support, medical assisting, and medical office administration as well as opportunities to earn a second A.A.S. degree or certificate in CISCO and Microsoft Windows networking technology or in business accounting. Special diploma and certificate programs in medical assisting and office skills are also offered at some campuses.

Program Description
Heald College programs include both professional and general education courses, which together allow students to experience the integration of knowledge and skills. The general education courses offer students breadth in their experiences by introducing them to major areas of knowledge, thus expanding their understanding of the world and cultures around them. Furthermore, these courses foster a spirit of inquiry and provide for students' development of the skills, knowledge, and intellectual habits necessary to support their personal, professional, and public lives. Heald also provides hands-on training in all of its programs to ensure that students can successfully apply the skills they learn in the workplace after graduation.

Adviser to the Campus Director. Students should contact the Admissions Department for additional information.

Graduation Requirements
To be eligible for graduation, students must successfully complete all classes with a minimum 2.0 cumulative grade point average and complete all program, unit, and course requirements.

Contact
Carolyn Kuralski
255 West Bullard Avenue
Fresno, CA 93704
Phone: (559) 438-4222
(800) 755-3550 (toll-free)
Fax: (559) 438-6368
E-mail: fresnoinfo@heald.edu
Web: www.heald.edu

Heald College, Hayward Campus, Hayward

About Our Institution
Heald College is a nonprofit, WASC-accredited institution with eleven campuses located in northern California, Hawaii, and Oregon. Heald College was founded in 1863 by Edward Payson Heald and for more than 140 years has helped students prepare for successful business, technical, and health-care careers.

Heald College–Hayward has successfully served students for more than fifty years. It has a 58,000-square-foot facility that provides hands-on learning and advanced networking labs. It also offers a convenient student lounge, a Learning Resource Center with access to online databases, and fiber-optic data communications throughout all classrooms. There are many opportunities for qualified graduates in the area. Programs in technology, business, and health care are offered.

Special Features
Heald College provides focused programs in business, technology, and health care that prepare students for success in the workplace in the shortest practical time. Heald College also provides personal attention every step of the way. From completion of the admissions application through navigation of financial aid options to ongoing academic assistance programs (workshops, individual tutoring, learning resource centers) to job placement assistance, the College believes that it succeeds only when its students succeed.

Financial Aid/Scholarships
A Financial Aid Adviser meets with students to assess each person's individual situation and eligibility for assistance. The adviser explains each option, guides the student to those that are appropriate, and assists in the proper completion of all the necessary paperwork. Financial aid options available include Federal Pell Grants, Federal SEOG, scholarships, state Cal Grants and private grants, Federal Work-Study, Federal Stafford Student Loans (subsidized and unsubsidized), Federal PLUS Loans, private loans, Workforce Investment Act (WIA) grants, and veterans' educational benefits. Students must qualify for financial aid and meet specific academic progress requirements to obtain and remain eligible for all federal and state financial assistance programs.

Tuition and Fees
Tuition and fees vary by program length. Students should contact the Admissions Department for additional information.

Accreditation
Heald is accredited by the Accrediting Commission for Community and Junior Colleges of the Western Association of Schools and Colleges (WASC). Heald's medical assisting program and its medical office program have both been approved by the American Medical Technologists (AMT), a nonprofit certification agency, and by the National Center for Competency Testing. These partnerships allow Heald's health-care graduates to sit for appropriate certification examinations. The Heald College accounting curriculum has been approved by the California Tax Education Council (CTEC) to offer course work that fulfills the 60-hour qualifying education requirement, imposed by the state, to become a tax preparer.

Admissions
Applicants must interview with an Admissions Adviser, indicate that they have a high school diploma or GED equivalent, complete an

Program Content
Most Heald campuses offer Associate in Applied Science (A.A.S.) degrees and diploma programs in accounting, business administration, criminal justice, office skills, office technologies, sales and marketing, software technologies, network systems administration, technical support, medical assisting, and medical office administration as well as opportunities to earn a second A.A.S. degree or certificate in CISCO and Microsoft Windows networking technology or in business accounting. Special diploma and certificate programs in medical assisting and office skills are also offered at some campuses.

Program Description
Heald College programs include both professional and general education courses, which together allow students to experience the integration of knowledge and skills. The general education courses offer students breadth in their experiences by introducing them to major areas of knowledge, thus expanding their understanding of the world and cultures around them. Furthermore, these courses foster a spirit of inquiry and provide for students' development of the skills, knowledge, and intellectual habits necessary to support their personal, professional, and public lives. Heald also provides hands-on training in all of its programs to ensure that students can successfully apply the skills they learn in the workplace after graduation.

application, pass an admissions examination, and be recommended by an Admissions Adviser to the Campus Director. Students should contact the Admissions Department for additional information.

Graduation Requirements
To be eligible for graduation, students must successfully complete all classes with a minimum 2.0 cumulative grade point average and complete all program, unit, and course requirements.

Contact
Cheryl Valente, Director of Admissions
25500 Industrial Boulevard
Hayward, CA 94525
Phone: (510) 783-2100
       (800) 755-3550 (toll-free)
Fax: (510) 783-3287
E-mail: cvalente@heald.edu
Web: www.heald.edu

Heald College, Rancho Cordova Campus, Sacramento

About Our Institution
Heald College is a nonprofit, WASC-accredited institution with eleven campuses located in northern California, Hawaii, and Oregon. Heald College was founded in 1863 by Edward Payson Heald and for more than 140 years has helped students prepare for successful business, technical, and health-care careers.

Heald College Rancho Cordova builds upon a legacy of teaching that started in 1912. Today, this campus offers high-demand career programs in business, technology, and health care. The school occupies a 46,000-square-foot building located near Highway 50. The classrooms are fully networked with Internet access for all students. The campus's proximity to Sacramento, California's state capital, makes it part of an area that attracts businesses from all around the world. This community encourages the growth of small businesses as well as emerging technologies.

Special Features
Heald College provides focused programs in business, technology, and health care that prepare students for success in the workplace in the shortest practical time. Heald College also provides personal attention every step of the way. From completion of the admissions application through navigation of financial aid options to ongoing academic assistance programs (workshops, individual tutoring, learning resource centers) to job placement assistance, the College believes that it succeeds only when its students succeed.

Financial Aid/Scholarships
A Financial Aid Adviser meets with students to assess each person's individual situation and eligibility for assistance. The adviser explains each option, guides the student to those that are appropriate, and assists in the proper completion of all the necessary paperwork. Financial aid options available include Federal Pell Grants, Federal SEOG, scholarships, state Cal Grants and private grants, Federal Work-Study, Federal Stafford Student Loans (subsidized and unsubsidized), Federal PLUS Loans, private loans, Workforce Investment Act (WIA) grants, and veterans' educational benefits. Students must qualify for financial aid and meet specific academic progress requirements to obtain and remain eligible for all federal and state financial assistance programs.

Tuition and Fees
Tuition and fees vary by program length. Students should contact the Admissions Department for additional information.

Accreditation
Heald is accredited by the Accrediting Commission for Community and Junior Colleges of the Western Association of Schools and Colleges (WASC). Heald's medical assisting program and its medical office program have both been approved by the American Medical Technologists (AMT), a nonprofit certification agency, and by the National Center for Competency Testing. These partnerships allow Heald's health-care graduates to sit for appropriate certification examinations. The Heald College accounting curriculum has been approved by the California Tax Education Council (CTEC) to offer course work that fulfills the 60-hour qualifying education requirement, imposed by the state, to become a tax preparer.

Admissions
Applicants must interview with an Admissions Adviser, indicate that they have a high school diploma or GED equivalent, complete an application,

Program Content
Most Heald campuses offer Associate in Applied Science (A.A.S.) degrees and diploma programs in accounting, business administration, criminal justice, office skills, office technologies, sales and marketing, software technologies, network systems administration, technical support, medical assisting, and medical office administration as well as opportunities to earn a second A.A.S. degree or certificate in CISCO and Microsoft Windows networking technology or in business accounting. Special diploma and certificate programs in medical assisting and office skills are also offered at some campuses.

Program Description
Heald College programs include both professional and general education courses, which together allow students to experience the integration of knowledge and skills. The general education courses offer students breadth in their experiences by introducing them to major areas of knowledge, thus expanding their understanding of the world and cultures around them. Furthermore, these courses foster a spirit of inquiry and provide for students' development of the skills, knowledge, and intellectual habits necessary to support their personal, professional, and public lives. Heald also provides hands-on training in all of its programs to ensure that students can successfully apply the skills they learn in the workplace after graduation.

pass an admissions examination, and be recommended by an Admissions Adviser to the Campus Director. Students should contact the Admissions Department for additional information.

Graduation Requirements
To be eligible for graduation, students must successfully complete all classes with a minimum 2.0 cumulative grade point average and complete all program, unit, and course requirements.

Contact
Cindi Stevens, Director of Admissions
2910 Prospect Park Drive
Rancho Cordova, CA 95670
Phone: (916) 638-1616
　　　(800) 755-3550 (toll-free)
Fax: (916) 638-1580
E-mail: cstevens@heald.edu
Web: www.heald.edu

Heald College, Roseville Campus, Sacramento

About Our Institution

Heald College is a nonprofit, WASC-accredited institution with eleven campuses located in northern California, Hawaii, and Oregon. Heald College was founded in 1863 by Edward Payson Heald and for more than 140 years has helped students prepare for successful business, technical, and health-care careers.

Heald College–Roseville was originally situated in Sacramento, where it served valley residents since 1986. Today, this high-tech campus is conveniently located along the Interstate 80 corridor in the center of the Roseville/Rocklin area, renowned for computer and electronic manufacturing and development. Occupying more than 50,000 square feet, the campus is fully networked and offers students a variety of programs in business, technology, and health-care fields.

Special Features

Heald College provides focused programs in business, technology, and health care that prepare students for success in the workplace in the shortest practical time. Heald College also provides personal attention every step of the way. From completion of the admissions application through navigation of financial aid options to ongoing academic assistance programs (workshops, individual tutoring, learning resource centers) to job placement assistance, the College believes that it succeeds only when its students succeed.

Financial Aid/Scholarships

A Financial Aid Adviser meets with students to assess each person's individual situation and eligibility for assistance. The adviser explains each option, guides the student to those that are appropriate, and assists in the proper completion of all the necessary paperwork. Financial aid options available include Federal Pell Grants, Federal SEOG, scholarships, state Cal Grants and private grants, Federal Work-Study, Federal Stafford Student Loans (subsidized and unsubsidized), Federal PLUS Loans, private loans, Workforce Investment Act (WIA) grants, and veterans' educational benefits. Students must qualify for financial aid and meet specific academic progress requirements to obtain and remain eligible for all federal and state financial assistance programs.

Tuition and Fees

Tuition and fees vary by program length. Students should contact the Admissions Department for additional information.

Accreditation

Heald is accredited by the Accrediting Commission for Community and Junior Colleges of the Western Association of Schools and Colleges (WASC). Heald's medical assisting program and its medical office program have both been approved by the American Medical Technologists (AMT), a nonprofit certification agency, and by the National Center for Competency Testing. These partnerships allow Heald's health-care graduates to sit for appropriate certification examinations. The Heald College accounting curriculum has been approved by the California Tax Education Council (CTEC) to offer course work that fulfills the 60-hour qualifying education requirement, imposed by the state, to become a tax preparer.

Admissions

Applicants must interview with an Admissions Adviser, indicate that they have a high school diploma or GED equivalent, complete an

Program Content

Most Heald campuses offer Associate in Applied Science (AAS) degrees and diploma programs in accounting, business administration, criminal justice, office skills, office technologies, sales and marketing, software technologies, network systems administration, technical support, medical assisting, and medical office administration as well as opportunities to earn a second AAS degree or certificate in CISCO and Microsoft Windows networking technology or in business accounting. Special diploma and certificate programs in medical assisting and office skills are also offered at some campuses.

Program Description

Heald College programs include both professional and general education courses, which together allow students to experience the integration of knowledge and skills. The general education courses offer students breadth in their experiences by introducing them to major areas of knowledge, thus expanding their understanding of the world and cultures around them. Furthermore, these courses foster a spirit of inquiry and provide for students' development of the skills, knowledge, and intellectual habits necessary to support their personal, professional, and public lives. Heald also provides hands-on training in all of its programs to ensure that students can successfully apply the skills they learn in the workplace after graduation.

application, pass an admissions examination, and be recommended by an Admissions Adviser to the Campus Director. Students should contact the Admissions Department for additional information.

Graduation Requirements

To be eligible for graduation, students must successfully complete all classes with a minimum 2.0 cumulative grade point average and complete all program, unit, and course requirements.

Contact

Cindi Stevens, Director of Admissions
7 Sierra Gate Plaza
Roseville, CA 95678
Phone: (916) 789-8600
　　　　(800) 755-3550 (toll-free)
Fax: (916) 789-8616
E-mail: cstevens@heald.edu
Web: www.heald.edu

Heald College, Salinas Campus, Salinas

About Our Institution
Heald College is a nonprofit, WASC-accredited institution with eleven campuses located in northern California, Hawaii, and Oregon. Heald College was founded in 1863 by Edward Payson Heald and for more than 140 years has helped students prepare for successful business, technical, and health-care careers.

Heald College–Salinas was founded in 1990 and is conveniently located in a recently expanded location on North Main Street. The campus, serving the central coast, occupies 36,000 square feet and offers programs in business, technology, and health care. The instructors at the high-tech, fully networked campus specialize in hands-on learning and education. Heald–Salinas offers a variety of business, technology, and health-care programs.

Special Features
Heald College provides focused programs in business, technology, and health care that prepare students for success in the workplace in the shortest practical time. Heald College also provides personal attention every step of the way. From completion of the admissions application through navigation of financial aid options to ongoing academic assistance programs (workshops, individual tutoring, learning resource centers) to job placement assistance, the College believes that it succeeds only when its students succeed.

Financial Aid/Scholarships
A Financial Aid Adviser meets with students to assess each person's individual situation and eligibility for assistance. The adviser explains each option, guides the student to those that are appropriate, and assists in the proper completion of all the necessary paperwork. Financial aid options available include Federal Pell Grants, Federal SEOG, scholarships, state Cal Grants and private grants, Federal Work-Study, Federal Stafford Student Loans (subsidized and unsubsidized), Federal PLUS Loans, private loans, Workforce Investment Act (WIA) grants, and veterans' educational benefits. Students must qualify for financial aid and meet specific academic progress requirements to obtain and remain eligible for all federal and state financial assistance programs.

Tuition and Fees
Tuition and fees vary by program length. Students should contact the Admissions Department for additional information.

Accreditation
Heald is accredited by the Accrediting Commission for Community and Junior Colleges of the Western Association of Schools and Colleges (WASC). Heald's medical assisting program and its medical office program have both been approved by the American Medical Technologists (AMT), a nonprofit certification agency, and by the National Center for Competency Testing. These partnerships allow Heald's health-care graduates to sit for appropriate certification examinations. The Heald College accounting curriculum has been approved by the California Tax Education Council (CTEC) to offer course work that fulfills the 60-hour qualifying education requirement, imposed by the state, to become a tax preparer.

Admissions
Applicants must interview with an Admissions Adviser, indicate that they have a high school diploma or GED equivalent, complete an application, pass an admissions examination, and be recommended by an Admissions

Program Content
Most Heald campuses offer Associate in Applied Science (AAS) degrees and diploma programs in accounting, business administration, criminal justice, office skills, office technologies, sales and marketing, software technologies, network systems administration, technical support, medical assisting, and medical office administration as well as opportunities to earn a second AAS degree or certificate in CISCO and Microsoft Windows networking technology or in business accounting. Special diploma and certificate programs in medical assisting and office skills are also offered at some campuses.

Program Description
Heald College programs include both professional and general education courses, which together allow students to experience the integration of knowledge and skills. The general education courses offer students breadth in their experiences by introducing them to major areas of knowledge, thus expanding their understanding of the world and cultures around them. Furthermore, these courses foster a spirit of inquiry and provide for students' development of the skills, knowledge, and intellectual habits necessary to support their personal, professional, and public lives. Heald also provides hands-on training in all of its programs to ensure that students can successfully apply the skills they learn in the workplace after graduation.

Adviser to the Campus Director. Students should contact the Admissions Department for additional information.

Graduation Requirements
To be eligible for graduation, students must successfully complete all classes with a minimum 2.0 cumulative grade point average and complete all program, unit, and course requirements.

Contact
Jason Ferguson, Director of Admissions
1450 North Main Street
Salinas, CA 93906
Phone: (831) 443-1700
       (800) 755-3550 (toll-free)
Fax: (831) 443-1050
E-mail: jason_ferguson@heald.edu
Web: www.heald.edu

Heald College, San Francisco Campus, San Francisco

About Our Institution

Heald College is a nonprofit, WASC-accredited institution with eleven campuses located in northern California, Hawaii, and Oregon. Heald College was founded in 1863 by Edward Payson Heald and for more than 140 years has helped students prepare for successful business, technical, and health-care careers.

San Francisco is the original home of Heald College. The campus's convenient financial district location provides students with easy access to Bay Area Rapid Transit (BART) and the Transbay bus terminal. The 60,000-square-foot campus features fully networked computers and labs. Programs in business, technology, and health care are offered.

Special Features

Heald College provides focused programs in business, technology, and health care that prepare students for success in the workplace in the shortest practical time. Heald College also provides personal attention every step of the way. From completion of the admissions application through navigation of financial aid options to ongoing academic assistance programs (workshops, individual tutoring, learning resource centers) to job placement assistance, the College believes that it succeeds only when its students succeed.

Financial Aid/Scholarships

A Financial Aid Adviser meets with students to assess each person's individual situation and eligibility for assistance. The adviser explains each option, guides the student to those that are appropriate, and assists in the proper completion of all the necessary paperwork. Financial aid options available include Federal Pell Grants, Federal SEOG, scholarships, state Cal Grants and private grants, Federal Work-Study, Federal Stafford Student Loans (subsidized and unsubsidized), Federal PLUS Loans, private loans, Workforce Investment Act (WIA) grants, and veterans' educational benefits. Students must qualify for financial aid and meet specific academic progress requirements to obtain and remain eligible for all federal and state financial assistance programs.

Tuition and Fees

Tuition and fees vary by program length. Students should contact the Admissions Department for additional information.

Accreditation

Heald is accredited by the Accrediting Commission for Community and Junior Colleges of the Western Association of Schools and Colleges (WASC). Heald's medical assisting program and its medical office program have both been approved by the American Medical Technologists (AMT), a nonprofit certification agency, and by the National Center for Competency Testing. These partnerships allow Heald's health-care graduates to sit for appropriate certification examinations. The Heald College accounting curriculum has been approved by the California Tax Education Council (CTEC) to offer course work that fulfills the 60-hour qualifying education requirement, imposed by the state, to become a tax preparer.

Admissions

Applicants must interview with an Admissions Adviser, indicate that they have a high school diploma or GED equivalent, complete an application, pass an admissions examination, and be recommended by an Admissions Adviser to the Campus Director. Students should contact the Admissions Department for additional information.

Program Content

Most Heald campuses offer Associate in Applied Science (AAS) degrees and diploma programs in accounting, business administration, criminal justice, office skills, office technologies, sales and marketing, software technologies, network systems administration, technical support, medical assisting, and medical office administration as well as opportunities to earn a second AAS degree or certificate in CISCO and Microsoft Windows networking technology or in business accounting. Special diploma and certificate programs in medical assisting and office skills are also offered at some campuses.

Program Description

Heald College programs include both professional and general education courses, which together allow students to experience the integration of knowledge and skills. The general education courses offer students breadth in their experiences by introducing them to major areas of knowledge, thus expanding their understanding of the world and cultures around them. Furthermore, these courses foster a spirit of inquiry and provide for students' development of the skills, knowledge, and intellectual habits necessary to support their personal, professional, and public lives. Heald also provides hands-on training in all of its programs to ensure that students can successfully apply the skills they learn in the workplace after graduation.

Graduation Requirements

To be eligible for graduation, students must successfully complete all classes with a minimum 2.0 cumulative grade point average and complete all program, unit, and course requirements.

Contact

Jeanette Lewis, Director of Admissions
350 Mission Street
San Francisco, CA 94105
Phone: (415) 808-3000
        (800) 755-3550 (toll-free)
Fax: (415) 808-3005
E-mail: jeanette_lewis@heald.edu
Web: www.heald.edu

Heald College, San Jose/Milpitas Campus, Milpitas

About Our Institution

Heald College is a nonprofit, WASC-accredited institution with eleven campuses located in Northern California, Hawaii, and Oregon. Heald College was founded in 1863 by Edward Payson Heald and for more than 140 years has helped students prepare for successful business, technical, and health-care careers.

Heald College–San Jose has served as a leading business, technology, and health-care career college since 1907. Located in the heart of Silicon Valley, the campus features a 56,000-square-foot, fully networked facility next to the Great Mall in Milpitas. Even though Silicon Valley is the center of the global technology market, there is also a strong demand for business and health-care graduates.

Special Features

Heald College provides focused programs in business, technology, and health care that prepare students for success in the workplace in the shortest practical time. Heald College also provides personal attention every step of the way. From completion of the admissions application through navigation of financial aid options to ongoing academic assistance programs (workshops, individual tutoring, learning resource centers) to job placement assistance, the College believes that it succeeds only when its students succeed.

Financial Aid/Scholarships

A Financial Aid Adviser meets with students to assess each person's individual situation and eligibility for assistance. The adviser explains each option, guides the student to those that are appropriate, and assists in the proper completion of all the necessary paperwork. Financial aid options available include Federal Pell Grants, Federal SEOG, scholarships, state Cal Grants and private grants, Federal Work-Study, Federal Stafford Student Loans (subsidized and unsubsidized), Federal PLUS Loans, private loans, Workforce Investment Act (WIA) grants, and veterans' educational benefits. Students must qualify for financial aid and meet specific academic progress requirements to obtain and remain eligible for all federal and state financial assistance programs.

Tuition and Fees

Tuition and fees vary by program length. Students should contact the Admissions Department for additional information.

Accreditation

Heald is accredited by the Accrediting Commission for Community and Junior Colleges of the Western Association of Schools and Colleges (WASC). Heald's medical assisting program and its medical office program have both been approved by the American Medical Technologists (AMT), a nonprofit certification agency, and by the National Center for Competency Testing. These partnerships allow Heald's health-care graduates to sit for appropriate certification examinations. The Heald College accounting curriculum has been approved by the California Tax Education Council (CTEC) to offer course work that fulfills the 60-hour qualifying education requirement, imposed by the state, to become a tax preparer.

Admissions

Applicants must interview with an Admissions Adviser, indicate that they have a high school diploma or GED equivalent, complete an application, pass an admissions examination, and be recommended by an

Program Content

Most Heald campuses offer Associate in Applied Science (A.A.S.) degrees and diploma programs in accounting, business administration, criminal justice, office skills, office technologies, sales and marketing, electronics technology, software technologies, network systems administration, technical support, medical assisting, and medical office administration as well as opportunities to earn a second A.A.S. degree or certificate in CISCO and Microsoft Windows networking technology or in business accounting. Special diploma and certificate programs in medical assisting and office skills are also offered at some campuses.

Program Description

Heald College programs include both professional and general education courses, which together allow students to experience the integration of knowledge and skills. The general education courses offer students breadth in their experiences by introducing them to major areas of knowledge, thus expanding their understanding of the world and cultures around them. Furthermore, these courses foster a spirit of inquiry and provide for students' development of the skills, knowledge, and intellectual habits necessary to support their personal, professional, and public lives. Heald also provides hands-on training in all of its programs to ensure that students can successfully apply the skills they learn in the workplace after graduation.

Admissions Adviser to the Campus Director. Students should contact the Admissions Department for additional information.

Graduation Requirements

To be eligible for graduation, students must successfully complete all classes with a minimum 2.0 cumulative grade point average and complete all program, unit, and course requirements.

Contact

Jade Muranaka
341 Great Mall Parkway
Milpitas, CA 95035
Phone: (408) 934-4900
    (800) 755-3550 (toll-free)
Fax: (408) 934-7777
E-mail: jade_muranaka@heald.edu
Web: www.heald.edu

Heald College, Stockton Campus, Stockton

About Our Institution

Heald College is a nonprofit, WASC-accredited institution with eleven campuses located in northern California, Hawaii, and Oregon. Heald College was founded in 1863 by Edward Payson Heald and for more than 140 years has helped students prepare for successful business, technical, and health-care careers.

Heald's Stockton campus began as a business college in 1906. Today, the campus offers programs in business, technology, and health care. Heald College–Stockton resides between Interstate 5 and Route 99 in a recently remodeled building that covers more than 34,000 square feet. Fully networked computers and a comprehensive Learning Resource Center are provided. Located in an office-park setting designed to replicate the professional environment where many Heald graduates will work, the campus offers programs that meet the needs of today's employers in technology, business, and health care.

Special Features

Heald College provides focused programs in business, technology, and health care that prepare students for success in the workplace and in the shortest practical time. Heald College also provides personal attention every step of the way. From completion of the admissions application through navigation of financial aid options to ongoing academic assistance programs (workshops, individual tutoring, learning resource centers) to job placement assistance, the College believes that it succeeds only when its students succeed.

Financial Aid/Scholarships

A Financial Aid Adviser meets with students to assess each person's individual situation and eligibility for assistance. The adviser explains each option, guides the student to those that are appropriate, and assists in the proper completion of all the necessary paperwork. Financial aid options available include Federal Pell Grants, Federal SEOG, scholarships, state Cal Grants and private grants, Federal Work-Study, Federal Stafford Student Loans (subsidized and unsubsidized), Federal PLUS Loans, private loans, Workforce Investment Act (WIA) grants, and veterans' educational benefits. Students must qualify for financial aid and meet specific academic progress requirements to obtain and remain eligible for all federal and state financial assistance programs.

Tuition and Fees

Tuition and fees vary by program length. Students should contact the Admissions Department for additional information.

Accreditation

Heald is accredited by the Accrediting Commission for Community and Junior Colleges of the Western Association of Schools and Colleges (WASC). Heald's medical assisting program and its medical office program have both been approved by the American Medical Technologists (AMT), a nonprofit certification agency, and by the National Center for Competency Testing. These partnerships allow Heald's health-care graduates to sit for appropriate certification examinations. The Heald College accounting curriculum has been approved by the California Tax Education Council (CTEC) to offer course work that fulfills the 60-hour qualifying education requirement, imposed by the state, to become a tax preparer.

Admissions

Applicants must interview with an Admissions Adviser, indicate that they have a high school diploma or GED equivalent, complete an application, pass an admissions examination, and be recommended by an Admissions Adviser

Program Content

Most Heald campuses offer Associate in Applied Science (AAS) degrees and diploma programs in accounting, business administration, criminal justice, office skills, office technologies, sales and marketing, software technologies, network systems administration, technical support, medical assisting, and medical office administration as well as opportunities to earn a second AAS degree or certificate in CISCO and Microsoft Windows networking technology or in business accounting. Special diploma and certificate programs in medical assisting and office skills are also offered at some campuses.

Program Description

Heald College programs include both professional and general education courses, which together allow students to experience the integration of knowledge and skills. The general education courses offer students breadth in their experiences by introducing them to major areas of knowledge, thus expanding their understanding of the world and cultures around them. Furthermore, these courses foster a spirit of inquiry and provide for students' development of the skills, knowledge, and intellectual habits necessary to support their personal, professional, and public lives. Heald also provides hands-on training in all of its programs to ensure that students can successfully apply the skills they learn in the workplace after graduation.

to the Campus Director. Students should contact the Admissions Department for additional information.

Graduation Requirements

To be eligible for graduation, students must successfully complete all classes with a minimum 2.0 cumulative grade point average and complete all program, unit, and course requirements.

Contact

Sandy Allen, Director of Admissions
1605 East March Lane
Stockton, CA 95210
Phone: (209) 473-5200
(800) 755-3550 (toll-free)
Fax: (209) 477-2739
E-mail: sandy-allen@heald.edu
Web: www.heald.edu

ITT Technical Institute, Anaheim

About Our Institution
The company: ITT Technical Institute is owned and operated by ITT Educational Services, Inc. (ITT/ESI), a leading private college system offering on technology-influenced programs of study. ITT/ESI operates seventy-seven ITT Technical Institutes in thirty states, providing career-focused degree programs to approximately 39,000 students as of spring 2004. Headquartered in Carmel, Indiana, ITT/ESI has been actively involved in the higher education community in the United States since 1969.

Curricula: Curriculum offerings are designed to prepare students for career opportunities in fields of technology. Students attend classes year-round, with convenient breaks provided throughout the year. A full-time student course load can have class meetings as often as three days per week and are typically available in the morning, afternoon, and evening, depending on student enrollment. General education courses may be available online. This class schedule offers students the flexibility to pursue part-time employment opportunities.

ITT Technical Institute, Anaheim, awards the Associate of Science and the Bachelor of Science degrees.

Special Features
Most ITT Technical Institute programs of study blend traditional academic content with applied learning concepts, with a significant portion devoted to practical study in a lab environment. Advisory committees, made up of representatives of local businesses help each ITT Technical Institute periodically review and update curricula, equipment, and laboratory design.

Financial Aid/Scholarships
ITT Technical Institute maintains a Financial Aid Department on the campus. The campus is designated as an eligible institution by the U.S. Department of Education for participation in the following programs: Federal Stafford Student Loan Program, Federal PLUS Loan Program, and Federal Work-Study Program. The school also offers nonfederal loans through Bank One for eligible students.

Tuition and Fees
March 2005 tuition is $386 per credit hour.

Accreditation
The Institute is accredited by the Accrediting Council for Independent Colleges and Schools (ACICS).

Admissions
For admission requirements, students should consult the school catalog.

Graduation Requirements
For graduation requirements, students should consult the school catalog.

Program Content
School of Information Technology: Information Systems Security, Data Communications Systems Technology, Software Engineering Technology, Information Technology–Computer Network Systems, Information Technology–Software Applications and Programming, Information Technology–Web Development

School of Electronics Technology: Electronics and Communications Engineering Technology, Computer and Electronics Engineering Technology

School of Drafting and Design: Digital Entertainment and Game Design, Computer Drafting and Design, Information Technology–Multimedia Option

School of Business: Business Administration, Business Accounting Technology, Technical Project Management

Contact
Lou Osborn, Director
ITT Technical Institute
525 North Muller Avenue
Anaheim, CA 92801
Phone: (714) 535-3700
Fax: (714) 535-1802

ITT Technical Institute, Oxnard

About Our Institution
The company: ITT Technical Institute is owned and operated by ITT Educational Services, Inc. (ITT/ESI), a leading private college system that offers technology-influenced programs of study. ITT/ESI operates seventy-seven ITT Technical Institutes in thirty states; they provide career-focused degree programs to approximately 39,000 students as of spring 2004. Headquartered in Carmel, Indiana, ITT/ESI has been actively involved in the higher education community in the United States since 1969.

Curricula: Curriculum offerings are designed to help students begin to prepare for career opportunities in the fields of technology. Students attend classes year-round, with convenient breaks provided throughout the year. A full-time student can have class meetings as often as three days a week, and they are typically available in the morning, afternoon, and evening, depending on student enrollment. General education courses may be available online. This schedule offers flexibility to allow students to pursue part-time employment opportunities.

ITT Technical Institute, Oxnard, awards Associate of Science and Bachelor of Science degrees.

Special Features
Most ITT Technical Institute programs of study blend traditional academic content with applied learning concepts, with a significant portion devoted to practical study in a lab environment. Advisory committees, made up of representatives of local businesses help each ITT Technical Institute periodically review and update curricula, equipment, and laboratory design.

Financial Aid/Scholarships
ITT Technical Institute maintains a Financial Aid Department on campus. The campus is designated as an eligible institution by the U.S. Department of Education for participation in the following programs: Federal Stafford Student Loan, Federal PLUS Loan, and Federal Work-Study. The school also participates in the California Grant Program and offers nonfederal loans through Bank One for eligible students.

Tuition and Fees
March 2005 tuition is $386 per credit hour.

Accreditation
Accrediting Council for Independent Colleges and Schools (ACICS).

Admissions
For admission requirements, students should contact the school for a catalog.

Graduation Requirements
For graduation requirements, students should consult the school catalog.

Program Content
School of Information Technology: Information Systems Security, Data Communication Systems Technology, Software Engineering Technology, Information Technology–Computer Network Systems, Information Technology–Software Applications and Programming, Information Technology–Web Development.

School of Electronics Technology: Electronics and Communications Engineering Technology, Computer and Electronics Engineering Technology.

School of Drafting and Design: Digital Entertainment and Game Design, Computer Drafting and Design, Information Technology–Multimedia Option.

School of Business: Business Administration, Business Accounting Technology, Technical Project Management.

School of Criminal Justice: Criminal Justice.

Contact
Lorraine Bunt, Director
ITT Technical Institute
2051 Solar Drive
Oxnard, CA 93036
Phone: (805) 988-0143
Fax: (805) 988-1813

ITT Technical Institute, Rancho Cordova

About Our Institution

ITT Technical Institute is owned and operated by ITT Educational Services, Inc. (ITT/ESI), a leading private college system that offers technology-influenced programs of study. ITT/ESI operates seventy-seven ITT Technical Institutes in thirty states; they provide career-focused degree programs to approximately 39,000 students as of spring 2004. Headquartered in Carmel, Indiana, ITT/ESI has been actively involved in the higher education community in the United States since 1969.

Curriculum offerings are designed to help students begin to prepare for career opportunities in the fields of technology. Students attend classes year-round, with convenient breaks provided throughout the year. A full-time student can have class meetings as often as three days a week, and they are typically available in the morning, afternoon, and evening, depending on student enrollment. General education courses may be available online. This schedule offers flexibility to allow students to pursue part-time employment opportunities.

ITT Technical Institute, Rancho Cordova, awards Associate of Science and Bachelor of Science degrees.

Special Features

Most ITT Technical Institute programs of study blend traditional academic content with applied learning concepts, with a significant portion devoted to practical study in a lab environment. Advisory committees, made up of representatives of local businesses help each ITT Technical Institute periodically review and update curricula, equipment, and laboratory design.

Financial Aid/Scholarships

ITT Technical Institute maintains a Financial Aid Department on campus. The campus is designated as an eligible institution by the U.S. Department of Education for participation in the following programs: Federal Stafford Student Loan, Federal PLUS Loan, and Federal Work-Study. The school also participates in the California Grant Program and offers nonfederal loans through Bank One for eligible students.

Tuition and Fees

March 2005 tuition is $386 per credit hour.

Accreditation

Accrediting Council for Independent Colleges and Schools (ACICS).

Admissions

For admission requirements, students should contact the school for a catalog.

Graduation Requirements

For graduation requirements, students should consult the school catalog.

Program Content

School of Information Technology: Information Systems Security, Data Communication Systems Technology, Software Engineering Technology, Information Technology–Computer Network Systems, Information Technology–Software Applications and Programming, Information Technology–Web Development.

School of Electronics Technology: Electronics and Communications Engineering Technology, Computer and Electronics Engineering Technology.

School of Drafting and Design: Digital Entertainment and Game Design, Computer Drafting and Design, Information Technology–Multimedia Option.

School of Business: Business Administration, Business Accounting Technology, Technical Project Management.

School of Criminal Justice: Criminal Justice.

Contact

Mark Garland, Director
ITT Technical Institute
10863 Gold Center Drive
Rancho Cordova, CA 95670
Phone: (916) 851-3900
Fax: (916) 851-9225

ITT Technical Institute, San Bernardino

About Our Institution

ITT Technical Institute is owned and operated by ITT Educational Services, Inc. (ITT/ESI), a leading private college system that offers technology-influenced programs of study. ITT/ESI operates seventy-seven ITT Technical Institutes in thirty states; they provide career-focused degree programs to approximately 39,000 students as of spring 2004. Headquartered in Carmel, Indiana, ITT/ESI has been actively involved in the higher education community in the United States since 1969.

Curriculum offerings are designed to help students begin to prepare for career opportunities in the fields of technology. Students attend classes year-round, with convenient breaks provided throughout the year. A full-time student can have class meetings as often as three days a week, and they are typically available in the morning, afternoon, and evening, depending on student enrollment. General education courses may be available online. This schedule offers flexibility to allow students to pursue part-time employment opportunities.

ITT Technical Institute, San Bernardino, awards Associate of Science and Bachelor of Science degrees.

Special Features

Most ITT Technical Institute programs of study blend traditional academic content with applied learning concepts, with a significant portion devoted to practical study in a lab environment. Advisory committees, made up of representatives of local businesses help each ITT Technical Institute periodically review and update curricula, equipment, and laboratory design.

Financial Aid/Scholarships

ITT Technical Institute maintains a Financial Aid Department on campus. The campus is designated as an eligible institution by the U.S. Department of Education for participation in the following programs: Federal Stafford Student Loan, Federal PLUS Loan, and Federal Work-Study. The school also participates in the California Grant Program and offers nonfederal loans through Bank One for eligible students.

Tuition and Fees

March 2005 tuition is $386 per credit hour.

Accreditation

Accrediting Council for Independent Colleges and Schools (ACICS).

Admissions

For admission requirements, students should contact the school for a catalog.

Graduation Requirements

For graduation requirements, students should consult the school catalog.

Program Content

School of Information Technology: Information Systems Security, Data Communication Systems Technology, Software Engineering Technology, Information Technology–Computer Network Systems, Information Technology–Software Applications and Programming, Information Technology–Web Development.

School of Electronics Technology: Electronics and Communications Engineering Technology, Computer and Electronics Engineering Technology.

School of Drafting and Design: Digital Entertainment and Game Design, Computer Drafting and Design, Information Technology–Multimedia Option.

School of Business: Business Administration, Business Accounting Technology, Technical Project Management.

School of Criminal Justice: Criminal Justice.

Contact

Terry Lorenz, Director
ITT Technical Institute
630 East Brier Drive
San Bernardino, CA 92408
Phone: (909) 889-3800
Fax: (909) 888-6970

CALIFORNIA

ITT Technical Institute, San Diego

About Our Institution
The company: ITT Technical Institute is owned and operated by ITT Educational Services, Inc. (ITT/ESI), a leading private college system offering technology-influenced programs of study. ITT/ESI operates seventy-seven ITT Technical Institutes in thirty states, providing career-focused degree programs to approximately 39,000 students as of spring 2004. Headquartered in Carmel, Indiana, ITT/ESI has been actively involved in the higher education community in the United States since 1969.

Curricula: Curriculum offerings are designed to help students begin to prepare for career opportunities in fields of technology. Students attend classes year-round, with convenient breaks provided throughout the year. A full-time student course load can have class meetings as often as three days a week and are typically available in the morning, afternoon, and evening, depending on student enrollment. General education courses may be available online. This class schedule offers flexibility to students to pursue part-time employment opportunities.

ITT Technical Institute, San Diego, awards the Associate of Science and the Bachelor of Science degrees.

Special Features
Most ITT Technical Institute programs of study blend traditional academic content with applied learning concepts, with a significant portion devoted to practical study in a lab environment. Advisory committees composed of representatives of local businesses help each ITT Technical Institute periodically review and update curricula, equipment, and laboratory design.

Financial Aid/Scholarships
ITT Technical Institute maintains a Financial Aid Department on campus. The campus is designated as an eligible institution by the U.S. Department of Education for participation in the following programs: Federal Stafford Student Loan Program, Federal PLUS Loan Program, and Federal Work-Study Program. The school also offers nonfederal loans available through Bank One for eligible students.

Tuition and Fees
March 2005 tuition is $386 per credit hour.

Accreditation
The school is accredited by the Accrediting Council for Independent Colleges and Schools (ACICS).

Admissions
For admission requirements, students should contact the school for a catalog.

Graduation Requirements
For graduation requirements, students should contact the school for a catalog.

Program Content
School of Information Technology: Data Communication Systems Technology, Information Systems Security, Information Technology–Computer Network Systems, Information Technology–Software Applications and Programming, Information Technology–Web Development, Software Engineering Technology

School of Electronics Technology: Computer and Electronics Engineering Technology, Electronics and Communications Engineering Technology

School of Drafting and Design: Computer Drafting and Design, Digital Entertainment and Game Design, Information Technology–Multimedia Option

School of Business: Business Accounting Technology, Business Administration, Technical Project Management

School of Criminal Justice: Criminal Justice

Contact
David Parker, Director
ITT Technical Institute
9680 Granite Ridge Drive
San Diego, CA 92123
Phone: (858) 571-8500
Fax: (858) 571-1277

ITT Technical Institute, Sylmar

About Our Institution
The company: ITT Technical Institute is owned and operated by ITT Educational Services, Inc. (ITT/ESI), a leading private college system that offers technology-influenced programs of study. ITT/ESI operates seventy-seven ITT Technical Institutes in thirty states; they provide career-focused degree programs to approximately 39,000 students as of spring 2004. Headquartered in Carmel, Indiana, ITT/ESI has been actively involved in the higher education community in the United States since 1969.

Curricula: Curriculum offerings are designed to help students begin to prepare for career opportunities in the fields of technology. Students attend classes year-round, with convenient breaks provided throughout the year. A full-time student can have class meetings as often as three days a week, and they are typically available in the morning, afternoon, and evening, depending on student enrollment. General education courses may be available online. This schedule offers flexibility to allow students to pursue part-time employment opportunities.

ITT Technical Institute, Sylmar, awards Associate of Science and Bachelor of Science degrees.

Special Features
Most ITT Technical Institute programs of study blend traditional academic content with applied learning concepts, with a significant portion devoted to practical study in a lab environment. Advisory committees, made up of representatives of local businesses help each ITT Technical Institute periodically review and update curricula, equipment, and laboratory design.

Financial Aid/Scholarships
ITT Technical Institute maintains a Financial Aid Department on campus. The campus is designated as an eligible institution by the U.S. Department of Education for participation in the following programs: Federal Stafford Student Loan, Federal PLUS Loan, and Federal Work-Study. The school also participates in the California Grant Program and offers nonfederal loans through Bank One for eligible students.

Tuition and Fees
March 2005 tuition is $386 per credit hour.

Accreditation
Accrediting Council for Independent Colleges and Schools (ACICS).

Admissions
For admission requirements, students should contact the school for a catalog.

Graduation Requirements
For graduation requirements, students should consult the school catalog.

Program Content
School of Information Technology: Information Systems Security, Data Communication Systems Technology, Software Engineering Technology, Information Technology–Computer Network Systems, Information Technology–Software Applications and Programming, Information Technology–Web Development.

School of Electronics Technology: Electronics and Communications Engineering Technology, Computer and Electronics Engineering Technology.

School of Drafting and Design: Digital Entertainment and Game Design, Computer Drafting and Design, Information Technology–Multimedia Option.

School of Business: Business Administration, Business Accounting Technology, Technical Project Management.

School of Criminal Justice: Criminal Justice.

Contact
Nader Mojtabai, Director
ITT Technical Institute
12669 Encinitas Avenue
Sylmar, CA 91342
Phone: (818) 364-5151
Fax: (818) 364-5150

ITT Technical Institute, Torrance

About Our Institution

The company: ITT Technical Institute is owned and operated by ITT Educational Services, Inc. (ITT/ESI), a leading private college system offering technology-influenced programs of study. ITT/ESI operates seventy-seven ITT Technical Institutes in thirty states, providing career-focused degree programs to approximately 39,000 students as of spring 2004. Headquartered in Carmel, Indiana, ITT/ESI has been actively involved in the higher education community in the United States since 1969.

Curricula: Curriculum offerings are designed to help students begin to prepare for career opportunities in fields of technology. Students attend classes year-round, with convenient breaks provided throughout the year. A full-time student course load can have class meetings as often as three days a week and are typically available in the morning, afternoon, and evening, depending on student enrollment. General education courses may be available online. This class schedule offers flexibility to students to pursue part-time employment opportunities.

ITT Technical Institute, Torrance, awards the Associate of Science and the Bachelor of Science degrees.

Special Features

Most ITT Technical Institute programs of study blend traditional academic content with applied learning concepts, with a significant portion devoted to practical study in a lab environment. Advisory committees composed of representatives of local businesses help each ITT Technical Institute periodically review and update curricula, equipment, and laboratory design.

Financial Aid/Scholarships

ITT Technical Institute maintains a Financial Aid Department on campus. The campus is designated as an eligible institution by the U.S. Department of Education for participation in the following programs: Federal Stafford Student Loan Program, Federal PLUS Loan Program, and Federal Work-Study Program. The school also offers nonfederal loans available through Bank One for eligible students.

Tuition and Fees

March 2005 tuition is $386 per credit hour.

Accreditation

The school is accredited by the Accrediting Council for Independent Colleges and Schools (ACICS).

Admissions

For admission requirements, students should contact the school for a catalog.

Graduation Requirements

For graduation requirements, students should contact the school for a catalog.

Program Content

School of Information Technology: Data Communication Systems Technology, Information Systems Security, Information Technology–Computer Network Systems, Information Technology–Software Applications and Programming, Information Technology–Web Development, Software Engineering Technology

School of Electronics Technology: Computer and Electronics Engineering Technology, Electronics and Communications Engineering Technology

School of Drafting and Design: Computer Drafting and Design, Digital Entertainment and Game Design, Information Technology–Multimedia Option

School of Business: Business Accounting Technology, Business Administration, Technical Project Management

School of Criminal Justice: Criminal Justice

Contact

Anne Marie Koerin, Director
ITT Technical Institute
20050 South Vermont Avenue
Torrance, CA 90502
Phone: (310) 380-1555
Fax: (310) 380-1557

ITT Technical Institute, West Covina

About Our Institution
ITT Technical Institute is owned and operated by ITT Educational Services, Inc. (ITT/ESI), a leading private college system that offers technology-influenced programs of study. ITT/ESI operates seventy-seven ITT Technical Institutes in thirty states; they provide career-focused degree programs to approximately 39,000 students as of spring 2004. Headquartered in Carmel, Indiana, ITT/ESI has been actively involved in the higher education community in the United States since 1969.

Curriculum offerings are designed to help students begin to prepare for career opportunities in the fields of technology. Students attend classes year-round, with convenient breaks provided throughout the year. A full-time student can have class meetings as often as three days a week, and they are typically available in the morning, afternoon, and evening, depending on student enrollment. General education courses may be available online. This schedule offers flexibility to allow students to pursue part-time employment opportunities.

ITT Technical Institute, West Covina, awards Associate of Science and Bachelor of Science degrees.

Special Features
Most ITT Technical Institute programs of study blend traditional academic content with applied learning concepts, with a significant portion devoted to practical study in a lab environment. Advisory committees, made up of representatives of local businesses help each ITT Technical Institute periodically review and update curricula, equipment, and laboratory design.

Financial Aid/Scholarships
ITT Technical Institute maintains a Financial Aid Department on campus. The campus is designated as an eligible institution by the U.S. Department of Education for participation in the following programs: Federal Stafford Student Loan, Federal PLUS Loan, and Federal Work-Study. The school also participates in the California Grant Program and offers nonfederal loans through Bank One for eligible students.

Tuition and Fees
March 2005 tuition is $386 per credit hour.

Accreditation
Accrediting Council for Independent Colleges and Schools (ACICS).

Admissions
For admission requirements, students should contact the school for a catalog.

Graduation Requirements
For graduation requirements, students should consult the school catalog.

Program Content
School of Information Technology: Information Systems Security, Data Communication Systems Technology, Software Engineering Technology, Information Technology–Computer Network Systems, Information Technology–Software Applications and Programming, Information Technology–Web Development.

School of Electronics Technology: Electronics and Communications Engineering Technology, Computer and Electronics Engineering Technology, Industrial Automation Engineering Technology.

School of Drafting and Design: Digital Entertainment and Game Design, Computer Drafting and Design, Information Technology–Multimedia Option.

School of Business: Business Administration, Business Accounting Technology, Technical Project Management.

School of Criminal Justice: Criminal Justice.

Contact
Maria Alamat, Director
ITT Technical Institute
1530 West Cameron Avenue
West Covina, CA 91790
Phone: (626) 960-8681
Fax: (626) 337-5271

National Institute of Technology, Long Beach

About Our Institution
The college was founded in 1969 as the Rosston School of Hair Design. In 1986 the school was acquired by Educorp, Inc., and renamed Educorp Career College. In 2000, Educorp Career College was purchased by Corinthian Schools, Inc., a division of Corinthian Colleges, Inc. The school's name was then changed to National Institute of Technology–Long Beach.

Special Features
The school's current facilities were constructed in 2003 and cover 42,712 square feet. There are seventeen lecture rooms, two combined-use lecture/laboratory spaces, two computer laboratories, four dedicated-use laboratories, and two warehouses, each containing a two-story framed house for practical applications of acquired skills. All necessary tools and equipment are available to students. Each lecture room accommodates 15 to 20 students. Ample parking is also available for students, with accessible handicap services provided.

Financial Aid/Scholarships
This campus offers students several options for payment of tuition, including a plan to help reduce their fees upon entry. The campus participates in several types of federal, state, and institutional financial aid programs.

Accreditation
The Institute maintains all approvals from the Bureau for Private Postsecondary and Vocational Education as well as its accreditation by the Accrediting Commission of Career Schools and Colleges of Technology (ACCSCT).

Admissions
All applicants must have a high school diploma or equivalent. However, the educational requirement may also be met if the applicant is at least 18 years of age and can demonstrate the "Ability to Benefit" from the training. The "Ability to Benefit" is determined by passing the admission examination and by a personal interview with the school administrator. Applicants who possess a high school diploma or equivalent take the PAR Aptitude Test published by the Irwin Corporation. Applicants without a high school diploma or equivalent take the CPAt. Applicants may apply for diploma, certificate, or accelerated programs. All applicants for degree programs must have a high school diploma or equivalent. All applications are taken in person, with appointment. Successful completion of an entrance examination is necessary.

Graduation Requirements
To qualify for graduation and a diploma, a student must complete a prescribed course of study with a minimum average of 70 percent (C), meet the credit-hour and skill requirements for the program, meet the school's attendance and conduct policies, and satisfy the financial obligations to the school.

Enrollment
There are 600 students enrolled.

Program Content
Electrical Technology; Electrician; Industrial Electrical Technology; Massage Therapist; Medical Assisting; Plumber; Residential Heating, Ventilation, and Air Conditioning

Contact
Therese El Khoury, Director of Admissions
2161 Technology Place
Long Beach, CA 90810
Phone: (562) 437-0501
Fax: (562) 432-3721
Web: www.nitschools.com

Programs Eligible for Scholarship	Tuition and Fees	Course Length/Credit Hours	Credential Earned
Electrical Technology	$23,238	18 months/108 credit hours	Diploma
Electrician	$11,790	648 clock hours/54 credit hours	Diploma
Industrial Electrical Technology	$15,900	864 clock hours/72 credit hours	Diploma
Massage Therapist	$10,520	648 clock hours/54 credit hours	Diploma
Medical Assisting	$ 9,630	648 clock hours/54 credit hours	Diploma
Plumber	$11,050	648 clock hours/54 credit hours	Diploma
Residential Heating, Ventilation, and Air Conditioning	$12,433	600 clock hours/45 credit hours	Diploma

NewSchool of Architecture & Design, San Diego

About Our Institution
NewSchool of Architecture & Design was established in 1980 as one of the nation's few private independent schools granting the Bachelor of Architecture degree. NewSchool provides pioneering academic leadership free from the structured environments found in larger traditional institutions. NewSchool takes great pride in its distinguished faculty members who interact with students in small groups or individual settings. A well-rounded curriculum provides students with a broad general education as well as discipline competencies.

Special Features
NewSchool believes that many individuals can find reward and fulfillment in the study of architecture. The instructional program at NewSchool helps students nurture their artistic passion into professional excellence. Students at NewSchool are challenged with rigorous advancement standards. The faculty includes experienced architects and practicing professionals who develop creative mentorship. NewSchool subscribes to the "learn by doing" method. Students are encouraged to intern as soon as possible, and the urban San Diego community is an ideal laboratory for architecture students.

Financial Aid/Scholarships
Financial aid is available to students who qualify. NewSchool has been approved by the Department of Education and the California Student Aid Commission to participate in Title IV and state programs.

Accreditation
The Bachelor of Architecture and Master of Architecture degrees are accredited by the National Architecture Accrediting Board and NewSchool is accredited by the Accrediting Council for Independent Colleges and Schools.

Admissions
All students must complete an application and pay the required admission fee for consideration. Graduation from a recognized high school or acceptable evidence of comparable academic achievement and a cumulative grade point average of 2.5 (for those applying for freshman year) or 2.5 (for transfer students) are required. In addition, transfer students must submit transcripts, and a portfolio review is required for all students seeking placement in second year or above.

Graduation
Students qualify for graduation once the following requirements are met: a 2.0 cumulative grade point average for undergraduate students; a 3.0 cumulative grade point average for graduate students; settlement of all financial obligations, including library charges and clearance from the librarian; maintenance of satisfactory attendance (70 percent); successful completion of the course of study, with acceptance of the thesis or graduation project (if applicable); and clearance from the Financial Aid Office.

Program Content
Degree programs leading to the Associate of Arts in Architecture, Bachelor of Arts in Architecture (four-year degree), Bachelor of Architecture (five-year degree), Master of Architecture (I, II, III), Master of Science in Architecture

Program Description
The Associate of Arts degree program prepares students for entry-level positions in architectural firms. It typically requires two to three academic years of full-time study to complete.

The Bachelor of Arts degree in architecture program prepares the student to enter a Master of Architecture program. It typically requires four to five academic years of full-time study to complete.

The Bachelor of Architecture degree is the first-professional degree. It provides the foundation required to prepare students for an internship in an architectural firm and for eventual licensing as a California architect. It typically requires five to six academic years of full-time study to complete.

The Master of Science in architecture degree program requires a bachelor's degree. It typically requires one to two academic years of full-time study. This degree is intended for students who do not plan on becoming registered architects.

The Master of Architecture first-professional degree program requires a bachelor's degree plus two to four academic years of full-time study. Related undergraduate degrees are defined by the National Architectural Accrediting Board (NAAB). The Master of Architecture second professional degree program requires a Bachelor of Architecture degree.

Contact
Gil Cooke
Director
NewSchool of Architecture & Design
1249 F Street
San Diego, CA 92101
Phone: (619) 235-4100 Ext. 103
Fax: (619) 235-9049
E-mail: gcooke@newschoolarch.edu

Platt College, Los Angeles

About Our Institution
Platt College is a private institution specializing in graphic design, information technology, multimedia, and paralegal studies. Platt's curriculum provides a balanced program of instruction necessary to succeed in today's high-technology industries. The dynamic requirements of employers as well as the personal needs of the student body mandate that Platt College upgrade and enhance each area of study on a continuing basis.

Special Features
Platt College's consistent pursuit of success for its graduates ensures that curriculum and course content be continually reviewed and updated based on industry standards. Platt's Career Services department, in part, facilitates these changes through the feedback it receives from employers of Platt graduates. Each program is geared to the specific needs of what is happening in the industry now. The accelerated nature of the programs benefits students by giving them consistent, real-world scenarios and classroom environments. The small class sizes and varied teaching styles, which incorporate lab and lecture in the same class, also provide an important groundwork for the student's ultimate goal of understanding a field of study and, finally, employment.

Financial Aid/Scholarships
Federal Pell Grants, Federal Work-Study, FSEOG, VA, WIA, GI Bill, I-20, scholarships, federal student loans, and alternative student loans are available to qualified students.

Accreditation
Platt College is accredited by ACCSCT.

Admissions
An applicant's past academic performance, test scores, work experience, and a general aptitude for professional success determine acceptance. To apply for admission, applicants should schedule an admissions interview. The admissions process consists of the submission and review of enrollment forms, appropriate tests, high school record, and a registration fee.

Graduation Requirements
In order to graduate, a student must complete all classes specified in Platt College's program catalog and maintain satisfactory academic progress throughout their tenure.

Contact
Manfred Rodriguez, Director
Platt College, Los Angeles
1000 South Fremont A9W
Alhambra, CA 91803
Phone: (626) 300-5444
Fax: (626) 300-3978
E-mail: mrodriguez@plattcollege.edu
Web: www.plattcollege.edu

Program Content
Graphic Design: The bachelor's degree program in visual communications and the associate degree program in graphic design are geared toward preparing students for the fields of visual and print media. Graduates can expect to exercise their skills in places such as advertising agencies, design studios, art departments, and printing houses.

Information Technology–Networking: This course is designed to give students the necessary tools to achieve success in the growing field of information technology. Students not only prepare for Microsoft certification and mastering networking techniques but also get hands-on exposure to the ever-changing needs that every company has in the area of data communications.

Multimedia: This program not only prepares students for the print media industry but also takes them to the next level of on-screen design. Graduates practice such skills as Web design, 3-D animation and modeling, video capture, and combining the mediums of graphics, motion, and sound.

Paralegal Studies: This program prepares graduates for entry-level positions, giving them the technical knowledge and work skills necessary for a career as a paralegal.

Platt College, Newport Beach

About Our Institution

Platt College is a private institution specializing in graphic design, information technology, multimedia, and paralegal studies. Platt College's curriculum provides a comprehensive program of instruction in each field, introducing students to both theory and practice. Qualified instructors stay current with changing industry trends and standards to impart the most relevant skills through their teaching.

Special Features

Platt College's class size allow students more time for one-on-one interaction with the instructors. These classes, coupled with valuable staff input and guidance, help students become proficient in their skills quickly. Through the accelerated programs, an associate degree can be earned in fifteen months. Platt College's application-based courses prime students for immediate integration into their industry upon graduation. Representatives from the Career Services Department constantly interact with students, graduates, and employers to maintain the high job-placement rates and student satisfaction on which Platt College prides itself.

Financial Aid/Scholarships

Platt College participates in financial assistance programs such as Pell, work-study, FSEOG, VA, WIA, Imagine America, CAPPs, and Presidential Scholarship. Financial aid officers meet with each student individually to discuss all of the available options.

Accreditation

Platt College is accredited by the Accrediting Commission of Career Schools and Colleges of Technology (ACCSCT). The school is also approved by the Bureau for Private Postsecondary and Vocational Education (BPPVE), pursuant to California Education Code Section 94310.

Admissions

Past academic performance, test scores, work experience, and a general aptitude for professional success determine an applicant's acceptance. To apply for admission, applicants must schedule an admissions interview for a personal tour of the College. At that time, prospective students have the opportunity to meet individually with representatives of each department to better acquaint themselves with Platt College and further shape their academic goals.

Graduation Requirements

In order to graduate, students must complete all classes specified in Platt College's program catalog and maintain satisfactory attendance and academic progress throughout their tenure.

Contact

Lisa Rhodes, Campus President
Platt College, Newport Beach
3901 MacArthur Boulevard
Newport Beach, CA 92660
Phone: (949) 833-2300
Fax: (949) 833-0269
E-mail: lrhodes@plattcollege.edu
Web: www.plattcollege.edu

Program Content

The bachelor's degree program in visual communications and the associate degree program in graphic design prepare students for the fields of visual and print media. Students learn the fundamentals of design and computer graphics. Ultimately, students develop a comprehensive portfolio which helps them find careers in places such as advertising agencies, design studios, art departments, and printing houses.

Graphic Design/Multimedia: The graphic design program with a multimedia emphasis not only prepares students for the print media industry, but also takes them to the level of on-screen design. Graduates develop and practice such skills as Web design, interactive design, 3-D animation and modeling, and video editing. Students learn how to most effectively combine the mediums of graphics, motion, and sound. Upon graduation, students possess two portfolios—one in print and the other an interactive CD.

Information Technology–Networking: The ITN program is designed to give students the necessary tools to achieve success in the growing field of information technology. Students prepare not only for Microsoft and CompTIA certifications, but also get hands-on training for the fast-paced technology industry.

Paralegal Studies: This program prepares graduates for entry-level positions, giving them the technical knowledge and work skills necessary for a career as a paralegal.

Platt College, Ontario

About Our Institution
Platt College is a private institution specializing in graphic design, information technology networking, multimedia, and paralegal studies. Platt's curriculum and class sizes provide a balanced program of instruction that students need to succeed in today's high-technology industry and meet their career goals. The ever-changing requirements of the industries served by Platt College, as well as the needs of the student body, mandate that Platt College upgrade and enhance its curriculum and equipment on a continuing basis.

Special Features
Platt Colleges has been helping students in local communities achieve success in meeting their career objectives. In addition to industry-professional faculty members, classes are designed to meet the educational and career needs of students by providing a balance of lectures and labs throughout their studies. Through constant input from industry specialists and potential employers, each program is geared to specific present and future needs of the respective industry. The accelerated nature of the programs benefits students by giving them consistent, real-world scenarios to prepare them for career success. Platt College's Career Services Department begins working with students at the time they start their first class to help prepare them to find employment in their field of study.

Financial Aid/Scholarships
Federal Pell Grants, Federal Work-Study, FSEOG, VA, WIA, Imagine America, CAPPS, and Presidential Scholarships are available to qualified students.

Accreditation
The Platt Colleges are accredited by the Accrediting Commission of Career Schools and Colleges of Technology (ACCSCT).

Admissions
Applicants are evaluated based on their past academic performance, college-administered test scores, work experience, and a general aptitude for professional success. To apply for admission, applicants should schedule an admissions interview and campus tour. The admissions process is consists of submission and review of enrollment forms, evaluation of appropriate tests, and confirmation of completion of high school record.

Graduation Requirements
In order to graduate, a student must complete all classes specified in Platt College's catalog and maintain satisfactory academic progress throughout their time on campus.

Contact
Joe Blackman, Director
Platt College, Ontario
3700 Inland Empire Boulevard
Ontario, CA 91764
Phone: (909) 941-9410
Fax: (909) 941-9660
E-mail: jblackman@plattcollege.edu
Web: www.plattcollege.edu

Program Content
The bachelor's degree program in visual communications and the associate degree program in graphic design help students acquire the technical knowledge, computer/software techniques, and creative skills necessary for entry-level positions and future growth potential in positions at advertising agencies, design studios, art departments, and related industries.

Information Technology Networking: Students who complete this program are able to plan, implement, maintain, and support information systems for numerous computer network configurations, as well as MCSE, MOUS, A+, Linux+, and Novell CAN operating environments.

Multimedia: This program provides students with the software techniques, terminology, and key concepts for multimedia video production, Internet/Web design, 3-D modeling/animation graphics, and sound sampling/editing.

Paralegal Studies: This program prepares graduates for entry-level positions, giving them the technical knowledge and legal-document preparation and work skills that are necessary to serve a variety of governmental, public, business, and private legal employers.

Remington College, San Diego Campus, San Diego

About Our Institution

Remington College–San Diego Campus was founded in 1995 as International University of Southern California, originally offering bachelor's and master's degree programs. The University was acquired by Education America (now known as Remington College) in 1999, adding associate degree programs to the existing bachelor's and master's degree programs during the same year. To date, Remington College consists of twenty campuses across the United States. Remington College teaches a "career first" curriculum that allows students to concentrate on learning the necessary technical skills early in their program and build on them as they progress toward graduation.

Special Features

Remington College is uncompromisingly dedicated to high-quality, postsecondary, career-oriented education. Its primary objectives are to graduate a high percentage of students who enter career programs and to help them achieve relevant employment at the highest possible starting salary. Remington College's philosophy is to provide high-quality programs that are sound in concept, implemented by a competent and dedicated faculty, and geared to serve those seeking a solid foundation in knowledge and skills required to gain employment in their chosen fields. The programs emphasize "hands-on" training, are relevant to employers' needs, and focus on areas that offer strong, long-term employment opportunities.

Financial Aid/Scholarships

Remington College firmly believes that continued education beyond high school is the right of every individual. Lack of financial resources alone should not be a barrier for attending the institution of the student's choice. Remington College–San Diego Campus maintains a Financial Aid Services Office on the campus. A variety of financial assistance is available for those who qualify, such as grants, loans, scholarships, work-study, veterans' benefits, vocational rehabilitation programs, and other aid programs.

Accreditation

Remington College–San Diego Campus is accredited by the Accrediting Council for Independent Colleges and Schools (ACICS). The Board of Behavioral Sciences and the Board of Psychology approve the Master of Arts degree in psychology with a specialization in marriage and family therapy. Upon completion of degree requirements and internship hours, graduates are eligible to sit for the State of California Marriage, Family and Child Counseling (MFCC) licensure exams.

Admissions

A high school diploma or GED, along with an acceptance interview, is used to determine a candidate's potential for success. Applicants to associate degree programs must obtain an acceptable score on the entrance test. For entrance to graduate programs, a bachelor's degree is required from an accredited college or university.

Graduation Requirements

In order to graduate, a student must complete all required courses with a passing grade and accumulate the total number of credits required for graduation from his or her course of study. The student must also maintain a cumulative grade point average of 2.0 or better.

Program Content

Associate of Applied Science degree programs in Business Information Systems, Computer Information Systems, and Computer Networking Technology

Bachelor of Arts degree program in Human Behavior

Bachelor of Science degree programs in Information Systems and Information Technology

Master of Arts degree programs in Human Behavior and Psychology, with a specialization in Marriage and Family Therapy

Master of Business Administration degree program

Contact

José Cisneros, Campus President
123 Camino de la Reina, Suite 100 North
San Diego, CA 92108
Phone: (619) 686-8600
Fax: (619) 686-8684
Web: www.remingtoncollege.edu

San Joaquin Valley College, Aviation Campus, Fresno

About Our Institution
San Joaquin Valley College (SJVC) is a private junior college that was founded in 1977 and is a recognized leader in providing high-quality degree curriculum in lower-division health, business, and technical fields. The college system has six campuses. Five campuses are located in the central San Joaquin Valley and enjoy the best qualities the California heartland has to offer. Bakersfield, Visalia, Fresno, and Modesto benefit from a valley perspective that offers an express corridor through the state and easy jaunts to scenic pockets of mountains and lakes for boating, camping, hiking, and other leisure activities. The newest campus in Rancho Cucamonga offers accessibility to many of California's most treasured points of interest. All of the campuses are in thriving business districts, close to food and shopping areas, and easily accessible by city transportation lines. Free parking is provided on campus and ride sharing is encouraged to benefit the student population.

Special Features
The campus is equipped with lecture halls, classrooms, and labs with specialty equipment and supplies that simulate actual working conditions. Health programs include clinical and/or extern experience in local health facilities. Employment services are provided to all students.

Financial Aid/Scholarships
Federal Pell Grant, FDSLP, work-study, FSEOG, VA, state grants, WIA, and bank loans on approval of credit are available. SJVC participates in Imagine America and California Association of Private Postsecondary Schools scholarship programs.

Tuition and Fees
In addition to tuition listed below, there is a $100 registration fee per academic year.

Accreditation
The College is accredited by the Accrediting Commission for Community and Junior Colleges of the Western Association of Schools and Colleges.

Admissions
Admission is open to men and women who possess a high school diploma or equivalent. Applicants must meet basic qualifications as determined through a personal interview with an Admissions Adviser.

Graduation Requirements
Satisfactory completion of at least 60 semester units of collegiate work with a minimum 2.0 grade point average is required. Some majors at SJVC require more than the minimum 60 units to complete. Students should see individual program requirements.

Program Content
Degree: Aviation Maintenance Technology

Program Description
Students develop proficiency in the technical skills necessary to work in the aviation maintenance technology field as well as a foundation of education that encourages critical thinking, social development, and life skills, all in as little as sixteen months.

Contact
Bob Loogman, Executive Director
4985 East Anderson Avenue
Fresno, CA 93727
Phone: (559) 453-0123
Fax: (559) 453-0133
E-mail: bobl@sjvc.com

Programs Eligible for Scholarship	Tuition and Fees	Course Length/Credit Hours	Credential Earned
Aviation Maintenance Technology	$21,080	67 weeks/88 credits	Degree

San Joaquin Valley College, Bakersfield

About Our Institution

San Joaquin Valley College (SJVC) is a private junior college that was founded in 1977 and is a recognized leader in providing high-quality degree curriculum in lower-division health, business, and technical fields. The college system has six campuses. Five campuses are located in the central San Joaquin Valley and enjoy the best qualities the California heartland has to offer. Bakersfield, Visalia, Fresno, and Modesto benefit from a valley perspective that offers an express corridor through the state and easy jaunts to scenic pockets of mountains and lakes for boating, camping, hiking, and other leisure activities. The newest campus in Rancho Cucamonga offers accessibility to many of California's most treasured points of interest. All of the campuses are in thriving business districts, close to food and shopping areas, and easily accessible by city transportation lines. Free parking is provided on campus and ride sharing is encouraged to benefit the student population.

Special Features

The campus is equipped with lecture halls, classrooms, and labs with specialty equipment and supplies that simulate actual working conditions. Health programs include clinical and/or extern experience in local health facilities. Employment services are provided to all students.

Financial Aid/Scholarships

Federal Pell Grant, FDSLP, work-study, FSEOG, VA, state grants, WIA, and bank loans on approval of credit are available. SJVC participates in Imagine America and California Association of Private Postsecondary Schools scholarship programs.

Tuition and Fees

There is a one-time registration fee of $200 included in the tuition listed below. Tuition is based on full-time enrollment; tuition varies for those attending less than full-time.

Accreditation

The College is accredited by the Accrediting Commission for Community and Junior Colleges of the Western Association of Schools and Colleges.

Admissions

Admission is open to men and women who possess a high school diploma or equivalent. Applicants must meet basic qualifications as determined through a personal interview with an Admissions Adviser.

Program Content

Degrees: Administrative Office Professional, Business Administration, Clinical and Administrative Medical Assisting, Corrections, Dental Assisting, Emergency Services and Safety Management, Health Care Administration, Health Care Insurance Specialist, Information Systems Engineer, Pharmacy Technology, Refrigeration and Air Conditioning Technology, Respiratory Care Practitioner, Surgical Technology

Program Description

Students develop proficiency in the technical skills necessary to work in a variety of business, health, or technical careers as well as a foundation of education that encourages critical thinking, social development, and life skills, all in as little as fifteen months.

Graduation Requirements

Satisfactory completion of at least 60 semester units of collegiate work with a minimum 2.0 grade point average is required. Some majors at SJVC require more than the minimum 60 units to complete. Students should see individual program requirements.

Contact

Michelle Hines, Enrollment Services Director
201 New Stine Road
Bakersfield, CA 93309
Phone: (661) 834-0126
Fax: (661) 834-1021
E-mail: michelle.hines@sjvc.edu

Programs Eligible for Scholarship	Tuition and Fees	Course Length/Credit Hours	Credential Earned
Administrative Office Professional	$21,080	65 weeks/66 credits	Degree
Business Administration	$21,080	65 weeks/66 credits	Degree
Clinical and Administrative Medical Assisting	$21,080	68 weeks/66 credits	Degree
Corrections	$21,080	65 weeks/66 credits	Degree
Dental Assisting	$21,080	68 weeks/66 credits	Degree
Emergency Services and Safety Management	$21,080	65 weeks/66 credits	Degree
Health Care Insurance Specialist	$21,080	65 weeks/66 credits	Degree
Information Systems Engineer	$22,400	60 weeks/60 credits	Degree
Pharmacy Technology	$21,080	68 weeks/66 credits	Degree
Refrigeration and Air Conditioning Technology	$21,080	60 weeks/61 credits	Degree
Respiratory Care Practitioner	$21,600	64 weeks/72 credits	Degree
Surgical Technology	$22,400	66 weeks/66 credits	Degree

San Joaquin Valley College, Fresno

About Our Institution

San Joaquin Valley College (SJVC) is a private junior college that was founded in 1977 and is a recognized leader in providing high-quality degree curriculum in lower-division health, business, and technical fields. The college system has six campuses. Five campuses are located in the central San Joaquin Valley and enjoy the best qualities the California heartland has to offer. Bakersfield, Visalia, Fresno, and Modesto benefit from a valley perspective that offers an express corridor through the state and easy jaunts to scenic pockets of mountains and lakes for boating, camping, hiking, and other leisure activities. The newest campus in Rancho Cucamonga offers accessibility to many of California's most treasured points of interest. All of the campuses are in thriving business districts, close to food and shopping areas, and easily accessible by city transportation lines. Free parking is provided on campus and car pooling is encouraged to benefit the student population.

Special Features

The campus is equipped with lecture halls, classrooms, and labs with specialty equipment and supplies that simulate actual working conditions. Health programs include clinical and/or extern experience in local health facilities. Employment services are provided to all students.

Financial Aid/Scholarships

Federal Pell Grant, FDSLP, work-study, FSEOG, VA, state grants, WIA, and bank loans on approval of credit are available. SJVC participates in Imagine America and California Association of Private Postsecondary Schools scholarship programs.

Tuition and Fees

There is a one-time registration fee of $200 included in the tuition listed below. Tuition is based on full-time enrollment; tuition varies for those attending less than full-time.

Accreditation

The College is accredited by the Accrediting Commission for Community and Junior Colleges of the Western Association of Schools and Colleges.

Admissions

Admission is open to men and women who possess a high school diploma or equivalent. Applicants must meet basic qualifications as determined through a personal interview with an Admissions Adviser.

Graduation Requirements

Satisfactory completion of a minimum of 60 semester units of collegiate work with a 2.0 grade point average or above is required. Some majors at

Program Content

Degrees: Business Administration, Clinical and Administrative Medical Assisting, Computer Support Technology, Corrections, Dental Assisting, Electronics Engineering Technology, Health Care Administration, Pharmacy Technology, and Refrigeration and Air Conditioning Technology

Program Description

Students develop proficiency in the technical skills necessary to work in a variety of business, health, or technical careers as well as a foundation of education that encourages critical thinking, social development, and life skills, all in as little as fifteen months.

SJVC require more than the minimum 60 units to complete. Students should see individual program requirements.

Contact

Susie Topjian, Enrollment Services Director
295 East Sierra Avenue
Fresno, CA 93710
Phone: (559) 448-8282
Fax: (559) 448-8250
E-mail: susiet@sjvc.edu

Programs Eligible for Scholarship	Tuition and Fees	Course Length/Credit Hours	Credential Earned
Business Administration	$21,080	65 weeks/66 credits	Degree
Clinical and Administrative Medical Assisting	$21,080	68 weeks/66 credits	Degree
Computer Support Technology	$24,570	75 weeks/75 credits	Degree
Corrections	$21,080	65 weeks/66 credits	Degree
Dental Assisting	$21,080	68 weeks/66 credits	Degree
Electronics Engineering Technology	$21,080	60 weeks/60 credits	Degree
Health Care Administration	$21,080	65 weeks/66 credits	Degree
Pharmacy Technology	$21,080	68 weeks/66 credits	Degree
Refrigeration and Air Conditioning Technology	$21,080	60 weeks/61 credits	Degree

San Joaquin Valley College, Rancho Cucamonga

About Our Institution

San Joaquin Valley College (SJVC) is a private junior college that was founded in 1977 and is a recognized leader in providing high-quality degree curriculum in lower-division health, business, and technical fields. The college system has six campuses. Five campuses are located in the central San Joaquin Valley and enjoy the best qualities the California heartland has to offer. Bakersfield, Visalia, Fresno, and Modesto benefit from a valley perspective that offers an express corridor through the state and easy jaunts to scenic pockets of mountains and lakes for boating, camping, hiking, and other leisure activities. The newest campus in Rancho Cucamonga offers accessibility to many of California's most treasured points of interest. All of the campuses are in thriving business districts, close to food and shopping areas, and easily accessible by city transportation lines. Free parking is provided on campus and car pooling is encouraged to benefit the student population.

Special Features

The campus is equipped with lecture halls, classrooms, and labs with specialty equipment and supplies that simulate actual working conditions. Health programs include clinical and/or extern experience in local health facilities. Employment services are provided to all students.

Financial Aid/Scholarships

The Federal Pell Grant Program, FDSLP, work-study programs, FSEOG, VA, state grants, WIA, and bank loans on approval of credit are available. SJVC participates in Imagine America and California Association of Private Postsecondary Schools scholarship programs.

Tuition and Fees

There is a one-time registration fee of $200 included in the tuition listed below. Tuition is based on full-time enrollment; tuition varies for those attending less than full-time.

Accreditation

The College is accredited by the Accrediting Commission for Community and Junior Colleges of the Western Association of Schools and Colleges.

Admissions

Admission is open to men and women who possess a high school diploma or equivalent. Applicants must meet basic qualifications as determined through a personal interview with an Admissions Adviser.

Graduation Requirements

Satisfactory completion of at least 60 semester units of collegiate work with a 2.0 grade point average or above is required. Some majors at SJVC require more than the minimum 60 units to complete. Students should see individual program requirements.

Program Content

Degrees: Business Administration, Clinical Medical Assisting, Corrections, Dental Assisting, Medical Office Administration, Pharmacy Technology, Respiratory Care Practice

Program Description

Students develop proficiency in the technical skills necessary to work in a variety of business, health, or technical careers as well as a foundation of education that encourages critical thinking, social development, and life skills, all in as little as fifteen months.

Contact

Ramon Abreu, Enrollment Services Director
10641 Church Street
Rancho Cucamonga, CA 91730
Phone: (909) 948-7582
Fax: (909) 948-3860
E-mail: ramona@sjvc.edu

Programs Eligible for Scholarship	Tuition and Fees	Course Length/Credit Hours	Credential Earned
Business Administration	$21,080	65 weeks/66 credits	Degree
Clinical Medical Assisting	$21,080	65–68 weeks/66 credits	Degree
Corrections	$21,080	65 weeks/66 credits	Degree
Dental Assisting	$21,080	65–68 weeks/66 credits	Degree
Medical Office Administration	$21,080	65 weeks/66 credits	Degree
Pharmacy Technology	$21,080	65–68 weeks/66 credits	Degree
Respiratory Care Practice	$25,000	64 weeks/72 credits	Degree

San Joaquin Valley College, Visalia

About Our Institution

San Joaquin Valley College (SJVC) is a private junior college that was founded in 1977 and is a recognized leader in providing high-quality degree curriculum in lower-division health, business, and technical fields. The college system has six campuses. Five campuses are located in the central San Joaquin Valley and enjoy the best qualities the California heartland has to offer. Bakersfield, Visalia, Fresno, and Modesto benefit from a valley perspective that offers an express corridor through the state and easy jaunts to scenic pockets of mountains and lakes for boating, camping, hiking, and other leisure activities. The newest campus in Rancho Cucamonga offers accessibility to many of California's most treasured points of interest. All of the campuses are in thriving business districts, close to food and shopping areas, and easily accessible by city transportation lines. Free parking is provided on campus and car pooling is encouraged to benefit the student population.

Special Features

The campus is equipped with lecture halls, classrooms, and labs with specialty equipment and supplies that simulate actual working conditions. Health programs include clinical and/or extern experience in local health facilities. Employment services are provided to all students.

Financial Aid/Scholarships

The Federal Pell Grant, FDSLP, work-study programs, FSEOG, VA, state grants, WIA, and bank loans on approval of credit are available. SJVC participates in Imagine America and California Association of Private Postsecondary Schools scholarship programs.

Tuition and Fees

There is a one-time registration fee of $200 included in the tuition listed below. Tuition is based on full-time enrollment; tuition varies for those attending less than full-time.

Accreditation

The College is accredited by the Accrediting Commission for Community and Junior Colleges of the Western Association of Schools and Colleges.

Admissions

Admission is open to men and women who possess a high school diploma or equivalent. Applicants must meet basic qualifications as determined through a personal interview with an Admissions Adviser.

Graduation Requirements

Satisfactory completion of at least 60 semester units of collegiate work with a minimum 2.0 grade point average is required. Some majors at

Program Content

Degrees: Business Administration, Clinical and Administrative Medical Assisting, Computer Support Technology, Corrections, Dental Assisting, Health Care Administration, Human Resource Administration, Pharmacy Technology, Respiratory Care Practitioner

Program Description

Students develop proficiency in the technical skills necessary to work in a variety of business, health, or technical careers as well as a foundation of education that encourages critical thinking, social development, and life skills, all in as little as fifteen months.

SJVC require more than the minimum 60 units to complete. Students should see individual program requirements.

Contact

Travis Sheridan, Enrollment Services Director
8400 West Mineral King Avenue
Visalia, CA 93291
Phone: (559) 651-2500
Fax: (559) 651-0574
E-mail: travis.sheridan@sjvc.edu

Programs Eligible for Scholarship	Tuition and Fees	Course Length/Credit Hours	Credential Earned
Business Administration	$21,080	65 weeks/66 credits	Degree
Clinical and Administrative Medical Assisting	$21,080	68 weeks/66 credits	Degree
Computer Support Technology	$24,570	75 weeks/75 credits	Degree
Corrections	$21,080	65 weeks/66 credits	Degree
Dental Assisting	$21,080	68 weeks/66 credits	Degree
Health Care Administration	$21,080	65 weeks/66 credits	Degree
Human Resource Administration	$21,080	65 weeks/66 credits	Degree
Pharmacy Technology	$21,080	68 weeks/66 credits	Degree
Respiratory Care Practitioner	$21,600	64 weeks/72 credits	Degree

Silicon Valley College, Emeryville

About Our Institution

Silicon Valley College (SVC) was founded in Fremont, California, in 1989 to provide students with the skills and knowledge necessary to start a successful career in health care, drafting, or graphics studies. A second campus, located in Walnut Creek, California, was opened in 1979. A third campus opened in San Jose, California, in January 1979, and a fourth campus was opened in Emeryville, California, in August 2001. In June 2002, SVC was purchased by U.S. Education Corporation (http://www.useducationcorp.com), a nationwide company established to acquire and manage similar institutions.

All SVC campuses have classrooms and laboratories containing the latest in equipment, administrative offices, computer labs, and attractively decorated and comfortably appointed student areas.

SVC is dedicated to providing the highest-quality education and training to prepare its graduates for entry-level careers in their respective fields. SVC keeps alert to industry needs and periodically revises its curriculum.

Special Features

Most programs require an externship, clinical rotation, and/or fieldwork experience that consists of unpaid work experience in a physician's office, hospital, clinic, or other appropriate work location. Students are eligible for graduation and employment assistance only after successful completion of the required number of hours for their field experience, externship, or clinical rotation. Employment assistance is available to all SVC graduates without charge. Part of every student's education involves job-search training, orientation to the job market, and help with resume writing and interview techniques. The College is open year-round, with programs starting on a regular basis throughout the year. Classes are offered in the morning, afternoon, and evening to accommodate work schedules.

Financial Aid/Scholarships

Financial aid programs include Federal Pell Grants, FFEL Stafford Loans, Perkins Loans, FSEOG, state grants, and work-study programs.

Tuition and Fees

Students should refer to the College's catalog for current tuition and fees.

Accreditation

Silicon Valley College is approved by California's Bureau for Private Postsecondary and Vocational Education (BPPVE) and is accredited by the Accrediting Commission of Career Schools and Colleges of Technology (ACCSCT). Silicon Valley College is categorized as an eligible

Program Content

Architectural Design Drafting, Biotechnology Lab Technician, Computer Graphics Design, Dental Assisting, Design and Visualization, Health Information Technology, Massage Therapy, Medical Assisting, Pharmacy Technician

institution by the U.S. Department of Education and provides training to veterans.

Contact

Elvie Engstrom, Executive Director
Silicon Valley College, Emeryville Campus
1400 65th Street, Suite 200
Emeryville, CA 94608
Phone: (510) 601-0133
Fax: (510) 601-0793
E-mail: emvwebleads@svcollege.com
Web: www.siliconvalley.edu

Programs Eligible for Scholarship*	Tuition and Fees	Credential Earned
Architectural Design Drafting	Varies	Certificate or degree
Biotechnology Lab Technician	Varies	Certificate or degree
Computer Graphics Design	Varies	Certificate or degree
Dental Assisting	Varies	Certificate or degree
Health Information Technology	Varies	Certificate or degree
Massage Therapy	Varies	Certificate or degree
Medical Assisting	Varies	Certificate or degree
Pharmacy Technician	Varies	Certificate or degree

*Not all programs offered at all locations

Silicon Valley College, Fremont

About Our Institution
Silicon Valley College (SVC) was founded in Fremont, California, in 1989 to provide students with the skills and knowledge necessary to start a successful career in health care, drafting, or graphics studies. A second campus, located in Walnut Creek, California, was opened in 1979. A third campus opened in San Jose, California, in January 1979, and a fourth campus was opened in Emeryville, California, in August 2001. In June 2002, SVC was purchased by U.S. Education Corporation (http://www.useducationcorp.com), a nationwide company established to acquire and manage similar institutions.

All SVC campuses have classrooms and laboratories containing the latest in equipment, administrative offices, computer labs, and attractively decorated and comfortably appointed student areas.

SVC is dedicated to providing the highest-quality education and training to prepare its graduates for entry-level careers in their respective fields. SVC keeps alert to industry needs and periodically revises its curriculum.

Special Features
Most programs require an externship, clinical rotation, and/or fieldwork experience that consists of unpaid work experience in a physician's office, hospital, clinic, or other appropriate work location. Students are eligible for graduation and employment assistance only after successful completion of the required number of hours for their field experience, externship, or clinical rotation. Employment assistance is available to all SVC graduates without charge. Part of every student's education involves job-search training, orientation to the job market, and help with resume writing and interview techniques. The College is open year-round, with programs starting on a regular basis throughout the year. Classes are offered in the morning, afternoon, and evening to accommodate work schedules.

Financial Aid/Scholarships
Financial aid programs include Federal Pell Grants, FFEL Stafford Loans, Perkins Loans, FSEOG, state grants, and work-study programs.

Tuition and Fees
Students should refer to the College's catalog for current tuition and fees.

Accreditation
Silicon Valley College is approved by California's Bureau for Private Postsecondary and Vocational Education (BPPVE) and is accredited by the Accrediting Commission of Career Schools and Colleges of Technology (ACCSCT). Silicon Valley College is categorized as an eligible

Program Content
Architectural Design Drafting, Biotechnology Lab Technician, Computer Graphics Design, Dental Assisting, Design and Visualization, Health Information Technology, Massage Therapy, Medical Assisting, Pharmacy Technician

institution by the U.S. Department of Education and provides training to veterans.

Contact
Chuck Ericson, Executive Director
Silicon Valley College, Fremont Campus
41350 Christy Street
Fremont, CA 94538
Phone: (510) 623-9966
Fax: (510) 623-9822
E-mail: fmtwebleads@svcollege.com
Web: www.siliconvalley.edu

Programs Eligible for Scholarship*	Tuition and Fees	Credential Earned
Architectural Design Drafting	Varies	Certificate or degree
Biotechnology Lab Technician	Varies	Certificate or degree
Computer Graphics Design	Varies	Certificate or degree
Dental Assisting	Varies	Certificate or degree
Health Information Technology	Varies	Certificate or degree
Massage Therapy	Varies	Certificate or degree
Medical Assisting	Varies	Certificate or degree
Pharmacy Technician	Varies	Certificate or degree

*Not all programs offered at all locations

Silicon Valley College, San Jose

About Our Institution
Silicon Valley College (SVC) was founded in Fremont, California, in 1989 to provide students with the skills and knowledge necessary to start a successful career in health care, drafting, or graphics studies. A second campus, located in Walnut Creek, California, was opened in 1979. A third campus opened in San Jose, California, in January 1979, and a fourth campus was opened in Emeryville, California, in August 2001. In June 2002, SVC was purchased by U.S. Education Corporation (http://www.useducationcorp.com), a nationwide company established to acquire and manage similar institutions.

All SVC campuses have classrooms and laboratories containing the latest in equipment, administrative offices, computer labs, and attractively decorated and comfortably appointed student areas.

SVC is dedicated to providing the highest-quality education and training to prepare its graduates for entry-level careers in their respective fields. SVC keeps alert to industry needs and periodically revises its curriculum.

Special Features
Most programs require an externship, clinical rotation, and/or fieldwork experience that consists of unpaid work experience in a physician's office, hospital, clinic, or other appropriate work location. Students are eligible for graduation and employment assistance only after successful completion of the required number of hours for their field experience, externship, or clinical rotation. Employment assistance is available to all SVC graduates without charge. Part of every student's education involves job-search training, orientation to the job market, and help with resume writing and interview techniques. The College is open year-round, with programs starting on a regular basis throughout the year. Classes are offered in the morning, afternoon, and evening to accommodate work schedules.

Financial Aid/Scholarships
Financial aid programs include Federal Pell Grants, FFEL Stafford Loans, Perkins Loans, FSEOG, state grants, and work-study programs.

Tuition and Fees
Students should refer to the College's catalog for current tuition and fees.

Accreditation
Silicon Valley College is approved by California's Bureau for Private Postsecondary and Vocational Education (BPPVE) and is accredited by the Accrediting Commission of Career Schools and Colleges of Technology (ACCSCT). Silicon Valley College is categorized as an eligible

Program Content
Architectural Design Drafting, Biotechnology Lab Technician, Computer Graphics Design, Dental Assisting, Design and Visualization, Health Information Technology, Massage Therapy, Medical Assisting, Pharmacy Technician

institution by the U.S. Department of Education and provides training to veterans.

Contact
Steve Ashab, Executive Director
Silicon Valley College, San Jose Campus
6201 San Ignacio Avenue
San Jose, CA 95119
Phone: (408) 360-0840
Fax: (408) 360-0848
E-mail: sjwebleads@svcollege.com
Web: www.siliconvalley.edu

Programs Eligible for Scholarship*	Tuition and Fees	Credential Earned
Architectural Design Drafting	Varies	Certificate or degree
Biotechnology Lab Technician	Varies	Certificate or degree
Computer Graphics Design	Varies	Certificate or degree
Dental Assisting	Varies	Certificate or degree
Health Information Technology	Varies	Certificate or degree
Massage Therapy	Varies	Certificate or degree
Medical Assisting	Varies	Certificate or degree
Pharmacy Technician	Varies	Certificate or degree

*Not all programs offered at all locations

Silicon Valley College, Walnut Creek

About Our Institution
Silicon Valley College (SVC) was founded in Fremont, California, in 1989 to provide students with the skills and knowledge necessary to start a successful career in health care, drafting, or graphics studies. A second campus, located in Walnut Creek, California, was opened in 1979. A third campus opened in San Jose, California, in January 1979, and a fourth campus was opened in Emeryville, California, in August 2001. In June 2002, SVC was purchased by U.S. Education Corporation (http://www.useducationcorp.com), a nationwide company established to acquire and manage similar institutions.

All SVC campuses have classrooms and laboratories containing the latest in equipment, administrative offices, computer labs, and attractively decorated and comfortably appointed student areas.

SVC is dedicated to providing the highest-quality education and training to prepare its graduates for entry-level careers in their respective fields. SVC keeps alert to industry needs and periodically revises its curriculum.

Special Features
Most programs require an externship, clinical rotation, and/or fieldwork experience that consists of unpaid work experience in a physician's office, hospital, clinic, or other appropriate work location. Students are eligible for graduation and employment assistance only after successful completion of the required number of hours for their field experience, externship, or clinical rotation. Employment assistance is available to all SVC graduates without charge. Part of every student's education involves job-search training, orientation to the job market, and help with resume writing and interview techniques. The College is open year-round, with programs starting on a regular basis throughout the year. Classes are offered in the morning, afternoon, and evening to accommodate work schedules.

Financial Aid/Scholarships
Financial aid programs include Federal Pell Grants, FFEL Stafford Loans, Perkins Loans, FSEOG, state grants, and work-study programs.

Tuition and Fees
Students should refer to the College's catalog for current tuition and fees.

Accreditation
Silicon Valley College is approved by California's Bureau for Private Postsecondary and Vocational Education (BPPVE) and is accredited by the Accrediting Commission of Career Schools and Colleges of Technology (ACCSCT). Silicon Valley College is categorized as an eligible

Program Content
Architectural Design Drafting, Biotechnology Lab Technician, Computer Graphics Design, Dental Assisting, Design and Visualization, Health Information Technology, Massage Therapy, Medical Assisting, Pharmacy Technician

institution by the U.S. Department of Education and provides training to veterans.

Contact
Bill Grady, Executive Director
Silicon Valley College, Walnut Creek Campus
2800 Mitchell Drive
Walnut Creek, CA 94598
Phone: (925) 280-0235
Fax: (925) 280-0267
E-mail: wcwebleads@svcollege.com
Web: www.siliconvalley.edu

Programs Eligible for Scholarship*	Tuition and Fees	Credential Earned
Architectural Design Drafting	Varies	Certificate or degree
Biotechnology Lab Technician	Varies	Certificate or degree
Computer Graphics Design	Varies	Certificate or degree
Dental Assisting	Varies	Certificate or degree
Health Information Technology	Varies	Certificate or degree
Massage Therapy	Varies	Certificate or degree
Medical Assisting	Varies	Certificate or degree
Pharmacy Technician	Varies	Certificate or degree

*Not all programs offered at all locations

Universal Technical Institute, Rancho Cucamonga

About Our Institution

UTI Rancho Cucamonga is a private postsecondary technical school that has provided students with the technical education needed for a successful career in the automotive industry since opening in 1998. UTI provides full student services, housing assistance, financial aid to those who qualify, campus activities, and both part-time and graduate employment assistance for as long as it is needed.

Special Features

UTI has developed strong industry relations with manufacturers such as Audi, BMW, Ford, International Trucks, Jaguar, Mercedes-Benz, NASCAR, Porsche, Volkswagen, and Volvo. These partnerships have created incredible training and career opportunities for UTI automotive and diesel graduates. From excellent electives for upgraded UTI training to fully paid manufacturer-specific graduate training, UTI's connections and commitment to excellence place its graduates in the driver's seat in a career field that is in demand. Many manufacturers and dealers, in addition to those listed above, also participate in UTI's TRIP program, wherein these companies agree to pay back the student tuition loans for the graduates they hire.

Financial Aid/Scholarships

UTI students are eligible to apply for various federal grants and loans. These include Pell Grants, FSEOG, and Stafford, Perkins, and PLUS Loans. UTI also sponsors, as well as administers, various scholarship programs and awards more than $500,000 in scholarships annually, including ones from SkillsUSA, CCA, Imagine America, Ford/AAA, FFA, and UTI's National High School Scholarship competition.

Tuition and Fees

Tuition and fees vary by course content. Tuition prices include all workbooks, textbooks, and uniforms; there are no hidden costs. For specific tuition information, students should contact the Rancho Cucamonga Admissions Office.

Accreditation

Universal Technical Institute is accredited by the Accrediting Commission of Career Schools and Colleges of Technology (ACCSCT), which is listed by the U.S. Department of Education as a nationally recognized accrediting agency.

Admissions

Each individual applying for admission must be at least 16 years of age, have a high school diploma or equivalent, and submit a completed application, a signed enrollment agreement, a registration fee, and any other information that the applicant or the Institute feels is pertinent to admission. Each applicant's qualifications for enrollment are reviewed and either approved, approved with stipulations, or denied.

Graduation Requirements

Students must achieve a minimum overall 2.0 cumulative GPA and receive a "satisfactory" in all required courses in their selected program. Graduation must be achieved within a ratio of 1:5 attempted courses in a student's program. Students must have a zero balance in their student account and have attended UTI's Career Development Classes.

Program Content

Automotive Technology

Program Description

UTI's Automotive Technology program prepares the graduate to diagnose, troubleshoot, service, and repair foreign and domestic automobiles. Students work in a professional, shoplike environment using the latest engine analyzers, handheld scanners, and other computerized diagnostic equipment. Students learn everything from basic engine systems to computerized engine controls. Graduates have all the skills needed to start a challenging and rewarding career in the automotive service industry.

Contact

Eric Oster, School Director
9494 Haven Avenue
Rancho Cucamonga, CA 91730
Phone: (909) 484-1929
      (888) 692-7800 (toll-free)
Fax: (909) 484-6639
E-mail: eoster@uticorp.com

Western Career College, Pleasant Hill

About Our Institution
Western Career College was founded in 1967 in Sacramento, California. In 1983, the College was purchased by the Education Corporation of America (EdCOA). A second campus, located in San Leandro, California, was opened in 1986, and a third campus opened in Pleasant Hill, California, in 1997. In Feburary 2003, Western Career College was purchased by U.S. Education Corporation (http://www.useducationcorp.com). All campuses have classrooms and laboratories containing the latest in health-care equipment, administrative offices, computer labs, and attractively decorated and comfortably appointed student unions. Libraries are maintained on all campuses of the College.

The mission of Western Career College is to provide education in the health-care field leading to an Associate in Science degree and/or a Certificate of Achievement. Western Career College is committed to a skills-based approach to education that prepares graduates for employment in entry-level positions in the health-care field and affords them the opportunity to obtain the credentials they need for advancement.

The Western Career College philosophy is to create an outcome-based learning environment. The College's focus is on retention, placement, and job performance, which results in graduates who are highly qualified and motivated employees. In addition to skills training, Western Career College students learn how to think critically, make decisions, gain independence, organize work, take initiative, supervise others, and be responsible employees. In a broad base of general education, course offerings provide students with communication, critical-thinking, mathematical, and computer skills, as well as perspectives from the sciences, humanities, and social sciences.

Special Features
All programs require an externship, clinical rotation, and/or fieldwork experience that consists of unpaid work experience in a physician's office, hospital, clinic, or other appropriate work location. Students are eligible for graduation and employment assistance only after successful completion of the required number of hours for their externship, clinical rotation, and/or fieldwork experience. Employment assistance is available to all Western Career College graduates without charge. Part of every student's education involves job search training, orientation to the job market, resume writing, and interview techniques.

Not all of Western Career College's programs are available at all of its locations.

Financial Aid/Scholarships
Financial aid programs include Federal Pell Grants, FFEL Stafford Loans, Perkins Loans, FSEOG, state grants, and JTPA.

Tuition and Fees
Students should refer to the school catalog, as tuition and fees vary by program.

Program Content
Dental Assisting, Massage Therapy, Medical Administrative Assisting, Medical Assisting, Medical Billing, Pharmacy Technician, Veterinary Technology, Vocational Nurse

Program Description
Western Career College specializes in education and skills training tailored to the needs of the health-care industry. The College has helped to shape the careers of thousands of health-care professionals.

Accreditation
Western Career College is accredited by the Western Association of Schools and Colleges and licensed by California's Bureau for Private Postsecondary and Vocational Education (BPPVE).

Admissions
All applicants must be at least 17 years of age. The College admits high school graduates or those who are beyond the age of compulsory school attendance and who have a GED credential or Proficiency Certificate as an equivalency to high school graduation. All applicants must take an entrance test administered by Western Career College. Upon the successful completion of this test, the applicant may be considered for enrollment in a particular certificate or degree program.

Contact
LaShawn Wells, Executive Director
Western Career College
380 Civic Drive, Suite 300
Pleasant Hill, CA 94523
Phone: (925) 609-6650
Fax: (925) 609-6666
E-mail: phwebleads@westerncollege.com
Web: www.westerncollege.com

Programs Eligible for Scholarship	Course Length/Credit Hours	Credential Earned
Dental Assisting	60 credit hours	AS
Massage Therapy	63 credit hours	AS
Medical Administrative Assistant	60 credit hours	AS
Medical Assisting	60 credit hours	AS
Medical Billing	60 credit hours	AS
Pharmacy Technician	60 credit hours	AS
Veterinary Technology	61 credit hours	AS

Western Career College, Sacramento

About Our Institution
Western Career College was founded in 1967 in Sacramento, California. In 1983, the College was purchased by the Education Corporation of America (EdCOA). A second campus, located in San Leandro, California, was opened in 1986, and a third campus opened in Pleasant Hill, California, in 1997. In Feburary 2003, Western Career College was purchased by U.S. Education Corporation (http://www.useducationcorp.com). All campuses have classrooms and laboratories containing the latest in health-care equipment, administrative offices, computer labs, and attractively decorated and comfortably appointed student unions. Libraries are maintained on all campuses of the College.

The mission of Western Career College is to provide education in the health-care field leading to an Associate in Science degree and/or a Certificate of Achievement. Western Career College is committed to a skills-based approach to education that prepares graduates for employment in entry-level positions in the health-care field and affords them the opportunity to obtain the credentials they need for advancement.

The Western Career College philosophy is to create an outcome-based learning environment. The College's focus is on retention, placement, and job performance, which results in graduates who are highly qualified and motivated employees. In addition to skills training, Western Career College students learn how to think critically, make decisions, gain independence, organize work, take initiative, supervise others, and be responsible employees. In a broad base of general education, course offerings provide students with communication, critical-thinking, mathematical, and computer skills, as well as perspectives from the sciences, humanities, and social sciences.

Special Features
All programs require an externship, clinical rotation, and/or fieldwork experience that consists of unpaid work experience in a physician's office, hospital, clinic, or other appropriate work location. Students are eligible for graduation and employment assistance only after successful completion of the required number of hours for their externship, clinical rotation, and/or fieldwork experience. Employment assistance is available to all Western Career College graduates without charge. Part of every student's education involves job search training, orientation to the job market, resume writing, and interview techniques.

Not all of Western Career College's programs are available at all locations.

Financial Aid/Scholarships
Financial aid programs include Federal Pell Grants, FFEL Stafford Loans, Perkins Loans, FSEOG, state grants, and JTPA.

Tuition and Fees
Students should refer to the school catalog, as tuition and fees vary by program.

Program Content
Dental Assisting, Massage Therapy, Medical Administrative Assisting, Medical Assisting, Medical Billing, Pharmacy Technician, Veterinary Technology, Vocational Nurse

Program Description
Western Career College specializes in education and skills training tailored to the needs of the health-care industry. The College has helped to shape the careers of thousands of health-care professionals.

Accreditation
Western Career College is accredited by the Western Association of Schools and Colleges and licensed by California's Bureau for Private Postsecondary and Vocational Education (BPPVE).

Admissions
All applicants must be at least 17 years of age. The College admits high school graduates or those who are beyond the age of compulsory school attendance and who have a GED credential or Proficiency Certificate as an equivalency to high school graduation. All applicants must take an entrance test administered by Western Career College. Upon the successful completion of this test, the applicant may be considered for enrollment in a particular certificate or degree program.

Contact
Sue Smith, Executive Director
Western Career College
8909 Folsom Boulevard
Sacramento, CA 95826
Phone: (916) 361-1660
Fax: (916) 361-6666
E-mail: sacwebleads@westerncollege.com
Web: www.westerncollege.com

Programs Eligible for Scholarship	Course Length/Credit Hours	Credential Earned
Dental Assisting	35 credit hours	Certificate of Achievement
Dental Assisting	60 credit hours	AS
Massage Therapy	38 credit hours	Certificate of Achievement
Massage Therapy	63 credit hours	AS
Medical Administrative Assistant	60 credit hours	AS
Medical Assisting	35 credit hours	Certificate of Achievement
Medical Assisting	60 credit hours	AS
Medical Billing	60 credit hours	AS
Pharmacy Technician	60 credit hours	AS
Veterinary Technology	61 credit hours	AS
Vocational Nurse	56.5 credit hours	Certificate of Achievement
Vocational Nurse	75.5 credit hours	AS

Western Career College, San Leandro

About Our Institution
Western Career College was founded in 1967 in Sacramento, California. In 1983, the College was purchased by the Education Corporation of America (EdCOA). A second campus, located in San Leandro, California, was opened in 1986, and a third campus opened in Pleasant Hill, California, in 1997. In Feburary 2003, Western Career College was purchased by U.S. Education Corporation (http://www.useducationcorp.com). All campuses have classrooms and laboratories containing the latest in health-care equipment, administrative offices, computer labs, and attractively decorated and comfortably appointed student unions. Libraries are maintained on all campuses of the College.

The mission of Western Career College is to provide education in the health-care field leading to an Associate in Science degree and/or a Certificate of Achievement. Western Career College is committed to a skills-based approach to education that prepares graduates for employment in entry-level positions in the health-care field and affords them the opportunity to obtain the credentials they need for advancement.

The Western Career College philosophy is to create an outcome-based learning environment. The College's focus is on retention, placement, and job performance, which results in graduates who are highly qualified and motivated employees. In addition to skills training, Western Career College students learn how to think critically, make decisions, gain independence, organize work, take initiative, supervise others, and be responsible employees. In a broad base of general education, course offerings provide students with communication, critical-thinking, mathematical, and computer skills, as well as perspectives from the sciences, humanities, and social sciences.

Special Features
All programs require an externship, clinical rotation, and/or fieldwork experience that consists of unpaid work experience in a physician's office, hospital, clinic, or other appropriate work location. Students are eligible for graduation and employment assistance only after successful completion of the required number of hours for their externship, clinical rotation, and/or fieldwork experience. Employment assistance is available to all Western Career College graduates without charge. Part of every student's education involves job search training, orientation to the job market, resume writing, and interview techniques.

Not all of Western Career College's programs are available at all locations.

Financial Aid/Scholarships
Financial aid programs include Federal Pell Grants, FFEL Stafford Loans, Perkins Loans, FSEOG, state grants, and JTPA.

Tuition and Fees
Students should refer to the school catalog, as tuition and fees vary by program.

Program Content
Dental Assisting, Massage Therapy, Medical Administrative Assisting, Medical Assisting, Medical Billing, Pharmacy Technician, Veterinary Technology, Vocational Nurse

Program Description
Western Career College specializes in education and skills training tailored to the needs of the health-care industry. The College has helped to shape the careers of thousands of health-care professionals.

Accreditation
Western Career College is accredited by the Western Association of Schools and Colleges and licensed by California's Bureau for Private Postsecondary and Vocational Education (BPPVE).

Admissions
All applicants must be at least 17 years of age. The College admits high school graduates or those who are beyond the age of compulsory school attendance and who have a GED credential or Proficiency Certificate as an equivalency to high school graduation. All applicants must take an entrance test administered by Western Career College. Upon the successful completion of this test, the applicant may be considered for enrollment in a particular certificate or degree program.

Contact
Dawn Matthews, Executive Director
Western Career College
170 Bayfair Mall
San Leandro, CA 94578
Phone: (510) 276-3888
Fax: (510) 276-3653
E-mail: slwebleads@westerncollege.com
Web: www.westerncollege.com

Programs Eligible for Scholarship	Course Length/Credit Hours	Credential Earned
Dental Assisting	35 credit hours	Certificate of Achievement
Dental Assisting	60 credit hours	AS
Massage Therapy	38 credit hours	Certificate of Achievement
Massage Therapy	63 credit hours	AS
Medical Administrative Assistant	60 credit hours	AS
Medical Assisting	35 credit hours	Certificate of Achievement
Medical Assisting	60 credit hours	AS
Medical Billing	60 credit hours	AS
Pharmacy Technician	60 credit hours	AS
Veterinary Technology	61 credit hours	AS
Vocational Nurse	56.5 credit hours	Certificate of Achievement
Vocational Nurse	75.5 credit hours	AS

Westwood College of Aviation Technology, Los Angeles, Inglewood

About Our Institution
The history of Westwood College of Aviation Technology–Los Angeles (WCAT-LAX) can be traced back more than sixty years. Formerly Northrop Rice Aviation, the school was originally founded in 1936. In 1999, the school changed ownership and subsequently changed its name to Westwood College of Aviation Technology. Over the years, the institution has focused on aircraft maintenance training, offering certificate programs in airframe and power plant maintenance. The school is highly committed to its mission of providing the aviation industry with technicians who become industry role models.

Special Features
The campus is conveniently located near Los Angeles International Airport. The facility is one of the largest of its kind and consists of two hangars and one administrative/classroom building. The school's program is certified by the Federal Aviation Administration (FAA).

Financial Aid/Scholarships
Westwood College participates in a variety of financial aid programs, including the Federal Pell Grant, the FFEL Stafford Student Loan (subsidized and unsubsidized), Plus loans, the Federal Perkins Loan, the Federal Supplemental Educational Opportunity Grant (FSEOG), the Westwood High School Scholarship Program, and educational assistance loans. Other types of financial aid may be available depending on individual student eligibility. Students should check with the Admissions Office for VA-approved benefits.

Tuition and Fees
Students should refer to the school catalog for detailed tuition and fee information.

Accreditation
The school is accredited by the Council on Occupational Education (COE). Westwood College of Aviation Technology, Inglewood, has a branch campus, Westwood College of Aviation Technology–Houston in Texas. The aviation programs at WCAT–LAX are approved, certified, and monitored by the Federal Aviation Administration, part 147.

Admissions
For aviation programs, successful candidates must have a high school diploma or GED credential. In accordance with FAA requirements, students must read, write, comprehend, and speak English proficiently.

Enrollment
To enroll, candidates must submit an application for admission, be interviewed by an admissions representative, submit a registration fee, and successfully complete the entrance exam.

Program Description
The Inglewood campus offers certificate programs in Airframe and Powerplant, Airframe Add-On, Airframe only, Powerplant only, and Powerplant Add-On.

Contact
Mitch Thomas
Executive Director
Westwood College of Aviation Technology
8911 Aviation Boulevard
Inglewood, CA 92801
Phone: (310) 337-4444
Fax: (310) 337-1176
E-mail: mthomas@westwood.edu
Web: Westwoodcollege.edu

Programs Eligible for Scholarships	Course Length/Credit Hours	Credential Earned
Airframe Add-On	*806.25 hours	Certificate
Airframe and Powerplant	17.5 months/2100 hours	Certificate
Airframe only	*1268.75 hours	Certificate
Powerplant Add-On	*831.25 hours	Certificate
Powerplant only	*1293.75 hours	Certificate

* Depends on class availability.

Westwood College, Anaheim

About Our Institution
Westwood College was founded in Denver, Colorado, in 1953 as the Radio and Television Repair Institute. In 1999, Westwood expanded into the southern California area and opened a campus in Anaheim, California. Committed to a positive and cooperative environment and working collaboratively with employers, the College is dedicated to high-quality, college-level, career-oriented education. Westwood's objective is to graduate confident, job-qualified individuals prepared to enter career fields of choice.

Special Features
Westwood College places a high value on the industry-experience faculty members bring to the classroom. While many faculty members have earned their bachelor's and master's degrees in their fields, Westwood looks for a combination of industry experience, educational training in the subject area, and prior teaching experience to ensure students receive a balanced, industry-relevant education.

Financial Aid/Scholarships
Westwood College participates in a variety of financial aid programs, including the Federal Pell Grant, the FFEL Stafford Student Loan (subsidized and unsubsidized), PLUS Loans, the Federal Perkins Loan, the Federal Supplemental Educational Opportunity Grant (FSEOG), the Westwood High School Scholarship Program, and educational assistance loans. Other types of financial aid may be available depending on individual student eligibility. Students should check with the Admissions Office for VA-approved benefits.

Tuition and Fees
Students should consult the school catalog for detailed tuition and fee information.

Accreditation
Westwood is accredited by the Accrediting Commission of Career Schools and Colleges of Technology (ACCSCT). This accreditation guides the College in its clearly defined mission and its aspirations to high standards to ensure quality programs and the human, physical, and financial resources to accomplish its mission. In addition, the Anaheim campus has received approval to operate within the state of California.

Admissions
Successful candidates for Westwood are required to have a high school diploma or GED certificate. Applicants must complete an acceptance application and either receive a composite minimum score of 17 on the ACT or 920 on the SAT or achieve the required scores on the Accuplacer Computerized Placement Test. Successful completion of a bachelor's degree is accepted in lieu of an admissions test. To

Program Content
Westwood College–Anaheim offers Associate of Science (AS) degree programs in Computer-Aided Design (CAD)/Architectural Drafting, Computer Network Engineering, Graphic Design and Multimedia, and Software Engineering, and Bachelor of Science (BS) degree programs in Animation, Business Administration: Concentration in Accounting, Business Administration: Concentration in Marketing and Sales, Criminal Justice, Computer Network Management, E-Business Management, Game Art and Design, Game Software Development, Information Systems Security, Interior Design, Visual Communications, and Web Design and Multimedia.

enroll, candidates submit an application for admission, are interviewed by an admissions representative, submit a registration fee, and, upon completion of testing, attend an acceptance interview to verify their commitment to begin training.

Contact
Frederick Holland
Executive Director
Westwood College
1551 South Douglass Road
Anaheim, CA 92806
Phone: (714) 704-2720
Fax: (714) 456-9971
E-mail: fholland@westwood.edu
Web: www.westwood.edu

Programs Eligible for Scholarship	Course Length/Credit Hours	Credential Earned
Animation	36 months/200 credit hours	BS
Business Administration: Concentration in Accounting	36 months/209.5 credit hours	BS
Business Administration: Concentration in Marketing and Sales	36 months/209.5 credit hours	BS
Computer-Aided Design/Architectural Drafting	20 months/101.5 credit hours	AS
Computer Network Engineering	20 months/114.5 credit hours	AS
Computer Network Management	36 months/202.5 credit hours	BS
Criminal Justice	36 months/209.5 credit hours	BS
E-Business Management	36 months/200.5 credit hours	BS
Game Art and Design	36 months/193 credit hours	BS
Game Software Development	36 months/195.5 credit hours	BS
Graphic Design and Multimedia	20 months/107 credit hours	AS
Information Systems Security	36 months/202.5 credit hours	BS
Interior Design	36 months/189.5 credit hours	BS
Software Engineering	20 months/107 credit hours	AS
Visual Communications	36 months/200 credit hours	BS
Web Design and Multimedia	36 months/200 credit hours	BS

Westwood College, Inland Empire, Upland

About Our Institution

Westwood College was founded in 1953 in Denver, Colorado, as the Radio and Television Repair Institute. Committed to a positive and cooperative environment and working collaboratively with employers, the College is dedicated to high quality, college-level, career-oriented education. Its objective is to graduate confident, job-qualified individuals prepared to enter career fields of choice.

Special Features

Westwood College places a high value on the industry experience faculty members bring to the classroom. While many faculty members have earned bachelor's and master's degrees in their fields, Westwood looks for a combination of industry experience, educational training in the subject area, and prior teaching experience to ensure that students receive a balanced, industry-relevant education.

Financial Aid/Scholarships

Westwood College participates in a variety of financial aid programs, including the Federal Pell Grant, the FFEL Stafford Student Loan (subsidized and unsubsidized), PLUS Loans, the Federal Perkins Loan, the Federal Supplemental Educational Opportunity Grant (FSEOG), the Westwood High School Scholarship Program, and educational assistance loans. Other types of financial aid may be available depending on individual student eligibility. Students should check with the Admissions Office for VA-approved benefits.

Tuition and Fees

Students should consult the school catalog for detailed tuition and fee information.

Accreditation

Westwood College is accredited by the Accreditation Commission of Career Schools and Colleges of Technology (ACCSCT). This accreditation guides the College, in that it has a clearly defined mission and aspires to high standards to ensure quality programs. Westwood has the human, physical, and financial resources to accomplish its mission. In addition, Westwood is approved and regulated by the Bureau for Private Postsecondary and Vocational Education.

Admissions

Successful candidates for Westwood are required to have a high school diploma or GED certificate. Applicants must complete an acceptance application and either receive a composite minimum score of 17 on the ACT or 920 on the SAT or achieve the required scores on the Accuplacer Computerized Placement Test. To enroll, candidates make an application of admission, are interviewed by an admissions representative, submit a registration fee, and, upon completion of

Program Content

Over the past forty-five years, in response to innovative requirements of industry, Westwood has grown into an institution offering Associate of Science (A.S.) degree programs in Computer-Aided Design (CAD)/Architectural Drafting, Computer Network Engineering, Graphic Design and Multimedia, and Software Engineering. Westwood also offers bachelor's degree programs in Animation, Business Administration: Concentration in Accounting, Business Administration: Concentration in Marketing and Sales, Computer Network Management, Criminal Justice, E-Business Management, Game Art and Design, Game Software Development, Information Systems Security, Interior Design, Visual Communications, and Web Design and Multimedia.

testing, attend an acceptance interview to verify their commitment to begin training.

Contact

Kathy Allin
Executive Director
Westwood College
20 West 7th Street
Upland, CA 91786-7148
Phone: (909) 931-7550
      (800) 221-5632 (toll-free)
Fax: (909) 931-9195
E-mail: kallin@westwood.edu
Web: www.westwood.edu

Programs Eligible for Scholarship	Course Length/Credit Hours	Credential Earned
Animation	36 months/200 credit hours	BS
Business Administration: Concentration in Accounting	36 months/209.5 credit hours	BS
Business Administration: Concentration in Marketing and Sales	36 months/209.5 credit hours	BS
Computer-Aided Design/Architectural Drafting	20 months/101.5 credit hours	AS
Computer Network Engineering	20 months/114.5 credit hours	AS
Computer Network Management	36 months/202.5 credit hours	BS
Criminal Justice	36 months/209.5 credit hours	BS
E-Business Management	36 months/200.5 credit hours	BS
Game Art and Design	36 months/193 credit hours	BS
Game Software Development	36 months/195.5 credit hours	BS
Graphic Design and Multimedia	20 months/107 credit hours	AS
Information Systems Security	36 months/202.5 credit hours	BS
Interior Design	36 months/189.5 credit hours	BS
Software Engineering	20 months/107 credit hours	AS
Visual Communications	36 months/200 credit hours	BS
Web Design and Multimedia	36 months/200 credit hours	BS

Westwood College, Long Beach

About Our Institution
Westwood College, Long Beach, is accredited by the Accrediting Commission of Career Schools and Colleges of Technology (ACCSCT). Westwood is committed to maintaining a positive and cooperative environment and to working collaboratively with employers to ensure a high-quality, college-level, career-oriented education. The objective is to graduate confident, job-qualified individuals prepared to enter their career fields of choice.

Special Features
Westwood College places a high value on the industry experience faculty members bring to the classroom. While many faculty members have earned bachelor's and master's degrees in their fields, Westwood looks for a combination of industry experience, educational training in the subject area, and prior teaching experience to ensure that students receive a balanced, industry-relevant education.

Financial Aid/Scholarships
Westwood College participates in a variety of financial aid programs, including the Federal Pell Grant, FFEL, Stafford Student Loan (subsidized and unsubsidized), Plus loans, Federal Perkins Loan, the Federal Supplemental Educational Opportunity Grant (FSEOG), the Westwood High School Scholarship Program, and educational assistance loans. Other types of financial aid may be available depending on individual student eligibility. Students should check with the Admissions Office for VA-approved benefits.

Tuition and Fees
Students should consult the school catalog for detailed tuition and fee information.

Accreditation
Westwood is accredited by by the Accrediting Commission of Career Schools and Colleges of Technology (ACCSCT). This accreditation guides the College, in that it has a clearly defined mission and aspires to high standards to ensure high-quality programs and has the human, physical, and financial resources to accomplish its mission.

Admissions
Successful candidates for Westwood are required to have a high school diploma or GED. Applicants must submit an application and receive a minimum score of 17 on the ACT or 920 on the SAT or achieve the required scores on the Accuplacer Computerized Placement Test. Candidates must also have an interview with an admissions representa-

Program Content
Associate Degrees: Computer-Aided Design/Architecural Drafting, Computer Network Engineering, Graphic Design and Multimedia, Software Engineering.

Bachelor's Degrees: Animation, Criminal Justice, Computer Network Management, Game Art and Design, Game Software Development, Information Systems Security, Interior Design, Visual Communications.

tive and submit a registration fee. Upon completion of testing, candidates must attend an acceptance interview to verify their commitment to begin training.

Contact
Vicki Bowles
Executive Director
3901 Via Ora Avenue, #103
Long Beach, CA 90810
Phone: (888) 403-3339 (toll-free)
Fax: (310) 522-2093
E-mail: vbowles@westwood.edu
Web: www.westwood.edu

Programs Eligible for Scholarship	Course Length/Credit Hours	Credential Earned
Animation	36 months/200 credit hours	BS
Computer Network Engineering	20 months/114.5 credit hours	AAS
Computer Network Management	36 months/202.5 credit hours	BS
Criminal Justice	36 months/209.5 credit hours	BS
Game Art and Design	36 months/193 credit hours	BS
Game Software Development	36 months/195.5 credit hours	BS
Graphic Design and Multimedia	20 months/107 credit hours	AAS
Information Systems Security	36 months/202.5 credit hours	BS
Software Engineering	20 months/107 credit hours	AAS
Visual Communications	36 months/200 credit hours	BS

Westwood College, Los Angeles

About Our Institution
Westwood College, Los Angeles, is committed to a positive and cooperative environment and, working collaboratively with employers, is dedicated to high-quality, college-level, career-oriented education. Its objective is to graduate confident, job-qualified individuals prepared to enter career fields of their choice. The College is affiliated with other Westwood Colleges, the first of which was founded in Denver, Colorado, in 1953.

Special Features
Westwood College places a high value on the industry experience faculty members brings to the classroom. While many faculty members have earned their bachelor's and master's degrees in their fields, Westwood looks for a combination of industry experience, educational training in the subject area, and prior teaching experience to ensure that students receive a balanced education utilizing industry-relevant equipment.

Financial Aid/Scholarships
Westwood College participates in a variety of financial aid programs, including the Federal Pell Grant, the FFEL Stafford Student Loan (subsidized and unsubsidized), PLUS Loans, the Federal Perkins Loan, the Federal Supplemental Educational Opportunity Grant (FSEOG), the Westwood High School Scholarship Program, and educational assistance loans. Other types of financial aid may be available depending on individual student eligibility. Students should check with the Admissions Office for VA-approved benefits.

Tuition and Fees
Students should consult the school catalog for detailed tuition and fee information.

Accreditation
Westwood College, Los Angeles, is accredited by the Accrediting Council of Independent Colleges and Schools (ACICS). This accreditation guides the College in its clearly defined mission and its aspirations to high standards to ensure high-quality programs and the human, physical, and financial resources to accomplish its mission.

Admissions
Successful candidates for Westwood are required to have a high school diploma or GED certificate. Applicants must complete an acceptance application and either receive a composite minimum score of 17 on the ACT or 920 on the SAT or achieve the required scores on the Accuplacer Computerized Placement Test. To enroll, candidates complete an admissions application, are interviewed by an admissions representative, submit a registration fee, and upon completion of testing, attend an acceptance interview to verify their commitment to begin training.

Program Description
The Los Angeles campus offers associate degree programs in Computer Network Engineering, Graphic Design and Multimedia, and Software Engineering, and bachelor's degree programs in Animation, Business Administration: Concentration in Accounting, Business Administration: Concentration in Marketing and Sales, Computer Network Management, Criminal Justice, E-Business Management, Game Art and Design, Game Software Development, Information Systems Security, Visual Communications, and Web Design and Multimedia.

Contact
William Frank, Executive Director
Westwood College
One Park Plaza
3250 Wilshire Boulevard, Suite 700
Los Angeles, CA 90067
Phone: (213) 739-9999
Fax: (213) 382-2468
E-mail: bfrank@westwood.edu
Web: www.westwood.edu

Programs Eligible for Scholarships	Course Length/Credit Hours	Credential Earned
Animation	36 months/200 credit hours	BS
Business Administration: Concentration in Accounting	36 months/209.5 credit hours	BS
Business Administration: Concentration in Marketing/Sales	36 months/209.5 credit hours	BS
Computer Network Engineering	20 months/114.5 credit hours	AS
Computer Network Management	36 months/202.5 credit hours	BS
Criminal Justice	36 months/209.5 credit hours	BS
E-Business Management	36 months/200.5 credit hours	BS
Game Art and Design	36 months/193 credit hours	BS
Game Software Development	36 months/195.5 credit hours	BS
Graphic Design and Multimedia	20 months/107 credit hours	AS
Information Systems Security	36 months/202.5 credit hours	BS
Software Engineering	20 months/107 credit hours	AS
Visual Communications	36 months/200 credit hours	BS
Web Design and Multimedia	36 months/200 credit hours	BS

WyoTech, Fremont

About Our Institution
WyoTech began operations under the name Sequoia Institute in 1962 to serve its students and industry by providing graduates with appropriate entry-level skills in the fields of automotive technology; heating, ventilation and air-conditioning (HVAC) technology; and plumbing technology. Depending upon the chosen field of study and specific program length, the school provides certificates, diplomas, and occupational degrees to motivated individuals. The primary objective of all WyoTech programs is to provide a solid base of knowledge and skills that lead to successful employment. WyoTech is one of more than eighty schools owned and operated by Corinthian Colleges, Inc.

Special Features
WyoTech's ASE Master Certified Automotive Program is dedicated to preparing well-trained individuals to meet the challenges of California's automotive industry. The Automotive Technology Program is NATEF approved as a Master Certified Automotive Training Program. Wyotech is an official ASE Test Center as well as an official EPA Technician Certification Test Center. The HVAC Technology Program participates in the ARI/GAMA Competency Exams Program.

Financial Aid/Scholarships
Pell Grants, FFEL, FWS, FSEOG, Sallie Mae, and institutional payment plans are offered.

Accreditation
WyoTech is accredited by the Accrediting Commission of Career Schools and Colleges of Technology (ACCSCT).

Admissions
Successful candidates are selected based on approval of the application, passing the school entrance exam, and documented proof of high school graduation or the equivalent.

Enrollment
Current enrollment in certificate and diploma programs is 935 in automotive technology, 181 in HVAC technology, and 22 in plumbing technology. Associate of Occupational Studies degree programs have 493 students.

Contact
Joe File, Director of Admissions
WyoTech
200 Whitney Place
Fremont, CA 94539
Phone: (800) 248-8585 (toll-free)
Fax: (510) 490-8599
E-mail: jfile@sequoiainstitute.edu
Web: www.wyotech.com

Program Content
Automotive Technology, Automotive Technology with a concentration in automotive diagnostics, Automotive Technology with a concentration in service management, HVAC Technology, HVAC Technology with a concentration in service systems, Plumbing Technology

Program Description
Automotive Technology: This program is designed for the individual who has a desire for a "bumper-to-bumper" education in the automotive repair industry. It represents a combination of WyoTech's Automotive Technology I and Automotive Technology II programs. Graduates are well prepared for employment in many dynamic, high-priority areas of the automotive industry.

HVAC Technology: This program is designed for the individual who has a desire to work with heating, ventilation, air conditioning, and refrigeration. In order to cover all of the necessary areas, WyoTech has developed a course of study that prepares students for both the residential and commercial areas of the HVAC industry. Graduates of this program are prepared to seek employment as entry-level technicians in the food industry, construction industry, healthcare industry, HVAC service organizations, and a host of other types of companies.

Plumbing Technology: This program's primary objective is to provide graduates with the knowledge necessary to pursue employment in the plumbing field as entry-level technicians. The program is designed to present a solid background in the theory and technology of the field, which can help graduates advance quickly in their chosen profession. Graduates are able to work in service and repair as well as new construction, restoration, and remodeling plumbing.

Programs Eligible for Scholarship	Tuition and Fees	Course Length/Credit Hours	Credential Earned
Automotive Technology	$21,950	1,200 hours	Diploma
Automotive Technology (automotive diagnostics)	$27,725	1,500 hours	AOS
Automotive Technology (service management)	$27,725	1,500 hours	AOS
HVAC Technology	$21,950	1,200 hours	Diploma
HVAC Technology (service systems)	$27,725	1,500 hours	AOS
Plumbing Technology	$12,150	648 hours	Diploma

The Art Institute of Colorado, Denver

About Our Institution
Founded in 1952, the Art Institute of Colorado is recognized as a leading postsecondary institution in the creative, applied, and culinary arts. Attracting half of its students from out-of-state and abroad, the Institute has a student body committed to pursuing creative careers. Students have hands-on training with industry-current technology from instructors, many of whom are working professionals in their fields.

Special Features
In addition to classrooms, students find studios, laboratories, a library, an academic services center for special academic assistance, an exhibition gallery, and a supply store. Equipment includes still and video cameras; editing decks; audio consoles; camcorders; modern computer labs, printers, and software; light tables; various sanding, milling, cutting, and modeling tools; and commercially equipped kitchens as well as a restaurant.

Financial Aid/Scholarships
The following financial assistance is available: Pell Grants, FFEL, FDSLP, Perkins, Work-Study, SEOG, SSIG, VA, Colorado State Grants, Colorado State Loans, JTFA, and institutional merit/need-based programs. Student Financial Services works with each student to develop an individualized financial plan.

Tuition and Fees
The Institute charges a $50 application fee and a $100 enrollment fee. Tuition charges are estimated at $375 per credit from November 1, 2004 to April 30, 2005. Students lock in a tuition rate at the time of enrollment; their rate does not increase as long as they stay in school and complete their program within 150 percent of the program length. Bachelor's degree students are permitted one quarter off during their program of study.

Accreditation
The Institute is approved by the Colorado Commission on Higher Education and is authorized by the Colorado Department of Higher Education to award diplomas and the AAS and BA degrees. It is accredited by the Accrediting Council for Independent Colleges and Schools.

Program Content
Advertising, Catering and Banquet Operations, Culinary Arts, Culinary Management, Digital Media Production, Graphic Design, Illustration and Design, Industrial Design, Interactive Media Design, Interior Design, Media Arts and Animation, Photography, Video Production, Visual Effects and Motion Graphics

Admissions
A final high school transcript or GED results, an essay, and a $50 application fee are required along with the application of admission.

Graduation Requirements
To graduate from the Art Institute, students must have a minimum CGPA of 2.0; receive a passing grade or credit for all required course work; meet portfolio or other requirements, if applicable; satisfy all financial obligations with the Institute; and earn at least 25 percent of the required credits at the Institute.

Contact
Brian A. Parker
The Art Institute of Colorado
1200 Lincoln Street
Denver, CO 80203
Phone: (303) 837-0825
(800) 275-2420 (toll-free)
Fax: (303) 860-8520
E-mail: baparker@aii.edu
Web: www.aic.aii.edu

Programs Eligible for Scholarship	Tuition and Fees	Course Length/Credit Hours	Credential Earned
Advertising	$72,401	132 weeks/192 credits	BA
Catering and Banquet Operations	$41,744	77 weeks/108 credits	AAS
Culinary Arts	$40,625	77 weeks/105 credits	AAS
Culinary Management	$73,076	143 weeks/192 credits	BA
Digital Media Production	$72,581	132 weeks/192 credits	BA
Graphic Design	$42,228	77 weeks/111 credits	AAS
Graphic Design	$72,441	132 weeks/192 credits	BA
Illustration and Design	$72,401	132 weeks/192 credits	BA
Industrial Design	$72,436	132 weeks/192 credits	BA
Interactive Media Design	$42,178	77 weeks/111 credits	AAS
Interactive Media Design	$72,341	132 weeks/192 credits	BA
Interior Design	$72,911	132 weeks/192 credits	BA
Media Arts and Animation	$72,341	132 weeks/192 credits	BA
Photography	$44,213	77 weeks/111 credits	AAS
Photography	$74,401	132 weeks/192 credits	BA
Video Production	$42,223	111 credits/77 weeks	AAS
Visual Effects and Motion Graphics	$72,716	132 weeks/192 credits	BA

Bel-Rea Institute of Animal Technology, Denver

About Our Institution
Animal technology is the only subject taught at Bel-Rea. The Institute's program is conducted at its own facility. Students come to Bel-Rea from all parts of the United States. The students range from 18 to 55 years of age. Some students have a previous college background, while others are right out of high school.

Bel-Rea prides itself on its faculty. Five members are veterinarians, and the remaining 12 have academic qualifications as well as experience in the field of veterinary medicine. Half of the staff, including members of the core curriculum faculty, have advanced degrees. The ratio of students to faculty members and staff members (full-time equivalents) is 25:1.

Bel-Rea awards the Associate of Applied Science degree.

Special Features
Student body representatives meet on a regular basis with the Student Services Director. Bel-Rea also has a student chapter of the North American Veterinary Technician Association. Bel-Rea has a trained counselor on staff. There is also placement assistance upon graduation.

The facilities of the Institute are all housed within one building, which contains five classrooms, a teaching laboratory, three demonstration rooms, a library, a student lounge, administrative offices, and kennel areas for dogs, cats, birds, and laboratory animals. The large-animal facility adjoins the teaching facility. This areas comprises a stable, a tack room, and a holding area for large animals. The school's facilities are available for student use, both in and out of class, between 7 a.m. and 7 p.m., Monday through Friday.

Internships take place at a variety of veterinary hospitals and clinics. A special five-week externship may also be pursued after graduation at Colorado State University's veterinary school. Students interested in working with exotic animals may take a special elective evening course.

Financial Aid/Scholarships
Financial aid is available to those who qualify; about 70 percent of Bel-Rea's students receive some form of financial aid. Financial aid packages consist of loans, grants, and jobs. Grant and loan awards are provided on the basis of the analysis of the Free Application for Federal Student Aid (FAFSA). Financial aid applications are accepted on a rolling basis.

Tuition and Fees
For students entering in the 2004–05 academic year, tuition for the full eighteen-month program is $18,750. Books and supplies come to about $1,200. Other expenses vary, depending on residence. The Institute does not provide room and board but assists students in finding accommodations in the community. Students who live in apartments or other housing may expect to spend about $4,500 for room and board in a twelve-month period. In addition, personal expenditures are likely to run about $1,000 per year.

Accreditation
American Veterinary Medical Association (AVMA), Accrediting Commission of Career Schools/Colleges of Technology (ACCSCT), and approval

Program Content
Animal Technology

by the Colorado Department of Higher Education, Division of Private Occupational Schools.

Admissions
Applicants must hold a high school or equivalency diploma and must have earned an average grade of C or better. High school and college transcripts (if applicable) must be sent to the Institute by the respective schools. Students with a high school GPA below 2.5 or a GED certificate must take an aptitude test before entering the program. Assurance of a desire to work in the veterinary medical profession is required. A health history is also required. Applicants are encouraged to have a personal interview and a tour of the facilities.

Applicants wishing to transfer credits from accredited colleges or universities should submit a transcript immediately following their application. Credits can be accepted only when the courses that have been taken duplicate the Institute's courses and the level of achievement in the courses taken was a grade of C or above. College classes that typically transfer are algebra, chemistry, humanities, and English.

Enrollment
The current enrollment is more than 600 women and men.

Contact
Admissions Department
Bel-Rea Institute of Animal Technology
1681 South Dayton Street
Denver, CO 80247
Phone: (303) 751-8700
        (800) 950-8001 (toll-free)
Fax: (303) 751-9969
E-mail: kaufman@bel-rea.com
Web: www.bel-rea.com

Blair College, Colorado Springs

About Our Institution
Blair College, founded in 1897, prepares graduates for entry-level positions within their field of training. The College is located on a 5-acre site with beautiful mountain views in eastern Colorado Springs, Colorado. The College occupies an attractive building containing 30,000 square feet, with spacious classrooms, seven computer labs containing state-of-the-art equipment, a student lounge, a library resource center, and ample parking surrounding the building. Blair College is one of more than eighty schools owned and operated by Corinthian Colleges, Inc., in the United States.

Special Features
The College provides a positive, student-oriented environment conducive to learning and academic achievement. Career planing and placement is available to assist graduates become successfully employed within their field of training.

Financial Aid/Scholarships
Blair College participates in various federal and state grants, loans, and assistance programs. Financial aid is available for those who qualify.

Tuition and Fees
Per-credit hours are assessed based on amount of classes taken per quarter. A $25 registration fee and $20 technology fee are charged quarterly.

Accreditation
Blair College is accredited by the Accrediting Council for Independent Colleges and Schools (ACICS) and the Commission on Accreditation of Allied Health Education Programs (CAAHEP). The Medical Assisting program is accredited by AAMA, a division of CAAHEP.

Admissions
Applicants must be a high school graduate or have a GED equivalent and successfully complete an entrance exam.

Graduation Requirements
Students must have earned a minimum of a 2.0 GPA and successfully complete all required credits.

Enrollment
There are 584 students enrolled.

Program Content
Accounting, Business Administration, Administrative Assistant, Computer Information Systems, Criminal Justice, Homeland Security Specialist, Legal Assistant/Paralegal, Medical Administrative Assistant, Medical Assisting, Medical Insurance Billing/Coding, Network Administration

Contact
Dawn Collins, Director of Admissions
828 Wooten Road
Colorado Springs, CO 80915
Phone: (719) 574-1082
Fax: (719) 574-4493
E-mail: mcollins@cci.edu
Web: www.blair-college.com

Programs Eligible for Scholarship	Tuition and Fees	Course Length/Credit Hours	Credential Earned
Accounting	$260/credit hour	96 credit hours	AAS
Administrative Assistant	$260/credit hour	96 credit hours	AAS
Business Administration	$260/credit hour	96 credit hours	AAS
Computer Information Systems	$260/credit hour	96 credit hours	AAS
Criminal Justice	$260/credit hour	96 credit hours	AAS
Homeland Security Specialist	$9,951 plus uniform	7 modules/48 credit hours	Diploma
Legal Assistant/Paralegal	$260/credit hour	96 credit hours	AAS
Medical Assisting	$260/credit hour	97 credit hours	AAS
Medical Administrative Assistant	$10,665	8 modules/47 credit hours	Diploma
Medical Insurance Billing/Coding	$9,557	6 modules/29 credit hours	Diploma
Network Administration	$308/credit hour	98 credit hours	AAS

Denver Automotive and Diesel College, Denver

About Our Institution
Denver Automotive and Diesel College (DADC) is dedicated to educating students for technical positions to help them realize their dreams and achieve their goals. It has been DADC's job for more than thirty-five years to know what specialized technology employers need, to develop automotive and diesel programs, to update equipment, and to revise curricula to stay current with industry standards. The DADC staff is committed to offering a positive training atmosphere to the current and future student body, as it has done for its 20,000 graduates.

At DADC, students are encouraged to utilize the job placement program to help them gain employment in their field of study, both while in school and upon graduation; the Automotive Service Excellence (ASE) Master Certified automotive training, along with the field experience, helps lead some DADC students to excellent career employment opportunities upon graduation.

Financial Aid/Scholarships
Students at DADC can utilize funding included under the Federal Title IV funding program as they qualify. Included are Federal Pell Grants, FSEOG, FFEL loans, and Federal Perkins Loans. VA benefits, institutional loans, and scholarships are also offered.

Tuition and Fees
Students should refer to the school catalog for tuition and fees for individual programs.

Accreditation
DADC is accredited by the Accrediting Commission of Career Schools and Colleges of Technology (ACCSCT).

Admissions
An applicant must possess a high school diploma, GED certificate, or its equivalent; achieve a passing score on the college entrance assessment test; and complete an interview.

Graduation Requirements
Students who have completed their prescribed program of study with a 2.0 GPA or better, earned the required credit hours, and paid all tuition and fees are eligible for graduation.

Contact
Executive Director
Denver Automotive and Diesel College
460 South Lipan Street
Denver, CO 80223
Phone: (303) 722-5724
Fax: (303) 778-8264
E-mail: execdirdenver@lincolntech.com
Web: www.dadc.com

Program Content
Associate of Applied Science Degree Programs: Diesel Technology, Master Technician

Diploma Program: Automotive Technology

ITT Technical Institute, Thornton

About Our Institution
The company: ITT Technical Institute is owned and operated by ITT Educational Services, Inc. (ITT/ESI), a leading private college system offering technology-influenced programs of study. ITT/ESI operates seventy-seven ITT Technical Institutes in thirty states, providing career-focused degree programs to approximately 39,000 students as of spring 2004. Headquartered in Carmel, Indiana, ITT/ESI has been actively involved in the higher education community in the United States since 1969.

Curricula: Curriculum offerings are designed to prepare students for career opportunities in fields of technology. Students attend classes year-round, with convenient breaks provided throughout the year. A full-time student course load can have class meetings as often as three days a week and are typically available in the morning, afternoon, and evening, depending on student enrollment. General education courses may be available online. This class schedule offers students the flexibility to pursue part-time employment opportunities.

ITT Technical Institute, Thornton, awards the Associate in Applied Science and Bachelor of Science degrees.

Special Features
Most ITT Technical Institute programs of study blend traditional academic content with applied learning concepts, with a significant portion devoted to practical study in a lab environment. Advisory committees, made up of representatives of local businesses, help each ITT Technical Institute periodically review and update curricula, equipment, and laboratory design.

Financial Aid/Scholarships
ITT Technical Institute maintains a Financial Aid Department on the campus. The campus is designated as an eligible institution by the U.S. Department of Education for participation in the following programs: Federal Stafford Student Loan Program, Federal PLUS Loan Program, and Federal Work-Study Program. The school also offers nonfederal loans through Bank One for eligible students.

Tuition and Fees
March 2005 tuition is $386 per credit hour.

Accreditation
The Institute is accredited by the Accrediting Council for Independent Colleges and Schools (ACICS).

Admissions
For admission requirements, prospective students should consult the school catalog.

Graduation Requirements
For graduation requirements, prospective students should consult the school catalog.

Program Content
School of Information Technology: Information Systems Security, Data Communications Systems Technology, Software Engineering Technology, Information Technology–Computer Network Systems, Information Technology–Software Applications and Programming, Information Technology–Web Development

School of Electronics Technology: Electronics and Communications Engineering Technology, Computer and Electronics Engineering Technology

School of Drafting and Design: Digital Entertainment and Game Design, Computer Drafting and Design, Information Technology–Multimedia Option

School of Business: Business Administration, Business Accounting Technology, Technical Project Management

School of Criminal Justice: Criminal Justice

Contact
Fred Hansen, Director
ITT Technical Institute
500 East 84th Avenue
Thornton, CO 80229
Phone: (303) 288-4488
Fax: (303) 288-8166

Parks College, Aurora

About Our Institution
Parks College, Aurora, is a branch of Parks College, Denver, founded in 1895. The institution, accredited by the Accrediting Council for Independent Colleges and Schools (ACICS), provides students with entry-level skills in a variety of occupational programs. This campus was opened in 1984, complete with laboratories, classrooms, a resource center, administrative offices, and student services. Parks College is one of more than eighty schools owned and operated by Corinthian Colleges, Inc., in the United States.

Special Features
Parks College has successfully trained and placed Colorado students for more than 100 years. Parks College provides a friendly, small-campus atmosphere. Its dedicated faculty and staff members take personal interest in student progress. The College provides career planning and placement services and offers placement assistance to graduates throughout their careers.

Financial Aid/Scholarships
Parks College offers financial aid programs such as Federal Pell Grants, FFEL, work-study, FSEOG, VA, and state grants. Financial aid is available for those who qualify.

Tuition and Fees
Per-credit-hour fees are assessed based on the number of classes taken per quarter. A quarterly registration fee is assessed for all nonmedical students.

Accreditation
Accrediting Council for Independent Colleges and Schools (ACICS).

Admissions
Graduation from high school or its equivalency (such as the GED program) is the minimum requirement for admission to the College. Successful completion of the assessment examination is a prerequisite for admission. Applicants who have completed at least one academic year of credits at another postsecondary institution are not required to complete the test.

Program Content
Accounting/Computer Applications, Business Administration, Computer Technology, Criminal Justice, Homeland Security Specialist, Medical Administrative Assistant, Medical Assisting, Medical Insurance Billing/Coding, Network Administration, Paralegal/Legal Assistant

Graduation Requirements
Students are required to earn a minimum 2.0 cumulative grade point average in their major, as well as a minimum 2.0 overall cumulative grade point average. Students must also meet specific program requirements.

Enrollment
700 students enrolled.

Contact
Rick Harding, Director of Admissions
14280 East Jewell Avenue, Suite 100
Aurora, CO 80012
Phone: (303) 745-6244
Fax: (303) 745-6245
E-mail: rharding@cci.edu
Web: www.parks-college.com

Programs Eligible for Scholarship	Tuition and Fees	Course Length/Credit Hours	Credential Earned
Accounting/Computer Applications	$260/credit hour	96 credit hours	AAS
Business Administration	$260/credit hour	96 credit hours	AAS
Computer Technology	$260/credit hour	96 credit hours	AAS
Criminal Justice	$260/credit hour	96 credit hours	AAS
Massage Therapy	$10,212	57 credit hours	Diploma
Medical Administrative Assistant	$9,765	47 credit hours	Diploma
Medical Assisting	$9,765	47 credit hours	Diploma
Medical Insurance Billing/Coding	$8,656	35 credit hours	Diploma
Paralegal/Legal Assistant	$260/credit hour	96 credit hours	AAS
Web Administration	$7,105	36 credit hours	Diploma
Web Design	$7,105	36 credit hours	Diploma
Web Development	$7,105	36 credit hours	Diploma

Parks College, Denver

About Our Institution
Parks College, currently located in the north suburban Denver community of Thornton, was founded in 1895. The modern facility houses classrooms, microcomputer labs, medical labs, keyboarding labs, a library, student lounge, career development center, and administrative offices. Parks College is one of more than eighty schools owned and operated by Corinthian Colleges, Inc., in the United States.

Special Features
Parks College has successfully trained and placed Colorado students for more than 100 years. Parks College provides a friendly, small-campus atmosphere. Its dedicated faculty and staff members take personal interest in student progress. The College provides career planning and placement services, offering placement assistance to graduates throughout their careers.

Financial Aid/Scholarships
The College participates in various programs: Federal Pell, Federal Family Educational Loan (FFEL), Federal Work-Study, Federal Supplemental Educational Opportunity Grants (FSEOG), VA, and state grants. Financial aid is available for those who qualify.

Tuition and Fees
Tuition is assessed based on the number of classes taken per quarter. There is a quarterly registration fee and a quarterly technology fee of $25 for all AAS programs.

Accreditation
The College is accredited by the Accrediting Council for Independent Colleges and Schools (ACICS). The Medical Assisting program is AAMA accredited, a division of the Commission on Accreditation of Allied Health Education Programs (CAAHEP).

Admissions
Graduation from high school or its equivalency (GED) is the minimum requirement for admission to the College. Successful completion of the assessment examination is a prerequisite for admission. Applicants who have completed 24 semester hours or 36 quarter hours at another postsecondary institution, and/or applicants who have completed the ACT with a minimum score of 15 or the SAT with a minimum score of 700 (except those interested in the Network Administration Program) are not required to complete the test.

Program Content
Accounting/Computer Applications, Business Administration, Computer Technology, Criminal Justice, Homeland Security Specialist, Medical Administrative Assistant, Medical Assisting, Medical Insurance Billing/Coding, Network Administration, Paralegal/Legal Assistant, Surgical Technologist

Graduation Requirements
Students are required to earn a minimum 2.0 cumulative grade point average in their major, as well as a 2.0 overall cumulative grade point average. Students must also meet specific program requirements.

Enrollment
There are 923 students enrolled.

Contact
James Henig, Director of Admissions
9065 Grant Street
Denver, CO 80229
Phone: (303) 457-2757
Fax: (303) 457-4030
E-mail: jhenig@cci.edu
Web: www.parks-college.com

Programs Eligible for Scholarship	Tuition and Fees	Course Length/Credit Hours	Credential Earned
Accounting/Computer Applications	$260/credit hour	96 credit hours	AAS
Business Administration	$260/credit hour	96 credit hours	AAS
Computer Technology	$260/credit hour	96 credit hours	AAS
Criminal Justice	$260/credit hour	96 credit hours	AAS
Homeland Security Specialist	$8,450	48 credit hours	Diploma
Medical Administrative Assistant	$9,765	47 credit hours	Diploma
Medical Assisting	$260/credit hour	97 credit hours	AAS
Medical Insurance Billing/Coding	$9,089	29 credit hours	Diploma
Network Administration	$308/credit hour	100 credit hours	AAS
	$277/credit hour	72 credit hours	Diploma
Paralegal/Legal Assistant	$260/credit hour	96 credit hours	AAS
Surgical Technologist	$308/credit hour	103 credit hours	AAS

Remington College, Colorado Springs Campus, Colorado Springs

About Our Institution
Remington College–Colorado Springs Campus is part of an twenty-campus network that stretches across the United States. The Colorado Springs Campus was originally a part of the Commonwealth International University system and became part of Education America in December 1998. The campus offers associate degrees in business information systems, computer information systems, computer network technology, Internet information systems, and criminal justice and bachelor's degrees in criminal justice.

Special Features
Remington College is uncompromisingly dedicated to providing high-quality, career-oriented education. Its primary objectives are to graduate a high percentage of students who enter career programs, to help them achieve relevant employment, and to prepare them for lifelong learning and leadership roles in their chosen professions. The programs offer hands-on training relevant to employers' needs.

Financial Aid/Scholarships
Remington College–Colorado Springs Campus offers a variety of grants, loans, scholarships, work-study, and veteran's benefits programs. The campus is approved by the Colorado State Approval Agency for veterans and eligible dependent students.

Accreditation
The Colorado Springs Campus of Remington College is accredited by the Accrediting Council for Independent Colleges and Schools (ACICS) and is licensed by the State of Colorado Department of Higher Education, Division of Private Occupational Schools.

Admissions
Applicants for admission must have a high school diploma or its equivalent (GED) or be a high school senior on track to graduate. Applicants must take an admission interview and an acceptance interview. Applicants for criminal justice programs must sign a release for a background check, showing evidence that they have not been convicted of any felony offenses.

Graduation Requirements
In order to graduate, a student must maintain an overall cumulative grade point average of 2.0 or better for the entire program and complete all courses specified in the program catalog.

Contact
Shibu Thomas, Campus President
Remington College–Colorado Springs Campus
6050 Erin Park Drive, Suite 250
Colorado Springs, CO 80918-3401
Phone: (719) 532-1234
Fax: (719) 264-1234
Web: www.remingtoncollege.edu

Program Description
Business Information Systems (A.A.S.): This program provides students with the tools necessary to use computer programs that address a broad spectrum of business applications and issues.

Computer Information Systems (A.A.S.): This program provides comprehensive training in three major areas: technical analysis, programming, and local area networks (LANs). Languages include Visual Basic, C++, Java, and more.

Computer Networking Technology (A.A.S.): This program provides comprehensive instruction in installing, configuring, maintaining, and troubleshooting local area networks, wide area networks, and Intranets.

Criminal Justice (A.A.S.): This program is designed to prepare the student for entry into the criminal justice system. Areas within this career field include, but are not limited to, law enforcement, public safety, corrections, court administration, crime prevention, juvenile justice, victim assistance, and loss prevention.

Criminal Justice (B.S.): This program is designed to provide specific, in-depth professional courses as well as general education courses. Theoretical knowledge is integrated with applied techniques. The curriculum is structured for the student seeking either preservice or in-service education. At the conclusion of this program, students are prepared to pursue employment or advancement in several criminal specialties, including law enforcement, courts, and corrections.

Internet Information Systems (A.A.S.): This program provides comprehensive training in the technology and techniques necessary to create, develop, market, and maintain a professional corporate Web site. The program emphasizes Java, HTML, Visual Basic, Visual InterDev, Internet Information Server, Apache Server, and principles of Web design and marketing.

Remington College, Denver Campus, Lakewood

About Our Institution
Remington College–Denver Campus is one of twenty Remington College campuses located across the United States. The Denver Campus is located in a newly remodeled 32,904-square-foot building in the suburban community of Lakewood. The campus opened for students in April 2000. The facility offers spacious classrooms and networked labs with Internet access for mobile computing. In addition, the campus offers the Information Resource Center, which features high-speed Internet access and other resources to support and enhance student learning.

Special Features
Remington College is dedicated to providing high-quality, postsecondary, career-oriented education that is designed to prepare graduates for lifelong learning and leadership roles upon graduation. Program offerings may include certificate, diploma, Associate of Applied Science, and baccalaureate degrees, with the primary objective of preparing graduates for relevant employment within their field of study. Specific programs are offered through distance learning. All programs focus on disciplines that offer strong, long-term employment opportunities through curricula that emphasize hands-on training that is relevant to employers' needs. Residential students receive a laptop computer while in training to help enhance computer skills and support learning. Residential students receive the added incentive of being able to keep their assigned laptops upon graduation.

Financial Aid/Scholarships
Remington College–Denver Campus maintains a Student Financial Services Department on the campus to help students obtain information about various financing options that may be available to them. Financial assistance is available to those who qualify.

Accreditation
Remington College–Denver Campus is accredited by the Accrediting Council for Independent Colleges and Schools (ACICS).

Admissions
Final acceptance to the Denver Campus requires completion of a high school diploma or the equivalent, such as the General Education Development (GED) test, and an acceptable score on the entrance test. The entrance exam may be waived with a minimum ACT score of 18 or minimum SAT subtest scores of 390 in math, 340 in reading, and 340 in English.

Contact
Shibu Thomas, Campus President
11011 West 6th Avenue
Lakewood, CO 80215
Phone: (303) 445-0500
Fax: (303) 445-0090
Web: www.remingtoncollege.edu

Program Content
Bachelor of Arts in Operations Management (Distance Learning)
Bachelor of Science in Criminal Justice
Bachelor of Science in Information Systems (Distance Learning)
Bachelor of Science in Information Technology (Distance Learning)
Associate of Applied Science in Computer Information Systems
Associate of Applied Science in Computer Networking Technology
Associate of Applied Science in Criminal Justice
Associate of Applied Science in Criminal Justice with Specialization in P.O.S.T.
Associate of Applied Science in Internet Information Systems

Westwood College of Aviation Technology, Denver

About Our Institution

Westwood College of Aviation Technology–Denver (WCAT), accredited by the Accrediting Commission of Career Schools and Colleges of Technology (ACCSCT) and certified by the FAA, was founded in Denver, Colorado, in 1965 as Colorado Aero Tech. Westwood College trains students in airframe and powerplant technology. In 1989, WCAT expanded its curriculum to include advanced electronics technology (avionics) training. Committed to providing students with a positive and cooperative environment and working collaboratively with employers, the College is dedicated to high-quality, college-level, career-oriented education. WCAT's objective is to produce confident, qualified graduates who are prepared to enter the aviation career field.

Special Features

Westwood College of Aviation Technology–Denver places a high value on the industry experience that faculty members bring to the classroom. While many faculty members have earned associate degrees in their fields as well as their airframe and powerplant licenses, Westwood looks for a combination of industry experience, educational training in the subject area, and prior teaching experience to ensure that students receive a well-balanced education.

Financial Aid/Scholarships

Westwood College participates in a variety of financial aid programs, including Federal Pell Grants, Perkins loans, Federal PLUS loans, Federal Stafford Student Loans, FSEOG, Westwood High School Scholarship program, and educational assistance loans. Other types of financial aid may be available depending on an individual student's eligibility. Students should check with the admissions office for approved VA benefits.

Tuition and Fees

Students should refer to the school catalog for detailed tuition and fee information.

Accreditation

Westwood College of Aviation Technology–Denver is accredited by the Accrediting Commission of Career Schools and Colleges of Technology. This accreditation means the College has a clearly defined mission, aspires to high standards to ensure quality programs, and has the human, physical, and financial resources to accomplish its mission. The programs at WCAT are approved, certified, and monitored by the Federal Aviation Administration, Part 147.

Program Description

The Denver campus offers AOS degree programs in Airframe and Powerplant Technology and Advanced Electronics Technology. Certificate programs in Airframe, Powerplant, Airframe Add-On, Powerplant Add-On, and Basic Electronics are also offered.

Admissions

To enroll at Westwood College of Aviation Technology–Denver, students should possess a high school diploma or its equivalent (or completed the GED) and be at least 17 years of age. Prospective students must be able to speak, read, and write English proficiently. Candidates must be interviewed by an admissions representative, complete an application for admission, submit a registration/application fee, and attend a mandatory orientation.

Contact

Kevin Paveglio
Executive Director
Westwood College of Aviation Technology
10851 West 120th Avenue
Denver, CO 80021
Phone: (303) 466-1714
        (800) 888-3995 (toll-free)
Fax: (303) 469-3797
E-mail: kpaveglio@westwood.edu
Web: www.westwood.edu

Programs Eligible for Scholarship	Course Length/Credit Hours	Credential Earned
Advanced Electronics Technology	17.5 months/2,100 clock hours	AOS
Airframe and Powerplant	17.5 months/2,100 clock hours	AOS
Airframe Add-On	6.5 months/806.25 clock hours	Certificate
Airframe Only	10.2 months/1,268.75 clock hours	Certificate
Basic Electronics	8.75 months/1,050 clock hours	Certificate
Powerplant Add-On	6.7 months/831.25 clock hours	Certificate
Powerplant Only	10.4 months/1,293.75 clock hours	Certificate

Westwood College, Denver North, Denver

About Our Institution

Westwood College was founded in Denver, Colorado, in 1953 as the Radio and Television Repair Institute. Committed to a positive and cooperative environment and working collaboratively with employers, the College is dedicated to high-quality, college-level, career-oriented education. Westwood's objective is to use up-to-date technologies, hands-on training in a modern facility, intern and extern opportunities, and graduate placement assistance to help students become confident, job-qualified individuals who are prepared to enter the career fields of their choice.

Special Features

Westwood College places a high value on the industry experience its faculty members bring to the classroom. While many faculty members have earned bachelor's and master's degrees in their fields, Westwood looks for a combination of industry experience, educational training in the subject area, and prior teaching experience to ensure that students receive a balanced, industry-relevant education.

Financial Aid/Scholarships

Westwood College participates in a variety of financial aid programs, including the Federal Pell Grant, the FFEL Stafford Student Loan (subsidized and unsubsidized), PLUS Loans, the Federal Perkins Loan, the Federal Supplemental Educational Opportunity Grant (FSEOG), the Westwood High School Scholarship Program, and educational assistance loans. Other types of financial aid may be available depending on individual student eligibility. Students should check with the Admissions Office for VA-approved benefits.

Tuition and Fees

Students should consult the school catalog for detailed tuition and fee information.

Accreditation

Westwood is accredited by the Accrediting Commission of Career Schools and Colleges of Technology (ACCSCT). This accreditation means the College has a clearly defined mission, aspires to high standards that ensure high-quality programs, and has the human, physical, and financial resources to accomplish its mission.

Admissions

Successful candidates for Westwood are required to have a high school diploma or GED certificate. Applicants must complete an acceptance application and either receive a minimum composite score of 17 on the ACT or 920 on the SAT or achieve the required scores on the Accuplacer Computerized Placement Test. To enroll, candidates complete an application for admission, are interviewed by an admissions representative, submit a registration fee, and upon completion of testing, attend an acceptance interview to verify their commitment to begin training.

Program Description

Over the past forty-five years, in response to innovative requirements of industry, Westwood has grown into an institution offering Bachelor of Science degree programs in Animation, Business Administration: Concentration in Accounting, Business Administration: Concentration in Marketing and Sales, Computer Network Management, E-Business Management, Electronic Engineering Technology, Information Systems Security, Interior Design, Technical Management, Visual Communications, and Web Design and Multimedia. Associate degrees are awarded in Automotive Technology, Computer-Aided Design/Architectural or Mechanical Drafting, Computer Network Management, Criminal Justice, Electronic Engineering Technology, Game Art and Design, Graphic Design and Multimedia, Game Software Development, Heating/Ventilation/Air Conditioning/Refrigeration, Hotel and Restaurant Management, Medical Assisting, Medical Transcription, Software Engineering, and Surveying.

Contact

Anthony Caggiano, President
Westwood College of Technology
7350 North Broadway
Denver, CO 80221
Phone: (303) 650-5050
        (800) 875-6050 (toll-free)
Fax: (303) 426-4647
E-mail: tcaggiano@westwood.edu
Web: www.westwood.edu

Programs Eligible for Scholarship	Course Length/Credit Hours	Credential Earned
Animation	36 months/195 credit hours	BS
Automotive Technology	17–24 months/90.5 credit hours	AOS
Business Administration: Concentration in Accounting	36 months/180 credit hours	BS
Business Administration: Concentration in Marketing and Sales	36 months/180 credit hours	BS
Computer-Aided Design/Architectural Drafting	20 months/101 credit hours	AAS
Computer-Aided Design/Mechanical Drafting	20 months/101 credit hours	AAS
Computer Network Management	36 months/192 credit hours	BS
Computer Network Engineering	20 months/108 credit hours	AAS
Criminal Justice	36 months/183 credit hours	BS
E-Business Management	36 months/187.5 credit hours	BS
Electronic Engineering Technology	36 months/180 credit hours	BS
Electronic Engineering Technology	20 months/99 credit hours	AS
Game Art and Design	36 months/193 credit hours	BS
Game Software Development	36 months/193.5 credit hours	BS
Graphic Design and Multimedia	20 months/105 credit hours	AAS
Heating/Ventilation/Air Conditioning/Refrigeration	17 months/92 credit hours	AOS
Hotel and Restaurant Management	20 months/105 credit hours	AAS
Information Systems Security	36 months/192 credit hours	BS
Interior Design	36 months/190 credit hours	BS
Medical Assisting	15 months/91 credit hours	AAS
Medical Transcription	22 months/96 credit hours	AAS
Software Engineering	20 months/97.5 credit hours	AAS
Surveying	17 months/93 credit hours	AAS
Technical Management	17 months/180 credit hours	BS
Visual Communications	36 months/192 credit hours	BS
Web Design and Multimedia	36 months/192 credit hours	BS

Westwood College, Denver North, Online Program, Denver

About Our Institution
Westwood College–Denver North was founded in 1953 as the Radio and Television Repair Institute. Almost fifty years later, with the growth of the Internet, Denver North established Westwood's first online degree program. The program is accredited through Denver North by the Accrediting Commission of Career Schools and Colleges of Technology (ACCSCT). The Online Program is committed to maintaining a positive and cooperative environment and to working collaboratively with employers to ensure a high-quality, college-level, career-oriented education. The objective is to graduate confident, job-qualified individuals prepared to enter their career fields of choice.

Special Features
Westwood College places a high value on the industry experience faculty members bring to the classroom. While many faculty members have earned bachelor's and master's degrees in their fields, Westwood looks for a combination of industry experience, educational training in the subject area, and prior teaching experience to ensure that students receive a balanced, industry-relevant education.

Financial Aid/Scholarships
Westwood College participates in a variety of financial aid programs, including the Federal Pell Grant, FFEL, Stafford Student Loan (subsidized and unsubsidized), Plus loans, Federal Perkins Loan, the Federal Supplemental Educational Opportunity Grant (FSEOG), the Westwood High School Scholarship Program, and educational assistance loans. Other types of financial aid may be available depending on individual student eligibility. Students should check with the Admissions Office for VA-approved benefits.

Tuition and Fees
Students should consult the school catalog for detailed tuition and fee information.

Accreditation
Westwood is accredited by the Accrediting Commission of Career Schools and Colleges of Technology (ACCSCT). This accreditation guides the College, in that it has a clearly defined mission and aspires to high standards to ensure high-quality programs and has the human, physical, and financial resources to accomplish its mission.

Program Content
Associate Degrees: Computer Network Engineering, Graphic Design and Multimedia, Software Engineering.

Bachelor's Degrees: Animation, Computer Network Management, Criminal Justice, E-Business Management, Game Software Development, Information Systems Security, Interior Design, Visual Communications, Web Design and Multimedia.

Admissions
Successful candidates for Westwood are required to have a high school diploma or GED. Applicants must submit an application and receive a minimum score of 17 on the ACT or 920 on the SAT or achieve the required scores on the Accuplacer Computerized Placement Test. In addition, successful candidates must pass the Computer Literacy Test. Candidates must also have an interview with an admissions representative and submit a registration fee. Upon completion of testing, candidates must attend an acceptance interview to verify their commitment to begin training.

Contact
Shaun McAlmont
President
Westwood College–Denver North
7350 North Broadway
Denver, CO 80221
Phone: (720) 887-8011
Fax: (303) 410-7996
E-mail: smcalmont@westwood.edu
Web: www.westwoodonline.edu

Programs Eligible for Scholarship	Course Length/Credit Hours	Credential Earned
Computer Network Engineering	20 months/108 credit hours	AAS
Graphic Design and Multimedia	20 months/105 credit hours	AAS
Software Engineering	20 months/97.5 credit hours	AAS
Animation	36 months/195 credit hours	BS
Computer Network Management	36 months/192 credit hours	BS
Criminal Justice	36 months/183 credit hours	BS
E-Business Management	36 months/187.5 credit hours	BS
Game Software Development	36 months/193.5 credit hours	BS
Information Systems Security	36 months/192 credit hours	BS
Interior Design	36 months/190 credit hours	BS
Visual Communications	36 months/192 credit hours	BS
Web Design and Media	36 months/192 credit hours	BS

Westwood College, Denver South, Denver

About Our Institution

Westwood College was founded in Denver, Colorado, in 1953 as the Radio and Television Repair Institute. Committed to a positive and cooperative environment and working collaboratively with employers, the College is dedicated to high-quality, college-level, career-oriented education. Westwood's objective is to graduate confident, job-qualified individuals prepared to enter career fields of choice.

Special Features

Westwood College places a high value on the industry experience faculty members bring to the classroom. While many faculty members have earned their bachelor's and master's degrees in their fields, Westwood looks for a combination of industry experience, educational training in the subject area, and prior teaching experience to ensure that students receive a balanced, industry-relevant education.

Financial Aid/Scholarships

Westwood College participates in a variety of financial aid programs, including the Federal Pell Grant, FFEL Stafford Student Loan (subsidized and unsubsidized), PLUS Loans, Federal Perkins Loan, the Federal Supplemental Educational Opportunity Grant (FSEOG), the Westwood High School Scholarship Program, and educational assistance loans. Other types of financial aid may be available depending on individual student eligibility. Students should check with the Admissions Office for VA-approved benefits.

Tuition and Fees

Students should consult the school catalog for detailed tuition and fee information.

Accreditation

Westwood is accredited by the Accrediting Commission of Career Schools and Colleges of Technology (ACCSCT). This accreditation indicates that the College has a clearly defined mission, aspires to high standards to ensure quality programs, and has the human, physical, and financial resources to accomplish its mission.

Admissions

Successful candidates for Westwood are required to have a high school diploma or GED certificate. Applicants must complete an acceptance application and either receive a composite minimum score of 17 on the ACT or 920 on the SAT or achieve the required scores on the Accuplacer Computerized Placement Test. To enroll, candidates complete an admissions application, are interviewed by an admissions representative, submit a registration fee, and upon completion of testing, attend an acceptance interview to verify their commitment to begin training.

Program Description

Over the past fifty years, in response to the innovative requirements of industry, Westwood has grown into an institution offering the Associate in Applied Science (A.A.S.) degree in Computer Network Engineering and in Graphic Design and Multimedia, and the Bachelor of Science (B.S.) degree in Animation, Business Administration: Concentration in Accounting, Business Administration: Concentration in Marketing and Sales, Computer Network Management, Criminal Justice, E-Business Management, Game Art and Design, Game Software Development, Information Systems Security, Interior Design, Visual Communications, and Web Design and Multimedia.

Contact

Wayne Fletcher
Executive Director
Westwood College
3150 South Sheridan Boulevard
Denver, CO 80227
Phone: (303) 650-5050
     (800) 875-6050 (toll-free)
Fax: (303) 426-4647
E-mail: wfletcher@westwood.edu
Web: www.westwood.edu

Programs Eligible for Scholarship	Course Length/Credit Hours	Credential Earned
Animation	36 months/195 credit hours	BS
Business Administration: Concentration in Accounting	36 months/180 credit hours	BS
Business Administration: Concentration in Marketing/Sales	36 months/180 credit hours	BS
Computer-Aided Design/Architectural Drafting	20 months/98 credit hours	AAS
Computer Network Engineering	20 months/108 credit hours	AAS
Computer Network Management	36 months/192 credit hours	BS
Criminal Justice	36 months/183 credit hours	BS
E-Business Management	36 months/187.5 credit hours	BS
Game Art and Design	36 months/193 credit hours	BS
Game Software Development	36 months/193.5 credit hours	BS
Graphic Design and Multimedia	20 months/105 credit hours	AAS
Information Systems Security	36 months/192 credit hours	BS
Interior Design	36 months/190 credit hours	BS
Software Engineering	20 months/97.5 credit hours	AAS
Visual Communications	36 months/192 credit hours	BS
Web Design and Multimedia	36 months/192 credit hours	BS

AMI, Inc., Daytona Beach

About Our Institution

Since 1972, AMI has trained entry-level technicians for the motorcycle, marine, and personal watercraft industries. AMI offers student services that include financial aid to those who qualify, housing assistance in the Daytona Beach area, and job placement assistance throughout the United States.

Special Features

AMI programs provide the student with an in-depth understanding of theory and principles in each career program, with an emphasis on hands-on training. All major manufacturers in the motorcycle, marine, and personal watercraft industries are represented. All AMI training programs are scheduled at 40 hours per week to give the graduate the benefit of employment opportunities without costly delay.

Financial Aid/Scholarships

AMI students are eligible to apply for various federal grants and loans. These include Pell Grants and Stafford and PLUS Loans. AMI also participates in various scholarship programs. Additional student loans are also possible through Key Bank and Sallie Mae. Vocational rehabilitation offices nationwide have also sponsored students to attend AMI via a variety of career retraining programs.

Tuition and Fees

Tuition and fees vary by program of choice. Tuition and supplemental fee cover all textbooks, handouts, shop supplies, uniform shirts, and graduation luncheon. All tools are provided for training. There are no additional charges.

Accreditation

AMI, Inc., is accredited by the Accrediting Commission of the Accrediting Council for Continuing Education and Training (ACCET), which is listed by the U.S. Secretary of Education as a nationally recognized accrediting agency.

Admissions

The entrance requirements for all programs are an accepted application for enrollment; a minimum age of 16; the ability to read, write, and speak English; and a high school diploma, its recognized equivalent, or a passing score on an independently administered Ability to Benefit test, approved by the Secretary of the U.S. Department of Education. A GED program is available.

Graduation Requirements

All students must maintain and complete training with a minimum 2.0 grade point average, which is 80 percent on a 100 percent system.

Contact

Carey Brown, Director of Admissions
3042 West International Speedway Blvd.
Daytona Beach, FL 32124
Phone: (386) 255-0295
        (800) 881-2AMI (toll-free)
E-mail: carey@amiwrench.com
Web: http://amiwrench.com

Program Content

Marine Technician Career Program, Motorcycle Technician Career Programs, Watercraft Technician Career Program

Program Description

AMI's career programs are designed to provide learning experiences that enable the student to develop the skill and knowledge to become an entry-level service technician in the powersports industry. The successful student develops additional managerial skills and knowledge that broadens the graduate's employment potential and assists in future advancement to parts or service management positions.

The Art Institute of Fort Lauderdale, Fort Lauderdale

About Our Institution
The Art Institute of Fort Lauderdale (AIFL), has as its primary purpose the training and education of individuals for careers in the design, practical arts, and business-related fields. With a student-faculty ratio of 20:1, the Art Institute prepares students with the knowledge and skills necessary to enter their chosen fields. All degree programs include course work in academic areas important to the overall growth of the individual. The Art Institute encourages the professional development of its students through curricula that emphasize the creative, communication, interpersonal, reasoning, and technical skills necessary for success.

AIFL opened its doors in September 1968, offering diploma programs in commercial art, interior design, and fashion illustration. The Art Institute received state approval for veterans' training in September 1970, and was accredited by the Accrediting Commission for Trade and Technical Schools of the Career College Association in April 1971. In 1979, the Art Institute was recognized as a two-year, degree-granting institution in the state of Florida, authorized to confer the Associate of Science degree by the State Board of Independent Colleges and Universities. In November 1987, the State Board of Independent Colleges and Universities approved the conferring of the Bachelor of Professional Studies degree. As of January 2004, the Art Institute offered twelve bachelor's degree programs. Currently, the Art Institute offers bachelor's and associate degrees and diploma programs.

The Art Institute of Fort Lauderdale occupies approximately 160,000 square feet of space in three separate buildings. The main facility is a 72,000-square-foot, four-story building. The Harbor Walk Annex, located at 1650 SE 17th Street, comprises approximately 35,000 square feet. Harbor Walk West houses the library and other facilities in 9,500 square feet of space.

Special Features
The library is located in the Harbor Walk West Building. It occupies about 5,000 square feet and is equipped with reading tables, computer stations with Internet access, a photocopier, and a laser printer. Computer labs are equipped with IBM-compatible workstations and Macintosh Power PC workstations. The video postproduction labs occupy 2,500 square feet and are equipped with editing stations. Two professionally designed broadcasting studios and a working newsroom are also part of the media space. The fashion design area consists of sewing rooms containing power sewing machines, cutting tables, power cutters, dressmakers forms, and steam irons. In addition, there is one design lab equipped with a computer-driven design workstation. The photography area contains the darkrooms with film processors, enlarger stations, and digital equipment.

The Art Institute's educational processes are supplemented by the Student Affairs Department. The mission of the Student Affairs Department is to support its stated purpose by providing assistance and services to the student body in the areas of employment, counseling, international advising, housing, food service, and bookstore supplies.

Financial Aid/Scholarships
At the time of initial enrollment, the student works with a financial planner to develop a financial plan to meet expenses involved in the education process (tuition, fees, supplies, cost of living, etc.). The Art Institute is eligible to offer its students the opportunity to apply for a variety of financial-assistance programs. These programs include loans, grants, and work-study assistance for qualified applicants. All eligible students may apply for financial assistance under various federal and state programs, such as institutional grants/awards, the Art Institute's National Scholarships, the AIFL Institutional Scholarship, and agency-related scholarships.

Tuition and Fees
For students who enroll from May 1, 2004, through October 31, 2004, tuition is charged at $365 per credit (with an average of 9 credits per quarter). An application fee of $50 is paid by new and transfer students only. Books, supplies, and lab fees vary according to program.

Accreditation
The Art Institute of Fort Lauderdale's degree programs are licensed by the State Board of Independent Colleges and Universities and authorized to confer Associate of Science and Bachelor of Science degrees. The Art Institute of Fort Lauderdale is accredited by the Accrediting Council of Independent Colleges and Schools, recognized by the U.S. Department of Education.

Admissions
All applicants of AIFL must demonstrate proof of high school graduation or its equivalent prior to receiving final acceptance. Applicants must submit a copy of their high school transcript. Applicants who have obtained their GED certificate must submit a transcript evidencing completion of such.

Graduation Requirements
To be qualified to graduate (and for those programs requiring a portfolio, become eligible to participate in Portfolio Review), a student must fulfill the following requirements: receive a passing grade or credit for all required course work, achieve a minimum CGPA of 2.0, maintain satisfactory academic progress standards, satisfy all financial obligations to the Art Institute, and receive a passing grade on the portfolio thesis, if required.

Contact
The Director of Admissions
The Art Institute of Fort Lauderdale
1799 SE 17th Street
Fort Lauderdale, FL 33316-3000
Phone: (954) 527-1799
(800) 275-7603 (toll-free)
Fax: (954) 728-8637
Web: www.aifl.edu

ATI College of Health, Miami

About Our Institution

ATI College of Health is a private institution founded in 1976. Graduates are prepared for entry-level positions as respiratory therapists, medical assisting technicians, diagnostic ultrasound technicians, pharmacy technicians, and dental assistants.

Special Features

Each program is a combination of both didactic (classroom) training and clinical or externship rotations.

Financial Aid/Scholarships

The school participates in a variety of financial assistance programs, including Federal Pell Grant and FSEOG, among others.

Accreditation

ATI College of Health is accredited by the Accrediting Commission of Career Schools and Colleges of Technology (ACCSCT) and the Commission on Accreditation of Allied Health Education Programs (CAAHEP). The school is licensed by the Florida State Board of Independent Post-Secondary Vocational, Technical, Trade, and Business Schools.

Admissions

Admissions requirements include a high school diploma or GED certificate, a personal interview with the Admissions Office, and the school director's approval.

Enrollment

There are 300 students enrolled.

Contact

Barbara Woosley
School Director
1395 Northwest 167th Street
Miami, FL 33169
Phone: (305) 628-1000
Fax: (305) 628-1461
Web: www.aticareertraining.com

Program Content

Dental Assistant, Diagnostic Ultrasound Technician, Medical Assisting Technician, Pharmacy Technician, Respiratory Therapy

Program Description

These programs provide students with the ability, through technical education and practical training, to begin careers as health-care professionals in their chosen areas of specialization.

Programs Eligible for Scholarship	Tuition and Fees	Course Length/Credit Hours	Credential Earned
Dental Assistant	$22,895	80 weeks/1,470 clock hours	AS
Diagnostic Ultrasound Technology	$33,295	110 weeks/1,920 clock hours	AS
Medical Assisting Technician	$18,295	60 weeks/1,200 clock hours	OAD
Pharmacy Technician	$18,295	60 weeks/1,200 clock hours	OAD
Respiratory Therapy	$33,295	110 weeks/2,185 clock hours	AS

ATI–Career Training Center, Fort Lauderdale

About Our Institution
The philosophy of ATI–Career Training Center, Fort Lauderdale, is "helping people achieve a better lifestyle by preparing them, through education, for a career in their chosen field."

Special Features
ATI is committed to providing assistance with total job market readiness, high-quality skills training, and job search skills. Classes are less than eighteen months in duration and are kept small for individualized attention. With hands-on training, students actually work with the equipment and software they will use in the workplace.

Financial Aid/Scholarships
ATI participates in the following programs: Pell Grant, FFEL, FDSLP, Federal Perkins Loan, work-study, FSEOG, and VA.

Accreditation
ATI is nationally accredited by the Accrediting Commission of Career Schools and Colleges of Technology (ACCSCT) and is licensed by the Commission for Independent Education, Florida Department of Education.

Admissions
A high school diploma or GED certificate, along with a personal interview, determine an applicant's potential for success.

Enrollment
350 students enrolled.

Contact
Connie Bailus, Executive Director
2880 Northwest 62nd Street
Fort Lauderdale, FL 33309
Phone: (954) 973-4760
Fax: (954) 973-6422
E-mail: cbailus@atienterprises.edu

Program Content
Drafting and Computer-Assisted Design, Electronics Engineering Technology, Information Technology and Network Administration, Medical Administrative Associate, Medical Assisting

Program Description
Drafting and Computer-Assisted Design: This program prepares graduates for civil, mechanical, architectural, and electronic design.

Electronics Engineering Technology: This program prepares graduates for positions in telecommunications, networking, aviation electronics, computer service, and related fields.

Information Technology and Network Administration: This program prepares graduates for computer network administration.

Medical Administrative Associate: This program prepares graduates for medical records, billing, coding, insurance, and transcription.

Medical Assisting: This program prepares graduates for positions as a medical assistant, receptionist, or insurance clerk/processor in a medical office, hospital, or clinic.

Programs Eligible for Scholarship	Tuition and Fees	Course Length/Credit Hours	Credential Earned
Drafting/Computer-Assisted Design	$18,293	60 weeks/90 credit hours	OAD
Electronics Engineering Technology	$23,295	80 weeks/122.5 credit hours	OAD
Info Technol/Network Admin	$19,770	60 weeks/90 credit hours	OAD
Medical Administrative Associate	$18,705	60 weeks/90 credit hours	OAD
Medical Assisting	$19,994	72 weeks/104 credit hours	OAD

ATI–Career Training Center, Miami

About Our Institution
ATI–Career Training Center is a private institution, accredited by ACCSCT, that was founded in 1954 to provide students with the skills required for entry-level positions in the electronics, air-conditioning, automotive, and drafting and CAD fields. The school occupies 32,000 square feet of well-equipped facilities on three floors.

Financial Aid/Scholarships
ATI–Career Training Center maintains a financial aid office on campus and provides a variety of available programs, including grants, loans, scholarships, and veterans' educational benefits.

Tuition and Fees
Tuition averages $2,500 per quarter for the six- or eight-quarter programs. Costs include application, books, materials, uniforms, tools, and all tuition fees.

Accreditation
ATI is accredited by ACCSCT.

Admissions
The school admits as regular students applicants having a high school diploma or the recognized equivalent (GED). ATI is open to nonresident alien students.

Graduation Requirements
To graduate from any program, a student must complete all required assignments and class work with a cumulative grade average of 70 percent, receive a passing grade on all individual subjects, and maintain an attendance record of 85 percent of required class time.

Contact
Errol Stephenson
School Director
ATI–Career Training Center
1 Northeast 19th Street
Miami, FL 33132
Phone: (305) 573-1600
Fax: (305) 576-8365
E-mail: estephenson@atienterprises.com

Program Content
Electronics Engineering Technology; Drafting and Computer-Assisted Design (CAD); Information Technology and Network Administration; Automotive Service Technology; Air-Conditioning, Refrigeration, and Major Appliance Service Technology

Program Description
Electronics Engineering Technology— The objective of the program is to prepare the students for entry-level positions as general electronic engineering technicians.

Drafting and Computer-Assisted Design— This program is designed to prepare students for an exciting entry-level position in drafting, design layout, and similar occupations using AutoCad.

Information Technology and Network Administration— This program prepares graduates for network administration.

Automotive Service Technology— The objective of this program is to prepare students for an entry-level position in the automotive maintenance field as well as prepare them for ASE certification.

Air-Conditioning, Refrigeration, and Major Appliance Service Technology— The objective is to prepare students for a position in the A/C, refrigeration, and major appliance repair fields.

Programs Eligible for Scholarship	Tuition and Fees	Course Length/Credit Hours	Credential Earned
Electronics Engineering Technology	$21,788	80 weeks	OAD
Drafting and Computer-Assisted Design	$17,368	60 weeks	OAD
Information Technology/Network Admin.	$16,995	60 weeks	OAD
Automotive Service Technology	$16,690	60 weeks	OAD
A/C, Refrigeration & Major Appliance	$17,248	60 weeks	OAD

ATI–Career Training Center, Oakland Park

About Our Institution
This private institution has been in existence since 1981 and was acquired by ATI Career Training Center in 1990. ATI's philosophy is to help people achieve a better lifestyle by preparing them, through education, for a career in their chosen field. The administrative offices and classrooms are housed in two 1-story buildings of approximately 22,000 square feet. The school occupies both buildings, which are air conditioned, well lit, and well equipped. Ample parking for students surrounds the buildings. The business office is open from 9 a.m. to 8 p.m. Monday through Thursday, 9 a.m. to 5 p.m. on Friday, and 9 a.m. to 1 p.m. on Saturday.

Special Features
ATI is approved to enroll nonimmigrant alien students and is approved for veterans' educational benefits.

Financial Aid/Scholarships
Pell, FFEL, Perkins, work-study, SEOG, VA, JTPA, and campus-based scholarships are available.

Accreditation
ATI is accredited by the Accrediting Commission of Career Schools and Colleges of Technology (ACCSCT).

Admissions
The school admits regular student applicants having a high school diploma or the recognized equivalent (GED). The applicant must be capable of performing the tasks involved at the school that will result in employment in their chosen career field. Final acceptance of each student must be given by the school director or the director's designee. The applicant's appearance and physical condition must be consistent with general employment situations.

Enrollment
A total of 240 students are enrolled.

Contact
Cindy Gordon
3501 NW 9th Avenue
Oakland Park, FL 33300
Phone: (954) 563-5899
Fax: (954) 568-0874
E-mail: cgordon@atienterprises.edu
Web: www.aticareertraining.edu

Program Content
Air Conditioning/Refrigeration/Major Appliances Technology, Automotive Service

Programs Eligible for Scholarship	Tuition and Fees	Course Length	Credential Earned
Air Conditioning/Refrigeration/Major Appliance Technology	$18,313	60 weeks	OA
Automotive Service	$18,010	60 weeks	OA

Florida College of Natural Health, Fort Lauderdale, Pompano Beach

About Our Institution

Florida College of Natural Health (FCNH) has four campuses in Fort Lauderdale, Miami, Orlando, and Sarasota. FCNH was founded in 1986 and is corporately owned and governed by Steiner Education Group, Inc., along with three other schools in Maryland, Pennsylvania, and Virginia. All locations have convenient day and evening schedules with monthly start dates.

Special Features

All campuses have a Student Clinic, where students have the opportunity to work with the public while attending school, and an extensive continuing education program, which enables students to enhance their skills and learn new modalities after graduation. The schools have a fully stocked Natural Health Shoppe on the campus that carries everything from massage creams and oils to music and school uniforms. All Steiner Education Group campuses employ a Career Services Coordinator who assists graduates in achieving their goals. The Career Services Departments have built relationships with some of the most successful employers in the industry, and graduates of the Steiner Education Group schools are given priority consideration when Steiner Leisure Ltd., a global provider of spa services, recruits for their maritime or land-based spas.

Financial Aid/Scholarships

FCNH is approved by the Department of Education for Title IV Funds, and federal financial aid is available to those who qualify, including Pell Grants and Stafford Student Loans.

Tuition and Fees

Students should call the campus for current pricing information.

Accreditation

FCNH is accredited by the Accrediting Commission of Career Schools and Colleges of Technology (ACCSCT) and is programmatically accredited by the Commission on Massage Therapy Accreditation (COMTA)

Contacts

Florida College of Natural Health
Fort Lauderdale (Main Campus)
2001 West Sample Road #100
Pompano Beach, FL 33064
Phone: (800) 541-9299 (toll-free)
E-mail: ftlauderdale@fcnh.com

FCNH Miami (Branch Campus)
7925 NW 12 Street #201
Miami, FL 33126
Phone: (800) 599-9599 (toll-free)
E-mail: miami@fcnh.com

FCNH Orlando (Branch Campus)
2600 Lake Lucien Drive #140
Maitland, FL 32751
Phone: (800) 393-7337 (toll-free)
E-mail: orlando@fcnh.com

Program Content

Advanced Therapeutic Massage, Massage and Spa , Medical Massage, Paramedical Skin Care, Skin Care, Therapeutic Massage, Therapeutic Massage and Physical Fitness, Therapeutic Massage and Skin Care.

Program Description

Advanced Therapeutic Massage combines the students' knowledge of massage with specific training in the treatment of sports injuries, pathology, medical terminology and documentation, and massage interventions.

The Massage Therapy and Physical Fitness Program combines the students' knowledge of massage therapy with specific instruction in health-related physical fitness. This program addresses the four entities of fitness: cardiorespiratory endurance, muscle strength, nutrition (body composition), and flexibility.

Massage Therapy and Spa Training augments the students' knowledge of massage with specific training in spa treatments and spa operations. Students learn body treatments, including body exfoliations, body masks, hydrotherapy, and body wraps.

The Medical Massage Program combines the students' knowledge of Swedish massage and human anatomy and physiology with specific training in treatment of injuries, pathologies, medical terminology, medical documentation, and massage interventions.

Paramedical Skin Care provides hands-on training to prepare the skin-care student to be marketable in the medical community.

The Therapeutic Massage and Skin Care concentration prepares the graduate to assume the responsibilities of both professions.

FCNH Sarasota (Branch Campus)
616 67th Street Circle East
Bradenton, FL 34236
Phone (800) 966-7117 (toll-free)
E-mail: sarasota@fcnh.com

Web: www.steinered.com (all campuses)

Programs Eligible for Scholarship	Course Length/Credit Hours	Credential Earned
Medical Massage	900 hours/46 credits	Diploma
Skin Care	300 hours/15 credits	Diploma
Therapeutic Massage	624 hours/34.5 credits	Diploma
Advanced Therapeutic Massage	1149 hours/64.5 credits	AS
Advanced Therapeutic Massage	1149 hours/64.5 credits	AS
Massage and Spa	1149 hours/64.5 credits	AS
Paramedical Skin Care	1201 hours/64.5 credits	AS
Therapeutic Massage and Physical Fitness	1149 hours/64.5 credits	AS
Therapeutic Massage and Skin Care	1149 hours/64.5 credits	AS

Florida Metropolitan University, Brandon, Tampa

About Our Institution
Florida Metropolitan University–Brandon Campus (FMU–Brandon) is one of ten institutions that make up Florida Metropolitan University, a division of Corinthian Colleges, Inc., which operates more than eighty such schools nationwide. FMU–Brandon was founded as Tampa College in 1890, making it the oldest business college in the state of Florida.

Special Features
FMU–Brandon prides itself on being student oriented. It prepares students for employment and productive lives. Students are provided the skills and knowledge to enter the workforce with confidence. The University has its computer labs connected to the Internet, allowing students access to a vast source of information and research materials. Faculty members are experienced in their particular academic field beyond teaching, thus bringing a real-world atmosphere into the classroom.

Financial Aid/Scholarships
Federal Pell Grant, Federal Supplemental Educational Opportunity Grant (FSEOG), Federal Work-Study Program (FWS), Florida Student Assistance Grant (FSAG), Federal Family Educational Loan Program (FFELP), Subsidized and Unsubsidized Federal Stafford Loans, and institutional scholarships are available. Financial aid is available for those who qualify.

Tuition and Fees
Per-credit hours are assessed based on the amount of classes taken per quarter and differ for selected programs. A registration fee of $25 is assessed per quarter. Books average $200 per quarter.

Accreditation
The University is accredited by the Accrediting Council for Independent Colleges and Schools (ACICS). The Medical Assisting program and the Surgical Technologist program are accredited by the Commission on Accreditation of Allied Health Education Programs (CAAHEP).

Program Content
Accounting, Assisting Living Administrator, Business, Computer Information Science, Computer Office Technologies & Applications, Criminal Justice, Homeland Security, Management/Marketing, Master of Business Administration, Master of Science in Criminal Justice, Medical Assisting, Medical Insurance Billing & Coding, Paralegal, Pharmacy Technician, Surgical Technologist

Admissions
Graduation from high school, or its equivalent (GED), is a prerequisite for admission. All applicants are required to successfully complete an assessment examination.

Graduation Requirements
A 2.0 or better cumulative grade point average and successful completion of all required courses for the particular program and degree level.

Enrollment
There are 1500–1600 students enrolled.

Contact
Steve Backman, President
Florida Metropolitan University
3924 Coconut Palm Drive
Tampa, FL 33619
Phone: (813) 621-0041
Fax: (813) 623-0919
E-mail: sbackman@cci.edu
Web: www.fmu.edu

Programs Eligible for Scholarship	Tuition and Fees	Course Length/Credit Hours	Credential Earned
Accounting	$250/credit hour	96 credit hours	AS
		192 credit hours	BS
Assisted Living Administrator	$250/credit hour	96 credit hours	AS
Business	$250/credit hour	96 credit hours	AS
		192 credit hours	BBA
Computer Information Science	$235/credit hour	96 credit hours	AS
		192 credit hours	BS
Computer Office Technologies & Applications	$260/credit hour	94 credit hours	AS
Criminal Justice	$250/credit hour	96 credit hours	AS
		192 credit hours	BS
Homeland Security	$250/credit hour	96 credit hours	AS
		192 credit hours	BS
Management/Marketing	$250/credit hour	96 credit hours	AS
		192 credit hours	BS
Master of Business Administration	$390/credit hour	56 credit hours	MBA
Master of Science Criminal Justice	$390/credit hour	54 credit hours	MS
Medical Assisting	$260/credit hour	97 credit hours	AS
Medical Insurance Billing & Coding	$260/credit hour	90 credit hours	AS
Paralegal	$250/credit hour	96 credit hours	AS
		192 credit hours	BS
Pharmacy Technician	$260/credit hour	97 credit hours	AS
Surgical Technologist	$290/credit hour	98 credit hours	AS

Florida Metropolitan University, Jacksonville

About Our Institution
Founded in 2000, Jacksonville is one of the newest of the ten Florida Metropolitan University (FMU) campuses. The newly renovated campus includes eighteen comfortable and spacious lecture rooms, four computer labs, a medical-assisting lab, a Learning Resource Center, bookstore, and student lounge, as well as administrative and student services offices.

Special Features
The Jacksonville campus offers various associate, bachelor's, and master's degrees in the business, criminal justice, computer, and medical fields. FMU's strength is its instructors, who bring years of real-world experience and education into the classroom to enhance the students' education. Jacksonville enjoys a high quality of living with a blend of cultural, entertainment, and recreational activities. In addition to the Jacksonville Symphony Orchestra, there are community theater groups, dozens of local art galleries, the Cummer Museum of Art and Gardens, the Jacksonville Jazz Festival, the Jacksonville Museum of Contemporary Art, the Museum of Science and History, and the Jacksonville Jaguars football team. There are appealing downtown riverside areas, handsome residential neighborhoods, and the region's only skyscrapers. Because Jacksonville was settled along both sides of the St. John's River, many attractions are on or near the riverbanks with beautiful vistas across the wide waterway.

Financial Aid/Scholarships
Information regarding the Pell Grant, Federal Supplemental Educational Opportunity Grant (FSEOG), Federal Work-Study (FWS), and scholarships can be obtained from the finance office on campus. Financial aid is available for those who qualify.

Accreditation
The Accrediting Council for Independent Colleges and Schools (ACICS) accredits all campuses of Florida Metropolitan University. All campuses are accredited to award associate degrees, bachelor's degrees, and master's degrees.

Admissions
Graduation from high school or its equivalent is a prerequisite for admission to the University. Applicants not completing a secondary program or not having a diploma will be considered for admission on the basis of the General Education Development (GED) test or other equivalency. All applicants are required to successfully complete an assessment examination. This standardized, nationally-normed test is administered by the college,

Program Content
Accounting, Business, Computer Information Science, Criminal Justice, Medical Assisting, Medical Insurance Billing/Coding, Paralegal, Pharmacy Technician

and is designed to further ensure that the applicant has the skills necessary to pursue a college-level program. Transfer students who are high school graduates or GED certificate holders (or other equivalency) and who can submit proof of successfully completing a minimum of 36 quarter hours or 24 semester hours of earned college credit at an accredited postsecondary institution will not be required to complete the above referenced test. Applicants who have completed the ACT with a score of at least 15 or the SAT with a score of a least 700 will not be required to complete the above referenced test.

Graduation Requirements
In order to graduate, a student must have earned a minimum GPA of 2.0 and have successfully completed all required credits within the maximum credits that may be attempted.

Enrollment
There are 900 students enrolled.

Contact
Robin Manning, Director of Admissions
Florida Metropolitan University
8226 Phillips Hwy.
Jacksonville, FL 32256
Phone (904) 731-4949
Fax: (904) 731-0599
E-mail: rmanning@cci.edu
Web: www.fmu.edu

Programs Eligible for Scholarship	Tuition and Fees	Course Length/Credit Hours	Credential Earned
Accounting	$250/credit hour	96 credit hours	AS
	$250/credit hour	192 credit hours	BS
Business	$250/credit hour	96 credit hours	AS
	$250/credit hour	192 credit hours	BS
Computer Information Science	$250/credit hour	96 credit hours	AS
	$250/credit hour	192 credit hours	BS
Criminal Justice	$250/credit hour	96 credit hours	AS
	$250/credit hour	192 credit hours	BS
Master of Business Administration	$390/credit hour	56 credit hours	MBA
Master of Science, Criminal Justice	$390/credit hour	54–58 credit hours	MS
Medical Assisting	$260/credit hour	97 credit hours	AS
Medical Insurance Billing/Coding	$7,500, including books	6 months	Certificate
Paralegal	$250/credit hour	96 credit hours	AS
Pharmacy Technician	$260/credit hour	97 credit hours	AS

Florida Metropolitan University, Lakeland

About Our Institution

Florida Metropolitan University (FMU), Lakeland, is one of nine institutions that comprise Florida Metropolitan University, a division of Corinthian Colleges, Inc., which operates more than eighty schools nationwide. FMU was founded in 1890 as Tampa College, making it the oldest business college in the state of Florida. FMU Lakeland prides itself in being student-oriented in preparing people for employment and productive lives. The University operates in a 26,000-square-foot facility that houses two computer labs, a medical assisting lab, M.B.A. labs, and a pharmacy technician lab. In addition, there are sixteen general purpose classrooms, a Learning Resource Center, a bookstore, and a student lounge.

Special Features

Students are provided the skills and knowledge to enter the workforce with confidence. The University's computer lab is connected to the Internet, allowing students access to a vast source of information and research materials. Faculty members are experienced in their particular academic field beyond teaching, thus bringing a real-world atmosphere to the instruction. The staff and faculty members are committed to helping each student reach his or her full potential by starting their experience off with a confidence building seminar and a mentoring program that help students realize they always have someone to assist them.

Financial Aid/Scholarships

Federal Pell Grant, Federal Supplemental Educational Opportunity Grant (FSEOG), Federal Work-Study Program (FWS), Florida Student Assistance Grant (FSAG), Federal Family Educational Loan Program (FFELP), Subsidized and Unsubsidized Federal Stafford Loans, and institutional scholarships. Financial aid is available for those who qualify.

Tuition and Fees

Per-credit hours are assessed based on the number of classes taken per quarter and differ for selected programs. A registration fee of $25 is assessed per quarter. Books average $200 per quarter.

Accreditation

The school is accredited by the Accrediting Council for Independent Colleges and Schools (ACICS).

Admissions

Graduation from high school, or its equivalent (GED), is a prerequisite for admission. Applicants not completing a secondary program or not having a diploma are considered for admission on the basis of the GED test or other equivalency. All applicants are required to successfully complete an assessment examination.

Program Content

Accounting, Assisted Living Administrator, Business, Computer Information Science, Computer Office Technologies and Applications, Criminal Justice, Health Care Administration, Legal Assistant/Paralegal, Management/Marketing, Massage Therapy, Master of Business Administration, Master of Science in Criminal Justice, Medical Assisting, Medical Insurance Billing and Coding, Pharmacy Technician

Graduation Requirements

A 2.0 cumulative grade point average and successful completion of all required courses for the particular program and degree level are required.

Enrollment

There are 757 students enrolled.

Contact

Jodi De La Garza, Director of Admissions
Florida Metropolitan University
995 East Memorial Boulevard
Suite 110
Lakeland, FL 33801
Phone: (863) 686-1444
Fax: (863) 688-9881
E-mail: fdelagar@cci.edu
Web: www.fmu.edu

Programs Eligible for Scholarship	Tuition and Fees	Course Length/Credit Hours	Credential Earned
Accounting	$235/credit hour	96 credit hours	AS
	$235/credit hour	192 credit hours	BS
Business	$235/credit hour	192 credit hours	BBA
Computer Information Science	$235/credit hour	96 credit hours	AS
	$235/credit hour	192 credit hours	BS
Computer Office Technologies and Applications	$260/credit hour	192 credit hours	BS
Criminal Justice	$235/credit hour	192 credit hours	BS
Health Care Administration	$235/credit hour	192 credit hours	BS
Management/Marketing	$235/credit hour	96 credit hours	AS
Master of Business Administration	$370/credit hour	54–56 credit hours	MBA
Master of Science in Criminal Justice	$370/credit hour	54–58 credit hours	MS
Medical Assisting	$245/credit hour	96 credit hours	AS
Medical Insurance Billing and Coding	$245/credit hour	90 credit hours	AS
Paralegal	$235/credit hour	96 credit hours	AS
Pharmacy Technician	$245/credit hour	96 credit hours	AS

Florida Metropolitan University, Melbourne

About Our Institution
Florida Metropolitan University (FMU)–Melbourne, is one of nine institutions that make up Florida Metropolitan University, a division of Corinthian Colleges, Inc., which operates more than eighty schools nationwide. FMU–Melbourne was established as a branch campus of Orlando College in 1995. The University is located on the east coast of central Florida. It is easily accessible to all central Florida attractions and is 5 minutes from the sandy beaches of the Atlantic Ocean. The campus has a single-story building on 5½ acres of land, tropically landscaped and located across the street from the Intracoastal Waterway. In 2001, FMU–Melbourne expanded its facilities to include a 5,500-square-foot learning site located at 2190 Sarno Road in Melbourne, Florida.

Special Features
The University's faculty members bring to the classroom the added educational tool of working in their field of instruction. This enables the students to receive real-life instruction as well as traditional textbook instruction.

Financial Aid/Scholarships
Federal Pell Grant, Federal Supplemental Educational Opportunity Grant (FSEOG), Federal Work-Study (FWS), Florida Student Assistance Grant (FSAG), Federal Family Educational Loan Program (FFELP), subsidized and unsubsidized Federal Stafford Student Loans, and institutional scholarships are available. Financial aid is available for those who qualify.

Tuition and Fees
Per-credit hours are assessed based on the number of classes taken per quarter and differ for selected programs. A registration fee of $25 and a technical fee of $35 are assessed per quarter. Books average $200 per quarter.

Accreditation
FMU–Melbourne is accredited by the Accrediting Council for Independent Colleges and Schools (ACICS). The Medical Assisting program is also accredited by the Commission on Accreditation of Allied Health Education Programs (CAAHEP) and the American Society of Health-System Pharmacists (ASHP).

Program Content
Accounting, Assisted Living, Business Administration, Computer Information Science, Criminal Justice, Film and Video, Health Care Administration, Master of Business Administration, Medical Assisting, Paralegal, Pharmacy Technician

Admissions
Graduation from high school, or its equivalent (GED), is a prerequisite for admission. Applicants not completing a secondary program or not having a diploma are considered for admission on the basis of the GED test or other equivalency. All applicants are required to successfully complete an assessment examination.

Graduation Requirements
A 2.0 or better cumulative grade point average and successful completion of all required courses for the particular program and degree level are required to graduate.

Enrollment
There are 900–975 students enrolled.

Contact
Timothy Alexander, Director of Admissions
2401 North Harbor City Blvd.
Melbourne, FL 32935
Phone: (321) 253-2929
Fax: (321) 255-2017
E-mail: talexand@cci.edu
Web: www.fmu.edu

Programs Eligible for Scholarship	Tuition and Fees	Course Length/Credit Hours	Credential Earned
Accounting	$250/credit hour	96 credit hours	AS
		192 credit hours	BS
Assisted Living	$250/credit hour	96 credit hours	AS
Business Administration	$250/credit hour	96 credit hours	AS
		192 credit hours	BBA
Computer Information Science	$250/credit hour	96 credit hours	AS
		192 credit hours	BS
Criminal Justice	$250/credit hour	96 credit hours	AS
		192 credit hours	BS
Film and Video	$270/credit hour	96 credit hours	AS
Health Care Administration	$250/credit hour	192 credit hours	BS
Master of Business Administration	$390/credit hour	54–56 credit hours	MBA
Medical Assisting	$260/credit hour	97 credit hours	AS
Paralegal	$250/credit hour	96 credit hours	AS
		192 credit hours	BS
Pharmacy Technician	$260/credit hour	97 credit hours	AS

Florida Metropolitan University, North Orlando Campus, Orlando

About Our Institution
Florida Metropolitan University–North Orlando Campus, is one of nine institutions that make up Florida Metropolitan University (FMU), a division of Corinthian Colleges, Inc., which operates more than eighty schools nationwide. FMU, Orlando North, formerly known as Orlando College, was established in Orlando in 1953 as Jones College and in 1981 became Orlando College. Graduates are prepared for a wide range of entry-level positions in various fields.

Special Features
Facilities include twenty modern lecture classrooms, nine labs with the latest computers, medical, commercial art and video production equipment, a modern Library Resource Center, and a student lounge. Students may attend and transfer to any Florida Metropolitan University campus and, upon graduation, receive placement assistance from any campus site.

Financial Aid/Scholarships
FMU–North Orlando participates in Federal Pell Grant, Federal Supplemental Educational Opportunity Grant (FSEOG), Federal Work-Study (FWS), Florida Student Assistance Grant (FSAG), Federal Family Educational Loan Program (FFELP), Subsidized and Unsubsidized Federal Stafford Loans, and institutional scholarship programs. Financial aid is available for those who qualify.

Accreditation
FMU–North Orlando, is accredited by the Accrediting Council for Independent Colleges and Schools (ACICS). The Medical Assisting program is also accredited by the Commission on Accreditation of Allied Health Education Programs (CAAHEP).

Admissions
Graduation from high school, or its equivalent (GED), is a prerequisite for admission. Applicants not completing a secondary program or not having a diploma are considered for admission on the basis of the GED test or other equivalency. All applicants are required to successfully complete an assessment examination.

Graduation Requirements
Requirements for graduation include a 2.0 cumulative grade point average and successful completion of all required courses for the particular program and degree level.

Program Content
Accounting, Business Administration, Commercial Art, Computer Information Science, Criminal Justice, Film and Video, Health-Care Administration, Legal Assistant/Paralegal, Management/Marketing, Massage Therapy, Master of Business Administration, Medical Assisting, Web Engineering

Enrollment
There are 1,500 students enrolled.

Contact
Dave Ritchie, Director of Admissions
5421 Diplomat Circle
Orlando, FL 32810
Phone: (407) 628-5870
Fax: (407) 628-1344
E-mail: dritchie@cci.edu
Web: www.fmu.edu

Programs Eligible for Scholarship	Tuition and Fees	Course Length/Credit Hours	Credential Earned
Accounting	$250/credit hour	96 credit hours	AS
		192 credit hours	BS
Business Administration	$250/credit hour	96 credit hours	AS
		192 credit hours	BBA
Commercial Art	$270/credit hour	96 credit hours	AS
		192 credit hours	BS
Computer Information Science	$250/credit hour	96 credit hours	AS
		192 credit hours	BS
Criminal Justice	$250/credit hour	96 credit hours	AS
		192 credit hours	BS
Film and Video	$270/credit hour	96 credit hours	AS
Health-Care Administration	$250/credit hour	192 credit hours	BS
Legal Assistant/Paralegal	$250/credit hour	96 credit hours	AS
Management/Marketing	$250/credit hour	96 credit hours	AS
		192 credit hours	BS
Massage Therapy	$10,300 total cost	54 credit hours	Diploma
Master of Business Administration	$390/credit hour	54–56 credit hours	MBA
Medical Assisting	$260/credit hour	97 credit hours	AS
Web Engineering	$250/credit hour	98 credit hours	AS

A registration fee of $25 per quarter and a tech fee of $35 per quarter are assessed.

Florida Metropolitan University, Orange Park

About Our Institution
Founded in 2004, Orange Park is the newest of the ten Florida Metropolitan University (FMU) campuses. The newly renovated campus includes twelve comfortable and spacious lecture rooms, five computer labs, a medical assisting lab, a Learning Resource Center, bookstore, and student lounge, as well as administrative and student services offices.

Special Features
The Orange Park campus offers various associate and bachelor's degrees in the business, criminal justice, and medical fields. FMU's strength is its instructors, who bring years of real-world experience and education into the classroom to enhance the students' education. Orange Park enjoys a high quality of living with a blend of cultural, entertainment, and recreational activities.

Financial Aid/Scholarships
Information regarding the Pell Grant, Federal Supplemental Educational Opportunity Grant (FSEOG), Federal Work-Study (FWS), and scholarships can be obtained from the finance office on campus. Financial aid is available for those who qualify.

Accreditation
The Accrediting Council for Independent Colleges and Schools (ACICS) accredits all campuses of Florida Metropolitan University. All campuses are accredited to award associate and bachelor's degrees.

Admissions
Graduation from high school or its equivalent is a prerequisite for admission to the University. Applicants not completing a secondary program or not having a diploma are considered for admission on the basis of the General Education Development (GED) test or other equivalency. All applicants are required to successfully complete an assessment examination. This standardized, nationally normed test is administered by the college and is designed to further ensure that the applicant has the skills necessary to pursue a college-level program. Transfer students who are high school graduates or GED certificate holders (or other equivalency) and who can submit proof of successfully completing a minimum of 36 quarter hours or 24 semester hours of earned college credit at an accredited postsecondary institution are not required to complete the above referenced test. Applicants who have completed the ACT with a score of at least 15 or the SAT with a score of at least 700 are not required to complete the above referenced test.

Graduation Requirements
In order to graduate, a student must have earned a minimum GPA of 2.0 and have successfully completed all required credits within the maximum credits that may be attempted.

Program Content
Business, Criminal Investigation, Criminal Justice, Medical Assisting

Enrollment
There are 200 students enrolled.

Contact
Roxanne Jordan, President
Florida Metropolitan University
805 Wells Road
Orange Park, FL 32073
Phone: (904) 264-9122
Fax: (904) 264-9952
E-mail: rjordan@cci.edu
Web: www.fmu.edu

Programs Eligible for Scholarship	Tuition and Fees	Course Length/Credit Hours	Credential Earned
Business	$250/credit hour	96 credit hours	AS
	$250/credit hour	192 credit hours	BS
Criminal Investigation	$250/credit hour	96 credit hours	AS
Criminal Justice	$250/credit hour	96 credit hours	AS
	$250/credit hour	192 credit hours	BS
Medical Assisting	$260/credit hour	97 credit hours	AS

Florida Metropolitan University, Pinellas, Clearwater

About Our Institution

Florida Metropolitan University (FMU), Pinellas, is one of ten institutions that comprise Florida Metropolitan University, a division of Corinthian Colleges, Inc., which operates more than eighty schools nationwide. FMU was founded as Tampa College in 1890, making it the oldest business college in the state of Florida. The University is located in Clearwater, in Pinellas County. All facilities are housed in one building and include comfortable classrooms, computer labs, a medical lab, library, student canteen, and administrative offices. Facilities are handicap accessible and ample parking is available.

Special Features

FMU, Pinellas, prides itself on being student-oriented. The school prepares people for employment and productive lives. Students are provided the skills and knowledge to enter the work force with confidence. The University has its computer labs connected to the Internet, allowing students access to a vast source of information and research materials. Faculty members are experienced in their particular academic field beyond teaching, thus bringing a real-world atmosphere to the instruction. Distance education is provided online.

Financial Aid/Scholarships

The Federal Pell Grant, the Federal Supplemental Educational Opportunity Grant (FSEOG), the Federal Work-Study Program (FWS), the Florida Student Assistance Grant (FSAG), the Federal Family Educational Loan Program (FFELP), Subsidized and Unsubsidized Federal Stafford Student Loans, and institutional scholarships are available to those who qualify.

Tuition and Fees

Per-credit hours are assessed based on the number of classes taken per quarter and differ for selected programs. A registration fee of $25 is assessed per quarter. Books average $200 per quarter.

Accreditation

The University is accredited by the Accrediting Council for Independent Colleges and Schools (ACICS).

Program Content

Accounting, Business Administration, Computer Information Science, Criminal Justice, Health-Care Administration, Homeland Security, Legal Assistant/Paralegal, Management/Marketing, Master of Business Administration, Medical Assisting, Medical Insurance Billing and Coding

Admissions

Graduation from high school, or its equivalent (GED), is a prerequisite for admission. Applicants not completing a secondary program or not having a diploma are considered for admission on the basis of the GED test or other equivalency. All applicants are required to complete an assessment examination successfully.

Graduation Requirements

Students must have a 2.0 cumulative grade point average and have successfully completed all required courses for the particular program and degree level.

Enrollment

There are 1,100–1,200 students enrolled.

Contact

Yvonne Hunter, Director of Admissions
2471 McMullen Booth Road
Clearwater, FL 33759
Phone: (727) 725-2688
(800) 353-3687 (toll-free)
Fax: (727) 796-3722
E-mail: yhunter@cci.edu
Web: www.fmu.edu

Programs Eligible for Scholarship	Tuition and Fees	Course Length/Credit Hours	Credential Earned
Accounting	$250/credit hour	96 credit hours	AS
		192 credit hours	BS
Business Administration	$250/credit hour	96 credit hours	AS
		192 credit hours	BBA
Computer Information Science	$250/credit hour	96 credit hours	AS
		192 credit hours	BS
Criminal Justice	$250/credit hour	96 credit hours	AS
		192 credit hours	BS
Management/Marketing	$250/credit hour	96 credit hours	AS
		192 credit hours	BS
Health-Care Administration	$250/credit hour	192 credit hours	BS
Homeland Security	$250/credit hour	96 credit hours	AS
		192 credit hours	BS
Legal Assistant/Paralegal	$250/credit hour	96 credit hours	AS
Master of Business Administration	$390/credit hour	56 credit hours	MBA
Medical Assisting	$260/credit hour	97 credit hours	AS
Medical Insurance Billing and Coding	$260/credit hour	96 credit hours	AS

Florida Metropolitan University, Pompano Beach

About Our Institution
Florida Metropolitan University, Pompano Beach, is one of ten institutions that comprise Florida Metropolitan University, a division of Corinthian Colleges, Inc., which owns and operates more than eighty schools nationwide. Its roots date back to its founding in 1940. One of the unique characteristics is its international orientation; students from more than forty different countries participate in learning together. In today's world of international business and finance, students can gain first-hand knowledge by working together with individuals from all around the world.

Special Features
The University's location in one of the major tourist areas in Florida, on the Atlantic Ocean, provides students with the opportunity for an excellent career education while enjoying the beauty of Fort Lauderdale.

Financial Aid/Scholarships
Federal Pell Grant, Federal Supplemental Educational Opportunity Grant (FSEOG), Federal Work-Study Program (FWS), Florida Student Assistance Grant (FSAG), Federal Family Educational Loan Program (FFELP), Subsidized and Unsubsidized Federal Stafford Loans, and institutional scholarships and loan plans are available to those who qualify.

Tuition and Fees
Per credit hours are assessed based on number of courses taken per quarter and differ for selected programs. A $25 registration fee and a technology fee of $25 are assessed per quarter. Books average $200 per quarter.

Accreditation
The Universtiy is accredited by the Accrediting Council for Independent Colleges and Schools (ACICS).

Admissions
Graduation from high school, or its equivalent (GED), is a prerequisite for admission. All applicants are required to successfully complete an assessment examination.

Program Content
Accounting, Assisted Living Administrator, Business, Computer Information Science, Criminal Investigations, Criminal Justice, Homeland Security, Hospitality Management, International Business, Legal Assistant/Paralegal, Management, Marketing, Master of Business Administration, Master of Science in Criminal Justice, Medical Assisting, Paralegal

Graduation Requirements
Students must have a minimum 2.0 cumulative grade point average and have successfully completed all required courses for the particular program and degree level.

Enrollment
There are 1,450 students enrolled.

Contact
Fran Heaston, Director of Admissions
Florida Metropolitan University
225 North Federal Highway
Pompano Beach, FL 33062
Phone: (800) 468-0168
(954) 783-7339
Fax: (954) 783-7964
E-mail: fheaston@cci.edu
Web: www.fmu.edu

Programs Eligible for Scholarship	Tuition and Fees	Course Length/Credit Hours	Credential Earned
Accounting	$250/credit hour	96 credit hours	AS
		192 credit hours	BS
Assisted Living Administrator	$250/credit hour	96 credit hours	AS
Business	$250/credit hour	96 credit hours	AS
		192 credit hours	BBA
Computer Information Science	$250/credit hour	96 credit hours	AS
		192 credit hours	BS
Criminal Investigations	$250/credit hour	96 credit hours	AS
Criminal Justice	$250/credit hour	96 credit hours	AS
		192 credit hours	BS
Homeland Security	$250/credit hour	96 credit hours	AS
		192 credit hours	BS
Hospitality Management	$250/credit hour	96 credit hours	AS
		192 credit hours	BS
International Business	$250/credit hour	96 credit hours	AS
		192 credit hours	BS
Legal Assistant/Paralegal	$250/credit hour	96 credit hours	AS
Management	$250/credit hour	96 credit hours	AS
		192 credit hours	BS
Marketing	$250/credit hour	192 credit hours	AS
		96 credit hours	BS
Master of Business Administration	$390/credit hour	56 credit hours	MBA
Master of Science in Criminal Justice	$390/credit hour	54 credit hours	MS
Medical Assisting	$260/credit hour	97 credit hours	AS
Paralegal	$250/credit hour	97 credit hours	BS

Florida Metropolitan University, South Orlando Campus, Orlando

About Our Institution
Florida Metropolitan University, South Orlando, is one of nine institutions that make up Florida Metropolitan University (FMU), a division of Corinthian Colleges, Inc., which operates more than eighty schools nationwide. FMU (previously known as Orlando College) was established in Orlando in 1953 as Jones College. In 1981, the college became Orlando College. In 1987, FMU South Orlando campus was established. The University has six computer labs, two medical labs, and twenty-two classrooms of varying sizes.

Special Features
The University's faculty members bring the added educational tool of working in their field of instruction to the classroom. This enables the students to receive real-life instruction as well as the traditional textbook instruction.

Financial Aid/Scholarships
The Federal Pell Grant, the Federal Supplemental Educational Opportunity Grant (FSEOG), Federal Work-Study Program (FWS), Florida Student Assistance Grant (FSAG), Federal Family Educational Loan Program (FFELP), Subsidized and Unsubsidized Federal Stafford Loans, and institutional scholarships are available to those who qualify.

Tuition and Fees
Per-credit-hour fees are assessed based on the amount of classes taken per quarter and differ for selected programs. A registration fee of $25 is assessed each quarter. All programs have a quarterly $35 lab fee. Books average $250 per quarter.

Accreditation
The University is accredited by the Accrediting Council for Independent Colleges and Schools (ACICS). The Medical Assisting program is also accredited by the Commission on Accreditation of Allied Health Education Programs.

Admissions
Graduation from high school, or its equivalent (GED), is a prerequisite for admission. Applicants not completing a secondary program or not having a diploma are considered for admission on the basis of the GED test or other equivalency. All applicants are required to successfully complete an assessment examination.

Program Content
Accounting, Business, Computer Information Science/Concentration in Network Administration or Web Engineering, Criminal Justice, Health Care Administration, Legal Assistant/Paralegal, Management/Marketing, Massage Therapy, Master of Business Administration, Medical Assisting, Medical Insurance Billing and Coding

Graduation Requirements
Students must have a minimum 2.0 cumulative grade point average and have successfully completed all required courses for their particular program and degree level.

Enrollment
There are 1,822 students enrolled.

Contact
Annette Cloin, Director of Admissions
Florida Metropolitan University
9200 South Park Center Loop
Orlando, FL 32819
Phone: (407) 851-2525
Fax: (407) 354
E-mail: acloin@cci.edu
Web: www.fmu.edu

Programs Eligible for Scholarship	Tuition and Fees*	Course Length/Credit Hours	Credential Earned
Accounting	$250/credit hour	96 credit hours	AS
		192 credit hours	BS
Assisted Living Administrator	$250/credit hour	96 credit hours	AS
Business	$250/credit hour	96 credit hours	AS
		192 credit hours	BBA
Computer Information Science	$250/credit hour	96 credit hours	AS
		192 credit hours	BS
Criminal Investigations	$250/credit hour	96 credit hours	AS
Criminal Justice	$250/credit hour	96 credit hours	AS
		192 credit hours	BS
Health Care Administration	$250/credit hour	192 credit hours	BS
Homeland Security	$250/credit hour	192 credit hours	BS
		192 credit hours	BS
Legal Assistant/Paralegal	$250/credit hour	96 credit hours	AS
		192 credit hours	BS
Management/Marketing	$250/credit hour	96 credit hours	AS
		192 credit hours	BS
Massage Therapy	$10,300 total	54 credit hours	Diploma
Master of Business Administration	$370/credit hour	56 credit hours	MBA
Medical Assisting	$260/credit hour	97 credit hours	AS
Medical Insurance Billing and Coding	$260/credit hour	90 credit hours	AS

*Tuition is $9,100 for 720 clock hours.

Florida Metropolitan University, Tampa

About Our Institution
Florida Metropolitan University, Tampa, is one of nine institutions that comprise Florida Metropolitan University (FMU), a division of Corinthian Colleges, Inc., which operates more than eighty schools nationwide. FMU was founded as Tampa College in 1890, making it the oldest business college in the state of Florida.

Special Features
Students are provided the skills and knowledge to enter the work force with confidence. The University has its computer lab connected to the Internet, allowing students access to a vast source of information and research materials. Faculty members are experienced in their particular academic field beyond teaching, thus bringing a real-world atmosphere into the classroom.

Financial Aid/Scholarships
The Federal Pell Grant, the Federal Supplemental Educational Opportunity Grant (FSEOG), the Federal Work-Study Program (FWS), the Florida Student Assistance Grant (FSAG), the Federal Family Educational Loan (FFEL) Program, Subsidized and Unsubsidized Federal Stafford Loans, and institutional scholarships are available to those who qualify.

Tuition and Fees
Per credit hours are assessed based on the amount of classes taken per quarter and differ for selected programs. A registration fee of $25 is assessed per quarter. Books average $200 per quarter.

Accreditation
The University is accredited by the Accrediting Council for Independent Colleges and Schools (ACICS).

Admissions
Graduation from high school, or its equivalent (GED), is a prerequisite for admission. Applicants not completing a secondary program or not having a diploma will be considered for admission on the basis of the GED test or other equivalency. All applicants are required to successfully complete an assessment examination.

Program Content
Accounting, Business, Commercial Art, Computer Information Science, Criminal Investigations, Criminal Justice, Health Care Administration, Homeland Security, Legal Assistant/Paralegal, Management/Marketing, Massage Therapy, Master of Business Administration, Medical Assisting, Medical Insurance Billing and Coding, Paralegal, Pharmacy Technician

Graduation Requirements
Students must have a 2.0 cumulative grade point average and have successfully completed all required courses for the particular program and degree level.

Enrollment
There are 1,704 students enrolled.

Contact
Donnie Broughton, Director of Admissions
Florida Metropolitan University
3319 West Hillsborough Avenue
Tampa, FL 33614
Phone: (813) 879-6000
Fax: (813) 871-2063
E-mail: dbrought@cci.edu
Web: www.fmu.edu

Programs Eligible for Scholarship	Tuition and Fees	Course Length/Credit Hours	Credential Earned
Accounting	$250/credit hour	96 credit hours	AS
		192 credit hours	BS
Business	$250/credit hour	96 credit hours	AS
		192 credit hours	BBA
Commercial Art	$270/credit hour	96 credit hours	AS
Computer Information Science	$250/credit hour	96 credit hours	AS
		192 credit hours	BS
Criminal Investigations	$250/credit hour	96 credit hours	AS
Criminal Justice	$250/credit hour	96 credit hours	AS
		192 credit hours	BS
Health Care Administration	$250/credit hour	192 credit hours	BS
Homeland Security	$250/credit hour	96 credit hours	AS
		192 credit hours	BS
Legal Assistant/Paralegal	$250/credit hour	96 credit hours	AS
Management/Marketing	$250/credit hour	96 credit hours	AS
		192 credit hours	BS
Massage Therapy	$9,100 total cost	57 credit hours	Diploma
Master of Business Administration	$390/credit hour	54–56 credit hours	MBA
Medical Assisting	$260/credit hour	96 credit hours	AS
Medical Insurance Billing and Coding	$250/credit hour	90 credit hours	AS
Paralegal	$250/credit hour	192 credit hours	BS
Pharmacy Technician	$260/credit hour	96 credit hours	AS

Florida Technical College, Auburndale

About Our Institution

Florida Technical College was established in 1982 to provide postsecondary training in specialized careers. Florida Technical College at Auburndale provides career training that matches the student's career goals with the needs of employers. In 2000, Florida Technical College became a part of ForeFront Education Inc., a national network of postsecondary schools dedicated to high-quality career education and student achievement.

Special Features

Florida Technical College at Auburndale provides specialized career education in many of the fastest-growing career fields and offers degree and diploma programs in the fields of medical administrative assistant, medical assistant, computer drafting and design, electronics/computer technology, network administration, programming, and Web site and graphic design. Florida Technical College at Auburndale provides student support services such as career services and placement and professional career assistance service.

Financial Aid/Scholarships

Financial assistance is available to qualified students. Florida Technical College at Auburndale maintains a financial aid office that provides a variety of programs, including Pell Grants, Subsidized Stafford Student Loan Program, Unsubsidized Stafford Student Loan Program, and Parents Auxiliary Loan.

Accreditation

Florida Technical College is accredited by the Accrediting Council for Independent Colleges and Schools (ACICS) to award specialized associate degrees and academic diplomas.

Admissions

A high school diploma or GED certificate is required for admission, in addition to passing an admissions test and meeting academic and financial criteria. International students from non-English-speaking countries must attain an ELS Language Center level of at least 108 or a minimum TOEFL score of 500 and submit proof of such scores. All applicants are required to attain a minimum score of 15 on the Wonderlic Scholastic Level Exam.

Graduation Requirements

A student must attain a 2.0 cumulative GPA or greater, conclude all arrangements necessary with the finance office, and successfully complete all specialized field requirements.

Contact

Chris Georgetti, Director
298 Havendale Boulevard
Auburndale, FL 33823
Phone: (863) 967-8822
Fax: (863) 967-4972
E-mail: cgeorgetti@flatech.edu
Web: www.flatech.edu

Program Content

Degrees: Computer Drafting and Design, Electronics/Computer Technology, Medical Administrative Assistant, Medical Assistant, Network Administration, Programming, and Web Site and Graphic Design.

Program Description

The Computer Drafting and Design curricula provides students with knowledge of architectural, electronic, and mechanical drafting and design; CAD; and LAN analysis and design.

In the Medical Administrative Assistant program, students gain skills for careers performing administrative functions in medical offices.

The Medical Assistant degree program provides training to become a medical assistant to work in a doctor's office or health-care facility performing clinical and administrative duties.

The Network Administration and Programming curricula provides students with knowledge of computer network design and administration as well as computer programming languages such as C++ and Java and Microsoft Windows applications for networks.

Florida Technical College, DeLand

About Our Institution

Florida Technical College was established in 1982 to provide postsecondary training in specialized careers. Florida Technical College–DeLand provides career training that matches the student's career goals with the needs of employers. In 2000, Florida Technical College became a part of ForeFront Education Inc., a national network of postsecondary schools dedicated to quality career education and student achievement.

Special Features

Florida Technical College–DeLand provides specialized career education in many of the fastest-growing career fields and offers degree and diploma programs in the fields of computer drafting and design, electronics/computer technology, medical administrative assistant, medical assistant, network administration, programming, and Web site and graphic design. Florida Technical College–DeLand provides student support services including career services and placement and professional career assistance.

Financial Aid/Scholarships

Financial assistance is available to qualified students. Florida Technical College–DeLand maintains a financial aid office providing a variety of programs, including Pell Grants, Subsidized Stafford Student Loan Program, Unsubsidized Stafford Student Loan Program, and Parents Auxiliary Loan.

Accreditation

Florida Technical College is accredited by the Accrediting Council for Independent Colleges and Schools (ACICS) to award Associate of Science degrees and academic diplomas.

Admissions

A high school diploma or GED certificate is required for admission in addition to passing an admissions test and meeting academic and financial criteria. Foreign students from non-English-speaking countries must attain an ELS Language Center level of 108 or a TOEFL level of 500 and submit proof of such scores. All applicants are required to attain a minimum score of 15 on the Wonderlic Scholastic Level Exam.

Graduation Requirements

A student must attain a 2.0 cumulative GPA or greater, conclude all arrangements necessary with the finance office, and successfully complete all specialized field requirements.

Contact

Bill Atkinson, Director
1199 South Woodland Boulevard
DeLand, FL 32720
Phone: (386) 734-3303
Fax: (386) 734-5150
E-mail: batkinson@flatech.edu
Web: www.flatech.edu

Program Content

Degrees: Computer Drafting and Design, Electronics/Computer Technology, Medical Administrative Assistant, Medical Assistant, Network Administration, Programming, and Web Site and Graphic Design.

Program Description

The computer information science (computer drafting and design) curricula provides students with knowledge of architectural, electronic, and mechanical drafting and design; CAD; and LAN analysis and design.

In the Medical Administrative Assistant program, students gain skills for careers performing administrative functions in medical offices.

The Medical Assistant degree program provides training to become a medical assistant to work in a doctor's office or health-care facility performing clinical and administrative duties.

The network administration/programming curricula provides students with knowledge of computer network design and administration as well as computer programming languages such as C++ and JAVA and Microsoft Windows applications for networks.

Florida Technical College, Jacksonville

About Our Institution

Florida Technical College was established in 1982 to provide postsecondary training in specialized careers. Florida Technical College–Jacksonville provides career training that matches the student's career goals with the needs of employers. In 2000, Florida Technical College became a part of ForeFront Education Inc., a national network of postsecondary schools dedicated to high-quality career education and student achievement.

Special Features

Florida Technical College–Jacksonville provides specialized career education in many of the fastest-growing career fields and offers degree and diploma programs in the fields of computer drafting and design, electronics/computer technology, medical assistant, network administration, and programming. Florida Technical College–Jacksonville provides student support services, including career services and placement and professional career assistance.

Financial Aid/Scholarships

Financial assistance is available to qualified students. Florida Technical College–Jacksonville maintains a financial aid office providing a variety of programs, including Pell Grants, Subsidized Stafford Student Loan Program, Unsubsidized Stafford Student Loan Program, and Parents Auxiliary Loan.

Accreditation

Florida Technical College is accredited by the Accrediting Council for Independent Colleges and Schools (ACICS) to award Specialized associate degrees and academic diplomas.

Admissions

A high school diploma or GED certificate is required for admission, in addition to passing an admissions test and meeting academic and financial criteria. Foreign students from non-English-speaking countries must attain an ELS Language Center level of 108 or a TOEFL level of 500 and submit proof of such scores. All applicants are required to attain a minimum score of 15 on the Wonderlic Scholastic Level Exam.

Graduation Requirements

A student must attain a 2.0 cumulative GPA or greater, conclude all arrangements necessary with the finance office, and successfully complete all specialized field requirements.

Contact

Barry Durden, Director
8711 Lone Star Road
Jacksonville, FL 32211
Phone: (904) 724-2229
Fax: (904) 720-0920
E-mail: bdurden@flatech.edu
Web: www.flatech.edu

Program Content

Degrees: Computer Drafting and Design, Electronics/Computer Technology, Medical Assistant, Network Administration, and Programming.

Program Description

The computer drafting and design curricula provides students with knowledge of architectural, electronic, and mechanical drafting and design; CAD; and LAN analysis and design.

The electronics/computer technology curricula provides students with knowledge of PC hardware and software in a variety of platforms—electronics, networking, and LAN analysis and design.

The medical assistant degree program provides training to become a medical assistant to work in a doctor's office or health-care facility performing clinical and administrative duties.

The network administration and programming curricula provides students with knowledge of computer network design and administration as well as computer programming languages such as C++ and JAVA and Microsoft Windows applications for networks.

Florida Technical College, Orlando

About Our Institution

Florida Technical College was established in 1982 to provide postsecondary training in specialized careers. Florida Technical College–Orlando provides career training that matches the student's career goals with the needs of employers. In 2000, Florida Technical College became a part of ForeFront Education Inc., a national network of postsecondary schools dedicated to high-quality career education and student achievement.

Special Features

Florida Technical College–Orlando provides specialized career education in many of the fastest-growing career fields and offers degree and diploma programs in the fields of computer drafting and design, electronics/computer technology, medical administrative assistant, medical assistant, network administration, programming, and Web site and graphic design. Florida Technical College–Orlando provides student support services, including career services and placement and professional career assistance.

Financial Aid/Scholarships

Financial assistance is available to qualified students. Florida Technical College–Orlando maintains a financial aid office providing a variety of programs, including Pell Grants, Subsidized Stafford Student Loan Program, Unsubsidized Stafford Student Loan Program, and Parents Auxiliary Loan.

Accreditation

Florida Technical College is accredited by the Accrediting Council for Independent Colleges and Schools (ACICS) to award Specialized associate degrees and academic diplomas.

Admissions

A high school diploma or GED certificate is required for admission in addition to passing an admissions test and meeting academic and financial criteria. Foreign students from non-English-speaking countries must attain an ELS Language Center level of 108 or a TOEFL level of 500 and submit proof of such scores. All applicants are required to attain a minimum score of 15 on the Wonderlic Scholastic Level Exam.

Graduation Requirements

A student must attain a 2.0 cumulative GPA or greater, conclude all arrangements necessary with the finance office, and successfully complete all specialized field requirements.

Contact

Ann Melone, Director
12689 Challenger Parkway
Orlando, FL 32826
Phone: (407) 447-7300
Fax: (407) 447-7301
E-mail: amelone@flatech.edu
Web: www.flatech.edu

Program Content

Degrees: Computer Drafting and Design, Electronics/Computer Technology, Medical Administrative Assistant, Medical Assistant, Network Administration, Programming, and Web Site and Graphic Design.

Program Description

The computer information science (computer drafting and design) curricula provides students with knowledge of architectural, electronic, and mechanical drafting and design; CAD; and LAN analysis and design.

In the Medical Administrative Assistant program, students gain skills for careers performing administrative functions in medical offices.

The Medical Assistant degree program provides training to become a medical assistant to work in a doctor's office or health-care facility performing clinical and administrative duties.

The network administration/programming curricula provides students with knowledge of computer network design and administration as well as computer programming languages such as C++ and JAVA and Microsoft Windows applications for networks.

Herzing College, Orlando

About Our Institution
The Winter Park campus is one of six campuses that make up the Herzing College system in the United States. The Herzing College system has been providing high-quality training to students since 1965. The College provides a solid postsecondary education in the areas of business, technology, and health care. Students can earn a bachelor's degree, an associate degree, or a diploma in a highly focused, student-centered learning environment, using state-of-the-industry equipment.

Special Features
The Winter Park campus is situated in the beautiful Lake View Office Park, surrounded by green space and a small lake, making the campus an excellent setting for student learning. Staff and faculty members are hired and evaluated according to their commitment to providing an environment that is both friendly and professional; students regularly comment that the one thing that makes Herzing College different from others they may have attended is the caring attitude of the staff and faculty members. Herzing students also have the benefit of a full-time Career Services Office that assists students with job placement while they are in school and upon graduation.

Financial Aid/Scholarships
The College helps students develop individual financial plans to pay for their education through a combination of financial aid (if qualified), family contributions, and/or employer tuition-reimbursement plans. The campus participates in the Imagine America Scholarship and the Military Assistance Program through the Career College Foundation. Herzing College also has a number of institutional scholarships available.

Tuition and Fees
Tuition costs are $200 per semester credit hour (SCH) for professional development classes and $275 per SCH for all other courses. The use of textbooks is included in the tuition for all courses except those taken online. There may also be separate program fees ranging from $75 to $295, depending on the program of study.

Accreditation
Herzing College is accredited by the Higher Learning Commission of the North Central Association of Colleges and Schools. For more information students should contact the Higher Learning Commission (telephone: 800-621-7440; Web site: http://www.ncahigherlearningcommission.org).

Admissions
Herzing does not have an open admissions policy. Prospective students are selected on the basis of their application, a personal interview and campus tour, the results of appropriate college placement tests, and the

Program Content

Bachelor of Science: Technology Management

Associate of Science: Business Administration and Computer Network Technology

Diploma Programs: Medical Assisting, Medical Billing and Insurance Coding, Network Management, Therapeutic Message, and Web Site Design

recommendation of the Director of Admissions. Information about specific programs, start dates, student services, and employment opportunities for graduates are provided during the interview, thus allowing candidates to make informed decisions. There is a $25 enrollment fee.

Graduation Requirements
Candidates for graduation must complete the required number of credit hours, maintain a cumulative grade point average of at least a 2.0 or higher, and pass all required courses. All financial obligations to the College must also be finalized with the business office.

Contact
Karen Mohamad, Vice President/Director of Admission
1595 South Semoran Boulevard, Suite 1501
Winter Park, FL 32792
Phone: (407) 478-0500
Fax: (407) 478-0501
E-mail: info@orl.herzing.edu
Web: www.herzing.edu

Programs Eligible for Scholarship	Tuition and Fees*	Course Length/Credit Hours	Credential Earned
Business Administration	$4,400/semester	70 credit hours	AS
Computer Network Technology	$4,400/semester	79 credit hours	AS
Medical Assisting	$4,400/semester	40 credit hours	Diploma
Medical Billing and Insurance Coding	$4,400/semester	48 credit hours	Diploma
Network Management (MCSE)	$4,400/semester	24 credit hours	Diploma
Technology Management	$4,400/semester	129 credit hours	BS
Therapeutic Massage	$4,400/semester	35 credit hours	Diploma
Web Site Design	$4,400/semester	27 credit hours	Diploma

*Semesters at Herzing College are sixteen weeks long. A full-time student generally completes 16 credits a semester.

International Academy of Design and Technology, Orlando

About Our Institution

The International Academy of Design and Technology (IADT) is for students who are looking for exciting and rewarding careers in today's rapidly expanding fields.

The Academy strives to stay attuned to students' personal, academic, and career goals and helps students pursue studies geared toward realizing their full potential. IADT's goal is to provide students with every advantage possible. Students study with highly qualified industry professionals, using industry-driven curriculum, software, and equipment in order to enable students to move into their desired field of study from the moment they step through IADT's doors. Students can expect to find project-oriented classes in their major from the first week. The Academy recognizes that hands-on learning experience is critical in the student's field. That is why IADT is are centered around giving each student opportunities to gain skills by working on relevant, industry-related projects while earning a marketable degree.

IADT is a vibrant and growing premier design college, providing an education that brings today's technology into the classroom. The Orlando branch campus was established in 2000. This 31,000-square-foot facility has nine computer labs and seven theory labs along with the administrative areas. The overwhelming success with the school's degree programs prompted the school to add another building with 45,000 square feet of space in 2003.

Special Features

IADT-Orlando students learn in industry-current classrooms and labs. An effective mix of lecture/conference instruction is reinforced by focused, hands-on exercises to insure understanding and to promote retention of information. The Academy's Career Services department provides advice and placement assistance for active students and graduates.

Financial Aid/Scholarships

IADT maintains a financial aid office on campus to help with a variety of programs, including grants, loans, scholarships, work-study, veteran benefits, and deferred payment for all students who qualify.

Tuition and Fees

Tuition averages $325 per credit hour for degree programs. Tuition is exclusive of the cost of books, supplies, lab fees, equipment, and professional development functions. Each student is required to pay a $100 registration fee upon enrollment.

Accreditation

IADT-Orlando is accredited by the Accrediting Council for Independent Colleges and Schools (ACICS). ACICS is listed as a nationally recognized accrediting agency by the United States Department of Education.

Admissions

To apply, students should complete the Academy's application form and schedule a personal interview with an admissions representative. Students may apply online at http://www.iadt.edu.

Graduation Requirements

In order to graduate, a student must earn a minimum CGPA of 2.0 and successfully complete all required credits within the maximum credits that may be attempted. Students meeting the CGPA or Rate of Progress requirements applicable to the total credits attempted, and meeting specific course requirements as defined in the program descriptions in the catalog, are deemed to have academic standing consistent with the Academy's graduation requirements.

Contact

John Dietrich
Vice President of Admissions
International Academy of Design and Technology
5959 Lake Ellenor Drive
Orlando, FL 32809
Phone: (877) 753-0007 (toll-free)
Fax: (407) 251-0465
Web: www.iadt.edu
    www.goiadtorlando.com (for high school students)

Program Content

Bachelor of Fine Arts (BFA): Computer Graphics, Digital Media Production, Fashion Design and Merchandising, Interior Design, Multimedia Design, Web Development
Bachelor of Science (BS): Network Design and Administration
Associate of Science (AS): Computer Graphics, Marketing and Advertising, Network Administration

Program Description

The BFA in Computer Graphics balances the principles of advertising and design with advanced training in technology and production. Students gain a strong understanding of industry standard software packages while mastering the various steps of design from the creative spark to the final product.

The BFA in Digital Media Production offers students the opportunity to develop both theoretical knowledge and practical skills in the use of digital media technology. Students learn concepts, techniques, and tools related to digital media design, interface design, audio/video editing, and Web design. Project management, creative design, and communication skills are integrated throughout the curriculum.

In the BFA in Fashion Design and Merchandising, students learn about fashion illustration, pattern drafting, design, draping, clothing construction, textiles, fashion history, fashion merchandising, and production techniques. The program also focuses on the global fashion and merchandising industry, addressing market and trend research, design development, visual displays, sales and business practices, and production management.

The BFA in Interior Design is designed to prepare students for professional opportunities in the field of interior design in order to enhance the function, quality, and safety of interior spaces. Students experiment with form, space, texture, and color. Design solutions are tested against a backdrop of knowledge acquired from codes and laws with attention given to the preparation of technical drawings and contracts. Skills such as drafting, computer-aided drawing, and rendering are mastered in order to provide final design recommendations and vehicles for the estimation and execution of the work.

The BFA in Multimedia Design trains students in Web design, print media, 3-D modeling and animation, and digital audio and video production. Special emphasis is placed on the effective integration of sight and sound and the process of creating multimedia presentations from storyboarding techniques to final delivery.

The BFA in Web Development prepares students for professional opportunities in the information technology area. The program focuses on the use of electronic technology while incorporating the basic theories of graphics, text, audio, video, and interactivity. The program provides advanced studies in director and postproduction techniques while supplementing those skills with such subjects as special effects, programming, action scripting, database management, and network design.

The BS in Network Design and Administration provides students with the knowledge and skills necessary to analyze, plan, design, implement, and manage enterprise networks. Students gain an understanding of the networking technology concepts of local area networks (LANs), wide area networks (WANs), and storage area networks (SANs). The program also provides students with an understanding of network security concepts, issues, and solutions as well as exposure to PC troubleshooting, applications, operating systems, network configuration, administration, hardware, maintenance, and security.

The AS in Computer Graphics provides students with the skills necessary to function as a graphic designer, package/product designer, marketing/advertising designer, illustrator, or media designer. It also focuses on the use of electronic technology while incorporating the basic theories of advertising, layout, type, color, and illustration.

The AS in Marketing and Advertising is designed to prepare students for various marketing, sales, and retail store management positions; to assist existing marketing managers and sales professionals in upgrading their skills; and to open up new career opportunities within the marketing field. Program content includes selection and buying of merchandise, advertising, sales, product distribution, customer relations, pricing, Internet marketing, and advertising.

The AS in Network Administration is designed to prepare students for entry into the computer networking field for network administration positions and to assist existing technology professionals in upgrading their skills. Program content includes networking fundamentals, CISCO equipment management, Windows server management, Windows networking design, network security, UNIX, and exchange mail server.

ITT Technical Institute, Lake Mary

About Our Institution

The company: ITT Technical Institute is owned and operated by ITT Educational Services, Inc. (ITT/ESI), a leading private college system offering technology-influenced programs of study. ITT/ESI operates seventy-seven ITT Technical Institutes in thirty states, providing career-focused degree programs to approximately 39,000 students as of spring 2004. Headquartered in Carmel, Indiana, ITT/ESI has been actively involved in the higher education community in the United States since 1969.

Curricula: Curriculum offerings are designed to help students begin to prepare for career opportunities in fields of technology. Students attend classes year-round, with convenient breaks provided throughout the year. A full-time student course load can have class meetings as often as three days a week and are typically available in the morning, afternoon, and evening, depending on student enrollment. General education courses may be available online. This class schedule offers flexibility to students to pursue part-time employment opportunities.

ITT Technical Institute, Lake Mary, awards the Associate of Science and the Bachelor of Science degrees.

Special Features

Most ITT Technical Institute programs of study blend traditional academic content with applied learning concepts, with a significant portion devoted to practical study in a lab environment. Advisory committees composed of representatives of local businesses help each ITT Technical Institute periodically review and update curricula, equipment, and laboratory design.

Financial Aid/Scholarships

ITT Technical Institute maintains a Financial Aid Department on campus. The campus is designated as an eligible institution by the U.S. Department of Education for participation in the following programs: Federal Stafford Student Loan Program, Federal PLUS Loan Program, and Federal Work-Study Program. The school also offers nonfederal loans available through Bank One for eligible students.

Tuition and Fees

March 2005 tuition is $386 per credit hour.

Accreditation

The school is accredited by the Accrediting Council for Independent Colleges and Schools (ACICS).

Admissions

For admission requirements, students should contact the school for a catalog.

Graduation Requirements

For graduation requirements, students should contact the school for a catalog.

Program Content

School of Information Technology: Data Communication Systems Technology, Information Systems Security, Information Technology–Computer Network Systems, Information Technology–Software Applications and Programming, Information Technology–Web Development, Software Engineering Technology

School of Electronics Technology: Computer and Electronics Engineering Technology, Electronics and Communications Engineering Technology

School of Drafting and Design: Computer Drafting and Design, Digital Entertainment and Game Design, Information Technology–Multimedia Option

School of Business: Business Accounting Technology, Business Administration, Technical Project Management

School of Criminal Justice: Criminal Justice

Contact

Gary Cosgrove, Director
ITT Technical Institute
1400 International Parkway South
Lake Mary FL 32746
Phone: (407) 660-2900
Fax: (407) 660-2566

ITT Technical Institute, Tampa

About Our Institution
The company: ITT Technical Institute is owned and operated by ITT Educational Services, Inc. (ITT/ESI), a leading private college system offering technology-influenced programs of study. ITT/ESI operates seventy-seven ITT Technical Institutes in thirty states, providing career-focused degree programs to approximately 39,000 students as of spring 2004. Headquartered in Carmel, Indiana, ITT/ESI has been actively involved in the higher education community in the United States since 1969.

Curricula: Curriculum offerings are designed to help students begin to prepare for career opportunities in fields of technology. Students attend classes year-round, with convenient breaks provided throughout the year. A full-time student course load can have class meetings as often as three days a week and are typically available in the morning, afternoon, and evening, depending on student enrollment. General education courses may be available online. This class schedule offers flexibility to students to pursue part-time employment opportunities.

ITT Technical Institute, Tampa, awards the Associate of Science and the Bachelor of Science degrees.

Special Features
Most ITT Technical Institute programs of study blend traditional academic content with applied learning concepts, with a significant portion devoted to practical study in a lab environment. Advisory committees composed of representatives of local businesses help each ITT Technical Institute periodically review and update curricula, equipment, and laboratory design.

Financial Aid/Scholarships
ITT Technical Institute maintains a Financial Aid Department on campus. The campus is designated as an eligible institution by the U.S. Department of Education for participation in the following programs: Federal Stafford Student Loan Program, Federal PLUS Loan Program, and Federal Work-Study Program. The school also offers nonfederal loans available through Bank One for eligible students.

Tuition and Fees
March 2005 tuition is $386 per credit hour.

Accreditation
The school is accredited by the Accrediting Council for Independent Colleges and Schools (ACICS).

Admissions
For admission requirements, students should contact the school for a catalog.

Graduation Requirements
For graduation requirements, students should contact the school for a catalog.

Program Content

School of Information Technology: Data Communication Systems Technology, Information Systems Security, Information Technology–Computer Network Systems, Information Technology–Software Applications and Programming, Information Technology–Web Development, Software Engineering Technology

School of Electronics Technology: Computer and Electronics Engineering Technology, Electronics and Communications Engineering Technology

School of Drafting and Design: Computer Drafting and Design, Digital Entertainment and Game Design, Information Technology–Multimedia Option

School of Business: Business Accounting Technology, Business Administration, Technical Project Management

School of Criminal Justice: Criminal Justice

Contact
Denny Alspaugh, Director
ITT Technical Institute
4809 Memorial Highway
Tampa, FL 33634
Phone: (813) 885-2244
Fax: (813) 888-8451

Motorcycle and Marine Mechanics Institute, Orlando

About Our Institution

MMI Florida is a private postsecondary technical school that provides students with the technical education needed for a successful career in the motorcycle, marine, and automotive industries since opening in 1973. MMI provides full student services, housing assistance, financial aid to those who qualify, campus activities, and both part-time and graduate employment assistance for as long as it is needed.

Special Features

MMI has developed strong and ongoing relationships with American Suzuki; Kawasaki Motors Corp., U.S.A.; Bombardier Motor Corp. of America; Mercury; OMC; and many other accessory, parts, and tool manufacturers. These relationships have created incredible training and career opportunities for MMI graduates. MMI's connections and commitment to excellence place graduates in the driver's seat in a career field that is in high demand.

Financial Aid/Scholarships

MMI students are eligible to apply for various federal grants and loans. These include Pell Grants, FSEOG, and Stafford, Perkins, and PLUS Loans. MMI also participates in various scholarship programs and awards more than $500,000 in scholarships annually. These programs include SkillsUSA, CCA, Imagine America, Ford/AAA, FFA, and Universal Technical Institute's National High School Scholarship competition.

Tuition and Fees

Tuition and fees vary by course content. Tuition prices include all workbooks, textbooks, and uniforms; there are no hidden costs. For specific tuition information, students should contact the Orlando Admissions Office.

Accreditation

Motorcycle and Marine Mechanics Institute is accredited by the Accrediting Commission of Career Schools and Colleges of Technology (ACCSCT), which is listed by the U.S. Department of Education as a nationally recognized accrediting agency.

Admissions

Each individual applying for admission must be at least 16 years of age, have a high school diploma or equivalent, and submit a completed application, a signed enrollment agreement, a registration fee, and any other information that the applicant or the Institute feels is pertinent to admission. Each applicant's qualifications for enrollment are reviewed and either approved, approved with stipulations, or denied.

Graduation Requirements

Students must receive a passing grade in each three-week course in order to be considered a graduate. All students are required to attend exit talks with Employment Services and Financial Aid. All monies owed must be paid in full three weeks prior to the student's graduation date.

Program Content

Automotive Technology, Marine Technology, Motorcycle Technology, Watercraft Technology

Program Description

MMI's marine programs prepare the graduate to service, repair, diagnose, and troubleshoot marine engines and watercraft vehicles. Students work in a professional, shoplike environment using the necessary equipment to prepare for an entry-level position in the industry. Students are trained in everything from lower units and powerheads to engine configurations and electrical, ignition, and charging systems. Graduates have all the skills needed to start a challenging and rewarding career in the marine industry.

Contact

Dianne Ely, School Director
9751 Delegates Drive
Orlando, FL 32837
Phone: (407) 240-2422
        (800) 342-9253 (toll-free)
Fax: (407) 240-1318
E-mail: dely@uticorp.com

National School of Technology, Fort Lauderdale

About Our Institution
National School of Technology–Fort Lauderdale is one of four institutions that make up the National School of Technology (NST), a division of Corinthian Colleges, Inc., which operates more than eighty such schools nationwide. NST was founded as the National School of Health Technology, Inc., of Florida in 1977. The Fort Lauderdale campus opened in September 2003. The purpose of the School is to provide high-quality education to students who seek careers in medically related fields. NST is constantly updating its curricula, recognizing its obligation to the students and the professions they serve.

Special Features
Located in one of the major tourist areas in Florida on the Atlantic Ocean, the School is located close to public transportation, shopping centers, restaurants, banks, and the beach.

Tuition and Fees
Tuition and fees vary by program.

Admissions
Candidates must have a high school diploma or the equivalent. Prospective students must complete an application for enrollment, which is reviewed by a director. Applicants are notified whether they have been accepted prior to the start date of the program and must sign an enrollment agreement with the School.

Graduation Requirements
Upon successful completion of all prescribed subjects of instruction with a minimum cumulative average of 70 percent and a demonstrated ability to perform all required competencies, satisfaction of all financial obligations to the School, and an exit interview, the student is awarded a credential as stated in the catalog program information.

Contact
Guy Jackson, School President
1040 Bayview Drive
Fort Lauderdale, FL 33304
Phone: (954) 630-0066
Fax: (954) 630-0076
Web: www.nst.cc

Program Content
Advanced Massage Therapist, Medical Assistant, Medical Coding Specialist

Programs Eligible for Scholarship	Tuition and Fees	Course Length/Credit Hours	Credential Earned
Medical Coding Specialist	$10,002	900 clock hours	refer to School catalog

National School of Technology, Hialeah

About Our Institution

National School of Technology, Hialeah, is one of four institutions that make up National School of Technology (NST), a division of Corinthian Colleges, Inc. (CCi), which operates more than eighty such schools nationwide. NST was founded as National School of Health Technology, Inc. of Florida in 1977. CCi acquired National School of Technology in April 2002. The purpose of the School is to provide high-quality education to students who seek careers in medically related fields. NST is constantly updating its curricula, recognizing its obligation to the students and the professions they serve.

Special Features

National School of Technology, Hialeah's location is convenient to public transportation, shopping centers, restaurants, and banks. The facility consists of classrooms, medical and computer laboratories, School offices, and financial aid offices. The medical classrooms and labs contain equipment commonly found in the medical environment. The campus provides a career and learning resource center, which contains reference materials for student use.

Financial Aid/Scholarships

Financial aid offered at the School include Federal Pell Grants, Federal Supplemental Educational Opportunity Grants (FSEOG), the Federal Work-Study Program, the Federal Family Educational Loan Program (FFELP), and Subsidized and Unsubsidized Federal Stafford Student Loans. Financial aid is available for those students who qualify.

Tuition and Fees

Tuition and fees vary by program and are as follows: cardiovascular technologist, $18,106 (1,500 clock hours); massage therapy, $7673 (600 clock hours); medical assisting, $12,679 (1,200 clock hours); medical insurance billing/coding, $10,002 (900 clock hours); pharmacy technician, $11,240 (1,200 clock hours); and surgical technologist, $16,456 (1,200 clock hours).

Accreditation

National School of Technology, Inc. is accredited by the Accrediting Bureau of Health Education Schools (ABHES) to award diplomas and associate degrees. NST is also accredited by the Commission on Accreditation of Allied Health Education Programs (CAAHEP) for its surgical technologist program.

Admissions

Applicants must be high school graduates or the equivalent. Prospective students must complete an application for enrollment, which is reviewed by the Director. Applicants are notified whether they have been accepted prior to the start date of the program and must sign an enrollment agreement with the School.

Graduation Requirements

Upon the successful completion of all prescribed subjects of instruction with a minimum cumulative average of 70 percent and a demonstrated ability to perform all required competencies, satisfaction of all financial obligations to the School, and an exit interview, the student is awarded a credential as stated in the catalog program information.

Enrollment

The total number of students enrolled is 707.

Contact

Gilbert Delgado, School President
National School of Technology, Hialeah
4410 West 16th Avenue, Suite 52
Hialeah, FL 33012
Phone: (305) 558–9500
Fax: (305) 558–4419
E-mail: gdelgado@cci.edu
Web: www.nst.cc

National School of Technology, Kendall

About Our Institution

National School of Technology (NST), Kendall, is one of four institutions that comprise the National School of Technology, a division of Corinthian Colleges, Inc. (CCi), which operates more than eighty such schools nationwide. NST, founded as National School of Health Technology, Inc., of Florida, was founded in 1977. CCi acquired the National School of Technology in April 2002. The purpose of the School is to provide high-quality education to students seeking careers in medically related fields. NST is constantly updating its curricula, recognizing its obligation to the students and the professions they serve.

Special Features

The campus is convenient to public transportation, shopping centers, restaurants, and banks. All facilities are accessible to people with disabilities. The campus consists of classrooms, medical and computer laboratories, school offices, and financial aid offices. The medical classrooms and labs contain equipment that is commonly found in the medical environment, such as ECG machines, microscopes, phlebotomy equipment, examining tables, blood cell counters, and other diagnostic equipment. The microcomputer labs are equipped with IBM-compatible computers that allow students to receive hands-on training. The surgical laboratories contain surgical instruments, trays, scrub stations, anatomical mannequins, surgical drapes, and other equipment for practicing techniques. The massage therapy clinical laboratories contain massage tables and chairs with accessories, adjustable face cradles, massage stools, and hydrotherapy equipment. The campus has a student lounge and a career and learning resource center.

Financial Aid/Scholarships

The School offers the Federal Pell Grant, Federal Supplemental Educational Opportunity Grant (FSEOG), Federal Work-Study Program, Federal Family Educational Loan Program (FFELP), and Subsidized and Unsubsidized Federal Stafford Student Loans. Federal Parent Loans for Undergraduate Students (PLUS) may be available to parents of dependent students. Financial aid is available for those who qualify.

Accreditation

National School of Technology, Inc., is accredited by the Accrediting Bureau of Health Education Schools (ABHES) to award diplomas and associate degrees. NST is also accredited by the Commission on Accreditation of Allied Health Education Programs (CAAHEP) for its surgical technologist program.

Admissions

Applicants must be high school graduates or the equivalent. Prospective students must complete an application for enrollment, which is reviewed by the Director. Applicants are notified as to whether they have been accepted prior to the start date of the program and must sign an enrollment agreement with the School.

Graduation Requirements

Upon successful completion of all prescribed subjects of instruction with a cumulative grade average of 70 percent or better, demonstration of the ability to perform all required competencies, satisfaction of all financial obligations to the School, and an exit interview, the student is awarded a credential, as stated in the catalog program information.

Enrollment

There are 1050 students currently enrolled.

Contact

National School of Technology, Kendall
9020 Southwest 137th Avenue
Miami, FL 33186
Phone: (305) 386-9900
Fax: (305) 388-1740
Web: www.nst.cc

Programs Eligible for Scholarship	Tuition, Fees, and Books	Course Length/Credit Hours
Assisted Living Administration	$225/ch	96 credit hours
Cardiovascular Technologist	$ 17,000	80 clock hours
Massage Therapy	$ 9,700	54 credit hours
Medical Assisting	$ 10,250	47 credit hours
Medical Insurance Billing/Coding	$ 7,500	35 credit hours
Paralegal	$225/ch	96 credit hours
Pharmacy Technician	$ 10,250	58 credit hours
Surgical Technologist	$ 18,000	75 credit hours

National School of Technology, Miami

About Our Institution

National School of Technology, Miami, is one of four institutions that compose National School of Technology (NST), a division of Corinthian Colleges, Inc. (CCi), which operates more than eighty such schools nationwide. NST, founded as National School of Health Technology, Inc. of Florida, was founded in 1977. CCi acquired National School of Technology in April 2002. The purpose of the School is to provide high-quality education to students seeking careers in medically related fields. NST is constantly updating its curricula, recognizing its obligation to the students and the professions they serve.

Special Features

National School of Technology consists of classrooms, medical and computer laboratories, school offices, and financial aid offices. The medical classrooms and labs contain equipment commonly found in the medical environment. The campus provides a career and learning resource center, which contains reference materials for student use.

Students attending the Miami campus may have classes offered at its additional classroom facility located nearby at 16150 Northeast 17th Avenue, Miami, Florida 33162.

Financial Aid/Scholarships

Financial aid is available for those who qualify and includes the Federal Pell Grant, Federal Supplemental Educational Opportunity Grant (FSEOG), Federal Work-Study Program, Federal Family Educational Loan Program (FFELP), and Subsidized and Unsubsidized Federal Stafford Loans.

Tuition and Fees

Tuition and fees for the massage therapy program (54 credits) are $9,700; medical assisting program (47 credits), $10,250; medical insurance billing/coding program (35 credits), $7,500; patient care technician program (51 credits), $9,100; pharmacy technician program (58 credits), $10,250; and surgical technologist program (75 credits), $18,000.

Accreditation

National School of Technology, Inc., is accredited by the Accrediting Bureau of Health Education Schools (ABHES) to award diplomas and associate degrees. NST is also accredited by the Commission on Accreditation of Allied Health Education Programs (CAAHEP) for its surgical technologist program.

Admissions

Applicants must be high school graduates or the equivalent. Prospective students must complete an application for enrollment, which is reviewed by the Director. Applicants are notified whether they have been accepted prior to the start date of the program and must sign an enrollment agreement with the School.

Graduation Requirements

Students are required to successfully complete all prescribed subjects of instruction with a cumulative average of 70 percent or better and demonstrate the ability to perform all required competencies.

Enrollment

The total number of students enrolled is 635.

Contact

Mario Miro, School President
National School of Technology, Miami
111 Northeast 183rd Street Suite 200
Miami, FL 33169
Phone: (305) 949–9500
Fax: (305) 949-7303
E-mail: nmiro@cci.edu
Web: www.nst.cc

Remington College, Jacksonville Campus, Jacksonville

About Our Institution
Remington College–Jacksonville Campus is located in one of Jacksonville's newest business complexes. The 25,000-square-foot space is minutes from regional recreational, hospitality, and waterfront amenities. The campus is divided into administrative and training areas. The training area includes approximately twenty classrooms with computer labs, an Informational Resource Center, and other specialized classrooms. The campus contains adequate, well-lit parking in an area adjacent to the building. The business complex provides security for the evening classes.

Remington College–Jacksonville Campus is an institution dedicated solely to technical education and is uncompromisingly dedicated to high-quality, college-level, career-oriented education. The College's primary objectives are to graduate a high percentage of students who enter career programs and to assist them with relevant employment at the highest possible starting salary.

The Jacksonville Campus opened its doors in 2000 as a branch of Education America–Tampa Technical Institute. It offers four associate degree programs: business information systems, computer information systems, computer network engineering technology, and Internet information systems. The College also offers three bachelor's degree programs: information systems, information technology, and operations management.

Special Features
Remington College–Jacksonville Campus focuses upon hands-on training that provides maximum opportunity for immediate entry-level employment upon graduation. Students are provided with a training environment that is physically comfortable, mentally stimulating, and conducive to acquiring knowledge. The campus utilizes a state-of-the-art facility to deliver technical training. All students receive a laptop computer to use while completing their program of study.

All faculty members are seasoned personnel possessing pertinent field experience in addition to holding a bachelor's or master's degree. The faculty members continue to develop their teaching skills through in-service training sessions and certification courses.

Tuition and Fees
Students should contact the campus for current tuition pricing. Textbook costs and lab fees are included in the tuition rate. A $50 registration fee is required for all programs.

Accreditation
The College's programs are accredited by the Accrediting Commission of Career Schools and Colleges of Technology (ACCSCT).

Admissions
Individuals applying to the programs must possess a high school diploma or GED. Remington College–Jacksonville Campus has a two-part personal interview admissions process. The initial interview is with a campus recruiter who determines the applicant's qualifications for enrollment. If both the applicant and recruiter are confident that the applicant has the desire and motivation to be successful, the applicant may complete the enrollment paperwork and pay the enrollment fee. Once the enrollment

Program Content
Associate degree programs: Business Information Systems, Computer Information Systems, Computer Network Engineering Technology, and Internet Information Systems

Bachelor's degree programs: Information Systems, Information Technology, and Operations Management

paperwork has been completed, an acceptance interview is scheduled with one of the administrators of the campus. It is the intent of the campus not to accept applicants unless it can determine that there is a strong likelihood the applicant has all of the necessary qualifications to be successful. Upon completion of the two-part personal interview application process, the applicants should have a thorough understanding of the campus, the curriculum, employment assistance, and financial assistance programs available to them.

Graduation Requirements
Students must complete all required classroom training with a cumulative grade point average of at least 2.0.

Contact
Anthony Galang, Campus President
7011 A. C. Skinner Parkway, Suite 140
Jacksonville, FL 32256
Phone: (904) 296-3435
Fax: (904) 296-9097
Web: www.remingtoncollege.edu

Remington College, Largo Campus, Largo

About Our Institution
Remington College was founded in 1985 in an effort to meet the growing need for computer-related education and training in the technical and business fields. To date, Remington College consists of twenty campuses across the United States. Remington College teaches a "career first" curriculum that allows students to concentrate on learning the necessary technical skills early in their program and build on them as they progress toward graduation.

Special Features
Remington College is uncompromisingly dedicated to high-quality, college-level, career-oriented education. Its primary objectives are to graduate a high percentage of students who enter career programs and to help them achieve relevant employment at the highest possible starting salary. Remington College's hands-on training is the foundation of its educational structure. Practical application in well-equipped labs, coupled with theoretical reinforcement in the classroom, allows students to acquire substantial knowledge in their chosen career field. When appropriate, externships are used to provide the student with real-world experience.

Financial Aid/Scholarships
Remington College participates in Pell, FFEL, FDSLP, Perkins, Work-Study, SEOG, SSIG, VA, state grants, and JTPA programs.

Accreditation
Remington College–Tampa Campus is accredited by the Accrediting Commission of Career Schools and Colleges of Technology (ACCSCT).

Admissions
A high school diploma or GED, along with an acceptance interview, is used to determine a candidate's potential success. At some sites, an entrance test is also required.

An associate degree in a technical field, with a minimum of 90 quarter credit hours (at least 24 of which are in general education courses), is required for Bachelor of Science programs.

Contact
Edna Higgins, Campus President
8550 Ulmerton Road, Unit 100
Largo, FL 33771
Phone: (727) 532-1999
Fax: (727) 530-7710
Web: www.remingtoncollege.edu

Program Description

Computer Information Systems: The program provides comprehensive training in three major areas: technical analysis, programming architecture, and local area networks (LAN).

Computer Networking Technology: The program is designed to prepare students for employment in the field of computer networking.

Electronic and Computer Engineering Technology: Students are trained to qualify for career positions, such as computer service technicians, electronic laboratory technicians, field service engineers, installation technicians, and as technicians in communications instrumentation and digital and computer electronics.

Internet Information Systems: The program provides comprehensive training in the technology and techniques necessary to create, develop, market, and maintain a professional, corporate Web site.

Information Systems: The program provides comprehensive training in technology necessary to design, implement, and administer information systems solutions.

Information Technology: The program prepares students to undertake twenty-first century information system challenges, emphasizing internetworking communications, telecommunications, computer telephony integration, Internet security, routing, project management, and e-business strategies.

Operations Management: The program is designed to prepare students for business and industry.

Remington College, Tampa Campus, Tampa

About Our Institution
Remington College–Tampa Campus was established in 1948 and is the oldest private technical college in the state of Florida. Tampa Campus is part of an twenty-campus network that stretches across the United States. Teaching a "career first" curriculum offering both Associate of Science and Bachelor of Science degrees, programs are focused on students acquiring the necessary technical skills early in the program and building on these skills as the students progress toward graduation.

Special Features
Remington College–Tampa Campus is uncompromisingly dedicated to high-quality, college-level, career-oriented education. Its primary objectives are to graduate a high percentage of students who enter career programs and to help them secure employment at the highest possible starting salary. Tampa Campus's hands-on training is the foundation of its educational structure. Practical application in well-equipped labs, coupled with theoretical reinforcement in the classroom, allows students to acquire substantial knowledge in their chosen career field. When appropriate, externships are used to provide the student with real-world experience. Remington College–Tampa Campus's student body comprises individuals from every state in the U.S. and more than seventy other countries.

Financial Aid/Scholarships
Remington College–Tampa Campus maintains a Financial Services Office on the campus, providing a variety of grants, loans, scholarships, work-study, veterans' benefits, and vocational rehabilitation programs.

Accreditation
Tampa Technical Institute is licensed by the Commission for Independent Education/Colleges and Universities (CIECU) and is accredited by the Accrediting Commission of Career Schools and Colleges of Technology (ACCSCT).

Admissions
Applicants for admission must have a high school diploma or GED certificate or be a high school senior on track to graduate. Applicants must take an admission interview and an acceptance interview.

Graduation Requirements
In order to graduate, students must maintain an overall cumulative grade point average of 2.0 or better for the entire program and complete all courses specified in the program catalog.

Contact
William Polmear, Campus President
2410 East Busch Boulevard
Tampa, FL 33612
Phone: (813) 932-0701
Fax: (813) 935-7415
Web: www.remingtoncollege.edu

Program Description
Business Information Systems: The program provides the student with the tools of technology for today's modern office environment.

Computer Information Systems: This program provides comprehensive training in three major areas: Technical Analysis, Programming, and Local Area Networks (LAN). Languages include Visual Basic, C++, COBOL, Java, and more.

Computer Networking Technology: This program provides comprehensive instruction in both Microsoft Windows NT® and Novell's NetWare®.

Digital Graphic Arts: This program provides comprehensive instruction in visualization, creative processing, graphic design, digital imaging, Web site design, and more.

Electronic and Computer Engineering Technology: This program explores both the fundamentals and advanced theory in electronics, integrated circuits, microprocessors, and computer technology.

Southwest Florida College, Fort Myers and Tampa

About Our Institution
Southwest Florida College is a private not-for-profit institution of higher learning authorized to award degrees, certificates, and diplomas in business and related areas. Southwest Florida College recognizes the ever-increasing need for postsecondary education and strives to provide opportunities for individuals to pursue their educational goals through career-focused training. The College is committed to providing an equal educational opportunity environment conducive to lifelong learning where individuals can acquire knowledge, build skills, and develop attitudes that help prepare them for rewarding careers in fields with high-growth potential.

Special Features
Southwest Florida College has two locations. The main campus is located in Fort Myers, Florida, and the branch campus is located in Tampa, Florida.

Tuition and Fees
Tuition and fees are determined each quarter and are based on the number of credits for which the student is enrolled. Tuition is $215 per credit hour. The estimated cost of books and supplies in a degree program is $300 per quarter.

Accreditation
Southwest Florida College is accredited as a junior college by the Accrediting Council for Independent Colleges and Schools (ACICS). ACICS is an independent, national, institutional accrediting agency recognized by the United States Department of Education and is a member of the Council for Higher Education Accreditation (CHEA).

Admissions
Southwest Florida College has an open admissions policy that allows all people who are high school graduates or who have successfully completed equivalent education as certified by state departments of education to be admitted. The College seeks individuals who have a genuine desire for practical career preparation.

Graduation Requirements
To qualify for graduation, students must have successfully completed all courses in their program and have a cumulative grade point average of 2.0 or higher. In addition, all financial obligations must have been satisfied.

Program Content

Associate in Science Degree Programs: Accounting Technology, Computer-Aided Drafting and Design, Criminal Justice, Graphic Design, Hospitality Management, Information Technology Management, Management and Marketing, Medical Administration, Medical Assistant, Medical Transcription, Microsoft Network Engineer with concentration in Network Security, Paralegal Studies, Pharmacy Technician, Surgical Technician, Technical Administration and Management

Diploma Programs: Medical Assistant, Medical Records and Coding, Microsoft Network Engineer with concentration in Network Security

Certificate Programs: Microsoft Network Engineer, Microsoft Systems Administrator

Contact
Carmen King
Director of Admissions
Southwest Florida College
Fort Myers Campus
1685 Medical Lane
Fort Myers, FL 33907
Phone: (239) 939-4766
        (866) SWFC-NOW (toll-free)
Fax: (239) 936-4040
E-mail: cking@swfc.edu
Web: www.swfc.edu

Stephanie Schweihofer
Director of Admissions
Southwest Florida College
Tampa Campus
3910 Riga Boulevard
Tampa, FL 33619
Phone: (813) 630-4401
Fax: (813) 630-4272
E-mail: sschweihofer@swfc.edu
Web: www.swfc.edu

Programs Eligible for Scholarship	Tuition and Fees	Course Length/Credit Hours	Credential Earned
Accounting Technology	$215/credit	96 credit hours	AS
Computer-Aided Drafting and Design	$215/credit	96 credit hours	AS
Criminal Justice	$215/credit	96 credit hours	AS
Graphic Design	$215/credit	96 credit hours	AS
Hospitality Management	$215/credit	96 credit hours	AS
Information Technology Management	$215/credit	96 credit hours	AS
Management and Marketing	$215/credit	96 credit hours	AS
Medical Administration	$215/credit	96 credit hours	AS
Medical Assistant	$215/credit	96 credit hours	AS
Medical Transcription	$215/credit	96 credit hours	AS
Microsoft Network Eng w/ Network Security	$215/credit	96 credit hours	AS
Paralegal Studies	$215/credit	96 credit hours	AS
Pharmacy Technician	$215/credit	96 credit hours	AS
Surgical Technician	$215/credit	96 credit hours	AS
Technical Administration and Management	$215/credit	96 credit hours	AS

Tulsa Welding School, Jacksonville

About Our Institution
Tulsa Welding School, Jacksonville (TWS–JAX) campus, started its first training class in November 2001. It is a branch campus of the main campus in Tulsa, Oklahoma, which has been graduating professional, entry-level welders since 1949. The welder programs in Jacksonville are identical in content and length to those in Tulsa. The School is located in the southeastern sector of the city near a major thoroughfare and is in a 41,000-square-foot building that has parking for more than 200 vehicles.

Special Features
Industry-specified training in structural, pipe, pipeline, and thin alloy welding are the major aspects of the curriculum.

Financial Aid/Scholarships
TWS–JAX is designated by the U.S. Department of Education as an eligible institution for participation in the following programs: Federal Pell Grant, Federal Supplemental Educational Opportunity Grant (FSEOG), subsidized and unsubsidized FFEL Stafford Student Loans, Plus Loans, and veterans' educational benefits. Along with the Tulsa campus, the School provides four $1,000 scholarships in each of the fifty states as well as Puerto Rico and the U.S. Virgin Islands for the 4 outstanding high school seniors chosen by the Future Farmers of America organizations within each locale. All TWS scholarships are awarded on a pro rata basis for each of the ten phases of training.

Tuition and Fees
The total cost for the seven-month Master Welder Program is $11,810, which includes tuition, fees, books, welding gear, accident insurance, and all welding supplies.

Accreditation
TWS is accredited by the Accrediting Commission of Career Schools and Colleges of Technology (ACCSCT).

Admissions
Applicants are required to be high school graduates or have a GED.

Graduation Requirements
Students who satisfactorily complete all specified phase courses within the program of enrollment, earn a CGPA of 2.0 out of a possible 4.0, and complete all TWS graduate clearance requirements are awarded a TWS diploma.

Contact
Bob Lutz
Director of Admissions
Tulsa Welding School
3500 Southside Boulevard
Jacksonville, FL 32216
Phone: (877) 935-3529 (toll-free)
Fax: (904) 646-9956
Web: www.weldingschool.edu

Program Content
Master Welder Program

Program Description
The Master Welder Program consists of ten 3-week phases of instruction, so graduation is possible within seven months. Instruction occurs 5 hours a day, five days a week.

Programs Eligible for Scholarship	Tuition and Fees	Course Length/Credit Hours	Credential Earned
Master Welder Program	$11,810	30 weeks/30 semester credits	Diploma

CEI (Career-Ed Institute), Marietta

About Our Institution

Since 1982, Career-Ed Institute (CEI) has been providing high-quality, postsecondary training in Massachusetts and Rhode Island. In 2001, CEI added two campuses in the Atlanta, Georgia, area and one campus in Henderson (Las Vegas), Nevada. All CEI locations offer focused programs that help its students receive the skills and confidence essential for success in their chosen field of study.

Special Features

CEI is dedicated and committed to providing an industry-standard and quality-driven instructional program, designed for students. The philosophy of CEI extends beyond the teaching of technical proficiencies and practical knowledge. CEI is committed to serving its students with concern and respect.

Financial Aid/Scholarships

CEI maintains a financial aid office at each location. A variety of available programs including grants, loans, scholarships, work-study, veteran's and vocational rehabilitation are available to qualified applicants. CEI provides two full and two half-tuition scholarships at each of its campuses. They are awarded annually to winners of the Scholarship Awards Program. Preliminary scholarship competition is conducted in the form of aptitude testing at each campus location. On the basis of test results, finalists are selected and invited to return for an interview conducted by the Scholarship Committee, which is made up of volunteers who represent business, industry, education, and/or government.

Accreditation

CEI is accredited by the Accrediting Council for Independent Colleges and Schools (ACICS), Washington, D.C., and is approved by a number of respective state and federal organizations. Further information is available from the school catalog.

Admissions

An applicant must satisfy the requirements of possessing a high school diploma or GED. A passing score on the CEI Entrance Examination is necessary for acceptance.

Graduation Requirements

Graduation requirements mandate that a student complete all required courses and achieve an overall grade point average of at least 2.0.

Contact

Executive Director
Career-Ed Institute
2359 Windy Hill Road
Marietta, GA 30067
Phone: 770-226-0056
Fax: 770-226-0084
E-mail: execdirmarietta@lincolntech.com
Web: www.ceitraining.com

Program Content

Medical Administrative Assistant, Medical Assistant, Network Systems Administrator

CEI (Career-Ed Institute), Norcross

About Our Institution
Since 1982, Career-Ed Institute (CEI) has been providing high-quality, postsecondary training in Massachusetts and Rhode Island. In 2001, CEI added two campuses in the Atlanta, Georgia, area and one campus in Henderson (Las Vegas), Nevada. All CEI locations offer focused programs that help its students receive the skills and confidence essential for success in their chosen field of study.

Special Features
CEI is dedicated and committed to providing an industry-standard and quality-driven instructional program, designed for students. The philosophy of CEI extends beyond the teaching of technical proficiencies and practical knowledge. CEI is committed to serving its students with concern and respect.

Financial Aid/Scholarships
CEI maintains a financial aid office at each location. A variety of available programs including grants, loans, scholarships, work-study, veteran's and vocational rehabilitation are available to qualified applicants. CEI provides two full and two half-tuition scholarships at each of its campuses. They are awarded annually to winners of the Scholarship Awards Program. Preliminary scholarship competition is conducted in the form of aptitude testing at each campus location. On the basis of test results, finalists are selected and invited to return for an interview conducted by the Scholarship Committee, which is made up of volunteers who represent business, industry, education, and/or government.

Accreditation
CEI is accredited by the Accrediting Council for Independent Colleges and Schools (ACICS), Washington, D.C., and is approved by a number of respective state and federal organizations. Further information is available from the school catalog.

Admissions
An applicant must satisfy the requirements of possessing a high school diploma or GED. A passing score on the CEI Entrance Examination is necessary for acceptance.

Graduation Requirements
Graduation requirements mandate that a student complete all required courses and achieve an overall grade point average of at least 2.0.

Contact
Executive Director
Career-Ed Institute
5675 Jimmy Carter Boulevard
Norcross, GA 30071
Phone: 678-966-9411
Fax: 678-966-9687
E-mail: execdirnorcross@lincolntech.com
Web: www.ceitraining.com

Program Content
Business Administration Specialist, Medical Administrative Assistant, Medical Assistant, Network Systems Administrator, PC Support Technician, Therapeutic Massage and Bodywork Technology

Georgia Medical Institute, Atlanta

About Our Institution

Georgia Medical Institute (GMI) was founded in 1977 by Ms. Ginger Gibbs and was, at that time, named Georgia Medical Employment Preparatory Center. Ms. Gibbs guided Georgia Medical to become a primary training school for medical personnel in the Atlanta area. In 1986 the school was acquired by Mr. Dominic J. Dean, Mr. Arthur Cuff, and Ms. Linda Lippmann-Cuff, and the school was renamed Georgia Medical Institute and expanded to three campuses. In 2000, it was purchased by Corinthian Schools, Inc. (CSi), a division of Corinthian Colleges, Inc. (CCi). CCi is one of the largest postsecondary school organizations in the United States, operating eighty-nine colleges and institutions nationwide.

Special Features

The founder's goal of providing quality medical education continues while Georgia Medical Institute and those who attend grow. The Downtown campus is one of five GMI school locations in the greater Atlanta metropolitan area. Each school contains spacious modern classrooms with attached laboratories, computer and typing labs, and a student lounge. All labs are properly equipped and meet OSHA safety guidelines.

Financial Aid/Scholarships

GMI participates in the Title IV Financial Aid Programs. Under these programs, students may apply for Federal Pell Grants and FFEL, depending on their educational needs. Certain eligible students may also participate in the Federal Supplemental Education Opportunity Grant (FSEOG) and Federal Work-Study (FWS) programs.

Accreditation

The Institute is accredited by the Accrediting Bureau of Health Education Schools (ABHES).

Admissions

All applicants are required to complete a personal interview with an admissions representative. Parents and spouses are encouraged to attend. This gives applicants and their families an opportunity to see the school's equipment and facilities, meet the staff and faculty, and ask questions relating to the campus, curriculum, and career objectives. Interviews also enable school administrators to determine whether an applicant is acceptable for enrollment in the program. Once an applicant has completed and submitted the Enrollment Agreement, the school reviews the information and informs the applicant of its decision. Prospective students must have a high school diploma or a recognized equivalency certificate (GED) and are required to furnish proof by providing the school with the diploma, an official transcript, or the GED certificate. A copy of the document will be placed in the student's file. Also, the student must achieve a passing score on a nationally normed, standardized test.

Program Content

Massage Therapy, Medical Administrative Assistant, Medical Assisting, Medical Insurance Billing/Coding, Patient Care Technician, Pharmacy Technician

Graduation Requirements

Students must pass all required courses and maintain at least a 70 percent overall grade average in their courses. The student must successfully complete the required clinical experience or externship, and must satisfy all school obligations, including academic, attendance, and current in-school financial payments.

Contact

Sonya Jabriel, Director of Admissions
Georgia Medical Institute
101 Marietta Street, Suite 600
Atlanta, GA 30303
Phone: (404) 525-1111
Fax: (404) 525-0966
E-mail: sjabriel@cci.edu
Web: www.georgia-med.com

Programs Eligible for Scholarship	Tuition and Fees	Course Length/Credit Hours	Credential Earned
Medical Administrative Assistant	$10,764	32 weeks	Diploma
Medical Assisting	$10,569	32 weeks	Diploma
Medical Insurance Billing/Coding	$ 7,491	20 weeks	Diploma
Patient Care Technician	$10,621	36 weeks	Diploma
Pharmacy Technician	$ 9,457	32 weeks	Diploma

Georgia Medical Institute, DeKalb

About Our Institution
Georgia Medical Institute (GMI), formerly the National Institute of Technology (NIT) in Atlanta, Georgia, opened in April 2000 as a branch campus of National Institute of Technology in Cross Lanes, West Virginia, to serve the growing educational needs of the Atlanta metropolitan area. NIT, Cross Lanes, opened in 1968 as a member of United Electronics Institute. In July 1995, the school was purchased by Corinthian Schools, Inc. (CSi), a division of Corinthian Colleges, Inc. (CCi). CCi is one of the largest postsecondary school organizations in the United States, operating eighty-nine colleges and institutions nationwide.

Special Features
The remodeled facility contains 20,000 square feet on the first and second floors of the stand-alone building, with six classrooms, two medical labs, four computer labs, and a library.

Financial Aid/Scholarships
GMI participates in the Title IV Financial Aid Programs. Under these programs, students may apply for Federal PELL Grants and Federal Family Education Loans. Certain eligible students may also participate in Federal Supplemental Education Opportunity Grants (FSEOG) and Federal Work-Study Program.

Accreditation
Georgia Medical Institute–DeKalb is accredited by the Accrediting Commission of Career Schools and Colleges of Technology (ACCSCT) and is a branch campus of NIT, Cross Lanes, West Virginia.

Admissions
Prospective students must have a high school diploma or a recognized equivalency certificate (GED) and are required to furnish proof by providing the school with the diploma, official transcript, or GED certificate. A copy of the document is placed in the student's file. Also, the student must achieve a passing score on a nationally normed, standardized test.

Enrollment
There are 400 to 450 students enrolled.

Contact
Trisha Wright Sherwood
Director of Admissions
Georgia Medical Institute
1706 Northeast Expressway
Atlanta, GA 30329
Phone: (404) 327-8787
Fax: (404) 327-8980
E-mail: tsherwood@cci.edu
Web: www.georgia-med.com

Program Content
Dialysis Technician, Massage Therapy, Medical Assisting, Medical Insurance Billing/Coding, Respiratory Care

Programs Eligible for Scholarship	Tuition and Fees	Course Length/Credit Hours	Credential Earned
Dialysis Technician	$ 9,645	720 clock hours/46 credit hours	Diploma
Massage Therapy	$11,780	730 clock hours/57 credit hours	Diploma
Medical Insurance Billing/Coding	$ 7,520	480 clock hours/29 credit hours	Diploma
Respiratory Care	$26,375	1,670 clock hours/108 credit hours	AS

Georgia Medical Institute, Jonesboro

About Our Institution
Georgia Medical Institute (GMI) was founded in 1977 by Ms. Ginger Gibbs and was, at that time, named Georgia Medical Employment Preparatory Center. Ms. Gibbs guided Georgia Medical to become a primary training school for medical personnel in the Atlanta area. In 1986 the school was acquired by Mr. Dominic J. Dean, Mr. Arthur Cuff, and Ms. Linda Lippmann-Cuff, and the school was renamed Georgia Medical Institute and expanded to three campuses. In 2000, it was purchased by Corinthian Schools, Inc. (CSi), a division of Corinthian Colleges, Inc. (CCi). CCi is one of the largest postsecondary school organizations in the United States, operating eighty-nine colleges and institutions nationwide.

Special Features
The founder's goal of providing quality medical education continues while Georgia Medical Institute and those who attend grow. The Jonesboro campus is one of five GMI school locations in the greater Atlanta metropolitan area. Each school contains spacious modern classrooms with attached laboratories, computer and typing labs, and a student lounge. All labs are properly equipped and meet OSHA safety guidelines.

Financial Aid/Scholarships
GMI participates in the Title IV Financial Aid Programs. Under these programs, students may apply for Federal Pell Grants and FFEL, depending on their educational needs. Certain eligible students may also participate in the Federal Supplemental Education Opportunity Grants (FSEOG) and Federal College Work-Study (FCWS) programs.

Accreditation
The Institute is accredited by the Accrediting Bureau of Health Education Schools (ABHES).

Admissions
All applicants are required to complete a personal interview with an admissions representative. Parents and spouses are encouraged to attend. This gives applicants and their families an opportunity to see the school's equipment and facilities, meet the staff and faculty, and ask questions relating to the campus, curriculum, and career objectives. Interviews also enable school administrators to determine whether an applicant is acceptable for enrollment in the program. Once an applicant has completed and submitted the Enrollment Agreement, the school reviews the information and informs the applicant of its decision. Prospective students must have a high school diploma or a recognized equivalency certificate (GED) and are required to furnish proof by providing the school with the diploma, an official transcript, or the GED certificate. A copy of the document is placed in the student's file. Also, the student must achieve a passing score on a nationally normed, standardized test. Ability to Benefit (ABT) students without a high school diploma or GED equivalent can be accepted by passing the CPAT test.

Program Content
Dental Assisting, Massage Therapy, Medical Administrative Assistant, Medical Assisting, Medical Insurance Billing/Coding, Patient Care Technician, Pharmacy Technician

Graduation Requirements
Students must pass all required courses and maintain at least a 70 percent overall grade average in their courses. The student must successfully complete the required clinical experience or externship, and must satisfy all school obligations, including academic, attendance, and current in-school financial payments.

Enrollment
There are 550–600 students enrolled.

Contact
Victor Tedoff, Director of Admissions
Georgia Medical Institute
6431 Tara Boulevard
Jonesboro, GA 30236
Phone: (770) 603-0000
Fax: (770) 210-3259
E-mail: vtedoff@cci.edu
Web: www.georgia–med.com

Programs Eligible for Scholarship	Tuition and Fees	Course Length/Credit Hours	Credential Earned
Dental Assisting	$10,600	32 weeks	Diploma
Massage Therapy	$11,750	36 weeks	Diploma
Medical Administrative Assistant	$10,600	32 weeks	Diploma
Medical Assisting	$10,600	32 weeks	Diploma
Medical Insurance Billing/Coding	$ 8,500	24 weeks	Diploma
Patient Care Technician	$10,600	32 weeks	Diploma
Pharmacy Technician	$10,200	32 weeks	Diploma

Georgia Medical Institute, Marietta

About Our Institution

Georgia Medical Institute (GMI) was founded in 1977 by Ms. Ginger Gibbs as the Georgia Medical Employment Preparatory Center. Ms. Gibbs guided Georgia Medical to become a primary training school for medical personnel in the Atlanta area. In 1986, the school was acquired by Mr. Dominic J. Dean, Mr. Arthur Cuff, and Ms. Linda Lippmann-Cuff. The school was renamed Georgia Medical Institute and expanded to three campuses. In 2000, it was purchased by Corinthian Schools, Inc. (CSi), a division of Corinthian Colleges, Inc. (CCi). CCi is one of the largest postsecondary school organizations in the United States, operating eighty-nine colleges and institutions nationwide.

Special Features

The founder's goal of providing quality medical education continues while Georgia Medical Institute and those who attend grow. The Marietta campus is one of five GMI school locations in the greater Atlanta metropolitan area. Each school contains spacious modern classrooms with attached laboratories, computer and typing labs, and a student lounge. All labs are properly equipped and meet OSHA safety guidelines.

Financial Aid/Scholarships

GMI participates in the Title IV Financial Aid Programs. Under these programs, students may apply for Federal Pell grants and FFEL, depending on their educational needs. Certain eligible students may also participate in the Federal Supplemental Educational Opportunity Grant (FSEOG) and Federal College Work-Study (FCWS) programs.

Accreditation

The Institute is accredited by the Accrediting Bureau of Health Education Schools (ABHES).

Admissions

All applicants are required to complete a personal interview with an admissions representative. Parents and spouses are encouraged to attend. This gives applicants and their families an opportunity to see the school's equipment and facilities, meet the staff and faculty members, and ask questions relating to the campus, curriculum, and career objectives. Interviews also enable school administrators to determine whether an applicant is acceptable for enrollment in the program. Once an applicant has completed and submitted the Enrollment Agreement, the school reviews the information and informs the applicant of its decision. Prospective students must have a high school diploma or a recognized equivalency certificate (GED) and are required to furnish proof by providing the school with the diploma, an official transcript, or the GED certificate. A copy of the document is placed in the student's file. Also, the student must achieve a passing score on a nationally standardized test.

Program Content

Massage Therapy, Medical Administrative Assisting, Medical Assisting, Medical Insurance Billing/Coding, Patient Care Technician, Pharmacy Technician, Surgical Technology

Graduation Requirements

Students must pass all required courses and maintain at least a 70 percent overall grade average in their courses. The student must successfully complete the required clinical experience or externship and must satisfy all school obligations, including academic, attendance, and current in-school financial payments.

Enrollment

There are 532 students enrolled.

Contact

Lynn Jones, Director of Admissions
Georgia Medical Institute
1600 Terrell Mill Road, Suite G
Marietta, GA 30067
Phone: (770) 303-7797
Fax: (770) 303-4422
E-mail: lyjones@cci.edu
Web: www.georgia-med.com

Programs Eligible for Scholarship	Tuition and Fees	Course Length/Credit Hours	Credential Earned
Massage Therapy	$11,750	720 clock hours/50.5 credit hours	Diploma
Medical Administrative Assisting	$10,600	720 clock hours/47 credit hours	Diploma
Medical Assisting	$10,600	720 clock hours/47 credit hours	Diploma
Medical Insurance Billing/Coding	$ 8,500	484 clock hours/35 credit hours	Diploma
Patient Care Technician	$10,600	720 clock hours/51 credit hours	Diploma
Pharmacy Technician	$10,200	720 clock hours/58 credit hours	Diploma
Surgical Technology	$19,300	1,200 clock hours/71 credit hours	Diploma

Georgia Medical Institute, Norcross

About Our Institution
Georgia Medical Institute (GMI) is one of eighty-nine schools owned and operated by Corinthian Colleges, Inc. GMI's philosophy is to provide high-quality programs that are sound in concept, implemented by a competent and dedicated faculty, and geared to serve those seeking a solid foundation in knowledge and skills required to obtain employment in their chosen fields. GMI-Norcross is a branch campus of Bryman College, Gardena, California.

Special Features
The school is conveniently located just off the Beaver Ruin Road exit from I-85 in the city of Norcross, Georgia. The attractive facility includes 19,000 square feet of space that includes computer, massage, dental, and medical assisting laboratories; lecture rooms; a library; a student lounge; and administrative areas.

Financial Aid/Scholarships
Pell, FSL, FPLUS, FSEOG, high school, and other scholarships are available for those who qualify.

Accreditation
GMI-Norcross is accredited by the Accrediting Commission of Career Schools and Colleges of Technology (ACCSCT).

Admissions
Candidates must have a high school diploma or equivalent. Successful completion of the assessment examination is a prerequisite for admission. For more information, applicants should contact the school to speak with an admissions representative.

Graduation Requirements
Students are required to earn a minimum cumulative grade point average of 2.0 in their major. Students must also meet specific program requirements.

Contact
Sandra Williams, Director of Admissions
1750 Beaver Ruin Road, Suite 500
Norcross, GA 30093
Phone: (770) 921-1085
Fax: (770) 923-4533
E-mail: sawilliams@cci.edu
Web: www.georgia-med.com

Program Content
Dental Assisting, Massage Therapy, Medical Administrative Assisting, Medical Assisting

Programs Eligible for Scholarship	Tuition and Fees	Course Length/Credit Hours	Credential Earned
Dental Assisting	$10,600	8 months/47 credit hours	Diploma
Massage Therapy	$11,750	9 months/57 credit hours	Diploma
Medical Administrative Assisting	$10,600	8 months/47 credit hours	Diploma
Medical Assisting	$10,600	8 months/47 credit hours	Diploma

Herzing College, Atlanta

About Our Institution
Herzing College has been an integral part of the Atlanta community since 1949 and provides a meaningful, high-quality education that prepares graduates for successful careers in business, information technology, and the health-care industry. The College confers a variety of Associate of Science (AS) and Bachelor of Science (BS) degrees as well as diplomas in medical office administration and insurance coding specialist. Herzing College concentrates on providing real skills that enable students to be prepared for a competitive job market.

Special Features
Students entering into the bachelor's program have the opportunity to complete their degree in three years as opposed to four years at other colleges. Herzing has designed class schedules to complement work schedules for students by creating day, evening, and online course offerings. The College's Career Services Department assists graduates with resume, job search, and placement assistance, which translates into excellent employment rates for graduates. All classroom workstations are connected to the Internet and the campus has a computerized library. Advisory boards for each of the curricula review the courses that are offered throughout the school year.

Financial Aid/Scholarships
Students attending Herzing may qualify for various financial assistance programs, including the following: Federal Pell, FSEOG, Work-Study, Perkins, FFEL, Stafford Loan, FFEL PLUS, William D. Ford Direct Loan Program, Federal Direct Stafford/Ford Loan, Federal Direct Unsubsidized Stafford/Ford Loan, Federal Direct PLUS Loan, VA benefits, and several scholarship programs sponsored by the College. In addition, students can take advantage of tuition payment plans, employer tuition reimbursement, the Institutional Grant Program, and the newly created Herzing Adult Learner Scholarship.

Tuition and Fees
The tuition is $285 per credit hour for all courses. Laboratory fees for Electronics Technology are $300 and for all other programs there is a $100 technology fee. There is no application fee. A $25 enrollment fee is required once a student has been accepted to the College; it is due prior to the start of classes. The College provides students with the necessary textbooks at no additional cost.

Accreditation
Herzing College is accredited by the Higher Learning Commission of the North Central Association of Colleges and Schools. For more information

Program Content
Associate of Science Programs: Business Administration; Computer Information Systems; Computer Network Technology; Computers, Electronics, and Telecommunications Technology; Legal Assisting/Paralegal
Bachelor of Science Programs: Business Administration, Information Technology, Technology Management.
Diploma Programs: Insurance Coding Specialist, Medical Office Administration

students should contact the Higher Learning Commission (telephone: 800-621-7440; Web site: http://www.ncahigherlearning commission.org).

Admissions
Each student must have a high school diploma or General Educational Development (GED) certificate, a passing score on a nationally recognized qualifying entrance examination, and a successful interview with an Admissions Representative.

Graduation Requirements
In order to graduate, students must have a cumulative grade point average of 2.0 or better, complete the required number of credit hours, pass all required courses, and be current in all financial obligations with the Financial Aid Office.

Contact
Frank Webster, Campus President
Herzing College
3355 Lenox Road, Suite 100
Atlanta, GA 30326
Phone: (800) 573-4533 (toll-free)
Fax: (404) 816-5576
E-mail: info@atl.herzing.edu
Web: www.herzing.edu

Programs Eligible for Scholarship	Tuition and Fees*	Course Length/Credit Hours	Credential Earned
Business Administration	$4,560/semester	70/125 credits	AS/BS
Computer Information Systems	$4,560/semester	79 credits	AS
Computer Network Technology	$4,560/semester	79 credits	AS
Computers, Electronics, and Telecommunications Technology	$4,560/semester	79 credits	AS
Legal Assisting/Paralegal	$4,560/semester	63 credits	AS
Information Technology	$4,560/semester	138 credits	BS
Technology Management	$4,560/semester	129 credits	BS
Medical Billing and Insurance Coding	$4,560/semester	42 credits	Diploma
Medical Office Administration	$4,560/semester	39 credits	Diploma

*Semesters at Herzing College are sixteen weeks long. A full-time student generally completes 16 credits a semester.

ITT Technical Institute, Duluth

About Our Institution

The company: ITT Technical Institute is owned and operated by ITT Educational Services, Inc. (ITT/ESI), a leading private college system offering technology-influenced programs of study. ITT/ESI operates seventy-seven ITT Technical Institutes in thirty states, providing career-focused degree programs to approximately 39,000 students as of spring 2004. Headquartered in Carmel, Indiana, ITT/ESI has been actively involved in the higher education community in the United States since 1969.

Curricula: Curriculum offerings are designed to help students begin to prepare for career opportunities in fields of technology. Students attend classes year-round, with convenient breaks provided throughout the year. A full-time student course load can have class meetings as often as three days a week and are typically available in the morning, afternoon, and evening, depending on student enrollment. General education courses may be available online. This class schedule offers flexibility to students to pursue part-time employment opportunities.

ITT Technical Institute, Duluth, awards the Associate of Science and the Bachelor of Science degrees.

Special Features

Most ITT Technical Institute programs of study blend traditional academic content with applied learning concepts, with a significant portion devoted to practical study in a lab environment. Advisory committees composed of representatives of local businesses help each ITT Technical Institute periodically review and update curricula, equipment, and laboratory design.

Financial Aid/Scholarships

ITT Technical Institute maintains a Financial Aid Department on campus. The campus is designated as an eligible institution by the U.S. Department of Education for participation in the following programs: Federal Stafford Student Loan Program, Federal PLUS Loan Program, and Federal Work-Study Program. The school also offers nonfederal loans available through Bank One for eligible students.

Tuition and Fees

March 2005 tuition is $386 per credit hour.

Accreditation

The school is accredited by the Accrediting Council for Independent Colleges and Schools (ACICS).

Admissions

For admission requirements, students should contact the school for a catalog.

Graduation Requirements

For graduation requirements, students should contact the school for a catalog.

Program Content

School of Information Technology: Data Communication Systems Technology, Information Systems Security, Information Technology–Computer Network Systems, Information Technology–Software Applications and Programming, Information Technology–Web Development

School of Electronics Technology: Computer and Electronics Engineering Technology, Electronics and Communications Engineering Technology

School of Drafting and Design: Computer Drafting and Design, Information Technology–Multimedia Option

School of Business: Technical Project Management

Contact

Chip Hinton, Director of Recruitment
ITT Technical Institute
10700 Abbotts Bridge Road
Duluth, GA 30097
Phone: (678) 957-8510
Fax: (678) 417-2070

Kerr Business College, Augusta

About Our Institution
Kerr Business College was founded in 1983 to provide educational opportunities for students to develop the necessary skills, attitudes, knowledge, and ethics to be successful in the business world.

Special Features
Key features of the College are small classes, modern equipment, tutoring, student-oriented faculty and staff members, and graduate services. Kerr Business College is also an authorized on-site Prometric testing center and is Microsoft Academy certified.

Financial Aid/Scholarships
The following financial aid programs are available: Federal Pell Grant, FFEL, FDSLP, VA, FSEOG, FWS, Federal Perkins Loan, and Chester H. Kerr Memorial Scholarship.

Tuition and Fees
Tuition ranges from $5,245 to $17,945 plus a $35 registration fee.

Accreditation
Kerr Business College is accredited by the Accrediting Council for Independent Colleges and Schools (ACICS).

Admissions
A high school diploma or GED certificate is required. In addition, a personal interview and a passing grade on an entrance examination are required.

Graduation Requirements
All courses in each program must be satisfactorily completed with a minimum GPA of 2.0.

Contact
Dawn McCraith, Director
2528 Centerwest Parkway, Building A
Augusta, GA 30909
Phone: (706) 738-5046
Fax: (706) 736-3599
E-mail: mccraith@kerrbusinesscollege.com
Web: www.kerrbusinesscollege.com

Program Content
Accounting Specialist, Administrative Office Specialist, Business Management, Computer Help Desk Support Specialist, Computer Technical Support Specialist, Health Care Technician, Medical Assistant, Medical Billing Specialist, Medical Office Specialist, Microsoft Network Engineer.

Program Description
The Accounting Specialist program is designed to prepare students for entry-level careers in bookkeeping.

The Administrative Office Specialist program emphasizes office skills needed for employment as an administrative office professional.

The Business Management program is designed to prepare students for basic entry-level careers in business.

The Computer Help Desk Support Specialist program prepares students to enter the information system field as troubleshooters and provide technical support for hardware, software, and systems.

The Computer Technical Support Specialist program prepares students to install and maintain computer networks and to troubleshoot.

The Health Care Technician program develops the proper skills and knowledge to function as part of a medical facility. Skills such as taking vital signs, phlebotomy, EKGs, catheterization, wound care, and CPR are taught.

The Medical Assistant program prepares students to perform multiskilled tasks in primarily ambulatory settings.

The Medical Billing Specialist program is designed to provide specialized skills in billing, coding, and insurance claims.

The Medical Office Specialist program develops medical and secretarial skills for employment in a variety of medically related companies.

The Microsoft Network Engineer (Certificate) program prepares students to become officially certified as a Microsoft Certified Systems Engineer. Students learn to install, configure, manage, and maintain a network operating system.

The Microsoft Network Engineer (Diploma) program is designed to assist students in becoming certified as a Microsoft Certified Systems Engineer. Students also complete course work that allows them to obtain CompTIA, A+, N+, and 1-Net+ certification and to become certified in Microsoft Visual Basic. Students learn to install, configure, manage, and maintain both a desktop operating system and a network operating system.

Programs Eligible for Scholarship	Tuition and Fees	Course Length/Credit Hours	Credential Earned
Accounting Specialist	$ 8,195	36 weeks/ 61 credit hours	Diploma
Administrative Office Specialist	$ 8,195	36 weeks/56.7 credit hours	Diploma
Business Management	$ 8,195	36 weeks/63.5 credit hours	Diploma
Computer Help Desk Support Specialist	$12,065	48 weeks/77.4 credit hours	Diploma
Computer Technical Support Specialist	$12,115	48 weeks/75.4 credit hours	Diploma
Health Care Technician	$ 5,245	24 weeks/44.6 credit hours	Certificate
Medical Assistant	$ 8,595	42 weeks/71.7 credit hours	Diploma
Medical Billing Specialist	$ 8,935	36 weeks/58.9 credit hours	Diploma
Medical Office Specialist	$ 8,295	36 weeks/59.9 credit hours	Diploma
Microsoft Network Engineer	$12,065	48 weeks/77.1 credit hours	Certificate
Microsoft Network Engineer	$18,195	72 weeks/ 119 credit hours	Diploma

Medix School, Smyrna

About Our Institution

Medix School was founded in 1969 and has continued to produce qualified graduates for the health-care field. All courses are selected and scheduled to contribute to that objective. Surveys of the industries that employ Medix School graduates are conducted, and the results of those surveys, along with input from the School's Advisory Board, determine what changes or modifications should be made in the Schools' training in order to give students the best possible preparation for careers in their chosen fields.

Special Features

Graduates of the medical assistant program can sit for the Certified Medical Assistant Exam (CMA) and the Phlebotomy Certification Exam (CPT). Graduates of the dental assisting program can sit for the Certified Dental Assistant Exam (CDA), which includes radiology and expanded functions. Graduates of the medical office administration program can sit for the National Center for Competency Testing Certification Exam. EMT graduates are entitled to sit for the National Registry Exam. Massage therapy graduates may sit for the National Certification Board for Therapeutic Massage and Bodywork Exam (NCBTW).

Programs are designed to begin every five weeks and are available in the morning, afternoon, and evening.

Financial Aid/Scholarships

The financial aid programs at Medix are for persons from all classes of society who have the ability and desire to benefit from such education or training. Students attending Medix may qualify for various scholarships or forms of financial aid.

Accreditation

Medix School is accredited by the Accrediting Bureau of Health Education Schools (ABHES), the Commission on Dental Accreditation of the American Dental Association, the Commission on Accreditation of Allied Health Education Programs (CAAHEP), and the American Association of Medical Assistants' Endowment (AMAE).

Admissions

Applicants must possess a high school diploma or GED certificate and pass an entrance exam followed by a personal interview.

Contact

Crystal Henry, Director of Admissions
Medix School
2108 Cobb Parkway
Smyrna, GA 30080
Phone: (770) 980-0002
Fax: (770) 980-0811
E-mail: email@medixschool.com
Web: www.medixschool.edu

Program Content

Certified Nursing Assistant/Patient Care Technician, Dental Assistant, Emergency Medical Technician, Massage Therapy, Medical Assistant, Medical Office Administration, Paramedic-Advanced Emergency Medical Technician

Program Description

Certified Nursing Assistant/Patient Care Technology A graduate of this program is prepared to work in a variety of nursing assistant and chronic care facilities. Students sit for the Georgia Department of Human Resources State Examination.

Dental Assistant This program trains students in "four-handed" dental procedures, practicing their competence in dental office and laboratory and chairside employment.

Emergency Medical Technician The program is based on the U.S. Department of Transportation's guidelines for the EMT Intermediate course curriculum. Graduates of the program sit for the National Registry EMT Exam and receive their Georgia approval numbers upon passing the exam.

Massage Therapy Graduates of this program are qualified to work in private practices, chiropractic offices, wellness centers, health clinics, resorts, spas, physical therapy practices, pain management centers, and massage therapy establishments.

Medical Assistant Medical assistant graduates are multi-skilled allied health professionals who work primarily in ambulatory settings such as medical offices and clinics.

Medical Office Administration Graduates of this program are similar to a medical assistant, but receive a strong emphasis on front office duties, enabling them to work in a wider variety of fields.

Paramedic-Advanced EMT Training in this program qualifies graduates to take the NREMTP Exam.

Programs Eligible for Scholarship	Course Length/Credit Hours
Certified Nursing Assistant/Patient Care Technology	18 weeks
Dental Assistant	40 weeks
Emergency Medical Technician	20 weeks
Massage Therapy	30 weeks
Medical Assistant	40 weeks
Medical Office Administration	40 weeks
Paramedic-Advanced EMT	53 weeks

Westwood College, Atlanta Midtown, Atlanta

About Our Institution
Westwood College–Atlanta Midtown is committed to providing a positive and cooperative environment and to working collaboratively with employers to ensure a high-quality, college-level, career-oriented education. The College's objective is to graduate confident, job-qualified individuals prepared to enter their chosen career field.

Special Features
Westwood College places a high value on the industry experience faculty members bring to the classroom. While many faculty members have earned bachelor's and master's degrees in their fields, Westwood looks for a combination of industry experience, educational training in the subject area, and prior teaching experience to ensure that students receive a balanced, industry-relevant education.

Tuition and Fees
The school catalog contains detailed information about tuition and fees.

Accreditation
Westwood is accredited by the Accrediting Council for Independent Colleges and Schools (ACICS). This accreditation guides the College, in that Westwood has a clearly defined mission, aspires to high standards to ensure high-quality programs, and has the human, physical, and financial resources to accomplish its mission.

Admissions
Successful candidates for Westwood are required to have a high school diploma or GED. In addition to submitting a completed application, applicants must receive a score of at least 17 on the ACT or 920 on the SAT, or they must achieve the required scores on the Accuplacer Computerized Placement Test. An interview with an admissions representative is also required. Upon acceptance, students must submit a registration fee and attend an acceptance interview to verify their commitment to begin training.

Program Content

Associate Degrees: Computer-Aided Design/Architectural Drafting, Computer Network Engineering, Graphic Design and Multimedia, Software Engineering

Bachelor's Degrees: Animation, Business Administration with concentration in accounting, Business Administration with concentration in marketing and sales, Computer Network Management, E-Business Management, Game Art and Design, Game Software Development, Information Systems Security, Interior Design, Visual Communications, Web Design and Multimedia

Certificates: Medical Assisting, Medical Insurance Coding and Billing

Contact
Bill Armour
Executive Director
Westwood College–Atlanta Midtown
1100 Spring Street
Atlanta, GA 30309
Phone: (404) 745-9862
Fax: (404) 892-7253
E-mail: barmour@westwood.edu
Web: www.westwood.edu

Programs Eligible for Scholarship	Tuition and Fees	Course Length/Credit Hours	Credential Earned
Computer Aided Design/Architectural Drafting	refer to school	20 months/101 hours	AAS
Computer Network Engineering	catalog	20 months/114 hours	AAS
Graphic Design and Multimedia		20 months/105 hours	AAS
Software Engineering		20 months/100.5 hours	AAS
Animation		36 months/194 hours	BS
Business Administration (accounting)		36 months/189 hours	BS
Business Administration (marketing and sales)		36 months/189 hours	BS
Computer Network Management		36 months/198 hours	BS
E-Business Management		36 months/189 hours	BS
Game Art and Design		36 months/211 hours	BS
Game Software Development		36 months/198 hours	BS
Information Systems Security		36 months/204 hours	BS
Interior Design		36 months/186.5 hours	BS
Visual Communications		36 months/196 hours	BS
Web Design and Multimedia		36 months/193 hours	BS

Westwood College, Atlanta Northlake, Atlanta

About Our Institution
Westwood College–Atlanta Northlake is committed to a positive and cooperative environment and working collaboratively with employers to ensure a high-quality, college-level, career-oriented education. Westwood's objective is to graduate confident, job-qualified individuals who are prepared to enter their chosen career field.

Special Features
Westwood College places a high value on the industry experience faculty members bring to the classroom. While many faculty members have earned bachelor's and master's degrees in their fields, Westwood looks for a combination of industry experience, educational training in the subject area, and prior teaching experience to ensure that students receive a balanced, industry-relevant education.

Tuition and Fees
Students should see the College's catalog for detailed tuition and fee information.

Accreditation
Westwood is accredited by the Accrediting Council for Independent Colleges and Schools (ACICS). This accreditation shows that the College has a clearly defined mission, aspires to high standards in order to ensure high-quality programs, and has the human, physical, and financial resources to accomplish its mission.

Admissions
Successful candidates for Westwood are required to have a high school diploma or GED certificate. Applicants must complete an application and receive a score of at least 17 on the ACT or 920 on the SAT or achieve the required scores on the Accuplacer Computerized Placement Test. To enroll, candidates complete an application for admission, attend an interview by an admissions representative, submit a registration fee, and, upon completion of testing, attend an acceptance interview to verify their commitment to begin training.

Program Content
The Atlanta Northlake campus offers associate degrees in computer-aided design–architectural drafting, computer network engineering, graphic design and multimedia, and software engineering; bachelor's degrees in animation, business administration: concentration in accounting, business administration: concentration in marketing and sales, computer network management, e-business management, game art and design, game software development, information systems security, interior design, visual communications, and Web design and multimedia; and certificates in medical assisting and medical insurance coding and billing.

Contact
Scott Nelson
Executive Director
Westwood College–Atlanta Northlake
1100 Spring Street
Atlanta, GA 30309
Phone: (404) 745-9862
Fax: (404) 892-7253
E-mail: barmour@westwood.edu
Web: www.westwood.edu

Programs Eligible for Scholarship	Tuition and Fees	Course Length/Credit Hours	Credential Earned
Computer-Aided Design–Architectural Drafting	refer to school catalog	20 months/101 credit hours	AAS
Computer Network Engineering		20 months/114 credit hours	AAS
Graphic Design and Multimedia		20 months/105 credit hours	AAS
Software Engineering		20 months/100.5 credit hours	AAS
Animation		36 months/194 credit hours	BS
Business Administration: Concentration in Accounting		36 months/189 credit hours	BS
Business Administration: Concentration in Sales and Marketing		36 months/189 credit hours	BS
Computer Network Management		36 months/198 credit hours	BS
E-Business Management		36 months/189 credit hours	BS
Game Art and Design		36 months/211 credit hours	BS
Game Software Development		36 months/198 credit hours	BS
Information Systems Security		36 months/204 credit hours	BS
Interior Design		36 months/186.5 credit hours	BS
Visual Communications		36 months/196 credit hours	BS
Web Design and Multimedia		36 months/193 credit hours	BS

Heald College, Honolulu Campus, Honolulu

About Our Institution
Heald College is a nonprofit, WASC-accredited institution with eleven campuses located in northern California, Hawaii, and Oregon. Heald College was founded in 1863 by Edward Payson Heald and for more than 140 years has helped students prepare for successful business, technical, and health-care careers.

The Honolulu campus has a rich Hawaiian heritage, reaching back to 1917. This campus became part of the Heald College system in 1993. Located near Ala Moana Center in a facility of more than 50,000 square feet, the campus is fully networked with advanced technologies. New classrooms have recently been added to this beautiful campus. Heald Honolulu offers a variety of business, technology, and health-care programs as well as hospitality and tourism.

Special Features
Heald College provides focused programs in business, technology, and health care that prepare students for success in the workplace in the shortest practical time. Heald College also provides personal attention every step of the way. From completion of the admissions application through navigation of financial aid options to ongoing academic assistance programs (workshops, individual tutoring, learning resource centers) to job placement assistance, the College believes that it succeeds only when its students succeed.

Financial Aid/Scholarships
A Financial Aid Adviser meets with students to assess each person's individual situation and eligibility for assistance. The adviser explains each option, guides the student to those that are appropriate, and assists in the proper completion of all the necessary paperwork. Financial aid options available include Federal Pell Grants, Federal SEOG, scholarships, state and private grants, Federal Work-Study, Federal Stafford Student Loans (subsidized and unsubsidized), Federal PLUS Loans, private loans, Workforce Investment Act (WIA) grants, and veterans' educational benefits. Students must qualify for financial aid and meet specific academic progress requirements to obtain and remain eligible for all federal and state financial assistance programs.

Tuition and Fees
Tuition and fees vary by program length. Students should contact the Admissions Department for additional information.

Accreditation
Heald is accredited by the Accrediting Commission for Community and Junior Colleges of the Western Association of Schools and Colleges (WASC). Heald's medical assisting program and its medical office program have both been approved by the American Medical Technologists (AMT), a nonprofit certification agency, and by the National Center for Competency Testing. These partnerships allow Heald's health-care graduates to sit for appropriate certification examinations. The Heald College accounting curriculum has been approved by the California Tax Education Council (CTEC) to offer course work that fulfills the 60-hour qualifying education requirement, imposed by the state, to become a tax preparer.

Admissions
Applicants must interview with an Admissions Adviser, indicate that they have a high school diploma or GED equivalent, complete an application, pass an admissions examination, and be recommended by an Admissions

Program Content
Most Heald campuses offer Associate in Applied Science (A.A.S.) degrees and diploma programs in accounting, business administration, criminal justice, office skills, office technologies, sales and marketing, software technologies, network systems administration, technical support, medical assisting, and medical office administration as well as opportunities to earn a second A.A.S. degree or certificate in CISCO and Microsoft Windows networking technology or in business accounting. Honolulu also offers degrees in hospitality and tourism and electronics technology. Special diploma and certificate programs in medical assisting and office skills are offered at some campuses.

Program Description
Heald College programs include both professional and general education courses, which together allow students to experience the integration of knowledge and skills. The general education courses offer students breadth in their experiences by introducing them to major areas of knowledge, thus expanding their understanding of the world and cultures around them. Furthermore, these courses foster a spirit of inquiry and provide for students' development of the skills, knowledge, and intellectual habits necessary to support their personal, professional, and public lives. Heald also provides hands-on training in all of its programs to ensure that students can successfully apply the skills they learn in the workplace after graduation.

Adviser to the Campus Director. Students should contact the Admissions Department for additional information.

Graduation Requirements
To be eligible for graduation, students must successfully complete all classes with a minimum 2.0 cumulative grade point average and complete all program, unit, and course requirements.

Contact
Lon Ibaraki, Director of Admissions
1500 Kapiolani Boulevard
Honolulu, HI 96814
Phone: (808) 955-1500
        (800) 755-3550 (toll-free)
Fax: (808) 955-6964
E-mail: lon_ibaraki@heald.edu
Web: www.heald.edu

Remington College, Honolulu Campus, Honolulu

About Our Institution

Remington College–Honolulu Campus was established as a branch campus of Education America–Dallas Campus, Inc., in December 1998. In February 1999, the main campus was changed from Education America–Dallas Campus to Education America–Denver Campus. It is now Remington College–Honolulu Campus and is part of a nationwide twenty-campus network. Offering both Associate of Science and Bachelor of Science degrees in a variety of technical fields, Remington College aggressively prepares students to enter the job market by facilitating an academic and hands-on learning environment.

Special Features

Remington College–Honolulu Campus is dedicated to providing high-quality education and dynamic education programs. One of its primary objectives is to graduate a high percentage of students who enter career programs and to help them secure relevant employment at the highest possible starting salary. Practical application in well-equipped labs, coupled with theoretical reinforcement in the classroom, allows students to acquire substantial knowledge in their chosen career field. When appropriate, externships or internships are used to provide the student with real-world experience.

Financial Aid/Scholarships

The Financial Services Office provides a variety of financial assistance, including information on how to apply for grants, loans, scholarships, work-study, veterans' aid, and vocational rehabilitation programs.

Accreditation

Remington College–Honolulu Campus is accredited by the Accrediting Council for Independent Colleges and Schools (ACICS).

Admissions

Consideration for admission to Associate of Applied Science degree programs requires that the student be a high school graduate from a state or regionally accredited institution or an equivalent, such as the GED, and have an acceptable score on the entrance test. Bachelor of Science degree applicants should have an associate degree in a related field with a minimum of 24 quarter-credit hours in general education courses. The Academic Dean evaluates college transcripts to determine transfer credit. All applicants must complete an admissions interview and an acceptance interview. In addition, all applicants are required to present a valid certificate indicating that they are free of tuberculosis in a communicable form.

Graduation Requirements

A student is eligible for graduation if he or she completes all courses as specified in the program catalog and maintains a cumulative grade point average of 2.0 or better throughout the program.

Contact

Kenneth Heinemann, Campus President
1111 Bishop Street, Suite 400
Honolulu, HI 96813
Phone: (808) 942-1000
Fax: (808) 533-3064
Web: www.remingtoncollege.edu

Program Description

A.A.S. in Clinical Medical Assisting: The emphasis of this program is placed on administrative skills that include patient scheduling, patient record management, and clinical skills. Students apply the program skills in an externship at an approved facility.

A.A.S. in Computer Information Systems: This program provides comprehensive training in three major areas: Technical analysis, programming architecture, and local area networks. Languages included are Visual Basic, C++, COBOL, Java, and more.

A.A.S. in Computer Networking Technology: This program provides comprehensive instruction in both Microsoft Windows NT® and Novell's NetWare®.

A.A.S. in Criminal Justice: The field of criminal justice centers on the control of criminal behavior in the maintenance of public order and includes the primary functions of law enforcement, prosecution, trial, and corrections.

A.A.S. in International Business: The focus of this program is instruction in the functions of general business operations such as merchandising, administration, distribution, and service.

B.S. in Criminal Justice: This program is designed to provide specific, in-depth, theoretical knowledge integrated with applied techniques in law enforcement, the courts system, and corrections.

B.S. in Operations Management: Instructional methods integrate the latest technologies with creative thinking to provide students with the decision-making skills and problem-solving behaviors needed for a career in business administration.

American Institute of Health Technology, Boise

About Our Institution
American Institute of Health Technology is a proprietary institution of higher education specializing in health-care careers. The Institute offers both certificate and degree programs and takes pride in the success of its students from program completion through certification and licensure to job placement.

Special Features
American Institute was founded in 1980, occupying 800 square feet of space and offering two programs in health care. The Institute now occupies a total of five buildings on a 6½-acre campus and offers more than ten different health-care programs at both the certificate and associate degree levels. American Institute owes its exceptional growth and reputation to its graduates and their success.

Financial Aid/Scholarships
Pell, FFEL, WIA, Vocational Rehabilitation, Alaska Student Loan Program, TEC, SEOG, VA assistance, and scholarships for graduating high school seniors and single working parents are available.

Tuition and Fees
Tuition and fees vary by program. Students should refer to the school catalog.

Accreditation
The American Institute of Health Technology, Inc., is institutionally accredited by the Accrediting Bureau of Health Education Schools (ABHES), which is listed by the U.S. Department of Education as a nationally recognized accrediting agency under the provisions of Chapter 33, Title 38, U.S. Code, and subsequent legislation. The ABHES offices are located at 803 West Broad Street, Suite 730, Falls Church, Virginia, 22046; (703) 533-2082.

Certain health-care disciplines require "occupational specific" licensure or certification to practice within the state of Idaho. Laws, rules, and regulations governing certification or licensure require that the applicant for licensure or certification be a graduate of a program accredited by a specific organization. This procedure is called Programmatic Accreditation and applies to certain programs taught at the American Institute of Health Technology, as specified below.

The American Institute of Health Technology's Dental Hygiene and Dental Assisting Programs are programmatically accredited by the Commission on Dental Accreditation. The Commission is a specialized accrediting body recognized by the U.S. Department of Education. The Commission on Dental Accreditation can be contacted at 211 East Chicago Avenue, Chicago, Illinois 60611; (312) 440-4653.

Graduation Requirements
In order to graduate, a student must have earned a minimum cumulative grade point average of 2.0, maintained 85 percent attendance, earned the minimum credit hours as required by the program of study, and satisfied all financial obligations to the Institute.

Contact
American Institute of Health Technology
1200 North Liberty Street
Boise, ID 83704
Phone: (208) 377-8080
Fax: (208) 322-7658
Web: www.aiht.com

Programs Eligible for Scholarship	Tuition and Fees	Course Length/Credit Hours	Credential Earned
Dental Assisting	$10,025	38 credit hours	Certificate
Massage Therapy	$ 9,115	33 credit hours	Certificate
Medical Administrative Assisting	$ 9,115	36 credit hours	Certificate
Medical Assisting	$ 9,155	31 credit hours	Certificate
Medical Billing	$ 9,115	36 credit hours	Certificate
Pharmacy Technician	$ 9,115	33.5 credit hours	Certificate
Dental Assisting	$17,275	68 credit hours	AAS
Massage Therapy	$16,385	63 credit hours	AAS
Medical Administrative Assisting	$16,385	66 credit hours	AAS
Medical Assisting	$16,385	61 credit hours	AAS
Medical Billing	$16,385	66 credit hours	AAS
Pharmacy Technician	$16,365	63.5 credit hours	AAS
Dental Hygienist	$42,500	5 semesters/83 credit hours	AAS

ITT Technical Institute, Boise

About Our Institution

ITT Technical Institute is owned and operated by ITT Educational Services, Inc. (ESI), a leading private college system offering technology-influenced programs of study. ESI operates seventy-seven ITT Technical Institutes in thirty states, providing career-focused degree programs to approximately 39,000 students as of spring 2004. Headquartered in Carmel, Indiana, ESI has been actively involved in the higher education community in the United States since 1969. Curriculum offerings are designed to help students prepare for career opportunities in technology fields. Students attend classes year-round, with convenient breaks provided throughout the year. A full-time student's courses may meet as often as three days per week and are typically available in the morning, afternoon, and evening, depending on student enrollment. General education courses may be available online. This class schedule offers flexibility to students to pursue part-time employment.

Special Features

Most of the programs blend traditional academic content with applied learning concepts, with a significant portion devoted to practical study in a lab environment. Advisory committees, composed of local business representatives, help each ITT Technical Institute periodically review and update curricula, equipment, and lab design.

The Associate of Applied Science, Bachelor of Applied Science, and Bachelor of Science degrees are awarded.

Financial Aid/Scholarships

The Institute maintains a Financial Aid Department on campus. The campus is designated as an eligible institution by the U.S. Department of Education for participation in the following programs: Federal Perkins Loan, Federal Stafford Student Loan, Federal Direct PLUS loan, and Federal Work-Study Program. The school also offers eligible students nonfederal loans through Bank One.

Tuition and Fees

March 2005 tuition is $386 per credit hour.

Accreditation

The Institute is accredited by the Accrediting Council for Independent Colleges and Schools (ACICS).

Admissions

For admission requirements, students should consult the school catalog.

Graduation Requirements

For graduation requirements, students should consult the school catalog.

Contact

Jennifer Kandler, Director
ITT Technical Institute
12302 West Explorer Drive
Boise, ID 83713
Phone: (208) 322-8844
Fax: (208) 322-0173

Program Content

School of Information Technology: Data Communication Systems Technology, Information Systems Security, Information Technology–Computer Network Systems, Information Technology–Software Applications and Programming, Information Technology–Web Development, Software Engineering Technology

School of Electronics Technology: Computer and Electronics Engineering Technology, Electronics and Communications Engineering Technology

School of Drafting and Design: Computer Drafting and Design, Digital Entertainment and Game Design, Information Technology–Multimedia Option

School of Business: Business Accounting Technology, Business Administration, Technical Project Management

School of Criminal Justice: Criminal Justice

The Cooking and Hospitality Institute of Chicago, Chicago

About Our Institution

Since 1983, the mission of the Institute has been to prepare students to fulfill their career aspirations in the food service industry. Since that time, the Institute has educated thousands of students who are staffing some of the finest establishments in the Chicago area and across the country. The diverse student body represents numerous states and many other countries. In 2000, the Institute introduced the Le Cordon Bleu Culinary Arts Program, which leads to an Associate of Applied Science degree.

Special Features

The Institute features a Learning Resource Center, with a computer lab and full Internet access. There are numerous student organizations, ranging from the Student Advisory Board to the award-winning Culinary Competition Team. Career Services matches current students with employers while they attend school and provides graduates with career opportunities. Externships help provide a foundation for students to enter the food service industry.

Financial Aid/Scholarships

The Institute participates in Title IV grants, student loans, and work-study programs. Many culinary organizations offer scholarship opportunities to students, ranging from $500 to $10,000. The Cooking and Hospitality Institute of Chicago offers several institutional scholarships. Financial aid is available for those who qualify.

Tuition and Fees

Tuition is $12,750 per semester; there is also an activity fee of $300. The one-time registration fee is $100.

Accreditation

The Institute is accredited by the Accrediting Commission of Career Schools and Colleges of Technology (ACCSCT) and the American Culinary Federation (ACF). It is also accredited by the Higher Learning Commission of the North Central Association of Colleges and Schools.

Admissions

Prospective students must submit proof of a GED credential, a high school diploma, or higher-level degree and must either transfer credits in college English and/or math, submit ACT or SAT scores, or take the Institute's math and/or English evaluation.

Graduation Requirements

Students must earn all credits dictated by their program of study and maintain satisfactory academic progress with a cumulative GPA of 2.0 or better (on a 4.0 scale).

Program Content

Culinary Arts, Patisserie and Baking

Program Description

The Associate of Applied Science degree in Le Cordon Bleu Culinary Arts includes training in professional cooking, cooking skills, nutrition sciences, baking and pastry skills, restaurant management skills, and general education.

The Institute offers an Associate of Applied Science degree in Le Cordon Bleu Patisserie and Baking. This program teaches the principles and techniques of professional pastry and baking production and is intended for students who have an interest in large-quantity baking or who want to work for establishments that have in-house baking and pastry operations.

Contact

Catherine Brokenshire, Vice President of Admissions
Cooking and Hospitality Institute of Chicago
361 West Chestnut
Chicago, IL 60610
Phone: (877) 828-7772 (toll-free)
Fax: (312) 944-8557
E-mail: chic@chicnet.org
Web: www.chic.edu

Programs Eligible for Scholarship	Tuition and Fees	Course Length/Credit Hours	Credential Earned
Culinary Arts	$38,250	65 credits	AAS
Patisserie and Baking	$38,250	64 credits	AAS

Coyne American Institute, Chicago

About Our Institution
Coyne American Institute, founded in 1899, is one of the oldest electrical schools in the United States. The Institute prepares graduates for entry-level positions as electricians; heating, air-conditioning, and refrigeration technicians; and electronic technicians and for general office positions in businesses that use the latest computer software programs.

Special Features
Programs are taught by working professionals. The technical training programs consist of 40 percent hands-on laboratory assignments on a variety of today's equipment. Tutoring is available to all students. There are both full-time day classes and part-time evening classes available.

Financial Aid/Scholarships
Federal Pell Grants, FFEL, VA, JTPA, and Imagine America are offered.

Tuition and Fees
Tuition ranges from $7,350 to $10,400 for full-time programs. Part-time programs range from $6,800 to $8,050.

Accreditation
Coyne American Institute is accredited by the Accrediting Commission of Career Schools and Colleges of Technology (ACCSCT).

Admissions
All candidates must have graduated from high school or possess a GED certificate. Personal interviews are required for all applicants. All applicants must pass the Institute's entrance examination.

Graduation Requirements
All students must pass each module of their program with a grade of 75 or better and adhere to the Institute's policies.

Contact
Peter Pauletti, Admissions Director
Coyne American Institute
1235 West Fullerton Avenue
Chicago, IL 60614
Phone: (773) 935-2520
(800) 999-5220 (toll-free)
Fax: (773) 935-2920
E-mail: ppauletti@coyneamerican.edu
Web: www.coyneamerican.edu

Program Content
Air Conditioning, Refrigeration, and Heating; Electrical Maintenance; Electronics Technician; Office Administrative Assistant

Program Description
Air Conditioning, Refrigeration, and Heating: The program prepares graduates to work in entry-level positions as air-conditioning, refrigeration, and heating service technicians.

Electrical Maintenance: The program prepares graduates to work in entry-level positions as residential or industrial electricians.

Electronics Technician: The program prepares graduates for entry-level positions as electronic technicians and computer repair technicians.

Office Administrative Assistant: The program prepares graduates for general office positions using word processing and the latest software programs.

Programs Eligible for Scholarship	Tuition and Fees	Course Length/Credit Hours	Credential Earned
Air Conditioning/Refrigeration/Heating	$ 8,800	36 weeks/72 quarter credits	Diploma
Basic Air Conditioning/Refrigeration/Heating	$ 6,800	48 weeks/51 quarter credits	Diploma
Electrical Maintenance	$ 8,900	36 weeks/72 quarter credits	Diploma
Basic Electrical Maintenance	$ 6,900	48 weeks/51 quarter credits	Diploma
Electronics Technician	$10,400	48 weeks/96 quarter credits	Diploma
Basic Electronics Technician	$ 8,050	64 weeks/68 quarter credits	Diploma
Office Administrative Assistant	$ 7,350	36 weeks/72 quarter credits	Diploma

Harrington College of Design, Chicago

About Our Institution
Harrington College of Design (HCD) was founded in 1931 and is dedicated exclusively to professional education in interior design. HCD is recognized by the Illinois Board of Higher Education as a private college authorized to award the Bachelor of Fine Arts degree in interior design and Associate of Applied Science degree in interior design. HCD is accredited by the National Association of Schools of Art and Design (NASAD), and the bachelor's program is accredited by the Foundation for Interior Design Education Research (FIDER), the nationally recognized accrediting agency for interior design.

Harrington Institute's location in the heart of Chicago, a world center of design, is of inestimable value. Students have access to important designers' resources at the Chicago Merchandise Mart to supplement their studies. Its showroom galleries, exhibiting the best of contemporary furnishings, textiles, and accessories of every description, are a magnet for designers from around the world. Libraries, galleries, museums, theaters, the Chicago Symphony Orchestra, and the Lyric Opera are within easy walking distance, and the proximity of the campus to Grant Park, the landmark Buckingham Fountain, and Lake Michigan enhances its atmosphere of beauty and tradition.

Special Features
The American Society of Interior Designers (ASID) sponsors a student chapter at the Institute, which offers students opportunities to meet practicing professionals and gain a firsthand understanding of professional standards and practices. Harrington Institute students are frequent award winners in national competitions sponsored by ASID, the Institute of Store Planners, and the Institute of Business Designers.

The design library's collections consist of more than 22,000 volumes and 23,000 slides, which support every aspect of the curriculum. The library subscribes to ninety international and domestic professional journals, magazines, and indices in interior design, architecture, and art. It also houses the Products Library of current catalogs, product information, color and fabric samples, and tile and laminate samples from more than 3,000 manufacturers. The library holds memberships in ILLINET/OCLC and the Chicago Library System, which enable staff members to search and borrow nationwide, via computer, from the holdings of almost 5,000 libraries containing 14 million volumes.

HCD students may apply to participate in study-abroad opportunities that in the past have included such locations as Greece, Paris, and Italy.

Financial Aid/Scholarships
In 2002–03, more than 60 percent of the full-time student body received loans and grants to help them meet the costs of education. The Harrington Institute administers these funds through the Federal Pell Grant, Federal Supplemental Educational Opportunity Grant, Federal Stafford Student Loan, and Federal PLUS programs as well as the privately funded Excel Student Loan program. International students are not eligible for federal financial aid or for part-time employment. Students should contact the Office of Financial Aid for application materials.

Tuition and Fees
Tuition for the 2003 academic year was $475 per credit hour, with an additional studio/lab fee of $175. Students should budget an estimated $350 per semester for textbooks and materials and an estimated $600 for the initial purchase of equipment. A monthly tuition payment plan is available.

Admissions
HCD maintains a selective admission policy and encourages students with creative aptitude to apply. No previous training in art or design is required because the program assumes progression from beginner to advanced and professional proficiency. Proof of high school graduation or its equivalent, a personal interview, official transcripts, and the application and application fee are prerequisites for admission. Early application is advised. The Institute is also authorized under federal law to enroll international (alien nonimmigrant) students.

Contact
Director of Admissions
Harrington College of Design
410 South Michigan Avenue
Chicago, IL 60605-1496
Phone: (877) 939-4975 (toll-free)
Fax: 312-697-8032
E-mail: hiid@interiordesign.edu
Web: www.interiordesign.edu

Illinois School of Health Careers, Chicago

About Our Institution

Illinois School of Health Careers (ISHC) was first established in 1990. Illinois School of Health Careers, Inc., is a wholly owned subsidiary of ForeFront Education, Inc., which acquired the school in July 2003. The mission of Illinois School of Health Careers is to provide quality educational and training opportunities to those individuals seeking the knowledge and skills necessary to obtain entry-level employment in the allied health professions.

Special Features

Illinois School of Health Careers provides diploma programs in dental assistant, massage therapy, and medical assistant. The School consists of classrooms, laboratories, an X-ray room, a library, a computer room, and a student lounge. It is conveniently accessible by public transportation on world-renowned State Street in downtown Chicago, close to the Harold Washington Library, the Art Institute of Chicago, Michigan Avenue, and Grant Park.

Financial Aid/Scholarships

ISHC is approved by the U.S. Department of Education to participate in the following Federal Title IV programs: Federal Pell Grants, Federal Family Education Loans or William D. Ford Federal Direct Loans (Subsidized and Unsubsidized), Federal Stafford Student Loans (Subsidized and Unsubsidized), and Federal PLUS Programs.

Accreditation

ISHC is approved to operate by the Illinois State Board of Education. The School is a member of Career College Association and American Massage Therapy Association and an authorized provider of health education through the American Red Cross. ISHC is institutionally (nondegree) accredited by the Accrediting Bureau of Health Education Schools (ABHES), which is listed as a nationally recognized accrediting agency by the U.S. Department of Education.

Admissions

All applicants to Illinois School of Health Careers must be at least 17 years old. The School admits applicants who submit a diploma, certificate, or other proof of graduation from an institution providing secondary education or the relevant equivalent of such graduation, such as a GED certificate.

Graduation Requirements

In order to graduate from Illinois School of Health Careers, students must successfully complete all required classwork, successfully complete all clinical experience or externship (if required), successfully pass cardiopulmonary resuscitation certification (if required), earn a minimum grade point average of 70 percent, make up any missed attendance over the allowed excused amount, complete the program within 1½ times the normal program length, complete all essential forms and examinations, attend a student loan exit interview (if applicable), and fulfill all financial obligations to the School.

Program Content

Diplomas: Dental Assistant, Massage Therapy, Medical Assistant

Program Description

Dental Assistant: The Dental Assistant diploma program consists of classroom training combined with an externship at a dental office. The goal of the Dental Assistant program is to gain entry-level employment in the dental field as a dental assistant.

Massage Therapy: The goal of the Massage Therapy diploma program is to provide the student with the skills necessary to gain employment as an entry-level massage therapist in a private office, health club, resort, salon or health professional's office.

Medical Assistant: The Medical Assistant diploma program strongly emphasizes hands-on clinical skills. The goal of the Medical Assistant program is to provide the student with the skills, knowledge, and training necessary to be able to function successfully as an entry-level medical assistant and/or phlebotomist in a clinic, hospital, or physician's office. Highlights of this program include a phlebotomy (drawing blood) component, CPR certification, and an introduction to computers.

Contact

Jeffrey L. Jarmes
Executive Director
220 S. State Street
Suite 600
Chicago, IL 60604
Phone: (312) 913-1230
Fax: (312) 913-1113
E-mail: jjarmes@ishc.edu
Web: www.ishc.edu

ITT Technical Institute, Burr Ridge

About Our Institution
The company: ITT Technical Institute is owned and operated by ITT Educational Services, Inc. (ITT/ESI), a leading private college system that offers technology-influenced programs of study. ITT/ESI operates seventy-seven ITT Technical Institutes in thirty states; they provide career-focused degree programs to approximately 39,000 students as of spring 2004. Headquartered in Carmel, Indiana, ITT/ESI has been actively involved in the higher education community in the United States since 1969.

Curricula: Curriculum offerings are designed to help students begin to prepare for career opportunities in the fields of technology. Students attend classes year-round, with convenient breaks provided throughout the year. A full-time student can have class meetings as often as three days a week, and they are typically available in the morning, afternoon, and evening, depending on student enrollment. General education courses may be available online. This schedule offers flexibility to allow students to pursue part-time employment opportunities.

ITT Technical Institute, Burr Ridge, awards Associate of Applied Science and Bachelor of Applied Science degrees.

Special Features
Most ITT Technical Institute programs of study blend traditional academic content with applied learning concepts, with a significant portion devoted to practical study in a lab environment. Advisory committees, made up of representatives of local businesses help each ITT Technical Institute periodically review and update curricula, equipment, and laboratory design.

Financial Aid/Scholarships
ITT Technical Institute maintains a Financial Aid Department on campus. The campus is designated as an eligible institution by the U.S. Department of Education for participation in the following programs: Federal Stafford Student Loan, Federal PLUS Loan, and Federal Work-Study. The school also participates in the California Grant Program and offers nonfederal loans through Bank One for eligible students.

Tuition and Fees
March 2005 tuition is $389 per credit hour.

Accreditation
Accrediting Council for Independent Colleges and Schools (ACICS).

Admissions
For admission requirements, students should contact the school for a catalog.

Graduation Requirements
For graduation requirements, students should consult the school catalog.

Program Content
School of Information Technology: Information Systems Security, Information Technology–Computer Network Systems, Information Technology–Software Applications and Programming, Information Technology–Web Development.

School of Electronics Technology: Computer and Electronics Engineering Technology.

School of Drafting and Design: Computer Drafting and Design, Information Technology–Multimedia Option.

School of Business: Technical Project Management.

Contact
Alida Carpenter, Director
ITT Technical Institute
7040 High Grove Boulevard
Burr Ridge, IL 60527
Phone: (630) 455-6470
Fax: (630) 455-6476

ITT Technical Institute, Matteson

About Our Institution
The company: ITT Technical Institute is owned and operated by ITT Educational Services, Inc. (ITT/ESI), a leading private college system focused on technology-oriented programs of study. ITT/ESI operates seventy-six ITT Technical Institutes in twenty-nine states, providing career-focused degree programs to approximately 33,000 students as of spring 2003. Headquartered in Indianapolis, Indiana, ITT/ESI has been actively involved in the higher education community in the United States since 1969.

Curricula: Curriculum offerings are designed to prepare students for career opportunities in fields of technology. Students attend classes year-round, with convenient breaks provided throughout the year. Classes are generally scheduled three days a week and are typically available in the morning, afternoon, and evening, depending on student enrollment. This class schedule offers students the flexibility to pursue part-time employment opportunities.

The degree awarded is the Associate of Applied Science.

Special Features
Most ITT Technical Institute programs of study blend traditional academic content with applied learning concepts, with a significant portion devoted to practical study in a lab environment. Advisory committees, made up of representatives of local businesses and employers for each program of study, help each ITT Technical Institute periodically assess and update curricula, equipment, and laboratory design. Assistance with housing and part-time employment is available.

Financial Aid/Scholarships
ITT Technical Institute maintains a Finance Department on the campus. The campus is designated as an eligible institution by the U.S. Department of Education for participation in the following programs: Federal Pell Grant Program, Federal Stafford Student Loan Program, Federal PLUS Loan Program, and Federal Work-Study Program. The school also offers nonfederal loans through Bank One for eligible students.

Tuition and Fees
March 2004 tuition was $364 per credit hour.

Accreditation
The Institute is accredited by the Accrediting Council for Independent Colleges and Schools (ACICS).

Admissions
Admission requirements include having obtained a high school diploma or GED, passing an admission test (subject to being waived—students should refer to the school catalog), and passing, as determined at the school's discretion, an interview with the Registrar of the school, if the Registrar requests an interview with the student.

Graduation Requirements
For graduation requirements, students should consult the school catalog.

Program Content
Computer Drafting and Design, Computer and Electronics Engineering Technology, Information Technology: Computer Network Systems, Multimedia, Software Applications and Programming, Web Development

Program Description
The Computer Drafting and Design program combines computer-aided drafting with conventional methods of graphic communication to solve drafting and basic design-related problems.

The Computer and Electronics Engineering Technology program prepares students for careers in entry-level positions in modern electronics and computer technology.

The IT Computer Network Systems program helps prepare students to perform tasks associated with installing, upgrading, and maintaining computer network systems.

The IT Multimedia program helps students prepare to perform tasks associated with designing and creating interactive multimedia communications.

The IT Software Applications and Programming program helps students prepare to perform tasks associated with developing and modifying software applications.

The IT Web Development program helps students prepare to perform tasks associated with designing, creating, and maintaining Web sites.

Contact
Lillian Williams-McClain
Director
ITT Technical Institute
600 Holiday Plaza Drive
Matteson, IL 60443
Phone: (708) 747-2571
Fax: (708) 747- 0023

ITT Technical Institute, Mount Prospect

About Our Institution

The company: ITT Technical Institute is owned and operated by ITT Educational Services, Inc. (ITT/ESI), a leading private college system offering technology-influenced programs of study. ITT/ESI operates seventy-seven ITT Technical Institutes in thirty states, providing career-focused degree programs to approximately 39,000 students as of spring 2004. Headquartered in Carmel, Indiana, ITT/ESI has been actively involved in the higher education community in the United States since 1969.

Curricula: Curriculum offerings are designed to prepare students for career opportunities in fields of technology. Students attend classes year-round, with convenient breaks provided throughout the year. A full-time student course load can have class meetings as often as three days a week and are typically available in the morning, afternoon, and evening, depending on student enrollment. General education courses may be available online. This class schedule offers students the flexibility to pursue part-time employment opportunities.

ITT Technical Institute, Mount Prospect, awards the Associate in Occupational Studies and Bachelor of Applied Science degrees.

Special Features

Most ITT Technical Institute programs of study blend traditional academic content with applied learning concepts, with a significant portion devoted to practical study in a lab environment. Advisory committees, made up of representatives of local businesses, help each ITT Technical Institute periodically review and update curricula, equipment, and laboratory design.

Financial Aid/Scholarships

ITT Technical Institute maintains a Financial Aid Department on the campus. The campus is designated as an eligible institution by the U.S. Department of Education for participation in the following programs: Federal Stafford Student Loan Program, Federal PLUS Loan Program, and Federal Work-Study Program. The school also offers nonfederal loans through Bank One for eligible students.

Tuition and Fees

March 2005 tuition is $386 per credit hour.

Accreditation

The Institute is accredited by the Accrediting Council for Independent Colleges and Schools (ACICS).

Admissions

For admission requirements, prospective students should contact the school for a catalog.

Graduation Requirements

For graduation requirements, prospective students should contact the school for a catalog.

Program Content

School of Information Technology: Information Systems Security, Information Technology–Computer Network Systems, Information Technology–Software Applications and Programming, Information Technology–Web Development

School of Electronics Technology: Electronics and Communications Engineering Technology, Computer and Electronics Engineering Technology

School of Drafting and Design: Computer Drafting and Design, Information Technology–Multimedia Option

School of Business: Technical Project Management

Contact

Elvis Parker, Director
ITT Technical Institute
1401 Feehanville Drive
Mt. Prospect, IL 60056
Phone: (847) 375-8800
Fax: (847) 375-9022

Lincoln Technical Institute, Melrose Park

About Our Institution
The Melrose Park campus is the newest facility in the Lincoln Technical Institute system. This 70,000-square-foot campus is conveniently located only 8 miles from Chicago's downtown district and only minutes from O'Hare International Airport. The modern auto shop has fourteen equipped bays and nine drive-in classrooms to provide the hands-on training required for industry employment. This campus also includes an Auto Web Tech Lab with thirty computers to enable students to learn the curriculum prevalent in the high-technology automotive industry.

Special Features
Lincoln Tech instructors are ASE certified in the courses they teach. ASE certification is a nationally recognized credential of excellence in the automotive field. Lincoln Tech has established several programs with local employers and has developed strong relationships to help students succeed.

Financial Aid/Scholarships
The Melrose Park campus offers a variety of tuition scholarships available to graduating high school students. Awards include the Imagine America Scholarship, the Boys and Girls Clubs of America Scholarship, the VICA Scholarship, and the Veterans Scholarship, as well as others. To apply for most of these scholarships, students must fill out an application and take an aptitude-based scholarship test. A Scholarship Committee, made up of volunteers representing business, industry, education, and/or government, interviews the finalists and makes the award decision. In addition, Lincoln Tech maintains a Financial Aid Office on campus, which offers qualified students a variety of programs, including grants, loans, work-study, and veterans' and vocational rehabilitation.

Accreditation
Lincoln Tech is accredited by the Accrediting Commission of Career Schools and Colleges of Technology (ACCSCT) and certified by NATEF. The Electronic Systems Technician Program is accredited by the National Center for Construction Education and Research (NCCER).

Admissions
Students must have either a high school diploma or a GED certificate and pass an entrance exam.

Contact
Executive Director
Lincoln Technical Institute
8317 West North Avenue
Melrose Park, IL 60160
Phone: (708) 344-4700
Fax: (708) 345-4065
E-mail: hcarver@lincolntech.com
Web: www.lincolntech.com

Program Content
Automotive Technology, Electronic Systems Technician, Medical Assistant

Olympia College, Burr Ridge

About Our Institution
Olympia College–Burr Ridge, Illinois, is one of four campuses in the Chicago area. The Burr Ridge campus opened in September 2002 and is a branch campus of Olympia College–Skokie, Illinois. Olympia College's philosophy is to provide high-quality programs that are sound in concept and implemented by a competent and dedicated faculty. The programs emphasize hands-on training, are relevant to employers' needs, and focus on areas that offer strong, long-term employment opportunities. Olympia College is one of more than eighty schools owned and operated by Corinthian Colleges, Inc. (CCi).

Special Features
The College is conveniently located on Frontage Road, just north of I-55 and east of County Line Road in Cook County. The attractive facility of approximately 30,000 square feet includes a total of six laboratories, seven lecture rooms, a resource center, a student lounge, and administrative areas. Parking is available adjacent to the school building. This institution—the facilities it occupies and the equipment it uses—complies with all federal, state, and local ordinances and regulations, including those related to fire safety, building safety, and health.

Financial Aid/Scholarships
Financial aid is available for those who qualify. The College participates in the Federal Pell Grant, FFEL, work-study, Federal Perkins Loan, VA, and WIA. Funding through other agencies and high school and other scholarships are available.

Accreditation
The College is accredited by the Accrediting Commission of Career Schools and Colleges of Technology (ACCSCT).

Admissions
Successful candidates are selected based on interviews and the completion and presentation of required documents. Enrollment is open to all high school graduates as well as those holding a GED certificate or its equivalent. Under certain circumstances, students who do not have a high school diploma or its equivalent may still be accepted for admission. Prospective students should contact the Admissions Department for additional information.

Graduation Requirements
To be eligible for graduation, students must complete all required courses with a grade of C or better, have a cumulative grade point average (GPA) of 2.0 or higher, and complete an approved externship with a grade of C or better.

Contact
David Profita, Director of Admissions
6880 North Frontage Road, Suite 400
Burr Ridge, IL 60527
Phone: (630) 920-1102
Fax: (630) 920-9012
E-mail: dprofita@cci.edu
Web: www.olympia-college.com

Program Content
Massage Therapy, Medical Administrative Assistant, Medical Assisting

Olympia College, Chicago

About Our Institution
Olympia College is one of more than 150 schools owned and operated by Corinthian Colleges, Inc. (CCi). Olympia College, Chicago, opened its doors to meet the growing demands in the Chicago area for more career training. Olympia College's philosophy is to provide high-quality programs that are sound in concept and implemented by a competent and dedicated faculty. The programs emphasize hands-on training, are relevant to employers' needs, and focus on areas that offer strong, long-term employment opportunities.

Special Features
Olympia College, Chicago, is conveniently located on the corner of South State and East Jackson in the downtown Chicago loop. Close to public transportation, this modern facility has more than 45,000 square feet and houses laboratories, lecture rooms, a library, and administrative areas.

Financial Aid/Scholarships
Pell, FFEL, SEOG, VA, WIA, and funding through other agencies are available to those who qualify.

Accreditation
Olympia College, Chicago, is accredited by the Accrediting Commission of Career Schools and Colleges of Technology (ACCSCT) and is a branch campus of Bryman College, San Francisco.

Admissions
Successful candidates are selected based on interviews and the completion and presentation of required documents. Enrollment is open to all high school graduates as well as those holding a GED or its equivalent. Under certain circumstances, students who do not have a high school diploma or its equivalent may still be accepted for admission. Students should contact the Admissions Department for additional information.

Graduation Requirements
To be eligible for graduation, students must complete all required courses with a grade of C or above and have a cumulative grade point average (GPA) of 2.0 or above and complete an approved externship with a grade of C or above.

Enrollment
There are 450 students enrolled.

Program Content
Medical Administrative Assistant, Medical Assisting, Pharmacy Technician

Contact
Nikee Carnagey, Director of Admissions
Olympia College
247 South State Street, Suite 400
Chicago, IL 60604
Phone: (312) 913-1616
Fax: (312) 913-9422
E-mail: ncarnage@cci.edu
Web: www.olympia-college.com

Programs Eligible for Scholarship	Tuition and Fees	Course Length/Credit Hours	Credential Earned
Medical Administrative Assistant	$ 9,261	47 semester credits	Diploma
Medical Assisting	$ 9,335	47 semester credits	Diploma
Pharmacy Technician	$10,500	58 semester credits	Diploma

Olympia College, Skokie

About Our Institution
Olympia College is one of more than eighty-nine schools owned and operated by Corinthian Colleges, Inc. (CCi). Olympia College, formerly Grand Rapids Educational Center, was founded in 1972. CCi acquired Olympia College in February 2001. Olympia College's philosophy is to provide high-quality programs that are sound in concept and implemented by a competent and dedicated faculty. The programs emphasize hands-on training, are relevant to employers' needs, and focus on areas that offer strong, long-term employment opportunities.

Special Features
Olympia College is conveniently located on Woods Drive, just south of Old Orchard Road and west of I-94. The attractive facility of approximately 20,000 square feet includes massage therapy and medical assisting laboratories, lecture rooms, a library/student lounge, and administrative areas. Ample parking is available adjacent to the school building.

Financial Aid/Scholarships
The College participates in Pell, Parent Plus Loan, student loans, work-study, SEOG, VA, and WIA programs. Funding through other agencies is available. Financial aid is available for those who qualify.

Accreditation
The College is accredited by the Accrediting Commission of Career Schools and Colleges of Technology (ACCSCT).

Admissions
All applicants need not possess a high school diploma or its equivalent but must successfully complete a preadmissions examination.

Graduation Requirements
To be eligible for graduation, students must complete all required courses with a grade of C or better, have a cumulative grade point average (GPA) of 2.0 or above, and complete an approved externship with a grade of C or better.

Enrollment
There are 500 students enrolled.

Contact
Romona Ewing, Director of Admissions
9811 Woods Drive
Skokie, IL 60077
Phone: (847) 470-0277
Fax: (847) 470-0266
E-mail: rewing@cci.edu
Web: www.olympia-college.com

Program Content
Massage Therapy, Medical Assisting, Medical Insurance Billing/Coding

Programs Eligible for Scholarship	Tuition and Fees	Course Length/Credit Hours	Credential Earned
Massage Therapy	$10,771	9 months/57 credits	Diploma
Medical Assisting	$10,210	8 months/47 credits	Diploma
Medical Insurance Billing/Coding	$8,012	6 months/35 credits	Diploma

Universal Technical Institute, Glendale Heights

About Our Institution
UTI Glendale Heights is a private postsecondary technical school that has provided students with the technical education needed for a successful career in the automotive and diesel industry since opening in 1988. UTI provides full student services, housing assistance, financial aid to those who qualify, campus activities, and both part-time and graduate employment assistance for as long as it is needed.

Special Features
UTI has developed strong industry relations with manufacturers such as Audi, BMW, Ford, International Trucks, Jaguar, Mercedes Benz, NASCAR, Porsche, Volkswagen, and Volvo. These agreements have created excellent training and career opportunities for UTI automotive and diesel graduates. From excellent electives for upgraded UTI training to fully paid manufacturer-specific graduate training, UTI's connections and commitment to excellence places its graduates in the driver's seat in a career field that is in demand. Many manufacturers and dealers in addition to those listed above also participate in UTI's TRIP program, wherein these companies agree to pay back the student tuition loans for the graduates they hire.

Financial Aid/Scholarships
UTI students are eligible to apply for various federal grants and loans. These include Federal Pell Grants, FSEOG, and Federal Student Stafford Loans, Federal Perkins Loans, and PLUS Loans. UTI also sponsors, as well as administers, various scholarship programs and awards more than $500,000 in scholarships annually, including VICA, CCA, Imagine America, Ford AAA, FFA, and UTI's National High School Scholarship competition.

Tuition and Fees
Tuition and fees vary by course content. Tuition prices include all workbooks, textbooks, and uniforms; there are no hidden costs. For specific tuition information, students should contact the Glendale Heights Admissions Office.

Accreditation
Universal Technical Institute is accredited by the Accrediting Commission of Career Schools and Colleges of Technology (ACCSCT), which is listed by the U.S. Department of Education as a nationally recognized accrediting agency.

Admissions
Each individual applying for admission must be at least 16 years of age and must submit a completed application, a signed enrollment agreement, a registration fee, a high school diploma or equivalent, and any other information that the applicant or Institute feels is pertinent to admission. Each applicant's qualifications for enrollment are reviewed and either approved, approved with stipulations, or denied.

Graduation Requirements
Students must achieve at least an overall 2.0 cumulative GPA and receive a "satisfactory" in all required courses in their selected program. Graduation must be achieved within a ratio of 1:5 attempted courses in a student's program. Students must have a zero balance in their student account and have attended UTI's Career Development Classes.

Program Content
Automotive Technology, Diesel and Industrial Technology, Automotive/Diesel and Industrial Technology

Program Description
UTI's automotive and diesel programs prepare the graduate to diagnose, troubleshoot, service, and repair foreign and domestic automobiles and diesel engines. Students work in a professional, shop-like environment using the latest engine analyzers, handheld scanners, and other computerized diagnostic equipment. Students learn everything from basic engine systems and computerized engine controls to hydraulics and transport refrigeration. Graduates have all the skills needed to start a challenging and rewarding career in the automotive and/or diesel industries.

Contact
Karl Lewandowski, School Director
601 Regency Drive
Glendale Heights, IL 60139
Phone: (630) 529-2662
   (800) 441-4248 (toll-free)
E-mail: karllewandowski@uticorp.com

Vatterott College, Quincy

About Our Institution
All Vatterott College programs are based on a proven successful formula of specialized, technology-focused, hands-on training in the fastest-growing industries. The College was founded in 1969 and now serves nearly 9,000 students per year at sixteen Midwestern campuses. The Quincy campus offers programs focused on the information technology, health-care, and technical trade industries.

Special Features
Vatterott College's hands-on training method of instruction equips students with the specific skills that are desired by local employers. Courses are geared to the student's field of study. Classes are available in both morning and evening schedules.

Financial Aid/Scholarships
Vatterott College participates in a variety of financial aid and scholarship programs. The College's Make-the-Grade scholarship offers tuition credit to qualifying students based on high school grades. Vatterott College also participates in the Imagine America scholarship program. High school seniors are eligible to apply. Prospective students should contact the campus Financial Aid Representative for specific information.

Tuition and Fees
The campus Admissions Representatives can provide complete tuition information.

Accreditation
Vatterott College is nationally accredited by the Accrediting Commission of Career Schools and Colleges of Technology (ACCSCT).

Admissions
The application process includes a personal interview and entrance evaluation. A high school diploma or GED is required.

Graduation Requirements
Students must show satisfactory progress by maintaining a minimum grade of 70 percent and a minimum attendance record of 80 percent.

Contact
Office of Admissions
Vatterott College
501 North 3rd Street
Quincy, IL 62301
Phone: (217) 224-0600
        (800) 438-5621 (toll-free)
Fax: (217) 223-6771
E-mail: quincy@vatterott-college.edu
Web: www.vatterott-college.edu

Program Content
Diploma: Computer-Aided Drafting and Design; Computer Office Assistant; Computer Technology; Electrical Mechanics; Heating, Air Conditioning, and Refrigeration; Medical Assistant

Westwood College, Chicago Loop, Chicago

About Our Institution
Westwood College–Chicago Loop is accredited by the Accrediting Council for Independent Colleges and Schools (ACICS). Westwood is committed to maintaining a positive and cooperative environment and to working collaboratively with employers to ensure a high-quality, college-level, career-oriented education. The objective is to graduate confident, job-qualified individuals prepared to enter their career fields of choice.

Special Features
Westwood College places a high value on the industry experience faculty members bring to the classroom. While many faculty members have earned bachelor's and master's degrees in their fields, Westwood looks for a combination of industry experience, educational training in the subject area, and prior teaching experience to ensure that students receive a balanced, industry-relevant education.

Financial Aid/Scholarships
Westwood College participates in a variety of financial aid programs, including the Federal Pell Grant, FFEL, Stafford Student Loan (subsidized and unsubsidized), Plus loans, Federal Perkins Loan, the Federal Supplemental Educational Opportunity Grant (FSEOG), the Westwood High School Scholarship Program, and educational assistance loans. Other types of financial aid may be available depending on individual student eligibility. Students should check with the Admissions Office for VA-approved benefits.

Tuition and Fees
Students should consult the school catalog for detailed tuition and fee information.

Accreditation
Westwood is accredited by the Accrediting Council for Independent Colleges and Schools (ACICS). This accreditation guides the College, in that it has a clearly defined mission and aspires to high standards to ensure high-quality programs and has the human, physical, and financial resources to accomplish its mission.

Program Content
Associate Degrees: Computer-Aided Design/Architectural Drafting, Computer Network Engineering, Graphic Design and Multimedia, Software Engineering.

Bachelor's Degrees: Animation, Business Administration: Accounting, Business Administration: Marketing and Sales, Computer Network Management, Criminal Justice, E-Business Management, Game Art and Design, Game Software Development, Information Systems Security, Interior Design, Visual Communications, Web Design and Multimedia.

Admissions
Successful candidates for Westwood are required to have a high school diploma or GED. Applicants must submit an application and receive a minimum score of 17 on the ACT or 920 on the SAT or achieve the required scores on the Accuplacer Computerized Placement Test. Candidates must also have an interview with an admissions representative and submit a registration fee. Upon completion of testing, candidates must attend an acceptance interview to verify their commitment to begin training.

Contact
Tamara Rozhon
Executive Director
Westwood College
17 North State Street
Chicago, IL 60602
Phone: (800) 693-5411 (toll-free)
Fax: (312) 739-1004
E-mail: trozhon@westwood.edu
Web: www.westwood.edu

Programs Eligible for Scholarship	Course Length/Credit Hours	Credential Earned
Animation	36 months/194 credit hours	BAS
Business Administration: Accounting	36 months/189 credit hours	BAS
Business Administration: Marketing and Sales	36 months/189 credit hours	BAS
Computer-Aided Design/Architectural Drafting	20 months/101 credit hours	AAS
Computer Network Engineering	20 months/114 credit hours	AAS
Computer Network Management	36 months/198 credit hours	BAS
Criminal Justice	36 months/183 credit hours	BAS
E-Business Management	36 months/189 credit hours	BAS
Game Art and Design	36 months/211 credit hours	BAS
Game Software Development	36 months/198 credit hours	BAS
Graphic Design and Multimedia	20 months/105 credit hours	AAS
Information Systems Security	36 months/204 credit hours	BAS
Interior Design	36 months/186.5 credit hours	BAS
Software Engineering	20 months/100.5 credit hours	AAS
Visual Communications	36 months/196 credit hours	BAS
Web Design and Multimedia	36 months/196 credit hours	BAS

Westwood College, O'Hare Airport, Schiller Park

About Our Institution
Westwood College–O'Hare opened in January 2000 and expanded as the O'Hare Airport campus in 2002. Committed to a positive and cooperative environment and working collaboratively with employers, the College is dedicated to high-quality, college-level, career-oriented education. Its objective is to graduate confident, job-qualified individuals prepared to enter career fields of choice.

Special Features
Westwood College places a high value on the industry experience faculty members bring to the classroom. While many faculty members have earned their bachelor's and master's degrees in their fields, Westwood looks for a combination of industry experience, educational training in the subject area, and prior teaching experience to ensure that students receive a balanced, state-of-the-art education.

Financial Aid/Scholarships
Westwood College participates in a variety of financial aid programs, including the Federal Pell Grant, FFEL Stafford Student Loan (subsidized and unsubsidized), PLUS Loans, Federal Perkins Loan, the Federal Supplemental Educational Opportunity Grant (FSEOG), the Westwood High School Scholarship Program, and educational assistance loans. Other types of financial aid may be available depending on individual student eligibility. Students should check with the Admissions Office for VA-approved benefits.

Tuition and Fees
Students should consult the school catalog for detailed tuition and fee information.

Accreditation
Westwood is accredited by the Accrediting Council of Independent Colleges and Schools (ACICS). This accreditation guides the College in its clearly defined mission and its aspirations to high standards to ensure quality programs and the human, physical, and financial resources to accomplish its mission.

Admissions
Successful candidates for Westwood are required to have a high school diploma or GED certificate. Applicants must complete an acceptance application and either receive a minimum composite score of 17 on the ACT or 920

Program Description
Over the past 45 years, in response to innovative requirements of industry, Westwood has grown to include seventeen Westwood Colleges. The O'Hare Airport campus offers associate degree programs in Computer-Aided Design (CAD)/Architectural Drafting, Computer Network Engineering, Graphic Design and Multimedia, and Software Engineering. Bachelor's programs are offered in Animation, Business Administration: Accounting, Business Administration: Marketing and Sales, Computer Network Management, Criminal Justice, E-Business Management, Game Art and Design, Game Software Development, Information Systems Security, Interior Design, Visual Communications, and Web Design and Multimedia.

on the SAT or achieve the required scores on the Accuplacer Computerized Placement Test.

To enroll, candidates submit an application for admission, are interviewed by an admissions representative, submit a registration fee and, upon completion of testing, attend an acceptance interview to verify their commitment to begin training.

Contact
Lou Pagano, Executive Director
Westwood College
8501 West Higgins Road
Chicago, IL 60631
Phone: (847) 928-0200
        (877) 877-8857 (toll-free)
Fax: (847) 928-1748
E-mail: lpagano@westwood.edu
Web: www.westwood.edu

Programs Eligible for Scholarship	Course Length/Credit Hours	Credential Earned
Animation	36 months/194 credit hours	BAS
Business Administration: Accounting	36 months/189 credit hours	BAS
Business Administration: Marketing and Sales	36 months/189 credit hours	BAS
Computer-Aided Design/Architectural Drafting	20 months/101 credit hours	AAS
Computer Network Engineering	20 months/114 credit hours	AAS
Computer Network Management	36 months/198 credit hours	BAS
Criminal Justice	36 months/183 credit hours	BAS
E-Business Management	36 months/189 credit hours	BAS
Game Art and Design	36 months/211 credit hours	BAS
Game Software Development	36 months/198 credit hours	BAS
Graphic Design and Multimedia	20 months/105 credit hours	AAS
Information Systems Security	36 months/204 credit hours	BAS
Interior Design	36 months/186.5 credit hours	BAS
Software Engineering	20 months/100.5 credit hours	AAS
Visual Communications	36 months/196 credit hours	BAS
Web Design and Multimedia	36 months/196 credit hours	BAS

Westwood College, DuPage, Woodridge

About Our Institution

Westwood College, DuPage, is accredited by the Accrediting Council for Independent Colleges and Schools (ACICS) and is approved and regulated by the Illinois State Board of Education and the Illinois Board of Higher Education. The College is committed to a positive and cooperative environment. Working collaboratively with employers, the College is dedicated to high-quality, college-level, career-oriented education. Its objective is to graduate confident, job-qualified individuals prepared to enter their career field of choice.

Special Features

Westwood College places a high value on the industry experience faculty members bring to the classroom. While many faculty members have earned bachelor's and master's degrees in their fields, Westwood looks for a combination of industry experience, educational training in the subject area, and prior teaching experience to ensure that students receive a balanced, industry-relevant education.

Financial Aid/Scholarships

Westwood College participates in a variety of financial aid programs, including the Federal Pell Grant, the FFEL Stafford Student Loan (subsidized and unsubsidized), PLUS Loans, the Federal Perkins Loan, the Federal Supplemental Educational Opportunity Grant (FSEOG), the Westwood High School Scholarship Program, and educational assistance loans. Other types of financial aid may be available depending on individual student eligibility. Students should check with the Admissions Office for VA-approved benefits.

Tuition and Fees

Students should consult the school catalog for detailed tuition and fee information.

Accreditation

Westwood is accredited by the Accrediting Council of Independent Colleges and Schools (ACICS). This accreditation guides the College, in that it has a clearly defined mission and aspires to high standards to ensure quality programs. Westwood has the human, physical, and financial resources to accomplish its mission.

Admissions

Successful candidates for Westwood are required to have a high school diploma or GED certificate. Applicants must complete an acceptance application and either receive a composite minimum score of 17 on the ACT or 920 on the SAT or achieve the required scores on the Accuplacer Computerized Placement Test. To enroll, candidates submit an application for admission, are interviewed by an admissions representative, submit a registration fee, and upon completion of testing, attend an acceptance interview to verify their commitment to begin training.

Program Description

The DuPage campus has grown into an instituiton offering Associate of Applied Science (A.A.S.) degrees in Computer Aided Design/Architectural Drafting, Computer Network Engineering, Graphic Design and Multimedia, and Software Engineering, as well as Bachelor of Applied Science (B.A.S.) degrees in Animation, Business Administration: Concentration in Accounting, Business Administration: Concentration in Marketing and Sales, Computer Network Management, Criminal Justice, E-Business Management, Game Art and Design, Game Software Development, Information Systems Security, Interior Design, Visual Communications, and Web Design and Multimedia.

Contact

Kelly Moore
Executive Director
Westwood College
7155 Janes Avenue
Woodridge, IL 60517
Phone: (630) 434-8244
Fax: (630) 434-8250
E-mail: kmoore@westwood.edu
Web: www.westwood.edu

Programs Eligible for Scholarship	Course Length/Credit Hours	Credential Earned
Animation	36 months/194 credit hours	BAS
Business Administration: Concentration in Accounting	36 months/189 credit hours	BAS
Business Administration: Concentration in Marketing and Sales	36 months/189 credit hours	BAS
Computer-Aided Design/Architectural Drafting	20 months/101 credit hours	AAS
Computer Network Engineering	20 months/114 credit hours	AAS
Computer Network Management	36 months/198 credit hours	BAS
Criminal Justice	36 months/188 credit hours	BAS
E-Business Management	36 months/189 credit hours	BAS
Game Art and Design	36 months/211 credit hours	BAS
Game Software Development	36 months/198 credit hours	BAS
Graphic Design and Multimedia	20 months/105 credit hours	AAS
Information Systems Security	36 months/204 credit hours	BAS
Interior Design	36 months/186.5 credit hours	BAS
Software Engineering	20 months/100.5 credit hours	AAS
Visual Communications	36 months/196 credit hours	BAS
Web Design and Multimedia	36 months/196 credit hours	BAS

Westwood College, River Oaks, Calumet City

About Our Institution
Westwood College, River Oaks, is committed to a positive and cooperative environment and working collaboratively with employers. The College is dedicated to high-quality, college-level, career-oriented education. Westwood's objective is to graduate confident, job-qualified individuals who are prepared to enter the career fields of their choice. The College is affiliated with other Westwood Colleges, the first of which was founded in Denver, Colorado, in 1953.

Special Features
Westwood College of Technology places a high value on the industry experience faculty members bring to the classroom. While many faculty members have earned bachelor's and master's degrees in their fields, Westwood looks for a combination of industry experience, educational training in the subject area, and prior teaching experience to ensure that students receive a balanced education and utilize state-of-the-art equipment.

Financial Aid/Scholarships
Westwood College participates in a variety of financial aid programs, including the Federal Pell Grant, the FFEL Stafford Student Loan (subsidized and unsubsidized), PLUS Loans, the Federal Perkins Loan, the Federal Supplemental Educational Opportunity Grant (FSEOG), the Westwood High School Scholarship Program, and educational assistance loans. Other types of financial aid may be available depending on individual student eligibility. Students should check with the Admissions Office for VA-approved benefits.

Tuition and Fees
Students should consult the school catalog for detailed tuition and fee information.

Accreditation
Westwood College is accredited by the Accrediting Council of Independent Colleges and Schools (ACICS). This accreditation means that the College has a clearly defined mission, aspires to high standards that ensure high-quality programs, and has the human, physical, and financial resources to accomplish its mission.

Admissions
Successful candidates for Westwood are required to have a high school diploma or GED certificate. Applicants must complete an acceptance application and either receive a minimum composite score of 17 on the ACT or 920 on the SAT or achieve the required scores on the Accuplacer Computerized Placement Test. To enroll, candidates complete an application for admission, are interviewed by an admissions representative, submit a registration fee, and upon completion of testing, attend an acceptance interview to verify their commitment to begin training.

Program Description
The River Oaks campus offers associate programs in Computer-Aided Design–Architectural Drafting, Computer Network Engineering, Graphic Design and Multimedia, and Software Engineering, as well as bachelor's programs in Animation, Business Administration: Concentration in Accounting, Business Administration: Concentration in Marketing and Sales, Computer Network Management, Criminal Justice, E-Business Management, Game Art and Design, Game Software Development, Information Systems Security, Interior Design, Visual Communications, and Web Design and Multimedia.

Contact
Bruce McKenzie, Executive Director
Westwood College
80 River Oaks Center, Suite D-49
Calumet City, IL 60409
Phone: (708) 832-1988
(888) 547-4960 (toll-free)
Fax: (708) 832-9617
E-mail: bmckenzie@westwood.edu
Web: www.westwood.edu

Programs Eligible for Scholarship	Course Length/Credit Hours	Credential Earned
Animation	36 months/194 credit hours	BAS
Business Administration: Concentration in Accounting	36 months/189 credit hours	BAS
Business Administration: Concentration in Marketing and Sales	36 months/189 credit hours	BAS
Computer-Aided Design/Architectural Drafting	20 months/101 credit hours	AAS
Computer Network Engineering	20 months/114 credit hours	AAS
Computer Network Management	36 months/198 credit hours	BAS
Criminal Justice	36 months/188 credit hours	BAS
E-Business Management	36 months/189 credit hours	BAS
Game Art and Design	36 months/211 credit hours	BAS
Game Software Development	36 months/198 credit hours	BAS
Graphic Design and Multimedia	20 months/105 credit hours	AAS
Information Systems Security	36 months/204 credit hours	BAS
Interior Design	36 months/186.5 credit hours	BAS
Software Engineering	20 months/100.5 credit hours	AAS
Visual Communications	36 months/196 credit hours	BAS
Web Design and Multimedia	36 months/196 credit hours	BAS

Indiana Business College, Anderson

About Our Institution

Indiana Business College (IBC) was founded in 1902. IBC is one of the largest business schools in the Midwest with ten campus locations in the state of Indiana. The main campus is in Indianapolis; a list of additional campuses follows.

Anderson	(765) 644-7514	Indy Medical	(317) 375-8000
Columbus	(812) 379-9000	Lafayette	(765) 447-9550
Evansville	(812) 476-6000	Marion	(765) 662-7497
Fort Wayne	(219) 471-7667	Muncie	(765) 288-8681
Indianapolis	(800) 999-9229	Terre Haute	(812) 232-4458

Special Features

More than 200 students attend the Anderson campus of Indiana Business College. The annual graduate/placement rate exceeds 90 percent statewide. Online classes and programs are available.

Financial Aid/Scholarships

Approximately 85 percent of IBC students qualify for federal grants and loans, state grants, College work-study, and scholarships.

Accreditation

Accredited by the Accrediting Council for Independent Colleges and Schools.

Regulated by the Indiana Commission on Proprietary Education.

Contact

Charlene Stacy, Executive Director
Indiana Business College
140 East 53rd Street
Anderson, IN 46013-1717
Phone: (765) 644-7514
Fax: (765) 644-5724
Web: www.ibcschools.edu

Program Content

Accounting, Accounting Assistant, Administrative Assistant, Business Administration, Health Claims Examiner, Medical Assistant, Medical Coding Specialist, Office Assistant, Organizational Management

Indiana Business College, Columbus

About Our Institution

Indiana Business College (IBC) was founded in 1902. IBC is one of the largest business schools in the Midwest, with ten campus locations in the state of Indiana. The main campus is in Indianapolis; a list of additional campuses follows.

Anderson	(765) 644-7514	Indy Medical	(317) 375-8000
Columbus	(812) 379-9000	Lafayette	(765) 447-9550
Evansville	(812) 476-6000	Marion	(765) 662-7497
Fort Wayne	(219) 471-7667	Muncie	(765) 288-8681
Indianapolis	(800) 999-9229	Terre Haute	(812) 232-4458

Special Features

More than 245 students attend the Columbus campus of Indiana Business College. The annual graduate/placement rate exceeds 90 percent statewide. Online classes and programs are available.

Financial Aid/Scholarships

Approximately 75 percent of IBC students qualify for federal grants and loans, state grants, College work-study, and scholarships.

Accreditation

Indiana Business College is accredited by the Accrediting Council for Independent Colleges and Schools.

The College is regulated by the Indiana Commission on Proprietary Education.

Contact

Angela Rentmeesters, Assistant Executive Director
Indiana Business College
2222 Poshard Drive
Columbus, IN 47203
Phone: (812) 379-9000
Fax: (812) 375-0414
Web: www.ibcschools.edu

Program Content

Accounting, Accounting Assistant, Administrative Assistant, Business Administration, Business and Information Technology, Computer Network Technician, Health Claims Examiner, Medical Assistant, Medical Coding Specialist, Office Assistant

Indiana Business College, Evansville

About Our Institution

Indiana Business College was founded in 1902. IBC is one of the largest business schools in the Midwest, with ten campus locations in the state of Indiana. The main campus is in Indianapolis; a list of additional campuses follows.

Anderson	(765) 644-7514	Indy Medical	(317) 375-8000
Columbus	(812) 379-9000	Lafayette	(765) 447-9550
Evansville	(812) 476-6000	Marion	(765) 662-7497
Fort Wayne	(219) 471-7667	Muncie	(765) 288-8681
Indianapolis	(800) 999-9229	Terre Haute	(812) 232-4458

Special Features

More than 230 students attend the Evansville campus of Indiana Business College. The annual graduate/placement rate exceeds 90 percent statewide. Online classes and programs are available.

Financial Aid/Scholarships

Approximately 85 percent of IBC students qualify for federal grants and loans, state grants, College work-study, and scholarships.

Accreditation

Indiana Business College is accredited by the Accrediting Council for Independent Colleges and Schools.

IBC's programs are also accredited by the Commission on Accreditation of Allied Health Education Programs (CAAHEP), on the recommendation of the committee on Accreditation for Medical Assistant Education, also known as the Curriculum Review Board of the American Association of Medical Assistant's Endowment (AAMAE).

The College is regulated by the Indiana Commission on Proprietary Education.

Contact

Steve Hardin, Executive Director
Indiana Business College
4601 Theater Drive
Evansville, IN 47715
Phone: (812) 476-6000
Fax: (812) 471-8576
Web: www.ibcschools.edu

Program Content

Accounting, Accounting Assistant, Administrative Assistant, Business Administration, Business and Information Technology, Computer Network Technician, Health Claims Examiner, Medical Assistant, Medical Coding Specialist, Medical Records Technology, Office Assistant

Indiana Business College, Fort Wayne

About Our Institution
Indiana Business College (IBC) was founded in 1902. IBC is one of the largest business schools in the Midwest, with ten campus locations in the state of Indiana. The main campus is in Indianapolis; a list of additional campuses follows.

Anderson	(765) 644-7514	Indy Medical	(317) 375-8000
Columbus	(812) 379-9000	Lafayette	(765) 447-9550
Evansville	(812) 476-6000	Marion	(765) 662-7497
Fort Wayne	(219) 471-7667	Muncie	(765) 288-8681
Indianapolis	(800) 999-9229	Terre Haute	(812) 232-4458

Special Features
More than 280 students attend the Fort Wayne campus of Indiana Business College. The annual graduate/placement rate exceeds 90 percent statewide. Online classes and programs are available.

Financial Aid/Scholarships
Approximately 85 percent of IBC students qualify for federal grants and loans, state grants, College work-study, and scholarships.

Accreditation
Indiana Business College is accredited by the Accrediting Council for Independent Colleges and Schools.

IBC's programs are also accredited by the Commission on Accreditation of Allied Health Education Programs (CAAHEP), on the recommendation of the committee on Accreditation for Medical Assistant Education, also known as the Curriculum Review Board of the American Association of Medical Assistant's Endowment (AAMAE).

The College is regulated by the Indiana Commission on Proprietary Education.

Contact
Janet Hein, Executive Director
Indiana Business College
6413 North Clinton Street
Fort Wayne, IN 46825
Phone: (219) 471-7667
Fax: (219) 471-6918
Web: www.ibcschools.edu

Program Content
Accounting, Accounting Assistant, Administrative Assistant, Business Administration, Health Claims Examiner, Medical Assistant, Medical Coding Specialist, Medical Office Assistant, Office Assistant, Surgical Technician

Indiana Business College, Indianapolis

About Our Institution

Indiana Business College (IBC) was founded in 1902. IBC is one of the largest business schools in the Midwest, with ten campus locations in the state of Indiana. The main campus is in Indianapolis; a list of additional campuses follows.

Anderson	(765) 644-7514	Indy Medical	(317) 375-8000
Columbus	(812) 379-9000	Lafayette	(765) 447-9550
Evansville	(812) 476-6000	Marion	(765) 662-7497
Fort Wayne	(219) 471-7667	Muncie	(765) 288-8681
Indianapolis	(800) 999-9229	Terre Haute	(812) 232-4458

Special Features

More than 620 students the Indianapolis campus of Indiana Business College. The annual graduate/placement rate exceeds 90 percent statewide. Online classes and programs are available.

Financial Aid/Scholarships

Approximately 85 percent of IBC students qualify for federal grants and loans, state grants, College work-study, and scholarships.

Accreditation

Indiana Business College is accredited by the Accrediting Council for Independent Colleges and Schools.

The College is regulated by the Indiana Commission on Proprietary Education.

Contact

Pat Mozley, Executive Director
Indiana Business College
550 East Washington Street
Indianapolis, IN 46204
Phone: (317) 264-5656
Fax: (317) 264-5650
Web: www.ibcschools.edu

Program Content

Accounting, Accounting Assistant, Administrative Assistant, Business Administration, Business Administration/Network Technology, Business and Information Technology, Cisco Network Associate, Computer Network Technician, Fashion Merchandising, Home Technology Integrator, Legal Administrative Assistant, Medical Transcription, Office Assistant, Organizational Management

Indiana Business College, Indy Medical, Indianapolis

About Our Institution
Indiana Business College (IBC) was founded in 1902. IBC is one of the largest business schools in the Midwest, with ten campus locations in the state of Indiana. The main campus is in Indianapolis; a list of additional campuses follows.

Anderson	(765) 644-7514	Indy Medical	(317) 375-8000
Columbus	(812) 379-9000	Lafayette	(765) 447-9550
Evansville	(812) 476-6000	Marion	(765) 662-7497
Fort Wayne	(219) 471-7667	Muncie	(765) 288-8681
Indianapolis	(800) 999-9229	Terre Haute	(812) 232-4458

Special Features
More than 550 students attend the Indianapolis medical campus of Indiana Business College. The annual graduate/placement rate exceeds 90 percent statewide. Online classes and programs are available.

Financial Aid/Scholarships
Approximately 85 percent of IBC students qualify for federal grants and loans, state grants, College work-study, and scholarships.

Accreditation
Indiana Business College by the Accrediting Council for Independent Colleges and Schools.

IBC's programs are also accredited by the Commission on Accreditation of Allied Health Education Programs (CAAHEP), on the recommendation of the committee on Accreditation for Medical Assistant Education, also known as the Curriculum Review Board of the American Association of Medical Assistant's Endowment (AAMAE).

The College is regulated by the Indiana Commission on Proprietary Education.

Contact
Rod Allee, Director of Admissions
Indiana Business College
8150 Brookville Road
Indianapolis, IN 46239
Phone: (317) 375-8000
Fax: (317) 351-1871
Web: www.ibcschools.edu

Program Content
Health Claims Examiner, Medical Coding Specialist, Medical Office Assistant, Medical Records Technology, Medical Assistant, Therapeutic Massage and Bodyworks, Therapeutic Massage Practitioner

Indiana Business College, Lafayette

About Our Institution

Indiana Business College (IBC) was founded in 1902. IBC is one of the largest business schools in the Midwest, with ten campus locations in the state of Indiana. The main campus is in Indianapolis; a list of additional campuses follows.

Anderson	(765) 644-7514	Indy Medical	(317) 783-5100
Columbus	(812) 379-9000	Lafayette	(765) 447-9550
Evansville	(812) 476-6000	Marion	(765) 662-7497
Fort Wayne	(219) 471-7667	Muncie	(765) 288-8681
Indianapolis	(800) 999-9229	Terre Haute	(812) 232-4458

Special Features

More than 170 students attend the Lafayette campus of Indiana Business College. The annual graduate/placement rate exceeds 90 percent. Online classes and programs are available.

Financial Aid/Scholarships

Approximately 85 percent of the students qualify for federal grants and loans, College work-study, and scholarships.

Accreditation

Indiana Business College is accredited by the Accrediting Council for Independent Colleges and Schools.

The College is regulated by the Indiana Commission on Proprietary Education.

Contact

Gregory P. Reger, Executive Director
Indiana Business College
2 Executive Drive
Lafayette, IN 47905-4859
Phone: (765) 447-9550
Fax: (765) 447-0868
Web: www.ibcschools.edu

Program Content

Accounting Assistant, Accounting, Administrative Assistant, Business Administration, Business and Information Technology, Computer Network Technician, Office Assistant

Indiana Business College, Marion

About Our Institution

Indiana Business College (IBC) was founded in 1902. IBC is one of the largest business schools in the Midwest, with ten campus locations in the state of Indiana. The main campus is in Indianapolis; a list of additional campuses follows.

Anderson	(765) 644-7514	Indy Medical	(317) 375-8000
Columbus	(812) 379-9000	Lafayette	(765) 447-9550
Evansville	(812) 476-6000	Marion	(765) 662-7497
Fort Wayne	(219) 471-7667	Muncie	(765) 288-8681
Indianapolis	(800) 999-9229	Terre Haute	(812) 232-4458

Special Features

More than 160 students attend the Marion campus of Indiana Business College. The annual graduate/placement rate exceeds 90 percent statewide. Online classes and programs are available.

Financial Aid/Scholarships

Approximately 85 percent of IBC students qualify for federal grants and loans, state grants, College work-study, and scholarships.

Accreditation

Indiana Business College is accredited by the Accrediting Council for Independent Colleges and Schools.

The College is regulated by the Indiana Commission on Proprietary Education.

Contact

Richard Herman, Executive Director
Indiana Business College
830 North Miller Avenue
Marion, IN 46952
Phone: (765) 662-7497
Fax: (765) 651-9421
Web: www.ibcschools.edu

Program Content

Accounting Assistant, Accounting, Administrative Assistant, Business Administration, Medical Assistant, Medical Coding Specialist, Medical Records Technology, Office Assistant

Indiana Business College, Muncie

About Our Institution
Indiana Business College (IBC) was founded in 1902. IBC is one of the largest business schools in the Midwest, with ten campus locations in the state of Indiana. The main campus is in Indianapolis; a list of additional campuses follows.

Anderson	(765) 644-7514	Indy Medical	(317) 375-8000
Columbus	(812) 379-9000	Lafayette	(765) 447-9550
Evansville	(812) 476-6000	Marion	(765) 662-7497
Fort Wayne	(219) 471-7667	Muncie	(765) 288-8681
Indianapolis	(800) 999-9229	Terre Haute	(812) 232-4458

Special Features
More than 280 students attend the Muncie campus of Indiana Business College. The annual graduate/placement rate exceeds 90 percent statewide. Online classes and programs are available.

Financial Aid/Scholarships
Approximately 85 percent of IBC students qualify for federal grants and loans, College work-study, and scholarships.

Accreditation
Indiana Business College is accredited as a business school by the Accrediting Council for Independent Colleges and Schools.

The College is regulated by the Indiana Commission on Proprietary Education.

Contact
Greg Bond, Executive Director
Indiana Business College
411 West Riggin Road
Muncie, IN 47303-6413
Phone: (765) 288-8681
Fax: (765) 288-8797
Web: www.ibcschools.edu

Program Content
Accounting Assistant, Accounting, Administrative Assistant, Business Administration, Business Administration/ Network Technology, Business and Information Technology, Computer Network Technician, Medical Assistant, Medical Coding Specialist, Medical Records Technology, Office Assistant, Organizational Management

Indiana Business College, Terre Haute

About Our Institution
Indiana Business College (IBC) was founded in 1902. IBC is one of the largest business schools in the Midwest, with ten campus locations in the state of Indiana. The main campus is in Indianapolis; a list of additional campuses follows.

Anderson	(765) 644-7514	Indy Medical	(317) 375-8000
Columbus	(812) 379-9000	Lafayette	(765) 447-9550
Evansville	(812) 476-6000	Marion	(765) 662-7497
Fort Wayne	(219) 471-7667	Muncie	(765) 288-8681
Indianapolis	(800) 999-9229	Terre Haute	(812) 232-4458

Special Features
More than 250 students attend the Terre Haute campus of Indiana Business College. The annual graduate/placement rate exceeds 90 percent statewide. Online classes and programs are available.

Financial Aid/Scholarships
Approximately 85 percent of IBC students qualify for federal grants and loans, state grants, College work-study, and scholarships.

Accreditation
Accredited by the Accrediting Council for Independent Colleges and Schools.

Commission on Accreditation of Allied Health Education Programs (CAAHEP) on the recommendation of the Committee on Accreditation for Medical Assistant Education, also known as the Curriculum Review Board of the American Association of Medical Assistant's Endowment (AAMAE).

Regulated by the Indiana Commission on Proprietary Education.

Contact
Laura Hale, Executive Director
Indiana Business College
3175 South Third Place
Terre Haute, IN 47802
Phone: (812) 232-4458
Fax: (812) 234-2361
Web: www.ibcschools.edu

Program Content
Accounting, Accounting Assistant, Administrative Assistant, Business Administration, Business Administration/ Network Technology, Health Claims Examiner, Medical Assistant, Medical Coding Specialist, Medical Records Technology, Office Assistant

ITT Technical Institute, Fort Wayne

About Our Institution
The company: ITT Technical Institute is owned and operated by ITT Educational Services, Inc. (ITT/ESI), a leading private college system offering technology-influenced programs of study. ITT/ESI operates seventy-seven ITT Technical Institutes in thirty states, providing career-focused degree programs to approximately 39,000 students as of spring 2004. Headquartered in Carmel, Indiana, ITT/ESI has been actively involved in the higher education community in the United States since 1969.

Curricula: Curriculum offerings are designed to help students begin to prepare for career opportunities in fields of technology. Students attend classes year-round, with convenient breaks provided throughout the year. A full-time student course load can have class meetings as often as three days a week and are typically available in the morning, afternoon, and evening, depending on student enrollment. General education courses may be available online. This class schedule offers flexibility to students to pursue part-time employment opportunities.

ITT Technical Institute, Ft. Wayne, awards the Associate of Applied Science, the Bachelor of Applied Science, and the Bachelor of Science degrees.

Special Features
Most ITT Technical Institute programs of study blend traditional academic content with applied learning concepts, with a significant portion devoted to practical study in a lab environment. Advisory committees composed of representatives of local businesses help each ITT Technical Institute periodically review and update curricula, equipment, and laboratory design.

Financial Aid/Scholarships
ITT Technical Institute maintains a Financial Aid Department on campus. The campus is designated as an eligible institution by the U.S. Department of Education for participation in the following programs: Federal Stafford Student Loan Program, Federal PLUS Loan Program, and Federal Work-Study Program. The school also offers nonfederal loans available through Bank One for eligible students.

Tuition and Fees
March 2005 tuition is $386 per credit hour.

Accreditation
The school is accredited by the Accrediting Council for Independent Colleges and Schools (ACICS).

Admissions
For admission requirements, students should contact the school for a catalog.

Graduation Requirements
For graduation requirements, students should contact the school for a catalog.

Program Content
School of Information Technology: Data Communication Systems Technology, Information Systems Security, Information Technology–Computer Network Systems, Information Technology–Software Applications and Programming, Information Technology–Web Development, Software Engineering Technology

School of Electronics Technology: Computer and Electronics Engineering Technology, Electronics and Communications Engineering Technology, Industrial Automation Engineering Technology

School of Drafting and Design: Computer Drafting and Design, Digital Entertainment and Game Design, Information Technology–Multimedia Option

School of Business: Business Accounting Technology, Business Administration, Technical Project Management

School of Criminal Justice: Criminal Justice

Contact
Alois Johnson, Director
ITT Technical Institute
4919 Coldwater Road
Ft. Wayne, IN 46825
Phone: (260) 484-4107
Fax: (260) 484-0860

ITT Technical Institute, Indianapolis

About Our Institution

The company: ITT Technical Institute is owned and operated by ITT Educational Services, Inc. (ITT/ESI), a leading private college system offering technology-influenced programs of study. ITT/ESI operates seventy-seven ITT Technical Institutes in thirty states, providing career-focused degree programs to approximately 39,000 students as of spring 2004. Headquartered in Carmel, Indiana, ITT/ESI has been actively involved in the higher education community in the United States since 1969.

Curricula: Curriculum offerings are designed to help students begin to prepare for career opportunities in fields of technology. Students attend classes year-round, with convenient breaks provided throughout the year. A full-time student course load can have class meetings as often as three days a week and are typically available in the morning, afternoon, and evening, depending on student enrollment. General education courses may be available online. This class schedule offers flexibility to students to pursue part-time employment opportunities.

ITT Technical Institute, Indianapolis, awards the Associate in Occupational Studies degree.

Special Features

Most ITT Technical Institute programs of study blend traditional academic content with applied learning concepts, with a significant portion devoted to practical study in a lab environment. Advisory committees composed of representatives of local businesses help each ITT Technical Institute periodically review and update curricula, equipment, and laboratory design.

Financial Aid/Scholarships

ITT Technical Institute maintains a Financial Aid Department on campus. The campus is designated as an eligible institution by the U.S. Department of Education for participation in the following programs: Federal Stafford Student Loan Program, Federal PLUS Loan Program, and Federal Work-Study Program. The school also offers nonfederal loans available through Bank One for eligible students.

Tuition and Fees

March 2005 tuition is $386 per credit hour.

Accreditation

The school is accredited by the Accrediting Council for Independent Colleges and Schools (ACICS).

Admissions

For admission requirements, students should contact the school for a catalog.

Graduation Requirements

For graduation requirements, students should contact the school for a catalog.

Program Content

School of Information Technology: Data Communication Systems Technology, Information Systems Security, Information Technology–Computer Network Systems, Information Technology–Software Applications and Programming, Information Technology–Web Development, Software Engineering Technology

School of Electronics Technology: Computer and Electronics Engineering Technology, Electronics and Communications Engineering Technology, Industrial Automation Engineering Technology

School of Drafting and Design: Computer Drafting and Design, Digital Entertainment and Game Design, Information Technology–Multimedia Option

School of Business: Business Accounting Technology, Business Administration, Technical Project Management

School of Criminal Justice: Criminal Justice

Contact

Jim Horner, Director
ITT Technical Institute
9511 Angola Court
Indianapolis, IN 46268
Phone: (317) 875-8640
Fax: (317) 875-8641

ITT Technical Institute, Newburgh

About Our Institution
The company: ITT Technical Institute is owned and operated by ITT Educational Services, Inc. (ITT/ESI), a leading private college system offering technology-influenced programs of study. ITT/ESI operates seventy-seven ITT Technical Institutes in thirty states, providing career-focused degree programs to approximately 39,000 students as of spring 2004. Headquartered in Carmel, Indiana, ITT/ESI has been actively involved in the higher education community in the United States since 1969.

Curricula: Curriculum offerings are designed to help students begin to prepare for career opportunities in fields of technology. Students attend classes year-round, with convenient breaks provided throughout the year. A full-time student course load can have class meetings as often as three days a week and are typically available in the morning, afternoon, and evening, depending on student enrollment. General education courses may be available online. This class schedule offers flexibility to students to pursue part-time employment opportunities.

ITT Technical Institute, Newburgh, offers the Associate in Occupational Studies degree.

Special Features
Most ITT Technical Institute programs of study blend traditional academic content with applied learning concepts, with a significant portion devoted to practical study in a lab environment. Advisory committees composed of representatives of local businesses help each ITT Technical Institute periodically review and update curricula, equipment, and laboratory design.

Financial Aid/Scholarships
ITT Technical Institute maintains a Financial Aid Department on campus. The campus is designated as an eligible institution by the U.S. Department of Education for participation in the following programs: Federal Stafford Student Loan Program, Federal PLUS Loan Program, and Federal Work-Study Program. The school also offers nonfederal loans available through Bank One for eligible students.

Tuition and Fees
March 2005 tuition is $386 per credit hour.

Accreditation
The school is accredited by the Accrediting Council for Independent Colleges and Schools (ACICS).

Admissions
For admission requirements, students should contact the school for a catalog.

Graduation Requirements
For graduation requirements, students should contact the school for a catalog.

Program Content

School of Information Technology: Data Communication Systems Technology, Information Systems Security, Information Technology–Computer Network Systems, Information Technology–Software Applications and Programming, Information Technology–Web Development, Software Engineering Technology

School of Electronics Technology: Computer and Electronics Engineering Technology, Electronics and Communications Engineering Technology, Industrial Automation Engineering Technology

School of Drafting and Design: Computer Drafting and Design, Digital Entertainment and Game Design, Information Technology–Multimedia Option

School of Business: Technical Project Management

Contact
Ken Butler, Director
ITT Technical Institute
10999 Stahl Road
Newburgh, IN 47630
Phone: (812) 858-1600
Fax: (812) 858-0646

Lincoln Technical Institute, Indianapolis

About Our Institution

Lincoln Tech's Indianapolis campus consists of a 60,000-square-foot facility with dozens of classrooms, labs, and shops to accommodate the programs in automotive technology, diesel, and drafting. Because of its resources, this comprehensive facility is the destination for students from as far as Kentucky and Ohio. Approximately 85 percent of the students take advantage of the housing referral program, which helps to provide clean and comfortable housing for relocating students. The campus is just 10 minutes from the Indianapolis Motor Speedway, which is the home of the famous Indianapolis 500 and Brickyard 400 races. The Institute's prime location enables students to be part of the action. Lincoln Tech also offers exciting opportunities in various internship programs.

Special Features

Lincoln Technical Institute has working relationships with Indianapolis Raceway Park. Students have the opportunity to tour the facilities and, in some cases, participate as technical support for some of the NHRA events.

Financial Aid/Scholarships

The Indianapolis campus has a variety of half and full tuition scholarships available to graduating high school students. Lincoln Tech participates in the Imagine America Scholarship, as well as others. To apply for most scholarships, students must fill out an application and take an aptitude-based scholarship test. A Scholarship Committee, made up of volunteers representing business, industry, education, and/or government, interviews finalists and makes the award decision. Lincoln Tech maintains a Financial Aid Office on campus, which offers a variety of grants, loans, work-study, veterans' aid, and vocational rehabilitation programs to qualified students.

Accreditation

Lincoln Technical Institute is accredited by the Accrediting Commission of Career Schools and Colleges of Technology (ACCSCT) and certified by NATEF.

Admissions

Students must have either a high school diploma or GED certificate and pass an entrance exam.

Graduation Requirements

In order to graduate, students must successfully complete all courses in the program and all required comprehensive exams. In addition, students must maintain a minimum overall GPA of 2.0.

Contact

Executive Director
Lincoln Technical Institute
1201 Stadium Drive
Indianapolis, IN 46202
Phone: (317) 632-5553
Fax: (317) 687-0475
E-mail: execdirindy@lincolntech.com
Web: www.lincolntech.com

Program Content

Associate Degree Programs: Automotive Service Management, Diesel and Truck Service Management, Architectural Drafting Design and CAD Technology, Mechanical Drafting Design and CAD Technology

Diploma Programs: Automotive, Diesel, and Truck Technology; Automotive Technology; Collision Repair and Refininshing; Diesel and Truck Technology; Electronic Systems Technician

Program Description

The Automotive and the Diesel Truck Service Management programs offer training that enables graduates to seek employment in the wide variety of management, technical, and administrative positions available in the automotive or diesel truck parts and service industry. The Architectural and Mechanical Drafting, Design, and Computer-Aided Drafting programs provide students with the knowledge and skills to perform as entry-level draftspersons.

Olympia College, Merrillville

About Our Institution

Olympia College is one of more than eighty schools owned and operated by Corinthian Colleges, Inc. (CCi). Olympia College, Merrillville opened its doors in February 2001. Olympia College's philosophy is to provide quality programs that are sound in concept and implemented by a competent and dedicated faculty. The programs emphasize hands-on training, are relevant to employer's needs, and focus on areas that offer strong, long-term employment opportunities.

Special Features

Olympia College has plenty of free parking, is handicapped-accessible, and is located near public transportation. Olympia College is spacious (15,381 square feet) and offers air-conditioning, administrative offices, lecture rooms, medical and computer labs, and a student lounge. Class enrollment is limited and many classes have small sizes. There is also free tutoring available. All courses have hands-on training as well as classroom instruction.

Financial Aid/Scholarships

Federal Pell Grants, FFEL, work-study, FSEOG, VA, WIA, and funding through other agencies are available to those who qualify.

Accreditation

Olympia College is accredited by the Accrediting Committee of the Accrediting Bureau of Health Education Schools (ABHES). The Surgical Technologist program is AAMA accredited, a division of CAAHEP. The Practical Nurse program is accredited by the Indiana State Board of Nursing.

Admissions

Applicants must be high school graduates or the equivalent (GED). All applicants must complete a qualification questionnaire and take a standardized exam. Student health forms are required before participation in clinical labs. Some programs require additional prerequisites.

Graduation Requirements

To be eligible for graduation, students must complete all required courses with a grade of C or above and a cumulative grade point average (GPA) of 2.0 or above and complete an approved externship with a grade of C or above.

Enrollment

There are 435 students enrolled.

Program Content

Massage Therapy, Medical Administrative Assistant, Medical Assistant, Practical Nurse, Surgical Technologist

Contact

Sandy Kaup, Director of Admissions
Olympia College
707 East 80th Place, Suite 200
Merrillville, IN 46410
Phone: (219) 756-6811
E-mail: skaup@cci.edu
Web: www.olympia-college.com

Programs Eligible for Scholarship	Tuition and Fees	Course Length/Credit Hours	Credential Earned
Massage Therapy	$ 9,257	57 semester credits	Diploma
Medical Administrative Assistant	$ 9,257	47 semester credits	Diploma
Medical Assistant	$ 9,257	47 semester credits	Diploma
Practical Nurse	$19,845	85.5 semester credits	Diploma
Surgical Technologist	$15,750	86 semester credits	Diploma

Professional Careers Institute, Indianapolis

About Our Institution
Professional Careers Institute (PCI) was founded in 1967. PCI's size enables close student contact with the faculty and staff. The institution maintains up-to-date equipment utilized by employers in the field. PCI received a School of Distinction award in 2003 from the Accrediting Commission of Career Schools and Colleges of Technology (ACCSCT).

PCI is dedicated to assisting students in acquiring marketable skills for the workplace of today and the future. Programs include theory and practical hands-on application to help students develop newly acquired skills and gain confidence in their new abilities.

Special Features
All programs require an externship, clinical rotation, and/or fieldwork experience that consists of unpaid work experience in a medical practice, dental practice, business, government office, or other appropriate work location. Students are eligible for graduation and employment assistance only after successful completion of the required number of hours. Employment assistance is available to all Professional Career Institute graduates without charge. Part of every student's education involves job-search training, orientation to the job market, resume writing, and interview techniques.

Financial Aid/Scholarships
PCI participates in the following grant programs: Federal Pell, FSEOG, Twenty-First Century Scholarships, and the Indiana Higher Education Grant Program. PCI participates in the following loan programs: Subsidized/Unsubsidized Stafford, Federal PLUS, and alternative loans.

Tuition and Fees
Students should refer to the current catalog supplement.

Accreditation
Professional Careers Institute is regulated by the Indiana Commission on Proprietary Education (ICOPE) and accredited by the Accrediting Commission of Career Schools and Colleges of Technology (ACCSCT). The medical assisting program is accredited by the Commission on Accreditation of Allied Health Education Programs (CAAHEP) on the recommendation of the Curriculum Review Board of the American Association of Medical Assistants Endowment (AAMAE). PCI is accredited in dental assisting by the American Dental Association Commission on Accreditation of Dental and Dental Auxiliary Educational Programs.

Program Content
Computer Office Administration, Computer Programming, Dental Assisting, Dental Assisting/Administration, Massage Therapy, Massage Therapy/Medical Assisting, Medical Assisting, Medical Assisting/Administration, Medical/Dental Office Administration, Office Administration, Paralegal/Legal Assisting

Admissions
Graduates of accredited high schools or academies or individuals who have passed the General Educational Development (GED) test are considered for enrollment. Each program has specific requirements (detailed in the school catalog), including some or all of the following: personal interview, keyboarding test, entrance test, and health exam. Families are encouraged to visit so that they can see the equipment and facilities and ask questions about the curriculum and possible career opportunities.

Contact
Paulette Clay
Admissions Director
Professional Careers Institute
7302 Woodland Drive
Indianapolis, IN 46278
Phone: (317) 299-6001
Fax: (317) 298-6342
E-mail: paulette.clay@pcicareers.com
Web: www.pcicareers.com

Programs Eligible for Scholarship	Tuition and Fees	Course Length/Credit Hours	Credential Earned
Computer Office Administration	refer to school catalog	31 credit hours	Diploma
Computer Programming		65 credit hours	AAS
Dental Assisting		43 credit hours	Diploma
Dental Assisting/Administration		71 credit hours	AAS
Massage Therapy		38 credit hours	Diploma
Massage Therapy/Medical Assisting		68 credit hours	AAS
Medical Assisting		31 credit hours	Diploma
Medical Assisting/Administration		65 credit hours	AAS
Medical/Dental Office Administration		28 credit hours	Diploma
Office Administration		65 credit hours	AAS
Paralegal/Legal Assisting		70 credit hours	AA

Vatterott College, Des Moines

About Our Institution
All Vatterott College programs are based on a proven successful formula of specialized, technology-focused, hands-on training in the fastest-growing industries. The College was founded in 1969 and now serves nearly 9,000 students per year at sixteen Midwestern campuses. The Des Moines campus offers programs focused on the information technology industry.

Special Features
Vatterott College's hands-on training method of instruction equips students with the specific skills that are desired by local employers. Courses are geared to the student's field of study. Classes are available in both morning and evening schedules.

Financial Aid/Scholarships
Vatterott College participates in a variety of financial aid and scholarship programs. The College's Make-the-Grade scholarship offers tuition credit to qualifying students based on high school grades. Vatterott College also participates in the Imagine America scholarship program. High school seniors are eligible to apply. Students should contact the campus Financial Aid Representative for specific information.

Tuition and Fees
The campus Admissions Representatives can provide complete tuition information.

Accreditation
Vatterott College is nationally accredited by the Accrediting Commission of Career Schools and Colleges of Technology.

Admission
The application process includes a personal interview and entrance evaluation. A high school diploma or GED is required.

Graduation Requirements
Students must show satisfactory progress by maintaining a minimum grade of 70% and an 80% attendance record.

Contact
Office of Admissions
Vatterott College
6100 Thornton Avenue, Suite 290
Des Moines, IA 50321
Phone: (515) 309-9000
Fax: (515) 309-0366
E-mail: desmoines@vatterott-college.edu
Web: www.vatterott-college.edu

Program Content
Associate of Occupational Studies (AOS) Degree: Computer Systems and Network Technology, Computer Programming and Network Management, Computer-Aided Drafting Technology

Diploma: Computer Technology, Computer Programming and System Analysis, Computer-Aided Drafting, Medical Office Assistant

Pinnacle Career Institute, Lawrence

About Our Institution
Pinnacle Career Institute's (PCI) mission is to provide training and education that lead to direct entry-level employment. PCI believes that classes should be small, with the majority of time spent with a hands-on approach. The staff and faculty members at PCI are dedicated to assisting students in achieving their educational goals. PCI programs cover diverse professions and offer multiple opportunities for new careers.

Special Features
PCI is located in the heart of Lawrence, Kansas, with easy accessibility from K-10, and it is on the main bus route. The facility, which underwent a major renovation that was completed in January 2004, is housed in an 18,500-square foot space that includes lecture rooms; medical, computer, massage, and business labs; a student lounge; resource center; and administrative areas.

Financial Aid/Scholarships
Federal Stafford Loans and PLUS Loans, Federal Supplemental Educational Opportunity Grants (FSEOG) and Pell Grants, and high school and other scholarships are available for those students who qualify.

Tuition and Fees
Information regarding the tuition costs and fees for each of PCI's programs is available from the Institute.

Accreditation
PCI is accredited by the Accrediting Council for Independent Colleges and Schools (ACICS), which is based in Washington, D.C.

Admissions
Candidates for enrollment must have a high school diploma or its equivalent. The successful completion of an assessment examination is a prerequisite for admission. The admissions representatives at PCI are very helpful, and individuals seeking more information on the admissions process should contact one of them directly at the toll-free number listed below.

Graduation Requirements
In addition to earning a cumulative grade point average of 2.0 or above, students must meet all program requirements to be eligible for graduation.

Program Content
Certificate Programs: Business Office Assistant, Massage Therapy, Medical Assisting, Medical Office Assistant

Contact
Karen Stewart
Pinnacle Career Institute
1600 West 23rd Street, Suite 200
Lawrence, KS 66046
Phone: 800-360-9640 (toll-free)
Fax: 785-841-4854
E-mail: kstewart@pcitraining.com
Web: www.pcitraining.edu

Programs Eligible for Scholarship	Tuition and Fees	Course Length/Credit Hours	Credential Earned
Business Office Assistant	$10,195	36 weeks	Certificate
Massage Therapy	$ 9,895	36 weeks	Certificate
Medical Assisting	$11,295	44 weeks	Certificate
Medical Office Assistant	$10,195	36 weeks	Certificate

Vatterott College, Wichita

About Our Institution
All Vatterott College programs are based on a proven successful formula of specialized, technology-focused, hands-on training in the fastest-growing industries. The College was founded in 1969 and now serves nearly 9,000 students per year at sixteen midwestern campuses. The Wichita campus offers programs focused on the information technology and technical trade industries.

Special Features
Vatterott College's hands-on training method of instruction equips students with the specific skills that are desired by local employers. Courses are geared to the student's field of study. Classes are available in morning, afternoon, and evening schedules.

Financial Aid/Scholarships
Vatterott College participates in a variety of financial aid and scholarship programs. The College's Make-the-Grade Scholarship offers tuition credit to qualifying students based on high school grades. Vatterott College also participates in the Imagine America Scholarship program. High school seniors are eligible to apply. Students should contact the campus Financial Aid Representative for specific information.

Tuition and Fees
The campus Admissions Representatives can provide complete tuition information.

Accreditation
Vatterott College is nationally accredited by the Accrediting Commission of Career Schools and Colleges of Technology.

Admissions
The application process includes a personal interview and entrance evaluation. A high school diploma or GED is required.

Graduation Requirements
Students must show satisfactory progress by maintaining a minimum grade of 70 percent and an 80 percent attendance record.

Contact
Office of Admissions
Vatterott College
3639 North Comotora
Wichita, KS 67226
Phone: (316) 634-0066
Fax: (316) 634-0002
E-mail: wichita@vatterott-college.edu
Web: www.vatterott-college.edu
(branch of main campus in St. Ann, MO)

Program Content
Diploma Programs: Computer-Aided Drafting; Computer Programming; Computer Technology; Heating, Air-Conditioning and Refrigeration Mechanic; Medical Office Assistant

Daymar College, Louisville

About Our Institution
Daymar College, a private accredited institution, was founded in 1963 to provide students with a strong business background and the practical skills needed to succeed in today's business world. Graduates are prepared for entry-level positions in the computer, medical, or paralegal fields. In 2001, Daymar College opened its branch in Louisville, Kentucky. The College is a Microsoft IT Academy.

Special Features
Daymar College offers its students small, intimate classroom settings along with faculty and staff members who assist students in achieving their maximum potential. The College provides academic classrooms, computer labs, a learning resource center, a bookstore, and a student lounge. Daymar's computer labs are equipped with computer hardware and software necessary for hands-on instruction. State-of-the-art equipment is provided for all students. Job placement assistance is available to current and graduating students as well as alumni.

Financial Aid/Scholarships
Pell, FFEL, FDSLP, work-study, FSEOG, Veterans Administration (VA) benefits, state vocational rehabilitation, state grants, and scholarships are available for those who qualify.

Tuition and Fees
Prospective students should contact the Admissions Department listed in the Contact section for information on tuition and fees.

Accreditation
Daymar College is accredited by the Accrediting Council for Independent Colleges and Schools. The College is also a member of the Career College Association and the Kentucky Association of Career Colleges and Schools.

Admissions
Successful candidates are admitted based on a personal interview and assessment evaluation.

Graduation Requirements
Diploma programs require completion of 56 to 64 credit hours and associate degree programs, 96 to 104 credit hours.

Contact
Patrick J. Carney, Director of Admissions
4400 Breckenridge Lane, Suite 415
Louisville, KY 40218
Phone: (502) 495-1040
        (866) 250-2343 (toll-free)
Fax: (502) 495-1518
Web: www.daymarcollege.edu

Program Content
Business Administration Technology, Computer Network Administration, Computer Repair Technology, Medical Office Technology, Medical Records Technology, Medical Transcription, Paralegal Studies

Program Description
Diploma programs are 55 weeks and associate degree programs 88 weeks in length.

Programs Eligible for Scholarship	Tuition and Fees	Course Length/Credit Hours	Credential Earned
All programs	Contact Admissions Department	55 weeks/56–64 credit hours 88 weeks/96–104 credit hours	Diploma Associate

Daymar College, Owensboro

About Our Institution

Daymar College, a private accredited institution, was founded in 1963 to provide students with a strong business background and the practical skills needed to succeed in today's business world. Graduates are prepared for entry-level positions in the business, computer, medical, or paralegal fields. The College's two newest programs are E-Commerce Engineer and Microsoft Support Engineer, allowing students to gain access to the rapidly expanding IT market. The College's brand-new facility includes modern computer labs, lecture rooms, and a licensed child-care center. The College is a Microsoft IT Academy, offers Microsoft Office Specialist testing, is a Prometric Testing Site, and proctors the National Center for Competency Testing (NCCT) in medical office assistant and insurance and coding specialist studies.

Special Features

Daymar College offers its students small, intimate classroom settings along with faculty and staff members who assist students in achieving their maximum potential. A licensed child-care center is located on-site. Every student completes an internship, and job placement is available.

In 2002, Daymar College opened a temporary learning site in Morgantown, Kentucky, to serve traditional students as well as displaced workers in a nearby small community.

In 2003, Daymar College opened a learning site in Albany, Kentucky, to serve traditional students as well as displaced workers in nearby small communities.

Financial Aid/Scholarships

Pell, FFEL, FDSLP, work-study, FSEOG, state grants, and scholarships are available for those who qualify.

Tuition and Fees

Prospective students should contact the Admissions Department listed in the Contact section for information on tuition and fees.

Accreditation

Daymar College is accredited by the Accrediting Council for Independent Colleges and Schools. The College is also a member of the Career College Association and the Kentucky Association of Career Colleges and Schools.

Admissions

Successful candidates are admitted based on a personal interview and assessment evaluation.

Graduation Requirements

Certificate programs require completion of 44 to 52 credit hours; diploma programs, 72 credit hours; and associate degree programs, 96 to 104 credit hours.

Program Content

Business Office Management, Computer Office Professional, E-Commerce Engineer, Medical Office Assistant, Microsoft Support Engineer, Paralegal Studies

Program Description

Certificate programs are 52 weeks in length; diploma programs, 78 weeks; and associate degree programs, 104 weeks.

Contact

Vickie McDougal, Director of Admissions
3361 Buckland Square
Owensboro, KY 42301
Phone: (270) 926-4040
        (800) 960-4090 (toll-free)
Fax: (270) 685-4090
Web: www.daymarcollege.edu

Programs Eligible for Scholarship	Tuition and Fees	Course Length/Credit Hours	Credential Earned
All programs	Contact Admissions Department	52 weeks/44–52 credit hours 78 weeks/72 credit hours 104 weeks/96–104 credit hours	Certificate Diploma Associate

Draughons Junior College, Bowling Green

About Our Institution
Draughons Junior College located in Bowling Green, Kentucky, is a branch campus of Draughons Junior College located in Nashville, Tennessee. The Nashville Draughons location has been accredited as a junior college of business by the Accrediting Commission of the Association of Independent Colleges and Schools, now ACICS, since 1978. Classes began being offered at the Bowling Green location on 2424 Airway Drive in 1988. Due to increased growth, the College moved in September 2003 to a new location at 2421 Fitzgerald Industrial Drive. The College's conveniently located new facility includes modern computer labs and lecture rooms.

Even though the College is officially a branch campus, the Bowling Green location operates as an independent college and takes pride and ownership in the school and community. The mission of the school is to "change lives—one person at a time." Operating under the direct definition of teamwork, the faculty and staff members of the Bowling Green campus care about the students and each other. This teamwork atmosphere has helped the College to develop a positive reputation in the community, which in turn, helps their graduates have better success in the local job market.

Special Features
Draughons Junior College offers its students small, interactive classroom settings along with faculty and staff members who assist students in achieving their maximum potential. The Vision Statement of the college is "Our vision is to provide a warm, friendly, nurturing atmosphere where students can learn the skills required, to obtain the jobs they need, to have the lives they want".

Draughons Junior College strives to provide each student with the knowledge and specialized skills they need to succeed in the job market. The College teaches these skills in a nonthreatening environment, while promoting their self-esteem, confidence level, and personal and professional development. By hiring instructors and staff members who not only have the knowledge, credentials, and experience to instruct the students, but also have an "intelligent heart", the College realizes its vision and main objective. Career Placement assistance is available to current and graduating students as well as alumni.

Financial Aid/Scholarships
The College offers Federal Pell Grants, FSEOG, state grants, FFEL, work-study, VA, SEOG, other financial aid opportunities.

Tuition and Fees
Prospective students should contact the Admissions Department for information on tuition and fees.

Accreditation
Draughons Junior College is accredited as a junior college by the Accrediting Council for Independent Colleges and Schools (ACICS). In addition, the campus in Bowling Green is authorized and regulated by the Kentucky State Board for Proprietary Education and the Kentucky Approving Agency for Veterans' Education.

Admissions
Regular applicants must have a high school diploma or GED. Students must take an assessment test, with the exception of those who have a composite score of 18 on the ACT or who have transfer credits in English or math. International students should contact the Director of Admissions for admission procedures and application forms.

Graduation Requirements
Each student is responsible for meeting the requirements of the curriculum, as outlined in the catalog, at the time of the first registration in that program.

Program Content
Diploma: Billing and Coding Specialist, Bookkeeping, Computer Information Technology, E-Commerce Engineer, Medical Assisting, Medical Transcription Specialist, Microsoft Support Engineer

Associate of Science Degree: Accounting, Billing and Coding Specialist, Business Management, Computer Information Technology, Criminal Justice, E-Commerce Engineer, Legal Assisting, Medical Assisting, Microsoft Support Engineer, Pharmacy Technology

Program Description
The degree program is divided into two independent, yet interrelated, components. The general education requirements provide the basis for a well-rounded education. The program requirements for both a degree and diploma provide skills and knowledge in the specialized area of interest. An exceptional staff of instructors works closely with each student for personal attention. Students have the opportunity for hands-on training, an internship, and job placement assistance. Draughons offers a degree in only two years or a diploma in one year.

Contact
Amye Melton
Director of Admissions
2421 Fitzgerald Industrial Drive
Bowling Green, KY 42101
Phone: (270) 843-6750
(800) 541-0296 (toll-free)
Fax: (270) 843-6976
E-mail: amelton@draughons.edu
Web: www.draughons.edu

ITT Technical Institute, Louisville

About Our Institution

ITT Technical Institute is owned and operated by ITT Educational Services, Inc. (ITT/ESI), a leading private college system offering technology-influenced programs of study. ITT/ESI operates seventy-seven ITT Technical Institutes in thirty states, providing career-focused degree programs to approximately 39,000 students as of spring 2004. Headquartered in Carmel, Indiana, ITT/ESI has been actively involved in the higher education community in the United States since 1969.

ITT Technical Institute, Louisville features programs of study leading to the Associate of Applied Science and Bachelor of Science degrees. Curriculum offerings are designed to prepare students for career opportunities in fields of technology. Students attend classes year-round, with convenient breaks provided throughout the year. A full-time student course load can have class meetings as often as three days a week, and classes are typically available in the morning, afternoon, and evening, depending on student enrollment. This class schedule offers students the flexibility to pursue part-time employment opportunities. General education courses may be available online.

Special Features

Most ITT Technical Institute programs of study blend traditional academic content with applied learning concepts, with a significant portion devoted to practical study in a lab environment. Advisory committees, made up of representatives of local businesses, help each ITT Technical Institute periodically review and update curricula, equipment, and laboratory design.

Financial Aid/Scholarships

ITT Technical Institute maintains a Financial Aid Department on the campus. The campus is designated as an eligible institution by the U.S. Department of Education for participation in the following programs: Federal Stafford Student Loan Program, Federal PLUS Loan Program, and Federal Work-Study Program. The school also offers nonfederal loans through Bank One for eligible students.

Tuition and Fees

March 2005 tuition is $386 per credit hour.

Accreditation

The Institute is accredited by the Accrediting Council for Independent Colleges and Schools (ACICS).

Admissions

For admission requirements, students should contact the school for a catalog.

Graduation Requirements

For graduation requirements, students should consult the school catalog.

Contact

Alan Crews, Director
ITT Technical Institute
10509 Timberwood Circle
Louisville, KY 40223
Phone: (502) 327-7424
Fax: (502) 327-7624

Program Content

School of Information Technology: Information Systems Security, Data Communication Systems Technology, Software Engineering Technology, Information Technology–Computer Network Systems, Information Technology–Software Applications and Programming, Information Technology–Web Development

School of Electronics Technology: Electronics and Communications Engineering Technology, Computer and Electronics Engineering Technology

School of Drafting and Design: Digital Entertainment and Game Design, Computer Drafting and Design, Information Technology–Multimedia

School of Business: Business Administration, Business Accounting Technology, Technical Project Management

School of Criminal Justice: Criminal Justice

Louisville Technical Institute, Louisville

About Our Institution
Louisville Technical Institute is a private technical college offering associate degrees, certificates, and diplomas. Louisville Tech offers career programs in architectural and mechanical CADD, computer engineering technology, mechanical engineering technology (robotics), computer network administration, information systems security, computer graphic design, interior design, and marine mechanics.

Louisville Tech has a history of more than forty years in the Louisville area and has earned a reputation as one of the area's leading technical training centers. Louisville Tech is located near the heart of the city and is close to the airport, shopping malls, and entertainment attractions.

Special Features
Students attending Louisville Tech find many unique features. Small classes and individual attention are key to much of Louisville Tech's success. Its four-day school week allows students time for lecture and lab, with Friday set aside as the PLUS day. Fridays allow students the opportunity to meet one-on-one with their instructors for individual tutoring.

Louisville Tech's Graduate Employment Services Department assists students in finding a job in their chosen career field. This service is available to all graduates and is a lifetime and nationwide program.

Louisville Tech offers its students modern computer labs and utilizes some of the latest computer software. Students have access to a campus library, the Internet, and a campus bookstore.

Financial Aid/Scholarships
Louisville Tech offers a variety of tuition assistance programs, including federal and state grant and student loan programs, VA, and several campus-based scholarship programs.

Tuition and Fees
Tuition and fees vary by program of study and range from $250 to $290 per credit hour. This rate does not include other charges and fees, such as application fees, computer lab fees, student housing, and books.

Accreditation
Louisville Tech is accredited by the Accrediting Council for Independent Colleges and Schools (ACICS).

Program Content
The programs at Louisville Tech are designed for students who are seeking short-term, career education in a growing technical field. The "Career First" curriculum allows students the opportunity to take career-related classes immediately upon entry into school while taking only a small number of required general education courses throughout their program. Louisville Tech classes are focused on getting the graduate into a career job with a secure future.

Graduation Requirements
In order to graduate, a student must have earned at least a 2.0 cumulative grade point average, earned the minimum credit hours required by the program of study, and satisfied all financial obligations to the college.

Contact
David Ritz, Director of Admissions
3901 Atkinson Square Drive
Louisville, KY 40218
Phone: (502) 456-6509
        (800) 844-6528 (toll-free)
Fax: (502) 456-2341
E-mail: dritz@louisvilletech.com
Web: www.louisvilletech.com

Programs Eligible for Scholarship	Tuition and Fees	Course Length/Credit Hours	Credential Earned
Architectural CADD	$260/credit hour	102 credit hours	AS
Computer Engineering Technology	$260/credit hour	103 credit hours	AS
Computer Graphic Design	$300/credit hour	100 credit hours	AS
Computer Network Administration	$300/credit hour	104 credit hours	AOS
Drafting	$260/credit hour	51 credit hours	Certificate
Information Systems Security	$300/credit hour	108 credit hours	AS
Interior Design	$260/credit hour	54 credit hours	Diploma
Interior Design	$260/credit hour	106 credit hours	AS
Marine Mechanics Technology	$2,080/module	36 credit hours	Certificate
Mechanical CADD	$260/credit hour	102 credit hours	AS
Mechanical Engineering Technology	$260/credit hour	102 credit hours	AS

National College of Business and Technology, Danville

About Our Institution

National College of Business and Technology was established in 1886. The Danville campus, which is located in the Bluegrass region of Central Kentucky, opened in 1975. National College of Business and Technology's curriculum is specific and concentrates on essential professional skills that lead toward employment in a specific field. Programs are planned to offer the most effective methods in technology, business organization, and management, while consistently meeting the demands of the modern world. The College offers courses that cover a broad range of majors, including accounting, business management, medical assisting, and office technology as well as other fields. Students can complete programs in as little as one year or less.

Special Features

A major strength of National College of Business and Technology is its ability to quickly adjust the curriculum to changes in the employment needs of business and industry and to meet the career interest of students. Community representatives, serving as a Campus Advisory Board, provide current and timely advice relative to the employment needs of business, technical, and government organizations.

The Career Center is available to assist with the entire job-search process. Specialized staff members are available to help students prepare a resume and cover letter and interview effectively. They assist the student throughout the employment search.

Students who wish to demonstrate their current skill level in selected areas may take an Advanced Placement evaluation. If successful, the student receives credit for that particular course and may shorten his or her program accordingly.

Scholarships are available not only to students who performed well during their secondary education but also to current students who excel while pursuing their particular program of study.

Financial Aid/Scholarships

National College of Business and Technology makes available an extensive program of financial assistance, which includes Federal Stafford Loans, Federal Plus Loans, Federal Perkins Loans, the Federal Pell Grant, the Federal Supplemental Educational Opportunity Grant, the Workforce Development Grant, and the Business Partnership Grant, as well as several scholarship opportunities.

Tuition and Fees

Tuition is $162 per credit hour. National College of Business and Technology is among the least expensive private colleges in its area. Students should check the catalog for current application, student activities, or graduation fees.

Accreditation

National College of Business and Technology is accredited by the Accrediting Council for Independent Colleges and Schools (ACICS);

Program Content

Accounting, Business Management, Computer Applications Technology, Medical Assisting, Office Administration

Program Description

All programs listed above lead to an Associate of Science degree.

The programs offered at National College of Business and Technology give the graduate the training that is needed to take the first step into an entry position as well as the background necessary to grow professionally in that field.

individual programs such as Medical Assisting may have programmatic accreditation.

Admission

A prospective student must have a high school diploma or GED certificate and submit an application for admission together with the application fee.

Graduation Requirements

In order to be eligible for graduation, the student must complete all courses outlined in the program and earn the required number of credit hours. To graduate from any program, a minimum 2.0 overall grade point average must be achieved.

Contact

Admissions Department
National College of Business and
  Technology
115 East Lexington Avenue
Danville, KY 40422
Phone: (859) 236-6991
Fax: (859) 236-1063

Programs Eligible for Scholarship	Tuition and Fees	Course Length/Credit Hours	Credential Earned
All related program areas	$15,552	96 credit hours	AS

National College of Business and Technology, Florence

About Our Institution

National College of Business and Technology was established in 1886. The Florence campus, which serves the surrounding community, is located just minutes from downtown Cincinnati, Ohio. National College of Business and Technology's curriculum is specific and concentrates on essential professional skills that lead toward employment in a specific field. Programs are planned to offer the most effective methods in technology, business organization, and management while consistently meeting the demands of the modern world. The College offers courses that cover a broad range of majors, including accounting, business management, medical assisting, executive and legal secretarial, and computer applications as well as other fields. Students can complete programs in as little as one year or less.

Special Features

A major strength of National College of Business and Technology is its ability to quickly adjust the curriculum to changes in the employment needs of business and industry and to meet the career interest of students. Community representatives, serving as a Campus Advisory Board, provide current and timely advice relative to the employment needs of business, technical, and government organizations.

The Career Center is available to assist with the entire job search process. Specialized staff members are available to help students to prepare a resume and cover letter and interview effectively. They assist the student throughout the employment search.

Students who wish to demonstrate their current skill level in selected areas may take an Advanced Placement evaluation. If successful, the student receives credit for that particular course and may shorten his or her program accordingly.

Scholarships are available not only to students who performed well during their secondary education but also to current students who excel while pursuing their particular program of study.

Financial Aid/Scholarships

National College of Business and Technology makes available an extensive program of financial assistance, which includes Federal Stafford Student Loans, Federal PLUS loans, Federal Perkins Loans, the Federal Pell Grant, the Federal Supplemental Educational Opportunity Grant, the Workforce Development Grant, and the Business Partnership Grant as well as several scholarship opportunities.

Tuition and Fees

Tuition is $162 per credit hour. National College of Business and Technology is among the least expensive private colleges in its area. Students should check the catalog for current application, student activities, and graduation fees.

Program Content

Accounting, Business Management, Computer Applications Technology, Medical Assisting, Office Administration

Program Description

All programs listed above lead to an Associate of Science degree.

The programs offered at National College of Business and Technology give the graduate the training that is needed to take the first step into an entry position as well as the background necessary to grow professionally in that field.

Accreditation

National College of Business and Technology is accredited by the Accrediting Council for Independent Colleges and Schools (ACICS); individual programs such as Medical Assisting may have programmatic accreditation.

Admission

A prospective student must have a high school diploma or GED certificate and submit an application for admission together with the application fee.

Graduation Requirements

In order to be eligible for graduation, the student must complete all courses outlined in the program and earn the required number of credit hours. To graduate from any program, an overall grade point average of at least 2.0 must be achieved.

Contact

Admissions Department
7627 Ewing Boulevard
Florence, KY 41042
Phone: (859) 525-6510
Fax: (859) 525-8961

Programs Eligible for Scholarship	Tuition and Fees	Course Length/Credit Hours	Credential Earned
All related program areas	$15,552	96 credit hours	AS

National College of Business and Technology, Lexington

About Our Institution

National College of Business and Technology was established in 1886. The Lexington campus, which is located close to the main business center of Lexington, Kentucky, opened in 1941. National College of Business and Technology's curriculum is specific and concentrates on essential professional skills that lead toward employment in a specific field. Programs are planned to offer the most effective methods in technology, business organization, and management while consistently meeting the demands of the modern world. The College offers courses that cover a broad range of majors, including accounting, business management, medical assisting, office technology, and radio and television broadcasting as well as other fields. Students can complete programs in as little as one year.

Special Features

A major strength of National College of Business and Technology is its ability to quickly adjust the curriculum to changes in the employment needs of business and industry and to meet the career interest of students. Community representatives, serving as a Campus Advisory Board, provide current and timely advice relative to the employment needs of business, technical, and government organizations.

The Career Center is available to assist with the entire job search process. Specialized staff members are available to help students to prepare a resume and cover letter and interview effectively. They assist the student throughout the employment search.

Students who wish to demonstrate their current skill level in selected areas may take an Advanced Placement evaluation. If successful, the student receives credit for that particular course and may shorten his or her program accordingly.

Scholarships are available not only to students who performed well during their secondary education but also to current students who excel while pursuing their particular program of study.

Financial Aid/Scholarships

National College of Business and Technology makes available an extensive program of financial assistance which includes Federal Stafford Loans, Federal Plus Loans, Federal Perkins Loans, the Federal Pell Grant, the Federal Supplemental Educational Opportunity Grant, the Workforce Development Grant, and the Business Partnership Grant, as well as several scholarship opportunities.

Tuition and Fees

Tuition is $170 per credit hour. National College of Business and Technology is among the least expensive private colleges in its area. Students should check the catalog for current application, student activities, or graduation fees.

Program Content

Accounting, Business Management, Computer Applications Technology, Medical Assisting, Office Administration, Radio and Television Broadcasting

Program Description

All programs listed above lead to an Associate of Science degree.

The programs offered at National College of Business and Technology give the graduate the training that is needed to take the first step into an entry position as well as the background necessary to grow professionally in that field.

Accreditation

National College of Business and Technology is accredited by the Accrediting Council for Independent Colleges and Schools (ACICS); individual programs such as Medical Assisting may have programmatic accreditation.

Admission

A prospective student must have a high school diploma or GED and submit an application for admission together with the application fee.

Graduation Requirements

In order to be eligible for graduation, the student must complete all courses outlined in the program and earn the required number of credit hours. To graduate from any program, a 2.0 overall grade point average must be achieved.

Contact

Admissions Department
628 East Main Street
Lexington, KY 40508
Phone: (859)253-0621
Fax: (859) 254-7664

Programs Eligible for Scholarship	Tuition and Fees	Course Length/Credit Hours	Credential Earned
All related program areas	$16,320	96 credit hours	AS

National College of Business and Technology, Louisville

About Our Institution

National College of Business and Technology was established in 1886. The Louisville campus is conveniently located in Southwest Jefferson and Shively and draws students from a wide area. National College of Business and Technology's curriculum is specific and concentrates on essential professional skills that will lead toward employment in a specific field. Programs are planned to offer the most effective methods in technology, business organization, and management while consistently meeting the demands of the modern world. The College offers courses that cover a broad range of majors, including accounting, business management, medical assisting, and office technology, as well as other fields. Students can complete programs in as little as one year or less.

Special Features

A major strength of National College of Business and Technology is its ability to quickly adjust the curriculum to changes in the employment needs of business and industry and to meet the career interest of students. Community representatives, serving as a Campus Advisory Board, provide current and timely advice relative to the employment needs of business, technical, and government organizations.

The Career Center is available to assist with the entire job search process. Specialized staff members are available to help students to prepare a resume and cover letter and interview effectively. They assist the student throughout the employment search.

Students who wish to demonstrate their current skill level in selected areas may take an Advanced Placement evaluation. If successful, the student receives credit for that particular course and may shorten their program accordingly.

Scholarships are available not only to students who performed well during their secondary education but also to current students who excel while pursuing their particular program of study.

Financial Aid/Scholarships

National College of Business and Technology makes available an extensive program of financial assistance which includes Federal Stafford Loans, Federal Plus Loans, Federal Perkins Loans, the Federal Pell Grant, the Federal Supplemental Educational Opportunity Grant, and the Workforce Development Grant, as well as several scholarship opportunities.

Tuition and Fees

Tuition is $170 per credit hour. National College of Business and Technology is among the least expensive private colleges in its area. Students should check the catalog for current application, student activities, or graduation fees.

Accreditation

National College of Business and Technology is accredited by the Accrediting Council for Independent Colleges and Schools (ACICS);

Program Content

Accounting, Business Management, Computer Applications Technology, Health Information Technology, Medical Assisting, Office Administration

Program Description

All programs listed above lead to an Associate of Science degree.

The programs offered at National College of Business and Technology give the graduate the training that is needed to take the first step into an entry position as well as the background necessary to grow professionally in that field.

individual programs such as Medical Assisting may have programmatic accreditation.

Admission

A prospective student must have a high school diploma or GED and submit an application for admission together with the application fee.

Graduation Requirements

In order to be eligible for graduation, the student must complete all courses outlined in the program and earn the required number of credit hours. To graduate from any program, a 2.0 overall grade point average must be achieved.

Contact

Admissions Department
4205 Dixie Highway
Louisville, KY 40216
Phone: (502) 447-7634
Fax: (502) 447-7665

Programs Eligible for Scholarship	Tuition and Fees	Course Length/Credit Hours	Credential Earned
All related program areas	$16,680	96 credit hours	AS

National College of Business and Technology, Pikeville

About Our Institution
National College of Business and Technology was established in 1886. The Pikeville campus is located in the heart of the coal-rich eastern Kentucky area. National College of Business and Technology's curriculum is specific and concentrates on essential professional skills that will lead toward employment in a specific field. Programs are planned to offer the most effective methods in technology, business organization, and management while consistently meeting the demands of the modern world. The College offers courses that cover a broad range of majors, including accounting, business management, medical assisting, and office technology as well as other fields. Students can complete programs in as little as one year or less.

Special Features
A major strength of National College of Business and Technology is its ability to quickly adjust the curriculum to changes in the employment needs of business and industry and to meet the career interest of students. Community representatives, serving as a Campus Advisory Board, provide current and timely advice relative to the employment needs of business, technical, and government organizations.

The Career Center is available to assist with the entire job search process. Specialized staff members are available to help students to prepare a resume and cover letter and interview effectively. They assist the student throughout the employment search.

Students who wish to demonstrate their current skill level in selected areas may take an Advanced Placement evaluation. If successful, the student receives credit for that particular course and may shorten his or her program accordingly.

Scholarships are available not only to students who performed well during their secondary education but also to current students who excel while pursuing their particular program of study.

Financial Aid/Scholarships
National College of Business and Technology makes available an extensive program of financial assistance, which includes Federal Stafford Student Loans, Federal PLUS loans, Federal Perkins Loans, the Federal Pell Grant, the Federal Supplemental Educational Opportunity Grant, the Workforce Development Grant, and the Business Partnership Grant as well as several scholarship opportunities.

Tuition and Fees
Tuition is $162 per credit hour. National College of Business and Technology is among the least expensive private colleges in its area. Students should check the catalog for current application, student activities, or graduation fees.

Accreditation
National College of Business and Technology is accredited by the Accrediting Council for Independent Colleges and Schools (ACICS);

Program Content
Accounting, Business Management, Computer Applications Technology, Health Information Technology, Medical Assisting, Office Administration

Program Description
All programs listed above lead to an Associate of Science degree.

The programs offered at National College of Business and Technology give the graduate the training that is needed to take the first step into an entry position as well as the background necessary to grow professionally in that field.

individual programs such as Medical Assisting may have programmatic accreditation.

Admission
A prospective student must have a high school diploma or GED certificate and submit an application for admission together with the application fee.

Graduation Requirements
In order to be eligible for graduation, the student must complete all courses outlined in the program and earn the required number of credit hours. To graduate from any program, an overall grade point average of at least 2.0 must be achieved.

Contact
Admissions Department
288 South Mayo Trail, Suite 2
Pikeville, KY 41501
Phone: (859) 432-5477
Fax: (859) 437-4952

Programs Eligible for Scholarship	Tuition and Fees	Course Length/Credit Hours	Credential Earned
All related program areas	$15,552	96 credit hours	AS

National College of Business and Technology, Richmond

About Our Institution
National College of Business and Technology was established in 1886. The Richmond campus is located just minutes from downtown Richmond and historical Madison County and proudly serves the Central Kentucky area. National College of Business and Technology's curriculum is specific and concentrates on the essential professional skills that lead toward employment in a specific field. Programs are planned to offer the most effective methods in technology, business organization, and management while consistently meeting the demands of the modern world. The College offers courses that cover a broad range of majors, including accounting, business management, medical assisting, and office technology as well as other fields. Students can complete programs in as little as one year or less.

Special Features
A major strength of National College of Business and Technology is its ability to quickly adjust the curriculum to changes in the employment needs of business and industry and to meet the career interest of students. Community representatives, serving as a Campus Advisory Board, provide current and timely advice relative to the employment needs of business, technical, and government organizations.

The Career Center is available to assist with the entire job-search process. Specialized staff members are available to help students prepare a resume and cover letter and interview effectively. They assist the student throughout the employment search.

Students who wish to demonstrate their current skill level in selected areas may take an Advanced Placement evaluation. If successful, the student receives credit for that particular course and may shorten his or her program accordingly.

Scholarships are available not only to students who performed well during their secondary education but also to current students who excel while pursuing their particular program of study.

Financial Aid/Scholarships
National College of Business and Technology makes available an extensive program of financial assistance which includes Federal Stafford Loans, Federal Plus Loans, Federal Perkins Loans, the Federal Pell Grant, the Federal Supplemental Educational Opportunity Grant, the Workforce Development Grant, and the Business Partnership Grant, as well as several scholarship opportunities.

Tuition and Fees
Tuition is $162 per credit hour. National College of Business and Technology is among the least expensive private colleges in its area. Students should check the catalog for current application, student activities, or graduation fees.

Program Content
Accounting, Business Management, Computer Applications Technology, Medical Assisting, Office Administration

Program Description
All programs listed above lead to an Associate of Science degree.

The programs offered at National College of Business and Technology give the graduate the training that is needed to take the first step into an entry position as well as the background necessary to grow professionally in that field.

Accreditation
National College of Business and Technology is accredited by the Accrediting Council for Independent Colleges and Schools (ACICS); individual programs such as Medical Assisting may have programmatic accreditation.

Admission
A prospective student must have a high school diploma or GED certificate and complete an application for admission together with the application fee.

Graduation Requirements
In order to be eligible for graduation, the student must complete all courses outlined in the program and earn the required number of credit hours. To graduate from any program, a minimum 2.0 overall grade point average must be achieved.

Contact
Admissions Department
National College of Business and
 Technology
139 South Killarney Lane
Richmond, KY 40475
Phone: (859) 623-8956
Fax: (859) 624-5544

Programs Eligible for Scholarship	Tuition and Fees	Course Length/Credit Hours	Credential Earned
All related program areas	$15,552	96 credit hours	AS

Southwestern College, Florence

About Our Institution

The Northern Kentucky Campus of Southwestern College is located in Florence, Kentucky, just ten minutes south of Cincinnati, Ohio. Located near the Florence Mall, the Northern Kentucky Campus is part of Antique Center, a shopping center just off the Route 75 expressway. Ample free parking is available. The facility is surrounded by local businesses and restaurants and is easily accessible via bus transportation. The facility includes lecture classrooms, computer lab, and a medical lab to assist in student learning.

Southwestern College is committed to the educational and personal enrichment of its students. It is the College's philosophy to establish and maintain standards that foster the training, advancement, welfare, and best interest of its students. Each program is designed to help provide students with the entry-level employment skills necessary to meet the requirements of industry, government, allied health, and business offices today and in the future. At Southwestern, a student learns the skills needed to advance in his or her career. The College strives to develop student attitudes and habits that can help lead to promotions and success.

Financial Aid/Scholarships

Southwestern College understands that its students' education is an investment in their future. Southwestern's financial aid office is there to help students finance that future in the easiest way possible, because affordability should never be an issue when making the decision to get an education.

Southwestern can help in putting together a financial assistance plan to help students manage the cost of their education, including books and equipment. A Financial Aid Advisor can assist students in choosing from the many options that are available to help cover their educational expenses.

Tuition and Fees

For current tuition and fees, students should contact Southwestern College.

Accreditation

Southwestern College is accredited by the Accrediting Council for Independent Colleges and Schools (ACICS).

Admissions

Students must have either a high school diploma or GED certificate and pass an entrance exam for acceptance.

Contact

Executive Director
Southwestern College
8095 Connector Drive
Florence, KY 41042
Phone: (859) 282-9999
Fax: (859) 282-7940
E-mail: execdirflorence@lincolntech.com
Web: www.swcollege.net/

Program Content

Accounting, Administrative Assistant, Business Administration, Computer Applications, Computer Information Specialist, Computerized Accounting, Medical Administrative Assistant, Medical Assistant, Medical Coding and Billing, Phlebotomy

Sullivan University, Louisville

About Our Institution

Founded in 1962, A. O. Sullivan, a postsecondary educator since 1926, and his son, A. R. Sullivan, decided to form a higher education institution founded on the highest ideals and standards to prepare students for successful careers. Since that time, the University has earned a reputation as one of the leading career institutions in the nation. Sullivan offers master's baccalaureate, associate, and diploma programs. Since achieving Level III accreditation in December 1996 and baccalaureate accreditation in January 1992, Sullivan has grown to become both Kentucky's newest four-year university and its largest independent college or university. The University also has a branch at Lexington and an extension at Fort Knox.

Special Features

Sullivan students study practical courses designed to build a foundation for their careers. Just the opposite of most colleges and universities, Sullivan students begin by concentrating specifically on their areas of interest; then, their general and advanced education courses are taken within the final few quarters of the degree program. The University operates on a quarter-hour system of four 11-week sessions, which allows baccalaureate students to finish their degrees in as little as thirty-six months. Day classes are offered every day of the week except Friday. "Plus Friday" is a free day when students may utilize the facilities and equipment for individual study and practice and faculty members are available to give students special assistance.

Financial Aid/Scholarships

Students attending Sullivan have access to federal and state financial aid programs, such as all Title IV programs. Many loans, grants, work-study programs, academic scholarships, and private scholarships are also available. As directed by the Department of Education, federal funds are allotted to the lowest-income families first, but funds are also available for middle- and upper-income families.

Tuition and Fees

Expenses for the 2004–05 academic year ranged from $12,240 to $13,260 for tuition and from $200 to $400 for first-quarter books. Housing cost $3,690; the general fee was $415; a parking merit was $24 per quarter. An additional comprehensive fee is applied for some hospitality programs.

Accreditation

Sullivan University is accredited by the Commission on Colleges of the Southern Association of Colleges and Schools to award associate, bachelor's, and master's degrees.

Admissions

To be considered for admission to Sullivan University, a student is required to demonstrate the appropriate aptitude and background for his or her anticipated field of study by successful completion of an entrance test and/or submission of ACT or SAT test scores. Students also must have a high school diploma or its equivalent, such as a GED certificate. Sullivan has a rolling admissions policy.

Graduation Requirements

For undergraduate programs, all students must attain a minimum cumulative GPA of 2.0 to qualify for a certificate, diploma or degree. In addition, a grade of C or higher is required for satisfactory completion of certain courses in each program as designated by the student's planner (available in the Registrar's Office). Dual associate degree attainment requires completion of a varying number of credit hours depending on the student's program of study. A minimum of 20 additional hours is required. Transfer students must complete a minimum of 25 percent of the credits required for graduation in a degree program at Sullivan. Dual options may be obtained by satisfactorily completing the option courses in another area plus any prerequisite courses.

Contacts

Stephen Coppock, Ed.D.
Sullivan University
3101 Bardstown Road
Louisville, KY 40205
Phone: (502) 456-6506
(800) 844-1354 (toll-free)
Fax: (502) 456-0040
E-mail: gscoppock@sullivan.edu

Dr. David McGuire
Sullivan University
2355 Harrodsburg Road
Lexington, KY 40504
Phone: (859) 276-4357
(800) 467-6281 (toll-free)
Fax: (859) 276-1153
E-mail: dmcguire@sullivan.edu

Barbara Dean
Sullivan University
P.O. Box 998
Ft. Knox, KY 40121
Phone: (502) 942-8503
(800) 562-6713 (toll-free)
Fax: (502) 942-3640
E-mail: bdean@sullivan.edu

Web: www.sullivan.edu

Programs Eligible for Scholarship	Tuition and Fees	Course Length/Credit Hours	Credential Earned
Certificate programs	$8,160–$12,240	6–9 months/39–58	Certificate
Diploma programs	$12,240–$16,320	9–12 months/54–82	Diploma
Associate in Science programs	$24,480–$25,704	18 months/94–126	AS
Baccalaureate programs	$36,720	180 credit hours	BS/BSBA/BSPS

Bryman College, New Orleans

About Our Institution
The Bryman Schools were founded in 1960 by Mrs. Esther Bryman as the Los Angeles Colleges of Medical and Dental Assistants. The Los Angeles campus was the original school. In December 1995, Corinthian Schools, Inc. (CSi), a division of Corinthian Colleges, Inc. (CCi), acquired the schools. CCi is one of the largest postsecondary school organizations in the United States, operating more than eighty colleges and institutions nationwide. The College is a branch campus of Bryman College, Hayward, in California.

The College's philosophy is to provide high-quality programs that are sound in concept, implemented by a competent and dedicated faculty, and geared to serve those seeking a solid foundation in the health-care field. The programs emphasize hands-on training, are relevant to the needs of employers, and focus on areas that offer strong long-term employment opportunities. Upon completion, graduates are prepared for entry-level positions in the medical and dental fields.

The College is conveniently located near public transportation and is easily accessible from the interstate. The downtown area, French Quarter, and the New Orleans Superdome are within 12 miles of the College.

Financial Aid/Scholarships
Information regarding Federal Pell Grants, Federal Stafford Student Loans, FSEOG, Federal Perkins Loans, Federal Work-Study, VA funds, Vocational Rehabilitation, and other assistance can be obtained from the Finance Office. Financial aid is available for those who qualify.

Accreditation
The Accrediting Commission of Career Schools and Colleges of Technology (ACCSCT) accredits all programs. The Medical Assisting program is accredited by AAMA, a division of the Commission on Accreditation of Allied Health Education Programs (CAAHEP).

Admissions
Successful candidates are selected based on interviews and the completion and presentation of required documents. Enrollment is open to all high school graduates as well as those holding a GED certificate or its equivalent. Under certain circumstances, students who do not have a high school diploma or its equivalent may still be accepted for admission. Students should contact the Admissions Department for additional information.

Graduation Requirements
To be eligible for graduation, students must successfully complete all classroom modules with a grade of at least 70 percent, finish an approved externship, and complete all other program requirements.

Program Content
Dental Assisting, Medical Administrative Assistant, Medical Assisting, Medical Insurance Billing/Coding, Pharmacy Technician

Enrollment
There are 200–400 students enrolled.

Contact
Tom Bonesteel, President
Bryman College
1201 Elmwood Park Boulevard, Suite 600
New Orleans, LA 70123
Phone: (504) 733-7117
Fax: (504) 734-1217
E-mail: mbonesteel@cci.edu
Web: www.bryman-college.com

Programs Eligible for Scholarship	Tuition and Fees	Course Length/Credit Hours	Credential Earned
Dental Assisting	$9,025	720 clock hours/47 credit hours	Diploma
Medical Administrative Assistant	$9,356	720 clock hours/47 credit hours	Diploma
Medical Assisting	$9,350	720 clock hours/47 credit hours	Diploma
Medical Insurance Billing/Coding	$6,026	480 clock hours/29 credit hours	Diploma
Pharmacy Technician	$9,208	720 clock hours/58 credit hours	Diploma

Delta School of Business and Technology, Lake Charles

About Our Institution

Delta Tech provides an atmosphere of growth and achievement. Founded in 1970, Delta is housed at 517 Broad Street in the Lake Charles historical district. The School offers nine-month diploma programs in accounting, administrative assistant studies, and medical office assistant studies. Eighteen-month associate degree programs are offered in accounting, administrative assistant studies, drafting, medical office assistant studies, business management, and information technology.

Special Features

Delta Tech is a certified Microsoft Office User Specialist training center. Hands-on computer training incorporated into every curriculum, extensive job search training, on-campus interviewing, and on-the-job training increases every graduate's skill and confidence levels. Tutoring, "Friday Plus," lifetime placement assistance, and refresher courses are added bonuses to Delta's "You Will Succeed" attitude.

Financial Aid/Scholarships

A variety of loans, grants, scholarships, work-study, veterans', vocational rehabilitation, and workforce programs are available for those who qualify. On-campus financial aid officers are available through the financial aid process, explaining and applying for the aid that is right for the student.

Tuition and Fees

Tuition averages $2480 per quarter for all courses available except information technology. A $150 registration fee is not included in tuition averages. Textbook fees are included in the financial aid package.

Accreditation

Delta Tech is accredited by the Accrediting Council for Independent Colleges and Schools to award diplomas and specialized associate degrees.

Admissions

Applicants must achieve a minimum score on an approved entrance exam. All students entering Delta Tech meet with admissions personnel to pinpoint current and future goals.

Graduation Requirements

Students must complete all courses specified in the catalogued curriculum with a minimum cumulative 2.0 grade point average.

Contact

Susan Ardoin, Admissions
517 Broad Street
Lake Charles, LA 70601
Phone: (337) 439-5765
        (800) 259-JOBS (toll-free)
Fax: (337) 436-5151
Web: www.deltatech.edu

Program Content

Accounting, Associate Accounting, Administrative Assistant, Associate Administrative Assistant Computer, Associate Administrative Assistant Legal, Associate Drafting, Medical Office Assistant, Associate Medical Office Assistant, Associate Business Management, Associate Information Technology

Program Description

The accounting curriculum provides entry-level bookkeeping training. The associate accounting curriculum enables graduates to extend career goals beyond entry-level bookkeeping into the management arena. The administrative assistant curriculum provides entry-level secretarial skills needed in business and legal offices. The associate administrative assistant curriculum provides skills necessary to become part of a decision-making team. The drafting curriculum offers careers that include, but are not limited to, engineering assistants, and architectural and engineering draftsmen. The medical office assistant program cross-trains students for positions in clerical and clinical medical offices. The associate medical office assistant program provides students with the skills necessary to become part of a medical office decision-making team. The associate business management offers business, decision-making, and human relations skills to enter into the business world. The associate information technology covers all aspects of managing and processing information. It offers careers in technical support as well as network administration.

Programs Eligible for Scholarship	Tuition and Fees	Course Length/Credit Hours	Credential Earned
Accounting	$ 8,500	51.6 credits	Diploma
Accounting	$17,000	100.6 credits	Associate
Administrative Assistant	$ 8,500	52.2 credits	Diploma
Administrative Assistant Computer	$17,000	102.4 credits	Associate
Administrative Assistant Legal	$17,000	102 credits	Associate
Business Management	$17,000	100.8 credits	Associate
Drafting	$17,000	97.2 credits	Associate
Information Technology	$19,400	102 credits	Associate
Medical Office Assistant	$ 8,500	51.6 credits	Diploma
Medical Office Assistant	$17,000	99.6 credits	Associate

Herzing College, New Orleans

About Our Institution
Herzing College is focused on adult education and training in diploma, associate, and bachelor's degree programs. The College is student centered in that its programs and schedules are designed to fit into the lifestyles of adults. Programs can be taken during the day or in the evening and are conveniently scheduled so that the students can meet their career goals in a shorter time than is possible in traditional four-year colleges.

Special Features
A typical Herzing student desires the interaction, personal touch, and small classes that allow and encourage personal and educational development. The staff and faculty members are hired and evaluated on the basis of their commitment to providing this environment. Herzing College has a three-year Bachelor of Science degree-completion policy for students meeting specific conditions. Herzing students also have the benefit of a full-time Career Services Office that assists students with job placement while they are in school and upon graduation.

Financial Aid/Scholarships
Students attending Herzing may qualify for various financial assistance programs, including the Federal Pell Grant, Federal Supplemental Educational Opportunity Grant, Federal Perkins Loan, and the William D. Ford Direct Loan programs. The federal funds available vary from year to year and are based on changes in federal appropriations and regulations. Applications for financial assistance should be made at the Financial Aid Office on the campus. Herzing College offers several types of institutional scholarships to adult learners and high school seniors. Students should contact the College for more information.

Tuition and Fees
Tuition is charged per semester hour: $255 per credit hour for general education, business, legal, and medical classes; $300 per credit hour for computer and technical classes. Textbooks are loaned to students at no charge.

Accreditation
Herzing College is accredited by the Higher Learning Commission of the North Central Association of Colleges and Schools. For more information, students should contact the Higher Learning Commission (telephone: 800-621-7440; Web site: http://www.ncahigherlearningcommission.org).

Program Content
Bachelor of Science Programs: Business Administration, Information Technology, Technology Management

Associate of Science Programs: Business Administration, Computer-Aided Drafting, Computer Information Systems, Computer Network Technology, Legal Assistant/Paralegal

Diploma Programs: Medical Billing and Insurance Coding, Medical Office Administration (MCSE)

Admissions
All applicants seeking admission to Herzing College must be high school graduates or the equivalent (GED). Applicants must be interviewed by an Admissions Representative, complete a Herzing entrance examination, and pay a $25 enrollment fee.

Graduation Requirements
In order to graduate, a student must maintain an overall cumulative grade point average of 2.0 or better, pass all program-required courses, and complete the required total number of credit hours. A minimum skill level is applicable in some courses. All financial obligations to the College must also be finalized with the Business Office.

Contact
Genny Boredelon, Director of Admissions
Herzing College
2400 Veteran's Boulevard, #410
Kenner, LA 70062
Phone: (504) 733-0074
　　　　(866) HERZING (toll-free)
Fax: (504) 733-0020
E-mail: genny@nor.herzing.edu
Web: www.herzing.edu

Programs Eligible for Scholarship	Tuition and Fees*	Course Length/Credit Hours	Credential Earned
Business Administration	$4,149	125 credits	Bachelor's
Information Technology	$4,554	138 credits	Bachelor's
Technology Management	$4,392	129 credits	Bachelor's
Business Administration	$4,193	70 credits	Associate
Computer Information Systems	$4,590	79 credits	Associate
Computer Network Technology	$4,590	79 credits	Associate
Computer-Aided Drafting	$4,590	79 credits	Associate
Legal Assistant/Paralegal	$4,080	63 credits	Associate
Medical Billing and Insurance Coding	$4,080	48 credits	Diploma
Medical Office Administration	$4,153	39 credits	Diploma

*Semesters at Herzing College are sixteen weeks long. A full-time student in the associate and bachelor's programs generally completes 16 credits a semester.

ITT Technical Institute, Saint Rose

About Our Institution

The company: ITT Technical Institute is owned and operated by ITT Educational Services, Inc. (ITT/ESI), a leading private college system that offers technology-influenced programs of study. ITT/ESI operates seventy-seven ITT Technical Institutes in thirty states; they provide career-focused degree programs to approximately 39,000 students as of spring 2004. Headquartered in Carmel, Indiana, ITT/ESI has been actively involved in the higher education community in the United States since 1969.

Curricula: Curriculum offerings are designed to help students begin to prepare for career opportunities in the fields of technology. Students attend classes year-round, with convenient breaks provided throughout the year. A full-time student can have class meetings as often as three days a week, and they are typically available in the morning, afternoon, and evening, depending on student enrollment. General education courses may be available online. This schedule offers flexibility to allow students to pursue part-time employment opportunities.

ITT Technical Institute, Saint Rose, awards Associate of Science and Bachelor of Science degrees.

Special Features

Most ITT Technical Institute programs of study blend traditional academic content with applied learning concepts, with a significant portion devoted to practical study in a lab environment. Advisory committees, made up of representatives of local businesses help each ITT Technical Institute periodically review and update curricula, equipment, and laboratory design.

Financial Aid/Scholarships

ITT Technical Institute maintains a Financial Aid Department on campus. The campus is designated as an eligible institution by the U.S. Department of Education for participation in the following programs: Federal Stafford Student Loan, Federal PLUS Loan, and Federal Work-Study. The school also participates in the California Grant Program and offers nonfederal loans through Bank One for eligible students.

Tuition and Fees

March 2005 tuition is $386 per credit hour.

Accreditation

Accrediting Council for Independent Colleges and Schools (ACICS).

Admissions

For admission requirements, students should contact the school for a catalog.

Graduation Requirements

For graduation requirements, students should consult the school catalog.

Program Content

School of Information Technology: Information Systems Security, Data Communication Systems Technology, Software Engineering Technology, Information Technology–Computer Network Systems, Information Technology–Software Applications and Programming, Information Technology–Web Development.

School of Electronics Technology: Electronics and Communications Engineering Technology, Computer and Electronics Engineering Technology.

School of Drafting and Design: Digital Entertainment and Game Design, Computer Drafting and Design, Information Technology–Multimedia Option.

School of Business: Technical Project Management.

Contact

Heidi Munoz, Director of Recruitment
ITT Technical Institute
140 James Drive East
Saint Rose, LA 70087
Phone: (504) 463-0338
Fax: (504) 463-0979

Remington College, Baton Rouge Campus, Baton Rouge

About Our Institution

Remington College was founded in 1985 in an effort to meet the growing need for computer-related education and training in the technical and business fields. To date, Remington College consists of twenty campuses across the United States. Remington College teaches a "career first" curriculum that allows students to concentrate on learning the necessary technical skills early in their program and build on them as they progress toward graduation.

Special Features

Remington College is uncompromisingly dedicated to high-quality, college-level, career-oriented education. Its primary objectives are to graduate a high percentage of students who enter career programs and to help them achieve relevant employment at the highest possible starting salary. Remington College's hands-on training is the foundation of its educational structure. Practical application in well-equipped labs, coupled with theoretical reinforcement in the classroom, allows students to acquire substantial knowledge in their chosen career field. When appropriate, externships are used to provide the student with real-world experience.

Financial Aid/Scholarships

Remington College–Baton Rouge Campus maintains a Financial Services Office on the campus, providing a variety of grants, loans, scholarships, work-study, veterans' benefits, and vocational rehabilitation programs.

Tuition and Fees

Students should contact the campus for current tuition pricing. Textbook cost and lab fees are included in tuition. A $50 registration fee is required for all programs.

Accreditation

Programs are accredited by the Accrediting Council for Independent Colleges and Schools (ACICS).

Admissions

A high school diploma or GED certificate, along with an acceptance interview, is used to determine a candidate's potential for success. At some sites, an entrance test is also required.

Graduation Requirements

In order to graduate, a student must maintain a minimum overall 2.0 cumulative grade point average for the entire program and complete all courses specified in the program catalog.

Contact

Midge Jacobson, Campus President
1900 North Lobdell
Baton Rouge, LA 70806
Phone: (225) 922-3990
Fax: (225) 922-9569
Web: www.remingtoncollege.edu

Program Content

Business Information Systems, Computer Networking Technology, Criminal Justice, Electronic Computer Technology, Medical Assisting, Medical Insurance and Coding, Pharmacy Technician

Program Description

Business Information Systems: The Business Information Systems program provides comprehensive training in the operation and effective use of various computer systems and software in DOS and Windows.

Computer Networking Technology: The Computer Networking Technology program provides comprehensive training in computer networking.

Criminal Justice: The Criminal Justice program trains students in the history and background of criminal justice, including the different types of law and judicial systems. Graduates are prepared for entry-level positions in law enforcement, correctional systems, security management, and criminology.

Electronic Computer Technology: The Electronic Computer Technology program provides training and develops technical skills for computer servicing and digital and computer electronics.

Medical Assisting: The objective of the Medical Assisting program is to prepare students for employment in a physician's office or a medical clinic. It emphasizes the development of both administrative and clinical skills.

Medical Insurance and Coding: The Medical Insurance and Coding program provides training in state and federal regulations, medical coding for procedures and diagnoses, and correct procedures for filing medical claims for optimal reimbursement for the clinic and/or hospital.

Pharmacy Technician: The Pharmacy Technician program provides students with knowledge and skills that enable them to apply to the Louisiana Pharmacy Board for certification as they learn medical abbreviations, prescription writing and interpretation, and drug forms, dosage, and administration.

Programs Eligible for Scholarship	Tuition and Fees	Course Length	Credential Earned
All	varies by program	32–96 weeks	Diploma/AS

Remington College, Lafayette Campus, Lafayette

About Our Institution
Remington College was founded in 1985 in an effort to meet the growing need for computer-related education and training in the technical and business fields. To date, Remington College consists of twenty campuses across the United States. Remington College teaches a "career-first" curriculum that allows students to concentrate on learning the necessary technical skills early in their program and building on these skills as they progress toward graduation.

Special Features
Remington College is uncompromisingly dedicated to high-quality, college-level, career-oriented education. Its primary objectives are to graduate a high percentage of students who enter career programs and to help them achieve relevant employment at the highest possible starting salary. Remington College's hands-on training is the foundation of its educational structure. Practical application in well-equipped labs, coupled with theoretical reinforcement in the classroom, allows students to acquire substantial knowledge in their chosen career field. When appropriate, externships are used to provide the student with real-world experience.

Financial Aid/Scholarships
Remington College–Lafayette Campus maintains a Financial Services Office on campus, providing a variety of grants, loans, scholarships, work-study, veterans' aid, and vocational rehabilitation programs.

Tuition and Fees
Students should contact the campus for current tuition pricing. Textbook cost and lab fees are included in tuition. A $50 registration fee is required for all programs.

Accreditation
Remington College–Lafayette Campus programs are accredited by the Accrediting Council for Independent Colleges and Schools (ACICS).

Admissions
A high school diploma or satisfactory GED test score, along with an acceptance interview, is used to determine a candidate's potential for success. An entrance test is also required.

Graduation Requirements
In order to graduate, a student must maintain an overall cumulative grade point average of 2.0 for the entire program and complete all courses specified in the program catalog.

Contact
Dr. Rosalie Lampone, Campus President
303 Rue Louis XIV
Lafayette, LA 70508
Phone: (337) 981-4010
Fax: (337) 983-7130
Web: www.remingtoncollege.edu

Program Content
Business Information Systems, Computer Networking Technology, Electronics and Computer Technology, Medical Assisting, and Medical Insurance Coding

Program Description
Business Information Systems: (A.S.): This program provides comprehensive training in the operation and effective use of various computer systems and software in DOS and Windows environments.

Computer Networking Technology (A.S.): Upon completion of the program, each student is able to install, configure, maintain, and troubleshoot local area networks and wide area networks that use DOS- and Window's-based network operating systems.

Electronics and Computer Technology (A.S.): The curriculum explores both the fundamentals and advanced theory in electronics, integrated circuits, microprocessors, and computer technology.

Medical Assistant (Diploma): The objective of the program is to provide graduates with the skills and knowledge that enable them to qualify for entry-level positions as medical assistants.

Medical Insurance and Coding (Diploma): Upon completion, graduates are able to process insurance claims and code from charts and billing.

Remington College, New Orleans Campus, New Orleans

About Our Institution
Remington College was founded in 1985 in an effort to meet the growing need for computer-related education and training in the technical and business fields. To date, Remington College consists of twenty campuses across the United States. Remington College teaches a "career first" curriculum that allows students to concentrate on learning the necessary technical skills early in their program and builds on them as they progress toward graduation.

Special Features
Remington College is uncompromisingly dedicated to high-quality, college-level, career-oriented education. Its primary objectives are to graduate a high percentage of students who enter career programs and to help them achieve relevant employment at the highest possible starting salary. Remington College's hands-on training is the foundation of its educational structure. Practical application in well-equipped labs and laptop computers for students, coupled with theoretical reinforcement in the classroom, allows students to acquire substantial knowledge in their chosen career field.

Financial Aid/Scholarships
Remington College–New Orleans Campus maintains a Financial Services Office on the campus, providing a variety of grants, loans, scholarships, work study, veterans' aid, and vocational rehabilitation programs.

Tuition and Fees
Students should contact the campus for current tuition pricing. Textbook cost and lab fees are included in tuition. A $50 registration fee is required for all programs.

Accreditation
Remington College–New Orleans Campus programs are accredited by the Accrediting Commission of Career Schools and Colleges of Technology (ACCSCT).

Admissions
A high school diploma or GED, along with an acceptance interview, is used to determine a candidate's potential for success. At some sites, an entrance test is also included.

Graduation Requirements
In order to graduate, a student must maintain an overall 2.0 cumulative grade point average for the entire program and complete all courses specified in the program catalog.

Contact
Gregg Falcon, Campus President
321 Veterans Memorial Blvd.
New Orleans, LA 70005
Phone: (504) 831-8889
Fax: (504) 831-6803
Web: www.remingtoncollege.edu

Program Content
Business Information Systems, Computer-Aided Drafting, Computer Graphic Design, Computer Network Technology, Computer Information Systems, Electronics Engineering Technology

Program Description
Business Information Systems: This program is designed to advance the student's knowledge in today's business office environments.

Computer-Aided Drafting: This program is designed to provide the student with experience in applying drafting skills to Mechanical, Electrical, Piping, Civil, Structural, and Architectural disciplines.

Computer Graphic Design: This program prepares students for work in the fast-paced world of commercial art and advertising.

Computer Networking Technology: This program is designed to prepare students for employment in the field of computer electronics. Students learn to troubleshoot, install, and maintain computer networks.

Computer Information Systems: The Computer Information Systems Program curriculum explores both the fundamentals and advanced theory in computer and programming, computer operations, system analysis, and system design.

Electronics Engineering Technology: This program provides students with a theoretical and practical understanding of basic electricity and electronics, semiconductors, digital logic gates, IC chips, basic circuit construction, communication, automated control systems, and computer architecture.

Baltimore School of Massage, Baltimore

About Our Institution

Baltimore School of Massage (BSM) has two locations, the main campus in Baltimore, Maryland, and a branch campus in York, Pennsylvania. Baltimore School of Massage is corporately owned and governed by Steiner Education Group, Inc., along with six other schools in Pennsylvania, Virginia, and Florida. BSM was founded in 1981 and moved to its present location in 1992. The School is located in the Woodlawn section of Baltimore County and is convenient to Baltimore City, Annapolis, and surrounding suburban areas. Maryland's Eastern Shore; Washington, D.C.; and Northern Virginia can be reached in about 1 to 1½ hours. All locations have full-time as well as part-time schedules, with day and evening classes to make it easy for students to fulfill their dreams of becoming massage therapists.

Special Features

The field of massage therapy is one of the fastest growing in the country, and the Baltimore School of Massage can thoroughly prepare a student for this exciting and rewarding career. The massage therapy programs are designed to give a thorough and comprehensive education in massage therapy in a positive learning environment. All campuses also have a Student Clinic where students have the opportunity to work with the public while attending school. BSM offers an extensive Continuing Education Program, which enables students to enhance their skills and learn new modalities after graduation. BSM also has a fully stocked Natural Health Shoppe on campus that carries everything students may need to enhance their practice, from massage creams and oils to music and school uniforms. All Steiner Education Group campuses employ a Career Services Coordinator that is available to assist graduates in achieving their goals. Whether graduates are interested in seeing the world by working aboard a cruise ship or would prefer a land-based position, the Career Services Department has built a relationship with some of the most successful employers in the industry. Graduates of the Steiner Education Group schools are given priority consideration when Steiner Leisure, Ltd., a global provider of spa services, is recruiting for their maritime or land-based spas.

Financial Aid/Scholarships

Baltimore School of Massage is approved by the Department of Education for Title IV funds, and federal financial aid is available to those who qualify. This may be in the form of Pell Grants and Stafford Loans. The Financial Aid Office is available to help guide students through this process.

Tuition and Fees

Students should call the campus for current pricing information.

Accreditation

Baltimore School of Massage is accredited by the Accrediting Commission of Career Schools and Colleges of Technology (ACCSCT) and programmatically accredited by the Commission on Massage Therapy Accreditation (COMTA). BSM is approved by the Maryland Higher Education Commission, the National Certification Board for Therapeutic Massage and Bodywork (NCBTMB) and the American Massage Therapy Association (AMTA) as a Category A Continuing Education Provider. The School is approved for the training of veterans and is a member of the AMTA Council of Schools. BSM is authorized to enroll nonimmigrant alien students by the Department of Justice and the Division of Homeland Security. The School is a member of the Maryland Association of Private Colleges and Career Schools (MAPCCS) and the Career College Association (CCA).

Program Content

Professional Program in Comprehensive Massage Therapy, Professional Program in Shiatsu and Asian Bodywork.

Program Description

Professional Program in Comprehensive Massage Therapy: The 637-hour program includes extensive lecture and hands-on training and prepares the student for a variety of settings. This program includes three major systems of bodywork: Swedish, deep tissue, and myofascial release; human anatomy; and physiology as well as additional modalities complete the curriculum.

Professional Program in Shiatsu and Asian Bodywork: The 620-hour program is designed to teach students the techniques of traditional Asian bodywork and how to apply those techniques as a Shiatsu practitioner. Whether students are already therapists or have no experience with Eastern or Western massage, they are able to graduate with an education in the art of Shiatsu as well as a working understanding of its practical application.

Admissions

Prospective students must complete an application, schedule an interview with an admissions representative, and be at least 18 years of age by the expected graduation date. A prospective student must display a genuine interest in becoming part of a learning atmosphere. Admissions requirements include evidence of high school graduation or GED equivalent. Upon acceptance, prior to starting classes, students are required to complete a physician's statement, signed by a licensed physician, indicating they are in good health and able to participate in the programs.

Contact

Baltimore School of Massage
6401 Dogwood Road
Baltimore, MD 21207
Phone: 410-944-8855
    877-944-8855 (toll-free)
Fax: 410-944-8859
Web: www.steinered.com

Broadcasting Institute of Maryland, Baltimore

About Our Institution

The Broadcasting Institute of Maryland (BIM) has been in existence since 1969 and believes a broadcasting education should focus on "hands-on" experience. With that in mind, BIM's facility includes three fully equipped radio studios, an AM and FM radio station (WBIM), and a full-service television studio that includes audio and video equipment, cameras, lighting, and editing capabilities. At BIM, there are no textbooks. Students study how to be a broadcaster by being a broadcaster. Whether it's on-air radio, TV, or radio or TV production, BIM students spend a great deal of their 600 hours in the "hands-on" mode.

Special Features

BIM's job placement service has been responsible for placing nearly 70 percent of its graduates in 2004 who majored in either radio or TV. Since 1969, BIM has graduated more than 2,000 students, including Robin Quivers (The Howard Stern Show), Lou Mann (President, House of Blues Media Properties), and numerous on-air radio and TV personalities throughout the country. BIM also streams its radio station on the Internet and offers a great early enrollment program, internships, and placement assistance.

Financial Aid/Scholarships

BIM elects not to participate in federal financial aid programs but does accept VA and other military-related funds. Most importantly, BIM has instituted its own form of financial aid, in which students may pay for their tuition over a period of time that extends past their graduation date. There are instances where BIM students can pay for their tuition on an interest-free basis, depending on the duration of time needed to make final payment. BIM does accept a variety of state and federal grants as well.

Tuition

Tuition at BIM is $10,900.

Accreditation

BIM is fully accredited by ACCSCT (Accrediting Commission of Career Schools and Colleges of Technology) and is one of only ten such fully accredited broadcasting schools in the entire country.

Admissions

To be admitted, students must visit the BIM campus, complete a personal interview with a grade of at least 70, complete a voice audition with a grade of at least 70, complete the Wonderlic Scholastic Level Exam with a grade of at least 18, complete an application form (available during the personal visit), and provide proof of a high school diploma or a satisfactory score on the GED test.

Enrollment

BIM enrolls no more than 30 students per class.

Program Content

On-air TV and radio, radio and TV production, media promotions, sales, and public relations

Program Description

The Broadcasting Institute of Maryland (BIM) helps prepare graduates for entry-level positions in a variety of media/communications fields, including on-air radio and TV, radio and TV production, media promotions, sales, and public relations.

BIM's educational program is 600 hours in length. There are four different starting points—day and evening during the fall and day and evening during the spring.

Contact

Robert Mathers
Broadcasting Institute of Maryland
7200 Harford Road
Baltimore, MD 21234
Phone: (410) 254-2770
          (800) 942-9246 (toll-free)
Fax: (410) 254-5357
E-mail: rm@bim.org
Web: www.bim.org

Hagerstown Business College, Hagerstown

About Our Institution

Hagerstown Business College (HBC) is a private junior college that has been providing high-quality career-oriented education for more than sixty years. HBC offers degree and certificate programs. Graduates receive lifetime career placement services. HBC is located on a 7.5-acre campus just 70 miles from Washington, D.C.; Baltimore, Maryland; and Harrisburg, Pennsylvania.

Special Features

Hagerstown Business College features a new 10,000-square-foot satellite campus in Frederick, Maryland and a 32,000-square-foot Career Technology Center. The College also offers an on-campus apartment-style residence hall as well as spacious outdoor areas for studying, relaxation, and sports activities. HBC's faculty members are credentialed professionals who have had practical and relevant experience in their fields. HBC is a Microsoft Certified Academic Training Provider.

Financial Aid/Scholarships

Pell Grants, FDSLP, FSEOG, work-study, VA benefits, state grants, and numerous scholarships are available to those who qualify.

Tuition and Fees

Tuition varies according to program.

Accreditation

The College is accredited by the Accrediting Council for Independent Colleges and Schools (ACICS), Commission on Accreditation of Allied Health Education Programs (CAAHEP), and National Accrediting Agency for Clinical Laboratory Sciences (NAACLS).

Admissions

Applicants must have a high school diploma or GED. All students must complete an application and complete the academic placement assessments.

Graduation Requirements

Candidates for graduation must complete all requirements for their program of study and maintain a CGPA of 2.0 or better, return all property belonging to the College, fulfill all financial obligations to the College prior to graduation, and attend graduate and financial aid exit interviews, if applicable.

Contact

Mr. James Klein
Director of Admissions
Hagerstown Business College
18618 Crestwood Drive
Hagerstown, MD 21742
Phone: (800) HBC-2670 (toll-free)
Fax: (301) 791-7661
E-mail: info@hagerstownbusinesscol.org
Web: www.hagerstownbusinesscol.org

Program Content

Degree: Accounting, Administrative Professional, Business Administration, Computer Applications, Computer Forensics, Criminal Justice, Graphic Design, Health Information Technology, Legal Assistant, Medical Receptionist/Transcriptionist, Medical Secretary/Assistant, Network Systems Programming, Network Systems Technology

Certificate: Computerized Accounting, Computer Network Technology, Computer Office Specialist, Legal Secretary, Medical Assistant, Medical Billing/Coding, Medical Receptionist, Medical Transcriptionist, Phlebotomist

Program Description

All career programs provide specialized or technical training for today's fastest-growing career fields. Each program includes computer training, an exceptional staff of credentialed faculty members, an internship, and job placement assistance.

Lincoln Technical Institute, Columbia

About Our Institution

The Columbia campus is one of the newest and largest facilities in the Lincoln Technical Institute system. The 75,300-square-foot campus is conveniently located between Baltimore and Washington, D.C., and is just off of I-95. There is ample parking for students on the premises. In addition, housing assistance is available. Instructional classrooms are equipped with industry-current equipment for students to practice their skills. The automotive program has a 10,000-square-foot auto shop consisting of sixteen bays, computerized diagnostic equipment, and specialty tools to ensure sufficient hands-on training. The air conditioning, refrigeration, and heating technology classrooms are self-contained, with equipment equivalent to industry standards today. Lincoln Tech has also introduced information technology programs. In addition, eight new and fully equipped computer labs feature twenty-nine individual workstations with Internet access.

Special Features

The Institute features twelve fully equipped classrooms and an eighteen-bay automotive shop for the automotive program. The shop was specifically designed to mirror an auto service repair facility and includes the newest automotive diagnostic and repair equipment. The air conditioning, refrigeration, and heating program includes eight fully equipped classrooms to teach the installation and servicing of commercial and residential environmental control systems. All of the faculty members are certified in their field, most at the master technician level.

Financial Aid/Scholarships

The Columbia campus has a variety of tuition scholarships available to graduating high school students. Awards include the Imagine America Scholarship, the County Executive Scholarship, and the MAPCS Scholarships, as well as others. To apply for most of these scholarships, students must fill out an application and take an aptitude-based scholarship test. A Scholarship Committee, made up of volunteers representing business, industry, education, and/or government, interviews the finalists and makes the award decision. In addition, Lincoln Tech maintains a Financial Aid Office on campus, which offers qualified students a variety of programs, including grants, loans, work-study, veterans' aid, and vocational rehabilitation.

Accreditation

The Institute is accredited by the Accrediting Commission of Career Schools and Colleges of Technology (ACCSCT) and certified by NATEF.

Admissions

Students may enroll at any time by contacting the school for admissions information. The applicant must have an interview with an admissions representative, complete an enrollment agreement and pay the registration fee, attain a passing score on the assessment test, submit evidence of a high school diploma or equivalent, and submit other information that may be required to determine qualification for admission.

Graduation Requirements

In order to graduate, students must complete all required courses in the program and all required comprehensive exams, attain a minimum overall grade point average of 2.0, not be on probation, have an overall 85

Program Content

Air Conditioning, Refrigeration, and Heating Technology; Automotive Technology; Computer Programming with Web Technology; PC Support Technician

Program Description

Automotive Technology: The program provides the graduate with the entry-level knowledge and skills required to correctly test, diagnose, replace, repair, and adjust as necessary the components of the mechanical, electronic, hydraulic, and accessories systems on current automobiles.

Air Conditioning, Refrigeration, and Heating Technology: The program provides the graduate with the entry-level skills required to install and service complete commercial and residential environmental control systems.

percent cumulative attendance average, and meet all financial obligations to the Institute.

Enrollment

Currently, 800 students are enrolled at the Institute.

Contact

Executive Director
9325 Snowden River Parkway
Columbia, MD 21046
Phone: (410) 290-7100
        (800) 924-9325 (toll-free)
Fax: (410) 309-6076
E-mail: execdircolumbia@lincolntech.com
Web: www.lincolntech.com

Medix School, Towson

About Our Institution
The School was founded in 1969 and has continued to produce qualified graduates for the health-care field. All the courses are selected and scheduled to contribute to that objective. Surveys of the industries that employ the School's graduates and input from its Advisory Board are used to determine what changes or modifications should be made in Medix School's training to give the best possible preparation for careers in the fields in which it trains.

Special Features
Graduates of the Medical Assistant Program can sit for the Certified Medical Assistant exam (CMA) and the Phlebotomy Certification exam. Graduates of the Dental Assistant Program can sit for the Certified Dental Assistant exam (CDA), which includes Radiology and Expanded Junctions. Graduates of the Medical Office Assistant Program can sit for the National Center for Competency Testing Certified Medical Office Assistant Exam.

Financial Aid/Scholarships
Financial aid programs offered include Federal Pell Grants, FFEL, FDLSP, Federal Perkins Loans, work-study, FSEOG, VA, state grants, and WIA.

Accreditation
Programs are accredited by the Accrediting Bureau of Health Education Schools, Commission on Dental Accreditation of the American Dental Association, and the Commission on Accreditation of Allied Health Education Programs (CAAHEP).

Admissions
A high school diploma or a GED certificate is required. In addition, applicants must successfully complete a standardized entrance exam and a personal interview.

Contact
Joan Verfuerth, Director of Admissions
Medix School
700 York Road
Towson, MD 21204
Phone: (410) 337-5155
Fax: (410) 337-5104
E-mail: admissions@medixschool.com
Web: www.medixschooltowson.edu

Program Content
Dental Assistant II, Medical Assistant, Medical Office Assistant

Programs Eligible for Scholarship	Tuition and Fees	Course Length/Credit Hours	Credential Earned
Dental Assistant II	$9180	40 weeks, 1,030 hours/42 credits	Certificate
Medical Assistant	$8892	40 weeks, 1,000 hours/45 credits	Certificate
Medical Office Assistant	$8892	40 weeks, 1,000 hours/45 credits	Certificate

Bryman Institute, Brighton

About Our Institution

The Bryman Schools were founded in 1960 by Mrs. Esther Bryman as the Los Angeles Colleges of Medical and Dental Assistants. The Los Angeles campus was the original school. In December 1995, Corinthian Schools, Inc. (CSi), a division of Corinthian Colleges, Inc. (CCi), acquired the schools. CCi is one of the largest postsecondary school organizations in the United States, operating more than eighty colleges and institutions nationwide.

The Institute's philosophy is to provide quality programs that are sound in concept, implemented by a competent and dedicated faculty, and geared to serve those seeking a solid foundation in the health-care field. The programs emphasize hands-on training, are relevant to the needs of employers, and focus on areas that offer strong long-term employment opportunities. Upon completion, graduates are prepared for entry-level positions in the medical and dental fields.

Financial Aid/Scholarships

Information regarding Federal Pell Grants, Federal Supplemental Educational Opportunity Grants, Federal Stafford Student Loans, Federal Perkins Loans, FPLUS, JTPA, and other assistance can be obtained from the Finance Office. Financial aid is available for those who qualify.

Accreditation

All programs are accredited by the Accrediting Commission of Career Schools and Colleges of Technology (ACCSCT).

Admissions

Successful candidates are selected based on interviews and the completion and presentation of required documents. Enrollment is open to all high school graduates as well as those holding a GED or its equivalent. Under certain circumstances, students who do not have a high school diploma or its equivalent may still be accepted for admission. Interested people should contact the Admissions Department for additional information.

Graduation Requirements

To be eligible for graduation, students must successfully complete all classroom modules with a grade of at least 70 percent, finish an approved externship of 160 hours for the medical and dental programs, and complete all other program requirements.

Enrollment

There are 500 students enrolled.

Program Content

Dental Assisting, Massage Therapy, Medical Administrative Assistant, Medical Assisting

Contact

Arthur Banaster, Director of Admissions
1505 Commonwealth Avenue
Brighton, MA 02135
Phone: (617) 783-9955
Fax: (617) 783-1166
E-mail: abanaste@cci.edu
Web: www.bryman-institute.com

Programs Eligible for Scholarship	Tuition and Fees	Course Length/Credit Hours	Credential Earned
Dental Assisting	$10,375	47 credit hours	Diploma
Massage Therapy	$10,500	47 credit hours	Diploma
Medical Administrative Assistant	$10,375	47 credit hours	Diploma
Medical Assisting	$10,375	47 credit hours	Diploma

Bryman Institute, Chelsea

About Our Institution

The Bryman Schools were founded in 1960 by Mrs. Esther Bryman as the Los Angeles Colleges of Medical and Dental Assistants. The Los Angeles campus was the original school. In December 1995, Corinthian Schools, Inc. (CSi), a division of Corinthian Colleges, Inc. (CCi), acquired the schools. CCi is one of the largest postsecondary school organizations in the United States, operating more than eighty colleges and institutions nationwide.

The Institute's philosophy is to provide quality programs that are sound in concept, implemented by a competent and dedicated faculty, and geared to serve those seeking a solid foundation in the health-care field. The programs emphasize hands-on training, are relevant to the needs of employers, and focus on areas that offer strong long-term employment opportunities. Upon completion, graduates are prepared for entry-level positions in the medical fields.

Financial Aid/Scholarships

Information regarding Federal Pell Grants, Federal Supplemental Educational Opportunity Grants, Federal Stafford Student Loans, Federal Perkins Loans, FPLUS, JTPA, and other assistance can be obtained from the Finance Office. Financial aid is available for those who qualify.

Accreditation

All programs are accredited by the Accrediting Commission of Career Schools and Colleges of Technology (ACCSCT).

Admissions

Successful candidates are selected based on interviews and the completion and presentation of required documents. Enrollment is open to all high school graduates as well as those holding a GED or its equivalent. Under certain circumstances, students who do not have a high school diploma or its equivalent may still be accepted for admission. Interested people should contact the Admissions Department for additional information.

Graduation Requirements

To be eligible for graduation, students must successfully complete all classroom modules with a grade of at least 70 percent, finish an approved externship of 160 hours for the medical and pharmacy technician programs, and complete all other program requirements.

Contact

Carl Williams, Director of Admissions
70 Everett Avenue
Chelsea, MA 02150
Phone: (617) 889-5999
Fax: (617) 889-0340
E-mail: cawilliams@cci.edu
Web: www.bryman-institute.com

Program Content

Massage Therapy, Medical Assisting, Pharmacy Technician

Programs Eligible for Scholarship	Tuition and Fees	Course Length/Credit Hours	Credential Earned
Massage Therapy	$12,045	57 credit hours	Diploma
Medical Assisting	$10,925	47 credit hours	Diploma
Pharmacy Technician	$10,780	58 credit hours	Diploma

CEI (Career-Ed Institute), Brockton

About Our Institution
Since 1982, Career-Ed Institute (CEI) has provided quality, postsecondary training in Massachusetts and Rhode Island. In 2001, CEI added two campuses in the Atlanta, Georgia, area and one campus in Henderson (Las Vegas), Nevada. All CEI locations offer focused programs designed to help students develop the skills and confidence essential for success in their chosen field of study.

Special Features
CEI is dedicated and committed to providing industry-standard, quality-driven instructional programs designed for serious-minded students. The philosophy of CEI extends beyond the teaching of technical proficiencies and practical knowledge. CEI is committed to serving its students with concern and respect.

Financial Aid/Scholarships
CEI maintains a financial aid office at each location. A variety of available programs, including grants, loans, scholarships, work-study, veteran's, and vocational rehabilitation, are available to qualified applicants. CEI provides two full-tuition and two half-tuition scholarships at each of its campuses. They are awarded annually to winners of the Scholarship Awards Program. Preliminary scholarship competition is conducted in the form of aptitude testing at each campus location. On the basis of test results, finalists are selected and invited to return for an interview conducted by the Scholarship Committee, composed of volunteers representing business, industry, education, and/or government.

Accreditation
CEI is accredited by the Accrediting Council for Independent Colleges and Schools, Washington, D.C., and is approved by a number of state and federal organizations. Additional information is available in the school catalog.

Admissions
An applicant must possess a high school diploma, GED certificate, or the equivalent. A passing score on the CEI Entrance Examination is necessary for acceptance.

Graduation Requirements
Graduation requirements mandate that a student complete all required courses and achieve an overall grade point average of at least 2.0.

Contact
Executive Director
Career-Ed Institute
375 Westgate Avenue
Brockton, MA 02301
Phone: 508-941-0730
Fax: 508-589-8436
E-mail: execdirbrockton@lincolntech.com
Web: www.ceitraining.com

Program Content
Medical Administrative Assistant, Network Systems Administrator, Therapeutic Massage and Bodywork Technology

CEI (Career-Ed Institute), Lowell

About Our Institution
Since 1982, Career-Ed Institute (CEI) has been providing high-quality, postsecondary training in Massachusetts and Rhode Island. In 2001, CEI added two campuses in the Atlanta, Georgia, area and one campus in Henderson (Las Vegas), Nevada. All CEI locations offer focused programs that help its students receive the skills and confidence essential for success in their chosen field of study.

Special Features
CEI is dedicated and committed to providing an industry-standard and quality-driven instructional program, designed for students. The philosophy of CEI extends beyond the teaching of technical proficiencies and practical knowledge. CEI is committed to serving its students with concern and respect.

Financial Aid/Scholarships
CEI maintains a financial aid office at each location. A variety of available programs including grants, loans, scholarships, work-study, veteran's and vocational rehabilitation are available to qualified applicants. CEI provides two full and two half-tuition scholarships at each of its campuses. They are awarded annually to winners of the Scholarship Awards Program. Preliminary scholarship competition is conducted in the form of aptitude testing at each campus location. On the basis of test results, finalists are selected and invited to return for an interview conducted by the Scholarship Committee, which is made up of volunteers who represent business, industry, education, and/or government.

Accreditation
CEI is accredited by the Accrediting Council for Independent Colleges and Schools (ACICS), Washington, D.C., and is approved by a number of respective state and federal organizations. Further information is available from the school catalog.

Admissions
An applicant must satisfy the requirements of possessing a high school diploma or GED. A passing score on the CEI Entrance Examination is necessary for acceptance.

Graduation Requirements
Graduation requirements mandate that a student complete all required courses and achieve an overall grade point average of at least 2.0.

Contact
Executive Director
Career-Ed Institute
211 Plain Street
Lowell, MA 01852
Phone: 978-458-4800
Fax: 978-458-1287
E-mail: execdirlowell@lincolntech.com
Web: www.ceitraining.com

Program Content
Medical Administrative Assistant, Medical Assistant, Network Systems Administrator, PC Support Technician, Pharmacy Technician, Therapeutic Massage and Bodywork Technology

CEI (Career-Ed Institute), Somerville

About Our Institution
Since 1982, Career-Ed Institute (CEI) has been providing high-quality, postsecondary training in Massachusetts and Rhode Island. In 2001, CEI added two campuses in the Atlanta, Georgia, area and one campus in Henderson (Las Vegas), Nevada. All CEI locations offer focused programs that help its students receive the skills and confidence essential for success in their chosen field of study.

Special Features
CEI is dedicated and committed to providing an industry-standard and quality-driven instructional program, designed for students. The philosophy of CEI extends beyond the teaching of technical proficiencies and practical knowledge. CEI is committed to serving its students with concern and respect.

Financial Aid/Scholarships
CEI maintains a financial aid office at each location. A variety of available programs including grants, loans, scholarships, work-study, veteran's and vocational rehabilitation are available to qualified applicants. CEI provides two full and two half-tuition scholarships at each of its campuses. They are awarded annually to winners of the Scholarship Awards Program. Preliminary scholarship competition is conducted in the form of aptitude testing at each campus location. On the basis of test results, finalists are selected and invited to return for an interview conducted by the Scholarship Committee, which is made up of volunteers who represent business, industry, education, and/or government.

Accreditation
CEI is accredited by the Accrediting Council for Independent Colleges and Schools (ACICS), Washington, D.C., and is approved by a number of respective state and federal organizations. Further information is available from the school catalog.

Admissions
An applicant must satisfy the requirements of possessing a high school diploma or GED. A passing score on the CEI Entrance Examination is necessary for acceptance.

Graduation Requirements
Graduation requirements mandate that a student complete all required courses and achieve an overall grade point average of at least 2.0.

Contact
Executive Director
Career-Ed Institute
5 Middlesex Avenue
Somerville, MA 02145
Phone: 617-776-3500
Fax: 617-766-1899
E-mail: execdirsomerville@lincolntech.com
Web: www.ceitraining.com

Program Content
Medical Administrative Assistant, Medical Assistant, Network Systems Administrator, PC Support Technician, Pharmacy Technician, Therapeutic Massage and Bodywork Technology

Hallmark Institute of Photography, Turners Falls

About Our Institution
Hallmark Institute of Photography was incorporated in 1974 and enrolled its first class in 1975. The program of study was designed by a team of highly successful professional photographers and grew from the realization that the career field of professional photography was in need of a different kind of educational program than that offered by the majority of photography schools and colleges. The basic philosophy is that the professional photographer should possess the business management skills needed to effectively market visual images and operate a photographic studio or to secure and hold meaningful employment with an established photographic concern.

Special Features
Hallmark Institute's unique ten-month, career-minded program approaches learning with a hands-on technique, quickly building from beginning to advanced photographic skills. Committed staff and faculty prepare an individual to handle photographic assignments of great diversity in a professional manner, including portraiture; catalog and advertising illustration; aerial and location; studio and environmental product; group and candid; industrial; photojournalism; and digital capture, manipulation, and restoration. With a well-rounded curriculum emphasizing the technical, artistic, and business aspects of photography, Hallmark graduates are ready to secure meaningful employment with established photographers or to begin plans for a successful photographic business of their own.

Financial Aid/Scholarships
A variety of financial assistance programs are available, such as Pell, FDSLP, work-study (not federally funded), SEOG, VA, state grants, state loans, and many alternative financial programs.

Tuition and Fees
The total tuition and fees are $30,950—this charge includes a $25 application fee, $100 enrollment fee (confirming deposit), $4,900 supplies and materials fee (film, paper, chemistry, books, facility and lab fees, etc.), and $25,925 for tuition.

Accreditation
The Institute is accredited by the Accrediting Commission of Career Schools and Colleges of Technology (ACCSCT).

Admissions
The Admissions Office requires an application, $25 application fee, two letters of recommendation and a personal interview to determine acceptance. The applicant must be at least a high school graduate or GED holder to attend. (High school seniors may submit an application prior to graduation, but will have to submit documentation of graduation before permission to enter class is granted.)

Graduation Requirements
A Certificate of Completion is awarded to those students who maintain satisfactory attendance during the school year, obtain a minimum of 75

Program Content
Professional Photography

Program Description
This ten-month resident program prepares the career-minded individual for the technical, artistic, and business demands of Professional Photography and Imaging.

percent of potential academic credit, and satisfy all obligations to the school.

Enrollment
Up to 250 students are accepted for the school year.

Contact
Tammy Murphy
Director of Admissions
241 Millers Falls Road
P.O. Box 308
Turners Falls, MA 01376
Phone: (413) 863-2478
Fax: (413) 863-4118
E-mail: info@hallmark.edu
Web: www.hallmark.edu

Programs Eligible for Scholarship	Tuition and Fees	Course Length/Credit Hours	Credential Earned
Professional Photography	$30,950	40 weeks/1,400 clock hours	Certificate

ITT Technical Institute, Norwood

About Our Institution

ITT Technical Institute is owned and operated by ITT Educational Services, Inc. (ITT/ESI), a leading private college system offering technology-influenced programs of study. ITT/ESI operates seventy-seven ITT Technical Institutes in thirty states, providing career-focused degree programs to approximately 39,000 students as of spring 2004. Headquartered in Carmel, Indiana, ITT/ESI has been actively involved in the higher education community in the United States since 1969.

ITT Technical Institute, Norwood offers programs of study leading to the Associate of Applied Science degree. Curriculum offerings are designed to prepare students for career opportunities in fields of technology. Students attend classes year-round, with convenient breaks provided throughout the year. A full-time student course load can have class meetings as often as three days a week, and classes are typically available in the morning, afternoon, and evening, depending on student enrollment. This class schedule offers students the flexibility to pursue part-time employment opportunities. General education courses may be available online.

Special Features

Most ITT Technical Institute programs of study blend traditional academic content with applied learning concepts, with a significant portion devoted to practical study in a lab environment. Advisory committees, made up of representatives of local businesses, help each ITT Technical Institute periodically review and update curricula, equipment, and laboratory design.

Financial Aid/Scholarships

ITT Technical Institute maintains a Financial Aid Department on the campus. The campus is designated as an eligible institution by the U.S. Department of Education for participation in the following programs: Federal Stafford Student Loan Program, Federal PLUS Loan Program, and Federal Work-Study Program. The school also offers nonfederal loans through Bank One for eligible students.

Tuition and Fees

March 2005 tuition is $386 per credit hour.

Accreditation

The Institute is accredited by the Accrediting Council for Independent Colleges and Schools (ACICS).

Admissions

For admission requirements, students should contact the school for a catalog.

Graduation Requirements

For graduation requirements, students should consult the school catalog.

Contact

Dennis Saccoia, Director
ITT Technical Institute
333 Providence Highway
Norwood, MA 02062
Phone: (781) 278-7200
Fax: (781) 278-0766

Program Content

School of Information Technology: Information Technology–Computer Network Systems, Information Technology–Software Applications and Programming, Information Technology–Web Development

School of Electronics Technology: Computer and Electronics Engineering Technology

School of Drafting and Design: Computer Drafting and Design, Information Technology–Multimedia Option

ITT Technical Institute, Woburn

About Our Institution

The company: ITT Technical Institute is owned and operated by ITT Educational Services, Inc. (ITT/ESI), a leading private college system offering technology-influenced programs of study. ITT/ESI operates seventy-seven ITT Technical Institutes in thirty states, providing career-focused degree programs to approximately 39,000 students as of spring 2004. Headquartered in Carmel, Indiana, ITT/ESI has been actively involved in the higher education community in the United States since 1969.

Curricula: Curriculum offerings are designed to prepare students for career opportunities in fields of technology. Students attend classes year-round, with convenient breaks provided throughout the year. A full-time student's courses may meet as often as three days per week and are typically available in the morning, afternoon, and evening, depending on student enrollment. General education courses may be available online. This class schedule offers students the flexibility to pursue part-time employment opportunities.

The Institute awards the Associate of Applied Science.

Special Features

Most ITT Technical Institute programs of study blend traditional academic content with applied learning concepts, with a significant portion devoted to practical study in a lab environment. Advisory committees, composed of representatives of local businesses, help each ITT Technical Institute periodically review and update curricula, equipment, and laboratory design.

Financial Aid/Scholarships

ITT Technical Institute maintains a Financial Aid Department on campus. The campus is designated as an eligible institution by the U.S. Department of Education for participation in the following programs: Federal Stafford Student Loan, Federal PLUS loan, and Federal Work-Study Program. The school also offers nonfederal loans through Bank One for eligible students.

Tuition and Fees

March 2005 tuition is $386 per credit hour.

Accreditation

The Institute is accredited by the Accrediting Council for Independent Colleges and Schools (ACICS).

Admissions

For admission requirements, students should consult the school catalog.

Graduation Requirements

For graduation requirements, students should consult the school catalog.

Program Content

School of Information Technology: Information Technology–Computer Network Systems Option, Software Applications and Programming Option, and Web Development Option

School of Electronics Technology: Computer and Electronics Engineering Technology

School of Drafting and Design: Computer Drafting and Design, Information Technology–Multimedia Option

Contact

Stephen Carter, Director
ITT Technical Institute
10 Forbes Road
Woburn, MA 01801
Phone: (781) 937-8324
Fax: (781) 937-3402

WyoTech, Bedford

About Our Institution
WyoTech, formerly East Coast Aero Tech, is one of more than eighty schools owned and operated by Corinthian Colleges, Inc. Founded in 1932 by John T. Griffin, Sr., WyoTech seeks students with the ability, curiosity, and motivation to be successful in the highly technical program of aviation maintenance. WyoTech is committed to providing a top-notch technical education for an elite student body, providing them with the marketable skills necessary to secure a position in a variety of exceptional career opportunities in aviation and related industries.

Special Features
WyoTech is based at Hanscom Air Field and is composed of 55,000 square feet of space for labs, shops, classrooms, and administrative offices. Located just 15 miles northwest of Boston, Massachusetts, the school is in the town of Bedford, an attractive historic area between the towns of Lexington and Concord. Shops and labs are equipped with aircraft and aircraft system mock-ups used to train students in the repair of today's state-of-the-art aircraft.

Financial Aid/Scholarships
Federal Pell Grants, Federal Stafford Student Loans, Federal PLUS loans, Federal Supplemental Educational Opportunity Grants, VA benefits, and high school and other scholarships are available for those who qualify.

Accreditation
WyoTech is accredited by the Accrediting Council of Career Schools and Colleges of Technology (ACCSCT).

Admissions
Candidates must have a high school diploma or the equivalent. A personal admissions interview is normally required.

Graduation Requirements
Students are required to earn a minimum cumulative grade point average of 2.0 in their major. Students must also meet specific program requirements.

Enrollment
There are 250 to 300 students enrolled.

Contact
Don Keeney, Director of Admissions
150 Hanscom Drive
Bedford, MA 01730
Phone: (781) 274-8448
Fax: (781) 274-8490
E-mail: dkeeney@cci.edu
Web: www.wyotech.com

Program Content
Aeronautical Maintenance Technology

Programs Eligible for Scholarship	Tuition and Fees	Course Length/Credit Hours
Aeronautical Maintenance Technology	$25,000	15 months/2,100 clock hours

Carnegie Institute, Troy

About Our Institution
Carnegie Institute, founded in 1947, is a private, accredited, postsecondary training institute. Through technically acquired knowledge and hands-on training, students develop competence in career-related skills. By keeping the curriculum relevant to career requirements, students are able to see the direct relationship between program objectives and employer expectations.

Special Features
A low student-teacher ratio and direct supervision by experienced subject specialists enables students to learn technical skills in Carnegie's well-equipped laboratories and classrooms. Students are assigned to approved externship facilities as final preparation for job placement.

Carnegie Institute's Medical Assistant Program is accredited by the Commission on Accreditation of Allied Health Education Programs (CAAHEP). Therefore, Medical Assistant graduates are eligible for the AAMA National Certification Exam immediately after successful completion of their training.

Financial Aid/Scholarships
Carnegie Institute participates in many financial aid programs, including Federal Pell Grants, Federal Supplemental Educational Opportunity Grants, Federal Family Education Loan Programs, Veterans Administration Benefits, Michigan Rehabilitation, Career Training Foundation Imaging America Scholarship, United Auto Workers Tuition Assistance programs, Michigan Merit Awards, Maxine Williams Scholarship, and the Massage Magazine Schools Program.

Tuition and Fees
For tuition, see the chart below. All supplies, lab fees, and books are included in the tuition.

Accreditation
Carnegie Institute has program accreditation through CAAHEP and institutional accreditation through the Accrediting Commission of Career Schools and Colleges of Technology (ACCSCT).

Admissions
Applicants are required to be high school graduates or its equivalent, with documentation of high school transcripts or GED. Also required is a personal interview with an admissions officer and satisfactory completion of program entry testing.

Graduation Requirements
In order to graduate, the student must have satisfactorily completed the program, have a combined average grade of not less than 70 percent, have

Program Content
Massage Therapist, Medical Administrative Assistant, Medical Assistant, Medical Business Specialist, Medical Insurance Biller, Medical Records Transcriptist

Program Description
Massage Therapist: A specialist in combining scientific concepts with professional applications of quality therapeutic massage and bodyworks.

Medical Administrative Assistant: A specialist on administrative and office management skills.

Medical Assistant: The most multiskilled professional on today's health-care team.

Medical Business Specialist: A medical office specialist with office automation skills.

Medical Insurance Biller: A medical billing specialist.

Medical Records Transcriptionist: A medical language and word-processing specialist.

recommendation of the faculty, satisfied indebtedness to the school, and have a satisfactory record of attendance.

Contact
Linda M. Ingraham
Chief Administrator and Director of Student Services
550 Stephenson Highway, Suites 100–109
Troy, MI 48083
Phone: (248) 589-1078
Fax: (248) 589-1631
E-mail: Carnegie47@aol.com
Web: www.carnegie-institute.com

Programs Eligible for Scholarship	Tuition and Fees	Course Length/Credit Hours	Credential Earned
Massage Therapist	$7,265	48 weeks/66.5 credit hours	Diploma
Medical Administrative Assistant	$8,225	48 weeks/75.5 credit hours	Diploma
Medical Assistant	$8,470	48 weeks/82 credit hours	Diploma
Medical Business Specialist	$6,480	48 weeks/46 credit hours	Diploma
Medical Insurance Biller	$5,990	36 weeks/33.5 credit hours	Diploma
Medical Records Transcriptionist	$8,205	48 weeks/69 credit hours	Diploma

ITT Technical Institute, Canton

About Our Institution
The company: ITT Technical Institute is owned and operated by ITT Educational Services, Inc. (ITT/ESI), a leading private college system offering technology-influenced programs of study. ITT/ESI operates seventy-seven ITT Technical Institutes in thirty states, providing career-focused degree programs to approximately 39,000 students as of spring 2004. Headquartered in Carmel, Indiana, ITT/ESI has been actively involved in the higher education community in the United States since 1969.

Curricula: Curriculum offerings are designed to help students begin to prepare for career opportunities in fields of technology. Students attend classes year-round, with convenient breaks provided throughout the year. A full-time student course load can have class meetings as often as three days a week and are typically available in the morning, afternoon, and evening, depending on student enrollment. General education courses may be available online. This class schedule offers flexibility to students to pursue part-time employment opportunities.

ITT Technical Institute, Canton, awards the Associate of Applied Science degree.

Special Features
Most ITT Technical Institute programs of study blend traditional academic content with applied learning concepts, with a significant portion devoted to practical study in a lab environment. Advisory committees composed of representatives of local businesses help each ITT Technical Institute periodically review and update curricula, equipment, and laboratory design.

Financial Aid/Scholarships
ITT Technical Institute maintains a Financial Aid Department on campus. The campus is designated as an eligible institution by the U.S. Department of Education for participation in the following programs: Federal Stafford Student Loan Program, Federal PLUS Loan Program, and Federal Work-Study Program. The school also offers nonfederal loans available through Bank One for eligible students.

Tuition and Fees
March 2005 tuition is $386 per credit hour.

Accreditation
The school is accredited by the Accrediting Council for Independent Colleges and Schools (ACICS).

Admissions
For admission requirements, students should contact the school for a catalog.

Graduation Requirements
For graduation requirements, students should contact the school for a catalog.

Program Content
School of Information Technology: Information Technology–Computer Network Systems, Information Technology–Software Applications and Programming, Information Technology–Web Development

School of Electronics Technology: Computer and Electronics Engineering Technology

School of Drafting and Design: Computer Drafting and Design, Information Technology–Multimedia Option

Contact
Nadine Palazzolo, Director
ITT Technical Institute
1905 South Haggerty Road
Canton, MI 48188
Phone: (734) 397-7800
Fax: (734) 397-1945

ITT Technical Institute, Grand Rapids

About Our Institution

The company: ITT Technical Institute is owned and operated by ITT Educational Services, Inc. (ITT/ESI), a leading private college system offering technology-influenced programs of study. ITT/ESI operates seventy-seven ITT Technical Institutes in thirty states, providing career-focused degree programs to approximately 39,000 students as of spring 2004. Headquartered in Carmel, Indiana, ITT/ESI has been actively involved in the higher education community in the United States since 1969.

Curricula: Curriculum offerings are designed to prepare students for career opportunities in fields of technology. Students attend classes year-round, with convenient breaks provided throughout the year. A full-time student's classes may meet as often as three days per week and are typically available in the morning, afternoon, and evening, depending on student enrollment. General education courses may be available online. This class schedule offers the flexibility to students to pursue part-time employment opportunities.

The Institute awards the Associate of Applied Science.

Special Features

Most ITT Technical Institute programs of study blend traditional academic content with applied learning concepts, with a significant portion devoted to practical study in a lab environment. Advisory committees, made up of representatives of local businesses, help each ITT Technical Institute periodically review and update curricula, equipment, and laboratory design.

Financial Aid/Scholarships

ITT Technical Institute maintains a Financial Aid Department on campus. The campus is designated as an eligible institution by the U.S. Department of Education for participation in the following programs: Federal Stafford Student Loan, Federal PLUS loan, and Federal Work-Study Program. The school also offers nonfederal loans through Bank One for eligible students.

Tuition and Fees

March 2005 tuition is $386 per credit hour.

Accreditation

The Institute is accredited by the Accrediting Council for Independent Colleges and Schools (ACICS).

Admissions

For information on admission requirements, students should consult the school catalog.

Graduation Requirements

For information on graduation requirements, students should consult the school catalog.

Program Content

School of Information Technology: Information Technology–Computer Network Systems, Information Technology–Software Applications and Programming, Information Technology–Web Development

School of Electronics Technology: Computer and Electronics Engineering Technology

School of Drafting and Design: Computer Drafting and Design, Information Technology–Multimedia Option

Contact

Dennis Hormel, Director
ITT Technical Institute
4020 Sparks Drive, SE
Grand Rapids, MI 49546
Phone: (616) 956-1060
Fax: (616) 956-5606

ITT Technical Institute, Troy

About Our Institution

ITT Technical Institute is owned and operated by ITT Educational Services, Inc. (ITT/ESI), a leading private college system offering technology-influenced programs of study. ITT/ESI operates seventy-seven ITT Technical Institutes in thirty states, which provide career-focused degree programs to approximately 39,000 students as of spring 2004. Headquartered in Carmel, Indiana, ITT/ESI has been actively involved in the higher education community in the United States since 1969.

Curriculum offerings are designed to help prepare students for career opportunities in fields of technology. Students attend classes year-round, with convenient breaks provided throughout the year. A student with a full-time course load can have class meetings as often as three days a week. Classes are typically available in the morning, afternoon, and evening, depending on student enrollment. General education courses may be available online. This class schedule offers students the flexibility to pursue part-time employment opportunities.

Special Features

Most ITT Technical Institute programs of study blend traditional academic content with applied learning concepts, with a significant portion devoted to practical study in a lab environment. Advisory committees, made up of representatives of local businesses, help each ITT Technical Institute periodically review and update curricula, equipment, and laboratory design.

Financial Aid/Scholarships

ITT Technical Institute maintains a Financial Aid Department on campus. The campus is designated as an eligible institution by the U.S. Department of Education for participation in the following programs: Federal Stafford Student Loan, Federal PLUS Loan, and Federal Work-Study. The school also offers nonfederal loans made available through Bank One for eligible students.

Tuition and Fees

March 2005 tuition was $386 per credit hour.

Admissions

For admissions requirements, students should contact the school for a catalog.

Graduation Requirements

For graduation requirements, students should contact the school for a catalog.

Contact

Steve Goddard, Director
ITT Technical Institute
1522 East Big Beaver Road
Troy, MI 48083
Phone: (248) 524-1800
Fax: (248) 524-1965

Program Content

ITT Technical Institute, Troy, offers the Associate of Applied Science in drafting and design, electronics technology, and information technology.

Program Description

School of Drafting and Design: Computer Drafting and Design, Information Technology-Multimedia option)

School of Electronics Technology: Computer and Electronics Engineering Technology

School of Information Technology: Information Technology-Computer Network Systems, Information Technology-Software Applications and Programming, and Information Technology-Web Development)

National Institute of Technology, Dearborn

About Our Institution

National Institute of Technology (NIT) is one of more than eighty schools owned and operated by Corinthian Colleges, Inc. (CCi). NIT–Dearborn is a branch campus of NIT in Southfield, Michigan. The main campus was originally a member of RETS Electronic School, which was established in 1935. NIT's philosophy is to provide high-quality programs that are sound in concept and implemented by a competent and dedicated faculty. The programs emphasize hands-on training, are relevant to employers' needs, and focus on areas that offer strong, long-term employment opportunities.

Special Features

The school is conveniently located on Michigan Avenue in Dearborn, Michigan. The attractive facility includes computer and medical assisting laboratories, lecture rooms, a career-services and resource center, a student lounge, and administrative areas. The campus is located close to public transportation.

Financial Aid/Scholarships

Financial aid is available for those who qualify. The school participates in Pell, FFEL, work-study, SEOG, VA, and WIA programs. Funding is also available through the Michigan Jobs Commission, UAW/TAP programs, Michigan Merit Awards, Michigan Rehabilitation Services, and a number of other agencies. High school and other scholarships are available.

Accreditation

Accredited by the Accrediting Commission of Career Schools and Colleges of Technology (ACCSCT).

Admissions

All applicants for the Network Systems Support program must possess a high school diploma or its equivalent and successfully complete the CPAt preadmissions examination. Applicants for all other programs need not possess a high school diploma or its equivalent but must successfully complete a preadmissions examination.

Graduation Requirements

Technical: Students must complete all program requirements and classroom training with a cumulative grade point average of at least 2.0. Medical: Students must complete all program requirements and classroom modules with a grade of at least 70 percent.

Enrollment

Six hundred thirty students are enrolled.

Program Content

Massage Therapy, Medical Assisting, Medical Insurance Billing/Coding, Network Systems Support

Contact

Kathy Galasso, Director of Admissions
23400 Michigan Avenue, Suite 200
Dearborn, MI 48124
Phone: (313) 562-4228
(888) 463-0494 (toll-free)
Fax: (313) 562-5774
E-mail: kgalasso@cci.edu
Web: www.nitschools.com

Programs Eligible for Scholarship	Tuition and Fees	Course Length/Credit Hours
Massage Therapy	$12,200	9 months
Medical Assisting	$10,750	8 months
Medical Insurance Billing/Coding	$ 8,300	6 months
Network Systems Support	$13,750	9 months

National Institute of Technology, Detroit

About Our Institution

The National Institute of Technology (NIT)–Detroit campus is a branch campus of the NIT–Southfield campus. The National Institute of Technology–Southfield is one of more than eighty schools owned and operated by a division of Corinthian Colleges, Inc.

Special Features

NIT–Detroit's facilities and equipment are excellent, and the years of field experience of the faculty members make career training an exceptional experience. There is placement assistance upon graduation.

Financial Aid/Scholarships

Available to students are Federal Pell Grants, FFEL, work-study, FSEOG, and WIA. Funding is also available through Michigan Works Agencies, UAW/TAP programs, Michigan Merit Awards, Michigan Rehabilitation Services, and a number of other agencies. High school and other scholarships are available. Financial aid is available for those who qualify.

Accreditation

The Institute holds accreditation by the Accrediting Commission of Career Schools and Colleges of Technology (ACCSCT).

Admissions

All applicants for the pharmacy technician program must possess a high school diploma or equivalent and successfully complete the CPAt preadmissions examination. Applicants for all other programs need not possess a high school diploma or its equivalent but must successfully complete a preadmissions examination.

Graduation Requirements

Students must complete all program requirements and classroom modules with a grade of at least 70 percent.

Enrollment

There are 365 students enrolled.

Contact

Mike Draheim, Director of Admissions
300 River Place Drive, Suite 1000
Detroit, MI 48207
Phone: (313) 567-5350
Fax: (313) 567-2095
E-mail: mdraheim@cci.edu
Web: www.nitschools.com

Program Content

Medical Assisting, Medical Insurance Billing/Coding, Pharmacy Technician

Programs Eligible for Scholarship	Tuition and Fees	Course Length/Credit Hours	Credential Earned
Medical Assisting	$10,750	8 months	Diploma
Medical Insurance Billing/Coding	$ 8,300	6 months	Diploma
Pharmacy Technician	$10,750	8 months	Diploma

National Institute of Technology, Southfield

About Our Institution
National Institute of Technology (NIT) was founded as RETS Electronics School in 1935 in Detroit, Michigan. It relocated to Livonia, Michigan, in 1983 and to Southfield in 1996. Branch campuses of NIT–Southfield are located in Dearborn, Michigan, and downtown Detroit. National Institute of Technology–Southfield is one of more than eighty schools owned and operated by a division of Corinthian Colleges, Inc.

Special Features
NIT–Southfield's facilities and equipment are excellent, and the years of field experience of the faculty members make career training an exceptional experience. There is placement assistance upon graduation.

Financial Aid/Scholarships
Federal Pell Grants, FFEL, Federal Perkins Loans, work-study, FSEOG, VA, WIA; funding also available through Michigan Jobs Commission, UAW/TAP programs, Michigan Merit Awards, Michigan Rehabilitation Services, and a number of other agencies. High school and other scholarships available. Financial aid available for those who qualify.

Accreditation
The Institute holds accreditation by the Accrediting Commission of Career Schools and Colleges of Technology (ACCSCT) and Microsoft IT Academy. The Medical Assisting Program is accredited by the AAMA, a division of the Commission on Accreditation of Allied Health Education Programs (CAAHEP).

Admissions
Applicants for all programs need not possess a high school diploma or its equivalent but must successfully complete a preadmissions examination.

Graduation Requirements
Technical: Students must complete all required program requirements and classroom training with a cumulative grade point average of at least 2.0. Medical: Students must complete all required program requirements and classroom modules with a grade of at least 70 percent.

Enrollment
There are 850 students enrolled.

Program Content
Computer Technology, Electronics and Computer Technology, Massage Therapy, Medical Administrative Assistant, Medical Assisting, Medical Insurance Billing/Coding

Contact
Joe Rocha
Director of Admissions
26111 Evergreen Road
Southfield, MI 48076
Phone: (248) 799-9933
         (877) 782-1290 (toll-free)
Fax: (248) 799-2912
E-mail: srocha@cci.edu
Web: www.nitschools.com

Programs Eligible for Scholarship	Tuition and Fees	Course Length/Credit Hours	Credential Earned
Computer Technology	$11,800	9 months	Diploma
Electronics and Computer Technology	$23,000	18 months	Diploma
Massage Therapy	$12,100	9 months	Diploma
Medical Administrative Assistant	$10,650	8 months	Diploma
Medical Assisting	$10,650	8 months	Diploma
Medical Insurance Billing/Coding	$ 8,300	6 months	Diploma

Olympia Career Training Institute, Grand Rapids

About Our Institution

Olympia Career Training Institute (OCTI) is one of more than 140 schools owned and operated by Corinthian Colleges, Inc. (CCi). OCTI, formerly Grand Rapids Educational Center, was founded in 1972. CCi acquired Olympia Career Training Institute in February 2001. OCTI's philosophy is to provide high-quality programs that are sound in concept and implemented by a competent and dedicated faculty. The programs emphasize hands-on training, are relevant to employers' needs, and focus on areas that offer strong, long-term employment opportunities.

Special Features

The school is conveniently located near the Route 131 and I-96 expressways and provides free parking, is handicapped accessible, and is near public transportation. OCTI is spacious (15,000 square feet), modern, and air conditioned. Facilities include administrative offices; lecture rooms; medical, dental, and computer labs; examination rooms; business labs; and student lounges.

Financial Aid/Scholarships

The school participates in Federal Pell Grant, FFEL, work-study, FSEOG, VA, WIA, and MEAP programs. Funding is also available through other agencies. High school and other scholarships are available. Financial aid is available for those who qualify.

Accreditation

Programs are accredited by the Accrediting Committee of the Accrediting Bureau of Health Education Schools (ABHES).

Admissions

Applicants must possess a high school diploma or its equivalent. All applicants must complete a qualification questionnaire and achieve a passing score on a nationally standardized test. This test measures an applicant's basic skills in reading and arithmetic. Student health forms are required before students may participate in clinical labs. Some programs have additional prerequisites.

Graduation Requirements

To be eligible for graduation, students must complete all required courses with a grade of C or better, have a cumulative grade point average (GPA) of 2.0 or higher, and complete an approved externship with a grade of C or above.

Enrollment

There are 800 students enrolled.

Program Content

Dental Assistant, Massage Therapy, Medical Administrative Assistant, Medical Assistant, Medical Insurance Billing/Coding, Network Systems Support, Pharmacy Technologist, Practical Nurse

Contact

Bobbi Block, Director of Admissions
1750 Woodworth Street, NE
Grand Rapids, MI 49525
Phone: (616) 364-8464
Fax: (616) 364-5404
E-mail: rblok@cci.edu
Web: www.olympia-institute.com

Programs Eligible for Scholarship	Tuition and Fees	Course Length/Credit Hours
Dental Assistant	$ 9,724.00	8 months/47 credit units
Massage Therapy	$11,210.70	3 months/60 credit units
Medical Assistant	$ 9,293.00	8 months/47 credit units
Medical Administrative Assistant	$10,218.13	8 months/47 credit units
Medical Insurance Billing/Coding	$ 7,995.85	6 months/35 credit units
Pharmacy Technologist	$10,464.71	9 months/58 credit units
Practical Nurse	$17,215.20	12 months/78 credit units

Olympia Career Training Institute, Kalamazoo

About Our Institution
Olympia Career Training Institute (OCTI) is one of more than eighty schools owned and operated by Corinthian Colleges, Inc. (CCi). OCTI, formerly Grand Rapids Educational Center, was founded in 1972. CCi acquired Olympia Career Training Institute in February 2001. OCTI's philosophy is to provide high-quality programs that are sound in concept and implemented by a competent and dedicated faculty. The programs emphasize hands-on training, are relevant to employers' needs, and focus on areas that offer strong, long-term employment opportunities.

Special Features
The school is conveniently located near the Route 131 and I-94 expressways and provides free parking, is handicapped accessible, and is near public transportation. OCTI is spacious (12,000 square feet), modern, smoke-free, and air conditioned. Facilities include administrative offices; lecture rooms; medical, dental, and computer labs; examination rooms; business labs; and student lounges. Class enrollment is limited, and some classes have fewer than 18 students.

Financial Aid/Scholarships
Financial aid is available for those who qualify. The school participates in Federal Pell Grant, FFEL, work-study, FSEOG, VA, and WIA programs. Funding also available through other agencies. High school and other scholarships are available.

Accreditation
The school is accredited by the Accrediting Committee of the Accrediting Bureau of Health Education Schools (ABHES).

Admissions
Applicants must possess a high school diploma or its equivalent. All applicants must complete a qualification questionnaire and achieve a passing score on a nationally standardized test. This test measures an applicant's basic skills in reading and arithmetic. Some programs have additional prerequisites.

Graduation Requirements
To be eligible for graduation, students must complete all required courses with a grade of C or better and a cumulative grade point average (GPA) of 2.0 or above and complete an approved externship with a grade of C or better.

Program Content
Dental Assistant, Massage Therapy, Medical Administrative Assistant, Medical Assisting, Medical Insurance Billing/Coding, Pharmacy Technician

Contact
Susan Smith, Director of Admissions
5349 West Main Street
Kalamazoo, MI 49009
Phone: (269) 381-9616
Fax: (269) 381-2513
E-mail: susans@cci.edu
Web: www.olympia-institute.com

Programs Eligible for Scholarship	Tuition and Fees	Course Length/Credit Hours
Dental Assistant	$9,340	8 months/47 credit units
Massage Therapy	$9,925	9 months/60 credit units
Medical Administrative Assistant	$9,340	8 months/47 credit units
Medical Assisting	$9,340	8 months/47 credit units
Medical Insurance Billing/Coding	$7,345	6 months/35 credit units
Pharmacy Technician	$9,870	8 months/58 credit units

Specs Howard School of Broadcast Arts, Southfield

About Our Institution

Founded on January 14, 1970, the Specs Howard School has spent more than three decades dedicated to high-quality hands-on training of broadcast professionals. The Specs Howard School has grown to become one of the nation's leading communications training centers and graduates approximately 400 students into the industry each year. The School has had a profound impact on the face of broadcasting in Michigan and throughout the United States.

Special Features

The Specs Howard School trains students in its audio practice studios and in-house radio stations, as well as the television studios, control rooms, and online video editing suites. Actual radio and television station situations are simulated in keeping with the hands-on philosophy of the School. All faculty members are experienced in the industry, and many are Specs Howard School graduates as well. The School's 35,000-square-foot facility features high-quality audio and video equipment, including digital editing suites for both audio and video.

Financial Aid/Scholarships

Federal programs available are FSEOG, Federal Pell Grant, Federal Subsidized Stafford Student Loans, Federal Unsubsidized Stafford Student Loans, Federal Parent Loans for Undergraduate Students, VA, and WIA. Available scholarships include Imagine America Scholarship (CCF), Detroit Area Film and Television (DAFT), Upper Midwest Communications Conclave Scholarship, Specs Howard School Scholarship Program, Specs Howard Industry Scholarship, and Michigan Merit Award Scholarship (MEAP).

Tuition and Fees

The Radio and Television Broadcasting Course is $9,995. All books and supplies are included.

The Radio and Television Broadcasting Comprehensive Course is $12,995. All books and supplies are included.

Accreditation

The Specs Howard School is accredited by the Accrediting Commission of Career Schools and Colleges of Technology (ACCSCT).

Admissions

The Specs Howard School is an equal opportunity educational facility. An Admissions Representative interviews all applicants. Application to the School's programs is open to persons who have graduated from high school or who have obtained a GED equivalency. High school seniors and GED candidates who satisfy all other requirements may register for SHS classes, but their enrollment is contingent upon receiving a high school diploma or GED certificate. All applicants must take and pass an entrance evaluation. Applicants for the Radio and Television Comprehensive Course may also be required to pass a proficiency examination prior to entering their second area of concentration.

Program Content

Radio and Television Broadcasting Comprehensive Course, Radio and Television Broadcasting Course

Program Description

The focus of all aspects of the courses at Specs Howard is hands-on. Students learn by doing. Courses include radio and television performance and production, commercial copywriting, newswriting, camera operation, radio and television studio operation, career perspectives, resume writing, and job interviews.

Graduation Requirements

Students graduating from the Specs Howard School programs must have completed all areas of training and must have attained satisfactory academic progress in all marking areas.

Enrollment

There are 535 students enrolled.

Contact

Admissions Department
19900 West Nine Mile Road
Southfield, MI 48075-3953
Phone: (248) 358-9000
Fax: (248) 746-9772
E-mail: info@specshoward.edu
Web: www.specshoward.edu

Programs Eligible for Scholarship	Tuition and Fees	Course Length/Credits/Hours	Credential Earned
Radio and Television Broadcasting Comprehensive Course	$12,995	48 weeks/36 credits/1,080 clock hours	Diploma

The Art Institutes International Minnesota, Minneapolis

About Our Institution

The purpose of the Art Institutes International Minnesota (Ai Minnesota) is to educate and train current or future design or business-related professionals using high-quality educational programs created to instruct students in skills useful in everyday performance in the workplace. The goal is to provide an employable graduate with the skills necessary for long-term success. Ai Minnesota is one of the Art Institutes, a system of thirty-one schools located across the U.S., providing an important source of design, media arts, fashion, and culinary professionals. Ai Minnesota offers certificate, Associate of Applied Science, Bachelor of Fine Arts, and Bachelor of Science degree programs.

Financial Aid/Scholarships

Student Financial Services assists students and their families with financial plans to help ensure the students' completion of their programs. Specialists from this department also help in the completion of federal and state applications for grants and loans. Once the students' eligibility for financial aid is determined, they receive help to develop plans for meeting educational expenses.

Admissions

A prospective student seeking admission to Ai Minnesota must be a high school graduate or hold a General Educational Development (GED) certificate as a prerequisite for admission. Students who have completed high school or its equivalent yet cannot provide the necessary documentation may provide alternate documentation to satisfy this requirement. The Ai Minnesota President must approve all exceptions. A student may submit proof of a degree from any accredited postsecondary school to satisfy the high school or GED requirement.

Graduation Requirements

Graduating students from all art-based/design programs must pass a required course in which a portfolio is produced. The portfolio must be to the standard established by the faculty for entry-level employment. A committee may evaluate the portfolio in some departments.

Contact

The Art Institutes International Minnesota
15 South 9th Street
Minneapolis, MN 55402
Phone: (612) 332-3361
Fax: (612) 332-3934
Web: www.aim.artinstitutes.edu

Program Description

Advertising: Presents a fundamental grounding in advertising with a foundation in design, copy writing, advertising campaign, marketing, business, and life skills needed to develop and sustain a career in advertising and related fields. Graduates are likely to find an entry-level positon in an advertising agency, an advertiser's company, a media buying or media planning company, or other related communications companies. (Bachelor's degree.)

Culinary Arts: Provides hands-on training in basic food-preparation skills through advanced culinary arts techniques. Programs include a foundation in health, safety, and nutrition studies as well as a solid business background in cost control, supervision of food-service personnel, and management of a commercial kitchen. Graduates have joined the staffs of luxury resorts, fine-dining restaurants, and contract food-service companies. (One-year certificates and associate and bachelor's degrees.)

Graphic Design: Emphasizes foundation art skills; conceptual thinking; technology-based creative execution, including digital imaging and illustration; production skills; and business practices. Students acquire and apply creative thinking, layout, typography, production, and art direction skills to develop a marketable portfolio. Graduates are prepared to enter an increasingly technical and competitive industry and join the creative staffs of advertising agencies, design studios, digital production studios, publishing houses, and corporate communications departments. (Associate and bachelor's degrees.)

Interior Design: Nurtures creativity while giving practical experience and technique in space planning, human factors, color, pattern, lighting, furniture, and materials. Building on a foundation of drawing, drafting, color, and design, students learn three-dimensional design, perspective, safety codes, computer-aided design (CAD), and other skills that enable them to develop thoughtful, substantive design solutions with market reality. Course work focuses on issues relevant to current design practice—conservation, preservation, cultural diversity, the needs of various economic and age groups, and changing technology. Graduates are qualified for entry-level positions with interior design firms or companies specializing in facilities or space planning. (Associate and bachelor's degrees.)

Media Arts and Animation: Presents a firm foundation in color, design, video production, and computer applications. Students learn to conceptualize and design 3-D images freehand and on the computer, and then learn script development and storyboarding, background and scenic layout, and special effects. With these skills, they produce a digital portfolio to show to potential employers. Students are prepared to enter this high-tech field as modelers, storyboard artists, animation artists, 3-D illustrators, digital artists, FX artists, video postproduction artists, and broadcast graphics designers as well as game designers and film animators. (Bachelor's degree.)

Multimedia and Web Design: Teaches how to use the Web to communicate effectively by organizing information into intuitive navigation structures and by developing creative interfaces using the most appropriate combination of media (text, graphics, photographs, animation, audio, and video). The students develop skills that prepare them for careers in the fast-paced, high-tech Web field. The program starts with an art foundation in drawing and design, then progresses through various aspects of graphic design, interface design, media production and manipulation, information design, and Web technologies. (Associate and bachelor's degrees.)

Photography: Provides a fundamental grounding in photography. The program is meant for those with creativity, imagination, an eye for color, attention to detail, and a degree of selective critical judgment. The program prepares graduates for entry-level positions in traditional and digital imaging. Emphasis is placed on the development of skills needed to produce compelling imagery appropriate to market needs. (Bachelor's degree.)

Visual Effects and Motion Graphics: Teaches the use of digital compositing to create layered and textural landscapes that engage both the mind and the emotions. Students learn how to build a seamless presentation that is both visually arresting and commercially effective through the integration of live-action footage, programming clips, graphic elements, and sound. In addition, they become knowledgeable about the stages of the production process and learn what it means to be part of a creative team working to meet a goal. (Bachelor's degree.)

Bryman Institute, Eagan

About Our Institution

The Bryman Schools were founded in 1960 by Mrs. Esther Bryman as the Los Angeles Colleges of Medical and Dental Assistants. The Los Angeles campus was the original school. In December 1995, Corinthian Schools, Inc. (CSi), a division of Corinthian Colleges, Inc. (CCi), acquired the schools. CCi is one of the largest postsecondary school organizations in the United States, operating more than eighty colleges and institutions nationwide.

The Institute's philosophy is to provide quality programs that are sound in concept, implemented by a competent and dedicated faculty, and geared to serve those seeking a solid foundation in the health-care field. The programs emphasize hands-on training, are relevant to the needs of employers, and focus on areas that offer strong long-term employment opportunities. Upon completion, graduates are prepared for entry-level positions in the medical fields.

Financial Aid/Scholarships

Information regarding Federal Pell Grants, Federal Stafford Student Loans, FPLUS, WIA, and other assistance can be obtained from the Finance Office. Financial aid is available for those who qualify.

Accreditation

All programs are accredited by the Accrediting Commission of Career Schools and Colleges of Technology (ACCSCT).

Admissions

Successful candidates are selected based on interviews and the completion and presentation of required documents. Enrollment is open to all high school graduates as well as those holding a GED or its equivalent. Under certain circumstances, students who do not have a high school diploma or its equivalent may still be accepted for admission. Interested people should contact the Admissions Department for additional information.

Graduation Requirements

To be eligible for graduation, students must successfully complete all classroom modules with a grade of at least 70 percent, finish an approved externship of 160 hours for the medical programs, and complete all other program requirements.

Enrollment

There are 125 students enrolled.

Program Content

Massage Therapy, Medical Assisting, Medical Insurance Billing and Coding

Contact

Douglas Lockwood, Director of Admissions
Bryman Institute
1000 Blue Gentian Road, Suite 250
Eagan, MN 55121
Phone: (651) 688-2145
Fax: (651) 686-8029
E-mail: dlockwood@cci.edu
Web: www.bryman-institute.com

Programs Eligible for Scholarship	Tuition and Fees	Course Length/Credit Hours	Credential Earned
Massage Therapy	$9,950	57 credit hours	Diploma
Medical Assisting	$9,250	47 credit hours	Diploma
Medical Insurance Billing/Coding	$7,250	35 credit hours	Diploma

Duluth Business University, Duluth

About Our Institution

DBU was formed as a private business school in 1891 in an effort to meet increasing demands for highly educated, skilled men and women. The University prides itself on providing specialized business, computer technology, and medical training as well as college-level general education for today's jobs.

Special Features

DBU is a private college specializing in skill-specific training. Programs are conveniently scheduled with day and evening classes and are designed for new students and/or working adults. The average enrollment is 300 students, with a student-faculty ratio of 8:1. The average placement rate of DBU graduates is more than 90 percent. DBU's programs emphasize hands-on training, are relevant to employers' needs, and focus on areas that offer strong, long-term employment opportunities. Small class sizes provide students with more one-on-one time with instructors. DBU is open year-round, with programs starting on a quarterly basis. All programs are fully accredited by the Accrediting Council for Independent Colleges and Schools, which is nationally recognized by the United States Department of Education and the Council for Higher Education Accreditation. Financial aid is available for those who qualify.

Financial Aid/Scholarships

DBU maintains a financial planning office on campus to assist students in applying for grants, loans, scholarships, work-study, veterans' benefits, and community resource assistance.

Tuition and Fees

Business and medical programs cost $239–$259 per credit; graphic design media classes, $299 per credit; and the registration fee, $35. Lab fees vary by program but range from $80 to $200 per quarter. Book costs generally range from $150 to $300 per quarter.

Accreditation

DBU is accredited by the Accrediting Council for Independent Colleges and Schools (ACICS), licensed by the Minnesota Higher Education Services Office (MHESO), granted approval for a dental assistant program by the Commission on Dental Accreditation, and accredited by the Commission of Accreditation of Allied Health Education Programs (CAAHEP) for medical assisting and is a Microsoft Authorized Academic Training Program (AATP) training center.

Program Content

Accounting, Billing and Coding Specialist, Business Administration, Business Office Specialist, Graphic Design Media, Massage Therapy, Medical Assistant, Veterinary Clinical Assistant, Veterinary Technology

Admissions

DBU admits those with a certificate of high school graduation or GED completion who also meet program admission standards by completing a pre-enrollment academic entrance exam. Applicants must achieve a minimum career program assessment test score. All prospective students should plan a personal interview at the school.

Graduation Requirements

Students must attain a cumulative grade point average of at least 2.0, attain minimum skill requirements in the selected program, and successfully complete all required credit work. Candidates for graduation must be free of debt to the school.

Contact

Admissions Department
Duluth Business University
4729 Mike Colalillo Drive
Duluth, MN 55807
Phone: (218) 722-4000
(800) 777-8406 (toll-free)
E-mail: dbu@cpinternet.com
Web: www.dbumn.edu

Programs Eligible for Scholarship	Tuition and Fees	Course Length/Credit Hours	Credential Earned
Accounting	$239 credit/$80 quarter	7–9 quarters/96–126 credits	Diploma/AAS
Billing and Coding Specialist	$259 credit/$80 quarter	3–6 quarters/47–90 credits	Diploma/AAS
Business Administration	$239 credit/$80 quarter	8 quarters/106 credits	AAS
Business Office Specialist	$259 credit/$80 quarter	3–6 quarters/42–90 credits	Diploma/AAS
Graphic Design Media	$299 credit/$110 quarter	6 quarters/94 credits	AAS
Massage Therapy	$259 credit/$95 quarter	3–6 quarters/44–91 credits	Diploma/AAS
Medical Assistant	$239 credit/$200 quarter	6–8 quarters/73–103 credits	Diploma/AAS
Veterinary Clinical Assistant	$239 credit/$80 quarter	4–6 quarters/54–91 credits	Diploma/AAS
Veterinary Technology	$259 credit/$140 quarter	7 quarters/111 credits	AAS

Herzing College, Lakeland Medical-Dental Academy Division, Minneapolis

About Our Institution
Herzing College, Lakeland Medical-Dental Academy (MDA) Division became part of Herzing College in May 2002. Established in 1958, Lakeland Medical-Dental Academy has trained and placed its graduates in all phases of allied health professions for more than 45 years.

Special Features
Herzing College, Lakeland MDA Division is focused on adult education and training for diplomas and AAS degrees in the allied health field. Programs are offered both during the day and in the evening and are conveniently scheduled so that students can meet their career goals in a shorter time than at traditional four-year colleges. Placement assistance is available to graduates who qualify. To gain real-world experience, all students participate in an internship/externship or directed practice before graduation.

Financial Aid/Scholarships
Herzing College offers Pell Grants, federal loans, VA assistance, state grants, WIA assistance, and Herzing Scholarships for those who qualify. Herzing College also has a number of institutional scholarships available.

Tuition and Fees
Tuition varies by program. Textbooks are included in the tuition charges, except for online courses.

Accreditation
Herzing College is accredited by the Higher Learning Commission of the North Central Association of Colleges and Schools. The Higher Learning Commission can be contacted at 800-621-7440 (toll-free) or via their Web site at www.ncahigherlearningcommission.org. Herzing is licensed by the Minnesota Higher Education Services Office. It is a member of the Minnesota Career Colleges Association (MCCA).

Herzing College, Lakeland Academy Division's Medical Assistant program is accredited by the Commission on Accreditation of Allied Health Programs (CAAHEP, 35 W. Wacker Drive, Suite 1970, Chicago, Illinois 60601-2208, telephone: 312-553-9355), on the recommendation of the Curriculum Review Board of the American Association of Medical Assistants Endowment.

The Dental Assistant and Dental Hygiene programs are accredited by the Commission on Dental Accreditation of the American Dental Association, a specialized body recognized by the Council of Post-Secondary Accreditation and by the United States Department of Education.

Program Content
Associate of Applied Science Degree Programs: Dental Assistant, Dental Hygiene, Medical Assistant, Medical Billing and Insurance Coding, Therapeutic Massage

Diploma Programs: Dental Assistant, Medical Assistant, Medical Billing and Insurance Coding, Therapeutic Massage

Admissions
All applicants seeking admission to Herzing College, Lakeland MDA Division must have a high school diploma or the equivalent (GED). Applicants must be interviewed by an admissions representative, complete a Herzing entrance examination, and pay a $25 enrollment fee.

Graduation Requirements
The requirements for graduation are a cumulative grade point average of 2.0 or higher, completion of the required number of credit hours, passing of all required courses, and satisfaction of all financial obligations with the business office.

Contact
Jim Decker, Director of Admissions
5700 West Broadway
Minneapolis, MN 55428
Phone: (763) 535-3000
Fax: (763) 535-9205
E-mail: info@mpls.herzing.edu
Web: www.herzing.edu

Programs Eligible for Scholarship	Tuition and Fees*	Course Length/Credit Hours	Credential Earned
Dental Assistant	$5,280/semester	46/67 credits	Diploma/AAS
Dental Hygiene	$8,400/semester	90 credits	AAS
Medical Assistant	$5,280/semester	40/67 credits	Diploma/AAS
Medical Billing and Insurance Coding	$5,280/semester	48/67 credits	Diploma/AAS
Therapeutic Massage	$5,280/semester	33/68 credits	Diploma/AAS

*Semesters at Herzing College are sixteen weeks long. A full-time student generally completes 16 credits in a semester.

Herzing College, Minneapolis Drafting School Division, Minneapolis

About Our Institution
Herzing College, Minneapolis Drafting School (MDS) Division, became part of Herzing College in June 2000. Established in 1961, the Minneapolis Drafting School has trained and placed its graduates in all phases of drafting and design for almost 45 years. The College has recently added programs in Computer Network Technology (AAS degree) and Web Site Design (diploma).

Special Features
Herzing College, MDS Division, is focused on providing Associate of Applied Science and Bachelor of Technology Management degree programs. Programs are conveniently scheduled with day and evening classes and are designed for new students and/or working adults. Herzing College has a three-year Bachelor of Science degree completion policy for students meeting specific conditions. Therefore, students can meet their career goals in a shorter time than at traditional four-year institutions. Placement assistance is available to graduates who qualify.

Financial Aid/Scholarships
Herzing College offers Pell Grants, federal loans, VA, state grants, JTPA, and Herzing Scholarships for those who qualify. Herzing College also has a number of institutional scholarships available.

Tuition and Fees
Tuition varies by program; see below for more information. Textbooks are included in the tuition charges, with the exception of online courses.

Accreditation
Herzing College is accredited by the Higher Learning Commission and a member of the North Central Association. The Higher Learning Commission can be contacted by telephone at 800-621-7440 (toll-free) or visited on the Web at http://www.ncahigherlearningcommission.org. Herzing College is licensed by the Minnesota Higher Education Services Office. It is a member of the Minnesota Career Colleges Association (MCCA).

Admissions
All applicants seeking admission to Herzing College, MDS Campus, must have a high school diploma or the equivalent (GED). Applicants must be interviewed by an Admission Representative, complete a Herzing entrance examination, and pay a $25 enrollment fee.

Graduation Requirements
The requirements for graduation are a cumulative grade point average of 2.0 or higher, completion of the required number of credit hours, passing of all required courses, and satisfaction of all financial obligations with the business office.

Program Content
Associate of Applied Science Programs: Computer Network Technology, CAD Drafting

Bachelor of Science Program: Technology Management

Diploma Programs: CAD Drafting, Web Site Design

Contact
Jim Decker, Director of Admissions
5700 West Broadway
Minneapolis, MN 55428
Phone: (763) 535-3000
Fax: (763) 535-9205
E-mail: info@mpls.herzing.edu
Web: www.herzing.edu

Programs Eligible for Scholarship	Tuition and Fees	Course Length/Credit Hours	Credential Earned
CAD Drafting	$4,400 per semester	50/79 credits	Diploma/AAS
Computer Network Technology	$4,400 per semester	79 credits	AAS
Technology Management	$4,400 per semester	129 credits	BS
Web Site Design	$4,400 per semester	32 credits	Diploma

Virginia College at Jackson, Jackson

About Our Institution
Virginia College is a private, proprietary institution of higher education committed to offering associate degree programs and diploma courses that strengthen the student's ability to enter or maintain a chosen career.

Special Features
Virginia College maintains vigilance over the ever-changing job market requirements and expands its program offerings accordingly. The College supports a progressive policy to prepare students as competitive employees in the local, regional, and multistate job markets.

Financial Aid/Scholarships
The College offers Pell Grants, FFEL, FDSLP, work-study, FSEOG, VA, and scholarships for graduated high school seniors and single working parents.

Tuition and Fees
Tuition and fees vary depending on the program and range from $8980 to $27,050, which includes books and fees.

Accreditation
The College is accredited by the Accrediting Council for Independent Colleges and Schools (ACICS).

Admissions
An entrance exam and a high school diploma or GED certificate are required.

Graduation Requirements
In order to graduate, a student must have earned a minimum 2.0 cumulative grade point average, earned the minimum credit hours required by the program of study, and satisfied all financial obligations to the College.

Contact
Bill Milstead, Director of Admissions
Virginia College at Jackson
5360 I-55 North
Jackson, MS 39211
Phone: (601) 977-0960
Fax: (601) 956-4325
Web: www.vc.edu

Program Content
Business Office Administration, Computer Network Administration, Medical Office Administration

Program Description
Business Office Administration: These programs prepare students in computerized office systems, office management, basic business operations, computer software applications, accounting procedures, and computer-based accounting transactions. The students also learn word processing, spreadsheets, database management, desktop publishing, accounting, payroll accounting, and professional career management.

Computer Network Administration: These programs offer students practical, hands-on training in operating, troubleshooting, configuring, upgrading, and maintaining microcomputers and complex networks. Students are trained for computer service, network administration, and technical support and prepared for obtaining certifications.

Medical Office Administration: These programs are designed to prepare students for positions in the medical field, combining a knowledge of automated medical office administration, medical reimbursement procedures, and patient contact. Students also become skilled in working in a physician's office or other medical setting, the fundamentals of medical office protocol, and insurance billing and coding.

Programs Eligible for Scholarship	Tuition and Fees	Course Length/Credit Hours	Credential Earned
Accounting Assistant	$ 8,980	48 credit hours	Diploma
Administrative Assistant	$10,090	54 credit hours	Diploma
Administrative Office Management	$17,120	92 credit hours	AAS
Cisco Network Associate	$12,840	48 credit hours	Diploma
Computer Network Technician	$ 9,410	38 credit hours	Diploma
Electronic Technology	$11,860	48 credit hours	Diploma
Electronic Technology	$24,600	100 credit hours	OA
Human Resource Management	$17,120	92 credit hours	AS
Medical Assistant	$10,460	56 credit hours	Diploma
Medical Billing and Coding	$10,090	54 credit hours	Diploma
Medical Office Administration and Assisting	$16,935	91 credit hours	AAS
Microsoft Network Engineer	$10,390	42 credit hours	Diploma
Network Engineering	$27,050	110 credit hours	OA
Surgical Technology	$18,500	92 credit hours	AAS
Therapeutic Massage	$19,300	96 credit hours	OA

ITT Technical Institute, Arnold

About Our Institution
The company: ITT Technical Institute is owned and operated by ITT Educational Services, Inc. (ITT/ESI), a leading private college system that offers technology-focused programs of study. ITT/ESI operates seventy-seven ITT Technical Institutes in thirty states, providing career-focused degree programs to approximately 39,000 students as of spring 2004. Headquartered in Carmel, Indiana, ITT/ESI has been actively involved in the higher education community in the United States since 1969.

Curricula: Curriculum offerings are designed to help students begin to prepare for career opportunities in the fields of technology. Students attend classes year-round, with convenient breaks provided throughout the year. A full-time student can have class meetings as often as three days a week, and they are typically available in the morning, afternoon, and evening, depending on student enrollment. General education courses may be available online. This schedule offers flexibility to allow students to pursue part-time employment opportunities.

ITT Technical Institute, Arnold, awards Associate of Applied Science and Bachelor of Science degrees.

Special Features
Most ITT Technical Institute programs of study blend traditional academic content with applied learning concepts, with a significant portion devoted to practical study in a lab environment. Advisory committees, made up of representatives of local businesses help each ITT Technical Institute periodically review and update curricula, equipment, and laboratory design.

Financial Aid/Scholarships
ITT Technical Institute maintains a Financial Aid Department on campus. The campus is designated as an eligible institution by the U.S. Department of Education for participation in the following programs: Federal Stafford Student Loan, Federal PLUS Loan, and Federal Work-Study. The school also participates in the California Grant Program and offers nonfederal loans through Bank One for eligible students.

Tuition and Fees
March 2005 tuition is $386 per credit hour.

Accreditation
Accrediting Council for Independent Colleges and Schools (ACICS).

Admissions
For admission requirements, students should contact the school for a catalog.

Graduation Requirements
For graduation requirements, students should consult the school catalog.

Program Content
School of Information Technology: Information Systems Security, Data Communication Systems Technology, Software Engineering Technology, Information Technology–Computer Network Systems, Information Technology–Software Applications and Programming, Information Technology–Web Development.

School of Electronics Technology: Electronics and Communications Engineering Technology, Computer and Electronics Engineering Technology.

School of Drafting and Design: Digital Entertainment and Game Design, Computer Drafting and Design, Information Technology–Multimedia Option.

School of Business: Business Administration, Business Accounting Technology, Technical Project Management.

School of Criminal Justice: Criminal Justice.

Contact
Paula Jerden, Director
ITT Technical Institute
1930 Meyer Drury Drive
Arnold, MO 63010
Phone: (636) 464-6600
Fax: (636) 464-6611

ITT Technical Institute, Earth City

About Our Institution

The company: ITT Technical Institute is owned and operated by ITT Educational Services, Inc. (ITT/ESI), a leading private college system offering technology-influenced programs of study. ITT/ESI operates seventy-seven ITT Technical Institutes in thirty states, providing career-focused degree programs to approximately 39,000 students as of spring 2004. Headquartered in Carmel, Indiana, ITT/ESI has been actively involved in the higher education community in the United States since 1969.

Curricula: Curriculum offerings are designed to help students begin to prepare for career opportunities in fields of technology. Students attend classes year-round, with convenient breaks provided throughout the year. A full-time student course load can have class meetings as often as three days a week and are typically available in the morning, afternoon, and evening, depending on student enrollment. General education courses may be available online. This class schedule offers flexibility to students to pursue part-time employment opportunities.

ITT Technical Institute, Earth City, awards the Associate of Applied Science, the Bachelor of Applied Science, and the Bachelor of Science degrees.

Special Features

Most ITT Technical Institute programs of study blend traditional academic content with applied learning concepts, with a significant portion devoted to practical study in a lab environment. Advisory committees composed of representatives of local businesses help each ITT Technical Institute periodically review and update curricula, equipment, and laboratory design.

Financial Aid/Scholarships

ITT Technical Institute maintains a Financial Aid Department on campus. The campus is designated as an eligible institution by the U.S. Department of Education for participation in the following programs: Federal Stafford Student Loan Program, Federal PLUS Loan Program, and Federal Work-Study Program. The school also offers nonfederal loans available through Bank One for eligible students.

Tuition and Fees

March 2005 tuition is $386 per credit hour.

Accreditation

The school is accredited by the Accrediting Council for Independent Colleges and Schools (ACICS).

Admissions

For admission requirements, students should contact the school for a catalog.

Graduation Requirements

For graduation requirements, students should contact the school for a catalog.

Program Content

School of Information Technology: Data Communication Systems Technology, Information Systems Security, Information Technology–Computer Network Systems, Information Technology–Software Applications and Programming, Information Technology–Web Development, Software Engineering Technology

School of Electronics Technology: Computer and Electronics Engineering Technology, Electronics and Communications Engineering Technology

School of Drafting and Design: Computer Drafting and Design, Digital Entertainment and Game Design, Information Technology–Multimedia Option

School of Business: Business Accounting Technology, Business Administration, Technical Project Management

School of Criminal Justice: Criminal Justice

Contact

Karen Finkenkeller, Director
ITT Technical Institute
13505 Lakefront Drive
Earth City, MO 63045
Phone: (314) 298-7800
Fax: (314) 298-0559

Missouri College, St. Louis

About Our Institution
Missouri College, founded in 1963, is a private career college located in St. Louis, Missouri. The College offers degree and diploma programs in the fields of computers, health care, and business. Its mission is to provide high-quality career education in a supportive learning environment to qualified and motivated students so that they may become professional employees in high-demand career fields.

Special Features
Missouri College's programs are career-focused and taught by professionals in their field. Students receive a hands-on education where they learn by doing. Whether it is in the computer lab or medical lab, the dental operatory or the massage clinic, students get plenty of experience practicing what they learn. In most programs, students gain valuable experience from an externship or clinical practice.

Financial Aid/Scholarships
Education is affordable; Missouri College has a financial plan for everyone. The Financial Assistance Department helps students apply for federal grants and loans for which they may qualify, including Pell Grants, Federal Stafford Student Loans, direct loans, and the Federal Work-Study Program. Missouri College offers a variety of scholarship opportunities, including the Imagine America Scholarship and the Missouri College Make the Grade Scholarship for high school students. Other loan options are available to cover all or part of the cost of education.

Accreditation
Missouri College is accredited by the Accrediting Commission of Career Schools and Colleges of Technology (ACCSCT) and is an American Massage Therapy Association (AMTA) School Member.

Admissions
All applicants must have documented proof of high school graduation or a GED certificate. Applicants are required to come to the College and complete an admissions interview.

Program Content
Business: Business Administration with a Concentration in Health-Care Management, Computer Administrative Assistant

Computers: Computer Network Administration, Information Technology, Visual Communications

Health Care: Dental Assistant, Dental Office Administration, Health Business Office Administration, Massage Therapy, Medical Administrative Assistant, Medical Assistant, Medical Massage Science, Medical Office Administration

Contact
Erin Cunningham, Admissions Director
10121 Manchester Road
St. Louis, MO 63122
Phone: (314) 821-7700
        (800) 216-6732 (toll-free)
Fax: (314) 821-0891
E-mail: info@missouricollege.com
Web: www.missouricollege.com

Programs Eligible for Scholarship	Tuition and Fees	Course Length/Credit Hours	Credential Earned
Business Administration with a Concentration in Health-Care Management	$44,000	126 weeks/120 credit hours	BA
Computer Administrative Assistant	$14,107	40 weeks/34 credit hours	Diploma
Computer Network Administration	$31,776	60 weeks/67 credit hours	AAS
Dental Assistant	$14,442	48 weeks/35 credit hours	Diploma
Dental Office Administration	$26,242	80 weeks/69 credit hours	AOS
Health Business Office Administration	$25,523	80 weeks/68 credit hours	AOS
Information Technology	$15,383	48 weeks/30 credit hours	Diploma
Massage Therapy	$14,252	30 weeks/31.5 credit hours	Diploma
Medical Administrative Assistant	$14,147	40 weeks/34 credit hours	Diploma
Medical Assistant	$14,412	40 weeks/34.5 credit hours	Diploma
Medical Massage Science	$26,205	66 weeks/66 credit hours	AOS
Medical Office Administration	$25,976	80 weeks/68.5 credit hours	AOS
Visual Communications	$36,008	60 weeks/60 credit hours	AAS

Missouri Tech, St. Louis

About Our Institution

Now primarily a college of computer technology, Missouri Tech has specialized in educating students for technical professions since 1932. Today, Missouri Tech offers degree programs in computer programming and networking, engineering management, and electronics, including instruction in programmable logical controllers. Students attend Missouri Tech because it provides hands-on training, offers tightly focused, professional programs, hires highly qualified instructors with field experience, schedules small classes, and places graduates successfully in professional positions. Missouri Tech is a proprietary college with a student body of approximately 200. The college is located in Creve Coeur, a suburb on the prosperous west side of St. Louis. Situated less than 7 miles south of Lambert-St. Louis International Airport, the college grounds are landscaped with lawns, trees, and a lake. The metropolitan area offers many attractions, including professional sports teams—the Cardinals for baseball, the Rams for football, and the Blues for hockey. Other attractions include the Gateway Arch, Six Flags, the St. Louis Science Center, the Missouri Historical Society, the St. Louis Art Museum, the St. Louis Zoo, entertainment at Laclede's Landing, shows at the Fox Theatre, and many others.

Special Features

Missouri Tech's computer lab contains 100 workstations, each connected as a client to the college's SQL server and operating under the Windows XP operating system. Visual Studio (including Visual C++ and Visual Basic), AutoCAD, Visio, Publisher, FrontPage, Access, Excel, Word, and PowerPoint are installed on the lab computers, which also have Internet access. Electronics students may look forward to using many training devices to gain hands-on experience. All students are taught by instructors with field experience, who bring their real-world knowledge into the classroom. The instructors also give plenty of personal attention since the college has an exceptionally low overall student-teacher ratio of 12:1 and does not require instructors to publish.

Financial Aid/Scholarships

Various loans, grants, and scholarships are available. Missouri Tech is approved by Vocational Rehabilitation, National Guard educational assistance, and VA. Many employers also sponsor their employees' education.

Tuition and Fees

Tuition is $398 per credit hour plus a laboratory/resource fee of $190 per semester.

Accreditation

Missouri Tech is accredited by the Accrediting Commission of Career Schools and Colleges of Technology (ACCSCT).

Admissions

Missouri Tech is open to qualified men and women regardless of religion, race, color, handicap, or national origin. Applicants must either submit an ACT score of 20 or better or pass an entrance examination. In addition, applicants must complete an assessment instrument to determine their placement in courses. An on-campus admissions interview must be completed before the beginning of classes. There are no deadlines for submitting applications.

Program Content

Electronics Engineering, Electronics Engineering Technology, Electronic Service Technician, Engineering Management, Information Technology, Network Administration, Software Engineering

Program Description

Offering diploma, associate, and bachelor's degree programs, Missouri Tech prepares students for entry into technical professions without requiring them to take many general education courses. In addition to providing them with knowledge, instructors develop students' problem-solving skills, recognizing that such skills are highly sought by employers. Instructors teach the basics of subjects and then assign hands-on projects requiring students to find solutions. As they work on the projects, students develop the mental tools they need to solve a much broader array of technical problems. The college's programs are built on the belief that students need confidence and motivation as well as a technical grounding to succeed professionally. Therefore, instructors encourage students to develop in the areas included in the five A's: Ambition, Attendance (responsibility), Academics, Attitude (engineering attitude), and Appearance (presence and confidence). The five A's converge to form the star that is Missouri Tech's logo.

Contact

Mr. Bob Honaker
Missouri Tech
1167 Corporate Lake Drive
St. Louis, MO 63132
Phone: (314) 569-3600
(800) 960-TECH (toll-free from Missouri only)
Fax: (314) 569-1167
E-mail: Bob@motech.edu
Web: www.motech.edu

Sanford-Brown College, Fenton

About Our Institution
Sanford-Brown College is a private, coeducational institution that was founded in 1866 for the purpose of offering business and career training following the American Civil War. Currently, Sanford-Brown College is a system of five campuses located in Fenton, Missouri; North Kansas City, Missouri; St. Charles, Missouri; Hazelwood, Missouri; and Granite City, Illinois. The College awards bachelor's and associate degrees in the areas of business, information technology, and allied health care. The mission of Sanford-Brown College is to provide fast, focused, hands-on training in a caring and supportive environment in order to enhance student success and prepare students for employment in an ever-changing job market.

Special Features
Sanford-Brown College utilizes a wide variety of student resources to prepare students to succeed in their chosen career paths. In spacious, comfortable campuses, students access the latest technology in the classroom and Learning Resource Center. Qualified instructors bring real, hands-on experience to each student in the class to build the confidence and skills necessary to perform well in the competitive job market. Dedicated Career Service personnel work individually with each student in preparation for seeking and interviewing for a chosen profession. The relationship between Career Services and the student continues after graduation; it is a lifetime service that the College provides. Sanford-Brown College also grants the privilege for any graduate to return to audit classes or take refresher courses at no additional charge.

Financial Aid/Scholarships
Sanford-Brown College maintains a financial aid office on campus, which provides a variety of programs that include grants, loans, work-study, veteran's benefits, and vocational rehabilitation. The College's advisers work with each student one-on-one, examining the student's individual financial situation and exploring which of these programs are best for the student.

Sanford-Brown College also offers $1 million in scholarships as part of a Legislative Scholarship program. For the 2004–05 academic year, eligible 2004 high school graduates are awarded scholarships in each of the programs for the five campuses.

All programs are eligible for scholarship.

Tuition and Fees
Tuition costs for the diploma and associate degree programs range from $1,400 to $3,875 per quarter, depending upon the program of study. Books and supplies are estimated on a program basis. Each student is required to pay a $25 application fee.

Accreditation
Sanford-Brown College's Missouri campuses are accredited by the Accrediting Council for Independent Colleges and Schools (ACICS). The nursing programs are approved by the Missouri State Board of Nursing. The radiography program is accredited by the Joint Review Committee on Education in Radiologic Technology (JRCERT). The medical assistant program is accredited by the Accrediting Bureau of Health Education Schools (ABHES). The respiratory therapy program is accredited by the Commission on Accreditation of Allied Health Education Programs (CAAHEP).

Program Content
Bachelor of Applied Science Degree: Business Administration, Criminal Justice, Health-Care Management, Information Technology Management

Associate of Applied Science Degree: Business Administration (Accounting, Management, Sales and Marketing), Computer and Internet Programming, Computer Support Administration, Health Information Technology, Massage Therapy, Medical Assistant, Network Administration, Nursing, Office Administration, Paralegal Studies, Radiography, Respiratory Therapy, Surgical Technology, Video Game Design, Web Programming

Diploma: Computer and Internet Programming, Computer Support Specialist, Medical Assistant, Medical Billing and Coding Specialist, Network Technology, Office Technology, Practical Nursing

Program availability varies by campus.

Admissions
An entrance exam, a high school diploma or GED certificate, and an interview by an admissions representative are required for admittance to Sanford-Brown College.

Graduation Requirements
To graduate, students must earn a cumulative grade point average of at least 2.0. Students must satisfy all academic, attendance, and financial aid requirements before a diploma or degree is awarded. Students must also attend all required career services workshops.

Contact
Sarah Squires
Director of High School Admissions Support
Sanford-Brown College
1203 Smizer Mill Road
Fenton, MO 63026
Phone: (636) 349-4900
(800) 456-7222 (toll-free)
Fax: (636) 349-9317
Web: www.sanford-brown.edu

MISSOURI

Springfield College, Springfield

About Our Institution
Springfield College is an institution that serves the multipurpose of offering Associate of Applied Science degrees, diploma programs, and a bachelor's degree in business administration. The associate degree programs are designed for those who desire collegiate education providing career-oriented training coupled with general education. The diploma programs are designed for those who desire short-term training specifically tailored to entry-level career preparation in specified fields. The bachelor's degree program is designed for those who seek advancement in training that enables them to further their current level of education and/or employment. Springfield College is one of eighty-nine schools owned and operated by Corinthian Colleges, Inc., in the United States.

Special Features
Springfield College offers specific and practical educational services designed to meet the demands of business and technology in the Springfield area. Programs of study provide a quality occupational education and prepare students for immediate job entry.

Financial Aid/Scholarships
Springfield College participates in Pell, FFEL, work-study, FSEOG, VA, JTPA, and other programs. High school and other scholarships are available for those who qualify.

Tuition and Fees
Per credit hours are assessed based on amount of classes taken per quarter. There is a quarterly registration fee of $25.

Accreditation
Springfield College is accredited by the Accrediting Council of Independent Colleges and Schools (ACICS). The medical assisting program is accredited by AAMA Accredited, a division of the Commission on Accreditation of Allied Health Education Programs (CAAHEP).

Admissions
Candidates must have a high school diploma or equivalent. However, the requirement may also be met if the applicant is at least 21 years of age and can demonstrate the ability to benefit from training. Springfield College only accepts students after a personal interview, which is designed to help students select the program of study best suited to their needs and future goals. All students entering the college are required to meet the Standards of Evaluation for admission.

Program Content
Accounting, Business Accounting, Business Administration, Computer Information Science, Dental Assisting, Medical Assisting, Medical Insurance Billing/Coding, Medical Office Assistant, Medical Transcription, Paralegal, Paralegal/Legal Assistant

Graduation Requirements
Students must have a minimum 2.0 CGPA and must have successfully completed all required credits with the maximum credits attempted. All financial obligations must be fulfilled before graduation.

Enrollment
There are 625 students enrolled.

Contact
Scott Lester, Director of Admissions
Springfield College
1010 West Sunshine
Springfield, MO 65807
Phone: (417) 864-7220
Fax: (417) 864-5697
E-mail: slester@cci.edu
Web: www.springfield-college.com

Programs Eligible for Scholarship	Tuition and Fees	Course Length/Credit Hours	Credential Earned
Business Administration	$202 per credit hour	96 credit hours	AAS
Business Administration	$202 per credit hour	192 credit hours	BBA
Computer Information Science	$202 per credit hour	96 credit hours	AAS
Medical Assisting	$202 per credit hour	97 credit hours	AAS
Paralegal/Legal Assistant	$202 per credit hour	96 credit hours	AAS
Medical Insurance Billing/Coding	$7,070	6 months	Certificate
Medical Office Assistant	$202 per credit hour	60 credit hours	Diploma
Medical Transcription	$202 per credit hour	48 credit hours	Diploma

Vatterott College, Joplin

About Our Institution
All Vatterott College programs are based on a proven successful formula of specialized, technology-focused, hands-on training in the fastest-growing industries. The College was founded in 1969 and now serves nearly 9,000 students per year at sixteen Midwestern campuses. The Joplin campus offers programs focused on the information technology, health care, cosmetology, and technical trade industries.

Special Features
Vatterott College's hands-on training method of instruction equips students with the specific skills that are desired by local employers. All courses are geared to the student's field of study. Classes are available in both morning and evening schedules.

Financial Aid/Scholarships
Vatterott College participates in a variety of financial aid and scholarship programs. The College's Make-the-Grade scholarship offers tuition credit to qualifying students based on high school grades. Vatterott College also participates in the Imagine America scholarship program. High school seniors are eligible to apply. Students should contact the campus Financial Aid Representative for specific information.

Tuition and Fees
The campus Admissions Representative can provide complete tuition information.

Accreditation
Vatterott College is nationally accredited by the Accrediting Commission of Career Schools and Colleges of Technology.

Admission
The application process includes a personal interview and entrance evaluation. A high school diploma or GED is required.

Graduation Requirements
Students must show satisfactory progress by maintaining a minimum grade of 70 percent and an 80 percent attendance record.

Contact
Office of Admissions
Vatterott College
5898 North Main
Joplin, MO 64801
Phone: (417) 781-5633
(800) 934-6975 (toll-free)
Fax: (417) 781-6437
E-mail: joplin@vatterott-college.edu
Web: www.vatterott-college.edu

(branch of main campus in St. Ann, MO)

Program Content
Associate of Occupational Studies (AOS) Degree: Computer Systems and Network Technology

Diploma: Computer Technology, Computer Programming, Computer Applications Specialist, Accounting with Data Processing, Medical Office Assistant, Cosmetology, and Manicuring and Sculptured Nails

Vatterott College, Kansas City

About Our Institution

All Vatterott College programs are based on a proven successful formula of specialized, technology-focused, hands-on training in the fastest-growing industries. The College was founded in 1969 and now serves nearly 9,000 students per year at sixteen midwestern campuses. The Kansas City campus offers programs focused on the information technology, health-care, and technical trade industries.

Special Features

Vatterott College's hands-on training method of instruction equips students with the specific skills that are desired by local employers. Courses are geared to the student's field of study. Classes are available in both morning and evening schedules.

Financial Aid/Scholarships

Vatterott College participates in a variety of financial aid and scholarship programs. The College's Make-the-Grade Scholarship offers tuition credit to qualifying students based on high school grades. Vatterott College also participates in the Imagine America Scholarship program. High school seniors are eligible to apply. Students should contact the campus Financial Aid Representative for specific information.

Tuition and Fees

The campus Admissions Representatives can provide complete tuition information.

Accreditation

Vatterott College is nationally accredited by the Accrediting Commission of Career Schools and Colleges of Technology.

Admission

The application process includes a personal interview and entrance evaluation. A high school diploma or GED is required.

Graduation Requirements

Students must show satisfactory progress by maintaining a minimum grade of 70 percent and an 80 percent attendance record.

Contact

Office of Admissions
Vatterott College
8955 East 38th Terrace
Kansas City, MO 64129
Phone: (816) 861-1000
         (800) 466-3997 (toll-free)
Fax: (816) 861-1400
E-mail: kc@vatterott-college.edu
Web: www.vatterott-college.com

(branch of main campus in St. Ann, MO)

Program Content

Associate of Occupational Studies (AOS) Degree: Computer Systems and Network Technology; Computer Programming and Technology; Computer-Aided Drafting Technology; Heating, Air Conditioning, and Refrigeration Technology; Applied Electrical Technology; Administrative Office Specialist; Medical Assistant

Diploma: Computer Technology; Computer Programming and System Analysis; Heating, Air Conditioning and Refrigeration Mechanic; Electrical Mechanic; Medical Office Assistant; Pharmacy Office Assistant; Administrative Applications Specialist; Drafting

Vatterott College, O'Fallon Campus, O'Fallon

About Our Institution

All Vatterott College programs are based on a proven successful formula of specialized, technology-focused, hands-on training in the fastest-growing industries. The College was founded in 1969 and now serves nearly 10,000 students per year at eighteen campuses across nine Midwestern states.

Special Features

Vatterott College's hands-on training method of instruction equips students with the specific skills that are desired by local employers. Courses are geared to the student's field of study. Classes are available in both morning and evening schedules. Career services are also available to those students who choose to enroll at Vatterott College.

Financial Aid/Scholarships

Vatterott College participates in a variety of financial aid and scholarship programs. The College's Make-the-Grade Scholarship offers tuition assistance to qualifying students based on their financial need. The scholarship rewards each student up to $1,000 with $25 for every A and $20 for every B throughout their four years in high school. Vatterott College also participates in the Imagine America Scholarship program, which rewards high school students a $1,000 scholarship. Only high school seniors are eligible and there are certain rules that may apply. Students should contact the campus Financial Aid representative with any further questions.

Tuition and Fees

The High School Relations Representative (Denis Busque) can provide specific tuition information.

Accreditation

Vatterott College is nationally accredited by the Accrediting Commission of Career Schools and Colleges of Technology.

Admissions

The application process includes a personal interview and entrance evaluation. A high school diploma or GED is required.

Graduation Requirements

Students must show satisfactory progress by maintaining a minimum grade of 70 percent and an 80 percent attendance record.

Contact

Office of Admissions
Vatterott College–Branch of St. Ann
927 East Terra Lane
O'Fallon, MO 63366
Phone: (636) 978–7488
(888) 766–3601 (toll-free)
Fax: (636) 978–5121
E-mail: denis.busque@vatterott-college.edu
Web: www.vatterott-college.edu

Program Content

Associate of Occupational Studies (AOS) Degree: Computer Systems and Network Technology; Electrical Mechanics Technology; Heating, Ventilation, and Air Conditioning/Refrigeration Technology; Medical Assistant

Diploma: Computer Technology; Electrical Mechanics; Heating, Ventilation, and Air Conditioning/Refrigeration Mechanics; Medical Office Assistant

Program offerings vary at each campus.

Vatterott College, St. Ann Campus, St. Louis

About Our Institution

All Vatterott College programs are based on a proven successful formula of specialized, technology-focused, hands-on training in the fastest-growing industries. The College was founded in 1969 and now serves nearly 9,000 students per year at sixteen midwestern campuses. The St. Ann campus offers programs focused on the information technology and technical trade industries.

Special Features

Vatterott College's hands-on training method of instruction equips students with the specific skills that are desired by local employers. Courses are geared to the student's field of study. Classes are available in both morning and evening schedules.

Financial Aid/Scholarships

Vatterott College participates in a variety of financial aid and scholarship programs. The College's Make-the-Grade Scholarship offers tuition credit to qualifying students based on high school grades. Vatterott College also participates in the Imagine America Scholarship program. High school seniors are eligible to apply. Students should contact the campus Financial Aid Representative for specific information.

Tuition and Fees

The campus Admissions Representatives can provide complete tuition information.

Accreditation

Vatterott College is nationally accredited by the Accrediting Commission of Career Schools and Colleges of Technology.

Admissions

The application process includes a personal interview and entrance evaluation. A high school diploma or GED is required.

Graduation Requirements

Students must show satisfactory progress by maintaining a minimum grade of 70 percent and an 80 percent attendance record.

Program Content

Bachelor of Science: Computer Engineering and Networking Technology, Computer Programming and Systems Analysis

Associate of Occupational Studies (AOS) Degree: Computer-Aided Drafting Technology; Computer Programming and Network Management; Computer Systems and Network Technology; Electrical Mechanics Technology; Heating, Air Conditioning and Refrigeration Technology; Combination Welding Technology

Diploma: Computer Programming; Computer Technology; Computer-Aided Drafting; Electrical Mechanics; Heating, Air Conditioning, Refrigeration Mechanic; Combination Welding

Program offerings vary at each campus.

Contact

Office of Admissions
Vatterott College, Main Campus
3925 Industrial Drive
St. Ann, MO 63074
Phone: (314) 428-5900
        (888) 370-7955 (toll-free)
Fax: (314) 428-5956
E-mail: saintann@vatterott-college.edu
Web: www.vatterott-college.edu

Office of Admissions
Vatterott College
2953 Highway K
O'Fallon, MO 63366
Phone: (636) 978-7488
        (888) 370-7955 (toll-free)
Fax: (636) 978-5121
E-mail: ofallon@vatterott-college.edu
Web: www.vatterott-college.edu

Vatterott College, Springfield

About Our Institution
All Vatterott College programs are based on a proven successful formula of specialized, technology-focused, hands-on training in the fastest-growing industries. The College was founded in 1969 and now serves nearly 9,000 students per year at sixteen Midwestern campuses. The Springfield campus offers programs focused on the information technology, health care, and technical trade industries.

Special Features
Vatterott College's hands-on training method of instruction equips students with the specific skills that are desired by local employers. Courses are geared to the student's field of study. Classes are available in both morning and evening schedules.

Financial Aid/Scholarships
Vatterott College participates in a variety of financial aid and scholarship programs. The College's Make-the-Grade scholarship offers tuition credit to qualifying students based on high school grades. Vatterott College also participates in the Imagine America scholarship program. High school seniors are eligible to apply. Students should contact the campus Financial Aid Representative for specific information.

Tuition and Fees
The campus Admissions Representatives can provide complete tuition information.

Accreditation
Vatterott College is nationally accredited by the Accrediting Commission of Career Schools and Colleges of Technology.

Admission
The application process includes a personal interview and entrance evaluation. A high school diploma or GED is required.

Graduation Requirements
Students must show satisfactory progress by maintaining a minimum grade of 70 percent and an 80 percent attendance record.

Contact
Office of Admissions
Vatterott College
1258 East Trafficway
Springfield, MO 65802
Phone: (417) 831-8116
      (800) 766-5829 (toll-free)
Fax: (417) 831-5099
E-mail: springfield@vatterott-college.edu
Web: www.vatterott-college.edu

(branch of main campus in St. Ann, MO)

Program Content

Associate of Occupational Studies (AOS) Degree: Computer-Aided Drafting Technology, Computer Systems and Network Technology, Information Systems and Web Development, Medical Assistant Specialist, Pharmacy Technician

Diploma: Administrative Applications Specialist, Computer-Aided Drafting and Design, Computer Technology, Dental Assistant, Information Systems, Medical Assistant, Medical Office Assistant, Pharmacy Assistant

Vatterott College, St. Joseph

About Our Institution

All Vatterott College programs are based on a proven successful formula of specialized, technology-focused, hands-on training in the fastest-growing industries. The College was founded in 1969 and now serves nearly 9,000 students per year at seventeen Midwestern campuses. The St. Joseph campus offers programs focused on the information technology, health care, business, cosmetology, and technical trade industries.

Special Features

Vatterott College's hands-on training method of instruction equips students with the specific skills that are desired by local employers. Courses are geared to the student's field of study. Classes are available in both morning and evening schedules.

Financial Aid/Scholarships

Vatterott College participates in a variety of financial aid and scholarship programs. The College's Make-the-Grade scholarship offers tuition credit to qualifying students based on high school grades. Vatterott College also participates in the Imagine America scholarship program. High school seniors are eligible to apply. Students should contact the campus Financial Aid Representative for specific information.

Tuition and Fees

The campus Admissions Representatives can provide complete tuition information.

Accreditation

Vatterott College is nationally accredited by the Accrediting Commission of Career Schools and Colleges of Technology.

Admission

The application process includes a personal interview and entrance evaluation. A high school diploma or GED is required.

Graduation Requirements

Students must show satisfactory progress by maintaining a minimum grade of 70% and an 80% attendance record.

Contact

Office of Admissions
Vatterott College
3131 Frederick Avenue
St. Joseph, MO 64506
Phone: (816) 364-5399
        (800) 282-5327 (toll-free)
Fax: 816-364-1593
E-mail: stjoe@vatterott-college.edu
Web: www.vatterott-college.edu

(branch of main campus in St. Ann, MO)

Program Content

Associate of Occupational Studies (AOS) Degree: Computer-Aided Drafting Technology, Computer Programming and Network Management, Computer Systems and Network Technology, Medical Assistant.

Diploma: Administrative Applications Specialist, Computer-Aided Drafting, Computer Programming and Systems Analysis, Computer Technology, Cosmetology, Cosmetology Instructor's Training, Manicuring and Sculptured Nails, Massage Therapy, Medical Office Assistant.

Online classes are available.

Vatterott College, Sunset Hills Campus, St. Louis

About Our Institution
All Vatterott College programs are based on a proven successful formula of specialized, technology-focused, hands-on training in the fastest-growing industries. The College was founded in 1969 and now serves nearly 9,000 students per year at eighteen Midwestern campuses. The Sunset Hills campus offers programs focused on the information technology, technical trade, and medical assistant fields.

Special Features
Vatterott College's hands-on training method of instruction equips students with the specific skills that are desired by local employers. Courses are geared to the student's field of study. Classes are available in both morning and evening schedules.

Financial Aid/Scholarships
Vatterott College participates in a variety of financial aid and scholarship programs. The College's Make-the-Grade scholarship offers tuition credit to qualifying students based on high school grades. Vatterott College also participates in the Imagine America scholarship program. High school seniors are eligible to apply. Students should contact the campus Financial Aid Representative for specific information.

Tuition and Fees
The campus Admissions Representatives can provide complete tuition information.

Accreditation
Vatterott College is nationally accredited by the Accrediting Commission of Career Schools and Colleges of Technology.

Admissions
The application process includes a personal interview and entrance evaluation. A high school diploma or GED is required.

Graduation Requirements
Students must show satisfactory progress by maintaining a minimum grade of 70 percent and an 80 percent attendance record.

Contact
Office of Admissions
Vatterott College
12970 Maurer Industrial Drive
St. Louis, MO 63127
Phone: (314) 843-4200
        (888) 828-8376 (toll-free)
Fax: (314) 843-1709
E-mail: sunsethills@vatterott-college.edu
Web: www.vatterott-college.edu

(branch of main campus in St. Ann, MO)

Program Content

Associate of Occupational Studies (AOS) Degree: Applied Electrical Technology; Building Maintenance Technology; Computer-Aided Drafting Technology; Computer Systems and Network Technology; Heating, Air Conditioning, and Refrigeration Technology; Information Systems Technology; Medical Assistant

Diploma Programs: Computer-Aided Drafting; Building Maintenance Mechanic; Computer Technology; Electrical Mechanic; Heating, Air Conditioning, and Refrigeration Mechanic; Medical Office Assistant; Network and Information Systems

Hamilton College, Omaha

About Our Institution

Hamilton College–Omaha is an institution of higher education offering quality programs that integrate general education, professional skills, and career-focused education to empower students to develop and achieve their personal and career potentials. Hamilton College–Omaha is owned by Kaplan Higher Education Corporation, a division of Kaplan Learning.

Accreditation

Hamilton College is accredited by the North Central Association to award diplomas and associate degrees. Hamilton College–Omaha is authorized to operate and is regulated by the Nebraska Commissioner of Education, is authorized to award associate degrees by the Nebraska Department of Education, and is approved under the provisions of Title 38, United States Code, to train eligible persons and veterans. All medical assistant programs are accredited by the Commission on Accreditation of Allied Health Education Programs (CAAHEP). The practical nurse program is approved by the Nebraska Board of Nursing and the Nebraska Department of Health and Human Services. Hamilton College is a Microsoft IT Academy.

Admissions

An entrance exam, a high school diploma or GED, and an informational interview are required.

Contact

Mark Stoltenberg, Executive Director
Hamilton College
3350 N. 90th Street
Omaha, NE 68134
Phone: (402) 572-8500
        (800) 642-1456 (toll-free)
Fax: (402) 573-1341
E-mail: mstoltenberg@hamiltonomaha.edu
Web: www.ncbedu.com

Program Content

Associate of Applied Science: Accounting Specialist, Business Administration, Computer Information Systems, Criminal Justice, Medical Assistant, Paralegal

Diploma: Dental Assistant, Massage Therapist, Practical Nursing

Vatterott College, Deerfield Campus, Omaha

About Our Institution
All Vatterott College programs are based on a proven successful formula of specialized, technology-focused, hands-on training in the fastest-growing industries. The College was founded in 1969 and now serves nearly 9,000 students per year at sixteen Midwestern campuses. The Omaha-Deerfield campus offers programs focused on the information technology and technical trade industries.

Special Features
Vatterott College's hands-on training method of instruction equips students with the specific skills that are desired by local employers. Courses are geared to the student's field of study. Classes are available in both morning and evening schedules.

Financial Aid/Scholarships
Vatterott College participates in a variety of financial aid and scholarship programs. The College's Make-the-Grade scholarship offers tuition credit to qualifying students based on high school grades. Vatterott College also participates in the Imagine America scholarship program. High school seniors are eligible to apply. Students should contact the campus Financial Aid Representative for specific information.

Tuition and Fees
The campus Admissions Representatives can provide complete tuition information.

Accreditation
Vatterott College in nationally accredited by the Accrediting Commission of Career Schools and Colleges of Technology (ACCSCT).

Admission
The application process includes a personal interview and entrance evaluation. A high school diploma or GED is required.

Graduation Requirements
Students must show satisfactory progress by maintaining a minimum grade of 70 percent and an 80 percent attendance record.

Contact
Office of Admissions
Vatterott College
5318 South 136th Street
Omaha, NE 68137
Phone: (402) 891-9411
Fax: (402) 891-9413
E-mail: deerfield@vatterott-college.edu
Web: www.vatterott-college.edu

Program Content

Associate of Occupational Studies (AOS) Degree: Computer-Aided Drafting, Computer Programming, Computer Systems and Network Technology, and Graphic Art and Design

Diploma Programs: Commercial Art, Computer-Aided Drafting, Computer Programming, and Computer Technology

Vatterott College, Spring Valley Campus, Omaha

About Our Institution
All Vatterott College programs are based on a proven successful formula of specialized, technology-focused, hands-on training in the fastest growing industries. The College was founded in 1969 and now serves nearly 9,000 students per year at sixteen midwestern campuses. The Vatterott College–Omaha (Dodge) campus offers programs focused on the health-care industry.

Special Features
Vatterott College's hands-on training method of instruction equips students with the specific skills that are desired by local employers. Courses are geared to the student's field of study. Classes are available in both morning and evening schedules.

Financial Aid/Scholarships
Vatterott College participates in a variety of financial aid and scholarship programs. The College's Make-the-Grade Scholarship offers tuition credit to qualifying students based on high school grades. Vatterott College also participates in the Imagine America scholarship program. High school seniors are eligible to apply. Applicants should contact the campus Financial Aid Representative for specific information.

Tuition and Fees
The campus Office of Admissions can provide complete tuition information.

Admissions
The application process includes a personal interview and entrance evaluation. A high school diploma or GED is required.

Graduation Requirements
Students must show satisfactory progress by maintaining a minimum grade of 70 percent and a minimum 80 percent attendance record.

Contact
Office of Admissions
Vatterott College
225 North 80th Street
Omaha, NE 68114
Phone: (402) 392-1300
Web: www.vatterott-college.edu

Program Content
Diploma: Dental Assistant; Heating, Air Conditioning, and Refrigeration Mechanic; Medical Administrative Assistant; Medical Assistant; Psychiatric Assistant

Associate of Applied Science: Veterinary Technician

Associate of Occupational Studies (AOS) Degree: Heating, Air Conditioning, and Refrigeration Technology

CEI (Career-Ed Institute), Henderson

About Our Institution
Since 1982, Career-Ed Institute (CEI) has been providing high-quality, postsecondary training in Massachusetts and Rhode Island. In 2001, CEI added two campuses in the Atlanta, Georgia, area and one campus in Henderson (Las Vegas), Nevada. All CEI locations offer focused programs that help its students receive the skills and confidence essential for success in their chosen field of study.

Special Features
CEI is dedicated and committed to providing an industry-standard and quality-driven instructional program, designed for students. The philosophy of CEI extends beyond the teaching of technical proficiencies and practical knowledge. CEI is committed to serving its students with concern and respect.

Financial Aid/Scholarships
CEI maintains a financial aid office at each location. A variety of available programs including grants, loans, scholarships, work-study, veteran's and vocational rehabilitation are available to qualified applicants. CEI provides two full and two half-tuition scholarships at each of its campuses. They are awarded annually to winners of the Scholarship Awards Program. Preliminary scholarship competition is conducted in the form of aptitude testing at each campus location. On the basis of test results, finalists are selected and invited to return for an interview conducted by the Scholarship Committee, which is made up of volunteers who represent business, industry, education, and/or government.

Accreditation
CEI is accredited by the Accrediting Council for Independent Colleges and Schools (ACICS), Washington, D.C., and is approved by a number of respective state and federal organizations. Further information is available from the school catalog.

Admissions
An applicant must satisfy the requirements of possessing a high school diploma or GED. A passing score on the CEI Entrance Examination is necessary for acceptance.

Graduation Requirements
Graduation requirements mandate that a student complete all required courses and achieve an overall grade point average of at least 2.0.

Contact
Executive Director
Career-Ed Institute
2290 Corporate Circle #100
Henderson, NV 89014
Phone: 702-269-7600
Fax: 702-269-7676
E-mail: execdirhenderson@lincolntech.com
Web: www.ceitraining.com

Program Content
Business Administration Specialist, Medical Administrative Assistant, Medical Assistant, Network Systems Administrator, Therapeutic Massage and Bodywork Technology

ITT Technical Institute, Henderson

About Our Institution

The company: ITT Technical Institute is owned and operated by ITT Educational Services, Inc. (ITT/ESI), a leading private college system offering technology-influenced programs of study. ITT/ESI operates seventy-seven ITT Technical Institutes in thirty states, providing career-focused degree programs to approximately 39,000 students as of spring 2004. Headquartered in Carmel, Indiana, ITT/ESI has been actively involved in the higher education community in the United States since 1969.

Curricula: Curriculum offerings are designed to help students begin to prepare for career opportunities in fields of technology. Students attend classes year-round, with convenient breaks provided throughout the year. A full-time student course load can have class meetings as often as three days a week and are typically available in the morning, afternoon, and evening, depending on student enrollment. General education courses may be available online. This class schedule offers flexibility to students to pursue part-time employment opportunities.

ITT Technical Institute, Henderson, awards the Associate of Applied Science and the Bachelor of Science degrees.

Special Features

Most ITT Technical Institute programs of study blend traditional academic content with applied learning concepts, with a significant portion devoted to practical study in a lab environment. Advisory committees composed of representatives of local businesses help each ITT Technical Institute periodically review and update curricula, equipment, and laboratory design.

Financial Aid/Scholarships

ITT Technical Institute maintains a Financial Aid Department on campus. The campus is designated as an eligible institution by the U.S. Department of Education for participation in the following programs: Federal Stafford Student Loan Program, Federal PLUS Loan Program, and Federal Work-Study Program. The school also offers nonfederal loans available through Bank One for eligible students.

Tuition and Fees

March 2005 tuition is $386 per credit hour.

Accreditation

The school is accredited by the Accrediting Council for Independent Colleges and Schools (ACICS).

Admissions

For admission requirements, students should contact the school for a catalog.

Graduation Requirements

For graduation requirements, students should contact the school for a catalog.

Program Content

School of Information Technology: Data Communication Systems Technology, Information Systems Security, Information Technology–Computer Network Systems, Information Technology–Software Applications and Programming, Information Technology–Web Development, Software Engineering Technology

School of Electronics Technology: Computer and Electronics Engineering Technology, Electronics and Communications Engineering Technology

School of Drafting and Design: Computer Drafting and Design, Digital Entertainment and Game Design, Information Technology–Multimedia

School of Business: Business Accounting Technology, Business Administration, Technical Project Management

School of Criminal Justice: Criminal Justice

Contact

Donn Nimmer, Director
ITT Technical Institute
168 North Gibson Road
Henderson, NV 89014
Phone: (702) 558-5404
Fax: (702) 558-5412

Las Vegas College, Henderson

About Our Institution
Las Vegas College was founded by Betty Krolak in 1979, under the name of Krolak Business Institute. The College was acquired by Rhodes Colleges, Inc., in October 1996, and the name was changed to Las Vegas College. Las Vegas College is one of more than eighty schools owned and operated by Corinthian Colleges, Inc., in the United States.

Financial Aid/Scholarships
Federal Pell Grants, FFEL, work-study, FSEOG, WIA, VA, and other programs are available. Financial aid is available for those who qualify.

Tuition and Fees
Per-credit-hour fees are assessed based on the number of classes taken per quarter. A $25 registration fee is charged each quarter.

Accreditation
The College is accredited by the Accrediting Council for Independent Colleges and Schools (ACICS).

Admissions
A high school diploma or GED certificate is required for admission. Those without a high school diploma or GED certificate may apply for some programs under the Ability to Benefit Provision, although space is limited. An admission interview is recommended with applicants so they may gain better understanding of the College.

Graduation Requirements
Students must successfully complete all classes required, achieve an overall grade point average of at least 2.0, and meet all financial obligations in order to graduate.

Enrollment
140 students enrolled.

Contact
Bart Van Ry, Director of Admissions
170 North Stephanie Street, #145
Henderson, NV 89010
Phone: (702) 567-1920
Fax: (702) 566-9725
Web: www.lasvegas-college.com

Program Content
Administrative Medical Assistant, Business Administration, Criminal Justice, Medical Assistant

Programs Eligible for Scholarship	Tuition and Fees	Course Length/Credit Hours	Credential Earned
Administrative Medical Assistant	$266/credit	48 credit hours	Diploma
Business Administration	$266/credit	96 credit hours	Associate
Criminal Justice	$266/credit	96 credit hours	Associate
Medical Assistant	$266/credit	97 credit hours	Associate

Las Vegas College, Las Vegas

About Our Institution
Las Vegas College was founded by Betty Krolak in 1979, under the name of Krolak Business Institute. The College was acquired by Rhodes Colleges, Inc., in October 1996, and the name was changed to Las Vegas College. Las Vegas College is one of more than eighty schools owned and operated by Corinthian Colleges, Inc., in the United States.

Special Features
The College offers the only court reporting program in Las Vegas and Nevada. Its paralegal program is taught by attorneys. Up-to-date computer training and externships are available.

Financial Aid/Scholarships
Federal Pell Grants, FFEL, work-study, FSEOG, WIA, VA, and other programs are available. Financial aid is available for those who qualify.

Tuition and Fees
Per-credit-hour fees are assessed based on the number of classes taken per quarter. A $25 registration fee is charged each quarter.

Accreditation
The College is accredited by the Accrediting Council for Independent Colleges and Schools (ACICS) and the National Court Reporters Association (NCRA). The Medical Assisting program is accredited by the AAMA, a division of the Commission on Accreditation of Allied Health Education Programs (CAAHEP).

Admissions
A high school diploma or GED certificate is required for admission. Those without a high school diploma or GED certificate may apply for some programs under the Ability to Benefit Provision, although space is limited. An admission interview is recommended with applicants so they may gain better understanding of the College.

Graduation Requirements
Students must successfully complete all classes required, achieve an overall grade point average of at least 2.0, and meet all financial obligations in order to graduate.

Program Content
Accounting, Administrative Assistant, Administrative Medical Assistant, Bookkeeping, Business Administration, Computer Office Technologies and Applications, Court Reporting, Criminal Justice, Homeland Security, Legal Administrative Assistant, Medical Assistant, Medical Insurance Billing/Coding, Paralegal, Scoping Technology

Enrollment
The number of students enrolled is 750.

Contact
Shawn Saunders, Director of Admissions
4100 Flamingo Road, Suite 2100
Las Vegas, NV 89103
Phone: (702) 368-6200
Fax: (702) 368-6464
E-mail: ssaunder@cci.edu
Web: www.lasvegas-college.com

Programs Eligible for Scholarship	Tuition and Fees	Course Length/Credit Hours	Credential Earned
Accounting	$239/credit	96 credit hours	Associate
Administrative Assistant	$239/credit	96 credit hours	Associate
Business Administration	$239/credit	96 credit hours	Associate
Court Reporting	$239/credit	140 credit hours	Associate
Criminal Justice	$239/credit	96 credit hours	Associate
Medical Assistant	$239/credit	97 credit hours	Associate
Paralegal	$239/credit	96 credit hours	Associate
Administrative Medical Assistant	$239/credit	48 credit hours	Diploma
Bookkeeping	$239/credit	48 credit hours	Diploma
Computer Office Technologies and Applications	$239/credit	68 credit hours	Diploma
Computer Office Technologies and Applications	$239/credit	96 credit hours	Diploma
Homeland Security	$239/credit	52 credit hours	Diploma
Legal Administrative Assistant	$239/credit	60 credit hours	Diploma
Medical Insurance Billing/Coding	$8,100	35 credit hours	Diploma
Scoping Technology	$239/credit	58 credit hours	Diploma

Berdan Institute, Totowa

About Our Institution
The purpose of Berdan Institute can best be described as the preparation of individuals for employment in positions related to the medical and dental professions. Students attending the school are assumed to have made a general selection of the career they wish to pursue. All of the courses given at the school are selected and scheduled to contribute to that objective.

Special Features
Programs are designed to begin every six weeks and are available in morning, afternoon, and evening sessions. The daytime program length is thirty-five weeks and the evening program length is forty-seven weeks, with a 160-hour externship at the completion of each program.

Financial Aid/Scholarships
The financial aid programs at Berdan are for persons from all classes of society who have the ability and desire to benefit from such education or training. Students attending Berdan may qualify for various financial aid programs or scholarships.

Tuition and Fees
The price of tuition and fees (textbook and lab/consumables fees plus a $100 registration fee) varies by program. Costs for the Certified Nurse's Assistant/Patient Care Technician (CNA/PCT) program total $2,625; the Dental Assistant program, $9,475; the Massage Therapy program, $7,850; the Medical Assistant program, $9,400; the Medical Billing program, $9,690; the Medical Office Administration program, $9,275; and the Pharmacy Technician program, $8,025. These figures do not include the application fee of $25.

Accreditation
Berdan's programs are accredited by the Accrediting Bureau of Health Education Schools (ABHES), the Commission on Dental Accreditation of the American Dental Association, the Commission on Accreditation of Allied Health Education Programs (CAAHEP), and the American Association of Medical Assistants Endowment (AAMAE).

Admissions
Students must possess a high school diploma or GED certificate and must pass the Wonderlic Admission Test.

Graduation Requirements
To be eligible for graduation, students must graduate with a GPA of 2.0 or above. Students must earn a minimum of C in each subject area and have a minimum attendance rate of 80 percent.

Contact
Alan Concha, Director of Admissions
Berdan Institute
265 Route 46, West
Totowa, NJ 07512
Phone: (973) 256-3444
Fax: (973) 256-0816
E-mail: aconcha21@aol.com
Web: www.berdaninstitute.com

Program Content
CNA/PCT (Certified Nurse's Assistant/Patient Care Technician), Dental Assistant, Massage Therapy, Medical Assistant, Medical Billing, Medical Office Administration, Pharmacy Technician

Program Description
CNA/PCT: The program objective is to train students to acquire satisfactory skills and demonstrate competence in a variety of nursing assistant and home health aide procedures and laboratory techniques.

Dental Assistant: The objective of the Dental Assistant Program is to train students to acquire satisfactory skills and demonstrate competence in a variety of dental office procedures and laboratory techniques.

Massage Therapy: The program objective is to equip participants with the necessary entry-level technical, business, and professional skills for achievement in the fields of massage therapy and body-work.

Medical Assistant: The medical assistant field is a multiskilled allied health profession whose practitioners work primarily in ambulatory settings such as medical offices and clinics.

Medical Office Administration: The objective of the Medical Office Administration Program is to train students to acquire satisfactory skills and demonstrate competence in a variety of medical/dental office administration procedures.

Medical Billing: Medical billers are responsible for properly filling out appropriate claim forms with all necessary information and submitting claim forms to the proper party for reimbursement.

Pharmacy Technician: This program provides students with the administrative and clinical skills needed for pharmacy positions in retail, hospital, clinic, and home IV facilities. Graduates receive a certificate and are prepared to take the national certification exam.

The Cittone Institute, Edison

About Our Institution

The first and largest of the Cittone locations, the Edison campus was established more than thirty-six years ago. Originally founded as a business training school, Cittone responded to the needs of the changing work environment and now offers programs that focus on the computer and allied health fields. The Edison campus boasts forty computer labs containing a total of nearly 800 Intel-based computers. This allows Cittone to offer students their own individual workstations for hands-on training. Cittone also has the added benefit of having high-speed, T1 Internet access at the campus for quicker and easier data transmission on the Web. There are laboratories for the allied health programs. Cittone's caring and supportive staff members help prepare students for their new careers.

Offering morning, afternoon, and evening classes, Cittone can accommodate the needs of those with the busiest of schedules. The school is conveniently located just off Exit 131 of the Garden State Parkway and is easily accessible via U.S. Route 1 and I-287. Plenty of student parking is available as well as free shuttle bus transportation to the Metro Park train station in Iselin, New Jersey.

Special Features

The Cittone Institute is dedicated and committed to providing industry-current and enriching instructional programs for the serious-minded student. Leading companies contract with Cittone in their search for well-trained prospective employees. At Cittone, every member of the student body is recognized and respected. As a member school of the Lincoln Educational Services parent organization, attention to individual needs, abilities, and interests is the hallmark of the Cittone philosophy of education.

Financial Aid/Scholarships

Cittone is a registered institution of learning, eligible to offer financial assistance to its students. Each campus maintains an active financial aid office dedicated to matching a variety of available programs, including grants, loans, work-study, and vocational rehabilitation, to those applicants who qualify, following established federal guidelines.

There are a variety of half- and full-tuition scholarships available to graduating high school students. To apply for these scholarships, prospective students must fill out an application and take an aptitude-based scholarship test. A Scholarship Committee, composed of volunteers representing business, industry, education, and/or government, interviews the finalists and makes the award decisions.

Accreditation

The Cittone Institute is accredited by the Accrediting Council for Independent Colleges and Schools (ACICS) in Washington, D.C., and is approved by a number of state and federal organizations. Additional information is available in the school catalog.

Admissions

Applicants must either have an associate or baccalaureate degree or possess a high school diploma, a GED certificate, or the equivalent and receive a passing score on the Cittone Entrance Examination.

Program Content

Business Administration Specialist, Graphic Web Design, Medical Administrative Assistant, Medical Assistant, Network Systems Administrator, Pharmacy Technician, Therapeutic Massage and Bodywork Technician

Graduation Requirements

Graduation requirements mandate that a student complete all required courses and achieve an overall grade point average of at least 2.0.

Contact

Executive Director
The Cittone Institute
1697 Oak Tree Road
Edison, NJ 08820
Phone: (732) 548-8798
Fax: (732) 548-9682
E-mail: execdiredison@lincolntech.com
Web: www.cittone.com

The Cittone Institute, Mount Laurel

About Our Institution

The Cittone Institute's Mount Laurel campus is located in a modern office-park setting. With multiple computer labs containing several hundred Intel-based computers, Cittone is the perfect place to receive computer training. Students train on their own individual workstations, and high-speed, T1 Internet access is available at the campus. There are also laboratories for the allied health programs. Students have the opportunity to learn from caring and supportive industry-experienced instructors, and Cittone's professional and courteous staff members are there to help.

Offering morning, afternoon, and evening classes, Cittone can accommodate the needs of those with the busiest of schedules. The school is conveniently located just off the New Jersey Turnpike on Route 73, near Interstate 295 and Routes 70 and 38. Plenty of student parking is available.

Financial Aid/Scholarships

Cittone is a registered institution of learning, eligible to offer financial assistance to its students. Each campus maintains an active financial aid office dedicated to matching a variety of available programs, including grants, loans, work-study, and vocational rehabilitation, to those applicants who qualify, following established federal guidelines. There are a variety of half- and full-tuition scholarships available to graduating high school students. To apply for these scholarships, prospective students must fill out an application and take an aptitude-based scholarship test. A Scholarship Committee, composed of volunteers representing business, industry, education and/or government, interviews the finalists and makes the award decisions.

Accreditation

The Cittone Institute is accredited by the Accrediting Council for Independent Colleges and Schools (ACICS) in Washington, D.C., and is approved by a number of state and federal organizations. Additional information is available in the school catalog.

Admissions

Applicants must either have an associate or baccalaureate degree or possess a high school diploma, a GED certificate, or the equivalent and receive a passing score on the Cittone Entrance Examination.

Graduation Requirements

Graduation requirements mandate that a student complete all required courses and achieve an overall grade point average of at least 2.0.

Contact

Executive Director
The Cittone Institute
1000 Howard Boulevard
Mount Laurel, NJ 08054
Phone: (856) 722-9333
Fax: (856) 722-1110
E-mail: execdirmtlaurel@lincolntech.com
Web: www.cittone.com

Program Content

Business Administration Specialist, Graphic Web Design, Medical Administrative Assistant, Medical Assistant, Network Systems Administrator, Pharmacy Technician

The Cittone Institute, Paramus

About Our Institution

The newest Cittone campus, the Paramus school is located in a modern building on Route 4 in Bergen County, New Jersey. The Cittone Institute is dedicated and committed to providing industry-current instructional programs for the serious-minded student. The facilities include laboratories for the allied health programs. To accommodate the needs of the students, the school contains a comfortable student lounge, complete with vending machines, a refrigerator, and microwave ovens. With the Bergen Mall located adjacent to the school, there are ample varieties of snacks and meals for students who choose not to bring their own lunch or dinner. Plenty of parking is available and, for students who wish to use public transportation, there are numerous bus routes with stops within walking distance of the school.

Students have chosen the Cittone Institute for their educational needs because of its more than thirty years of experience, flexible class starts, career services, financial aid for qualified applicants, high-quality training and equipment and for the potential for students to graduate in a matter of months.

Financial Aid/Scholarships

Cittone is a registered institution of learning, eligible to offer financial assistance to its students. Each campus maintains an active financial aid office dedicated to matching a variety of available programs, including grants, loans, work-study, and vocational rehabilitation, to those applicants who qualify, following established federal guidelines. There are a variety of half- and full-tuition scholarships available to graduating high school students. To apply for these scholarships, prospective students must fill out an application and take an aptitude-based scholarship test. A Scholarship Committee, composed of volunteers representing business, industry, education and/or government, interviews the finalists and makes the award decisions.

Accreditation

The Cittone Institute is accredited by the Accrediting Council for Independent Colleges and Schools (ACICS) in Washington, D.C., and is approved by a number of state and federal organizations. Additional information is available in the school catalog.

Admissions

Applicants must either have an associate or baccalaureate degree or possess a high school diploma, a GED certificate, or the equivalent and receive a passing score on the Cittone Entrance Examination.

Graduation Requirements

Graduation requirements mandate that a student complete all required courses and achieve an overall grade point average of at least 2.0.

Program Content

Business Administration Specialist, Graphic Web Design, Medical Administrative Assistant, Medical Assistant, Network Systems Administrator, Pharmacy Technician, Therapeutic Massage and Bodywork Technology

Contact

Executive Director
The Cittone Institute
160 East State Route 4
Paramus, NJ 07652
Phone: 201-845-6868
Fax: (210) 368-0736
E-mail: execdirparamus@lincolntech.com
Web: www.cittone.com

Lincoln Technical Institute, Mahwah

About Our Institution
The Mahwah campus is a comprehensive training facility. Lincoln Technical Institute currently maintains an extensive inventory of training equipment, vehicles, tools, and computer diagnostic equipment in order to ensure that students have sufficient hands-on training and experience on industry-standard equipment. The 53,000-square-foot location contains eighteen instructional areas and has an 11,000-square-foot automotive shop with sixteen auto bays for student learning. The campus also has an advanced technical training center for automotive studies and a new computer simulation technology lab to be used in the automotive and air conditioning, refrigeration, and heating programs. The newly renovated CAD drafting labs are currently equipped with AutoCAD 2000 software.

Special Features
The skills enhancement program provides students with math and reading skills tutoring as related to their technical training. A library is available for the use of the students and graduates. Employment assistance is provided to current students, as well as graduates. Some programs offer an internship component.

Financial Aid/Scholarships
The Mahwah campus has a variety of tuition scholarships available to graduating high school students. The Institute participates in the Imagine America Scholarship program, as well as others. To apply for most of these scholarships, students must fill out an application and take an aptitude-based scholarship test. A Scholarship Committee, made up of volunteers representing business, industry, education, and/or government, interviews the finalists and makes the award decision. In addition, Lincoln Tech maintains a Financial Aid Office on campus, which offers a variety of programs, including grants, loans, work-study, veterans' aid, and vocational rehabilitation, to qualified students.

Tuition and Fees
Lincoln Technical Institute has established a schedule of fees/cancellation and refund policy, which contains detailed information on these charges, as well as others.

Accreditation
Lincoln Technical Institute is accredited by the Accrediting Commission of Career Schools and Colleges of Technology (ACCSCT) and certified by NATEF.

Admissions
A student must have either a high school diploma or a GED certificate and pass an entrance exam.

Graduation Requirements
To graduate from Lincoln Technical Institute, all students must successfully complete all required courses and comprehensive exams, attain an overall grade point average of 2.0 or better, and satisfy all financial obligations.

Contact
Executive Director
70 McKee Drive
Mahwah, NJ 07430
Phone: (201) 529-1414
Fax: (201) 529-5295
E-mail: execdirmahwah@lincolntech.com
Web: www.lincolntech.com

Program Content
Air Conditioning, Refrigeration, and Heating Technology; Automotive Technology; Electronic Systems Technician

Lincoln Technical Institute, Union

About Our Institution

As one of Lincoln Tech's largest campuses, Union is able to offer a wide variety of training options for students. The 60,000-square-foot facility contains the training equipment students might expect from an industry leader. The auto shop has a total of twenty-four equipped work bays to provide the hands-on training required for industry employment. The Institute has individual labs for training on heating, residential air conditioning, commercial air conditioning, and refrigeration units. A new computer lab is equipped with various computer software and simulates automotive and HVAC environments. Lincoln Tech has an excellent reputation and has a long-term history in New Jersey, creating many opportunities for students and graduates with local employers familiar with the Institute's focused training programs.

Prospective students in the New York City area who want further information can visit the Admissions Office in Brooklyn, located at 81 Willoughby Street, and can be reached by telephone at (718) 246-4001 or toll-free at (800) 786-0644. In addition, bus transportation to and from Lincoln Tech is available from convenient locations in Brooklyn and Queens.

Special Features

The career services department provides employment assistance to students upon graduation.

Financial Aid/Scholarships

The Union campus has a variety of tuition scholarships available to graduating high school students. The Institute also participates in the Imagine America Scholarship program, as well as others. To apply for most of these scholarships, students must fill out an application and take an aptitude-based scholarship test. A Scholarship Committee, made up of volunteers representing business, industry, education, and/or government, interviews the finalists and makes the award decision. In addition, Lincoln Tech maintains a Financial Aid Office on campus, which offers a variety of programs, including grants, loans, work-study, veterans' aid, and vocational rehabilitation, to qualified applicants.

Accreditation

Lincoln Tech is accredited by the Accredited Commission of Career Schools and Colleges of Technology (ACCSCT) and certified by NATEF.

Admissions

Students must have either a high school diploma or GED certificate and pass an entrance exam.

Graduation Requirements

In order to graduate, students must successfully complete all courses in the program. In addition, students must maintain a minimum overall GPA of 2.0.

Contact

Executive Director
Lincoln Technical Institute
2299 Vauxhall Road
Union, NJ 07083
Phone: (908) 964-7800
Fax: (908) 964-3035
E-mail: execdirunion@lincolntech.com
Web: www.lincolntech.com

Program Content

Air Conditioning, Refrigeration, and Heating Technology; Automotive Technology; Electronic Systems Technician

Program Description

Air Conditioning, Refrigeration, and Heating Technology: The program provides students with entry-level skills required to install and service commercial and residential environmental control systems under the supervision of an experienced mechanic.

Automotive Technology: The program provides students with the entry-level knowledge and skills required to correctly test, diagnose, replace, repair, and adjust as necessary the components of the mechanical, electronic, hydraulic, and accessories systems on current automobiles.

RETS Institute, Nutley

About Our Institution
RETS Institute, established in 1957, has provided almost 50 years of career training in electronics, computer repair, business, and medical assisting. RETS is accredited by ACCSCT and is approved by the New Jersey Department of Education. The programs emphasize hands-on training that is relevant to employer needs and focuses on careers that offer strong long-term employment opportunities. The school is owned by M. Eastwick Colleges, Inc.

Special Features
The RETS electronics and computer technology program has been evaluated by the American Council on Education's College Credit Recommendation Service (ACE/CCRS), which determined that courses are equivalent to or similar to those taught at the college level. RETS is also approved by the National Center for Competency Testing (NCCT) to administer Phlebotomy Technician, ECG Technician, Medical Assistant (CMA), and Insurance and Coding Specialist Certification Examinations. In addition, RETS is a corporate member in good standing of the Computer Technology Industry Association (CompTIA), a Pearson VUE–authorized testing center, and an FOA-Approved Training Organization with the Fiber Optic Association.

Financial Aid/Scholarships
RETS Institute is approved for Pell Grants, Direct Student Loans, SEOG Grants, Parent Loans, VA benefits, Workforce, and RETS Institute Scholarships.

Tuition and Fees
Tuition ranges from $4,000 to $17,100, depending on the program and its length. Books and equipment are included in all program tuition prices. The one-time application/registration fee is $125 and is payable at the time of enrollment.

Accreditation
RETS Institute is accredited by the Accrediting Commission of Career Schools and Colleges of Technology.

Admissions
Candidates are selected through a personal interview with an admission representative, evaluation of high school transcripts, and a qualification questionnaire.

Graduation Requirements
Students must successfully complete all required classroom training with a cumulative grade point average of at least 2.0, meet all program requirements for attendance, complete all career planning and placement assistance requirements, and pay all monies due to the school.

Program Content
Electronics and Computer Technology, Business Operations, Medical Assistant

Program Description
Electronics and Computer Technology: The course of study includes both the fundamentals and the advanced theory of electronics, integrated circuits, and microprocessing. Students also receive hands-on training on test equipment and background in the fundamentals of digital computers. Preparation for the A+ and Microsoft Windows 2000 professional exam is included.

Business Operations: This program gives the student all the fundamental and computer skills necessary for an entry-level business career. Microsoft Office, MOUS certifications, computerized accounting, and e-mail applications are included.

Medical Assistant: This program gives students both the clinical and administrative office skills necessary to gain entry-level employment as a medical assistant. Students prepare for and receive CPR, first aid, and OSHA certifications while in school and are eligible for EKG, phlebotomy, and RMA certifications once graduated. Computer and medical office management skills are also emphasized, including basic billing and coding.

Contact
Martin Klangasky
103 Park Avenue
Nutley, NJ 07110
Phone: (973) 661-0600
Fax: (973) 661-2954
E-mail: retsfa@aol.com

Programs Eligible for Scholarship	Tuition and Fees	Course Length/Credit Hours	Credential Earned
Electronics and Computer Technology	$17,225	18 months/90 credit hours	Diploma
Business Operations	$ 8,165	9 months/54 credit hours	Certificate
Medical Assistant	$ 9,425	9 months/43 credit hours	Certificate

Apollo College, Albuquerque

About Our Institution

Apollo College, founded in 1976, is recognized in communities as a leader in high-quality career education, with a hands-on orientation. Since then, the College has enjoyed a proud history of assisting people in becoming skilled professionals who go on to assume important positions in their communities. Highly trained, experienced faculty members present course materials that are relevant to current workforce needs; small class sizes ensure individualized attention for students. Programs begin on a monthly basis, with day and evening classes offered to accommodate busy schedules.

Special Features

The College's Advisory Board, composed of industry professionals, keeps Apollo abreast of the latest advances in their respective fields. Classrooms and labs are equipped with the latest-technology equipment.

Career and academic counseling is available. Placement services, such as job fairs, assistance with resume and interview preparation, and on-campus recruiting are available through the Office of Student Services. The College also assists full-time students in finding part-time employment. Housing information is available through the Admissions Department. Apollo's Skills Advancement Program offers continuous refresher courses to graduates at no extra cost.

Financial Aid/Scholarships

Financial aid is available to those who qualify. Apollo participates in a variety of state and federal financial aid and alternate loan programs, including Pell, FFEL, FDSLP, SEOG, SSIG, and JTPA.

Tuition and Fees

There is a separate application fee.

Accreditation

Apollo is nationally accredited by the Accrediting Bureau of Education Schools to award diplomas and associate degrees. Additional accreditations and approvals include the American Association of Medical Assistants, ABHES, APSA, JRCERT, CoARC, CAAHEP, and AMTA.

Admissions

Students must submit a completed application and a registration fee. An interview with an admissions representative is required. For some programs, an interview with a program director or instructional staff member may also be required to determine eligibility.

Graduation Requirements

To graduate, students must have satisfied all financial obligations and successfully completed the course of study and externship, including course requirements.

Enrollment

There are 350 students enrolled.

Program Content

Dental Assistant, Massage Therapist, Medical Administrative Assistant (Computerized Medical Office Secretary), Medical Assistant, Medical Records Specialist, Pharmacy Technician, Veterinary Assistant

Program Description

Dental Assistant students are trained to work directly with patients and dentists and perform dental office administrative duties.

The Massage Therapist program, through classroom and clinical training, prepares students for the NCBTMB certification exam and rewarding careers as health-care professionals.

The Medical Administrative Assistant Program provides instruction in medical law, ethics, and terminology and computer and office skills that are critical to office practice.

Medical Assistant students are trained to aid physicians and other medical personnel as they treat patients and perform administrative tasks that keep a medical office running smoothly.

Medical Records Specialist students learn to maintain accurate, organized documentation of medical care to provide data for a variety of health information needs.

Pharmacy Technician students are provided a working knowledge of the pharmaceutical business and learn to apply technical and practical training in pharmaceutical and medical terminology, drug dispensing, and administration.

Veterinary Assistants achieve the skills needed to succeed in a career with animals, meeting the strong demand for qualified animal-care services. Students learn up-to-date career skills and hands-on experience in today's veterinary technology.

Contact

Deanna BakerEric Garcia, Campus Director
5301 Central Avenue N.E. Suite 101
Albuquerque, NM 87108-1513
Phone: (505) 254-7777
        (800) 36-TRAIN (toll-free)
Fax: (505) 254-1101
E-mail: dbaker@apollocollege.com
Web: www.apollocollege.com

Programs Eligible for Scholarship	Tuition and Fees	Course Length/Credit Hours	Credential Earned
Dental Assistant	Call campus for current pricing information.	720 hours/24 credits	Diploma
Massage Therapist		720 hours/36 credits	Diploma
Medical Administrative Assistant (Computerized Medical Office Secretary)		720 hours/24 credits	Diploma
Medical Assistant		720 hours/24 credits	Diploma
Medical Records Specialist		860 hours/27 credits	Diploma
Pharmacy Technician		836 hours/24 credits	Diploma
Veterinary Assistant		720 hours/24 credits	Diploma

ITT Technical Institute, Albuquerque

About Our Institution
The company: ITT Technical Institute is owned and operated by ITT Educational Services, Inc. (ITT/ESI), a leading private college system that offers technology-influenced programs of study. ITT/ESI operates seventy-seven ITT Technical Institutes in thirty states; they provide career-focused degree programs to approximately 39,000 students as of spring 2004. Headquartered in Carmel, Indiana, ITT/ESI has been actively involved in the higher education community in the United States since 1969.

Curricula: Curriculum offerings are designed to help students begin to prepare for career opportunities in the fields of technology. Students attend classes year-round, with convenient breaks provided throughout the year. A full-time student can have class meetings as often as three days a week, and they are typically available in the morning, afternoon, and evening, depending on student enrollment. General education courses may be available online. This schedule offers flexibility to allow students to pursue part-time employment opportunities.

ITT Technical Institute, Albuquerque, awards Associate of Applied Science, Bachelor of Applied Science, and Bachelor of Science degrees.

Special Features
Most ITT Technical Institute programs of study blend traditional academic content with applied learning concepts, with a significant portion devoted to practical study in a lab environment. Advisory committees, made up of representatives of local businesses help each ITT Technical Institute periodically review and update curricula, equipment, and laboratory design.

Financial Aid/Scholarships
ITT Technical Institute maintains a Financial Aid Department on campus. The campus is designated as an eligible institution by the U.S. Department of Education for participation in the following programs: Federal Stafford Student Loan, Federal PLUS Loan, and Federal Work-Study. The school also participates in the California Grant Program and offers nonfederal loans through Bank One for eligible students.

Tuition and Fees
March 2005 tuition is $407 per credit hour.

Accreditation
Accrediting Council for Independent Colleges and Schools (ACICS).

Admissions
For admission requirements, students should contact the school for a catalog.

Graduation Requirements
For graduation requirements, students should consult the school catalog.

Program Content
School of Information Technology: Information Systems Security, Data Communication Systems Technology, Software Engineering Technology, Information Technology–Computer Network Systems, Information Technology–Software Applications and Programming, Information Technology–Web Development.

School of Electronics Technology: Electronics and Communications Engineering Technology, Computer and Electronics Engineering Technology.

School of Drafting and Design: Digital Entertainment and Game Design, Computer Drafting and Design, Information Technology–Multimedia Option.

School of Business: Business Administration, Business Accounting Technology, Technical Project Management.

School of Criminal Justice: Criminal Justice.

Contact
Marianne Rittner, Director
ITT Technical Institute
5100 Masthead Street, NE
Albuquerque, NM 87109
Phone: (505) 828-1114
Fax: (505) 828-1849

Apex Technical School, New York

About Our Institution

Licensed by the State of New York and accredited by the Accrediting Commission of Career Schools and Colleges of Technology, Apex Tech is a recognized leader in its field. It has provided companies in the New York metropolitan area with more than 15,000 skilled graduates since its founding in 1961. Occupying 100,000 square feet, Apex Tech operates one of the largest and most complete training facilities in the area. Centrally located at 635 Avenue of the Americas, at West 19th Street, the School is readily accessible via both public and private transportation.

Special Features

Apex Tech takes a step-by-step approach to teaching course work, moving from the basics to more advanced levels of study. Taught in manageable "course segments" by instructors with firsthand experience in their fields, classes combine hands-on training and textbook theory to provide the most comprehensive education possible. The School offers a variety of day and evening classes to accommodate busy students' schedules. New classes begin every month.

Financial Aid/Scholarships

Pell, FFEL, Work-Study, SEOG, VA, WIA, and other financial aid assistance is available for those who qualify. Apex Tech's financial aid department assists students in determining the types of financial aid available and helps guide them through the application process. The department works with various state and federal agencies and lending institutions and provides assistance in applying for the various grants or loans available. Following an assessment of a student's individual needs, a counselor develops a financial aid package in accordance with School, state, and federal guidelines.

Tuition

Tuition ranges from $12,708 to $19,061. Books, tools, and fees range from $438 to $653.

Accreditation

ACCSCT.

Admissions

Successful candidates must interview with an admissions representative, have parental consent if under 18, and be in possession of a valid high school diploma or equivalency certificate. Students without a diploma may gain entry through a satisfactory score on a standardized test.

Graduation Requirements

In order to graduate, a student must attain an overall 2.0 cumulative grade point average for the entire program and complete all courses specified in the program.

Program Content

Auto Body Repair, Automotive Mechanics, Automotive Technician, Combination Welding Technology, Refrigeration & Air Conditioning

Program Description

Apex Tech offers a choice of four certificate courses that may be completed in little as five to ten months: Auto Body Repair, Automotive Mechanics, Refrigeration & Air Conditioning, and Welding Technology. Each is part of a focused, high-quality training program designed to get students an entrée into their fields of choice in a minimum amount of time.

Contact

William Ott, Admissions Director
635 Avenue of the Americas
New York, NY 10011
Phone: (212) 645-3300
Fax: (212) 645-6985
Web: www.apextechnical.com

Programs Eligible for Scholarship	Tuition and Fees	Course Length/Credit Hours	Credential Earned
Auto Body Repair	$14,014	900	Certificate
Automotive Mechanics	$13,320	900	Certificate
Automotive Technician	$19,819	1,350	Certificate
Combination Welding Technology	$15,140	900	Certificate
Refrigeration & Air Conditioning	$14,339	900	Certificate

Guide to Career Colleges 2005

The Art Institute of New York City, New York

About Our Institution

The Art Institute of New York City, formerly the New York Restaurant School, is one of the Art Institutes, a system of thirty-one educational institutions throughout the United States offering postsecondary education programs in the creative and culinary arts.

In the culinary field, the school offers the Associate in Occupational Studies degree in culinary management and certificates in culinary arts, pastry arts, and restaurant management.

In the visual arts, new offerings include the Associate in Occupational Studies in art and design technology, with a concentration in graphic design, interactive media design, fashion design, or video production.

Art Institute of New York City graduates are trained for entry-level positions through concentrated, highly structured programs of study that reflect the needs of a changing job market. Graduates are provided with assistance in securing employment that culminates in professional satisfaction and rewards. Curricula are taught by faculty members who are or have been working professionally in their fields.

The emphasis of the school has always been on high-quality education. The strong performance of graduates working in the field is a testament to the strength of its programs.

Financial Aid/Scholarships

Financial Aid: Federal Pell Grant, Federal Supplemental Educational Opportunity Grant (FSEOG), Federal Stafford Student Loans (subsidized and unsubsidized), Federal Parent Loan to Undergraduate Students (FPLUS), Federal Work-Study Program, Tuition Assistance Program (TAP), Veterans' Educational Act, Vocational Rehabilitation Programs.

Scholarships: The Art Institute of New York City encourages potential and current students to apply for scholarships to help them finance their education. During the admissions process, students can apply for the following scholarships in which the Art Institute of New York City actively participates: the Art Institutes Best Teen Chef Culinary Scholarship Competition, the James Beard Foundation Scholarship, C-Cap, Americans for the Arts and The Art Institutes Poser Design Competition "Life is Better with Art in It", National Art Honor Society Scholarship, Evelyn Keedy Memorial Scholarship, C-CAP, VICA Skills USA Championship, Technology Student Association Competition, IACP Foundation, ProStart, Scholastics Arts Competition, and the John Shields Scholarship.

Tuition and Fees

Tuition for the 2004 academic year is listed on the Enrollment Agreement and in the Tuition and Refund Policy section of the catalog. The Art Institute of New York City administration makes every effort to control costs; however, occasional increases in tuition and fees are necessary. Students are responsible for payment of tuition and fees according to the schedule on their Enrollment Agreement. Tuition and fees are charged per charge period only. The student is never obligated for any charges beyond the charge period during which the student is attending.

Accreditation

The Art Institute of New York City is accredited by the Accrediting Council for Independent Colleges and Schools (ACICS).

Admissions

A high school diploma or GED certificate is required for admission. Prospective students are asked to write a 150-word essay.

Graduation Requirements

In order to graduate, students must fulfill all program requirements, have a cumulative grade point average (CGPA) of at least 2.0, and fulfill all financial obligations to the school.

Contact

Director of Admissions
The Art Institute of New York City
75 Varick Street or 11 Beach Street
New York, NY 10013
Phone: (212) 226-5500 or 625-6762
        (800) 654-2433 (toll-free)
Fax: (212) 226-5664
Web: www.ainyc.aii.edu

Program Content

Associate in Occupational Studies degree in culinary management, art and design technology (with concentrations in graphic design, interactive media design, fashion design, and video production); certificate in culinary arts, restaurant management, pastry arts (Interior design and advertising is planned to be offered beginning January 2005.)

Program Description

The culinary arts management program culminates in an Associate in Occupational Studies degree and gives graduates a broad knowledge of the restaurant industry. It is a six-quarter (full-day) or eight-quarter (part-day) program that focuses on both cooking and management skills.

The culinary arts program provides hands-on instruction in fundamental cooking and culinary skills. The program is offered in full-day and part-day formats and can be completed in either four or six quarters. An externship during the last quarter brings theoretical examples and practical learning into a real-world setting.

The pastry arts program focuses on the basics of preparing pastry from scratch, with concentrated courses that give students a secure foundation. As in culinary arts, students work at an externship program during the last quarter. The program is offered in both full-time (three quarters) and part-time (four quarters) formats.

In the certificate program in restaurant management, students learn all aspects of the field, from efficient operation of a working kitchen to maintenance of the front of the house. The program is offered in both full-time (three quarters) and part-time (four quarters) formats.

In graphic design, students develop basic skills in design, illustration, painting, and typography. Emphasis is placed on learning the skills and techniques of both computer graphics and traditional design and production tools, such as the drawing board and drawing instruments. It is a full-time (seven quarters) program.

In the interactive media design program, students learn how a multimedia and design professional designs information with graphics, audio, video, photography, and animation, integrating them in innovative ways. Students are introduced to the fundamentals of drawing and design, digital image manipulation, multimedia system design, sound design, and scripting, video, and animation. The program is full-time (seven quarters).

The fashion design program emphasizes innovation and creativity in fashion while providing students with the professional skills and technical knowledge necessary for a successful entry into the fashion industry. Students are introduced to the basic skills of construction in sewing, flat pattern drafting, and draping. It is a full-time (seven quarters) program.

Video production students work with a faculty that includes experienced professionals to develop competence in using the video camera as a technical and imaginative tool for communications art. Students then progress to more advanced skills in multicamera production, postproduction techniques, nonlinear editing, and the creating of a video from initial idea to final, edited composition. It is a full-time (seven quarters) program.

The French Culinary Institute, New York

About Our Institution
The French Culinary Institute (FCI), founded in 1984, is recognized as one of the top professional culinary schools in the country. It offers a unique opportunity to study culinary and pastry arts, bread baking, and culinary business under the direction of some of the world's most legendary four-star chefs and culinary trendsetters—right in the heart of New York City's thriving culinary scene.

The Institute's Total Immersion[SM] curriculum is guided by masters of French technique: Alain Sailhac, Jacques Pépin, Jacques Torres, and André Soltner; Master Sommelier Andrea Immer; Wedding Cake Master Ron Ben-Israel; Chez Panisse's Alice Waters; and Food Journalist Alan Richman.

Special Features
The French Culinary Institute has an elegant International Culinary Theater; an in-house restaurant, L'Ecole, where students get hands-on training; a library; a Career Services department; an Alumni Affairs department; a computer lab; a student lounge; and student clubs. The FCI launched and supports www.PastryScoop.com, an online resource and community for pastry professionals and enthusiasts.

Financial Aid/Scholarships
The French Culinary Institute maintains a Financial Aid Office, providing financial assistance to those who qualify. The FCI has secured a number of scholarship opportunities for current and future students to choose from.

Tuition and Fees
The tuition for Classic Culinary Arts with bread baking (full-time) is $33,500. Classic Culinary Arts (part-time) is $29,500. Classic Pastry Arts (full-time and part-time) is $32,500. The tuition for Art of International Bread Baking is $6,150. Essentials of Restaurant Management is $6,900. Fundamentals of Wine is $895 and Craft of Food Writing is $895.

Accreditation
The French Culinary Institute is accredited by the Accrediting Commission of Career Schools and Colleges of Technology and is licensed by the New York State Education Department.

Admissions
An admission portfolio consisting of an essay, a resume, and proof of high school graduation or its equivalent is required.

Graduation Requirements
In order to graduate, every student must complete at least 90 percent of the required total hours of instruction and receive an average passing grade on written tests and a rating of Satisfactory on practical evaluations.

Program Content
Classic Culinary Arts, Classic Pastry Arts, Essentials of Restaurant Management, Fundamentals of Wine, The Art of International Bread Baking, The Craft of Food Writing

Program Description
Classic Culinary Arts Through the Total Immersion[SM] approach to training, this program teaches the classic French techniques of culinary arts in 6- or 9–months.

Classic Pastry Arts: Through the Total Immersion[SM] approach to training, this program teaches the classic French techniques of pastry arts in 6- or 9–months.

Essentials of Restaurant Management: In 90 course hours, this program teaches the skills and tools necessary to build and run a successful restaurant or culinary business.

Fundamentals of Wine: In 16 course hours this program teaches wine regions, tasting notes, purchasing and storing, and how to build a profitable wine service.

The Art of International Bread Baking: Through the Total Immersion[SM] approach to training, this program teaches artisanal techniques of bread baking in three 2-week sections: French breads, Italian breads, and German and European breads.

The Craft of Food Writing: This program teaches the elements of food journalism, including pitching to editors, food features, and restaurant reviewing in 15 course hours.

Contact
David Waggoner, Dean of Admission
The French Culinary Institute
462 Broadway
New York, NY 10013
Phone: (212) 219-8890
        (888) FCI-CHEF (toll-free)
Fax: (212) 226-0672
E-mail: admission@frenchculinary.com
Web: www.frenchculinary.com

Programs Eligible for Scholarship	Tuition and Fees	Course Length/Credit Hours	Credential Earned
Classic Culinary Arts Day	$33,500	6 months	Diploma
Classic Culinary Arts Evening	$29,500	6 months	Diploma
Classic Pastry Arts	$32,500	6 months	Diploma
Essentials of Restaurant Management	$ 6,900	90 course hours	Diploma
Fundamentals of Wine	$ 895	16 course hours	Diploma
The Art of International Bread Baking	$ 6,150	6 weeks	Diploma
The Craft of Food Writing	$ 895	15 course hours	Diploma

Island Drafting and Technical Institute, Amityville

About Our Institution

The Island Drafting and Technical Institute (IDTI) is a career college offering technical training in drafting, electronics, and computer technology. IDTI provides industry with fully trained graduates and also provides companies with specialized training for current employees. The Institute was founded in 1957 and is staffed by faculty members who have had professional and practical experience in the engineering, architectural, computer-aided drafting/design (CADD), computer, and electronics fields.

The Institute's aim is to graduate students well-trained and technically qualified so that they may enter their chosen field or continue their education at the baccalaureate or higher level. Island Drafting and Technical Institute has more than forty-five years of leadership and experience in preparing its students for careers. The faculty members have stayed abreast of the latest developments in the industry, and the College has continued to provide the personal attention students need to succeed.

Special Features

IDTI's programs offer both full- and part-time coed day and evening classes. The Institute is an AutoCAD-authorized training center and a Microsoft-authorized academic training provider.

Financial Aid/Scholarships

Island Drafting and Technical Institute provides individualized financial aid application assistance to each of its students, using the latest in Internet technology for filing and follow-up. School scholarships are available as well as grants and loans, including Pell, FFEL, FDSLP, Perkins, SEOG, SSIG, VA, state grants, and JTPA.

Accreditation

Accrediting Commission of Career Schools and Colleges of Technology (ACCSCT).

Admissions

A high school diploma or its equivalent is required.

Contact

James G. Di Liberto, President
128 Broadway
Amityville, NY 11701
Phone: (631) 691-8733
Fax: (631) 691-8738
E-mail: info@idti.edu
Web: www.idti.edu

Program Content

CADD-Architectural, CADD-Mechanical, Electronic and Computer Technology

Program Description

Associate (AOS) degree and diploma programs are offered in computers, electronics, drafting, electronic technician, CNE-certified NetWare engineer, MCSE, CISCO, and computer-aided drafting/design (CADD) in architecture or mechanical.

Programs Eligible for Scholarship	Tuition and Fees	Course Length/Credit Hours	Credential Earned
CADD-Architectural	varies	60 weeks/60 credit hours	AOS
CADD-Mechanical	varies	60 weeks/60 credit hours	AOS
Electronic and Computer Technology	varies	60 weeks/60 credit hours	AOS

ITT Technical Institute, Albany

About Our Institution
The company: ITT Technical Institute is owned and operated by ITT Educational Services, Inc. (ITT/ESI), a leading private college system that offers technology-influenced programs of study. ITT/ESI operates seventy-seven ITT Technical Institutes in thirty states; they provide career-focused degree programs to approximately 39,000 students as of spring 2004. Headquartered in Carmel, Indiana, ITT/ESI has been actively involved in the higher education community in the United States since 1969.

Curricula: Curriculum offerings are designed to help students begin to prepare for career opportunities in the fields of technology. Students attend classes year-round, with convenient breaks provided throughout the year. A full-time student can have class meetings as often as three days a week, and they are typically available in the morning, afternoon, and evening, depending on student enrollment. General education courses may be available online. This schedule offers flexibility to allow students to pursue part-time employment opportunities.

ITT Technical Institute, Albany, awards the Associate in Occupational Studies degree.

Special Features
Most ITT Technical Institute programs of study blend traditional academic content with applied learning concepts, with a significant portion devoted to practical study in a lab environment. Advisory committees, made up of representatives of local businesses help each ITT Technical Institute periodically review and update curricula, equipment, and laboratory design.

Financial Aid/Scholarships
ITT Technical Institute maintains a Financial Aid Department on campus. The campus is designated as an eligible institution by the U.S. Department of Education for participation in the following programs: Federal Stafford Student Loan, Federal PLUS Loan, and Federal Work-Study. The school also participates in the California Grant Program and offers nonfederal loans through Bank One for eligible students.

Tuition and Fees
March 2005 tuition is $386 per credit hour.

Accreditation
Accrediting Council for Independent Colleges and Schools (ACICS).

Admissions
For admission requirements, students should contact the school for a catalog.

Graduation Requirements
For graduation requirements, students should consult the school catalog.

Program Content
School of Information Technology: Information Technology–Computer Network Systems, Information Technology–Software Applications and Programming, Information Technology–Web Development.

School of Electronics Technology: Computer and Electronics Technology.

School of Drafting and Design: Computer Drafting and Design, Information Technology–Multimedia Option.

Contact
Christopher Chang, Director
ITT Technical Institute
13 Airline Drive
Albany, NY 12205
Phone: (518) 452-9300
Fax: (518) 452-9393

ITT Technical Institute, Getzville

About Our Institution
The company: ITT Technical Institute is owned and operated by ITT Educational Services, Inc. (ITT/ESI), a leading private college system offering technology-influenced programs of study. ITT/ESI operates seventy-seven ITT Technical Institutes in thirty states, providing career-focused degree programs to approximately 39,000 students as of spring 2004. Headquartered in Carmel, Indiana, ITT/ESI has been actively involved in the higher education community in the United States since 1969.

Curricula: Curriculum offerings are designed to help students begin to prepare for career opportunities in fields of technology. Students attend classes year-round, with convenient breaks provided throughout the year. A full-time student course load can have class meetings as often as three days a week and are typically available in the morning, afternoon, and evening, depending on student enrollment. General education courses may be available online. This class schedule offers flexibility to students to pursue part-time employment opportunities.

ITT Technical Institute, Getzville, awards the Associate in Occupational Studies degree.

Special Features
Most ITT Technical Institute programs of study blend traditional academic content with applied learning concepts, with a significant portion devoted to practical study in a lab environment. Advisory committees composed of representatives of local businesses help each ITT Technical Institute periodically review and update curricula, equipment, and laboratory design.

Financial Aid/Scholarships
ITT Technical Institute maintains a Financial Aid Department on campus. The campus is designated as an eligible institution by the U.S. Department of Education for participation in the following programs: Federal Stafford Student Loan Program, Federal PLUS Loan Program, and Federal Work-Study Program. The school also offers nonfederal loans available through Bank One for eligible students.

Tuition and Fees
March 2005 tuition is $386 per credit hour.

Accreditation
The school is accredited by the Accrediting Council for Independent Colleges and Schools (ACICS).

Admissions
For admission requirements, students should contact the school for a catalog.

Graduation Requirements
For graduation requirements, students should contact the school for a catalog.

Program Content
School of Information Technology: Information Technology–Computer Network Systems, Information Technology–Software Applications and Programming, Information Technology–Web Development

School of Electronics Technology: Computer and Electronics Technology

School of Drafting and Design: Computer Drafting and Design, Information Technology–Multimedia

Contact
Lester Burgess, Director
ITT Technical Institute
2295 Millersport Highway
Getzville, NY 14068
Phone: (716) 689-2200
Fax: (716) 689-2828

ITT Technical Institute, Liverpool

About Our Institution
The company: ITT Technical Institute is owned and operated by ITT Educational Services, Inc. (ITT/ESI), a leading private college system offering on technology-influenced programs of study. ITT/ESI operates seventy-seven ITT Technical Institutes in thirty states, providing career-focused degree programs to approximately 39,000 students as of spring 2004. Headquartered in Carmel, Indiana, ITT/ESI has been actively involved in the higher education community in the United States since 1969.

Curricula: Curriculum offerings are designed to prepare students for career opportunities in fields of technology. Students attend classes year-round, with convenient breaks provided throughout the year. A full-time student course load can have class meetings as often as three days per week and are typically available in the morning, afternoon, and evening, depending on student enrollment. General education courses may be available online. This class schedule offers students the flexibility to pursue part-time employment opportunities.

ITT Technical Institute, Liverpool, awards the Associate in Occupational Studies degree.

Special Features
Most ITT Technical Institute programs of study blend traditional academic content with applied learning concepts, with a significant portion devoted to practical study in a lab environment. Advisory committees, made up of representatives of local businesses help each ITT Technical Institute periodically review and update curricula, equipment, and laboratory design.

Financial Aid/Scholarships
ITT Technical Institute maintains a Financial Aid Department on the campus. The campus is designated as an eligible institution by the U.S. Department of Education for participation in the following programs: Federal Stafford Student Loan Program, Federal PLUS Loan Program, and Federal Work-Study Program. The school also offers nonfederal loans through Bank One for eligible students.

Tuition and Fees
March 2005 tuition is $386 per credit hour.

Accreditation
The Institute is accredited by the Accrediting Council for Independent Colleges and Schools (ACICS).

Admissions
For admission requirements, students should consult the school catalog.

Graduation Requirements
For graduation requirements, students should consult the school catalog.

Program Content
School of Information Technology: Information Technology–Computer Network Systems, Information Technology–Software Applications and Programming, Information Technology–Web Development

School of Electronics Technology: Computer and Electronics Technology

School of Drafting and Design: Computer Drafting and Design

Contact
Joseph Gustin, Director
ITT Technical Institute
235 Greenfield Parkway
Liverpool, NY 13088
Phone: (315) 461-8000
Fax: (315) 461-8008

Mandl School, New York

About Our Institution
Mandl School provides a direct path to challenging careers in the health-care industry, offering specialized programs in medical assistant with word processing, dental assistant with word processing, medical laboratory technician, phlebotomy and EKG technician, nursing assistant, certified ophthalmic assistant, medical billing and coding, and much more. Mandl School is New York City's oldest and largest allied health education facility. It has been operating for more than seventy-eight years. Mandl School is located in the famous Studio 54 Building, on six modern floors in the heart of Manhattan's business and theater district, and is easily accessible by all forms of transportation.

Special Features
The Mandl School has approximately 30,000 square feet of classroom space, laboratories, and student service areas, including a student lounge and word processing center. All of the instructional departments of the Mandl School are completely equipped with the necessary business, medical, dental, and ophthalmic laboratory equipment and the materials and supplies necessary for training in each specialty. Typical classrooms vary from 10 to 30 students per instructor, depending on the program and subject. Job placement assistance is available to all graduates.

Financial Aid/Scholarships
Financial aid is available for those who qualify.

Accreditation
Accrediting Commission of Career Schools and Colleges of Technology (ACCSCT) and Accrediting Bureau of Health Education Schools (ABHES).

Contact
Melvyn Weiner, Director
Mandl School
254 West 54th Street
New York, NY 10019
Phone: (212) 247-3434
Fax: (212) 247-3617
E-mail: stu.mandl@prodigy.net
Web: www.mandlschool.com

Program Content
Diploma: Certified Ophthalmic Assistant, Dental Assistant with Word Processing, Medical Assistant with Word Processing, Medical Laboratory Technician, Nursing Assistant, Surgical Technologist

Certificate: Medical Billing and Coding, Phlebotomy Technician

Program Description
Mandl's career-focused programs provide both the administrative and clinical skills needed to maximize the students' potential and give them a competitive edge in today's job market. Graduates of any of Mandl School's programs are eligible to sit for a national registry or certification examination.

Programs Eligible for Scholarship	Tuition and Fees	Course Length/Credit Hours	Credential Earned
Certified Ophthalmic Assistant	$ 9,895	900 hours	Diploma
Dental Assistant with Word Processing	$ 8,695	900 hours, 760 hours	Diploma
Medical Assistant with Word Processing	$ 8,695	900 hours, 760 hours	Diploma
Medical Laboratory Technician	$ 8,695	1,500 hours, 2,500 hours	Diploma
Nursing Assistant	$ 980	120 hours	Diploma
Surgical Technologist with Internship	$16,500	1,200 hours	Diploma
Medical Billing and Coding	$ 980	90 hours	Certificate
Phlebotomy Technician	$ 980	90 hours	Certificate

Rochester Business Institute, Rochester

About Our Institution
The institution was founded in 1863 and has offered quality career training for 141 years to those interested in business careers. Rochester Business Institute (RBI) is one of more than eighty schools owned and operated by Corinthian Colleges, Inc., in the United States.

Financial Aid/Scholarships
Pell, FFEL, work-study, SEOG, VA, state grants, and scholarships are available for those who qualify.

Tuition and Fees
Tuition is currently $250 per credit hour. A $25 registration fee is assessed per quarter.

Accreditation
Rochester Business Institute is accredited by the Accrediting Council for Independent Colleges and Schools (ACICS).

Admissions
Candidates must complete an enrollment agreement, attend a personal interview, complete a validated entrance examination.

Graduation Requirements
Students must have a grade point average of 2.0 or better and earn the required minimum number of quarter credits necessary. Graduates must fulfill all financial obligations prior to the degree/diploma being issued.

Enrollment
1,200 students enrolled.

Contact
Deanna Pfluke, Director of Admissions
1630 Portland Avenue
Rochester, NY 14621
Phone: (585) 266-0430
Fax: (585) 266-8243
E-mail: dpfluke@cci.edu
Web: www.rochester-institute.com

Program Content
Accounting, Administrative Information Processing, Business Accounting and Applications, Business Administration, Business Management, Computer Programming with Business Applications, Information Processing Specialist, Medical Assisting, Paralegal/Legal Assistant, Programming for Business

Programs Eligible for Scholarship	Tuition and Fees	Course Length/Credit Hours	Credential Earned
Accounting	$250/credit hour	96 credit hours	AOS
Administrative Information Processing	$250/credit hour	96 credit hours	AOS
Business Administration	$250/credit hour	96 credit hours	AOS
Computer Programming with Business Applications	$250/credit hour	96 credit hours	AOS
Medical Assisting	$250/credit hour	97 credit hours	AOS
Paralegal/Legal Assistant	$250/credit hour	96 credit hours	AOS
Business Accounting and Applications	$250/credit hour	64 credit hours	Diploma
Business Management	$250/credit hour	64 credit hours	Diploma
Information Processing Specialist	$250/credit hour	64/66 credit hours	Diploma
Programming for Business	$250/credit hour	32 credit hours	Certificate

The Art Institute of Charlotte, Charlotte

About Our Institution

The Art Institute of Charlotte, formerly the American Business and Fashion Institute, has been a member of the community since 1973. It became a part of the Art Institutes, a system of schools located in major urban areas nationwide, in 1999. The Charlotte area offers a wide variety of events, ranging from major sporting events to cultural activities such as art shows and theater productions. The Institute provides students with a strictly creative outlet.

Special Features

The school offers a unique curriculum to its students. One of the best examples is the number of full-time and adjunct faculty members who are also prominent members of the art community. Students are guaranteed hands-on assignments in their particular field of study beginning with their first semester of class. The Art Institute of Charlotte also offers a state-of-the-art library and an outstanding Student Services Department, which aids students with career placement assistance during and after graduation. Advisory boards for each curriculum have been established to review the courses offered at the Institute. Those who sit on the advisory boards are professionals from the Charlotte area who are dedicated to helping the Institute make immediate changes as the job market dictates.

Financial Aid/Scholarships

The Art Institute of Charlotte offers a variety of financial assistance programs and scholarships. Based on eligibility, students can qualify for a Federal Pell Grant, Federal Stafford Student Loan, Federal Unsubsidized Stafford Student Loan, Federal Perkins Loan, Federal Work-Study Program, FSEOG, Federal PLUS Loan, veterans' benefits, the Art Institute of Charlotte High School Senior Scholarships, and Merit Scholarships.

Tuition and Fees

Tuition was charged at $306 per credit hour, effective November 1, 2002.

Accreditation

The Art Institute of Charlotte is accredited by the Accrediting Council for Independent Colleges and Schools to award certificates, diplomas, and associate degrees; licensed by the North Carolina Board of Community Colleges to award certificates and diplomas; licensed by the Board of Governors of the University of North Carolina to award associate degrees; and approved for the training of veterans and other eligible persons under provisions §3676, Title 38, U.S. Code.

Admissions

To be admitted to the Art Institute of Charlotte, students must submit a completed application along with a $50 fee and meet with an Assistant Director of Admissions, who can answer any questions about the school as well as schedule the next steps, such as a meeting with a financial planner. This representative takes students through the entire admissions process, from start to finish.

Graduation Requirements

All students must complete their program credit hours (all required courses) with a minimum 2.0 cumulative grade point average and successfully complete all portfolio requirements.

Program Content

Culinary Arts, Fashion Marketing, Graphic Design, Interior Design, Multimedia and Web Design

Program Description

Culinary Arts: Graduates are prepared for entry-level positions, such as line cook, pantry cook, assistant pastry chef, assistant dining room manager, or sommelier. Students may gain experience in settings ranging from cruise ships and resorts to hotels, restaurants, and corporate dining rooms.

Graphic Design: Advertisements, magazines, books, and consumer packages are all composed of images and printed words, and all must be designed. In the Institute's program, students learn how to design by studying color, composition, typography, and drawing, as well as learning the skills and techniques of computer graphics, electronic imaging, and production. Students' ideas for magazine layouts, poster art, and more start as sketches and result in final designs for their portfolio.

Multimedia and Web Design: Research has shown that there is a strong demand for artists who can design, develop, and maintain effective Web sites. Businesses are particularly interested in people who can create graphics, code in HTML, write scripts, program in an Internet language, and determine server space.

Fashion Marketing: Students with an eye for style and head for numbers can study in the heart of the Southern fashion market. They learn how to generate consumer appeal through designs, displays, and purchasing and are trained in fashion merchandising, fashion coordination, fashion show production, buying and textiles, small-business management, advertising and retail management, and visual merchandising.

Interior Design: Interior designers must have a thorough understanding of efficient space planning, color, pattern, lighting, furniture, and materials. In early courses, students learn the basics of drawing, drafting, color, and design and the fundamentals of space planning and perspective.

Contact

David L. Loughry, Director of Admissions
The Art Institute of Charlotte
Three LakePointe Plaza
2110 Water Ridge Parkway
Charlotte, NC 28217
Phone: (800) 872-4417 (toll-free)
Fax: (704) 357-1133
E-mail: aichadm@aii.edu
Web: www.aich.artinstitutes.edu

Programs Eligible for Scholarship	Tuition and Fees	Course Length/Credit Hours	Credential Earned
Culinary Arts	$306/credit hour	21 months/108 credit hours	AAS
Fashion Marketing	$306/credit hour	21 months/112 credit hours	AAS
Graphic Design	$306/credit hour	21 months/112 credit hours	AAS
Interior Design	$306/credit hour	21 months/112 credit hours	AAS
Multimedia and Web Design	$306/credit hour	21 months/112 credit hours	AAS

Brookstone College of Business, Charlotte

About Our Institution

Established in 1939, Brookstone College of Business was previously known as Ashmore Business College and Asheboro Business College. Ashmore Business College was the first nationally accredited business college in North Carolina, while Asheboro College was the first junior college of business in North Carolina licensed to award degrees. In 1984, these two schools were combined and relocated to the Greensboro/High Point area. The new institution became Brookstone College of Business, and the programs of study were shortened to certificate and diploma programs to facilitate quicker entry into the job market. The Charlotte campus was opened in 1987.

Special Features

Brookstone's convenient day and evening class schedules allow students to attend classes while working full- or part-time or managing a home. Lifetime placement assistance is offered to all graduates.

Financial Aid/Scholarships

Federal Pell, FFEL, FDSLP, work-study, FSEOG, and others. Approved for veterans' training.

Tuition and Fees

The average cost for the 2004–05 academic program is $10,000 for tuition and books.

Accreditation

Brookstone is accredited by the Accrediting Council for Independent Colleges and Schools (ACICS).

Admissions

The admissions policy is designed to attract persons who have the capability and the desire to develop marketable skills in concentrated training programs. In order to be admitted into any program, a high school diploma or GED certificate is required. Candidates are interviewed and tested to determine their capabilities.

Graduation Requirements

A minimum 2.0 cumulative grade point average is required for graduation. In addition, students must meet all financial obligations to the College, and specific program requirements must be met, including completion of all required classes and credits.

Program Content

Accounting Systems Technology, Administrative Assisting, Computerized Accounting, Computer Technology, Information Processing Technology, Medical and Health Office Technology, and Medical Assisting and Office Technology

Program Description

Accounting Systems Technology: Emphasis in this program is training the student in advanced accounting principles, including payroll, while utilizing these principles on accounting software.

Administrative Assisting: Emphasis in this program is preparing the student for entry-level positions in office settings that include word processing/secretarial technology.

Computerized Accounting: Emphasis in this program is on basic accounting principles and accounting software.

Computer Technology: Emphasis in this program is on configuring, installing, diagnosing, repairing, upgrading, and maintaining microcomputers and their peripherals.

Information Processing Technology: Emphasis is on the prospective student who desires to specialize in automated office procedures through the use of integrated software applications.

Medical and Health Office Technology: Emphasis in this program is on medical information processing and medical administrative software.

Medical Assisting and Office Technology: Emphasis in this program is on both clinical and administrative functions in an ambulatory health facility.

Contact

Vanessa Gray
10125 Berkeley Place Drive
Charlotte, NC 28262
Phone: (704) 547-8600
Fax: (704) 547-8887
E-mail: admissions@brookstone.edu
Web: www.brookstone.edu

Programs Eligible for Scholarship	Tuition and Fees	Course Length/Credit Hours	Credential Earned
Accounting Systems Technology	$ 9,500	50 weeks/60 credit hours	Diploma
Administrative Assisting	$ 6,650	35 weeks/40 credit hours	Certificate
Computerized Accounting	$ 6,650	35 weeks/42 credit hours	Certificate
Computer Technology	$10,200	50 weeks/54 credit hours	Diploma
Information Processing Technology	$ 9,500	50 weeks/54 credit hours	Diploma
Medical and Health Office Technology	$ 9,500	50 weeks/62 credit hours	Diploma
Medical Assisting and Office Technology	$13,150	65 weeks/76 credit hours	Diploma

Brookstone College of Business, Greensboro

About Our Institution
Established in 1939, Brookstone College of Business was previously known as Ashmore Business College and Asheboro Business College. Ashmore Business College was the first nationally accredited business college in North Carolina, while Asheboro Business College was the first junior college of business in North Carolina licensed to award degrees. In 1984, these two schools were combined and relocated to the Greensboro/High Point area. The new institution became Brookstone College of Business, and the programs of study were shortened to certificate and diploma programs to facilitate quicker entry for graduates into the job market. A campus in Charlotte, North Carolina, was opened in 1987.

Special Features
Brookstone's convenient day and evening class schedules allow students to attend classes while working full-time or part-time or managing a home. Lifetime placement assistance is offered to all graduates.

Financial Aid/Scholarships
Pell Grants, FFEL, FDSLP, Work-Study, FSEOG, VA, JTPA, and other sources are available.

Tuition and Fees
The average cost for the 2004–05 academic program is $10,000 for tuition and books.

Accreditation
Brookstone is accredited by the Accrediting Council for Independent Colleges and Schools (ACICS).

Admissions
The admissions policy is designed to attract people who have the capability and desire to develop marketable skills in concentrated training programs. In order to be admitted into any program, a high school diploma or GED certificate is required. Candidates are interviewed and tested to determine their capabilities.

Graduation Requirements
In order to graduate, a student must have a minimum 2.0 cumulative grade point average, all required classes, and total credits earned and must have met all financial obligations to the college and specific program requirements.

Contact
Bridget Handley
Brookstone College of Business
7815 National Service Road, Suite 600
Greensboro, NC 27409
Phone: (800) 992-5515 (toll-free)
Fax: (336) 668-2627
Web: www.brookstone.edu

Program Content
Accounting Systems Technology, Administrative Assisting, Computerized Accounting, Computer Technology, Information Processing Technology, Medical Assisting and Office Technology, Medical and Health Office Technology

Program Description
Accounting Systems Technology: Emphasis in this program is to train the student in advanced accounting principles, including payroll, while utilizing these principles on accounting software.

Administrative Assisting: Emphasis in this program is to prepare the student for entry-level positions in office settings that include word processing/secretarial technology.

Computerized Accounting: Emphasis in this program is on basic accounting principles and accounting software.

Computer Technology: Emphasis in this program is on configuring, installing, diagnosing, repairing, upgrading, and maintaining microcomputers and their peripherals.

Information Processing Technology: Emphasis is designed for the prospective student who desires to specialize in automated office procedures through the use of integrated software applications.

Medical and Health Office Technology: Emphasis in this program is on medical information processing and medical administrative software.

Medical Assisting and Office Technology: Emphasis in this program is on both clinical and administrative functions in an ambulatory health facility.

Programs Eligible for Scholarship	Tuition and Fees	Course Length/Credit Hours	Credential Earned
Accounting Systems Technology	$ 9,500	50 weeks/60 hours	Diploma
Administrative Assisting	$ 6,650	35 weeks/40 hours	Certificate
Computerized Accounting	$ 6,650	35 weeks/42 hours	Certificate
Computer Technology	$10,200	50 weeks/54 hours	Diploma
Information Processing Technology	$ 9,500	50 weeks/54 hours	Diploma
Medical and Health Office Technology	$ 9,500	50 weeks/62 hours	Diploma
Medical Assisting and Office Technology	$13,150	65 weeks/76 hours	Diploma

ECPI College of Technology, Charlotte

About Our Institution

ECPI College of Technology, an on-campus and online private college, was established in 1966 and operates in Virginia Beach, Newport News, and Northern Virginia, Virginia; Greensboro, Charlotte, and Raleigh, North Carolina; and Greenville, South Carolina. The College has an outstanding reputation for providing high-quality graduates to employers, including many Fortune 500 companies.

Special Features

ECPI provides high-quality technical, business, and health science education in a student-centered environment. The College prepares graduates to meet the needs of employers by offering classroom and hands-on instruction with industry-standard equipment. A valuable combination of technical and general education courses in degree programs enables graduates to advance quickly and to continue their lifelong pursuit of knowledge. Low faculty-student ratios facilitate instruction, and tutorial assistance is available at no additional charge. Programs are kept up-to-date with the input of advisory boards made up of leading employers and graduates. Job placement assistance is provided to qualified graduates, and students have the opportunity to interview for employment at job fairs held on campus.

Financial Aid/Scholarships

The College maintains a financial aid office providing a variety of financial aid programs, including Pell Grants, FFEL, Perkins Loans, work-study, FSEOG, VA, and scholarships.

Tuition and Fees

Tuition and fees vary by program.

Accreditation

The College is accredited by the Commission on Colleges of the Southern Association of Colleges and Schools.

Admissions

A high school diploma or GED certificate is required for admission, in addition to passing an admissions test and meeting academic and financial criteria.

Graduation Requirements

A student must attain a minimum 2.0 cumulative GPA for the entire program, achieve all applicable skill proficiencies, and complete all courses specified for the program.

Program Content

A.A.S. Degrees: Business Systems Administration, Computer Network Technology, IT/ Networking and Security Management, IT/ Web Design, Medical Administration, Medical Assisting

Diplomas: Business Administration, Computer Network Technology II, Information Technology/Networking and Security Management, Information Technology/Web Design, Medical Administration, Medical Assisting, Practical Nursing

Program Description

The Computer Science and Information Science programs prepare students for a variety of employment opportunities that include network administration, Web site development, and software applications. Hands-on instruction is featured whenever practical in both case study and laboratory settings. Faculty members use program advisory committees to identify and focus on current industry needs.

The Computer Electronics Technology programs prepare students for a variety of employment opportunities that include computer networks, telecommunications, electronics, and computer technology. Students receive hands-on instruction in these programs.

Program content has been carefully developed by faculty members using recommendations of employers and advisory board members to best meet industry needs.

Contact

Victor Riley, Provost
4800 Airport Center Parkway
Charlotte, NC 28208
Phone: (704) 399-1010
Fax: (704) 399-9144
E-mail: vriley@ecpi.edu
Web: www.ecpi.edu

Programs Eligible for Scholarships	Course Length/Credit Hours	Credential Earned
Business Systems Administration	67 credits	AAS
Business Systems Administration	45 credits	Diploma
Computer Network Technology	73 credits	AAS
Computer Network Technology II	52 credits	Diploma
IT/Networking and Security Management	73 credits	AAS
IT/Networking and Security Management	52 credits	Diploma
IT/Web Design	73 credits	AAS
IT/Web Design	52 credits	Diploma
Medical Administration	67 credits	AAS
Medical Administration	48 credits	Diploma
Medical Assisting	64 credits	AAS
Medical Assisting	53 credits	Diploma
Practical Nursing	46 credits	Diploma

ECPI College of Technology, Greensboro

About Our Institution
ECPI College of Technology, an on-campus and online private college, was established in 1966 and operates in Virginia Beach, Newport News, and Northern Virginia, Virginia; Greensboro, Charlotte, and Raleigh, North Carolina; and Greenville and Charleston, South Carolina. The College has an outstanding reputation for providing high-quality graduates to employers, including many Fortune 500 companies.

Special Features
ECPI provides high-quality technical, business, and health science education in a student-centered environment. The College prepares graduates to meet the needs of employers by offering classroom and hands-on instruction with industry-standard equipment. A valuable combination of technical and general education courses in degree programs enables graduates to advance quickly and to continue their lifelong pursuit of knowledge. Low faculty-student ratios facilitate instruction, and tutorial assistance is available at no additional charge. Programs are kept up-to-date with the input of advisory boards made up of leading employers and graduates. Job placement assistance is provided, and students may interview for employment at job fairs held on campus.

Financial Aid/Scholarships
The College maintains a financial aid office providing a variety of financial aid programs, including Pell Grants, FFEL, Perkins Loans, work-study, FSEOG, VA, and scholarships.

Tuition and Fees
Tuition and fees vary by program.

Accreditation
The College is accredited by the Commission on Colleges of the Southern Association of Colleges and Schools.

Admissions
A high school diploma or GED certificate is required in addition to passing an admissions test and meeting academic and financial criteria.

Graduation Requirements
A student must attain a minimum 2.0 cumulative GPA for the entire program, achieve all applicable skill proficiencies, and complete all courses specified for the program.

Program Content

A.A.S. Degrees: Business Systems Administration, Computer Network Technology, IT/Networking and Security Management, IT/Web Design, Medical Administration, Medical Assisting

Diplomas: Business Systems Administration, Computer Network Technology II, Information Technology/Networking and Security Management, Information Technology/Web Design, Medical Administration, Medical Assisting

Program Description

The Computer Science and Information Science programs prepare students for a variety of employment opportunities that include network administration, Web site development, and software applications. Hands-on instruction is featured whenever practical in both case study and laboratory settings. Faculty members use program advisory committees to identify and focus on current industry needs.

The Computer Electronics Technology programs prepare students for a variety of employment opportunities that include computer networks, telecommunications, electronics, and computer technology. Students receive hands-on instruction in these programs. Program content has been carefully developed by faculty members using recommendations of employers and advisory board members to best meet industry needs.

Contact
Melinda Catron, Provost
ECPI College of Technology
7802 Airport Center Drive
Greensboro, NC 27409
Phone: (336) 665-1400
Fax: (336) 664-0801
E-mail: mcatron@ecpi.edu
Web: www.ecpi.edu

Programs Eligible for Scholarship	Course Length/Credit Hours	Credential Earned
Business Systems Administration	67 credits	AAS
Business Systems Administration	45 credits	Diploma
Computer Network Technology	73 credits	AAS
Computer Network Technology II	52 credits	Diploma
IT/Networking and Security Management	73 credits	AAS
IT/Networking and Security Management	52 credits	Diploma
IT/Web Design	73 credits	AAS
IT/Web Design	52 credits	Diploma
Medical Administration	67 credits	AAS
Medical Administration	48 credits	Diploma
Medical Assisting	64 credits	AAS
Medical Assisting	53 credits	Diploma

ECPI College of Technology, Raleigh

About Our Institution
ECPI College of Technology, an on-campus and online private college, was established in 1966 and operates in Virginia Beach, Newport News, and Northern Virginia, Virginia; Greensboro, Charlotte, and Raleigh, North Carolina; and Greenville and Charleston, South Carolina. The College has an outstanding reputation for providing high-quality graduates to employers, including many Fortune 500 companies.

Special Features
ECPI provides high-quality technical, business, and health science education in a student-centered environment. The College prepares graduates to meet the needs of employers by offering classroom and hands-on instruction with industry-standard equipment. A valuable combination of technical and general education courses in degree programs enables graduates to advance quickly and to continue their lifelong pursuit of knowledge. Low faculty-student ratios facilitate instruction, and tutorial assistance is available at no additional charge. Students in degree programs can participate in an externship course that provides valuable experience in an employment setting. Programs are kept up-to-date with the input of advisory boards made up of leading employers and graduates. Job placement assistance is provided to qualified graduates, and students have the opportunity to interview for employment at job fairs held on campus.

Financial Aid/Scholarships
The College maintains a financial aid office, providing a variety of financial aid programs, including Pell Grants, FFEL, Perkins Loans, work-study, FSEOG, VA, and scholarships.

Tuition and Fees
Tuition and fees vary by program.

Accreditation
The College is accredited by the Commission on Colleges of the Southern Association of Colleges and Schools to award associate and baccalaureate degrees.

Admissions
A high school diploma or GED certificate is required for admission; in addition, applicants must pass an admissions test and meet academic and financial criteria.

Graduation Requirements
A student must attain a minimum 2.0 cumulative GPA, achieve all applicable skill proficiencies, and complete all courses specified for the program.

Program Content

A.A.S. Degree: Business Systems Administration, Computer Network Technology, IT/Networking and Security Management, IT/Web Design, Medical Administration, Medical Assisting

Diplomas: Business Administration, Computer Network Technology II, Information Technology/Networking and Security Management, Information Technology/Web Design, Medical Administration, Medical Assisting, Practical Nursing

Program Description
The Computer Science and Information Science programs prepare students for a variety of employment opportunities that include network administration, Web site development, and software applications. Hands-on instruction is featured whenever practical in both case study and laboratory settings. The degree program features an externship course that consists of both program competencies and actual work experience. Faculty members use the program advisory committees to identify and focus on the current needs of industry. General education courses enable students to continue their lifelong pursuit of knowledge and to demonstrate those characteristics expected of a college graduate.

The Computer Electronics Technology programs prepare students for a variety of employment opportunities that include computer networks, telecommunications, electronics, and computer technology. Students receive hands-on instruction in these programs, and degree students receive actual work experience in externship courses that require demonstration of program competencies.

Program content has been carefully developed by faculty members using recommendations of employers and advisory board members to best meet industry needs.

Contact
Susan Wells, Provost
Raleigh Branch Campus
4101 Doie Cope Road
Raleigh, NC 27613
Phone: (919) 571-0057
Fax: (919) 571-0780
E-mail: swells@ecpi.edu
Web: www.ecpi.edu

Programs Eligible for Scholarship	Course Length/Credit Hours	Credential Earned
Business Systems Administration	45/67 credits	Diploma/AAS
Computer Network Technology	73 credits	AAS
Computer Network Technology II	45 credits	Diploma
IT/Networking and Security Management	52/73 credits	Diploma/AAS
IT/Web Design	52/73 credits	Diploma/AAS
Medical Administration	48/67 credits	Diploma/AAS
Medical Assisting	53/64 credits	Diploma/AAS
Practical Nursing	46 credits	Diploma

NASCAR Technical Institute, Mooresville

About Our Institution
Opened in 2001, NTI Mooresville is a private postsecondary technical school that provides students with the technical education needed for a successful career in the automotive industry. NTI provides full student services: housing assistance, financial aid to those who qualify, campus activities, and both part-time and graduate employment assistance for as long as it is needed.

Special Features
NTI is an affiliate of Universal Technical Institute, Inc., and operates in a strategic relationship with NASCAR. This strategic relationship, formed in 1999, was developed to provide high-quality entry-level technicians to NASCAR and related automotive industry companies. UTI has trained high-quality technicians for the automotive industry since it was founded in 1965. This 146,000-square-foot training facility contains laboratories and classrooms for automotive training, NASCAR-specific training, and Ford elective training; administration facilities; and NASCAR's NASCAR TECH television studio.

Financial Aid/Scholarships
NTI students are eligible to apply for various federal grants and loans. These include Federal Pell Grants, FSEOG, Federal Stafford Student Loans, Federal Perkins Loans, and Federal PLUS loans. NTI also participates in various scholarship programs, such as VICA, CCA, Dodge Diversity, Imagine America, Ford AAA, the UPS Racing Technical Edge Scholarship Program, and UTI's National High School Senior Scholarship Program.

Tuition and Fees
Tuition and fees vary by course content. Tuition prices include all workbooks, textbooks, and uniforms; there are no hidden costs. For specific tuition information, students should contact the NTI Mooresville Admissions Office.

Accreditation
NTI is accredited by the Accrediting Commission of Career Schools and Colleges of Technology (ACCSCT), which is listed by the U.S. Department of Education as a nationally recognized accrediting agency and is also a member of the Council on Postsecondary Accreditation.

Admissions
Applicants must be at least 16 years of age and submit a completed application, a signed enrollment agreement, a registration fee, a high school diploma or equivalent, and any other information that the applicant or Institute feels is pertinent to admission. Each applicant's qualifications for enrollment are reviewed and either approved, approved with stipulation, or denied.

Graduation Requirements
Students must achieve at least an overall 2.0 cumulative GPA and receive a satisfactory grade in all required courses in their selected program. Graduation must be achieved within a ratio of 1½ attempted courses in a student's program. Candidates for graduation must also have a zero balance in their student account and have attended NTI's Career Development classes.

Program Content
Automotive/NASCAR Technology, Automotive/NASCAR/Ford FACT Technology

Program Description
The objective of NTI's automotive/NASCAR programs is to qualify students as entry-level automotive technicians equipped with the basic knowledge and skills required to diagnose malfunctions in the complete mechanical and electrical systems and make necessary repairs and replacements. Students are also prepared with specific skills for possible entry-level positions in NASCAR-related employment opportunities. The program is intended for the qualified novice who wishes to learn the trade or the practicing technician who wishes to upgrade their skill in the trade. The addition of the Ford FACT provides students with Ford-specific training, providing additional employment opportunities with the Ford Motor Company.

Contact
Mike Fritz
School Director
220 Byers Creek Road
Mooresville, NC 28117
Phone: (704) 658-1950
(866) 316-2722 (toll-free)
(866) 416-2722 (toll-free)
Fax: (704) 658-1952
E-mail: mfritz@uticorp.com
Web: www.uticorp.com

Akron Institute, Cuyahoga Falls

About Our Institution
Founded in 1970 as the Akron Medical Dental Institute, the Akron Institute currently offers programs in allied health and business careers. Akron Institute occupies 20,000 square feet of space for training and administration purposes in a building previously used as medical offices but now adapted for educational use.

Special Features
Akron Institute offers associate degree and diploma programs in the technology, business, and health-care fields. All diploma programs build toward an associate degree. A unique feature of Akron Institute programs is the preparation for industry certifications that is embedded in the curriculum, providing students with the opportunity to test for nationally and internationally recognized certifications in information technology and allied health. Employment assistance services are provided to graduates.

Financial Aid/Scholarships
Akron Institute maintains a financial aid team on campus, providing a variety of available programs, including grants, loans, veterans' benefits, and vocational rehabilitation. Akron Institute also has a number of institutional scholarships available.

Tuition and Fees
The tuition of $3,066 to $3,726 per semester includes the use of all books. A one-time-only uniform fee of $55 applies to the allied-health programs.

Accreditation
Akron Institute is a private college that is accredited by the Accrediting Commission of Career Schools and Colleges of Technology (ACCSCT) and is approved by the Ohio State Board of Career Colleges and Schools.

Admissions
Interested candidates should contact the Akron Institute Admissions Office to arrange an appointment. A high school diploma or the equivalency (GED) is required. Acceptance is based on a testing and interviewing process. Successful candidates must pass a scholastic-level exam and receive a recommendation from an admissions representative for admission to the college. There is a $25 enrollment fee.

Graduation Requirements
In order to graduate, a student must have a cumulative grade point average of at least 2.0 and pass all required courses. All incomplete and failed required courses must be successfully completed before graduation.

Program Content
Business Administration, Computer Network Technology, Dental Assisting, Medical Assisting, Medical Billing and Insurance Coding

Contact
Richard Fuller, Director of Admissions
Akron Institute
1625 Portage Trail
Cuyahoga Falls, OH 44223
Phone: (330) 928-3400
        (800) 311-0512 (toll free)
E-mail: info@akroninstitute.com

Programs Eligible for Scholarship	Tuition and Fees	Course Length/Credit Hours	Credential Earned
Business Administration	$3,404/semester	71 semester credit hours	AAS
Computer Network Technology	$3,726/semester	79 semester credit hours	AAS
Dental Assisting	$3,527/semester	46/64 semester credit hours	Diploma/AAS
Medical Assisting	$3,066/semester	40/61 semester credit hours	Diploma/AAS
Medical Billing and Insurance Coding	$3,680/semester	48/63 semester credit hours	Diploma/AAS

ETI Technical College, Niles

About Our Institution

It is the purpose of ETI Technical College of Niles to provide sound educational programs in the fields of computerized office technology, electronic engineering, legal assistant studies, medical assistant studies, and refrigeration, air conditioning, and heating. The College's "learn by doing" method of instruction provides the student with a proportional amount of time in theory and in lab to enable a graduate to enter a high-tech career.

Special Features

Through close association with instructors and fellow students, the student grows in maturity and obtains the confidence necessary for advancement in today's highly competitive world. ETI provides small classes, free tutoring, financial aid, and placement assistance to those who qualify.

Financial Aid/Scholarships

ETI maintains a financial aid department that provides one-on-one service to students. Students can apply for Federal Pell Grants, OIG, FEOG, Federal Stafford Student Loans, PLUS Loans, and several scholarships.

Tuition and Fees

Tuition averages approximately $2,800 per semester for each program available. ETI programs can be completed in three, four, or five semesters. Total fees for all programs vary.

Accreditation

ETI Technical College of Niles is accredited by the Accrediting Commission of Career Schools and Colleges of Technology (ACCSCT).

Admissions

All individuals applying to ETI must have graduated from high school or have successfully taken the GED test and passed an admissions test.

Graduation Requirements

Candidates for graduation must have a GPA of 2.0 or higher and have satisfied all the course requirements.

Contact

Diane Marsteller
Director of Admissions
2076 Youngstown-Warren Road
Niles, OH 44446
Phone: 330-652-9919
Fax: 330-652-4399
E-mail: etiadmissionsdir@hotmail.com

Program Content

Computer Electronic Engineering Technology; Computer Electronic Engineering Technology with a major in information technology and networking; Computerized Office Technology; Computerized Office Technology with a major in web design or accounting; Electronic Technology; Legal Assistant; Medical Assistant; Medical Assistant with a major in medical secretary; Refrigeration, Air Conditioning, and Heating

Program Description

Computer Electronic Engineering Technology provides the technical skills necessary for entry-level jobs in electronic engineering fields. Students majoring in information technology and networking learn how to install, configure, and troubleshoot computer networks.

Computerized Office Technology prepares students to become proficient in software applications and to compete in an office environment. Students may major in Web design or accounting.

Electronic Technology prepares the student for entry-level positions in electronic technology fields.

Legal Assistant studies provides legal skills necessary for entry-level employment in legal and business environments.

Medical Assistant studies prepares the student for employment in the dual (clinical/clerical) role of a medical assistant. The major in medical secretary specializes in the medical office.

Refrigeration, Air Conditioning, and Heating prepares students for entry-level employment in the domestic, commercial, and industrial fields of HVAC.

Programs Eligible for Scholarship	Tuition and Fees	Course Length/Credit Hour	Credential Earned
Computer Electronic Engineering Technology	$17,930	75 weeks/72 credit hours	Associate
Computer Electronic Engineering Technology (information technology and networking)	$17,930	75 weeks/70 credit hours	Associate
Computerized Office Technology	$16,090	75 weeks/75 credit hours	Associate
Computerized Office Technology (accounting)	$16,090	75 weeks/77 credit hours	Associate
Computerized Office Technology (Web design)	$16,090	75 weeks/78 credit hours	Associate
Electronic Technology	$ 8,765	45 weeks/30 credit hours	Diploma
Legal Assistant	$16,400	75 weeks/87 credit hours	Associate
Medical Assistant	$16,480	75 weeks/76 credit hours	Associate
Medical Assistant (medical secretary)	$16,480	75 weeks/77 credit hours	Associate
Refrigeration, Air Conditioning, and Heating	$ 8,765	48 weeks/37 credit hours	Diploma

International College of Broadcasting, Dayton

About Our Institution
International College of Broadcasting (ICB) is a private, proprietary institution of higher education committed to offering associate degrees and diploma programs, which strengthens the student's ability to learn the hands-on skills that spell success in today's fast-paced communications industry.

Special Features
ICB realizes the need for trained personnel, both behind the scenes and in front of the audience. This is evidenced by the strong demand for qualified individuals in the technical and highly competitive fields of radio and television. As one of the few colleges in the country offering a two-year intensive training program, the industry counts on graduates to fill the ever-present positions in all areas of broadcasting.

Financial Aid/Scholarships
ICB participates in Pell, OIG, FFEL, FDSLP, SEOG, BVR, VA, and scholarship programs.

Tuition and Fees
Tuition and fees vary based on program, ranging from $7,680 to $16,200 including books.

Accreditation
ICB is accredited by the Accrediting Commission of Career Schools and Colleges of Technology (ACCSCT).

Admissions
An entrance exam and a high school diploma or GED are required.

Graduation Requirements
In order to graduate, a student must have earned a minimum 2.0 cumulative grade point average, earned the minimum credit hours as required by the program of study, and satisfied all financial obligations to the College.

Contact
Chuck O. Oesterle
Director of Admissions
6 South Smithville
Dayton, OH 45431
Phone: (937) 258-8251
        (800) 517-7284 (toll-free)
Fax: (937) 258-8714

Program Content
Recording Audio Engineering/Video Production, Television and Radio Broadcasting, Recording/Audio Engineering

Program Description
Recording Audio Engineering/Video Production This associate degree program includes the emergence of new technologies and program forms, such as music videos. These new technologies and program forms bring the need for well-rounded, versatile professionals, trained in both video and audio. This program achieves this through a combination of lecture and in-studio experience, with the emphasis placed on hands-on training. Students learn to take projects from their initial concepts to finished production.

Television and Radio Broadcasting This associate degree program includes courses designed to give students a full understanding of radio and television, as well as to prepare them for employment in the expanding area of business and industrial communications. Basic and general educational courses enhance the technical education and enable students to advance toward career objectives.

Recording/Audio Engineering The primary educational goal of the Recording/Audio Engineering Program is to teach the operation of professional recording and sound reinforcement equipment, as well as to prepare the student for the many aspects of the music industry known today. This includes theory, music history, the music industry, songwriting, publishing, copywriting, and business communications.

Programs Eligible for Scholarship	Tuition and Fees	Course Length/Credits	Credential Earned
Recording Audio Engineering/Video	$15,700	60 credit hours	AAS
Television and Radio Broadcasting	$15,700	60 credit hours	AAS
Recording/Audio Engineering	$ 7,380	28 credit hours	Diploma

ITT Technical Institute, Dayton

About Our Institution

ITT Technical Institute is owned and operated by ITT Educational Services, Inc. (ITT/ESI), a leading private college system that offers technology-influenced programs of study. ITT/ESI operates seventy-seven ITT Technical Institutes in thirty states; they provide career-focused degree programs to approximately 39,000 students as of spring 2004. Headquartered in Carmel, Indiana, ITT/ESI has been actively involved in the higher education community in the United States since 1969.

Curriculum offerings are designed to help students begin to prepare for career opportunities in the fields of technology. Students attend classes year-round, with convenient breaks provided throughout the year. A full-time student can have class meetings as often as three days a week, and they are typically available in the morning, afternoon, and evening, depending on student enrollment. General education courses may be available online. This schedule offers flexibility to allow students to pursue part-time employment opportunities.

ITT Technical Institute, Dayton, awards Associate of Applied Science degrees.

Special Features

Most ITT Technical Institute programs of study blend traditional academic content with applied learning concepts, with a significant portion devoted to practical study in a lab environment. Advisory committees, made up of representatives of local businesses help each ITT Technical Institute periodically review and update curricula, equipment, and laboratory design.

Financial Aid/Scholarships

ITT Technical Institute maintains a Financial Aid Department on campus. The campus is designated as an eligible institution by the U.S. Department of Education for participation in the following programs: Federal Stafford Student Loan, Federal PLUS Loan, and Federal Work-Study. The school also participates in the California Grant Program and offers nonfederal loans through Bank One for eligible students.

Tuition and Fees

March 2005 tuition is $386 per credit hour.

Accreditation

Accrediting Council for Independent Colleges and Schools (ACICS).

Admissions

For admission requirements, students should contact the school for a catalog.

Graduation Requirements

For graduation requirements, students should consult the school catalog.

Program Content

School of Information Technology: Information Technology–Computer Network Systems, Information Technology–Software Applications and Programming, Information Technology–Web Development.

School of Electronics Technology: Computer and Electronics Engineering Technology.

School of Drafting and Design: Computer Drafting and Design, Information Technology–Multimedia Option.

Contact

Mike Shaffer, Director
ITT Technical Institute
3325 Stop 8 Road
Dayton, OH 45414
Phone: (937) 454-2267
Fax: (937) 454-2278

ITT Technical Institute, Hilliard

About Our Institution

The company: ITT Technical Institute is owned and operated by ITT Educational Services, Inc. (ITT/ESI), a leading private college system offering technology-influenced programs of study. ITT/ESI operates seventy-seven ITT Technical Institutes in thirty states, providing career-focused degree programs to approximately 39,000 students as of spring 2004. Headquartered in Carmel, Indiana, ITT/ESI has been actively involved in the higher education community in the United States since 1969.

Curricula: Curriculum offerings are designed to help students begin to prepare for career opportunities in fields of technology. Students attend classes year-round, with convenient breaks provided throughout the year. A full-time student course load can have class meetings as often as three days a week and are typically available in the morning, afternoon, and evening, depending on student enrollment. General education courses may be available online. This class schedule offers flexibility to students to pursue part-time employment opportunities.

ITT Technical Institute, Hilliard, offers the Associate of Applied Science and the Associate of Applied Business degrees.

Special Features

Most ITT Technical Institute programs of study blend traditional academic content with applied learning concepts, with a significant portion devoted to practical study in a lab environment. Advisory committees composed of representatives of local businesses help each ITT Technical Institute periodically review and update curricula, equipment, and laboratory design.

Financial Aid/Scholarships

ITT Technical Institute maintains a Financial Aid Department on campus. The campus is designated as an eligible institution by the U.S. Department of Education for participation in the following programs: Federal Stafford Student Loan Program, Federal PLUS Loan Program, and Federal Work-Study Program. The school also offers nonfederal loans available through Bank One for eligible students.

Tuition and Fees

March 2005 tuition is $386 per credit hour.

Accreditation

The school is accredited by the Accrediting Council for Independent Colleges and Schools (ACICS).

Admissions

For admission requirements, students should contact the school for a catalog.

Graduation Requirements

For graduation requirements, students should contact the school for a catalog.

Program Content

School of Information Technology: Information Technology–Computer Network Systems, Information Technology–Software Applications and Programming, Information Technology–Web Development

School of Electronics Technology: Computer and Electronics Engineering Technology

School of Drafting and Design: Computer Drafting and Design, Information Technology–Multimedia Option

School of Business: Business Accounting Technology, Business Administration

School of Criminal Justice: Criminal Justice

Contact

Jim Vaas, Director
ITT Technical Institute
3781 Park Mill Run Drive
Hilliard, OH 43026
Phone: (614) 771-4488
Fax: (614) 921-4179

ITT Technical Institute, Norwood

About Our Institution
The company: ITT Technical Institute is owned and operated by ITT Educational Services, Inc. (ITT/ESI), a leading private college system that offers technology-influenced programs of study. ITT/ESI operates seventy-seven ITT Technical Institutes in thirty states; they provide career-focused degree programs to approximately 39,000 students as of spring 2004. Headquartered in Carmel, Indiana, ITT/ESI has been actively involved in the higher education community in the United States since 1969.

Curricula: Curriculum offerings are designed to help students begin to prepare for career opportunities in the fields of technology. Students attend classes year-round, with convenient breaks provided throughout the year. A full-time student can have class meetings as often as three days a week, and they are typically available in the morning, afternoon, and evening, depending on student enrollment. General education courses may be available online. This schedule offers flexibility to allow students to pursue part-time employment opportunities.

ITT Technical Institute, Norwood, awards the Associate of Applied Science degree.

Special Features
Most ITT Technical Institute programs of study blend traditional academic content with applied learning concepts, with a significant portion devoted to practical study in a lab environment. Advisory committees, made up of representatives of local businesses help each ITT Technical Institute periodically review and update curricula, equipment, and laboratory design.

Financial Aid/Scholarships
ITT Technical Institute maintains a Financial Aid Department on campus. The campus is designated as an eligible institution by the U.S. Department of Education for participation in the following programs: Federal Stafford Student Loan, Federal PLUS Loan, and Federal Work-Study. The school also participates in the California Grant Program and offers nonfederal loans through Bank One for eligible students.

Tuition and Fees
March 2005 tuition is $386 per credit hour.

Accreditation
Accrediting Council for Independent Colleges and Schools (ACICS).

Admissions
For admission requirements, students should contact the school for a catalog.

Graduation Requirements
For graduation requirements, students should consult the school catalog.

Program Content
School of Information Technology: Information Technology–Computer Network Systems, Information Technology–Software Applications and Programming, Information Technology–Web Development.

School of Electronics Technology: Computer and Electronics Engineering Technology.

School of Drafting and Design: Computer Drafting and Design, Information Technology–Multimedia Option.

Contact
Bill Bradford, Director
ITT Technical Institute
4750 Wesley Avenue
Norwood, OH 45212
Phone: (513) 531-8300
Fax: (513) 531-8368

ITT Technical Institute, Strongsville

About Our Institution

The company: ITT Technical Institute is owned and operated by ITT Educational Services, Inc. (ITT/ESI), a leading private college system offering technology-influenced programs of study. ITT/ESI operates seventy-seven ITT Technical Institutes in thirty states, providing career-focused degree programs to approximately 39,000 students as of spring 2004. Headquartered in Carmel, Indiana, ITT/ESI has been actively involved in the higher education community in the United States since 1969.

Curricula: Curriculum offerings are designed to help students begin to prepare for career opportunities in fields of technology. Students attend classes year-round, with convenient breaks provided throughout the year. A full-time student course load can have class meetings as often as three days a week and are typically available in the morning, afternoon, and evening, depending on student enrollment. General education courses may be available online. This class schedule offers flexibility to students to pursue part-time employment opportunities.

ITT Technical Institute, Strongsville, awards the Associate of Applied Science degree.

Special Features

Most ITT Technical Institute programs of study blend traditional academic content with applied learning concepts, with a significant portion devoted to practical study in a lab environment. Advisory committees composed of representatives of local businesses help each ITT Technical Institute periodically review and update curricula, equipment, and laboratory design.

Financial Aid/Scholarships

ITT Technical Institute maintains a Financial Aid Department on campus. The campus is designated as an eligible institution by the U.S. Department of Education for participation in the following programs: Federal Stafford Student Loan Program, Federal PLUS Loan Program, and Federal Work-Study Program. The school also offers nonfederal loans available through Bank One for eligible students.

Tuition and Fees

March 2005 tuition is $384 per credit hour.

Accreditation

The school is accredited by the Accrediting Council for Independent Colleges and Schools (ACICS).

Admissions

For admission requirements, students should contact the school for a catalog.

Graduation Requirements

For graduation requirements, students should contact the school for a catalog.

Contact

Scott Behmer, Director
ITT Technical Institute
14955 Sprague Road
Strongsville, OH 44136
Phone: (440) 234-9091
Fax: (440) 234-7568

Program Content

Business Accounting Technology, Business Administration, Computer Drafting and Design, Computer and Electronics Engineering Technology, Criminal Justice, Information Technology: Computer Network Systems, Multimedia, Software Applications and Programming, Web Development

Program Description

The Business Accounting Technology program prepares students for a business accounting career. The program includes instruction on basic accounting technology. Professional and interpersonal communication are also elements of this program.

The Business Administration program offers students an opportunity to develop knowledge and skills that can help them begin careers in a variety of entry-level business and related positions. The program also offers instruction on teamwork, technology, and problem-solving and includes general education course work.

The Computer Drafting and Design program combines computer-aided drafting with conventional methods of graphic communication to solve drafting and basic design-related problems.

The Computer and Electronics Engineering Technology program prepares students for careers in entry-level positions in modern electronics and computer technology.

The Criminal Justice program prepares students for careers in the fields of law enforcement, community corrections, private investigation, and security. This program also offers the academic preparation that can help students pursue a broad spectrum of criminal justice careers in the private sector involving workplace security, safety officers, and security patrol officers.

The IT Computer Network Systems program helps prepare students to perform tasks associated with installing, upgrading, and maintaining computer network systems.

The IT Multimedia program helps students prepare to perform tasks associated with designing and creating interactive multimedia communications.

The IT Software Applications and Programming program helps students prepare to perform tasks associated with developing and modifying software applications.

The IT Web Development program helps students prepare to perform tasks associated with designing, creating, and maintaining Web sites.

ITT Technical Institute, Youngstown

About Our Institution
The company: ITT Technical Institute is owned and operated by ITT Educational Services, Inc. (ITT/ESI), a leading private college system offering technology-influenced programs of study. ITT/ESI operates seventy-seven ITT Technical Institutes in thirty states, providing career-focused degree programs to approximately 39,000 students as of spring 2004. Headquartered in Carmel, Indiana, ITT/ESI has been actively involved in the higher education community in the United States since 1969.

Curricula: Curriculum offerings are designed to help students begin to prepare for career opportunities in fields of technology. Students attend classes year-round, with convenient breaks provided throughout the year. A full-time student course load can have class meetings as often as three days a week and are typically available in the morning, afternoon, and evening, depending on student enrollment. General education courses may be available online. This class schedule offers flexibility to students to pursue part-time employment opportunities.

ITT Technical Institute, Youngstown, awards the Associate of Applied Science degree.

Special Features
Most ITT Technical Institute programs of study blend traditional academic content with applied learning concepts, with a significant portion devoted to practical study in a lab environment. Advisory committees composed of representatives of local businesses help each ITT Technical Institute periodically review and update curricula, equipment, and laboratory design.

Financial Aid/Scholarships
ITT Technical Institute maintains a Financial Aid Department on campus. The campus is designated as an eligible institution by the U.S. Department of Education for participation in the following programs: Federal Stafford Student Loan Program, Federal PLUS Loan Program, and Federal Work-Study Program. The school also offers nonfederal loans available through Bank One for eligible students.

Tuition and Fees
March 2005 tuition is $386 per credit hour.

Accreditation
The school is accredited by the Accrediting Council for Independent Colleges and Schools (ACICS).

Admissions
For admission requirements, students should contact the school for a catalog.

Graduation Requirements
For graduation requirements, students should contact the school for a catalog.

Program Content
School of Information Technology: Information Technology–Computer Network Systems, Information Technology–Software Applications and Programming, Information Technology–Web Development

School of Electronics Technology: Computer and Electronics Engineering Technology

School of Drafting and Design: Computer Drafting and Design, Information Technology–Multimedia Option

Contact
Frank Quartini, Director
ITT Technical Institute
1030 North Meridian Road
Youngstown, OH 44509
Phone: (330) 270-1600
Fax: (330) 270-8333

Ohio Institute of Photography and Technology, Dayton

About Our Institution
Ohio Institute of Photography and Technology (OIP&T) has been training students for thirty-one years. Originally established by a group of photographers from the Midwest, the school began as a highly specialized and innovative photographic training center located in Dayton, Ohio. In 1991, OIP&T began exploring other possible programs. As a result, the school expanded its curricula over the next few years to include medical assisting, medical office management, and desktop media. More recently, graphic design was added. OIP&T offers both diploma and degree programs. Employees are proud of the unique blend of art and technology on which the curricula are based.

Special Features
OIP&T has modern computer labs and equipment that is representative of that existing in industry. OIP&T is owned by Quest Education Corporation, based in Atlanta, Georgia. Quest currently operates forty-five schools and colleges nationwide, and is Kaplan, Inc.'s higher education division. The division includes campus-based schools and online postsecondary and career schools, including Concord Law School and Kaplan College. Kaplan is a wholly-owned subsidiary of The Washington Post Company (NYSE: WPO).

Financial Aid/Scholarships
Federal Pell Grants, FFEL, Ohio Instructional Grant (OIG), Work-Study, FSEOG, VA, WIA, and other programs are available.

Tuition and Fees
Tuition and fees vary by program.

Accreditation
OIP&T's programs are accredited by the Accrediting Commission of Career Schools and Colleges of Technology (ACCSCT) and the Commission on Accreditation of Allied Health Education Programs (CAAHEP).

Admissions
Applicants must possess a high school diploma or pass the GED test, successfully pass the entrance evaluation, and complete a tour of the college.

Graduation Requirements
Candidates for graduation must complete all requirements for their program of study, attain a cumulative GPA of 2.0 or better, return all property belonging to the college, and fulfill all financial obligations to the college.

Contact
David McDaniel
OIP&T
2029 Edgefield Road
Dayton, OH 45439
Phone: (800) 932-9698 (toll-free)
Fax: (937) 294-2259
Web: www.oipt.com

Program Content
Diploma: Desktop Media, Medical Assisting, Professional Photography

Associate Degree: Graphic Design, Medical Office Management, Photographic Technology (including Multimedia)

Ohio Technical College, Cleveland

About Our Institution
Since its founding in 1969, Ohio Technical College (OTC) has been dedicated to providing premier training to prepare students for challenging, rewarding careers in modern technologies. This is accomplished by pursuing industry alliances, training students on the most-up-to-date equipment, and focusing on individual needs of students. OTC is a medium-sized institution where students are treated as individuals and are known by their names rather than by a number.

Special Features
The total area of its half-million-square-foot facility makes Ohio Technical College one of the largest training centers in the United States. OTC boasts one of the highest student retention and job placement rates in the country. The College is linked to BMW of North America, Mercedes Benz, Firestone, and Ryder Transportation, among others, in cooperative educational programs. Perhaps the most unique aspect of training at OTC is that all training is performed on live equipment. The College has more than sixty tractor units and eighty automobiles. In addition, students in the auto/diesel program have the apparatus to obtain their CDL and drive trailer units as well as repair them.

Financial Aid/Scholarships
OTC participates in all Federal Title IV financial aid programs. These include grants, loans, and work-study. OTC also offers the Julius A. Brenner Founders Grant and the Roger Penske Scholarship and awards scholarships to selected participants of the VICA, GNYADA, and FORD/AAA Troubleshooting Competitions at the national and regional levels.

Accreditation
OTC holds accreditation and/or certification from ACCSCT, Ryder Logistics, EETC, OPE, NATEF/ASF, and I-CAR.

Admissions
All applicants are required to complete a personal interview with an Admissions Representative. Prospective students must be high school graduates, have a GED certificate, or pass an Ability to Benefit Test.

Contact
Tom King
Director of Admissions
1374 East 51st Street
Cleveland, OH 44103
Phone: (216) 881-1700
Fax: (216) 881-9145
E-mail: ohioauto@aol.com
Web: www.ohiotechnicalcollege.com

Program Content
Alternative Fuel Vehicle Technology, Autobody Technology, Auto-Diesel Master Vehicle Technology, Automotive Technician, Automotive Technology, Diesel Equipment Technology, Diesel Technician, High-Performance Vehicle Technology, Outdoor Power Equipment, Outdoor Power Equipment and Management Technology, Stationary Standby Generator Technician, Commercial Truck Driving Training (CDL), Associate of Applied Science in Auto-Diesel Technology, Associate of Applied Science in Diesel Equipment Technology

Program Description
Eighteen-Month Degree Program: Associate of Applied Science in Auto-Diesel Technology, Associate of Applied Science in Diesel Equipment Technology

Eighteen-Month Diploma Program: Auto-Diesel Master Vehicle Technology, Diesel Equipment Technology

Twelve-Month Diploma Program: Auto Technology, Auto Body Technology, Outdoor Power Equipment and Technology

Three-Month Certificate Program: Alternative Fuel Vehicle Technology, Generator Power Systems, High-Performance Vehicle Technology

80-Hour Licensing Program: CDL

Programs Eligible for Scholarship	Tuition and Fees	Course Length/Credit Hours	Credential Earned
Alternative Fuel Vehicle Technology	$ 4,320	12 weeks/300 clock hours	Diploma
Autobody Technology	$18,800	48 weeks/1,200 clock hours	Diploma
Auto-Diesel Technology	$22,200	72 weeks/134.5 credit hours	AAS
Auto-Diesel Master Vehicle Technology	$19,300	72 weeks/1,800 clock hours	Diploma
Automotive Technology	$17,600	48 weeks/1,200 clock hours	Diploma
Diesel Equipment Technology	$22,700	72 weeks/134.5 credit hours	AAS
Diesel Equipment Technology	$19,800	72 weeks/1,800 clock hours	Diploma
High-Performance Vehicle Technology	$ 4,827	12 weeks/300 clock hours	Diploma
Outdoor Power Equipment and Technology	$15,600	48 weeks/1,200 clock hours	Diploma

Ohio Valley College of Technology, East Liverpool

About Our Institution
Ohio Valley College of Technology (OVCT) is a private, technology-oriented career college. The College specializes in associate degrees in four concentrations: medical assisting or medical office administration, dental assisting, computer technology, and accounting management. Originally founded in 1886, the College has well-established relationships with area employers. Located in a small-town setting midway between Youngstown, Ohio, and Pittsburgh, Pennsylvania, the College is strategically located for convenient access.

Special Features
Structured scheduling allows students to earn an associate degree in as little as sixteen months. All graduates of the College earn lifetime career placement and training assistance, allowing graduates to return to the classroom to brush up skills at no cost. The OVCT philosophy is powerful training with personal attention, and the College emphasizes the small classroom setting as the best learning environment.

Financial Aid/Scholarships
All associate degree programs at Ohio Valley College of Technology are eligible for scholarships. The College participates in major federal financial aid programs, including grants, scholarships, and loans. Ohio residents may also be eligible for state-funded grants. The College also provides high school senior scholarships and participates in the Ohio legislative scholarship program. Other approved funding sources include Workforce Investment Act programs, TAA, Vocational Rehabilitation, and veterans training programs.

Accreditation
The College is accredited by the Accrediting Council for Independent Colleges and Schools (ACICS). Additional accreditation for the Medical Assisting Program is provided through the Commission on Accreditation of Allied Health Education Programs (CAAHEP).

Admissions
A high school diploma or GED is required for admission. In addition, prospective students must meet with an admissions representative for a career-planning session. The College may take into consideration other appropriate factors bearing on the applicant's potential for success.

Graduation Requirements
Students must maintain a minimum overall 2.0 cumulative grade point average, successfully complete all courses required in their program, and meet any specific program requirements listed in the College catalog.

Contact
Scott S. Rogers, Director
Ohio Valley College of Technology
16808 St. Clair Avenue
P.O. Box 7000
East Liverpool, OH 43920
Phone: (330) 385-1070
Fax: (330) 385-4606
E-mail: info@ovct.edu
Web: www.ovct.edu

Program Content
Accounting Management, Computer Technology, Dental Assisting, Medical Assisting, Medical Office Administration

Program Description
Accounting Management: This program emphasizes both accounting theory and practical application of accounting fundamentals. It includes computerized accounting, taxation, payroll, and cost accounting.

Computer Technology: This program is designed to prepare students for entry-level positions in computer operations/business settings. Students may choose either the software or technical emphasis, depending on their interests and goals.

Dental Assisting: This curriculum is designed to train the graduate to work with a dentist in patient procedures, as well as take radiographs, perform lab functions, and manage a dental office.

Medical Assisting: This program is designed to prepare graduates for the clinical skills necessary to work in hospitals, clinics, doctors' offices, and related fields. Administrative duties are also covered in the program.

Medical Office Administration: This program prepares students for administrative/clerical functions in the medical field, including terminology, transcription, medical office procedures, and insurance.

Remington College, Cleveland Campus, Cleveland

About Our Institution
Remington College was founded in 1985 in an effort to meet the growing need for computer-related education and training in the technical and business fields. To date, Remington College consists of twenty campuses across the United States. It teaches a "career first" curriculum that allows students to concentrate on learning the necessary technical skills early in their program and build on these skills as they progress toward graduation.

Special Features
Remington College is uncompromisingly dedicated to high-quality, college-level, career-oriented education. Its primary objectives are to graduate a high percentage of students who enter career programs and to help them achieve relevant employment at the highest possible starting salary. Remington College's hands-on training is the foundation of its educational structure. Practical application in well-equipped labs, coupled with theoretical reinforcement in the classroom, allows students to acquire substantial knowledge in their chosen career field. When appropriate, externships are used to provide the student with real-world experience.

Financial Aid/Scholarships
Remington College–Cleveland Campus maintains a Financial Services Office on the campus, providing a variety of grants, loans, scholarships, work-study, veterans' benefits, and vocational rehabilitation programs.

Tuition and Fees
Students should contact the campus for current tuition pricing. Textbook costs and lab fees are included in the tuition. A $50 registration fee is required for all programs.

Accreditation
Remington College–Cleveland Campus programs are accredited by the Accrediting Commission of Career Schools and Colleges of Technology (ACCSCT).

Admissions
A high school diploma or GED certificate, along with an acceptance interview, is used to determine a candidate's potential for success. At some sites, an entrance test is also included.

Graduation Requirements
In order to graduate, a student must maintain an overall cumulative grade point average of at least 2.0 for the entire program, complete all courses specified in the program catalog, and meet all financial obligations to the College.

Contact
Todd Zvaigzne, Campus President
14445 Broadway Avenue
Cleveland, OH 44125
Phone: (216) 475-7520
Fax: (216) 475-6055
Web: www.remingtoncollege.edu

Program Content
Business Information Systems, Computer Information Systems, Computer Networking Technology, Criminal Justice, Internet Information Systems, Laptop Programs, Medical Assisting, and Medical Insurance Coding

Program Description
Business Information Systems (A.A.S.): Training teaches the application of computer hardware and software to business functions in accounting, document processing, Internet research and Web site development, and marketing.

Computer Information Systems (A.A.S.): This program provides comprehensive training on PCs and networks, with an emphasis on developing programming skills.

Computer Networking Technology (A.A.S.): Training focuses on how to install, configure, maintain, and troubleshoot local area networks, wide area networks, and intranets that use DOS- and Windows-based network operating systems.

Criminal Justice (A.A.S.): This program is designed to prepare the student for entry into the criminal justice system. Areas within this career field include, but are not limited to, law enforcement, public safety, corrections, court administration, crime prevention, juvenile justice, victim assistance, and loss prevention.

Internet Information Systems (A.A.S.): Training focuses on Java, HTML, Visual Basic, Apache Server, principles of Web design, and e-commerce.

Medical Assisting (Diploma): Training focuses on both administrative and clinical procedures used in medical settings.

Medical Insurance Coding (Diploma): This program provides the basic elements of the field of insurance coding, such as medical abbreviations, computerized medical billing, medical records management, compliance, medical terminology, and office and hospital applications. Methods of coding and billing are taught as necessary for the student to become a successful medical insurance coder.

Remington College, Cleveland West Campus, North Olmsted

About Our Institution

Remington College was founded in 1985 in an effort to meet the growing need for computer-related education and training in the technical and business fields. To date, Remington College consists of twenty campuses across the United States. It teaches a "career first" curriculum that allows students to concentrate on learning the necessary technical skills early in their program and build on these skills as they progress toward graduation.

Special Features

Remington College is uncompromisingly dedicated to high-quality, college-level, career-oriented education. Its primary objectives are to graduate a high percentage of students who enter career programs and to help them achieve relevant employment at the highest possible starting salary. Remington College's hands-on training is the foundation of its educational structure. Practical application in well-equipped labs, coupled with theoretical reinforcement in the classroom, allows students to acquire substantial knowledge in their chosen career field. When appropriate, externships are used to provide the student with real-world experience.

Financial Aid/Scholarships

Remington College–Cleveland West Campus maintains a Financial Services Office on the campus, providing a variety of grants, loans, scholarships, work-study, veterans' benefits, and vocational rehabilitation programs.

Tuition and Fees

Students should contact the campus for current tuition pricing. Textbook costs and lab fees are included in the tuition. A $50 registration fee is required for all programs.

Accreditation

Remington College–Cleveland West Campus programs are accredited by the Accrediting Commission of Career Schools and Colleges of Technology (ACCSCT).

Admissions

A high school diploma or GED certificate, along with an acceptance interview, is used to determine a candidate's potential for success. At some sites, an entrance test is also included.

Graduation Requirements

In order to graduate, a student must maintain an overall cumulative grade point average of at least 2.0 for the entire program, complete all courses specified in the program catalog, and meet all financial obligations to the College.

Contact

Gary Azotea, Campus President
26350 Brookpark Road
North Olmsted, OH 44070
Phone: (440) 777-2560
Fax: (440) 777-3238
Web: www.remingtoncollege.edu

Program Content

Business Information Systems, Computer Networking Technology, Criminal Justice, Dental Assisting, Medical Assisting, Pharmacy Technician

Program Description

Business Information Systems (AAS): Training teaches the application of computer hardware and software to business functions in accounting, documents processing, Internet research and Web site development, and marketing.

Computer Networking Technology (AAS): Training focuses on how to install, configure, maintain, and troubleshoot local area networks, wide area networks, and intranets that use DOS- and Windows-based network operating systems.

Criminal Justice (AAS): This program is designed to prepare the student for entry into the criminal justice system. Areas within this career field include, but are not limited to, law enforcement, public safety, corrections, court administration, crime prevention, juvenile justice, victim assistance, and loss prevention.

Dental Assisting (Diploma): This program prepares graduates to work chairside with the dentist as well as in the business office and dental laboratory. Graduates prepare instrument trays, process x-rays, perform instrument and operatory infection control, perform oral hygiene instruction, and maintain patient records.

Medical Assisting (Diploma): Training in both administrative and clinical procedures used in medical settings.

Pharmacy Technician (Diploma): Medical abbreviations, prescription writing and interpretation, drug forms and administration, relationship between pharmacist and pharmacy technician.

RETS Tech Center, Centerville

About Our Institution
RETS was founded in Dayton, Ohio, in 1953 and has worked steadily to keep program offerings on the leading edge of technological advancement.

Special Features
The school is situated on 12.5 acres in suburban Centerville. The classroom building, which contains more than 45,000 square feet of space, opened in 1999, and there is free parking for more than 350 cars.

Financial Aid/Scholarships
Federal Pell Grants, FFEL, FDSLP, Federal Perkins Loans, FSEOG, SSIG, VA, state grants, WIA, Imagine America Scholarships.

Tuition and Fees
Tuition varies from $2,580 to $3,815 per semester, depending on the program. Book fees average $300 per semester, and lab fees average $85 per semester. Students should refer to the school catalog for tuition and fees for individual programs.

Admissions
Applicants must be high school graduates or have a GED certificate. A personal interview on campus, with both the admissions department and the financial aid office, is required before final admission is granted. All applicants are required to take the school's entrance examination.

Graduation Requirements
The school awards a diploma, an Associate of Applied Business, or an Associate of Applied Science degree upon completion of all required course work with a minimum GPA of 2.0.

Contact
Admissions Office
555 East Alex Bell Road
Centerville, OH 45459-2712
Phone: (937) 433-3410
　　　　(800) 837-7387 (toll-free)
Fax: (937) 435-6516
E-mail: kcmiller@retstechcenter.com
Web: www.retstechcenter.com

Program Content
Computer Applications Administration; Computer Information Technologies; Electronics Engineering Technology; Heating, Ventilating, Air Conditioning, and Refrigeration (HVACR); Legal Assisting/Paralegal; Medical Assisting; Medical Coding Specialist; Practical Nursing; Travel and Tourism

Program Description
Computer Applications Administration graduates typically serve in system interfacing, analysis, and programming. The program includes accounting.

Computer Information Technologies graduates are equipped to enter fields that include networking, programming, systems maintenance technology, graphics, and desktop publishing. Their skills include PC Technician, C++, Visual Basic, A++, and Network+.

Electronics Engineering Technology graduates are prepared for positions as programmers and technicians. They also serve as engineering aides and associate engineers and in the computer repair and maintenance, fiber-optic, and electronic communications fields.

Heating, Ventilating, Air Conditioning, and Refrigeration program graduates serve as installers, service techs, sales reps, refrigeration mechanics, and residential air conditioning and heating contractors. The HVACR program is only the third program in the nation to achieve accreditation by PAHRA.

Legal Assisting/Paralegal graduates serve in private law firms, government agencies, legal aid offices, corporate law departments, insurance companies, prosecutors' and public defenders' offices, etc. Offered in the evenings only. This program has received accreditation by the American Bar Association (ABA).

Medical Assisting graduates sit for the CMA examination and work in clinical or office settings. The program includes an externship.

Medical Coding Specialist graduates work as coders, claims specialists, ICD9/CPT. The program includes terminology, anatomy/physiology, etiology, pathology, symptoms, diagnostics, and treatments. Offered in the evenings only.

Practical Nursing graduates sit for their licenses and enter the medical field as LPNs, ready to become a member of a medical heath-care team that is predicted to continue to experience severe shortages of nurses for the foreseeable future.

Travel and Tourism graduates work in agencies, for carriers, or in the hospitality field in reservations, ticketing, etc.

Programs Eligible for Scholarship	Course Length/Credit Hours	Credential Earned
Computer Applications Administration	five 15-week semesters/81 credit hours	AAB
Electronics Engineering Technology	five 15-week semesters/73 credit hours	AAS
HVAC/R	three 12-week quarters/36 credit hours	Diploma
Legal Assisting/Paralegal (evenings only)	five 15-week semesters, 80 credit hours	AAB
Medical Assisting	four 15-week semesters/63 credit hours	AAS
Medical Coding Specialist (evenings only)	three 15-week semesters	Diploma
Travel and Tourism	two 15-week semesters	Diploma

Southwestern College, Dayton

About Our Institution

The Dayton campus is located on the eleventh floor of the 111 Building, a major office building in downtown Dayton, Ohio. It is easily accessible via a major interstate highway and public transportation. There are lecture classrooms, spacious computer rooms, and a medical lab to assist in student learning. The school also offers a beautiful view of the nearby river and the city of Dayton.

Southwestern College is committed to the educational and personal enrichment of its students. It is the College's philosophy to establish and maintain standards that foster the training, advancement, welfare, and best interest of its students. Each program is designed to help provide students with the entry-level employment skills necessary to meet the requirements of industry, government, allied health, and business offices today and in the future. At Southwestern, a student learns the skills needed to advance in his or her career. The College strives to develop student attitudes and habits that can help lead to promotions and success.

Financial Aid/Scholarships

Southwestern College understands that its students' education is an investment in their future. Southwestern's financial aid office is there to help students finance that future in the easiest way possible, because affordability should never be an issue when making the decision to get an education.

Southwestern can help in putting together a financial assistance plan to help students manage the cost of their education, including books and equipment. A Financial Aid Advisor can assist students in choosing from the many options that are available to help cover their educational expenses.

Tuition and Fees

For current tuition and fees, students should contact Southwestern College.

Accreditation

Southwestern College is accredited by the Accrediting Council for Independent Colleges and Schools (ACICS).

Admissions

Students must have either a high school diploma or GED certificate and pass an entrance exam for acceptance.

Contact

Executive Director
Southwestern College
111 West First Street
Dayton, OH 45402
Phone: (937) 224-0061
Fax: (937) 224-0065
E-mail: execdirdayton@lincolntech.com
Web: www.swcollege.net/

Program Content

Accounting, Administrative Assistant, Business Administration, Computer Applications, Computer Information Specialist, Computerized Accounting, Legal Secretary, Medical Administrative Assistant, Medical Assistant, Medical Coding and Billing, Phlebotomy

Southwestern College, Franklin

About Our Institution

The Franklin campus, in Franklin, Ohio, is just minutes south of Dayton. Located in a suburban neighborhood, the classically structured educational building has large windows, providing for well-lit, comfortable classrooms. Ample free parking is available. This location offers large lecture classrooms, computer labs, and a medical lab to assist in student learning.

Southwestern College is committed to the educational and personal enrichment of its students. It is the College's philosophy to establish and maintain standards that foster the training, advancement, welfare, and best interest of its students. Each program is designed to help provide students with the entry-level employment skills necessary to meet the requirements of industry, government, allied health, and business offices today and in the future. At Southwestern, a student learns the skills needed to advance in his or her career. The College strives to develop student attitudes and habits that can help lead to promotions and success.

Financial Aid/Scholarships

Southwestern College understands that its students' education is an investment in their future. Southwestern's financial aid office is there to help students finance that future in the easiest way possible, because affordability should never be an issue when making the decision to get an education.

Southwestern can help in putting together a financial assistance plan to help students manage the cost of their education, including books and equipment. A Financial Aid Advisor can assist students in choosing from the many options that are available to help cover their educational expenses.

Tuition and Fees

For current tuition and fees, students should contact Southwestern College.

Accreditation

Southwestern College is accredited by the Accrediting Council for Independent Colleges and Schools (ACICS).

Admissions

Students must have either a high school diploma or GED certificate and pass an entrance exam for acceptance.

Contact

Executive Director
Southwestern College
201 East Second Street
Franklin, OH 45005
Phone: (937) 746-6633
Fax: (937) 746-6754
E-mail: execdirfranklin@lincolntech.com
Web: www.swcollege.net/

Program Content

Administrative Assistant, Business Administration, Computer Applications, Computer Information Specialist, Computerized Accounting, Legal Secretary, Medical Administrative Assistant, Medical Assistant, Medical Coding and Billing, Phlebotomy

Southwestern College, Tri-County, Cincinnati

About Our Institution

The Tri-County campus occupies two floors of a recently renovated office building in a suburb of northern Cincinnati and is easily accessible via several major interstate and intrastate highways. Available bus transportation drops students off right in front of the school. Located just off of Route 275 (near the Tri-County Mall), there is ample free parking around the building. There are lecture classrooms, spacious computer labs, and a medical lab to assist in student learning.

Southwestern College is committed to the educational and personal enrichment of its students. It is the College's philosophy to establish and maintain standards that foster the training, advancement, welfare, and best interest of its students. Each program is designed to help provide students with the entry-level employment skills necessary to meet the requirements of industry, government, allied health, and business offices today and in the future. At Southwestern, a student learns the skills needed to advance in his or her career. The College strives to develop student attitudes and habits that can help lead to promotions and success.

Financial Aid/Scholarships

Southwestern College understands that its students' education is an investment in their future. Southwestern's financial aid office is there to help students finance that future in the easiest way possible, because affordability should never be an issue when making the decision to get an education.

Southwestern can help in putting together a financial assistance plan to help students manage the cost of their education, including books and equipment. A Financial Aid Advisor can assist students in choosing from the many options that are available to help cover their educational expenses.

Tuition and Fees

For current tuition and fees, students should contact Southwestern College.

Accreditation

Southwestern College is accredited by the Accrediting Council for Independent Colleges and Schools (ACICS).

Admissions

Students must have either a high school diploma or GED certificate and pass an entrance exam for acceptance.

Contact

Executive Director
Southwestern College
149 Northland Boulevard
Cincinnati, OH 45246
Phone: (513) 874-0432
Fax: (513) 874-0123
E-mail: execdirtri-county@lincolntech.com
Web: www.swcollege.net/

Program Content

Accounting, Administrative Assistant, Business Administration, Computer Applications, Computer Information Specialist, Computerized Accounting, Legal Secretary, Medical Administrative Assistant, Medical Assistant, Medical Coding and Billing, Phlebotomy

Southwestern College, Vine Street, Cincinnati

About Our Institution

The Vine Street campus occupies the second floor of the Provident Bank building on Vine Street in Cincinnati. Located in the heart of the downtown area and a block up from Fountain Square, the Vine Street Campus is easily accessible via a major interstate highway and public bus transportation. There are lecture classrooms, spacious computer labs, and a medical lab to assist in student learning.

Southwestern College is committed to the educational and personal enrichment of its students. It is the College's philosophy to establish and maintain standards that foster the training, advancement, welfare, and best interest of its students. Each program is designed to help provide students with the entry-level employment skills necessary to meet the requirements of industry, government, allied health, and business offices today and in the future. At Southwestern, a student learns the skills needed to advance in his or her career. The College strives to develop student attitudes and habits that can help lead to promotions and success.

Financial Aid/Scholarships

Southwestern College understands that its students' education is an investment in their future. Southwestern's financial aid office is there to help students finance that future in the easiest way possible, because affordability should never be an issue when making the decision to get an education.

Southwestern can help in putting together a financial assistance plan to help students manage the cost of their education, including books and equipment. A Financial Aid Advisor can assist students in choosing from the many options that are available to help cover their educational expenses.

Tuition and Fees

For current tuition and fees, students should contact Southwestern College.

Accreditation

Southwestern College is accredited by the Accrediting Council for Independent Colleges and Schools (ACICS).

Admissions

Students must have either a high school diploma or GED certificate and pass an entrance exam for acceptance.

Contact

Executive Director
Southwestern College
632 Vine Street
Cincinnati, OH 45202
Phone: (513) 421-3212
Fax: (513) 421-8325
E-mail: execdirvinestreet@lincolntech.com
Web: www.swcollege.net/

Program Content

Administrative Assistant, Business Administration, Computer Applications, Computer Information Specialist, Computerized Accounting, Legal Secretary, Medical Administrative Assistant, Medical Assistant, Medical Coding and Billing, Phlebotomy

Trumbull Business College, Warren

About Our Institution
Trumbull Business College, established in 1972, offers a professional college atmosphere. The facility occupies more than 60,000 square feet, with computer labs, library, student lounge, and spacious classrooms. Graduates are trained on the most popular business software programs available.

Special Features
Students benefit from the services of a full-time on-site tutor. A lifetime brush-up policy gives graduates the opportunity to come back and monitor a previously taken class at no expense.

Financial Aid/Scholarships
Financial assistance is provided to those who qualify through a variety of programs that include state grants, scholarships, work-study, veterans programs, vocational rehabilitation, Pell, FFEL, FDSLP, Perkins, SEOG, and JTPA.

Tuition and Fees
Depending on the type and length of the program, tuition and fees range from $15,330 to less than $21,365.

Accreditation
Accrediting Council for Independent Colleges and Schools (ACICS).

Admissions
All applicants must possess a high school diploma or GED and be available for a personal interview.

Graduation Requirements
Students must meet the course and credit requirements specified for their curriculum in addition to a minimum of a 2.0 accumulative GPA.

Contact
Amy Gazdik, High School Coordinator
3200 Ridge Avenue, SE
Warren, OH 44484
Phone: (330) 369-3200 Ext. 14

Program Content
Associate of Applied Business in Accounting, Associate of Applied Business in Business Administration, Associate of Applied Business in Business Computer Applications, Associate of Applied Business in Secretarial Science in Office Administration, Associate of Applied Business in Secretarial Science in Medical Secretarial, Associate of Applied Business in Secretarial Science in Legal Secretarial, Accounting Diploma, Business Computer Applications Diploma, Executive Secretarial Diploma, Computerized Office Specialist Diploma, Medical Secretarial Diploma, Legal Secretarial Diploma, Junior Accounting Diploma, Clerk/Typist Diploma

Programs Eligible for Scholarship	Tuition and Fees	Course Length/Credit Hours	Credential Earned
Accounting	$20,495	18 months	Associate
Business Administration	$21,165	18 months	Associate
Business Computer Applications	$20,490	18 months	Associate
Legal Secretarial	$20,520	18 months	Associate
Medical Secretarial	$21,365	18 months	Associate
Office Administration	$20,520	18 months	Associate
Accounting	$15,665	12 months	Diploma
Business Computer Applications	$15,710	12 months	Diploma
Computerized Office Specialist	$15,330	12 months	Diploma
Executive Secretarial	$15,330	12 months	Diploma
Legal Secretarial	$15,380	12 months	Diploma
Medical Secretarial	$15,430	12 months	Diploma

Vatterott College, Cleveland Campus, Broadview Heights

About Our Institution
All Vatterott College programs are based on a proven successful formula of specialized, technology-focused, hands-on training in the fastest-growing industries. The College was founded in 1969 and now serves nearly 9,000 students per year at sixteen Midwestern campuses. The Cleveland campus offers programs focused on the information technology and technical trade industries.

Special Features
Vatterott College's hands-on training method of instruction equips students with the specific skills that are desired by local employers. Courses are geared to the student's field of study. Classes are available in both morning and evening schedules.

Financial Aid/Scholarships
Vatterott College participates in a variety of financial aid and scholarship programs. The College's Make-the-Grade scholarship offers tuition credit to qualifying students based on high school grades. Vatterott College also participates in the Imagine America scholarship program. High school seniors are eligible to apply. Students should contact the campus Financial Aid Representative for specific information.

Tuition and Fees
The campus Admissions Representatives can provide complete tuition information.

Accreditation
Vatterott College is nationally accredited by the Accrediting Commission of Career Schools and Colleges of Technology.

Admissions
The application process includes a personal interview and entrance evaluation. A high school diploma or GED is required.

Graduation Requirements
Students must show satisfactory progress by maintaining a minimum grade of 70 percent and an 80 percent attendance record.

Contact
Kevin Pugely, High School Admissions Coordinator
Vatterott College
5025 East Royalton Road
Broadview Heights, OH 44147
Phone: (440) 526-1660
        (800) 864-5644 (toll-free)
Fax: (440) 526-1933
E-mail: cleveland@vatterott-college.edu
Web: www.vatterott-college.edu

(branch of main campus in St. Ann, MO)

Program Content
Associate of Applied Science (AAS) Degree: Building Maintenance Technology, Computer Systems and Network Technology, Electrical Technology, Environmental Systems Technology

Diploma: Building Maintenance Mechanic, Computer Technology, Electrical Mechanic, HVAC Mechanic

Virginia Marti College of Art and Design, Lakewood

About Our Institution

Virginia Marti College was founded in 1966. Mrs. Marti started the College while operating a bridal salon. Her first class was made up of 5 students. The College moved to its current location in 1985. The College offers excellent training in the areas of fashion design, fashion merchandising, graphic design, and interior design. What makes the school appealing is that students get four years of training in just two years. The College is located just 10 minutes from downtown Cleveland. The neighborhood surrounding the College has a blend of small businesses, resale boutiques, restaurants, homes, and apartments.

There are many main highways close to the College as well as public transportation. Cleveland Hopkins Airport is a short drive from the College. The College is minutes away from Cleveland's many cultural sites, including the Cleveland Museum of Art, Playhouse Square, the Cleveland Orchestra, the Rock and Roll Hall of Fame, and the Science Center.

Special Features

Virginia Marti College is located in a newly remodeled 22,000-square-foot building. The College has twelve classrooms/labs in addition to administrative and clerical areas. The equipment consists of PCs, network hardware, and laser printers. Other items include overhead projectors, TV/VCR's, tape players, computer projectors, and copiers. The student-faculty ratio is 15:1. Job placement is 90 percent.

Financial Aid/Scholarships

Virginia Marti College offers students a variety of ways to pay tuition. The College realizes that student's often lack the funds to begin college. The College has a financial aid office that participates in different types of federal, state, and institutional financial aid programs, most of which are based on financial need.

Accreditation

Virginia Marti College is accredited by the Accrediting Commission of Career Schools and Colleges of Technology (ACCSCT). The College is approved by the State Board of Property School Registration.

Admissions

Admission requirements include having a high school diploma or GED and submitting a completed application form, a letter of recommendation, and a letter written to the president of College on why they want to attend and why they should be accepted. Applicants must also complete an informational interview and take an entrance exam.

Graduation Requirements

Requirements in all programs include the accumulation of the minimum number of credits for the major course of study with final quarterly and cumulative grade point average of not less than 2.0 and also maintain

Program Content

Associate of Applied Business (AAB): Fashion Design, Fashion Merchandising, Graphic Design, Interior Design

satisfactory attendance in scheduled classes. Students must fulfill all financial obligations.

Enrollment

There are 260 students enrolled.

Contact

Quinn Marti, Admissions
John Minkiewicz, Admissions
11724 Detroit Ave.
Lakewood, OH 44107
Phone: (216) 221-8584
Fax: (216) 221-2311
Web: www.virginiamarticollege.com

Programs Eligible for Scholarship	Tuition and Fees	Course Length/Credit Hours	Credential Earned
Fashion Design	$31,350	1,540 clock hours	AAB
Fashion Merchandising	$31,350	1,340 clock hours	AAB
Graphic Design	$31,350	1,530 clock hours	AAB
Interior Design	$31,350	1,390 clock hours	AAB

Platt College, Oklahoma City

About Our Institution

Platt College, Oklahoma, was the branch of a proprietary institution that began in 1879 and is known as one of the first business colleges west of the Mississippi. To keep abreast of the fast-occurring changes in occupational trends, Platt College opened in Tulsa, Oklahoma, in 1979, offering courses in drafting and design. In 1981, Platt College began offering the same courses in Oklahoma City. At the Tulsa and Oklahoma City campuses, Platt College now offers courses in drafting and design, commercial art and graphic design, medical assisting/phlebotomy, dental assisting, practical nursing, pharmacy technician studies, and visual communications. Platt College is dedicated to providing to each of its students an environment that is conducive to growth, not only in skill training but also in personal growth. It is with this growth that students are able to pursue their career choices and meet the demands of the industry.

Special Features

Platt College has a small teacher-student ratio. The College offers placement and counseling assistance.

Financial Aid/Scholarships

During the admission process, students seeking financial assistance are required to see a Financial Aid Officer. Students who are enrolled at least half-time, show financial need, and continue to make satisfactory progress may be eligible for FFEL Stafford Student Loans, Federal Pell Grants, FSEOG, scholarships, and funds from various state agencies.

Tuition and Fees

Tuition averages approximately $7,000 per course. Tuition includes a $100 registration fee as well as books and supplies.

Accreditation

Platt College is licensed by the Oklahoma Board of Private Vocational Schools (OBPVS) and is approved for training by the Bureau of Indian Affairs (BIA), the Job Training Partnership Act (JTPA), the State Accrediting Agency for the training of eligible veterans, and veterans eligible for vocational rehabilitation. Platt College is accredited by the Accrediting Commission of Career Schools and Colleges of Technology (ACCSCT).

Admissions

Enrollment is open to men and women past the age of compulsory education. The school considers the following in evaluating applicants: graduation from an approved high school program or successful completion of a GED program (applicants without a high school diploma or GED certificate are required to take a Department of Education–

Program Content

Culinary Arts, Dental Assistant, Medical Assistant/Phlebotomy, Pharmacy Technician, Practical Nursing, Registered Nurse, Surgical Technologist Studies

approved evaluation to determine ability to benefit) and determination of purpose and attitude conducive to success.

Contact

Renee Jackson
Director of Admissions
Platt College Central
309 South Ann Arbor
Oklahoma City, OK 73128
Phone: (405) 946-7799
Fax: (405) 943-2150

Platt College North
2727 West Memorial
Oklahoma City, OK 73134
Phone: (405) 749-2433
Fax: (405) 748-4150

Platt College
3801 South Sheridan
Tulsa, OK 74145
Phone: (918) 663-9000
Fax: (918) 622-1240

Platt College
112 Southwest 11th
Lawton, OK 73501
Phone: (580) 355-4416
Fax: (580) 355-4526

Programs Eligible for Scholarship	Tuition and Fees	Course Length/Credit Hours
Culinary Arts/AS	$19,500	1,680 clock hours/105.45 quarter ch
Dental Assistant	$ 7,845	800 clock hours/37 quarter ch
Medical Assistant	$ 8,345	840 clock hours/39.5 quarter ch
Pharmacy Technician	$ 7,845	810 clock hours/36.5 quarter ch
Practical Nursing/AOS	$14,745	1,570 clock hours/102.75 quarter ch
Registered Nurse	$15,895	1,575 clock hours/108 quarter ch
Surgical Technologist Studies	$12,445	1,145 clock hours/76.5 quarter ch

Platt College, Tulsa

About Our Institution

Platt College, Oklahoma, was the branch of a proprietary institution that began in 1879 and is known as one of the first business colleges west of the Mississippi. To keep abreast of the fast-occurring changes in occupational trends, Platt College opened in Tulsa, Oklahoma, in 1979, offering courses in drafting and design. In 1981, Platt College began offering the same courses in Oklahoma City. At the Tulsa and Oklahoma City campuses, Platt College now offers courses in drafting and design, commercial art and graphic design, medical assisting/phlebotomy, dental assisting, practical nursing, pharmacy technician studies, and visual communications. Platt College is dedicated to providing to each of its students an environment that is conducive to growth, not only in skill training, but also in personal growth. It is with this growth that students are able to pursue their career choices and meet the demands of the industry.

Special Features

Platt College has a small teacher-student ratio. The College offers placement and counseling assistance.

Financial Aid/Scholarships

During the admission process, students seeking financial assistance are required to see a Financial Aid Officer. Students who are enrolled at least half-time, show financial need, and continue to make satisfactory progress may be eligible for Federal Stafford Student Loans, Federal Pell Grants, FSEOG, scholarships, and financial assistance from various state agencies.

Tuition and Fees

Tuition averages approximately $7,000 per course. Tuition includes a $100 registration fee as well as books and supplies.

Accreditation

Platt College is licensed by the Oklahoma Board of Private Vocational Schools (OBPVS) and is approved for training by the Bureau of Indian Affairs (BIA), the Job Training Partnership Act (JTPA), the State Accrediting Agency for the training of eligible veterans, and veterans eligible for vocational rehabilitation. Platt College is accredited by the Accrediting Commission of Career Schools and Colleges of Technology (ACCSCT).

Admissions

Enrollment is open to men and women past the age of compulsory education. The school considers the following in evaluating applicants: graduation from an approved high school program or successful completion of a GED program (applicants without a high school diploma or GED certificate are required to take a Department of Education–

Program Content

Culinary Arts, Dental Assistant, Medical Assistant/Phlebotomy, Pharmacy Technician, Practical Nursing, Registered Nurse, Surgical Technologist Studies

approved evaluation to determine ability to benefit) and determination of purpose and attitude conducive to success.

Contact

Renee Jackson
Director of Admissions
Platt College Central
309 South Ann Arbor
Oklahoma City, OK 73128
Phone: (405) 946-7799
Fax: (405) 943-2150

Platt College North
2727 West Memorial
Oklahoma City, OK 73134
Phone: (405) 749-2433
Fax: (405) 748-4150

Platt College
3801 South Sheridan
Tulsa, OK 74145
Phone: (918) 663-9000
Fax: (918) 622-1240

Platt College
112 Southwest 11th
Lawton, OK 73501
Phone: (580) 355-4416
Fax: (580) 355-4526

Programs Eligible for Scholarship	Tuition and Fees	Course Length/Credit Hours
Culinary Arts/AS	$19,500	1,680 clock hours/105.45 quarter ch
Dental Assistant	$ 7,845	800 clock hours/37 quarter ch
Medical Assistant	$ 8,345	840 clock hours/39.5 quarter ch
Pharmacy Technician	$ 7,845	810 clock hours/36.5 quarter ch
Practical Nursing/AOS	$14,745	1,570 clock hours/102.75 quarter ch
Registered Nurse/AS	$15,895	1,575 clock hours/108 quarter ch
Surgical Technologist Studies	$12,445	1,145 clock hours/76.5 quarter ch

Tulsa Welding School, Tulsa

About Our Institution
Founded in 1949, Tulsa Welding School (TWS) is America's leader in welder training. TWS serves the serious student who desires to put forth a great deal of effort to achieve professional welding skills. Students attend from most of the states throughout America, plus Germany, Belgium, and England. Graduates can look forward to a wide range of career opportunities. During 2002, TWS graduates reported an average starting pay in excess of $3,900 per month, including overtime in some cases. TWS produces world-class welders.

Special Features
Industry-specified training in structural, pipe, pipeline, and thin-alloy welding. In addition, welding quality assurance/quality control inspection.

Financial Aid/Scholarships
TWS is designated as an eligible institution by the U.S. Department of Education for participation in the following programs: Federal Pell Grant, Federal SEOG Grant, subsidized and unsubsidized Federal Stafford Loan programs, and Federal PLUS Loan program. Along with the Jacksonville campus, the School annually provides four $1,000 scholarships in each of the fifty states of the U.S., Puerto Rico, and the U.S. Virgin Islands for the 4 outstanding high school seniors chosen by the Future Farmers of America organizations within each locale.

Tuition and Fees
The total cost for the Master Welder Program is $11,810, which includes tuition, fees, books, welding gear, accident insurance, and all welding supplies.

Accreditation
TWS is accredited by the Accrediting Commission of Career Schools and Colleges of Technology (ACCSCT).

Admissions
Applicants are required to be high school graduates or possess a General Equivalency Diploma (GED).

Graduation Requirements
Students who satisfactorily complete all specified phase courses within the program of enrollment, earn a CGPA of 2.0 out of a possible 4.0, and complete all TWS graduate clearance requirements are awarded a TWS diploma.

Program Content
Master Welder Program

Program Description
Master Welder Program: The Master Welder Program consists of ten 3-week phases of instruction. Thus, graduation is possible within seven months. Instruction occurs 5 hours per day, five days per week.

Contact
Mike Thurber
Director of Admissions
Tulsa Welding School
2545 East 11th Street
Tulsa, OK 74104-3909
Phone: (800) 331-2934 (toll-free)
Fax: (918) 587-8170
Web: www.weldingschool.edu

Programs Eligible for Scholarship	Tuition and Fees	Course Length/Credit Hours	Credential Earned
Master Welder Program	$11,810	30 weeks	Diploma

Vatterott College, Oklahoma City

About Our Institution

All Vatterott College programs are based on a proven successful formula of specialized, technology-focused, hands-on training in the fastest-growing industries. The College was founded in 1969 and now serves nearly 9,000 students per year at sixteen Midwestern campuses. The Oklahoma City campus offers programs focused on the information technology and technical trade industries.

Special Features

Vatterott College's hands-on training method of instruction equips students with the specific skills that are desired by local employers. Courses are geared to the student's field of study. Classes are available in both morning and evening schedules.

Financial Aid/Scholarships

Vatterott College participates in a variety of financial aid and scholarship programs. The College's Make-the-Grade scholarship offers tuition credit to qualifying students based on high school grades. Vatterott College also participates in the Imagine America scholarship program. High school seniors are eligible to apply. Students should contact the campus Financial Aid Representative for specific information.

Tuition and Fees

The campus Admissions Representatives can provide complete tuition information.

Accreditation

Vatterott College is nationally accredited by the Accrediting Commission of Career Schools and Colleges of Technology.

Admission

The application process includes a personal interview and entrance evaluation. A high school diploma or GED is required.

Graduation Requirements

Students must show satisfactory progress by maintaining a minimum grade of 70 percent and an 80 percent attendance record.

Contact

Office of Admissions
Vatterott College
4629 Northwest 23rd Street
Oklahoma City, OK 73127
Phone: (405) 945-0088
         (888) 948-0088 (toll-free)
Fax: (405) 945-0788
E-mail: okcity@vatterott-college.edu
Web: www.vatterott-college.edu

Program Content

Associate of Occupational Studies (AOS) Degree: Applied Electrical Technology; Computer-Aided Drafting Technology; Computer Programming and Technology; Computer Systems and Network Technology; Heating, Air Conditioning, and Refrigeration Technology; and Medical Assistant Technology

Diploma: Computer-Aided Drafting; Computer Office Assistant; Computer Programming; Computer Technology; Electrical Mechanic; Heating, Air Conditioning, and Refrigeration Technology; and Medical Office Assistant

Vatterott College, Tulsa

About Our Institution

All Vatterott College programs are based on a proven successful formula of specialized, technology-focused, hands-on training in the fastest-growing industries. The College was founded in 1969 and now serves nearly 9,000 students per year at sixteen Midwestern campuses. The Tulsa campus offers programs focused on the information technology, technical trade, and medical industries.

Special Features

Vatterott College's hands-on training method of instruction equips students with the specific skills that are desired by local employers. Courses are geared to the student's field of study. Classes are available in both morning and evening schedules.

Financial Aid/Scholarships

Vatterott College participates in a variety of financial aid and scholarship programs. The College's Make-the-Grade scholarship offers tuition credit to qualifying students based on high school grades. Vatterott College also participates in the Imagine America scholarship program. High school seniors are eligible to apply. Students should contact the campus Financial Aid Representatives for specific information.

Tuition and Fees

The campus Admissions Representatives can provide complete tuition information.

Accreditation

Vatterott College is nationally accredited by the Accrediting Commission of Career Schools and Colleges of Technology. Vatterott College, Tulsa is licensed by the Oklahoma Board of Private Vocational Schools.

Admission

The application process includes a personal interview and entrance evaluation. A high school diploma or GED is required.

Graduation Requirements

Students must show satisfactory progress by maintaining a minimum grade of 70 percent and an 80 percent attendance record.

Contact

Office of Admissions
Vatterott College
555 South Memorial Drive
Tulsa, OK 74112
Phone: (918) 835-8288
        (888) 857–4016 (toll-free)
Fax: (918) 836-9698
E-mail: tulsa@vatterott-college.edu
Web: www.vatterott-college.edu

(branch of main campus in St. Ann, MO)

Program Content

Associate of Occupational Studies (AOS) Degree: Computer Systems and Network Technology; Electrical Technology; Heating, Air Conditioning, and Refrigeration Technology; Medical Assistant; Web Design, Gaming, and Multimedia Programming

Diploma: Computer Technology; Electrical Mechanic; Heating, Air Conditioning, and Refrigeration Mechanic; Medical Office Assistant; Web Design and Software Development

Apollo College, Portland

About Our Institution
Apollo College, founded in 1976, is recognized as a leader in communities for high-quality career education, with hands-on orientation. Since then, the College has enjoyed a proud history of assisting people in becoming skilled professionals who go on to assume important positions in their communities. Highly trained, experienced faculty members present course materials that are relevant to current workforce needs; small class sizes ensure individualized attention for students. Programs begin on a monthly basis, with day and evening classes offered to accommodate busy schedules.

Special Features
The College's Advisory Board, composed of industry professionals, keeps Apollo abreast of the latest advances in their respective fields. Classrooms and labs are equipped with the latest technological equipment.

Career and academic counseling is available. Placement services, such as job fairs, assistance with resume and interview preparation, and on-campus recruiting are available through the Office of Student Services. The College also assists full-time students in finding part-time employment. Housing information is available through the Admissions Department.

Apollo's Skills Advancement Program offers continuous refresher courses to graduates at no extra cost.

Financial Aid/Scholarships
Financial aid is available to those who qualify. Apollo participates in a variety of state and federal financial aid and alternate loan programs, including Pell, FFEL, FDSLP, SEOG, SSIG, and JTPA.

Tuition and Fees
There is a separate application fee.

Accreditation
Apollo is nationally accredited by the Accrediting Bureau of Education Schools to award diplomas and associate degrees. Additional accreditations and approvals include the American Association of Medical Assistants, ABHES, APSA, JRCERT, CoARC, CAAHEP, and AMTA.

Admissions
Students must submit a completed application and a registration fee. An interview with an admissions representative is required. For some programs, and interview with a program director or instructional staff member may also be required to determine eligibility.

Enrollment
There are 500 students enrolled.

Graduation Requirements
To graduate, students must have satisfied all financial obligations and successfully completed the course of study and externship, including course requirements.

Program Content
Dental Assistant, Health Claims Exmaniner, Medical Administrative Assistant, Medical Assistant, Medical Assistant w/Limited X-Ray, Pharmacy Technician, Veterinary Assistant

Program Description
Dental Assistant students are trained to work directly with patients and dentists and perform dental office administrative duties.

The Health Claims Examiner/Medical Biller Program provides students with classroom instruction and the practical experience needed to report, transmit, and track claims in a medical or insurance office setting.

The Medical Administrative Assistant Program provides instruction in medical law, ethics, and terminology and computer and office skills that are critical to office practice.

Medical Assistant students are trained to aid physicians and other medical personnel as they treat patients and perform administrative tasks that keep a medical office running smoothly.

The Limited X-Ray Program, combined with the Medical Assistant Program, provides a full scope of training in anatomy and physiology, clinical and office procedures, and limited X-ray services.

Pharmacy Technician students are provided a working knowledge of the pharmaceutical business and learn to apply technical and practical training in pharmaceutical and medical terminology, drug dispensing, and administration.

Veterinary Assistants achieve the skills needed to succeed in a career with animals, meeting the strong demand for qualified animal-care services. Students learn up-to-date career skills and hands-on experience in today's veterinary technology.

Contact
Micaela Sieraki, Campus Director
2004 Lloyd Center
Portland, OR 97232
Phone: (503) 761-6100
     (800) 36-TRAIN (toll-free)
Fax: (503) 761-3351
E-mail: msieracki@apollocollege.com
Web: www.apollocollege.com

Programs Eligible for Scholarship	Tuition and Fees	Course Length/Credit Hours	Credential Earned
Dental Assistant	Call campus for current pricing information.	720 hours/24 credits	Diploma
Health Claims Examiner		840 hours/24 credits	Diploma
Medical Administrative Assistant		720 hours/24 credits	Diploma
Medical Assistant		720 hours/24 credits	Diploma
Medical Assistant w/Limited X-Ray		880 hours/29 credits	Diploma
Pharmacy Technician		836 hours/24 credits	Diploma
Veterinary Assistant		720 hours/24 credits	Diploma

Ashmead College, Portland

About Our Institution

Ashmead College was founded in 1974 as the Seattle Massage School to teach massage skills to people wishing to practice professional massage. With programs in massage, fitness training, and advanced studies, Ashmead College provides students with an interactive learning environment that has a firm foundation in both practical and theoretical education. Graduates are prepared to become successful practitioners in their fields. Ashmead College is dedicated to providing qualified and skilled professionals for the health and wellness industry. Ashmead College is a member of the American Massage Therapy Association's (AMTA) Council of Schools.

Special Features

Ashmead College recognizes the importance of a strong support system for its students. Programs feature classroom lectures, hands-on practice, and real-life experience. In the Student Clinic, massage students experience working with the public. A Student Services Adviser provides resources, encouragement, and advice. The Graduate Services Department provides assistance with job searches and professional and business development throughout the graduates' careers in health and wellness.

Financial Aid/Scholarships

Ashmead College features a financial aid office on each campus, and a Financial Aid Officer is available to help students determine eligibility. Title IV Federal Financial Aid is available for those who qualify. Ashmead College participates in the Washington State Need Grant, Federal Pell Grant, Federal Stafford Student Loan, and Federal PLUS Loan programs and offers additional financing options.

Tuition and Fees

Tuition for the Massage Professional Licensing Program is $12,507 and includes fees and textbooks. Tuition for the Massage Professional Licensing and Spa Specialist Program is $15,791 and includes fees and textbooks. Other supplies are variable, depending on the program, and range from free of charge up to $1,000.

Accreditation

Ashmead College is fully accredited by the Accrediting Council for Continuing Education and Training (ACCET).

Admissions

Applicants must pass an entrance interview, be a high school graduate or have a GED certificate, and be a minimum of 18 years of age upon graduation from Ashmead College.

Graduation Requirements

Students must have attended a minimum of 75 percent of the total program in which they were enrolled, completed all required course work, achieved a cumulative grade point average of at least 2.0, met all financial obligations to the school, met Graduate Services exit interview

Program Content

Professional Licensing, Professional Licensing and Spa and Aromatherapy

Program Description

Professinal Licensing prepares students to become successful massage professionals. Graduates are prepared to test for the Washington and Oregon State Massage Licensing Exams as well as the National Certification Examination for Therapeutic Massage and Body Work/National Licensing Examination.

Professional Licensing and Spa and Aromatherapy provides training in massage spa treatments, and aromatherapy.

requirements and completed all relevant paperwork, and completed the financial aid exit interview and all related materials (applies to federal–student-loan borrowers only).

Contact

Director of Admissions
Ashmead College
9600 Southwest Oak Street, Suite 400
Tigard, OR 97223
Phone: (503) 892-8100
Fax: (503) 892-8871
Web: www.ashmeadcollege.com

Programs Eligible for Scholarship	Tuition and Fees	Course Length/Credit Hours	Credential Earned
Professional Licensing	$12,507	12 months/805.5 hours	Certificate
Professional Licensing and Spa and Aromatherapy	$15,291	15 months/979.75 hours	Certificate

Heald College, Portland Campus, Portland

About Our Institution
Heald College is a nonprofit, WASC-accredited institution with eleven campuses located in northern California, Hawaii, and Oregon. Heald College was founded in 1863 by Edward Payson Heald and for more than 140 years has helped students prepare for successful business, technical, and health-care careers.

Heald College–Portland is located in the heart of downtown near Pioneer Square. This central location gives the campus a high profile in the business community as well as offers students convenient access to public transportation. The Portland campus offers career programs in business, technology, and health care to fit the needs of the College's growing employer base.

Special Features
Heald College provides focused programs in business, technology, and health care that prepare students for success in the workplace in the shortest practical time. Heald College also provides personal attention every step of the way. From completion of the admissions application through navigation of financial aid options to ongoing academic assistance programs (workshops, individual tutoring, learning resource centers) to job placement assistance, the College believes that it succeeds only when its students succeed.

Financial Aid/Scholarships
A Financial Aid Adviser meets with students to assess each person's individual situation and eligibility for assistance. The adviser explains each option, guides the student to those that are appropriate, and assists in the proper completion of all the necessary paperwork. Financial aid options available include Federal Pell Grants, Federal SEOG, scholarships, state and private grants, Federal Work-Study, Federal Stafford Student Loans (subsidized and unsubsidized), Federal PLUS Loans, private loans, Workforce Investment Act (WIA) grants, and veterans' educational benefits. Students must qualify for financial aid and meet specific academic progress requirements to obtain and remain eligible for all federal and state financial assistance programs.

Tuition and Fees
Tuition and fees vary by program length. Students should contact the Admissions Department for additional information.

Accreditation
Heald is accredited by the Accrediting Commission for Community and Junior Colleges of the Western Association of Schools and Colleges (WASC). Through an interregional accreditation agreement with WASC, the Northwest Association of Schools and Colleges recognizes Heald's Portland campus. Heald–Portland is also approved by the Oregon Student Assistance Commission. Heald's medical assisting program and its medical office program have both been approved by the American Medical Technologists (AMT), a nonprofit certification agency, and by the National Center for Competency Testing. These partnerships allow Heald's health-care graduates to sit for appropriate certification examinations. The Heald College accounting curriculum has been approved by the California Tax Education Council (CTEC) to offer course work that fulfills the 60-hour qualifying education requirement, imposed by the state, to become a tax preparer.

Admissions
Applicants must interview with an Admissions Adviser, indicate that they have a high school diploma or GED equivalent, complete an application, pass an admissions examination, and be recommended by an Admissions

Program Content
Most Heald campuses offer Associate in Applied Science (A.A.S.) degrees and diploma programs in accounting, business administration, criminal justice, office skills, office technologies, sales and marketing, software technologies, network systems administration, technical support, medical assisting, and medical office administration as well as opportunities to earn a second A.A.S. degree or certificate in CISCO and Microsoft Windows networking technology or in business accounting. Special diploma and certificate programs in medical assisting and office skills are also offered at some campuses.

Program Description
Heald College programs include both professional and general education courses, which together allow students to experience the integration of knowledge and skills. The general education courses offer students breadth in their experiences by introducing them to major areas of knowledge, thus expanding their understanding of the world and cultures around them. Furthermore, these courses foster a spirit of inquiry and provide for students' development of the skills, knowledge, and intellectual habits necessary to support their personal, professional, and public lives. Heald also provides hands-on training in all of its programs to ensure that students can successfully apply the skills they learn in the workplace after graduation.

Adviser to the Campus Director. Students should contact the Admissions Department for additional information.

Graduation Requirements
To be eligible for graduation, students must successfully complete all classes with a minimum 2.0 cumulative grade point average and complete all program, unit, and course requirements.

Contact
Phal Seth, Director of Admissions
625 Southwest Broadway, Suite 200
Portland, OR 97205
Phone: (503) 229-0492
        (800) 755-3550 (toll-free)
Fax: (503) 229-0498
E-mail: phal_seth@heald.edu
Web: www.heald.edu

ITT Technical Institute, Portland

About Our Institution
The company: ITT Technical Institute is owned and operated by ITT Educational Services, Inc. (ITT/ESI), a leading private college system offering technology-influenced programs of study. ITT/ESI operates seventy-seven ITT Technical Institutes in thirty states that provide career-focused degree programs to approximately 39,000 students as of spring 2004. Headquartered in Carmel, Indiana, ITT/ESI has been actively involved in the higher education community in the United States since 1969.

Curricula: Curriculum offerings are designed to help students begin to prepare for career opportunities in fields of technology. Students attend classes year-round, with convenient breaks provided throughout the year. A student with a full-time course load can have class meetings as often as three days a week. Classes are typically available in the morning, afternoon, and evening, depending on student enrollment. General education courses may be available online. This class schedule offers students the flexibility to pursue part-time employment opportunities.

Special Features
Most ITT Technical Institute programs of study blend traditional academic content with applied learning concepts, with a significant portion devoted to practical study in a lab environment. Advisory committees, made up of representatives of local businesses, help each ITT Technical Institute periodically review and update curricula, equipment, and laboratory design.

Financial Aid/Scholarships
ITT Technical Institute maintains a Financial Aid Department on campus. The campus is designated as an eligible institution by the U.S. Department of Education for participation in the following programs: Federal Stafford Student Loan Program, Federal PLUS Loan Program, and Federal Work-Study Program. The school also offers nonfederal loans made available through Bank One for eligible students.

Tuition and Fees
March 2005 tuition was $386 per credit hour.

Admissions
Interested students should contact the school for specific admission requirements and for a catalog.

Graduation Requirements
Interested students should contact the school for a catalog and for graduation requirements for specific programs.

Contact
Wayne Matulich, Director
ITT Technical Institute
6035 Northeast 78th Court
Portland, OR 97218
Phone: (503) 255-6500
Fax: (503) 255-8381

Program Description
ITT Technical Institute in Portland offers the Associate of Applied Science. The Institute's four schools teach the skills and knowledge used to begin careers in a global, technology-driven culture. The schools offer the following programs.

School of Business: Technical Project Management

School of Drafting and Design: Computer Drafting and Design, Digital Entertainment and Game Design, Information Technology (with an option in Multimedia)

School of Electronics Technology: Computer and Electronics Engineering Technology, Electronics and Communications Engineering Technology, Industrial Automation Engineering Technology

School of Information Technology: Data Communication Systems Technology, Information Systems Security, Information Technology (with options in Computer Network Systems, Software Applications and Programming, and Web Development), Software Engineering Technology

Pioneer Pacific College, Springfield

About Our Institution

Pioneer Pacific College (PPC) is a highly focused private career college offering programs that prepare traditional and adult students for exciting jobs in business, information technology, health, and legal careers. Day classes meet four days a week for approximately 20 hours, making part-time employment, child care, and location manageable. Most programs are also offered evenings for students who wish to maintain full-time employment while attending school. Day and evening programs are available at locations in Clackamas, Springfield, and Wilsonville. Diploma programs can be completed in as few as forty weeks, and A.A.S. degrees can be earned in only seventy weeks.

Special Features

All programs have a heavy emphasis on appropriate computer skills to maximize job placement and are selected, designed, and updated to assure a high level of employability. Students work with the modern, up-to-date hardware, software, and networks that are commonly found in industry today. Students learn hands-on technical job skills, how to analyze and solve problems, and the communications and interpersonal relationship skills that enable them to work as effective members of a team. This is done in a friendly atmosphere of small classes, individualized attention, and heavy interaction between the students and faculty and staff members.

Financial Aid/Scholarships

Pioneer Pacific maintains a financial aid office on campus and offers a variety of programs that include grants, loans, scholarships, and veterans' benefits. PPC also offers a scholarship to each high school in Oregon and scholarships to community service organizations to award to qualified adult minorities and women in the Portland area.

Tuition and Fees

PPC's academic measurement system is quarter credit hours. Each program has an average tuition per credit as listed below. Fees for items such as application, registration, and graduation are approximately $200 and are included in the total program cost.

Accreditation

Pioneer Pacific is accredited by the Accrediting Council for Independent Colleges and Schools to award certificates, diplomas, and occupational associate degrees. The Accrediting Council for Independent Colleges and Schools is listed as a nationally recognized accrediting agency by the United States Department of Education and is recognized by the Council for Higher Education Accreditation. The College is also approved by the Oregon Office of Degree Authorization to offer and confer academic degrees.

Program Content

Degree: Business: Accounting, Business: Administration, Business: Marketing and Sales, Computer and Networking Technology, Criminal Justice, Health-Care Administration, Medical Assisting

Diploma: Medical Assisting, Medical Claims and Billing Specialist

Admissions

The general admissions requirement is a high school diploma or equivalent, such as a GED or an accredited home-study course. In addition, applicants are required to achieve program-specific minimums on the ACT Career Programs Assessment Test (CPAt). Candidates must also complete a two-part personal interview process, first with an Admissions Officer and then with an official authorized to accept students.

Graduation Requirements

Students are eligible to receive the graduation reward stipulated for a program if they have completed all required courses, accumulated the total number of credits required for their course of study with a passing grade, attained a cumulative GPA of at least 2.0, and met all financial obligations to the school.

Contact

Debra Marcus
Pioneer Pacific College
3800 Sports Way
Springfield, OR 97477
Phone: (541) 684-4644
        (866) PPC-INFO (toll-free)
Fax: (541) 684-0655
E-mail: inquiries@pioneerpacific.edu
Web: http://pioneerpacific.edu

Programs Eligible for Scholarship	Tuition and Fees	Course Length/Credit Hours	Credential Earned
Business: Accounting	$156 per credit hour	90.5 credit hours	AAS
Business: Administration	$156 per credit hour	90 credit hours	AAS
Business: Marketing and Sales	$156 per credit hour	91 credit hours	AAS
Computer and Networking Technology	$175 per credit hour	90.5 credit hours	AAS
Criminal Justice	$165 per credit hour	90 credit hours	AAS
Health-Care Administration	$156 per credit hour	90.5 credit hours	AAS
Medical Assisting	$152 per credit hour	90 credit hours	AAS
Medical Assisting	$152 per credit hour	63.5 credit hours	Diploma
Medical Claims and Billing Specialist	$156 per credit hour	55.5 credit hours	Diploma

Pioneer Pacific College, Wilsonville

About Our Institution

Pioneer Pacific College (PPC) is a highly focused private career college offering programs that prepare traditional and adult students for exciting jobs in business, information technology, health, and legal careers. Day classes meet four days a week for approximately 20 hours, making part-time employment, child care, and location manageable. Most programs are also offered evenings and Saturdays for students who wish to maintain full-time employment while attending school. Diploma programs can be completed in as few as forty weeks, A.A.S. degrees in only seventy weeks, and bachelor's degrees in less than four years.

Special Features

All programs have a heavy emphasis on appropriate computer skills to maximize job placement and are selected, designed, and updated to assure a high level of employability. Students work with the modern, up-to-date hardware, software, and networks that are commonly found in industry. Students learn hands-on technical job skills, how to analyze and solve problems, and the communications and interpersonal relationship skills that enable them to work as effective members of a team. This is done in a friendly atmosphere of small classes, individualized attention, and heavy interaction between the students the faculty and staff members.

Financial Aid/Scholarships

Pioneer Pacific maintains a financial aid office on campus and offers a variety programs, including grants, loans, scholarships, and veterans' benefits. PPC also offers a scholarship to each high school in Oregon and scholarships to community service organizations to award to qualified adult minorities and women in the Portland area.

Tuition and Fees

PPC's academic measurement system is quarter credit hours. Each program has an average tuition per credit as listed below. Fees for application, registration, graduation, etc. are approximately $200 and are included in the total program cost.

Accreditation

Pioneer Pacific is accredited by the Accrediting Council for Independent Colleges and Schools to award certificates, diplomas, and degrees. The Accrediting Council for Independent Colleges and Schools is listed as a nationally recognized accrediting agency by the United States Department of Education and is recognized by the Council for Higher Education Accreditation. The College is also approved by the Oregon Office of Degree Authorization to offer and confer academic degrees.

Program Content

Degree: Business: Accounting, Business: Administration, Business: Marketing and Sales, Computer and Networking Technology, Criminal Justice, Health-care Administration, Legal Assisting/Paralegal, Medical Assisting, Web Site Design and Administration

Diploma: Medical Assisting, Medical Claims and Biling Specialist, Pharmacy Technician

Admissions

The general admissions requirement is a high school diploma or equivalent, such as a GED or an accredited home-study course. In addition, applicants are required to achieve program-specific minimums on the ACT Career Programs Assessment Test (CPAt). Candidates must also complete a two-part personal interview process, first with an Admissions Officer and then with an official authorized to accept students.

Graduation Requirements

A student is eligible to receive the graduation reward stipulated for a program if he or she has completed all required courses, accumulated the total number of credits required for his or her course of study with a passing grade, attained a cumulative GPA of at least 2.0, and met all financial obligations to the school.

Contact

Mary Harris
Pioneer Pacific College
27501 Southwest Parkway Avenue
Wilsonville, OR 97070
Phone: (503) 682-3903
        (866) PPC-INFO (toll-free)
Fax: (503) 682-1514
E-mail: inquiries@pioneerpacific.edu
Web: pioneerpacific.edu

Programs Eligible for Scholarship	Tuition and Fees	Course Length/Credit Hours	Credential Earned
Business: Accounting	$156/credit hour	90.5 credit hours	AAS
Business: Administration	$156/credit hour	90.0 credit hours	AAS
Business: Marketing and Sales	$156/credit hour	91.0 credit hours	AAS
Computer and Networking Technology	$175/credit hour	90.5 credit hours	AAS
Computer and Networking Technology	$225/credit hour	183.5 credit hours	BS
Criminal Justice	$165/credit hour	90.0 credit hours	AAS
Health-care Administration	$156/credit hour	90.5 credit hours	AAS
Legal Assisting/Paralegal	$165/credit hour	93.5 credit hours	AA
Medical Assisting	$152/credit hour	63.5 credit hours	Diploma
Medical Assisting	$152/credit hour	90.0 credit hours	AAS
Medical Assisting w/Limited X-ray	$152/credit hour	73.5 credit hours	Diploma
Medical Assisting w/Limited X-ray	$152/credit hour	100.0 credit hours	AAS
Medical Claims and Billing Specialist	$156/credit hour	55.5 credit hours	Diploma
Pharmacy Technician	$156/credit hour	60.0 credit hours	Diploma
Web Site Design and Administration	$175/credit hour	90.0 credit hours	AAS
Web Site Design and Administration	$225/credit hour	182 credit hours	BS

Western Business College, Portland

About Our Institution
Western Business College was founded in 1955. A leader right from the start, it became the first college in Oregon to offer data processing employment training. Situated in the heart of downtown Portland, the College occupies 34,000 square feet in a six-floor building. It has been at its present location since 1992. The building includes twenty-four classrooms and a student lounge. The College continually updates its curriculum and facilities to successfully meet ever-changing employment needs. Western Business College is one of more than eighty schools owned and operated by Corinthian Colleges, Inc., in the United States.

Special Features
The College is dedicated to the ideal that students should have the opportunity to reach their full potential. The high quality of instruction and program content provides solid career training designed to prepare men and women to enter and prosper in the employment community.

Financial Aid/Scholarships
Pell Grants, FFEL, work-study, SEOG, VA Scholarships, and state loans are available to those who qualify.

Tuition and Fees
Per-credit-hour fees are assessed based on the number of classes taken per quarter. There is a registration fee of $25 per term.

Accreditation
All programs are accredited by the Accrediting Council for Independent Colleges and Schools (ACICS), except the Medical Assisting Program, which is accredited by the AAMA, a division of the Commission on Accreditation of Allied Health Education Programs (CAAHEP).

Admissions
Graduation from high school or its equivalent (GED or ATB) is a prerequisite for admission. High school transcripts or equivalency documentation must be submitted by all applicants. International students are accepted with a TOEFL score of at least 450 (or 133 for the computer-based TOEFL).

Graduation Requirements
Students must complete the required number of credits for their program of study with passing grades in all required courses and a minimum 2.0 (C) cumulative grade point average.

Program Content
Accounting, Accounting/Business Administration, Administrative Assistant, Administrative Medical Assistant, Advanced Computer Applications, Automated Office Technology, Bookkeeping, Executive Assistant, Legal Administrative Assistant, Medical Administrative Assistant, Medical Assistant, Medical Insurance Billing/Coding, Microcomputer Applications, Operations Specialist, Paralegal/Legal Assistant, Pharmacy Technician, Receptionist/General Office Assistant, Travel/Hospitality

Enrollment
778 students are enrolled at the College.

Contact
Laurel Buchanan, Director of Admissions
425 SW Washington Street
Portland, OR 97204
Phone: (503) 222-3225
Fax: (503) 228-6926
E-mail: lbuchana@cci.edu
Web: www.western-college.com

Programs Eligible for Scholarship	Tuition and Fees	Course Length/Credit Hours	Credential Earned
Accounting	$234/credit hour	96 credits	AAS
Accounting/Business Administration	$234/credit hour	64 credits	Diploma
Administrative Assistant	$234/credit hour	64 credits	Diploma
Administrative Medical Assistant	$234/credit hour	48 credits	Diploma
Advanced Microcomputer Applications	$234/credit hour	90 credits	AAS
Automated Office Technology	$234/credit hour	48 credits	Diploma
Bookkeeping	$234/credit hour	48 credits	Diploma
Executive Assistant	$234/credit hour	90 credits	Diploma
Legal Administrative Assistant	$234/credit hour	64 credits	Diploma
Medical Administrative Assistant	$7,700	47 credits	Diploma
Medical Assistant	$234/credit hour	75 credits	Diploma
Medical Assistant	$234/credit hour	97 credits	AAS
Medical Insurance Billing/Coding	$7,700	35 credits	Diploma
Microcomputer Applications	$234/credit hour	64 credits	Diploma
Operations Specialist	$234/credit hour	48 credits	Diploma
Paralegal/Legal Assistant	$234/credit hour	96 credits	Diploma
Pharmacy Technician	$234/credit hour	60 credits	Diploma
Pharmacy Technician	$234/credit hour	97 credits	AAS
Receptionist/General Office Assistant	$234/credit hour	36 credits	Diploma
Travel/Hospitality	$234/credit hour	48 credits	Diploma
Travel/Hospitality Administration	$234/credit hour	64 credits	Diploma
Travel/Hospitality Management	$234/credit hour	90 credits	AAS

Academy of Medical Arts and Business, Harrisburg

About Our Institution

Academy of Medical Arts and Business has been training men and women for more than twenty-two years to become skilled and motivated workers in the child-care, computer, culinary, dental, legal, medical, and professional massage therapy fields. Graduates of the Academy have served internships and have been hired at more than 1,000 Pennsylvania businesses and corporations. The Academy has won dozens of national, state, and local awards for best teachers, best students, and best school. The Academy campus is located in the foothills of the Blue Mountains outside the city of Harrisburg, Pennsylvania. It is readily accessible from Routes 11, 15, 22, 81, 230, and 322 and the Pennsylvania Turnpike. Harrisburg International Airport is 15 minutes to the south. Washington, D.C., and Philadelphia are 2 hours away; Gettysburg is 35 minutes away; and Hershey is 15 minutes away.

Special Features

Academy of Medical Arts and Business features an on-site child-care center and cafeteria as well as modern medical, dental, child-care, and computer labs; Internet classrooms; and spacious outdoor areas for studying, relaxation, and sports activities. Classes are held to a minimum for maximum individual attention, and all programs include specialized internships.

Financial Aid/Scholarships

Financial aid sources include Pell Grants, FFELP, FDSLP, the Federal Work-Study Program, FSEOG, VA, PHEAA Grants, TAA, WIB, OVR, and other sources.

Tuition and Fees

Tuition is $4325 per semester; fees are $350 per semester. The Academy offers an affordable tuition payment plan.

Accreditation

Academy of Medical Arts and Business is accredited by the Accrediting Commission of Career Schools and Colleges of Technology (ACCSCT). The Academy is authorized under federal law to enroll nonimmigrant alien students.

Admissions

Applicants must have a high school diploma or GED certificate. They must have a personal interview and tour with a representative of the Academy.

Program Content

Degree: Child-Care Specialist, Culinary Arts Specialist, Data Processing Technology Specialist, Dental Assistant Specialist, Medical Assistant Specialist, Medical Office Management, Paralegal Specialist, Professional Massage Therapy Specialist

Diploma: Data Processing Technology, Dental Assistant, Digital Arts Specialist, Medical Assistant, Medical Secretary, Paralegal, Professional Massage Therapist

Program Description

All career programs provide specialized or technical training for today's fastest-growing career fields. Each program includes computer training, an exceptional staff of instructors who work closely with each student for personal attention and hands-on training, and internship and job placement assistance. The Academy offers a degree in fifteen months or a diploma in nine months.

Graduation Requirements

All students must complete all required courses and attain satisfactory completion of an internship. All monetary obligations must be paid in full, and all loaned books and equipment must be returned in acceptable condition.

Contact

Gary Kay
Academy of Medical Arts and Business
2301 Academy Drive
Harrisburg, PA 17112-1012
Phone: (717) 545-4747
Fax: (717) 901-9090
E-mail: info@acadcampus.com
Web: www.acadcampus.com

Programs Eligible for Scholarship	Tuition and Fees	Course Length/Credit Hours	Credential Earned
Child-Care Specialist	$17,870	60 weeks/69 credits	Degree
Culinary Arts Specialist	$17,870	60 weeks/65 credits	Degree
Data Processing Technology Specialist	$17,870	60 weeks/64 credits	Degree
Dental Assistant Specialist	$17,870	60 weeks/70 credits	Degree
Digital Arts Specialist	$17,870	60 weeks/65 credits	Diploma
Medical Assistant Specialist	$17,870	60 weeks/69 credits	Degree
Medical Office Management	$17,870	60 weeks/69 credits	Degree
Paralegal Specialist	$17,870	60 weeks/74 credits	Degree
Professional Massage Therapy Specialist	$17,870	60 weeks/70 credits	Degree

The Art Institute of Philadelphia, Philadelphia

About Our Institution

The Art Institute of Philadelphia (AIPH) is one of The Art Institutes, a system of thirty schools nationwide that provide an important source of design, media arts, fashion, and culinary professionals. The parent company of The Art Institutes, Education Management Corporation (EDMC), is among the largest providers of proprietary postsecondary education in the United States, offering doctoral, bachelor's, and associate degrees and nondegree programs. EDMC has provided career-oriented education programs for more than forty years, and its schools have graduated more than 150,000 students.

AIPH maintains a Career Services Center for graduates and students. Of all graduates available for placement in 2002, 85.8 percent were working in their field within six months of graduation, earning an average salary of $26,262.

Special Features

AIPH occupies five facilities conveniently located in downtown Philadelphia. The main building is an 80,000-square-foot facility originally designed in 1928 as CBS's flagship radio station affiliate. Designated as a historical site by the Philadelphia Historical Commission, the Art Deco building became home to AIPH in 1982. Students who choose school-sponsored housing are assigned to the facility located on the Avenue of the Arts at the southeast corner of Broad and Chestnut Streets, two blocks from the school.

Financial Aid/Scholarships

AIPH participates in the following financial assistance programs: Federal Pell Grant, work-study, FSEOG, Pennsylvania State Grant Program, Merit Scholarship Program, and the Art Institute of Philadelphia High School Senior Scholarship for Graduating High School Seniors.

Tuition and Fees

Tuition and fees are $13,356 for a diploma program, from $33,390 to $443,520 for an Associate of Science degree, and $66,780 for a Bachelor of Science degree, not including books and miscellaneous fees.

Accreditation

AIPH is accredited by the Accrediting Council for Independent Colleges and Schools (ACICS) to award the Associate of Science and the Bachelor of Science degrees and is authorized by the Commonwealth of Pennsylvania Department of Education to confer both degrees. It is also approved for training veterans and eligible veterans' dependents and is authorized under federal law to enroll nonimmigrant alien students.

Admissions

An applicant must submit a high school diploma or GED certificate and an essay and interview with an admissions representative.

Program Content

A.S. Degrees: Computer Animation, Culinary Arts, Fashion Design, Fashion Marketing, Graphic Design, Interactive Media Design, Interior Design, Photography, Video Production, Visual Merchandising

B.S. Degrees: Digital Media Production, Fashion Design, Fashion Marketing, Graphic Design, Industrial Design Technology, Interactive Media Design, Interior Design, Media Arts and Animation, Visual Effects and Motion Graphics

Diploma Program: Baking and Pastry

Program Description

Classes are structured to be like real-world situations, and their environments are as close to professional as possible. Computer lab facilities include Intergraph visual workstations, Pentium-based and Macintosh G-4 PCs, Avid video labs, Adobe Premier, a PAD lab (computerized pattern making), and a TV studio equipped with current technology, including digital applications and equipment.

Contact

Tim Howard, Director of Admissions
The Art Institute of Philadelphia
1622 Chestnut Street
Philadelphia, PA 19103-5119
Phone: (215) 567-7080
        (800) 275-2474 (toll-free)
Fax: (215) 405-6399
Web: www.aiph.artinstitutes.edu

The Art Institute of Pittsburgh, Pittsburgh

About Our Institution
On October 1, 1921, the Art Institute of Pittsburgh officially opened its doors to 9 students in a single room in the heart of downtown Pittsburgh. Even in its earliest days, the Art Institute of Pittsburgh operated with an eye toward employers' needs, graduating commercial artists responsive to industry trends. More than eighty years later, the Art Institute's mission to train students for creative careers remains exactly the same.

The Art Institute of Pittsburgh's historic impact on American culture is a story best told through the successes of more than 40,000 alumni. Graduates influence daily life as photojournalists for major metropolitan newspapers and interior designers for major firms and hotels and hospitals. They entertain as animators on feature films, television shows, and video games. Art Institute of Pittsburgh industrial design graduates create innovative new products. Video and digital media specialists bring the news and other television programs. The advertising and graphic design industry is influenced by Art Institute graduates who create visual communications for agencies, corporations, and nonprofit organizations all over the world.

The Art Institute's curriculum has expanded from traditional associate degrees to the offering of academic bachelor's degrees. The addition of new academic programs and the need for streamlined technology precipitated the school's move into a fully renovated landmark facility in downtown Pittsburgh. Through its online division, the Art Institute of Pittsburgh offers the convenience of many online courses and full degree programs, creating flexible schedules to meet student work, study, and commuting needs.

The Art Institute of Pittsburgh has expanded to include the culinary arts—now occupying an entire floor of brand-new kitchens and industry-standard equipment.

Students find Pittsburgh to be an exciting urban campus situated in a thriving metropolis that sprawls over 55 square miles. The city is situated halfway between New York City and Chicago and is within a 2-hour flight or a day's drive of more than 70 percent of the U.S. population. The city is the headquarters for Alcoa, Heinz, and many new technology-driven businesses and is well known for health-care excellence with many highly reputable university and community hospitals. There are free summer concerts in downtown's Market Square, an abundance of theaters, thriving nightlife districts and eclectic coffee shops, and meeting places on every corner.

Special Features
Students at the Art Institute of Pittsburgh can find reasonably priced housing through the services of the school's Housing Department. School-sponsored housing is available at Allegheny Center Apartment Complex, which offers newly furnished, networked units on the city's North Side. Downtown Pittsburgh is serviced by Port Authority Transit and a subway system making all of Allegheny County's surrounding neighborhoods easily accessible to students of the Art Institute of Pittsburgh. Activities, entertainment, events, special interest clubs, and student chapters of professional organizations are offered through the school's Student Services Department. As students near graduation, the Art Institute provides important assistance in career planning, job-search strategies, interview techniques, and resume development. The school's Career Services Department undertakes graduate placement as a sophisticated marketing effort and works closely with each student to achieve field-related employment within six months of graduation.

Financial Aid/Scholarships
The school participates in the following financial assistance programs: Federal Stafford Student Loan, Federal Pell Grant, Federal Supplemental Educational Opportunity Grant (FSEOG), Federal Perkins Loan, Federal Work-Study Program, Federal PLUS/SLS Loans, state-funded student assistance programs, Vocational Rehabilitation Assistance, and Veterans Administration benefits. Various merit-based and need-based scholarships are available at the Art Institute of Pittsburgh. Information about the school's scholarships can be obtained in the Admissions Office.

Program Content
B.S. Degrees: Advertising*, Culinary Management, Game Art and Design*, Graphic Design*, Digital Media Production, Industrial Design, Interior Design*, Media Arts and Animation, Multimedia and Web Design*, Photography, Visual Effects and Motion Graphics

A.S. Degrees: Culinary Arts, Graphic Design*, Industrial Design, Multimedia and Web Design, Photography, Video Production

Diplomas: The Art of Cooking, Digital Design*, Residential Design*, Web Design*

*Degrees also offered online

Tuition and Fees
Tuition for all degree programs is charged at $354 per credit (with an average of 15 credits per quarter). There are a $50 application fee and a $100 enrollment fee. Upon enrollment, each student receives a program-specific starting supply kit, with prices ranging from $155 to $900, depending on the program of study.

Accreditation
The Art Institute of Pittsburgh is accredited by the Accrediting Council of Independent Colleges and Schools (ACICS). The Art Institute of Pittsburgh is a candidate for Accreditation by the Commission of Higher Education of the Middle States Association of Colleges and Schools. Candidacy for Middle States Accreditation was granted in June 2003.

Admissions
A prospective student seeking admission to the Art Institute of Pittsburgh must be a high school graduate with a GPA of at least 2.0, hold a GED certificate, or hold a bachelor's degree or higher as a prerequisite for admission. Interested students should contact an admissions representative for a tour.

Graduation Requirements
To be qualified to graduate, a student must receive a passing grade or credit for all required course work, earn the minimum required credits for the program, achieve a minimum GPA of 2.0, meet portfolio or other requirements, and satisfy all financial obligations to the Art Institute of Pittsburgh. Completion of a bachelor's degree requires 180 credits and thirty-six months; an associate degree, 105 credits and twenty-one months; and a diploma, 36 credits and twelve months.

Contact
Newton Myvett, Director of Admissions
The Art Institute of Pittsburgh
420 Boulevard of the Allies
Pittsburgh, PA 15219
Phone: (412) 263-6600
(800) 275-2470 (toll-free)
Fax: (412) 291-3715
E-mail: nmyvett@aii.edu
Web: www.aip.aii.edu

Automotive Training Center, Exton

About Our Institution

Since 1917, Automotive Training Center (ATC) has offered high-quality career education for automotive, diesel, and collision repair technicians. ATC's NATEF/ASE modular curriculum allows a student to study one vehicle system at a time. Each specialty area has its own ASE-certified instructor specialist who teaches the academic and hands-on sections of the class. Small classes of usually no more than 25 students ensure close instructor supervision. Most programs are fifteen months long.

Special Features

- Extensive hands-on training in seventeen specialty shops
- No unrelated subjects (English, math, humanities)
- National winner, 1st Place Award for Excellence in Automotive Technician Education, 1999–2004
- Member of the I-CAR Industry Training Alliance using the ADVANCE-TECH Curriculum
- Dell Computer Lab with twenty-six stations for interactive CD, online, and instructor-led classes
- Computer Diagnostic Center equipped with a Maxwell Vehicle Chassis Dynamometer
- Fully equipped high-performance machine shop with a 2,000-horsepower SuperFlow Engine Dynamometer and electronic Flowbench
- Ford Motor Company–authorized training partner; students can earn Ford credentials while in school
- Career and Student Services department that provides advising and assistance with transportation, housing, and employment

Financial Aid/Scholarships

Federal Pell Grants, PHEAA state grants, Federal Stafford Student Loans, and Federal PLUS loans are available to those who qualify. ATC offers institutional scholarships to current-year high school graduates based upon testing and evaluation. Students may be eligible for Imagine America, Hope, ATC institutional, ADAGP, and NJCIE scholarships.

Tuition and Fees

Tuition is $11,360 per academic year. The registration fee is $150. Books average $125 per course. There are no material fees or shop/lab fees.

Accreditation

Automotive Training Center is accredited by the Accrediting Commission of Career Schools and Colleges of Technology (ACCSCT).

Admissions

Interested students should contact the school for a personal interview and tour of the facility. Applicants must possess a high school diploma or GED certificate or pass a nationally recognized exam for the ability to benefit and obtain a satisfactory score on the school's entrance exam.

Program Content

Automotive and Diesel Technology, Automotive Technology (evening), Collision Reconditioning Technology, and Collision Repair Technology (evening). Specialty courses are offered in Computer Controls and On-Board Diagnosis, High-Performance, and Pennsylvania Safety and Emission Certification.

Program Description

The core of all programs models the eight ASE specialty areas. All programs are NATEF/ASE certified. The collision repair programs utilize the I-CAR ADVANCE-TECH Curriculum.

Graduation Requirements

Students must complete all program requirements with a C (2.0) average or above and attend 90 percent or more of the program hours.

Contact

Donald S. VanDemark Jr.
Vice President/COO
Automotive Training Center
114 Pickering Way
Exton, PA 19341
Phone: (800) 411-8031 (toll-free)
Fax: (610) 363-8524
E-mail: atc@autotraining.edu
Web: www.autotraining.edu

Programs Eligible for Scholarship	Tuition and Fees	Course Length/Credit Hours	Credential Earned
Advanced Automotive Technology	$28,400	2,400	Diploma
Automotive Technology	$22,720	1,920	Diploma
Automotive Technology (evening)	$16,420	1,344	Diploma
Collision Reconditioning Technology	$22,720	1,920	Diploma
Collision Repair Technology (evening)	$16,420	1,344	Diploma
Specialized Automotive Technology	$25,560	2,160	Diploma

Baltimore School of Massage, York Campus, York

About Our Institution
Baltimore School of Massage (BSM) has two locations, a branch campus in York, Pennsylvania, and the main campus in Baltimore, Maryland. The York Campus was opened in 1999 and moved to its current location in 2000. The School is close enough to Philadelphia, Washington, and Baltimore to enjoy big city events and far enough away from the cities for residents to enjoy the comfort, safety, and sense of community that is found in smaller towns. BSM–York Campus is corporately owned and governed by Steiner Education Group, Inc., along with six other schools in Maryland, Virginia, and Florida. All locations have full-time as well as part-time schedules with day and evening classes to make it easy for students to fulfill their dreams of becoming massage therapists.

Special Features
The field of massage therapy is one of the fastest growing in the country, and the Baltimore School of Massage–York Campus can thoroughly prepare students for this exciting and rewarding career. All campuses also have a Student Clinic where students have the opportunity to work with the public while they attend school. BSM–York Campus offers an extensive Continuing Education Program, which enables students to enhance their skills and learn new modalities after graduation. BSM–York Campus also has a fully stocked Natural Health Shoppe on campus that carries everything from massage creams and oils to music and school uniforms. All Steiner Education Group campuses employ a Career Services Coordinator who is available to assist graduates in achieving their goals. Whether they are interested in seeing the world by working aboard a cruise ship or would prefer a land-based position, the Career Services Department at BSM–York Campus has built a relationship with some of the most successful employers in the industry. Graduates of the Steiner Education Group schools are given priority consideration when Steiner Leisure Ltd., a global provider of spa services, is recruiting for their maritime or land-based spas.

Financial Aid/Scholarships
Baltimore School of Massage–York Campus is approved by the Department of Education for Title IV Funds and Federal Financial Aid is available to those who qualify. This may be in the form of Pell Grants and Stafford Loans. The Financial Aid Office is available to help guide students through this process.

Tuition and Fees
Students should call the campus for current pricing information.

Accreditation
Baltimore School of Massage–York Campus is accredited by the Accrediting Commission of Career Schools and Colleges of Technology (ACCSCT) and programmatically accredited by the Commission on Massage Therapy Accreditation (COMTA). The School is approved by the Pennsylvania Higher Education Commission, the Pennsylvania Association of Private Schools Administrators (PAPSA), and the National Certification Board for Therapeutic Massage and Bodywork (NCBTMB) as a Category A Continuing Education Provider. BSM–York Campus is approved for the training of veterans and is authorized to enroll nonimmigrant alien students by the Department of Justice and the Division of Homeland Security. The School is a member of the

Program Content
Professional Program in Comprehensive Massage Therapy

Program Description
Professional Program in Comprehensive Massage Therapy: The massage therapy program is designed to give a thorough education in massage therapy in a positive learning environment. It includes extensive lecture and hands-on training and prepares the student for a variety of settings. This program includes three major systems of bodywork: Swedish, deep tissue, and myofascial release; human anatomy; and physiology as well as additional modalities. The curriculum provides the student the skills necessary to be successful as an entry-level massage therapist in spa, medical, or private practice.

American Massage Therapy Association (AMTA) Council of Schools and the Career College Association (CCA).

Admissions
Prospective students must complete an application, schedule an interview with an admissions representative, and be at least 18 years of age by the expected graduation date. A prospective student must display a genuine interest in becoming part of a learning atmosphere. Admissions requirements include evidence of high school graduation or GED equivalent. Upon acceptance, prior to starting classes, students are required to complete a physician's statement, signed by a licensed physician, indicating they are in good health and able to participate in the programs.

Contact
Baltimore School of Massage–York Campus
170 Red Rock Road
York, PA 17402
Phone: (717) 268-1881
 (866) 699-1881 (toll-free)
Fax: 717-268-1991
Web: www.steinered.com

Programs Eligible for Scholarship	Tuition and Fees	Course Length/Credit Hours	Credential Earned
Professional Program in Comprehensive Massage Therapy	Call campus for current pricing information	637 hours/49 credits	Diploma

Berks Technical Institute, Wyomissing

About Our Institution

Berks Technical Institute was established in 1974. Berks provides career training that matches the student's career goals with the needs of employers. In 2000, Berks became a part of ForeFront Education, Inc., a national network of postsecondary schools dedicated to high-quality career education and student achievement.

Special Features

Berks provides specialized career education in many of the fastest growing career fields and offers degree and diploma programs in the fields of medical assisting, computer programming, electronics technology, networking, graphic design, paralegal, office assisting, business, accounting, Web design, and drafting technology. Berks provides student support services, including career services and placement.

Financial Aid/Scholarships

Berks maintains a financial aid office that provides a variety of programs, including FFELP, Federal Stafford Student Loan, Federal PLUS loan, Federal Pell Grant, HELP, PHEAA Grants, and FSEOG.

Accreditation

Berks is accredited by the Accrediting Commission of Career Schools and Colleges of Technology (ACCSCT).

Admissions

A high school diploma or GED certificate is required for admission, in addition to passing an admissions test and meeting academic and financial criteria.

Graduation Requirements

A student must attain a minimum 2.0 cumulative GPA, maintain satisfactory attendance, complete all designated requirements of the program, satisfy financial obligations to Berks, and complete exit interviews.

Contact

Adrian Clark, Executive Director
2205 Ridgewood Road
Wyomissing, PA 19610
Phone: (610) 372-1722
Fax: (610) 376-4684
E-mail: aclark@berks.edu
Web: www.berks.edu

Program Content

Degrees: Accounting, Business Management, Drafting Technology, Electronics Technology, Graphic Design, Internet/Network Engineering, Medical Assisting, Network/Internet Professional, Paralegal, and Web Design

Diplomas: Computer Programming Science, Medical Assistant, and Professional Massage Therapy

Program Description

Medical assistant science provides students with clinical and administrative skills and preparation for careers in doctors' offices and other health-care facilities.

The networking and computer programming curricula provide students with knowledge of computer programming languages, such as C++, JAVA, and Microsoft Access, and programs to perform computer operations on PCs and midrange computers.

The graphic design curricula provide students with knowledge of desktop publishing, graphic design, and commercial art. The drafting technology curricula provide students with knowledge in architectural or mechanical drafting.

PENNSYLVANIA

Bradley Academy for the Visual Arts, York

About Our Institution
Bradley Academy, one of the Art Institutes and a national leader in creative education, was established to meet the community's need for well-trained visual artists. It is Bradley Academy's mission to be responsive to the needs of employers by teaching, within a supportive environment, the creative, technical, and workplace skills required for a successful career. Bradley's success is measured by the number of students who complete their programs and get jobs in their chosen fields.

Special Features
In 1997, Bradley Academy moved into a totally new facility in a suburban area on the eastern edge of York, Pennsylvania. Features include a community gallery, a student gallery, four desktop computer labs, an open lab for student use, and a campuswide wireless network. A two-week Student Success program is held to provide an opportunity for review of basic skills to those who need it.

Financial Aid/Scholarships
Bradley Academy participates in the Federal Pell Grant, Federal Stafford Student Loan, PLUS Loan, FSEOG, College Work-Study, VA, state grant for Pennsylvania residents, JTPA, and OVR programs. Bradley Academy also offers monthly payment plans, financial planning assistance, and some institutional aid.

Accreditation
Bradley Academy is accredited by the Accrediting Commission of Career School and Colleges of Technology (ACCSCT) and is licensed by the Pennsylvania State Board of Private Licensed Schools.

Admissions
Applicants must be high school graduates or have a GED certificate prior to the start of classes. High school seniors can apply during their senior year. There is no formal application deadline. Students are encouraged to begin the process with a personal interview by the fall of their senior year. Class sizes are small, and classes sometimes fill well in advance of the starting date. A portfolio review is required for graphic design and animation applicants.

Contact
Bradley Academy for the Visual Arts
1409 Williams Road
York, PA 17402
Phone: (800) 864-7725 (toll-free)
Fax: (717) 840-1951
E-mail: info@bradleyacademy.net
Web: www.bradleyacademy.net

Program Content
Animation, Digital Arts, Fashion Marketing, Graphic Design, Interior Design, Web Design

Programs Eligible for Scholarship	Tuition and Fees	Course Length/Credit Hours	Credential Earned
Animation	$28,080	18 months/72 credits	AST
Digital Arts	$28,080	18 months/72 credits	AST
Fashion Marketing	$28,080	18 months/72 credits	ASB
Graphic Design	$28,080	18 months/72 credits	AST
Interior Design	$28,080	18 months/72 credits	AST
Web Design	$28,080	18 months/72 credits	AST

CHI Institute, Southampton

About Our Institution

CHI Institute was founded in 1981, and classes in computer technology started in spring 1982 at its present facility. In the ensuing years, programs were added due to industry needs and student interest. In 1985, CHI Institute achieved degree-granting status. In February 1998, the school was purchased by Education Medical, Inc. (EMI). In September 1998, EMI changed its name to Quest Education Corporation. Quest was purchased in July 2000 by Kaplan, Inc. Quest and Kaplan are dedicated to continuing the same excellent education for which CHI Institute is known.

Special Features

CHI Institute offers valuable preparation for those seeking their Microsoft Certified Systems Engineer (MCSE), Microsoft Certified Professional (MCP), Microsoft Office User Specialist (MOUS), and A+ certifications. CHI is an Authorized Academic Training Provider (AATP) of Microsoft and uses the Official Microsoft Curriculum. CHI Institute is an approved testing site for the National Center for Competency Testing (NCCT) for those Medical Assistant students seeking this national recognition. Students in the Medical Assistant program can also apply for membership to the National Registry of Medical Assistants.

Financial Aid/Scholarships

CHI Institute offers many sources of financial aid for those who qualify. Students can apply for William D. Ford Subsidized Loans, Unsubsidized Loans, and Parent Loans (PLUS). Also offered for those who qualify are Federal Pell, Federal Supplemental Educational Opportunity (FSEOG), and PHEEA State Grants. Eligible students can also apply for the Federal Work-Study Program. CHI Institute offers seven tuition scholarships to graduating seniors; one full, two half, and four quarter scholarships.

Tuition and Fees

Total program costs, including application fee, tuition, lab fee, and textbooks and tools, are shown in the table (below). The $100 application fee is due when the student has been accepted for admission and signs the enrollment agreement. The lab fee is due at orientation. Tuition payments are due on a term basis, with the first payment due on or before orientation day. Students should consult the school catalog for detailed information.

Accreditation

CHI is accredited by the Accrediting Commission of Career Schools and Colleges of Technology (ACCSCT) and is licensed by the Pennsylvania State Board of Private Licensed Schools. CHI Institute is also a member of the Career College Association and is approved by the Veterans Administration (VA) to train eligible participants.

Admissions

An applicant to the school must be a high school graduate or possess a GED. Proof of a high school diploma or GED must be presented to the school. Transcript requests can be filled out at CHI Institute and sent to the high school that the individual graduated from. Credit for prior education/training is determined by the Education Department at the campus. An applicant to the Elec-

Program Content

Degree Programs Computer Engineering Technology, Computer Programming, Criminal Justice, Graphic Design, Network Engineering Technology

Diploma Programs Application and Internet Programming, Cable Network Technician, Computer Networking, Computerized Office Applications, Electrician (Residential, Commercial, and Industrial), Medical Assistant with Phlebotomy

trician Program is not required to be a high school graduate or possess a GED but must successfully complete an approved Ability to Benefit test administered and scored by a third party. The test is arranged by the school.

Graduation Requirements

Candidates for graduation must complete all requirements for their program of study, attain a minimum GPA of 2.0, return any property belonging to the school, and fulfill all financial obligations prior to graduation.

Contact

Eric Heller, Director of Admissions
CHI Institute, Southampton Campus
520 Street Road
Southampton, PA 18966
Phone: (215) 357-5100
Fax: (215) 357-4212
E-mail: eheller@chicareers.com
Web: www.CHItraining.com

Programs Eligible for Scholarship	Tuition and Fees	Course Length/Credit Hours	Credential Earned
Computer Engineering Technology	$22,091	90 credits	AST
Computer Programming	$24,237	94 credits	AST
Criminal Justice	$20,598	95 credits	ASB
Graphic Design	$24,707	93 credits	AST
Network Engineering Technology	$24,357	94 credits	AST
Application and Internet Programming	$12,161	45 credits	Diploma
Cable Network Technician	$ 3,345	6 credits	Diploma
Computer Networking	$13,053	47 credits	Diploma
Computerized Office Applications	$ 6,889	24 credits	Diploma
Electrician	$14,390	72 credits	Diploma
Medical Assistant with Phlebotomy	$11,224	45 credits	Diploma

The Cittone Institute, Center City, Philadelphia

About Our Institution

Since 1967, The Cittone Institute has provided quality postsecondary training to students from the mid-Atlantic states. The Cittone Institute has campuses in Edison, Mount Laurel, and Paramus, New Jersey; Center City and Northeast Philadelphia, Pennsylvania; and Plymouth Meeting, Pennsylvania. The schools offer a variety of programs designed to help students develop the skills and confidence essential for success in their chosen field os study.

Special Features

The Cittone Institute is dedicated and committed to providing industry-current instructional programs for serious-minded students. Leading companies contract with the Cittone Institute in their search for qualified entry-level employees. At Cittone, students are recognized and respected. As a member school of the Lincoln Educational Services parent organization, attention to individual needs, abilities, and interests is the hallmark of the Cittone philosophy of education.

Financial Aid/Scholarships

Cittone is a registered institution of learning, eligible to offer financial assistance to its students. Each campus maintains an active financial aid office dedicated to matching a variety of available programs, including grants, loans, work-study, and vocational rehabilitation, to those applicants who qualify, following established federal guidelines.

Accreditation

The Cittone Institute is accredited by Accrediting Council for Independent Colleges and Schools (ACICS) in Washington, D.C., and is approved by a number of state and federal organizations. Additional information is available in the school catalog.

Admissions

Applicants must either have an associate or baccalaureate degree or possess a high school diploma, a GED certificate, or the equivalent and receive a passing score on the Cittone Entrance Examination.

Graduation Requirements

Graduation requirements mandate that a student complete all required courses and achieve an overall grade point average of at least 2.0.

Contact

Executive Director
The Cittone Institute
3600 Market Street
Philadelphia, PA 19104
Phone: (215) 382-1553
Fax: (215) 382-3875
E-mail: execdirccphilly@lincolntech.com
Web: www.cittone.com

Program Content

Medical Administrative Assistant, Medical Assistant, Network Systems Administrator, PC Support Technician

The Cittone Institute, Northeast, Philadelphia

About Our Institution

Since 1967, The Cittone Institute has provided high-quality postsecondary training to students from the mid-Atlantic states. The Cittone Institute has campuses in Edison, Mount Laurel, and Paramus, New Jersey; Center City and Northeast Philadelphia, Pennsylvania; and Plymouth Meeting, Pennsylvania. The schools offer a variety of programs designed to help students develop the skills and confidence essential for success in their chosen field of study.

Special Features

The Cittone Institute is dedicated and committed to providing industry-current instructional programs for the serious-minded student. Leading companies contract with Cittone in their search for qualified entry-level employees. At Cittone, students are recognized and respected. As a member school of the Lincoln Educational Services parent organization, attention to individual needs, abilities, and interests is the hallmark of the Cittone philosophy of education.

Financial Aid/Scholarships

Cittone is a registered institution of learning, eligible to offer financial assistance to its students. Each campus maintains an active financial aid office dedicated to matching a variety of available programs, including grants, loans, work-study, and vocational rehabilitation, to those applicants who qualify, following established federal guidelines.

Accreditation

The Cittone Institute is accredited by the Accrediting Council for Independent Colleges and Schools (ACICS) in Washington, D.C., and is approved by a number of state and federal organizations. Additional information is available in the school catalog.

Admissions

Applicants must either have an associate or baccalaureate degree or possess a high school diploma, a GED certificate, or the equivalent and receive a passing score on the Cittone Entrance Examination.

Graduation Requirements

Graduation requirements mandate that a student complete all required courses and achieve an overall grade point average of at least 2.0.

Contact

Executive Director
The Cittone Institute
2180 Hornig Road, Bldg. A
Philadelphia, PA 19116
Phone: (215) 969-0869
Fax: (215) 969-3459
E-mail: execdirnephilly@lincolntech.com
Web: www.cittone.com

Program Content

Graphic Web Design, Medical Administrative Assistant, Medical Assistant, Network Systems Administrator, PC Systems and Networking Technology

The Cittone Institute, Plymouth Meeting

About Our Institution
Since 1967, The Cittone Institute has provided high-quality postsecondary training to students from the mid-Atlantic states. The Cittone Institute has campuses in Edison, Mount Laurel, and Paramus, New Jersey; Center City and Northeast Philadelphia, Pennsylvania; and Plymouth Meeting, Pennsylvania. The schools offer a variety of programs to help students develop the skills and confidence essential for success in their chosen field of study.

Special Features
The Cittone Institute is dedicated and committed to providing industry-current instructional programs for the serious-minded student. Leading companies contract with the Cittone Institute in their search for qualified entry-level employees. At Cittone, the students are recognized and respected. As a member of the Lincoln Educational Services parent organization, attention to individual needs, abilities, and interests is the hallmark of the Cittone philosophy of education.

Financial Aid/Scholarships
Cittone is a registered institution of learning, eligible to offer financial assistance to its students. Each campus maintains an active financial aid office dedicated to matching a variety of available programs, including grants, loans, work-study, and vocational rehabilitation, to those applicants who qualify, following established federal guidelines.

Accreditation
The Cittone Institute is accredited by the Accrediting Council for Independent Colleges and Schools (ACICS) in Washington, D.C., and is approved by a number of state and federal organizations. More information is available in the school catalog.

Admissions
Applicants must either have an associate or baccalaureate degree or possess a high school diploma, a GED certificate, or the equivalent and receive a passing score on the Cittone Entrance Examination.

Graduation Requirements
Graduation requirements mandate that a student complete all required courses and achieve an overall grade point average of at least 2.0.

Contact
Executive Director
The Cittone Institute
One Plymouth Meeting, #300
Plymouth Meeting, PA 19462
Phone: (610) 941-0319
Fax: (610) 941-3681
E-mail: execdirplymouth@lincolntech.com
Web: www.cittone.com

Program Content
Computer Programming and Applications Technology, Computer Programming and Internet Technology, Medical Administrative Assistant, Medical Assistant, Network Systems Administrator, PC Systems and Networking Technology, PC Systems Technology, Pharmacy Technician, Therapeutic Massage and Bodywork Technician

Computer Learning Network, Altoona

About Our Institution
Computer Learning Network has awarded short-term career training diplomas since 1982. Its programs offer training opportunities in the computer, business office, and medical professions. The programs are designed to provide technical knowledge and hands on learning to prepare students to begin careers upon graduation in entry level positions. Programs vary in length from six to nine months full-time and twelve to eighteen months part-time. Many program offerings provide the student for nationally recognized, industry standard certifications. Both day and evening programs are available.

Financial Aid/Scholarships
As an eligible institution, Computer Learning Network participates in the Federal Title IV financial aid programs, including Federal Pell Grants, Subsidized and Unsubsidized Stafford Loans, and Federal Plus Loans. All programs are eligible for military benefits. Tuition payment plans can be customized for the individual student.

Tuition and Fees
Tuition and fees vary by program; however, all fees are clearly outlined and a total program cost is provided to the prospective student. A $50 application fee is charged.

Accreditation
Computer Learning Network is accredited by the Accrediting Commission of Career Schools and Colleges of Technology.

Admissions
Applicants for admission are required to demonstrate an aptitude for success through personal assessment by school staff members, which includes an enrollment interview and an acceptable score on an entrance exam. A high school diploma or GED is required for admission. Students should ask about other requirements for individual programs. All applicants are required to visit the school prior to recommendation for acceptance.

Graduation Requirements
In order to graduate, the student must have satisfactorily completed all required courses in the program, have a combined average grade of not less than 70 percent, and have satisfied any indebtedness to the school.

Program Content
Administrative Assistant, Business Administration, Legal Assistant, Massage Therapist, Medical Administrative Assistant, Medical Assistant, Medical Office Professional, Network and Internet Security Administration, Network Technician, Office Professional, Pharmacy Technician, Software Application Specialist

Contact
Vickie J. Clements, Director
Computer Learning Network
2900 Fairway Drive
Altoona, PA 16602
Phone: 800-458-6706 (toll-free)
E-mail: director@cln.edu
Web: www.cln.edu

Programs Eligible for Scholarship	Tuition and Fees	Course Length/Credit Hours	Credential Earned
Administrative Assistant	$ 9,400	960 hours/40 credits	Diploma
Business Administration	$21,050	1,800 hours/90 credits	Diploma
Legal Assistant	$10,625	960 hours/45 credits	Diploma
Massage Therapist	$11,840	960 hours/48 credits	Diploma
Medical Administrative Assistant	$10,000	960 hours/40 credits	Diploma
Medical Assistant	$11,130	960 hours/46 credits	Diploma
Medical Office Professional	$ 8,770	720 hours/34 credits	Diploma
Network and Internet Security Administration	$11,590	960 hours/48 credits	Diploma
Network Technician	$11,590	960 hours/48 credits	Diploma
Office Professional	$ 8,170	720 hours/34 credits	Diploma
Pharmacy Technician	$10,625	960 hours/45 credits	Diploma
Software Application Specialist	$11,440	960 hours/48 credits	Diploma

Computer Learning Network, Mechanicsburg

About Our Institution
Computer Learning Network has provided short-term career training since 1982. Its programs offer training opportunities in the computer, office, and medical professions. The programs are designed to provide technical knowledge and hands-on training to prepare students to begin their careers upon graduation. Programs vary in length from ten months (full-time) to fifteen months (part-time). Many program offerings provide the opportunity for nationally recognized certifications.

Financial Aid/Scholarships
As an eligible institution, Computer Learning Network participates in the Federal Title IV financial aid programs, including Pell and Subsidized and Unsubsidized Stafford and PLUS Loans. Tuition payment plans can be customized for the individual student.

Tuition and Fees
Tuition and fees vary by program; however, all fees are clearly outlined and a total program cost is provided for the prospective student.

Accreditation
Computer Learning Network is accredited by the Accrediting Commission of Career Schools and Colleges of Technology.

Admissions
Admission is open to anyone with a high school diploma or GED who demonstrates the ability to benefit from a chosen program by obtaining the required cut score on a preadmissions evaluation. Students should ask about other requirements for some programs. All applicants are required to visit the school for a personal interview prior to recommendation for acceptance.

Graduation Requirements
Upon satisfactory completion of all course work with a 70 percent GPA and payment of all tuition and fees, the student is awarded a diploma for the program completed.

Contact
Terra Reider, Director of Admissions
401 East Winding Hill Road
Mechanicsburg, PA 17011
Phone: (717) 761-1481
E-mail: treider@clntraining.net
Web: www.clntraining.net

Program Description
Desktop Applications Specialist prepares students for software support specialist, word processor, and help desk support and Microsoft Office Specialist certifications.

Health Information Specialist provides in-depth course work in insurance and billing and medical transcription.

Massage Therapy Practitioner offers study in different massage modalities and necessary business skills.

Medical Assistant is intensive and prepares students for all procedures required for employment in a physician's office or clinic.

Network Administration Specialist offers hands-on training to enter the fields of network operations, security, and administration. Help for A+, Net+, MCP, and MCSA certification is provided.

Network and Internet Security Administration prepares students for network administration and network security. Help for Net+, Linux+, Security+, MCP, and CCNA certifications is provided.

Pharmacy Technician provides training for assuming employment in retail, hospital, or mail order pharmacies.

Webmaster provides the educational background and practical skills for Internet and Web site design and maintenance.

Programs Eligible for Scholarship	Tuition and Fees	Course Length/Credit Hours	Credential Earned
Desktop Applications Specialist	$11,125	960 hours	Diploma
Health Information Specialist	$11,800	960 hours	Diploma
Massage Therapy Practitioner	$13,205	960 hours	Diploma
Medical Assistant	$11,650	960 hours	Diploma
Network Administration Specialist	$11,440	960 hours	Diploma
Network and Internet Security Administration	$12,430	960 hours	Diploma
Pharmacy Technician	$12,037	960 hours	Diploma
Webmaster	$12,195	960 hours	Diploma

Duff's Business Institute, Pittsburgh

About Our Institution
Founded in 1840, Duff's Business Institute is recognized as the oldest private business school in the United States. Thousands of Duff's graduates have gone on to become recognized leaders of business and industry. Mr. H. J. Heinz, founder of the H. J. Heinz company, attended Duff's. The institution's graduates maintain a fine reputation among local employers. This reputation continues to ensure career placement success for Duff's graduates. Duff's Business Institute is one of more than eighty schools owned and operated by a division of Corinthian Colleges, Inc., in the United States.

Special Features
Duff's is proud of its caring, educated faculty and staff members. Students receive constant attention and assistance from their instructors and from the support staff. Centrally located in downtown Pittsburgh, Duff's is accessible to many forms of public transportation.

Financial Aid/Scholarships
Federal Pell Grants, Federal Work-Study Program, FSEOG, state grants, FFEL, Federal Stafford Student Loans, Federal PLUS Program, and other types of financial aid are available for those who qualify.

Tuition and Fees
Per-credit-hour fees are assessed based on the amount of classes taken per quarter. There is a $150 one-time student service fee, a quarterly registration fee of $15, and a $25 quarterly technology fee.

Accreditation
The Institute is accredited by the Accrediting Council for Independent Colleges and Schools (ACICS). The medical assistant program is accredited by AAMA, a division of the Commission on Accreditation of Allied Health Education Programs (CAAHEP).

Admissions
Applicants must provide proof of high school graduation or the equivalent (GED). Successful completion of an assessment examination is required for admission. Applicants who have completed the ACT test with a score of at least 15, or the SAT with a score of 700 or more, are not required to complete the test. In addition, applicants must complete a personal interview with an Admissions Representative.

Graduation Requirements
In order to graduate, students must attain an overall minimum 2.0 cumulative grade point average for the program and complete all courses specified in the program catalog. In addition, students must satisfy all financial obligations.

Enrollment
There are 643 students enrolled.

Contact
Lynn Fischer
Director of Admissions
100 Forbes Avenue, Suite 1200
Pittsburgh, PA 15222
Phone: (412) 261-4520
(888) 279-3314 (toll-free)
Fax: (412) 261-4546
E-mail: lfischer@cci.edu
Web: www.duffs-institute.com

Programs Eligible for Scholarship	Tuition and Fees	Course Length/Credit Hours	Credential Earned
Accounting	$223/credit hour	18–24 months/114 credit hours	ASB
Business Administration	$223/credit hour	18–24 months/109 credit hours	ASB
Legal Admin. Secretary	$223/credit hour	18–24 months/105 credit hours	ASB
Medical Admin. Secretary	$223/credit hour	18–24 months/106 credit hours	ASB
Paralegal	$223/credit hour	18–24 months/109 credit hours	ASB
Admin. Secretary	$223/credit hour	18–24 months/103 credit hours	ASB
Medical Assistant (day)	$223/credit hour	10 months/53 credit hours	Diploma
Medical Assistant (evening)	$223/credit hour	13 months/53 credit hours	Diploma
Career Access Program	$92/externship credit hour	6–9 months/34 credit hours	Diploma
Computer Operator	$92/externship credit hour	6–9 months/35 credit hours	Diploma
Criminal Justice	$152/credit hour	123 credit hours	Diploma
Medical Insurance Billing/Coding	$6,849	5 months	Diploma
Patient Care Technician	$10,701	9 months	Diploma

ICM School of Business & Medical Careers, Pittsburgh

About Our Institution
The ICM School of Business & Medical Careers is owned by Kaplan Higher Education Corporation. Established in 1963, ICM is one of the oldest proprietary schools in Pittsburgh, with a long legacy of employment success with Tri-State Area (Pennsylvania, West Virginia, and Ohio) employers. In nearly four decades of continuous operation, ICM has trained and placed thousands of students in fields ranging from computers to medical, travel, fashion, business, accounting, occupational therapy, and criminal justice. ICM's reputation and recognition among the area's major employers have enabled the School to grow and meet the demands of students graduating in the new millennium. Currently, Kaplan operates sixty-seven proprietary schools throughout the country.

Special Features
In addition to the School's outstanding curriculum and training, the ICM Advisory Boards, consisting of local representatives from employers and businesses for each program of study, meet regularly with the Education Department to assess curricula, equipment, and employers' needs. ICM students can thus be assured that their training reflects current trends/needs in their employment field. ICM is also a Microsoft IT Academy and as such teaches all Microsoft authorized curricula with certified instructors. ICM also is an Authorized Academic Testing Center, enabling students to take certified examinations on-site. Accordingly, its success rate for students taking Microsoft Certification exams far exceeds the national average. ICM also features one of the largest A+ labs in Pittsburgh for students interested in computer troubleshooting and repair. Candidates interested in student housing should contact an admissions representative for assistance. Students interested in part-time employment are encouraged to visit ICM's Career Center for one-on-one assistance. Graduates of ICM automatically qualify for its continuous placement program.

Financial Aid/Scholarships
The U.S. Department of Education recognizes ICM for participation in all major financial aid programs. As part of the admissions process, candidates participate in a financial aid interview with ICM's financial aid counselors who are committed to personalized service, and work to ensure that each student receives all the financial aid they qualify for. ICM also offers ten $6,500 scholarships to eligible high school seniors each year. To apply, candidates may call ICM, visit the ICM Web page, or complete an entry form at their school. Students enrolled at ICM also receive one-on-one assistance with scholarship opportunities indigenous to their location, nationality, or workplace.

Accreditation
ICM is accredited by the Accrediting Council for Independent Colleges and Schools (ACICS), the Accreditation Council for Occupational Therapy Education (ACOTE) of the American Occupational Therapy Association (AOTA), and the Commission on Accreditation of Allied Health Education Programs (CAAHEP).

Program Content
Accounting Management, Business Administration/Management, Computer Management, Computer Management–Database Administration, Computer Management–Network Administration, Computer Management–Network Engineering Technology, Computer Management–Solutions Development, Computer Network Technician, Criminal Justice, Criminal Justice–Cybercrime, Fashion Merchandising, Legal Office Administration, Medical Assisting Management, Medical Office Administration, Network Administration, Occupational Therapy Assistant, Office Administration, Webmaster (ASB, AST, or Diploma)

Admissions
All students must have a high school diploma or pass the GED test to be accepted by ICM. Each candidate participates in a personal interview, where the School learns of the candidate's interest and motivation and where the candidate is provided an overview of the curriculum, the School, financial requirements, and possible financial assistance available. Candidates must take the School's entrance examination and, if applicable, meet with the Acceptance Committee before acceptance can be granted.

Enrollment
A total of 1,044 students are enrolled.

Contact
Marcia Rosenberg
10 Wood Street
Pittsburgh, PA 15222
Phone: (800) 441-5222 (toll-free)
Fax: (412) 261-0998
Web: www.icmschool.com

Programs Eligible for Scholarship	Tuition and Fees	Course Length/Credit Hours	Credential Earned
All Degree Programs	Refer to school catalog	3–18 months	Diploma, Associate in Specialized Business degree, or Associate in Specialized Technology degree

International Academy of Design and Technology, Pittsburgh

About Our Institution

The International Academy of Design and Technology (IADT) is a career-oriented college located in Pittsburgh, Pennsylvania, dedicated to providing academic excellence in a professional environment. IADT prepares students for exciting and rewarding careers in rapidly expanding computer-driven fields. The goal of IADT is to educate individuals to be self-reliant, confident and skilled, and capable of performing successfully in today's workplace. IADT prepares students with the knowledge and skills necessary for a dynamic career in design and technology. Each student in the Academy is given an excellent opportunity to grow vocationally, intellectually, emotionally, and professionally.

Special Features

Students learn through a combination of practical hands-on courses and demonstration classes. Taught in professionally equipped, modern classrooms with the computer equipment, programs at IADT are designed to promote creativity and teach problem-solving skills while preparing students for rewarding careers in a variety of industries. Courses are taught at succeeding levels under the guidance of instructors with solid professional experience. IADT also features full-service career placement for its students and professionally places a high percentage of its graduates.

Financial Aid/Scholarships

IADT maintains a financial aid office on campus and offers a variety of programs. The school participates in various federal and state student financial assistance programs. There are also nongovernment student loan programs available if the student qualifies. Federal government aid includes Pell Grants, FSEOG, Federal Stafford Student Loans, and Federal PLUS Loans. Scholarships of varying amounts are awarded each year.

Tuition and Fees

Tuition is $3,800 to $4,900 per term, depending on the program.

Accreditation

IADT is accredited by the Accrediting Council for Independent Colleges and Schools and licensed by the Pennsylvania State Board of Private Licensed Schools.

Admissions

A high school diploma or equivalent is required. Students should apply for admission as soon as possible in order to be officially accepted for a specific program and starting date. An application for admission and personal interview must be completed. An entrance exam may be required. Students should call the admissions office to begin the application process.

Graduation Requirements

A student must have earned a minimum 2.0 grade point average and must have successfully completed every course within the program. The normal program length is eighteen months.

Contact

Mr. Robert Cappel, Vice President of Admissions
International Academy of Design and Technology
555 Grant Street
Oliver Avenue Entrance
Pittsburgh, PA 15219
Phone: (800) 447-8324 (toll-free)
Fax: (412) 391-4224
Web: www.iadt-pitt.com

Program Content

Diploma: Business Administration, E-Commerce, Justice Technology, PC/LAN
A.S.B./A.S.T. Degree: Computer Information Management, Visual Communications

Program Description

Business Administration: This program prepares students for entry-level positions in marketing, advertising, or other business industries. The program emphasizes training in software applications used in a modern office and in marketing, advertising, and management areas. General education requirements broaden the student's course of study beyond technical training.
Computer Information Management (CIM): CIM is a comprehensive course in microcomputer software and hardware, networking, telecommunications, and programming. The program is designed to provide students with the knowledge and skills necessary for employment in the microcomputer/telecommunications industry and is taught on a professional level.
E-Commerce: This curriculum exposes students to a fast-paced, intensive training program that combines theory and concepts with hands-on computer experience. Classroom instructors are well trained and utilize a combination of practical examples and business-based solutions.
Justice Technology: This program prepares the graduate to enter the justice profession. The course includes studies such as crime scene investigation and management, forensics, evidence processing, computer forensics, and law enforcement.
PC/LAN: This program focuses on the skills necessary to utilize current network technology, integrating microcomputers to share peripheral devices and communicating with each other in local area, wide-area, and enterprise networks. Microcomputer hardware is examined using diagnostic and troubleshooting tools to enable the student to understand how a microcomputer operates and how it can be integrated into a local area and/or wide-area network.
Visual Communications: Courses in this program stimulate and develop conceptualization and design capabilities, while practical hands-on lab classes emphasize critical production skills. The program begins with a core of basic skills and gradually builds to more advanced techniques. Students develop computer skills utilizing the equipment and software currently used in the field. Various business subjects are also integrated into the curriculum to provide additional structure and support.

Programs Eligible for Scholarship	Tuition and Fees	Course Length/Credit Hours	Credential Earned
Business Administration	$4,100/term	6 terms/18 months/100 credits	Diploma
Computer Information Management	$4,650/term	6 terms/18 months/97 credits	ASB
E-Commerce	$4,100/term	6 terms/18 months/101 credits	Diploma
Justice Technology		7 terms/21 months	Diploma
PC/LAN	$4,900/term	3 terms/9 months/36 credits	Diploma
PC/LAN (weekend)	$3,800/term	4 terms/12 months/36 credits	Diploma
Visual Communications	$4,800/term	6 terms/18 months/98 credits	AST

Lansdale School of Business, North Wales

About Our Institution

Lansdale School of Business (LSB) is a private institution founded in 1918 to prepare servicemen to reenter the job force after military service. Although times have changed, the School's philosophy has remained the same: to prepare students for the rapidly changing world of business.

Special Features

LSB is a junior college accredited by ACICS. All classrooms are furnished according to the needs of each specialized program area. Small classrooms reflect the desire to provide individual attention to all students. Facilities include five state-of-the-art computer labs, a medical lab that provides medical assistant students with well-lit work space and equipment, and a library with materials on numerous subjects and Internet access.

Financial Aid/Scholarships

Lansdale School of Business administers a variety of assistance programs to help students finance their education. Financial aid is usually offered through a package that consists of some combination of grants and loans. Programs offered include grants, loans, veterans' aid, trade rehabilitation, and vocational rehabilitation.

Accreditation

LSB is accredited by the Accrediting Council for Independent Colleges and Schools (ACICS).

Admissions

Each applicant participates in a career evaluation interview. To qualify for acceptance, applicants must be interviewed by an admissions representative and have a high school diploma or GED certificate. Acceptance is based on the applicant's meeting the above requirements, a review of the education records, and a review of career interests.

Program Content

Allied Health–Medical Assistant, Allied Health–Pharmacy Technician, Business Administration–Accounting/Management, Business Administration–Criminal Justice, Business Administration–Marketing/Management, Business Administration–Office Operations Management, Business Administration–Paralegal, Computer Technologies–Computer Applications Management, Computer Technologies–Computer Graphics and Design, Computer Technologies–Network Administration, Computer Technologies–Web Administration, Computer Technologies–Web Design

Contact

Marianne H. Johnson
Director of Admissions
Lansdale School of Business
Church Road
North Wales, PA 19454
Phone: (215) 699-5700
Fax: (215) 699-8770
E-mail: mjohnson@lsb.edu
Web: www.lsb.edu

Programs Eligible for Scholarship	Tuition and Fees	Course Length/Credit Hours

In the following programs, students may earn an Associate in Specialized Business degree or a diploma. Lansdale School of Business offers many options to students continuing their education.

Programs Eligible for Scholarship	Tuition and Fees	Course Length/Credit Hours
Allied Health–Medical Assistant	$13,030	17 months/70 credits
Allied Health–Pharmacy Technician	$13,030	17 months/70 credits
Business Administration–Accounting/ Management	$13,030	17 months/70 credits
Business Administration–Criminal Justice	$13,030	17 months/70 credits
Business Administration–Marketing/ Management	$13,030	17 months/70 credits
Business Administration–Office Operations Management	$13,030	17 months/70 credits
Business Administration–Paralegal	$13,030	17 months/70 credits
Computer Technologies–Computer Applications Management	$13,030	17 months/70 credits
Computer Technologies–Computer Graphics and Design	$13,030	17 months/70 credits
Computer Technologies–Network Administration	$14,780	17 months/70 credits
Computer Technologies–Web Administration	$14,780	17 months/70 credits
Computer Technologies–Web Design	$13,030	17 months/70 credits

Lincoln Technical Institute, Allentown

About Our Institution

The Allentown facility is located on a 10-acre campus in a building of approximately 26,000 square feet of comfortable, air-conditioned classrooms, laboratories, drafting and CAD rooms, and administrative offices. Excellent parking is available on the grounds. Interstate and major traffic routes are nearby, offering convenient travel to and from the Institute.

The Institute features electronic test equipment and computer equipment, which affords students the opportunity to train on equipment used in industry. Mechanical and architectural drafting classes currently utilize AutoCAD 2000 software.

Lincoln Tech has a basketball court and a multipurpose sports field on campus for student activities. Some activities are generated and run by the student council. These activities include cookouts, volleyball tournaments, flag football, ski trips, and other related activities throughout the year.

Special Features

A revision to the free course certificate policy offers each student who successfully completes their training a free course certificate. This certificate may be redeemed to repeat a course already taken or to take a new course in the program for which they trained that was not offered prior to graduation.

Financial Aid/Scholarships

The Allentown campus has a variety of half and full tuition scholarships available to graduating high school students. Awards include the Imagine America Scholarship and the Lincoln Tech Scholarship, among others. To apply for most of these scholarships, students must fill out an application and take an aptitude-based scholarship test. A Scholarship Committee, made up of volunteers representing business, industry, education, and/or government, interviews the finalists and makes the award decision. In addition, Lincoln Tech maintains a Financial Aid Office on campus, which offers qualified students a variety of programs, including grants, loans, work-study, veterans' aid, and vocational rehabilitation.

Accreditation

The Institute is accredited by the Accrediting Commission for Career School and Colleges of Technology (ACCSCT).

Admissions

Students must have either a high school diploma or a GED certificate and pass an entrance exam.

Contact

Executive Director
Lincoln Technical Institute
5151 Tilghman Street
Allentown, PA 18104
Phone: (610) 398-5300
Fax: (610) 395-2706
E-mail: execdirallentown@lincolntech.com
Web: www.lincolntech.com

Program Content

Electronic Engineering Technology, Electronic Servicing, Medical Administrative Assistant, Medical Assistant, Medical Assisting and Administrative Technology, PC Support Technician, PC Systems and Networking Technology, Pharmacy Technician

Lincoln Technical Institute, Philadelphia

About Our Institution

Lincoln Tech has a simple focus: to better prepare and train students to become qualified and knowledgeable entry-level auto/diesel technicians. To achieve this goal, the automotive students learn in an ASE master-certified program. The Institute offers hands-on training on educational and industry materials from experienced instructors. The programs have gained industry recognition for producing well-trained individuals who are prepared to join the workforce. Lincoln Tech's location in Philadelphia allows students to take advantage of internships and postgraduation opportunities in dealerships.

In addition, Lincoln Tech offers an associate degree program in service management for students who would like to train at the next level. The Institute offers both day and evening classes, and convenient public transportation options are available. There are several ways to create a schedule that suits individual needs.

Special Features

Lincoln Tech is authorized to award the Associate in Specialized Technology degree by Pennsylvania's Department of Education. The Institute is licensed by the State Board of Private Licensed Schools and is approved for the training of veterans and others who are eligible. An internship program is also offered.

Financial Aid/Scholarships

The Philadelphia campus has a variety of tuition scholarships available to graduating high school students. Awards include the Imagine America Scholarship, the Automotive Dealer Association of Greater Philadelphia Scholarship, and the PA Cooperative Vocational Education Association Scholarship as well as others. To apply for most of these scholarships, students must fill out an application and take an aptitude-based scholarship test. A Scholarship Committee, made up of volunteers representing business, industry, education, and/or government, interviews the finalists and makes the award decision. In addition, Lincoln Tech maintains a Financial Aid Office on campus, which offers qualified students a variety of programs, including grants, loans, work-study, veterans' aid, and vocational rehabilitation.

Accreditation

Lincoln Tech is accredited by the Accrediting Commission of Career Schools and Colleges of Technology (ACCSCT). The Institute is certified by the National Automotive Technical Education Foundation (NATEF).

Admissions

Students must have either a high school diploma or GED certificate and pass an entrance exam.

Graduation Requirements

In order to graduate, students must attain a minimum cumulative grade point average of 2.0, earn 75.5 credits for Automotive Service Management or 59 credits for Automotive Technology, and successfully complete all required courses in the program. Students must not be on probation. In addition, students must satisfy all financial obligations.

Program Content

Automotive Service Management, Automotive Technology

Program Description

Lincoln Tech programs are designed to provide graduates with the entry-level skills and knowledge required to diagnose, test, replace, repair, and adjust as necessary the components of the mechanical, electronic, hydraulic, and accessory systems on current automobiles. Upon completion of these programs, graduates are qualified for entry into the automotive field as a mechanic or technician, performing many of the common service operations and, under supervision, more specialized or involved tasks with a dealer, independent shop, or other service outlet.

Contact

Executive Director
Lincoln Technical Institute
9191 Torresdale Avenue
Philadelphia, PA 19136
Phone: (215) 335-0800
Fax: (215) 335-1443
E-mail: execdirphilly@lincolntech.com
Web: www.lincolntech.com

The New Castle School of Trades, Pulaski

About Our Institution
The New Castle School of Trades was founded in 1945 and is a multipurpose technical and trade institution. It is the School's philosophy to service with excellence the needs of students and the community by matching skills. Training programs are kept practical, intense, and results-oriented in the attainment of viable, measurable skills that graduates can use.

Special Features
Classes begin every five weeks and are available in both morning and evening. Associate degree programs are fifteen months and diploma programs range from six to fifty weeks in length.

Financial Aid/Scholarships
Financial aid programs are available at the New Castle School of Trades for those who qualify. Various scholarship opportunities are also available.

Tuition and Fees
In addition to tuition (listed in the table below), students are charged an application fee of $25 and a registration fee of $75. Books, tools, and workshops are available at extra cost.

Accreditation
The New Castle School of Trades is accredited by the Accrediting Commission of Career Schools and Colleges of Technology. The School is also a member of the Greater New Castle Chamber of Commerce, the Better Business Bureau of Western Pennsylvania, the Pennsylvania Association of Student Financial Aid, the National Institute of Metalworking Skills, the Pennsylvania Manufacturer's Association, the Career College Association, the Pennsylvania Association of Private School Administrators, the National Home Builders Association, the Air Conditioning Contractors of America, the American Welding Society, the National Automotive Technicians Education Foundation, the Mercer County Builders Association, and the Lawrence County Builders Association.

Admissions
Students must pass the Wonderlic Admissions Test to enter all programs. In addition, a high school diploma or GED is required for entry into degree programs.

Graduation Requirements
To be eligible for graduation, students must have a GPA of 2.0 or above, no failing grades in any course, and a minimum of 85 percent attendance.

Program Content
Associate in Specialized Technology (AST): Automotive Technology, Building Technology, Electrical Technology, Machine Technology, Refrigeration and Air Conditioning Technology

Diploma: Combination Welding, Commercial Truck Driving, Refrigeration and Climate Control

Contact
Jim Catheline
New Castle School of Trades
RD 1
Pulaski, PA 16143
Phone: (800) 837-8299 (toll-free)

Programs Eligible for Scholarship	Tuition and Fees	Course Length/Credit Hours	Credential Earned
Automotive Technology	$15,295	60 weeks/1,500 hours	AST
Building Technology	$14,395	60 weeks/1,500 hours	AST
Combination Welding	$10,100	40 weeks/1,000 hours	Diploma
Commercial Truck Driving	$4,100	6 weeks/240 hours	Diploma
Electrical Technology	$14,020	60 weeks/1,500 hours	AST
Machine Technology	$14,095	60 weeks/1,500 hours	AST
Refrigeration and Air Conditioning Technology	$14,095	60 weeks/1,500 hours	AST
Refrigeration and Climate Control	$11,762	50 weeks/1,250 hours	Diploma

The PJA School, Upper Darby

About Our Institution
The PJA School is a practical school for the practical student who seeks strong career skills and rapid entry into the fields of law, business, accounting, and computer applications. Students may earn their Associate in Specialized Business (ASB) degree in a streamlined manner and then take advantage of PJA's outstanding employment assistance. Upon completion of their ASB degree, students may continue on toward a bachelor's degree right on PJA's campus through the PJA School's partnership with Chestnut Hill College and Immaculata University. Since 1981, PJA students have been successfully training for careers as paralegals, accountants, legal secretaries, and much more.

Special Features
The PJA School has developed a strong reputation as a leader in the training of paralegals, business and accounting personnel, legal secretaries, and specialists in computer applications for the business world. More than 90 percent of the largest law firms in the Delaware Valley have hired PJA's graduates as have prominent firms in the accounting and corporate world. The School and its staff have won numerous awards, and the School is one of few nationwide to receive "no stipulations" in each of its last three accreditation cycles. This is a strong and rare vote of confidence by the accrediting commission and reflects that the School was found to be outstanding among its peers.

Financial Aid/Scholarships
Pell Grants, PHEAA Grants, FFEL, Direct Loan, WIA, OVR, VA, and Imagine America Scholarships are available. All graduates of the paralegal, business and accounting specialist, and legal/accounting paraprofessional programs who continue on to Chestnut Hill College through the partnership program receive a 10 percent discount on tuition for all bachelor's degree courses taken at PJA, as well as a 15 percent discount from Immaculata University for their courses.

Accreditation
The School is accredited by the Accrediting Commission of Career Schools and Colleges of Technology (ACCSCT) and is recommended for college credit acceptance by the American Council on Education (ACE).

Admissions
Applicants must meet a variety of criteria depending on the program for which they are applying. No SATs or other standardized testing is required. PJA considers each applicant based on total background, including education, experience, communication skills, speech, appearance, and maturity.

Program Content
Paralegal, Business and Accounting Specialist, Legal/Accounting Paraprofessional, Legal Secretary, Para-Accountant, Paralegal Including Computer Applications, Computerized Office Specialist.

Program Description
The PJA School believes that its highest goal must be to graduate competent, skilled professionals who are truly prepared, both personally and professionally, to fill the employment needs of today and the future.

Both task-specific and personal skill development form the basis of PJA's training. Indeed the guiding force behind every policy, effort, and activity of the School is to encourage such growth in our students.

By striving for this goal, the PJA School believes it is making a difference in the lives of its students and graduates as well as the broader community.

Contact
Daniel A. Alpert
Director of Institutional Development
7900 West Chester Pike
Upper Darby, PA 19082
Phone: (610) 789-6700
(800) RING-PJA (toll-free)
E-mail: pjaschool@dvol.com
Web: www.pjaschool.com

Programs Eligible for Scholarship	Tuition and Fees	Course Length/Credit Hours	Credential Earned
Paralegal	refer to school catalog	84 credit hours	ASB
Business and Accounting Specialist	refer to school catalog	84 credit hours	ASB
Legal/Accounting Paraprofessional	refer to school catalog	86 credit hours	ASB

The Restaurant School at Walnut Hill College, Philadelphia

About Our Institution

The Restaurant School at Walnut Hill College is an accredited, independent, degree-granting institution dedicated to educating those who wish to pursue careers in the hospitality industry. The School offers specialized Associate in Science and Bachelor of Science degrees in four majors: culinary arts, pastry arts, restaurant management, and hotel management.

Special Features

The School's programs combine intensive academic studies with practical experience, including a tour of France or cruise and resort tour. Students have the opportunity to learn the art of true hospitality in the City of Lights or behind the scenes of Walt Disney World.

Financial Aid/Scholarships

Pell Grants, PHEAA state grants, and Federal Family Education Loans (FFEL) are available to those who qualify. Scholarship information is also available through the School's student services department.

Tuition and Fees

Tuition and fees are approximately $13,200 per academic year for one of the four majors. This cost does not include books and equipment.

Admissions

Admissions requirements include an application, goal statement, references, high school transcript or GED certificate, and an achievement analysis or SAT with a combined score of at least 900.

Contact

Office of Admissions
4207 Walnut Street
Philadelphia, PA 19104
Phone: (215) 222-4200
Fax: 215-222-4219
Web: www.walnuthillcollege.edu

Program Description

Culinary Arts This program is designed to provide students with the essential foundation for a culinary arts career. The curriculum combines fundamental and advanced culinary courses with relevant academic classes to allow students to develop the creative, professional, and leadership skills necessary for successful careers in the hospitality industry.

Hotel Management Courses such as Introduction to Hospitality, Front Office Management, and Hotel Management and Operations as well as practical experience are designed to equip students with the pertinent industry knowledge and managerial and administrative skills required to excel in the growing hospitality field.

Pastry Arts Fundamental and advanced pastry techniques are skills necessary for a career in the pastry arts profession. Introductory courses include Pastry Techniques, Professional Bread Baking, Cake Baking and Decorating. Students progress to specialized courses, such as Chocolate and Candies, European Tortes and Gateaux, and Wedding Cakes.

Restaurant Management This program is structured to integrate traditional classroom learning with unique practical experiences. Students develop the industry knowledge, administration, and leadership required for positions in restaurants, hotels, resorts, corporate dining, and other food-service facilities.

Programs Eligible for Scholarship	Tuition and Fees	Course Length/Credits	Credential Earned
Culinary Arts	$13,200/year	64 credit hours	AS
Culinary Arts	$13,200/year	123 credit hours	BS
Pastry Arts	$13,200/year	64 credit hours	AS
Pastry Arts	$13,200/year	120.5 credit hours	BS
Restaurant Management	$13,200/year	63 credit hours	AS
Restaurant Management	$13,200/year	122 credit hours	BS
Hotel Management	$13,200/year	65.5 credit hours	AS
Hotel Management	$13,200/year	122.5 credit hours	BS

Rosedale Technical Institute, Pittsburgh

About Our Institution
Rosedale Technical Institute is a private technical institute devoted to the training of personnel for the automotive, electrical, truck, and transportation industries. The school was founded in 1949 and has been in continuous operation since. In July 1969, the school was incorporated as Rosedale Technical Institute, Inc. On October 1, 1977, the school moved to its present location. As of January 1, 1987, Rosedale became a division of Electronic Institutes, Inc., and is now a nonprofit institution.

Special Features
The school offers complete programs in automotive technology, diesel technology, and electrical technology as day programs; automotive technician studies is also offered as an evening program. The programs are designed to prepare individuals for entry-level employment as automotive mechanics, diesel and truck mechanics, and electricians.

The school's 250 students occupy approximately 90,000 square feet of space in an educational center located on a 6-acre campus in the Squirrel Hill district of Pittsburgh. The automotive shop area contains tune-up bays, service lifts, and stalls similar to those found in commercial garages and auto dealerships. Various tune-up machines, brake machines, and two alignment machines are located in the shop area. The electrical shop area contains an indoor two-story house frame used for residential and construction wiring. There are stations for motor repair, commercial circuitry, electronic machine control, and programmable logic controllers. The diesel shop contains trucks, transmissions, drive trains, and a number of diesel engines for students to learn troubleshooting and repair. Students learn the proper use of hand tools, pneumatic tools, diagnostic meters, scan tools, oscilloscopes, and measuring equipment.

Financial Aid/Scholarships
The school is an eligible institution for federal Title IV financial aid programs and for the Pennsylvania State Grant and Loan Program. Students and parents who feel they need financial assistance with tuition and related costs have the opportunity to meet with a financial aid officer to determine the financial aid the family may qualify for.

Tuition and Fees
Tuition costs are shown in the accompanying table.

Accreditation
Rosedale Technical Institute is accredited by the Accrediting Commission of Career Schools and Colleges of Technology. The school received its initial accreditation in 1974. The Institute is licensed by the Pennsylvania Board of Private Licensed Schools. It has been granted ASE Master Certification for Automotive Training Programs.

Admissions
To be accepted for admission, an applicant must have a standard high school diploma or a high school equivalency certificate and must successfully complete a recognized entrance exam. This exam is administered by the Director of Education or a member of the staff at the school. Each applicant must submit a final high school transcript or a copy of his or her high school diploma or equivalency certificate. Applications are accepted from high school seniors who are expected to graduate; however, their graduation must be confirmed before they enter school. Students wishing to apply for admission should arrange for an interview with the Admissions Department. The interview can be scheduled either at the school or in the student's home. Out-of-town students may use the toll-free number to contact the Institute to set up an appointment (telephone: 800-521-6262, toll-free).

Applicants with previous training or applicable experience may enter with advanced standing, and the course will be shortened proportionally with approval of the Director of Education.

Graduation Requirements
To graduate, students must complete all required assignments and class work with a final quality point average (QPA) of 2.0 or above. Students must have a minimum attendance rate of 85 percent of the scheduled class time. Tuition accounts must be satisfied prior to graduation. A student who satisfactorily completes a program receives a degree.

Program Content
Automotive Technology, Diesel Technology, Electrical Technology

Contact
Kevin Auld
Director of Admissions
4634 Browns Hill Road
Pittsburgh, PA 15217
Phone: (412) 521-6200
Fax: (412) 521-2520

Programs Eligible for Scholarship	Tuition and Fees	Course Length/Credit Hours	Credential Earned
Automotive Technology	$17,990	16 months/96 credits	Degree
Diesel Technology	$17,990	16 months/90 credits	Degree
Electrical Technology	$17,990	16 months/96 credits	Degree

Schuylkill Institute of Business & Technology, Pottsville

About Our Institution

Schuylkill Institute of Business & Technology (SIBT) was established in 1977 in Pottsville, Pennsylvania. SIBT provides career training that matches the student's career goals with the needs of employers. In 2000, SIBT became a part of ForeFront Education Inc., a national network of postsecondary schools dedicated to quality career education and student achievement.

Special Features

SIBT provides specialized career education in many of the fastest-growing career fields and offers degree and diploma programs in the fields of drafting technology, electronics technology, graphic design, medical assisting, and networking. SIBT provides student support services, including career services and placement.

Financial Aid/Scholarships

SIBT maintains a financial aid office providing a variety of programs, including FFELP, Stafford Loan, Federal Plus Loan, Pell Grants, HELP, PHEAA Grants, and SEOG. Some students may also be eligible for educational benefits under programs administered by the Veterans Administration, Pennsylvania Office of Vocational Rehabilitation, or for benefits under the Job Training Partnership Act (JTPA).

Accreditation

The Institute is accredited by the Accrediting Council for Independent Colleges and Schools (ACICS) to award Associate in Specialized Business degrees and diplomas.

Admissions

A high school diploma or GED certificate is required for admission, in addition to passing an admissions test and meeting academic and financial criteria.

Graduation Requirements

A student must attain a minimum 2.0 cumulative GPA, maintain satisfactory attendance, complete all designated requirements of the program, satisfy financial obligations to SIBT, and complete exit interviews.

Contact

Tony Dooley, Director
171 Red Horse Road
Pottsville, PA 17901
Phone: (570) 622-4835
Fax: (570) 622-6563
E-mail: tdooley@sibt.edu
Web: www.sibt.edu

Program Content

Degrees: Drafting, Graphic Design, Medical Assisting, Network/Internet Professional, and Paralegal/Legal Secretary.

Diplomas: PC Network/Internet Technician and Professional Massage Therapist.

Program Description

Medical assistant science provides students with clinical and administrative skills and preparation for careers in doctors' offices and health-care facilities.

The PC network and Internet professional curricula provide students with knowledge of PC hardware and software in a variety of platforms, as well as networking, home page production, and Internet access.

The graphic design curricula provide students with the knowledge of desktop publishing, graphic design, and commercial art.

Thompson Institute, Harrisburg

About Our Institution
Thompson Institute is conveniently located near good public transportation and is easily accessible from Routes 81 and 83. Parking is available on campus. The campus consists of three separate buildings housing the dormitories, administrative offices, and educational facilities. A large open field with sand volleyball and other recreational activities is adjacent to the buildings. Picnic tables are available throughout the campus.

Special Features
The Institute's Career Services Department actively assists students with job placement upon graduation. Assistance in seeking part-time employment while in school is also available. Throughout the school year, student activities that encourage school spirit are offered. Externships are available for different programs in career-related positions.

Accreditation
Thompson Institute is accredited by the Accrediting Council for Independent Colleges and Schools (ACICS).

Admissions
Applicants must be high school graduates or have a GED certificate and furnish proof by providing the school with an official copy of the high school transcript or GED certificate.

Enrollment
There are 550 students enrolled at Thompson Institute.

Contact
Charles Zimmerman
5650 Derry Street
Harrisburg, PA 17111
Phone: (717) 564-4112
Fax: (717) 564-3779
E-mail: czimmerman@thompson.edu
Web: www.thompson.edu

Program Content
Accounting, Business Administration, Computer-Aided Drafting, Computer Graphics, Digital Arts, Medical Assisting, Medical Billing and Coding Specialist, Network Administration

Program Description
Thompson Institute's mission is to provide high-quality programs that are sound in concept, implemented by a competent and dedicated faculty, and geared to serve those seeking a solid foundation in knowledge and skills required to obtain employment in their chosen fields. The programs emphasize hands-on training that is relevant to employers' needs and focuses on areas that offer strong employment opportunities.

Programs Eligible for Scholarship	Course Length/Credit Hours	Credential Earned
Accounting	72 weeks/1,792 hours	Associate
Business Administration	72 weeks/1,792 hours	Associate
Computer-Aided Drafting	72 weeks/1,904 hours	Associate
Criminal Justice	60 weeks/1,500 hours	Associate
Medical Assistant	72 weeks/1,792 hours	Associate
Computer Network Administration	72 weeks/1,856 hours	Diploma
Computer Network Technology	48 weeks/1,008 hours	Diploma
Digital Arts	72 weeks/2,016 hours	Diploma
Medical Assisting	32 weeks/730 hours	Diploma
Medical Billing and Coding Specialist	42 weeks/870 hours	Diploma

Thompson Institute, Philadelphia

About Our Institution

Established in 1982, Thompson Institute–Philadelphia is a branch campus of the main campus in Harrisburg that was founded in 1918. Thompson–Philadelphia has a modern air-conditioned facility occupying 14,000 square feet and containing ten classrooms, administrative offices, a resource center with an electronic library, and full Internet access. In January 2002, the school was acquired by Quest Education Corporation. Quest Education Corporation is a subsidiary of Kaplan, Inc. Quest and Kaplan are dedicated to continuing the same excellent education for which the school is known.

Special Features

The school is located in the University City's prestigious Science Center, with easy access to the Market Frankford El train (Blue line to 34th Street).

Financial Aid/Scholarships

Federal Pell Grant, FFEL, Federal Perkins Loan, FSEOG, VA, JTPA.

Accreditation

Accrediting Council for Independent Colleges and Schools (ACICS), Commission on Accreditation of Allied Health Education Programs (CAAHEP), and approved by American Association of Medical Assistants Endowment (AAMAE). For memberships/affiliations, students should refer to the school's catalog.

Admissions

Applicants must be high school seniors and are required to complete a personal interview with an admissions representative.

Contact

Scott Dams, Director of Admissions
3010 Market Street, 2nd Floor
Philadelphia, PA 19104-3325
Phone: (215) 594-4000
Fax: (215) 594-4088
E-mail: sdams@thompsoninstitute.org
Web: www.thompsoninstitute.org

Program Content

Medical Assisting, Medical Office Management

Program Description

Medical Assisting: 720 clock hours/ modular diploma program. Graduates can qualify for entry-level positions as medical assistants, phlebotomists, and physical therapy assistants.

Medical Office Management: 720 clock hours/modular diploma program. Graduates can qualify for entry-level positions as medical receptionists, insurance processors, medical records clerks, and medical office managers.

Programs Eligible for Scholarship	Tuition and Fees	Course Length/Credit Hours	Credential Earned
Medical Assisting	$8,000	32 weeks/47 credit units	Diploma
Medical Office Management	$8,000	32 weeks/47 credit units	Diploma

Triangle Tech, DuBois

About Our Institution

Triangle Tech is a well-established, multipurpose institution that is committed to offering comprehensive training programs designed to help students develop their abilities to receive greater employment opportunities. Emphasis is on acquisition of knowledge and skills by students to deal with the rigors of professional life. The DuBois school is located in Sandy Township on Route 830W, just off of Route 219 and I-80 at Exit 16. Triangle Tech's facilities occupy a total of approximately 32,000 square feet. Classrooms accommodate 15–30 students; labs and shops are generally limited to 20. Parking is available on the premises.

Special Features

The objectives at Triangle Tech are to provide students with a practical, technical education using classroom lectures and extensive hands-on training and to help students prepare for a meaningful entry-level career. Programs are maintained in accordance with the standards of industry, business, and education. Day and evening classes are offered. Curricula include the Associate in Specialized Technology degree and diploma programs. Triangle Tech provides students with a variety of advisory services, including tutorial assistance, career advising, financial aid, and housing.

Financial Aid/Scholarships

Programs are available to qualified students, including Federal Pell Grants, FSEOG, PHEAA, OIG, VA Dependents Educational Assistance Program, Vocational Rehabilitation Program, Federal Perkins Loans, Federal and Direct Stafford Loans, Federal PLUS Loans, Triangle Tech's Installment Payment Plan, Triangle Tech Scholarships, and private scholarships.

Tuition and Fees

Tuition is $5,432 per term. Fees vary according to the program.

Accreditation

Triangle Tech, DuBois, is accredited by the Accrediting Commission of Career Schools and Colleges of Technology (ACCSCT).

Admissions

Applicants must have graduated from an accredited high school or have earned a GED prior to admission, and they must participate in a personal interview at the school prior to enrollment. Applicants are encouraged to visit Triangle Tech to tour the facilities and meet faculty members and students.

Graduation Requirements

Students must complete all of the required subjects in the prescribed curriculum or have been granted credit under Advanced Standing, attain a cumulative minimum GPA of 2.0 (with no grades of F), meet minimum attendance requirements, and settle all financial obligations to the school.

Program Content

Degree: Architectural CADD Technology, Carpentry and Construction Technology, Maintenance Electricity and Construction Technology, Mechanical CADD Technology, Welding and Fabrication Technology

Program Description

Architectural Computer-Aided Drafting and Design Technology This curriculum provides a well-rounded program of basic manual drafting courses coupled with extensive CADD instruction. Emphasis is placed on drafting and design of commercial and residential buildings.

Carpentry and Construction Technology This curriculum provides training on residential and light commercial construction inclusive of each stage of building development. Emphasis is placed on hands-on construction techniques, including site layout, foundations and form work, framing, and interior and exterior finishing techniques.

Maintenance Electricity and Construction Technology This curriculum places emphasis on residential, commercial, and industrial construction and maintenance electricity. Along with electrical construction techniques, the ability to design control circuits, repair motors, and troubleshoot electrical equipment is covered in detail.

Mechanical Computer-Aided Drafting and Design Technology This curriculum provides a well-rounded program of manual drafting courses coupled with extensive CADD instruction. The curriculum emphasizes all phases of mechanical design, including drafting fundamentals, structural design, piping, fabrication and welding, machines, jigs and fixtures, springs, gears, and computers.

Welding and Fabrication Technology This curriculum provides training on plate and pipe welding, including TIG, MIG, and Core Wire production processes. Architectural and structural steel drawings, pipe drawings, and layout work are covered. Students take the AWS and ASME certification exams as part of the training program.

Contact

Deborah Hepburn, School Director
Triangle Tech
P.O. Box 551
DuBois, PA 15801
Phone: (814) 371-2090
Fax: (814) 371-9227
E-mail: dhepburn@triangle-tech.edu
Web: www.triangle-tech.edu

Programs Eligible for Scholarship	Tuition and Fees	Course Length/Credits	Credential Earned
Architectural CADD Technology	$21,728	16 months/72 credits	Degree
Carpentry and Construction Technology	$21,728	16 months/72 credits	Degree
Maintenance Electricity and Construction	$21,728	16 months/72 credits	Degree
Mechanical CADD Technology	$21,728	16 months/72 credits	Degree
Welding and Fabrication Technology	$21,728	16 months/72 credits	Degree

Triangle Tech, Erie

About Our Institution

Triangle Tech is a well-established, multipurpose institution that is committed to offering comprehensive training programs designed to help students develop their abilities to receive greater employment opportunities. Emphasis is on acquisition of knowledge and skills by students to deal with the rigors of professional life. The Erie school is located on the west side, minutes from downtown Erie. Triangle Tech's facilities occupy a total of approximately 22,000 square feet. Classrooms accommodate 15–30 students; labs and shops are generally limited to 20. Parking is available on the premises with complete security provided.

Special Features

The objectives at Triangle Tech are to provide students with a practical, technical education using classroom lectures and extensive hands-on training and to help students prepare for a meaningful career. Programs are maintained in accordance with the standards of industry, business, and education. Day and evening classes are offered. Curricula include the Associate in Specialized Technology degree and diploma programs. Triangle Tech provides students with a variety of advisory services, including tutorial assistance, career advising, financial aid, and housing.

Financial Aid/Scholarships

Programs are available to qualified students, including Federal Pell Grants, FSEOG, PHEAA, OIG, VA Dependents Educational Assistance Program, Vocational Rehabilitation Program, Federal Perkins Loans, Federal and Direct Stafford Loans, Federal PLUS Loans, Triangle Tech's Installment Payment Plan, Triangle Tech Scholarships, and private scholarships.

Tuition and Fees

Tuition is $5,432 per term. Fees vary according to the program.

Accreditation

Triangle Tech, Erie, is accredited by the Accrediting Commission of Career Schools and Colleges of Technology (ACCSCT).

Admissions

Applicants must have graduated from an accredited high school or have earned a GED prior to admission, and they must participate in a personal interview at the school prior to enrollment. Applicants are encouraged to visit Triangle Tech to tour the facilities and meet faculty members and students.

Graduation Requirements

Students must complete all of the required subjects in the prescribed curriculum or have been granted credit under Advanced Standing, attain a cumulative minimum GPA of 2.0 (with no grades of F), meet minimum attendance requirements, and settle all financial obligations to the school.

Program Content

Degree: Architectural CADD Technology, Carpentry and Construction Technology, Maintenance Electricity and Construction Technology, Mechanical CADD Technology

Program Description

Architectural Computer-Aided Drafting and Design Technology This curriculum provides a well-rounded program of basic manual drafting courses coupled with extensive CADD instruction. Emphasis is placed on drafting and design of commercial and residential buildings.

Carpentry and Construction Technology This curriculum provides training on residential and light commercial construction inclusive of each stage of building development. Emphasis is placed on hands-on construction techniques, including site layout, foundations and form work, framing, and interior and exterior finishing techniques.

Maintenance Electricity and Construction Technology This curriculum places emphasis on residential, commercial, and industrial construction and maintenance electricity. Along with electrical construction techniques, the ability to design control circuits, repair motors, and troubleshoot electrical equipment is covered in detail.

Mechanical Computer-Aided Drafting and Design Technology This curriculum provides a well-rounded program of manual drafting courses coupled with extensive CADD instruction. The curriculum emphasizes all phases of mechanical design, including drafting fundamentals, structural design, piping, fabrication and welding, machines, jigs and fixtures, springs, gears, and computers.

Contact

Dave McMutrie
Triangle Tech
2000 Liberty Street
Erie, PA 16502
Phone: (814) 453-6016
Fax: (814) 454-2818
E-mail: dmcmutrie@triangle-tech.edu
Web: www.triangle-tech.edu

Programs Eligible for Scholarship	Tuition and Fees	Course Length/Credits	Credential Earned
Architectural CADD Technology	$21,728	16 months/72 credits	Degree
Carpentry and Construction Technology	$21,728	16 months/72 credits	Degree
Maintenance Electricity and Construction	$21,728	16 months/72 credits	Degree
Mechanical CADD Technology	$21,728	16 months/72 credits	Degree

Triangle Tech, Greensburg

About Our Institution

Triangle Tech is an institution that is committed to offering comprehensive training programs designed to help students develop their abilities to receive greater employment opportunities. The school is located in downtown Greensburg. The RHVAC department is located 2 miles north of downtown. Triangle Tech's Business Careers Institute, a satellite location, is equipped to provide business administration training programs.

Special Features

The objectives at Triangle Tech are to provide students with a practical, technical education using classroom lectures and hands-on training and to help students prepare for a meaningful career. Programs are maintained in accordance with the standards of industry, business, and education. Day and evening classes are offered. Curricula include the Associate in Specialized Technology degree and diploma programs. Triangle Tech provides students with a variety of advisory services, including tutorial assistance, career advising, financial aid, and housing.

Financial Aid/Scholarships

Programs are available to qualified students, including Federal Pell Grants, FSEOG, PHEAA, OIG, VA Dependents Educational Assistance Program, Vocational Rehabilitation Program, Federal Perkins Loans, Federal and Direct Stafford Loans, Federal PLUS Loans, Triangle Tech's Installment Payment Plan, Triangle Tech Scholarships, and private scholarships.

Tuition and Fees

Tuition is $5,432 per term. Fees vary according to the program.

Accreditation

Triangle Tech, Greensburg, is accredited by the Accrediting Commission of Career Schools and Colleges of Technology (ACCSCT).

Admissions

Applicants must have graduated from an accredited high school or have earned a GED prior to admission, and they must participate in a personal interview at the school prior to enrollment. Applicants are encouraged to visit Triangle Tech to tour the facilities and meet faculty members and students.

Graduation Requirements

Students must complete all of the required subjects in the prescribed curriculum or have been granted credit under Advanced Standing, attain a cumulative minimum GPA of 2.0 (with no grades of F), meet minimum attendance requirements, and settle all financial obligations to the school.

Program Content

Degree: Architectural CADD Technology; Maintenance Electricity and Construction Technology; Mechanical CADD Technology; Refrigeration, Heating, Ventilation, and Air Conditioning Technology

Diploma: Carpentry and Construction Technology

Program Description

Architectural Computer-Aided Drafting and Design Technology Basic manual drafting courses and extensive CADD instruction are provided.

Carpentry and Construction Technology Residential and light commercial construction of each stage of building development is emphasized.

Maintenance Electricity and Construction Technology Residential/commercial/industrial construction and maintenance electricity are covered.

Mechanical Computer-Aided Drafting and Design Technology Manual drafting courses and extensive CADD instruction are provided.

Refrigeration, Heating, Ventilation, and AC Technology Training is provided on refrigeration, heating, ventilation, air-conditioning systems, and preparing for the EPA certification exam.

Contact

Kurt Stridinger, School Director
Triangle Tech
222 East Pittsburgh Street, Suite A
Greensburg, PA 15601
Phone: (724) 832-1050
Fax: (724) 834-0325
E-mail: kstridinger@triangle-tech.edu
Web: www.triangle-tech.edu

Programs Eligible for Scholarship	Tuition and Fees	Course Length/Credits	Credential Earned
Architectural CADD Technology	$21,728	16 months/72 credits	Degree
Carpentry and Construction Technology	$21,728	16 months/72 credits	Diploma
Maintenance Electricity and Construction	$21,728	16 months/72 credits	Degree
Mechanical CADD Technology	$21,728	16 months/72 credits	Degree
Refrigeration, Heating, Ventilation, and AC Technology	$21,728	16 months/72 credits	Degree

Triangle Tech, Pittsburgh

About Our Institution

Triangle Tech is a well-established, multipurpose institution that is committed to offering comprehensive training programs designed to help students develop their abilities to receive greater employment opportunities. Emphasis is on acquisition of knowledge and skills by students to deal with the rigors of professional life. The school is located on the Northside, minutes from downtown Pittsburgh. Triangle Tech occupies an 8-acre, 51,000-square-foot complex of nine buildings. Classrooms accommodate 15–30 students; labs and shops are generally limited to 20. Triangle Tech's Machine Shop Technologies Institute (MSTI), a satellite location at Pittsburgh's West End (110 South Main Street), is an 18,000-square-foot facility that houses a carpentry shop, classrooms, and lab facilities.

Special Features

The objectives at Triangle Tech are to provide students with a practical, technical education using classroom lectures and extensive hands-on training and to help students prepare for a meaningful career. Programs are maintained in accordance with the standards of industry, business, and education. Day and evening classes are offered. Curricula include the Associate in Specialized Technology degree and diploma programs. Triangle Tech provides students with a variety of advisory services, including tutorial assistance, career advising, financial aid, and housing.

Financial Aid/Scholarships

Programs are available to qualified students, including Federal Pell Grants, FSEOG, PHEAA, OIG, VA Dependents Educational Assistance Program, Vocational Rehabilitation Program, Federal Perkins Loans, Federal and Direct Stafford Loans, Federal PLUS Loans, Triangle Tech's Installment Payment Plan, Triangle Tech Scholarships, and private scholarships.

Tuition and Fees

Tuition is $5,432 per term. Fees vary according to the program.

Accreditation

Triangle Tech, Pittsburgh, is accredited by the Accrediting Commission of Career Schools and Colleges of Technology (ACCSCT).

Admissions

Applicants must have graduated from an accredited high school or have earned a GED prior to admission, and they must participate in a personal interview at the school prior to enrollment. Applicants are encouraged to visit Triangle Tech to tour the facilities and meet faculty members and students.

Graduation Requirements

Students must complete all of the required subjects in the prescribed curriculum or have been granted credit under Advanced Standing, attain a cumulative minimum GPA of 2.0 (with no grades of F), meet minimum attendance requirements, and settle all financial obligations to the school.

Program Content

Degree: Architectural CADD Technology; Carpentry and Construction Technology; Maintenance Electricity and Construction Technology; Mechanical CADD Technology; Refrigeration, Heating, Ventilation, and Air Conditioning Technology; Welding and Fabrication Technology

Program Description

Architectural Computer-Aided Drafting and Design Technology Basic manual drafting courses and extensive CADD instruction are provided.
Carpentry and Construction Technology Residential and light commercial construction of each stage of building development is emphasized.
Maintenance Electricity and Construction Technology Emphasis is on residential, commercial, and industrial construction and maintenance electricity.
Mechanical Computer-Aided Drafting and Design Technology Manual drafting courses and extensive CADD instruction are provided.
Refrigeration, Heating, Ventilation, and AC Technology Training is provided on refrigeration, heating, ventilation, air-conditioning systems, and preparing for the EPA certification exam.
Welding and Fabrication Technology Training is provided on plate and pipe welding and preparing for the AWS and ASME certification exams.

Contact

Stacie Hendrickson, School Director
Triangle Tech
1940 Perrysville Avenue
Pittsburgh, PA 15214
Phone: (412) 359-1000
Fax: (412) 359-1012
E-mail: shendrickson@triangle-tech.edu
Web: www.triangle-tech.edu

Programs Eligible for Scholarship	Tuition and Fees	Course Length/Credits	Credential Earned
Architectural CADD Technology	$21,728	16 months/72 credits	Degree
Carpentry and Construction Technology	$21,728	16 months/72 credits	Degree
Maintenance Electricity and Construction	$21,728	16 months/72 credits	Degree
Mechanical CADD Technology	$21,728	16 months/72 credits	Degree
Refrigeration, Heating, Ventilation, and AC Technology	$21,728	16 months/72 credits	Degree
Welding and Fabrication Technology	$21,728	16 months/72 credits	Degree

Triangle Tech, Sunbury

About Our Institution

Triangle Tech is a well-established, multipurpose institution that is committed to offering comprehensive training programs designed to help students develop their abilities to receive greater employment opportunities. Emphasis is on the acquisition of knowledge and skills by students to deal with the rigors of professional life. The Sunbury school is located on Performance Drive, 1 mile east of Sunbury at the intersection of Routes 890 and 61. Triangle Tech's facilities occupy a total of approximately 10,000 square feet. Classrooms accommodate from 15 to 30 students, and labs and shops are generally limited to a maximum of 20 students. Parking is available on the premises.

Special Features

The objectives at Triangle Tech are to provide students with a practical, technical education using classroom lectures and extensive hands-on training and to help the students prepare for a meaningful career. Programs are maintained in accordance with the standards of industry, business, and education. Day and evening classes are offered. Curricula include Associate in Specialized Technology degree and diploma programs. Triangle Tech provides students with a variety of advisory services, including tutorial assistance, career advising, financial aid, and housing.

Financial Aid/Scholarships

Programs are available to qualified students, including Federal Pell Grants, Federal Supplemental Education Opportunity Grants, Pennsylvania Higher Education Assistance Agency (PHEAA) grant programs, Ohio Instructional Grant Program (OIG), VA Dependents Educational Assistance Program, Vocational Rehabilitation Program, Federal Perkins Loans, Federal and Direct Stafford Student Loans, Federal PLUS Loans, Triangle Tech's Installment Payment Plan (IPP), Triangle Tech scholarships, and private scholarships.

Tuition and Fees

Tuition at Triangle Tech is $5,432 per term. Fees vary according to the program.

Accreditation

Triangle Tech, located in Sunbury, Pennsylvania, is accredited by the Accrediting Commission of Career Schools and Colleges of Technology (ACCSCT).

Admissions

Applicants must have graduated from an accredited high school or have earned a GED certificate prior to admission and must have a personal interview at the school prior to enrollment. Applicants are encouraged to visit Triangle Tech to tour the facilities and meet faculty members and students.

Program Content

Degrees: Carpentry and Construction Technology, Maintenance Electricity and Construction Technology

Program Description

Carpentry and Construction Technology This curriculum provides training in residential and light commercial construction inclusive of each stage of building development. Emphasis is placed on hands-on construction techniques, including site layout, foundations and form work, framing, and interior and exterior finishing techniques.

Maintenance Electricity and Construction Technology This curriculum places emphasis on residential, commercial, and industrial construction and maintenance electricity. Along with electrical construction techniques, the ability to design control circuits, repair motors, and troubleshoot electrical equipment is covered in detail.

Graduation Requirements

Students must complete all of the required subjects in the prescribed curriculum or have been granted credit under Advanced Standing, attain a cumulative minimum GPA of 2.0 (with no grades of F), meet the minimum attendance requirements, and settle all financial obligations to the school.

Contact

Jess Null, School Director
Triangle Tech
RR#1, Box 51, Route 890
Sunbury, PA 17801
Phone: (570) 988-0700
Fax: (570) 988-4641
E-mail: jnull@triangle-tech.edu
Web: www.triangle-tech.edu

Programs Eligible for Scholarship	Tuition and Fees	Course Length/Credit Hours	Credential Earned
Carpentry and Construction Technology	$21,728	16 months/72 credits	Degree
Maintenance Electricity and Construction Technology	$21,728	16 months/72 credits	Degree

Universal Technical Institute, Exton

About Our Institution
Opened in 2004, UTI Exton is a private postsecondary technical school that provides students with the technical education needed for a successful career in the automotive industry. UTI provides full student services, housing assistance, financial aid to those who qualify, campus activities, and both part-time and graduate employment assistance for as long as it is needed.

Special Features
UTI has developed strong industry relations with manufacturers such as Audi, BMW, Ford, International Trucks, Jaguar, Mercedes-Benz, NASCAR, Porsche, Volkswagen, and Volvo. These agreements have created excellent training and career opportunities for UTI automotive and diesel graduates nationwide. From excellent electives for upgraded UTI training to fully paid manufacturer-specific graduate training, UTI's connections and commitment to excellence places its graduates in the driver's seat in a career field that is in demand. Many manufacturers and dealers in addition to those listed above also participate in UTI's TRIP program, wherein these companies agree to pay back the student tuition loans for the graduates they hire.

Financial Aid/Scholarships
At approved campuses, UTI students are eligible to apply for various federal grants and loans. These include Federal Pell Grants, FSEOG, and Federal Student Stafford Loans, Federal Perkins Loans, and PLUS Loans. UTI also sponsors, as well as administers, various scholarship programs and awards more than $500,000 in scholarships annually, including SkillsUSA, CCA, Imagine America, Ford/AAA, FFA, and UTI's National High School Scholarship competition.

Tuition and Fees
Tuition and fees vary by course content. Tuition prices include all workbooks, textbooks, and uniforms; there are no hidden costs. For specific tuition information, students should contact the Exton Admissions Office.

Accreditation
Universal Technical Institute is accredited by the Accrediting Commission of Career Schools and Colleges of Technology (ACCSCT), which is listed by the U.S. Department of Education as a nationally recognized accrediting agency.

Admissions
Each individual applying for admission must be at least 16 years of age, must have a high school diploma or equivalent, and must submit a completed application, a signed enrollment agreement, a registration fee, and any other information that the applicant or the Institute feels is pertinent to admission. Each applicant's qualifications for enrollment are reviewed and either approved, approved with stipulations, or denied.

Graduation Requirements
Students must achieve at least an overall 2.0 cumulative GPA and receive a satisfactory grade in all required courses in their selected program. Graduation must be achieved within a ratio of 1:5 attempted courses in a student's program. Students must have a zero balance in their student account and have attended UTI's Career Development Classes.

Program Content
Automotive Technology; Ford Technology elective available

Program Description
UTI's automotive and diesel programs prepare the graduate to diagnose, troubleshoot, service, and repair foreign and domestic automobiles and diesel engines. Students work in a professional, shoplike environment using the latest engine analyzers, handheld scanners, and other computerized diagnostic equipment. Students learn everything from basic engine systems and computerized engine controls to hydraulics and transport refrigeration. Graduates have all the skills needed to start a challenging and rewarding career in the automotive and diesel repair industries.

Contact
Ken Lewandowski, School Director
750 Pennsylvania Drive
Exton, PA 19341
Phone: (610) 458-5595
         (877) 884-3986 (toll-free)
E-mail: klewandowski@uticorp.com
Web: www.uticorp.com

West Virginia Career Institute, Uniontown, Mount Braddock

About Our Institution
West Virginia Career Institute (WVCI) is a technologically oriented institute located on a spacious 4½-acre campus on the Mount Braddock Road. The campus includes networked computer and medical labs, a resource center, and related facilities. An Internet accessibility expansion project and an additional computer lab were completed in early 1999, with expanded up-to-date computer technology training resources. Registered Medical Assistants extern at local medical facilities as well as Ruby Memorial Hospital in Morgantown.

Special Features
Founded in 1922, the West Virginia Junior College (WVJC) main campus in Morgantown has decades-old relationships with employers in southwestern Pennsylvania and northern West Virginia. Qualified WVCI students can utilize the employer network for college work-study jobs, medical externships, and employment after graduation.

Financial Aid/Scholarships
WVCI participates in all major federal financial aid programs, including grants, scholarships, and loans. WVCI also provides high school senior scholarships, participates in the Pennsylvania vocational rehabilitation program, and is approved for the training of veterans.

Tuition and Fees
Tuition is $2,850 per term. In addition, there is a $25 application fee.

Accreditation
WVCI is accredited by the Accrediting Council for Independent Colleges and Schools (ACICS).

Admissions
Admission requires a high school diploma or a satisfactory GED test score. In addition, WVCI may take into consideration other appropriate factors bearing on the applicant's potential for success.

Graduation Requirements
Students must maintain an overall minimum 2.0 cumulative grade point average, successfully complete all courses required in their program, and meet any specific program requirements listed in the catalog.

Contact
Stephanie Franks, Admissions Representative
West Virginia Career Institute
P.O. Box 278
Mount Braddock, PA 15465
Phone: (724) 437-4600
Fax: (724) 437-6053
Web: www.wvjcmorgantown.edu

Program Content
Executive Office Administration, Information Technology/Accounting, Medical Assistant, Medical Office Administration

Program Description
Computers: WVCI's computer-oriented programs are designed to combine a variety of information technology skills with business training to prepare graduates for a wide variety of occupations.

MOA: Medical Office Assistant/Medical Assistant training is designed to prepare graduates with the clinical and administrative skills necessary to work in hospitals, clinics, doctors' offices, and related fields.

IT/A: This training is designed to combine computer skills with business/accounting to prepare graduates to work in today's accounting and business offices.

EOA: This program is designed to prepare graduates to work in secretarial positions in offices requiring both office and computer skills.

For specific program titles, content, and objectives, students should refer to the school's catalog.

WyoTech, Blairsville

About Our Institution
WyoTech, Blairsville, offers degree and diploma programs in automotive technology and collision/refinishing technology. WyoTech's primary objectives are to impart specific knowledge and skills, to graduate each student, and to help place graduates in their chosen fields. WyoTech, Blairsville, is a branch of WyoTech, Laramie. WyoTech is one of more than eighty schools owned and operated by Corinthian Colleges, Inc.

Special Features
Students receive hands-on learning from certified technicians and work with the most modern equipment in an atmosphere designed to simulate industry conditions.

Financial Aid/Scholarships
WyoTech offers Federal Pell Grants, Federal Supplemental Educational Opportunity Grants (FSEOG), Federal Perkins Loans, Federal Stafford Student Loans (Subsidized and Unsubsidized), and veterans' benefits. Financial aid is available for those who qualify.

Tuition and Fees
Tuition varies based on programs and ranges from $22,000 to $29,300. Books and tools are loaned to students at no additional charge. Tuition includes a $100 deposit that is required at the time of application. In addition, there is a $100 refundable tool desposit.

Accreditation
WyoTech is accredited by the Accrediting Commission of Career Schools and Colleges of Technology (ACCSCT).

Admissions
In order to be admitted to WyoTech, an applicant must submit an application for admission, be interviewed and recommended for admission by a school representative, and provide proof of high school graduation or its equivalent.

Graduation Requirements
To be eligible for graduation, the student must complete each course in the program with a minimum grade of 70 percent.

Enrollment
There are 996 students enrolled.

Contact
Wendy Hauser, Director of Admissions
500 Innovation Drive
Blairsville, PA 15717
Phone: (724) 459-3286
E-mail: whauser@wyotech.com
Web: www.wyotech.com

Programs Eligible for Scholarship	Tuition and Fees	Course Length/Credit Hours	Credential Earned
Auto Tech w/Specialty Auto Fabrication	$29,300	12 months/91 ch	Diploma
Chassis Fab & High Perf Engines w/Auto Tech	$22,000	9 months/71 ch	Diploma
Chassis Fab & High Perf Engines w/Coll Refin Technology	$22,000	9 months/67 ch	Diploma
Collision/Refin & Upholstery Technology	$22,000	9 months/63 ch	Diploma
Collision/Refin Tech w/Specialty Auto Fabrication	$29,300	12 months/87 ch	Diploma
Street Rod & Custom Fab w/Auto Technology	$22,000	9 months/68 ch	Diploma
Street Rod & Custom Fab w/Coll Refin Tech	$22,000	9 months/64 ch	Diploma
Auto Technology & Management	$20,400	9 months/73 ch	AAS
Auto Tech w/Chassis Fab & Management	$27,700	12 months/96 ch	AAS
Auto Tech w/Street Rod & Management	$27,700	12 months/93 ch	AAS
Collision/Refin Technology & Management	$20,400	9 months/69 ch	AAS
Collision/Refin Tech w/Chassis Fab & Management	$27,700	12 months/92 ch	AAS
Collision/Refin Tech w/Street Rod & Management	$27,700	12 months/89 ch	AAS
WyoTech Graduate Online Applied Service Management	$ 5,700	9 months/72 ch	AST

Yorktowne Business Institute, York

About Our Institution

In 1976, Yorktowne Business Institute was incorporated under the Business Corporation Law of the Commonwealth of Pennsylvania. Since its beginning, Yorktowne Business Institute has grown and developed into a high-quality alternative for a four-year college program. The Institute was founded with the intent of providing the business, allied health, and food service communities with highly skilled paraprofessionals. To accomplish this goal in the shortest amount of time, the Yorktowne Business Institute curriculum includes only those subjects that are practical and relevant in nature. Programs and individual courses continually change to meet the needs of the business community. Every year brings new dimensions in Yorktowne Business Institute's development, yet the original goal of training for job skills remains at the core of its endeavors.

Special Features

Yorktowne Business Institute is proud to have five state-of-the-art computer labs, including Internet labs with full student access. In addition, there is a full functioning medical lab for clinical experience. The Institute has recently added a new student-run restaurant to enhance the culinary arts program.

Financial Aid/Scholarships

Federal Pell Grant, FFEL, FSEOG, VA, state grants, and Office of Vocational Rehabilitation programs are offered.

Tuition and Fees

Programs range from $3,787 per term to $6,690 per term. Fees are based on the course of study chosen.

Accreditation

Yorktowne Business Institute is accredited by the Accrediting Council for Independent Colleges and Schools (ACICS).

Admissions

The Institute enrolls persons having a high school diploma or the recognized equivalent of a high school diploma (GED). The admissions decision is based on the results of an admissions test and interest expressed in the student interview. Yorktowne Business Institute welcomes applications from men and women who are interested in acquiring employable business, allied health, or culinary skills. All individuals who follow the requested application procedures and meet the above requirements are considered without discrimination based on race, religion, physical handicap, socioeconomic status, sex, or age.

Program Content

Administrative Assistant; Business Management; Computer Applications Specialist; Computerized Accounting; Culinary Arts; Medical Assistant; Medical Billing Specialist; Medical Secretary; Professional Baking and Pastry

Graduation Requirements

Students must successfully complete all requirements of their chosen course of study and be in good financial standing.

Contact

Deborah Bostic
West 7th Avenue
York, PA 17404
Phone: (717) 846-5000
        (800) 840-1004 (toll-free)
Fax: (717) 848-4584
Web: www.ybi.edu
        www.yorkchef.com

Programs Eligible for Scholarship	Tuition and Fees	Course Length/Credit Hours	Credential Earned
Medical Billing Specialist	$ 7,575	30 weeks/37.5 credits	Diploma
Professional Baking and Pastry	$13,068	45 weeks/36 credits	Diploma
Administrative Assistant	$15,600	60 weeks/75 credits	ASB
Business Management	$15,600	60 weeks/75 credits	ASB
Computer Applications Specialist	$15,600	60 weeks/75 credits	ASB
Computerized Accounting	$15,600	60 weeks/75 credits	ASB
Medical Secretary	$15,600	60 weeks/75 credits	ASB
Culinary Arts	$26,760	60 weeks/75 credits	AST
Medical Assistant	$19,344	75 weeks/93 credits	AST

Columbia College, Caguas

About Our Institution

Columbia College is a private college offering collegiate and noncollegiate levels of study in the fields of business and management, and it also offers programs of study in the allied health fields and in computer science and technology. The institution's main campus is located in Caguas, and a branch campus is located in Yauco on the island of Puerto Rico.

Special Features

Columbia College has an on-site cafeteria, library, and computer labs as well as a spacious outdoor area for studying and activities.

Financial Aid/Scholarships

Columbia College participates in financial aid programs such as Federal Pell Grants, FSEOG, work-study, state grants, and veterans' benefits.

Tuition and Fees

Tuition is $130 per credit. Fees are $75. Lab fees range from $100 to $150.

Accreditation

Columbia College is accredited by the Accrediting Council for Independent Colleges and Schools (ACICS), the Council of Higher Education, and the General Council on Education. It has also attained candidacy status through the Middle States Association of Colleges and Schools.

Admissions

Applicants must have a high school diploma or its equivalent. Some programs of study, however, have additional entrance requirements that must also be met.

Graduation Requirements

All students must meet the required number of courses set forth in their program of study. They must have achieved a general minimum GPA of 2.25 in all baccalaureate studies and 2.0 in all studies under the bachelor's level. Students must also settle all financial obligations with the institution.

Contact

Ana R. Burgos
Columbia College–Caguas Campus
P.O. Box 8517
Caguas, PR 00726
Phone: (787) 743-4041 Ext. 223
Fax: (787) 746-5616
Web: www.columbiaco.edu

Program Content

Graduate: Business Administration

Bachelor's: Business Administration and Nursing Sciences

Associate: Business Administration in Management, Business Administration in Information Systems, Retail Marketing, Secretarial Sciences, Digital Electronics and Microprocessors, and Nursing

Certificates: Basic and Advanced Entrepreneurship

Programs Eligible for Scholarship	Tuition and Fees	Course Length/Credit Hours	Credential Earned
Business Administration	$15,600*	120 credits	Bachelor's
Nursing Sciences	$ 8,840*	68 cr w/Associate	Bachelor's
Business Administration in Information Systems	$10,010*	77 credits	Associate
Business Administration in Management	$10,010*	77 credits	Associate
Digital Electronics and Microprocessors	$ 9,490*	73 credits	Associate
Nursing	$ 9,230*	71 credits	Associate
Retail Marketing	$10,010*	77 credits	Associate
Secretarial Sciences	$ 9,750*	75 credits	Associate

* Subject to the number of terms taken and tuition increases. Extra fees are added for labs taken and general fees.

ICPR Junior College, Arecibo

About Our Institution

ICPR Junior College is a proprietary, nonsectarian, coeducational institution founded in Hato Rey, Puerto Rico, in 1946. Two other campuses are located in Mayagüez (since 1955) and in Arecibo (since 1976). For fifty-six years, the College has served its community well, providing high-quality educational services to students in urban areas. Programs are offered in Spanish at regular and extended hours for those students wishing to work while they go to school or for returning students who want to retrain or sharpen their skills. English courses are required for graduation. The quality of the programs has made ICPR Junior College a popular choice of students. From Arecibo campus, there is an excellent view of the Atlantic Ocean.

Special Features

ICPR Junior College spares no effort to keep up with technological and educational changes that benefit its philosophy and goals. Under the motto Education is Growth, the College has maintained it position in the foreground of education with new programs, modern computer laboratories, and the Information Access and Learning Resources Center (library) with Internet access.

Financial Aid/Scholarships

A Financial Aid Office is available at each campus. Students may receive Federal Pell Grants, FDSLP, Federal Work-Study, FSEOG, LEAP, VA, or WIA assistance if they qualify. In addition, students may apply for state and institutional scholarships.

Accreditation

ICPR Junior College is accredited by the Commission on Higher Education of the Middle States Association of Colleges and Schools.

Admissions

The Institution admits persons with a high school diploma or a recognized equivalent to a high school diploma (GED). ICPR Junior College accepts all students who fulfill the requirements and follow admission procedures, without discrimination based on race, religion, physical handicap, socioeconomic status, sex, or age.

Program Content

Associate Degrees in Business Administration: Accounting, Computer Repair and Maintenance, Computerized Information Systems, Hotel Management, Management and Marketing, Tourism

Associate Degrees in Office Systems: Administrative Assistant, Administrative Clerk, Bilingual Clerk, Medical Billing Services

Contact

Mrs. Elsa N. Baños
Dean Director
20 San Patricio Avenue
P.O. Box 140067
Arecibo, PR 00614-0067
Phone: (787) 878-6000
Fax: (787) 878-7750
E-mail: icprar@icprjc.edu
Web: www.icprjc.edu

Programs Eligible for Scholarship	Tuition and Fees	Course Length/Credit Hours	Credential Earned
Business Administration			
Accounting	$9,595	90 weeks (2 years)	AS
Computer Repair and Maintenance	$9,595	90 weeks (2 years)	AS
Computerized Information Systems	$9,595	90 weeks (2 years)	AS
Hotel Management	$9,595	90 weeks (2 years)	AS
Management and Marketing	$9,595	90 weeks (2 years)	AS
Tourism	$9,595	90 weeks (2 years)	AS
Office Systems			
Administrative Assistant	$9,595	90 weeks (2 years)	AS
Administrative Clerk	$9,595	90 weeks (2 years)	AS
Bilingual Clerk	$9,595	90 weeks (2 years)	AS
Medical Billing Services	$9,595	90 weeks (2 years)	AS

ICPR Junior College, Mayagüez

About Our Institution
ICPR Junior College is a proprietary, nonsectarian, coeducational institution founded in Hato Rey, Puerto Rico, in 1946. Two other campuses are located in Mayagüez (since 1955) and in Arecibo (since 1976). For fifty-eight years the College has served its community well, providing quality educational services to students in urban areas. Programs are offered in Spanish at regular and extended hours for those students wishing to work while they go to school or for returning students who want to retrain or sharpen their skills. English courses are required for graduation. The quality of its programs has made ICPR Junior College a popular choice of students.

Special Features
ICPR Junior College spares no effort to keep up with technological and educational changes that benefit its philosophy and goals. Under the motto Education is Growth, the College has maintained itself in the foreground with new programs, modern computer laboratories, and the Information Access and Learning Resources Center (library) with Internet access.

Financial Aid/Scholarships
A Financial Aid Office is available at each campus. Students may receive Federal Pell Grants, FDSLP, Federal Work-Study, FSEOG, LEAP, VA, or WIA if they qualify. In addition, students may apply for state and institutional scholarships.

Accreditation
ICPR Junior College is accredited by the Commission on Higher Education of the Middle States Association of Colleges and Schools.

Admissions
The institution admits persons with a high school diploma or the recognized equivalent to a high school diploma (GED). ICPR Junior College accepts all students that fulfill the requirements and follow admission procedures, without discrimination based on race, religion, physical handicap, socioeconomic status, sex, or age.

Program Content
Associate Degrees in Business Administration: Accounting, Computer Repair and Maintenance, Computerized Information Systems, Hotel Management, Management and Marketing, Tourism

Associate Degrees in Office Systems: Administrative Assistant, Administrative Clerk, Bilingual Clerk, Medical Billing Services

Contact
Mrs. Dorca Acosta, Dean/Director
80 West McKinley Street
P.O. Box 1108
Mayagüez, PR 00681-1108
Phone: (787) 832-6000
Fax: (787) 833-2237
E-mail: icprma@icprjc.edu
Web: www.icprjc.edu

Programs Eligible for Scholarship	Tuition and Fees	Course Length/Credit Hours	Credential Earned
Business Administration			
Accounting	$9,595	90 weeks (2 years)	AS
Computer Repair and Maintenance	$9,595	90 weeks (2 years)	AS
Computerized Information Systems	$9,595	90 weeks (2 years)	AS
Hotel Management	$9,595	90 weeks (2 years)	AS
Management and Marketing	$9,595	90 weeks (2 years)	AS
Tourism	$9,595	90 weeks (2 years)	AS
Office Systems			
Administrative Assistant	$9,595	90 weeks (2 years)	AS
Administrative Clerk	$9,595	90 weeks (2 years)	AS
Bilingual Clerk	$9,595	90 weeks (2 years)	AS
Medical Billing Services	$9,595	90 weeks (2 years)	AS

ICPR Junior College, San Juan

About Our Institution

ICPR Junior College is a proprietary, nonsectarian, coeducational institution founded in Hato Rey, Puerto Rico, in 1946. Two other campuses are located in Mayagüez (since 1955) and in Arecibo (since 1976). For fifty-eight years, the College has served its community well, providing quality educational services to students in urban areas. Programs are offered in Spanish at regular and extended hours for those students wishing to work while they go to school or for returning students who want to retrain or sharpen their skills. English courses are required for graduation. The quality of the programs has made ICPR Junior College a popular choice of students.

Special Features

ICPR Junior College spares no effort to keep up with technological and educational changes that benefit its philosophy and goals. Under the motto Education is Growth, the College has maintained itself in the foreground with new programs, modern computer laboratories, and the Information Access and Learning Resources Center (library) with Internet access.

Financial Aid/Scholarships

A Financial Aid Office is available at each campus. Students may receive Federal Pell Grants, FDSLP, Federal Work-Study, FSEOG, LEAP, VA, or WIA if they qualify. In addition, students may apply for state and institutional scholarships.

Accreditation

Commission on Higher Education of the Middle States Association of Colleges and Schools.

Admissions

The Institution admits persons with a high school diploma or the recognized equivalent to a high school diploma (GED). ICPR Junior College accepts all students who fulfill the requirements and follow admission procedures, without discrimination based on race, religion, physical handicap, socioeconomic status, sex, or age.

Program Content

Associate Degrees in Business Administration: Accounting, Computer Repair and Maintenance, Computerized Information Systems, Hotel Management, Management and Marketing, Tourism

Associate Degrees in Office Systems: Administrative Assistant, Administrative Clerk, Bilingual Clerk, Medical Billing Services

Contact

Ms. Maria Rivera Cancel, Dean/Director
558 Muñoz Rivera Avenue
P.O. Box 190304
San Juan, PR 00919-0304
Phone: (787) 753-6000
Fax: (787) 763-7249
E-mail: icprhr@icprjc.edu
Web: www.icprjc.edu

Programs Eligible for Scholarship	Tuition and Fees	Course Length/Credit Hours	Credential Earned
Business Administration			
Accounting	$9,595	90 weeks (2 years)	AS
Computer Repair and Maintenance	$9,595	90 weeks (2 years)	AS
Computerized Information Systems	$9,595	90 weeks (2 years)	AS
Hotel Management	$9,595	90 weeks (2 years)	AS
Management and Marketing	$9,595	90 weeks (2 years)	AS
Tourism	$9,595	90 weeks (2 years)	AS
Office Systems			
Administrative Assistant	$9,595	90 weeks (2 years)	AS
Administrative Clerk	$9,595	90 weeks (2 years)	AS
Bilingual Clerk	$9,595	90 weeks (2 years)	AS
Medical Billing Services	$9,595	90 weeks (2 years)	AS

CEI (Career-Ed Institute), Lincoln

About Our Institution
Since 1982, Career-Ed Institute (CEI) has been providing high-quality, postsecondary training in Massachusetts and Rhode Island. In 2001, CEI added two campuses in the Atlanta, Georgia, area and one campus in Henderson (Las Vegas), Nevada. All CEI locations offer focused programs that help its students receive the skills and confidence essential for success in their chosen field of study.

Special Features
CEI is dedicated and committed to providing an industry-standard and quality-driven instructional program, designed for students. The philosophy of CEI extends beyond the teaching of technical proficiencies and practical knowledge. CEI is committed to serving its students with concern and respect.

Financial Aid/Scholarships
CEI maintains a financial aid office at each location. A variety of available programs including grants, loans, scholarships, work-study, veteran's and vocational rehabilitation are available to qualified applicants. CEI provides two full and two half-tuition scholarships at each of its campuses. They are awarded annually to winners of the Scholarship Awards Program. Preliminary scholarship competition is conducted in the form of aptitude testing at each campus location. On the basis of test results, finalists are selected and invited to return for an interview conducted by the Scholarship Committee, which is made up of volunteers who represent business, industry, education, and/or government.

Accreditation
CEI is accredited by the Accrediting Council for Independent Colleges and Schools (ACICS), Washington, D.C., and is approved by a number of respective state and federal organizations. Further information is available from the school catalog.

Admissions
An applicant must satisfy the requirements of possessing a high school diploma or GED. A passing score on the CEI Entrance Examination is necessary for acceptance.

Graduation Requirements
Graduation requirements mandate that a student complete all required courses and achieve an overall grade point average of at least 2.0.

Contact
Executive Director
Career-Ed Institute
Lincoln Mall
622 George Washington Hwy.
Lincoln, RI 02865
Phone: 401-334-2430
Fax: 401-334-5087
E-mail: execdirlincoln@lincolntech.com
Web: www.ceitraining.com

Program Content
Medical Administrative Assistant, Medical Assistant, Network Systems Administrator, PC Support Technician, Therapeutic Massage and Bodywork Technology

New England Institute of Technology, Warwick

About Our Institution
Founded in 1940 as the New England Technical Institute, New England Institute of Technology (NEIT) began as a certificate-granting trade school. The Board of Regents of Rhode Island granted the institution the authority to offer Associate in Science degree programs in 1977, at which time its name was changed to New England Institute of Technology. In 1982, NEIT was accredited by the New England Association of Schools and Colleges (NEASC). In 1984, the state of Rhode Island authorized NEIT to offer Bachelor of Science degree programs. Today, enrollment has grown from 70 students in 1971 to more than 2,700 students. The original educational programs have increased to twenty-eight associate and eight bachelor's degree programs. The campus now has two locations, 2500 Post Road and 100 Access Road, and includes twelve buildings with more than 250,000 square feet of state-of-the-art classroom, laboratory, faculty, and administrative office space.

Special Features
Facilities   The Julian B. Gouse Campus on Post Road consists of nine buildings containing more than 164,000 square feet of offices, classroom and laboratory space, and a Learning Resources Center, a student lounge, and a cafeteria. The nearby Access Road campus comprises more than 36,000 square feet of office, classroom, and laboratory space and a student lounge. In January 2005, the NEIT Center for Automotive Technology opens. It is the largest facility of its kind in New England, featuring 53,000 square feet of shop, laboratory, and classroom space dedicated to automotive technology.

Objective   The mission of NEIT is to provide specialized associate and bachelor's degree programs that prepare students for technical careers. Through technical courses and an integrated liberal arts core, the programs emphasize the relevance of continuous learning to personal and professional growth. Graduates are prepared to enter the workforce or to continue their education. As an extension of the primary mission, NEIT offers the opportunity to pursue technical studies to satisfy personal interests.

Faculty   The faculty members in the technical programs have at least three years' experience in their fields and bring work-based experience into the classrooms and the labs.

Financial Aid/Scholarships
All applicants are required to meet with a financial aid officer. The officer assists the applicant in arranging an individual payment schedule. Financial aid programs available are the Federal Pell Grant; FSEOG; Federal Work-Study Program; the FFEL Stafford Student Loan; Federal PLUS loans; state grants; Citizens Scholarship Foundation of America, Inc.; private scholarships and loans; and institutional scholarships and loans.

Tuition and Fees
$13,200 annually.

Accreditation
New England Institute of Technology is accredited by NEASC. Individually accredited programs are Electronics Engineering Technology, by the Technology Accreditation Commission of the Accreditation Board for Engineering and Technology (ABET); Surgical Technology, by the Commission on Accreditation of Allied Health Education Programs (CAAHEP); Automotive Technology, by the National Automotive Technician's Education Foundation (NATEF); and Occupational Therapy Assistant Technology, by the Accreditation Council for Occupational Therapy Education (ACOTE).

Admissions
A candidate must have a high school diploma, have earned a recognized equivalency diploma, or, if beyond the age of compulsory school atten-

Program Content
Associate in Science Degree Programs: Advanced Automotive Technology, Architectural Building and Engineering Technology, Auto Body Technology, Automotive Technology, Building Construction and Cabinetmaking Technology, Business Software Applications Technology, Clinical Medical Assistant Technology, Computer-Aided Design–Mechanical Technology, Computer and Network Servicing Technology, Computer Information Systems Technology, Computerized Business Management Technology, Electrical Technology, Electronics Engineering Technology, Electronics Technology, Information Technology, Interior Design Technology, Internet Communications Technology, Manufacturing Engineering Technology, Marine Technology, Mechanical Design Technology, Mechanical Engineering Technology, Multimedia and Web Design, Multimedia Technology, Occupational Therapy Assistant Technology, Plumbing/Heating/Gas Technology, Refrigeration/Air Conditioning/Heating/Gas Technology, Surgical Technology, Video and Radio Production Technology.

Bachelor of Science Degree Programs: Architectural Building and Engineering Technology, Business Management Technology, Digital Recording Arts Technology, Electronics Engineering Technology, Information Technology, Interior Design Technology, Mechanical Engineering Technology, Telecommunications Technology.

dance, pass a standardized test at NEIT. Applicants must schedule an interview. Students entering the bachelor's degree program are required to have an associate degree or to be otherwise eligible for junior-level standing and to have a cumulative GPA of at least 2.0.

Graduation Requirements
To graduate, a student must successfully complete all courses listed in the curriculum, have a cumulative grade point average of at least 2.0, complete the last 34 quarter credit hours (associate degree) or 60 quarter credit hours (bachelor's degree) at NEIT and have received credit for the balance of the program, successfully complete TEC 102 through community service (associate degree), and fulfill all financial obligations to the college.

Contact
Michael D. Kwiatkowski
Director of Admissions
2500 Post Road
Warwick, RI 02886
Phone: (401) 739-5000
Fax: (401) 738-5122
E-mail: mickey_k@neit.edu
Web: www.neit.edu

ECPI College of Technology, Charleston

About Our Institution

ECPI College of Technology, an on-campus and online private college, was established in 1966 and operates in Virginia Beach, Newport News, and Northern Virginia, Virginia; Greensboro, Charlotte, and Raleigh, North Carolina; and Greenville and Charleston, South Carolina. The College has an outstanding reputation for providing high-quality graduates to employers, including many Fortune 500 companies.

Special Features

ECPI provides high-quality technical and business education in a student-centered environment. The College prepares graduates to meet the needs of employers by offering classroom and hands-on instruction with industry-standard equipment. A valuable combination of technical and general education courses in degree programs enables graduates to advance quickly and to continue their lifelong pursuit of knowledge. Low faculty-student ratios facilitate instruction, and tutorial assistance is available at no additional charge. Students in degree programs can participate in an externship course that provides valuable experience in an employment setting. Programs are kept up-to-date with the input of advisory boards made up of leading employers and graduates. Job placement assistance is provided to qualified graduates.

Financial Aid/Scholarships

The College maintains a financial aid office providing assistance with a variety of financial aid programs, including Pell Grants, FFEL, Perkins Loans, work-study, FSEOG, VA, NexStep, and scholarships.

Tuition and Fees

Tuition and fees vary by program.

Accreditation

The College is accredited by the Commission on Colleges of the Southern Association of Colleges and Schools to award associate and baccalaureate degrees.

Admissions

A high school diploma or GED certificate is required for admission, in addition to passing an admissions test and meeting academic and financial criteria.

Graduation Requirements

A student must attain a minimum 2.0 cumulative GPA for the entire program, achieve all applicable skill proficiencies, and complete all courses specified for the program.

Program Content

Diplomas: Computer Network Technology, Information Technology/Networking and Security Management, Medical Administration, Medical Assisting

Program Description

The programs at ECPI College of Technology prepare students for a variety of employment opportunities, such as network administration, computer network development, criminal justice technology, network security, electronics, computer technology, and medical assisting.

Program content has been carefully developed by faculty members using recommendations of employers and advisory board members to best meet industry needs.

Contact

Shirley Long, Admissions Director
7410 Northside Drive #G101
Charleston, SC 29420
Phone: (843) 414-0350
Fax: (843) 572-8085
E-mail: slong@ecpi.edu
Web: www.ecpi.edu

Programs Eligible for Scholarship	Course Length/Credit Hours	Credential Earned
Computer Network Technology	52 credits	Diploma
IT/Networking and Security Management	52 credits	Diploma
Medical Administration	48 credits	Diploma
Medical Assisting	41 credits	Diploma

ECPI College of Technology, Greenville

About Our Institution
ECPI College of Technology (an online and on-campus private college) was established in 1966 and operates in Virginia Beach, Newport News, and Northern Virginia, Virginia; Greensboro, Charlotte, and Raleigh, North Carolina; and Greenville and Charleston, South Carolina. The College has an outstanding reputation for providing high-quality graduates to employers, including many Fortune 500 companies.

Special Features
ECPI provides high-quality technical, business, and health science education in a student-centered environment. The College prepares graduates to meet the needs of employers by offering classroom and hands-on instruction with industry-standard equipment. A valuable combination of technical and general education courses in degree programs enables graduates to advance quickly and to continue their lifelong pursuit of knowledge. Low faculty-student ratios facilitate instruction, and tutorial assistance is available at no additional charge. Students in degree programs can participate in an externship course that provides valuable experience in an employment setting. Programs are kept up-to-date with the input of advisory boards made up of leading employers and graduates. Job placement assistance is provided to graduates.

Financial Aid/Scholarships
The College maintains a financial aid office providing a variety of financial aid programs, including Pell Grants, FFEL, Perkins Loans, work-study, FSEOG, VA, and scholarships.

Tuition and Fees
Tuition and fees vary by program.

Accreditation
The College is accredited by the Commission on Colleges of the Southern Association of Colleges and Schools.

Admissions
A high school diploma or GED certificate is required in addition to passing an admissions test and meeting academic and financial criteria.

Graduation Requirements
A student must attain a minimum 2.0 cumulative GPA for the entire program, achieve all applicable skill proficiencies, and complete all courses specified for the program.

Program Content
A.A.S. Degrees: Business Systems Administration, Computer Network Technology, IT/Networking and Security Management, IT/Web Design, Medical Administration

Diplomas: Business Systems Administration, Computer Technology, Medical Administration

Program Description
The programs at ECPI College of Technology prepare students for a variety of employment opportunities, such as network administration, Web site development, software or accounting applications, computer network development, wireless communications, electronics, and computer technology. Program content has been carefully developed by faculty members using recommendations of employers and advisory board members to best meet industry needs.

Contact
Patrick Donivan, Provost
ECPI College of Technology
15 Brendan Way, #120
Greenville, SC 29615-3514
Phone: (864) 288-2828
Fax: (864) 288-2930
E-mail: pdonivan@ecpi.edu
Web: www.ecpi.edu

Programs Eligible for Scholarship	Course Length/Credit Hours	Credential Earned
Business Systems Administration	68 credits	AAS
Business Systems Administration	45 credits	Diploma
Computer Network Technology	74 credits	AAS
Computer Technology	42 credits	Diploma
IT/Networking and Security Management	74 credits	AAS
IT/Web Design	74 credits	AAS
Medical Administration	68 credits	AAS
Medical Administration	48 credits	Diploma

ITT Technical Institute, Greenville

About Our Institution

The company: ITT Technical Institute is owned and operated by ITT Educational Services, Inc. (ITT/ESI), a leading private college system offering technology-influenced programs of study. ITT/ESI operates seventy-seven ITT Technical Institutes in thirty states, providing career-focused degree programs to approximately 39,000 students as of spring 2004. Headquartered in Carmel, Indiana, ITT/ESI has been actively involved in the higher education community in the United States since 1969.

Curricula: Curriculum offerings are designed to help students begin to prepare for career opportunities in fields of technology. Students attend classes year-round, with convenient breaks provided throughout the year. A full-time student course load can have class meetings as often as three days a week and are typically available in the morning, afternoon, and evening, depending on student enrollment. General education courses may be available online. This class schedule offers flexibility to students to pursue part-time employment opportunities.

ITT Technical Institute, Greenville, awards the Associate of Applied Science and the Bachelor of Science degrees.

Special Features

Most ITT Technical Institute programs of study blend traditional academic content with applied learning concepts, with a significant portion devoted to practical study in a lab environment. Advisory committees composed of representatives of local businesses help each ITT Technical Institute periodically review and update curricula, equipment, and laboratory design.

Financial Aid/Scholarships

ITT Technical Institute maintains a Financial Aid Department on campus. The campus is designated as an eligible institution by the U.S. Department of Education for participation in the following programs: Federal Stafford Student Loan Program, Federal PLUS Loan Program, and Federal Work-Study Program. The school also offers nonfederal loans available through Bank One for eligible students.

Tuition and Fees

March 2005 tuition is $386 per credit hour.

Accreditation

The school is accredited by the Accrediting Council for Independent Colleges and Schools (ACICS).

Admissions

For admission requirements, students should contact the school for a catalog.

Graduation Requirements

For graduation requirements, students should contact the school for a catalog.

Program Content

School of Information Technology: Data Communication Systems Technology, Information Systems Security, Information Technology–Computer Network Systems, Information Technology–Software Applications and Programming, Information Technology–Web Development, Software Engineering Technology

School of Electronics Technology: Computer and Electronics Engineering Technology, Electronics and Communications Engineering Technology

School of Drafting and Design: Computer Drafting and Design, Digital Entertainment and Game Design, Information Technology–Multimedia

School of Business: Technical Project Management

Contact

David Murray, Director
ITT Technical Institute
6 Independence Point
Independence Corporate Park
Greenville, SC 29615
Phone: (864) 288-0777
Fax: (864) 297-0930

Draughons Junior College, Clarksville

About Our Institution

In 1879, Professor John F. Draughon, who was living in Adams, Tennessee, in Robertson County, realized the need for business-trained people. With very little capital, a horse, a wagon, and the teaching materials that were available at that time, he founded Draughons Practical Business College on wheels. He made a monthly circuit of towns in north-central Tennessee and southern Kentucky for several years before opening his permanent school in Nashville. After Professor Draughon's death in 1921, many of the business schools he established merged with other schools or went out of business. Draughons Business College in Nashville survived the Depression and World War II and, after the war and under new management, again assumed its role in the community to train qualified business personnel. In 1954, the Accrediting Commission for Business Schools accredited Draughons. In 1978, the Accrediting Commission of the Association of Independent Colleges and Schools accredited Draughons as a junior college of business. Draughons Junior College (DJC) has a rich history of serving the educational needs of students since 1884. Currently, Draughons Junior College has four campuses (Nashville, Clarksville, and Murfreesboro, Tennessee, and Bowling Green, Kentucky) that teach and train individuals in eleven professional careers. Draughons Junior College offers financial aid for those who qualify and is also approved for VA training. In addition, Draughons Junior College offers flexible scheduling and job placement assistance.

Special Features

Through the Lifetime Audit Privilege program, DJC allows a graduate to return at any time, and as many times as desired, to review any lecture course or identical skills course taken previously, without any additional tuition charge, with the exception of the cost of the textbooks and fees associated with that particular course. The College offers a flexible six-day school week, in which classes are offered Monday through Saturday during the day, afternoon, late afternoon, and night sessions. The daily course schedule is divided into four blocks of 3 hours per class. This allows a student to attend school for only four days and carry a full-time course load, allowing for other educational activities as the student desires. Facilities and equipment are available for individual study and practice during class time and/or times that a class is not scheduled during campus operating hours. Faculty members are available by appointment for advisement, counseling, course scheduling, and approved make-up work. Free tutors and tutoring are available on request. In DJC's Be Your Own Success Story program, the curriculum is purposely designed to help students meet their career goals. This can mean immediate employment after fulfilling the requirements for the Associate of Science degree or the diploma programs. Career services include a lifetime placement service at no additional cost as well as assistance in obtaining part-time positions for students who are attending school.

Financial Aid/Scholarships

The College offers Federal Pell Grants, FSEOG, state grants, FFEL, work-study, VA, SEOG, other financial aid opportunities. Draughons Junior College also offers scholarship opportunities, including the CCA Imagine America Scholarship Program.

Tuition and Fees

Prospective students should contact the admissions department for information on tuition and fees.

Accreditation

Draughons Junior College is accredited as a junior college by the Accrediting Council for Independent Colleges and Schools (ACICS). The College is chartered by the state of Tennessee as a privately owned nondenominational, coeducational school of business and is authorized by the Tennessee Higher Education Commission (THEC) and the Kentucky State Board for proprietary education.

Program Content

Diploma: Bookkeeping, Computer Information Technology, E-Commerce Engineer, Health Information Technology, Medical Assisting, Microsoft Support Engineer

Associate of Science Degree: Accounting, Business Management, Computer Information Technology, Computer Network Technology, Criminal Justice, E-Commerce Engineer, Health Information Technology, Legal Assisting, Medical Assisting, Microsoft Support Engineer, Pharmacy Technology

Prospective students should contact the admissions department for current list of programs.

Program Description

The degree program is divided into two independent, yet interrelated, components. The general education requirements provide the basis for a well-rounded education. The program requirements for both a degree and diploma provide skills and knowledge in the specialized area of interest. An exceptional staff of instructors works closely with each student for personal attention. Students have the opportunity for hands-on training, an internship, and job placement assistance. Draughons offers a degree in only two years or a diploma in one year.

Admissions

Regular applicants must have a high school diploma or GED. Students must take an assessment test, with the exception of those who have a composite score of 18 on the ACT or who have transfer credits in English or math. International students should contact the Director of Admissions for admission procedures and application forms.

Graduation Requirements

Each student is responsible for meeting the requirements of the curriculum, as outlined in the catalog, at the time of the first registration in that program.

Contact

Christi Nolder
Director of Admissions
Draughons Junior College
1860 Wilma Rudolph Boulevard
Clarksville, TN 37040
Phone: (931) 552-7600
Fax: (931) 552-3624
E-mail: cnolder@draughons.edu
Web: www.draughons.edu

Draughons Junior College, Nashville

About Our Institution

In 1879, Professor John F. Draughon, who was living in Adams, Tennessee, in Robertson County, realized the need for business-trained people. With very little capital, a horse, a wagon, and the teaching materials that were available at that time, he founded Draughons Practical Business College on wheels. He made a monthly circuit of towns in north-central Tennessee and southern Kentucky for several years before opening his permanent school in Nashville. After Professor Draughon's death in 1921, many of the business schools he established merged with other schools or went out of business. Draughons Business College in Nashville survived the Depression and World War II and, after the war and under new management, again assumed its role in the community to train qualified business personnel. In 1954, the Accrediting Commission for Business Schools accredited Draughons. In 1978, the Accrediting Commission of the Association of Independent Colleges and Schools accredited Draughons as a junior college of business. Draughons Junior College (DJC) has a rich history of serving the educational needs of students since 1884. Currently, Draughons Junior College has four campuses (Nashville, Clarksville, and Murfreesboro, Tennessee, and Bowling Green, Kentucky) that teach and train individuals in eleven professional careers. Draughons Junior College offers financial aid for those who qualify and is also approved for VA training. In addition, Draughons Junior College offers flexible scheduling and job placement assistance.

Special Features

Through the Lifetime Audit Privilege program, DJC allows a graduate to return at any time and, as many times as desired, to review any lecture course or identical skills course taken previously, without any additional tuition charge, with the exception of the cost of the textbooks and fees associated with that particular course. The College offers a flexible six-day school week, in which classes are offered Monday through Saturday during the day, afternoon, late afternoon, and night sessions. The daily course schedule is divided into four blocks of 3 hours per class. This allows a student to attend school for only four days and carry a full-time course load, allowing for other educational activities as the student desires. Facilities and equipment are available for individual study and practice during class time and/or times that a class is not scheduled during campus operating hours. Faculty members are available by appointment for advisement, counseling, course scheduling, and approved make-up work. Free tutors and tutoring are available on request. In DJC's Be Your Own Success Story program, the curriculum is purposely designed to help students meet their career goals. This can mean immediate employment after fulfilling the requirements for the Associate of Science degree or the diploma programs. Career services include a lifetime placement service at no additional cost as well as assistance in obtaining part-time positions for students who are attending school.

Financial Aid/Scholarships

The College offers Federal Pell Grants, FSEOG, state grants, FFEL, work-study, VA, and other financial aid opportunities. Draughons Junior College also offers scholarship opportunities, including the CCA Imagine America Scholarship Program.

Tuition and Fees

Tuition for the Legal Assisting Program is $275 per semester credit hour; for specific courses for the Microsoft Support Engineer Program, $300 per semester credit hour; and for all other programs, $250 per semester credit hour. In addition, there are a $20 application fee (initial semester; for international students, $75), $125 matriculation fee (initial semester), $75 graduation fee (final semester), $75 technology fee (per class), and $5 transcript fee (after one transcript).

Accreditation

Draughons Junior College is accredited as a junior college by the Accrediting Council for Independent Colleges and Schools (ACICS). The College is chartered by the state of Tennessee as a privately owned nondenomina-

Program Content

Diploma: Bookkeeping, Computer Information Technology, E-Commerce Engineer, Health Information Technology, Medical Assisting, Microsoft Support Engineer

Associate of Science Degree: Accounting, Business Management, Computer Information Technology, Computer Network Technology, Criminal Justice, E-Commerce Engineer, Health Information Technology, Legal Assisting, Medical Assisting, Microsoft Support Engineer, Pharmacy Technology

Program Description

The degree program is divided into two independent, yet interrelated, components. The general education requirements provide the basis for a well-rounded education. The program requirements for both a degree and diploma provide skills and knowledge in the specialized area of interest. An exceptional staff of instructors works closely with each student for personal attention. Students have the opportunity for hands-on training, an internship, and job placement assistance. Draughons offers a degree in only two years or a diploma in one year.

tional, coeducational school of business and is authorized by the Tennessee Higher Education Commission (THEC) and the Kentucky State Board for proprietary education.

Admissions

Regular applicants must have a high school diploma or GED certificate. Students must take an assessment test, with the exception of those who have a composite score of at least 18 on the ACT or who have transfer credits in English or math. International students should contact the Director of Admissions for admission procedures and application forms.

Graduation Requirements

Each student is responsible for meeting the requirements of the curriculum, as outlined in the catalog, at the time of the first registration in that program.

Contact

Darrel Hanbury
Director of Admissions
340 Plus Park Boulevard
Nashville, TN 37217
Phone: (615) 361-7555
Fax: (615) 367-2736
E-mail: admissions@draughons.edu
Web: www.draughons.edu

ITT Technical Institute, Knoxville

About Our Institution
The company: ITT Technical Institute is owned and operated by ITT Educational Services, Inc. (ITT/ESI), a leading private college system offering technology-influenced programs of study. ITT/ESI operates seventy-seven ITT Technical Institutes in thirty states, providing career-focused degree programs to approximately 39,000 students as of spring 2004. Headquartered in Carmel, Indiana, ITT/ESI has been actively involved in the higher education community in the United States since 1969.

Curricula: Curriculum offerings are designed to prepare students for career opportunities in fields of technology. Students attend classes year-round, with convenient breaks provided throughout the year. A full-time student course load can have class meetings as often as three days a week and are typically available in the morning, afternoon, and evening, depending on student enrollment. General education courses may be available online. This class schedule offers students the flexibility to pursue part-time employment opportunities.

ITT Technical Institute, Knoxville, awards the Associate of Applied Science and Bachelor of Applied Science degrees.

Special Features
Most ITT Technical Institute programs of study blend traditional academic content with applied learning concepts, with a significant portion devoted to practical study in a lab environment. Advisory committees, made up of representatives of local businesses, help each ITT Technical Institute periodically review and update curricula, equipment, and laboratory design.

Financial Aid/Scholarships
ITT Technical Institute maintains a Financial Aid Department on the campus. The campus is designated as an eligible institution by the U.S. Department of Education for participation in the following programs: Federal Stafford Student Loan Program, Federal PLUS Loan Program, and Federal Work-Study Program. The school also offers nonfederal loans through Bank One for eligible students.

Tuition and Fees
March 2005 tuition is $386 per credit hour.

Accreditation
The Institute is accredited by the Accrediting Council for Independent Colleges and Schools (ACICS).

Admissions
For admission requirements, prospective students should consult the school catalog.

Graduation Requirements
For graduation requirements, prospective students should consult the school catalog.

Program Content
School of Information Technology: Information Systems Security, Data Communications Systems Technology, Information Technology–Computer Network Systems, Information Technology–Software Applications and Programming, Information Technology–Web Development

School of Electronics Technology: Electronics and Communications Engineering Technology, Computer and Electronics Engineering Technology

School of Drafting and Design: Computer Drafting and Design, Information Technology–Multimedia

School of Business: Technical Project Management

Contact
Dave Reynolds, Director
ITT Technical Institute
10208 Technology Drive
Knoxville, TN 37932
Phone: (865) 671-2801
Fax: (865) 671-2811

ITT Technical Institute, Memphis

About Our Institution
The company: ITT Technical Institute is owned and operated by ITT Educational Services, Inc. (ITT/ESI), a leading private college system offering technology-influenced programs of study. ITT/ESI operates seventy-seven ITT Technical Institutes in thirty states, providing career-focused degree programs to approximately 39,000 students as of spring 2004. Headquartered in Carmel, Indiana, ITT/ESI has been actively involved in the higher education community in the United States since 1969.

Curricula: Curriculum offerings are designed to prepare students for career opportunities in fields of technology. Students attend classes year-round, with convenient breaks provided throughout the year. A full-time student course load can have class meetings as often as three days a week and are typically available in the morning, afternoon, and evening, depending on student enrollment. General education courses may be available online. This class schedule offers students the flexibility to pursue part-time employment opportunities.

ITT Technical Institute, Memphis, awards the Associate in Applied Science and Bachelor of Applied Science degrees.

Special Features
Most ITT Technical Institute programs of study blend traditional academic content with applied learning concepts, with a significant portion devoted to practical study in a lab environment. Advisory committees, made up of representatives of local businesses, help each ITT Technical Institute periodically review and update curricula, equipment, and laboratory design.

Financial Aid/Scholarships
ITT Technical Institute maintains a Financial Aid Department on the campus. The campus is designated as an eligible institution by the U.S. Department of Education for participation in the following programs: Federal Stafford Student Loan Program, Federal PLUS Loan Program, and Federal Work-Study Program. The school also offers nonfederal loans through Bank One for eligible students.

Tuition and Fees
March 2005 tuition is $386 per credit hour.

Accreditation
The Institute is accredited by the Accrediting Council for Independent Colleges and Schools (ACICS).

Admissions
For admission requirements, prospective students should consult the school catalog.

Graduation Requirements
For graduation requirements, prospective students should consult the school catalog.

Program Content
School of Information Technology: Information Systems Security, Data Communications Systems Technology, Software Engineering Technology, Information Technology–Computer Network Systems, Information Technology–Software Applications and Programming, Information Technology–Web Development

School of Electronics Technology: Electronics and Communications Engineering Technology, Computer and Electronics Engineering Technology

School of Drafting and Design: Digital Entertainment and Game Design, Computer Drafting and Design, Information Technology–Multimedia Option

School of Business: Business Administration, Business Accounting Technology, Technical Project Management

School of Criminal Justice: Criminal Justice

Contact
Brenda Nash, Director
ITT Technical Institute
1255 Lynnfield Road
Memphis, TN 38119
Phone: (901) 762-0556
Fax: (901) 762-0566

ITT Technical Institute, Nashville

About Our Institution

ITT Technical Institute is owned and operated by ITT Educational Services, Inc. (ITT/ESI), a leading private college system offering technology-influenced programs of study. ITT/ESI operates seventy-seven ITT Technical Institutes in thirty states, which provide career-focused degree programs to approximately 39,000 students as of spring 2004. Headquartered in Carmel, Indiana, ITT/ESI has been actively involved in the higher education community in the United States since 1969.

Curriculum offerings are designed to help prepare students for career opportunities in fields of technology. Students attend classes year-round, with convenient breaks provided throughout the year. A student with a full-time course load can have class meetings as often as three days a week. Classes are typically available in the morning, afternoon, and evening, depending on student enrollment. General education courses may be available online. This class schedule offers students the flexibility to pursue part-time employment opportunities.

The degrees awarded are the Associate of Applied Science and the Bachelor of Applied Science.

Special Features

Most ITT Technical Institute programs of study blend traditional academic content with applied learning concepts, with a significant portion devoted to practical study in a lab environment. Advisory committees, made up of representatives of local businesses, help each ITT Technical Institute periodically review and update curricula, equipment, and laboratory design.

Financial Aid/Scholarships

ITT Technical Institute maintains a Financial Aid Department on campus. The campus is designated as an eligible institution by the U.S. Department of Education for participation in the following programs: Federal Pell Grant, Federal Stafford Student Loan, Federal PLUS Loan, and Federal Work-Study. The school also offers nonfederal loans made available through Bank One for eligible students.

Tuition and Fees

March 2004 tuition was $364 per credit hour.

Admissions

For admissions requirements, students should contact the school for a catalog.

Graduation Requirements

For graduation requirements, students should contact the school for a catalog.

Contact

Jim Coakley, Director
ITT Technical Institute
2845 Elm Hill Pike
Nashville, TN 37214
Phone: (615) 889-8700
Fax: (615) 872-7209

Nashville Auto-Diesel College, Nashville

About Our Institution

Nashville Auto-Diesel College (NADC) strives to meet its mission of excellence by offering the comprehensive training and education necessary to prepare graduates for initiating a lifelong career in their chosen technical area. NADC also serves those individuals who wish to upgrade and/or broaden their technical and academic knowledge and skills. The College is committed to providing high-quality education and experience and helping to instill within its students the qualities that employers need, such as accuracy, precision, respect, and dependability. At NADC, students not only receive hands-on training in the auto-diesel, collision and refinishing repair, or high-performance industries—they also build a solid foundation for a successful and rewarding future. NADC staff members are committed to offering a positive training atmosphere to its more than 1,300 full-time undergraduates, who come from all fifty states and sixty-two countries. NADC's 13-acre campus has computers for general students use with Internet access available.

Financial Aid/Scholarships

Financial help is available for qualified students. Using federal programs, NADC offers financial aid plans that covers tuition, including Federal Pell Grants, Federal Supplemental Educational Opportunity Grants (FSEOG), Federal Work-Study Programs (FWS), Federal Stafford Student Loans (Subsidized and Unsubsidized), Federal Parent Loan (PLUS) Programs, Vocational Rehabilitiation, and veteran's benefits.

Accreditation

NADC is accredited by the Accrediting Commission of Career Schools and Colleges of Technology (ACCSCT).

Admissions

An applicant must possess a high school transcript and must complete an interview.

Contact

Executive Director
Nashville Auto-Diesel College
1524 Gallatin Road
Nashville, TN 37206
Phone: (615) 226-3990
       (800) 228-NADC (toll-free)
Fax: (615) 262-8466
E-mail: execdirnashville@lincolntech.com
Web: www.nadcedu.com

Program Content

Associate of Applied Science Degree Programs: Automotive and Diesel Technology, Collision Repair and Refinishing

National College of Business and Technology, Knoxville

About Our Institution

National College of Business and Technology was established in 1886. The Knoxville campus joined the National family in 2003. National College of Business and Technology's curriculum is specific and concentrates on essential professional skills that lead toward employment in a specific field. Programs are planned to offer the most effective methods in technology, business organization, and management while consistently meeting the demands of the modern world. The College offers courses that cover a broad range of majors, including accounting, management, and office technology as well as other fields. Students can complete programs in as little as one year or less.

Special Features

A major strength of National College of Business and Technology is its ability to quickly adjust the curriculum to respond to changes in the employment needs of business and industry and to meet the career interests of students. Community representatives, serving as a Campus Advisory Board, provide current and timely advice relative to the employment needs of business, technical, and government organizations.

The Career Center is available to assist with the entire job search process. Specialized staff members are available to help students prepare a resume and cover letter and to interview effectively. They assist the student throughout the employment search.

Students who wish to demonstrate their current skill level in selected areas may take an Advanced Placement evaluation. If successful, the student receives credit for that particular course and may shorten his or her program accordingly.

Financial Aid/Scholarships

National College of Business and Technology makes available an extensive program of financial assistance that includes Federal Stafford Loans, Federal Plus Loans, Federal Perkins Loans, Federal Pell Grants, Federal Supplemental Educational Opportunity Grants, Workforce Development Grants, and the Business Partnership Grant as well as several scholarship opportunities.

Scholarships are available not only to students who performed well in secondary school but also to current students who excel while pursuing their particular program of study.

Tuition and Fees

Tuition is $170 per credit hour. National College of Business and Technology is among the least expensive private colleges in its area. Students should check the catalog for the current application, student activities, and graduation fees.

Accreditation

National College of Business and Technology is accredited by the Accrediting Council for Independent Colleges and Schools (ACICS); individual programs may have programmatic accreditation.

Program Content

Accounting, Business Management, Medical Assisting

Program Description

The programs offered at National College of Business and Technology give the graduate the training that is needed to take the first step into an entry position as well as the background necessary to grow professionally in that field.

Admission

A prospective student must have a high school diploma or GED certificate and submit an application for admission together with the application fee.

Graduation Requirements

In order to be eligible for graduation, the student must complete all courses outlined in the program and complete the required number of credit hours. To graduate from any program, at least a 2.0 overall grade point average must be achieved.

Contact

Admissions Department
8415 Kingston Pike
Knoxville, TN 37919
Phone: (865) 539-2011
Fax: (865) 824-2778

Programs Eligible for Scholarship	Tuition and Fees	Course Length/Credit Hours	Credential Earned
All related program areas	$16,320	96	AS

National College of Business and Technology, Nashville

About Our Institution

National College of Business and Technology was established in 1886. The Nashville campus, which is located on a major thoroughfare southeast of the downtown area, opened its new location in July 2001. National College of Business and Technology's curriculum is specific and concentrates on essential professional skills that lead toward employment in a specific field. Programs are planned to offer the most effective methods in technology, business organization, and management, which consistently meet the demands of the modern world. The College offers courses that cover a broad range of majors, including business management, medical assisting studies, computer applications technology, and office technology as well as other fields. Students can complete programs in as little as one year or less.

Special Features

A major strength of National College of Business and Technology is its ability to quickly adjust the curriculum to changes in the employment needs of business and industry and to meet the career interest of students. Community representatives, serving as a Campus Advisory Board, provide current and timely advice relative to the employment needs of business, technical, and government organizations.

The Career Center is available to assist with the entire job-search process. Specialized staff members are available to help students to prepare a resume, cover letter, and interview effectively. Staff members assist the student throughout the employment search.

Students who wish to demonstrate their current skill level in selected areas may take an Advanced Placement evaluation. If successful, the student receives credit for that particular course and may shorten their program accordingly.

Financial Aid/Scholarships

National College of Business and Technology makes available an extensive program of financial assistance that includes Federal Stafford Loans, Federal Plus Loans, Federal Perkins Loans, the Federal Pell Grant, the Federal Supplemental Educational Opportunity Grant, the Workforce Development Grant, and the Business Partnership Grant, as well as several scholarship opportunities. Scholarships are available not only to students who performed well during their secondary education, but also to current students who excel while pursuing their particular program of study.

Tuition and Fees

Tuition is $170 per credit hour. National College of Business and Technology is among the least expensive private colleges in its area. Students should check the catalog for current application, student activities, or graduation fees.

Program Content

Associate of Science: Business Management, Computer Applications Technology, Medical Assisting, Office Administration

Program Description

The programs offered at National College of Business and Technology give the graduate the training that is needed to take the first step into an entry position as well as the background necessary to grow professionally in that field.

Accreditation

The College is accredited by the Accrediting Council for Independent Colleges and Schools (ACICS). In addition, individual programs such as medical assisting studies may have programmatic accreditation.

Admission

A prospective student must have a high school diploma or GED and complete an application for admission accompanied with the application fee.

Graduation Requirements

In order to be eligible for graduation, students must complete all courses studies in the program and earn the required number of credit hours. In addition, a minimum 2.0 overall grade point average must be maintained.

Contact

Admissions Department
3748 Nolensville Pike
Nashville, TN 37211
Phone: (615) 333-3344
Fax: (615) 333-3429

Programs Eligible for Scholarship	Tuition and Fees	Course Length/Credit Hours	Credential Earned
All related program areas	$16,320	96 credit hours	AS

Remington College, Memphis Campus, Memphis

About Our Institution
Remington College was founded in 1985 in an effort to meet the growing need for computer-related education and training in the technical and business fields. To date, Remington College consists of twenty-two campuses across the United States. The Memphis campus was opened in 1987. Remington College teaches a "career first" curriculum that allows students to concentrate on learning the necessary technical skills early in their program and building on these skills as they progress toward graduation.

Special Features
Remington College is uncompromisingly dedicated to high-quality, college-level, career-oriented education. Its primary objectives are to graduate a high percentage of students who enter career programs and to help them achieve relevant employment at the highest possible starting salary. Remington College's hands-on training is the foundation of its educational structure. Practical application in well-equipped labs, coupled with theoretical reinforcement in the classroom, allows students to acquire substantial knowledge in their chosen career field. When appropriate, externships are used to provide the student with real-world experience.

Financial Aid/Scholarships
Remington College–Memphis Campus maintains a Financial Services Office on campus, providing a variety of grants, loans, scholarships, work-study, veterans' aid, and vocational rehabilitation programs.

Tuition and Fees
Students should contact the campus for current tuition pricing. Textbook cost and lab fees are included in tuition. A $50 registration fee is required for all programs.

Accreditation
Remington College–Memphis programs are accredited by the Accrediting Commission of Career Schools and Colleges of Technology (ACCSCT).

Admissions
A high school diploma or GED, along with an acceptance interview, is used to determine a candidate's potential for success. An entrance test is also required.

Graduation Requirements
In order to graduate, a student must maintain an overall cumulative grade point average of 2.0 or better for the entire program and complete all courses specified in the program catalog.

Contact
Dr. Lori May, Campus President
2731 Nonconnah Boulevard
Memphis, TN 38132
Phone: (901) 345-1000
Fax: (901) 396-8310
Web: www.remingtoncollege.edu

Program Content
Business Information Systems, Computer Networking Technology, Criminal Justice, Electronics and Computer Technology, Medical Assisting, Operations Management, Pharmacy Technician

Program Description
Business Information Systems: Comprehensive curriculum includes an extensive study of the application of computer hardware and software to business functions, such as accounting, document processing, Internet research, and Web site development and marketing.

Computer Networking Technology: Comprehensive training in computer networking. Graduates can install, configure, maintain, and troubleshoot local area and wide area networks and Intranets that use DOS and Windows network operating systems.

Criminal Justice: Prepares students for entry into or advancement within any one of the many career fields in the criminal justice system.

Electronics and Computer Technology: Theoretical and practical understanding of basic electricity and electronics, semiconductors, digital gates in IC chips, and basic circuit construction of audio amplifiers, radios, switching circuits, and timing circuits.

Medical Assisting: Prepares students to work in administrative and clinical positions.

Operations Management: Prepares students for entry-level management career positions in business and industry and develops decision-making and problem-solving skills needed for professional administrators.

Pharmacy Technician: Prepares students for entry-level positions in pharmacies. The curriculum includes pharmacology, dosage calculation, pharmacy technology, and drug-supply maintenance.

Remington College, Nashville Campus, Nashville

About Our Institution

Remington College was founded in 1985 in an effort to meet the growing need for computer-related education and training in the technical and business fields. To date, Remington College consists of twenty campuses across the United States. Remington College teaches a "career first" curriculum that allows students to concentrate on learning the necessary technical skills early in their program and build on them as they progress toward graduation.

Special Features

Remington College is uncompromisingly dedicated to high-quality, college-level, career-oriented education. Its primary objectives are to graduate a high percentage of students who enter the career programs and to help them achieve relevant employment at the highest possible starting salary. Remington College's hands-on training is the foundation of its educational structure. Practical application in well-equipped labs, coupled with theoretical reinforcement in the classroom, allows students to acquire substantial knowledge in their chosen career field. When appropriate, externships are used to provide the student with real-world experience.

Financial Aid/Scholarships

Remington College–Nashville Campus maintains a Financial Services Office on the campus, providing a variety of grants, loans, scholarships, work-study, veterans' aid, and vocational rehabilitation programs.

Tuition and Fees

Students should contact the campus for current tuition pricing. Textbook cost and lab fees are included in tuition. A $50 registration fee is required for all programs.

Accreditation

Remington College–Nashville's programs are accredited by the Accrediting Commission of Career Schools and Colleges of Technology (ACCSCT).

Admissions

A high school diploma or GED, along with an acceptance interview, is used to determine a candidate's potential for success. At some sites, an entrance test is also required.

Graduation Requirements

In order to graduate, a student must maintain a minimum 2.0 cumulative grade point average for the entire program and complete all courses specified in the program catalog.

Contact

Joseph Rossberger, Campus President
441 Donnelson Pike, Suite 150
Nashville, TN 37214
Phone: (615) 889-5520
Fax: (615) 889-5528
Web: www.remingtoncollege.edu

Program Description

Business Information Systems (A.A.S.): The program provides comprehensive training in the operation and effective use of various computer systems and software in DOS and Windows environments.

Computer Information Systems (A.A.S.): This program provides comprehensive training on PCs and networks, with an emphasis on developing programming skills.

Computer Networking Technology (A.A.S.): Upon completion of the program, each student is able to install, configure, maintain, and troubleshoot local area networks, wide area networks, and intranets that use DOS and Windows-based network operating systems.

Electronics Engineering Technology (A.A.S.): The curriculum explores both the fundamentals and advanced theory in electronics, integrated circuits, microprocessors, and computer technology.

Internet Information Systems (A.A.S.): This program provides training in Java, HTML, Visual Basic, Apache server, and principles of Web design and e-commerce.

Medical Assisting (Diploma): The objective of the program is to provide graduates with the skills and knowledge that will enable them to qualify for entry-level positons as medical assistants.

Operations Management (B.A.S.): The program is designed to prepare students for business and industry.

Vatterott College, Memphis

About Our Institution
All Vatterott College programs are based on a proven successful formula of specialized, technology-focused, hands-on training in the fastest-growing industries. The College was founded in 1969 and now serves nearly 9,000 students per year at sixteen Midwestern campuses. The Memphis campus offers programs focused on the information technology and technical trade industries.

Special Features
Vatterott College's hands-on training method of instruction equips students with the specific skills that are desired by local employers. Courses are geared to the student's field of study. Classes are available in both morning and evening schedules.

Financial Aid/Scholarships
Vatterott College participates in a variety of financial aid and scholarship programs. The College's Make-the-Grade scholarship offers tuition credit to qualifying students based on high school grades. Vatterott College also participates in the Imagine America scholarship program. High school seniors are eligible to apply. Students should contact the campus Financial Aid Representative for specific information.

Tuition and Fees
The campus Admissions Representatives can provide complete tuition information.

Accreditation
Vatterott College is nationally accredited by the Accrediting Commission of Career Schools and Colleges of Technology.

Admissions
The application process includes a personal interview and entrance evaluation. A high school diploma or GED is required.

Graduation Requirements
Students must show satisfactory progress by maintaining a minimum grade of 70 percent and an 80 percent attendance record.

Contact
Office of Admissions
Vatterott College
6152 Macon Road
Memphis, TN 38134
Phone: (901) 761-5730
Fax: (901) 763-2897
E-mail: memphis@vatterott-college.edu
Web: www.vatterott-college.edu

(branch of main campus in St. Ann, MO)

Program Content
Associate Degree Programs: Computer-Aided Drafting Technology; Computer Systems and Network Technology; Heating, Air-Conditioning, and Refrigeration Technology

Diploma Programs: Computer-Aided Drafting; Computer Technology; Electrical Mechanic; Heating, Air-Conditioning, and Refrigeration Mechanic; Medical Assistant

West Tennessee Business College, Jackson

About Our Institution

For more than 100 years, West Tennessee Business College (WTBC) has been providing high-quality education to students seeking relevant career training. The programs are designed to provide students with the skills necessary to meet the demands of today's fast-paced, competitive job market. West Tennessee Business College's faculty consists of professionals with extensive experience in each specialized field. A supportive classroom environment allows for personalized instruction and individual attention. The curriculum is career-oriented and is enhanced by externships.

Special Features

The computer program at WTBC ensures that business students receive the competitive edge needed for current employment opportunities. Computer labs are equipped with current software applications and modern equipment, and computer stations are networked and Internet accessible. The College has a modern medical laboratory and twenty-station cosmetology clinic. From the time a student enrolls at WTBC, the primary emphasis is on employability. All graduates are eligible for placement assistance.

Financial Aid/Scholarships

The financial aid officers help prospective students identify the different types of federal funds available. WTBC offers scholarships.

Tuition and Fees

Tuition ranges from $4420 to $14,940, depending upon the program selected. The tuition cost includes all textbooks and instructional material.

Admissions

An entrance exam and a regular high school diploma or GED, along with a personal interview, is used to determine entrance eligibility.

Accreditation

WTBC is accredited by ACICS. The medical assisting program has a dual accreditation through ACICS and CAAHEP.

Graduation Requirements

To meet the requirements for receiving a diploma, students must complete the required courses in a program within the contracted time frame with an 80 GPA or above and pay all College financial obligations.

Contact

Ann Record, Director of Admissions
West Tennessee Business College
1186 Highway 45 Bypass
Jackson, TN 38302
Phone: (731) 668-7240
        (800) 737-9822 (toll-free)
Fax: (731) 668-3824
E-mail: arecord@wtbc.com
Web: www.wtbc.com

Program Content

AAS Degree Programs: Administrative Assistant, Medical Administrative Assistant

Diploma Programs: Accounting Clerk, Administrative Assistant, Cosmetology, Esthetician, General Office Clerk, Manicure, Medical Assisting, Medical Office Specialist

Program Description

Administrative Assistant (AAS): Leading to the occupational Associate of Applied Science degree, the Administrative Assistant program prepares students to perform administrative tasks for a modern office, to assume responsibilities, to make decisions, and to work independently.

Medical Administrative Assistant (AAS): Leading to the occupational Associate of Applied Science degree, the Medical Administrative Assistant program prepares students to perform administrative tasks in a physician's office, hospital, or other medical facility.

Administrative Assistant: The vocational objective of this program is to prepare students for office and administrative support positions in a wide variety of office environments.

Cosmetology: Cosmetologists cut, style, color, and perm hair, and advise patrons on how to care for their hair.

Esthetician: Estheticians provide nonmedical care of the human skin to keep it healthy and beautiful.

General Office Clerk: Instruction in records management, office machines, and using microcomputers as a business tool prepares the student for an entry-level position.

Manicure: Provides instruction in the care and improvement of the hands and nails and the composition of the cosmetics used; develops the student's ability to give a good manicure and apply sculptured nails.

Medical Assisting: Medical Assisting provides a current knowledge base, task requirements, and skill development procedures that the medical assistant needs to qualify for entry-level employment in a physician's office, a medical clinic, or any appropriate health-care facility.

Medical Office Specialist: A medical office specialist must possess human relations skills and be proficient in performing administrative duties in a medical office. Transcription and insurance coding are emphasized.

Programs Eligible for Scholarship	Tuition and Fees	Course Length/Credit Hours	Credential Earned
Administrative Assistant	$13,860	77 semester credits	AAS
Medical Administrative Assistant	$14,940	83 semester credits	AAS
Administrative Assistant	$ 9,975	37 semester credits	Diploma
Cosmetology	$ 8,950	1,500 clock hours	Diploma
Esthetician	$ 5,850	750 clock hours	Diploma
General Office Clerk	$ 6,975	24 semester credits	Diploma
Manicure	$ 4,850	600 clock hours	Diploma
Medical Assisting	$ 9,975	37 semester credits	Diploma
Medical Office Specialist	$ 8,975	30 semester credits	Diploma

American InterContinental University, Houston

About Our Institution

American InterContinental University (AIU) was founded in Europe in 1970 on the premise that universities should transcend the bounds of the traditional, theoretical approach to education by providing students with a curriculum that prepares them for successful, productive careers. For many years, AIU has offered this innovative approach to education at its campuses in London, established in 1973; Atlanta Buckhead, 1977; Los Angeles, 1982; Dubai, United Arab Emirates, 1995; Atlanta Dunwoody, 1998; and Fort Lauderdale, 1998. In 2003, the Houston campus was established.

In 2001, Career Education Corporation (CEC) acquired the University. CEC is one of North America's largest providers of private, postsecondary education.

Special Features

Houston, America's fourth-largest city, is a center of international business and high technology and home to many of the largest corporate names in the country. The campus is located in the Westchase District—Houston's distinctive business community that is home to more than 1,500 businesses. This area has excellent public transportation and highway access (just off the Sam Houston Tollway between I-10 and Westpark).

The campus is a 68,000-square-foot freestanding, air-conditioned building at the corner of Richmond Avenue and Briar Park. It has ample gated parking. It houses classrooms, labs, team rooms, the Library/Learning Center, the Technology Center, the bookstore, lounges, and an administrative/clerical area. The facility is equipped for wireless laptop use in all student areas.

AIU's accelerated programs provide a fast-track approach for students to their career path. The exclusive team-based learning model is one that provides students with skills that can mean success in today's business world.

Students attending the University may opt to study at another AIU campus in the U.S. or participate in an exciting study-abroad program to London or Dubai for a term or an academic year.

Upon graduation, AIU's full-time Career Placement Department works individually with students to get them started on their path to success. This assistance is available throughout a graduate's career.

Financial Aid/Scholarships

The campus offers a variety of scholarships, grants, loans, and part-time work-study employment to help defray the cost of education. Financial aid is available to those who qualify. University-administered federal funding includes Federal Supplemental Educational Opportunity Grants and Federal Work-Study Program awards. Additional federal funding includes Federal Pell Grants, Federal Subsidized and Unsubsidized Stafford Student Loans, and Federal PLUS loans.

The University participates in the Career Colleges and Schools of Texas Scholarship Program and the Imagine America Scholarship Program. AIU also directly administers its own scholarship program. For scholarship information, students should contact the campus or consult the campus catalog. Other sources of aid to students may include vocational rehabilitation firms, veterans' benefits, and private scholarships.

Accreditation

American InterContinental University–Houston Campus is accredited by the Commission on Colleges of the Southern Association of Colleges and Schools (1866 Southern Lane, Decatur, Georgia, 20022-4097; telephone: 404-679-4501) to award associate, bachelor's, and master's degrees.

Admissions

A major difference between AIU and many other colleges and universities is the culturally diverse student population. AIU students come from many different countries and backgrounds and bring a wide range of viewpoints, special interests, and talents to enrich the learning community. Selection of students is based on an individual assessment of each applicant. There are four start dates for new students each year.

Graduation Requirements

In order to qualify for graduation, students must have a minimum GPA of 2.0 for undergraduate programs or 3.0 for graduate programs, clearance by the Student Affairs Department that all program requirements have been met, clearance by the Financial Aid Department for all financial aid requirements, clearance by the Student Accounts Department for all financial obligations, and clearance by the Learning Resource Center and Housing for all financial obligations (if applicable).

Contact

Greg Garrett
Director of Admissions
American InterContinental University–
  Houston Campus
9999 Richmond Avenue
Houston, TX 77042
Phone: (866) 792-5500 (toll-free)
Fax: (832) 201-3637
E-mail: ggarrett@aiuhouston.com
Web: www.aiuhouston.com

Programs Eligible for Scholarship	Tuition and Fees	Course Length/Credit Hours	Credential Earned
Business Administration	$26,675	5 ten-week quarters/90 cr	AA
Business Administration (Enterprise Management)	$55,275	10 ten-week quarters/180 cr	BBA
Information Technology	$55,275	10 ten-week quarters/180 cr	BIT
Visual Communications	$55,275	10 ten-week quarters/180 cr	BFA
Business Administration	$20,950	4 ten-week quarters/48 cr	MBA

The Art Institute of Dallas, Dallas

About Our Institution
The Art Institute of Dallas began in 1964 as the Dallas Fashion Merchandising College. In 1978, it changed location and became the Fashion and Art Institute of Dallas. Following another relocation, the Fashion and Art Institute of Dallas expanded its programs in fashion merchandising and interior design and added a commercial art program. In 1979, the Institute was approved to grant an Associate of Applied Arts degree in each of its programs. In October 1984, the Institute became a member of the Design Schools. Continuing with the same student body, faculty members, and curriculum, the school then changed its name to the Art Institute of Dallas. In September 1988, the school moved to its present facilities at Two NorthPark East, 8080 Park Lane, in North Dallas.

Special Features
The Art Institute of Dallas is a private college for creative professional studies, based upon focused and balanced curricula. The college prepares students for careers in design, media arts, and culinary arts by providing an intensive educational environment and by responding to changing technology in order to meet the opportunities of a global economy. The school measures its success by its ability to provide a learning-centered climate fostered by dedicated and knowledgeable faculty members, prepare students for career entry and professional growth in their respective fields, and maintain a systematic approach to institutional improvement through assessment and long-range planning.

Financial Aid/Scholarships
Federal Work-Study, Federal Unsubsidized Stafford Student Loan, Federal Subsidized Stafford Student Loan, Federal PLUS Loan, Federal Pell Grant, Federal SEOG, and other financial assistance programs are offered. Students should call Student Financial Services (SFS) for details.

Tuition and Fees
Tuition is $369 per credit hour. There is an application fee, student activity fee, graduation fee, and culinary lab fee.

Accreditation
The Art Institute of Dallas is accredited by the Commission on Colleges of the Southern Association of Colleges and Schools to award the Associate of Applied Arts, Associate of Applied Sciences, and Bachelor of Fine Arts degrees. The culinary arts and the art of cooking programs are accredited by the American Culinary Federation (ACF). The interior design program awards a Bachelor of Fine Arts degree in interior design and is accredited by the Foundation for Interior Design Education Research (FIDER) using the Professional Standards 2002.

Admissions
High school graduation or a General Educational Development (GED) credential is a prerequisite for admission. All Institute applicants are evaluated on the basis of their previous education, their background, and their stated or demonstrated interest in their creative professional studies. Portfolios may also be requested for evaluation. Applicants who have taken the SAT or ACT are encouraged to submit scores to the Admissions Office for evaluation.

Program Content
Advertising Design, Animation Art and Design, Culinary Arts, Digital Media Production, Fashion Design, Graphic Design, Interactive Media Design, Interior Design, Restaurant and Catering Management

Graduation Requirements
A student must receive a passing grade or credit for all required course work, achieve a minimum CGPA of 2.0, and satisfy all financial obligations with the Institute in order to participate in the graduation ceremony and to receive a diploma and/or academic transcript from the Institute.

Contact
Maggie Crum
Director of Admissions
The Art Institute of Dallas
Two NorthPark East
8080 Park Lane, Suite 100
Dallas, TX 75231
Phone: (214) 692-8080
        (800) 275-4243 (toll-free)
Fax: (214) 750-9460
E-mail: crispm@aii.edu
Web: www.aid.edu

Programs Eligible for Scholarship	Tuition and Fees	Course Length/Credit Hours	Credential Earned
Advertising Design	$73,288	132 weeks/180 credit hours	BFA
Animation Art and Design	$43,567	77 weeks/105 credit hours	AAA
Culinary Arts	$43,626	77 weeks/105 credit hours	AAS
Digital Media Production	$73,936	132 weeks/180 credit hours	BFA
Fashion Design	$42,195	77 weeks/105 credit hours	AAA
Graphic Design	$43,294	77 weeks/105 credit hours	AAA
Graphic Design	$73,000	132 weeks/180 credit hours	BFA
Interactive Media Design	$73,252	132 weeks/180 credit hours	BFA
Interior Design	$71,597	132 weeks/180 credit hours	BFA
Restaurant and Catering Management	$43,626	77 weeks/105 credit hours	AAS
Video Production	$41,897	77 weeks/105 credit hours	AAS

The Art Institute of Houston, Houston

About Our Institution

The mission of the Art Institute of Houston is to provide a quality collaborative academic environment for individuals seeking creative careers through higher education. Baccalaureate and associate degrees are competency based, incorporating traditional liberal arts and hands-on instruction. Faculty members use learning-centered methodology that prepares students for career entry in the design, visual, and culinary arts fields as well as for continued professional development.

Financial Aid/Scholarships

Financial assistance is available for those who qualify. Scholarships are available.

Tuition and Fees

Tuition was $363 per credit hour, effective May 1, 2004, for those who enrolled after April 27, 2004. Kits are optional, although books for general education and supplies must be purchased at the student's expense.

Accreditation

The Art Institute of Houston is accredited by the Commission on Colleges of the Southern Association of Colleges and Schools (1866 Southern Lane, Decatur, Georgia 30033-4097, telephone: (404) 679-4501) to award the Associate of Applied Science degree and the Bachelor of Fine Arts degree. It is authorized by the Texas Higher Education Coordinating Board to award the Associate of Applied Arts degree and the Bachelor of Fine Arts degree. The Institute is approved for the training of veterans and eligible veterans' dependents and is authorized under federal law to enroll nonimmigrant alien students. The Associate of Applied Science degree offered by the culinary arts program is also accredited by the American Culinary Federation (ACF).

Admissions

Prospective students must have a high school diploma or a GED and meet all admission requirements.

Graduation Requirements

Students must receive a passing grade or credit for all course work, achieve a minimum cumulative GPA of 2.0, satisfy the requirements of the Texas Success Initiative, complete a clearance process, and satisfy all financial obligations to the Art Institute of Houston.

Program Content

Animation Art and Design, Culinary Arts, Graphic Design, Interactive Media Design, Interior Design, Media Arts and Animation, Multimedia and Web Design, Restaurant and Catering Management, Culinary Arts Diploma Program

Contact

Aaron McCardell III
Director of Admissions
The Art Institute of Houston
1900 Yorktown
Houston, TX 77056
Phone: (800) 275-4244 (toll-free)
Fax: (713) 966-2797
E-mail: mccardea@aii.edu

Programs Eligible for Scholarship	Course Length/Credit Hours	Credential Earned
Animation Art and Design	8 quarters/108 credit hours	AAS
Culinary Arts	7 quarters/108 credit hours	AAS
Graphic Design	7 quarters/105 credit hours	AAS
Graphic Design	12 quarters/180 credit hours	BFA
Interactive Media Design	7 quarters/105 credit hours	AAS
Interior Design	12 quarters/180 credit hours	BFA
Media Arts and Animation	12 quarters/180 credit hours	BFA
Multimedia and Web Design	7 quarters/105 credit hours	AAS
Restaurant and Catering Management	6 quarters/90 credit hours	AAS
Culinary Arts Diploma Program	5 quarters/61 credit hours	Diploma

ATI–Career Training Center, Dallas

About Our Institution

The ATI chain of schools was founded in the late 1960s and was acquired in 1985 by ATI Enterprises, Inc. ATI–Career Training Center was opened in 1986 and is now located in a beautiful 36,000-square-foot building in a business park near I-35 (Stemmons Freeway) in northwest Dallas. The school consists of twenty-nine classrooms and labs, a resource center, and administrative offices. An additional 12,000-square-foot facility is located nearby and contains eight classrooms and a spa.

Special Features

ATI provides job placement assistance, tutoring, and student advising. The ATI Student Association gives students the opportunity to help others by participating in activities that benefit nonprofit organizations such as Ronald McDonald House.

Financial Aid/Scholarships

ATI participates in a variety of financial assistance programs, including Pell, FFEL, PDSLP, Perkins, Federal Work-Study, SEOG, and VA.

Accreditation

ATI is accredited by the Accrediting Commission of Career Schools and Colleges of Technology (ACCSCT).

Admissions

The school admits regular student applicants having a high school diploma or the recognized equivalent (GED). Persons desiring to apply to ATI should contact the school directly.

Enrollment

There are 800 students enrolled.

Contact

Debra Chapman, Director of Admissions
ATI–Career Training Center
10003 Technology Boulevard, West
Dallas, TX 75220
Phone: (214) 902-8191
Fax: (214) 358-7500
Web: www.aticareertraining.com

Program Content

Diploma: Business Administration Technology, Computer-Assisted Design, Dental Assisting, Electronic Technology, Graphic Design, Massage Therapy, Medical Assisting, Network Administration

Associate of Applied Science: Respiratory Therapy Technology

Programs Eligible for Scholarship	Tuition and Fees	Course Length/Credit Hours	Credential Earned
Business Administration Technology	$14,846	48 weeks/70 quarter credit hours	Diploma
Computer-Assisted Design	$13,246	48 weeks/64.5 quarter credit hours	Diploma
Dental Assisting	$11,995	48 weeks/58 quarter credit hours	Diploma
Electronic Technology	$18,035	60 weeks/95 quarter credit hours	Diploma
Graphic Design	$16,570	60 weeks/90.5 quarter credit hours	Diploma
Massage Therapy	$ 3,715	12 weeks/20 quarter credit hours	Diploma
Medical Assisting	$11,995	48 weeks/58 quarter credit hours	Diploma
Network Administration	$19,995	60 weeks/90.5 quarter credit hours	Diploma
Respiratory Therapy Technology	$31,243	96 weeks/96 quarter credit hours	AAS

ATI–Career Training Center, Hurst

About Our Institution
ATI–Career Training Center is accredited by ACCSCT and has been in operation since 1986. It is part of a group of technical schools whose primary objectives are to prepare their graduates for careers and, at the same time, develop their students' motivation so they will continue to progress in their chosen fields.

Special Features
ATI provides job placement assistance, tutoring, and advising for students. The ATI Student Association gives students an opportunity to help others by participating in activities that benefit nonprofit community service organizations.

Financial Aid/Scholarships
Pell Grant, Federal Family Educational Loan Program (FFEL), Federal Direct Student Loan Program (FDSLP), Federal Perkins Loan Program, work-study, Supplemental Educational Opportunity Grant (SEOG), Veterans Benefits (VA), Texas Rehabilitation Commission (TRC), and scholarships.

Accreditation
ATI–Career Training Center is accredited by the Accrediting Commission of Career Schools and Colleges of Technology (ACCSCT).

Admissions
The school admits as regular students applicants having a high school diploma or the recognized equivalent (GED). Applicants must be capable of performing the tasks involved at the school and in the resultant employment in their chosen career field.

Graduation Requirements
Students must pass each course in their program of study, maintain a minimum of 2.0 GPA, and complete all program requirements within 1.5 times the program length.

Contact
Joe P. Mehlmann, Executive Director
ATI–Career Training Center
6351 Grapevine Highway, #100
North Richland Hills, TX 76180
Phone: (817) 284-1141
Fax: (817) 284-2107

Program Content
Business Administration Technology (BAT), Dental Assisting (DA), Electronic Technology (ET), Graphic Design (GD), Medical Assisting (MA), Network Administration (NA)

Program Description
The BAT program is intended for persons who desire a career working with computers (PCs) in an office environment.

The DA and MA programs include an externship and prepare graduates for careers in the allied health fields in private practices, clinics, and hospitals.

The ET program is intended for persons who desire a career in electronics and computer technology.

The GD program is intended for persons who desire a career in visual communications.

The NA program is intended for persons who desire a career in network administration and computer support areas.

Programs Eligible for Scholarship	Tuition and Fees	Course Length/Credit Hours	Credential Earned
Business Administration Technology	$14,114	960 cl hrs/70 quarter ch	Diploma
Dental Assisting/Medical Assisting	$11,327	960 cl hrs/58 quarter ch	Diploma
Electronic Technology	$17,100	1,200 cl hrs/95 quarter ch	Diploma
Graphic Design	$15,655	1,200 cl hrs/86 quarter ch	Diploma
Network Administration	$17,975	1,200 cl hrs/90 quarter ch	Diploma

ATI Technical Training Center, Dallas

About Our Institution
ATI Technical Training Center was founded in the late 1960s and is conveniently located near Dallas Love Field, public transportation, and major freeways. The campus consists of two buildings totaling approximately 60,000 square feet of space. These buildings house classrooms, administrative offices, and four separate lab areas. The philosophy is to help people achieve a better lifestyle by preparing them, through education, for a career of their choice. Graduates are prepared for entry-level positions in their chosen field.

Financial Aid/Scholarships
ATI Technical Training Center maintains a business office staffed by professionals and has a variety of funding programs available to students. The following programs are available: Federal Pell Grant Program, Federal Family Education Loan Program, Federal Direct Student Loan Program, Federal Perkins Loan Program, Federal Supplemental Educational Opportunity Grant Program, Federal Work-Study Program, Job Training Partnership Act, Texas Rehabilitation Commission, and Veterans Administration educational benefits.

Tuition and Fees
Total program costs range from $12,000 to $14,780; tools, uniforms, books, and tuition are included.

Accreditation
ATI Technical Training Center is accredited by the Accrediting Commission of Career Schools and Colleges of Technology (ACCSCT).

Admissions
The school admits applicants with a high school diploma or the recognized equivalent (G.E.D.). Applicants must be capable of performing the tasks involved at the school and in the resultant employment in their chosen field. Prior to being accepted, an applicant must be interviewed by an admissions officer, complete an enrollment agreement, pay a registration fee, and submit any other information that may be required to determine qualifications.

Graduation Requirements
To graduate and be awarded a diploma, students must pass each course in their program of study, have an overall grade point average of 2.0, attend no fewer than 80 percent of their scheduled program hours, and complete all program requirements within a period of time that does not exceed 1.5 times the program length.

Program Content
Air Conditioning, Heating, and Refrigeration (ACHR); Automotive Service Technician (AST); Combination Welding (CW)

Program Description
ACHR: This program prepares graduates for entry-level positions as service technicians in the residential and commercial air conditioning, heating, and refrigeration field.

AST: This program prepares graduates for entry-level positions in the automotive service industry.

CW: This program prepares graduates for entry-level welding positions in a variety of industries.

Contact
Darrell Testerman, Executive Director
ATI Technical Training Center
6627 Maple Avenue
Dallas, TX 75235
Phone: (214) 352-2222
Fax: (214) 350-3951
Web: www.aticareertraining.com

Programs Eligible for Scholarship	Tuition and Fees	Course Length/Credit Hours	Credential Earned
Air Conditioning, Heating, and Refrigeration	$14,400	48 weeks/960 clock hours/ 72 quarter credit hours	Diploma
Automotive Service Technician	$14,780	48 weeks/960 clock hours/ 72 quarter credit hours	Diploma
Combination Welding	$12,000	36 weeks/720 clock hours/ 54 quarter credit hours	Diploma

Court Reporting Institute of Dallas, Dallas

About Our Institution

Since 1978, the Court Reporting Institute of Dallas (CRID) has produced the finest court reporters in the nation. The school is presently the largest and most successful court reporting school in Texas. An outstanding faculty, coupled with state-of-the-art training facilities, make CRID an ideal place to become a court reporter.

Special Features

CRID's program is one of the few programs in Texas to offer an Associate of Applied Science degree in court reporting. CRID's student services department assists students with part-time jobs, housing, and day-care needs. CRID also maintains an articulation agreement with Northwood University and the University of Phoenix, allowing students to earn their bachelor's degree.

Financial Aid/Scholarships

CRID is accredited by the Accrediting Council for Independent Colleges and Schools (ACICS), and financial aid is available to those who qualify. CRID participates in the following federal aid programs: Pell Grants, SEOG Grants, Stafford Loans, Direct Loans, Plus Loans, and Perkins Loans. CRID participates in the Imagine America Scholarship Program and the Career Colleges and Schools of Texas Scholarship Program.

Tuition and Fees

Tuition for day school is $2,220 per quarter. Night school tuition is $1,500 per quarter. The school's registration fee is $100.

Admissions

Students must possess a high school diploma or GED to be accepted into the program.

Contact

Eric S. Juhlin, Director
Pamela K. Bennett, Academic Dean
Debra Smith-Armstrong, Director of Admissions
Linda Craft, Director of Financial Aid
8585 North Stemmons Freeway
Suite 200 North Tower
Dallas, TX 75247
Phone: (800) 880-9722 (toll-free)
Fax: (214) 631-0143
E-mail: darmstrong@crid.com
Web: www.crid.com

Program Content

Court Reporting

Programs Eligible for Scholarship	Tuition and Fees	Course Length/Credit Hours	Credential Earned
Court Reporting	$2,220/quarter (day)/ $1,500/quarter (night)	108 quarter credit hours	AAS

Court Reporting Institute of Houston, Houston

About Our Institution
The Court Reporting Institute of Houston (CRIH) is the newest location of the Court Reporting Institute of Dallas (CRID), which since 1978 has produced the finest court reporters in the nation. An outstanding faculty, coupled with state-of-the-art training facilities, make CRIH an ideal place to become a court reporter.

Special Features
CRIH's program is one of the few programs in Texas to offer an Associate of Applied Science degree in court reporting. CRIH's student services department assists students with part-time jobs, housing, and day-care needs. CRIH also maintains an articulation agreement with Northwood University and the University of Phoenix, allowing students to earn their bachelor's degree.

Financial Aid/Scholarships
CRIH is accredited by the Accrediting Council for Independent Colleges and Schools (ACICS), and financial aid is available to those who qualify. CRIH participates in the following federal aid programs: Pell Grants, FSEOG, Stafford Student Loans, Direct Loans, Plus Loans, and Perkins Loans. CRIH participates in the Imagine America Scholarship Program and the Career Colleges and Schools of Texas Scholarship Program.

Tuition and Fees
Tuition for day school is $2,220 per quarter. Night school tuition is $1,500 per quarter. The school's registration fee is $100.

Admissions
Students must possess a high school diploma or GED certificate to be accepted into the program.

Contact
Cindy Smith, Director
13101 Northwest Freeway
Suite 100
Houston, TX 77040
Phone: (866) 996-8300 (toll-free)
Fax: (713) 996-8360
E-mail: csmith@crid.com
Web: www.crid.com

Program Content
Court Reporting

Programs Eligible for Scholarship	Tuition and Fees	Course Length/Credit Hours	Credential Earned
Court Reporting	$2,220/quarter (day)/ $1,500/quarter (night)	108 quarter credit hours	AAS

Everest College, Dallas

About Our Institution

Everest College, Dallas, offers Associate of Applied Science degrees in business administration, criminal justice, and medical assisting. Everest College, Dallas, is one of more than eighty schools in the United States that are owned and operated by Corinthian Colleges, Inc. (CCi). The Everest College campus in Dallas opened in February 2003 and is a branch campus of Western Business College in Portland, Oregon.

Special Features

The College is close to public transportation, including the Mockingbird DART station. All classrooms are spacious, modern, and comfortable. In addition, the campus is wheelchair accessible.

Financial Aid/Scholarships

Pell, FSL, FPLUS, FSEOG, VA, VOC REHAB, and WIA are offered. High school and other scholarships are available for those who qualify.

Tuition and Fees

Tuition is charged per credit hour and does not include books. A $25 registration fee is assessed per quarter.

Accreditation

Everest College, Dallas, is accredited by the Accrediting Council for Independent Colleges and Schools (ACICS).

Admissions

Candidates must have a high school diploma or the equivalent. Successful completion of the assessment examination is a prerequisite for admission. Applicants who have completed one academic year of credits at another postsecondary institution are not required to complete the test.

Graduation Requirements

Students are required to earn a minimum cumulative grade point average of 2.0 in their major. Students must also meet specific program requirements.

Enrollment

Eight hundred seventy-five students are enrolled.

Contact

Jae Lee, Director of Admissions
Everest College, Dallas
6060 North Central Expressway, Suite 101
Dallas, TX 75206
Phone: (214) 234-4850
Fax: (214) 696-6208
E-mail: jlee@cci.edu
Web: www.everest-college.com

Program Content

Business Administration, Criminal Justice, Medical Assisting, Medical Insurance Billing/Coding

Programs Eligible for Scholarship	Tuition and Fees	Course Length/Credit Hours	Credential Earned
Business Administration	$24/credit hour	96 credit hours	AAS
Criminal Justice	$245/credit hour	96 credit hours	AAS
Medical Assisting	$245/credit hour	97 credit hours	AAS
Medical Insurance Billing/Coding	$8465 with books	35 credit hours	Diploma

Everest College, Mid Cities, Arlington

About Our Institution

Everest College–Mid Cities in suburban Dallas, Texas, offers Associate of Applied Science degrees in business administration, criminal justice, and medical assisting as well as a diploma in medical insurance billing/coding. Everest College opened its doors in June 2003. Located in Arlington's Six Flags Mall, the campus represents one of more than eighty schools owned and operated by Corinthian Colleges, Inc., in the United States. Everest College–Mid Cities is a branch campus of Rochester Business Institute in Rochester, New York.

Special Features

The campus is located on the second floor of the Six Flags Shopping Mall. The 25,000-square-foot campus is conveniently located alongside state highway 360, and just south of Interstate 30. Within 1 mile of the campus are Ameriquest Field in Arlington and Six Flags over Texas.

Financial Aid/Scholarships

Pell, FSL, PLUS, FSEOG, and VA financial aid programs as well as high school and other scholarships are available for those who qualify.

Tuition and Fees

Per credit hours are assessed based on the number of classes taken per quarter. A $25 registration fee is assessed per quarter.

Accreditation

Everest College–Mid Cities is accredited by the Accrediting Council for Independent Colleges and Schools (ACICS).

Admissions

Candidates must have a high school diploma or equivalent. Successful completion of the COMPASS assessment examination is a prerequisite for admission. Applicants with previous college experience who have completed 24 semester credit hours or 36 quarter credit hours with a CGPA of 2.0 or better are not required to complete the test.

Graduation Requirements

Students are required to earn a minimum cumulative grade point average of 2.0 and must have successfully completed all required credits within the maximum timeframe attempted.

Enrollment

There are 530 students enrolled.

Program Content

Business Administration, Criminal Justice, Medical Assisting, Medical Insurance Billing/Coding

Contact

Bruce J. Schlee, Director of Admissions
2801 East Division Street, Ste. 250
Arlington, TX 76011
Phone: (817) 652-7790
Fax: (817) 649-6033
E-mail: bschlee@cci.edu
Web: www.everest-college.com

Programs Eligible for Scholarship	Tuition and Fees	Course Length/Credit Hours	Credential Earned
Business Administration	$206/credit hour	96 credit hours	AAS
Criminal Justice	$206/credit hour	96 credit hours	AAS
Medical Assisting	$206/credit hour	97 credit hours	AAS
Medical Insurance Billing/Coding	$8,065	35 credit hours	Diploma

ITT Technical Institute, Arlington

About Our Institution
The company: ITT Technical Institute is owned and operated by ITT Educational Services, Inc. (ITT/ESI), a leading private college system offering technology-influenced programs of study. ITT/ESI operates seventy-seven ITT Technical Institutes in thirty states, providing career-focused degree programs to approximately 39,000 students as of spring 2004. Headquartered in Carmel, Indiana, ITT/ESI has been actively involved in the higher education community in the United States since 1969.

Curricula: Curriculum offerings are designed to help students begin to prepare for career opportunities in fields of technology. Students attend classes year-round, with convenient breaks provided throughout the year. A full-time student course load can have class meetings as often as three days a week and are typically available in the morning, afternoon, and evening, depending on student enrollment. General education courses may be available online. This class schedule offers flexibility to students to pursue part-time employment opportunities.

ITT Technical Institute, Arlington, awards the Associate of Applied Science degree.

Special Features
Most ITT Technical Institute programs of study blend traditional academic content with applied learning concepts, with a significant portion devoted to practical study in a lab environment. Advisory committees composed of representatives of local businesses help each ITT Technical Institute periodically review and update curricula, equipment, and laboratory design.

Financial Aid/Scholarships
ITT Technical Institute maintains a Financial Aid Department on campus. The campus is designated as an eligible institution by the U.S. Department of Education for participation in the following programs: Federal Stafford Student Loan Program, Federal PLUS Loan Program, and Federal Work-Study Program. The school also offers nonfederal loans available through Bank One for eligible students.

Tuition and Fees
March 2005 tuition is $386 per credit hour.

Accreditation
The school is accredited by the Accrediting Council for Independent Colleges and Schools (ACICS).

Admissions
For admission requirements, students should contact the school for a catalog.

Graduation Requirements
For graduation requirements, students should contact the school for a catalog.

Program Content
School of Information Technology: Information Technology–Computer Network Systems, Information Technology–Software Applications and Programming, Information Technology–Web Development

School of Electronics Technology: Computer and Electronics Engineering Technology

School of Drafting and Design: Computer Drafting and Design, Information Technology–Multimedia Option

Contact
Paulette Gallerson, Director
ITT Technical Institute
551 Ryan Plaza Drive
Arlington, TX 76011
Phone: (817) 794-5100
Fax: (817) 275-8446

ITT Technical Institute, Austin

About Our Institution
The company: ITT Technical Institute is owned and operated by ITT Educational Services, Inc. (ITT/ESI), a leading private college system offering technology-influenced programs of study. ITT/ESI operates seventy-seven ITT Technical Institutes in thirty states, providing career-focused degree programs to approximately 39,000 students as of spring 2004. Headquartered in Carmel, Indiana, ITT/ESI has been actively involved in the higher education community in the United States since 1969.

Curricula: Curriculum offerings are designed to help students begin to prepare for career opportunities in fields of technology. Students attend classes year-round, with convenient breaks provided throughout the year. A full-time student course load can have class meetings as often as three days a week and are typically available in the morning, afternoon, and evening, depending on student enrollment. General education courses may be available online. This class schedule offers flexibility to students to pursue part-time employment opportunities.

ITT Technical Institute, Indianapolis, awards the Associate of Applied Science degree.

Special Features
Most ITT Technical Institute programs of study blend traditional academic content with applied learning concepts, with a significant portion devoted to practical study in a lab environment. Advisory committees composed of representatives of local businesses help each ITT Technical Institute periodically review and update curricula, equipment, and laboratory design.

Financial Aid/Scholarships
ITT Technical Institute maintains a Financial Aid Department on campus. The campus is designated as an eligible institution by the U.S. Department of Education for participation in the following programs: Federal Stafford Student Loan Program, Federal PLUS Loan Program, and Federal Work-Study Program. The school also offers nonfederal loans available through Bank One for eligible students.

Tuition and Fees
March 2005 tuition is $386 per credit hour.

Accreditation
The school is accredited by the Accrediting Council for Independent Colleges and Schools (ACICS).

Admissions
For admission requirements, students should contact the school for a catalog.

Graduation Requirements
For graduation requirements, students should contact the school for a catalog.

Program Content
School of Information Technology: Information Technology–Computer Network Systems, Information Technology–Software Applications and Programming, Information Technology–Web Development

School of Electronics Technology: Computer and Electronics Engineering Technology

School of Drafting and Design: Computer Drafting and Design, Information Technology–Multimedia Option

Contact
Barbara Anthony, Director
ITT Technical Institute
6330 Highway 290 E
Austin, TX 78723
Phone: (512) 467-6800
Fax: (512) 467-6677

ITT Technical Institute, Houston North, Houston

About Our Institution
The company: ITT Technical Institute is owned and operated by ITT Educational Services, Inc. (ITT/ESI), a leading private college system offering technology-influenced programs of study. ITT/ESI operates seventy-seven ITT Technical Institutes in thirty states, providing career-focused degree programs to approximately 39,000 students as of spring 2004. Headquartered in Carmel, Indiana, ITT/ESI has been actively involved in the higher education community in the United States since 1969.

Curricula: Curriculum offerings are designed to help students begin to prepare for career opportunities in fields of technology. Students attend classes year-round, with convenient breaks provided throughout the year. A full-time student course load can have class meetings as often as three days a week and are typically available in the morning, afternoon, and evening, depending on student enrollment. General education courses may be available online. This class schedule offers flexibility to students to pursue part-time employment opportunities.

ITT Technical Institute, Houston North, awards the Associate of Applied Science degree.

Special Features
Most ITT Technical Institute programs of study blend traditional academic content with applied learning concepts, with a significant portion devoted to practical study in a lab environment. Advisory committees composed of representatives of local businesses help each ITT Technical Institute periodically review and update curricula, equipment, and laboratory design.

Financial Aid/Scholarships
ITT Technical Institute maintains a Financial Aid Department on campus. The campus is designated as an eligible institution by the U.S. Department of Education for participation in the following programs: Federal Stafford Student Loan Program, Federal PLUS Loan Program, and Federal Work-Study Program. The school also offers nonfederal loans available through Bank One for eligible students.

Tuition and Fees
March 2005 tuition is $386 per credit hour.

Accreditation
The school is accredited by the Accrediting Council for Independent Colleges and Schools (ACICS).

Admissions
For admission requirements, students should contact the school for a catalog.

Graduation Requirements
For graduation requirements, students should contact the school for a catalog.

Program Content
School of Information Technology: Information Technology–Computer Network Systems, Information Technology–Software Applications and Programming, Information Technology–Web Development

School of Electronics Technology: Computer and Electronics Engineering Technology

School of Drafting and Design: Computer Drafting and Design, Information Technology–Multimedia Option

Contact
David Champlin, Director
ITT Technical Institute
15621 Blue Ash Drive
Houston, TX 77090
Phone: (281) 873-0512
Fax: (281) 873-0518

ITT Technical Institute, Houston South, Houston

About Our Institution

ITT Technical Institute is owned and operated by ITT Educational Services, Inc. (ITT/ESI), a leading private college system focused on technology-oriented programs of study. ITT/ESI operates seventy-eight ITT Technical Institutes in twenty-nine states, providing career-focused degree programs to approximately 38,000 students as of March 2004. Headquartered in Indianapolis, Indiana, ITT/ESI has been actively involved in the higher education community in the United States since 1969. Curriculum offerings are designed to help students begin to prepare for career opportunities in fields of technology. Students attend classes year-round, with convenient breaks provided throughout the year. Classes are generally scheduled three days a week and are typically available in the morning, afternoon, and evening, depending on student enrollment. This class schedule gives students the flexibility to pursue part-time employment opportunities.

Special Features

Most ITT Technical Institute programs of study blend traditional academic content with applied learning concepts, with a significant portion devoted to practical study in a lab environment. Advisory committees, made up of representatives of local businesses and employers for each program of study, help each ITT Technical Institute periodically assess and update curricula, equipment, and laboratory design. Assistance with housing and part-time employment is available.

The Institute awards the Associate of Applied Science.

Financial Aid/Scholarships

ITT Technical Institute maintains a Finance Department on the campus. The campus is designated as an eligible institution by the U.S. Department of Education for participation in the following programs: Federal Pell Grant, Federal Stafford Student Loan, Federal PLUS Loan, and Federal Work-Study. The school also offers nonfederal loans through Bank One for eligible students.

Tuition and Fees

September 2004 tuition is $368 per credit hour.

Accreditation

Accrediting Council for Independent Colleges and Schools (ACICS).

Admissions

Admission requirements include having obtained a high school diploma or GED, passing an admission test (subject to being waived—students should refer to the school catalog), and passing, as determined at the school's discretion, an interview with the Registrar of the school, if the Registrar requests an interview with the student.

Graduation Requirements

For graduation requirements, students should consult the school catalog.

Program Content

Computer Drafting and Design, Computer and Electronics Engineering Technology, Information Technology: Computer Network Systems, Multimedia, Software Applications and Programming, Web Development

Program Description

The Computer Drafting and Design program combines computer-aided drafting with conventional methods of graphic communication to solve drafting and basic design-related problems.

The Computer and Electronics Engineering Technology program prepares students for careers in entry-level positions in modern electronics and computer technology.

The IT Computer Network Systems program helps prepare students to perform tasks associated with installing, upgrading, and maintaining computer network systems.

The IT Multimedia program helps students prepare to perform tasks associated with designing and creating interactive multimedia communications.

The IT Software Applications and Programming program helps students prepare to perform tasks associated with developing and modifying software applications.

The IT Web Development program helps students prepare to perform tasks associated with designing, creating, and maintaining Web sites.

Contact

Bob Jeffords, Director
ITT Technical Institute
2222 Bay Area Boulevard
Houston, TX 77058
Phone: (281) 486-2630
Fax: (281) 486-6099

ITT Technical Institute, Houston West, Houston

About Our Institution

The company: ITT Technical Institute is owned and operated by ITT Educational Services, Inc. (ITT/ESI), a leading private college system focused on technology-influenced programs of study. ITT/ESI operates seventy-seven ITT Technical Institutes in thirty states, providing career-focused degree programs to approximately 39,000 students as of spring 2004. Headquartered in Carmel, Indiana, ITT/ESI has been actively involved in the higher education community in the United States since 1969.

Curricula: Curriculum offerings are designed to help students begin to prepare for career opportunities in fields of technology. Students attend classes year-round, with convenient breaks provided throughout the year. A student with a full-time course load can have class meetings as often as three days a week. Classes are generally scheduled three days a week and are typically available in the morning, afternoon, and evening, depending on student enrollment. General education courses may be available online. This class schedule offers students the flexibility to pursue part-time employment opportunities.

Special Features

Most ITT Technical Institute programs of study blend traditional academic content with applied learning concepts, with a significant portion devoted to practical study in a lab environment. Advisory committees, made up of representatives of local businesses, help each ITT Technical Institute periodically review and update curricula, equipment, and laboratory design.

Financial Aid/Scholarships

ITT Technical Institute maintains a Finance Department on the campus. The campus is designated as an eligible institution by the U.S. Department of Education for participation in the following programs: Federal Stafford Student Loan Program, Federal PLUS Loan Program, and Federal Work-Study Program. The school also offers nonfederal loans made available through Bank One for eligible students.

Tuition and Fees

March 2005 tuition is $386 per credit hour.

Accreditation

Accrediting Council for Independent Colleges and Schools (ACICS).

Admissions

For admission requirements, students should contact the school for a catalog.

Graduation Requirements

For graduation requirements, students should consult the school catalog.

Contact

Robert Van Elsen, Director
ITT Technical Institute
2950 South Gessner
Houston, TX 77063
Phone: (713) 952-2294
Fax: (713) 952-2393

Program Content

ITT Technical Institute, Houston West, offers the Associate of Applied Science in drafting and design, electronics technology, and information technology.

Program Description

School of Drafting and Design: Information Technology-Multimedia option

School of Electronics Technology: Computer and Electronics Engineering Technology

School of Information Technology: Information Technology-Computer Network Systems, Information Technology-Software Applications and Programming, and Information Technology-Web Development)

ITT Technical Institute, San Antonio

About Our Institution
The company: ITT Technical Institute is owned and operated by ITT Educational Services, Inc. (ITT/ESI), a leading private college system offering technology-influenced programs of study. ITT/ESI operates seventy-seven ITT Technical Institutes in thirty states, providing career-focused degree programs to approximately 39,000 students as of spring 2004. Headquartered in Carmel, Indiana, ITT/ESI has been actively involved in the higher education community in the United States since 1969.

Curricula: Curriculum offerings are designed to help students begin to prepare for career opportunities in fields of technology. Students attend classes year-round, with convenient breaks provided throughout the year. A full-time student course load can have class meetings as often as three days a week and are typically available in the morning, afternoon, and evening, depending on student enrollment. General education courses may be available online. This class schedule offers flexibility to students to pursue part-time employment opportunities.

ITT Technical Institute, San Antonio, awards the Associate of Applied Science degree.

Special Features
Most ITT Technical Institute programs of study blend traditional academic content with applied learning concepts, with a significant portion devoted to practical study in a lab environment. Advisory committees composed of representatives of local businesses help each ITT Technical Institute periodically review and update curricula, equipment, and laboratory design.

Financial Aid/Scholarships
ITT Technical Institute maintains a Financial Aid Department on campus. The campus is designated as an eligible institution by the U.S. Department of Education for participation in the following programs: Federal Stafford Student Loan Program, Federal PLUS Loan Program, and Federal Work-Study Program. The school also offers nonfederal loans available through Bank One for eligible students.

Tuition and Fees
March 2005 tuition is $386 per credit hour.

Accreditation
The school is accredited by the Accrediting Council for Independent Colleges and Schools (ACICS).

Admissions
For admission requirements, students should contact the school for a catalog.

Graduation Requirements
For graduation requirements, students should contact the school for a catalog.

Program Content

School of Information Technology: Information Technology–Computer Network Systems, Information Technology–Software Applications and Programming, Information Technology–Web Development

School of Electronics Technology: Computer and Electronics Engineering Technology

School of Drafting and Design: Computer Drafting and Design, Information Technology–Multimedia

Contact
Steve Marks, Director
ITT Technical Institute
5700 Northwest Parkway
San Antonio, TX 78249
Phone: (210) 694-4612
Fax: (210) 694-4651

Lincoln Technical Institute, Grand Prairie

About Our Institution
Located in the center of the Dallas–Fort Worth Metroplex, the Lincoln Tech campus has 44,000 square feet of building space with adequate shop space to hold twenty-five automobiles and four class-eight trucks simultaneously. Lincoln Tech currently maintains an impressive inventory of training equipment, vehicles, tools, and computer diagnostic equipment, ensuring that students get sufficient hands-on experience on industry-standard equipment. In addition, a new PC lab in the center of the facility is used to enhance the computer literacy skills of the students and provide an environment to practice advanced repairs using computer simulation software. Grand Prairie's faculty members have collectively amassed more than 300 years of field experience. Auto/Diesel instructors hold more than 150 ASE certifications.

Unique to the campus is the involvement in the local race scene. Currently, selected students get to work on a pit crew for a local driver and travel to weekend race events. The Institute's racing program recently became the first member of Team ASE racing and currently campaigns a NHRA Super-Comp Dragster. The campus also serves as a destination school and offers housing assistance to out-of-area students.

Special Features
Lincoln Tech offers student assistance in many areas, including career assistance tutoring, skills enhancement, financial aid, and housing assistance. Lincoln also has a free course certificate policy offered to graduates. The certificate may be used by the graduate to repeat a course already taken or take a new course that was not previously offered.

Financial Aid/Scholarships
The Grand Prairie campus has a variety of tuition scholarships available to graduating high school students. Awards include the Imagine America Scholarship, the Automobile Association of America Scholarship, the Martin Frost Congressional Scholarship, the Charles England Scholarship, the CCST Scholarship, and the Mayoral Scholarship, as well as others. To apply for most of these scholarships, students must fill out an application and take an aptitude-based scholarship test. A Scholarship Committee, made up of volunteers representing business, industry, education, and/or government, interviews the finalists and makes the award decision. In addition, Lincoln Tech maintains a Financial Aid Office on campus, which offers to qualified students a variety of programs, including grants, loans, work-study, veterans' aid, and vocational rehabilitation.

Accreditation
Lincoln Tech is accredited by the Accrediting Commission of Career Schools and Colleges of Technology (ACCSCT) and certified by NATEF.

Admissions
Students must have either a high school diploma or GED certificate and pass an entrance exam.

Program Content
Automotive Technology; Diesel and Truck Technology; Heating, Air Conditioning, and Refrigeration Service

Program Description
Automotive Technology: The program provides graduates with entry-level skills and knowledge to test, diagnose, replace, and repair mechanical and electronic components of current automobiles.

Diesel and Truck Technology: The program provides graduates with entry-level skills to test, diagnose, replace, and repair components on medium- or heavy-duty trucks.

Heating, Air Conditioning, and Refrigeration Service: The program provides graduates with entry-level skills required to install and service heating, comfort-cooling, and refrigeration systems.

Contact
Executive Director
Lincoln Technical Institute
2501 East Arkansas Lane
Grand Prairie, TX 75052
Phone: 972-660-5701
Fax: 972-660-6148
E-mail: execdirgrandprairie@lincolntech.com
Web: www.lincolntechracing.com
www.lincolntech.com

MTI College of Business and Technology, Eastside, Houston

About Our Institution
MTI College of Business and Technology, a private institution, was founded in 1980 for the purpose of providing industry-based training programs in business and computer systems technology. Graduates are prepared to enter career fields such as computer repair, networking, and business administration. MTI College of Business and Technology has three locations—southwest Houston, southeast Houston in the NASA area, and East Houston. Facilities include a resource library with Internet access, 63,000 square feet of classroom space at the southwest location, 33,000 square feet of classroom space at the NASA area location, and 33,600 square feet of classroom space at the Eastside location. Each facility is equipped with leading-edge business and computer technology.

Special Features
At MTI College of Business and Technology, students learn how to apply broad business and computer theories to real-world situations using leading-edge software and computer technology as their primary instruments for learning. The College's Career Services department provides advising and placement assistance for active students and graduates.

Financial Aid/Scholarships
MTI College of Business and Technology maintains a financial aid office on campus, which provides a variety of programs that include grants, loans, scholarships, course-credit programs, work-study, veterans' benefits, and vocational rehabilitation.

Tuition and Fees
Tuition averages $3,700 per semester. Total tuition includes books, supplies, and lab fees.

Accreditation
MTI is accredited by the Accrediting Commission of Career Schools and Colleges of Technology (ACCSCT).

Admissions
Applicants for certificate programs must have a high school diploma or equivalency certificate (GED) or prove their ability to benefit by obtaining a satisfactory score on the Ability to Benefit Examination (ATB), which is provided on campus. Students must be beyond the age of compulsory education. Successful completion of an entrance examination administered by MTI is also a prerequisite for admission. There are additional admissions requirements for the ESL program. Students should contact MTI for details.

Graduation Requirements
To graduate and qualify for a certificate, students must earn a cumulative grade point average of at least 2.0. Students must satisfy all academic, attendance, and financial aid requirements before a certificate is awarded.

Program Content
Certificates: Computer Medical Bulling and Coding, English as a Second Language, English as a Second Language (competency certificate), Medical Billing and Coding, Microcomputer Applications Occupational Technology

Program Description
Computer Medical Billing and Coding: Designed for students who do not possess computer and keyboarding skills, this program provides students with the skills and basic working knowledge to attain entry-level employment in a medical-related office, such as a private physician's office, medical clinic, hospital clerical department, insurance company, or nursing care facility.

English as a Second Language: This program focuses on building English language competencies and the development of English language skills for students whose native language is not English.

Medical Billing and Coding: Designed for students with basic computer skills and knowledge of office computer applications, this program provides students with the skills and basic working knowledge required to attain entry-level employment in a medical-related office, such as a private physician's office, medical clinic, hospital clerical department, insurance company, or nursing care facility.

Microcomputer Applications Occupational Technology: This program prepares students for an entry-level position in an office or business environment.

Contact
Ed Kessing, Director
MTI College of Business and Technology
11420 East Freeway
Houston, TX 77029
Phone: (877) 543-7894 (toll-free)
Fax: (713) 979-1818
E-mail: ed@mti.edu
Web: http://www.mti.edu

Programs Eligible for Scholarship	Tuition and Fees	Course Length/Credit Hours	Credential Earned
Computer Medical Billing and Coding	$11,100	45 weeks/795 hours	Certificate
Medical Billing and Coding	$ 7,400	30 weeks/530 hours	Certificate
Microcomputer Applic. Occup. Technology	$ 7,400	30 weeks/530 hours	Certificate

MTI College of Business and Technology, Houston

About Our Institution

MTI College of Business and Technology, a private institution, was founded in 1980 for the purpose of providing industry-based training programs in business and computer systems technology. Graduates are prepared to enter career fields such as computer repair, networking, and business administration. MTI College of Business and Technology has three locations, one in southwest Houston, one in southeast Houston in the NASA area, and one in east Houston Facilities include a resource library with Internet access, 63,000 square feet of classroom space at the southwest location, 33,000 square feet of classroom space at the NASA area location, and 33,600 square feet of classroom space at the Eastside location, which are filled with leading-edge business and computer technology.

Special Features

At MTI College of Business and Technology, students learn how to apply broad business and computer theories to real-world situations using leading-edge software and computer technology as primary instruments for learning. The College's Career Services Department provides advising and placement assistance for active students and graduates.

Financial Aid/Scholarships

MTI College of Business and Technology maintains a financial aid office on campus, which provides a variety of programs that include grants, loans, scholarships, course credit programs, work-study, veterans benefits, and vocational rehabilitation.

Tuition and Fees

Tuition averages $4020 per module for the five-semester Associate of Occupational Studies degree programs. Total tuition includes books, supplies, and lab fees.

Accreditation

MTI is accredited by the Accrediting Commission of Career Schools and Colleges of Technology (ACCSCT).

Admissions

Applicants for certificate programs must have a high school diploma or recognized equivalency certificate (GED) or prove their ability to benefit by obtaining a satisfactory score on the Ability to Benefit (ATB) Examination, which is provided on campus. Students must be beyond the age of compulsory education.

Applicants for degree programs must have a high school diploma, GED, or evidence of successful completion of at least two years of study at an accredited college or university toward a bachelor's degree.

Program Content

Associate of Occupational Studies (AOS) Degrees: Business Technology, Business Technology–Bilingual Subspecialty, Business Technology–Medical Subspecialty), Computer Systems Technology, Computer Systems Technology–Web Technology Subspecialty

Diplomas: LAN Technology, Medical Insurance Claims Procedures

Certificates: Computer Technology, Microcomputer Applications Occupational Technology, Network Technology, Medical Billing and Coding, Computer Medical Billing and Coding, Medical Office Procedures and Transcription, English as a Second Language (competency certificate)

Successful completion of an entrance examination administered by MTI is also a prerequisite for admission. There are additional admission requirements for the ESL program. Students should contact MTI for details.

Graduation Requirements

To graduate, students must earn a cumulative grade point average of 2.0 to qualify for a certificate, diploma, or degree. Students must satisfy all academic, attendance, and financial aid requirements before a certificate, diploma, or degree is awarded.

Contact

David Wood, Director of Admissions
MTI College of Business and Technology
7277 Regency Square Blvd.
Houston, TX 77036
Phone: (800) 344-1990 (toll-free)
Fax: (713) 974-2090
E-mail: davidw@mti.edu
Web: www.mti.edu

Programs Eligible for Scholarship	Tuition and Fees	Course Length/Credit hours	Credential Earned
Business Technology	$18,500	75 weeks/1,325 hours	AOS
Business Technology–Bilingual Subspecialty	$19,500	75 weeks/1,325 hours	AOS
Business Technology–Medical Subspecialty	$18,500	75 weeks/1,325 hours	AOS
Computer Medical Billing and Coding	$11,100	45 weeks/795 hours	Certificate
Computer Systems Technology	$21,500	75 weeks/1,325 hours	AOS
Computer Systems Technology–Web Technology	$22,500	75 weeks/1,325 hours	AOS
Computer Technology	$ 8,600	30 weeks/530 hours	Certificate
LAN Technology	$17,200	60 weeks/1,060 hours	Diploma
Medical Billing and Coding	$ 7,400	30 weeks/530 hours	Certificate
Medical Insurance Claims Procedures	$14,800	60 weeks/1,060 hours	Diploma
Medical Office Procedures and Transcription	$11,100	45 weeks/795 hours	Certificate
Microcomputer Applications Occupational Tech.	$ 7,400	30 weeks/530 hours	Certificate
Network Technology	$12,900	45 weeks/795 hours	Certificate

MTI College of Business and Technology, NASA, Houston

About Our Institution

MTI College of Business and Technology, a private institution, was founded in 1980 for the purpose of providing industry-based training programs in business and computer systems technology. Graduates are prepared to enter career fields such as computer repair, networking, and business administration. MTI College of Business and Technology has three locations—one in southwest Houston, one in southeast Houston in the NASA area, and one in east Houston. Facilities include a resource library with Internet access, 63,000 square feet of classroom space at the southwest Houston location, 33,000 square feet of classroom space at the NASA-area location, and 33,600 square feet of classroom space at the Eastside location, which are filled with leading-edge business and computer technology.

Special Features

At MTI College of Business and Technology, students learn how to apply broad business and computer theories to real-world situations using leading-edge software and computer technology as primary instruments for learning. The College's Career Services department provides advising and placement assistance for active students and graduates.

Financial Aid/Scholarships

MTI College of Business and Technology maintains a financial aid office on campus, which provides a variety of programs that include grants, loans, scholarships, course-credit programs, work-study, veterans' benefits, and vocational rehabilitation.

Tuition and Fees

Tuition averages $3,900 per module for the five-semester Associate of Occupational Studies degree programs. Total tuition includes books, supplies, and lab fees.

Accreditation

MTI is accredited by the Accrediting Commission of Career Schools and Colleges of Technology (ACCSCT).

Admissions

Applicants for certificate programs must have a high school diploma or equivalency certificate (GED) or prove their ability to benefit by obtaining a satisfactory score on the Ability to Benefit Examination (ATB), which is provided on campus. Students must be beyond the age of compulsory education.

Applicants for degree programs must have a high school diploma, a recognized equivalency certificate (GED), or evidence of successful completion of at least two years of study at an accredited college or university toward a bachelor's degree.

Program Content

Associate of Occupational Studies Degrees: Computer Systems Technology, Business Technology, Business Technology–Medical Subspecialty

Diplomas: LAN Technology, Medical Insurance Claims Procedures

Certificates: Medical Billing and Coding, Computer Medical Billing and Coding, Medical Office Procedures and Transcription, Computer Technology, Microcomputer Applications Occupational Technology, Network Technology, English as a Second Language (competency certificate)

Successful completion of an entrance examination administered by MTI is also a prerequisite for admission. There are additional admissions requirements for the ESL program. Students should contact MTI for details.

Graduation Requirements

To graduate, students must earn a cumulative grade point average of at least 2.0 to qualify for a certificate, diploma, or degree. Students must satisfy all academic, attendance, and financial aid requirements before a certificate, diploma, or degree will be awarded.

Contact

Derrell Beck
Director of Admissions
MTI College of Business and Technology
1275 Space Park Drive
Houston, TX 77058
Phone: (888) 532-7675 (toll-free)
Fax: (281) 333-4118
E-mail: derrell@mti.edu
Web: www.mti.edu

Programs Eligible for Scholarship	Tuition and Fees	Course Length/Credit Hours	Credential Earned
Business Technology	$18,500	75 weeks/1,325 hours	AOS
Business Technology–Medical Subspecialty	$18,500	75 weeks/1,325 hours	AOS
Computer Medical Billing and Coding	$11,100	45 weeks/795 hours	Certificate
Computer Systems Technology	$21,500	75 weeks/1,325 hours	AOS
Computer Technology	$ 8,600	30 weeks/530 hours	Certificate
LAN Technology	$17,200	60 weeks/1,060 hours	Diploma
Medical Billing and Coding	$ 7,400	30 weeks/530 hours	Certificate
Medical Insurance Claims Procedures	$14,800	60 weeks/1,060 hours	Diploma
Medical Office Procedures and Transcription	$11,100	45 weeks/795 hours	Certificate
Microcomputer Applic. Occup. Technology	$ 7,400	30 weeks/530 hours	Certificate
Network Technology	$12,900	45 weeks/795 hours	Certificate

National Institute of Technology, Austin

About Our Institution

National Institute of Technology (NIT) in Austin, Texas, was formed in September 2002 to meet the expanding needs of the local market. NIT–Austin is a branch campus of NIT–Southfield, Michigan. NIT is owned and operated by a division of Corinthian Colleges, Inc. (CCi). CCi, one of the largest postsecondary school organizations in the United States, owns and operates more than 80 colleges and institutions nationwide.

Special Features

The school is conveniently located in Austin on U.S. Highway 290 East. The attractive facility includes computer and medical assisting laboratories, lecture rooms, a library, a student lounge, and administrative areas. The modern, air-conditioned facility is designed for training students for the working world. Several classrooms are designed and equipped for laboratory instruction.

Financial Aid/Scholarships

NIT–Austin offers several options for payment of tuition. Those able to pay tuition are given a plan that helps reduce their fees upon entry. In addition, because NIT recognizes that many students lack the resources to begin their educational training, the school participates in several types of federal, state, and institutional financial aid programs, most of which are based on financial need.

Tuition and Fees

The Medical Administrative Assistant, Medical Assisting, Pharmacy Technician, and Residential Heating, Ventilation, and Air Conditioning Technician (RHVAC) programs can be completed in less than one year. The all-inclusive tuition for each program is as follows: Electronics, Computer, and Communications Technology, $19,952; Medical Administrative Assistant, $11,140; Medical Assisting, $10,924; Pharmacy Technician, $10,889; and RHVAC, $11,561.

Accreditation

NIT–Austin is accredited by the Accrediting Commission of Career Schools and Colleges of Technology (ACCSCT).

Admissions

Candidates must have a high school diploma or its equivalent. Successful completion of the assessment examination is a prerequisite for admission. Applicants who do not have a high school diploma, official transcripts, or a GED certificate may apply for some programs under the Ability to Benefit Provision.

Graduation Requirements

Students are required to earn a minimum cumulative grade point average of 2.0 in their major and must meet specific program requirements.

Program Content

Electronics, Computer, and Communications Technology; Medical Administrative Assistant; Medical Assisting; Pharmacy Technician; Residential Heating, Ventilation, and Air Conditioning Technician

Contact

Kim Whitehead, Director of Admissions
9100 U.S. Hwy 290 East, Suite 100
Austin, TX 78754
Phone: (512) 928–1933
Fax: (512) 927–8587
E-mail: kwhitehe@cci.edu
Web: www.nitschools.com

National Institute of Technology, Bissonnet

About Our Institution
The National Institute of Technology–Bissonnet (NIT–Bissonnet) opened its doors in 2004 to meet the expanding needs of the local Houston market, joining its three existing schools, NIT–Galleria, NIT–Greenspoint, and NIT–Hobby. NIT is owned and operated by Corinthian Colleges, Inc., one of the largest postsecondary school organizations in the United States, operating more than eighty colleges and institutions nationwide.

Special Features
The NIT–Bissonnet campus is conveniently located on the southwest side of Houston just off U.S. Highway 59 at the Bissonnet exit, with immediate access to major freeways and the Metro bus route. Its 28,400-square-foot facility contains administrative offices, classrooms, computer labs, a student lounge, restrooms, and a Resource Center that contains reference and reading materials related to the academic programs.

Financial Aid/Scholarships
The school offers several options for payment of tuition. Those able to pay tuition are given a plan to help reduce their fees upon entry. In addition, the school recognizes that many students lack the resources to begin their educational training, so NIT participates in several types of federal, state, and institutional financial aid programs, most of which are based on financial need.

Tuition and Fees
The Medical Assistant program costs $11,179, the Medical Insurance Billing/Coding program costs $8,631, and the Pharmacy Technician program costs $10,763.

Accreditation
National Institute of Technology is accredited by the Accrediting Commission of Career Schools and Colleges of Technology (ACCSCT).

Admissions
All applicants are required to complete a personal interview with an Admission representative. Parents and spouses are encouraged to attend. Personal interviews enable the school administrators to determine whether an applicant is acceptable for enrollment into the desired program. The following items must be completed at the time of application: administration and evaluation of an applicable entrance examination, the Enrollment Agreement (if applicant is under 18 years of age, it must be signed by a parent or guardian), and financial aid forms (if applicant wishes to apply for financial aid).

Applicants who do not have a high school diploma, official transcripts, or a GED credential may also apply for some programs under the Ability-to-Benefit program. The number of students enrolled under this program is limited.

Graduation Requirements
To be eligible for graduation in allied health programs, students must complete all required classroom modules with a grade of at least 2.0; meet the grade requirements for the modules' components, if applicable; complete all program requirements; pass the graduate exam, if applicable; and successfully complete all extern requirements.

Program Content
Medical Assistant, Medical Insurance Billing/Coding, Pharmacy Technician

To be eligible for graduation in business and technical programs, students must complete all required classroom training with a cumulative grade point average of at least 2.0 and complete all program requirements.

Contact
Vanessa Smith, Director of Admissions
9700 Bissonnet, Suite 1400
Houston, TX 77036
Phone: (713) 772-4200
Fax: (713) 772-4204
E-mail: vasmith@cci.edu
Web: www.nitschools.com

National Institute of Technology, Galleria

About Our Institution
To meet the expanding needs of the local market, National Institute of Technology–Galleria (NIT–Galleria) opened in April 1999. Two additional campuses have opened in Houston since then: NIT–Greenspoint and NIT–Hobby. All three Houston locations are branch campuses of NIT in San Antonio, Texas. NIT is owned and operated by Corinthian Schools, Inc. (CSi), which is a division of Corinthian Colleges, Inc., one of the largest postsecondary school organizations in the United States, operating more than eighty colleges and institutions nationwide.

Special Features
The school is located in a modern air-conditioned building about 1 mile inside the "Loop," the main artery that encircles the city of Houston. The building has more than 20,000 square feet containing fifteen classrooms, administrative offices, a student lounge, restrooms, and a library containing reference and reading materials related to the academic programs.

Financial Aid/Scholarships
NIT provides a financial aid office on the campus that offers a variety of available programs, including grants, loans, scholarships, and work-study. Financial aid is available for those who qualify.

Tuition and Fees
The tuition ranges from $8,505 to $21,361 and includes books and services provided by the school. The Enrollment Agreement obligates the student and the school for the entire program of instruction. A tuition deposit of $50 is also included in the final program price entered in the Enrollment Agreement.

Accreditation
NIT–Galleria is accredited by the Accrediting Commission of Career Schools and Colleges of Technology (ACCSCT) and is approved and regulated by the Texas Workforce Commission.

Admissions
All applicants are required to complete a personal interview with an admissions representative. Parents and spouses are encouraged to attend. Personal interviews also enable school administrators to determine whether an applicant is acceptable for enrollment into the program.

The school follows an open enrollment system. The following items must be completed at the time of application: administration and evaluation of the applicant's entrance examination, a tour of the facility with an admissions representative, the enrollment agreement (if the applicant is under 18 years of age, it must be signed by a parent or guardian), and a $50 tuition deposit (must accompany the enrollment agreement to get a firm commitment from the applicant about the seriousness of interest in the college).

Prospective students must have a high school diploma or a recognized equivalency certificate (GED). All prospective students are required to achieve a passing score on a nationally normed, standardized test. This test measures an applicant's basic skills in reading and arithmetic.

Program Content
Electronics and Computer Engineering Technology, Medical Assisting, Medical Insurance Billing/Coding, Network Systems Support

Graduation Requirements
To be eligible for graduation, students in allied health programs must complete all required classroom modules with a grade of at least 70 percent; meet the grade requirements for the module components, if applicable; complete all program requirements; and successfully complete all extern requirements.

Students in business and technical programs must complete all required classroom training with a cumulative grade point average of at least 2.0; pass the graduate exam, if applicable; and complete all program requirements.

Contact
Scott Morris
Director of Admissions
4150 Westheimer, Suite 200
Houston, TX 77027
Phone (713) 629-1637
Fax: (713) 629-1643
E-mail: smorris@cci.edu
Web: www.nitschools.com

Programs Eligible for Scholarship	Tuition and Fees	Course Length/Credit Hours	Credential Earned
Electronics and Computer Engineering Technology	$21,361	52 weeks/1,500 clock hours	Diploma
Medical Assisting	$11,100	32 weeks/720 clock hours	Diploma
Medical Insurance Billing/Coding	$ 8,508	28 weeks/560 clock hours	Diploma
Network Systems Support	$14,200	36 weeks/720 clock hours	Diploma

National Institute of Technology, Greenspoint

About Our Institution

National Institute of Technology–Greensport (NIT–Greensport) opened its doors in January 2000 to meet the expanding needs of the local market. NIT–Greensport, along with two additional schools, NIT–Galleria and NIT–Hobby, are branch campuses of NIT–San Antonio. NIT is owned and operated by Corinthian Colleges, Inc., one of the largest postsecondary school organizations in the United States, operating more than 160 colleges and institutions in North America.

Special Features

The National Institute of Technology campus on the north side of Houston, Texas, comprises 23,000 square feet of classrooms, laboratories, and administrative offices. The campus is conveniently located at the intersection of Northpoint Drive and Northchase Drive one-half mile south of the Greenspoint Shopping Mall. Major freeways in the immediate area are Beltway 8 and I-45. Bus transportation is available.

Financial Aid/Scholarships

This campus offers students several options for payment of tuition. Those able to pay tuition are given a plan to help reduce their fees upon entry. In addition, the school recognizes that many students lack the resources to begin their educational training, so the campus participates in several types of federal, state, and institutional financial aid programs, most of which are based on financial need.

Accreditation

National Institute of Technology is accredited by the Accrediting Commission of Career Schools and Colleges of Technology (ACCSCT).

Admissions

Prospective students must have a high school diploma or a recognized equivalency certificate. The student must also achieve a passing score on a nationally normed, standardized test. Applicants who do not have a high school diploma or GED may apply under the Ability to Benefit Provision (not available to Pharmacy Technician applicants). However, the number of students enrolled under the Ability to Benefit Provision is limited.

Graduation Requirements

Students may qualify for graduation if they meet the Satisfactory Academic Progress requirements. Students in allied health must complete all required classroom modules with a grade of at least 70 percent, meet the grade requirements for the module components, complete all program requirements, and successfully complete all extern requirements. Students in business and technical programs must complete all required classroom training with a cumulative grade point average of at least 2.0, pass the graduate exam, if applicable, and complete all program requirements.

Program Content

Dental Assisting, Medical Assisting, Medical Insurance Billing/Coding, Pharmacy Technician

Enrollment

Enrollment is 600–650 students.

Contact

Jeff Brown
Director of Admissions
255 Northpoint Drive, Suite 100
Houston, TX 77060
Phone (281) 447-7037
Fax: (281) 447-6937
E-mail: jbrown@cci.edu
Web: www.nitschools.com

Programs Eligible for Scholarship	Tuition and Fees	Course Length/Credit Hours	Credential Earned
Dental Assisting	$10,422	8 months	Diploma
Medical Assisting	$10,422	8 months	Diploma
Medical Insurance Billing/Coding	$ 8,159	6 months	Diploma
Pharmacy Technician	$10,422	8 months	Diploma

National Institute of Technology, Hobby

About Our Institution

National Institute of Technology (NIT) in Houston–Hobby opened its doors in 2001 to meet the expanding needs of the local market. NIT–Hobby, along with two additional schools, NIT–Galleria and NIT–Greenspoint, are branch campuses of NIT–San Antonio. NIT is owned and operated by Corinthian Colleges, Inc., one of the largest postsecondary school organizations in the United States, operating more than 130 colleges and institutions nationwide.

Special Features

The NIT–Hobby campus opened in October 2001 and is conveniently located on the southeast side of Houston just off I-45 at the Woodridge Exit, with immediate access to major freeways and the Metro bus route. Its 17,890-square-foot facility contains administrative offices, classrooms, computer labs, a student lounge, restrooms, and a Resource Center that contains reference and reading materials related to the academic programs.

Financial Aid/Scholarships

The campus offers several options for payment of tuition. Those able to pay tuition are given a plan to help reduce their fees upon entry. In addition, the school recognizes that many students lack the resources to begin their educational training, so NIT participates in several types of federal, state, and institutional financial aid programs, most of which are based on financial need.

Tuition and Fees

The Medical Assisting program costs $11,364, the program in Medical Insurance Billing/Coding costs $8,627, and the Pharmacy Technician program costs $10,841.

Accreditation

National Institute of Technology is accredited by the Accrediting Commission of Career Schools and Colleges of Technology (ACCSCT).

Admissions

All applicants are required to complete a personal interview with an admissions representative. Parents and spouses are encouraged to attend. Personal interviews enable the school administrators to determine whether an applicant is acceptable for enrollment into the desired program. The school follows an open-enrollment system. The following items must be completed at the time of application: administration and evaluation of an applicable entrance examination, the Enrollment Agreement (if applicant is under 18 years of age, it must be signed by a parent or guardian), and financial aid forms (if applicant wishes to apply for financial aid).

Applicants who do not have a high school diploma, official transcripts, or a GED certificate may also apply for some programs under the Ability to Benefit Provision. The number of students enrolled under the Ability to Benefit Provision is limited.

Graduation Requirements

To be eligible for graduation, students in allied health programs must complete all required classroom modules with a grade of at least 70 percent; meet the grade requirements for the module components, if

Program Content

Medical Assisting, Medical Insurance Billing/Coding, Pharmacy Technician

applicable; complete all program requirements; pass the graduate exam, if applicable; and successfully complete all extern requirements.

To be eligible for graduation, students in business and technical programs must complete all required classroom training with a cumulative grade point average of at least 2.0 and complete all program requirements.

Enrollment

There are 315 students enrolled at NIT–Hobby.

Contact

Greg Lotz, Director of Admissions
7151 Office City Drive
Houston, TX 77087
Phone: (713) 645-7404
Fax: (713) 645-7346
E-mail: glotz@cci.edu
Web: www.nitschools.com

National Institute of Technology, San Antonio

About Our Institution

National Institute of Technology (NIT) is one of more than eighty schools owned and operated by a division of Corinthian Colleges, Inc. NIT–San Antonio was established in 1935 as an electronics school. Today, along with teaching an Electronics, Computer, and Communications Technology program, the school teaches Medical Administrative Assistant; Medical Assisting; Network Systems Support; Pharmacy Technician; Computerized Business Applications; and Residential Heating, Ventilation, and Air Conditioning Technician. The curricula have been developed based on employer needs. Students use modern equipment and facilities similar to the kind they can expect to find on the job. By emphasizing focused training, NIT provides people entering or reentering today's competitive market with practical, skill-specific training vital to their success.

Special Features

The school is located in a modern air-conditioned building and is specifically designed for training students for the working world. The building has 66,000 square feet, containing thirty-seven classrooms, administrative offices, a student lounge, restrooms, and a resource center containing reference and reading materials related to the academic programs. Several of the classrooms are designed and equipped for laboratory instruction.

Financial Aid/Scholarships

NIT provides a financial aid office on campus, providing a variety of available programs, including grants, loans, scholarships, work-study, VA, VAR, JTPA, and TRC.

Tuition and Fees

The tuition ranges from $11,500 to $21,000 and includes books and services provided by the school. The Enrollment Agreement obligates the student and the school for the entire program of instruction.

Accreditation

NIT–San Antonio is accredited by the Accrediting Commission of Career Schools and Colleges of Technology (ACCSCT) and approved and regulated by the Texas Workforce Commission.

Admissions

Successful candidates must have a high school diploma or a recognized equivalency certificate (GED) and be able to achieve a passing score on a nationally normed, standardized test.

Graduation Requirements

To be eligible for graduation, students must:

Program Content

Computerized Business Applications; Electronics, Computer, and Communications Technology; Medical Administrative Assistant; Medical Assisting; Pharmacy Technician; Residential Heating, Ventilation, and Air Conditioning Technician

- Complete all required classroom modules with a grade of at least 70 percent or a GPA of at least 2.0, as applicable.
- Pass the graduate exam, if applicable.
- Complete all program requirements.
- Successfully complete all extern requirements (Medical Assisting).

Contact

Jimmy Clontz, Director of Admissions
6510 First Park Ten Blvd.
San Antonio, TX 78213
Phone: (210) 733-6000
(210) 738-7800
Fax: (210) 733-3300
Web: www.nitschools.com

Programs Eligible for Scholarship	Tuition and Fees	Course Length/Credit Hours	Credential Earned
Computerized Business Applications	$11,500	9 months/720 clock hours	Diploma
Electronics, Computer, and Communications Technology	$20,959	13 months/1,500 clock hours	Diploma
Medical Assisting	$10,683	8 months/720 clock hours	Diploma
Medical Administrative Assistant	$10,853	8 months/720 clock hours	Diploma
Pharmacy Technician	$14,190	8 months/720 clock hours	Diploma
Residential Heating, Ventilation, and Air Conditioning	$11,621	9 months/810 clock hours	Diploma

The Ocean Corporation, Houston

About Our Institution
The Ocean Corporation has been in the education field since 1969, providing instruction in commercial diving and nondestructive testing. Courses include the Ultimate Diver Training Course, Nondestructive Testing/Inspection Training Course, and Medical Technician Training Course. The campus is on 4.2 acres located in Houston on the Gulf of Mexico in the hub of the diving industry. Houston also has the reputation of being the world center for nondestructive testing. The school draws students nationally and internationally and offers job placement assistance.

Special Features
The Ocean Corporation helps men and women turn their dreams into reality. After a brief thirty weeks of instruction, they are able to enter the respective field in which they were trained. Both industries are unique and offer higher than average pay, excitement, and travel opportunities.

Financial Aid/Scholarships
From its on-campus office, the Ocean Corporation offers Title IV Funding through the Federal Government—the subsidized and unsubsidized Stafford Loans, the Plus Loan, and the Pell Grant. The school also participates in the Veterans' Administration Educational Benefits, JTPA, Vocational Rehabilitation Educational Programs, Imagine America, and CCSCT.

Tuition and Fees
The Ocean Corporation's Ultimate Diver Training program is $14,000. The cost includes books, tools, and supplies. The Nondestructive Testing/Inspection Training Course is $12,500 and the Medical Technician Training Course is $4500.

Accreditation
The Ocean Corporation is accredited by the Accrediting Commission of Career Schools and Colleges of Technology.

Admissions
A prospective student who chooses a career as a diver must have a high school diploma or a GED certificate, be 18 years old, and pass a medical examination and an assessment test.

A prospective student who chooses a career as an inspection technician must have a high school diploma or GED certificate, be 18 years old, and pass an assessment test.

Graduation Requirements
The student must show a satisfactory progress by maintaining a minimum grade of 70 percent in all subjects except where outside certifying agencies require a higher score.

Program Content
The Ultimate Diver Training Course, Nondestructive Testing/Inspection Training Course, Medical Technician Training Course

Program Description
The Ultimate Diver Training Course trains students to be able to enter the commercial diving industry.

The Nondestructive Testing/Inspection Training Course trains students to be able to enter any industry that uses nondestructive testing.

The Medical Technician Training is further education for commercial divers.

Contact
John Wood, President
10840 Rockley Road
Houston, TX 77099
Phone: (800) 321-0298
Fax (281) 530-9143
E-mail: admissions@oceancorp.com
Web: www.oceancorp.com

Programs Eligible for Scholarship	Tuition and Fees	Course Length/Credit Hours	Credential Earned
Ultimate Diver Training	$14,000	750 clock hours/ 25 semester credit hours	Certificate
Nondestructive Testing/Inspector Training	$12,500	750 clock hours/ 25 semester credit hours	Certificate
Medical Technician Training	$ 4,500	215 clock hours/ 8 semester credit hours	Certificate

Remington College, Dallas Campus, Garland

About Our Institution

Remington College–Dallas Campus is located at 1800 Eastgate Drive in Garland, Texas. The professional environment in which the school is located provides an ideal setting for students to receive their orientation into the business world. Instructional areas include an industry-standard personal computer laboratory equipped with IBM-compatible computers, medical classrooms and laboratories, and a resource center. A resource area with periodicals and books is also provided for the students.

Special Features

Remington College–Dallas Campus has a full-time Student Services Coordinator who assists students with any of their immediate needs. The campus also has a full-time Career Services Coordinator who assists students with part-time and full-time placement.

Financial Aid/Scholarships

Remington College–Dallas Campus maintains a Financial Aid Office on campus, providing a variety of grants, loans, vocational rehabilitation, and scholarships programs.

Tuition and Fees

Students should contact the campus for current tuition pricing. Textbook cost and lab fees are included in the tuition. A $50 registration fee is required for all programs.

Accreditation

Remington College–Dallas Campus is accredited by the Accrediting Council for Independent Colleges and Schools (ACICS) and approved and regulated by the Texas Workforce Commission, Proprietary Schools Section, Austin, Texas. Degree programs are approved by the Texas Higher Education Coordinating Board, Community and Technical Colleges Division.

Admissions

All applicants must have a high school diploma or its equivalent, such as the GED. Applicants are required to complete a personal interview with an admissions representative. An entrance exam is administered to determine a candidate's potential for success.

Graduation Requirements

To be eligible for graduation, students must complete all classroom work each grading period with a cumulative point average of at least 2.0, complete all program requirements, and pay all monies due to the school.

Contact

Greenie "Skip" Walls III, Campus President
1800 Eastgate Drive
Garland, TX 75041
Phone: (972) 686-7878
Fax: (972) 686-5116
Web: www.remingtoncollege.edu

Program Content

Business Information Systems, Computer Network Technology, Criminal Justice, Electronics and Computer Technology, Medical Assisting, Pharmacy Technician

Program Description

Business Information Systems: Graduates of the program are qualified for entry-level positions in the office environment.

Computer Networking Technology: Graduates of the program have the skills and knowledge for entry-level positions in network operations and related fields.

Criminal Justice: Graduates of the program are prepared for entry into or advancement within the criminal justice system.

Electronics and Computer Technology: Graduates of the program are qualified for entry-level positions in computer services and related fields.

Medical Assisting: Graduates of the program have the skills and knowledge for entry-level positions in the health-care field.

Pharmacy Technician: Graduates of the program have the skills to obtain entry-level positions in pharmacies.

Remington College, Fort Worth Campus, Fort Worth

About Our Institution
Remington College–Fort Worth Campus was founded in 1988 in an effort to meet the growing need for computer-related education and training in the technical, business, and allied health fields. To date, Remington College consists of twenty-two campuses across the United States. Remington College teaches a "career first" curriculum that allows students to concentrate on learning the necessary technical skills early in their program and build on these skills as they progress toward graduation.

Special Features
Remington College is uncompromisingly dedicated to high-quality, college-level, career-oriented education. Its primary objectives are to graduate a high percentage of students who enter career programs and to help them achieve relevant employment at the highest possible starting salary. Remington College's hands-on training is the foundation of its educational structure. Practical application in well-equipped labs, coupled with theoretical reinforcement in the classroom, allows students to acquire substantial knowledge in their chosen career field. When appropriate, externships are used to provide the student with real-world experience.

Financial Aid/Scholarships
Remington College–Fort Worth Campus maintains a Financial Services Office on the campus, providing a variety of grants, loans, scholarships, work-study, veterans' benefits, and vocational rehabilitation programs.

Tuition and Fees
Students should contact the campus for current tuition pricing. Textbook cost and lab fees are included in tuition. A $50 registration fee is required for all programs.

Accreditation
Remington College–Fort Worth Campus programs are accredited by the Accrediting Commission of Career Schools and Colleges of Technology (ACCSCT) and the Texas Higher Education Coordinating Board (THECB).

Admissions
A high school diploma or its equivalent (GED), along with an entrance test and acceptance interview, is used to determine a candidate's potential for success.

Graduation Requirements
In order to graduate, a student must maintain an overall cumulative grade point average of 2.0 or better for the entire program and complete all courses specified in the program catalog.

Contact
Linda Wey, Campus President
300 E. Loop 820
Fort Worth, TX 76112
Phone: (817) 451-0017
　　　(800) 336-6668
Fax: (817) 496-1257
Web: www.remingtoncollege.edu

Program Content
Accounting, Business Administration and Management, Business Systems Analysis and Design, Criminal Justice, Data Processing Technology, Graphic Art and Design, Information Sciences and Systems, Medical Assistant

Program Description
Business Technology Program: The curriculum is designed to satisfy students' desire to learn a technical skill in a field that has experienced rapid growth.

Computer Networking Systems Technology Program: The curriculum explores both the fundamental and advanced theory in network installations, server administration, and local and wide area networks. The program prepares students to take the Microsoft Certified Systems Engineer Exams.

Criminal Justice: The curriculum is designed to prepare the student in many ways that exist within the career field, such as loss prevention, private investigation, and corrections.

Digital Graphic Art: This program prepares students for entry-level positions in desktop publishing, computer graphics, digital imaging, production art, and Web site design.

Medical Assisting Program: The program provides graduates with the skills and knowledge that will enable them to qualify for entry-level positions in the health-care field.

Remington College, Houston Campus, Houston

About Our Institution
Remington College was founded in 1985 in an effort to meet the growing need for computer-related education and training in the technical and business fields. To date, Remington College consists of twenty campuses across the United States. Remington College teaches a "career first" curriculum that allows students to concentrate on learning the necessary technical skills early in their program and build on them as they progress toward graduation.

Special Features
Remington College is uncompromisingly dedicated to high-quality, college-level, career-oriented education. Its primary objectives are to graduate a high percentage of students who enter career programs and to help them achieve relevant employment at the highest possible starting salary. Remington College's hands-on training is the foundation of its educational structure. Practical application in well-equipped labs, coupled with theoretical reinforcement in the classroom, allows students to acquire substantial knowledge in their chosen career field. When appropriate, externships are used to provide the student with real-world experience.

Financial Aid/Scholarships
Remington College–Houston Campus maintains a Financial Services Office on the campus, providing a variety of grants, loans, scholarships, work-study, veterans' aid, and vocational rehabilitation programs.

Tuition and Fees
Students should contact the campus for current tuition pricing. Textbook costs and lab fees are included in the tuition. A $50 registration fee is required for all programs.

Accreditation
Remington College–Houston Campus programs are accredited by the Accrediting Commission of Career Schools and Colleges of Technology (ACCSCT).

Admissions
A high school diploma or GED certificate, along with an acceptance interview, is used to determine a candidate's potential for success. An entrance test is also required.

Graduation Requirements
In order to graduate, a student must maintain a minimum overall 2.0 cumulative grade point average for the entire program and complete all courses specified in the program catalog. Degree-seeking students must pass the Texas Higher Education Assessment (THEA) test.

Contact
Chris Tilley, Campus President
Remington College–Houston Campus
3110 Hayes Road, Suite 380
Houston, TX 77082
Phone: (281) 899-1240
Fax: (281) 597-8466
Web: www.remingtoncollege.edu

Program Content
Business Information Systems, Computer Information Systems, Computer Network Systems Technology, Electronics and Computer Engineering Technology, Internet Information Systems, Medical Assisting

Program Description
Business Information Systems: The program is designed to provide comprehensive training in a variety of computer software applicable to business applications, accounting, document processing, Internet research, and Web site development.

Computer Information Systems: The Computer Information Systems Program curriculum explores both the fundamentals and advanced theory in computers and programming, computer operations, system analysis, and system design.

Computer Network Systems Technology: The curriculum explores PC troubleshooting, network installations, server administration, and wide-area networks.

Electronics and Computer Engineering Technology: The curriculum explores both the fundamentals and advanced theory in electronics, integrated circuits, microprocessors, and computer technology.

Medical Assisting: The objective of the Medical Assisting Program is to provide graduates with the skills and knowledge that enable them to qualify for entry-level positions as medical assistants.

Universal Technical Institute, Houston

About Our Institution

UTI Houston is a private postsecondary technical school that has provided students with the technical education needed for a successful career in the automotive, diesel, and collision repair and refinishing industries since opening in 1983. UTI provides full student services, housing assistance, financial aid to those who qualify, campus activities, and both part-time and graduate employment assistance for as long as needed.

Special Features

UTI has strong industry relations with international companies such as Audi, BMW, Ford, International Trucks, Jaguar, Mercedes-Benz, NASCAR, Porsche, Volkswagen, and Volvo. These agreements have created excellent training and career opportunities for UTI automotive and diesel graduates. From electives for upgraded UTI training to fully paid manufacturer-specific graduate training, UTI's connections and commitment to excellence place its graduates in the driver's seat in a career field that is in demand. Many manufacturers and dealers in addition to those listed above also participate in UTI's TRIP program, wherein these companies agree to pay back the student tuition loans for the graduates they hire.

Financial Aid/Scholarships

UTI students are eligible to apply for various federal grants and loans. These include Pell Grants, FSEOG, and Stafford, Perkins, and PLUS loans. UTI also sponsors, as well as administers, various scholarship programs and awards more than $500,000 in scholarships annually, including ones from SkillsUSA, CCA, Imagine America, Ford/AAA, FFA, and UTI's National High School Scholarship competition.

Tuition and Fees

Tuition and fees vary by course content. Tuition prices include all workbooks, textbooks, and uniforms; there are no hidden costs. For specific tuition information, students should contact the Houston Admissions Office.

Accreditation

UTI is accredited by the Accrediting Commission of Career Schools and Colleges of Technology (ACCSCT), which is listed by the U.S. Department of Education as a nationally recognized accrediting agency.

Admissions

Applicants must be at least 16 years of age, have a high school diploma or equivalent, and submit a completed application, a signed enrollment agreement, a registration fee, and any other information that the applicant or the Institute feels is pertinent to admission. Each applicant's qualifications for enrollment are reviewed and either approved, approved with stipulations, or denied.

Graduation Requirements

Students must achieve at least an overall 2.0 cumulative GPA and receive a satisfactory grade in all required courses in the selected program. Graduation must be achieved within a ratio of 1:5 attempted courses in a student's program. Students must have a zero balance in their student account and have attended UTI's Career Development Classes.

Program Content

Automotive Technology, Diesel and Industrial Technology, Automotive/Diesel and Industrial Technology, Collision Repair and Refinish Technology, Toyota Professional Collision Training, and Ford Technology elective available.

Program Description

UTI's Automotive and Diesel ASE Master Certified programs prepare the graduate to diagnose, troubleshoot, service, and repair foreign and domestic automobiles and diesel engines. Students work in a professional, shoplike environment using the latest engine analyzers, handheld scanners, and other computerized diagnostic equipment. Students learn everything from basic engine systems to computerized engine controls and from hydraulics to transport refrigeration. UTI's ASE Master Certified, I-CAR-based Collision Repair and Refinish Technology program covers it all, from welding and cutting to frame alignment and paint color theory, providing the specialized hands-on training needed to repair structural and nonstructural damage on cars and trucks. Graduates of this program are DuPont-certified in color theory. UTI graduates have all the skills needed to start a challenging and rewarding career in the automotive, diesel, and collision repair industries.

Contact

Ken Golaszewski, School Director
721 Lockhaven Drive
Houston, TX 77073
Phone: (281) 443-6262
(800) 325-0354 (toll-free)
Fax: (281) 443-1866
E-mail: kgolaszewski@uticorp.com
Web: www.uticorp.com

Virginia College at Austin, Austin

About Our Institution
Virginia College at Austin is a private, proprietary institution of higher education committed to offering associate degrees and diploma courses that strengthen the student's ability to enter or maintain a chosen career.

Special Features
Virginia College maintains vigilance on the ever-changing job market requirements and expansion of its program offerings. The College supports a progressive policy to prepare students as competitive employees in the local, regional, and multistate job markets.

Financial Aid/Scholarships
Virginia College at Austin participates in the Federal Pell Grant, FFEL, FDSLP, Federal Work-Study Program, FSEOG, and scholarships for graduating high school seniors and single, working parents.

Tuition and Fees
Tuition and fees vary depending on the program, ranging from $9,000 to $24,000, which includes books and fees.

Accreditation
Virginia College at Austin is accredited by the Accrediting Council for Independent Colleges and Schools (ACICS).

Admissions
An entrance exam and a high school diploma or GED certificate are required for admission.

Graduation Requirements
In order to graduate, a student must have earned a minimum 2.0 cumulative grade point average, earned the minimum credit hours as required by the program of study, satisfied all financial obligations to the school, fulfilled attendance requirements, and completed an application for graduation and all exit interview requirements with the School Student Finance Department and Graduate Career Services Department. Students in the Associate of Applied Science (A.A.S.) degree programs must pass the TASP test or an alternative test approved by the Texas Higher Education Coordinating Board. Students who do not complete all graduation requirements by the end of the following quarter's add/drop period are not certified as graduates of a particular quarter. Those students must reapply for graduation during the quarter in which all requirements are met.

Contact
Charlotte A. Frohnhoefer, Director of Admissions
Virginia College at Austin
6301 East Highway 290
Austin, TX 78723
Phone: (512) 371-3500
Fax: (512) 371-3502
Web: www.vc.edu

Program Content
Accounting Associate, Administrative Assistant, Administrative Office Management, Bilingual Business Administration, Cisco Network Administration, Computer Network Technician, Diagnostic Medical Sonography, Linux Network Administration, Medical Assistant, Medical Assisting and Office Administration, Medical Billing and Coding, Microsoft Network Engineer, Paralegal Studies

Program Description
Administrative Assistant This program is designed to prepare graduates to work in business offices of all sizes. Students learn to perform various computer and basic accounting operations.
Administrative Office Management This program is designed for students interested in entering the business world as specialists in computerized office systems and office management.
Cisco Network Administration This program prepares students for a technical career in the Wide Area Network administration field.
Computer Network Technician This program prepares students for a career in the computer network and microcomputer service and repair fields. Students learn skills that prepare them to take the A+ and Network+ Certification exams.
Diagnostic Medical Sonography Students trained in this degree program are prepared to assist physicians by performing high-frequency sound wave patient examinations to image internal structures.
Linux Network Administration This program prepares students for a technical career in the computer network administration field directly related to the Linux computer network.
Medical Assistant Graduates of this specialized program are able to perform basic first aid and CPR, perform routine laboratory procedures, administer medications as directed by a physician, and perform administrative functions and duties in a health-care facility.
Medical Assisting and Office Administration This program is designed to prepare students for the medical field, combining knowledge of automated medical office and patient contact.
Medical Billing and Coding This program is designed to serve those students who are interested in a medical field position related to reimbursement procedures. Students learn fundamentals of medical office protocol and specialized training.
Microsoft Network Engineer This program prepares students for a career in the Microsoft computer network engineering field.

Programs Eligible for Scholarship	Tuition and Fees	Course Length/Credit Hours	Credential Earned
Accounting Associate	$19,200	96 credit hours	AAS
Administrative Office Management	$19,200	96 credit hours	AAS
Bilingual Business Administration	$19,200	96 credit hours	AAS
Cisco Network Administration	$24,000	96 credit hours	AAS
Diagnostic Medical Sonography	$20,160	96 credit hours	AAS
Linux Network Administration	$24,000	96 credit hours	AAS
Medical Assisting and Office Administration	$19,200	96 credit hours	AAS
Microsoft Network Engineer	$24,000	96 credit hours	AAS
Paralegal Studies	$19,200	96 credit hours	AAS
Administrative Assistant	$10,400	52 credit hours	Diploma
Computer Network Technician	$ 9,000	36 credit hours	Diploma
Medical Assistant	$10,800	52 credit hours	Diploma
Medical Billing and Coding	$ 9,600	50 credit hours	Diploma

Western Technical Institute, El Paso

About Our Institution
Western Technical Institute (WTI) started serving the needs of industry on January 1, 1970. The institution enjoys an excellent reputation within the community, among its leaders, and among industry employers. WTI is proud of its heritage and enjoys third-generation family ownership. WTI is very active in the arena of contract training.

Special Features
Western Technical Institute offers short-term, intensive hands-on training. This allows its students to obtain their career goals and get out in the workforce faster. WTI offers tutoring and ongoing placement.

Financial Aid/Scholarships
Since WTI is an accredited institution, students are eligible to apply for a range of federal student aid programs. WTI participates in numerous scholarship programs. Interested parties should contact the school for details or visit the Web site listed below.

Tuition and Fees
Tuition and fees vary depending on which course and schedule a student decides to take. Costs are comparable to industry numbers and, in most cases, are a little lower than those at other institutions. The school offers a payment plan to fit just about anyone's budget. Each student is required to pay a $100 registration fee upon enrolling.

Accreditation
ACCSCT, CAAHEP.

Admissions
Prospective students must have a high school diploma or GED certificate and must be able to meet the entrance exam score requirement on the CPAT or Wonderlic Assessment. Some courses require a typing proficiency of at least 25 words per minute. Automotive and refrigeration students must have a current driver's license prior to starting classes. Applicants must be at least 17 years of age.

Graduation Requirements
In order to graduate and qualify for a certificate, diploma, or degree, a student must receive a passing grade for each course and have a grade point average of at least 2.0. Students must also satisfy all academic, attendance, and financial aid requirements before a certificate, diploma, or degree will be awarded.

Program Content

AOS Degree: Automotive Technology, Microcomputer Technology, Microcomputer Technology/Electronics, Refrigeration HVAC Technology

Certificate: Combination Welding, GED, Health Information Technology, Information Technology, Medical Assisting

Contact
Bill Terrell, Chief Administrative Officer
1000 Texas Avenue
El Paso, TX 79901
Phone: (915) 532-3737
Fax: (915) 532-6946
E-mail: bterrell@wti-ep.com
Web: www.wti-ep.com

Programs Eligible for Scholarship	Tuition and Fees	Course Length/Credit Hours	Credential Earned
Automotive Technology	$19,050	71 credit units	AOS
Microcomputer Technology	$23,346	85 credit units	AOS
Microcomputer Technology/Electronics	$19,455	72 credit units	AOS
Refrigeration HVAC Technology	$19,050	71 credit units	AOS
Combination Welding	$11,271	29.5 credit units	Certificate
Health Information Technology	$11,673	41 credit units	Certificate
Information Technology	$14,267	49 credit units	Certificate
Medical Assisting	$ 9,090	34 credit units	Certificate

All courses offered at WTI are eligible for the Imagine America Scholarship.

Westwood Aviation Institute, Houston

About Our Institution

Westwood Aviation Institute–Houston is focused on aircraft maintenance training, offering programs in Airframe and Powerplant maintenance. Committed to a positive and cooperative environment and working in collaboration with employers, the Institute is dedicated to high-quality, college-level, career-oriented education. Westwood's objective is to graduate confident, qualified individuals prepared to enter the aviation career field.

Special Features

Westwood Aviation Institute–Houston places a high value on the industry experience faculty members bring to the classroom. While several faculty members have earned their associate degrees in their fields, as well as their Airframe and Powerplant licenses, Westwood looks for a combination of industry experience, educational training in the subject area, and prior teaching experience to ensure that students receive a balanced education.

Financial Aid/Scholarships

Westwood Aviation Institute participates in a variety of financial aid programs, including Federal Pell Grants, Perkins loans, Federal PLUS loans, Federal Stafford Student Loans, FSEOG, Westwood High School Scholarship program, and educational assistance loans. Other types of financial aid may be available depending on an indivdual student's eligibility. Students should check with the admissions office for approved VA benefits.

Tuition and Fees

Students should consult the school catalog for detailed tuition and fee information.

Accreditation

Westwood Aviation Institute–Houston is accredited by the Council on Occupational Education (COE). This accreditation means the Institute has a clearly defined mission, aspires to high standards to ensure high-quality programs, and has the human, physical, and financial resources to accomplish its mission. The school's program is certified by the Federal Aviation Administration (FAA).

Admissions

To enroll at Westwood Aviation Institute–Houston, students should possess a high school diploma or GED and be at least 17 years of age. Prospective students must be able to speak, read, and write English proficiently. Applicants must complete an enrollment application and interview with an admissions representative.

Program Content

The Houston campus offers certificate programs in Airframe and Powerplant Technology, Airframe Only, Powerplant Only, Airframe Add-On, and Powerplant Add-On.

Contact

Bob Pim
Executive Director
8880 Telephone Road
Houston, TX 77061
Phone: (713) 644-7777
　　　　(800) 776-7423 (toll-free)
Fax: 713-644-0902
E-mail: rpim@westwood.edu
Web: www.westwood.edu

Programs Eligible for Scholarship	Course Length/Credit Hours	Credential Earned
Airframe and Powerplant	16.5 months/2048 hours/59 credits	Certificate
Airframe Only*	1280 hours/39 credits	Certificate
Powerplant Only*	1248 hours/34 credits	Certificate
Airframe Add-On*	800 hours/25 credits	Certificate
Powerplant Add-On*	768 hours/20 credits	Certificate

* Depends on class availability.

Westwood College, Dallas

About Our Institution

Westwood College–Dallas is accredited by ACICS and approved and regulated by the Texas Workforce Commission and the Texas Higher Education Coordinating Board. The College is committed to a positive and cooperative environment. Working collaboratively with employers, the College is dedicated to high-quality, college-level, career-oriented education. Our objective is to graduate confident, job-qualified individuals who are prepared to enter career fields of their choice.

Special Features

Westwood College places a high value on the industry experience faculty members bring to the classroom. While many faculty members have earned bachelor's and master's degrees in their fields, Westwood looks for a combination of industry experience, educational training in the subject area, and prior teaching experience to ensure that students receive a balanced, industry-relevant education.

Financial Aid/Scholarships

Westwood College participates in a variety of financial aid programs, including the Federal Pell Grant, Federal Stafford Student Loan (subsidized and unsubsidized), Federal PLUS loan, Federal Perkins Loan, FSEOG, the Westwood High School Scholarship program, and educational assistance loans. Other types of financial aid may be available, depending on individual student eligibility. Check with the admissions office for VA-approved benefits.

Tuition and Fees

Students should consult the school catalog for detailed tuition and fee information.

Accreditation

Westwood is accredited by the Accrediting Council for Independent Colleges and Schools (ACICS). This accreditation shows that the College has a clearly defined mission, aspires to high standards to ensure high-quality programs, and has the human, physical, and financial resources to accomplish its mission.

Admissions

Successful candidates for Westwood are required to have a high school diploma or GED. Applicants must submit an application and receive a minimum score of 17 on the ACT or 920 on the SAT or achieve the required scores on the Accuplacer Computerized Placement Test. Candidates must also have an interview with an admissions representative and submit a registration fee. Upon completion of testing, candidates must attend an acceptance interview to verify their commitment to begin training.

Program Content

The Dallas campus offers associate degrees in Computer Network Engineering, Computer-Aided Design: Architectural Drafting, Computer-Aided Design: Interior Finishes, Graphic Design and Multimedia, and Software Engineering and a diploma program for Medical Assisting.

Contact

Vince Thomae
Executive Director
8390 LBJ Freeway
Dallas, TX 75243
Phone: (214) 570-0100
Fax: (214) 570-8502
E-mail: vthomae@westwood.edu
Web: www.westwood.edu

Programs Eligible for Scholarship	Course Length/Credit Hours	Credential Earned
Computer-Aided Design: Architectural Drafting	20 months/103.5 credit hours	AAS
Computer-Aided Design: Interior Finishes	20 months/102 credit hours	AAS
Computer Network Engineering	20 months/102 credit hours	AAS
Graphic Design and Multimedia	20 months/105 credit hours	AAS
Software Engineering	20 months/101.5 credit hours	AAS
Medical Assisting	12 months/76.5 credit hours	Diploma

Westwood College, Fort Worth, Euless

About Our Institution

Westwood College–Ft. Worth is accredited by the Accrediting Council for Independent Colleges and Schools (ACICS) and approved and regulated by the Texas Workforce Commission and the Texas Higher Education Coordinating Board. The College is committed to a positive and cooperative environment. Working collaboratively with employers, the College is dedicated to high-quality, college-level, career-oriented education. The objective is to graduate confident, job-qualified individuals prepared to enter career fields of choice.

Special Features

Westwood College places a high value on the industry experience faculty members bring to the classroom. While many faculty members have earned bachelor's and master's degrees in their fields, Westwood looks for a combination of industry experience, educational training in the subject area, and prior teaching experience to ensure that students receive a balanced, industry-relevant education.

Financial Aid/Scholarships

Westwood College participates in a variety of financial aid programs, including the Federal Pell Grant, FFEL, Stafford Student Loan (subsidized and unsubsidized), Plus loans, Federal Perkins Loan, the Federal Supplemental Educational Opportunity Grant (FSEOG), the Westwood High School Scholarship Program, and educational assistance loans. Other types of financial aid may be available depending on individual student eligibility. Students should check with the Admissions Office for VA-approved benefits.

Tuition and Fees

Students should consult the school catalog for detailed tuition and fee information.

Accreditation

Westwood is accredited by ACICS. This accreditation guides the College, in that it has a clearly defined mission and aspires to high standards to ensure quality programs. The school has the human, physical, and financial resources to accomplish its mission.

Admissions

Successful candidates for Westwood are required to have a high school diploma or GED. Applicants must submit an application and receive a minimum score of 17 on the ACT or 920 on the SAT or achieve the required scores on the Accuplacer Computerized Placement Test. Candidates must also have an interview with an admissions representative and submit a registration fee. Upon completion of testing, candidates must attend an acceptance interview to verify their commitment to begin training.

Program Content

The Ft. Worth campus offers associate degrees in Computer-Aided Design/Architectural Drafting, Computer-Aided Design/Interior Finishes, Computer Network Engineering, Graphic Design and Multimedia, and Software Engineering.

Contact

Kelly Coates
Executive Director
Westwood College–Ft. Worth
1331 Airport Freeway
Euless, TX 76040
Phone: (817) 685-9994
Fax: (817) 685-8929
E-mail: kcoates@westwood.edu
Web: www.westwood.edu

Programs Eligible for Scholarship	Course Length/Credit Hours	Credential Earned
Computer-Aided Design/Architectural Drafting	20 months/103.5 credits	AAS
Computer-Aided Design/Interior Finishes	20 months/102 credits	AAS
Computer Network Engineering	20 months/102 credits	AAS
Graphic Design and Multimedia	20 months/105 credits	AAS
Software Engineering	20 months/101.5 credits	AAS

Westwood College, Houston South, Houston

About Our Institution
Westwood College–Houston South is committed to maintaining a positive and cooperative environment and to working collaboratively with employers to ensure a high-quality, college-level, career-oriented education. The objective is to graduate confident, job-qualified individuals prepared to enter their career fields of choice.

Special Features
Westwood College places a high value on the industry experience faculty members bring to the classroom. While many faculty members have earned bachelor's and master's degrees in their fields, Westwood looks for a combination of industry experience, educational training in the subject area, and prior teaching experience to ensure that students receive a balanced, industry-relevant education.

Financial Aid/Scholarships
Westwood College participates in a variety of financial aid programs, including the Federal Pell Grant, FFEL, Stafford Student Loan (subsidized and unsubsidized), Plus loans, Federal Perkins Loan, the Federal Supplemental Educational Opportunity Grant (FSEOG), the Westwood High School Scholarship Program, and educational assistance loans. Other types of financial aid may be available depending on individual student eligibility. Students should check with the Admissions Office for VA-approved benefits.

Tuition and Fees
Students should consult the school catalog for detailed tuition and fee information.

Accreditation
Westwood is accredited by the Accrediting Commission of Career Schools and Colleges of Technology (ACCSCT). This accreditation guides the College, in that it has a clearly defined mission and aspires to high standards to ensure high-quality programs and has the human, physical, and financial resources to accomplish its mission. In addition, the College is approved and regulated by the Texas Workforce Commission.

Admissions
Successful candidates for Westwood are required to have a high school diploma or GED. Applicants must submit an application and receive a minimum score of 17 on the ACT or 920 on the SAT or achieve the required scores on the Accuplacer Computerized Placement Test. Candidates must also have an interview with an admissions representative and submit a registration fee. Upon completion of testing, candidates must attend an acceptance interview to verify their commitment to begin training.

Program Content
Associate Degrees: Computer-Aided Design/Architecural Drafting, Computer-Aided Design/Concentration in Interior Finishes, Computer Network Engineering, Graphic Design and Multimedia, Software Engineering.

Contact
Rick Skinner
Executive Director
7322 Southwest Freeway
Houston, TX 77074
Phone: (713) 777-4433
Fax: (713) 219-2088
E-mail: cjones@westwood.edu
Web: www.westwood.edu

Programs Eligible for Scholarship	Course Length/Credit Hours	Credential Earned
Computer-Aided Design/Architectural Drafting	20 months/103.5 credit hours	AAS
Computer-Aided Design/Concentration in Interior Finishes	20 months/102 credit hours	AAS
Computer Network Engineering	20 months/102 credit hours	AAS
Graphic Design and Multimedia	20 months/105 credit hours	AAS
Software Engineering	20 months/101.5 credit hours	AAS

ITT Technical Institute, Murray

About Our Institution

ITT Technical Institute is owned and operated by ITT Educational Services,
Inc. (ITT/ESI), a leading private college system offering technology-influenced programs of study. ITT/ESI operates seventy-seven ITT Technical Institutes in thirty states; they provide career-focused degree programs to approximately 39,000 students as of spring 2004. Headquartered in Carmel, Indiana, ITT/ESI has been actively involved in the higher education community in the United States since 1969. Curriculum offerings are designed to help students begin to prepare for career opportunities in fields of technology. Students attend classes year-round, with convenient breaks provided throughout the year. A full-time student course load can have class meetings as often as three days per week, and classes are typically available in the morning, afternoon, and evening, depending on student enrollment. General education courses may be available online. This class schedule offers flexibility to students to pursue part-time employment opportunities.

Special Features

Most ITT Technical Institute programs of study blend traditional academic content with applied learning concepts, with a significant portion devoted to practical study in a lab environment. Advisory committees, made up of representatives of local businesses, help each ITT Technical Institute periodically review and update curricula, equipment, and laboratory design.

The Institute awards the Associate in Occupational Studies.

Financial Aid/Scholarships

ITT Technical Institute maintains a Financial Aid Department on the campus. The campus is designated as an eligible institution by the U.S. Department of Education for participation in the following programs: Federal Stafford Student Loan, Federal PLUS Loan, and Federal Work-Study. The school also offers nonfederal loans through Bank One for eligible students.

Tuition and Fees

March 2005 tuition is $386 per credit hour.

Accreditation

Accrediting Council for Independent Colleges and Schools (ACICS).

Graduation Requirements

For graduation requirements, students should consult the school catalog.

Contact

Dr. Mike Linzmaier, Director
ITT Technical Institute
920 West LeVoy Drive
Murray, UT 84123
Phone: (801) 263-3497
Fax: (801) 263-3497

Program Content

School of Information Technology: Data Communication Systems Technology, Information Systems Security, Information Technology (Computer Network Systems Option, Software Applications and Programming Option, Web Development Option), Software Engineering Technology

School of Electronics Technology: Computer and Electronics Engineering Technology, Electronics and Communications Engineering Technology, Industrial Automation Engineering Technology

School of Drafting and Design: Computer Drafting and Design, Digital Entertainment and Game Design, Information Technology-Multimedia Option

School of Business: Business Accounting Technology, Business Administration, Technical Project Management

School of Criminal Justice: Criminal Justice

Mountain West College, West Valley City

About Our Institution
Mountain West College was founded in 1982 as a computer school. It has since grown into a full-fledged college of business-related programs. Graduates are prepared for entry-level positions. Mountain West College is one of more than eighty schools owned and operated by Corinthian Colleges, Inc., in the United States.

Special Features
Facilities include four computer labs, a modern resource learning center, and numerous classrooms, lounges, and offices.

Financial Aid/Scholarships
Mountain West College participates in Federal Pell Grants, Federal Family Educational Loan (FFEL) Program, work-study, Federal Supplemental Educational Opportunity Grants (FSEOG), VA, and high school scholarships. Financial aid is available for those who qualify.

Tuition and Fees
Per-credit-hour fees are assessed based on the amount of classes taken per quarter.

Accreditation
Mountain West College is accredited by the Accrediting Council for Independent Colleges and Schools (ACICS). The Medical Assisting Program is accredited by AAMA, a division of the Commission on Accreditation of Allied Health Education Programs (CAAHEP).

Admissions
An applicant must be a high school graduate or have a GED certificate and successfully complete an assessment exam.

Graduation Requirements
To graduate, students must have earned a minimum of a 2.0 CGPA and must successfully complete all required credits within the maximum credits that may be attempted.

Enrollment
There are 715 students enrolled.

Program Content
Accounting, Business, Business Accounting, Computer Information Systems, Criminal Justice, Medical Assisting, Medical Insurance Billing and Coding, Paralegal, Professional Office Administration, Surgical Technologist, Travel and Tourism

Contact
Jason Peterson, Director of Admissions
Mountain West College
3280 West 3500 South
West Valley City, UT 84119
Phone: (801) 840-4800
Fax: (801) 969-0828
E-mail: jasonp@cci.edu
Web: www.mwcollege.com

Programs Eligible for Scholarship	Tuition and Fees	Course Length/Credit Hours	Credential Earned
Accounting	$267/credit hour	72 weeks/96 credit hours	AS
Business	$267/credit hour	72 weeks/96 credit hours	AA
Computer Information Systems	$267/credit hour	72 weeks/90 credit hours	AS
Medical Assisting	$267/credit hour	72 weeks/97 credit hours	Diploma/AS
Medical Insurance Billing and Coding	$8,269	6 months/35 credit hours	Diploma
Paralegal	$267/credit hour	72 weeks/96 credit hours	AA
Professional Office Administration	$267/credit hour	72 weeks/90 credit hours	AS
Surgical Technologist	$267/credit hour	72 weeks/107 credit hours	AS
Travel and Tourism	$267/credit hour	72 weeks/90 credit hours	Diploma/AA

New England Culinary Institute, Montpelier

About Our Institution

New England Culinary Institute (NECI) has been training chefs and food and beverage professionals since 1980. NECI students learn in the Institute's restaurants and food service operations under the supervision of its highly trained chefs. NECI's small class size, averaging 7 students to 1 instructor, sets it apart from other culinary and food and beverage programs.

Special Features

NECI is located in beautiful, safe Vermont. Its students learn by doing. The unique, intensive training prepares graduates for success in the industry because the education takes place in actual restaurants and other food service facilities, such as a cafeteria, a bakery, and a banquet/catering facility. Paid internships outside the school continue the hands-on, on-the-job training. All students are provided with single-occupancy housing and membership at a local fitness center. NECI has a partnership arrangement with the Council of Independent Restaurants of America (CIRA) for the benefit of students and interns.

Financial Aid/Scholarships

NECI's financial planner assists students and their families in coming up with a personalized plan geared toward each individual's circumstances. Federal financial aid is available for those who qualify. NECI participates in many scholarship programs.

Tuition and Fees

There are no application fees for any programs. The first-year tuition and fees for students enrolling prior to September 1, 2005, in the associate programs in culinary arts or baking and pastry arts are: tuition, $20,995; room and board, $6,055; and all other fees and deposits, $2,240. For the associate and bachelor's programs in food and beverage management, tuition is $18,650; room and board, $6,985; and all other fees and deposits, $1,925. For the certificate programs in baking, pastry, or basic cooking, tuition is $8,875; room and board, $3,490; and all other fees and deposits, $1,615.

Accreditation

NECI is accredited by the Accrediting Commission of Career Schools and Colleges of Technology (ACCSCT).

Admissions

The culinary arts and baking and pastry arts programs enroll four times each year: March, June, September, and December. Both food and beverage management programs enroll twice yearly, in March and September.

For the certificate and associate programs, applicants must submit an originally signed application, a minimum of one letter of recommendation, a one- to two-page essay (double-spaced), and an official high school transcript. For the bachelor's degree program, applicants must submit an originally signed application, a minimum of two letters of recommendation, a three- to four-page essay (double-spaced), and official high school and college transcripts. An admissions interview must also be completed for all programs.

It is strongly recommended that prospective students visit the school and attend one of the twice-weekly tours prior to enrolling.

Graduation Requirements

To graduate, students must make satisfactory academic progress, which includes the completion of credit or clock hours within a specific time period as well as earning acceptable class evaluations.

Contact

Dawn Hayward, Director of Admissions
New England Culinary Institute
250 Main Street
Montpelier, VT 05602
Phone: 877-223-6324 (toll-free)
E-mail: info@neci.edu
Web: http://www.neci.edu

Program Content

Associate Degree in Culinary Arts Cooking theory and food science; the history, flavor and culture of food; knife skills; a la carte cooking; baking; health and wellness; communications; storeroom management; career development; table service; introduction to wines; catering and banquets; garde manger; meat fabrication and charcuterie; operations management; pastries; confections and plated desserts; computer studies.

Associate Degree in Baking and Pastry Arts Baking theory; food science; the history, flavor and culture of food; knife skills; career development; introduction to computers; operations management for the bakeshop; foundations in the pastry arts; health and wellness; communications; storeroom management; customer and table service; visual arts and principles of design; beverages for the pastry menu.

Associate Degree in Food and Beverage Management Food and beverage math, computers, health and wellness, writing, psychology and its professional applications, food production management, food history, legal issues and regulatory affairs, purchasing, physiology of taste and flavor, food production, marketing, beverage and catering operations, professional presentations, human resources management, service management, public speaking, nutrition, social sciences and industry applications, financial management and accounting.

Bachelor's Degree in Food and Beverage Management Accounting; marketing; computer systems; food and beverage management; reading and writing; effective and ethical communication; human resource management; physiology of taste and flavor; Spanish; concept development and business planning; labor, management, and the organization; applied marketing for the food service industry; food writing; financial analysis; multiunit operations management; wine business; health and wellness; nutrition; visual design in the hospitality industry; corporate management and finance; entrepreneurship; food and culture; applied research methods. Many of these courses have additional levels of advanced instruction.

Program Description

Associate Degree in Culinary Arts In each of the two years of this program, students have six months of residency and an additional six months to complete 700 hours of paid internship. Students are trained for all types of culinary careers.

Associate Degree in Baking and Pastry Arts In each of the two years of this program, students have six months of residency and an additional six months to complete 700 hours of paid internship. Students are trained for culinary careers in the areas of baking and pastry.

Associate Degree in Food and Beverage Management This program is organized as a 1½-year program with a one-year residency and a six-month paid internship. It includes a culinary component so that students have a mastery of both "back of the house" (kitchens) and "front of the house" (dining room management) careers.

Bachelor's Degree in Food and Beverage Management This eighteen-month program (beyond the associate degree or other qualifying educational credits) includes classroom work, intensive hands-on, and project-based learning in a variety of settings as well as a six-month paid internship. It is designed for those who want to advance their careers in "top-of-the-house" roles (the business and entrepreneurial aspects of the industry).

Certificate in Basic Cooking This fifteen-week residency is followed by one 6-month, 700-hour paid internship. The program is designed to prepare students to start a career as a prep, line, or banquet cook. The certificate program can also serve as preparation for the associate degree program in culinary arts.

Certificate in Baking This fifteen-week residency is followed by one 6-month, 700-hour paid internship. The program is designed to prepare students to start a career as bakers in bakeshops, restaurants, or other commercial kitchens. The certificate program can also serve as preparation for the associate degree program in baking and pastry arts.

Certificate in Pastry This fifteen-week residency is followed by one 6-month, 700-hour paid internship. The program is designed to prepare students to start a career as pastry cooks in bakeshops, restaurants, or other commercial kitchens. The certificate program can also serve as preparation for the associate degree program in baking and pastry arts.

ECPI College of Technology, Newport News

About Our Institution

ECPI College of Technology (an on-campus and online private college) was established in 1966 and operates in Virginia Beach, Newport News, and Northern Virginia, Virginia; Greensboro, Charlotte, and Raleigh, North Carolina; and Greenville and Charleston, South Carolina. The College has an outstanding reputation for providing high-quality graduates to employers, including many Fortune 500 companies.

Special Features

ECPI provides high-quality technical and business education in a student-centered environment. The College prepares graduates to meet the needs of employers by offering classroom and hands-on instruction with industry-standard equipment. A valuable combination of technical and general education courses in degree programs enables graduates to advance quickly and to continue their lifelong pursuit of knowledge. Low faculty-student ratios facilitate instruction, and tutorial assistance is available at no additional charge. Students in degree programs can participate in an externship course that provides valuable experience in an employment setting. Programs are kept up-to-date with the input of advisory boards made up of leading employers and graduates. Job placement assistance is provided to qualified graduates, and students have the opportunity to interview for employment at job fairs held on campus.

Financial Aid/Scholarships

The College maintains a Financial Aid Office providing a variety of financial aid programs, including Federal Pell Grants, FFEL, Perkins Loans, work-study, FSEOG, VA, NexStep, and scholarships.

Tuition and Fees

Tuition and fees vary by program.

Accreditation

The College is accredited by the Commission on Colleges of the Southern Association of Colleges and Schools to award associate and baccalaureate degrees.

Admissions

A high school diploma or GED certificate is required for admission, in addition to passing an admissions test and meeting academic and financial criteria.

Graduation Requirements

A student must attain a minimum 2.0 cumulative GPA for the entire program, achieve all applicable skill proficiencies, and complete all courses specified for the program.

Program Content

A.A.S. Degrees: Accounting Administration, Business Systems Administration, Computer Network Technology, Criminal Justice Technology, Information Technology/Computer Programming, Information Technology/Networking and Security Management, Information Technology/Web Design, Medical Administration, Wireless Communications

Diplomas: Accounting Administration, Business Administration, Computer Technology, Information Technology/Computer Programming, Medical Administration

Program Description

The Computer Science and Information Science programs and the Computer Electronics Technology programs prepare students for a variety of employment opportunities, such as network administration, Web site development, computer programming, software or accounting applications, computer network development, wireless communications, electronics, computer technology, and criminal justice technology.

Program content has been carefully developed by faculty members using recommendations of employers and advisory board members to best meet industry needs.

Contact

John Olson, Provost
ECPI College of Technology
1001 Omni Boulevard, #100
Newport News, VA 23606
Phone: (757) 838-9191
Fax: (757) 827-5351
E-mail: jolson@ecpi.edu
Web: www.ecpi.edu

Programs Eligible for Scholarship	Course Length/Credit Hours	Credential Earned
Accounting Administration	68 credits	AAS
Accounting Administration	45 credits	Diploma
Business Systems Administration	68 credits	AAS
Business Systems Administration	45 credits	Diploma
Computer Network Technology	74 credits	AAS
Computer Technology	42 credits	Diploma
IT/Computer Programming	74 credits	AAS
IT/Computer Programming	45 credits	Diploma
IT/Networking and Security Management	74 credits	AAS
IT/Web Design	74 credits	AAS
Medical Administration	68 credits	AAS
Medical Administration	48 credits	Diploma
Wireless Communications	74 credits	AAS

ECPI College of Technology, Northern Virginia, Manassas

About Our Institution

The College, an on-campus and online private college, was established in 1966 and operates in Virginia Beach, Newport News, and Northern Virginia, Virginia; Greensboro, Charlotte, and Raleigh, North Carolina; and Greenville and Charleston, South Carolina. The College has an outstanding reputation for providing high-quality graduates to employers, including many Fortune 500 companies.

Special Features

ECPI provides high-quality technical, business, and health science education in a student-centered environment. The College prepares graduates to meet the needs of employers by offering classroom and hands-on instruction with industry-standard equipment. A valuable combination of technical and general education courses in degree programs enables graduates to advance quickly and continue their lifelong learning. Programs are kept up-to-date using the input of advisory boards that consist of leading employers and graduates. Hands-on instruction is featured whenever possible to increase the ability of students to move from theory to practical application. Low faculty-student ratios are maintained to facilitate instruction, and tutorial assistance is available at no additional charge. Students in degree programs have the opportunity to participate in an externship course that provides valuable experience in an employment setting. Job placement assistance is provided to qualified graduates, and many students have an opportunity to interview for employment in Job Fairs that are held on campus.

Financial Aid/Scholarships

The College maintains a financial aid office providing a variety of programs, including Pell Grants, FFEL, Perkins Loans, work-study, FSEOG, VA, and scholarships.

Tuition and Fees

Tuition and fees vary by program.

Accreditation

The College is accredited by the Commission on Colleges of the Southern Association of Colleges and Schools to award associate and baccalaureate degrees.

Admissions

A high school diploma or GED is required for admission in addition to passing an admissions test and meeting academic and financial criteria.

Graduation Requirements

A student must attain a 2.0 cumulative GPA for the entire program, achieve all applicable skill proficiencies, and complete all courses specified for the program.

Program Content

A.A.S. Degrees: Business Systems Administration, Computer Network Technology, Criminal Justice Technology, IT/Computer Programming, IT/Networking and Security Management, IT/Web Design, Medical Administration, Medical Assisting, Wireless Communications

Diplomas: Business Systems Administration, Computer Technology, IT/Computer Programming, Medical Administration, Medical Assisting, Practical Nursing

Program Description

The Computer Science and Information Science programs prepare students for a variety of employment opportunities that include network administration, Web site development, computer programming, and software or accounting applications. Degree programs feature an externship course that consists of both program competencies and actual work experience. The faculty utilizes program advisory committees to identify and focus on current needs of industry. General education courses enable students to continue their lifelong pursuit of knowledge and to demonstrate those characteristics expected of a college graduate.

The Computer Electronics Technology programs prepare students for a variety of employment opportunities that include computer networks, telecommunications, electronics, and computer technology.

Contact

Judi Hughes, Provost
ECPI College of Technology
10021 Balls Ford Road, #100
Manassas, VA 20109
Phone: (703) 330-5300
E-mail: jhughes@ecpi.edu
Web: www.ecpi.edu

Programs Eligible for Scholarship	Course Length/Credit Hours	Credential Earned
Business Systems Administration	45/68 credits	Diploma/AAS
Computer Network Technology	74 credits	AAS
Computer Technology	42 credits	Diploma
Criminal Justice Technology	74 credits	AAS
IT/Computer Programming	45/74 credits	Diploma/AAS
IT/Networking and Security Management	74 credits	AAS
IT/Web Design	74 credits	AAS
Medical Administration	41/68 credits	Diploma/AAS
Medical Assisting	46/65 credits	Diploma/AAS
Practical Nursing	74 credits	Diploma

ECPI College of Technology, Virginia Beach

About Our Institution

ECPI College of Technology, an on-campus and online private college, was established in 1966 and operates in Virginia Beach, Newport News, and Northern Virginia, Virginia; Greensboro, Charlotte, and Raleigh, North Carolina; and Greenville and Charleston, South Carolina. The College has an outstanding reputation for providing high-quality graduates to employers, including many Fortune 500 companies.

Special Features

ECPI provides high-quality technical and business education in a student-centered environment. The College prepares graduates to meet the needs of employers by offering classroom and hands-on instruction with industry-standard equipment. A valuable combination of technical and general education courses in degree programs enables graduates to advance quickly and to continue their lifelong pursuit of knowledge. Low faculty-student ratios facilitate instruction, and tutorial assistance is available at no additional charge. Students in degree programs can participate in an externship course that provides valuable experience in an employment setting. Programs are kept up-to-date with the input of advisory boards made up of leading employers and graduates. Job placement assistance is provided to qualified graduates.

Financial Aid/Scholarships

The College maintains a financial aid office providing assistance with a variety of financial aid programs, including Pell Grants, FFEL, Perkins Loans, work-study, FSEOG, VA, NexStep, and scholarships.

Tuition and Fees

Tuition and fees vary by program.

Accreditation

The College is accredited by the Commission on Colleges of the Southern Association of Colleges and Schools to award associate and baccalaureate degrees.

Admissions

A high school diploma or GED certificate is required for admission, in addition to passing an admissions test and meeting academic and financial criteria.

Graduation Requirements

A student must attain a minimum 2.0 cumulative GPA for the entire program, achieve all applicable skill proficiencies, and complete all courses specified for the program.

Program Content

A.A.S. Degrees: Accounting Administration, Business Systems Administration, Computer Network Technology, Criminal Justice Technology, Information Technology/Computer Programming, Information Technology/Networking and Security Management, Information Technology/Web Design, Wireless Communications

Diplomas: Accounting Administration, Business Administration, Computer Technology, Information Technology/Computer Programming, Medical Administration

Program Description

The programs at ECPI College of Technology prepare students for a variety of employment opportunities, such as network administration, Web site development, computer programming, software or accounting applications, computer network development, criminal justice technology, network security, wireless communications, electronics, and computer and biomedical technology.

Program content has been carefully developed by faculty members using recommendations of employers and advisory board members to best meet industry needs.

Contact

R. J. Ballance, Vice President
5555 Greenwich Road
Virginia Beach, VA 23462
Phone: (757) 490-9090
Fax: (757) 671-8661
E-mail: rballance@ecpi.edu
Web: www.ecpi.edu

Programs Eligible for Scholarship	Course Length/Credit Hours	Credential Earned
Accounting Administration	68 credits	AAS
Accounting Administration	45 credits	Diploma
Biomedical Equipment Technology	74 credits	AAS
Business Systems Administration	68 credits	AAS
Business Systems Administration	45 credits	Diploma
Computer Network Technology	74 credits	AAS
Computer Technology	42 credits	Diploma
Criminal Justice Technology	74 credits	AAS
Information Systems	127 credits	BS
IT/Computer Programming	74 credits	AAS
IT/Computer Programming	42 credits	Diploma
IT/Networking and Security Management	74 credits	AAS
IT/Web Design	74 credits	AAS
Wireless Communications	74 credits	AAS

ECPI Technical College, Glen Allen

About Our Institution
The College was established in 1966 and operates in Richmond (main campus) and Glen Allen (branch), Virginia. The College has an outstanding reputation for providing high-quality graduates to employers, including many Fortune 500 companies.

Special Features
ECPI provides high-quality technical and business education in a student-centered environment. The College prepares graduates to meet the needs of employers by offering classroom and application-oriented instruction with industry-standard equipment. A valuable combination of technical and general education courses in degree programs enables graduates to advance quickly and to continue their lifelong pursuit of knowledge. Low faculty-student ratios facilitate instruction, and tutorial assistance is available at no additional charge. Students in degree programs can participate in an externship course that provides valuable experience in an employment setting. Programs are kept up-to-date with the input of advisory boards made up of leading employers and graduates. Job placement assistance is provided to qualified graduates, and students have the opportunity to interview for employment at job fairs held on campus.

Financial Aid/Scholarships
The College maintains a financial aid office providing a variety of programs including Pell Grants, FFEL, Perkins Loans, work-study, FSEOG, VA, and scholarships.

Tuition and Fees
Tuition and fees vary by program.

Accreditation
The College is accredited by the Accrediting Commission of Career Schools and Colleges of Technology (ACCSCT).

Admissions
A high school diploma or GED certificate is required for admission, in addition to passing an admissions test and meeting academic and financial criteria.

Graduation Requirements
A student must attain a minimum 2.0 cumulative GPA for the entire program, achieve all applicable skill proficiencies, and complete all courses specified for the program.

Program Content
BS Degree: Management Information Systems

AAS Degrees (Computer and Information Science): Business Administration, Criminal Justice Technology, Information Technology/Computer Programming, Information Technology/Networking and Security Management, Information Technology/Web Design, Medical Administration

AAS Degrees (Computer Electronics Technology): Computer Electronics Engineering Technology, Wireless Communications

Diplomas: Business Administration, Computer Electronics Engineering Technology, Information Technology/Computer Programming

Program Description
The programs at ECPI Technical College prepare students for a variety of employment opportunities, such as network administration, Web site development, computer programming, software or accounting applications, computer network development, criminal justice technology, telecommunications, electronics, and computer technology.

Program content has been carefully developed by faculty members using recommendations of employers and advisory board members to best meet industry needs.

Contact
Loretta Pully, Financial Aid Director
ECPI Technical College, Branch Campus
4305 Cox Road
Glen Allen, VA 23060
Phone: (804) 934-0100
Fax: (804) 934-0054
E-mail: lpully@ecpitech.edu
Web: www.ecpitech.edu

Programs Eligible for Scholarship	Course Length/Credit Hours	Credential Earned
Business Administration	68 credits	AAS
Business Administration	45 credits	Diploma
Computer Electronics Engineering Technology	74 credits	AAS
Computer Electronics Engineering Technology	45 credits	Diploma
Criminal Justice Technology	74 credits	AAS
IT/Computer Programming	74 credits	AAS
IT/Computer Programming	45 credits	Diploma
IT/Networking and Security Management	74 credits	AAS
IT/Web Design	74 credits	AAS
Management Information Systems	120 credits	BS
Medical Administration	68 credits	AAS
Wireless Communications	74 credits	AAS

ECPI Technical College, Richmond

About Our Institution
The College was established in 1966 and operates in Richmond and Glen Allen, Virginia. The College has an outstanding reputation for providing high-quality graduates to employers, including many Fortune 500 companies.

Special Features
ECPI provides high-quality technical and business education in a student-centered environment. The College prepares graduates to meet the needs of employers by offering classroom and application-oriented instruction with industry-standard equipment. A valuable combination of technical and general education courses in degree programs enables graduates to advance quickly and to continue their lifelong pursuit of knowledge. Low faculty-student ratios facilitate instruction, and tutorial assistance is available at no additional charge. Students in degree programs can participate in an externship course that provides valuable experience in an employment setting. Programs are kept up-to-date with the input of advisory boards made up of leading employers and graduates. Job placement assistance is provided to qualified graduates, and students have the opportunity to interview for employment at job fairs held on campus.

Financial Aid/Scholarships
The College maintains a financial aid office providing a variety of programs including Pell Grants, FFEL, Perkins Loans, work-study, FSEOG, VA, and scholarships.

Tuition and Fees
Tuition and fees vary by program.

Accreditation
The College is accredited by the Accrediting Commission of Career Schools and Colleges of Technology (ACCSCT).

Admissions
A high school diploma or GED certificate is required for admission, in addition to passing an admissions test and meeting academic and financial criteria.

Graduation Requirements
A student must attain a minimum 2.0 cumulative GPA for the entire program, achieve all applicable skill proficiencies, and complete all courses specified for the program.

Program Content
B.S. Degree: Management Information Systems

A.A.S. Degrees: Business Administration, Computer Network Technology, Criminal Justice Technology, Information Technology/Computer Programming, Information Technology/Networking and Security Management, Information Technology/Web Design, Medical Administration, Wireless Communications

Diplomas: Business Administration, Computer Technology, Information Technology/Computer Programming, Medical Administration

Program Description
The programs at ECPI Technical College prepare students for a variety of employment opportunities, such as network administration, Web site development, computer programming, software or accounting applications, computer network development, wireless communications, electronics, computer technology, and criminal justice technology.

Program content has been carefully developed by faculty members using recommendations of employers and advisory board members to best meet industry needs.

Contact
Ada Gerard, Director
ECPI Technical College, Main Campus
800 Moorefield Park Drive
Richmond, VA 23236
Phone: (804) 330-5533
Fax: (804) 330-5577
E-mail: agerard@ecpitech.edu
Web: www.ecpitech.edu

Programs Eligible for Scholarship	Course Length/Credit Hours	Credential Earned
Management Information Systems	120 credits	BS
Business Administration	45/68 credits	Diploma/AAS
Computer Electronics Engineering Technology	74 credits	AAS
Computer Electronics Engineering Technology	42 credits	Diploma
Criminal Justice Technology	74 credits	AAS
IT/Computer Programming	45/74 credits	Diploma/AAS
IT/Networking and Security Management	74 credits	AAS
IT/Web Design	74 credits	AAS
Medical Administration	48/68 credits	Diploma/AAS
Wireless Communications	74 credits	AAS

ECPI Technical College, Roanoke

About Our Institution
The College was established in 1966. The College has an outstanding reputation for providing high-quality graduates to employers, including many Fortune 500 companies.

Special Features
ECPI provides high-quality technical, business, and health science education in a student-centered environment. The College prepares graduates to meet the needs of employers by offering classroom and hands-on instruction with industry-standard equipment. A valuable combination of technical and general education courses in degree programs enables graduates to advance quickly and continue their lifelong learning. Programs are kept up-to-date using the input of advisory boards that consist of leading employers and graduates. Hands-on instruction is featured whenever possible to increase the ability of students to move from theory to practical application. Low faculty-student ratios are maintained to facilitate instruction, and tutorial assistance is available at no additional charge. Students in degree programs have the opportunity to participate in an externship course that provides valuable experience in an employment setting. Job placement assistance is provided to qualified graduates, and many students have an opportunity to interview for employment in job fairs that are held on campus.

Financial Aid/Scholarships
The College maintains a Financial Aid Office providing a variety of programs, including Federal Pell Grants, FFEL, Perkins Loans, work-study, FSEOG, VA benefits, and scholarships.

Tuition and Fees
Tuition and fees vary by program.

Accreditation
The College is accredited by the Accrediting Commission of Career Schools and Colleges of Technology (ACCSCT).

Admissions
A high school diploma or GED is required for admission in addition to passing an admissions test and meeting academic and financial criteria.

Graduation Requirements
A student must attain a 2.0 cumulative GPA for the entire program, achieve all applicable skill proficiencies, and complete all courses specified for the program.

Program Content

A.A.S. Degrees (Computer and Information Science curricula): Business Administration, Information Technology/Networking and Security Management

A.A.S. Degrees (Computer Electronics Technology curricula): Computer Network Technology, Wireless Communications

A.A.S. Degrees (Health Sciences curricula): Medical Administration, Medical Assisting

Diploma: Practical Nursing

Program Description
The Computer Science and Information Science programs prepare students for a variety of employment opportunities that include network administration, Web site development, and software or accounting applications. Degree programs feature an externship course that consists of both program competencies and actual work experience. The faculty utilizes program advisory committees to identify and focus on current needs of industry.

The Computer Electronics Technology programs prepare students for a variety of employment opportunities that include computer networks, wireless communications, electronics, and computer technology.

Contact
Elmer Haas, Director
5234 Airport Road
Roanoke, VA 24012
Phone: (540) 563-8080
Fax: (540) 362-5400
E-mail: ehaas@ecpitech.edu
Web: www.ecpitech.edu

Programs Eligible for Scholarship	Course Length/Credit Hours	Credential Earned
Business Administration	72 credits	AAS
Computer Electronics Engineering Technology	78 credits	AAS
IT/Networking and Security Management	78 credits	AAS
Medical Administration	72 credits	AAS
Medical Assisting	74 credits	AAS
Wireless Communications	78 credits	AAS
Practical Nursing	46 credits	Diploma

ITT Technical Institute, Richmond

About Our Institution
The company: ITT Technical Institute is owned and operated by ITT Educational Services, Inc. (ITT/ESI), a leading private college system offering technology-influenced programs of study. ITT/ESI operates seventy-seven ITT Technical Institutes in thirty states that provide career-focused degree programs to approximately 39,000 students as of spring 2004. Headquartered in Carmel, Indiana, ITT/ESI has been actively involved in the higher education community in the United States since 1969.

Curricula: Curriculum offerings are designed to help students begin to prepare for career opportunities in fields of technology. Students attend classes year-round, with convenient breaks provided throughout the year. A full-time student course load can have class meetings as often as three days a week and are typically available in the morning, afternoon, and evening, depending on student enrollment. General education courses may be available online. This class schedule offers flexibility to students to pursue part-time employment opportunities.

Special Features
Most ITT Technical Institute programs of study blend traditional academic content with applied learning concepts, with a significant portion devoted to practical study in a lab environment. Advisory committees, made up of representatives of local businesses, help each ITT Technical Institute periodically review and update curricula, equipment, and laboratory design.

The Richmond campus offers Associate of Applied Science and Bachelor of Science degrees.

Financial Aid/Scholarships
ITT Technical Institute maintains a Financial Aid Department on campus. The campus is designated as an eligible institution by the U.S. Department of Education for participation in the Federal Stafford Student Loan, Federal PLUS Loan, and Federal Work-Study Programs. The school also offers nonfederal loans available through Bank One for eligible students.

Tuition and Fees
March 2005 tuition is $386 per credit hour.

Accreditation
The Institute is accredited by the Accrediting Council for Independent Colleges and Schools (ACICS).

Admissions
For admission requirements, students should consult the school catalog.

Graduation Requirements
For graduation requirements, students should consult the school catalog.

Program Content
School of Business: Business Accounting Technology, Business Administration, Technical Project Management

School of Criminal Justice: Criminal Justice

School of Drafting and Design: Computer Drafting and Design, Digital Entertainment and Game Design, Information Technology–Multimedia

School of Electronics Technology: Computer and Electronics Engineering Technology, Electronics and Communications Engineering Technology

School of Information Technology: Data Communication Systems Technology, Information Systems Security, Information Technology–Computer Network Systems, Information Technology–Software Applications and Programming, Information Technology–Web Development, Software Engineering Technology

Contact
Doug Howard, Director
ITT Technical Institute
300 Gateway Centre Parkway
Richmond, VA 23235
Phone: (804) 330-4992
Fax: (804) 330-4993

ITT Technical Institute, Springfield

About Our Institution

The company: ITT Technical Institute is owned and operated by ITT Educational Services, Inc. (ITT/ESI), a leading private college system offering technology-influenced programs of study. ITT/ESI operates seventy-seven ITT Technical Institutes in thirty states, providing career-focused degree programs to approximately 39,000 students as of spring 2004. Headquartered in Carmel, Indiana, ITT/ESI has been actively involved in the higher education community in the United States since 1969.

Curricula: Curriculum offerings are designed to help students begin to prepare for career opportunities in fields of technology. Students attend classes year-round, with convenient breaks provided throughout the year. A full-time student course load can have class meetings as often as three days a week and are typically available in the morning, afternoon, and evening, depending on student enrollment. General education courses may be available online. This class schedule offers flexibility to students to pursue part-time employment opportunities.

ITT Technical Institute, Springfield, awards the Associate of Applied Science degree.

Special Features

Most ITT Technical Institute programs of study blend traditional academic content with applied learning concepts, with a significant portion devoted to practical study in a lab environment. Advisory committees composed of representatives of local businesses help each ITT Technical Institute periodically review and update curricula, equipment, and laboratory design.

Financial Aid/Scholarships

ITT Technical Institute maintains a Financial Aid Department on campus. The campus is designated as an eligible institution by the U.S. Department of Education for participation in the following programs: Federal Stafford Student Loan Program, Federal PLUS Loan Program, and Federal Work-Study Program. The school also offers nonfederal loans available through Bank One for eligible students.

Tuition and Fees

March 2005 tuition is $386 per credit hour.

Accreditation

The school is accredited by the Accrediting Council for Independent Colleges and Schools (ACICS).

Admissions

For admission requirements, students should contact the school for a catalog.

Graduation Requirements

For graduation requirements, students should contact the school for a catalog.

Program Content

School of Information Technology: Data Communication Systems Technology, Information Systems Security, Information Technology–Computer Network Systems, Information Technology–Software Applications and Programming, Information Technology–Web Development

School of Electronics Technology: Computer and Electronics Engineering Technology, Electronics and Communications Engineering Technology

School of Drafting and Design: Computer Drafting and Design, Information Technology–Multimedia Option

School of Business: Business Accounting Technology, Business Administration, Technical Project Management

School of Criminal Justice: Criminal Justice

Contact

Kurt Thompson, Director
ITT Technical Institute
7300 Boston Boulevard
Springfield, VA 22153
Phone: (703) 440-9535
Fax: (703) 440-9561

Kee Business College, Chesapeake

About Our Institution
Kee Business College, formerly known as College of Hampton Road, was founded in 1941. The school name was changed to Kee Business College in 1996, and the Chesapeake branch campus of Kee Business College–Newport News, Virginia, was established in 1999. The school is one of more than eighty colleges and institutions nationwide owned and operated by Corinthian Colleges, Inc.

Special Features
The modern facility is equipped with both medical and computer labs to provide students with the hands-on experience and training they need to function effectively in their professions. The air-conditioned building has approximately 21,300 square feet, including five lecture rooms, five computer laboratories, two medical laboratories, one massage therapy laboratory, one dental laboratory, a library/resource center, administrative offices, a student lounge, and restrooms.

Financial Aid/Scholarships
The College participates in various programs: Federal Pell, Federal Family Educational Loan (FFEL), Federal Direct Student Loan (FDSL), Perkins, work-study, Federal Supplemental Educational Opportunity (FSEOG), and veterans benefits. Financial aid is available for those who qualify.

Accreditation
Kee Business College is accredited by the Accrediting Council for Independent Colleges and Schools (ACICS). The Medical Assisting program is accredited by AAMA, a division of the Commission on Accreditation of Allied Health Education Programs (CAAHEP).

Admissions
The school follows an open-enrollment system. Individuals may apply up to one year in advance of a scheduled class start. All applicants are required to complete a personal interview with an admissions representative, pass an entrance evaluation, and complete an application for enrollment. A high school diploma or GED credential is required.

Graduation Requirements
Medical programs: Complete all required classroom modules with a grade of at least 70 percent and successfully complete 160 clock hours in an approved externship. Computerized Office Applications and Massage Therapy Programs: Complete all required classroom training with a cumulative grade point average of at least 2.0 and complete all program requirements.

Enrollment
There are 400–500 students enrolled.

Program Content
Computerized Office Applications, Computer Office Technologies and Applications, Dental Assisting, Homeland Security Specialist, Massage Therapy, Medical Administrative Assistant, Medical Assisting, Medical Insurance Billing/Coding

Contact
Ed Flores, Director of Admissions
Kee Business College
825 Greenbrier Circle
Chesapeake, VA 23320
Phone: (757) 361-3900
Fax: (757) 361-3917
E-mail: eflores@cci.edu
Web: www.cci.edu

Programs Eligible for Scholarship	Tuition and Fees	Course Length/Credit Hours	Credential Earned
Computerized Office Applications	$10,390	10 months/840 hours	Diploma
Dental Assisting	$ 9,975	8 months/720 hours	Diploma
Massage Therapy	$10,615	9 months/720 hours	Diploma
Medical Administrative Assistant	$10,575	8 months/720 hours	Diploma
Medical Assisting	$10,575	8 months/720 hours	Diploma
Medical Insurance Billing/Coding	$ 7,475	6 months/650 hours	Diploma

Kee Business College, Newport News

About Our Institution

Kee Business College, formerly known as College of Hampton Road, was founded in 1941. The school's name was changed to Kee Business College in 1996, and the Chesapeake branch campus of Kee Business College–Newport News, Virginia, was established in 1999. The school is one of more than eighty colleges and institutions nationwide owned and operated by Corinthian Colleges, Inc.

Special Features

The modern facility is equipped with both medical and computer labs to provide students with the hands-on experience and training they need to function effectively in their professions. The air-conditioned building has approximately 29,000 square feet, including five lecture rooms, five computer laboratories, two medical laboratories, one massage therapy laboratory, one dental laboratory, a library/resource center, administrative offices, a student lounge, and restrooms.

Financial Aid/Scholarships

The College participates in various programs: Federal Pell, Federal Family Educational Loan (FFEL), Federal Direct Student Loan (FDSL), Perkins, Federal Work-Study, Federal Supplemental Educational Opportunity (FSEOG), and veterans benefits. Financial aid is available for those who qualify.

Accreditation

Kee Business College is accredited by the Accrediting Council for Independent Colleges and Schools (ACICS). The Medical Assisting program is accredited by American Association of Medical Assistants (AAMA), a division of the Commission on Accreditation of Allied Health Education Programs (CAAHEP).

Admissions

The school follows an open-enrollment system. Individuals may apply up to one year in advance of a scheduled class start. All applicants are required to complete a personal interview with an admissions representative, pass an entrance evaluation, and complete an application for enrollment. A high school diploma or GED credential is required.

Graduation Requirements

Students enrolled in medical programs must complete all required classroom modules with a grade of at least 70 percent and successfully complete 160 clock hours in an approved externship. Students enrolled in programs in computerized office applications and massage therapy must complete all required classroom training with a cumulative grade point average of at least 2.0 and complete all program requirements.

Program Content

Computerized Office Applications, Dental Assisting, Homeland Security Specialist, Massage Therapy, Medical Administrative Assistant, Medical Assisting, Medical Insurance Billing/Coding

Enrollment

There are 341 students enrolled.

Contact

Margaret Ortiz
Kee Business College
825 Greenbrier Circle
Chesapeake, VA 23320
Phone: 757-361-3900
Fax: 757-361-3917
E-mail: mortiz@cci.edu
Web: www.cci.edu

Programs Eligible for Scholarship	Tuition and Fees	Course Length/Credit Hours	Credential Earned
Computerized Office Applications	$13,427	10 months/840 hours	Diploma
Dental Assisting	$11,284	8 months/720 hours	Diploma
Homeland Security Specialist	$ 8,998	7 months/640 hours	Diploma
Massage Therapy	$11,890	9 months/720 hours	Diploma
Medical Administrative Assistant	$12,313	8 months/720 hours	Diploma
Medical Assisting	$12,300	8 months/720 hours	Diploma
Medical Insurance Billing/Coding	$ 9,254	6 months/650 hours	Diploma

Medical Careers Institute, Newport News

About Our Institution
Initially established in 1978, this private, postsecondary career training institution has a certificate to operate issued by the Commonwealth of Virginia, Board of Education. MCI has authority from the Commonwealth of Virginia, Department of Health Regulatory Board's State Board of Nursing, to conduct a practical nursing program. Facilities include a well-equipped dental laboratory and operatory, medical laboratory, and simulated clinical nursing environment. MCI also has numerous lecture/demonstration classrooms as well as computer labs. MCI has an extension campus in Virginia Beach and a branch in Richmond.

Special Features
The medical assisting department head is a registered medical assistant. The Placement Director assists students in obtaining externship experience while in school and assists graduates in securing employment in full-time health-care positions. Part-time jobs are available to students while attending MCI.

Financial Aid/Scholarships
The Institute maintains a financial aid office that provides a variety of aid programs, including Pell Grants, FFEL, Perkins, work-study, FSEOG, VA, TA, Vocational Rehabilitation, NeXStep, Imagine America Scholarships, and JTPA.

Tuition and Fees
Tuition and fees vary by program.

Accreditation
The Institute is accredited by the Commission of the Council on Occupational Education. The medical assisting program is accredited by the Commission on Accreditation of Allied Health Education Programs.

Admissions
A diploma or GED is required in addition to passing an admissions test and meeting academic and financial criteria. Practical nursing applicants must interview with the Practical Nursing Director. The practical nursing, medical assistant, and dental assistant programs require a complete physical examination.

Graduation Requirements
A student must attain a minimum overall 2.0 cumulative GPA for the entire program, achieve all required skill proficiencies, and complete all courses specified in the catalog.

Program Content
Associate of Applied Science (A.A.S.) in Health Science Programs in Massage Therapy, Medical Assisting

Diploma Programs in Dental Assistant, Massage Therapy, Medical Assisting, Medical Office Specialist, Medical Transcriptionist, Practical Nursing

Program Description
The Practical Nursing program prepares students to perform as members of a health-care team and to function under the supervision of a physician and/or a registered nurse in providing nursing care and provides extensive clinical experience.

The Medical/Dental programs prepare students without related backgrounds to meet the requirements for entry-level employment as dental assistants, medical assistants, medical office specialists, or medical transcriptionists.

The Massage Therapy programs teach the art and science of massage therapy, while focusing on the medical and rehabilitative effects of massage for employment in private clinics, chiropractic clinics, medical and health centers, spas, or private physician's offices.

Contact
Laura Egatz, Director
1001 Omni Boulevard #200
Newport News, VA 23606
Phone: (757) 873-2423
Fax: (757) 873-2472
E-mail: legatz@medical.edu
Web: www.medical.edu

Programs Eligible for Scholarship	Course Length/Credit Hours	Credential Earned
Dental Assistant	32 credits	Diploma
Massage Therapy	44/61 credits	Diploma/AAS
Medical Assisting	39/60 credits	Diploma/AAS
Medical Office Specialist	35 credits	Diploma
Medical Transcriptionist	35 credits	Diploma
Practical Nursing	46 credits	Diploma

Medical Careers Institute, Richmond

About Our Institution

Initially established in 1978, this private, postsecondary career-training institution has a certificate to operate issued by the Commonwealth of Virginia Board of Education. Medical Career Institute (MCI) has the authority, given by the Commonwealth of Virginia Department of Health Regulatory Board's State Board of Nursing, to conduct a practical nursing program. Facilities include a well-equipped medical laboratory and simulated clinical nursing environment. MCI also has numerous lecture/demonstration classrooms as well as computer labs. MCI has its main campus in Newport News, an extension campus in Virginia Beach, and a branch in Richmond.

Special Features

The medical assisting department head is a registered medical assistant. The Placement Director assists students in obtaining externship experience while in school and assists graduates in securing employment in full-time health-care positions. Part-time jobs are available to students while attending MCI.

Financial Aid/Scholarships

The Institute maintains a Financial Aid Office that provides a variety of aid programs, including Pell Grants, FFEL, Perkins, Work-Study, FSEOG, VA, TA, Vocational Rehabilitation, NEXStep, Imagine America Scholarships, and WIA.

Tuition and Fees

Tuition and fees vary by program.

Accreditation

MCI is accredited by the Accrediting Commission of the Council on Occupational Education. Its medical assisting program is accredited by the Commission on Accreditation of Allied Health Education Programs.

Admissions

A high school diploma or GED certificate is required in addition to passing an admissions test and meeting academic and financial criteria. Practical nursing applicants must interview with the Practical Nursing Director. The practical nursing and medical assisting programs require a complete physical examination.

Graduation Requirements

A student must attain a minimum overall 2.0 cumulative GPA for the entire program, achieve all required skill proficiencies, and complete all courses specified in the catalog.

Program Content

Associate of Applied Science (A.A.S.) Degree Programs: Health Science with a major in medical assisting, Massage Therapy

Diploma Programs: Medical Assisting, Medical Office Specialist, Practical Nursing

Program Description

The Practical Nursing Program prepares students to perform as members of a health-care team and to function under the supervision of a physician and/or a registered nurse in providing nursing care and provides extensive clinical experience.

The medical programs prepare students without related backgrounds to meet the requirements for entry-level employment as medical assistants or medical office specialists.

Contact

Jeff Muroski, Director
Medical Careers Institute
800 Moorefield Park Drive, #302
Richmond, VA 23236
Phone: (804) 521-0400
Fax: (804) 521-0406
E-mail: jmuroski@medical.edu
Web: www.medical.edu

Programs Eligible for Scholarship	Course Length/Credit Hours	Credential Earned
Health Science (medical assisting)	60 credits	AAS
Massage Therapy	61 credits	AAS
Medical Assisting	39 credits	Diploma
Medical Office Specialist	35 credits	Diploma
Practical Nursing	46 credits	Diploma

Medical Careers Institute, Virginia Beach

About Our Institution

Initially established in 1978, this private, postsecondary career training institution has a certificate to operate issued by the Commonwealth of Virginia, Board of Education. Medical Career Institute (MCI) has authority from the Commonwealth of Virginia, Department of Health Regulatory Board's State Board of Nursing to conduct a practical nursing program and a registered nursing program. Facilities include a well-equipped medical laboratory and simulated clinical nursing environment. MCI also has numerous lecture/demonstration classrooms as well as computer labs. MCI has its main campus in Newport News, an extension campus in Virginia Beach, and a branch in Richmond.

Special Features

The medical assisting department head is a certified medical assistant. The Placement Director assists students in obtaining externship experience while in school and assists graduates in securing employment in full-time health-care positions. Part-time jobs are available to students while attending MCI.

Financial Aid/Scholarships

The Institute maintains a Financial Aid Office that provides a variety of aid programs, including Pell Grants, FFEL, Perkins, Work-Study, FSEOG, VA, TA, Vocational Rehabilitation, NeXStep, Imagine American Scholarships, and JTPA.

Tuition and Fees

Tuition and fees vary by program.

Accreditation

The Institute is accredited by the Commission of the Council on Occupational Education.

The medical assisting program is accredited by the Commission on Accreditation of Allied Health Education Programs.

Admissions

A diploma or GED certificate is required in addition to passing an admissions test and meeting academic and financial criteria. Practical nursing applicants must interview with the Practical Nursing Director. The practical nursing, registered nursing, and medical assisting programs require a complete physical examination.

Graduation Requirements

A student must attain a minimum overall 2.0 cumulative GPA for the entire program, achieve all required skill proficiencies, and complete all courses specified in the catalog.

Program Content

Associate of Applied Science (A.A.S.) Degree Program in Health Science, with a major in medical assisting, physical therapy, and registered nursing

Diploma Programs in Medical Assisting, Medical Office Specialist, Practical Nursing

Program Description

The Practical Nursing Program prepares students to perform as members of a health-care team and to function under the supervision of a physician and/or a registered nurse in providing nursing care and provides extensive clinical experiences.

The Medical Programs prepare students without related backgrounds to meet the requirements for entry-level employment as medical assistants, medical office specialists, physical therapists, practical nurses, or registered nurses.

Contact

Joyce Wheatley, Director
Medical Careers Institute
5501 Greenwich Road, #100
Virginia Beach, VA 23462
Phone: (757) 497-8400
Fax: (757) 497-8473
E-mail: jwheatley@medical.edu
Web: www.medical.edu

Programs Eligible for Scholarship	Course Length/Credit Hours	Credential Earned
Medical Assisting	39/60 credits	Diploma/AAS
Medical Office Specialist	35 credits	Diploma
Medical Transcriptionist	35 credits	Diploma
Practical Nursing	46 credits	Diploma

National College of Business and Technology, Bluefield

About Our Institution

National College of Business and Technology was established in 1886. The Bluefield campus, which proudly overlooks the heart of Bluefield, Virginia, opened in 1981. National College of Business and Technology's curriculum is specific and concentrates on essential professional skills that will lead toward employment in a specific field. Programs are planned to offer the most effective methods in technology, business organization, and management while consistently meeting the demands of the modern world. The College offers courses that cover a broad range of majors, including accounting, management, medical assisting, and office technology as well as other fields. Students can complete programs in as little as one year or less.

Special Features

A major strength of National College of Business and Technology is its ability to quickly adjust the curriculum to changes in the employment needs of business and industry and to meet the career interest of students. Community representatives, serving as a Campus Advisory Board, provide current and timely advice relative to the employment needs of business, technical, and government organizations.

The Career Center is available to assist with the entire job search process. Specialized staff members are available to help students to prepare a resume and cover letter and interview effectively. They assist the student throughout the employment search.

Students who wish to demonstrate their current skill level in selected areas may take an Advanced Placement evaluation. If successful, the student receives credit for that particular course and may shorten his or her program accordingly.

Scholarships are available not only to students who performed well during their secondary education but also to current students who excel while pursuing their particular program of study.

Financial Aid/Scholarships

National College of Business and Technology makes available an extensive program of financial assistance, which includes the Federal Stafford Loan, Federal Plus Loan, Federal Perkins Loan, Federal Pell Grant, Federal Supplemental Educational Opportunity Grant, Workforce Development Grant, and Business Partnership Grant as well as several scholarship opportunities.

Tuition and Fees

Tuition is $170 per credit hour. National College of Business and Technology is among the least expensive private colleges in its area. Students should check the catalog for current application, student activities, or graduation fees.

Accreditation

National College of Business and Technology is accredited by the Accrediting Council for Independent Colleges and Schools (ACICS);

Program Content

Accounting, Administrative Office Professional, Computer Applications Technology, Management, Medical Assisting

Program Description

All programs listed above lead to an Associate of Science degree.

The programs offered at National College of Business and Technology give the graduate the training that is needed to take the first step into an entry position as well as the background necessary to grow professionally in that field.

individual programs such as Medical Assisting may have programmatic accreditation.

Admission

A prospective student must have a high school diploma or GED certificate and submit an application for admission together with the application fee.

Graduation Requirements

In order to be eligible for graduation, the student must complete all courses outlined in the program and earn the required number of credit hours. To graduate from any program, a 2.0 overall grade point average must be achieved.

Contact

Admissions Department
100 Logan Street
Bluefield, VA 24605
Phone: (276) 326-3621
Fax: (276) 322-5731

Programs Eligible for Scholarship	Tuition and Fees	Course Length/Credit Hours	Credential Earned
All related program areas	$16,320	96 credit hours	AOS

National College of Business and Technology, Bristol

About Our Institution

National College of Business and Technology was established in 1886. The Bristol campus, which is located in the heart of Bristol, Virginia, opened in 1992. National College of Business and Technology's curriculum is specific and concentrates on essential professional skills that lead toward employment in a specific field. Programs are planned to offer the most effective methods in technology, business organization, and management while consistently meeting the demands of the modern world. The College offers courses that cover a broad range of majors including accounting, management, medical assisting, and office technology as well as other fields. Students can complete programs in as little as one year or less.

Special Features

A major strength of National College of Business and Technology is its ability to quickly adjust the curriculum to changes in the employment needs of business and industry and to meet the career interest of students. Community representatives, serving as a Campus Advisory Board, provide current and timely advice relative to the employment needs of business, technical, and government organizations.

The Career Center is available to assist with the entire job-search process. Specialized staff members are available to help students prepare a resume and cover letter and interview effectively. They assist the student throughout the employment search.

Students who wish to demonstrate their current skill level in selected areas may take an Advanced Placement evaluation. If successful, the student receives credit for that particular course and may shorten his or her program accordingly.

Scholarships are available not only to students who performed well during their secondary education, but also to current students who excel while pursuing their particular program of study.

Financial Aid/Scholarships

National College of Business and Technology makes available an extensive program of financial assistance, which includes Federal Stafford Loans, Federal Plus Loans, Federal Perkins Loans, the Federal Pell Grant, the Federal Supplemental Educational Opportunity Grant, the Workforce Development Grant, and the Business Partnership Grant, as well as several scholarship opportunities.

Tuition and Fees

Tuition is $162 per credit hour. National College of Business and Technology is among the least expensive private colleges in its area. Students should check the catalog for current application, student activities, or graduation fees.

Accreditation

National College of Business and Technology is accredited by the Accrediting Council for Independent Colleges and Schools (ACICS);

Program Content

Accounting, Computer Applications Technology, Management, Office Administration, Medical Assisting

Program Description

All programs listed above lead to an Associate of Science degree.

The programs offered at National College of Business and Technology give the graduate the training that is needed to take the first step into an entry position as well as the background necessary to grow professionally in that field.

individual programs such as Medical Assisting may have programmatic accreditation.

Admission

A prospective student must have a high school diploma or GED certificate and submit an application for admission together with the application fee.

Graduation Requirements

In order to be eligible for graduation, the student must complete all courses outlined in the program and earn the required number of credit hours. To graduate from any program, a minimum 2.0 overall grade point average must be achieved.

Contact

Admissions Department
National College of Business and
   Technology
300 A Piedmont Avenue
Bristol, VA 24201
Phone: (540) 669-5333
Fax: (540) 669-4793

Programs Eligible for Scholarship	Tuition and Fees	Course Length/Credit Hours	Credential Earned
All related program areas	$15,552	96 credit hours	AOS

National College of Business and Technology, Charlottesville

About Our Institution
National College of Business and Technology was established in 1886. The Charlottesville campus, located on U.S. Highway 29, opened in 1979. National College of Business and Technology's curriculum is specific and concentrates on essential professional skills that lead toward employment in a specific field. Programs are planned to offer the most effective methods in technology, business organization, and management, while consistently meeting the demands of the modern world. The College offers courses that cover a broad range of majors, including accounting, management, medical assisting, and office technology as well as other fields. Students can complete programs in as little as one year or less.

Special Features
A major strength of National College of Business and Technology is its ability to quickly adjust the curriculum to changes in the employment needs of business and industry and to meet the career interest of students. Community representatives, serving as a Campus Advisory Board, provide current and timely advice relative to the employment needs of business, technical, and government organizations.

The Career Center is available to assist with the entire job search process. Specialized staff members are available to help students to prepare a resume and cover letter and interview effectively. They assist the student throughout the employment search.

Students who wish to demonstrate their current skill level in selected areas may take an Advanced Placement evaluation. If successful, the student receives credit for that particular course and may shorten his or her program accordingly.

Scholarships are available not only to students who performed well during their secondary education but also to current students who excel while pursuing their particular program of study.

Financial Aid/Scholarships
National College of Business and Technology makes available an extensive program of financial assistance which includes the Federal Stafford Loan, Federal Plus Loan, Federal Perkins Loan, Federal Pell Grant, Federal Supplemental Educational Opportunity Grant, Workforce Development Grant, and Business Partnership Grant as well as several scholarship opportunities.

Tuition and Fees
Tuition is $170 per credit hour. National College of Business and Technology is among the least expensive private colleges in its area. Check the catalog for current application, student activities, or graduation fees.

Accreditation
National College of Business and Technology is accredited by the Accrediting Council for Independent Colleges and Schools (ACICS);

Program Content
Accounting, Computer Applications Technology, Management, Medical Assisting, Office Administration, Tourism and Hospitality

Program Description
All programs listed above lead to an Associate of Science degree.

The programs offered at National College of Business and Technology give the graduate the training that is needed to take the first step into an entry position as well as the background necessary to grow professionally in that field.

individual programs such as Medical Assisting may have programmatic accreditation.

Admission
A prospective student must have a high school diploma or GED certificate and submit an application for admission together with the application fee.

Graduation Requirements
In order to be eligible for graduation, the student must complete all courses outlined in the program and earn the required number of credit hours. To graduate from any program, a 2.0 overall grade point average must be achieved.

Contact
Admissions Department
1819 Emmet Street
Charlottesville, VA 22901
Phone: (434) 295-0136
Fax: (434) 979-8061

Programs Eligible for Scholarship	Tuition and Fees	Course Length/Credit Hours	Credential Earned
All related program areas	$16,320	96 credit hours	AOS

National College of Business and Technology, Danville

About Our Institution
National College of Business and Technology was established in 1886. The Danville campus, which offers students a central location in the heart of the business and financial districts, opened in 1982. National College of Business and Technology's curriculum is specific and concentrates on the essential professional skills that will lead toward employment in a specific field. Programs are planned to offer the most effective methods in technology, business organization, and management, while consistently meeting the demands of the modern world. The College offers courses that cover a broad range of majors, including accounting, management, medical assisting, and office technology as well as other fields. Students can complete programs in as little as one year or less.

Special Features
A major strength of National College of Business and Technology is its ability to quickly adjust the curriculum to changes in the employment needs of business and industry and to meet the career interest of students. Community representatives, serving as a Campus Advisory Board, provide current and timely advice relative to the employment needs of business, technical, and government organizations.

The Career Center is available to assist with the entire job-search process. Specialized staff members are available to help students prepare a resume and cover letter and interview effectively. They assist the student throughout the employment search.

Students who wish to demonstrate their current skill level in selected areas may take an Advanced Placement evaluation. If successful, the student receives credit for that particular course and may shorten his or her program accordingly.

Scholarships are available not only to students who performed well during their secondary education but also to current students who excel while pursuing their particular program of study.

Financial Aid/Scholarships
National College of Business and Technology makes available an extensive program of financial assistance, which includes Federal Stafford Loans, Federal Plus Loans, Federal Perkins Loans, the Federal Pell Grant, the Federal Supplemental Educational Opportunity Grant, the Workforce Development Grant, and the Business Partnership Grant, as well as several scholarship opportunities.

Tuition and Fees
Tuition is $162 per credit hour. National College of Business and Technology is among the least expensive private colleges in its area. Students should check the catalog for current application, student activities, or graduation fees.

Accreditation
National College of Business and Technology is accredited by the Accrediting Council for Independent Colleges and Schools (ACICS);

Program Content
Accounting, Computer Applications Technology, Management, Medical Assisting, Office Administration

Program Description
All programs listed above lead to an Associate of Science degree.

The programs offered at National College of Business and Technology give the graduate the training that is needed to take the first step into an entry position as well as the background necessary to grow professionally in that field.

individual programs such as Medical Assisting may have programmatic accreditation.

Admission
A prospective student must have a high school diploma or GED certificate and submit an application for admission together with the application fee.

Graduation Requirements
In order to be eligible for graduation, the student must complete all courses outlined in the program and earn the required number of credit hours. To graduate from any program, a minimum 2.0 overall grade point average must be achieved.

Contact
Admissions Department
National College of Business and Technology
734 Main Street
Danville, VA 24541
Phone: (434) 793-6822
Fax: (434) 793-3634

Programs Eligible for Scholarship	Tuition and Fees	Course Length/Credit Hours	Credential Earned
All related program areas	$15,552	96 credit hours	AOS

National College of Business and Technology, Harrisonburg

About Our Institution

National College of Business and Technology was established in 1886. The Harrisonburg campus, which features all the modern amenities conducive to study in a businesslike environment while keeping the charm of a collegiate atmosphere, opened in 1989. National College of Business and Technology's curriculum is specific and concentrates on essential professional skills that lead toward employment in a specific field. Programs are planned to offer the most effective methods in technology, business organization, and management while consistently meeting the demands of the modern world. The College offers courses that cover a broad range of majors, including accounting, management, medical assisting, and office technology, as well as other fields. Students can complete programs in as little as one year or less.

Special Features

A major strength of National College of Business and Technology is its ability to quickly adjust the curriculum to changes in the employment needs of business and industry and to meet the career interest of students. Community representatives, serving as a Campus Advisory Board, provide current and timely advice relative to the employment needs of business, technical, and government organizations.

The Career Center is available to assist with the entire job search process. Specialized staff members are available to help students to prepare a resume and cover letter and interview effectively. They assist the student throughout the employment search.

Students who wish to demonstrate their current skill level in selected areas may take an Advanced Placement evaluation. If successful, the student receives credit for that particular course and may shorten his or her program accordingly.

Scholarships are available not only to students who performed well during their secondary education but also to current students who excel while pursuing their particular program of study.

Financial Aid/Scholarships

National College of Business and Technology makes available an extensive program of financial assistance, which includes Federal Stafford Student Loans, Federal PLUS loans, Federal Perkins Loans, the Federal Pell Grant, the Federal Supplemental Educational Opportunity Grant, the Workforce Development Grant, and the Business Partnership Grant as well as several scholarship opportunities.

Tuition and Fees

Tuition is $162 per credit hour. National College of Business and Technology is among the least expensive private colleges in its area. Students should check the catalog for current application, student activities, and graduation fees.

Program Content

Accounting, Computer Applications Technology, Management, Medical Assisting, Office Administration

Program Description

All programs listed above lead to an Associate of Science degree.

The programs offered at National College of Business and Technology give the graduate the training that is needed to take the first step into an entry position as well as the background necessary to grow professionally in that field.

Accreditation

National College of Business and Technology is accredited by the Accrediting Council for Independent Colleges and Schools (ACICS); individual programs such as Medical Assisting may have programmatic accreditation.

Admission

A prospective student must have a high school diploma or GED certificate and submit an application for admission together with the application fee.

Graduation Requirements

In order to be eligible for graduation, the student must complete all courses outlined in the program and earn the required number of credit hours. To graduate from any program, an overall grade point average of at least 2.0 must be achieved.

Contact

Admissions Department
51B Burgess Road
Harrisonburg, VA 22801
Phone: (540) 432-0943
Fax: (540) 432-1133

Programs Eligible for Scholarship	Tuition and Fees	Course Length/Credit Hours	Credential Earned
All related program areas	$15,552	96 credit hours	AOS

National College of Business and Technology, Lynchburg

About Our Institution
National College of Business and Technology was established in 1886. The Lynchburg campus, which is situated in the Timberlake area of the city, opened in 1979. National College of Business and Technology's curriculum is specific and concentrates on essential professional skills that will lead toward employment in a specific field. Programs are planned to offer the most effective methods in technology, business organization, and management, consistently meeting the demands of the modern world. The College offers courses that cover a broad range of majors including Accounting, Management, Medical Assisting, Computer Systems Management, and Office Technology as well as other fields. Students can complete programs in as little as one year or less.

Special Features
A major strength of National College of Business and Technology is its ability to quickly adjust the curriculum to changes in the employment needs of business and industry and to meet the career interest of students. Community Representatives, serving as a Campus Advisory Board, provide current and timely advice relative to the employment needs of business, technical, and government organizations.

The Career Center is available to assist with the entire job search process. Specialized staff members are available to help students to prepare a resume and cover letter and interview effectively. They assist the student throughout the employment search.

Students who wish to demonstrate their current skill level in selected areas may take an Advanced Placement Evaluation. If successful, the student receives credit for that particular course and may shorten his or her program accordingly.

Scholarships are available not only to students who performed well during their secondary education but also to current students who excel while pursuing their particular program of study.

Financial Aid/Scholarships
National College of Business and Technology makes available an extensive program of financial assistance which includes the Federal Stafford Loan, Federal Plus Loan, Federal Perkins Loan, Federal Pell Grant, Federal Supplemental Educational Opportunity Grant, Workforce Development Grant, and Business Partnership Grant as well as several scholarship opportunities.

Tuition and Fees
Tuition is $170 per credit hour. National College of Business and Technology is among the least expensive private colleges in its area. Students should check the catalog for current application, student activities, or graduation fees.

Accreditation
National College of Business and Technology is accredited by the Accrediting Council for Independent Colleges and Schools (ACICS);

Program Content
Accounting, Computer Applications Technology, Management, Office Administration, Medical Assisting

Program Description
All programs listed above lead to an Associate of Science degree.

The programs offered at National College of Business and Technology give the graduate the training that is needed to take the first step into an entry position as well as the background necessary to grow professionally in that field.

individual programs such as Medical Assisting may have programmatic accreditation.

Admission
A prospective student must have a high school diploma or GED certificate and submit an application for admission together with the application fee.

Graduation Requirements
In order to be eligible for graduation, the student must complete all courses outlined in the program and earn the required number of credit hours. To graduate from any program, a 2.0 overall grade point average must be achieved.

Contact
Admissions Department
104 Candlewood Court
Lynchburg, VA 24502
Phone: (434) 239-3500
Fax: (434) 239-3948

Programs Eligible for Scholarship	Tuition and Fees	Course Length/Credit Hours	Credential Earned
All related program areas	$16,320	96 credit hours	AOS

National College of Business and Technology, Martinsville

About Our Institution

National College of Business and Technology was established in 1886. The Martinsville campus, which proudly offers career-oriented education to residents of the city and surrounding areas, opened in 1978. National College of Business and Technology's curriculum is specific and concentrates on the essential professional skills that lead toward employment in a specific field. Programs are planned to offer the most effective methods in technology, business organization, and management while consistently meeting the demands of the modern world. The College offers courses that cover a broad range of majors, including accounting, management, and office technology as well as other fields. Students can complete programs in as little as one year or less.

Special Features

A major strength of National College of Business and Technology is its ability to quickly adjust the curriculum to changes in the employment needs of business and industry and to meet the career interest of students. Community representatives, serving as a Campus Advisory Board, provide current and timely advice relative to the employment needs of business, technical, and government organizations.

The Career Center is available to assist with the entire job-search process. Specialized staff members are available to help students prepare a resume and cover letter and interview effectively. They assist the student throughout the employment search.

Students who wish to demonstrate their current skill level in selected areas may take an Advanced Placement evaluation. If successful, the student receives credit for that particular course and may shorten his or her program accordingly.

Scholarships are available not only to students who performed well during their secondary education but also to current students who excel while pursuing their particular program of study.

Financial Aid/Scholarships

National College of Business and Technology makes available an extensive program of financial assistance which includes Federal Stafford Loans, Federal Plus Loans, Federal Perkins Loans, the Federal Pell Grant, the Federal Supplemental Educational Opportunity Grant, the Workforce Development Grant, and the Business Partnership Grant as well as several scholarship opportunities.

Tuition and Fees

Tuition is $162 per credit hour. National College of Business and Technology is among the least expensive private colleges in its area. Check the catalog for current application, student activities or graduation fees.

Program Content

Accounting, Computer Applications Technology, Management, Medical Assisting, Office Administration

Program Description

All programs listed above lead to an Associate of Science degree.

The programs offered at National College of Business and Technology give the graduate the training that is needed to take the first step into an entry position as well as the background necessary to grow professionally in that field.

Accreditation

National College of Business and Technology is accredited by the Accrediting Council for Independent Colleges and Schools (ACICS); individual programs may have programmatic accreditation.

Admission

A prospective student must have a high school diploma or GED certificate and submit an application for admission together with the application fee.

Graduation Requirements

In order to be eligible for graduation, the student must complete all courses outlined in the program and earn the required number of credit hours. To graduate from any program, a minimum 2.0 overall grade point average must be achieved.

Contact

Admissions Department
National College of Business and
  Technology
10 Church Street
Martinsville, VA 24114
Phone: (276) 632-5621
Fax: (276) 632-7915

Programs Eligible for Scholarship	Tuition and Fees	Course Length/Credit Hours	Credential Earned
All related program areas	$15,552	96 credit hours	AOS

National College of Business and Technology, Salem

About Our Institution
National College of Business and Technology was established in 1886. The Roanoke Valley campus, which first opened its doors in 1886, offers students a central location in the heart of a young, vigorous and optimistic trade, banking and medical center for Southwest Virginia. National College of Business and Technology's curriculum is specific and concentrates on essential professional skills that will lead toward employment in a specific field. Programs are planned to offer the most effective methods in technology, business organization, and management while consistently meeting the demands of the modern world. The College offers courses that cover a broad range of majors, including accounting, management, medical assisting, and office technology as well as other fields. Students can complete programs in as little as one year or less.

Special Features
A major strength of National College of Business and Technology is its ability to quickly adjust the curriculum to changes in the employment needs of business and industry and to meet the career interest of students. Community representatives, serving as a Campus Advisory Board, provide current and timely advice relative to the employment needs of business, technical, and government organizations.

The Career Center is available to assist with the entire job search process. Specialized staff members are available to help students to prepare a resume and cover letter and interview effectively. They assist the student throughout the employment search.

Students who wish to demonstrate their current skill level in selected areas may take an Advanced Placement evaluation. If successful, the student receives credit for that particular course and may shorten his or her program accordingly.

Scholarships are available not only to students who performed well during their secondary education but also to current students who excel while pursuing their particular program of study.

Financial Aid/Scholarships
National College of Business and Technology makes available an extensive program of financial assistance which includes Federal Stafford Loans, Federal Plus Loans, Federal Perkins Loans, the Federal Pell Grant, the Federal Supplemental Educational Opportunity Grant, the Workforce Development Grant, and the Business Partnership Grant, as well as several scholarship opportunities.

Tuition and Fees
Tuition is $170 per credit hour for the BA and AOS and $215 per credit hour for the MBA. National College of Business and Technology is among the least expensive private colleges in its area. Students should check the catalog for current application, student activities, or graduation fees.

Program Content
Accounting, Computer Applications Technology, Information Systems Engineering, Management, Master of Business Administration, Medical Assisting, Office Administration, Paralegal, Tourism and Hospitality

Program Description
All programs listed above lead to an Associate of Science, a Bachelor of Arts, or a Master of Business degree.

The programs offered at National College of Business and Technology give the graduate the training that is needed to take the first step into an entry position as well as the background necessary to grow professionally in that field.

Accreditation
National College of Business and Technology is accredited by the Council for Independent Colleges and Schools (ACICS); individual programs such as Medical Assisting may have programmatic accreditation.

Admission
A prospective student must have a high school diploma or GED and submit an application for admission together with the application fee.

Graduation Requirements
In order to be eligible for graduation, the student must complete all courses outlined in the program and earn the required number of credit hours. To graduate from any program, a 2.0 overall grade point average must be achieved.

Contact
Admissions Department
1813 East Main Street
Salem, VA 24153
Phone: (540) 986-1800
Fax: (540) 986-1344

Programs Eligible for Scholarship	Tuition and Fees	Course Length/Credit Hours	Credential Earned
All related program areas	$16,320	96 credit hours	AOS
All related program areas	$30,600	180 credit hours	BA
All related program areas	$12,040	56 credit hours	MBA

Parks College, Arlington

About Our Institution

Parks College, Arlington, offers associate degree and diploma programs in the business administration, criminal justice, homeland security, and paralegal fields. Parks College, Arlington, is one of more than eighty schools owned and operated by Corinthian Colleges, Inc. (CCi), in the United States and is a branch campus of Parks College, Denver. Historically, the roots of Parks College, Denver, extend back to 1859. The Parks College campus in Arlington was opened in May 2002.

Special Features

The College is close to public transportation, both bus and metro. All classrooms have panoramic city views. The campus is wheelchair accessible.

Financial Aid/Scholarships

The College participates in the following programs: Federal Pell, Federal Stafford Loan (FSL), Federal PLUS, Federal Supplemental Educational Opportunity Grants (FSEOG), and VA. High school and other scholarships are available for those who qualify.

Tuition and Fees

Tuition is based upon the number of classes taken per quarter. A $25 registration fee is assessed each quarter.

Accreditation

The College is accredited by the Accrediting Council of Independent Colleges and Schools (ACICS).

Admissions

Candidates must have a high school diploma or equivalent. Successful completion of the assessment examination is a prerequisite for admission. Applicants who have completed one academic year of credits at another postsecondary institution are not required to complete the test.

Graduation Requirements

Students are required to earn a minimum cumulative grade point average of 2.0 in their major. Students must also meet specific program requirements.

Enrollment

There are 420 students enrolled.

Contact

Lachelle Green, Director of Admissions
801 North Quincy Street, Suite 500
Arlington, VA 22203
Phone: (703) 248-8887
Fax: (703) 351-2202
Web: www.parks-college.com

Program Content

Business Administration, Criminal Justice, Homeland Security Specialist, Paralegal/Legal Assistant

Programs Eligible for Scholarship	Tuition and Fees	Course Length/Credit Hours	Credential Earned
Business Administration	$220/credit hour	18 months/96 credit hours	AAS
Criminal Justice	$220/credit hour	18 months/96 credit hours	AAS
Homeland Security Specialist	$ 8,950	9 months/48 credit hours	Diploma
Paralegal/Legal Assistant	$220/credit hour	18 months/96 credit hours	AAS

Stratford University, Falls Church

About Our Institution
Since 1976, the mission of Stratford University has been to provide students with the skills, tools, and education needed to reach their potential in the field of their choice. The institution serves a diverse student body with two campuses in northern Virginia. Both facilities feature advanced technology and equipment.

Special Features
Stratford University offers master's degrees, bachelor's degrees, Associate of Applied Science degrees, and diplomas in a classroom environment sensitive to individual differences and desires. Faculty and staff members place value on each student and encourage each student's pursuit of educational goals. The University's Career Services Center provides a variety of activities and placement opportunities. In addition, the externship component in selected programs provides hands-on experience, which may lead to permanent job opportunities.

Financial Aid/Scholarships
Stratford University offers an array of financial aid opportunities, including federal student loans, Pell Grants, FSEOG grants, college work-study, veterans' education benefits, vocational rehabilitation, third-party financing, and scholarships.

Accreditation
Stratford University is accredited by the Accrediting Council for Independent Colleges and Schools. The advanced culinary arts program has programmatic accreditation through the American Culinary Federation.

Admissions
An entrance exam or an SAT score (1000 minimum) or an ACT score (21 minimum) and a high school diploma or GED are used to determine the potential for a student's success and acceptance into a program of study.

Graduation Requirements
An undergraduate student must attain a minimum cumulative grade point average of 2.0 and accumulate the required credits for the program as listed in the catalog. A graduate student must attain a minimum cumulative GPA of 3.0 and accumulate the required credits for the program as listed in the catalog.

Contact
Director of Admissions
Tysons Corner Campus
Stratford University
7777 Leesburg Pike, Lobby North
Falls Church, VA 22043
Phone: (703) 821-8570
Web: www.stratford.edu

Program Content
Master of Science Degrees (54 quarter credits): Telecommunications Systems, Enterprise Business Management, Entrepreneurial Business

Associate of Applied Science and Bachelor's Degrees (90 quarter credits for associate's; 180 quarter credits for bachelor's): Digital Design and Animation, Network Management and Security, Advanced Culinary Arts, Hotel and Restaurant Management, Business Administration

Diploma Programs (60 quarter credits): Digital Design and Animation, Network Management and Security Professional, Advanced Culinary Arts Professional

Program Description
Digital Design and Animation: Students are prepared to design interactive, animated Web pages, CDs, or videos, taking an artistic expression and translating it into a banner ad, an animated GIF, a 3-D rendering, or a complete project. This program allows students to fulfill their love of art with the use of computers.

Networking and Security: Students are prepared to design, install, support, maintain, and manage secure computer networks. They may also be certified in MCSE, CCNA, and CISSP.

Culinary Arts: Students focus on culinary skills, food science, nutrition, and the business end of catering and restaurant management in this American Culinary Federation–accredited program.

Hospitality: Students gain a foundation in hotel and event management skills to enhance their careers. Upon successful completion, students receive various certifications through the American Hotel and Lodging Association.

Business: Students learn the fundamentals, principles, techniques, and skills necessary to the theory and effective practice of various business environments.

Stratford University, Woodbridge

About Our Institution

Since 1976, the mission of Stratford University has been to provide students with the skills, tools, and education needed to reach their potential in the field of their choice. The institution serves a diverse student body with two campuses in northern Virginia. Both facilities feature advanced technology and equipment.

Special Features

Stratford University offers bachelor's degrees, Associate of Applied Science degrees, and diplomas in a classroom environment sensitive to individual differences and desires. Faculty and staff members place value on each student and encourage each student's pursuit of educational goals. The University's Career Services Center provides a variety of activities and placement opportunities. In addition, the externship component of the programs provides hands-on experience, which may lead to permanent job opportunities.

Financial Aid/Scholarships

Stratford University offers an array of financial aid opportunities, including federal student loans, Pell Grants, FSEOG grants, college work-study, veterans' education benefits, vocational rehabilitation, third-party financing, and scholarships.

Accreditation

Stratford University is accredited by the Accrediting Council for Independent Colleges and Schools.

Admissions

An entrance exam or an SAT (1000 minimum) or ACT (21 minimum) score and a high school diploma or GED are used to determine the potential for a student's success and acceptance into a program of study.

Graduation Requirements

A student must attain a minimum cumulative grade point average of 2.0 and accumulate the required credits for the program as listed in the catalog.

Contact

Admissions Department
Woodbridge Campus
Stratford University
13576 Minnieville Road
Woodbridge, VA 22192
Phone: (703) 897-1982
Web: www.stratford.edu

Program Content

Associate of Applied Science and Bachelor's Degrees (90 quarter credits for associate, 180 quarter credits for bachelor's): Digital Design and Animation, Network Management and Security, Business Administration

Diploma Program (60 quarter credits): Digital Design and Animation, Network Management and Security Professional

Program Description

Digital Design and Animation: Students are prepared to design interactive, animated Web pages, CDs, or videos, taking an artistic expression and translating it into a banner ad, an animated GIF, a 3-D rendering, or a complete project. This program allows students to fulfill their love of art with the use of computers.

Networking and Security: Students are prepared to design, install, support, maintain, and manage secure computer networks. They may also be certified in MCSE, CCNA, and CISSP.

Business: Students learn the fundamentals, principles, techniques, and skills necessary for the theory and effective practice of various business environments.

Virginia School of Massage, Charlottesville

About Our Institution
Virginia School of Massage (VSM) is nestled in the foothills of the Blue Ridge Mountains in picturesque Charlottesville, Virginia. VSM has been accredited since 1998 and is corporately owned and governed by Steiner Education Group, Inc., along with six other schools in Florida, Maryland, and Pennsylvania. The School is close to Shenandoah National Park as well as several regional and state parks. Charlottesville is a beautiful college town that is home to the University of Virginia; the town offers hiking and mountain biking trails in the summer and ski slopes in the winter. VSM offers full-time as well as part-time schedules with day and evening classes to make it easy for students to fulfill their dream of becoming a massage therapist.

Special Features
The field of massage therapy is one of the fastest growing in the country, and the Virginia School of Massage can thoroughly prepare students for this exciting and rewarding career. All campuses also have a Student Clinic where students have the opportunity to work with the public while they attend school. VSM is proud to offer an extensive continuing education program, which enables students to enhance their skills and learn new modalities after graduation. VSM also has a fully stocked Natural Health Shoppe on campus that carries everything from massage creams and oils to music and school uniforms—anything students may need to enhance their practice. All Steiner Education Group campuses employ a Career Services Coordinator who is available to assist graduates in achieving their goals. Whether students are interested in seeing the world by working aboard a cruise ship or would prefer a land-based position, the Career Services Department has built relationships with some of the most successful employers in the industry. Graduates of the Steiner Education Group schools are given priority consideration when Steiner Leisure Ltd., a global provider of spa services, is recruiting for their maritime or land-based spas.

Financial Aid/Scholarships
Virginia School of Massage is approved by the Department of Education for Title IV funds, and federal financial aid is available to qualified applicants in the form of Federal Pell Grants and Federal Stafford Student Loans. The Financial Aid Office helps guide students through this process.

Tuition and Fees
Students should call the campus for current pricing information.

Accreditation
Virginia School of Massage is accredited by the Accrediting Commission of Career Schools and Colleges of Technology (ACCSCT) and is programmatically accredited by the Commission on Massage Therapy Accreditation (COMTA). VSM is approved by the Commonwealth of Virginia Department of Education and the National Certification Board for Therapeutic Massage and Bodywork (NCBTMB). The School is a member of the American Massage Therapy Association (AMTA) Council of Schools (Category A Continuing Education Provider) and is a member in good standing of the Virginia Association of Massage Schools, Virginia Career College Association (VCCA), and the Career College Association (CCA). VSM is authorized by the Department of Justice, Division of Homeland Security, to enroll nonimmigrant alien students and is approved for veterans' training.

Admissions
Prospective students must complete an application, schedule an interview with an admissions representative, and be at least 18 years of age by the expected graduation date. Prospective students must display a genuine interest in becoming part of a learning atmosphere. Admissions requirements include evidence of high school graduation or GED equivalent. Upon acceptance, prior to starting

Program Content
Professional Program in Comprehensive Massage Therapy, Professional Program in Shiatsu and Asian Bodywork

Program Description
VSM offers a 637-hour Professional Program in Comprehensive Massage Therapy and a 620-hour Professional Program in Shiatsu and Asian Bodywork.

The Professional Program in Comprehensive Massage Therapy includes extensive lecture and hands-on training, preparing students to work in hospitals, medical clinics, and doctors' offices as well as spa and resort settings. This program includes three major systems of bodywork: Swedish, deep tissue, and myofascial release. Human anatomy and physiology and additional modalities complete the curriculum and add further depth to the training. The entire program is designed to refine the students' sense of touch (for palpation skills) and to synthesize all of the program elements.

The Professional Program in Shiatsu and Asian Bodywork is designed to teach students the techniques of traditional Asian bodywork and how to apply those techniques as a shiatsu practitioner. Whether students are already therapists or have no experience with Eastern or Western massage, they graduate with both an education in the art of shiatsu as well as a working understanding of its practical application. Upon completion of this program, students have gained a thorough knowledge of human anatomy and physiology as it applies to shiatsu and Asian bodywork, the communication skills needed to relate well with clients, and an understanding of the ethical issues related to shiatsu and Asian bodywork.

classes, students are required to complete a physician's statement that is signed by a licensed physician, indicating that they are in good health and able to participate in the programs.

Contact
Virginia School of Massage
2008 Morton Drive
Charlottesville, VA 22903
Phone: (434) 293-4031
        (888) 599-2001 (toll-free)
Fax: (434) 293-4190
Web: www.steinered.com

Programs Eligible for Scholarship	Tuition and Fees	Course Length/Credit Hours	Credential Earned
Massage Therapy	Call the campus	637 hours/49 credits	Diploma
Shiatsu and Asian Bodywork	for current fees	620 hours/49 credits	Diploma

Apollo College, Spokane

About Our Institution
Apollo College, founded in 1976, is recognized in communities as a leader in high-quality career education, with hands-on orientation. Since then, the College has enjoyed a proud history of assisting people in becoming skilled professionals who go on to assume important positions in their communities. Highly trained, experienced faculty members present course materials that are relevant to current workforce needs; small class sizes ensure individualized attention for students. Programs begin on a monthly basis, with day and evening classes offered to accommodate busy schedules.

Special Features
The College's Advisory Board, composed of industry professionals, keeps Apollo abreast of the latest advances in their respective fields. Classrooms and labs are equipped with the latest-technology equipment.

Career and academic counseling is available. Placement services, such as job fairs, assistance with resume and interview preparation, and on-campus recruiting are available through the Office of Student Services. The College also assists full-time students in finding part-time employment. Housing information is available through the Admissions Department. Apollo's Skills Advancement Program offers continuous refresher courses to graduates at no extra cost.

Financial Aid/Scholarships
Financial aid is available to those who qualify. Apollo participates in a variety of state and federal financial aid and alternate loan programs, including Pell, FFEL, FDSLP, SEOG, SSIG, and JTPA.

Tuition and Fees
There is a separate application fee.

Accreditation
Apollo is nationally accredited by the Accrediting Bureau of Education Schools to award diplomas and associate degrees. Additional accreditations and approvals include the American Association of Medical Assistants, ABHES, APSA, JRCERT, CoARC, CAAHEP, and AMTA.

Admissions
Students must submit a completed application and a registration fee. An interview with an admissions representative is required. For some programs, an interview with a program director or instructional staff member may also be required to determine eligibility.

Enrollment
There are 500 students enrolled.

Graduation Requirements
To graduate, students must have satisfied all financial obligations and successfully completed the course of study and externship, including course requirements.

Program Content
Dental Assistant, Medical Administrative Assistant (Computerized Medical Office Secretary), Medical Assistant, Medical Radiography, Medical Records, and Pharmacy Technician

Program Description
Dental Assistant students are trained to work directly with patients and dentists and perform dental office administrative duties.

The Medical Administrative Assistant Program provides instruction in medical law, ethics, and terminology and computer and office skills that are critical to office practice.

Medical Assistant students are trained to aid physicians and other medical personnel as they treat patients and perform administrative tasks that keep a medical office running smoothly.

Medical Radiography students attend three 16-week semesters of classroom training that prepares them for an additional sixteen-week externship and a national certification examination.

Students in the Medical Records Specialist Program learn to maintain accurate, organized documentation of medical care to provide data for a variety of health information needs.

Pharmacy Technician students are provided a working knowledge of the pharmaceutical business and learn to apply technical and practical training in pharmaceutical and medical terminology, drug dispensing, and administration.

Contact
Ray Keevy, Campus Director
10102 East Knox Suite #200
Spokane, WA 99206
Phone: (509) 532-8888
        (800) 36-TRAIN (toll-free)
Fax: (509) 433-5983
E-mail: rkeevy@apollocollege.com
Web: www.apollocollege.com

Programs Eligible for Scholarship	Tuition and Fees	Course Length/Credit Hours	Credential Earned
Dental Assistant	Call campus for current pricing information.	720 hours/24 credits	Diploma
Medical Administrative Assistant (Computerized Medical Office Secretary)		720 hours/24 credits	Diploma
Medical Assistant		720 hours/24 credits	Diploma
Medical Radiography (X-Ray)		2,752 hours/104 credits	Diploma
Medical Records Specialist		860 hours/27 credits	Diploma
Pharmacy Technician		836 hours/24 credits	Diploma

The Art Institute of Seattle, Seattle

About Our Institution
Originally founded in 1946 as the Burnley School of Professional Art, The Art Institute of Seattle has a proud history in the Seattle community as a contributor to the creative industries in the Northwest. From the early days of 1200 students in attendance to today's enrollment of approximately 2500, The Art Institute remains committed to offering quality programs based on the real-world needs of business.

Special Features
The Art Institute of Seattle is an urban campus composed of three facilities that include classrooms, audio and video studios, photography studios and labs, fabric sample rooms, airbrush studios, student store, student lounges, copy centers, gallery, woodshop, sculpture room, fashion display windows, resource center, culinary facilities with professionally equipped kitchens and a public restaurant, and a technology center equipped with PC and Macintosh computers. The faculty includes both part-time and full-time instructors. Services available to students include student housing, counseling, part-time job assistance (pregraduation), tutoring and learning services, special needs services, and career assistance (postgraduation).

Financial Aid/Scholarships
The Art Institute of Seattle students are eligible for Pell, SEOG, Perkins, Stafford, Work-Study, FPLUS, VA, Bureau of Indian Affairs, Washington State Need grants, Alaska State Student Loan, Vocational Rehabilitation Assistance, and institutional merit scholarships.

Tuition and Fees
Tuition is $360 per credit hour. Additional fees include a $50 application fee and a $100 tuition deposit. Students lock in their tuition rate at the time of enrollment. The rate does not increase as long as students stay in school and complete their programs within a maximum of 1½ times the normal program length.

Accreditation
The Art Institute of Seattle is accredited by the Northwest Commission of Schools and of Colleges and Universities and is licensed by the Washington Workforce Training and Education Coordinating Board. The Culinary Arts program is accredited by the American Culinary Federation.

Admissions
Admission requirements are: an admissions interview (in person or by phone), proof of high school graduation or GED, admissions application and $50 application fee, essay, enrollment agreement, and $100 tuition deposit.

Program Content
Animation Art and Design, The Art of Cooking, Audio Production, Baking & Pastry, Computer Design Technology, Culinary Arts, Desktop Production, Fashion Design, Fashion Marketing, Graphic Design, Industrial Design Technology, Interior Design, Media Arts & Animation, Multimedia and Web Design, Photography, Residential Design, Video Production

Program Description
The Art Institute's programs have been designed and are continually reviewed with the assistance of industry representatives. Classes are taught year-round and are offered during the day and evening.

Graduation Requirements
To qualify for graduation, a student must receive a passing grade or credit for all required course work, earn the required credits in each of the disciplines for their major, achieve a minimum CGPA of 2.0, meet portfolio and other requirements as outlined by the student's program, satisfy all financial obligations to The Art Institute, and earn at least one quarter of the required credits at The Art Institute of Seattle.

Enrollment
2500 students enrolled.

Contact
Karen Shea, Director of Admissions
The Art Institute of Seattle
2323 Elliott Avenue
Seattle, WA 98122
Phone: (206) 448-6600
        (800) 275-2471
Fax: (206) 269-0275
E-mail: aisadm@aii.edu
Web: www.ais.edu

Programs Eligible for Scholarship	Tuition and Fees	Course Length/Credit Hours	Credential Earned
Animation Art and Design	refer to school catalog	24 months/120 credits	AAA
The Art of Cooking		12 months/36 credits	Diploma
Audio Production		18 months/90 credits	AAA
Baking & Pastry		12 months/36 credits	Diploma
Computer Design Technology		12 months/36 credits	Diploma
Culinary Arts		21 months/99 credits	AAA
Desktop Production		12 months/36 credits	Diploma
Fashion Design		18 months/90 credits	AAA
Fashion Marketing		18 months/90 credits	AAA
Graphic Design		24 months/120 credits	AAA
Graphic Design		36 months/180 credits	BFA
Industrial Design Technology		24 months/120 credits	AAA
Interior Design		27 months/135 credits	AAA
Interior Design		36 months/180 credits	BFA
Media Arts & Animation		36 months/180 credits	BFA
Multimedia and Web Design		24 months/120 credits	AAA
Photography		24 months/120 credits	AAA
Residential Design		12 months/36 credits	Diploma
Video Production		18 months/90 credits	AAA

Ashmead College, Everett

About Our Institution

Ashmead College was founded in 1974 as the Seattle Massage School to teach massage skills to people wishing to practice professional massage. With programs in massage, fitness training, and advanced studies, Ashmead College provides students with an interactive learning environment that has a firm foundation in both practical and theoretical education. Graduates are prepared to become successful practitioners in their fields. Ashmead College is dedicated to providing qualified and skilled professionals for the health and wellness industry. Ashmead College is a member of the American Massage Therapy Association's (AMTA) Council of Schools.

Special Features

Ashmead College recognizes the importance of a strong support system for its students. Programs feature classroom lectures, hands-on practice, and real-life experience. In the Student Clinic, massage students experience working with the public. Tutoring is available throughout the programs as are teaching assistants. A Student Services Adviser provides resources, encouragement, and advice. The Graduate Services Department provides assistance with job searches and professional and business development throughout the graduates' careers in health and wellness.

Financial Aid/Scholarships

Ashmead College features a financial aid office on each campus, and a Financial Aid Officer is available to help students determine eligibility. Title IV Federal Financial Aid is available for those who qualify. Ashmead College participates in the Washington State Need Grant, Federal Pell Grant, Federal Stafford Student Loan, and Federal PLUS Loan programs and offers additional financing options.

Tuition and Fees

Tuition for the Professional Licensing Program is $12,007 and includes fees and textbooks. The Professional Licensing Program and Spa Specialist tuition is $15,291, which includes textbooks and spa kits. Other supplies are variable and range from free of charge up to $1,000.

Accreditation

Ashmead College is fully accredited by the Accrediting Council for Continuing Education and Training (ACCET).

Admissions

Applicants must pass an entrance interview, be a high school graduate or have a GED certificate, and be a minimum of 18 years of age upon graduation from Ashmead College.

Graduation Requirements

Students must have attended a minimum of 75 percent of the total program in which they were enrolled, completed all required course work, achieved a cumulative grade point average of at least 2.0, met all financial obligations to the school, met Graduate Services exit interview

Program Content

Professional Licensing, Professional Licensing and Spa and Aromatherapy

Program Description

The Professional Licensing program prepares students to become successful massage professionals. Graduates are prepared to test for National Certification Examination for Therapeutic Massage and Body Work/National Licensing Examination.

The Professional Licensing and Spa and Aromatherapy program provides training in massage, spa treatments, and aromatherapy.

requirements and completed all relevant paperwork, and completed the financial aid exit interview and all related materials (applies to federal–student-loan borrowers only).

Contact

Admissions Representative
Ashmead College
3019 Colby Avenue
Everett, WA 98201
Phone: (425) 339-2678
Fax: (425) 258-2620
Web: www.ashmeadcollege.com

Programs Eligible for Scholarship	Tuition and Fees	Course Length/Credit Hours	Credential Earned
Professional Licensing	$12,007	12 months/805.5 hours	Certificate
Professional Licensing and Spa and Aromatherapy	$15,291	12 months/979.75 hours	Certificate

Ashmead College, Seattle

About Our Institution

Ashmead College was founded in 1974 as the Seattle Massage School to teach massage skills to people wishing to practice professional massage. With programs in massage, aromatherapy/spa therapies, and fitness training, Ashmead College provides students with an interactive learning environment that has a firm foundation in both practical and theoretical education. Graduates are prepared to become successful practitioners in their fields. Ashmead College is dedicated to providing qualified and skilled professionals for the health and wellness industry. Ashmead College is a member of the American Massage Therapy Association's (AMTA) Council of Schools.

Special Features

Ashmead College recognizes the importance of a strong support system for its students. Programs feature classroom lectures, hands-on practice, and real-life experience. In the Student Clinic, massage students experience working with the public. Fitness trainer students participate in internships in a variety of fitness settings. Tutoring is available throughout the programs as are teaching assistants. A Student Services Adviser provides resources, encouragement, and advice. The Career Services Department provides assistance with job searches and professional and business development throughout the graduates' careers in health and wellness.

Financial Aid/Scholarships

Ashmead College features a financial aid office on each campus, and a Financial Aid Officer is available to help students determine eligibility. Title IV Federal Financial Aid is available for those who qualify. Ashmead College participates in the Washington State Need Grant, Federal Pell Grant, Federal Stafford Student Loan, and Federal PLUS Loan programs and offers additional financing options.

Tuition and Fees

Tuition for the four-term programs is $12,507 and includes fees and textbooks. The Professional Licensing, Aromatherapy, and Spa program adds one additional day and a cost of $3,284, which includes fees and textbooks. Other supplies are variable, depending on the program, and range from free of charge up to $1,050.

Accreditation

Ashmead College is fully accredited by the Accrediting Council for Continuing Education and Training (ACCET).

Admissions

Applicants must pass an entrance interview, be a high school graduate or have a GED certificate, and be a minimum of 18 years of age upon graduation from Ashmead College.

Program Content

Fitness Trainer Program (FTP); Professional Licensing; Professional Licensing and Spa and Aromatherapy

Program Description

Graduates of the FTP are prepared to work successfully in the fitness industry in a variety of health and wellness facilities and environments. They are also prepared to test for major fitness certifications.

Professional Licensing prepares students to become successful massage professionals. Graduates are prepared to test for the Washington and Oregon State Massage Licensing Exams.

Professional Licensing and Spa and Aromatherapy prepares students for practical usage of aromatic oils and spa therapies.

Graduation Requirements

Students must have attended a minimum of 75 percent of the total program in which they were enrolled, completed all required course work, achieved a cumulative grade point average of at least 2.0, met all financial obligations to the school, met Graduate Services exit interview requirements and completed all relevant paperwork, and completed the financial aid exit interview and all related materials (applies to federal–student-loan borrowers only).

Contact

Julianne Lau
Director of Admissions
Ashmead College
2111 North Northgate Way, Suite 218
Seattle, WA 98133
Phone: (206) 440-3090
Fax: (206) 440-3239
Web: www.ashmeadcollege.com

Programs Eligible for Scholarship	Tuition and Fees	Course Length/Credit Hours	Credential Earned
Fitness Trainer Program	$12,507	12 months/759.75 hours	Certificate
Professional Licensing	$12,507	12 months/805.5 hours	Certificate
Professional Licensing and Spa and Aroma Therapy	$15,791	12 months/979.75 hours	Certificate

Ashmead College, Tacoma

About Our Institution

Ashmead College was founded in 1974 as the Seattle Massage School to teach massage skills to people wishing to practice professional massage. With programs in massage, fitness training, and advanced studies, Ashmead College provides students with an interactive learning environment that has a firm foundation in both practical and theoretical education. Graduates are prepared to become successful practitioners in their fields. Ashmead College is dedicated to providing qualified and skilled professionals for the health and wellness industry. Ashmead College is a member of the American Massage Therapy Association's (AMTA) Council of Schools.

Special Features

Ashmead College recognizes the importance of a strong support system for its students. Programs feature classroom lectures, hands-on practice, and real-life experience. In the Student Clinic, massage students experience working with the public. Tutoring is available throughout the programs as are teaching assistants. A Student Services Adviser provides resources, encouragement, and advice. The Graduate Services Department provides assistance with job searches and professional and business development throughout the graduates' careers in health and wellness.

Financial Aid/Scholarships

Ashmead College features a financial aid office on each campus, and a Financial Aid Officer is available to help students determine eligibility. Title IV Federal Financial Aid is available for those who qualify. Ashmead College participates in the Washington State Need Grant, Federal Pell Grant, Federal Stafford Student Loan, and Federal PLUS Loan programs and offers additional financing options.

Tuition and Fees

Tuition for the four-term programs is $12,007 and includes fees and textbooks. Tuition for the Professional Licensing Program/Spa Specialist is $15,291 and includes an $800 supply fee, which is completed in the four-term format. Other supplies are variable, depending on the program, and range from free of charge up to $1,000.

Accreditation

Ashmead College is fully accredited by the Accrediting Council for Continuing Education and Training (ACCET).

Admissions

Applicants must pass an entrance interview, be a high school graduate or have a GED certificate, and be a minimum of 18 years of age upon graduation from Ashmead College.

Graduation Requirements

Students must have attended a minimum of 75 percent of the total program in which they were enrolled, completed all required course work, achieved a cumulative grade point average of at least 2.0, met all

Program Content

Professional Licensing, Professional Licensing and Spa and Aromatherapy

Program Description

The Professional Licensing program prepares students to become successful massage professionals. Graduates are prepared to test for the Washington and Oregon State Massage Licensing Exams as well as the National Certification Examination for Therapeutic Massage and Body Work/National Licensing Examination.

The Professional Licensing and Spa and Aromatherapy program provides training in massage, spa treatments, and aromatherapy.

financial obligations to the school, met Graduate Services exit interview requirements and completed all relevant paperwork, and completed the financial aid exit interview and all related materials (applies to federal–student-loan borrowers only).

Contact

Director of Admissions
Ashmead College
5005 Pacific Highway, East
Suite 20
Fife, WA 98424
Phone: (253) 926-1435
Fax: (253) 926-0651
Web: www.ashmeadcollege.com

Programs Eligible for Scholarship	Tuition and Fees	Course Length/Credit Hours	Credential Earned
Professional Licensing	$12,007	12 months/805.5 hours	Certificate
Professional Licensing and Spa and Aromatherapy	$15,291	12 months/979.75 hours	Certificate

Ashmead College, Vancouver

About Our Institution
Ashmead College was founded in 1974 as the Seattle Massage School to teach massage skills to people wishing to practice professional massage. With programs in massage, fitness training, and advanced studies, Ashmead College provides students with an interactive learning environment that has a firm foundation in both practical and theoretical education. Graduates are prepared to become successful practitioners in their fields. Ashmead College is dedicated to providing qualified and skilled professionals for the health and wellness industry. Ashmead College is a member of the American Massage Therapy Association's (AMTA) Council of Schools.

Special Features
Ashmead College recognizes the importance of a strong support system for its students. Programs feature classroom lectures, hands-on practice, and real-life experience. In the Student Clinic, massage students experience working with the public. Tutoring is available throughout the programs as are teaching assistants. A Student Services Adviser provides resources, encouragement, and advice. The Graduate Services Department provides assistance with job searches and professional and business development throughout the graduates' careers in health and wellness.

Financial Aid/Scholarships
Ashmead College features a financial aid office on each campus, and a Financial Aid Representative is available to help students determine eligibility. Title IV Federal Financial Aid is available for those who qualify. Ashmead College participates in the Washington State Need Grant, Federal Pell Grant, Federal Stafford Student Loan, Federal Supplemental Educational Opportunity Grant, Work-Study, and Federal PLUS Loan programs and offers additional financing options.

Tuition and Fees
Tuition for the four-term programs is $12,507 and includes fees and textbooks. The Clinical and Sports Massage Specialist program adds one additional term and a cost of $3,639, which includes fees and textbooks. Other supplies are variable, depending on the program, and range from free of charge up to $1,000.

Accreditation
Ashmead College is fully accredited by the Accrediting Council for Continuing Education and Training (ACCET).

Admissions
Applicants must pass an entrance interview, be a high school graduate or have a GED certificate, and be a minimum of 18 years of age upon graduation from Ashmead College.

Graduation Requirements
Students must have attended a minimum of 75 percent of the total program in which they were enrolled, completed all required course work, achieved a

Program Description
The Clinical and Sports Massage Specialist Program prepares students for specialty work in both clinical and sports massage settings.

The Professional Licensing Program prepares students to become successful massage professionals. Graduates are prepared to test for the Washington and Oregon State Massage Licensing Exams.

The Professional Licensing and Spa and Aromatherapy Program prepares students for practical usage of aromatic oils, including how to use them for health and well-being.

cumulative grade point average of at least 2.0, met all financial obligations to the school, met Graduate Services exit interview requirements and completed all relevant paperwork, and completed the financial aid exit interview and all related materials (applies to federal–student-loan borrowers only).

Contact
Lalitha Pataki
Director of Admissions
Ashmead College
120 Northeast 136th Avenue, Suite 220
Vancouver, WA 98684
Phone: (360) 885-3152
Fax: (360) 885-3151
Web: www.ashmeadcollege.com

Programs Eligible for Scholarship	Tuition and Fees	Course Length/Credit Hours	Credential Earned
Clinical and Sports Massage Specialist	$16,301	15 months/1,048.75 hours	Certificate
Professional Licensing	$12,507	12 months/805.5 hours	Certificate
Professional Licensing and Spa and Aromatherapy	$15,791	12 months/979.25 hours	Certificate

Bryman College, Everett

About Our Institution

Bryman College, formerly Eton Technical Institute, was founded in 1922 as the Bremerton Business College. Since then it has served the Puget Sound region by providing quality training for students in the health field. Students learn theory and skills from classroom lectures, laboratory work, and hands-on practice. Students also receive extensive experience in private practices and medical settings during the externship portion of their training. Bryman College's warm atmosphere and professional staff and faculty members help students reach their dreams.

Special Features

Bryman College recognizes the importance of a strong support system for students. Programs feature classroom lecture, hands-on practice, and real-life experience. Classes feature laboratories with quality equipment and tools. Tutoring is available throughout the programs. A student services adviser provides resources, encouragement, and advice. The Graduate Services Department provides assistance with job-search and professional skills that help graduates find their first job in a health field.

Financial Aid/Scholarships

Bryman College features a Financial Aid Office on each campus, and a financial aid representative is available to help students determine eligibility. Title IV federal financial aid is available for those who qualify. Bryman College participates in Federal Pell Grant, Federal Stafford Student Loan, and Federal Plus Loan programs as well as additional financing options.

Tuition and Fees

Tuition for the Medical Billing Program is $9,728 and includes all lab fees, books, and miscellaneous supplies. The program consists of five modules plus an externship.

The tuition for the Dental Assisting Program is $10,650; it is $11,427 for the Pharmacy Technician Program. This includes all lab fees, books, miscellaneous supplies, and uniform. These programs each consist of six modules plus an externship. The tuition for the Medical Assisting Program is $11,100 and includes all lab fees, miscellaneous supplies, and uniforms. Books are charged separately. The Medical Assisting Program consists of seven 4-week modules plus an externship.

Accreditation

Bryman College is accredited by the Accrediting Council for Independent Colleges and Schools (ACICS). The Medical Assisting Program is also accredited by the Commission on Accreditation of Allied Health Education Programs (CAAHEP).

Admissions

Applicants must pass an entrance exam and be a high school graduate or have a GED certificate. However, individuals interested in the Medical

Program Content

Dental Assisting (DA), Medical Assisting (MA), Medical Billing (MB), Pharmacy Technician (PhT)

Program Description

The Dental Assisting Program is designed to prepare the student for a career as a dental assistant.

The Medical Assisting Program is designed to prepare the student for a career as a medical assistant.

The Medical Billing Program is designed to prepare the student for a career as a medical biller.

The Pharmacy Technician Program is designed to prepare the student for a career as a pharmacy technician.

Assisting Program can take an Ability to Benefit test for admittance if he or she does not have a high school diploma or a GED.

Graduation Requirements

Students must attain required competency or speed levels in all courses, fulfill all clinical and externship requirements, have a cumulative grade point average of at least 2.0, satisfy all other academic requirements for graduation, and satisfy all nonacademic requirements such as payment of tuition and fees.

Contact

Admissions Representative
Bryman College
906 SE Everett Mall Way, Suite 600
Everett, WA 98208
Phone: 425-789-7960
Fax: 425-789-7989
Web: http://brymancollege.com

Programs Eligible for Scholarship	Tuition and Fees	Course Length/Credit Hours	Credentials Earned
Dental Assisting	$10,650	36 weeks plus externship/880 hours	Certificate
Medical Assisting	$11,100	28 weeks plus externship/720 hours	Certificate
Medical Billing	$ 9,728	30 weeks plus externship/780 hours	Certificate
Pharmacy Technician	$11,427	36 weeks plus externship/880 hours	Certificate

Guide to Career Colleges 2005

Bryman College, Lynnwood

About Our Institution
The Bryman Schools were founded in 1962 by Mrs. Esther Bryman as the Los Angeles Colleges of Medical and Dental Assistants. The Los Angeles campus was the original school. In December 1995, Corinthian Schools Inc. (CSi), a division of Cornithian Colleges, Inc. (CCi), acquired the schools. CCi is one of the largest postsecondary school organizations in the United States, operating more than eighty colleges and institutions nationwide.

Special Features
The College's philosophy is to provide high-quality programs that are sound in concept, implemented by a competent and dedicated faculty, and geared to serve those seeking a solid foundation in the health-care field. The programs emphasize hands-on training, are relevant to the needs of employers, and focus on areas that offer strong long-term employment positions in the medical and dental fields.

Financial Aid/Scholarships
Information regarding Pell Grants, FFEL, state grants, and other assistance can be obtained from the Finance Office. Financial aid is available for those who qualify.

Accreditation
All programs are accredited by the Accrediting Commission of Career Schools and Colleges of Technology (ACCSCT).

Admissions
Successful candidates are selected based on admissions tests, interviews, and the completion and presentation of required documents. Enrollment is open to all high school graduates as well as those holding a GED certificate or its equivalent. Under certain circumstances, students who do not have a high school diploma or its equivalent may still be accepted for admission. Students should contact the Admissions Department for additional information.

Graduation Requirements
To be eligible for graduation, students must successfully complete all classroom modules with a grade of at least 70 percent, finish an approved externship of 160 hours, and complete all other program requirements.

Contact
Gynger Steele, Director of Admissions
19020 33rd Avenue West
Suite 250
Lynnwood, WA 98036
Phone (425) 778-9894
Fax: (425) 778-9794
E-mail: gsteele@cci.edu
Web: www.bryman-college.com

Program Content
Dental Assisting, Homeland Security Specialist, Medical Administrative Assistant, Medical Assisting, Medical Insurance Billing/Coding

Programs Eligible for Scholarship	Tuition and Fees	Course Length/Credit Hours	Credential Earned
Dental Assisting	$10,364	8 months/47 credit hours	Diploma
Medical Administrative Assistant	$10,299	8 months/47 credit hours	Diploma
Medical Assisting	$10,244	8 months/47 credit hours	Diploma

Bryman College, Port Orchard

About Our Institution
Bryman College, formerly Eton Technical Institute, was founded in 1922 as the Bremerton Business College. Since then it has served the Puget Sound region by providing quality training for students in the health field. Students learn theory and skills from classroom lectures and laboratory and hands-on practice. Students also receive extensive experience in private practices and medical settings during the externship portion of their training. Bryman College's warm atmosphere and professional staff and faculty members help students reach their dreams.

Special Features
Bryman College recognizes the importance of a strong support system for students. Programs feature classroom lecture, hands-on practice, and real-life experience. Classes feature laboratories with quality equipment and tools. Tutoring is available throughout the programs. A student services adviser provides resources, encouragement, and advice. The Graduate Services Department provides assistance with job-search and professional and business development throughout the graduates' careers in health.

Financial Aid/Scholarships
Bryman College features a Financial Aid Office on each campus, and a financial aid representative is available to help students determine eligibility. Title IV federal financial aid is available for those who qualify. Bryman College participates in Federal Pell Grant, Federal Stafford Student Loan, and Federal Plus Loan programs as well as additional financing options.

Tuition and Fees
Tuition for the Medical Billing Program is $9,727, including all lab fees, books, and miscellaneous supplies. The program consists of four modules plus an externship.

The tuition for the Dental Assisting Program is $10,883.71; the Medical Assisting Program is $11,657; and the Pharmacy Technician Program is $11,716.45. This includes all lab fees, books, miscellaneous supplies, and uniforms. The Dental Assisting and Pharmacy Technician programs each consist of five modules plus an externship. The Medical Assisting Program consists of seven modules plus an externship.

Accreditation
Bryman College is accredited by the Accrediting Council for Independent Colleges and Schools (ACICS). The Medical Assisting Program is also accredited by the Commission on Accreditation of Allied Health Education Programs (CAAHEP).

Admissions
Applicants must pass an entrance exam and be a high school graduate or have a GED certificate for the Dental Assisting, Medical Assisting, Medical

Program Content
Dental Assisting (DA), Medical Assisting (MA), Medical Billing (MB), Pharmacy Technician (PhT)

Program Description
The Dental Assisting Program is designed to prepare the student for a career as a dental assistant.

The Medical Assisting Program is designed to prepare the student for a career as a medical assistant.

The Medical Billing Program is designed to prepare the student for a career as a medical biller.

The Pharmacy Technician Program is designed to prepare the student for a career as a pharmacy technician.

Billing, and Pharmacy Technician programs. However, individuals interested in the Medical Assisting Program can take an Ability to Benefit (ATB) test for admittance if they do not have a high school diploma or a GED.

Graduation Requirements
Students must attain required competency or speed levels in all courses, fulfill all clinical and externship requirements, have achieved a cumulative grade point average of at least 2.0, satisfy all other academic requirements for graduation, and satisfy all nonacademic requirements such as payment of tuition and fees.

Contact
Sheila Austin
Director of Admissions
Bryman College
3649 Frontage Road
Port Orchard, WA 98367
Phone: (360) 473-1120
Fax: (360) 792-2404
Web: http://brymancollege.com

Programs Eligible for Scholarship	Tuition and Fees	Course Length/Credit Hours	Credential Earned
Dental Assisting	$10,883.71	44 weeks plus externship/880 hours	Certificate
Medical Assisting	$10,657.00	32 weeks plus externship/880 hours	Certificate
Medical Billing	$ 9,727.00	36 weeks plus externship/780 hours	Certificate
Pharmacy Technician	$11,716.45	44 weeks plus externship/960 hours	Certificate

Bryman College, Renton

About Our Institution

The Bryman Schools were founded in 1962 by Mrs. Esther Bryman as the Los Angeles Colleges of Medical and Dental Assistants. The Los Angeles campus was the original school. In December 1995, Corinthian Schools, Inc. (CSi), a division of Corinthian Colleges, Inc. (CCi), acquired the schools. CCi is one of the largest postsecondary school organizations in the United States, operating more than eighty colleges and institutions nationwide.

The College's philosophy is to provide high-quality programs that are sound in concept, implemented by a competent and dedicated faculty, and geared to serve those seeking a solid foundation in the health-care field. The programs emphasize hands-on training, are relevant to the needs of employers, and focus on areas that offer strong long-term employment opportunities. Upon completion, graduates are prepared for entry-level positions in the medical and dental fields.

Financial Aid/Scholarships

Information regarding Federal Pell Grants, WIA, FFEL, state grants, and other assistance can be obtained from the Finance Office. Financial aid is available for those who qualify.

Accreditation

All programs are accredited by the Accrediting Commission of Career Schools and Colleges of Technology (ACCSCT).

Admissions

Successful candidates are selected based on admissions tests, interviews, and the completion and presentation of required documents. Enrollment is open to all high school graduates as well as those holding a GED certificate or its equivalent. Under certain circumstances, students who do not have a high school diploma or its equivalent may still be accepted for admission. Students should contact the Admissions Department for additional information.

Graduation Requirements

To be eligible for graduation, students must successfully complete all classroom modules with a grade of at least 70 percent, finish an approved externship of 160 to 240 hours, and complete all other program requirements.

Enrollment

There are 760 students enrolled.

Program Content

Dental Assisting, Medical Administrative Assistant, Medical Assisting, Medical Lab Assistant, Pharmacy Technician

Contact

Paige Mathis, Director of Admissions
981 Powell Avenue SW, Suite 200
Renton, WA 98055
Phone: (425) 255-3281
(888) 741-4271 (toll-free)
Fax: (425) 255-9327
E-mail: pmathis@cci.edu
Web: www.bryman-college.com

Programs Eligible for Scholarship	Tuition and Fees	Course Length/Credit Hours	Credential Earned
Dental Assisting	$11,628	720 clock hours/47 credit hours	Diploma
Medical Administrative Assistant	$11,809	720 clock hours/47 credit hours	Diploma
Medical Assisting	$11,708	720 clock hours/47 credit hours	Diploma
Medical Lab Assistant	$11,441	720 clock hours/47 credit hours	Diploma
Pharmacy Technician	$11,941	800 clock hours/61 credit hours	Diploma

Bryman College, Tacoma

About Our Institution
Bryman College, formerly known as Eton Technical Institute was founded in 1922 as the Bremerton Business College. Since then it has served the Puget Sound region, providing quality training for students in the health field. Students learn theory and skills from classroom lectures, laboratory work, and hands-on practice. Students also receive extensive experience in private practices and medical settings during the externship portion of their training. Bryman College's warm atmosphere and professional staff and faculty members help students reach their dreams.

Special Features
Bryman College recognizes the importance of a strong support system for students. Programs feature classroom lecture, hands-on practice, and real-life experience. Classes feature laboratories with quality equipment and tools. Tutoring is available throughout the programs. A student services adviser can provide resources, encouragement, and advice. The Graduate Services Department provides assistance with job-search and professional and business development throughout the graduates' careers in health.

Financial Aid/Scholarships
Bryman College features a Financial Aid Office on each campus, and a financial aid representative is available to help students determine eligibility. Title IV federal financial aid is available for those who qualify. Bryman College participates in Federal Pell Grant, Federal Stafford Student Loan, and Federal Plus Loan programs as well as additional financing options.

Tuition and Fees
Tuition for the Medical Billing Program includes all lab fees, books, and miscellaneous supplies. The program consists of five modules plus an externship.

The tuition for the Dental Assisting, Medical Assisting, and Pharmacy Technician programs includes all lab fees, books, miscellaneous supplies, and uniform. The Dental Assisting and Pharmacy Technician programs each consist of six modules plus an externship. The Medical Assisting Program consists of seven modules plus an externship.

Accreditation
Bryman College is accredited by the Accrediting Council for Independent Colleges and Schools (ACICS).

Admissions
Applicants must pass an entrance exam and be a high school graduate or have a GED certificate.

Program Content
Dental Assisting (DA), Medical Assisting (MA), Medical Billing (MB), Pharmacy Technician (PhT)

Program Description
The Dental Assisting Program is designed to prepare the student for a career as a dental assistant.

The Medical Assisting Program is designed to prepare the student for a career as a medical assistant.

The Medical Billing Program is designed to prepare the student for a career as a medical biller.

The Pharmacy Technician Program is designed to prepare the student for a career as a pharmacy technician.

Graduation Requirements
Students must attain required competency or speed levels in all courses, fulfill all clinical and externship requirements, achieve a cumulative grade point average of at least 2.0, satisfy all other academic requirements for graduation, and satisfy all nonacademic requirements, such as payment of tuition and fees.

Contact
Lynette Rickman
Director of Admissions
Bryman College
2156 Pacific Avenue
Tacoma, WA 98402
Phone: (253) 207-4000
Fax: (253) 207-4031
Web: http://brymancollege.com

Programs Eligible for Scholarship	Tuition and Fees	Course Length/Credit Hours	Credentials Earned
Dental Assisting	$11,657.00	44 weeks with externship/880 hours	Diploma of Completion
Medical Assisting	$10,883.71	23 weeks with externship/720 hours	Diploma of Completion
Medical Billing	$ 9,727.00	36 weeks with externship/880 hours	Diploma of Completion
Pharmacy Technician	$11,716.45	44 weeks with externship/960 hours	Diploma of Completion

Gene Juarez Academy of Beauty, North Seattle Campus, Seattle

About Our Institution
Founded in 1987, Gene Juarez Academy of Beauty prepares students for a successful career in the cosmetology and manicuring industry. The campus features a modern salon-like atmosphere where hands-on learning combines with cosmetology arts and sciences instruction.

Special Features
As part of an internationally recognized salon organization founded in 1972, the Academy draws resources from 1,100 employees and attract clientele based upon a world-class reputation. An ever-growing, always-improving learning organization, the Academy focuses on continually developing faculty members so that they may facilitate the finest cosmetology education. Gene Juarez Academy of Beauty graduates are successful and sought after.

Financial Aid/Scholarships
Students attending the Academy may qualify for various financial assistance programs, including PELL, FFEL, FDSLP, SEOG, VA, State Grants, JTPA, and the Worker Retraining Program.

Tuition and Fees
Tuition averages $5.50 per clock hour. Fees for the application, books, and materials total approximately $800.

Accreditation
Gene Juarez Academy of Beauty is accredited by the National Accrediting Commission of Cosmetology Arts and Sciences (NACCAS).

Admissions
A personal interview and high school diploma or GED are used to determine potential success in the beauty industry.

Graduation Requirements
Graduation requirements include completing 600 hours for Manicuring and Instructor Training or 1,800 hours for Cosmetology, appropriate course work, and written and practical examinations.

Contact
India Jenson
Admissions Representative
10715 8th Avenue, NE
Seattle, WA 98125
Phone: (206) 368-0210
Fax: (206) 364-8953
E-mail: indiaj@genejuarez.com

Program Content
Cosmetology, Manicuring, and Instructor Training

Program Description
Cosmetology: Trains students in haircutting, hairstyling, chemical processing of the hair, and basic introduction to manicuring and aesthetics as well as client satisfaction and business practices.

Manicuring: Trains students in all nail techniques normally offered in the cosmetology field as well as business practices.

Instructor Training: Trains student instructors in basic instructional methods needed to teach cosmetology school students.

Programs Eligible for Scholarship	Tuition and Fees	Course Length/Clock Hours	Credential Earned
Cosmetology	$10,400	52 weeks/1,800 clock hours	Diploma
Manicuring	$ 4,600	16 weeks/600 clock hours	Diploma
Instructor Training	$ 4,600	16 weeks/600 clock hours	Diploma

Gene Juarez Academy of Beauty, South Seattle/Tacoma Campus, Federal Way

About Our Institution
Founded in 1987, Gene Juarez Academy of Beauty prepares students for a successful career in the cosmetology and manicuring industry. The campus features a modern salon-like atmosphere where hands-on learning combines with cosmetology arts and sciences instruction.

Special Features
As part of an internationally recognized salon organization founded in 1972, the Academy draws resources from 1,100 employees and attracts clientele based upon a world-class reputation. An ever-growing, always-improving learning organization, the Academy focuses on continually developing faculty members so that they may facilitate the finest cosmetology education. Gene Juarez Academy of Beauty graduates are successful and sought after.

Financial Aid/Scholarships
Students attending the Academy may qualify for various financial assistance programs, including the Federal Pell Grant, FFEL, FDSLP, FSEOG, VA, state grants, and Worker Retraining Program.

Tuition and Fees
Tuition averages $5.77 to $7.50 per clock hour. Fees for registration, books, and materials total approximately $800.

Accreditation
Gene Juarez Academy of Beauty is accredited by the National Accrediting Commission of Cosmetology Arts and Sciences (NACCAS).

Admissions
A personal interview and high school diploma or GED certificate are used to determine potential success in the beauty industry.

Graduation Requirements
Graduation requirements include completing 600 hours for Manicuring and Instructor Training or 1,800 hours for Cosmetology, appropriate course work, and written and practical examinations.

Contact
Maryann Brathwaite
Admissions Representative
2222 S. 314th Street
Federal Way, WA 98003
Phone: (253) 839-4338
Fax: (253) 946-6560
E-mail: maryannb@genejuarez.com

Program Content
Cosmetology, Manicuring, and Instructor Training

Program Description
Cosmetology: Trains students in haircutting, hairstyling, chemical processing of the hair, basic introduction to manicuring and esthetics, and client satisfaction and business practices.

Manicuring: Trains students in all nail techniques normally offered in the cosmetology field as well as business practices.

Instructor Training: Trains student instructors in basic instructional methods needed to teach cosmetology school students.

Programs Eligible for Scholarship	Tuition and Fees	Course Length/Clock Hours	Credential Earned
Cosmetology	$10,500	52 weeks/1,800 clock hours	Diploma
Manicuring	$4,500	16 weeks/600 clock hours	Diploma
Instructor Training	$4,500	16 weeks/600 clock hours	Diploma

International Air Academy, Vancouver

About Our Institution
International Air Academy (IAA) was founded in 1979 by a retired airline executive who appreciated the growing need within the airline industry for qualified and trained customer service personnel and the great lack of high-quality airline training anywhere in the United States. Since then, International Air Academy has trained and placed more than 22,000 young men and women in positions with all the leading airlines as flight attendants, ticket agents, and reservationists, to name a few. No travel school has documented more job opportunities with more airlines than IAA. Choose the school the airlines use.

Special Features
Short-term programs of twenty weeks or less have led graduates on to careers in advanced positions, including flight service crew chiefs, station managers, and corporate management. Concentrated training and high standards mean that successful students must have desire and commitment, love working with people, and have the flexibility to go where the opportunities are.

Financial Aid/Scholarships
Applicants should contact the Admissions Department for complete information regarding funding sources, especially for information about the Imagine America Scholarship. The Academy does not limit the number of students accepted who receive Imagine America Scholarships.

Tuition and Fees
Tuition and fees run from $3700 to $6100, depending on the program. Applicants should contact Admissions Department for complete information.

Graduation Requirements
The school catalog is available to all interested parties. Students should contact the Admissions Department for assistance.

Contact
Colleen Piller, Director of Admissions
2901 E. Mill Plain Blvd.
Vancouver, WA 98661
Phone: (360) 695-2500
        (800) 234-1350 (toll-free)
Fax: (360) 992-4340
E-mail: admissions@airacademy.com
Web: www.airacademy.com

Program Content
Airline/Travel Specialist

Program Description
The Airline/Travel Specialist program prepares individuals for positions in airline reservations and airport customer service and also qualifies the student for interviews for in-flight service positions through the school's Career Development Department.

Programs Eligible for Scholarship	Tuition and Fees	Course Length/Credit Hours	Credential Earned
Airline/Travel Specialist	$6,300	20 weeks/28.5 credits	Diploma

For complete information regarding fees, tuition, course descriptions, and more, students should contact the Admissions Department at International Air Academy and request a current school catalog.

ITT Technical Institute, Bothell

About Our Institution

ITT Technical Institute is owned and operated by ITT Educational Services, Inc. (ITT/ESI), a leading private college system focused primarily on technology-oriented programs of study as well as business and criminal justice. ITT/ESI operates seventy-six ITT Technical Institutes in twenty-nine states, providing career-focused degree programs to approximately 40,000 students as of spring 2004. Headquartered in Indianapolis, Indiana, ITT/ESI has been actively involved in the higher education community in the United States since 1969. Curriculum offerings are designed to help students begin to prepare for career opportunities in the fields of technology, business, and criminal justice. Students attend classes year-round, with convenient breaks provided throughout the year. Classes are generally scheduled three days a week and are typically available in the morning, afternoon, and evening, depending on student enrollment. This class schedule offers flexibility to students to pursue part-time employment opportunities.

Special Features

ITT Technical Institute, Bothell, awards Associate of Applied Science, Bachelor of Science, and Master of Business Administration degrees. Most ITT Technical Institute programs of study blend traditional academic content with applied learning concepts, with a significant portion devoted to practical study in a lab environment. Advisory committees, made up of representatives of local businesses and employers for each program of study, help each ITT Technical Institute periodically assess and update curricula, equipment, and laboratory design. Assistance with housing and part-time employment is available.

Financial Aid/Scholarships

ITT Technical Institute maintains a Finance Department on campus. The campus is designated as an eligible institution by the U.S. Department of Education for participation in the following federal programs: Pell Grant, Stafford Student Loan, PLUS Loan, and Work-Study. The school also offers nonfederal loans through Bank One for eligible students.

Tuition and Fees

March 2005 tuition is $392 per credit hour.

Accreditation

Accrediting Council for Independent Colleges and Schools (ACICS).

Admissions

Admission requirements include having obtained a high school diploma or GED, passing an admission test (subject to being waived—students should refer to the school catalog), and passing, as determined at the school's discretion, an interview with the Registrar of the school, if the Registrar requests an interview with the student.

Graduation Requirements

For graduation requirements, students should consult the school catalog.

Contact

Mike Milford, Director
ITT Technical Institute
2525 223rd Street, S.E.
Bothell, WA 98021
Phone: (425) 485-0303
Fax: (425) 485-3438
Web: www.itt-tech.edu

Program Content

Business Accounting, Business Administration, Computer Drafting and Design, Computer and Electronics Engineering Technology, Criminal Justice, Data Communication Systems Technology, Digital Entertainment and Game Design, Electronics and Communications Engineering Technology, Information Systems Security, Information Technology (Computer Network Systems, Multimedia, Software Applications and Programming, Web Development), Software Engineering Technology, Technical Project Management

Program Description

The Computer Drafting and Design program combines computer-aided drafting with conventional methods of graphic communication to solve drafting and basic design-related problems.

The Computer and Electronics Engineering Technology program prepares students for careers in entry-level positions in modern electronics and computer technology.

The Data Communication System Technology program prepares students to design, deploy, and manage data communication systems and infrastructures.

The Digital Entertainment and Game Design program helps graduates prepare for career opportunities involving technology associated with designing and developing digital games and multimedia applications.

The Electronics and Communications Engineering Technology program prepares graduates for careers in entry-level positions involving electronics engineering technology, including communication systems.

The Information Systems Security program gives students the opportunity to study the essentials of information security and the security aspects of common information technology platforms.

The IT Computer Network Systems program helps prepare students to perform tasks associated with installing, upgrading, and maintaining computer network systems.

The IT Multimedia program helps students prepare to perform tasks associated with designing and creating interactive multimedia communications.

The IT Software Applications and Programming program helps students prepare to perform tasks associated with developing and modifying software applications.

The IT Web Development program helps students prepare to perform tasks associated with designing, creating, and maintaining Web sites.

The Software Engineering Technology program emphasizes technical skills that are used to design and implement software-based solutions for business and consumer markets.

The Technical Project Management Bachelor's program teaches students IT/e-commerce project management skills.

ITT Technical Institute, Seattle

About Our Institution

The company: ITT Technical Institute is owned and operated by ITT Educational Services, Inc. (ITT/ESI), a leading private college system offering technology-influenced programs of study. ITT/ESI operates seventy-seven ITT Technical Institutes in thirty states, providing career-focused degree programs to approximately 39,000 students as of spring 2004. Headquartered in Carmel, Indiana, ITT/ESI has been actively involved in the higher education community in the United States since 1969.

Curricula: Curriculum offerings are designed to help students begin to prepare for career opportunities in fields of technology. Students attend classes year-round, with convenient breaks provided throughout the year. A full-time student course load can have class meetings as often as three days a week and are typically available in the morning, afternoon, and evening, depending on student enrollment. General education courses may be available online. This class schedule offers flexibility to students to pursue part-time employment opportunities.

ITT Technical Institute, Seattle, awards the Associate of Applied Science, the Bachelor of Applied Science, and the Bachelor of Science degrees.

Special Features

Most ITT Technical Institute programs of study blend traditional academic content with applied learning concepts, with a significant portion devoted to practical study in a lab environment. Advisory committees composed of representatives of local businesses help each ITT Technical Institute periodically review and update curricula, equipment, and laboratory design.

Financial Aid/Scholarships

ITT Technical Institute maintains a Financial Aid Department on campus. The campus is designated as an eligible institution by the U.S. Department of Education for participation in the following programs: Federal Stafford Student Loan Program, Federal PLUS Loan Program, and Federal Work-Study Program. The school also offers nonfederal loans available through Bank One for eligible students.

Tuition and Fees

March 2005 tuition is $392 per credit hour.

Accreditation

The school is accredited by the Accrediting Council for Independent Colleges and Schools (ACICS).

Admissions

For admission requirements, students should contact the school for a catalog.

Graduation Requirements

For graduation requirements, students should contact the school for a catalog.

Program Content

School of Information Technology: Data Communication Systems Technology, Information Systems Security, Information Technology–Computer Network Systems, Information Technology–Software Applications and Programming, Information Technology–Web Development, Software Engineering Technology

School of Electronics Technology: Computer and Electronics Engineering Technology, Electronics and Communications Engineering Technology

School of Drafting and Design: Computer Drafting and Design, Digital Entertainment and Game Design, Information Technology–Multimedia Option

School of Business: Business Accounting Technology, Business Administration, Technical Project Management

School of Criminal Justice: Criminal Justice

Contact

Jack Kempt, Director of Recruitment
ITT Technical Institute
12720 Gateway Drive
Seattle, WA 98168
Phone: (206) 244-3300
Fax: (206) 246-7635

Western Business College, Vancouver

About Our Institution
In 1979, Western Business College in Portland, Oregon established a new branch school in Vancouver, Washington to meet the growing business training and employment needs of southwest Washington. In 1998, the school moved to a beautiful new site on the rapidly expanding east side of the county. The building has 16,000 square feet and includes ten classrooms, four computer labs, two well-equipped medical labs, a library, a student lounge, and administrative offices. Western Business College is one of more than eighty schools owned and operated by Corinthian Colleges, Inc., in the United States.

Special Features
The college is dedicated to the ideal that students should have the opportunity to reach their full potential. The quality of instruction and program content provides quality career training, designed to prepare men and women to enter and prosper in the employment community. The college stands behind this philosophy by offering graduate placement assistance upon program completion.

Financial Aid/Scholarships
Pell, FFEL, SEOG, work-study, and VA scholarships are available to those who qualify.

Tuition and Fees
Per credit hours are assessed based on amount of classes taken per quarter. There is a registration fee of $25 per term.

Accreditation
The College is accredited by the Accrediting Council for Independent Colleges and Schools (ACICS). The Medical Assisting program is accredited by the Commission on Accreditation of Allied Health Education Programs (CAAHEP).

Admissions
Successful candidates must be high school graduates or have a GED or have passed an Ability to Benefit (ATB) test.

Program Content
Accounting, Accounting/Business Administration, Administrative Assistant, Administrative Medical Assistant, Advanced Microcomputer Applications, Automated Office Technology, Bookkeeping, Executive Administrative Assistant, Legal Administrative Assistant, Medical Assistant, Medical Insurance Billing/Coding, Microcomputer Applications, Operations Specialist, Paralegal/Legal Assistant, Receptionist/General Office Assistant

Graduation Requirements
To be eligible for graduation, students must complete the required number of credits for their program with passing grades in all required courses, and earn a minimum of a 2.0 (C) cumulative grade point average.

Enrollment
450 students enrolled.

Contact
Renee Schiffhauer, Director of Admissions
120 NE 136th Avenue
Suite 130
Vancouver, WA 98684
Phone: (360) 254-3282
Fax: (360) 254-3035.
E-mail: rschiffauer@cci.edu
Web: www.western-college.com

Programs Eligible for Scholarship	Tuition and Fees	Course Length/Credit Hours	Credential Earned
Accounting	$220/credit hour	64/96 credit hours	Diploma/Degree
Accounting/Business Administration	$234/credit hour	64 credit hours	Diploma
Administrative Assistant	$234/credit hour	64 credit hours	Diploma
Administrative Medical Assistant	$234/credit hour	48 credit hours	Diploma
Advanced Microcomputer Applications	$234/credit hour	90 credit hours	Degree
Automated Office Technology	$234/credit hour	48 credit hours	Diploma
Bookkeeping	$234/credit hour	64 credit hours	Diploma
Executive Administrative Assistant	$234/credit hour	90 credit hours	Diploma
Legal Administrative Assistant	$234/credit hour	64 credit hours	Diploma
Medical Assistant	$234/credit hour	75/97 credit hours	Diploma/Degree
Medical Insurance Billing/Coding	$7,700	35 credit hours	Diploma
Microcomputer Applications	$234/credit hour	64/90 credit hours	Diploma/Degree
Operations Specialist	$234/credit hour	48 credit hours	Diploma
Paralegal/Legal Assistant	$234/credit hour	96 credit hours	Diploma

National Institute of Technology, Cross Lanes

About Our Institution
National Institute of Technology–Cross Lanes (NIT–Cross Lanes) is one of more than 150 schools owned and operated by Corinthian Colleges, Inc. The Cross Lanes campus was founded in 1968.

Special Features
The school has 26,000 square feet and contains seventeen classrooms designed for theory and laboratory instruction, administrative offices, a library, a study area, a break room, and rest rooms. Classrooms contain computers, medical materials, and resources to train for additional certifications.

Financial Aid/Scholarships
Financial aid includes Federal Pell Grant, Federal Stafford Student Loan, Federal Perkins Loan, Federal Work-Study, FSEOG, VA, WIA (financial aid available for those who qualify), WV Higher Education Grant, and the HEAPS Scholarship. Scholarships exist for graduating high school seniors. Applicants should talk with a financial aid representative for more information.

Accreditation
Accrediting Commission of Career Schools and Colleges of Technology (ACCSCT).

Admissions
Applicants must be a high school graduate or have a GED certificate or its equivalent. Under certain circumstances, students without a GED certificate or its equivalent may apply under the Ability to Benefit Provision. Students then must interview with an admissions representative and have an enrollment application reviewed by the Admissions Director and school president.

Graduation Requirements
Medical programs: Students should complete all required classroom modules with a grade of at least 70 percent and meet the grade requirements for the module components. Technical programs: Students should complete all required classroom training with a cumulative grade point average of at least 2.0.

Enrollment
There are 550 students enrolled at the National Institute of Technology–Cross Lanes.

Program Content
Electronics, Computer and Communications Technology; Homeland Security Specialist; Massage Therapy; Medical Business and Clinical Specialist; Pharmacy Technician

Contact
John L. Good, Senior HS Admissions Counselor
5514 Big Tyler Road
Cross Lanes, WV 25313
Phone: (304) 776-6290
Fax: (304) 776-6262
E-mail: jgood@cci.edu
Web: www.nitschools.com

Programs Eligible for Scholarship	Tuition and Fees	Course Length/Credit Hours	Credential Earned
Electronics, Computer and Communications Technology	$20,342	20 months/124 credit hours	Special AA
Homeland Security Specialist	$ 8,300	7 months/48 credit hours	Diploma
Massage Therapy	$10,900	9 months/57 credit hours	Diploma
Medical Business and Clinical Specialist	$10,690	12 months/65 credit hours	Diploma
Pharmacy Technician	$ 9,592	9 months/58 credit hours	Diploma

West Virginia Junior College, Charleston

About Our Institution
West Virginia Junior College's (WVJC) programs are focused on computer technology, allied health, legal office, and general business training. The College houses several computer and medical labs. WVJC prides itself on having high-tech programs, facilities, and equipment. West Virginia Junior College was established on September 1, 1892. As such, it has long-term relationships with employers throughout the community. WVJC uses these relationships to assist graduates in achieving their career goals.

Special Features
WVJC in Charleston offers short-term, high-tech training. Both day and night classes are available. Together with a four-day school week, students can design schedules to meet their needs. WVJC prides itself in providing a small-college atmosphere with personal attention.

Financial Aid/Scholarships
WVJC participates in all major federal financial aid programs, including grants, college work-study, and loans. WVJC also provides high school senior scholarships; participates in the West Virginia vocational rehabilitation program, Workforce Investment Act programs, West Virginia Higher Education Grant, and TAA; and is approved for the training of veterans.

Accreditation
WVJC is accredited by the Accrediting Council for Independent Colleges and Schools (ACICS).

Admissions
Admission requires a high school diploma or GED certificate. In addition, WVJC may take into consideration other appropriate factors bearing on the applicant's potential for success.

Graduation Requirements
Students must maintain a minimum overall 2.0 cumulative grade point average, successfully complete all courses required in the program, and meet any specific program requirements listed in the catalog.

Contact
Lucinda Curry, Associate Director
West Virginia Junior College
1000 Virginia Street, East
Charleston, WV 25301
Phone: (304) 345-2820
Fax: (304) 345-1425
Web: www.wvjc.edu

Program Content
Computer Information Technology/Technical Emphasis, Legal Office Assisting, Medical Assisting/Office Technology, Medical Secretarial/Office Technology

All associate degree programs are eligible for scholarships.

West Virginia Junior College, Morgantown

About Our Institution
West Virginia Junior College (WVJC) is a technology-oriented junior college that provides training in three fields—computer technology, medical assisting, and business. The main campus building includes networked computer labs, an Internet-accessible resource center, and a medical laboratory. Registered Medical Assistants may qualify to extern at Ruby Memorial Hospital and other medical facilities.

Special Features
Founded in 1922, WVJC has decades-old relationships with employers throughout the area, including WVU, Ruby Memorial Hospital, NIOSH, and other federal facilities, as well as with small local employers. WVJC graduates have exclusive access to the WVJC employer network. College work-study jobs and medical externships are available to qualified students. A four-day school week and day and night classes provide students with flexible schedules.

Financial Aid/Scholarships
WVJC participates in all major federal financial aid programs, including grants, scholarships, college work-study, and loans. WVJC also provides high school senior scholarships; participates in the West Virginia vocational rehabilitation program, Workforce Investment Act programs, TAA, and JTPA; and is approved for the training of veterans.

Tuition and Fees
Tuition is $3,000 per term. In addition, there is a $25 application fee.

Accreditation
WVJC is accredited by the Accrediting Council for Independent Colleges and Schools (ACICS).

Admissions
Admission requires a high school diploma or GED. In addition, WVJC may take into consideration other appropriate factors bearing on the applicant's potential for success.

Graduation Requirements
Students must maintain an overall 2.0 cumulative grade point average, successfully complete all courses required in the students program, and meet any specific program requirements listed in the catalog.

Contact
Stephanie Franks
West Virginia Junior College
148 Willey Street
Morgantown, WV 26505
Phone: (304) 296-8282
Fax: (304) 296-5612
Web: www.wvjcmorgantown.edu

Program Content
Information Technology, Internet Technology, Legal Office Assistant, Management, Medical Assisting,

Program Description
Computer: These programs are designed to combine a variety of information technology skills with business training to prepare graduates a wide variety of occupations.

LOA: The Legal Office Assistant Program is designed to prepare students to work in a wide variety of legal and other offices/business where a knowledge of legal forms and procedures would be helpful.

Management/Accounting: This training is designed for students with a strong interest in business or accounting. A computer component is included in course work.

RMA: Registered Medical Assistant training is designed to prepare graduates with both clinical and administrative skills necessary to work in hospitals, clinics, doctor's offices and related fields.

For specific program titles, content, and objectives, see the school catalog.

All associate degree programs are eligible for scholarships.

Herzing College, Madison

About Our Institution
Founded in 1948 as one of the state's first electronics schools, Herzing College has evolved into a degree-granting senior college. Herzing College currently occupies 30,000 square feet of space for training and administration purposes in a building that is specifically adapted for educational use.

Special Features
Herzing College offers associate degree, bachelor's degree, and diploma programs in the technology, business, and health care fields. All associate degree programs build toward a bachelor's degree. Under certain conditions, students are guaranteed a three-year completion of any Herzing bachelor's degree. A unique feature of Herzing programs is the preparation for industry certifications that is embedded in the curriculum. This provides students with the opportunity to test for nationally and internationally recognized certifications in IT and electronics, e.g. Microsoft Certified Systems Engineer (MCSE), A+, Network+, Cisco CCNA, Novell CNA, UNIX CUSA, and Certified Electronics Technician (CEA). Employment assistance services are provided to graduates. The placement rate for the reporting year 2003 was 92.3 percent.

Financial Aid/Scholarships
Herzing College maintains a financial aid team on campus, providing a variety of available programs, including grants, loans, work-study, veterans, and vocational rehabilitation. Herzing College also has a number of institutional scholarships available.

Tuition and Fees
The tuition of $4,044 to $4,569 per semester includes all books. A one-time-only equipment and supply fee of $350 applies to associate-level computer, electronics, and telecommunications technology and CAD students.

Accreditation
Herzing College is accredited by the Higher Learning Commission of the North Central Association of Colleges and Schools. For more information, students should contact the Higher Learning Commission (telephone: 800-621-7440; Web site: http://www.ncahigherlearning commission.org).

Program Content
Associate of Science Programs: Business Administration; Computer-Aided Drafting; Computers, Electronics, and Telecommunications Technology; Computer Information Systems; Computer Network Technology

Associate of Applied Science Program: Health Care

Bachelor of Science Programs: Business Administration, Information Technology, and Technology Management

Diploma Programs: Medical Billing and Insurance Coding, Web Site Design

Admissions
Interested candidates should contact Herzing Admissions to arrange an appointment. Acceptance is based on a testing and interviewing process. Successful candidates must pass a scholastic level exam and receive a recommendation from an Admissions Representative for admission to the college.

Graduation Requirements
In order to graduate, a student must have a cumulative grade point average of at least 2.0 and pass required courses. All incomplete and failed required courses must be successfully completed before graduation.

Contact
Director of Admissions
Herzing College
5218 East Terrace Drive
Madison, WI 53718
Phone: (608) 249-6611
      (800) 582-1227 (toll-free)
E-mail: info@msn.herzing.edu
Web: www.herzing.edu

Programs Eligible for Scholarship	Tuition and Fees*	Course Length/Credit Hours	Credential Earned
Business Administration	$4,400/semester	70/125 credit hours	AS/BS
CAD Drafting	$4,569/semester	79 credit hours	AS
Computer Information Systems	$4,569/semester	79 credit hours	AS
Computer Network Technology	$4,569/semester	79 credit hours	AS
Computers, Electronics, and Telecommunications Technology	$4,400/semester	79 credit hours	AS
Health Care	$4,400/semester	63 credit hours	AAS
Information Technology	$4,443/semester	138 credit hours	BS
Medical Billing and Insurance Coding	$4,400/semester	42 credit hours	Diploma
Technology Management	$4,066/semester	129 credit hours	BS
Web Site Design (online only)	$5,040/semester	31 credit hours	Diploma

*Semesters at Herzing College are sixteen weeks long. A full-time student generally completes 16 credits a semester.

ITT Technical Institute, Green Bay

About Our Institution
The company: ITT Technical Institute is owned and operated by ITT Educational Services, Inc. (ITT/ESI), a leading private college system offering technology-influenced programs of study. ITT/ESI operates seventy-seven ITT Technical Institutes in thirty states, providing career-focused degree programs to approximately 39,000 students as of spring 2004. Headquartered in Carmel, Indiana, ITT/ESI has been actively involved in the higher education community in the United States since 1969.

Curricula: Curriculum offerings are designed to help students begin to prepare for career opportunities in fields of technology. Students attend classes year-round, with convenient breaks provided throughout the year. A full-time student course load can have class meetings as often as three days a week and are typically available in the morning, afternoon, and evening, depending on student enrollment. General education courses may be available online. This class schedule offers flexibility to students to pursue part-time employment opportunities.

ITT Technical Institute, Green Bay, awards the Associate of Applied Science and the Bachelor of Science degrees.

Special Features
Most ITT Technical Institute programs of study blend traditional academic content with applied learning concepts, with a significant portion devoted to practical study in a lab environment. Advisory committees composed of representatives of local businesses help each ITT Technical Institute periodically review and update curricula, equipment, and laboratory design.

Financial Aid/Scholarships
ITT Technical Institute maintains a Financial Aid Department on campus. The campus is designated as an eligible institution by the U.S. Department of Education for participation in the following programs: Federal Stafford Student Loan Program, Federal PLUS Loan Program, and Federal Work-Study Program. The school also offers nonfederal loans available through Bank One for eligible students.

Tuition and Fees
March 2005 tuition is $386 per credit hour.

Accreditation
The school is accredited by the Accrediting Council for Independent Colleges and Schools (ACICS).

Admissions
For admission requirements, students should contact the school for a catalog.

Graduation Requirements
For graduation requirements, students should contact the school for a catalog.

Program Content
School of Information Technology: Data Communication Systems Technology, Information Systems Security, Information Technology–Computer Network Systems, Information Technology–Software Applications and Programming, Information Technology–Web Development, Software Engineering Technology

School of Electronics Technology: Computer and Electronics Engineering Technology, Electronics and Communications Engineering Technology

School of Drafting and Design: Computer Drafting and Design, Digital Entertainment and Game Design, Information Technology–Multimedia Option

School of Business: Business Accounting Technology, Business Administration, Technical Project Management

School of Criminal Justice: Criminal Justice

Contact
Ray Sweetman, Director of Recruitment
ITT Technical Institute
470 Security Boiulevard
Green Bay, WI 54313
Phone: (920) 662-9000
Fax: (920) 662-9384

ITT Technical Institute, Greenfield

About Our Institution

The company: ITT Technical Institute is owned and operated by ITT Educational Services, Inc. (ITT/ESI), a leading private college system offering technology-influenced programs of study. ITT/ESI operates seventy-seven ITT Technical Institutes in thirty states, providing career-focused degree programs to approximately 39,000 students as of spring 2004. Headquartered in Carmel, Indiana, ITT/ESI has been actively involved in the higher education community in the United States since 1969.

Curricula: Curriculum offerings are designed to help students begin to prepare for career opportunities in fields of technology. Students attend classes year-round, with convenient breaks provided throughout the year. A full-time student course load can have class meetings as often as three days a week and are typically available in the morning, afternoon, and evening, depending on student enrollment. General education courses may be available online. This class schedule offers flexibility to students to pursue part-time employment opportunities.

ITT Technical Institute, Greenfield, awards the Associate of Applied Science, the Bachelor of Science, and the Bachelor of Applied Science degrees.

Special Features

Most ITT Technical Institute programs of study blend traditional academic content with applied learning concepts, with a significant portion devoted to practical study in a lab environment. Advisory committees composed of representatives of local businesses help each ITT Technical Institute periodically review and update curricula, equipment, and laboratory design.

Financial Aid/Scholarships

ITT Technical Institute maintains a Financial Aid Department on campus. The campus is designated as an eligible institution by the U.S. Department of Education for participation in the following programs: Federal Stafford Student Loan Program, Federal PLUS Loan Program, and Federal Work-Study Program. The school also offers nonfederal loans available through Bank One for eligible students.

Tuition and Fees

March 2005 tuition is $386 per credit hour.

Accreditation

The school is accredited by the Accrediting Council for Independent Colleges and Schools (ACICS).

Admissions

For admission requirements, students should contact the school for a catalog.

Graduation Requirements

For graduation requirements, students should contact the school for a catalog.

Program Content

School of Information Technology: Data Communication Systems Technology, Information Systems Security, Information Technology–Computer Network Systems, Information Technology–Software Applications and Programming, Information Technology–Web Development, Software Engineering Technology

School of Electronics Technology: Computer and Electronics Engineering Technology, Electronics and Communications Engineering Technology

School of Drafting and Design: Computer Drafting and Design, Digital Entertainment and Game Design, Information Technology–Multimedia

School of Business: Business Accounting Technology, Business Administration, Technical Project Management

School of Criminal Justice: Criminal Justice

Contact

Jon Patterson, Director
ITT Technical Institute
6300 West Layton Avenue
Greenfield, WI 53220
Phone: (414) 282-9494
Fax: (414) 282-9698

Madison Media Institute, Madison

About Our Institution

Madison Media Institute (MMI), located on the east side of Madison, Wisconsin, has been preparing students for jobs in electronic media since 1969. MMI is recognized as a leading resource for technical information and training in electronic media.

Through the years, there has been an increasing dependence on communications technology, especially electronic media. Today, when one refers to the communications economy, the reference is to electronic media in all of its forms. The latest trends—DVD authoring, streaming video, high-definition television, and digital recording—are reshaping the entertainment and communications industries. Those who possess the necessary skills and experience by using the latest technology are positioned to lead the communications revolution.

Electronic media is the most dynamic and influential industry of the twenty-first century. Prospective students are encouraged to accept the challenges and embrace the opportunities offered by MMI's programs.

Madison Media Institute strives to provide the highest-quality media career training programs available. MMI does this by keeping in close touch with the real-world requirements of the industries that employ MMI graduates. The Institute's goal is to offer training on the most efficient and cost-effective basis possible. This provides real value to the students taking courses at the Institute.

MMI believes that career training is best done through hands-on training with real-world equipment in real-world job situations. The curriculum and facilities are continually upgraded to reflect current industry standards.

Special Features

The school offers 19,200 square feet of classroom, computer lab, and studio space. The video production facility is equipped with digital video editing systems, computer graphics software, professional digital field cameras, lighting equipment, special effects generators, and digital audio production equipment.

The Recording and Music Technology program utilizes a MIDI and synthesizer lab complete with twenty-four Macintosh® computer/MIDI/synthesizer workstations, Reason® and Digital Performer® software packages, Digidesign's Pro Tools System® digital audio workstations, and video postproduction facilities, including surround sound-mixing capabilities. In addition, there is a fully equipped forty-eight-track recording studio. The control room features a forty-input SSL 4000 console with G+ computer as well as a 2-inch, twenty-four-track analog machine.

The Digital Art and Animation program trains its students using labs equipped with computer workstations loaded and configured with Dreamweaver®, Flash®, 3D Studio Max®, Adobe After Effects®, Adobe PhotoShop®, Adobe Premiere®, Adobe Illustrator®, Quark®, and various other audio and video-editing software.

The maximum class sizes are 36 students for lecture settings, 14 students for a studio section, and 24 students for a computer lab.

Financial Aid/Scholarships

Assistance in paying educational-related expenses is available to qualified students from federal financial aid programs, including Federal Pell Grants,

Program Content

Associate of Arts (AA): Multimedia Technology, Recording and Music Technology

Diploma: Video Production

Federal Family Education Loans, and Federal Supplemental Educational Opportunity Grants (FSEOG). Students may also qualify for funding through DWD, VA, BIA, private scholarships, or private loan programs.

Tuition and Fees

Tuition is $338 per credit. The application fee is $30. Costs for books and other materials vary.

Accreditation

Madison Media Institute is approved by the Wisconsin Educational Approval Board (EAB) and is accredited by the Accrediting Commission of Career Schools and Colleges of Technology (ACCSCT). The Institute is approved by EAB and ACCSCT to offer occupational associate degrees and diplomas.

Admissions

A high school diploma or its equivalent is required for admission to Madison Media Institute. Applicants must also submit two letters of recommendation and a brief essay outlining their education objectives and career goals.

The admissions office conducts an in-depth interview with candidates to determine their suitability for admission to a prospective student's chosen program.

All persons meeting the entrance requirements are accepted for admission regardless of sex, race, age, or religion.

Contact

Madison Media Institute
2702 Agriculture Drive
Madison, WI 53718
Phone: (608) 663-2000
         (800) 236-4997 (toll-free)
Web: www.madisonmedia.com

WyoTech, Laramie

About Our Institution
WyoTech, Laramie, offers degree and diploma programs in automotive technology, diesel technology, and collision/refinishing technology. WyoTech's primary objectives are to impart specific knowledge and skills, to graduate each student, and to help place graduates in their chosen fields. WyoTech has several satellite campuses and is one of more than eighty schools owned and operated by Corinthian Colleges, Inc.

Special Features
Students receive hands-on learning from certified technicians and work with the most modern equipment in an atmosphere designed to simulate industry conditions.

Financial Aid/Scholarships
WyoTech offers Federal Pell Grants, Federal Supplemental Educational Opportunity Grants (FSEOG), Federal Perkins Loans, Federal Stafford Student Loans (Subsidized and Unsubsidized), and veterans' benefits. Financial aid is available for those who qualify.

Tuition and Fees
Tuition varies based on programs and ranges from $20,400 to $29,300. Books and tools are loaned to students at no additional charge. Tuition includes a $100 deposit that is required at the time of application. In addition, there is a $100 refundable tool desposit and a $50 nonrefundable housing reservation fee. Rent per month is $275.

Accreditation
WyoTech is accredited by the Accrediting Commission of Career Schools and Colleges of Technology (ACCSCT).

Admissions
In order to be admitted to WyoTech, an applicant must submit an application for admission, be interviewed and recommended for admission by a school representative, and provide proof of high school graduation or its equivalent.

Graduation Requirements
To be eligible for graduation, the student must complete each course in the program with a minimum grade of 70 percent.

Enrollment
There are 2,051 students enrolled.

Contact
Glenn R. Halsey, Director of Admissions
4373 North Third Street
Laramie, WY 82072
Phone: (307) 742-3776
E-mail: ghalsey@wyotech.com
Web: www.wyotech.com

Programs Eligible for Scholarship	Tuition and Fees	Course Length/Credit Hours	Credential Earned
Advanced Diesel Technology	$22,000	9 months/67ch	Diploma
Auto/Diesel Vehicle Technology	$22,000	9 months/71 ch	Diploma
Auto Tech w/Specialty Auto Fab	$29,300	12 months/91 ch	Diploma
Collision/Refin & Upholstery Technology	$22,000	9 months/63 ch	Diploma
Collision/Refin Tech w/Specialty Auto Fab	$29,300	12 months/87 ch	Diploma
Chassis Fab & High Perf Engines w/Auto Technology	$22,000	9 months/71 ch	Diploma
Chassis Fab & High Perf Engines w/Coll Refin Technology	$22,000	9 months/67 ch	Diploma
Chassis Fab & High Perf Engines w/Diesel Technology	$22,000	9 months/70 ch	Diploma
Diesel/Auto Vehicle Technology	$22,000	9 months/71 ch	Diploma
Street Rod & Custom Fab w/Auto Tech	$22,000	9 months/68 ch	Diploma
Street Rod & Custom Fab w/Coll Refin Tech	$22,000	9 months/64 ch	Diploma
Street Rod & Custom Fab w/Diesel Tech	$22,000	9 months/67 ch	Diploma
Auto Technology & Management	$20,400	9 months/73 ch	AAS
Auto Tech w/Chassis Fab & Management	$27,700	12 months/96 ch	AAS
Auto Tech w/Street Rod & Management	$27,700	12 months/93 ch	AAS
Collision/Refin Technology & Management	$20,400	9 months/69 ch	AAS
Collision/Refin Tech w/Chassis Fab & Manage	$27,700	12 months/92 ch	AAS
Collision/Refin Tech w/Street Rod & Manage	$27,700	12 months/89 ch	AAS
Diesel Technology and Management	$20,400	9 months/72 ch	AAS
WyoTech Graduate Online Applied Service Management	$ 5,700	9 months/72 ch	AST

Indexes

Alphabetical Listing of
Career Colleges

Boldface type indicates that the school is a participating institution in the Ⓐ *Imagine America* Scholarship Program.

Boldface type indicates that the school is a participating institution in the ⓝ *Imagine America* Scholarship Program.

Boldface type indicates that the school is a participating institution in the ⊕ *Imagine America* Scholarship Program.

Boldface type indicates that the school is a participating institution in the ◉ *Imagine America* Scholarship Program.

Boldface type indicates that the school is a participating institution in the ⓐ *Imagine America* Scholarship Program.

Boldface type indicates that the school is a participating institution in the Ⓝ *Imagine America* Scholarship Program.

Boldface type indicates that the school is a participating institution in the 🅐 *Imagine America* Scholarship Program.

Boldface type indicates that the school is a participating institution in the ⓐ *Imagine America* Scholarship Program.

ALPHABETICAL LISTING OF CAREER COLLEGES

Boldface type indicates that the school is a participating institution in the ⊕ *Imagine America* Scholarship Program.

Geographical Listing of Career Colleges

Boldface type indicates that the school is a participating institution in the Ⓐ *Imagine America* Scholarship Program.

Boldface type indicates that the school is a participating institution in the **Ⓐ** *Imagine America* Scholarship Program.

Boldface type indicates that the school is a participating institution in the ⓝ *Imagine America* Scholarship Program.

Boldface type indicates that the school is a participating institution in the 🄐 *Imagine America* Scholarship Program.

Boldface type indicates that the school is a participating institution in the Ⓝ *Imagine America* Scholarship Program.

Boldface type indicates that the school is a participating institution in the Ⓝ *Imagine America* Scholarship Program.

Boldface type indicates that the school is a participating institution in the ⊗ *Imagine America* Scholarship Program.

Boldface type indicates that the school is a participating institution in the ✪ *Imagine America* Scholarship Program.

Boldface type indicates that the school is a participating institution in the Ⓝ *Imagine America* Scholarship Program.

Boldface type indicates that the school is a participating institution in the ⊛ *Imagine America* Scholarship Program.

Alphabetical Listing of Programs

Boldface type indicates that the school is a participating institution in the Ⓐ *Imagine America* Scholarship Program.

Boldface type indicates that the school is a participating institution in the ⦿ *Imagine America* Scholarship Program.

Guide to Career Colleges 2005

Accounting and Business/Management

Boldface type indicates that the school is a participating institution in the ⒶImagine America Scholarship Program.

Accounting and Finance

Accounting Related

Accounting Technology and Bookkeeping

Acupuncture

Administrative Assistant and Secretarial Science

Boldface type indicates that the school is a participating institution in the 🟊 *Imagine America* Scholarship Program.

Boldface type indicates that the school is a participating institution in the Ⓐ *Imagine America* Scholarship Program.

Adult and Continuing Education

Adult Development and Aging

Advanced/Graduate Dentistry and Oral Sciences Related

Advertising

Aesthetician/Esthetician and Skin Care

Aircraft Pilot (Private)

Aircraft Powerplant Technology

Airframe Mechanics and Aircraft Maintenance Technology

Airline Flight Attendant

Airline Pilot and Flight Crew

Air Traffic Control

Allied Health and Medical Assisting Services Related

Boldface type indicates that the school is a participating institution in the ⓘ *Imagine America* Scholarship Program.

Alternative and Complementary Medical Support Services Related

Anatomy

Animation, Interactive Technology, Video Graphics and Special Effects

Boldface type indicates that the school is a participating institution in the Ⓐ *Imagine America* Scholarship Program.

Boldface type indicates that the school is a participating institution in the ⓘ *Imagine America* Scholarship Program.

Boldface type indicates that the school is a participating institution in the ⓐ *Imagine America* Scholarship Program.

Boldface type indicates that the school is a participating institution in the ❶ *Imagine America* Scholarship Program.

Boldface type indicates that the school is a participating institution in the Ⓐ *Imagine America* Scholarship Program.

Boldface type indicates that the school is a participating institution in the ⊛ *Imagine America* Scholarship Program.

Business Administration, Management and Operations Related

Business Automation/Technology/Data Entry

Boldface type indicates that the school is a participating institution in the 🄐 *Imagine America* Scholarship Program.

Business/Commerce

Business/Corporate Communications

Business Machine Repair

Business, Management, and Marketing Related

Business Operations Support and Secretarial Services Related

Cabinetmaking and Millwork

CAD/CADD Drafting/Design Technology

Boldface type indicates that the school is a participating institution in the 🄐 *Imagine America* Scholarship Program.

Boldface type indicates that the school is a participating institution in the ⒶⒶ*Imagine America* Scholarship Program.

Cardiovascular Technology

Carpentry

Ceramic Arts and Ceramics

Child Care and Support Services Management

Child Care Provision

Cinematography and Film/Video Production

Civil Drafting and CAD/CADD

Civil Engineering Technology

Clinical Laboratory Science/Medical Technology

Boldface type indicates that the school is a participating institution in the Ⓝ *Imagine America* Scholarship Program.

Boldface type indicates that the school is a participating institution in the ⓐ *Imagine America* Scholarship Program.

Commercial Photography

Communications Systems Installation and Repair Technology

Communications Technology

Boldface type indicates that the school is a participating institution in the Ⓐ *Imagine America* Scholarship Program.

Computer and Information Sciences

Computer and Information Sciences and Support Services Related

Computer and Information Sciences Related

Boldface type indicates that the school is a participating institution in the ⓐ *Imagine America* Scholarship Program.

Boldface type indicates that the school is a participating institution in the ⓐ *Imagine America* Scholarship Program.

Boldface type indicates that the school is a participating institution in the ◑ *Imagine America* Scholarship Program.

Computer Graphics

Boldface type indicates that the school is a participating institution in the ⓝ *Imagine America* Scholarship Program.

Computer/Information Technology Services Administration Related

Boldface type indicates that the school is a participating institution in the Ⓐ *Imagine America* Scholarship Program.

Computer Installation and Repair Technology

Boldface type indicates that the school is a participating institution in the Ⓝ *Imagine America* Scholarship Program.

Computer Programming

Boldface type indicates that the school is a participating institution in the Ⓐ *Imagine America* Scholarship Program.

Computer Programming Related

AEC Southern Ohio College, Akron Campus, Akron,
    OH... 198

Boldface type indicates that the school is a participating institution in the Ⓝ *Imagine America* Scholarship Program.

Computer Programming (Specific Applications)

Computer Programming (Vendor/Product Certification)

Boldface type indicates that the school is a participating institution in the Ⓐ *Imagine America* Scholarship Program.

Boldface type indicates that the school is a participating institution in the Ⓐ *Imagine America* Scholarship Program.

Computer Software and Media Applications Related

Computer Software Engineering

Boldface type indicates that the school is a participating institution in the Ⓐ *Imagine America* Scholarship Program.

Computer Software Technology

Computer Systems Analysis

Boldface type indicates that the school is a participating institution in the ⓐ *Imagine America* Scholarship Program.

Computer Systems Networking and Telecommunications

Boldface type indicates that the school is a participating institution in the ⓐ *Imagine America* Scholarship Program.

Boldface type indicates that the school is a participating institution in the ❶ *Imagine America* Scholarship Program.

Computer/Technical Support Specialist

Boldface type indicates that the school is a participating institution in the ⓐ *Imagine America* Scholarship Program.

Computer Technology/Computer Systems Technology

Boldface type indicates that the school is a participating institution in the ⓐ *Imagine America* Scholarship Program.

Construction Engineering Technology

Corrections

Cosmetology

Cosmetology, Barber/Styling, and Nail Instruction

Boldface type indicates that the school is a participating institution in the ⓐ *Imagine America* Scholarship Program.

Boldface type indicates that the school is a participating institution in the ⊕ *Imagine America* Scholarship Program.

Boldface type indicates that the school is a participating institution in the ⓐ *Imagine America* Scholarship Program.

Boldface type indicates that the school is a participating institution in the ⊕ *Imagine America* Scholarship Program.

Boldface type indicates that the school is a participating institution in the ⓐ *Imagine America* Scholarship Program.

Boldface type indicates that the school is a participating institution in the 🅐 *Imagine America* Scholarship Program.

Desktop Publishing and Digital Imaging Design

Diagnostic Medical Sonography and Ultrasound Technology

Dialysis Technology

Diesel Mechanics Technology

Digital Communication and Media/ Multimedia

Boldface type indicates that the school is a participating institution in the Ⓐ *Imagine America* Scholarship Program.

Diving, Professional and Instruction

Drafting and Design Technology

Boldface type indicates that the school is a participating institution in the ⬤ *Imagine America* Scholarship Program.

Boldface type indicates that the school is a participating institution in the ⓐ *Imagine America* Scholarship Program.

Boldface type indicates that the school is a participating institution in the ⊛ *Imagine America* Scholarship Program.

Electrical/Electronics Drafting and CAD/CADD

Electrical/Electronics Equipment Installation and Repair

Electrician

Boldface type indicates that the school is a participating institution in the ⓐ *Imagine America* Scholarship Program.

Boldface type indicates that the school is a participating institution in the ⓐ *Imagine America* Scholarship Program.

Boldface type indicates that the school is a participating institution in the ⓐ *Imagine America* Scholarship Program.

Boldface type indicates that the school is a participating institution in the ⓐ *Imagine America* Scholarship Program.

Health Information/Medical Records Administration

Health Information/Medical Records Technology

Boldface type indicates that the school is a participating institution in the ⓐ *Imagine America* Scholarship Program.

Heating, Air Conditioning, Ventilation and Refrigeration Maintenance Technology

Heavy Equipment Maintenance Technology

Hematology Technology

Home Health Aide/Home Attendant

Horseshoeing

Hospital and Health Care Facilities Administration

Hospitality Administration

Boldface type indicates that the school is a participating institution in the ⬤ *Imagine America* Scholarship Program.

Boldface type indicates that the school is a participating institution in the ⓝ *Imagine America* Scholarship Program.

Information Technology

Boldface type indicates that the school is a participating institution in the ⓐ *Imagine America* Scholarship Program.

Boldface type indicates that the school is a participating institution in the Ⓐ *Imagine America* Scholarship Program.

Boldface type indicates that the school is a participating institution in the ⍟ *Imagine America* Scholarship Program.

Boldface type indicates that the school is a participating institution in the ⓝ *Imagine America* Scholarship Program.

Legal Assistant/Paralegal

Boldface type indicates that the school is a participating institution in the ⊛ *Imagine America* Scholarship Program.

Logistics and Materials Management

Machine Shop Technology

Machine Tool Technology

Make-Up Artist

Management Information Systems

Management Information Systems and Services Related

Management Science

Marine Maintenance and Ship Repair Technology

Marine Technology

Marketing/Marketing Management

Marketing Related

Massage Therapy

Boldface type indicates that the school is a participating institution in the Ⓐ *Imagine America* Scholarship Program.

Boldface type indicates that the school is a participating institution in the ⊕ *Imagine America* Scholarship Program.

Boldface type indicates that the school is a participating institution in the ① *Imagine America* Scholarship Program.

Boldface type indicates that the school is a participating institution in the **◑** *Imagine America* Scholarship Program.

Boldface type indicates that the school is a participating institution in the ⊗ *Imagine America* Scholarship Program.

Boldface type indicates that the school is a participating institution in the ⊕ *Imagine America* Scholarship Program.

Boldface type indicates that the school is a participating institution in the **◐** *Imagine America* Scholarship Program.

National College of Business and Technology, Kettering, OH 202
National Institute of Technology, Long Beach, CA 86
National Institute of Technology, Detroit, MI 160
National Institute of Technology, Southfield, MI 160
National Institute of Technology, Austin, TX 249
National Institute of Technology, Houston, TX 249
National Institute of Technology, Houston, TX 250
National Institute of Technology, San Antonio, TX 250
National Institute of Technology, Cross Lanes, WV 274
National Institute of Technology–Dearborn, Dearborn, MI 160
National Institute of Technology–Greenspoint, Houston, TX 250
National Institute of Technology–Hobby, Houston, TX . 250
National School of Technology, Inc., Fort Lauderdale, FL 117
National School of Technology, Inc., Hialeah, FL 117
National School of Technology, Inc., Miami, FL 117
National School of Technology, Inc., North Miami Beach, FL 118
Nevada Career Academy, Sparks, NV 178
Nevada Career Institute, Las Vegas, NV 178
New England Institute of Technology, Warwick, RI 234
New England Institute of Technology at Palm Beach, West Palm Beach, FL 118
North Florida Institute, Orange Park, FL 118
Ohio Institute of Photography and Technology, Dayton, OH 202
Ohio Valley College of Technology, East Liverpool, OH 202
Olympia Career Training Institute, Grand Rapids, MI . . 160
Olympia Career Training Institute, Kalamazoo, MI 161
Olympia College, Burr Ridge, IL 134
Olympia College, Chicago, IL 134
Olympia College, Skokie, IL 134
Olympia College, Merrillville, IN 140
Parks College, Aurora, CO 99
Parks College, Denver, CO 99
Parks College, McLean, VA 266
PCI Health Training Center, Dallas, TX 250
Pennco Tech, Bristol, PA 221
Pima Medical Institute, Mesa, AZ 71
Pima Medical Institute, Tucson, AZ 71
Pima Medical Institute, Chula Vista, CA 87
Pima Medical Institute, Colorado Springs, CO 99
Pima Medical Institute, Denver, CO 99
Pima Medical Institute, Las Vegas, NV 178
Pima Medical Institute, Albuquerque, NM 187
Pima Medical Institute, Renton, WA 273
Pima Medical Institute, Seattle, WA 274
Pinnacle Career Institute, Kansas City, MO 171
Pinnacle Career Institute, Lawrence, KS 142
Pioneer Pacific College, Clackamas, OR 208
Pioneer Pacific College, Wilsonville, OR 208
Pioneer Pacific College-Eugene/Springfield Branch, Springfield, OR 209
Pittsburgh Technical Institute, Oakdale, PA 221
Platt College, Lawton, OK 206
Platt College, Oklahoma City, OK 206
Platt College, Oklahoma City, OK 206
Platt College, Tulsa, OK 207
Porter and Chester Institute, Enfield, CT 102
Porter and Chester Institute, Stratford, CT 102
Porter and Chester Institute, Watertown, CT 102
Porter and Chester Institute, Wethersfield, CT 102
Porter and Chester Institute, Chicopee, MA 157
Professional Careers Institute, Indianapolis, IN 140

Provo College, Provo, UT 256
Remington College, Houston, TX 251
Remington College–Baton Rouge Campus, Baton Rouge, LA 150
Remington College–Cleveland Campus, Cleveland, OH 202
Remington College–Cleveland West Campus, North Olmstead, OH 202
Remington College–Colorado Springs Campus, Colorado Springs, CO 100
Remington College–Dallas Campus, Garland, TX 251
Remington College–Denver Campus, Lakewood, CO . . . 100
Remington College–Fort Worth Campus, Fort Worth, TX 251
Remington College–Honolulu Campus, Honolulu, HI . . 128
Remington College–Houston Campus, Houston, TX 251
Remington College–Jacksonville Campus, Jacksonville, FL 119
Remington College–Lafayette Campus, Lafayette, LA . . 150
Remington College–Little Rock Campus, Little Rock, AR 73
Remington College–Memphis Campus, Memphis, TN . . 239
Remington College–Nashville Campus, Nashville, TN . 239
Remington College–Pinellas Campus, Largo, FL 119
RETS Institute, Nutley, NJ 185
RETS Medical and Business Institute, Hopkinsville, KY . . 146
RETS Tech Center, Centerville, OH 203
RETS Technical Center, Boston, MA 157
Rochester Business Institute, Rochester, NY 192
Rockford Business College, Rockford, IL 134
Ross Medical Education Center, Hollywood, FL 119
Ross Medical Education Center, West Palm Beach, FL . . . 120
Ross Medical Education Center, Decatur, GA 126
Ross Medical Education Center, Smyrna, GA 126
Ross Medical Education Center, Ann Arbor, MI 161
Ross Medical Education Center, Brighton, MI 161
Ross Medical Education Center, Flint, MI 161
Ross Medical Education Center, Grand Rapids, MI 161
Ross Medical Education Center, Lansing, MI 161
Ross Medical Education Center, Port Huron, MI 161
Ross Medical Education Center, Redford, MI 161
Ross Medical Education Center, Roosevelt Park, MI 161
Ross Medical Education Center, Warren, MI 161
Ross Medical Education Center–Saginaw Campus, Saginaw, MI 162
St. Louis College of Health Careers, St. Louis, MO 171
St. Louis College of Health Careers, St. Louis, MO 171
San Antonio College of Medical and Dental Assistants, San Antonio, TX 251
Sanford-Brown College, Collinsville, IL 134
Sanford-Brown College, Fenton, MO 172
Sanford-Brown College, Hazelwood, MO 172
Sanford-Brown College, North Kansas City, MO 172
Sanford-Brown Institute, Jacksonville, FL 120
Sanford-Brown Institute, Lauderdale Lakes, FL 120
Sanford-Brown Institute, Tampa, FL 120
Sanford-Brown Institute, Atlanta, GA 126
Sanford-Brown Institute, Landover, MD 152
Sanford-Brown Institute, Springfield, MA 157
Sanford-Brown Institute, Iselin, NJ 185
Sanford-Brown Institute, Garden City, NY 193
Sanford-Brown Institute, New York, NY 193
Sanford-Brown Institute, White Plains, NY 193
Sanford-Brown Institute, Middleburg Heights, OH 203
Sanford-Brown Institute, Bensalem, PA 222
Sanford-Brown Institute, Dallas, TX 252
Sanford-Brown Institute, Houston, TX 252
San Joaquin Valley College, Bakersfield, CA 88

Boldface type indicates that the school is a participating institution in the Ⓐ *Imagine America* Scholarship Program.

Medical/Health Management and Clinical Assistant

Medical Insurance Coding

Boldface type indicates that the school is a participating institution in the Ⓐ *Imagine America* Scholarship Program.

Boldface type indicates that the school is a participating institution in the ◐ *Imagine America* Scholarship Program.

Medical Insurance/Medical Billing

Boldface type indicates that the school is a participating institution in the Ⓘ *Imagine America* Scholarship Program.

Medical Office Assistant

Boldface type indicates that the school is a participating institution in the Ⓐ *Imagine America* Scholarship Program.

Medical Office Computer Specialist

Medical Office Management

Boldface type indicates that the school is a participating institution in the Ⓐ *Imagine America* Scholarship Program.

Medical Pharmacology and Pharmaceutical Sciences

Medical Radiologic Technology

Medical Reception

Boldface type indicates that the school is a participating institution in the ⒶImagine America Scholarship Program.

Boldface type indicates that the school is a participating institution in the ◐ *Imagine America* Scholarship Program.

Boldface type indicates that the school is a participating institution in the 🛈 *Imagine America* Scholarship Program.

Boldface type indicates that the school is a participating institution in the Ⓐ *Imagine America* Scholarship Program.

Operations Management

Ophthalmic and Optometric Support Services and Allied Professions Related

Ophthalmic Technology

Opticianry

Optometric Technician

Painting

Petroleum Technology

Pharmacy (B.Pharm., Pharm.D.)

Pharmacy Administration and Pharmaceutics

Pharmacy Technician

Boldface type indicates that the school is a participating institution in the ⓐ *Imagine America* Scholarship Program.

Boldface type indicates that the school is a participating institution in the ⓐ *Imagine America* Scholarship Program.

Phlebotomy

Photographic and Film/Video Technology

Photography

Physical Therapist Assistant

Boldface type indicates that the school is a participating institution in the ⓢ *Imagine America* Scholarship Program.

Medical Careers Institute, Virginia Beach, VA **264**
Michiana College, South Bend, IN 140
Pima Medical Institute, Mesa, AZ 71
Pima Medical Institute, Tucson, AZ 71
Pima Medical Institute, Denver, CO 99
Pima Medical Institute, Albuquerque, NM 187
Provo College, Provo, UT 256
South College, Knoxville, TN 240
South University, Montgomery, AL. 63
South University, West Palm Beach, FL 120
South University, Savannah, GA 126
Stevens-Henager College–Provo, Provo, UT 257

Physician Assistant
Career Education Institute, Brockton, MA 155
San Joaquin Valley College, Visalia, CA 89
South University, Savannah, GA 126
Stevens-Henager College–Provo, Provo, UT 257

Pipefitting and Sprinkler Fitting
New England Institute of Technology, Warwick, RI 234
TCI-The College of Technology, New York, NY 193

Plumbing Technology
Instituto Banca y Comercio, Manati, PR 230
National Institute of Technology, Long Beach, CA 86
New England Institute of Technology, Warwick, RI 234
Orleans Technical Institute, Philadelphia, PA 220
WyoTech, Fremont, CA 95

Pre-Law Studies
AEC Texas Institute, Garland, TX 241
The Brown Mackie College–Lenexa Campus, Lenexa, KS 141
Empire College, Santa Rosa, CA 80
Herzing College, Kenner, LA. 149
ICM School of Business & Medical Careers,
  Pittsburgh, PA. **217**
Michiana College, Fort Wayne, IN. 140
National American University–Sioux Falls Branch, Sioux
  Falls, SD. 236
RETS Institute of Technology, Louisville, KY 146
South University, Montgomery, AL. 63
South University, Savannah, GA 126
South University, Columbia, SC. 235
Western State University College of Law, Fullerton, CA . 94

Printmaking
Academy of Art University, San Francisco, CA......... 73

Psychiatric/Mental Health Services Technology
PCI Health Training Center, Dallas, TX 250

Purchasing, Procurement/Acquisitions and Contracts Management
Strayer University, Washington, DC 103
Strayer University, Memphis, TN 240
Strayer University, Nashville, TN 240
Strayer University at Alexandria Campus, Alexandria,
  VA. 267
Strayer University at Anne Arundel Campus,
  Millersville, MD 152
Strayer University at Arlington Campus, Arlington, VA . 267
Strayer University at Cary, Morrisville, NC 196
Strayer University at Chesapeake Campus, Chesapeake,
  VA. 267
Strayer University at Chesterfield Campus, Midlothian,
  VA. 268
Strayer University at Delaware County, Springfield, PA . 223

Strayer University at Fredericksburg Campus,
  Fredericksburg, VA. 268
Strayer University at Henrico Campus, Glen Allen, VA.. 268
Strayer University at Loudoun Campus, Ashburn, VA... 268
Strayer University at Lower Bucks County, Feasterville
  Trevose, PA. 223
Strayer University at Manassas Campus, Manassas, VA . 269
Strayer University at Montgomery Campus,
  Germantown, MD 153
Strayer University at Newport News Campus, Newport
  News, VA 269
Strayer University at North Charlotte, Charlotte, NC 197
Strayer University at Owings Mills Campus, Owings
  Mills, MD. 153
Strayer University at Prince George's County, Suitland,
  MD 153
Strayer University at Raleigh, Raleigh, NC 197
Strayer University at South Charlotte, Charlotte, NC 197
Strayer University at Takoma Park, Washington, DC 103
Strayer University at White Marsh Campus, Baltimore,
  MD 153
Strayer University at Woodbridge Campus, Woodbridge,
  VA. 269

Quality Control Technology
Capella University, Minneapolis, MN................. 163
Ocean Corporation, Houston, TX 250

Radio and Television
Academy of Radio Broadcasting, Phoenix, AZ 65
Academy of Radio Broadcasting, Huntington Beach, CA. 74
Brown College, Mendota Heights, MN................. 162
Hesser College, Manchester, NH 178
International College of Broadcasting, Dayton, OH 200
International College of Broadcasting, Dayton, OH 200
Madison Media Institute, Madison, WI 276
The New England Institute of Art, Brookline, MA....... 157
New England Institute of Technology, Warwick, RI 234
Specs Howard School of Broadcast Arts Inc.,
  Southfield, MI 162

Radio and Television Broadcasting Technology
Brown College, Mendota Heights, MN................. 162
New England Institute of Technology, Warwick, RI 234
New England School of Communications, Bangor, ME .. 151

Radiologic Technology/Science
Apollo College–Westside, Inc., Phoenix, AZ 66
Career Technical College, Monroe, LA 148
Instituto Vocational y Commercial EDIC, Caguas, PR.... 231
Keiser College, Daytona Beach, FL 114
Keiser College, Fort Lauderdale, FL 114
Keiser College, Lakeland, FL. 114
Keiser College, Melbourne, FL 114
Keiser College, Miami, FL. 115
Keiser College, Orlando, FL 115
Keiser College, Sarasota, FL 115
Keiser College, Tallahassee, FL..................... 116
Maric College, North Hollywood, CA................. 85
MedVance Institute, Baton Rouge, LA 150
MedVance Institute, Cookeville, TN 238
MedVance Institute, Houston, TX 248
Pima Medical Institute, Mesa, AZ 71
Pima Medical Institute, Tucson, AZ 71
Pima Medical Institute, Chula Vista, CA 87
Pima Medical Institute, Denver, CO 99
Pima Medical Institute, Las Vegas, NV............... 178
Pima Medical Institute, Albuquerque, NM 187

Boldface type indicates that the school is a participating institution in the Ⓝ *Imagine America* Scholarship Program.

Boldface type indicates that the school is a participating institution in the ⓝ *Imagine America* Scholarship Program.

Boldface type indicates that the school is a participating institution in the ⊕ *Imagine America* Scholarship Program.

Survey Technology

System Administration

System, Networking, and LAN/WAN Management

Boldface type indicates that the school is a participating institution in the ⓐ *Imagine America* Scholarship Program.

Taxation

Teacher Assistant/Aide

Technology Management

Boldface type indicates that the school is a participating institution in the ⓘ *Imagine America* Scholarship Program.

Telecommunications

Telecommunications Technology

Tool and Die Technology

Tourism and Travel Services Management

Boldface type indicates that the school is a participating institution in the Ⓝ *Imagine America* Scholarship Program.

Boldface type indicates that the school is a participating institution in the ◐ *Imagine America* Scholarship Program.

Boldface type indicates that the school is a participating institution in the Ⓐ *Imagine America* Scholarship Program.

Welding Technology

Word Processing

Boldface type indicates that the school is a participating institution in the ⊘ *Imagine America* Scholarship Program.

Alphabetical Listing of Allied Members

ALPHABETICAL LISTING OF ALLIED MEMBERS

Alphabetical Listing of *Imagine America* Scholarship Program Participants

ALPHABETICAL LISTING OF *IMAGINE AMERICA* SCHOLARSHIP PROGRAM PARTICIPANTS

Alphabetical Listing of Military Recruiting Programs

Boldface type indicates that the school is a participating institution in the Ⓝ *Imagine America* Scholarship Program.

Boldface type indicates that the school is a participating institution in the ⊛ *Imagine America* Scholarship Program.

ALPHABETICAL LISTING OF MILITARY RECRUITING PROGRAMS

Boldface type indicates that the school is a participating institution in the ⓐ *Imagine America* Scholarship Program.

NOTES

MAY   2007

NOTES